Multinational Business Finance

TENTH EDITION

The Addison-Wesley Series in Finance

Chambers/Lacey
Modern Corporate Finance:
Theory and Practice

Copeland/Weston
Financial Theory
and Corporate Policy

Dufey/Giddy
Cases in International Finance

Eakins
Finance: Investments,
Institutions, and Management

Eiteman/Stonehill/Moffett
Multinational Business Finance

Gitman
Principles of Managerial Finance

Gitman
Principles of Managerial Finance
—Brief Edition

Gitman/Joehnk
Fundamentals of Investing

Gitman/Madura
Introduction to Finance

Hughes/MacDonald
International Banking:
Text and Cases

Madura
Personal Finance

McDonald
Derivatives Markets

Megginson
Corporate Finance Theory

Melvin
International Money and Finance

Mishkin/Eakins
Financial Markets and Institutions

Moffett
Cases in International Finance

Moffett/Stonehill/Eiteman
Fundamentals of
Multinational Finance

Rejda
Principles of Risk Management
and Insurance

Solnik/Mcleavey
International Investments

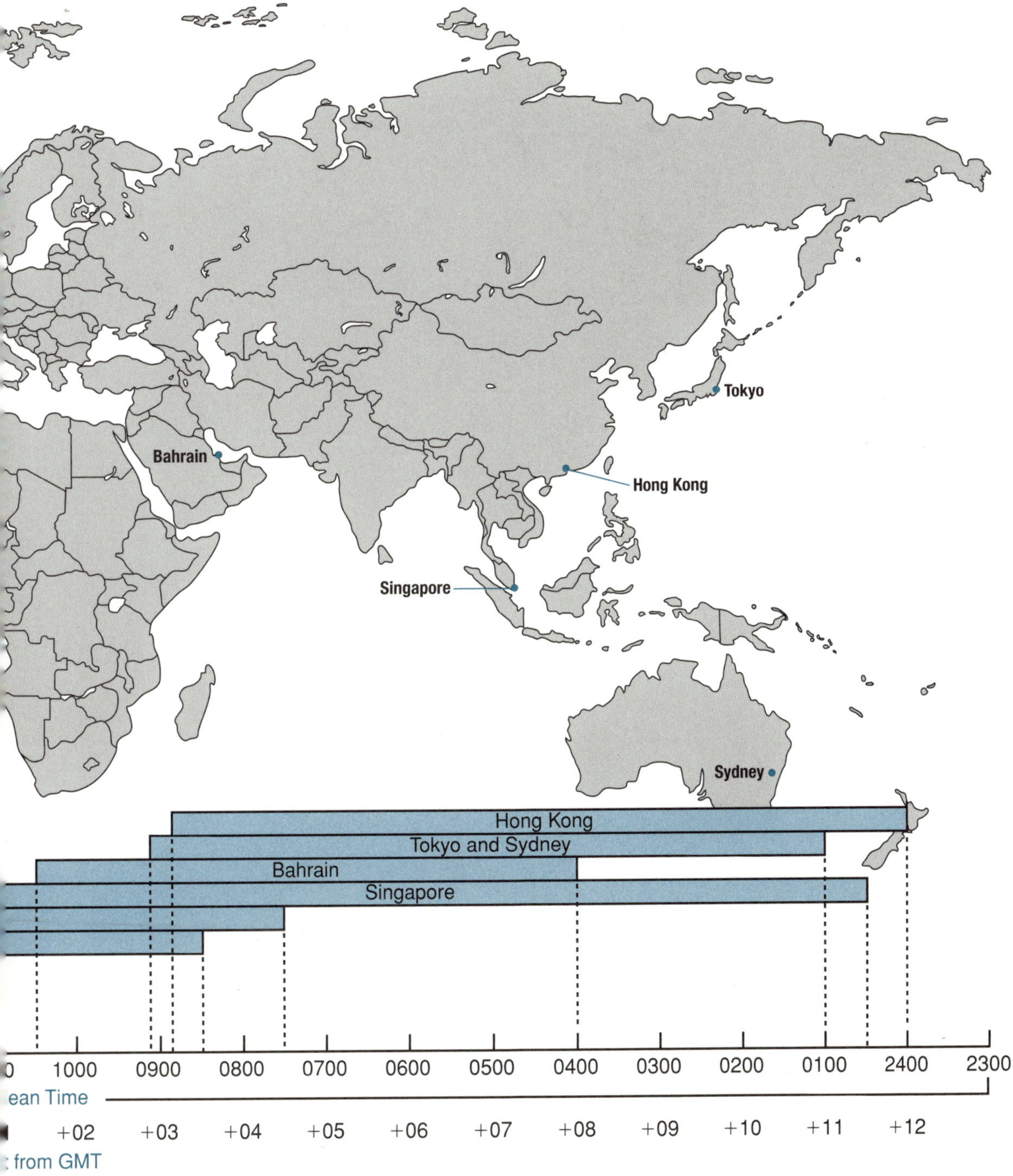

Tokyo
Bahrain
Hong Kong
Singapore
Sydney
Hong Kong
Tokyo and Sydney
Bahrain
Singapore
0
1000
0900
0800
0700
0600
0500
0400
0300
0200
0100
2400
2300
ean Time
+02
+03
+04
+05
+06
+07
+08
+09
+10
+11
+12
: from GMT

Multinational Business Finance

TENTH EDITION

David K. **EITEMAN** • *Arthur I.* **STONEHILL** • *Michael H.* **MOFFETT**

University of California, Los Angeles

University of Hawaii at Manoa

Thunderbird—The American Graduate School of International Management

PEARSON
Addison Wesley

Boston San Francisco New York
London Toronto Sydney Tokyo Singapore Madrid
Mexico City Munich Paris Cape Town Hong Kong Montreal

Editor-in-Chief: Denise Clinton
Acquisitions Editor: Donna Battista
Senior Project Manager: Mary Clare McEwing
Managing Editor: James Rigney
Senior Production Supervisor: Katherine Watson
Marketing Manager: Barbara LeBuhn
Design Manager: Regina Hagen Kolenda
Cover Designer: Regina Hagen Kolenda
Cover Image: © Masterfile
Digital Assets Manager: Jason Miranda
Media Producer: Jennifer Pelland
Media Manager: Michelle Neal
Senior Manufacturing Buyer: Hugh Crawford
Project Management and Composition: Argosy Publishing
Printer and Binder: R.R. Donnelley

Library of Congress Cataloging-In-Publication Data

Eiteman, David, K
Multinational business finance.—10th ed. / by David K. Eiteman, Arthur I. Stonehill, Michael H. Moffett
p.cm.
Rev. ed. Of: Multinational business finance / David K. Eiteman, Arthur I. Stonehill, Michael H. Moffett.
Includes bibliographical references and index.
ISBN 0-201-78567-6
1. International business enterprises—Finance. I. Stonehill, Arthur I. II. Eiteman, David K. III. Multinational business finance. IV. Title
HG4027.5.E36 2004
658.15'99—dc21

ISBN: 0-201-78567-6

2 3 4 5 6 7 8 9 10—DOC—07 06 05 04

Preface

AS THE FIELD OF INTERNATIONAL FINANCE HAS EVOLVED, SO HAS THE CONTENT OF *Multinational Business Finance.* As in previous editions, we perceive the multinational enterprise to be a unique institution that acts as a catalyst and a facilitator of international trade and as an important producer and distributor in host countries where its subsidiaries are located. The success of a multinational enterprise continues to be dependent on its ability to recognize and benefit from imperfections in national markets for products, factors of production, and financial assets.

Also carried over from earlier editions is the theme that volatile exchange rates may increase risk, but they also create opportunities for both investors and firms to profit, given a proper understanding of exchange rate risk management.

The tenth edition continues to recognize the increasing importance of global integration of money and capital markets, a trend that is creating expanded opportunities for both investors and organizations that need to raise capital. Although global integration of financial markets removes some market imperfections that impede the flow of capital internationally, excellent opportunities continue to exist for investors to increase their returns while lowering their risk through international portfolio diversification and for firms to lower their cost of capital by sourcing it internationally.

What Is New in the Tenth Edition?

- The chapter sequence has been reordered as a response to reviewer comments, with the balance of payments now added as a standalone chapter, followed by foreign exchange markets, derivatives, parity conditions, and foreign exchange rate determination.
- We have added three new decision cases—Stanley Works (taxation), Beijing International Club Corporation (international capital budgeting), and Gucci versus LVMH (hostile takeover bid)—and retained three others from the ninth edition.
- We have expanded the number of mini-cases to fifteen, and have continued to expand the number of comprehensive illustrative cases, as well as the number of practical global financial perspectives.
- End-of-chapter materials have been greatly enhanced, with new and expanded qualitative questions and quantitative problems for student review. The tenth edition of *Multinational Business Finance* now has over 300 questions and over 260 problems for review and testing purposes.
- All chapters have a separate set of Internet exercises in which students are directed to specific sources of information on the World Wide Web about current company, market, and business events. Many of these exercises have been designed to require the student to use real-time resources in the preparation of executive briefings and decision-based support.

- We have changed the focus of Chapter 1 to corporate financial goals and corporate governance, highlighting the global controversy following the Enron and WorldCom corporate failures.
- We have added a new chapter on political risk rather than having that material spread throughout the book.
- Emerging markets are emphasized throughout the book, including extensive coverage of the emerging market crises of 1997–2002. The perspective of multinational firms operating in emerging markets is included in chapters on cost and availability of capital, sourcing equity globally, capital budgeting, political risk, international acquisition, evaluation of performance, and working capital management.
- We have also written a shorter version of *Multinational Business Finance* entitled *Fundamentals of Multinational Finance* (2003, Addison Wesley Publishing). This shorter version allowed us to experiment with a number of new pedagogical features, some of which are incorporated into the tenth edition of *Multinational Business Finance.*

Supplements

The tenth edition features an enhanced supplements package. An Instructor's Resource Disk includes an Instructor's Manual, Test Bank, PowerPoint slides, and spreadsheet solutions to end-of-chapter problems and case material. A significantly expanded Test Bank includes multiple-choice and short-essay questions. The PowerPoint slides now constitute an even more useful teaching tool with the addition of lecture outlines.

In addition, students now have access to spreadsheet solutions to a selected set of end-of-chapter problems. They can download these spreadsheets from our Web site at www.aw.com/eiteman. Instructors have access to spreadsheet solutions for all problems via the Web site and the Instructor's Resource Disk.

Audience

The tenth edition of *Multinational Business Finance* is appropriate for the same audiences as those of the previous editions. Earlier editions have been widely used in international financial management courses in university degree programs, university-run executive education programs, and company management development programs.

Readers will find *Multinational Business Finance* most meaningful if they have the background knowledge or experience equivalent to a basic finance course. A previous course in international economics is desirable, but the text and web site supplements are designed to cover sufficient economic material so that a separate background is not essential.

Acknowledgments

The authors are very grateful to the numerous persons who have provided reviews as well as critical comments and suggestions to improve both the current and earlier editions of this book. The tenth edition has benefited immensely from comments we received on previous editions, both from formal reviews and from colleagues' replies to our surveys. The names of our reviewers and survey respondents appears on page viii through xiii.

Gratitude

Woven into the fabric of this book are ideas received from faculty and students at institutions all over the world where we have taught. These include our home universities of University of California, Los Angeles; Oregon State University; University of Hawaii; and Thunderbird. Our visiting stints have been at the Hong Kong University of Science and Technology; University of California, Berkeley; University of Michigan, Ann Arbor; Cranfield School of Management, United Kingdom; University of Hawaii at Manoa; Northern European Management Institute, Norway; Copenhagen Business School, Denmark; Aarhus School of Business, Denmark; Helsinki School of Economics and Business Administration, Finland; Institute for the Development of Executives, Argentina; National University of Singapore; International Centre for Public Enterprises, Yugoslavia; Beijing Institute of Chemical Engineering and Management; and Dalian University of Science & Technology, China. Further ideas came from consulting assignments in Argentina, Belgium, Canada, Denmark, Finland, Guatemala, Hong Kong, Indonesia, Japan, Malaysia, Mexico, the Netherlands, Norway, People's Republic of China, Peru, Sweden, Taiwan, the United Kingdom, and Venezuela.

We would like to extend our deep appreciation to our supplements authors for their excellent work: to Curt Bacon, Southern Oregon University, for his significant expansion of the Test Bank, and to Mark Bradt for his fine work in enhancing our PowerPoint slides with lecture outlines. We also give special thanks to Senior Adjunct Professor Frank Clauss, Ph.D., of Golden Gate University, for his development of the excellent spreadsheet exhibits in the text.

We would also like to thank all those with Addison Wesley who have worked so diligently on this tenth edition: Donna Battista, MaryClare McEwing, and Katherine Watson, as well as the superb team led by Sally Boylan at Argosy Publishing.

Finally, we would like to rededicate this book to our parents, the late Wilford and Sylvia Eiteman, the late Harold and Norma Stonehill, and Bennie Ruth and Hoy Moffett, who gave us the motivation to become academicians and authors. We thank our wives, Keng-Fong, Kari, and Megan, for their patience through the years spent preparing this edition.

Pacific Palisades, California D.K.E.
Honolulu, Hawaii A.I.S.
Glendale, Arizona M.H.M

LIST OF REVIEWERS

Special thanks to those who provided detailed input into the construction of the tenth edition through detailed book evaluations.

Bala Arshanapalli
Indiana University Northwest

Morten Balling
Arhus School of Business, Denmark

Kam C. Chan
University of Dayton

Chun Chang
University of Minnesota

San Chee
Boston University Metropolitan College

Nikolai Chuvakhin
Pepperdine University

Mara Faccio
University of Notre Dame

Anthony Matias
Palm Beach Atlantic College

Lawrence Tai
Loyola Marymount University

Sean Toohey
University of Western Sydney, Australia

ACADEMIC ADOPTERS SURVEYED

We take this opportunity to thank the following people for their responses to surveys of adopters of previous editions (affiliations are those at the time they provided their response):

Otto Adleberger
Essen University, Germany

Alan Alford
Northeastern University

Stephen Archer
Williamette University

Bala Arshanapalli
Indiana University, Northwest

Hossein G. Askari
George Washington University

Robert T. Aubey
University of Wisconsin at Madison

David Babbel
University of Pennsylvania

James Baker
Kent State University

Morten Balling
Aarhus School of Business, Denmark

Arindam Bandopadhyaya
University of Massachusetts at Boston

Ari Beenhakker
University of South Florida

Carl Beidleman
Lehigh University

Robert Boatler
Texas Christian University

Nancy Bord
University of Hartford

Finbarr Bradley
University of Dublin, Ireland

Tom Brewer
Georgetown University

Robert Carlson
Assumption University, Thailand

San Chee
Boston University Metropolitan College

Kevin Cheng
New York University

It-Keong Chew
University of Kentucky

Frederick D.S. Choi
New York University

Jay Choi
Temple University

Nikolai Chuvakhin
Pepperdine University

Mark Ciechon
University of California, Los Angeles

J. Markham Collins
University of Tulsa

Alan N. Cook
Baylor University

Kerry Cooper
Texas A&M University

Robert Cornu
Cranfield School of Management, U.K.

Roy Crum
University of Florida

Steven Dawson
University of Hawaii at Manoa

David Distad
University of California, Berkeley

Gunter Dufey
University of Michigan, Ann Arbor

Mark Eaker
Duke University

Rodney Eldridge
George Washington University

Vihang Errunza
McGill University

Cheol S. Eun
Georgia Tech University

Laura Field
Pennsylvania State University

William R. Folks, Jr.
University of South Carolina

Lewis Freitas
University of Hawaii at Manoa

Anne Fremault
Boston University

Fariborg Ghadar
George Washington University

Ian Giddy
New York University

Martin Glaum
Justus-Lievig-Universitat Giessen, Germany

Manolete Gonzales
Oregon State University

Deborah Gregory
University of Georgia

Robert Grosse
Thunderbird

Christine Hekman
Georgia Tech University

James Hodder
University of Wisconsin, Madison

Alfred Hofflander
University of California, Los Angeles

Janice Jadlow
Oklahoma State University

Veikko Jaaskelainen
Helsinki School of Economics and Business Administration

Ronald A. Johnson
Northeastern University

Joan Junkus
DePaul University

Fred Kaen
University of New Hampshire

Charles Kane
Boston College

Robert Kemp
University of Virginia

W. Carl Kester
Harvard Business School

Seung Kim
St. Louis University

Yong Kim
University of Cincinnati

Gordon Klein
University of California, Los Angeles

Steven Kobrin
University of Pennsylvania

Paul Korsvold
Norwegian School of Management

Chris Korth
University of South Carolina

Chuck C. Y. Kwok
University of South Carolina

Sarah Lane
Boston University

Martin Laurence
William Patterson College

Eric Y. Lee
Fairleigh Dickinson University

Donald Lessard
Massachusetts Institute of Technology

Wilbur G. Lewellen
Purdue University

Pat Maddox
Argelo State University

Arvind Mahajan
Texas A&M University

Rita Maldonado-Baer
New York University

Anthony Matias
Palm Beach Atlantic College

Charles Maxwell
Murray State University

Sam McCord
Auburn University

Tom McCurdy
University of Toronto

Jeanette Medewitz
University of Nebraska at Omaha

Robert Mefford
University of San Francisco

Paritash Mehta
Temple University

Antonio Mello
University of Wisconsin at Madison

Eloy Mestre
American University

Kenneth Moon
Suffolk University

Gregory Noronha
Arizona State University

John P. Olienyk
Colorado State University

Edmund Outslay
Michigan State University

Lars Oxelheim
Lund University, Sweden

Yoon S. Park
George Washington University

Harvey Poniachek
New York University

Yash Puri
University of Massachusetts at Lowell

Kumoli Ramakrishnan
University of South Dakota

R. Ravichandrarn
University of Colorado at Boulder

Scheherazade Rehman
George Washington University

Jeff Rosenlog
Emory University

David Rubinstein
University of Houston

Alan Rugman
Oxford University, U.K.

R.J. Rummel
University of Hawaii at Manoa

Mehdi Salehizadeh
San Diego State University

Charles Schell
University of Northern British Columbia

Lemma Senbet
University of Maryland

Roland Schmidt
Erasmus University, The Netherlands

Alan Shapiro
University of Southern California

Hany Shawky
State University of New York, Albany

Hamid Shomali
Golden Gate University

Vijay Singal
Virginia Tech University

Luc Soenen
California Polytechnic State University

Michael Salt
San Jose State University

Marjorie Stanley
Texas Christian University

Lawrence Tai
Loyola Marymount University

Jahangir Sultan
Bentley College

Kishore Tandon
CUNY - Bernard Baruch College

Russell Taussig
University of Hawaii at Manoa

Lee Tavis
University of Notre Dame

Norman Toy
Columbia University

Miguel Villanueva
Brandeis University

K.G. Viswanathan
Hofstra University

Joseph D. Vu
University of Illinois, Chicago

Michael Williams
University of Texas at Austin

Brent Wilson
Brigham Young University

Alexander Zamperion
Bentley College

Emilio Zarruk
Florida Atlantic University

Tom Zwirlein
University of Colorado, Colorado Springs

Industry (present or former affiliation)

Paul Adaire
Philadelphia Stock Exchange

Barbara Block
Tektronix, Inc.

Holly Bowman
Bankers Trust

Payson Cha
HKR International, Hong Kong

John A. Deuchler
Private Export Funding Corporation

Kåre Dullum
Gudme Raaschou Investment Bank, Denmark

Steven Ford
Hewlett Packard

David Heenan
Campbell Estate, Hawaii

Sharyn H. Hess
Foreign Credit Insurance Association

Aage Jacobsen
Gudme Raaschou Investment Bank, Denmark

Ira G. Kawaller
Chicago Mercantile Exchange

Kenneth Knox
Tektronix, Inc.

Arthur J. Obesler
Eximbank

I. Barry Thompson
Continental Bank

Gerald T. West
Overseas Private Investment Corporation

Willem Winter
First Interstate Bank of Oregon

David K. Eiteman

David K. Eiteman is Professor of Finance Emeritus at the John E. Anderson Graduate School of Management at UCLA. He has also held teaching or research appointments at the Hong Kong University of Science & Technology, Showa Academy of Music (Japan), the National University of Singapore, Dalian University (China), the Helsinki School of Economics and Business Administration (Finland), University of Hawaii at Manoa, University of Bradford (U.K.), Cranfield School of Management (U.K.), and IDEA (Argentina). He is a former president of the International Trade and Finance Association, Society for Economics and Management in China, and Western Finance Association.

Professor Eiteman received a B.B.A. (Business Administration) from the University of Michigan, Ann Arbor (1952); M.A. (Economics) from the University of California, Berkeley (1956); and a Ph.D. (Finance) from Northwestern University (1959).

He has authored or co-authored four books and twenty-nine other publications. His articles have appeared in *The Journal of Finance*, *The International Trade Journal*, *Financial Analysts Journal*, *Journal of World Business*, *Management International*, *Business Horizons*, *MSU Business Topics*, *Public Utilities Fortnightly*, and others. In addition to *Multinational Business Finance*, tenth edition, he has coauthored *Fundamentals of Multinational Finance* (first edition) with Arthur Stonehill and Michael Moffett.

Arthur I. Stonehill

Arthur I. Stonehill is a Professor of Finance and International Business, Emeritus, at Oregon State University, where he taught for 24 years (1966–1990). During 1991–1997 he held a split appointment at the University of Hawaii at Manoa and Copenhagen Business School. From 1997 to 2001 he continued as a Visiting Professor at the University of Hawaii at Manoa. He has also held teaching or research appointments at the University of California, Berkeley, Cranfield School of Management (U.K.); and the North European Management Institute (Norway). He was a former president of the Academy of International Business and was a western director of the Financial Management Association.

Professor Stonehill received a B.A. (History) from Yale University (1953); an M.B.A. from Harvard Business School (1957), and a Ph.D. from the University of California, Berkeley (1965). He was awarded honorary doctorates from the Aarhus School of Business (Denmark, 1989), the Copenhagen Business School (Denmark, 1992), and Lund University (Sweden, 1998).

He has authored or co-authored nine books and twenty-five other publications. His articles have appeared in *Financial Management*, *Journal of International Business Studies*, *California Management Review*, *Journal of Financial and Quantitative Analysis*, *Journal of International Financial Management and Accounting*, *The Investment Analyst* (U.K.), *Nationaløkonomisk Tidskrift* (Denmark), *Sosialøkonomen* (Norway), *Journal of Financial Education*, and others. In addition to *Multinational Business Finance*, tenth edition, he has coauthored *Fundamentals of Multinational Finance* (first edition) with David Eiteman and Michael Moffett.

Michael H. Moffett

Michael H. Moffett is Associate Professor of Finance at Thunderbird, the American Graduate School of International Management. He was formerly Associate Professor of Finance at Oregon State University (1985–1993). He has also held teaching or research appointments at the University of Michigan, Ann Arbor (1991–1993); the Brookings Institution, Washington, D.C., the University of Hawaii at Manoa; the Aarhus School of Business (Denmark); the Helsinki School of Economics and Business Administration (Finland); the International Centre for Public Enterprises (Yugoslavia); and the University of Colorado, Boulder.

Professor Moffett received a B.A. (Economics) from the University of Texas at Austin (1977); an M.S. (Resource Economics) from Colorado State University (1979); an M.A. (Economics) from the University of Colorado, Boulder (1983); and a Ph.D. (Economics) from the University of Colorado, Boulder (1985).

He has authored, co-authored, or contributed to eight books and a dozen other publications. His articles have appeared in the *Journal of Financial and Quantitative Analysis*, *Journal of Applied Corporate Finance*, *Journal of International Money and Finance*, *Journal of International Financial Management and Accounting*, *Contemporary Policy Issues*, *Brookings Discussion Papers in International Economics*, and others. He has contributed to a number of collected works, including the *Handbook of Modern Finance*, the *International Accounting and Finance Handbook*, and the *Encyclopedia of International Business.* He is also co-author of two books in multinational business with Michael Czinkota and Ilkka Ronkainen, *International Business* (seventh edition); *Global Business* (second edition); and *Fundamentals of International Business.* In addition to *Multinational Business Finance*, tenth edition, he has coauthored *Fundamentals of Multinational Finance* (first edition) with Arthur Stonehill and David Eiteman.

BRIEF CONTENTS

CONTENTS

PART 1

Global Financial Environment

PART 1

Part 1 is an introduction to the global financial environment in which the multinational enterprise (MNE) exists.

Chapter 1 describes what is different about international financial management. It starts with an analysis of the goals of management from an international perspective. The *shareholder wealth maximization* philosophy that is prevalent in the Anglo-American markets is compared to the *corporate wealth maximization* philosophy that is prevalent in many non-Anglo-American markets. The next section analyzes corporate governance, also from an international perspective. *Corporate governance* is the relationship among stakeholders used to determine and control the strategic direction and performance of an organization. It includes the role of agency theory, composition and control of boards of directors, and takeover defenses. Corporate governance varies by country because of cultural, historical, and institutional variables. Failures in corporate governance are common, as highlighted recently by examples in the United States. The final section explains how corporate governance is regulated in the United States, including the recent Sarbanes-Oxley Act of 2002.

Chapter 2 defines currency terminology. It describes the history of the international monetary system from 1876 to the present. It then compares contemporary currency regimes (systems) and the special case of emerging market currency regimes, including currency boards and dollarization. Chapter 2 concludes with a detailed examination of European monetary unification resulting in the launch of the new currency—the euro.

Chapter 3 examines the balance of payments. We analyze each account and the most important summary accounts. We explain why the balance of payments always "balances." It does so because of the net errors and omissions account and the official reserves account. We present the detailed U.S. balance of payments accounts for the 1993–2000 period. Chapter 3 ends with a description of historical patterns of capital mobility and capital flight, key components within the balance of payments.

Chapter 1

Financial Goals and Corporate Governance

THE BOOK IS ABOUT INTERNATIONAL FINANCIAL MANAGEMENT WITH SPECIAL EMPHASIS ON THE *multinational enterprise*. The multinational enterprise (MNE) is defined as one that has operating subsidiaries, branches, or affiliates located in foreign countries. It also includes firms in service activities such as consulting, accounting, construction, legal, advertising, entertainment, banking, telecommunications, and lodging.

MNEs are headquartered all over the world. Many of them are owned by a mixture of domestic and foreign stockholders. The ownership of some firms is so dispersed internationally that they are known as *transnational corporations*. The transnationals are usually managed from a global perspective rather than from the perspective of any single country.[1]

Although *Multinational Business Finance* (MBF) emphasizes MNEs, purely domestic firms also often have significant international activities. These include the import and export of products, components, and services. Domestic firms can also license foreign firms to conduct their foreign business. They have exposure to foreign competition in their domestic market. They also have indirect exposure to international risks through their relationships with customers and suppliers. Therefore domestic firm managers need to understand international financial risks, especially those related to foreign exchange rates and the credit risks related to trade payments.

What Is Different About Global Financial Management?

Exhibit 1.1 details some of the main differences between international and domestic financial management. These component differences include institutions, foreign exchange and political risks, and the required modifications of financial theory and financial instruments.

International financial management requires an understanding of cultural, historical, and institutional differences such as those affecting corporate governance.

1. Although *Multinational Business Finance* (MBF) is written in English and usually uses the U.S. dollar in the exposition, the authors have tried to make it relevant for all MNEs by using numerous non-U.S.-based MNEs as examples. In fact, almost half of MBF's sales are outside of the United States. Sales of MBF in the emerging markets of Asia, Latin America, and Eastern Europe make up a growing market segment.

Exhibit 1.1 What Is Different About International Financial Management?

Concept	International	Domestic
Culture, history, and institutions	Each foreign country is unique and not always understood by MNE management	Each country has a known environment; base case
Corporate governance	Foreign countries' regulations and institutional practices are all uniquely different	Regulations and institutions are well known
Foreign exchange risk	MNEs face foreign exchange risks due to their subsidiaries, as well as import/export and foreign competitors	Foreign exchange risks from import/export and foreign competition, but not from subsidiaries
Political risk	MNEs face political risks because of their foreign subsidiaries and high profile	Negligible political risks
Modification of domestic finance theories	MNEs must modify finance theories like capital budgeting and cost of capital because of foreign complexities	Base case
Modification of domestic financial instruments	MNEs utilize modified financial instruments such as options, futures, swaps, and letters of credit	Base case

Although both domestic firms and MNEs are exposed to foreign exchange risks, MNEs alone face certain unique risks that are not normally a threat to domestic operations, such as political risks.

MNEs also face other risks that can be classified as extensions of domestic finance theory. For example, the normal domestic approach to the cost of capital, sourcing debt and equity, capital budgeting, working capital management, taxation, and credit analysis needs to be modified to accommodate foreign complexities. Moreover, a number of financial instruments that are used in domestic financial management have been modified for use in international financial management. Examples are foreign currency options and futures, interest rate and currency swaps, and letters of credit.

In the rest of this chapter we examine how cultural, historical, and institutional differences affect a firm's choice of financial goals and corporate governance.

What Is the Goal of Management?

The introductory course in finance is usually taught within the framework of maximizing shareholders' wealth as *the goal of management*. This perspective is dominant not only in the Anglo-American-based courses, but also, to some extent, in basic finance courses taught in the rest of the world.[2] One has only to observe that the same textbooks, or translated versions, are used worldwide. Even when local authors write basic finance textbooks for their own national markets, they still often adopt the same prescriptive model that is used in the Anglo-American markets.

Although the idea of maximizing shareholder wealth is probably realistic both in theory and in practice in the Anglo-American markets, it is not always realistic elsewhere. Some basic

2. *Anglo-American* is defined to include the United States, United Kingdom, Canada, Australia, and New Zealand.

differences in corporate and investor philosophies exist between the Anglo-American markets and those in the rest of the world. Therefore one must realize that the so-called ***universal truths*** taught in basic finance courses are actually ***culturally determined norms.***

Shareholder Wealth Maximization

The Anglo-American markets are characterized by a philosophy that a firm's objective should follow the *shareholder wealth maximization* (SWM) model. More specifically, the firm should strive to maximize the return to shareholders, as measured by the sum of capital gains and dividends, for a given level of risk. Alternatively, the firm should minimize the risk to shareholders for a given rate of return.

The SWM model assumes as a universal truth that the stock market is efficient. The share price is always correct because it captures all the expectations of return and risk as perceived by investors. It quickly incorporates new information into the share price. Share prices, in turn, are deemed the best allocators of capital in the macro economy.

The SWM model also treats its definition of risk as a universal truth. *Risk* is defined as the added risk that the firm's shares bring to a diversified portfolio. The total operational risk of the firm can be eliminated through portfolio diversification by the investors. Therefore this *unsystematic risk*, the risk of the individual security, should not be a prime concern for management unless it increases the prospect of bankruptcy. *Systematic risk*, the risk of the market in general, cannot be eliminated. This reflects risk that the share price will be a function of the stock market.

Agency theory. The field of *agency theory* is the study of how shareholders can motivate management to accept the prescriptions of the SWM model.[3] For example, liberal use of stock options should encourage management to think like shareholders. Whether these inducements succeed is open to debate. However, if management deviates too much from SWM objectives of working to maximize the returns to the shareholders, the board of directors should replace them. In cases where the board is too weak or ingrown to take this action, the discipline of the equity markets could do it through a takeover. This discipline is made possible by the one-share-one-vote rule that exists in most Anglo-American markets.

Long-term versus short-term value maximization. During the 1990s, the economic boom and rising stock prices in the United States and abroad exposed a flaw in the SWM model, especially in the United States. Instead of seeking long-term value maximization, several large U.S. corporations sought short-term value maximization (e.g., the continuing debate about meeting the market's expected quarterly earnings). This strategy was partly motivated by the overly generous use of stock options to motivate top management. In order to maximize growth in short-term earnings and to meet inflated expectations by investors, firms such as Enron, Global Crossing, Adelphia, Tyco, and WorldCom undertook risky, deceptive, and sometimes dishonest practices for the recording of earnings and/or obfuscation of liabilities, which ultimately led to their demise.

3. Michael C. Jensen and W. Meckling, "Theory of the Firm: Managerial Behavior, Agency Costs, and Ownership Structure," *Journal of Financial Economics*, 3, 1976, and Michael C. Jensen, "Agency Cost of Free Cash Flow, Corporate Finance and Takeovers," *American Economic Review*, 76, 1986, pp. 323–329.

This destructive short-term focus by both management and investors has been correctly labeled *impatient capitalism*. This point of debate is also sometimes referred to as the firm's *investment horizon* in reference to how long it takes the firm's actions, investments, and operations to result in earnings.

In contrast to impatient capitalism is *patient capitalism*, which focuses on long-term shareholder wealth maximization. Legendary investor Warren Buffett, through his investment vehicle Berkshire Hathaway, represents one of the best of the patient capitalists. Buffett has become a multibillionaire by focusing his portfolio on mainstream firms that grow slowly but steadily with the economy, such as Coca Cola. He was not lured into investing in the high-growth but risky dot.coms of 2000 or the "high-tech" sector that eventually imploded in 2001.

Corporate Wealth Maximization

In contrast to the SWM model, continental European and Japanese markets are characterized by a philosophy that a corporation's objective should be to maximize *corporate wealth*. Thus a firm should treat shareholders on a par with other corporate interest groups, such as management, labor, the local community, suppliers, creditors, and even the government. The goal is to earn as much as possible in the long run, but to retain enough to increase the corporate wealth for the benefit of all interest groups. This model has also been labeled the *stakeholder capitalism model*.

Definition. The definition of *corporate wealth* is much broader than just financial wealth, such as cash, marketable securities, and unused credit lines. It includes the firm's technical, market, and human resources. "Consequently, it goes beyond the wealth measured by conventional financial reports to include the firm's market position as well as the knowledge and skill of its employees in technology, manufacturing processes, marketing and administration of the enterprise."[4]

The corporate wealth maximization (CWM) model does not assume that equity markets are either efficient or inefficient. It does not really matter because the firm's financial goals are not exclusively shareholder-oriented. In any case, the model assumes that long-term "loyal" shareholders should influence corporate strategy, not the transient portfolio investor.

The CWM model assumes that *total risk*—that is, operating and financial risk—does count. It is a specific corporate objective to generate growing earnings and dividends over the long run with as much certainty as possible, given the firm's mission statement and goals. Risk is measured more by product market variability than by short-term variation in earnings and share price.

Single versus multiple goals. Although the CWM model typically avoids a flaw of the SWM model, namely impatient capital that is short-run-oriented, it has its own flaw. Trying to meet the desires of multiple stakeholders leaves management without a clear signal about the tradeoffs. Instead, management tries to influence the tradeoffs through written and oral disclosures and complex compensation systems.

4. Gordon Donaldson and Jay Lorsch, *Decision Making at the Top: The Shaping of Strategic Direction* (New York: Basic Books, 1983), pp. 162–163.

The score card. In contrast to the CWM model, the SWM model requires a single goal of value maximization with a well-defined score card. In the words of Michael Jensen:

> *Maximizing the total market value of the firm—that is, the sum of the market values of the equity, debt and any other contingent claims outstanding on the firm—is the objective function that will guide managers in making the optimal tradeoffs among multiple constituencies (or stakeholders). It tells the firm to spend an additional dollar of resources to satisfy the desires of each constituency as long as that constituency values the result at more than a dollar. In this case, the payoff to the firm from the investment of resources is at least a dollar (in terms of market value).*[5]

Although both forms of wealth maximization have their strengths and weaknesses, two trends in recent years have led to an increasing focus on the shareholder wealth form. First, as more of the non-Anglo-American markets have increasingly privatized their industries, the stockholder wealth focus is seemingly needed to attract international capital from outside investors, many of whom are from other countries. Second, and still quite controversial, many analysts believe that shareholder-based MNEs are increasingly dominating their global industry segments. Nothing attracts followers like success. Global Finance Perspective 1.1 illustrates the movement toward shareholder wealth in Germany.

Global Finance Perspective 1.1

Changing Values: Satisfying Shareholders

Ulrich Hartmann, the chief executive of industrial giant VebaAG, is doing something unheard of in Germany: he's worrying about shareholder value. He has laid off thousands of workers, fired longtime managers, and closed divisions that date back to Veba's beginnings—all in the name of investors. "Our commitment," he said in last year's annual report, "is to create value for you, our shareholders."

The developments at Veba, Germany's fourth-largest company in revenue terms, underscore a trend catching hold in German boardrooms. Mr. Hartmann believes the trend will pick up in Germany, if only because the pursuit of shareholder value is in everyone's interest. "Satisfying the shareholders is the best way to make sure that other stakeholders are served as well," he says. "It does no good when all the jobs are at sick companies."

But the German public—used to a fabled "German model" of management that advocates describe as "capitalism with a human face"—remains deeply suspicious of the alternative way of doing business. "A number of people are left behind," says Norbert Wieczorek, a member of Germany's lower house of parliament and an economic expert with the opposition Social Democratic Party. "That's not the German way."

Mr. Hartmann is one of a new breed of German managers who are enthusiastically embracing the shareholder-value concept. Others are Juergen Dormann at Hoescht AG and Juergen Schrempp at Daimler-Benz AG. During a recent interview, a secretary interrupted the conversation to notify Mr. Schrempp of Daimler's opening stock price. "A year ago, no one in the company knew what the stock price was," he says. Now, he adds, the company keeps stockholders in mind with everything it does.

Driving companies to change are ever-growing capital requirements. Unable to raise enough money in Germany, companies are turning to foreigners. Nearly half the shares of drug companies Hoechst, Bayer AG, and Schering AG are owned by non-Germans, who want more than just a dividend check. "There is no German or French or American capital market anymore," says Veba's Mr. Hartmann. "It is a global capital market, and we all have to play by the same rules."

Source: Greg Steinmetz, "Changing Values: Satisfying Shareholders Is a Hot New Concept at Some German Firms," *The Wall Street Journal*, 3/6/96, pp. A1, A10.

5. Michael C. Jensen, "Value Maximization, Stakeholder Theory, and the Corporate Objective Function," *Journal of Applied Corporate Finance,* Fall 2001, Volume 14, No. 3, p. 12.

Operational Goals for MNEs

Whether a MNE is trying to maximize shareholder wealth or to maximize corporate wealth, it must be guided by operational goals suitable for various levels of the firm. Even if the firm's goal is to maximize shareholder value, the manner in which investors value the firm is not always obvious to the firm's top management. Many top executives believe that the stock market moves in mysterious ways and is not always consistent in its conclusions. Therefore most firms hope to receive a favorable investor response to the achievement of operational goals that can be controlled by the way in which the firm performs.

The MNE, because it is a collection of many business units operating in a multitude of economic environments, must determine for itself the proper balance between three common operational financial objectives:

1. Maximization of consolidated after-tax income;
2. Minimization of the firm's effective global tax burden; and
3. Correct positioning of the firm's income, cash flows, and available funds as to country and currency.

These goals are frequently inconsistent, in that the pursuit of one may result in a less desirable outcome in regard to another. Management must make decisions about the proper tradeoffs between goals about the future (which is why people, rather than computers, are employed as managers). The operational goals should be guided by an understanding of what variables create or destroy value as detailed in Global Finance Perspective 1.2.

The primary operational goal of the MNE is to *maximize consolidated profits, after tax*. *Consolidated profits* are the profits of all the individual units of the firm originating in many different currencies expressed in the currency of the parent company. Each of a multinational's foreign subsidiaries has its own set of traditional financial statements: 1) a statement of income, summarizing the revenues and expenses experienced by the firm over the year; 2) a balance sheet, summarizing the assets employed in generating the unit's revenues, and the financing of those assets; and 3) a statement of cash flows, summarizing those activities of the firm that generate and then use cash flows over the year. These financial statements are expressed initially in the local currency of the unit for tax and reporting purposes to the local government, but must be consolidated with the parent company's financial statements for reporting to shareholders.

Corporate Governance

The relationship among stakeholders used to determine and control the strategic direction and performance of an organization is termed *corporate governance*. Corporate governance is, in essence, the method by which an organization establishes order among the various stakeholders to ensure that decisions are made and interests are represented in line with the firm's stated objectives.

Dimensions of Corporate Governance

Corporate governance has many meanings, depending on the context in which the term is used, as shown in Exhibit 1.2.

Global Finance Perspective 1.2

What Drives Value?

The concept of *shareholder value* is often misunderstood by business executives and investors alike. Measurements of capital gains (share price movements) and dividends (current income distributions) do not tell the entire story of how shareholder value is created. Analysts and investors, however, look far beyond the basics of financial performance in their assessment of corporate value. They look to the knowledge assets of the firm.

Knowledge assets are the company's intangible assets, the sources and uses of its intellectual talent—its competitive advantage. Experts argue that there are at least 10 categories of knowledge assets:

1. Innovation
2. Quality
3. Customer care
4. Management skill
5. Alliances
6. Research and product/service development
7. Technology to streamline operations
8. Brand value
9. Employee relations
10. Environmental and community awareness

The investor is not looking at past performance as demonstrated by the numbers, but the prospects for the future—and their probable returns on investment. It is therefore critical for management to communicate their vision regarding the prospects for the future to investors and analysts. And what is it the analyst and investor want? They want transparency, honesty, and openness. They want management to demonstrate their ability to do what they say they will do. They want clearly defined strategies, measurable results, and a value proposition.

What Destroys Value?

Sometimes the most important thing to know is what *not* to do. Although there are countless books, periodicals, courses, and seminars to help key decision-makers define and refine their strategies and implementation plans, there are still lessons to be learned from past mistakes. A recent Forrester survey of Fortune 1000 global companies separated the primary causes of stock value losses (25% or more) into four categories—Strategic (58%), Operational (31%), Financial (6%), and Hazard (5%):

Strategic	
Customer demand shortfall	24%
Competitive pressure	12%
M & A integration problems	7%
Misaligned products	6%
Customer pricing pressure	4%
Loss of key customer	2%
Regulatory problems	1%
R & D delays	1%
Supplier problems	1%
Operational	
Cost overruns	11%
Accounting irregularities	7%
Management ineffectiveness	7%
Supply chain issues	6%
Financial	
Foreign macroeconomic issues	3%
High-input commodity prices	2%
Interest rate fluctuations	1%
Hazard	
Lawsuits	1%
Natural disasters	1%

Source: http://www.forrester.com

Agency theory. The term "corporate governance" has traditionally been used to describe how shareholders can contract with management to act on their behalf (value maximization). Management is motivated by positive incentives (options) and negative incentives (getting fired). The term also is used to describe how shareholders can contract with creditors, especially bondholders. Agency theory needs to be modified considerably to handle the complexities facing MNEs in their relationships with their own subsidiaries, branches, and affiliates, as well as with host foreign governments.

Exhibit 1.2 Dimensions of Corporate Governance

Agency Theory	Composition and Control of Boards of Directors	Cultural, Historical, and Institutional Variables
1. Shareholders contract with management	1. How many members should be *outsiders* versus *insiders*?	1. Dual classes of voting stock
2. Shareholders contract with creditors	2. Who should be on the audit committee?	2. Takeover defenses
3. Management contracts with foreign subsidiaries, joint ventures, and affiliates	3. Who should be on the compensation committee?	3. Family and government ownership
4. Management contracts with foreign host governments	4. Who should be on the nominating committee?	4. Emerging market complexities
	5. How to constrain nepotism, insider trading, and corruption?	

Composition and control of boards of directors. Corporate governance is now in the spotlight, because of the composition and control of corporate boards of directors. How many board members should be outsiders (not employed by the firm) compared to insiders (employees of the firm, including CEOs, COOs, and CFOs)? Who should be on the board's compensation committee? How can board-level nepotism, corruption, and insider trading be constrained? These questions need to be answered in all countries, not just in the highly publicized current situation in the United States.

Cultural, historical, and institutional variables. In every country, cultural, historical, and institutional variables influence how each government attempts to regulate, or does not regulate, corporate governance. For example, one might wonder why shareholders do not enforce their own objectives when management does not act as their agent. The answer is that the non-Anglo-American markets are not characterized by the corporate one-share-one-vote rule. On the contrary, dual classes of voting shares and restrictions on how many shares can be voted are the norm. Furthermore, many other anti-takeover defenses exist that make it difficult to replace management except by internal pressure from the board of directors.

Even without formal takeover defenses, the pattern of ownership and corporate governance in many countries has prevented the successful development of a market for corporate control. For example, in Germany and France, the largest proportion of gross domestic product originates from firms that are not publicly listed and whose shares are concentrated in few hands. Many of these firms remain private. Others are controlled by banks, other financial institutions, or other corporations. The banks often have a disproportionate influence, because they can vote the proxies of their trust accounts. In Japan, ownership of many groups or keiretsus is internal to the group itself. Each member owns shares of other members. A bank is typically closely involved, both in cross-ownership and as a prime lender. Therefore, an unfriendly merger or acquisition would be very difficult to implement in the ownership environments typified by Germany, France, or Japan.[6]

6. Steven Kaplan, "Corporate Governance and Corporate Performance: A Comparison of Germany, Japan, and the U.S.," *Journal of Applied Corporate Finance*, Winter 1997, Volume 9, No. 4, pp. 86–93.

The emerging market case is even more illustrative. Many of the most prominent firms are owned by families or the government, or by the relatives or friends of top government officials (so-called cronyism). They are often overstaffed, because of nepotism and political payoffs. They are often over-financed by banks that are also owned by the same elite group. The emerging market crisis, starting in Asia in 1997 (see Chapter 2), may have shaken this situation considerably, thus leading to more shareholder-friendly behavior.

It should also be noted that a number of large multinationals resident outside the Anglo-American countries have had to tap global equity and debt markets to maintain a competitive cost and availability of capital. Since they need to attract international portfolio investors, their behavior has become more shareholder-friendly than before. Some of these firms have even converted to the one-share-one-vote system in response to shareholder demands.[7]

Failures in Corporate Governance

Failures in corporate governance are common. Recent examples of failures in the United States include:

1. Enron—lack of full disclosure of off-balance-sheet debt and manipulation of energy markets.
2. WorldCom—capitalizing over $7.0 billion that should have been written off as operating expenses.
3. Global Crossing—hiding its overinvestment and operating losses while still promoting the stock.
4. Adelphia—management looted the firm through loans from the firm backed by the firm's own stock.

In each case, prestigious auditing firms, such as Arthur Andersen, missed the violations or minimized them, presumably because of lucrative consulting relationships or other conflicts of interest. Moreover, security analysts urged investors to buy the shares of these and other firms that they knew to be highly risky or even close to bankruptcy. Even more egregious, most of the top executives that were responsible for the mismanagement that destroyed their firms walked away with huge gains on shares sold before the downfall, and even overly generous severance payments.

Poor performance of management usually requires changes to management, ownership, or both. Exhibit 1.3 illustrates some of the alternative paths available to shareholders when dissatisfied with firm performance.

Regulation of Corporate Governance

The recent failures in corporate governance in the United States have spawned a flurry of government and private initiatives to prevent the same kind of future failures. Exhibit 1.4 explains the regulatory pyramid as it exists in the United States.

7. For example, in 2001, Nokia, the Finnish telecommunications company, converted all its share classes to one class with one-share-one-vote voting rights.

Exhibit 1.3 Potential Responses to Shareholder Dissatisfaction

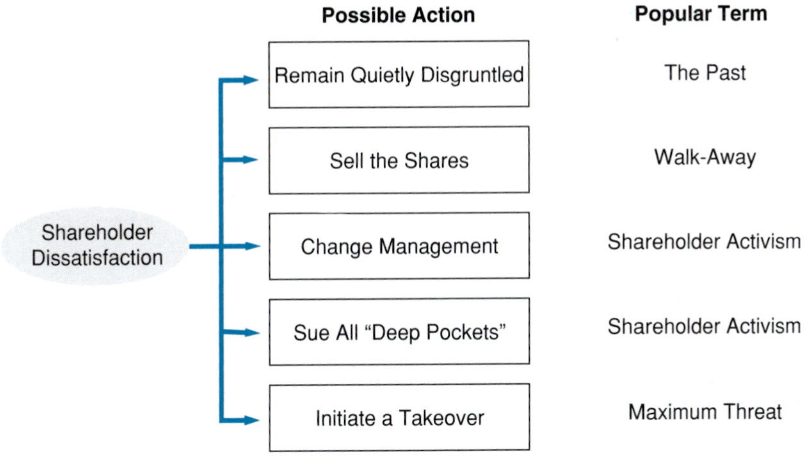

What counts is that the management of a publicly quoted company and its board of directors know that the company can become the subject of unfriendly legal suits or a hostile takeover bid if they fail to perform.

For a quick glimpse of who makes the rules that govern the markets, consult the regulatory pyramid.[8] The U.S. Congress sits on top and decides when the investment world (at least in the U.S.) requires new laws or organizations, such as the Securities Investor Protection Corporation (SIPC). Formed in 1971, the SIPC partially insures securities and cash in customer accounts against the failure of member brokerage firms. Down one level, the Securities and Exchange Commission (SEC) enforces anti-fraud statutes and policies, as well as compliance with laws that require the timely and accurate release of financial information by public companies. The SEC also regulates national exchanges, investment companies, over-the-counter brokerage firms, and all other participants in securities markets. The SEC also proposes new legislation, when necessary to protect the markets.

Self-regulatory organizations, including the New York Stock Exchange (NYSE), occupy the third tier. As self-regulator of the largest market center in the securities industry, the NYSE enforces standards of conduct for its members and member organizations. More than a third of the NYSE's employees work in regulation. The base of the pyramid consists of about 350 NYSE member brokerage firms, which buy and sell stocks for customers around the world and ensure that their employees are highly trained and meet rigorous industry standards. They are also responsible for obtaining the best execution for their customers.

8. This section is based on *Your Market: Straight Talk for Investors*, The New York Stock Exchange with Time, Inc. Custom Publishing, July 2002, p. 15.

Exhibit 1.4 The Corporate Regulatory Pyramid in the United States

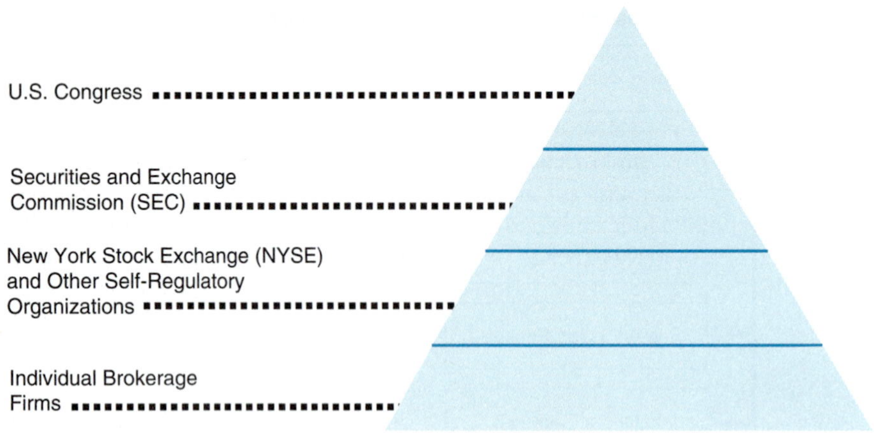

Source: Your Market: Straight Talk for Investors, The New York Stock Exchange with Time, Inc. Custom Publishing, July 2002, p. 15.

Beyond this framework, state regulators and attorneys general monitor and enforce business practices in their respective states. The Financial Accounting Standard Board (FASB) is an independent body that establishes and interprets conventions, rules, and procedures that the SEC expects public accountants to follow.

The Sarbanes-Oxley Act

The regulatory pyramid in the United States has already reacted to the recent failures in corporate governance. The United States Congress passed the Sarbanes-Oxley Act, which was subsequently signed by President George W. Bush on July 30, 2002. The Act has three major requirements: 1) the CEOs of publicly traded companies vouch for the veracity of the firm's published financial statements; 2) corporate boards must have audit committees drawn from independent directors; and 3) companies can no longer make loans to corporate directors. The Act goes on to spell out penalties for various levels of failure in corporate governance.

Although most of its terms are appropriate for the U.S. situation, Sarbanes-Oxley does conflict with some practices in other countries. For example, in Germany, supervisory board audit committees must include employee representatives—which by definition are therefore not independent. In fact, independent audit committees are almost unheard of in Europe or Asia. In Japan, outside auditors are chosen by shareholders, not the audit panel, as required by the Act.

Although a few companies such as Porsche have publicly decided not to list in the United States as a result of the requirements of Sarbanes-Oxley, a number of other major European and Asian multinationals—Unilever, Siemens, ST Microelectronics, ING, and Toyota, to name a few—have stated that they will be able to comply. A variety of German and Japanese lobbyists continue, however, to work toward amendments to the Act that would reduce those issues most troublesome for their constituent firms.

Governance, Rights, and the Future

The first years of the 21st century have seen a rebirth in society's reflections on business. One of the most audible debates has been that regarding sustainable development, the principle that economic development today does not compromise the ability of future generations to achieve and enjoy similar standards of living.[9] Although sustainable development initially focused on environmental concerns, it has evolved to include equal concerns that "incorporate the ambition for a just and caring society."[10] Although these debates have typically remained within areas of economic development, the debate in business circles has centered on corporate social responsibility. Global Finance Perspective 1.3 illustrates corporate social responsibility in practice.

Global Finance Perspective **1.3**

Corporate Sustainability

Recent reports from the Danish pharmaceuticals group Novo Nordisk, and Carrefour, a French food retailer, demonstrate the potentially wide practical impact of a company's commitment to sustainability.

Novo Nordisk (*Reporting on the Triple Bottom Line 2001*) identifies a wide range of "indicators" that measure its impact on the environment, people, and societies. Examples of areas covered include animal welfare, water and energy use efficiency, and compliance with regulatory limits. The report stresses the need to involve and educate employees; work internationally; define targets and report annually; balance financial, environmental, social, and health policies in the business decision processes; and conduct dialogue and partnerships with stakeholders.

The operational impact at Carrefour (*Sustainability Report 2001*) involves everything from fostering fair trade—the report cites 54 tonnes of "Carrefour organic" coffee sold in France last year that was bought in Mexico for 30 percent more than the market price—to reducing atmospheric emissions from cold storage units and a commitment to eliminate genetically modified organisms from animal feed in the company's product lines.

Source: Adapted from "Measuring the Impact of a New Approach," *Financial Times*, Monday, August 19, 2002, p. 5. Direct quote.

SUMMARY

- International financial management differs from domestic financial management because of differences in culture, history, and institutions; corporate governance; foreign exchange risk; political risk; and the need to modify domestic finance theories and financial instruments.
- The Anglo-American markets are characterized by a philosophy that a firm's objective should follow the *shareholder wealth maximization* (SWM) model.
- Agency theory is the study of how shareholders can motivate management to accept the prescriptions of the SWM model.

9. One of the first elaborations of the concept of sustainable development arose from the 1987 Brundtland Report sponsored by Gro Harlem Brundtland, Prime Minister of Norway.

10. Tim Dickson, "The Financial Case for Behaving Responsibly," *Financial Times*, Monday, August 19, 2002, p. 5.

- Firms that focus too much on short-term results are labeled *impatient capitalists*. Firms that focus on long-term shareholder wealth maximization are *patient capitalists*.
- In contrast to the SWM model, continental European and Japanese markets are characterized by a philosophy that a corporation's objective should be to *maximize corporate wealth* (CWM).
- The CWM model has multiple goals besides financial wealth, including maximizing the firm's technical, market, and human resources.
- Whether a MNE is trying to maximize shareholder wealth or corporate wealth, it must be guided by operational goals suitable for various levels of the firm. The most important operational goals are to maximize the firm's consolidated after-tax income; minimize its effective global tax burden; and correctly position the firm's income, cash flow, and available funds as to currency and country.
- The relationship among stakeholders used to determine and control the strategic direction and performance of an organization is termed *corporate governance*.
- Dimensions of corporate governance include agency theory; composition and control of boards of directors; and cultural, historical, and institutional variables.
- Failures in corporate governance, especially in the United States, have recently been in the spotlight and have been given partial blame for the decline in value of the U.S. stock markets.
- Shareholders who are dissatisfied with their firm's performance have five typical choices: remain quietly disgruntled; sell their shares; change management; sue all "deep pockets"; or initiate a takeover.
- The recent failures in corporate governance in the United States have spawned a flurry of government and private initiatives to prevent the same kind of future failures.
- The corporate regulatory pyramid in the United States includes the U.S. Congress, Securities and Exchange Commission (SEC), New York Stock Exchange (NYSE) and other self-regulatory organizations, and individual brokerage firms.
- The regulatory pyramid in the United States has already reacted to the recent failures in corporate governance by passing the Sarbanes-Oxley Act of 2002. The Act specifically asks the CEOs of firms to vouch for their financial statements and to create audit committees from independent directors. The Act, however, is inconsistent with the policies and practices employed in many other countries, and has been a point of contention for firms considering listing (or continued listings) in the United States.
- The coming decade may see a growing consensus of corporate leaders who see the objectives of the firm to include the environmental and social soundness of the firm's activities in addition to the pursuit of profit.

QUESTIONS

1. **Corporate goals: shareholder wealth maximization.** Explain the assumptions and objectives of the shareholder wealth maximization model.
2. **Corporate goals: corporate wealth maximization.** Explain the assumptions and objectives of the corporate wealth maximization model.
3. **Corporate governance.** Define the following terms
   a. Corporate governance
   b. The market for corporate control
   c. Agency theory
   d. Cronyism
   e. Stakeholder capitalism

4. **Operational goals.** What should be the primary operational goal of a MNE?

5. **Knowledge assets.** "Knowledge assets" are a firm's intangible assets, the sources and uses of its intellectual talent—its competitive advantage. What are some of the most important knowledge assets that create shareholder value?

6. **Labor unions.** In Germany and Scandinavia, among others, labor unions have representation on boards of directors or supervisory boards. How might such union representation be viewed under the shareholder wealth maximization model compared to the corporate wealth maximization model?

7. **Interlocking directorates.** In an interlocking directorate, members of the board of directors of one firm also sit on the board of directors of other firms. How would interlocking directorates be viewed by the shareholder wealth maximization model compared to the corporate wealth maximization model?

8. **Leveraged buyouts.** A leveraged buyout is a financial strategy in which a group of investors gain voting control of a firm and then liquidate its assets in order to repay the loans used to purchase the firm's shares. How would leveraged buyouts be viewed by the shareholder wealth maximization model compared to the corporate wealth maximization model?

9. **High leverage.** How would a high degree of leverage (debt/assets) be viewed by the shareholder wealth maximization model compared to the corporate wealth maximization model?

10. **Conglomerates.** Conglomerates are firms that have diversified into unrelated fields. How would a policy of conglomeration be viewed by the shareholder wealth maximization model compared to the corporate wealth maximization model?

11. **Risk.** How is risk defined in the shareholder wealth maximization model compared to the corporate wealth maximization model?

12. **Stock options.** How would stock options granted to a firm's management and employees be viewed by the shareholder wealth maximization model compared to the corporate wealth maximization model?

13. **Shareholder dissatisfaction.** If shareholders are dissatisfied with their company what actions can they take?

14. **Dual classes of common stock.** In many countries it is common for a firm to have two or more classes of common stock with differential voting rights. In the United States the norm is for a firm to have one class of common stock with one-share-one-vote rights. What are the advantages and disadvantages of each system?

15. **Emerging markets corporate governance failures.** It has been claimed that failures in corporate governance have hampered the growth and profitability of some prominent firms located in emerging markets. What are some typical causes of these failures in corporate governance?

16. **Emerging markets corporate governance improvements.** In recent years, emerging market MNEs have improved their corporate governance policies and become more shareholder-friendly. What do you think is driving this phenomenon?

17. **Corporate regulatory pyramid in the United States.** Describe the four tiers of regulators of U.S. securities markets.

PROBLEMS

Use the following formula for shareholder returns to answer questions 1 through 3, where P_t is the share price at time t, and D_t is the dividend paid at time t.

$$\text{Shareholder return} = \frac{P_2 - P_1 + D_2}{P_1}$$

1. **Shareholder returns.** If a share price rises from \$16 to \$18 over a one-year period, what was the rate of return to the shareholder if:
   a. The company paid no dividends?
   b. The company paid a dividend of \$1 per share?
2. **Shareholder choices.** Wilford Fong, a prominent investor, is evaluating investment alternatives. If he believes an individual equity will rise in price from \$62 to \$74 in the coming one-year period, and the share is expected to pay a dividend of \$2.25 per share, and he expects at least a 12% rate of return on an investment of this type, should he invest in this particular equity?
3. **Microsoft's dividend.** In January 2003, Microsoft announced that it would begin paying a dividend. The company stated that it would begin paying a dividend of \$0.16 per share beginning in 2003. Given the following share prices for Microsoft stock in the recent past, how would a constant dividend of \$0.16 per share per year have changed the company's return to its shareholders over this period?

First Trading Day	Closing Share Price
1998 (Jan 2)	\$131.13
1999 (Jan 4)	\$141.00
2000 (Jan 3)	\$116.56
2001 (Jan 2)	\$43.38
2002 (Jan 2)	\$67.04
2003 (Jan 2)	\$53.72

4. **Dual classes of common stock.** Dual classes of common stock are common in a number of countries. Assume that Powlitz Manufacturing has the following capital structure at book value:

Powlitz Manufacturing	Local Currency (millions)
Long-term debt	200
Retained earnings	300
Paid-in common stock: 1 million A shares	100
Paid-in common stock: 4 million B shares	400
Total long-term capital	1,000

The A shares each have 10 votes, the B shares each have 1 vote.

   a. What proportion of the total long-term capital has been raised by A shares?
   b. What proportion of voting rights is represented by A shares?
   c. What proportion of the dividends should the A shares receive?
5. **Corporate governance: Minority shareholder control.** In the mini-case following this chapter, "Corporate Governance at Brasil Telecom," voting control of Brasil Telecom was held by a partnership between Opportunity and Pension Funds. However, the Pension Funds were increasingly frustrated with Opportunity's leadership. Assume that the Pension Funds have decided to switch allegiance and align themselves with Telecom Italia.
   a. Calculate the new distribution of voting rights, preferred shares, and total shares in Solpart Participacoes.
   b. Which group would now control Brasil Telecom?
6. **Price/Earnings ratios and acquisitions.** During the 1960s, many conglomerates were created by a firm enjoying a high price/earnings ratio (P/E). They then used their highly valued stock to acquire other firms that had lower P/E ratios, usually in unrelated domestic industries. These conglomerates went out of fashion during the 1980s when they lost their high P/E ratios, thus making it more difficult to find other firms with lower P/E ratios to acquire.

   During the 1990s, the same acquisition strategy was possible for firms located in countries where high P/E ratios were common, compared to firms in other countries, where low P/E ratios were common. Assume the following hypothetical firms in the pharmaceutical industry.

   Pharm-USA wants to acquire Pharm-Italy. It offers 5,500,000 shares of Pharm-USA, with a current market value of \$220,000,000 and a

Pharm-Italy and Pharm-USA

	P/E ratio	Number of shares	Market Value per Share	Earnings	EPS	Total Market Value
Pharm-Italy	20	10,000,000	$20	$10,000,000	$1.00	$200,000,000
Pharm-USA	40	10,000,000	$40	$10,000,000	$1.00	$400,000,000

10% premium on Pharm-Italy's shares, for all of Pharm-Italy's shares.

a. How many shares would Pharm-USA have outstanding after the acquisition of Pharm-Italy?

b. What would be the consolidated earnings of the combined Pharm-USA and Pharm-Italy?

c. Assuming the market continues to capitalize Pharm-USA's earnings at a P/E ratio of 40, what would be the new market value for Pharm-USA?

d. What is the new earnings per share of Pharm-USA?

e. What is the new market value of a share of Pharm-USA?

f. How much did Pharm-USA's stock price increase?

g. Assume that the market takes a negative view of the merger and lowers Pharm-USA's P/E ratio to 30. What would be the new market price per share of stock? What would be its percentage loss?

7. **Corporate governance: overstating earnings.** A number of firms, especially in the United States, have had to lower their previously reported earnings due to accounting errors or fraud. Assume that Pharm-USA (in the previous problem) had to lower its earnings to $5,000,000 from the previously reported $10,000,000. What might be its new market value prior to the acquisition? Could it still do the acquisition?

Carlton Corporation

Problems 8 through 10 are based on the hypothetical MNE Carlton Corporation. Carlton is a U.S.-based multinational manufacturing firm, with wholly owned subsidiaries in Brazil, Germany, and China, in addition to domestic operations in the United States. Carlton is traded on the NYSE under the symbol CLT. Carlton currently has 650,000 shares outstanding. The basic operating characteristics of the various business units is shown in the table at the bottom of the page.

8. **Carlton Corporation's consolidated earnings.** Carlton must pay corporate income tax in each country in which it currently has operations.

   a. After deducting taxes in each country, what are Carlton's consolidated earnings and consolidated earnings per share in U.S. dollars?

   b. What proportion of Carlton's consolidated earnings arise from each individual country?

   c. What proportion of Carlton's consolidated earnings arise from outside the United States?

9. **Carlton EPS sensitivity to exchange rates.** Assume a major political crisis wracks Brazil, first affecting the value of the Brazilian real and subsequently inducing an economic recession in the country.

   a. What would be the impact on Carlton's consolidated earnings per share (EPS) if the Brazilian real were to fall to R$4.50/$, with all other earnings and exchange rates remaining the same?

Carlton Corporation

(000s, local currency)	USA (dollars, $)	Brazil (real, R$)	Germany (euros,€)	China (renminbi, Rmb)
Earnings before tax (EBT)	$4,500	R$6,250	€4,500	Rmb2,500
Corporate income tax rate	35%	25%	40%	30%
Average exchange rate for period	—	R$3.50/$	€0.9260/$	Rmb8.50/$

b. What would be the impact on Carlton's consolidated EPS if, in addition to the fall in the value of the real to R$4.50/$, earnings before taxes in Brazil fell to R$5,800,000 as a result of the recession?

10. Carlton's earnings and global taxation. All MNEs attempt to minimize their global tax liabilities. Return to the original set of baseline assumptions and answer the following questions regarding Carlton's global tax liabilities.

a. What is the total amount—in U.S. dollars—that Carlton is paying across its global business in corporate income taxes?

b. What is Carlton's effective tax rate on a global basis (total taxes paid as a percentage of pre-tax profits)?

c. What would be the impact on Carlton's EPS and global effective tax rate if Germany instituted a corporate tax reduction to 28%, and Carlton's earnings before tax in Germany rose to €5,000,000?

INTERNET EXERCISES

WWW.

1. **Multinational firms and global assets/income.** The differences across MNEs is striking. Using a sample of firms such as those listed here, pull from their individual web pages the proportions of their incomes which are earned outside their country of incorporation. (Note that Nestlé calls itself a "transnational company.")

Walt Disney	http://www.disney.com
Nestlé S.A.	http://www.nestle.com
Intel	http://www.intel.com
Daimler-Benz	http://www.daimlerchrysler.de
Mitsubishi Motors	http://www.mitsubishi.com
Nokia	http://www.nokia.com
Royal Dutch/Shell	http://www.shell.com

Also note the way in which international business is now conducted via the Internet. Several of the above listed pages allow the user to choose the language of the presentation viewed.

2. **Corporate governance.** There is no hotter topic in business today than corporate governance. Use the following site to view recent research, current events and news items, and other information related to the relationships between a business and its stakeholders.

Corporate Governance Net http://www.corpgov.net

3. **Fortune Global 500.** *Fortune* magazine is relatively famous for its listing of the Fortune 500 firms are in the global marketplace. Use *Fortune*'s web site to find the most recent listing of which firms from which countries are in this distinguished club.

Fortune http://www.fortune.com

4. ***Financial Times.*** The *Financial Times*, based in London (the global center of international finance), has a web site that possesses a wealth of information. After going to the home page, go to the Markets Data & Tools page, and examine recent stock market activity around the globe. Note the similarity in movement on a daily basis among the world's major equity markets.

Financial Times http://www.ft.com

SELECTED READINGS

Hofstede, Geert, Cheryl A. Van Deusen, Carolyn Mueller, Thomas A. Charles, and the Business Goals Network, "What Goals Do Business Leaders Pursue? A Study in Fifteen Countries," *Journal of International Business Studies*, Fourth Quarter, 2002, Volume 39, No. 4, pp. 785–803.

Jensen, Michael C., "Value Maximization, Stakeholder Theory, and the Corporate Objective Function," *Journal of Applied Corporate Finance*, Fall 2001, Volume 14, No. 3, pp. 8–21.

Kaplan, Steven, "Corporate Governance and Corporate Performance: A Comparison of Germany, Japan, and the U.S.," *Journal of Applied Corporate Finance*, Winter 1997, Volume 9, No. 4, pp. 86–93.

Pedersen, Torben, and Steen Thomsen, "European Patterns of Corporate Ownership," *Journal of International Business Studies*, Volume 28, No. 4, Fourth Quarter 1997, pp. 759–778.

MINI-CASE

Corporate Governance at Brasil Telecom

In the spring of 2001, the management of Brasil Telecom (BT) found itself in the middle of a bitter and disruptive competition—among its own owners. The two largest investors in BT, Telecom Italia and CVC/Opportunity (an investment banking firm), had very different ideas about where the Brazilian telecommunication industry was going, and how they as individual entities would attempt to exploit it. At a time when BT needed access to global capital markets, the in-fighting between owners was creating an image of a company not in control of its own destiny. BT's share price, listed on the New York Stock Exchange, was less than half of its peak of early 2000. BT's management team was faced with real challenges, in the marketplace and in the firm.

Privatization of the Brazilian Telecom Market

On July 29, 1998, Telebrás, the Brazilian telecom giant, was sold by the Brazilian government in 12 pieces to the highest bidders for a total of R$22 billion (US$19 billion). The auction, which was carried live on Brazilian television, yielded nearly US$5 billion more than expected. The sale of Telebrás was the second largest telecom privatization in history, falling second only to the US$70 billion sale of Japan's NTT in 1986.

The sale broke Telebrás into 12 separate units over the three basic dimensions of telecommunications services: 1) one long-distance and international operator, Embratel; 2) three fixed-line phone service companies; and 3) eight A-band cellular companies for mobile cellular communications. The bidding for Embratel became so heated and active between Sprint and MCI that the process reverted from sealed written bids to open outcry bidding on the floor of the Rio de Janeiro stock exchange. Each bidder sequentially bested the competitor in $8.5 million increments until Sprint withdrew at $2.2 billion.

Telebrás had a rather complex ownership structure, before and after privatization. The government of Brazil held 51.8% of the voting share rights to Telebrás, and sold this effective control through the auction. But most of Telebrás's equity (80%) was in the form of preferred non-voting shares. This meant that after privatization, roughly 49% of the voting shares and 80% of all shares would still be *free float* (traded publicly). This created a great deal of concern over what rights the minority shareholders would have in the post-privatization world. The government responded with additional restrictions and regulations requiring the new companies to hold votes of their entire shareholding body, voting and non-voting share owners, on any new service agreements.

Brasil Telecom

The Brazilian privatization process, meant to encourage diversity of ownership and a healthy competitive market, actually resulted in significant fragmentation. As a result of the Telebrás ownership structure and the auction process whereby a single buyer could purchase controlling interest, but not necessarily the entire business, a major bidder could gain control at roughly half the cost.

In the July 1998 sale, a consortium called Solpart purchased the Brazilian government's stake of Telebrás, gaining 51.8% control of the voting stock. Solpart was a consortium composed of Telecom Italia; a group of Brazilian pension funds who had partnered with CVC/Opportunity; and a telecom investment holding company owned outright by CVC/Opportunity. CVC/Opportunity was itself a partnership between Citibank Venture Capital (CVC) and the Brazilian investment banking firm Opportunity.

As a result, Brasil Telecom (BT) was controlled by two separate and powerful groups, Telecom Italia and CVC/Opportunity (Exhibit A). These two groups were increasingly at odds as to the appropriate growth strategies for BT, primarily because of the overall strategies of the two owners themselves. Although it appeared on a constructive voting-rights basis that Opportunity held control, this was dependent on its ability to maintain an alliance with the Pension Funds. The Pension Funds were increasingly frustrated with Opportunity's leadership.

Exhibit A The Ownership Structure of Brasil Telecom (BT)

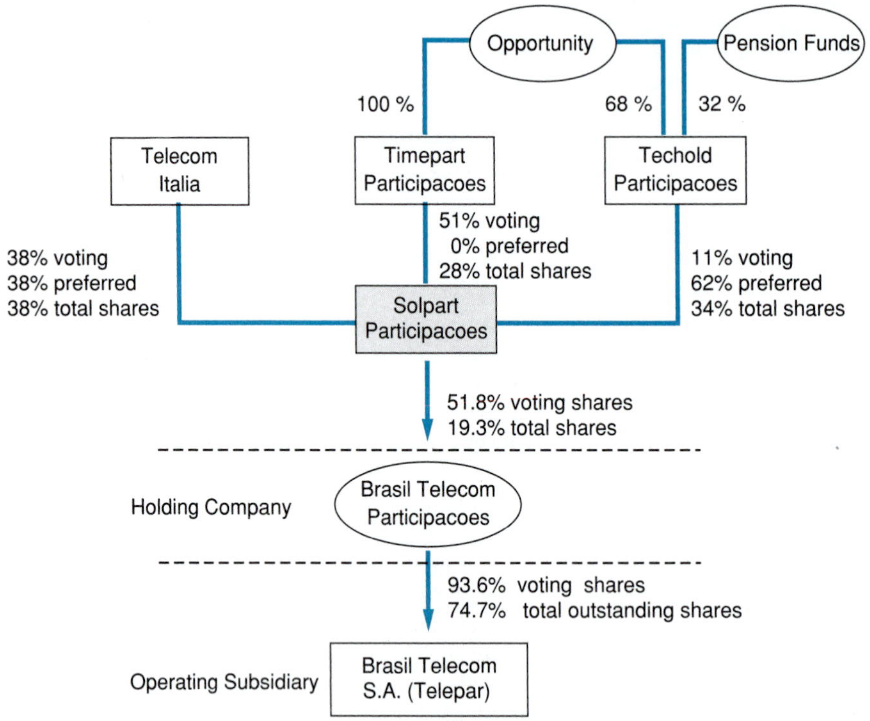

Growing Debate

BT had been very vocal throughout 2000 that it intended to meet government-mandated infrastructure targets early, probably by end of year 2001, so that it could expand services beyond its current coverage area to Regions I and III (Exhibit B), and international long distance early. Externally, the company planned a media campaign to promote its brand in new areas beyond current coverage. Internally, it was putting together an incentive plan for employees that would effectively double annual bonuses if the company met targets by end of year 2001.

Achieving the goals—either on-schedule or early—required BT to install lines in low population/low density areas, a high-cost low-return activity. If BT postponed these investments, it could redeploy the capital toward investments with higher expected returns. The $3 billion to $4 billion investment could not be postponed indefinitely, but time was money. The downside risk was that it could lose two years in its ability to expand to other areas and other telecom services.

By June 2001, BT's management was facing an industry in rapid consolidation and owners who could not agree on any avenue of action. Speculation turned from which directions in wireline and wireless to move to how to resolve the conflict between owners. The debate focused on meeting targets early and spending large sums of capital, versus staying on the previously accepted slower expansion schedule and allowing the market to continue its own consolidations and shakeouts. The first path was one of choice; the second appeared to be one of default.

Exhibit B **The Three Brazilian Wireline Regions**

Brasil Telecom recently confirmed market suspicions that there are differences of opinion among the company's main controllers—Telecom Italia and Opportunity—and the dispute has deepened over the last few months. This has generated uncertainty regarding the company's long-term operating strategy and whether it will be able to take part in the PCS [personal communication services] auction.

We believe that the conflict that exists between BT's controllers is negative for the company and adds to the risk associated with the share prices in the short term. In our opinion, these differences of opinion will not be resolved in the near future, as we believe that Telecom Italia will (1) wait until the PCS auctions are over to decide on whether or not it sells its stake in BT, and (2) make it as difficult as possible for BT to take part in the auctions . . .

As such, we are assuming a discount rate of 17% for BT, higher than the rate of 16% used for TNE [regional competitor]. Our target price of US$17.43 per ADR [American Depositary Receipt] indicates potential upside of 36%. However, we expect the performance of the stock to continue to be weak until conflicts between shareholders are solved.

Brazilian Telecoms, "Picking the Winners in Troubled Waters,"
Santander Central Hispano, January 2001

Case Questions

1. What do you believe a government expects to gain from privatizing major sectors like telecommunications?
2. Why would two major investors like CVC/Opportunity and Telecom Italia create a partnership to gain control of a firm and then be unable to agree on the firm's future strategy?
3. If you were in management at Brasil Telecom, how would the fighting between your owners alter your ability to do your job? What could you do to "manage your owners"?
4. If you were a minority investor in Brasil Telecom, holding some of the publicly traded shares, what rights do you believe you should have in the ownership-control debate?

Chapter 2

The International Monetary System

THE INCREASED VOLATILITY OF EXCHANGE RATES IS ONE OF THE MAIN ECONOMIC DEVELOPMENTS of the past 40 years. Under the current system of partly floating and partly fixed exchange rates, earnings of multinational firms, banks, and individual investors undergo real and paper fluctuations as a result of changes in exchange rates. Policies for forecasting and reacting to exchange rate fluctuations are still evolving as we improve our understanding of the international monetary system, accounting and tax rules for foreign exchange gains and losses, and the economic effect of exchange rate changes on future cash flows and market values.

Although volatile exchange rates increase risk, they also create profit opportunities for firms and investors, given a proper understanding of exchange risk management. In order to manage foreign exchange risk, however, management must first understand how the international monetary system functions. The international monetary system is the structure within which foreign exchange rates are determined, international trade and capital flows are accommodated, and balance-of-payments adjustments made. All of the instruments, institutions, and agreements that link together the world's currency, money markets, securities, real estate, and commodity markets are also encompassed within that term.

Currency Terminology

Let us begin with some basic terms in order to prevent confusion in reading this chapter:

- A *foreign currency exchange rate*, or simply *exchange rate*, is the price of one country's currency in units of another currency or commodity (typically gold or silver). If the government of a country—for example, Argentina—regulates the rate at which its currency—the peso—is exchanged for other currencies, the system or regime is classified as a fixed or managed exchange rate regime. The rate at which the currency is fixed, or pegged, is frequently referred to as its par value. If the government does not interfere in the valuation of its currency in any way, we classify the currency as *floating* or *flexible.*
- *Spot exchange rate* is the quoted price for foreign exchange to be delivered at once, or in two days for interbank transactions. For example, ¥114/$ is a quote for the exchange rate between the Japanese yen and the U.S. dollar. We would need 114 yen to buy one U.S. dollar for immediate delivery.

- *Forward rate* is the quoted price for foreign exchange to be delivered at a specified date in the future. For example, assume the 90-day forward rate for the Japanese yen is quoted as ¥112/$. No currency is exchanged today, but in 90 days it will take 112 yen to buy one U.S. dollar. This can be guaranteed by a *forward exchange contract.*

- *Forward premium* or *discount* is the percentage difference between the spot and forward exchange rate. To calculate this, using the quotes from the previous two examples, one formula is:

$$\frac{S-F}{F}\times\frac{360}{\text{n}}\times 100=\frac{¥114/\$-¥112/\$}{¥112/\$}\times\frac{360}{90}\times 100=7.14\%$$

  where S is the spot exchange rate, F is the forward rate, and n is the number of days until the forward contract becomes due.

- *Devaluation of a currency* refers to a drop in foreign exchange value of a currency that is pegged to gold or to another currency. In other words, the par value is reduced. The opposite of devaluation is *revaluation.* To calculate devaluation as a percentage, one formula is:

$$\text{Percentage change}=\frac{\text{Beginning rate}-\text{ending rate}}{\text{ending rate}}$$

- *Weakening*, *deterioration*, or *depreciation* of a currency refers to a drop in the foreign exchange value of a floating currency. The opposite of weakening is *strengthening* or *appreciating*, which refers to a gain in the exchange value of a floating currency.

- *Soft* or *weak* describes a currency that is expected to devalue or depreciate relative to major currencies. It also refers to currencies whose values are being artificially sustained by their governments. A currency is considered *hard* or *strong* if it is expected to revalue or appreciate relative to major trading currencies.

- Sometimes we view *Eurocurrencies* as another kind of money, although in reality they are domestic currencies of one country on deposit in a bank in a second country. Their value is identical to that of the same currency "at home." For example, a *Eurodollar* is a U.S. dollar–denominated interest-bearing deposit in a bank outside the United States. A *Euroyen* is a yen-denominated deposit in a bank outside Japan. The bank may be a foreign bank or the overseas branch of a U.S. or Japanese bank.

The next section presents a brief history of the international monetary system from the days of the classical gold standard to the present time. This history is followed by an analysis of contemporary currency regimes and the relative advantages of fixed versus floating rate systems. The most recent currency regime began with the launching of the euro, a common currency for 12 of the 15 countries that are members of the European Union. The chapter concludes with the regime choices facing emerging markets, including currency boards and dollarization.

History of the International Monetary System

Over the ages, currencies have been defined in terms of gold and other items of value, and the international monetary system has been the subject of a variety of international agreements. A review of these systems provides a useful perspective from which to understand today's system and to evaluate weaknesses and proposed changes in the present system.

The Gold Standard, 1876–1913

Since the days of the Pharaohs (about 3000 B.C.), gold has served as a medium of exchange and a store of value. The Greeks and Romans used gold coins and passed on this tradition through the mercantile era to the nineteenth century. The great increase in trade during the free-trade period of the late nineteenth century led to a need for a more formalized system for settling international trade balances. One country after another set a par value for its currency in terms of gold and then tried to adhere to the so-called "rules of the game." This later came to be known as the classical gold standard. The gold standard as an international monetary system gained acceptance in Western Europe in the 1870s. The United States was something of a latecomer to the system, not officially adopting the standard until 1879.

The "rules of the game" under the gold standard were clear and simple. Each country set the rate at which its currency unit (paper or coin) could be converted to a weight of gold. The United States, for example, declared the dollar to be convertible to gold at a rate of $20.67 per ounce of gold (a rate in effect until the beginning of World War I). The British pound was pegged at £4.2474 per ounce of gold. As long as both currencies were freely convertible into gold, the dollar/pound exchange rate was:

$$\frac{\$20.67\ /\ \text{ounce of gold}}{\pounds 4.2474\ /\ \text{ounce of gold}} = \$4.8665\ /\ \pounds$$

Because the government of each country on the gold standard agreed to buy or sell gold on demand with anyone at its own fixed parity rate, the value of each individual currency in terms of gold—and therefore exchange rates between currencies—was fixed. Maintaining adequate reserves of gold to back its currency's value was very important for a country under this system. The system also had the effect of implicitly limiting the rate at which any individual country could expand its money supply. Any growth in the amount of money was limited to the rate at which official authorities could acquire additional gold.

The gold standard worked adequately until the outbreak of World War I interrupted trade flows and the free movement of gold. This caused the main trading nations to suspend operation of the gold standard.

The Inter-War Years and World War II, 1914–1944

During World War I and the early 1920s, currencies were allowed to fluctuate over fairly wide ranges in terms of gold and each other. Theoretically supply and demand for a country's exports and imports caused moderate changes in an exchange rate about a central equilibrium value. This was the same function that gold had performed under the previous gold standard. Unfortunately, such flexible exchange rates did not work in an equilibrating manner. To the contrary, international speculators sold the weak currencies short, causing them to fall further in value than warranted by real economic factors. *Selling short* is a speculation technique in which an individual speculator sells an asset such as a currency to another party for delivery at a future date. The

Global Finance Perspective 2.1

Global Finance in History

The origins of the names of monies are sometimes not what one would guess. Here are the historical origins of a select few:

Name	Origins
krona	From the word meaning "crown" and simultaneously that of "gold" from the Latin *aureus.*
dollar	From the old German *Daler* or *Taler*, an abbreviation of the name given the silver coin *joachimsthaler*. The coin possessed the likeness of St. Joachim , and was first minted in 1519.
franc	From the Latin inscription of the coin first minted in 1360 by order of King John II of France, which read: *Johannes Dei Gracia Francorum Rex* (John by the Grace of God King of the Franks).
mark	From an old Norse term for unit of measure, a *mark*, used as early as the third century A.D. It was first employed by the Goths and later by the Germans.
peso	From the word meaning "weight." The *peso* was established in Spain in 1497 by King Ferdinand and Queen Isabella. The Spanish *peseta* was introduced as a companion coin to the *full peso* (the "piece of eight") referring to its value of eight *reales.*
pound	Pound is from the Roman *libra* or pound, money of account from early medieval times. The British pound is from the eighth century in Anglo-Saxon Britain, when the basic monetary unit called the *sterling* was defined as 1/240 of a pound of sterling silver.
lira	The Italian *lira* from *libra* was first minted in 1472 by the Doge Nicolas Tron of Venice. This was also known as the *testone* or "head" because it depicted the head of Doge Nicolas.
yen	From Japanese meaning "round," and basically borrowed from the Chinese term *yuan* also meaning round.

speculator, however, does not yet own the asset, expecting the price of the asset to fall by the date when the asset must be purchased in the open market by the speculator for delivery.

The reverse happened with strong currencies. Fluctuations in currency values could not be offset by the relatively illiquid forward exchange market except at exorbitant cost. The net result was that the volume of world trade did not grow in the 1920s in proportion to world gross national product, but instead declined to a very low level with the advent of the Great Depression in the 1930s.

The United States adopted a modified gold standard in 1934 when the U.S. dollar was devalued to $35 per ounce of gold from the $20.67 per ounce price in effect prior to World War I. Contrary to previous practice, the U.S. Treasury traded gold only with foreign central banks, not private citizens. From 1934 to the end of World War II, exchange rates were theoretically determined by each currency's value in terms of gold. During World War II and its chaotic aftermath, however, many of the main trading currencies lost their convertibility into other currencies. The dollar was the only major trading currency that continued to be convertible.

Bretton Woods and the International Monetary Fund, 1944

As World War II drew toward a close in 1944, the Allied Powers met at Bretton Woods, New Hampshire, in order to create a new post-war international monetary system. The Bretton Woods Agreement established a U.S. dollar–based international monetary system and provided for two new institutions, the International Monetary Fund and the World Bank. The International

Monetary Fund (IMF) aids countries with balance of payments and exchange rate problems. The International Bank for Reconstruction and Development (World Bank) helped fund post-war reconstruction and since then has supported general economic development.

The IMF was the key institution in the new international monetary system, and it has remained so to the present. The IMF was established to render temporary assistance to member countries trying to defend their currencies against cyclical, seasonal, or random occurrences. It also assists countries having structural trade problems if they promise to take adequate steps to correct their problems. If persistent deficits occur, however, the IMF cannot save a country from eventual devaluation. In recent years, it has attempted to help countries facing financial crises. It has provided massive loans as well as advice to Russia and other former Russian republics, Brazil, Indonesia, Turkey, Argentina, and South Korea, to name but a few.

Under the original provisions of the Bretton Woods Agreement, all countries fixed the value of their currencies in terms of gold but were not required to exchange their currencies for gold. Only the dollar remained convertible into gold (at $35 per ounce). Therefore each country established its exchange rate vis-à-vis the dollar, and then calculated the gold par value of its currency to create the desired dollar exchange rate. Participating countries agreed to try to maintain the value of their currencies within 1% (later expanded to 2¼%) of par by buying or selling foreign exchange or gold as needed. Devaluation was not to be used as a competitive trade policy, but if a currency became too weak to defend, a devaluation of up to 10% was allowed without formal approval by the IMF. Larger devaluations required IMF approval.

The *Special Drawing Right* (SDR) is an international reserve asset created by the IMF to supplement existing foreign exchange reserves. It serves as a unit of account for the IMF and other international and regional organizations and is also the base against which some countries peg the exchange rate for their currencies.

Defined initially in terms of a fixed quantity of gold, the SDR has been redefined several times. It is currently the weighted value of currencies of the U.S. dollar, euro, Japanese yen and U.K. pound. Individual countries hold SDRs in the form of deposits in the IMF. These holdings are part of each country's international monetary reserves, along with official holdings of gold, foreign exchange, and its reserve position at the IMF. Members may settle transactions among themselves by transferring SDRs.

Fixed Exchange Rates, 1945–1973

The currency arrangement negotiated at Bretton Woods and monitored by the IMF worked fairly well during the post–World War II period of reconstruction and rapid growth in world trade. However, widely diverging national monetary and fiscal policies, differential rates of inflation and various unexpected external shocks eventually resulted in the system's demise. The U.S. dollar was the main reserve currency held by central banks and was the key to the web of exchange rate values. Unfortunately the United States ran persistent and growing deficits in its balance of payments. A heavy capital outflow of dollars was required to finance these deficits and to meet the growing demand for dollars from investors and businesses. Eventually the heavy overhang of dollars held by foreigners resulted in a lack of confidence in the ability of the United States to meet its commitment to convert dollars to gold.

This lack of confidence forced President Richard Nixon to suspend official purchases or sales of gold by the U.S. Treasury on August 15, 1971, after the United States suffered outflows of roughly one-third of its official gold reserves in the first seven months of the year. Exchange rates of most of the leading trading countries were allowed to float in relation to the dollar and thus indirectly in relation to gold. By the end of 1971, most of the major trading currencies had appreciated vis-à-vis the dollar. This change was—in effect—a devaluation of the dollar.

A year and a half later the U.S. dollar once again came under attack, thereby forcing a second devaluation on February 12, 1973, this time by 10% to $42.22 per ounce of gold. By late February 1973, a fixed-rate system no longer appeared feasible given the speculative flows of currencies. The major foreign exchange markets were actually closed for several weeks in March 1973. When they reopened, most currencies were allowed to float to levels determined by market forces. Par values were left unchanged. The dollar floated downward approximately 10% by June 1973.

An Eclectic Currency Arrangement, 1973–Present

Since March 1973, exchange rates have become much more volatile and less predictable than they were during the "fixed" exchange rate period, when changes occurred infrequently. Exhibit 2.1 illustrates the wide swings exhibited by one of the oldest and fundamental currency rates, the U.S. dollar to British pound exchange rate. The dollar/pound rate has historically been called "cable" as a result of its early trading via the Trans-Atlantic cable that first connected London and New York over a century ago. The U.S. dollar to British pound exchange rate fluctuations mirror similar volatility between other exchange rate pairs.

Exhibit 2.2 summarizes the key events and external shocks that have affected currency values since March 1973. The most important shocks in recent years have been the European Monetary

Exhibit 2.1 The U.S. Dollar–British Pound Exchange Rate, 1971–2001

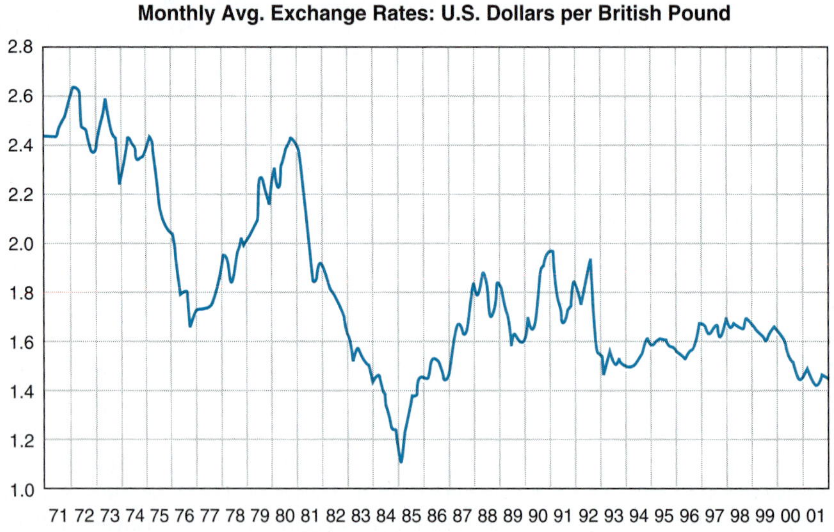

Source: Pacific Currency Exchange, http://pacific.commerce.ubc.ca/xr © 2001 by Prof. Werner Antweiler, University of British Columbia, Vancouver, BC, Canada.

Exhibit 2.2 World Currency Events, 1971–2002

Date	Event	Impact
August 1971	Dollar floated	Nixon closes the U.S. gold window, suspending purchases or sales of gold by U.S. Treasury; temporary imposition of 10% import surcharge
December 1971	Smithsonian Agreement	Group of Ten reaches compromise whereby the US$ is devalued to $38/oz. of gold; most other major currencies are appreciated versus US$
February 1973	U.S. dollar devalued	Devaluation pressure increases on US$ forcing further devaluation to $42.22/oz. of gold
Feb–March 1973	Currency markets in crisis	Fixed exchange rates no longer considered defensible; speculative pressures force closure of international foreign exchange markets for nearly two weeks; markets reopen on floating rates for major industrial currencies
June 1973	U.S. dollar depreciation	Floating rates continue to drive the now freely floating US$ down by about 10% by June
Fall 1973–1974	OPEC oil embargo	Organization of Petroleum Exporting Countries (OPEC) imposes oil embargo, eventually quadrupling the world price of oil; because world oil prices are stated in US$, value of US$ recovers some former strength
January 1976	Jamaica Agreement	IMF meeting in Jamaica results in the "legalization" of the floating exchange rate system already in effect; gold is demonetized as a reserve asset
1977–1978	U.S. inflation rate rises	Carter administration reduces unemployment at the expense of inflation increases; rising U.S. inflation causes continued depreciation of the US$
March 1979	EMS created	European Monetary System (EMS) is created, establishing a cooperative exchange rate system for participating members of the EEC
Summer 1979	OPEC raises prices	OPEC nations raise price of oil once again
Spring 1980	U.S. dollar begins rise	Worldwide inflation and early signs of recession coupled with real interest differential advantages for dollar-denominated assets contribute to increased demand for dollars
August 1982	Latin American Debt Crisis	Mexico informs U.S. Treasury that it will be unable to make debt service payments; Brazil and Argentina follow within months
February 1985	U.S. dollar peaks	The U.S. dollar peaks against most major industrial currencies, hitting record highs against the Deutschemark and other European currencies
February 1987	Louvre Accords	Group of Six members state they will "intensify" economic policy coordination to promote growth and reduce external imbalances
September 1992	EMS crisis	High German interest rates induce massive capital flows into Deutschemark-denominated assets causing the withdrawal of the Italian lira and British pound from the EMS's common float
July 31, 1993	EMS realignment	EMS adjusts allowable deviation band to ±15% for all member countries (except the Dutch guilder); U.S. dollar continues to weaken; Japanese yen reaches ¥100.25/$
January 1994	EMI founded	European Monetary Institute (EMI), the predecessor to the European Central Bank, is founded in Frankfurt, Germany

(continued)

Exhibit 2.2 World Currency Events, 1971–2002 (continued)

Date	Event	Impact
December 1994	Peso collapse	Mexican peso suffers major devaluation as a result of increasing pressure on the managed devaluation policy; peso falls from Ps3.46/$ to Ps5.50/$ within days; the peso's collapse results in a fall in most major Latin American exchanges in a contagion process—the tequila effect
August 1995	Yen peaks	Japanese yen reaches an all-time high versus the U.S. dollar of ¥79/$; yen slowly depreciates over the following two-year period, rising to over ¥130/$
June 1997	Asian crisis	Thai baht is devalued in July, followed soon after by the Indonesian rupiah, Korean won, Malaysian ringgit, and Philippine peso; following initial exchange rate devaluations, Asian economy plummets into recession
August 1998	Russian crisis	On Monday August 17, the Russian Central Bank devalues the rouble by 34%; rouble continues to deteriorate in the following days sending already weak Russian economy into recession
January 1, 1999	Euro launched	Official launch date for the single European currency, the euro; 11 European Union member states elect to participate in the system, which irrevocably locks their individual currencies rates between them
January 1999	Brazilian real crisis	Brazilian real, initially devalued 8.3% by the Brazilian government on January 12, is allowed to float against the world's currencies
February 2001	Turkish lira	Turkish lira floated due to balance of payments imbalances, rising external debt, and capital flight
January 1, 2002	Euro coinage	Euro coins and notes are introduced in parallel with home currencies; national currencies are phased out during the six-month period beginning January 1
January 8, 2002	Argentine peso crisis	Argentine peso, its value fixed to the U.S. dollar at 1:1 since 1991 through a currency board, is devalued to Ps1.4/$; the devaluation follows months of turmoil, the ouster of three presidents in three weeks, continuing bank holidays, and riots in the streets of Buenos Aires

System (EMS) restructuring in 1992 and 1993; the emerging market currency crises, including that of Mexico in 1994, Thailand (and a number of other Asian countries) in 1997, Russia in 1998, Brazil in 1999, and Turkey in 2001; the introduction of the euro in 1999; and Argentina and Venezuela in 2002.

Contemporary Currency Regimes

The international monetary system today is composed of national currencies, artificial currencies (such as the SDR), and one entirely new currency (the euro) that has now replaced 12 national European Union currencies. All of these currencies are linked to one another via a smorgasbord of currency regimes.

The IMF's Exchange Rate Regime Classifications

The International Monetary Fund classifies all exchange rate regimes into eight specific categories (listed here with the number of participating countries as of October 2001). The eight categories span the spectrum of exchange rate regimes from rigidly fixed to independently floating:

1. **Exchange Arrangements with No Separate Legal Tender (39):** The currency of another country circulates as the sole legal tender or the member belongs to a monetary or currency union in which the same legal tender is shared by the members of the union.

2. **Currency Board Arrangements (8):** A monetary regime based on an implicit legislative commitment to exchange domestic currency for a specified foreign currency at a fixed exchange rate, combined with restrictions on the issuing authority to ensure the fulfillment of its legal obligation.

3. **Other Conventional Fixed Peg Arrangements (44):** The country pegs its currency (formally or *de facto*) at a fixed rate to a major currency or a basket of currencies (a *composite*), where the exchange rate fluctuates within a narrow margin or at most ±1% around a central rate.

4. **Pegged Exchange Rates within Horizontal Bands (6):** The value of the currency is maintained within margins of fluctuation around a formal or *de facto* fixed peg that are wider than ±1% around a central rate.

5. **Crawling Pegs (4):** The currency is adjusted periodically in small amounts at a fixed, pre-announced rate or in response to changes in selective quantitative indicators.

6. **Exchange Rates within Crawling Pegs (5):** The currency is maintained within certain fluctuation margins around a central rate that is adjusted periodically at a fixed pre-announced rate or in response to change in selective quantitative indicators.

7. **Managed Floating with No Pre-Announced Path for the Exchange Rate (33):** The monetary authority influences the movements of the exchange rate through active intervention in the foreign exchange market without specifying or pre-committing to a pre-announced path for the exchange rate.

8. **Independent Floating (47):** The exchange rate is market-determined, with any foreign exchange intervention aimed at moderating the rate of change and preventing undue fluctuations in the exchange rate, rather than at establishing a level for it.

The most prominent example of a rigidly fixed system is the euro area, in which the euro is the single currency for its member countries. However, the euro itself is an independently floating currency against all other currencies. Other examples of rigidly fixed exchange regimes include Ecuador and Panama, which use the U.S. dollar as their official currency, the Central African Franc (CFA) zone, in which countries such as Mali, Niger, Senegal, Cameroon, and Chad, among others, use a single common currency (the franc, even though the French franc itself is no more), and the Eastern Caribbean Currency Union (ECCU), whose members use a single common currency (the Eastern Caribbean dollar).

At the other extreme are 47 countries with independently floating currencies. These include many of the most developed countries such as Japan, the United States, the United Kingdom,

Canada, Australia, New Zealand, Sweden, and Switzerland. However, this category also includes a number of unwilling participants—emerging market countries that tried to maintain fixed rates but were forced by the marketplace to let them float. Among these are Korea, the Philippines, Brazil, Indonesia, Mexico, and Thailand.

It is important to note that only the last two categories, 80 of the total 186 country-currencies listed, are actually "floating" in any real degree. Although the contemporary international monetary system is typically referred to as a "floating regime," it is clearly not the case for the majority of the world's nations.

Fixed Versus Flexible Exchange Rates

A nation's choice as to which currency regime to follow reflects national priorities about all facets of the economy, including inflation, unemployment, interest rate levels, trade balances, and economic growth. The choice between fixed and flexible rates may change over time as priorities change.

At the risk of overgeneralizing, the following points partly explain why countries pursue certain exchange rate regimes. They are based on the premise that, other things being equal, countries would prefer fixed exchange rates.

- Fixed rates provide stability in international prices for the conduct of trade. Stable prices aid in the growth of international trade and lessen risks for all businesses.
- Fixed exchange rates are inherently anti-inflationary, requiring the country to follow restrictive monetary and fiscal policies. This restrictiveness, however, can often be a burden to a country wishing to pursue policies that alleviate continuing internal economic problems, such as high unemployment or slow economic growth.
- Fixed exchange rate regimes necessitate that central banks maintain large quantities of international reserves (hard currencies and gold) for use in the occasional defense of the fixed rate. As international currency markets have grown rapidly in size and volume, increasing reserve holdings has become a significant burden to many nations.
- Fixed rates, once in place, can be maintained at rates that are inconsistent with economic fundamentals. As the structure of a nation's economy changes and its trade relationships and balances evolve, the exchange rate itself should change. Flexible exchange rates allow this to happen gradually and efficiently, but fixed rates must be changed administratively—usually too late, too highly publicized, and at too large a one-time cost to the nation's economic health.

Attributes of the "Ideal" Currency

If the ideal currency existed in today's world, it would possess three attributes (illustrated in Exhibit 2.3), often referred to as *the Impossible Trinity*:

1. **Exchange rate stability:** The value of the currency would be fixed in relationship to other major currencies, so traders and investors could be relatively certain of the foreign exchange value of each currency in the present and into the near future.

Exhibit 2.3 The Impossible Trinity

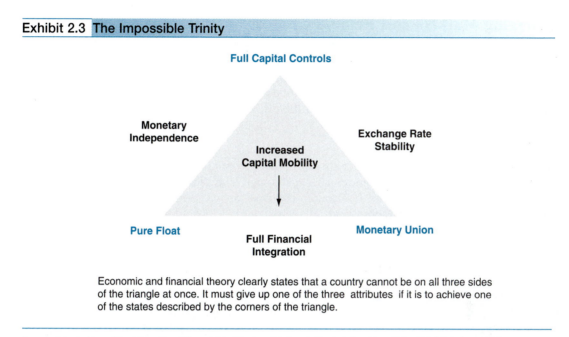

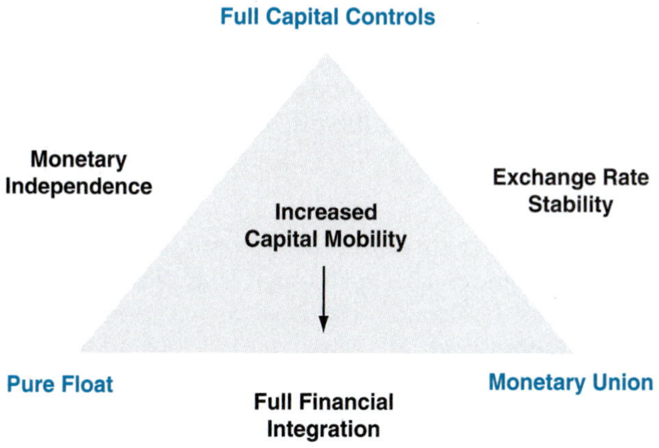

Economic and financial theory clearly states that a country cannot be on all three sides of the triangle at once. It must give up one of the three attributes if it is to achieve one of the states described by the corners of the triangle.

Source: Adapted from "The International Financial Architecture," Jeffrey A. Frankel, *Brookings Policy Brief #51*, June 1999.

2. **Full financial integration:** Complete freedom of monetary flows would be allowed, so traders and investors could willingly and easily move funds from one country and currency to another in response to perceived economic opportunities or risks.
3. **Monetary independence:** Domestic monetary and interest rate policies would be set by each individual country to pursue desired national economic policies, especially as they might relate to limiting inflation, combating recessions, and fostering prosperity and full employment.

The reason these qualities are termed "The Impossible Trinity" is that a country must give up one of the three goals described by the sides of the triangle: monetary independence, exchange rate stability, or full financial integration. The forces of economics do not allow the simultaneous achievement of all three. For example, a country with a pure float exchange rate regime can have monetary independence and a high degree of financial integration with the outside capital markets, but the result must be a loss of exchange rate stability (as in the case of the United States). Similarly, a country which maintains very tight controls over the inflow and outflow of capital will retain its monetary independence and a stable exchange rate, at the loss of being integrated with global financial and capital markets (as in the case of Malaysia in the 1998–2002 period).

As illustrated in Exhibit 2.3, the consensus of many experts is that the force of increased capital mobility has been pushing more and more countries toward full financial integration in an attempt to stimulate their domestic economies and feed the capital appetites of their own MNEs. As a result, their currency regimes are being "cornered" into being either purely floating (like the United States) or integrated with other countries in monetary unions (like the European Union).

Emerging Markets and Regime Choices

The 1997–2002 period saw increasing pressures on emerging market countries to choose among more extreme types of exchange rate regimes. The increased capital mobility pressures noted in the previous section have driven a number of countries to choose between a free-floating exchange rate (such as Turkey in February 2002) and the opposite extreme, a fixed-rate regime—a *currency board* (Argentina) or even *dollarization* (as in the case of Ecuador in 2000).

Currency Boards

A *currency board* exists when a country's central bank commits to back its monetary base—its money supply—entirely with foreign reserves at all times. This means that a unit of domestic currency cannot be introduced into the economy without an additional unit of foreign exchange reserves being obtained first. Eight countries, including Hong Kong, utilize currency boards as a means of fixing their exchange rates.

Argentina. In 1991, Argentina moved from its previous managed exchange rate of the Argentine peso to a currency board. The currency board structure fixed the Argentine peso's value to the U.S. dollar on a one-to-one basis. The Argentine government preserved the fixed rate of exchange by requiring that every peso issued through the Argentine banking system be backed by either gold or U.S. dollars held on account in banks in Argentina. This 100% reserve system made the monetary policy of Argentina depend on the country's ability to obtain U.S. dollars through trade or investment. Only after Argentina had earned these dollars through trade could its money supply be expanded. This eliminated the possibility of the nation's money supply growing too rapidly and causing inflation.

An additional feature of the Argentine currency board system was the ability of all Argentines or foreigners to hold dollar-denominated accounts in Argentine banks. These accounts were in actuality Eurodollar accounts—dollar-denominated deposits in non-U.S. banks. These accounts provided savers and investors the ability to choose whether to hold pesos.

From the very beginning, however, there was substantial doubt in the market that the Argentine government could maintain the fixed exchange rate. Argentine banks regularly paid slightly higher interest rates on peso-denominated accounts than on dollar-denominated accounts. This interest differential represented a market-determined risk premium of the system itself. Depositors were rewarded for accepting risk—for keeping their money in peso-denominated accounts. This was an explicit signal by the marketplace that there was a perceived possibility that what was then "fixed" would not always be so.

The market proved to be correct. In January 2002, after months of economic and political turmoil and nearly three years of economic recession, the Argentine currency board was ended. The peso was first devalued from Ps1.00/$ to Ps1.40/$, then floated completely. It fell in value dramatically within days. The Argentine decade-long experiment with a rigidly fixed exchange rate was over. The devaluation followed months of turmoil, the ouster of three presidents in three weeks, continuing bank holidays, and riots in the streets of Buenos Aires. The Argentina crisis is presented in detail later in Chapter 7.

Dollarization

Several countries have suffered currency devaluation for many years, primarily as a result of inflation, and have taken steps toward dollarization. *Dollarization* is the use of the U.S. dollar as the official currency of the country. Panama has used the dollar as its official currency since 1907.

Ecuador, after suffering a severe banking and inflationary crisis in 1998 and 1999, adopted the U.S. dollar as its official currency in January 2000. One of the primary attributes of dollarization was summarized well by *Business Week* in a December 11, 2000, article entitled "The Dollar Club":

> *One attraction of dollarization is that sound monetary and exchange-rate policies no longer depend on the intelligence and discipline of domestic policymakers. Their monetary policy becomes essentially the one followed by the U.S., and the exchange rate is fixed forever.*

The arguments for dollarization follow logically from the previous discussion of "The Impossible Trinity." A country that dollarizes removes any currency volatility (against the dollar), and would theoretically eliminate the possibility of future currency crises. Additional benefits are expectations of greater economic integration with the United States and other dollar-based markets, both product and financial markets. This last point has led many to argue in favor of regional dollarization, in which several countries that are highly economically integrated may benefit significantly from dollarizing together.

Three major arguments exist against dollarization. The first is the loss of sovereignty over monetary policy. This is, however, the point of dollarization. Secondly, the country loses the power of *seigniorage*, the ability to profit from its ability to print its own money. Third, the central bank of the country, because it no longer has the ability to create money within its economic and financial system, can no longer serve the role of lender of last resort. This role carries with it the ability to provide liquidity to save financial institutions that may be on the brink of failure during times of financial crisis.

Ecuador. Ecuador officially completed the replacement of the Ecuadorian sucre with the U.S. dollar as legal tender on September 9, 2000. This made Ecuador the largest national adopter of the U.S. dollar, and in many ways set it up as a test case of dollarization for other emerging market countries to watch closely. As illustrated by Exhibit 2.4, this was the last stage of a massive depreciation of the sucre in a brief two-year period.

During 1999, Ecuador suffered a rising rate of inflation and a falling level of economic output. In March 1999, the Ecuadorian banking sector was hit with a series of devastating *bank runs*, financial panics in which all depositors attempted to withdraw all of their funds simultaneously. Although there were severe problems in the Ecuadorian banking system, the truth was that even the healthiest financial institution would fail under the strain of this financial drain. Ecuador's president at that time, Jamil Mahuad, immediately froze all deposits (what was termed a "bank holiday" in the U.S. in the 1930s, in which banks closed their doors). The Ecuadorian sucre, which in January 1999 was trading at roughly Sucre 7,400/dollar, plummeted in early March to Sucre 12,500/dollar. Ecuador defaulted on more than $13.6 billion in foreign debt in 1999 alone. President Mahuad moved quickly to propose dollarization to save the failing Ecuadorian economy.

By January 2000, when the next president took office (after a rather complicated military coup and subsequent withdrawal), the sucre had fallen in value to Sucre 20,000/dollar. The new president, Gustavo Naboa, continued the dollarization initiative. Although not supported by either the United States government or the International Monetary Fund, Ecuador completed its replacement of its own currency with the dollar over the next nine months.

The results of dollarization in Ecuador are still unknown. Ecuadorian residents did immediately return over $600 million into the banking system, money which they had withheld from the

Exhibit 2.4 The Ecuadorian Sucre Exchange Rate, November 1998–March 2000

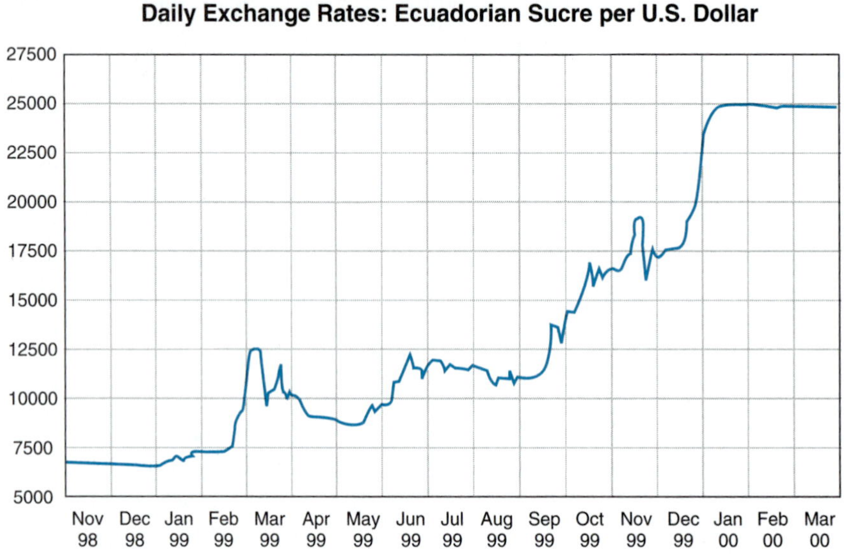

Source: Pacific Currency Exchange, http://pacific.commerce.ubc.ca/xr © 2001 by Prof. Werner Antweiler, University of British Columbia, Vancouver, BC, Canada.

banks in fear of bank failure. This added capital infusion, along with new IMF loans and economic restructurings, allowed the country to actually close 2000 with a small 1.0% economic gain. Inflation, however, remained high, closing the year at over 91% (up from 66% in 1999). Clearly, dollarization alone did not eliminate inflationary forces. Ecuador continues to struggle to find the balance both economically and politically with its new currency regime.

There is no doubt that for many emerging markets a currency board, dollarization, and freely floating exchange rate regimes are all extremes. In fact, many experts feel that the global financial marketplace will drive more and more emerging market nations towards one of these extremes. As illustrated by Exhibit 2.5, there is a distinct lack of "middle ground" between rigidly fixed and freely floating. In anecdotal support of this argument, a poll of the general population in Mexico in 1999 indicated that 9 out of 10 people would prefer dollarization over a floating-rate peso. Clearly, there are many in the emerging markets of the world who have little faith in their leadership and institutions to implement an effective exchange rate policy.

The Birth of a European Currency: The Euro

The 15 members of the European Union are also members of the European Monetary System (EMS). This group has tried to form an island of fixed exchange rates among themselves in a sea of major floating currencies. Members of the EMS rely heavily on trade with each other, so they perceive that the day-to-day benefits of fixed exchange rates between them are great. Nevertheless.

Exhibit 2.5 The Currency Regime Choices for Emerging Markets

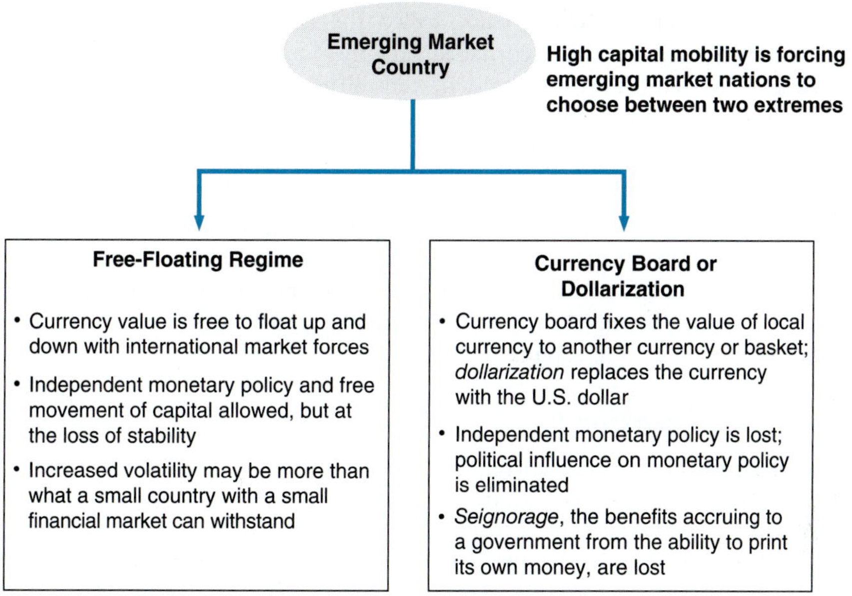

the EMS has undergone a number of major changes since its inception in 1979, including major crises and reorganizations in 1992 and 1993 and conversion of 11 members to the euro on January 1, 1999 (Greece joined in 2001). In December 1991, the members of the European Union met at Maastricht, the Netherlands, and finalized a treaty that changed Europe's currency future.

Emerging Market Country
High capital mobility is forcing emerging market nations to choose between two extremes
Free-Floating Regime
• Currency value is free to float up and down with international market forces
• Independent monetary policy and free movement of capital allowed, but at the loss of stability
• Increased volatility may be more than what a small country with a small financial market can withstand
Currency Board or Dollarization
• Currency board fixes the value of local currency to another currency or basket; *dollarization* replaces the currency with the U.S. dollar
• Independent monetary policy is lost; political influence on monetary policy is eliminated
• *Seignorage*, the benefits accruing to a government from the ability to print its own money, are lost

Timetable. The Maastricht Treaty specified a timetable and a plan to replace all individual ECU currencies with a single currency, called the euro. Other steps were adopted that would lead to a full European Economic and Monetary Union (EMU).

Convergence criteria. To prepare for the EMU, the Maastricht Treaty called for the integration and coordination of the member countries' monetary and fiscal policies. The EMU would be implemented by a process called *convergence*. Before becoming a full member of the EMU, each member country was originally expected to meet the following convergence criteria:

1. Nominal inflation should be no more than 1.5% above the average for the three members of the EU with the lowest inflation rates during the previous year.
2. Long-term interest rates should be no more than 2% above the average for the three members with the lowest interest rates.
3. The fiscal deficit should be no more than 3% of gross domestic product.
4. Government debt should be no more than 60% of gross domestic product.

The convergence criteria were so tough that few, if any, of the members could satisfy them at that time, but eleven countries managed to do so just prior to 1999.

Strong central bank. A strong central bank, called the European Central Bank (ECB), was established in Frankfurt, Germany, in accordance with the Treaty. The bank is modeled after the U.S. Federal Reserve System. This independent central bank dominates the countries' central banks, which continue to regulate banks resident within their borders; all financial market intervention and the issuance of euros will remain the sole responsibility of the ECB. The single most important mandate of the ECB is to promote price stability within the European Union.

As part of its development of cross-border monetary policy, the ECB has formed TARGET, the Transeuropean Automated Real-time Gross settlement Express Transfer system. TARGET is the mechanism by which the ECB will settle all cross-border payments in the conduct of EU banking business and regulation. It will allow the ECB to quickly and costlessly conduct monetary policy and other intra-banking system capital movements.

Why Monetary Unification?

According to the EU, EMU is a single currency area, now known informally as Euro Zone, within the EU single market in which people, goods, services, and capital are supposed to move without restrictions. Beginning with the Treaty of Rome in 1957 and continuing with the Single Europea Act of 1987, the Maastricht Treaty of 1991–1992, and the Treaty of Amsterdam of 1997, a core set of European countries worked steadily toward integrating their individual countries into one larger, more efficient, domestic market. Even after the launch of the 1992 Single Europe program, however, a number of barriers to true openness remained. The use of different currencies required both consumers and companies to treat the individual markets separately. Currency risk of cross-border commerce still persisted. The creation of a single currency is designed to move beyond these vestiges of separated markets.

The Launch of the Euro

On January 4, 1999, 11 member states of the EU initiated the EMU. They established a single currency, the euro, which replaced the individual currencies of the participating member states. The 11 countries were Austria, Belgium, Finland, France, Germany, Ireland, Italy, Luxembourg, the Netherlands, Portugal, and Spain. The United Kingdom, Sweden, and Denmark chose to maintain their individual currencies. Greece did not qualify for EMU but joined the Euro Zone in 2001. On December 31, 1998, the final fixed rates between the 11 participating currencies and the euro were put into place. On January 4, 1999, the euro was officially launched. Although the result of a long-term and methodical program for the alignment of all political and economic forces in the EU, the launch of the euro was only the first of many steps to come. The impacts of the euro on the economic environment and on society in general within the participating countries have been and will continue to be dramatic. It is only now becoming apparent what some of the impacts might be.

The euro affects markets in three ways: 1) countries within the Euro Zone enjoy cheaper transaction costs; 2) currency risks and costs related to exchange rate uncertainty are reduced; and 3) all consumers and businesses both inside and outside the Euro Zone enjoy price transparency and increased price-based competition.

Achieving Monetary Unification

If the euro is to be a successful replacement for the currencies of the participating EU states, it must have an economic foundation that is solid. The primary driver of a currency's value is its ability to maintain its purchasing power (money is worth what money can buy). The single largest threat to maintaining purchasing power is inflation. So, job one for the EU since the beginning has been to construct an economic system that would work to prevent inflationary forces from undermining the euro.

Fiscal policy and monetary policy. Monetary policy for the EMU is conducted by the European Central Bank (ECB), which has one responsibility: to preserve price stability. Following the basic structures that were used in the establishment of the Federal Reserve System in the United States and the Bundesbank in Germany, the ECB is free of political pressures that have historically caused monetary authorities to yield to employment pressures by inflating economies. The ECB's independence allows it to focus on price stability without falling victim to history's trap.

Fixing the value of the euro. The December 31, 1998, fixing of the rates of exchange between national currencies and the euro were permanent fixes for these currencies. The United Kingdom has been skeptical of increasing EU infringement on its sovereignty, and has opted not to participate. Sweden, which has failed to see significant benefits from EU membership (although it is one of the newest members), has also been skeptical of EMU participation. Denmark, like the U.K. and Sweden, has a strong political element that is highly nationalistic, and so far has opted not to participate.

On January 4, 1999, the euro began trading on world currency markets. Its introduction was a smooth one. The euro's value slid steadily following its introduction, however, primarily as a result of the robustness of the U.S. economy and U.S. dollar, and continuing sluggish economic sectors in the EMU countries. Exhibit 2.6 illustrates the euro's value, both before and after its official introduction on January 1, 1999. The euro declined in value from its original value of $1.19 in January 1999 to $0.87 in February 2002, but then strengthened dramatically to over $1.08 in the spring of 2003.

The official abbreviation of the euro, EUR, has been registered with the International Standards Organization (letter abbreviations are needed for computer-based worldwide trading). This is similar to the three-letter computer symbols used for the United States dollar, USD, and the British pound sterling, GBP. The official symbol of the euro is €. According to the EU, the symbol was inspired by the Greek letter epsilon, simultaneously referring to Greece's ancient role as the source of European civilization and recalling the first letters of the word Europe.

Exchange Rate Regimes: What Lies Ahead?

All exchange rate regimes must deal with the tradeoff between rules and discretion, as well as between cooperation and independence. Exhibit 2.7 illustrates the tradeoffs between exchange rate regimes based on rules, discretion, cooperation, and independence.

- Horizontally, the tradeoff for countries participating in a specific system is between consulting and acting in unison with other countries—cooperation—or operating as a member of the system, but acting on their own—independence.
- Vertically, different exchange rate arrangements may dictate whether the country's government has strict intervention requirements—rules—or whether it can choose whether, when, and to what degree to intervene in the foreign exchange markets—discretion.

Exhibit 2.6 The Dollar Value of the Euro, January 1999–February 2003

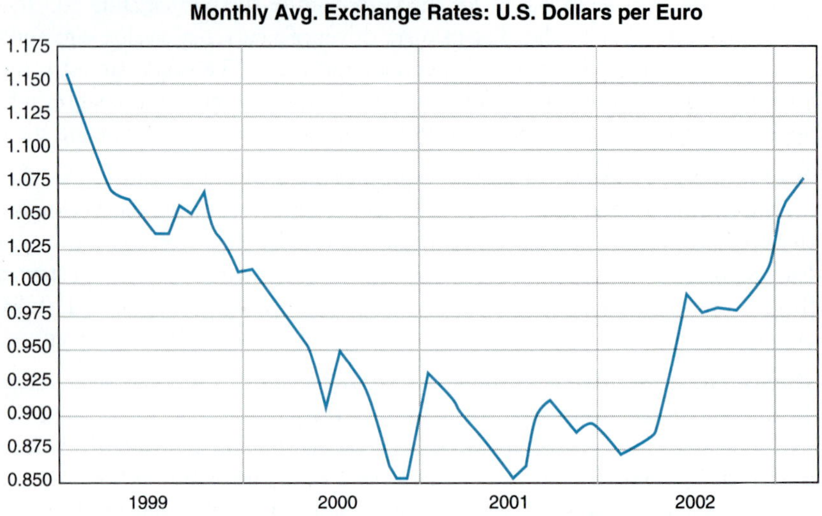

Source: Pacific Currency Exchange, http://pacific.commerce.ubc.ca/xr © 2003 by Prof. Werner Antweiler, University of British Columbia, Vancouver, BC, Canada. Time period shown in diagram 1/Jan/1999–24/Feb/2003.

Exhibit 2.7 The Tradeoffs Between Exchange Rate Regimes

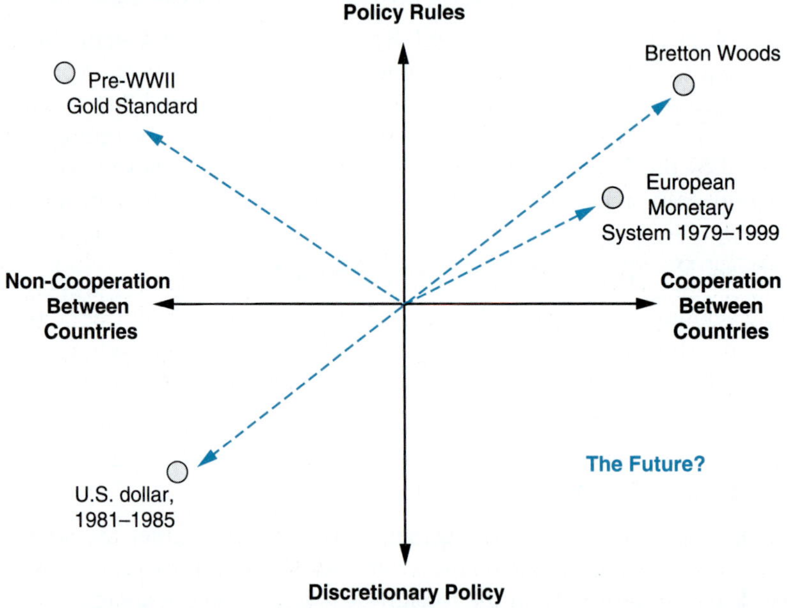

Regime structures like the gold standard required no cooperative policies among countries, only the assurance that all would abide by the "rules of the game." In the gold standard in effect prior to World War II, this translated into the willingness of governments to buy or sell gold at parity rates on demand. The Bretton Woods Agreement, the system in place between 1944 and 1973, required more in the way of cooperation in that gold was no longer the "rule," and countries were required to cooperate to a higher degree to maintain the dollar-based system. Exchange rate systems, like the European Monetary System's fixed exchange rate band system used from 1979 to 1999, were hybrids of these cooperative and rule regimes.

The present international monetary system is characterized by no rules, with varying degrees of cooperation. Although there is no present solution to the continuing debate over what form a new international monetary system should take, many believe that it could succeed only if it combined cooperation among nations with individual discretion to pursue domestic social, economic, and financial goals.

SUMMARY

- A foreign currency exchange rate, or simply exchange rate, is the price of one country's currency in units of another currency or commodity (typically gold or silver).
- Spot exchange rate is the quoted price for foreign exchange to be delivered at once, or in two days for interbank transactions. For example, ¥114/$ is a quote for the exchange rate between the Japanese yen and the U.S. dollar.
- Devaluation refers to a drop in foreign exchange value of a currency that is pegged to gold or to another currency. In other words, the par value is reduced. The opposite of devaluation is revaluation.
- Weakening, deterioration, or depreciation of a currency refers to a drop in the foreign exchange value of a floating currency. The opposite of weakening is strengthening or appreciating, which refers to a gain in the exchange value of a floating currency.
- If the ideal currency existed in today's world, it would possess three attributes: a fixed value, convertibility, and independent monetary policy.
- Emerging market countries must often choose between two extreme exchange rate regimes, either a free-floating regime or an extremely fixed regime such as a currency board or dollarization.
- The 15 members of the European Union are also members of the European Monetary System (EMS). This group has tried to form an island of fixed exchange rates among themselves in a sea of major floating currencies. Members of the EMS rely heavily on trade with each other, so the day-to-day benefits of fixed exchange rates between them are perceived to be great.
- The euro affects markets in three ways: (1) countries within the Euro Zone enjoy cheaper transaction costs; (2) currency risks and costs related to exchange rate uncertainty are reduced; and (3) all consumers and businesses both inside and outside the Euro Zone enjoy price transparency and increased price-based competition.

QUESTIONS

1. **The gold standard and the money supply.** Under the gold standard all national governments promised to follow the "rules of the game." This meant defending a fixed exchange rate. What did this promise imply about a country's money supply?
2. **Causes of devaluation.** If a country follows a fixed exchange rate regime, what macroeconomic

variables could cause the fixed exchange rate to be devalued?

3. **Fixed versus flexible exchange rates.** What are the advantages and disadvantages of fixed exchange rates?

4. **The Impossible Trinity.** Explain what is meant by the term "Impossible Trinity" and why the trinity is thought impossible.

5. **Currency board or dollarization.** Fixed exchange rate regimes are sometimes implemented through a *currency board* (as in Hong Kong) or *dollarization* (as in Ecuador). What is the difference between the two approaches?

6. **Emerging market exchange rate regimes.** High capital mobility is forcing emerging market nations to choose between free-floating regimes and currency board or dollarization regimes. What are the main outcomes of each of these regimes from the perspective of emerging market nations?

7. **Argentine currency board.** How did the Argentine currency board function from 1991 to January 2002 and why did it collapse?

8. **The euro.** On January 4, 1999, 11 member states of the European Union initiated the European Monetary Union (EMU) and established a single currency, the euro, which replaced the individual currencies of participating member states. Describe three of the main ways that the euro affects the members of the EMU.

9. **Mavericks.** The United Kingdom, Denmark, and Sweden have chosen not to adopt the euro but rather to maintain their individual currencies. What are the motivations of each of these three countries, which are also members of the European Union?

10. **International Monetary Fund (IMF).** The IMF was established by the Bretton Woods Agreement (1944). What were its original objectives?

11. **Special Drawing Rights.** What are Special Drawing Rights?

12. **Definitions.** Define the following currency terms:

    a. devaluation
    b. revaluation
    c. depreciation
    d. appreciation
    e. soft or weak
    f. hard or strong
    g. eurodollar
    h. euroyen

13. **Exchange rate regime classifications.** The IMF classifies all exchange rate regimes into eight specific categories that are summarized in this chapter. Under which exchange rate regime would you classify the following countries?

    a. France
    b. The United States
    c. Japan
    d. Thailand

14. **The ideal currency.** What are the attributes of the ideal currency?

15. **Bretton Woods failure.** Why did the fixed exchange rate regime of 1945–1973 eventually fail?

16. **Inter-war float.** What was the experience with floating exchange rates during the inter-war years and World War II, 1914–1944.

PROBLEMS

1. **Frankfurt and New York.** In Frankfurt, one can buy a U.S. dollar for €0.9200. In New York, one can buy a euro for $1.0870. What is the foreign exchange rate between the dollar and the euro?

2. **Peso exchange rate changes.** In December 1994 the government of Mexico officially changed the value of the Mexican peso from 3.2 pesos per dollar to 5.5 pesos per dollar. Was this a *devaluation*, *revaluation*, *depreciation*, or *appreciation*? What was the percentage change?

3. **Good as gold.** Under the gold standard, the price of an ounce of gold in U.S. dollars was $20.67, while the price of that same ounce in British pounds was £4.2474. What would the exchange rate between the dollar and the

pound be if the U.S. dollar price had been $38.00 per ounce?

4. **Gold standard.** Before World War I, $20.67 was needed to buy one ounce of gold. If, at the same time one ounce of gold could be purchased in France for FF310.00, what was the exchange rate between French francs and U.S. dollars?

5. **Spot rate customer.** The spot rate for Mexican pesos is Ps9.5200/$. If your company buys Ps100,000 spot from the bank on Monday, how much must your company pay and on what day?

6. **Forward rate.** The 180-day forward rate for the euro is quoted at €0.9210/$. If your company buys €100,000 forward 180 days on September 6, 2003, how much must your company pay and on what date to settle the forward agreement?

7. **Forward discount on the dollar.** What is the forward discount on the dollar if the spot rate is $1.0200/€ and the 180-day forward rate is $1.0858/€?

8. **Forward premium on the euro.** What is the forward premium on the euro if the spot rate on September 3, 2003 is €0.9804/$ and the 180-day forward rate is €0.9210/$?

9. **Iraqi import.** A European-based manufacturer ships a machine tool to a buyer in Jordan at a sales price of €375,000. Jordan imposes a 12% import duty on all products purchased from the European Union. The Jordanian importer then re-exports the product to an Iraqi importer, but only after imposing its own resale fee of 22%. Given the following spot exchange rates on January 30, 2003, what is the total cost to the Iraqi importer in Iraqi dinar, and what is the U.S. dollar equivalent of that price?

Spot rate, Jordanian dinar (JD) per euro (€)	JD 0.7597/€
Spot rate, Jordanian dinar (JD) per U.S. dollar ($)	JD 0.7051/$
Spot rate, Iraqi dinar (ID) per Jordanian dinar (JD)	ID 3,843/JD
Spot rate, Iraqi dinar (ID) per U.S. dollar ($)	ID 2,710/$

10. **Tsar Alexander III's Russian gold loan.** Countries and governments have been raising capital in the international financial markets for centuries. The Russian government of Tsar Alexander III issued a 100-year *bearer bond* in 1894 (the bond itself is reproduced on the following page). A *bearer bond* is a security sold to an investor in which the *bearer* of the bond, the holder, is entitled to receive an interest payment at regularly scheduled dates as listed on the bond. There is no record kept by any authority on who the owner of the bond is, allowing the investor to earn the interest payments without tax authorities knowing the investor's identity. This allowed the bond issuer, in this case the Tsar, to raise capital at lower interest rates because investors would most likely be able to avoid paying taxes on the interest income they received.

    This bond paid interest on a quarterly basis. Each bond contained a sheet of coupons that were numbered and dated. In order for an investor to redeem his coupons for cash payment, he would clip a coupon from the sheet and take it to one of the listed banks around the world to receive his interest payment. As noted on the coupon and on the bond itself, there were explicit dates on each individual coupon as to when it could be redeemed. The bond listed the cities and the amount of the interest payment in local currency terms. The 118th coupon in the series is reproduced below.

RUSSIAN 4% GOLD LOAN, SIXTH ISSUE, 1894

Talon of the Bond of 187 Rouble 50 Cop.
(1/Rouble = 1/15 Imper.)

118th Coupon of the Bond, due 18 June/1 July 1923:
in Paris 5 Francs, in Berlin 4 Mark 4 Pf.,
in London 3 Schill. 11 _ P.,
in Amsterdam 2 Flor. 39 C.,
in New York 96 1/4 Cents.

Valid for 10 years.

BOND

R. 125.

of one hundred and twenty five Gold Roubles

= 500 Francs = 404 German Marks = 19 Pounds Sterling 15 shill. 6 pence
= 239 Dutch Flor. = 96,25 United States Gold Dollars,
inscribed into the Great Book of the Public Debt at the Office of the Imperial Commission of the Sinking Fund
to Bearer.

The Bearer of this Bond is entitled to the amount of one hundred and twenty five Gold Roubles bearing interest at FOUR per cent per annum until its redemption by drawing.
This Bond is for ever exempt from every present and future Russian Tax whatever.

The interest will be paid against the coupons every three months viz: on the 20th March/1st April, 19th June/1st July, 19th September/1st October, 20th December/1st January of each year, at the choice of the Bearer:

in **ST.-PETERSBURG:**	at the State Bank, in Gold Roubles or Credit Roubles, at the rate of exchange of the day;
in **PARIS:**	at the Banque de Paris et des Pays-Bas, at the Crédit Lyonnais, at the Comptoir National d'Escompte de Paris, at the office of the Russian Bank for Foreign Trade and at Messrs Hottingeur & Co, in Francs;
in **LONDON:**	at the Russian Bank for Foreign Trade (London-branch), in Pounds Sterling;
in **BERLIN:**	at Messrs Mendelssohn & Co, in German Marks;
in **AMSTERDAM:**	at Messrs Lippmann, Rosenthal & Co, in Dutch Florins;
in **NEW-YORK:**	at Messrs Baring, Magoun & Co, in Gold Dollars.

These Bonds will be redeemed at par, within 81 years by drawings by lot, which will take place at the Imperial Commission of the Sinking Fund half yearly, the 20th March/1st April and 19th September/1st October, beginning from 19th September/1st October 1894. To the redemption of this Loan will be applied every half year 0,084281% of the nominal amount of the original issue together with 2% on the amount of the Bonds previously drawn.

Up to the 19th December/1st January 1904, the amount allotted for the amortization of this Loan, mentioned at the previous article, shall not be increased, not shall up to the said date be admitted reimbursement or conversion of the whole Loan. The payment of the drawn Bonds will take place on the date of payment of the next following coupon, at the same places and in the same currencies as the coupons. Coupons due after the date of payment of the drawn bonds must remain attached thereto, otherwise the amount of missing coupons will be deducted from the capital upon payment of the Bond. The drawn Bonds of this Loan not presented for payment within 30 years, from the date fixed for their reimbursement falling under prescription, shall be void; coupons not presented within 10 years after their due date will likewise be void through prescription.

The Bonds of this Loan bear coupons up to the 19th December 1903/1st January 1904 and a Talon, on presentation of which after the said date new coupon sheets will be delivered, free of charge, for the undrawn Bonds, at the places designated for the payment of the coupons. The Bonds of this Loan are issued either nominative or on Bearer. The rules for the nominative Bonds, their exchange for Bonds on Bearer and vice-versa are to be approved by the Minister of Finance.

We order:

1. to issue 4% Bonds for a nominal amount of one hundred and thirteen millions six hundred thousand (113,600,000) Gold Roubles and to inscribe this issue in the Great Book of the Public Debt under the denomination of Russian Four per cent Gold Loan, 6th issue, 1894;
2. the interest on these bonds to run from the 20th December 1893/1st January 1894 and their amortization to take place within 81 years from the 20th December 1894/1st January 1895;
3. to fix all other conditions of this issue in conformity with the ones established by Art. IV of Our Imperial Ukase of the 9th/21st August 1893 for the Russian Four per cent Gold Loan, 5th issue, 1893;
4. to determine simultaneously with the issue of these Bonds the right and privilege concerning their acceptance as security for State-contracts and as guarantee for due payment of accise-duties.

The 118th coupon, which the bearer can present for payment beginning June 18, 1923, indicates what payment the bearer can receive depending on which currency the bearer is receiving payment in. This obviously implies a set of fixed exchange rates in effect on the date of issuance (1894). Use the coupon and the bond on the preceding page to answer the following questions.

a. What is the value of the total bond as originally issued in French francs, German marks, British pounds, Dutch florins, and U.S. dollars?

b. Create a chart that shows the fixed rate of exchange implied by the coupon for the six different currencies.

c. Create a second chart which compares these exchange rates with these same exchange rates today (use the *Wall Street Journal* or *Financial Times* to find current exchange rates).

INTERNET EXERCISES

WWW.

1. **International Monetary Fund's Special Drawing Rights.** The Special Drawing Right (SDR) is a composite index of four key participant currencies. Use the IMF's web site to find the current weights and valuation of the SDR.

   International Monetary Fund http://www.imf.org/external/np/tre/sdr/basket.htm

2. **Capital controls.** One of the key "sides" of the Impossible Trinity discussed in the chapter is the degree of capital mobility into and out of a country. Use the International Finance subsection of Yahoo to determine the current state of capital movement freedom for the following countries: Chile, China, Malaysia, Taiwan, and Russia.

   Yahoo http://biz.yahoo.com/ifc

3. **Dollarization and currency boards.** Use the following web sites, and any others you may find, to track the ongoing debate of the relative success of dollarization and currency boards.

   International Monetary Fund http://www.imf.org/external/pubs

   National Bureau of Economic Research http://papers.nber.org/papers

   Cato Institute http://www.cato.org/pubs

4. **Malaysian currency controls.** The institution of currency controls by the Malaysian government in the aftermath of the Asian currency crisis is a classic response by government to unstable currency conditions. Use the following web site to increase your knowledge of how currency controls work.

   EconEdLink http://www.econedlink.org/lessons/index.cfm?lesson=EM25

5. **Personal transfers.** As anyone who has traveled internationally learns, the exchange rates available to private retail customers are not always as attractive as those accessed by companies and corporations. The OzForex web site contains a section on "customer rates" that illustrates the difference. Use the site to calculate what the percentage difference between Australian dollar/U.S. dollar spot exchange rates are for retail customers versus a bank.

   OzForex http://www.ozforex.com/cgi-bin/spotrates_transfers.asp

SELECTED READINGS

Miller, Merton H., "Financial Markets and Economic Growth," *Journal of Applied Corporate Finance*, Fall 1998, Volume 11, No. 3, pp. 8–15.

Rajan, Raghuram G., and Luigi Zingales, "Which Capitalism? Lessons From the East Asia Crisis," *Journal of Applied Corporate Finance*, Fall 1998, Volume 11, No. 3, pp. 40–48.

Singal, Vijay, "Floating Currencies, Capital Controls, or Currency Boards: What's the Best Remedy for the Currency Crisis," *Journal of Applied Corporate Finance*, Winter 1999, Volume 11, No. 4, pp. 49–56.

Chapter 3

The Balance of Payments

INTERNATIONAL BUSINESS TRANSACTIONS OCCUR IN MANY DIFFERENT FORMS OVER THE COURSE OF a year. The measurement of all international economic transactions between the residents of a country and foreign residents is called the *balance of payments* (BOP).[1] Government policymakers need such measures of economic activity in order to evaluate the general competitiveness of domestic industry, to set exchange rate or interest rate policies or goals, and for many other purposes. Multinational businesses use various BOP measures to gauge the growth and health of specific types of foreign trade or financial transactions against the home country.

Home-country and host-country BOP data are important to business managers, investors, consumers, and government officials because the data influence and are influenced by other key macroeconomic variables such as gross domestic product, employment, price levels, exchange rates, and interest rates. Monetary and fiscal policy must take the BOP into account at the national level. Business managers and investors need BOP data to anticipate changes in host country economic policies that might be driven by BOP events. BOP data might be important for any of the following reasons:

- The BOP is an important indicator of pressure on a country's foreign exchange rate and thus on the potential for a firm trading with or investing in that country to experience foreign exchange gains or losses. Changes in the BOP may predict the imposition or removal of foreign exchange controls.
- Changes in a country's BOP may signal the imposition or removal of controls over payment of dividends and interest, license fees, royalty fees, or other cash disbursements to foreign firms or investors.
- The BOP helps to forecast a country's market potential, especially in the short run. A country experiencing a serious trade deficit is not as likely to expand imports as it would if it were running a surplus. It may, however, welcome investments that increase its exports.

1. The official terminology used throughout this chapter is that of the International Monetary Fund (IMF). Because the IMF is the primary source of similar statistics for balance of payments and economic performance by nations worldwide, its language is more general than other terminology such as that employed by the United States Department of Commerce.

Typical BOP Transactions

International transactions take many forms. Each of the following examples is an international economic transaction that is counted and captured in the U.S. balance of payments:

- Honda U.S. is the U.S. distributor of automobiles manufactured in Japan by its parent company, Honda of Japan.
- A U.S.-based firm, Fluor Corporation, manages the construction of a major water treatment facility in Bangkok, Thailand.
- The U.S. subsidiary of a French firm, Saint Gobain, pays profits (dividends) back to its parent firm in Paris.
- Daimler-Chrysler, the well-known German/American automobile manufacturer, purchases a small automotive parts manufacturer outside Chicago, Illinois.
- An American tourist purchases a small Lapponia necklace in Finland.
- The U.S. government finances the purchase of military equipment for its NATO (North Atlantic Treaty Organization) military ally, Norway.
- A Mexican lawyer purchases a U.S. corporate bond through an investment broker in Cleveland.

This is a small sample of the hundreds of thousands of international transactions that occur each year. The balance of payments provides a systematic method for classifying these transactions. One rule of thumb always aids the understanding of BOP accounting: "Follow the cash flow."

The BOP is composed of a number of subaccounts that are watched quite closely by groups as diverse as investment bankers, farmers, politicians, and corporate executives. These groups track and analyze the two major subaccounts, the *Current Account* and the *Capital/Financial Account*, on a continuing basis. Exhibit 3.1 provides an overview of these major subaccounts of the BOP.

Fundamentals of Balance of Payments Accounting

The BOP must balance. If it does not, something has not been counted or has been counted improperly. It is therefore incorrect to state that the BOP is in disequilibrium. It cannot be. The supply and demand for a country's currency may be imbalanced, but supply and demand are not the same thing as the BOP. A subaccount of the BOP, such as the merchandise trade balance, may be imbalanced, but the entire BOP of a single country is always balanced.

There are three main elements of the actual process of measuring international economic activity: 1) identifying what is and is not an international economic transaction; 2) understanding how the flow of goods, services, assets, and money create debits and credits to the overall BOP; and 3) understanding the bookkeeping procedures for BOP accounting.

Defining International Economic Transactions

Identifying international transactions is ordinarily not difficult. The export of merchandise goods such as trucks, machinery, computers, telecommunications equipment, and so forth is obviously an international transaction. Imports such as French wine, Japanese cameras, and German auto-

Exhibit 3.1 Generic Balance of Payments

A.	***Current Account***	
	1. Net export/imports of goods (*trade balance*)	
	2. Net exports/imports of services	
	3. Net income (investment income from direct and portfolio investment plus employee compensation)	
	4. Net transfers (sums sent home by migrants and permanent workers abroad, gifts, grants, and pensions)	*A (1–4) = Current Account Balance*
B.	***Capital Account***	
	Capital transfers related to the purchase and sale of fixed assets such as real estate	
C.	***Financial Account***	
	1. Net foreign direct investment	
	2. Net portfolio investment	
	3. Other financial items	*A + B + C = Basic Balance*
D.	***Net Errors and Omissions Account***	
	Missing data such as illegal transfers	*A + B + C + D = Overall Balance*
E.	***Reserves and Related Items: Official Reserve Account***	
	Changes in official monetary reserves including gold, foreign exchange, and IMF position.	

mobiles are also clearly international transactions. But this merchandise trade is only a portion of the thousands of different international transactions that occur in the United States or any other country each year.

Many other international transactions are not so obvious. The purchase of a glass figure in Venice, Italy, by a U.S. tourist is classified as a U.S. merchandise import. In fact, all expenditures made by U.S. tourists around the globe for services (meals, hotel accommodations), but not for goods, are recorded in the U.S. balance of payments as imports of travel services in the Current Account. The purchase of a U.S. Treasury bill by a foreign resident is an international financial transaction and is duly recorded in the Capital/Financial Account of the U.S. balance of payments.

The BOP as a Flow Statement

The BOP is often misunderstood, because many people infer from its name that it is a balance sheet, whereas in fact it is a cash flow statement. By recording all international transactions over a period of time such as a year, it tracks the continuing flows of purchases and payments between a country and all other countries. It does not add up the value of all assets and liabilities of a country on a specific date like a balance sheet does for an individual firm.

Two types of business transactions dominate the balance of payments:

1. **Exchange of Real Assets:** The exchange of goods (for example: automobiles, computers, watches, textiles) and services (for example: banking services, consulting services, travel services) for other goods and services (barter) or for money.

2. **Exchange of Financial Assets:** The exchange of financial claims (for example: stocks, bonds, loans, purchases or sales of companies) for other financial claims or money.

Although assets can be identified as real or financial, it is often easier to think of all assets simply as goods that can be bought and sold. The purchase of a hand-woven area rug in a shop in Bangkok by a U.S. tourist is not all that different from a Wall Street banker buying a British government bond for investment purposes.

BOP Accounting

The measurement of all international transactions in and out of a country over a year is a daunting task. Mistakes, errors, and statistical discrepancies will occur. The primary problem is that double-entry bookkeeping is employed in theory, but not in practice. Individual purchase and sale transactions should—in theory—result in financing entries in the balance of payments that match. In reality, the entries are recorded independently. Current and Capital/Financial Account entries are recorded independently of one another, not together as double-entry bookkeeping would prescribe. Thus there will be serious discrepancies (to use a nice term for it) between debits and credits.

The Accounts of the Balance of Payments

The balance of payments is composed of two primary subaccounts, the Current Account and the Capital/Financial Account. In addition, the Official Reserves Account tracks government currency transactions, and a fourth statistical subaccount, the Net Errors and Omissions Account, is produced to preserve the balance in the BOP. The international economic relationships between countries do, however, continue to evolve, as the recent revision of the major accounts within the BOP discussed next indicates.

The Current Account

The Current Account includes all international economic transactions with income or payment flows occurring within the year, the current period. The Current Account consists of four subcategories:

1. **Goods trade and import of goods:** Merchandise trade is the oldest and most traditional form of international economic activity. Although many countries depend on imports of goods (as they should according to the theory of comparative advantage), they also normally work to preserve either a balance of goods trade or even a surplus.

2. **Services trade:** The export and import of services. Common international services are financial services provided by banks to foreign importers and exporters, travel services of airlines, and construction services of domestic firms in other countries. For the major industrial countries, this subaccount has shown the fastest growth in the past decade.

3. **Income:** Predominantly current income associated with investments that were made in previous periods. If a U.S. firm created a subsidiary in South Korea to produce metal parts in a pre-

vious year, the proportion of net income that is paid back to the parent company in the current year (the dividend) constitutes current investment income. Additionally, wages and salaries paid to nonresident workers are also included in this category.

4. **Current transfers:** The financial settlements associated with the change in ownership of real resources or financial items. Any transfer between countries that is one-way—a gift or grant—is termed a current transfer. For example, funds provided by the United States government to aid in the development of a less-developed nation would be a current transfer. Transfers associated with the transfer of fixed assets are included in a separate account, the Capital/Financial Account.

All countries participate in some amount of trade, most of which is merchandise. Many smaller and less-developed countries have little in the way of service trade, or items that fall under the income or transfers subaccounts.

The Current Account is typically dominated by the first component described, the export and import of merchandise. For this reason, the Balance of Trade (BOT), which is so widely quoted in the business press in most countries, refers specifically to the balance of exports and imports of goods trade only. If the country is a larger industrialized country, however, the BOT is somewhat misleading, in that service trade is not included.

Exhibit 3.2 summarizes the Current Account and its components for the United States for the 1996–2000 period. As illustrated, the U.S. goods trade balance has been consistently negative, but has been partially offset by the continuing surplus in Services Trade Balance.

Exhibit 3.3 places the current account values of Exhibit 3.2 in perspective over time by dividing the current account into its two major components: 1) goods trade and 2) services trade and

Exhibit 3.2 The United States Current Account, 1996–2000 (billions of U.S. dollars)

	1996	1997	1998	1999	2000
Goods exports	614	680	672	687	775
Goods imports	–803	–877	–917	–1030	–1224
Goods trade balance (BOT)	–189	–196	–245	–343	–450
Services trade credits	238	255	260	271	291
Services trade debits	–151	–166	–182	–189	–217
Services trade balance	87	88	78	81	74
Income receipts	226	261	259	285	353
Income payments	–205	–252	–265	–299	–368
Income balance	21	9	–6	–14	–15
Current transfers, credits	9	8	9	9	10
Current transfers, debits	–49	–49	–54	–58	–64
Net transfers	–40	–41	–44	–49	–54
Current Account Balance	–121	–140	–217	–324	–445

Source: Derived from International Monetary Fund, *Balance of Payments Statistics Yearbook*, 2001.

Exhibit 3.3 **U.S. Trade Balance and Balance on Services and Income, 1985–2000 (billions of U.S. dollars)**

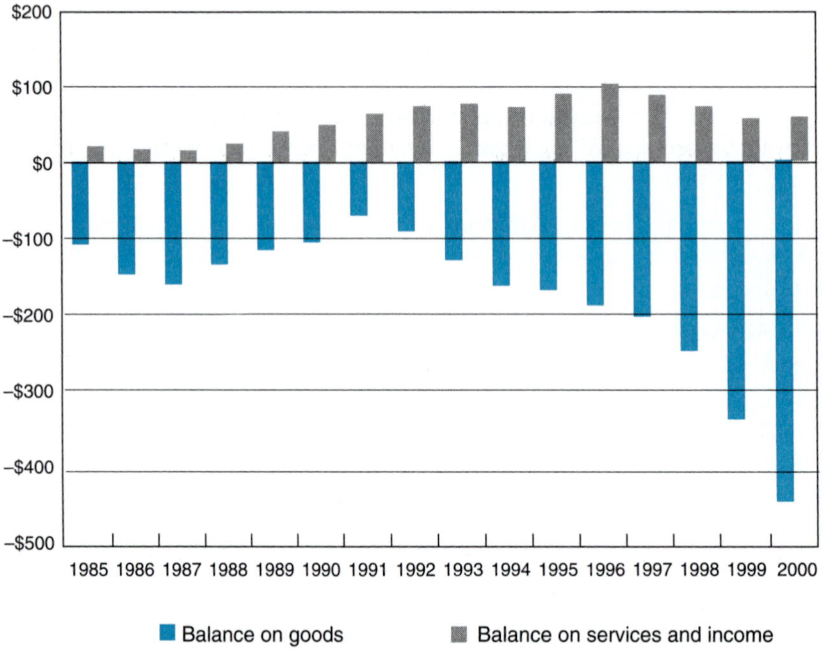

Source: International Monetary Fund, *Balance of Payments Statistics Yearbook,* 2001.

investment income. The first and most striking message is the magnitude of the goods trade deficit in the 1990s (a continuation of a position created in the early 1980s). The balance on services and income, although not large in comparison to net goods trade, has with few exceptions run a surplus over the past two decades.

The deficits in the BOT of the past decade have been an area of considerable concern for the United States, in both the public and private sectors. Merchandise trade is the original core of international trade. The manufacturing of goods was the basis of the industrial revolution, and the focus of the theory of comparative advantage in international trade to be reviewed in Chapter 15. Manufacturing is traditionally a sector of the economy that employs most of a country's workers. The goods trade deficit of the 1980s saw the decline of traditional heavy industries in the United States, industries that through history employed many U.S. workers. Declines in the BOT in areas such as steel, automobiles, automotive parts, textiles, and shoe manufacturing caused massive economic and social disruption.

Understanding merchandise import and export performance is much like understanding the market for any single product. The demand factors that drive both are income, the economic growth rate of the buyer, and price of the product in the eyes of the consumer after passing through an exchange rate. For example, U.S. merchandise imports reflect the income level of U.S. consumers and growth of industry. As income rises, so does the demand for imports.

Exports follow the same principles but in the reversed position. U.S. manufacturing exports depend not on the incomes of U.S. residents, but on the incomes of buyers of U.S. products in all other countries around the world. When these economies are growing, the demand for U.S. products will also rise.

The service component of the U.S. current account is a mystery to many. As illustrated in Exhibits 3.2 and 3.3, the U.S. has consistently achieved a surplus in services trade income. The major categories of services include travel and passenger fares, transportation services, expenditures by U.S. students abroad and foreign students pursuing studies in the U.S., telecommunications services, and financial services.

The Capital/Financial Account

The *Capital/Financial Account* of the balance of payments measures all international economic transactions of financial assets. It is divided into two major components, the Capital Account and the Financial Account.

Exhibit 3.4 shows the major subcategories of the U.S. financial account balance from 1996 to 2000: *direct investment*, *portfolio investment*, and *other long-term and short-term capital.*

Exhibit 3.5 shows how the major subaccounts of the U.S. financial account—*net direct investment*, *portfolio investment*, and *other investment*—have changed since 1985.

The Capital Account. The Capital Account is made up of transfers of financial assets and the acquisition and disposal of nonproduced/nonfinancial assets. This account has been introduced as a separate component in the International Monetary Fund's balance of payments only recently.

Exhibit 3.4 The United States Financial Account and Components (billions of U.S. dollars)

	1996	1997	1998	1999	2000
Direct Investment					
Direct investment abroad	–92	–105	–143	–155	–152
Direct investment in the US	87	106	178	301	288
Net direct investment	–5	1	36	146	135
Portfolio Investment					
Assets, net	–150	–119	–136	–131	–125
Liabilities, net	368	386	269	355	475
Net portfolio investment	218	267	133	224	350
Other Investment					
Other investment assets	–179	–263	–74	–159	–303
Other investment liabilities	132	268	57	158	262
Net other investment	–47	5	–17	–1	–41
Net Financial Account Balance	165	273	152	368	444

Source: Derived from International Monetary Fund, *Balance of Payments Statistics Yearbook*, 2001.

Exhibit 3.5 The United States Financial Account, 1985–2000 (billions of U.S. dollars)

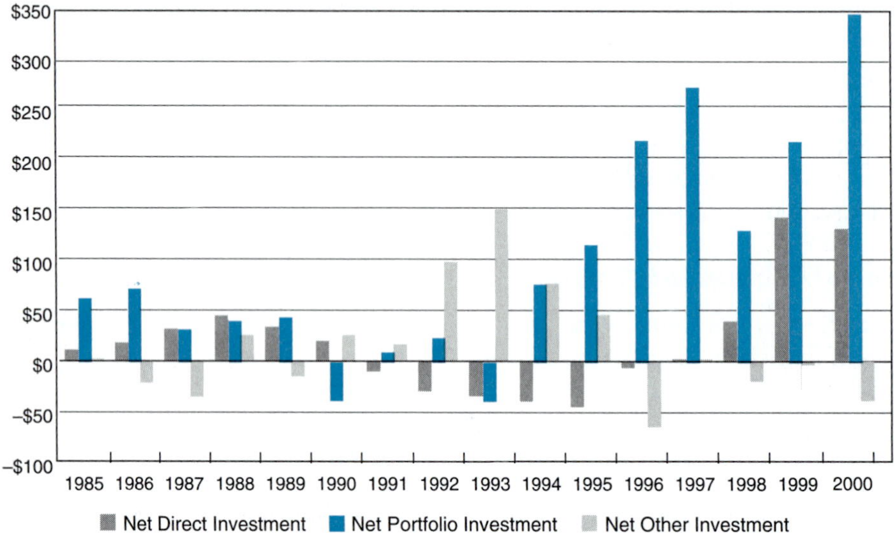

Source: International Monetary Fund, *Balance of Payments Statistics Yearbook,* 2001.

The magnitude of capital transactions covered is relatively minor, and we will include it in principle in all the following discussion of the Financial Account.

The Financial Account. Financial assets can be classified in a number of different ways including the length of the life of the asset (its maturity) and the nature of the ownership (public or private). The Financial Account, however, uses a third method to classify financial assets: the degree of investor control over the assets or operations. The Financial Account consists of three components thus classified: *direct investment,* in which the investor exerts some explicit degree of control over the assets; portfolio investment, in which the investor has no control over the assets; and other asset investment.

Direct investment. This is the net balance of capital dispersed from and into the United States for the purpose of exerting control over assets. If a U.S. firm builds a new automotive parts facility in another country or actually purchases a company in another country, this is a *direct investment* in the U.S. balance of payments accounts. When the capital flows out of the U.S., it enters the balance of payments as a negative cash flow. If, however, a foreign firm purchases a firm in the United States, it is a capital inflow and enters the balance of payments positively. Whenever 10% or more of the voting shares in a U.S. company are held by foreign investors, the company is classified as the U.S. affiliate of a foreign company, and a *foreign direct investment.* Similarly, if U.S. investors hold 10% or more of the control in a company outside the United States, that company is considered the foreign affiliate of a U.S. company.

The 1980s boom in foreign investment into the United States, or foreign resident purchases of assets in the United States, was extremely controversial. The source of concern over foreign investment in any country, including the United States, focuses on two topics: control and profit. Some countries possess restrictions on what foreigners may own in their country. This rule is based on the premise that domestic land, assets, and industry in general should be owned by residents of the country. On the other hand, the United States has traditionally had few restrictions on what foreign residents or firms can own or control; most restrictions remaining today relate to national security concerns. Unlike the case in the traditional debates over whether international trade should be free, there is no consensus that international investment should necessarily be free. This question is still very much a domestic political concern first, and an international economic issue second.

The second major source of concern over foreign direct investment is who receives the profits from the enterprise. Foreign companies owning firms in the United States will ultimately profit from the activities of the firms, or put another way, from the efforts of U.S. workers. In spite of evidence that indicates foreign firms in the United States reinvest most of their profits in their U.S. businesses (in fact at a higher rate than domestic firms), the debate on possible profit drains has continued. Regardless of the actual choices made, workers of any nation feel the profits of their work should remain in their own hands. Once again, this is in many ways a political and emotional concern more than an economic one.

The choice of words used to describe foreign investment can also influence public opinion. If these massive capital inflows are described as "capital investments from all over the world showing their faith in the future of U.S. industry," the net capital surplus is represented as decidedly positive. If, however, the net capital surplus is described as resulting in "the United States being the world's largest debtor nation," the negative connotation is obvious. Both are essentially spins on the economic principles at work. Capital, whether short-term or long-term, flows to where the investor believes it can earn the greatest return for the level of risk. And although in an accounting sense this is "international debt," when the majority of the capital inflow is in the form of direct investment, a long-term commitment to jobs, production, services, technological, and other competitive investments, the impact on the competitiveness of industry located within the U.S. is increased. When the "net debtor" label is applied to equity investment, it is misleading in that it invites comparison with large debt crisis conditions suffered by many countries in the past.

Portfolio investment. This is net balance of capital that flows in and out of the United States but does not reach the 10% ownership threshold of direct investment. If a U.S. resident purchases shares in a Japanese firm but does not attain the 10% threshold, we define the purchase as a *portfolio investment* (and in this case an outflow of capital). The purchase or sale of debt securities (like U.S. Treasury bills) across borders is also classified as *portfolio investment* because debt securities by definition do not provide the buyer with ownership or control.

Portfolio investment is capital invested in activities that are purely profit-motivated (return), rather than ones made to control or manage the investment. Purchases of debt securities, bonds, interest-bearing bank accounts, and the like are intended only to earn a return. They provide no vote or control over the party issuing the debt. Purchases of debt issued by the U.S. government (U.S. Treasury bills, notes, and bonds) by foreign investors constitutes *net portfolio investment* in the United States. It is worth noting that most U.S. debt purchased by foreigners is U.S. dollar–denominated—denominated in the currency of the issuing country. Most foreign debt issued by countries such as Russia, Mexico, Brazil, and Southeast Asian countries is also U.S. dollar–denominated—in this case, the currency of a foreign country. The foreign country must earn dollars to repay its foreign-held debt. The United States need not earn any foreign currency to repay its foreign debt.

As illustrated in Exhibit 3.5, portfolio investment has shown much more volatile behavior than net foreign direct investment over the past decade. Many U.S. debt securities such as U.S. Treasury securities and corporate bonds were in high demand in the late 1980s, while surging emerging markets in both debt and equities caused a reversal in direction in the 1990s. The motivating forces for portfolio investment flows are always the same—return and risk. This fact, however, does not make the flows any more predictable.

Other investment assets/liabilities. This final category consists of various short-term and long-term trade credits, cross-border loans from all types of financial institutions, currency deposits and bank deposits, and other accounts receivable and payable related to cross-border trade.

Current and Financial Account Balance Relationships

Exhibit 3.6 illustrates the Current and Financial Account balances for the United States over recent years. What the exhibit shows is one of the basic economic and accounting relationships of the balance of payments: the inverse relation between the Current and Financial Accounts. This inverse relationship is not accidental. The methodology of the balance of payments—double-entry bookkeeping, in theory—requires that the current and financial accounts be off-setting. Countries experiencing large current account deficits "finance" these purchases through equally large surpluses in the financial account, and vice versa.

Exhibit 3.6 **Current and Capital/Financial Account Balances for the United States, 1992–2000, (billions of U.S. dollars)**

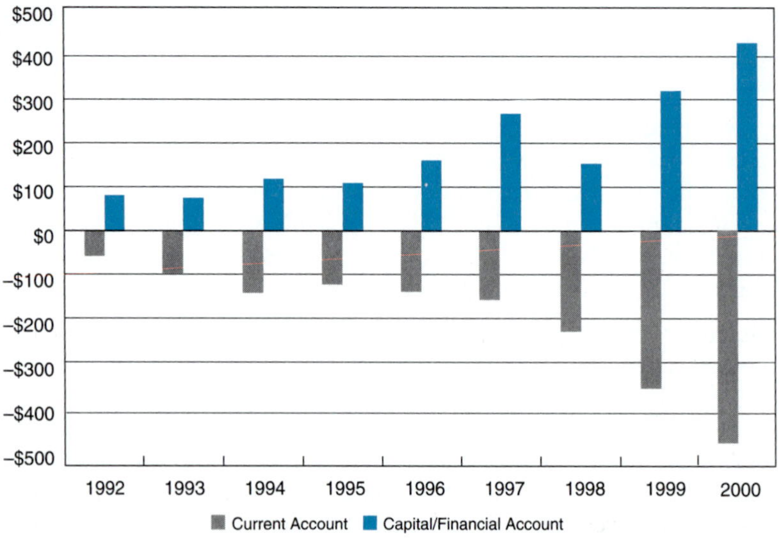

Source: International Monetary Fund, *Balance of Payments Statistics Yearbook,* 2001.

Net Errors and Omissions

As noted before, because current and financial account entries are collected and recorded separately, errors or statistical discrepancies will occur. The *Net Errors and Omissions Account* ensures that the BOP actually balances.

Official Reserves Account

The *Official Reserves Account* is the total reserves held by official monetary authorities within the country. These reserves are normally composed of the major currencies used in international trade and financial transactions (so-called "hard currencies" like the U.S. dollar, European euro, British pounds, and Japanese yen; gold; and special drawing rights, SDRs).

The significance of official reserves depends generally on whether the country is operating under a fixed exchange rate regime or a floating exchange rate system. If a country's currency is fixed, the government of the country officially declares that the currency is convertible into a fixed amount of some other currency. For example, the South Korean won was fixed to the U.S. dollar for many years. It was the Korean government's responsibility to maintain this fixed rate, also called *parity rate.* If for some reason there was an excess supply of Korean won on the currency market, to prevent the value of the won from falling, the South Korean government had to support the won's value by purchasing won on the open market (by spending its hard currency reserves, its official reserves) until the excess supply was eliminated. Under a floating rate system, the Korean government possesses no such responsibility and the role of official reserves is diminished.

The Balance of Payments in Total

Exhibit 3.7 provides the official balance of payments for the United States as presented by the International Monetary Fund (IMF), the multinational organization that collects these statistics for over 160 different countries around the globe. Now that the individual accounts and the relationships among the accounts have been discussed, Exhibit 3.7 allows us to take a comprehensive overview of how the individual accounts are combined to create some of the most useful summary measures for multinational business managers.

The Current Account (item A in Exhibit 3.7), the Capital Account (item B), and the Financial Account (item C) combine to form the Basic Balance (Total, Groups A through C). This balance is one of the most frequently used summary measures of the BOP. It describes the international economic activity of the nation, which is determined by market forces, not by government decisions (such as currency market intervention). The U.S. Basic Balance totaled a deficit of \$0.43 billion in 2000. A second frequently used measure, the Overall Balance, also called the official settlements balance (Total, Groups A through D in Exhibit 3.7), was at a surplus of \$0.30 billion in 2000.

The meaning of the BOP has changed over the past 30 years. As long as most of the major industrial countries were still operating under fixed exchange rates, the interpretation of the BOP was relatively straightforward:

- A surplus in the BOP implied that the demand for the country's currency exceeded the supply and that the government should allow the currency value to increase or intervene and accumulate additional foreign currency reserves in the Official Reserves Account. This

Exhibit 3.7 The United States Balance of Payments, Analytic Presentation, 1993–2000 (billions of U.S. dollars)

	1993	1994	1995	1996	1997	1998	1999	2000
A. Current Account	**–82.48**	**–118.20**	**–109.89**	**–120.94**	**–139.82**	**–217.41**	**–324.39**	**–444.69**
Goods: exports fob	458.84	504.93	577.05	614.02	680.33	672.39	686.86	774.86
Goods: imports fob	–589.41	–668.69	–749.38	–803.12	–876.51	–917.12	–1029.98	–1224.43
Balance on Goods	–130.57	–163.76	–172.33	–189.10	–196.18	–244.73	–343.12	–449.57
Services: credit	184.06	199.03	217.46	238.17	254.70	260.36	270.54	290.88
Services: debit	–122.28	–131.92	–141.50	–150.91	–166.28	–182.44	–189.27	–217.07
Balance on Goods and Services	–68.79	–96.65	–96.37	–101.84	–107.76	–166.81	–261.85	–375.76
Income: credit	134.21	165.44	211.54	225.86	260.58	259.27	285.32	352.90
Income: debit	–110.27	–148.75	–190.99	–204.87	–251.85	–265.45	–298.94	–367.68
Balance on Goods, Services, and Income	–44.85	–79.96	–75.82	–80.85	–99.03	–172.99	–275.47	–390.54
Current transfers: credit	5.93	6.49	7.68	8.89	8.49	9.20	9.27	10.24
Current transfers: debit	–43.56	–44.73	–41.75	–48.98	–49.28	–53.62	–58.19	–64.39
B. Capital Account	**–0.09**	**–0.46**	**0.37**	**0.69**	**0.35**	**0.64**	**–3.50**	**0.68**
Capital account: credit	0.37	0.31	0.67	0.69	0.35	0.64	0.49	0.68
Capital account: debit	–0.46	–0.77	–0.30	0.00	0.00	0.00	–3.99	0.00
Total, Groups A Plus B	***–82.57***	***–118.66***	***–109.52***	***–120.25***	***–139.47***	***–216.77***	***–327.89***	***–444.01***
C. Financial Account	**82.93**	**124.61**	**123.06**	**165.47**	**272.50**	**151.58**	**367.91**	**443.58**
Direct investment	–32.57	–34.05	–40.98	–5.36	0.77	35.69	145.61	135.24
Direct investment abroad	–83.95	–80.18	–98.78	–91.88	–104.82	–142.51	–155.41	–152.44
Direct investment in United States	51.38	46.13	57.80	86.52	105.59	178.20	301.02	287.68
Portfolio investment assets	–146.25	–60.31	–122.51	–149.83	–118.98	–136.13	–131.22	–124.94
Equity securities	–63.37	–48.10	–65.41	–82.85	–57.58	–101.28	–114.39	–99.74
Debt securities	–82.88	–12.21	–57.10	–66.98	–61.40	–34.85	–16.83	–25.20
Portfolio investment liabilities	111.00	139.41	237.48	367.73	385.61	269.35	354.75	474.59
Equity securities	20.94	0.89	16.56	11.13	67.85	41.96	112.34	193.85
Debt securities	90.06	138.52	220.92	356.60	317.76	227.39	242.41	280.74
Other investment assets	31.04	–40.90	–121.38	–178.90	–262.83	–74.21	–159.23	–303.27
Monetary authorities	0.00	0.00	0.00	0.00	0.00	0.00	0.00	0.00
General government	–0.34	–0.37	–0.98	–1.00	0.06	–0.42	2.75	–0.94
Banks	30.62	–4.20	–75.11	–91.56	–141.13	–35.58	–76.27	–138.49
Other sectors	0.76	–36.33	–45.29	–86.34	–121.76	–38.21	–85.71	–163.84
Other investment liabilities	119.71	120.46	170.45	131.83	267.93	56.88	158.00	261.96
Monetary authorities	68.00	9.59	46.73	56.88	–18.86	6.89	24.59	–6.80
General government	0.56	2.77	0.90	0.73	–2.86	–3.35	–0.97	–0.55
Banks	39.91	108.00	64.19	22.19	171.32	30.27	67.19	93.75
Other sectors	11.24	0.10	58.63	52.03	118.33	23.07	67.19	175.56
Total, Groups A Through C	***0.36***	***5.95***	***13.54***	***45.22***	***133.03***	***–65.19***	***40.02***	***–0.43***
D. Net Errors and Omissions	**1.01**	**–11.30**	**–3.79**	**–51.89**	**–132.01**	**71.94**	**–48.77**	**0.73**
Total, Groups A Through D	***1.37***	***–5.35***	***9.75***	***–6.67***	***1.02***	***6.75***	***–8.75***	***0.30***
E. Reserves and Related Items	**–1.38**	**5.35**	**–9.75**	**6.67**	**–1.02**	**–6.74**	**8.73**	**–0.30**

Source: International Monetary Fund, *Balance of Payments Statistics Yearbook*, 2001, p. 944.
Note: Totals may not match original source due to rounding.

intervention would occur as the government sold its own currency in exchange for other currencies, thus building up its stores of hard currencies.

- A deficit in the BOP implied an excess supply of the country's currency on world markets, and the government should then either devalue the currency or expend its official reserves to support its value.

The transition to floating exchange rate regimes in the 1970s (described in the previous chapter) changed the focus from the total BOP to its various subaccounts like the Current and Financial Account balances. These subaccounts are the indicators of economic activities and currency repercussions to come.

Capital Mobility

The degree to which capital moves freely across borders is critically important to a country's balance of payments. We have already seen how the United States, while experiencing a deficit in its Current Account balance over the past 20 years, has simultaneously enjoyed a Financial Account surplus. This Financial Account surplus has probably been one of the major reasons for the ability of the U.S. dollar to maintain its value over this period. Other countries however—for example, Brazil in 1998–1999 and Argentina in 2001–2002—have experienced massive Financial Account outflows, which were major components of their economic and financial crises. Before leaving our discussion of the balance of payments we need to gain additional insights into the history of capital mobility and the contribution of capital outflows—capital flight—to balance of payments crises.

Historical Patterns of Capital Mobility

Has capital always been free to move in and out of a country? Definitely not. The ability of foreign investors to own property, buy businesses, or purchase stocks and bonds in other countries has been controversial. Obstfeld and Taylor (2001) in a recent paper studied the globalization of capital markets and concluded that the pattern illustrated in Exhibit 3.8 is a fair representation of the "conventional wisdom" on the openness of global capital markets in recent history. Since 1860, the gold standard in use prior to the First World War and the post-1971 period of floating exchange rates saw the greatest ability of capital to flow cross-border. Note that Obstfeld and Taylor use no specific quantitative measure of mobility. The diagram uses only a stylized distinction between "low" and "high," combining two primary factors: the exchange rate regimes and the state of international political and economic relations.

The authors argue that the post-1860 era can be subdivided into four distinct periods:

1. The first period, 1860–1914, is a period characterized by continuously increasing capital openness as more and more countries adopted the gold standard and expanded international trade relations.
2. The second period, 1914–1945, is a period of global economic destruction. The combined destructive forces of two world wars and a worldwide depression led most nations to move toward highly nationalistic and isolationist political and economic policies, effectively eliminating any significant movement of capital between countries.
3. The third period, 1945–1971, or the Bretton Woods era, saw a great expansion of international trade in goods and services. This time also saw the slow but steady recovery of capital

Exhibit 3.8 A Stylized View of Capital Mobility in Modern History

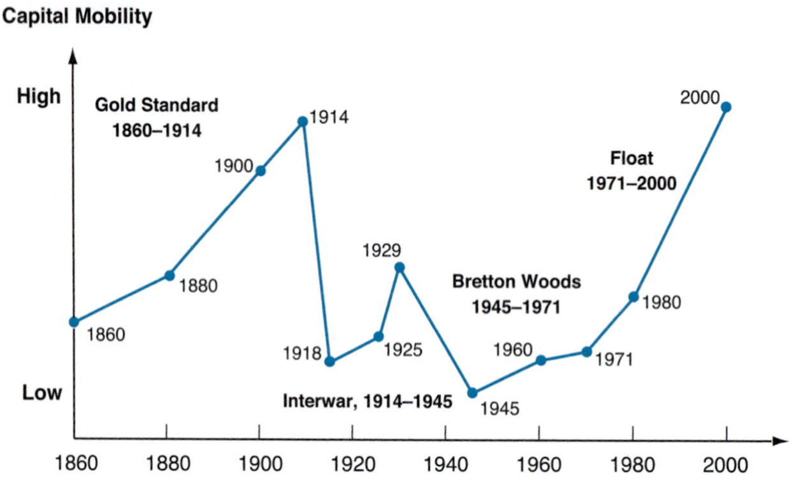

Source: "Globalization and Capital Markets," Maurice Obstfeld and Alan M. Taylor, NBER Conference Paper, May 4–5, 2001, p. 6.

markets. The fixed exchange rate regime of Bretton Woods may have failed because the sheer forces of global capital could no longer be held in check.

4. The fourth and current period, 1971–2000 [2002], is a period characterized by floating exchange rates and economic volatility, but rapidly expanding cross-border capital flows. The major industrial countries either no longer try to, no longer need to, or no longer can control the movement of capital. Because currency markets are free to reflect underlying economic fundamentals and investor sentiments about the future, capital movements increased in response to this openness.

The currency crises of the latter half of the 1990s and of the early 21st century may result in the reversal of this freedom of cross-border capital movement; it is still too early to tell. It is clear, however, that the ability of capital to move instantaneously and massively across borders has been one of the major factors in the severity of recent currency crises.

Capital Flight

A final issue is *capital flight*. Although no single accepted definition of capital flight exists, Ingo Walter's discussion has been one of the more useful:

> *International flows of direct and portfolio investments under ordinary circumstances are rarely associated with the capital flight phenomenon. Rather, it is when capital transfers by residents conflict with political objectives that the term "flight" comes into general usage.*

Ingo Walter, "The Mechanisms of Capital Flight," in *Capital Flight and Third World Debt*, edited by Donald R. Lessard and John Williamson, Institute for International Economics, Washington, D.C., 1987, p. 104.

Although it is not limited to heavily indebted countries, the rapid and sometimes illegal transfer of convertible currencies out of a country poses significant economic and political problems. Many heavily indebted countries have suffered significant capital flight, which has compounded their problems of debt service.

Five primary mechanisms exist by which capital may be moved from one country to another:

1. Transfers via the usual international payments mechanisms, regular bank transfers, are obviously the easiest and lowest cost, and are legal. Most economically healthy countries allow free exchange of their currencies, but of course for such countries "capital flight" is not a problem.
2. Transfer of physical currency by bearer (the proverbial smuggling out of cash in the false bottom of a suitcase) is more costly and, for transfers out of many countries, illegal. Such transfers may be deemed illegal for balance of payments reasons or to make difficult the movement of money from the drug trade or other illegal activities.
3. The transfer of cash into collectibles or precious metals, which are then transferred across borders.
4. Money laundering, the cross-border purchase of assets, which are then managed in a way that hide the movement of money and its ownership.
5. False invoicing of international trade transactions. Capital is moved through the under-invoicing of exports or the over-invoicing of imports, where the difference between the invoiced amount and the actually agreed-upon payment is deposited in banking institutions in a country of choice.

SUMMARY

- The balance of payments (BOP) is the summary statement of all international transactions between one country and all other countries.
- The BOP is a flow statement, summarizing all the international transactions that occur across the geographic boundaries of the nation over a period of time, typically a year.
- Although the BOP must always balance in theory, in practice there are substantial imbalances as a result of statistical errors and misreporting of Current Account and Capital/Financial Account flows.
- The two major subaccounts of the balance of payments, the Current Account and the Capital/Financial Account, summarize the current trade and international capital flows of the country respectively.
- The Current Account and Capital/Financial Account are typically inverse on balance; one is in surplus while the other experiences deficit.
- Although most nations strive for Current Account surpluses, it is not clear whether a balance on Current or Capital/Financial Account or a surplus on Current Account is either sustainable or desirable.
- Although merchandise trade is more easily observed (e.g., goods flowing through ports of entry), the growth of services trade is more significant to the balance of payments for many of the world's largest industrialized countries.
- Monitoring of the various subaccounts of a country's balance of payment activity is helpful to decision-makers and policymakers on all levels of government and industry in detecting

the underlying trends and movements of fundamental economic forces driving a country's international economic activity.

- The ability of capital to move instantaneously and massively across borders has been one of the major factors in the severity of recent currency crises.
- The rapid and sometimes illegal transfer of convertible currencies out of a country poses significant economic and political problems. Many heavily indebted countries have suffered significant capital flight, which has compounded their problems of debt service.

QUESTIONS

1. **Balance of payments defined.** The measurement of all international economic transactions between the residents of a country and foreign residents is called the balance of payments (BOP). What institution provides the primary source of similar statistics for balance of payments and economic performance worldwide?
2. **Importance of BOP.** Business managers and investors need BOP data to anticipate changes in host country economic policies that might be driven by BOP events. From the perspective of business managers and investors list three specific signals that a country's BOP data can provide.
3. **Economic activity.** What are the two main types of economic activity measured by a country's BOP?
4. **Balance.** Why does the BOP always "balance"?
5. **BOP accounting.** If the BOP were viewed as an accounting statement, would it be a balance sheet of the country's wealth, an income statement of the country's earnings, or a funds flow statement of money into and out of the country?
6. **Current account.** What are the main component accounts of the current account? Give one debit and one credit example for each component account for the United States.
7. **Real versus financial assets.** What is the difference between a "real" asset and a "financial" asset?
8. **Direct versus portfolio investments.** What is the difference between a direct foreign investment and a portfolio foreign investment? Give an example of each. Which type of investment is a multinational industrial company more likely to make?
9. **Capital and Financial accounts.** What are the main components of the Financial accounts? Give one debit and one credit example for each component account for the United States.
10. **Classifying transactions.** Classify the following as a transaction reported in a sub-component of the Current Account or the Capital and Financial Accounts of the two countries involved:
    a. A U.S. food chain imports wine from Chile.
    b. A U.S. resident purchases a euro-denominated bond from a German company.
    c. Singaporean parents pay for their daughter to study at a U.S. university.
    d. A U.S. university gives a tuition grant to a foreign student from Singapore.
    e. A British company imports Spanish oranges, paying with Eurodollars on deposit in London.
    f. The Spanish orchard deposits half the proceeds of its sale in a New York bank.
    g. The Spanish orchard deposits half the proceeds in a eurodollar account in London.
    h. A London-based insurance company buys U.S. corporate bonds for its investment portfolio.
    i. An American multinational enterprise buys insurance from a London insurance broker.
    j. A London insurance firm pays for losses incurred in the United States because of an international terrorist attack.

k. Cathay Pacific Airlines buys jet fuel at Los Angeles International Airport so it can fly the return segment of a flight back to Hong Kong.

l. A California-based mutual fund buys shares of stock on the Tokyo and London stock exchanges.

m. The U.S. army buys food for its troops in South Asia from local vendors.

n. A Yale graduate gets a job with the International Committee of the Red Cross in Bosnia and is paid in Swiss francs.

o. The Russian government hires a Norwegian salvage firm to raise a sunken submarine.

p. A Colombian drug cartel smuggles cocaine into the United States, receives a suitcase of cash, and flies back to Colombia with that cash.

q. The U.S. government pays the salary of a foreign service officer working in the U.S. embassy in Beirut.

r. A Norwegian shipping firm pays U.S. dollars to the Egyptian government for passage of a ship through the Suez canal.

s. A German automobile firm pays the salary of its executive working for a subsidiary in Detroit.

t. An American tourist pays for a hotel in Paris with his American Express card.

u. A French tourist from the provinces pays for a hotel in Paris with his American Express card.

v. A U.S. professor goes abroad for a year on a Fullbright grant.

11. **The Balance.** What are the main summary statements of the balance of payments accounts and what do they measure?

12. **Drugs and terrorists.** Where in the balance of payments accounts do the flows of "laundered" money by drug dealers and international terrorist organizations flow?

13. **Capital mobility – United States.** The US dollar has maintained or increased its value over the past 20 years despite running a gradually increasing current account deficit. Why has this phenomenon occurred?

14. **Capital mobility – Brazil.** Brazil has experienced periodic depreciation of its currency over the past 20 years despite occasionally running a current account surplus. Why has this phenomenon occurred?

15. **Capital flight.** Capital flight has historically weakened the currencies of many countries. What are five of the typical mechanisms by which flight capital can be moved from one currency to another?

16. **U.S. BOP and the U.S. dollar.** With reference to the U.S. balance of payments shown in Exhibit 3.7, identify the specific accounts that enable the U.S. dollar to maintain its value.

PROBLEMS

Australia's Current Account. Use the following data from the International Monetary Fund to answer questions 1 through 4.

Australia's Current Account

(Millions of US dollars)	1998	1999	2000
Goods: exports	55,884	56,096	64,041
Goods: imports	61,215	65,826	68,752
Services: credit	16,181	17,354	18,346
Services: debit	17,272	18,304	18,025
Income: credit	6,532	6,909	8,590
Income: debit	17,842	19,211	19,516
Current transfers: credit	2,651	3,003	2,629
Current transfers: debit	2,933	3,032	2,629

1. What is Australia's balance on goods?
2. What is Australia's balance on services?
3. What is Australia's balance on goods and services?
4. What is Australia's current account balance?

Uruguay's Balance of Payments. Use the following Uruguay balance of payments data from the IMF (all items are for the current account) to answer questions 5 through 9.

Uruguay's Current Account

(Millions of US dollars)	1998	1999	2000
Goods: exports	2,829	2,291	2,380
Goods: imports	3,601	3,187	3,316
Services: credit	1,319	1,262	1,354
Services: debit	884	802	900
Income: credit	608	736	761
Income: debit	806	879	937
Current transfers: credit	75	78	71
Current transfers: debit	16	5	5

5. What is Uruguay's Balance on Goods?
6. What is Uruguay's Balance on Services?
7. What is Uruguay's Balance on Goods and Services?
8. What is Uruguay's Balance on Goods, Services, and Income?
9. What is Uruguay's Current Account balance?

Myanmar. Use the following Myanmar balance of payments data to answer questions 10 through 13.

Myanmar's Current Account

(Millions of US dollars)	1998	1999	2000
A. Current account balance	–494.2	–281.9	–243.0
B. Capital account balance	0.0	0.0	0.0
C. Financial account balance	535.1	248.8	160.1
D. Net errors and omissions	18.8	–12.3	59.6
E. Reserves and related items	–59.7	45.4	23.3

10. Is Myanmar experiencing a net capital inflow or outflow?
11. What is Myanmar's total for Groups A and B?
12. What is Myanmar's total for Groups A through C?
13. What is Myanmar's total for Groups A through D?

Argentina's Balance of Payments. Argentina used a currency board to maintain its peso on a par with the U.S. dollar. However, in January 2002 the peso collapsed. Argentina's BOP could have signaled this event. Listed below is Argentina's BOP for the period 1998–2000. Use this data to answer questions 14 through 20.

Argentina's Current Account

(Millions of US dollars)	1998	1999	2000
A. Current Account			
Goods: exports	26,433	23,309	26,409
Goods: imports	29,532	24,103	23,851
Services: credit	4,618	4,446	4,536
Services: debit	9,127	8,601	8,871
Income: credit	6,121	6,085	7,397
Income: debit	13,537	13,557	14,879
Current transfers: credit	711	688	641
Current transfers: debit	313	306	352
B. Capital Account	73	88	87
C. Financial Account			
Direct investment abroad	2,326	1,354	1,113
Direct investment in Arg.	7,292	23,984	11,665
Portfolio invest. assets, net	–1,905	–2,129	–1,060
Portfolio invest. liab's, net	10,693	–4,782	–1,332
Balance on other invest, net	5,217	–1,026	–50
D. Net Errors and Omissions	–328	–729	–403
E. Reserves and Related Items	–4,090	–2,013	1,176

14. What is Argentina's Balance on Services?
15. What is Argentina's Current Account Balance?
16. What seems to have been the primary driver of Argentina's Current Account between 1998 and 2000?
17. What is Argentina's Financial Account balance?
18. What is Argentina's total for Groups A through C?
19. What is Argentina's total for Groups A through D?
20. Argentina's balance of payments was clearly deteriorating during this period. What does it forecast for the country's currency board regime?

INTERNET EXERCISES

WWW.

1. **World organizations and the economic outlook.** The IMF, World Bank, and United Nations are only a few of the major world organizations which track, report, and aid international economic and financial development. Using these web sites and others that may be linked, briefly summarize the economic outlook for the developed and emerging nations of the world. For example, the full text of chapter 1 of the *World Economic Outlook* published annually by the World Bank is available through the IMF's web page.

International Monetary Fund	http://www.imf.org
United Nations	http://www.unsystem.org
The World Bank Group	http:// www.worldbank.org
Europa (EU) Homepage	http://europa.eu.int
Bank for International Settlements	http:// www.bis.org

2. **St. Louis Federal Reserve.** The Federal Reserve Bank of St. Louis provides a large amount of recent open-economy macroeconomic data online. Use the following addresses to track down recent BOP and GDP data for the major industrial countries.

Recent international economic data	http:// research.stlouisfed.org/publications/iet
Balance of payments statistics	http:// research.stlouisfed.org/fred2/categories/14/ 41

3. **Capital controls.** All countries regulate in some form or fashion the flow of capital into and out of their country. Use the following web site to determine the current openness of the following countries to capital movements: Argentina, Colombia, Malaysia, Nepal, and Taiwan.

Yahoo International Finance Center	http:// biz.yahoo.com/ifc

4. **The Latest BOP numbers for the United States and Japan.** Use the following Bureau of Economic Analysis (U.S. government) and Ministry of Finance (Japanese government) web sites to find the most recent balance of payments statistics for both countries.

Bureau of Economic Analysis	http://www.bea.doc.gov/bea
Ministry of Finance	http://www.mof.go.jp

5. **World Trade Organization and Doha.** The World Trade Organization (WTO) is currently in a multiple-year round of negotiations on international trade. The current round is taking place in Doha, Qatar, and is scheduled to conclude most of its tasks by

January 1, 2005. Visit the WTO's web site and find the most recent evidence presented by the WTO on the progress of talks on issues, including international trade in services and international recognition of intellectual property.

World Trade Organization http:// www.wto.org

SELECTED READINGS

International Monetary Fund, *Balance of Payments Statistics Yearbook*, annual.

Obstfeld, Maurice, and Alan M. Taylor, "Globalization and Capital Markets," paper presented at NBER conference on Globalization in Historical Perspective, Santa Barbara, May 4–5, 2001.

Walter, Ingo, "The Mechanisms of Capital Flight," in *Capital Flight and Third World Debt*, edited by Donald R. Lessard and John Williamson, Institute for International Economics, Washington D.C., 1987, p. 104.

MINI-CASE

Turkey's Kriz (A): Deteriorating Balance of Payments

It was only when optimistic Turks started snapping up imports that investors began to doubt that foreign capital inflows would be sufficient to fund both spendthrift consumers and the perennially penurious government.

"On the Brink Again," *The Economist*, February 24, 2001.

In February 2001 Turkey's rapidly escalating economic kriz, or crisis, forced the devaluation of the Turkish lira. The Turkish government had successfully waged war on the inflationary forces embedded in the country's economy in 1999 and early 2000. But just as the economy began to boom in the second half of 2000, pressures on the country's balance of payments and currency rose. The question asked by many analysts in the months following the crisis was whether the crisis had been predictable, and what early signs of deterioration should have been noted by the outside world.

The Accounts

Exhibit A presents the Turkish balances on Current Account and Financial Account between 1993 and 2000 (ending less than two months prior to the devaluation). Several issues are immediately evident.

- First, Turkey seemingly suffered significant volatility in the balances on key international accounts. The Financial Account swung between surplus (1993) to deficit (1994), and back to surplus again (1995–1997). After plummeting in 1998, the financial surplus returned in 1999 and 2000.
- Secondly, as is typically the case, the Current Account behaved in a relatively inverse manner to the Financial Account, running deficits in most of the years shown. But significantly, the deficit on Current Account grew dramatically in 2000, to over $9.8 billion, from a deficit in 1999 of only $1.4 billion.

Many analysts are quick to point out that the sizeable increase in the Current Account deficit should have been seen as a danger signal of imminent collapse. Others, however, point out quite correctly that most national economies experience rapid increases in trade and Current Account deficits during rapid periods of economic growth. And to add weight to the argument, the net

Exhibit A **Turkey's Balance of Payments, 1993–2000**

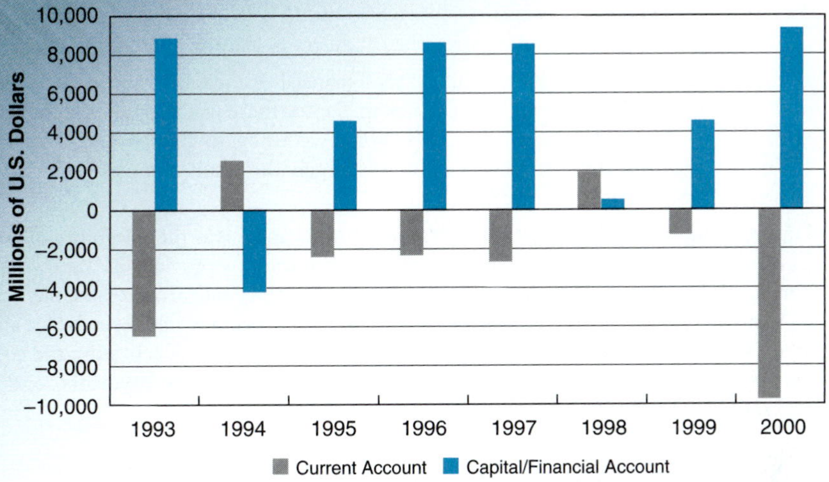

surplus on the Financial Account seemed to indicate a growing confidence in the Turkish economy's outlook by foreign investors.

An examination of the subcomponents of these major account balances is helpful. As illustrated in Exhibit B, the rapid deterioration of the Current Account in 2000 was largely the result of a

Exhibit B **Sub-Accounts of the Turkish Current Account, 1998–2000 (millions of U.S. dollars)**

	1998	1999	2000
Goods: exports	31,220	29,325	31,664
Goods: imports	–45,440	–39,768	–54,041
Balance on Goods	–14,220	–10,443	–22,377
Services: credit	23,321	16,398	19,484
Services: debit	–9,859	–8,953	–8,149
Balance on Services	13,462	7,445	11,335
Income: credit	2,481	2,350	2,836
Income: debit	–5,466	–5,887	–6,838
Balance on Income	–2,985	–3,537	–4,002
Current transfers: credit	5,860	5,294	5,317
Current transfers: debit	–133	–119	–92
Balance on Transfers	5,727	5,175	5,225
Balance on Current Account	1,984	–1,360	–9,819

Source: International Monetary Fund, *Balance of Payments Statistics Yearbook*, 2001, p. 913.

rapid jump in imported goods and merchandise. The goods import bill rose from $39.8 billion in 1999 to over $54.0 billion in 2000, an increase of 36% in one year. At the same time, services trade and current income accounts, both credits and debits subcomponents, showed little change. Unfortunately, the statistics reported to the IMF provide little in additional detail as to the composition of these rapid imports, their industry or nature, and their financing.

A similar decomposition of the surplus on the Financial Account also allows us to identify where in the various inflows and outflows of capital in Turkey there was a significant change. Exhibit C provides this Financial Account decomposition. According to Exhibit C, the doubling of the Turkish Financial Account surplus in 2000 was largely the result of a massive increase—over $7 billion—in "net other investment."

One very important determinant of these account balances was the telecommunications sector. Throughout 2000 TelSim, the national telecommunications provider in Turkey, imported billions of dollars worth of equipment from Nokia (Finland) and Motorola (United States). The equipment was purchased on trade credit, meaning that TelSim would repay Nokia and Motorola at a future date for the equipment, primarily from the proceeds of activating the equipment for telecommunications services. TelSim, however, defaulted on its payments, and Nokia and Motorola were left with billions of dollars in losses.

Exhibit C Sub-Accounts of the Turkish Financial Account, 1998–2000 (millions of U.S. dollars)

	1998	1999	2000
Net direct investment	573	138	112
Net portfolio investment	–6,711	3,429	1,022
Net other investment	6,586	1,103	8,311
Balance on Financial Account	448	4,670	9,445

Source: International Monetary Fund, *Balance of Payments Statistics Yearbook*, 2001, p. 913.

Case Questions

1. Where in the Current Account would the imported telecommunications equipment be listed? Would this correspond to the increase in magnitude and timing of the Financial Account?
2. Why do you think that net direct investment declined from $571 million in 1998 to $112 million in 2000?
3. Why do you think that TelSim defaulted on its payments for equipment imports from Nokia and Motorola?

PART 2

Foreign Exchange Theory and Markets

PART 2

Part 2 examines how foreign exchange theories and markets operate as background knowledge that must be understood by management of MNEs in order to measure and manage their firms' foreign exchange risks.

Chapter 4 describes the foreign exchange markets with respect to their geographical extent, functions performed, market participants, and size. The chapter ends with a detailed description of how *foreign exchange rates* are quoted, *cross rates* are determined, and *international arbitrage* occurs.

Chapter 5 explains the world of *foreign currency derivatives.* It starts with a description of *foreign currency futures* and how they compare to forward contracts. It then describes foreign currency *put and call options*, the markets on which they are traded, and how they are quoted. We then show how options can be used for speculation compared to speculating in the spot and forward markets. The chapter ends with an analysis of how we can price and value options. An interesting mini-case on Nicholas Leeson and Baring Brothers illustrates the potential danger if foreign currency futures and options are abused.

Chapter 6 examines international parity conditions that are the underlying determinants of foreign exchange rates. It explores the relationship between prices and exchange rates, defined as *purchasing power parity.* It then explains the relationship between interest and exchange rates through the *Fisher effect* and the *international Fisher effect.* It shows how *covered interest arbitrage* ensures that *interest rate parity* will hold. This means that the difference between short-term interest rates in two countries should be equal to the forward premium or discount on their currencies. It also shows how speculators can use *uncovered interest arbitrage* to gamble on their expectations about future spot exchange rates. The chapter then discusses whether the forward exchange rate is a good predictor of the future spot rate. It concludes with a model showing how prices, interest rates, and exchange rates should trend toward equilibrium.

Chapter 7 examines how to forecast foreign exchange rates. It describes the *balance of payments approach*, the *asset market approach*, and the *technical analysis approach*. It then describes how disequilibrium has characterized exchange rates in a number of emerging country markets. Chapter 7 presents detailed analyses of currency and economic crises in Asia starting in 1997, Russia in 1998, and Argentina in 2001–2002. The final section describes how foreign exchange rates are forecast in practice.

Chapter 4

The Foreign Exchange Market

THE *FOREIGN EXCHANGE MARKET* PROVIDES THE PHYSICAL AND INSTITUTIONAL STRUCTURE THROUGH which the money of one country is exchanged for that of another country, the rate of exchange between currencies is determined, and foreign exchange transactions are physically completed. *Foreign exchange* means the money of a foreign country; that is, foreign currency bank balances, banknotes, checks, and drafts. A *foreign exchange transaction* is an agreement between a buyer and seller that a fixed amount of one currency will be delivered for some other currency at a specified rate.

This chapter describes the following features of the foreign exchange market:

- Geographical extent
- Three main functions
- Participants
- Immense daily transaction volume
- Types of transactions, including spot, forward, and swap transactions
- Methods of stating exchange rates, quotations, and changes in exchange rates

Geographical Extent of the Foreign Exchange Market

The foreign exchange market spans the globe, with prices moving and currencies trading somewhere every hour of every business day. Major world trading starts each morning in Sydney and Tokyo; moves west to Hong Kong and Singapore; passes on to Bahrain; shifts to the main European markets of Frankfurt, Zurich, and London; jumps the Atlantic to New York; goes west to Chicago; and ends in San Francisco and Los Angeles. Many large international banks operate foreign exchange trading rooms in each major geographic trading center in order to serve important commercial accounts on a round-the clock-basis. Global currency trading is indeed a 24-hour-a-day process. As illustrated in Exhibit 4.1, the volume of currency transactions ebbs and flows across the globe as the major currency trading centers of London, New York, and Tokyo open and close throughout the day.

In some countries, a portion of foreign exchange trading is conducted on an official trading floor by open bidding. Closing prices are published as the official, or "fixing," price for the day, and certain commercial and investment transactions are based on

Exhibit 4.1 Measuring Foreign Exchange Market Activity: Average Electronic Conversations Per Hour

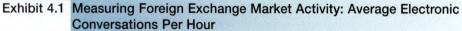

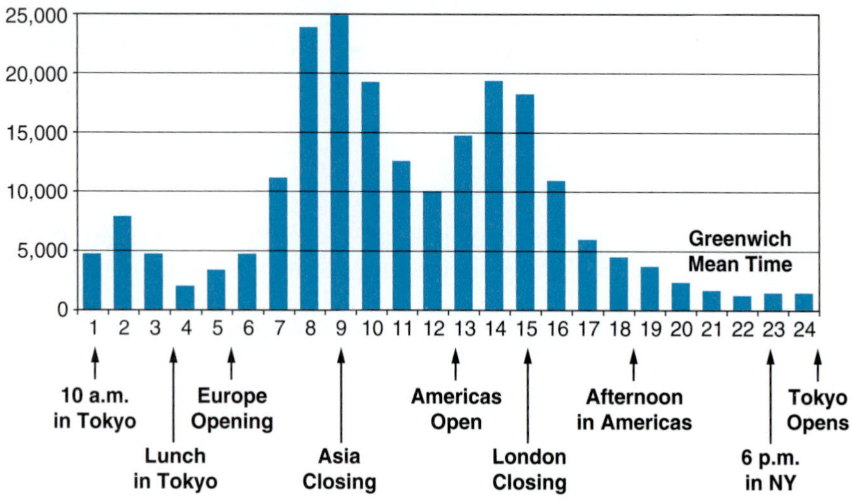

Source: Federal Reserve Bank of New York, "The Foreign Exchange Market in the United States," 2001, http://www.ny.frb.org.

this official price. Business firms in countries with exchange controls often must surrender foreign exchange earned from exports to the central bank at the daily fixing price.

Banks engaged in foreign exchange trading are connected by highly sophisticated telecommunications networks. Professional dealers and brokers obtain exchange rate quotes on desktop computer screens and communicate with each other by telephone, computer, fax, and telex. The foreign exchange departments of many nonbank business firms also use computer networks to keep in touch with the market and to seek out the best quotations. Reuters, Telerate, and Bloomberg are the leading suppliers of foreign exchange rate information and trading systems. A recent development has been the introduction of automated "matching" systems into computerized quotation systems. Many dealers think computer-executed transactions will replace other, more conventional, trading systems in the near future.

Functions of the Foreign Exchange Market

The foreign exchange market is the mechanism by which participants transfer purchasing power between countries, obtain or provide credit for international trade transactions, and minimize exposure to the risks of exchange rate changes.

- Transfer of purchasing power is necessary because international trade and capital transactions normally involve parties living in countries with different national currencies. Each party usually wants to deal in its own currency, but the trade or capital transaction can be invoiced in only one currency. Hence one party must deal in a foreign currency.

- Because the movement of goods between countries takes time, inventory in transit must be financed. The foreign exchange market provides a source of credit. Specialized instruments, such as bankers' acceptances and letters of credit, are available to finance international trade. These documents will be explained in Chapter 23.
- The foreign exchange market provides "hedging" facilities for transferring foreign exchange risk to someone else more willing to carry risk. These facilities are explained in Chapter 8.

Market Participants

The foreign exchange market consists of two tiers: the interbank or wholesale market and the client or retail market. Individual transactions in the interbank market are usually for large sums that are multiples of a million U.S. dollars or the equivalent value in other currencies. By contrast, contracts between a bank and its clients are usually for specific smaller amounts.

Five broad categories of participants operate within these two tiers: bank and nonbank foreign exchange dealers, individuals and firms conducting commercial or investment transactions, speculators and arbitragers, central banks and treasuries, and foreign exchange brokers.

Bank and Nonbank Foreign Exchange Dealers

Banks, and a few nonbank foreign exchange dealers, operate in both the interbank and client markets. They profit from buying foreign exchange at a "bid" price and reselling it at a slightly higher "offer" (also called "ask") price. Competition among dealers worldwide narrows the spread between bid and offer and so contributes to making the foreign exchange market "efficient" in the same sense as in securities markets.

Dealers in the foreign exchange departments of large international banks often function as "market makers." Such dealers stand willing at all times to buy and sell those currencies in which they specialize and thus maintain an "inventory" position in those currencies. They trade with other banks in their own monetary centers and with other centers around the world in order to maintain inventories within the trading limits set by bank policy. Trading limits are important because foreign exchange departments of many banks operate as profit centers, and individual dealers are compensated on a profit incentive basis.

Currency trading is quite profitable for commercial and investment banks. Many of the major currency-trading banks in the United States derive between 10% and 20% on average of their annual net income from currency trading. But currency trading is also very profitable for the bank's traders, who typically earn a bonus based on the profitability to the bank of their individual trading activities.

Small- to medium-size banks are likely to participate but not be market makers in the interbank market. Instead of maintaining significant inventory positions, they buy from and sell to larger banks to offset retail transactions with their own customers. Of course, even market-making banks do not make markets in every currency. They trade for their own account in those currencies of most interest to their customers and become participants when filling customer needs in less important currencies.

Individuals and Firms Conducting Commercial and Investment Transactions

Importers and exporters, international portfolio investors, MNEs, tourists, and others use the foreign exchange market to facilitate execution of commercial or investment transactions. Their use of the foreign exchange market is necessary but nevertheless incidental to their underlying commercial or investment purpose. Some of these participants use the market to "hedge" foreign exchange risk. As illustrated by Global Finance Perspective 4.1, however, there are a number of unconventional trading practices in the world today.

Speculators and Arbitragers

Speculators and arbitragers seek to profit from trading in the market itself. They operate in their own interest, without a need or obligation to serve clients or to ensure a continuous market. Whereas dealers seek profit from the spread between bid and offer in addition to what they might gain from changes in exchange rates, speculators seek all of their profit from exchange rate changes. Arbitragers try to profit from simultaneous exchange rate differences in different markets.

A large proportion of speculation and arbitrage is conducted on behalf of major banks by traders employed by those banks. Thus banks act both as exchange dealers and as speculators and arbitragers. (However, banks seldom admit to speculating; they characterize themselves as "taking an aggressive position"!) As illustrated in Global Finance Perspective 4.2, though, there are also many fraudulent currency dealers and funds.

Global Finance Perspective 4.1

Iraqi Dialing for Dinars

For years following the Persian Gulf War, the foreign exchange traders in the streets of Baghdad set the daily foreign exchange rates by listening to the radio. Because so much of the information that came out of the Iraqi Central Bank of the Ministry of Finance was widely assumed to be false, foreign exchange dealers dialed into the news from London or New York to know the latest regarding the continuing tensions between Iraq and Western nations.

To check the health of the Iraqi economy, "forget about visiting the Central Bank of the Ministry of Finance. Take a walk down a narrow side street behind the Shorja outdoor market instead, and watch the black-market money-changers hawk crumpled Ben Franklins."

The foreign exchange traders regularly tune in to the foreign news on their short-wave radios. What they hear—and how they interpret what they hear—will decide what they offer for dollars during their next venture onto the street-side trading floor.

The Iraqi dinar has always fluctuated wildly, because its worth is based on Iraqis' wavering expectations of when the country will be able again to export crude oil—the nation's vital foreign-currency earner—and because Iraq imports so many of its products. When oil flows, Iraq is awash in dollars, which the government sells to the people at inexpensive rates (more than three dollars to a dinar, for example, before the 1991 Gulf War). However, when the prospects for oil exports decrease, the demand for U.S. dollars on the black markets rises dramatically. In short, bad news makes the dollar rise against the dinar and good news makes it fall.

Source: Adapted from "Dialing for Dinars: Iraqis Turn On Radio To Set Exchange Rate," *Wall Street Journal*, Friday September 20, 1996, p. A8.

Global Finance Perspective **4.2**

Beware of Foreign Currency Trading Frauds

Have you been solicited to trade foreign currency contracts (also known as "forex")? If so, you need to know how to spot foreign currency trading frauds. The United States Commodity Futures Trading Commission (CFTC), the federal agency that regulates commodity futures and options markets in the United States, warns consumers to take special care to protect themselves from the various kinds of frauds being perpetrated in today's financial markets, including those involving so-called "foreign currency trading."

A new federal law, the Commodity Futures Modernization Act of 2000, makes clear that the CFTC has the jurisdiction and authority to investigate and take legal action to close down a wide assortment of unregulated firms offering or selling foreign currency futures and options contracts to the general public. In addition, the CFTC has jurisdiction to investigate and prosecute foreign currency fraud occurring in its registered firms and their affiliates.

The CFTC has witnessed the increasing numbers and growing complexity of financial investment opportunities in recent years, including a sharp rise in foreign currency trading scams. While much foreign currency trading is legitimate, various forms of foreign currency trading have been touted in recent years to defraud members of the public.

Warning Signs of Fraud

If you are solicited by a company that claims to trade foreign currencies and asks you to commit funds for those purposes, you should be very careful. Watch for the warning signs listed below, and take the following precautions before placing your funds with any currency trading company.

1. Stay away from opportunities that sound too good to be true
2. Avoid any company that predicts or guarantees large profits
3. Stay away from companies that promise little or no financial risk
4. Don't trade on margin unless you understand what it means
5. Question firms that claim to trade in the "interbank market"
6. Be wary of sending or transferring cash on the Internet, by mail, or otherwise
7. Currency scams often target members of Ethnic Minorities
8. Be sure you get the company's performance track record
9. Don't deal with anyone who won't give you their background

Source: Public warning issued by the U.S. Commodities and Futures Trading Commission. http://www.cftc.gov/opa/enf98/opaforexa15.htm, March 8, 2002.

Central Banks and Treasuries

Central banks and treasuries use the market to acquire or spend their country's foreign exchange reserves as well as to influence the price at which their own currency is traded. They may act to support the value of their own currency because of policies adopted at the national level or because of commitments entered into through membership in joint float agreements, such as the European Monetary System (EMS) central banks' agreement that preceded introduction of the euro. Consequently motive is not to earn a profit as such, but rather to influence the foreign exchange value of their currency in a manner that will benefit the interests of their citizens. In many instances, they do their job best when they willingly take a loss on their foreign exchange transactions. As willing loss takers, central banks and treasuries differ in motive and behavior from all other market participants.

Foreign Exchange Brokers

Foreign exchange brokers are agents who facilitate trading between dealers without themselves becoming principals in the transaction. For this service, they charge a small commission. They maintain instant access to hundreds of dealers worldwide via open telephone lines. At times a broker may maintain a dozen or more such lines to a single client bank, with separate lines for different currencies and for spot and forward markets.

It is a broker's business to know at any moment exactly which dealers want to buy or sell any currency. This knowledge enables the broker to find quickly an opposite party for a client without revealing the identity of either party until after a transaction has been agreed upon. Dealers use brokers for speed and because they want to remain anonymous, since the identity of participants may influence short-term quotes.

Transactions in the Interbank Market

Transactions in the interbank market are conducted via the latest technology in telecommunications. Since there is little face-to-face foreign exchange trading (except those few countries still using trading floors), complete trust between parties is critical. Nevertheless, as described in Global Finance Perspective 4.2, foreign exchange trading frauds have occurred. In the United States, the Commodity Futures Modernization Act of 2000 gives the responsibility to regulate foreign exchange trading fraud to the U.S. Commodity Futures Trading Commission (CFTC).

Transactions in the foreign exchange market can be executed on a "spot," "forward," or "swap" basis. A broader definition of the foreign exchange market includes foreign currency options and futures (covered in Chapter 5). A spot transaction requires almost immediate delivery of foreign exchange. A forward transaction requires delivery of foreign exchange at some future date, either on an "outright" basis or through a "futures" contract. A swap transaction is the simultaneous exchange of one foreign currency for another.

Spot Transactions

A *spot transaction* in the interbank market is the purchase of foreign exchange, with delivery and payment between banks to take place, normally, on the second following business day. The Canadian dollar settles with the U.S. dollar on the first following business day.

The date of settlement is referred to as the *value date*. On the value date, most dollar transactions in the world are settled through the computerized Clearing House Interbank Payments System (CHIPS) in New York, which provides for calculation of net balances owed by any one bank to another and for payment by 6:00 P.M. that same day in Federal Reserve Bank of New York funds.

A typical spot transaction in the interbank market might involve a U.S. bank contracting on a Monday for the transfer of £10,000,000 to the account of a London bank. If the spot exchange rate were \$1.6984/£, the U.S. bank would transfer £10,000,000 to the London bank on Wednesday, and the London bank would transfer \$16,984,000 to the U.S. bank at the same time. A spot transaction between a bank and its commercial customer would not necessarily involve a wait of two days for settlement.

Outright Forward Transactions

An *outright forward transaction* (usually called just "forward") requires delivery at a future value date of a specified amount of one currency for a specified amount of another currency. The exchange rate is established at the time of the agreement, but payment and delivery are not required until maturity. Forward exchange rates are normally quoted for value dates of one, two, three, six, and twelve months. Actual contracts can be arranged for other numbers of months or, on occasion, for periods of more than one year. Payment is on the second business day after the even-month anniversary of the trade. Thus a two-month forward transaction entered into on March 18 will be for a value date of May 20, or the next business day if May 20 falls on a weekend or holiday.

Note that as a matter of terminology we can speak of "buying forward" or "selling forward" to describe the same transaction. A contract to deliver dollars for euros in six months is both "buying euros forward for dollars" and "selling dollars forward for euros."

Swap Transactions

A *swap transaction* in the interbank market is the simultaneous purchase and sale of a given amount of foreign exchange for two different value dates. Both purchase and sale are conducted with the same counterparty. A common type of swap is a "spot against forward." The dealer buys a currency in the spot market and simultaneously sells the same amount back to the same bank in the forward market. Since this is executed as a single transaction with one counterparty, the dealer incurs no unexpected foreign exchange risk. Swap transactions and outright forwards combined made up 57% of all foreign exchange market activity in April 2001.

Forward-forward swaps. A more sophisticated swap transaction is called a *forward-forward* swap. A dealer sells £20,000,000 forward for dollars for delivery in, say, two months at $1.6870/£ and simultaneously buys £20,000,000 forward for delivery in three months at $1.6820/£. The difference between the buying price and the selling price is equivalent to the interest rate differential, i.e., interest rate parity, between the two currencies. Thus a swap can be viewed as a technique for borrowing another currency on a fully collateralized basis.

Nondeliverable forwards (NDFs). Created in the early 1990s, the *nondeliverable forward*, or NDF, is now a relatively common derivative offered by the largest providers of foreign exchange derivatives. NDFs possess the same characteristics and documentation requirements as traditional forward contracts except that they are settled only in U.S. dollars and the foreign currency being sold forward or bought forward is not delivered. The dollar-settlement feature reflects the fact that NDFs are contracted offshore, for example, in New York for a Mexican investor, and so are beyond the reach and regulatory frameworks of the home country governments (Mexico, in this case). NDFs are used primarily for emerging market currencies, currencies that typically do not have liquid money markets or eurocurrency interest rates. Pricing of NDFs reflects basic interest differentials, as with regular forward contracts, plus an additional premium charged by the bank for dollar settlement.

Size of the Market

The Bank for International Settlements (BIS), in conjunction with central banks around the world, conducts a survey of currency trading activity every three years. The most recent survey, conducted in April 2001, estimated daily global net turnover in traditional foreign exchange market activity to be $1,210 billion, the first decline observed by the BIS since it began surveying banks on foreign currency trading in the 1980s. BIS data is shown in Exhibit 4.2.

Exhibit 4.2 Global Foreign Exchange Market Turnover (daily averages in April, billions of U.S. dollars)

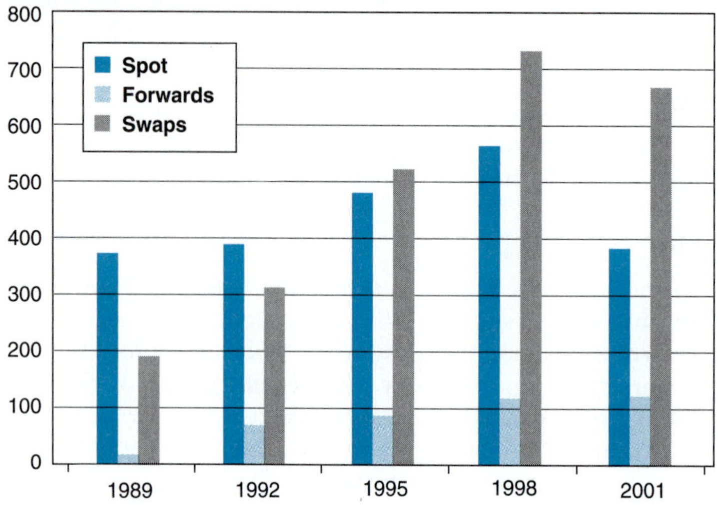

Source: Bank for International Settlements, "Central Bank Survey of Foreign Exchange and Derivatives Market Activity in April 2001," October 2001, http://www.bis.org.

Global foreign exchange turnover in Exhibit 4.2 is divided into three categories of currency instruments: spot transactions, forward transactions, and swap transactions. Two of the three categories of currency transactions fell between the 1998 and 2001 surveys. Spot market daily turnover fell the farthest, from $568 billion in 1998 to $387 billion in 2001. Forward transactions actually increased, rising slightly from $128 billion to $131 billion.

Foreign exchange swaps fell to $656 billion in 2001 from $734 billion in 1998.The BIS attributes the introduction of the euro (in place of the individual European currencies and intra–European Monetary System exchange), the growing share of electronic broking in the spot interbank market, and consolidation in banking in general as the likely explanations of this market reduction.

Exhibit 4.3 shows the proportionate share of foreign exchange trading for the most important national markets in the world in April 2001. (Note that although the data is collected and reported on a national basis, "the United States" should largely be interpreted as "New York," due to the fact that the great majority of foreign exchange trading takes place in the major city in each country.) The United Kingdom (London) continues to be the world's major foreign exchange market in traditional foreign exchange market activity with roughly $500 billion in average daily turnover. The U.K. is followed by the United States (New York), Japan (Tokyo), Singapore, and Germany (Frankfurt). Indeed, more than half of all world foreign exchange trading takes place in just those five countries. Foreign exchange trading in both Japan and Singapore each individually exceeds that in any European country except the United Kingdom, and Hong Kong (not shown) is seventh in the world.

Exhibit 4.4 summarizes the BIS April 2001 survey results by currency, rather than by country of traditional trading activity. Because every foreign exchange transaction involves two cur-

Exhibit 4.3 Geographic Distribution of Foreign Exchange Market Turnover (daily averages in April, billions of U.S. dollars)

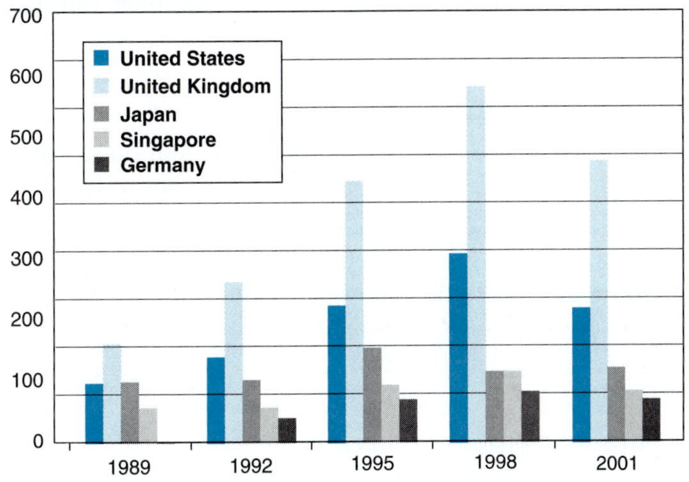

Source: Bank for International Settlements, "Central Bank Survey of Foreign Exchange and Derivatives Market Activity in April 2001," October 2001, http://www.bis.org.

Exhibit 4.4 Currency Distribution of Global Foreign Exchange Market Turnover (percentage shares of average daily turnover in April)

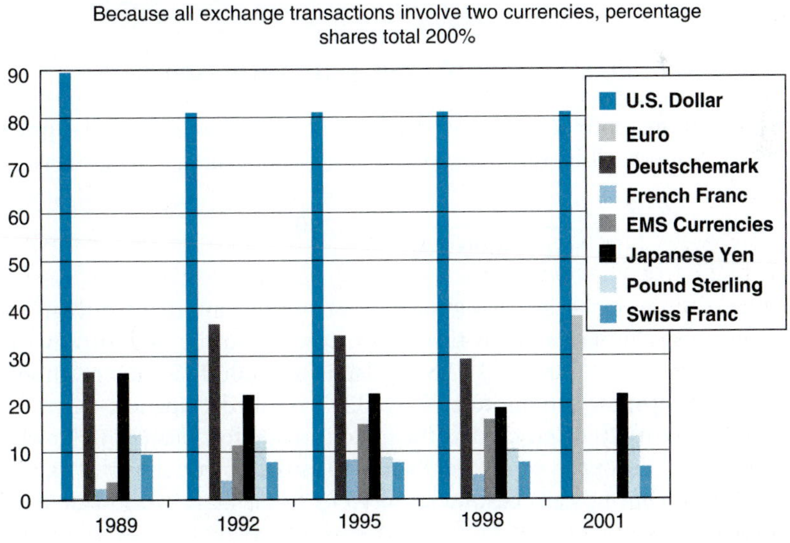

Source: Bank for International Settlements, "Central Bank Survey of Foreign Exchange and Derivatives Market Activity in April 2001," October 2001, http://www.bis.org.

rencies, the data cannot logically be broken down by single currency alone. Hence the sum of the world's reported transactions comes to twice the actual turnover, and the percent of total trades for each currency totals 200%. Net global turnover in April 2001 was dominated by trading in U.S. dollars, euros, and Japanese yen. The "big three," as they are often called, were followed by the U.K. pound sterling and the Swiss franc, in that order.

Foreign Exchange Rates and Quotations

A foreign exchange rate is the price of one currency expressed in terms of another currency. A foreign exchange quotation (or quote) is a statement of willingness to buy or sell at an announced rate.

In the retail market (including newspapers and foreign exchange booths at airports), quotes are most often given as the home currency price of the foreign currency and are also given for many currency pairs. However, this practice is not uniform worldwide. As described in the next section, the professional interbank market has standardized its quotation system.

Interbank Quotations

Recall from Exhibit 4.4 that most foreign exchange transactions involve the U.S. dollar. Professional dealers and brokers may state foreign exchange quotations in one of two ways: 1) the foreign currency price of one dollar, or 2) the dollar price of a unit of foreign currency. Most foreign currencies in the world are stated in terms of the number of units of foreign currency needed to buy one dollar. For example, the exchange rate between U.S. dollars and Swiss franc is normally stated:

SF1.6000/$, read as "1.6000 Swiss francs per dollar."

This method, called *European terms*, expresses the rate as the foreign currency price of one U.S. dollar. An alternative method is called *American terms*. The same exchange rate expressed in American terms is:

$0.6250/SF, read as "0.6250 dollars per Swiss franc."

Under American terms, foreign exchange rates are stated as the U.S. dollar price of one unit of foreign currency. Note that European terms and American terms are reciprocals:

$$\frac{1}{SF1.6000\,/\,\$} = \$0.6250\,/\,SF$$

With several exceptions, including two important ones, most interbank quotations around the world are stated in European terms. Thus throughout the world the normal way of quoting the relationship between the Swiss franc and U.S. dollar is SF1.6000/$; this method may also be called "Swiss terms." A Japanese yen quote of ¥118.32/$ is called "Japanese terms," although the expression "European terms" is often used as the generic name for Asian as well as European currency prices of the dollar. European terms were adopted as the universal way of expressing foreign exchange rates for most (but not all) currencies in 1978 to facilitate worldwide trading through telecommunications.

As mentioned, several exceptions exist to the use of European terms quotes. The two most important are quotes for the euro and for the U.K. pound sterling. The euro, first traded in

January 1999, and the U.K. pound sterling are both normally quoted in American terms; that is, the U.S. dollar price of a euro or a pound sterling. Additionally, Australian dollars and New Zealand dollars are normally quoted in American terms. Sterling is quoted as the foreign currency price of one pound for historical reasons. For centuries the British pound sterling consisted of 20 shillings, each of which had 12 pence. Multiplication and division with the nondecimal currency were difficult. The custom evolved for foreign exchange prices in London, then the undisputed financial capital of the world, to be stated in foreign currency units per pound. This practice remained even after sterling changed to decimals in 1971.

American terms are used in quoting rates for most foreign currency options and futures, as well as in retail markets that deal with tourists and personal remittances. Foreign exchange traders use nicknames for major currencies. "Cable" means the exchange rate between U.S. dollars and U.K. pound sterling, the name dating from the time when transactions in dollars and pounds were carried out over the Trans-Atlantic telegraph cable. A Canadian dollar is a "loonie," named after the water fowl on Canada's one-dollar coin. "Paris" means the French franc, while "Kiwi" stands for the New Zealand dollar, "Aussie" for the Australian dollar, "Swissie" for Swiss francs, and "Sing dollar" for the Singapore dollar.

Currency amounts must be precise in foreign exchange conversations to avoid major blunders. Unfortunately British and U.S. English meaning differs for the word "billion." For the British, "one billion" is 1 followed by 12 zeros; i.e., 1,000,000,000,000 or a million million. In the United States and France, where the system of numeration is based on groups of threes rather than fours, one billion is a thousand million, or 1,000,000,000. For the British, a "trillion" is a million billions, while in U.S. and French usage a "trillion" is a thousand billions; i.e., the same as one British billion.[1] To avoid confusion, foreign exchange traders use the word "yard" to describe a U.S. billion.

Direct and Indirect Quotes

Foreign exchange quotes are at times described as either *direct* or *indirect.* In this pair of definitions, the home or base country of the currencies being discussed is critical.

A *direct quote* is a home currency price of a unit of foreign currency, and an *indirect quote* is a foreign currency price of a unit of home currency. The form of the quote depends on what the speaker regards as "home."

The foreign exchange quote, "SF1.6000/\$" is a direct quote in Switzerland—it is the Swiss home currency (Swiss franc) price of a foreign currency (U.S. dollar). Exactly the same quotation, "SF1.6000/\$," is an indirect quotation when used in the United States—it is now the foreign currency (Swiss franc) price of the home currency (U.S. dollar). The reciprocal of this quote, "\$0.6250/SF," is a direct quote in the United States and an indirect quote in Switzerland.

The direct dollar quote against the Swiss franc, \$0.6250/SF in the previous example, can also be referred to as the "external value of the Swiss franc"—that is, the value of one Swiss franc outside of Switzerland. The "internal value of the Swiss franc" is SF1.6000/\$—the number of Swiss francs that can be purchased for one dollar.

1. *The Shorter Oxford English Dictionary on Historical Principles*, 3rd Edition, Volumes I and II, Oxford: Clarendon Press, 1973.

Bid and Ask Quotations

Interbank quotations are given as a bid and ask (also referred to as offer). A *bid* is the price (i.e., exchange rate) in one currency at which a dealer will buy another currency. An *ask* is the price (i.e., exchange rate) at which a dealer will sell the other currency. Dealers bid (buy) at one price and ask (sell) at a slightly higher price, making their profit from the spread between the buying and selling prices.

Bid and ask quotations in the foreign exchange markets are superficially complicated in that the bid for one currency is also the ask for the opposite currency. A trader seeking to buy dollars with Swiss francs is simultaneously offering to sell Swiss francs for dollars. Assume a bank makes the quotations shown in the top half of Exhibit 4.5 for the Japanese yen. The spot quotations on the first line indicate that the bank's foreign exchange trader will buy dollars (i.e., sell Japanese yen) at the bid price of ¥118.27 per dollar. The trader will sell dollars (i.e., buy Japanese yen) at the ask price of ¥118.37 per dollar.

As illustrated in Exhibit 4.5, however, the full outright quotation (the full price to all of its decimal points) is typically shown only for the current spot rate. Traders, however, tend to abbreviate when talking on the phone or putting quotations on a video screen. The first term, the bid, of a spot quotation may be given in full: that is, "118.27." However, the second term, the ask, will probably be expressed only as the digits that differ from the bid. Hence the bid and ask for spot yen would probably be shown "118.27-37" on a video screen.

Exhibit 4.5 Spot and Forward Quotations for the Euro and Japanese Yen

		Euro: Spot & Forward ($/€)			Yen: Spot & Forward (¥/$)		
	Term	**Mid Rates**	**Bid**	**Ask**	**Mid Rates**	**Bid**	**Ask**
	Spot	1.0899	1.0897	1.0901	118.32	118.27	118.37
Cash	1 week	1.0903	3	4	118.23	−10	−9
Rates	1 mo	1.0917	17	19	117.82	−51	−50
	2 mo	1.0934	35	36	117.38	−95	−93
	3 mo	1.0953	53	54	116.91	−143	−140
	4 mo	1.0973	72	76	116.40	−195	−190
	5 mo	1.0992	90	95	115.94	−240	−237
	6 mo	1.1012	112	113	115.45	−288	−287
	9 mo	1.1075	175	177	114.00	−435	−429
	1 yr	1.1143	242	245	112.50	−584	−581
Swap	2 yr	1.1401	481	522	106.93	−1150	−1129
Rates	3 yr	1.1679	750	810	101.09	−1748	−1698
	4 yr	1.1899	960	1039	96.82	−2185	−2115
	5 yr	1.2102	1129	1276	92.91	−2592	−2490

Note: mo is month, yr is year. Mid Rates are the numerical average of Bid and Ask.

Expressing Forward Quotations on a Points Basis

The spot quotations given in the top line for each currency in Exhibit 4.5 are "outright": ¥118.27/$ for the spot bid and ¥118.37/$ for the spot ask. The forward rates are, however, typically quoted in terms of points, also referred to as "cash rates" and "swap rates," depending on maturity. A point is the last digit of a quotation, with convention dictating the number of digits to the right of the decimal point. Currency prices for the U.S. dollar are usually expressed to four decimal points. Hence a point is equal to 0.0001 of most currencies. Some currencies, such as the Japanese yen shown in Exhibit 4.5, are quoted only to two decimal points. A forward quotation expressed in points is not a foreign exchange rate as such. Rather it is the *difference* between the forward rate and the spot rate. Consequently the spot rate itself can never be given on a points basis.

The three-month points quotations for the Japanese yen in Exhibit 4.5 are "–143" bid and "–140" ask. The first number ("–143") refers to points away from the spot bid, and the second number ("–140") to points away from the spot ask. Given the outright quotes of 118.27 bid and 118.37 ask, the outright three-month forward rates are calculated as follows:

	Bid	*Ask*
Outright spot:	¥118.27	¥118.37
plus points (3 months)	–1.43	–1.40
Outright forward:	¥116.84	¥116.97

The forward bid and ask quotations in Exhibit 4.5 for two years or longer are called *swap rates.* As mentioned earlier, many forward exchange transactions in the interbank market involve a simultaneous purchase for one date and sale (reversing the transaction) for another date. This "swap" is a way to borrow one currency for a limited time while giving up the use of another currency for the same time. In other words, it is a short-term borrowing of one currency combined with a short-term loan of an equivalent amount of another currency. The two parties could, if they wanted, charge each other interest at the going rate for each of the currencies. However, it is easier for the party with the higher-interest currency to simply pay the net interest differential to the other. The swap rate expresses this net interest differential on a points basis rather than as an interest rate.

Forward Quotations in Percentage Terms

As introduced in Chapter 2, forward quotations may also be expressed as the percent-per-annum deviation from the spot rate. This method of quotation facilitates comparing premiums or discounts in the forward market with interest rate differentials. However, the percent premium or discount depends on which currency is the *home*, or *base*, currency. Assume the following quotations, where the dollar is the home currency:

	Foreign currency/ home currency	*Home currency/ foreign currency*
Spot rate	¥105.65/$	$0.009465215/¥
3-month forward	¥105.04/$	$0.009520183/¥

Quotations expressed in foreign currency terms. (Indirect quotations.) When the foreign currency price of the home currency is used, the formula for the percent-per-annum premium or discount becomes:

$$f^{¥} = \frac{\text{spot} - \text{forward}}{\text{forward}} \times \frac{360}{n} \times 100$$

where n is the number of days in the contract (n may also be the number of months, in which case the numerator is 12).

Substituting ¥/$ spot and forward rates, as well as the number of days forward (90):

$$f^{¥} = \frac{105.65 - 105.04}{105.04} \times \frac{360}{90} \times 100 = +2.32\% \text{ per annum}$$

The sign is positive indicating that the forward yen is selling at a 2.32% per annum premium over the dollar.

Quotations expressed in home currency terms (Direct quotatons.) When the home currency price for a foreign currency is used, the formula for the percent premium or discount ($f^{¥}$) is:

$$f^{¥} = \frac{\text{forward} - \text{spot}}{\text{spot}} \times \frac{360}{n} \times 100$$

Substituting the $/¥ spot and forward rates, as well as the number of days forward (90):

$$f^{¥} = \frac{0.009520183 - 0.009465215}{0.009465215} \times \frac{360}{90} \times 100 = +2.32\% \text{ per annum}$$

The sign is positive, indicating that the forward yen is selling at a 2.32% per annum premium over the dollar.

Reading Newspaper Quotations

Foreign exchange rates are quoted in all major world newspapers. The manner of quotation in the *Wall Street Journal* and the *Financial Times*, two of the world's major English-language business newspapers, is shown in Exhibits 4.6 and 4.7. Although these quotes for the pound are for the same day, they are not identical because of time zone differences and because different banks were surveyed for the quotes.

The *Wall Street Journal* gives American terms quotes under the heading "U.S. $ equivalent" and European terms quotes under the heading "Currency per U.S. $." Quotes are for the past two trading days, and are given on an outright basis for spot, one-, three-, and six-month forwards (forwards are listed only for a few select currencies). The heading of the table states that quotes are "selling rates," i.e., ask rates. Bid rates are not given. Quotes are for trading among banks in amounts of $1 million or more, as quoted at 4 P.M. Eastern Standard Time by Reuters and other sources. The *Journal* states that retail transactions provide fewer units of foreign currency per dollar.

Exhibit 4.6 Exchange Rate Quotes from the *Wall Street Journal*

	U.S. $ equivalent		Currency per U.S. $	
	Thu	Wed	Thu	Wed
Britain (Pound)	1.4443	1.4475	.6924	.6908
1-month forward	1.4418	1.4452	.6936	.6919
3-months forward	1.4371	1.4401	.6958	.6944
6-months forward	1.4301	1.4336	.6993	.6975

Source: "Exchange Rates," The *Wall Street Journal*, Friday, October 19, 2001 (quotes for Thursday, October 18), p. C11.

Exhibit 4.7 Foreign Exchange Quotes from the *Financial Times*

	Closing mid-point	Change on day	Bid/offer spread	Day's mid high	Day's mid low	One month Rate	One month %PA	Three months Rate	Three months %PA	One year Rate	One year %PA
UK (£)	1.4446	-0.0066	444-447	1.4502	1.4419	1.4421	2.1	1.4374	2.0	1.4183	1.8

Source: "Dollar Spot, Forward Against The Dollar," The *Financial Times*, Friday, October 19, 2001 (quotes for Thursday, October 18), p. 31.

The *Financial Times* presents the latest day's spread and closing bid and ask quotes in its first three columns. One-month, three-month, and one-year forward rates are quoted in direct terms as well as expressed in terms of the percent per annum deviation from the spot rate.

Cross Rates

Many currency pairs are only inactively traded, so their exchange rate is determined through their relationship to a widely traded third currency (*cross rate*). For example, a Mexican importer needs Japanese yen to pay for purchases in Tokyo. Both the Mexican peso (Ps) and the Japanese yen (¥) are commonly quoted against the U.S. dollar. Assume the following quotes:

Japanese yen	¥121.13/$
Mexican peso	Ps9.1900/$

The Mexican importer can buy one U.S. dollar for Ps9.1900, and with that dollar buy ¥121.13. The cross rate calculation would be:

$$\frac{\text{Japanese yen / US dollar}}{\text{Mexican pesos / US dollar}} \times \frac{¥121.13 / \$}{\text{Ps}9.1900 / \$} = ¥13.1806 / \text{Ps}$$

The cross rate could also be calculated as the reciprocal:

$$\frac{\text{Mexican pesos / US dollar}}{\text{Japanese yen / US dollar}} \times \frac{\text{Ps}9.1900 / \$}{¥121.13 / \$} = \text{Ps}0.0759 / ¥$$

Cross rates often appear in financial publications in the form of a matrix such as is shown in Exhibit 4.8. This matrix shows the amount of each currency (columns) needed to buy a unit of the currency of the country on the row. For example, reading across the row labeled "Mexico," it takes 9.1900 Mexican pesos to buy one U.S. dollar, 8.3124 pesos to buy one euro, and 13.273 pesos to buy one U.K. pound.

Intermarket Arbitrage

Cross rates can be used to check on opportunities for intermarket arbitrage. Suppose the following exchange rates are quoted:

Citibank quotes U.S. dollars per euro:	\$0.9045/€
Barclays Bank quotes U.S. dollars per pound sterling	\$1.4443/£
Dresdner Bank quotes euros per pound sterling:	€1.6200/£

The cross rate between Citibank and Barclays Bank is:

$$\frac{\$1.4443 / £}{\$0.9045 / €} = €1.5968 / £$$

This cross rate is not the same as Dresdner Bank's quotation of €1.6200/£, so an opportunity exists to profit from arbitrage between the three markets. Exhibits 4.9A and 4.9B show the steps in what is called *triangular arbitrage.*

A market trader with \$1,000,000 can sell that sum spot to Barclays Bank for \$1,000,000 ÷ \$1.4443/£ = £692,377. Simultaneously these pounds can be sold to Dresdner Bank for £692,377 × €1.6200/£ = €1,121,651, and the trader can then immediately sell these euros to

Exhibit 4.8 Key Currency Cross Rates

	Dollar	Euro	Pound	Sfranc	Guilder	Peso	Yen	Lira	D-Mark	Ffranc	CdnDlr
Canada	1.5787	1.4279	2.2801	0.9655	.64796	.17178	.01303	.00074	.73010	.21769	....
France	7.2522	6.5596	10.4744	4.4353	2.9766	.78914	.05987	.00339	3.3539	....	4.5938
Germany	2.1623	1.9558	3.1230	1.3224	.88750	.23529	.01785	.00101	....	.29816	1.3697
Italy	2140.7	1936.3	3091.8	1309.2	878.63	232.94	17.673	....	990.00	295.18	1356.0
Japan	121.13	109.56	174.95	74.081	49.717	13.181	....	.05658	56.019	16.703	76.728
Mexico	9.1900	8.3124	13.273	5.6205	3.7720	....	.07587	.00429	4.2501	1.2672	5.8212
Netherlands	2.4364	2.2037	3.5189	1.4901	....	.26511	.02011	.00114	1.1268	.33595	1.5433
Switzerland	1.6351	1.4789	2.3616	....	.67111	.17792	.01350	.00076	.75619	.22546	1.0357
U.K.	.69240	.6263	....	.4234	.28418	.07534	.00572	.00032	.32020	.09547	.43857
Euro	1.10560	....	1.5968	.67616	.45378	.12030	.00913	.00052	.51130	.15245	.70031
U.S.	....	.9045	1.4443	.61158	.41044	.10881	.00826	.00047	.46247	.13789	.63343

Source: Reuters, as quoted in "Key Currency Cross Rates," the *Wall Street Journal*, Friday, October 19, 2001. Quotes are for late New York trading, Thursday, October 18, 2001.

Exhibit 4.9 A Triangular Arbitrage

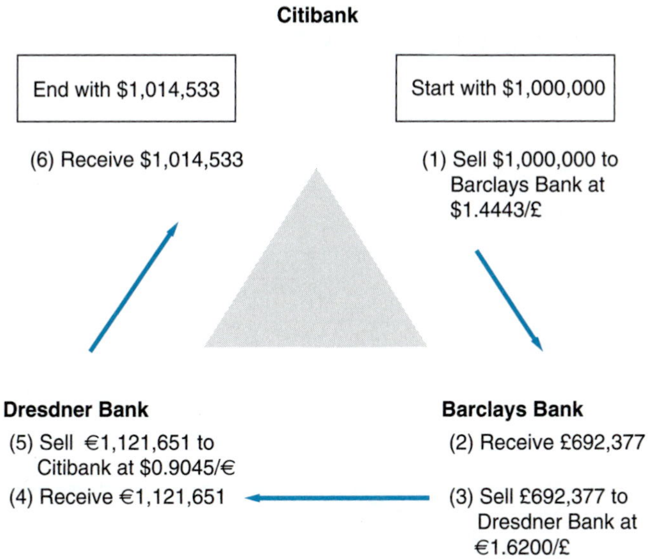

Citibank for dollars: €1,121,651 × $0.9045/€ = $1,014,533. The profit on one such "turn" is a risk-free $14,533. Such triangular arbitrage can continue until exchange rate equilibrium is reestablished; that is, until the calculated cross rate equals the actual quotation, less any tiny margin for transaction costs.

Exhibit 4.9B shows a sensitivity analysis and the equilibrium exchange rate (no gain or loss) for the triangular arbitrage in Exhibit 4.9A. Note that when the Dresdner quote is less than the Barclay/Citibank cross rate, the loss can be reversed by moving money counter-clockwise to the triangular flow shown in Exhibit 4.9A. Therefore it is always possible to profit when the intermediate quote and cross rate are different.

Exhibit 4.9B is the first time we use a spreadsheet construction of an exhibit. Spreadsheets have become a very common tool in all functional areas of business management—marketing, operations, etc.—in addition to their traditional uses in finance and accounting. Some exhibits in this book will use a spreadsheet form. The purpose is both to present important content and to give you some insight into how the content was constructed or calculated. We assume you are already familiar with basic spreadsheet operations calculation components are secondary to the purpose of the exhibit.

Two aspects should be noted: 1) Such arbitrage is practical only if the participants have instant access to quotes and executions. Hence, except in rare instances, such arbitrage is conducted only by foreign exchange traders. "Public" participation is most difficult. 2) Bank traders can conduct such arbitrage without an initial sum of money, other than their bank's credit standing, because the trades are entered into and subsequently "washed" (i.e., offset) by electronic means before the normal settlement two days later.

Exhibit 4.9 B Triangular Arbitrage

	A	B	C	D	E	F	G
1	Exhibit 4.9B Triangular Arbitrage						
2	Bank	Quote		Move	$1,000,000	Sensitivity Analysis	
3	Barclays	$/£	1.4443	$ to £	£692,377	Dresdner Quote	$ Gain or Loss
4	Dresdner	€/£	1.6200	£ to€	€1,121,651		
5	Citibank	$/€	0.9045	€to $	$1,014,533	1.5800	-$10,517
6		Cross Rate		$ Gain =	$14,533	1.5900	-$4,255
7	Barclays/Citibank	€/£	1.5968			1.6000	$2,008
8						1.6100	$8,270
9						1.6200	$14,533

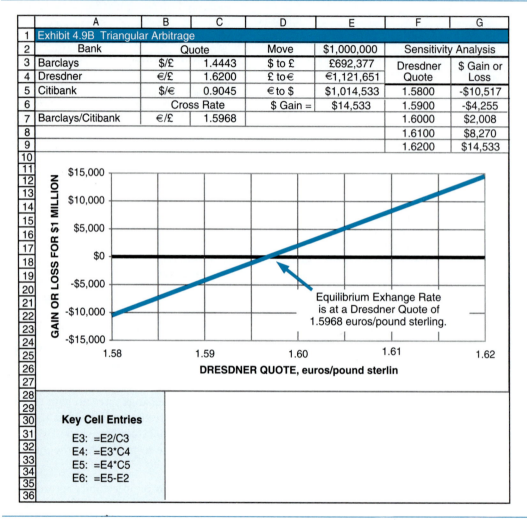

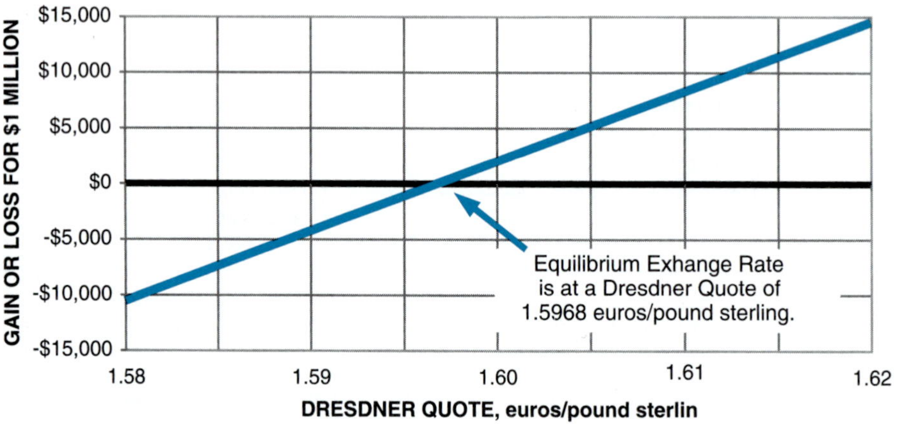

Key Cell Entries

E3: =E2/C3
E4: =E3*C4
E5: =E4*C5
E6: =E5-E2

Measuring a Change in Spot Exchange Rates

Assume that the Swiss franc, recently quoted at SF1.5625/$ (which is the same as $0.6400/SF), suddenly strengthens to SF1.2800/$ (which is the same as $0.78125/SF). What is the percent increase in the dollar value of the franc, and thus in the value of Swiss franc–denominated accounts receivable or payable? As with forward quotations in percentage form, the home currency is critical.

Quotations expressed in home currency terms. (Direct quotations.) When the home currency price for a foreign currency is used, the formula for the percent change in the foreign currency is:

$$\%\Delta = \frac{\text{Ending rate} - \text{Beginning rate}}{\text{Beginning rate}} \times 100 = \frac{\$0.78125\,/\,\text{SF} - \$06400\,/\,\text{SF}}{\$06400\,/\,\text{SF}} \times 100 = +22.07\%$$

In this instance, the Swiss franc is 22.07% stronger at the ending rate. Holders of U.S. dollar receivables will receive 22.07% more dollars—but those who owe Swiss francs will have to pay 22.07% more to buy them.

Quotations expressed in foreign currency terms. (Indirect quotations.) When the foreign currency price of the home currency is used, the formula for the percent change in the foreign currency becomes:

$$\%\Delta = \frac{\text{Beginning rate} - \text{Ending rate}}{\text{Ending rate}} \times 100 = \frac{\text{SF}1.5625\,/\,\$ - \text{SF}1.2800\,/\,\$}{\text{SF}1.2800\,/\,\$} \times 100 = +22.07\%$$

By both methods of calculation, the Swiss franc increased 22.07% in value relative to the dollar.

SUMMARY

- The three functions of the foreign exchange market are to transfer purchasing power, provide credit, and minimize foreign exchange risk.
- The foreign exchange market is composed of two tiers: the interbank market and the client market. Participants within these tiers include bank and nonbank foreign exchange dealers, individuals and firms conducting commercial and investment transactions, speculators and arbitragers, central banks and treasuries, and foreign exchange brokers.
- Geographically, the foreign exchange market spans the globe, with prices moving and currencies traded somewhere every hour of every business day.
- A foreign exchange rate is the price of one currency expressed in terms of another currency. A foreign exchange quotation is a statement of willingness to buy or sell currency at an announced price.
- Transactions within the foreign exchange market are executed either on a spot basis, requiring settlement two days after the transaction, or on a forward or swap basis, which requires settlement at some designated future date.
- European terms quotations are the foreign currency price of a U.S. dollar. American terms quotations are the dollar price of a foreign currency.
- Quotations can be direct or indirect. A direct quote is the home currency price of a unit of foreign currency, while an indirect quote is the foreign currency price of a unit of home currency.
- Direct and indirect are not synonyms for American and European terms, because the home currency will change depending on who is doing the calculation, while European terms are always the foreign currency price of a dollar.
- A cross rate is an exchange rate between two currencies, calculated from their common relationships with a third currency. When cross rates differ from the direct rates between two currencies, intermarket arbitrage is possible.

QUESTIONS

1. **Definitions.** Define the following terms:
   a. Foreign exchange market
   b. Foreign exchange transaction
   c. Foreign exchange
2. **Functions of the foreign exchange market.** What are the three major functions of the foreign exchange market?
3. **Market participants.** For each of the foreign exchange market participants identify their motive for buying or selling foreign exchange.
4. **Transaction.** Define each of the following types of foreign exchange transactions:
   a. Spot
   b. Outright forward
   c. Forward-forward swaps
   d. Non-deliverable forwards (NDFs)
5. **Foreign exchange market characteristics.** With reference to foreign exchange turnover in 2001:
   a. Rank the relative size of spot, forwards, and swaps.
   b. Rank the five most important geographic locations for foreign exchange turnover.
   c. Rank the three most important currencies of denomination.
6. **Foreign exchange rate quotations.** Define and give an example of each of the following quotes:
   a. Bid quote
   b. Ask quote
7. **Reciprocals.** Convert the following indirect quotes to direct quotes and direct quotes to indirect quotes:
   a. Euro: €1.02/$ (indirect quote)
   b. Russia: Rub 30/$ (indirect quote)
   c. Canada: $0.63/C$ (direct quote)
   d. Denmark: $0.1300/DKr (direct quote)
8. **Geographical extent of the foreign exchange market.**
   a. What is the geographical location of the foreign exchange market?
   b. What are the two main types of trading systems for foreign exchange?
   c. How are foreign exchange markets connected for trading activities?
9. **American and European terms.** With reference to interbank quotations, what is the difference between American terms and European terms?
10. **Direct and indirect quotes.**
    a. Define and give an example of a direct quote between the U.S. dollar and the Mexican peso, where the United States is designated as the home country.
    b. Define and give an example of an indirect quote between the Japanese yen and the Chinese renminbi (yuan), where China is designated as the home country.

PROBLEMS

1. **Ringgit up or down?** Before the Asian currency crisis the Malaysian ringgit traded at RM2.7000/$. It currently trades at RM3.8000/$. Did the ringgit appreciate or depreciate, and by what percentage?
2. **Forward premiums and discounts.** Spot and 180-day forward exchange rates for several major currencies follow. For each pair, calculate the percentage premium or discount, expressed as an annual rate.

	Quoted spot rate	180-day forward rate
European euro	$0.8000/€	$0.8160/€
British pound	$1.562/£	$1.5300/£
Japanese yen	¥120.00/$	¥118.00/$
Swiss franc	SF1.6000/$	SF1.6200/$
Hong Kong dollar	HK$8.0000/$	HK$7.8000/$

3. **Trading in Switzerland.** You receive the following quotes for Swiss francs against the dollar for spot, one-month, three months, and six months forward:

   1.6075 to 1.6085, 10 to 15, 14 to 22, 20 to 30

   a. Calculate the outright quotes for bid and ask, and the number of points spread between each bid and ask.

   b. What do you notice about the spread as quotes move from spot to six months forward? Why do you think this occurs?

4. **Yen forward premiums.** Using the midrate yen quotes in Exhibit 4.5:

   a. Calculate the forward premiums or discounts for all maturities listed.

   b. Explain how the forward premium or discount changes as the maturity gets longer.

5. **Euro forward premiums.** Using the midrate euro quotes in Exhibit 4.5:

   a. Calculate the forward premiums or discounts for all maturities listed.

   b. Explain how the forward premium or discount changes as the maturity gets longer.

6. **Traveling: Copenhagen to St. Petersburg.** On your post-graduation celebratory trip, you are leaving Copenhagen, Denmark, for St. Petersburg, Russia. Denmark's currency is the krone (Denmark, although an EU member, is not a participant in the euro.) You leave Copenhagen with 10,000 Danish kroner still in your wallet. Wanting to exchange all of these for Russian rubles, you obtain the following quotes:

Dkr 8.5515/$	R 30.962/$

   a. What is the Danish krone/Russian ruble cross rate?

   b. How many rubles will you obtain for your kroner?

7. **Riskless profit on the franc.** The following exchange rates are available to you.

Mt. Fuji Bank	¥120.00/$
Mt. Rushmore Bank	SF1.6000/$
Matterhorn Bank	¥80.00/SF

   Assume you have an initial SF10,000,000. Can you make a profit via triangular arbitrage? If so, show steps and calculate the amount of profit in Swiss francs.

8. **Trans-Atlantic arbitrage.** A corporate treasury with operations in New York simultaneously calls Citibank in midtown New York and Barclays in London. The two banks give the following quotes at the same time on the euro:

Citibank NY	*Barclays London*
$0.9650-70/€	$0.9640-60/€

   Explain, using $1 million or its euro equivalent, how the corporate treasury could make geographic arbitrage profit with the two different exchange rate quotes.

9. ***Wall Street Journal* quotes and premiums.** Using the *Wall Street Journal* quotes in Exhibit 4.6:

   a. Calculate the forward premiums or discounts for both quotation forms (U.S.$ equivalent and currency per U.S.$).

   b. Why are the forward premiums or discounts not identical? If you use the correct forward premium formulation, shouldn't the premiums be identical? Explain.

10. ***Financial Times* quotes.** Using the spot and forward quotes on the British pound in Exhibit 4.7 in the chapter, demonstrate how the *Financial Times* is calculating the forward premiums on the:

    one-month forward rate

    three-month forward rate

    one-year forward rate

11. **Venezuelan bolivar (A).** The Venezuelan government officially floated the Venezuelan bolivar (Bs) in February of 2002. Within weeks, its value had moved from the pre-float fix of Bs778/$ to Bs1025/$.

    a. Is this a devaluation or a depreciation of the bolivar?

    b. By what percentage did its value change?

12. **Venezuelan bolivar (B).** The Venezuelan political and economic crisis deepened in late 2002 and early 2003. On January 1, 2003, the bolivar

was trading at Bs1400/\$. By February 1, its value had fallen to Bs1950/\$. Many currency analysts and forecasters were predicting that the bolivar would fall an additional 40% from its February 1 value by early summer 2003.

a. By what percentage did the bolivar change in value in January 2003?

b. If the currency forecasters are correct, what would the Bolivar's value be against the dollar in June 2003?

13. **Indirect quotation.** Given the following quotations when the dollar is the home currency:

Spot rate: €1.0200/\$

three-month forward rate: €1.0300/\$

Calculate the forward premium on the dollar.

14. **Direct quotation on the dollar.** Given the following quotations where the dollar is the home currency:

Spot rate: \$1.5500/£

six-month forward rate: \$1.5600/£

Calculate the forward discount on the dollar.

15. **Mexican peso-European euro cross rates.** Given the following exchange rates:

Mexican peso Ps: 10.20/\$

euro: €1.02/\$

Calculate the cross rate between the Mexican peso and the euro.

16. **Around the horn.** Assume the following quotes:

Citibank quotes U.S. dollars per pound at \$1.5400/£

National Westminster quotes euro per pound at €1.6000/£

Deutschebank quotes dollars per euro at \$0.9700/€

Calculate how a market trader at Citibank with \$1,000,000 can make an inter-market arbitrage profit.

INTERNET EXERCISES

www.

1. **Forward quotes.** OzForex Foreign Exchange Services provides representative forward rates on a multitude of currencies on-line. Use the following web site to search out forward exchange rate quotations on a variety of currencies. (Note the London, New York, and Sydney times listed on the quotation screen.)

   OzForex http://www.ozforex.com.au/fxoptions/optiondynamics.htm

2. **Oanda.com currency services.** The Oanda.com company web site has a plethora of currency related data and services. Use the following specific Internet addresses to access some of these services, including the Trading Game.

   Trading game http://fxgame.oanda.com

   FX History http://www.oanda.com/convert/fxhistory

   Currency map http://www.oanda.com/products/fxmap/fxmap.shtml

3. **Emerging market currencies.** Although major currencies like the U.S. dollar and the Japanese yen dominate the headlines, there are nearly as many currencies as countries in the world. Many of these currencies are traded in extremely thin and highly regulated markets, making their convertibility suspect. Finding quotations for these currencies is sometimes very difficult. Using the web page listed below, see how many African currency quotes you can find.

   Emerging Markets http://emgmkts.com

4. **Exchange rate indices.** JP Morgan calculates and maintains indices of many of the world's major currencies' values relative to baskets of other major currencies. Like those published by the IMF, these indices serve as more fundamental and general indicators of relative currency value.

   JP Morgan Currency Indices http://jpmorgan.com/MarketDataInd/Forex/ CurrIndex.html

5. **Pacific Exchange Rate Service.** The Pacific Exchange Rate Service web site, headed by Professor Werner Antweiler of the University of British Columbia, contains a wealth of current information on currency exchange rates and related statistics. Use the service to plot the recent performance of currencies that have suffered recent significant devaluations or depreciations, such as the Argentine peso, the Venezuelan bolivar, the Turkish lira, and the Egyptian pound.

   Pacific Exchange Rate Service http://pacific.commerce.ubc.ca/xr

SELECTED READINGS

Bank for International Settlements, "Central Bank Survey of Foreign Exchange and Derivatives Market Activity in April 2004," October 2004.

Glassman, Debra, "Exchange Rate Risk and Transactions Costs: Evidence from Bid-Ask Spreads," *Journal of International Money and Finance*, Dec 1987, Volume 6, No. 4, pp. 479–491.

Zaheer, Srilata, "Circadian Rhythms: The Effects of Global Market Integration on the Currency Trading Industry," *Journal of International Business Studies*, Fourth Quarter 1995, Volume 26, No. 4, pp. 699–728.

Chapter 5

Foreign Currency Derivatives

FINANCIAL MANAGEMENT OF THE MULTINATIONAL ENTERPRISE IN THE 21ST CENTURY WILL INVOLVE *financial derivatives*. These derivatives, so named because their values are derived from an underlying asset like a stock or a currency, are a powerful tool used in business today for two very distinct management objectives: *speculation* and *hedging*. The financial manager of a MNE may purchase these financial derivatives in order to take positions in the expectation of profit (speculation) or may use these instruments to reduce the risks associated with the everyday management of corporate cash flow (hedging). Before these financial instruments can be used effectively, however, the financial manager must understand certain basics about their structure and pricing. We will cover two common foreign currency financial derivatives in this chapter: *foreign currency options* and *foreign currency futures*. We focus here on the fundamentals of their valuation and their use for speculative purposes. Chapter 8 will describe hedging, or how these foreign currency derivatives can be used to hedge commercial transactions. Chapter 14 will describe the valuation and use of interest rate swaps, the financial derivative most widely used by firms globally today.

A word of caution and reservation before proceeding further. Financial derivatives are a powerful tool in the hands of careful and competent financial managers. They can also be very destructive devices when used recklessly and carelessly. The 1990s were littered with cases in which financial managers lost control of their derivatives, resulting in significant losses for their companies and occasionally their outright collapse. In the right hands and with proper controls, however, financial derivatives can provide management with opportunities to enhance and protect their corporate financial performance. On the other hand, the mini-case at the end of this chapter describes how one rogue trader, Nicholas Leeson, brought down the historic Baring Brothers & Co. through uncontrolled speculation. We begin with the relatively easier foreign currency derivative, the foreign currency future.

Foreign Currency Futures

A *foreign currency futures contract* is an alternative to a forward contract that calls for future delivery of a standard amount of foreign exchange at a fixed time, place, and price. It is similar to futures contracts that exist for commodities (hogs, cattle, lumber, etc.), interest-bearing deposits, and gold.

Most world money centers have established foreign currency futures markets. In the United States, the most important market for foreign currency futures is the International Monetary Market (IMM) of Chicago, a division of the Chicago Mercantile Exchange.

Contract Specifications

Contract specifications are established by the exchange on which futures are traded. Using the Chicago IMM as an example, the major features that must be standardized are the following:

Size of the contract. Called the *notional principal*, trading in each currency must be done in an even multiple of currency units.

Method of stating exchange rates. "American terms" are used; that is, quotations are the U.S. dollar cost of foreign currency units, also known as *direct quotes.*

Maturity date. Contracts mature on the third Wednesday of January, March, April, June, July, September, October, or December.

Last trading day. Contracts may be traded through the second business day prior to the Wednesday on which they mature. Therefore, unless holidays interfere, the last trading day is the Monday preceding the maturity date.

Collateral and maintenance margins. The purchaser must deposit a sum as an initial margin or collateral. This requirement is similar to requiring a performance bond, and it can be met by a letter of credit from a bank, Treasury bills, or cash. In addition, a maintenance margin is required. The value of the contract is marked to market daily, and all changes in value are paid in cash daily. *Marked to market* means that the value of the contract is revalued using the closing price for the day. The amount to be paid is called the *variation margin.*

Settlement. Only about 5% of all futures contracts are settled by the physical delivery of foreign exchange between buyer and seller. Most often, buyers and sellers offset their original position prior to delivery date by taking an opposite position. That is, if one party buys a futures contract, that party will normally close out its position by selling a futures contract for the same delivery date. The complete buy/sell or sell/buy is called a *round turn.*

Commissions. Customers pay a commission to their broker to execute a round turn and a single price is quoted. This practice differs from that of the interbank market, where dealers quote a bid and an offer and do not charge a commission.

Use of a clearing house as a counterparty. All contracts are agreements between the client and the exchange clearing house, rather than between the two clients involved. Consequently clients need not worry that a specific counterparty in the market will fail to honor an agreement. The clearing house is owned and guaranteed by all members of the exchange.

Using Foreign Currency Futures

To illustrate the use of currency futures for speculating on currency movements, we will focus on the Mexican peso futures traded on the Chicago Mercantile Exchange (CME). Exhibit 5.1 presents typical Mexican peso (Ps) futures quotations from the *Wall Street Journal.* Each contract is for 500,000 "new Mexican pesos," and is quoted in U.S. dollars per Mexican peso.

Exhibit 5.1 Mexican Peso Futures, US$/peso (CME)

Maturity	Open	High	Low	Settle	Change	High	Low	Open Interest
Mar	.10953	.10988	.10930	.10958	...	.11000	.09770	34,481
June	.10790	.10795	.10778	.10773	...	.10800	.09730	3,405
Sept	.10615	.10615	.10610	.10573	...	.10615	.09930	1,481

Source: Wall Street Journal, February 22, 2002, p. C13.

All contracts are for 500,000 new Mexican pesos. "Open" means the opening price on the day. "High" means the high price on the day. "Low" indicates the lowest price on the day. "Settle" is the closing price on the day. "Change" indicates the change in the settle price from the previous day's close. "High" and "Low" to the right of "Change" indicate the highest and lowest prices this specific contract (as defined by its maturity) has experienced over its trading history. "Open Interest" indicates the number of contracts outstanding.

Any investor wishing to speculate on the movement of the Mexican peso versus the U.S. dollar could pursue one of the following strategies. Keep in mind that the principle of a futures contract is that if a speculator buys a futures contract, they are locking in the price at which they must buy that currency on the specified future date, and if they sell a futures contract, they are locking in the price at which they must sell that currency on that future date.

Short positions. If Amber McClain, a speculator working for International Currency Traders, believes the Mexican peso will fall in value versus the U.S. dollar by March, she could sell a March futures contract, taking a short position. By selling a March contract, Amber locks in the right to sell 500,000 Mexican pesos at a set price. If the price of the peso does fall by the maturity date as she expects, Amber has a contract to sell pesos at a price above their current price on the spot market. Hence, she makes a profit.

Using the quotes on Mexican peso futures in Exhibit 5.1, Amber sells one March futures contract for 500,000 pesos at the closing price, termed settle price, of \$0.10958/Ps. The value of her position at maturity—at the expiration of the futures contract in March—is then:

$$\text{value at maturity (short position)} = -\text{ notional principal} \times (\text{spot} - \text{futures})$$

Note that the short position is entered into the valuation as a negative notional principal. If the spot exchange rate at maturity is \$0.09500/Ps, the value of her position on settlement is:

$$\text{value} = -\text{ Ps}500{,}000 \times (\$0.09500/\text{Ps} - \$0.10958/\text{Ps}) = \$7{,}290$$

Amber's expectation proved correct; the Mexican peso fell in value versus the U.S. dollar. We could say that "Amber ends up buying at \$0.09500 and sells at \$0.10958 per peso."

All that was really required of Amber to speculate on the Mexican peso's value was that she formed an opinion on the Mexican peso's future exchange value versus the U.S. dollar. In this case, she opined that it would fall in value by the March maturity date of the futures contract.

Long positions. If Amber McClain expected the peso to rise in value versus the dollar in the near term, she could take a long position, by buying a March future on the Mexican peso. Buying a March future means that Amber is locking in the price at which she must buy Mexican pesos at the future's maturity date. Amber's futures contract at maturity would have the following value:

$$\text{value at maturity (long position)} = \text{notional principal} \times (\text{spot} - \text{futures})$$

Again using the March settle price on Mexican peso futures in Exhibit 5.1, \$0.10958/Ps, if the spot exchange rate at maturity is \$0.1100/Ps, Amber has indeed guessed right. The value of her position on settlement is then:

$$\text{value} = \text{Ps}500{,}000 \times (\$.11000/\text{Ps} - \$.10958/\text{Ps}) = \$210$$

In this case, Amber makes a profit in a matter of months of \$210 on the single futures contract. We could say that "Amber buys at \$0.10958 and sells at \$0.11000 per peso."

But what happens if Amber's expectation about the future value of the Mexican peso proves wrong? For example, if the Mexican government announces that the rate of inflation in Mexico has suddenly risen dramatically, and the peso falls to \$0.08000/Ps by the March maturity date, the value of Amber's futures contract on settlement is:

$$\text{value} = \text{Ps}500{,}000 \times (\$.08000/\text{Ps} - \$.10958/\text{Ps}) = (\$14{,}790)$$

In this case, Amber McClain suffers a major speculative loss. Such is the life of the currency speculator!

Futures contracts could obviously be used in combinations to form a variety of more complex positions. When we are combining contracts, however, valuation is fairly straightforward and additive in character.

Foreign Currency Futures Versus Forward Contracts

Foreign currency futures contracts differ from forward contracts in a number of important ways, as shown in Exhibit 5.2. Individuals find futures contracts useful for speculation because they usually do not have access to forward contracts. For businesses, futures contracts are often considered inefficient and burdensome because the futures position is marked to market on a daily basis over the life of the contract. Although this does not require the business to pay or receive cash on a daily basis, it does result in more frequent margin calls from its financial service providers than the business typically wants.

Currency Options

A *foreign currency option* is a contract giving the option purchaser (the buyer) the right, but not the obligation, to buy or sell a given amount of foreign exchange at a fixed price per unit for a specified time period (until the maturity date). The most important phrase in this definition is "but not the obligation"; this means that the owner of an option possesses a valuable choice.

In many ways, buying an option is like buying a ticket to a benefit concert. The buyer has the right to attend the concert, but does not have to do so. The buyer of the concert ticket risks nothing more than what she paid for the ticket. Similarly, the buyer of an option cannot lose anything more than what the buyer paid for the option. If the buyer of the ticket decides later not to attend the concert (prior to the day of the concert) the ticket can be sold to someone else who does wish to go.

- There are two basic types of options: *calls* and *puts*. A *call* is an option to buy foreign currency, and a *put* is an option to sell foreign currency.
- The buyer of an option is termed the *holder*, while the seller of an option is referred to as the *writer* or *grantor*.

Exhibit 5.2 Currency Futures and Forwards Compared

Characteristic	Foreign currency futures	Forward contracts
Size of contract	standardized contracts per currency	any size desired
Maturity	fixed maturities, longest typically being one year	any maturity up to one year, sometimes longer
Location	trading occurs on an organized exchange	trading occurs between individuals and banks with other banks by telecom linkages
Pricing	open outcry process on the exchange floor	prices are determined by bid and ask quotes
Margin/Collateral	initial margin that is marked to market on a daily basis	no explicit collateral, but standard bank relationship necessary
Settlement	rarely delivered upon; settlement normally takes place through purchase of offsetting position	contract is normally delivered upon, although the taking of offsetting positions is possible
Commissions	single commission covers both purchase and sale ("roundtrip")	no explicit commission; banks earn effective commissions through the bid-ask spreads
Trading hours	traditionally traded during exchange hours; some exchanges have moved to 24 hours	negotiated by phone or Internet 24 hours a day through bank global networks
Counterparties	unknown to each other due to the auction market structure	parties are in direct contact in settling forward specifications
Liquidity	liquid but relatively small in total sales volume and value	liquid and relatively large in sales volume compared to futures contracts

Every option has three different price elements: 1) the *exercise* or *strike price*, the exchange rate at which the foreign currency can be purchased (call) or sold (put); 2) the *premium*, the cost, price, or value of the option itself; and 3) the underlying or actual spot exchange rate in the market.

An *American option* gives the buyer the right to exercise the option at any time between the date of writing and the expiration or maturity date. A *European option* can be exercised only on its expiration date, not before. Nevertheless, American and European options are priced almost the same, because the option holder would normally sell the option itself before maturity. The option would then still have some "time value" above its "intrinsic value" if exercised (explained later in this chapter).

- The *premium* or *option price* is the cost of the option, usually paid in advance by the buyer to the seller. In the over-the-counter market (options offered by banks), premiums are quoted as a percentage of the transaction amount. Premiums on exchange-traded options are quoted as a domestic currency amount per unit of foreign currency.

- An option whose exercise price is the same as the spot price of the underlying currency is said to be *at-the-money (ATM)*. An option that would be profitable, excluding the cost of the premium, if exercised immediately is said to be *in-the-money (ITM)*. An option that would not be profitable, again excluding the cost of the premium, if exercised immediately is referred to as *out-of-the-money (OTM)*.

Foreign Currency Options Markets

In the past three decades, the use of foreign currency options as a hedging tool and for speculative purposes has blossomed into a major foreign exchange activity. A number of banks in the United States and other capital markets offer flexible foreign currency options on transactions of $1 million or more. The bank market, or *over-the-counter market* as it is called, offers custom-tailored options on all major trading currencies for any time period up to one year, and in some cases, two to three years.

In December 1982, the Philadelphia Stock Exchange introduced trading in standardized foreign currency option contracts in the United States. The Chicago Mercantile Exchange and other exchanges in the United States and abroad have followed suit. Exchange-traded contracts are particularly appealing to speculators and individuals who do not normally have access to the over-the-counter market. Banks also trade on the exchanges, because it is one of several ways they can offset the risk of options they have transacted with clients or other banks.

Increased use of foreign currency options is a reflection of the explosive growth in the use of other kinds of options and the resultant improvements in option pricing models. The original option pricing model developed by Black and Scholes in 1973 has been commercialized since then by numerous firms offering software programs and even built-in routines for handheld calculators. Several commercial programs are available for option writers and traders to utilize.

Options on the Over-the-Counter Market

Over-the-counter (OTC) options are most frequently written by banks for U.S. dollars against British pounds sterling, Swiss francs, Japanese yen, Canadian dollars, and most recently, the euro.

The main advantage of over-the-counter options is that they are tailored to the specific needs of the firm. Financial institutions are willing to write or buy options that vary by amount (notional principal), strike price, and maturity. Although the over-the-counter markets were relatively illiquid in the early years, the market has grown to such proportions that liquidity is now quite good. On the other hand, the buyer must assess the writing bank's ability to fulfill the option contract. Termed counterparty risk, the financial risk associated with the counterparty is an increasing issue in international markets as a result of the increasing use of financial contracts like options and swaps by MNE management. Exchange-traded options are more the territory of individuals and financial institutions themselves than of business firms.

If an investor wishes to purchase an option in the over-the-counter market, the investor will normally place a call to the currency option desk of a major money center bank; specify the currencies, maturity, strike rate(s); and ask for an *indication*—a bid-offer quote. The bank will normally take a few minutes to a few hours to price the option and return the call.

Options on Organized Exchanges

Options on the physical (underlying) currency are traded on a number of organized exchanges worldwide, including the Philadelphia Stock Exchange (PHLX) and the Chicago Mercantile Exchange.

Exchange-traded options are settled through a clearing house, so that buyers do not deal directly with sellers. The clearing house is the counterparty to every option contract and it guarantees fulfillment. Clearing-house obligations are in turn the obligation of all members of the exchange, including a large number of banks. In the case of the Philadelphia Stock Exchange, clearing house services are provided by the Options Clearing Corporation (OCC).

Currency Option Quotations and Prices

Typical quotes in the *Wall Street Journal* for options on Swiss francs are shown in Exhibit 5.3. The *Journal*'s quotes refer to transactions completed on the Philadelphia Stock Exchange on the previous day. Quotations usually are available for more combinations of strike prices and expiration dates than were actually traded and thus reported in the newspaper. Currency option strike prices and premiums on the U.S. dollar are typically quoted as direct quotations on the U.S. dollar and indirect quotations on the foreign currency ($/SF, $/¥, etc.).

Exhibit 5.3 illustrates the three different prices that characterize any foreign currency option. The three prices that characterize an "August 58½ call option" (highlighted in Exhibit 5.3) are the following:

1. *Spot rate.* In Exhibit 5.3, "Option & Underlying" means that 58.51 cents, or $0.5851, was the spot dollar price of one Swiss franc at the close of trading on the preceding day.
2. *Exercise price.* The exercise price, or "Strike price" listed in Exhibit 5.3, means the price per franc that must be paid if the option is exercised. The August call option on francs of 58½ means $0.5850/SF. Exhibit 5.3 lists nine different strike prices, ranging from $0.5600/SF to $0.6000/SF, although more were available on that date than are listed here.
3. *Premium.* The premium is the cost or price of the option. The price of the August 58½ call option on Swiss francs was 0.50 U.S. cents per franc, or $0.0050/SF. There was no trading of the September and December 58½ call on that day. The premium is the market value of

Exhibit 5.3 Swiss Franc Option* Quotations (U.S. cents/SF)

Option & Underlying	Strike price	Calls—Last Aug	Calls—Last Sep	Calls—Last Dec	Puts—Last Aug	Puts—Last Sep	Puts—Last Dec
58.51	56	—	—	2.76	0.04	0.22	1.16
58.51	56½	—	—	—	0.06	0.30	—
58.51	57	1.13	—	1.74	0.10	0.38	1.27
58.51	57½	0.75	—	—	0.17	0.55	—
58.51	58	0.71	1.05	1.28	0.27	0.89	1.81
58.51	**58½**	**0.50**	**—**	**—**	**0.50**	**0.99**	**—**
58.51	59	0.30	0.66	1.21	0.90	1.36	—
58.51	59½	0.15	0.40	—	2.32	—	—
58.51	60	—	0.31	—	2.32	2.62	3.30

*Each option = 62,500 Swiss francs. The August, September, and December listings are the option *maturities* or expiration dates.

the option, and therefore the terms premium, cost, price, and value are all interchangeable when referring to an option.

The August 58½ call option premium is 0.50 cents per franc, and in this case, the August 58½ put's premium is also 0.50 cents per franc. Since one option contract on the Philadelphia Stock Exchange consists of 62,500 francs, the total cost of one option contract for the call (or put, in this case) is SF62,500 × \$0.0050/SF = \$312.50.

Foreign Currency Speculation

Speculation is an attempt to profit by trading on expectations about prices in the future. In the foreign exchange markets, speculators take an open (unhedged) position in a foreign currency and then close that position after the exchange rate has—they hope—moved in the expected direction. In the following section, we analyze the manner in which speculation is undertaken in spot, forward, and options markets. It is important to understand this phenomenon, because it has a major impact on our inability to accurately forecast future exchange rates. As illustrated by Global Finance Perspective 5.1, however, many currency speculators still get it wrong.

Speculating in the Spot Market

Hans Schmidt is a currency speculator in Zurich, Switzerland. He is willing to risk money on his own opinion about future currency prices. Hans may speculate in the spot, forward, or options markets. To illustrate, assume the Swiss franc is currently quoted as follows:

spot rate:	\$0.5851/SF
six-month forward rate:	\$0.5760/SF

Global Finance Perspective 5.1

Rogue Currency Trader at Allied Irish Bank

John Rusnak, a currency trader at the U.S. Baltimore branch of Allied Irish Bank, became the newest member of the "rogue traders club" in February 2002 when it was disclosed he had lost \$691 million on the bank's behalf. It seems that Mr. Rusnak failed to hedge a series of currency futures contract positions against the potential fall of the Japanese yen. Currency traders typically take positions in the spot and futures markets for expected speculative profit. To protect or "cover" their speculation, however, they typically purchase currency option contracts as insurance against their getting it wrong. The yen fell, Rusnak failed to cover, and the bank suffered the losses.

Rusnak, 37, earned an annual salary of \$85,000, in addition to annual performance bonuses of between \$100,000 and \$150,000 per year over the past 5 years. Unfortunately, his losses—which did not enrich him personally other than his ability to keep his job while making such bad bets—cost Allied Irish Bank greatly. As a result of the losses revealed, Allied Irish's annual earnings for 2001 were reduced to \$424 million, less than half what was previously expected. The bank also had to restate its financial results as reported to the Securities and Exchange Commission in the United States as far back as 1997.

Rusnak's losses reached such astronomical proportions as a result of a complex combination of documents he falsified and a failure in the bank's own control and audit processes. Beginning in 1997, Rusnak had suffered continuing losses on currency positions he took for speculation purposes on behalf of the bank. Rather than acknowledge and report his losses, Rusnak wove a complex series of falsified documents that made it appear that he had been covering the positions throughout. Mr. Rusnak's services were terminated.

Hans has \$100,000 with which to speculate, and he believes that in six months the spot rate for the franc will be \$0.6000/SF. Speculation in the spot market requires only that the speculator believe the foreign currency will appreciate in value. Hans should take the following steps:

1. Use the \$100,000 today to buy SF170,910.96 spot at \$0.5851/SF.
2. Hold the SF170,910.96 indefinitely. Although the franc is expected to rise to the target value in six months, Hans is not committed to that time horizon.
3. When the target exchange rate has been reached, sell SF170,910.96 at the new spot rate of \$0.6000/SF, receiving SF170,910.96 × \$0.6000/SF = \$102,546.57.

This process results in a profit of \$2,546.57, or 2.5% on the \$100,000 committed for six months (5.0% per annum). This ignores for the moment interest income on the Swiss francs and opportunity cost on the dollars.

The potential maximum gain is unlimited, while the maximum loss will be \$100,000 if the francs purchased in step 1 drop in value to zero. Having initially undertaken a spot market speculation for six months, Hans is nevertheless not bound by that target date. He may sell the francs earlier or later if he wishes.

Speculating in the Forward Market

Forward market speculation occurs when the speculator believes that the spot price at some future date will differ from today's forward price for that same date. Success does not depend on the direction of movement of the spot rate, but on the relative position of the future spot rate and the current forward rate. Given the above data and expectations, Hans Schmidt should take the following steps:

1. Today buy SF173,611.11 forward six months at the forward quote of \$0.5760/SF. Note that this step requires no outlay of cash.
2. In six months, fulfill the forward contract, receiving SF173,611.11 at \$0.5760/SF for a cost of \$100,000.
3. Simultaneously sell the SF173,611.11 in the spot market, at Hans's expected future spot rate of \$0.6000/SF, receiving SF173,611.11 × \$0.6000/SF = \$104,166.67.

This results in a profit of \$4,166.67 (\$104,166.67 – \$100,000.00).

The profit of \$4,166.67 cannot be related to an investment base to calculate a return on investment, because the dollar funds were never needed. On the six-month anniversary, Hans simply crosses the payment obligation of \$100,000 with receipts of \$104,166.67, and accepts a net \$4,166.67. Nevertheless, some financial institutions might require him to deposit collateral as margin to ensure his ability to complete the trade.

In this particular forward speculation, the maximum loss is \$100,000, the amount needed to buy francs via the forward contract. This loss would be incurred only if the value of the spot franc in six months were zero. The maximum gain is unlimited, since francs acquired in the forward market can (in theory) rise to an infinite dollar value.

Forward market speculation cannot be extended beyond the maturity date of the forward contract. However, if Hans wants to close out his operation before maturity, he may buy an offsetting contract. In the previous example, after, say, four months, Hans could sell SF173,611.11 forward two months at whatever forward price then existed. Two months after that he would close the matured six-month contract to purchase francs against the matured two-month contract to sell francs, pocketing any profit or paying up any loss. The amount of profit or loss would be fixed by the price at which Hans sold forward two months.

The previous example is only one of several possible types of forward speculations, and ignores any interest earned. In a spot speculation, the speculator can invest the principal amount in the foreign money market to earn interest. In the various forward speculations, a speculator who is holding cash against the risk of loss can invest those funds in the home money market. Thus relative profitability will be influenced by interest differentials.

Speculating in Option Markets

Options differ from all other types of financial instruments in the patterns of risk they produce. The option owner has the choice of exercising the option or allowing it to expire unused. The owner will exercise it only when exercising is profitable, which means only when the option is in the money. In the case of a call option, as the spot price of the underlying currency moves up, the holder has the possibility of unlimited profit. On the downside, however, the holder can abandon the option and walk away with a loss never greater than the premium paid.

Buyer of a Call

The position of Hans as a buyer of a call is illustrated in Exhibit 5.4. Assume he purchases the August call option on Swiss francs described previously, the one with a strike price of 58½ ($0.5850/SF), and a premium of $0.005/SF. The vertical axis measures profit or loss for the option buyer at each of several different spot prices for the franc up to the time of maturity.

At all spot rates below the strike price of 58.5, Hans would choose not to exercise his option. This is obvious because at a spot rate of 58.0, for example, he would prefer to buy a Swiss franc for $0.580 on the spot market rather than exercising his option to buy a franc at $0.585. If the spot rate remains below 58.0 until August when the option expired, Hans would not exercise the option. His total loss would be limited to only what he paid for the option, the $0.005/SF purchase price. At any lower price for the franc, his loss would similarly be limited to the original $0.005/SF cost.

Alternatively, at all spot rates above the strike price of 58.5, Hans would exercise the option, paying only the strike price for each Swiss franc. For example, if the spot rate were 59.5 cents per franc at maturity, he would exercise his call option, buying Swiss francs for $0.585 each instead of purchasing them on the spot market at $0.595 each. He could sell the Swiss francs immediately in the spot market for $0.595 each, pocketing a gross profit of $0.010/SF, or a net profit of $0.005/SF after deducting the original cost of the option of $0.005/SF. Hans's profit, if the spot rate is greater than the strike price, with strike price $0.585, a premium of $0.005, and a spot rate of $0.595, is:

$$\begin{aligned} \text{Profit} &= \text{spot rate} - (\text{strike price} + \text{premium}) \\ &= \$0.595/\text{SF} - (\$0.585/\text{SF} + \$0.005/\text{SF}) \\ &= \$0.005/\text{SF} \end{aligned}$$

Exhibit 5.4 Profit and Loss for the Buyer of a Call Option on Swiss Francs

Exhibit 5.4 Profit and Loss for the Buyer of a Call Option on Swiss Francs

Cost of the Call Option, per Swiss Franc	$0.005					
Exercise or Strike Price, per Swiss Franc	$0.585					
Spot price of Swiss Franc	$0.570	$0.580	$0.585	$0.590	$0.600	$0.610
Buyer's Payoff for Call Option, U.S. cents per Swiss Franc	(0.500)	(0.500)	(0.500)	0.000	1.000	2.000

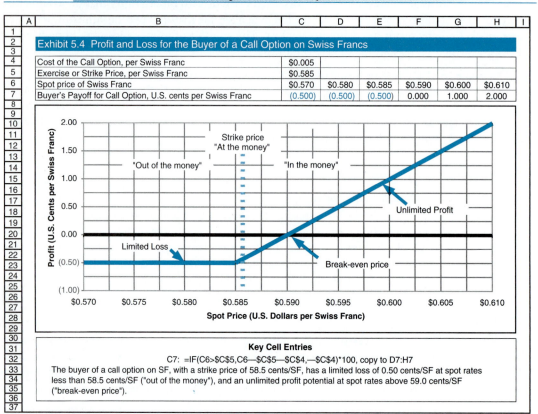

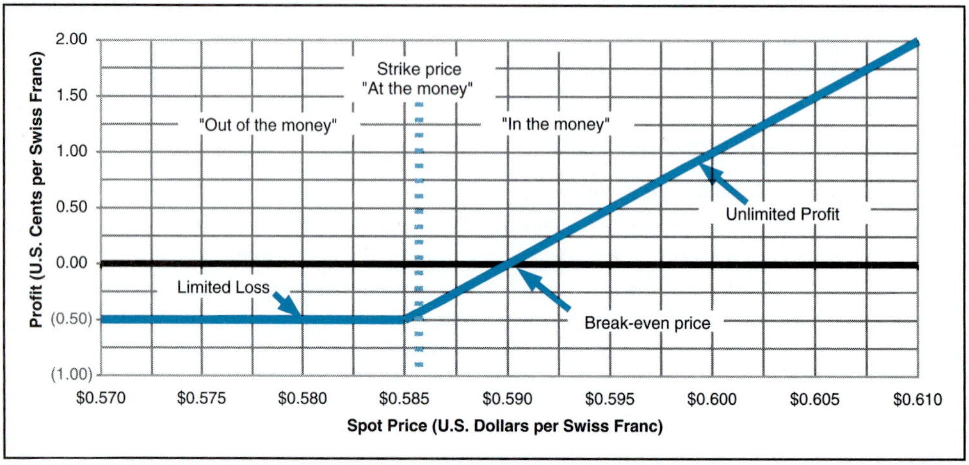

Key Cell Entries

C7: =IF(C6>$C$5,C6—$C$5—$C$4,—$C$4)*100, copy to D7:H7

The buyer of a call option on SF, with a strike price of 58.5 cents/SF, has a limited loss of 0.50 cents/SF at spot rates less than 58.5 cents/SF ("out of the money"), and an unlimited profit potential at spot rates above 59.0 cents/SF ("break-even price").

More likely, Hans would realize the profit through executing an offsetting contract on the options exchange rather than taking delivery of the currency. Because the dollar price of a franc could rise to an infinite level (off the upper right-hand side of the page in Exhibit 5.4), maximum profit is unlimited. The buyer of a call option thus possesses an attractive combination of outcomes: limited loss and unlimited profit potential.

Note that the *break-even price* of $0.590/SF is the price at which Hans neither gains nor loses on exercise of the option. The premium cost of $0.005, combined with the cost of exercising the option of $0.585, is exactly equal to the proceeds from selling the francs in the spot market at $0.590. Note that he will still exercise the call option at the break-even price. This is so because by exercising it he at least recoups the premium paid for the option. At any spot price above the exercise price but below the break-even price, the gross profit earned on exercising the option and selling the underlying currency covers part (but not all) of the premium cost.

Writer of a Call

The position of the writer (seller) of the same call option is illustrated in Exhibit 5.5. If the option expires when the spot price of the underlying currency is below the exercise price of 58.5, the

Exhibit 5.5 Profit and Loss for the Writer of a Call Option on Swiss Francs

Exhibit 5.5 Profit and Loss for the Writer of a Call Option on Swiss Francs

	C	D	E	F	G	H
Cost of the Call Option, per Swiss Franc	$0.005					
Exercise or Strike Price, per Swiss Franc	$0.585					
Spot price of Swiss Franc	$0.570	$0.580	$0.585	$0.590	$0.600	$0.610
Seller's Payoff for Call Option, U.S. cents per Swiss Franc	0.500	0.500	0.500	(0.000)	(1.000)	(2.000)

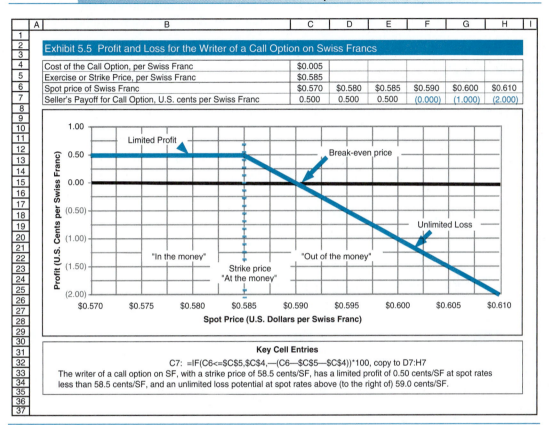

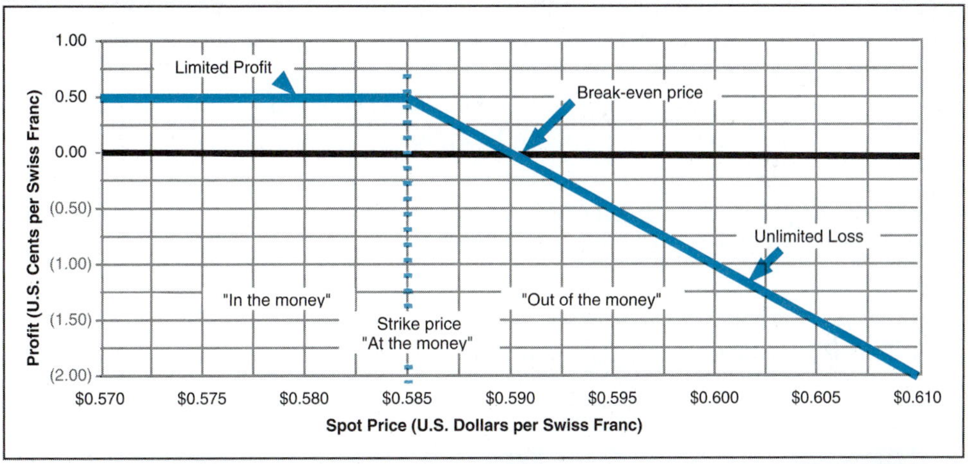

Key Cell Entries

C7: =IF(C6<=$C$5,$C$4,—(C6—$C$5—$C$4))*100, copy to D7:H7

The writer of a call option on SF, with a strike price of 58.5 cents/SF, has a limited profit of 0.50 cents/SF at spot rates less than 58.5 cents/SF, and an unlimited loss potential at spot rates above (to the right of) 59.0 cents/SF.

option holder does not exercise. What the holder loses, the writer gains. The writer keeps as profit the entire premium paid of $0.005/SF. Above the exercise price of 58.5, the writer of the call must deliver the underlying currency for $0.585/SF at a time when the value of the franc is above $0.585. If the writer wrote the option *naked*—that is, without owning the currency—that writer will now have to buy the currency at spot and take the loss. The amount of such a loss is unlimited and increases as the price of the underlying currency rises. Once again, what the holder gains, the writer loses, and vice versa. Even if the writer already owns the currency, the writer will experience an opportunity loss, surrendering against the option the same currency that could have been sold for more in the open market.

For example, the profit to the writer of a call option of strike price $0.585, premium $0.005, a spot rate of $0.595/SF is:

$$\begin{aligned}\text{Profit} &= \text{Premium} - (\text{spot rate} - \text{strike price})\\ &= \$0.005/\text{SF} - (\$0.595/\text{SF} - \$0.585/\text{SF})\\ &= -\ \$0.005/\text{SF}\end{aligned}$$

but only if the spot rate is greater than or equal to the strike rate. At spot rates less than the strike price, the option will expire worthless and the writer of the call option will keep the premium earned. The maximum profit that the writer of the call option can make is limited to the premium. The writer of a call option would have a rather unattractive combination of potential outcomes: limited profit potential and unlimited loss potential; but there are ways to limit such losses through other offsetting techniques.

Buyer of a Put

Hans's position as buyer of a put is illustrated in Exhibit 5.6. The basic terms of this put are similar to those we just used to illustrate a call. The buyer of a put option, however, wants to be able to sell the underlying currency at the exercise price when the market price of that currency drops (not rises as in the case of a call option). If the spot price of a franc drops to, say, $0.575/SF, Hans will deliver francs to the writer and receive $0.585/SF. The francs can now be purchased on the spot market for $0.575 each and the cost of the option was $0.005/SF, so he will have a net gain of $0.005/SF.

Explicitly, the profit to the holder of a put option if the spot rate is less than the strike price, with a strike price $0.585/SF, premium of $0.005/SF, and a spot rate of $0.575/SF, is:

Exhibit 5.6 Profit and Loss for the Buyer of a Put Option on Swiss Francs

Exhibit 5.6 Profit and Loss for the Buyer of a Put Option on Swiss Francs

Cost of the Put Option, per Swiss Franc	$0.005					
Exercise or Strike Price, per Swiss Franc	$0.585					
Spot price of Swiss Franc	$0.560	$0.570	$0.580	$0.585	$0.590	$0.600
Buyer's Payoff for Put Option, U.S. cents per Swiss Franc	2.000	1.000	0.000	(0.500)	(0.500)	(0.500)

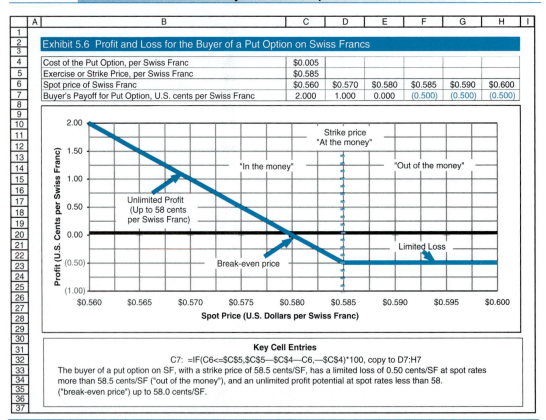

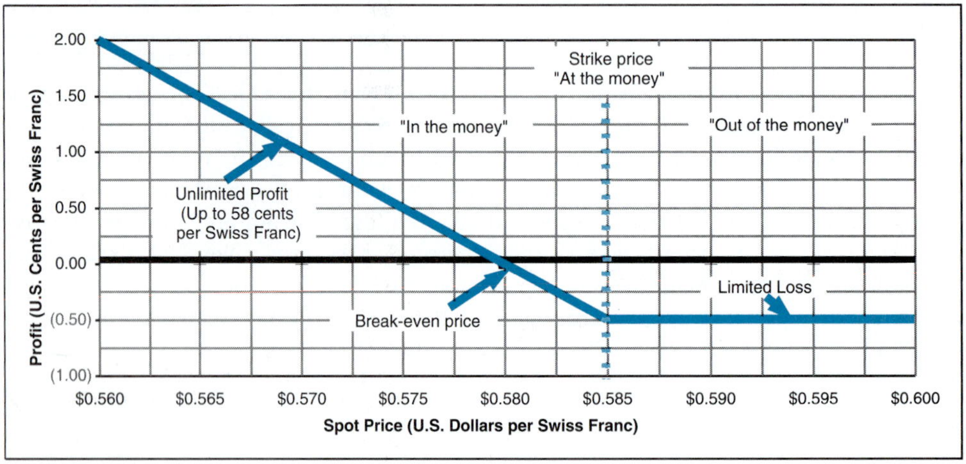

Key Cell Entries

C7: =IF(C6<=$C$5,$C$5—$C$4—C6,—$C$4)*100, copy to D7:H7

The buyer of a put option on SF, with a strike price of 58.5 cents/SF, has a limited loss of 0.50 cents/SF at spot rates more than 58.5 cents/SF ("out of the money"), and an unlimited profit potential at spot rates less than 58. ("break-even price") up to 58.0 cents/SF.

$$\begin{aligned} \text{profit} &= \text{strike price} - (\text{spot rate} + \text{premium}) \\ &= \$0.585/\text{SF} - (\$0.575/\text{SF} + \$0.005/\text{SF}) \\ &= \$0.005/\text{SF} \end{aligned}$$

The break-even price for the put option is the strike price less the premium, or $0.580/SF in this case. As the spot rate falls further and further below the strike price, the profit potential would continually increase, and Hans's profit could be unlimited (up to a maximum of $0.580/SF, when the price of a franc would be zero). At any exchange rate above the strike price of 58.5, Hans would not exercise the option, and so would lose only the $0.005/SF premium paid for the put option. The buyer of a put option has an almost unlimited profit potential with a limited loss potential. Like the buyer of a call, the buyer of a put can never lose more than the premium paid up front.

Writer of a Put

The position of the writer who sold the put to Hans is shown in Exhibit 5.7. Note the symmetry of profit/loss, strike price, and break-even prices between the buyer and the writer of the put. If

Exhibit 5.7 Profit and Loss for the Writer of a Put Option on Swiss Francs

Exhibit 5.7 Profit and Loss for the Writer of a Put Option on Swiss Francs

Cost of the Put Option, per Swiss Franc	$0.005					
Exercise or Strike Price, per Swiss Franc	$0.585					
Spot price of Swiss Franc	$0.560	$0.570	$0.580	$0.585	$0.590	$0.600
Seller's Payoff for Put Option, U.S. cents per Swiss Franc	(2.000)	(1.000)	0.000	0.500	0.500	0.500

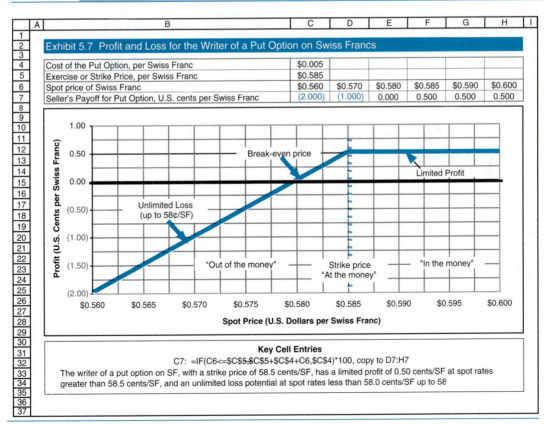

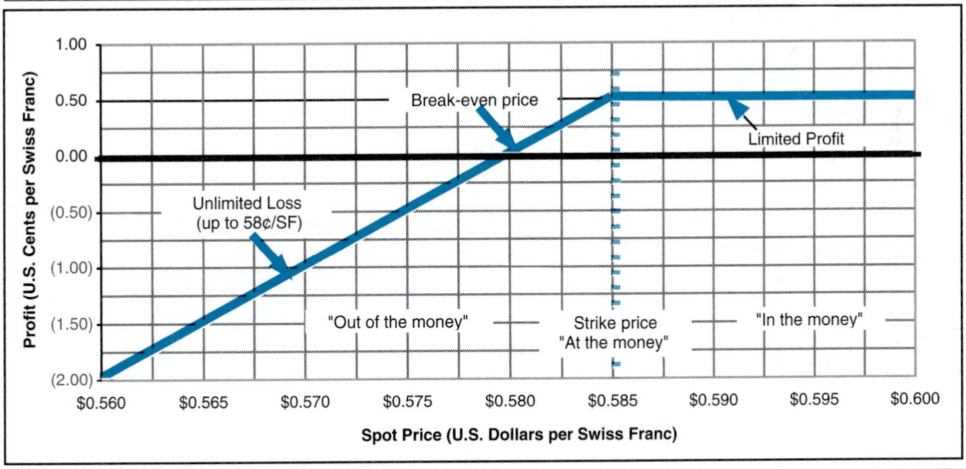

Key Cell Entries

C7: =IF(C6<=$C$5,$C$5+$C$4+C6,$C$4)*100, copy to D7:H7

The writer of a put option on SF, with a strike price of 58.5 cents/SF, has a limited profit of 0.50 cents/SF at spot rates greater than 58.5 cents/SF, and an unlimited loss potential at spot rates less than 58.0 cents/SF up to 58

the spot price of francs drops below 58.5 cents per franc, Hans will exercise the option. Below a price of 58.5 cents per franc, the writer will lose more than the premium received from writing the option ($0.005/SF), falling below break-even. Between $0.580/SF and $0.585/SF the writer will lose part, but not all, of the premium received. If the spot price is above $0.585/SF, Hans will not exercise the option, and the option writer will pocket the entire premium of $0.005/SF.

The profit (loss) earned by the writer of a $0.585 strike price put, premium $0.005, at a spot rate of $0.575, is:

$$\begin{aligned}\text{profit (loss)} &= \text{premium} - (\text{strike price} - \text{spot rate})\\ &= \$0.005/\text{SF} - (\$0.585/\text{SF} - \$0.575/\text{SF})\\ &= -\ \$0.005/\text{SF}\end{aligned}$$

but only for spot rates that are less than or equal to the strike price. At spot rates greater than the strike price, the option expires out-of-the-money and the writer keeps the premium. The writer of the put option has the same basic combination of outcomes available to the writer of a call: limited profit potential and unlimited loss potential.

Option Pricing and Valuation

Exhibit 5.8 illustrates the profit/loss profile of a European-style call option on British pounds. The call option allows the holder to buy British pounds at a strike price of $1.70/£. It has a 90-day maturity. The value of this call option is actually the sum of two components:

$$\text{total value (premium)} = \text{intrinsic value} + \text{time value}$$

The pricing of any currency option combines six elements. For example, this European-style call option on British pounds has a premium of $0.033/£ (3.3 cents per pound) at a spot rate of $1.70/ £. This premium is calculated using the following assumptions:

1. Present spot rate: $1.70/£
2. Time to maturity: 90 days
3. Forward rate for matching maturity (90 days): $1.70/£
4. U.S. dollar interest rate: 8.00% per annum
5. British pound sterling interest rate: 8.00% per annum
6. Volatility, the standard deviation of daily spot price movement: 10.00% per annum

Intrinsic value is the financial gain if the option is exercised immediately. It is shown by the solid line in Exhibit 5.8, which is zero until it reaches the strike price, then rises linearly (one cent for each one-cent increase in the spot rate). Intrinsic value will be zero when the option is out-of-the-money—that is, when the strike price is above the market price—as no gain can be derived from exercising the option. When the spot rate rises above the strike price, the intrinsic value becomes positive, because the option is always worth at least this value if exercised. On the date of maturity, an option will have a value equal to its intrinsic value (zero time remaining means zero time value).

Exhibit 5.8 Intrinsic Value, Time Value, and Total Value for a Call Option on British Pounds with a Strike Price of $1.70/£

Exhibit 5.8 Intrinsic Value,Time Value, and Total Value for a Call Option on British Pounds with a Strike Price of $1.70/ £

Input Data	
Present spot rate, $/£	$1.70
Time to maturity, days	90
Forward rate for matching maturity (90 days), $/£	$1.70
U.S. dollar interest rate, pct/yr	8.0%
British pound sterling interest rate, pct/yr	8.0%
Standard deviation of daily spot price movement, pct/yr	10.0%

Effect of Spot Rate on Intrinsic, Time, and Total Value

Spot rate, $/£	Intrinsic value, US cents/£	Time value, US cents/£	Total value, US cents/£
1.65	0.00	1.37	1.37
1.66	0.00	1.67	1.67
1.67	0.00	2.01	2.01
1.68	0.00	2.39	2.39
1.69	0.00	2.82	2.82
1.70	0.00	3.30	3.30
1.71	1.00	2.82	3.82
1.72	2.00	2.39	4.39
1.73	3.00	2.01	5.01
1.74	4.00	1.67	5.67

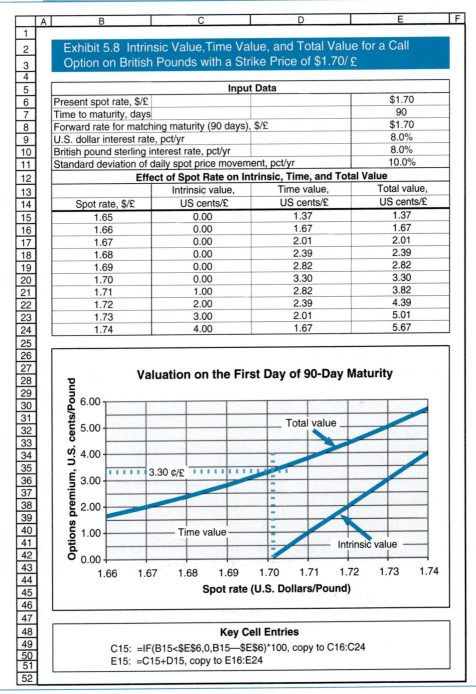

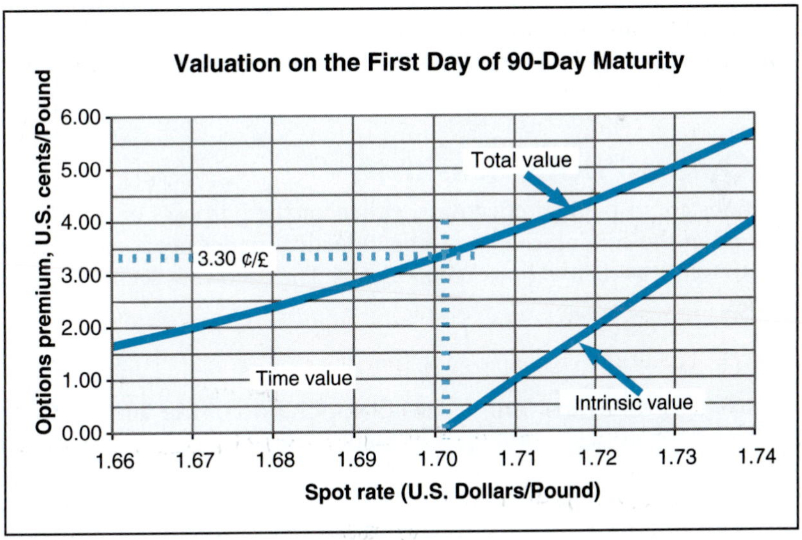

Key Cell Entries

C15: =IF(B15<$E$6,0,B15—$E$6)*100, copy to C16:C24
E15: =C15+D15, copy to E16:E24

- When the spot rate is \$1.74/£, the option is in-the-money and has an *intrinsic value* of \$1.74 – \$1.70/£, or 4 cents per pound.
- When the spot rate is \$1.70/£, the option is at-the-money and has an *intrinsic value* of \$1.70 – \$1.70/£, or zero cents per pound.
- When the spot rate is \$1.66/£, the option is out-of-the-money and has no intrinsic value. Only a fool would exercise this call option at this spot rate instead of buying pounds more cheaply on the spot market.

The *time value* of an option exists because the price of the underlying currency, the spot rate, can potentially move further and further into the money between the present time and the option's expiration date. Time value is shown in Exhibit 5.8 as the area between the *total value* of the option and its intrinsic value.

Exhibit 5.9 separates the total value into intrinsic and time values for the call option depicted in Exhibit 5.8. For example, at a spot rate of \$1.72/£, the option's total value is made up of 2 cents per pound intrinsic value and 2.39 cents per pound in time value for a total value of 4.39 cents per pound.

Note that the time value component is the same in value (symmetric) as you move in either direction away from the strike price of \$1.70/£. For example, the time value is 2.39 cents at spot rates of 1.68 (2 cents below strike) and 1.72 (2 cents above strike). This demonstrates the underlying principle that option pricing is based on an expected distribution of possible outcomes around the forward rate, which in this case is the same as the strike price, \$1.70.

An investor will pay something today for an out-of-the-money option (i.e., zero intrinsic value) on the chance that the spot rate will move far enough before maturity to move the option in-the-money. Consequently, the price of an option is always somewhat greater than its intrinsic value, since there is always some chance that the intrinsic value will rise between the present and the expiration date.

Currency Option Pricing Sensitivity

If currency options are to be used effectively, either for the purposes of speculation or risk management (covered in the coming chapters), the individual trader needs to know how option values —*premiums*—react to their various components. The following section will analyze these six basic sensitivities:

Exhibit 5.9 Intrinsic, Time, and Total Value Components of the 90-Day Call Option on British Pounds at Varying Spot Exchange Rates

					Strike				
Spot (\$/£)	**1.66**	**1.67**	**1.68**	**1.69**	**1.70**	**1.71**	**1.72**	**1.73**	**1.74**
Intrinsic	0.00	0.00	0.00	0.00	0.00	1.00	2.00	3.00	4.00
Time	1.67	2.01	2.39	2.82	3.30	2.82	2.39	2.01	1.67
Total value	1.67	2.01	2.39	2.82	3.30	3.82	4.39	5.01	5.67

1. The impact of changing forward rates
2. The impact of changing spot rates
3. The impact of time to maturity
4. The impact of changing volatility
5. The impact of changing interest differentials
6. The impact of alternative option strike prices

Forward Rate Sensitivity

Although rarely noted, standard foreign currency options are priced around the forward rate because the current spot rate and both the domestic and foreign interest rates (home currency and foreign currency rates) are included in the option premium calculation.[1] Regardless of the specific strike rate chosen and priced, the forward rate is central to valuation. The option-pricing formula calculates a subjective probability distribution centered on the forward rate. This approach does not mean that the market expects the forward rate to be equal to the future spot rate. It is simply a result of the arbitrage-pricing structure of options.

The forward rate focus also provides helpful information for the trader managing a position. When the market prices a foreign currency option, it does so without any bullish or bearish sentiment on the direction of the foreign currency's value relative to the domestic currency. If the trader has specific expectations about the future spot rate's direction, those expectations can be put to work. A trader will not be inherently betting against the market. In a following section, we will also describe how a change in the interest differential between currencies, the theoretical foundation of forward rates, also alters the value of the option.

Spot Rate Sensitivity (delta)

The call option on British pounds depicted in Exhibit 5.8 possesses a premium that exceeds the intrinsic value of the option over the entire range of spot rates surrounding the strike rate. As long as the option has time remaining before expiration, the option will possess this time value element. This characteristic is one of the primary reasons why an American-style option, which can be exercised on any day up to and including the expiration date, is seldom actually exercised prior to expiration. If the option holder wishes to liquidate it for its value, it would normally be sold, not exercised, so any remaining time value can also be captured by the holder. If the current spot rate

---

1. Recall from Chapter 4 that the forward rate is calculated from the current spot rate and the two subject currency interest rates for the desired maturity. For example, the 90-day forward rate for the call option on British pounds described earlier is calculated as follows:

$$F_{90} = \$1.70/£ \times \left[\frac{1 + 0.08\left(\frac{90}{360}\right)}{1 + 0.08\left(\frac{90}{360}\right)} \right] = \$1.70/£$$

falls on the side of the option's strike price which would induce the option holder to exercise the option upon expiration, the option also has an intrinsic value. The call option illustrated in Exhibit 5.8 is in-the-money (ITM) at spot rates to the right of the strike rate of \$1.70/£, at-the-money (ATM) at \$1.70/£, and out-of-the-money (OTM) at spot rates less than \$1.70/£.

The vertical distance between the market value and the intrinsic value of a call option on pounds is greatest at a spot rate of \$1.70/£. At \$1.70/£, the spot rate equals the strike price (at-the-money). This premium of 3.30 cents per pound consists entirely of time value. In fact, the value of any option which is currently out-of-the-money (OTM) is made up entirely of time value. The further the option's strike price is out-of-the-money, the lower the value or premium of the option. This is because the market believes the probability of this option actually moving into the exercise range prior to expiration is significantly less than one that is already at-the-money. If the spot rate were to fall to \$1.68/£, the option premium falls to 2.39 cents/£—again, entirely time value. If the spot rate were to rise above the strike rate to \$1.72/£, the premium rises to 4.39 cents/£. In this case, the premium represents an intrinsic value of 2.00 cents (\$1.72/£ – \$1.70/£) plus a time value element of 2.39 cents. Note the symmetry of time value premiums (2.39 cents) to the left and to the right of the strike rate.

The symmetry of option valuation about the strike rate is seen by decomposing the option premiums into their respective intrinsic and time values. Exhibit 5.10 illustrates how varying the current spot rate by ± \$0.05 about the strike rate of \$1.70/£ alters each option's intrinsic and time values.

The sensitivity of the option premium to a small change in the spot exchange rate is called the *delta*. For example, the delta of the \$1.70/£ call option, when the spot rate changes from \$1.70/£ to \$1.71/£, is simply the change in the premium divided by the change in the spot rate:

$$\text{delta} = \frac{\Delta \text{ premium}}{\Delta \text{ spot rate}} = \frac{\$0.038/£ - \$0.033/£}{\$1.71/£ - \$1.70/£} = 0.5$$

If the delta of the specific option is known, it is easy to determine how the option's value will change as the spot rate changes. If the spot rate changes by one cent (\$0.01/£), given a delta of 0.5, the option premium would change by 0.5 × \$0.01, or \$0.005. If the initial premium was \$0.033/£, and the spot rate increased by 1 cent (from \$1.70/£ to \$1.71/£), the new option premium would be \$0.033 + \$0.005 = \$0.038/£. Delta varies between +1 and 0 for a call option, and –1 and 0 for a put option.

Traders in options categorize individual options by their delta rather than in-the-money, at-the-money, or out-of-the-money. As an option moves further in-the-money, like the in-the-money

Exhibit 5.10 Decomposing Call Option Premiums: Intrinsic Value and Time Value

Strike Rate (\$/£)	Spot Rate (\$/£)	Money	Call Premium (cents/£)	=	Intrinsic Value (cents/£)	+	Time Value (cents/£)	Delta (0 to 1)
1.70	1.75	ITM	6.37		5.00		1.37	.71
1.70	1.70	ATM	3.30		0.00		3.30	.50
1.70	1.65	OTM	1.37		0.00		1.37	.28

option in Exhibit 5.10, delta rises toward 1.0 (in this case to .71). As an option moves further out-of-the-money, delta falls toward zero. Note that the out-of-the-money option in Exhibit 5.10 has a delta of only 0.28.[2]

> Rule of Thumb: The higher the delta (deltas of 0.7, or 0.8 and more are considered high), the greater the probability of the option expiring in-the-money.

Time to Maturity: Value and Deterioration (theta)

Option values increase with the length of time to maturity. The expected change in the option premium from a small change in the time to expiration is termed *theta*.

Theta is calculated as the change in the option premium over the change in time. If the \$1.70/£ call option were to age one day from its initial 90-day maturity, the theta of the call option would be the difference in the two premiums, 3.30 cents/£ and 3.28 cents/£ (assuming a spot rate of \$1.70/£):

$$\text{theta} = \frac{\Delta\,\text{premium}}{\Delta\,\text{time}} = \frac{\text{cents}3.30\,/\,£ - \text{cents}3.28\,/\,£}{90-89} = 0.02$$

Theta is based not on a linear relationship with time, but rather the square root of time. Exhibit 5.11 illustrates the time value deterioration for our same \$1.70/£ call option on pounds. The at-the-money strike rate is \$1.70/£, and the out-of-the- money and in-the-money spot rates are \$1.75/£ and \$1.65/£, respectively. Option premiums deteriorate at an increasing rate as they approach expiration. In fact, the majority of the option premium—depending on the individual option—is lost in the final 30 days prior to expiration.

This exponential relationship between option premium and time is seen in the ratio of option values between the three-month and the one-month at-the-money maturities. The ratio for the at-the-money call option is not 3 to 1 (holding all other components constant), but rather:

$$\frac{\text{premium of 3 month}}{\text{premium of 1 month}} = \frac{\sqrt{3}}{\sqrt{1}} = \frac{1.73}{1.00} = 1.73$$

The three-month option's price is only 1.73 times that of the one-month, not three times the price.

The rapid deterioration of option values in the last days prior to expiration is seen by once again calculating the theta of the \$1.70/£ call option, but now as its remaining maturity moves from 15 days to 14 days:

$$\text{theta} = \frac{\Delta\,\text{premium}}{\Delta\,\text{time}} = \frac{\text{cents}1.37\,/\,£ - \text{cents}1.32\,/\,£}{15-14} = 0.05$$

2. The expected change in the option's delta resulting from a small change in the spot rate is termed *gamma*. It is often used as a measure of the stability of a specific option's delta. Gamma is utilized in the construction of more sophisticated hedging strategies which focus on deltas (delta-neutral strategies).

Exhibit 5.11 Theta: Option Premium Time Value Deterioration

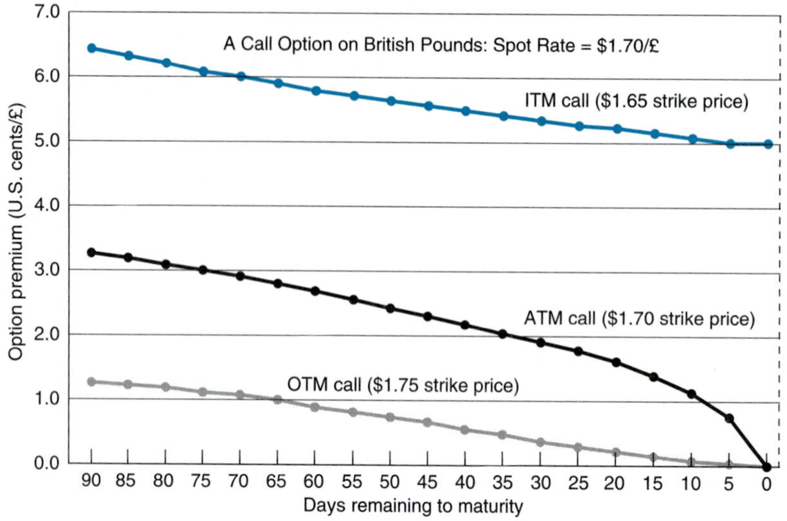

A decrease of one day in the time to maturity now reduces the option premium by 0.05 cents/£, rather than only 0.02 cents/£ as it did when the maturity was 90 days.

Exhibit 5.11 also illustrates the basic spot rate-option premium relations noted previously. The out-of-the-money call option's premium is logically smaller than the at-the-money option throughout its life, but deteriorates at a slower rate due to an initially smaller level to fall from. The in-the-money option is of greater value throughout its time-life relative to the at-the-money, falling toward its intrinsic value (5 cents/£) at expiration. The at-the-money option, however, falls particularly quickly in the final periods prior to expiration. As any specific option ages, moving continually towards expiration, the time value will constantly decrease (assuming nothing else has changed). This situation would be illustrated by the total value line of the call option initially shown in Exhibit 5.8 collapsing inward towards the strike price of $1.70.

The implications of time value deterioration for traders are quite significant. A trader purchasing an option with only one or two months until expiration will see the option's value deteriorate rapidly. If the trader were to then sell the option, it would have a significantly smaller market value in the periods immediately following its purchase.

At the same time, however, a trader who is buying options of longer maturities will pay more, but not proportionately more, for the longer maturity option. A six-month option's premium is approximately 2.45 times more expensive than the one-month, while the twelve-month option would be only 3.46 times more expensive than the one-month. This implies that 2 three-month options do not equal 1 six-month option.

Rule of Thumb: A trader will normally find longer-maturity options better values, giving the trader the ability to alter an option position without suffering significant time value deterioration.

Sensitivity to Volatility (lambda)

There are few words in the financial field more used and abused than *volatility.* Option volatility is defined as the standard deviation of daily percentage changes in the underlying exchange rate. Volatility is important to option value because of an exchange rate's perceived likelihood to move either into or out of the range in which the option would be exercised. If the exchange rate's volatility is rising, and therefore the risk of the option being exercised is increasing, the option premium would be increasing.

Volatility is stated in percent per annum. For example, an option may be described as having a 12.6% annual volatility. The percentage change for a single day can be found as follows:

$$\frac{12.6\%}{\sqrt{365}} = \frac{12.6\%}{19.105} = 0.66\% \text{ daily volatility}$$

For our \$1.70/£ call option, an increase in annual volatility of 1 percentage point—for example, from 10.0% to 11.0%—will increase the option premium from \$0.033/£ to \$0.036/£. The marginal change in the option premium is equal to the change in the option premium itself divided by the change in volatility:

$$\frac{\Delta \text{ premium}}{\Delta \text{ volatility}} = \frac{\$0.036/£ - \$0.033/£}{.11 - .10} = 0.30$$

The primary problem with volatility is that it is unobservable; it is the only input into the option pricing formula that is determined subjectively by the trader pricing the option. No single correct method for its calculation exists. The problem is one of forecasting; historical volatility is not necessarily an accurate predictor of the future volatility of the exchange rate's movement, yet there is little to go on except history.

Volatility is viewed three ways: *historic*, where the volatility is drawn from a recent period of time; *forward-looking*, where the historic volatility is altered to reflect expectations about the future period over which the option will exist; and implied, where the volatility is backed out of the market price of the option.

- *Historic volatility.* Historic volatility is normally measured as the percentage movement in the spot rate on a daily, 6-, or 12-hour basis over the previous 10, 30, or even 90 days.
- *Forward-looking volatility.* Alternatively, an option trader may adjust recent historic volatilities for expected market swings or events, either upward or downward.
- *Implied volatility.* Implied volatility is equivalent to having the answers to the test; implied volatilities are calculated by being backed out of the market option premium values traded. Since volatility is the only unobservable element of the option premium price, after all other components are accounted for, the residual value of volatility implied by the price is used.

If option traders believe that the immediate future will be the same as the recent past, the historic volatility will equal the forward-looking volatility. If, however, the future period is expected to experience greater or lesser volatility, the historic measure must be altered for option pricing.

Selected implied volatilities for a number of currency pairs on January 31, 2002, are listed in Exhibit 5.12. These volatilities are *mid-rates*, the average of the bid and ask rates quoted for option contracts. Exhibit 5.12 clearly illustrates that option volatilities vary considerably across currencies, and that the relationship between volatility and maturity (time to expiration) does not move in just one direction. For example, the first exchange rate quoted, the US$/euro cross-rate, rises from a 9.0% volatility at one week to 10.9% for the three-year maturity. The US$/Canadian dollar cross-rate, however, moves in the opposite direction; from 7.4% for one week to 6.3% for the three-year maturity.

Because volatilities are the only judgmental component that the option writer contributes, they play a critical role in the pricing of options. All currency pairs have historical series that contribute to the formation of the expectations of option writers. But in the end, the truly talented option writers are those with the intuition and insight to price the future effectively.

Like all futures markets, option volatilities react instantaneously and negatively to unsettling economic and political events (or rumor). A doubling of volatility for an at-the-money option will result in an equivalent doubling of the option's price. Most currency option traders focus their activities on predicting movements of currency volatility in the short run, because short-run movements move price the most. For example, option volatilities rose significantly in the months preceding the Persian Gulf War, in September 1992 when the European Monetary System was in crisis, in 1997 after the onset of the Asian financial crisis, and in the days following the terrorist attacks on the United States in September 2001. In all instances option volatilities for major cross-currency combinations such as the SF/$ rose to nearly 20% for extended periods. As a result, premium costs rose by corresponding amounts.

Rule of Thumb: Traders who believe that volatilities will fall significantly in the near-term will sell (write) options now, hoping to buy them back for a profit immediately after volatilities fall, causing option premiums to fall.

Exhibit 5.12 Foreign Exchange Implied Volatility, January 31, 2002

		Currency Option Maturity							
Currency (cross)	**Symbol**	**1 week**	**1 month**	**2 month**	**3 month**	**6 month**	**12 month**	**2 year**	**3 year**
European euro	EUR	9.0	9.2	9.4	9.8	10.5	10.8	10.9	10.9
Japanese yen	JPY	9.2	9.1	9.4	9.5	10.1	10.4	10.4	10.4
Swiss franc	CHF	9.0	9.2	9.5	9.9	10.5	10.8	10.9	10.9
British pound	GBP	7.3	7.6	7.8	8.0	8.5	8.9	9.1	9.3
Canadian dollar	CAD	7.4	6.8	6.7	6.5	6.5	6.4	6.4	6.3
Australian dollar	AUD	10.5	10.6	10.7	11.0	11.5	11.6	11.5	11.3
British pound/euro	GBPEUR	6.2	6.5	6.7	6.9	7.4	7.6	7.3	7.2
Euro/Japanese yen	EURJPY	10.3	10.3	10.4	10.7	11.0	11.2	11.3	11.3

Source: http://ny.frb.org/pihome/statistics/vrate.shtml. Notes: These Federal Reserve Bank of New York survey ranges are for implied volatilities, mid-rates, for at the money options at 11:00 a.m. Eastern Standard Time. Quotes are for contracts of $10 million with a prime counterparty.

Sensitivity to Changing Interest Rate Differentials (rho *and* phi)

At the start of this section, we pointed out that currency option prices and values are focused on the forward rate. The forward rate is in turn based on the theory of Interest Rate Parity discussed later in Chapter 6. Interest rate changes in either currency will alter the forward rate, which in turn will alter the option's premium or value. The expected change in the option premium from a small change in the domestic interest rate (home currency) is termed *rho*. The expected change in the option premium from a small change in the foreign interest rate (foreign currency) is termed *phi*.

Continuing with our numerical example, an increase in the U.S. dollar interest rate from 8.0% to 9.0% *increases* the ATM call option premium on British pounds from \$0.033/£ to \$0.035/£. This is a *rho* value of positive 0.2.

$$rho = \frac{\Delta \text{ premium}}{\Delta \text{ U.S. dollar interest rate}} = \frac{\$0.035/£ - \$0.033/£}{9.0\% - 8.0\%} = 0.2$$

A similar 1% increase in the foreign interest rate—the pound sterling rate, in this case—*reduces* the option value (premium) from \$0.033/£ to \$0.031/£. The *phi* for this call option premium is therefore – 0.2.

$$phi = \frac{\Delta \text{ premium}}{\Delta \text{ foreign interest rate}} = \frac{\$0.031/£ - \$0.033/£}{9.0\% - 8.0\%} = -0.2$$

For example, throughout the 1990s, U.S. dollar (domestic currency) interest rates were substantially lower than pound sterling (foreign currency) interest rates. This meant that the pound consistently sold forward at a discount versus the U.S. dollar. If this interest differential were to widen (either from U.S. interest rates falling or foreign currency interest rates rising, or some combination of both), the pound would sell forward at a larger discount. An increase in the forward discount is the same as a decrease in the forward rate (in U.S. dollars per unit of foreign currency). The option premium condition states that the premium must increase as interest rate differentials increase (assuming spot rates remain unchanged).

Exhibit 5.13 demonstrates how European call option premiums on the British pound change with interest differentials. If we use the same call option value assumptions as before, an increase in pound sterling interest rates relative to U.S. dollar interest rates, $i_{US\$} - i_{£}$, a movement from left to right results in a decline in call option premiums.

For the option trader, an expectation of the differential between interest rates can obviously help in the evaluation of where the option value is headed. For example, when foreign interest rates are higher than domestic interest rates, the foreign currency sells forward at a discount. This results in relatively lower call option premiums (and lower put option premiums).

Rule of Thumb: A trader who is purchasing a call option on foreign currency should do so before the domestic interest rate rises. This timing will allow the trader to purchase the option before its price increases.

Exhibit 5.13 Interest Differentials and Call Option Premiums

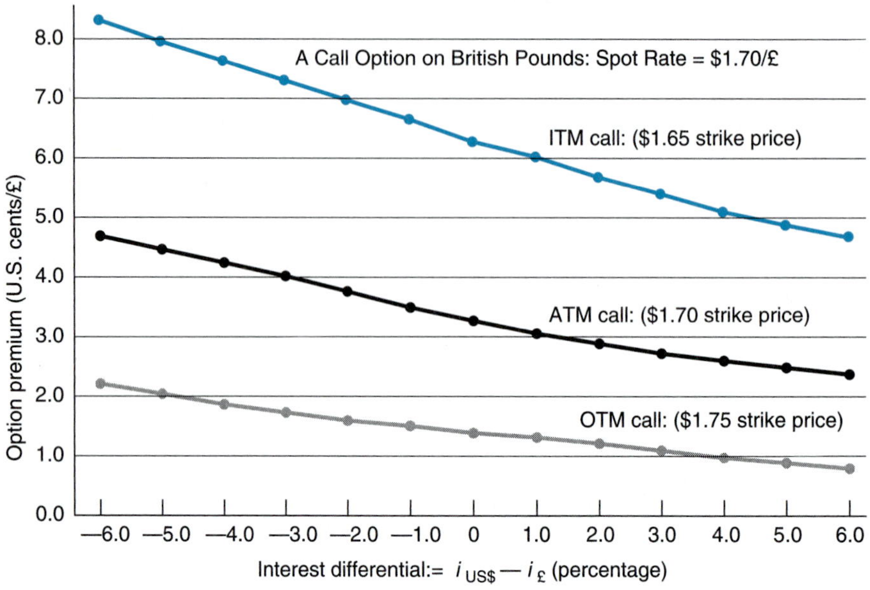

Alternative Strike Prices and Option Premiums

The sixth and final element that is important in option valuation (but, thankfully, has no Greek alias) is the selection of the actual strike price. Although we have conducted all of our sensitivity analysis using the strike price of $1.70/£ (a forward at-the-money strike rate), a firm purchasing an option in the over-the-counter market may choose its own strike rate. The question is how to choose?

Exhibit 5.14 illustrates call option premiums required for a series of alternative strike rates above and below the forward at-the-money strike rate of $1.70/£ using our benchmark example. The option premium for the call option used throughout, $1.70/£, is 3.3 cents/£. Call options written with strike prices less than $1.70/£, when the present spot rate is $1.70/ £, are already profitable or in-the-money. For example, a call option with a strike rate of $1.65/£ would have an intrinsic value of $0.05/£ ($1.70/£ – $1.65/£), which the option premium must cover. The call option premium for the $1.65/£ strike rate is 6.3 cents/£, which is higher than the benchmark.

Similarly, call options on pounds at strike rates above $1.70/£ become increasingly cheap as the underlying spot rate, which is presently $1.70/£, will have to move further to make them profitable. At present they have no intrinsic value. For example, a call option on pounds with a strike rate of $1.75/£ possesses a premium of only 1.5 cents/£, because the option is at present very much out-of-the-money. The option has no intrinsic value but time value only; intrinsic value is zero.

Exhibit 5.15 briefly summarizes the various "Greek" elements and impacts discussed in the previous sections. The option premium is one of the most complex concepts in financial theory, and the application of option pricing to exchange rates does not make it any simpler. Only with a

Exhibit 5.14 Option Premiums for Alternative Strike Rates

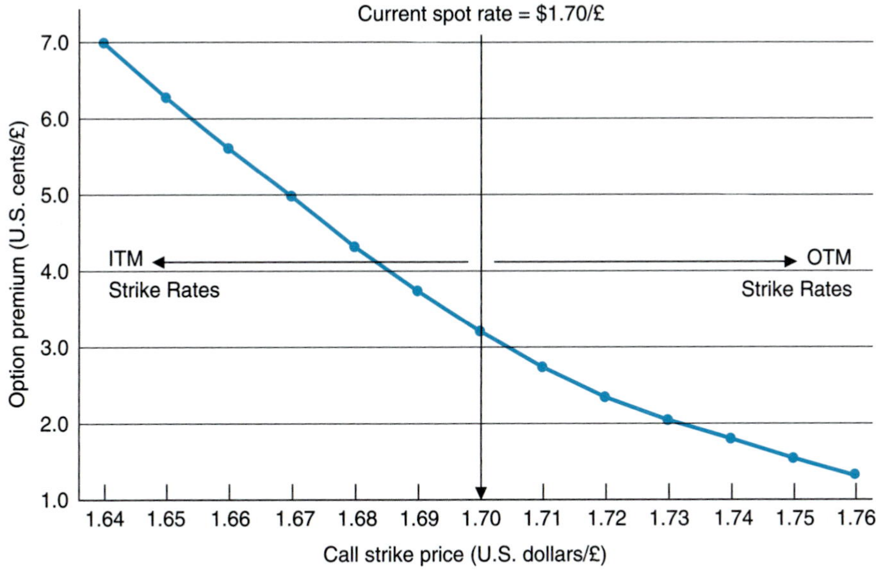

Exhibit 5.15 Summary of Option Premium Components

Greek	Definition	Interpretation
Delta	Expected change in the option premium for a small change in the **spot rate**	The higher the delta, the more likely the option will move in-the-money
Theta	Expected change in the option premium for a small change in **time to expiration**	Premiums are relatively insensitive until the final 30 or so days
Lambda	Expected change in the option premium for a small change in **volatility**	Premiums rise with increases in volatility
Rho	Expected change in the option premium for a small change in the **domestic interest rate**	Increases in domestic interest rates cause increasing call option premiums
Phi	Expected change in the option premium for a small change in the **foreign interest rate**	Increases in foreign interest rates cause decreasing call option premiums

considerable amount of time and effort can the individual be expected to attain a "second sense" in the management of currency option positions.

Prudence in Practice

In the following chapters, we will illustrate how currency options can be used to reduce the risks associated with the conduct of multinational financial management. It is critical, however, that the user of any financial tool or technique—including financial derivatives—follow sound principles and practices. Many a firm has been ruined as a result of the misuse of derivatives. A word to the wise: Do not fall victim to what many refer to as the gambler's dilemma—confusing luck with talent.

As illustrated in the Global Finance Perspective 5.2 box that follows, major corporate financial disasters related to financial derivatives continue to be a problem in global business. As is the case with so many issues in modern society, technology is not at fault, but, rather human error in its use. We conclude our discussion of financial derivatives with a note of caution and humility from an essay in the *Harvard Business Review* by Peter Bernstein:

> *More than any other development, the quantification of risk defines the boundary between modern times and the rest of history. The speed, power, movement, and instant communication that characterize our age would have been inconceivable before science replaced superstition as a bulwark against risks of all kinds.*
>
> *It is hubris that we believe that we can put reliable and stable numbers on the impact of a politician's power, on the probability of a takeover boom like the one that occurred in the 1980s, on the return on the stock market over the next 2, 20, or 50 years, or on subjective factors like utility and risk aversion. It is equally silly to limit our deliberations only to those variables that do lend themselves to quantification, excluding all serious consideration of the unquantifiable. It is irrational to confuse probability with timing and to assume that an event with low probability is therefore not imminent. Such confusion, however, is by no means unusual. And it surely is naïve to define discontinuity as anomaly instead of as normality; only the shape and the timing of the disturbances are hidden from us, not their inevitability.*
>
> *Finally, the science of risk management is capable of creating new risks even as it brings old risk under control. Our faith in risk management encourages us to take risk we otherwise would not take. On*

Global Finance Perspective 5.2

A Selected List of Derivative and Managerial Disasters

Date	Company	Description
1991	Allied-Lyons (UK)	Losses of £165 million related to speculation on currency options.
1993	Shell Showa Seikyu (Japan)	Over ¥1.5 billion in losses arising from recognition of cumulative losses on forward contracts continually rolled over between 1989 and 1993.
1993	Metallgesellschaft (Germany)	A flawed petroleum futures hedging strategy, which essentially caused the collapse of the organization.
1994	Codelco (Chile)	A copper futures trader for the national copper company of Chile, Codelco, losses approximately 0.5% of Chile's gross domestic product for 1994 through speculative futures trading.
1994	Kashima Oil (Japan)	Hundreds of millions of yen are lost on a failed forward speculation on the Japanese yen.
1994	Procter & Gamble (US) Gibson Greeting Cards (US) Air Products (US) Dharmala (Indonesia)	All suffer material losses in the millions of dollars on leveraged swap agreements with Bankers Trust of the United States.
1995	Barings Brothers (UK)	The oldest investment bank in London fails as a result of the losses on futures trading suffered by one trader in its Singapore office, a Mr. Nicholas Leeson. (See the mini-case at the end of this chapter.)
2002	Allied Irish Bank (US/UK)	A rogue currency trader in the Baltimore offices of Allied Irish Bank is credited with losing more than $691 million.

most counts, that is beneficial. But we should be wary of increasing the total amount of risk in the system. Research shows that the security of seat belts encourages drivers to behave more aggressively, with the result that the number of accidents rises even as the seriousness of injury in any one accident may diminish.[3]

SUMMARY

- A foreign currency futures contract is an exchange-traded agreement calling for future delivery of a standard amount of foreign exchange at a fixed time, place, and price.
- Foreign currency futures contracts are in reality standardized forward contracts.
- Unlike forward contracts, however, trading occurs on the floor of an organized exchange rather than between banks and customers. Futures also require collateral and are normally settled through the purchase of an offsetting position.
- As summarized in Exhibit 5.2, futures differ from forward contracts by size of contract, maturity, location of trading, pricing, collateral/margin requirements, method of settlement, commissions, trading hours, counterparties, and liquidity.
- Financial managers typically prefer foreign currency forwards over futures because of forwards' simplicity of use and position maintenance. Financial speculators typically prefer foreign currency futures over forwards because of the liquidity of the futures markets.
- Foreign currency options are financial contracts that give the holder the right, but not the obligation, to buy (in the case of calls) or sell (in the case of puts) a specified amount of foreign exchange at a predetermined price on or before a specified maturity date.
- The use of a currency option as a speculative device for the buyer of an option arises from the fact that an option gains in value as the underlying currency rises (for calls) or falls (for puts). The amount of loss when the underlying currency moves opposite to the desired direction is limited to the premium of the option.
- The use of a currency option as a speculative device for the writer (seller) of an option arises from the option premium. If the option—either a put or call—expires out-of-the-money (valueless), the writer of the option has earned, and retains, the entire premium.
- Speculation is an attempt to profit by trading on expectations about prices in the future. In the foreign exchange market, one speculates by taking a position in a foreign currency and then closing that position after the exchange rate has moved; a profit results only if the rate moves in the direction that the speculator expected.
- Currency option valuation, the determination of the option's premium, is a complex combination of the current spot rate, the specific strike rate, the forward rate (which itself is dependent on the current spot rate and interest differentials), currency volatility, and time to maturity.
- The total value of an option is the sum of its intrinsic value and time value. Intrinsic value depends on the relationship between the option's strike price and the current spot rate at any single point in time, whereas time value estimates how this current intrinsic value may change—for the better—prior to the option's maturity or expiration.

3. Reprinted by permission of *Harvard Business Review*. Excerpt from "The New Religion of Risk Management" by Peter L. Bernstein, March–April 1996. Copyright 1996 by the Harvard Business School Publishing Corporation; all rights reserved.

QUESTIONS

1. **Options versus futures.** Explain the difference between foreign currency options and futures and when either might be most appropriately used.

2. **Trading location for futures.** Check the *Wall Street Journal* to find where in the United States foreign exchange future contracts are traded.

3. **Futures terminology.** Explain the meaning and probable significance for international business of the following contract specifications:
   a. Specific-sized contract
   b. Standard method of stating exchange rates
   c. Standard maturity date
   d. Collateral and maintenance margins
   e. Counterparty

4. **A futures trade.** A newspaper shows the following prices for the previous day's trading in U.S. dollar-euro currency futures:

Month:	December
Open:	0.9124
Settlement:	0.9136
Change:	+0.0027
High:	0.9147
Low:	0.9098
Estimated volume	29,763
Open interest:	111,360
Contract size:	€125,000

   What do the above terms indicate?

5. **Puts and calls.** What is the basic difference between a *put* on British pounds sterling and a *call* on sterling?

6. **Call contract elements.** You read that exchange-traded American call options on pounds sterling having a strike price of $1.460 and a maturity of next March are now quoted at 3.67. What does this mean if you are a potential buyer?

7. **The option cost.** What happens to the premium you paid for the above option in the event you decide to let the option expire unexercised? What happens to this amount in the event you do decide to exercise the option?

8. **Buying a European option.** You have the same information as in question 4, except that the pricing is for a European option. What is different?

9. **Writing options.** Why would anyone write an option, knowing that the gain from receiving the option premium is fixed but the loss if the underlying price goes in the wrong direction can be extremely large?

10. **Option valuation.** The value of an option is stated to be the sum of its *intrinsic value* and its *time value*. Explain what is meant by these terms.

PROBLEMS

1. **Peso futures.** Amber McClain, the currency speculator we met earlier in the chapter, sells eight June futures contracts for 500,000 pesos at the closing price quoted in Exhibit 5.1.
   a. What is the value of her position at maturity if the ending spot rate is $0.12000/Ps?
   b. What is the value of her position at maturity if the ending spot rate is $0.09800/Ps?
   c. What is the value of her position at maturity if the ending spot rate is $0.11000/Ps?

2. **Pound futures.** Michael Palin, a currency trader for a New York investment firm, uses the following futures quotes on the British pound to speculate on the value of the British pound.
   a. If he buys 5 June pound futures and the spot rate at maturity is $1.3980/pound, what is the value of his position?
   b. If he sells 12 March pound futures and the spot rate at maturity is $1.4560/pound, what is the value of his position?

British Pound Futures, U.S.$/pound (CME) **Contract = 62,500 pounds**

Maturity	Open	High	Low	Settle	Change	High	Low	Open Interest
Mar	1.4246	1.4268	1.4214	1.4228	.0032	1.4700	1.3810	25,605
June	1.4164	1.4188	1.4146	1.4162	.0030	1.4550	1.3910	809

Abstracted from The *Wall Street Journal*, Friday February 22, 2002, p.C13. Quotations are for close of business on Thursday, February 21, 2002. All contracts are for 62,500 British pounds.

c. If he buys 3 March pound futures and the spot rate at maturity is $1.4560/pound, what is the value of his position?

d. If he sells 12 June pound futures and the spot rate at maturity is $1.3980/pound, what is the value of his position?

3. Hans Schmidt, euro speculator. Hans is once again speculating on the movement of currencies. Hans has $10 million to begin with, and he must state all profits at the end of any speculation in U.S. dollars. The spot rate on the euro is $0.8850/€, while the 30-day forward rate is $0.9000/€.

a. If Hans believes the euro will continue to slide in value against the U.S. dollar, so that he expects the spot rate to be $0.8440/€ at the end of 30 days, what should he do?

b. If Hans believes the euro will appreciate in value against the U.S. dollar, so that he expects the spot rate to be $0.9440/€ at the end of 30 days, what should he do?

4. Hans Schmidt, Swiss franc speculator. Similar to the situation Hans saw in the chapter, Hans believes the Swiss franc will appreciate versus the U.S. dollar in the coming three-month period. He has $100,000 to invest. The current spot rate is $0.5820/SF, the three-month forward rate is $0.5640/SF, and he expects the spot rate to reach $0.6250/SF in three months.

a. Calculate Hans's expected profit assuming a pure spot market speculation strategy.

b. Calculate Hans's expected profit assuming he buys or sells SF three months forward.

5. Katya and the yen. Katya Berezovsky works in the currency trading unit of Sumara Workers Bank in Togliatti, Russia. Her latest speculative position is to profit from her expectation that the U.S. dollar will rise significantly against the Japanese yen. The current spot rate is ¥120.00/$. She must choose between the following 90-day options on the Japanese yen:

Option	Strike price	Premium
Put on yen	¥125/$	$0.00003/¥
Call on yen	¥125/$	$0.00046/¥

a. Should Katya buy a put on yen or a call on yen?

b. Using your answer to part a, what is Katya's break-even price?

c. Using your answer to part a, what is Katya's gross profit and net profit (including the premium) if the spot rate at the end of the 90 days is ¥140/$?

6. Samuel's bet. Samuel Samosir, who trades currencies for Peregrine Investments in Jakarta, Indonesia, focuses nearly all of his time and attention on the U.S. dollar/Singapore dollar ($/S$) cross rate. The current spot rate is $0.6000/S$. After considerable study this week, he has concluded that the Singapore dollar will appreciate versus the U.S. dollar in the coming 90 days, probably to about $0.7000/S$. He has the following options on the Singapore dollar to choose from:

Option	Strike price	Premium
Put on S$	$0.6500/S$	$0.00003/S$
Call on S$	$0.6500/S$	$0.00046/S$

a. Should Samuel buy a put on Singapore dollars or a call on Singapore dollars?

b. Using your answer to part a, what is Samuel's break-even price?

c. Using your answer to part a, what is Samuel's gross profit and net profit (including the premium) if the spot rate at the end of the 90 days is indeed \$0.7000/S\$?

d. Using your answer to part a, what is Samuel's gross profit and net profit (including the premium) if the spot rate at the end of the 90 days is indeed \$0.8000/S\$?

7. **How much profit—calls?** Assume a call option on euros is written with a strike price of \$0.9400/€ at a premium of 0.9000¢ per euro (\$0.0090/€) and with an expiration date three months from now. The option is for €100,000. Calculate your profit or loss if you exercise before maturity at a time when the euro is traded spot at:

a. \$0.9000/€
b. \$0.9200/€
c. \$0.9400/€
d. \$0.9600/€
e. \$0.9800/€
f. \$1.0000/€
g. \$1.0200/€

8. **How much profit—puts?** Assume a put option on Japanese yen is written with a strike price of \$0.008000/¥ (¥125.00/\$) at a premium of 0.0080¢ per yen and with an expiration date six months from now. The option is for ¥12,500,000. Calculate your profit or loss if you exercise before maturity at a time when the yen is traded spot at ¥110/\$, ¥115/\$, ¥120/\$, ¥125/\$, ¥130/\$, ¥135/\$, and ¥140/\$.

9. **Falling Canadian dollar.** Giri Patel works for CIBC Currency Funds in Toronto. Giri is something of a *contrarian* — as opposed to most of the forecasts, he believes the Canadian dollar (C\$) will appreciate versus the U.S. dollar over the coming 90 days. The current spot rate is \$0.6750/C\$. Giri can choose between the following options on the Canadian dollar:

Option	Strike price	Premium
Put on C\$	\$0.7000	\$0.0003/C\$
Call on C\$	\$0.7000	\$0.0249/C\$

a. Should Giri buy a put on Canadian dollars or a call on Canadian dollars?

b. Using your answer to part a, what is Giri's break-even price?

c. Using your answer to part a, what is Giri's gross profit and net profit (including the premium) if the spot rate at the end of the 90 days is indeed \$0.7600/C\$?

d. Using your answer to part a, what is Giri's gross profit and net profit (including the premium) if the spot rate at the end of the 90 days is indeed \$0.8250/C\$?

10. **Braveheart's puts on pounds.** Andy Furstow is a speculator for a currency fund in London named Braveheart. Braveheart's clients are a collection of wealthy private investors who, with a minimum stake of £250,000 each, wish to speculate on the movement of currencies. The investors expect annual returns in excess of 25%. Although officed in London, all accounts and expectations are based in U.S. dollars.

Andy Furstow is convinced that the British pound will slide significantly — possibly to \$1.3200/£ — in the coming 30 to 60 days. The current spot rate is \$1.4260/£. Andy wishes to buy a put on pounds that will yield the 25% return expected by his investors. Which of the following put options would you recommend he purchase? Prove your choice is the preferable combination of strike price, maturity, and up-front premium expense.

Strike Price	Maturity	Premium
\$1.36/£	30 days	\$0.00081/£
\$1.34/£	30 days	\$0.00021/£
\$1.32/£	30 days	\$0.00004/£
Strike Price	**Maturity**	**Premium**
\$1.36/£	60 days	\$0.00333/£
\$1.34/£	60 days	\$0.00150/£
\$1.32/£	60 days	\$0.00060/£

Pricing Your Own Options (Option.xls)

The set of assumptions used throughout the second half of this chapter used in the pricing of a call option on British pounds were as follows:

Spot rate	\$1.70/£
Maturity	90 days
90-day eurodollar deposit rate	8.00% per annum
90-day euro-pound deposit rate	8.00% per annum
U.S. dollar/British pound 90-day volatility	10.0%

Simple Options Valuation Program

Parameters	
Current spot rate	170.0000
Foreign interest rate (5% as .05)	8.000%
Domestic interest rate (10% as .1)	8.000%
Option (1, CALL, -1, PUT)	1
Strike rate	170.0000
Days to maturity	90
Annual volatility (10% as .1)	10.00%

American model	
Price	3.289
Delta	0.5030
Gamma	0.0481
Theta	6.6954

European model	
Price	3.302
Delta	0.4999
Gamma	0.0463
Theta	6.4294

Source: Professor James N. Bodurtha. Reprinted with permission.

Use these assumptions and the option pricing spreadsheet (Option.xls)—which will calculate both European and American currency option premiums when you plug in values—to answer problems 11 through 15.

Note: Check that the spreadsheet is working correctly by first plugging in the baseline values pictured above and calculating the same option premiums. Also note that the $1.70/£ spot exchange rate should be entered as 170.00 U.S. cents per pound.

11. **Call options on British pounds.** Assuming the following inputs, calculate the European price (premium) for a call option on British pounds for 30, 60, 90, 120, 150, 180, 210, 240, 270, 300, 330, and 360 days in maturity. After calculating the premiums, graph the premium against maturity.

Current spot rate	$1.70/£
90-day europound deposit rate	8.00% per annum
90-day eurodollar deposit rate	8.00% per annum
Option	1 = CALL
Strike rate	$1.70/£
Annual volatility	10.00%

12. **Put options on euros.** Assuming the following inputs, calculate the European price (premium) for a put option on the European euro for both an 8.0% volatility and a 12.0% volatility.

Current spot rate	$1.0840/€
90-day euro-euro deposit rate	4.00% per annum
90-day eurodollar deposit rate	2.00% per annum
Option	–1 = PUT
Strike rate	$1.0400/€
Days to maturity	90 days
Annual volatility	8.00% and 12.00%

13. **Solar turbines and Venezuelan bolivares.** Financial derivatives are difficult to purchase on emerging market currencies—especially those that have recently suffered significant devaluations or depreciations. Solar Turbines, a U.S.–based gas turbine manufacturer, recently delivered $250,000 worth of gas pipeline compression turbines to the national petroleum company of Venezuela.

The Venezuelan government requires payees to accept payment in the Venezuelan bolivar, a currency that was recently devalued and is continuing to fall in value. Solar Turbines wishes to acquire a put option on bolivares. Assuming the following inputs, calculate the European price (premium) for a put option on the Venezuelan bolivar for the full amount of the sale. (Remember that spot rates and strike rates must be entered in domestic currency units per unit of foreign currency.)

Current spot rate	B1,600/$
90-day bolivar deposit rate	24.00% per annum
90-day eurodollar deposit rate	2.00% per annum
Option	–1 = PUT
Strike rate	B1,800/$
Days to maturity	90 days
Annual volatility	20.00%

14. **Vitro de Mexico.** The Mexican peso (Ps) has recently been appreciating versus the Canadian dollar. A Canadian firm that purchases specialty flat-panel glass for office buildings has ordered C$350,000 worth of glass from Vitro de Mexico. Assuming the following inputs, calculate the European price (premium) for a call option with a strike price of C$0.15/ Ps on the Mexican pesos needed for payment in 180 days.

Current spot rate	C$0.1390/Ps
90-day euro-Canadian dollar deposit rate	6.00% per annum
90-day Mexican peso deposit rate	12.00% per annum
Option	1 = CALL
Strike rate	C$0.1500/Ps
Days to maturity	180 days
Annual volatility	14.00%

15. **Put options on Chinese renminbi.** Many Western financial services providers would like to start offering put options on the Chinese renminbi (Rmb). The problem, as is often the case with regulated financial markets, is the multitude of restrictions on interest-bearing accounts in the subject currency. Assuming the following inputs, calculate the European price (premium) for a put option on the renminbi.

Current spot rate	Rmb8.500/$
90-day Rmb deposit rate	14.00% per annum
90-day eurodollar deposit rate	4.00% per annum
Option	–1 = PUT
Strike rate	Rmb9.000/$
Days to maturity	90 days
Annual volatility	4.00%

INTERNET EXERCISES

1. **Option pricing.** OzForex Foreign Exchange Services is a private firm with an enormously powerful foreign currency derivative-enabled web site. Use the following web site to evaluate the various "Greeks" related to currency option pricing.

   OzForex http://www.ozforex.com.au/fxoptions/optiondynamics.htm

2. **Brazilian real.** The Chicago Mercantile Exchange (CME) trades futures and options on the Brazilian real. Use the following Internet address to evaluate the uses of these currency derivatives.

   CME/Brazilian real http://www.cme.com/products/currency/brazilianreal.cfm

3. **Currency volatilities.** The single unobservable variable in currency option pricing is volatility, since volatility inputs are the expected standard deviation of the daily spot rate for the coming period of the option's maturity. Use the New York Federal Reserve's web site to obtain current currency volatilities.

   Federal Reserve Bank of New York http://ny.frb.org/pihome/statistics/vrate.shtml

4. **Currency options and futures exchanges.** Currency options and futures are traded in many exchanges (bolsas, bourses, etc.) around the world. Using the following list as a starting point, determine exactly which currencies are traded on exchanges in the forms of futures or options.

London Stock Exchange	http://www.stockex.co.uk/aim
Tokyo Stock Exchange	http://www.tse.or.jp/eindex.html
SBF–Paris Bourse	http://www.bourse-de-paris.fr/bourse/sbf/homesbf-gb.htlm
Bolsa de Bogota	http://www.bolsabogota.com.co
Singapore Exchange	http://www.simex.com.sg

Or, for a wider spectrum of global markets:

Investor Map http://invesotrmap.com/global.htm

5. **Philadelphia Stock Exchange.** The Philadelphia Stock Exchange (PSE) was the first major exchange to trade currency options. The following Internet address takes you to the PSE's currency option trading center. What are the latest developments in customized option notional principals and maturity dates?

   Philadelphia Stock Exchange http://www.phlx.com/products/currency.html

SELECTED READINGS

Giddy, Ian H., and Gunter Dufey, "Uses and Abuses of Currency Options," *Journal of Applied Corporate Finance*, Fall 1995, Volume 8, No. 3, pp. 49–57.

Huckins, Nancy White and Anoop Rai, "Market Risk for Foreign Currency Options: Basle's Simplified Model," *Financial Management*, Spring 1999, Volume 28, No. 1, pp. 99–109.

Melino, Angelo, and Stuart M. Turnbull, "Misspecification and the Pricing and Hedging of Long-Term Currency Options," *Journal of International Money and Finance,* June 1995, Volume 14, No. 3, pp. 373–393.

MINI-CASE

Rogue Trader, Nicholas Leeson[4]

Nicholas Leeson was a rogue trader who reduced the value of the venerable Baring Brothers & Co. (BB&Co) Bank from roughly \$500 million to \$1.60 million. Leeson traded futures contracts on the Nikkei 225 and on Japanese Government Bonds without authorization while management at Barings, the Singapore International Monetary Exchange, the Osaka Stock Exchange, and other governing bodies in Britain and Singapore disregarded or failed to recognize the potential for financial disaster. The failure of Barings Bank provides a lesson in the risks and responsibilities involved in organizing and monitoring derivatives trading.

Baring Brothers History

Baring Brothers had a long history in the London financial district with the distinction of having gone global with its operations in the eighteenth century. Founded in the late 1700s, the bank was turned into a general banking and mercantile operation by Sir Francis Baring. During his tenure, the bank developed several lines of business: underwriting bonds, accepting deposits, and trading commodities.

4. Abstracted from "Baring Brothers & Co., Technical Note on Rogue Trader Nicholas Leeson," by Professor Mark Griffiths, Thunderbird Case Series, A06-99-0021.

Baring Brothers reached the height of its reputation after the Napoleonic Wars in Europe. The bank led the funding of the French reparations to the victors and was lauded in 1817 by the French Duc de Richelieu as the "sixth power in Europe," after Great Britain, France, Russia, Austria, and Prussia. Baring Brothers helped finance the Louisiana Purchase for the United States, underwrote railroad construction in Canada, and financed other projects throughout the Americas. One of those other projects was underwriting a £2 million share issue for the Buenos Aires Water Supply and Drainage Co. in 1890. The issue did not sell, but Baring Brothers had already sent the money and was on the brink of failure when the Bank of England organized a consortium to bail it out.[5] Thereafter, it was known as Baring Brothers & Co.

For all its long history in cross-border transactions, the bank never grew along with the size of the markets it served. In 1995, Baring Brothers & Co. remained a small, family-controlled bank ranked 474th in the world banking market.

Barings entered the securities market in 1984 when it acquired the Far East department of Henderson Crothwaite (British stockbrokers). This new entity at Barings was called Baring Securities Ltd. (BSL). Christopher Heath, a specialist in Japanese instruments, managed to maintain independent control of BSL until 1993.

During eight consecutive profitable years, everyone at Barings became accustomed to large bonuses, largely funded by profits in Baring Securities. In 1989, BSL provided £50 million of £65 million total profit for Barings. Unfortunately, the losses incurred in 1992 lead to Heath being asked to resign in March 1993.

Nicholas Leeson

Nicholas Leeson was two days shy of his twenty-eighth birthday when his trading activities forced Baring Brothers & Co. into bankruptcy. Leeson left a note on his desk saying "I'm sorry" and bolted to Kuala Lumpur with his wife following shortly thereafter.

Nick Leeson was born in Watford, England, just outside of London. His father was a plasterer and his mother was a nurse. He was the oldest of four children. Leeson did not attend university; instead, he went directly to work in London upon completion of high school. He worked with a British bank, Coutts & Co., and then Morgan Stanley, before moving to Barings Securities London in 1989.

Nick Leeson was twenty-two years old when he was hired for the position at Baring Securities London (BSLL). BSLL was looking to fill a position settling trades completed in Japan. Leeson, who had experience at Morgan Stanley settling futures and options in Japan, was a good replacement. He worked hard, kept to himself, and was known as someone anxious to learn and eager to please. He was subsequently selected as a member of a team of four people assigned to straighten out some back office problems in Jakarta.

In 1992, he was selected to run the back office for the new Baring Futures Singapore (BFS), a subsidiary that would trade futures and options. His exact responsibilities were somewhat unclear, although they did include responsibility for both the back office accounting and control functions as well as for executing clients' orders. This was when Leeson's unauthorized trading activities began. On his initiative, Leeson sat for and passed the futures-trading exam to become registered as an associated person with the Singapore International Monetary Exchange (SIMEX). He did not need the license to fulfill his responsibilities, but he did need it to execute trades. To meet his Baring's responsibilities, he only needed to take orders from clients, and pass them to a trader for execution.

5. Stephen Fay, *The Collapse of Barings* (New York: W.W. Norton Co. Inc., 1997), p. 10.

In 1992, Leeson established the error account 88888 (eight is considered a lucky number by the Chinese), which, according to SIMEX investigators, he immediately began using to conceal unauthorized trading activities.[6] While a legitimate error account numbered 99002 was known to BSLL, the 88888 account did not show on files or statements transmitted from Singapore to London. Account 88888 was known to SIMEX, but as a customer account, not as an error account. Leeson had to represent it differently to each group because he could not hide the existence of 88888 from SIMEX, and he could not explain its volume and balance to BSLL (but he could hide it from them).

Derivatives

Since the early 1970s, derivatives have increasingly been used by firms to manage their exposure to risks. When purchasing a derivative, only part of the value of the underlying asset is at risk, while the opportunity to benefit from favorable price fluctuations is retained. Derivatives can offer potentially enormous gains, which can lead to their use as speculative instruments. They also offer potentially debilitating losses, depending on the positions taken.

Nick Leeson was trading futures and options on the Nikkei 225, an index of Japanese securities. Leeson was long Nikkei 225 futures, short Japanese government bond futures, and short both put and call options on the Nikkei index. He was betting that the Nikkei index would rise. He was wrong and ended up losing $1.39 billion. For Leeson to suffer losses of this magnitude in futures positions during January and February of 1995, he had to have held approximately one quarter of the entire open interest on the Osaka and Singapore stock exchanges. Unfortunately, since management had given such free rein to Leeson by allowing him to control both front and back office operations, this level of investment went undetected by the firm.[7]

Leeson offset any losses incurred on his long positions in Nikkei futures by writing Nikkei options. That is, when Leeson purchased futures contracts, he was required to pay cash—a margin of 15% of the contract's value to SIMEX—and when the losses on the contracts accumulated, additional margin was required, because futures contracts are marked-to-market on a daily basis. However, when he wrote the options, he received cash, in the form of premiums. The premiums from the Nikkei options served two purposes: 1) they were used to hide losses created by the futures, which would otherwise have shown in BFS's financial statements, and 2) the premiums served to cover the margin calls on the futures. Leeson was able to do this due to the nature of the Japanese futures market at this time. In Japan, margin is posted on a net basis for all customers. Therefore, if many customers were short index futures, the firm can take long positions without having to post cash margin. In addition, daily settlement was one-sided. That is, losers must cover their losses daily, but winners were not permitted to withdraw gains. Therefore, it was possible to cover the firm's losses with customer gains. Another aspect of the Japanese futures market that enabled Leeson to do this was that the exchange did not require a separation between customer and proprietary funds. Therefore, it was impossible to distinguish between the firm's and the customers' positions.

The Nikkei 225 experienced an extended bull run throughout the late 1980s, reaching a height of close to 40,000 in 1989. By mid-1994, Leeson was convinced that since the Nikkei had fallen to half of its 1989 high, and interest rates were low, it would likely recover in the near future. He was convinced it would not fall below 19,000 and he was willing to put a lot of

6. Fay, *Collapse*, p. 94.

7. Hans R. Stoll, "Lost Barings: A Tale in Three Parts Concluding with a Lesson," *The Journal of Derivatives,* Fall 1995, Volume 3, No.1.

Baring's money at risk based on that belief. However, a rise in interest rates would hurt him and, accordingly, he took short positions in Japanese Government Bonds futures contracts that would pay off if interest rates rose.

Leeson's options positions were founded on his belief that volatility would be low. In fact, he had traded enough contracts by the time of the collapse that he was *causing* volatility to remain low. Increasingly, he had to write a larger volume of options in order to get the same amount of premiums. When it became increasingly difficult for the options' premiums to cover the margin calls on the futures, Leeson requested money from London. By February 23, 1995, BSLL had sent approximately $600 million to BFS. BSLL funded his request with little information, and with the understanding that a portion of the money was "loans to clients," as portrayed on the BFS balance sheet.

The Losses

Leeson began trading futures in July 1992, and by the end of the month, he had bought and sold 2,051 Nikkei futures, suffering an immediate loss of approximately $64,000.[8] By the end of the year, his losses in account 88888 were more than $3.2 million. The numbers turned somewhat in his favor by mid-1993 when the losses amounted to only $40,000. Unfortunately, Leeson intended to keep trading until his numbers were positive. By the end of 1993, the losses were approximately $30 million. At this point, Leeson wrote options for approximately $35 million to offset the futures losses and to avoid suspicion from London and the auditors. Throughout this time period, Leeson was reporting record profits, and was being heralded as a superstar.

By the end of 1994, the Nikkei had fallen to just under 20,000 and Leeson's losses approached $330 million. Meanwhile, Barings executives were expecting an estimated $20 million in profits from BFS for 1994.

Leeson's activities in the first few months of 1995 were like those of any self-respecting speculator. On January 13, 1995, the Nikkei reached 19,331 and Barings was long 3,024 Nikkei futures contracts. But, on January 17, 1995, an earthquake measuring 7.2 devastated the Japanese city of Kobe. The Nikkei plummeted below 18,840 by January 20, at which point Leeson doubled his contracts to 7,135.[9] This process continued as the Nikkei fell to 18,000 on February 23, 1995, and Leeson's exposure grew to more than 55,399 unhedged Nikkei futures.[10] Compounding the problem, interest rates did not rise as Leeson had expected and he was losing on the Japanese Government Bond futures as well.

By Friday, February 24, 1995, Barings and the world discovered that Leeson had incurred losses approaching $1.1 billion,[11] more than double the capitalization of the bank. The bank was headed toward bankruptcy. When the markets opened in Singapore and Osaka on Monday, the exchanges would declare Barings in default on its margins.

Throughout that weekend, the Bank of England hosted meetings in London to try to form a consortium to bail out Barings. Barclays Bank assumed the leadership role and was able to attain commitments for $900 million for three months. Unfortunately for Barings, no one would assume the contingent risk of additional, but as yet undiscovered losses, and the efforts failed. At

8. Fay, *Collapse*, p. 97.
9. *Time*, "On Going Broke," p. 44.
10. Fay, *Collapse*, p. 275.
11. "Report of the Board of Banking Supervision Inquiry into the Circumstances of the Collapse of Barings," Bank of England, July 18, 1995 p. 2 (hereafter referred to as Bank of England).

Exhibit A Key Events: Nick Leeson and Baring Brothers & Co.

1989:	Nick Leeson is hired as a trade office clerk who settles accounts.
1992.	Leeson moves to Singapore where he is responsible for the back office of Baring Futures Singapore (BFS) and the execution of clients' trades.
June 1992:	Leeson obtains a license to trade for BFS in the Singapore International Monetary Exchange. He is not authorized by Barings to trade beyond execution of clients' requests.
July 1992:	Leeson sets up the error account 88888, used to conduct unauthorized trading.
October 1992:	Losses in 88888 reach £4.5 million.
June 1993:	Losses in 88888 reach a low point of £34,000.
October 1993:	Leeson is given discretion by Barings to decide when and at what price to trade on behalf of Barings. Losses in 88888 are at £24.39 million.
1993:	Baring Brothers & Co becomes one of the first banks to complete a solo-consolidation (merging its banking business with its securities business) under new regulations.
March 1994:	$40 million is lost by CS First Boston in a scheme that had the bank reimbursing a client for unauthorized money-losing derivative trades within its account.
April 1994:	Joseph Jett is exposed by his employer, Kidder Peabody, for $350 million of false profit. Procter & Gamble (P&G) joins the ranks of derivative losers. It loses $157 million in interest rate swaps. Bankers Trust is at the heart of the controversy. P&G refuses to pay arguing misrepresentation on the part of Bankers Trust.
October 1994:	Eastman Kodak loses $220 million in swaps and options.
August 1994:	Internal audit is conducted at BFS. It criticizes Leeson's control of back and front office activities and expresses concern over reconciliation of funds received from London.
December 1994:	Orange County loses $1.7 billion and goes bankrupt on inverse floaters. Merrill Lynch is sued and pays roughly $480 million to Orange County and fines to the SEC.
December 31, 1994:	Losses in account 88888 exceed £208 million. Baring executives expected an estimated $20–36 million in profits for the bank from BFS.
January 11, 1995:	SIMEX sends a letter to BFS explaining that the margin for account 88888 is short $100 million. It is referred to Leeson for a response.
January. 13, 1995:	The Nikkei is at 19,331 and Barings has 3,024 Nikkei futures contracts.
January 17, 1995:	Kobe, Japan, suffers a disastrous earthquake. The damage is estimated at over $100 billion. This drives down the Nikkei, causing the value of Barings' futures positions to drop precipitously.
January 20, 1995:	Leeson doubles down to 7,135 contracts in the Nikkei, hoping for a reversal of fortune.
January 25, 1995:	The Nikkei drops below 18,000. Leeson doubles again to 17,000 (est.) contracts on Jan. 27.
February 17, 1995:	Leeson increases the number of contracts to 20,076.
February 23, 1995:	Losses approach $1.1 billion, more than twice Baring Bank's capitalization. The bank goes bankrupt and Leeson flees Singapore, two days before his twenty-eighth birthday.

the time, it was already known that on Monday, February 27, 1995, there would be an additional $370 million in losses from Barings positions, bringing the total loss to $1.39 billion.[12] Barings was bankrupt. A detailed time-line is presented in Exhibit A.

Case Questions

1. What was Nick Leeson's strategy to earn trading profits on derivatives?
2. What went wrong that caused his strategy to fail?
3. Why did Nick Leeson establish a bogus error account (88888) when a legitimate account (99002) already existed?
4. Why did Barings and its auditors not discover that the error account was used by Leeson for unauthorized trading?
5. Why did none of the regulatory authorities in Singapore, Japan, and the United Kingdom discover the true use of the error account?
6. Why was Barings Bank willing to transfer large cash sums to Barings Futures Singapore?
7. Why did the attempt by the Bank of England to organize a bailout for Barings fail?
8. Suggest regulatory and management reforms that might prevent a future debacle of the type that bankrupted Barings.

12. Martin Mayer, *The Bankers: The Next Generation* (New York: Truman Talley Books/Plume, 1997), p. 335.

Chapter 6

International Parity Conditions

WHAT ARE THE DETERMINANTS OF EXCHANGE RATES? ARE CHANGES IN EXCHANGE RATES PREDICTABLE? These are fundamental questions that managers of multinational enterprises (MNEs), international portfolio investors, importers and exporters, and government officials must deal with every day. This chapter will describe the core financial theories surrounding the determination of exchange rates. Chapter 7 will introduce two other major theoretical schools of thought regarding currency valuation, and combine the three different theories in a variety of real-world applications.

The economic theories that link exchange rates, price levels, and interest rates together are called *international parity conditions.* In the eyes of many, these international parity conditions form the core of the financial theory that is considered unique to the field of international finance. These theories do not always work out to be "true" when compared to what students and practitioners observe in the real world, but they are central to any understanding of how multinational business is conducted and funded in the world today. And, as is often the case, the mistake is not always in the theory itself, but in the way it is interpreted or applied in practice.

Prices and Exchange Rates

If the identical product or service can be sold in two different markets, and no restrictions exist on the sale or transportation costs of moving the product between markets, the product's price should be the same in both markets. This is called the *law of one price.*

A primary principle of competitive markets is that prices will equalize across markets if frictions or costs of moving the products or services between markets do not exist. If the two markets are in two different countries, the product's price may be stated in different currency terms, but the price of the product should still be the same. Comparing prices would require only a conversion from one currency to the other. For example:

$$P^{\$} \times S = P^{¥}$$

where the price of the product in U.S. dollars ($P^{\$}$), multiplied by the spot exchange rate (S, yen per U.S. dollar), equals the price of the product in Japanese yen ($P^{¥}$). Conversely, if the prices of the two products were stated in local currencies, and markets were efficient at competing away a higher price in one market relative to the other, the exchange rate could be deduced from the relative local product prices:

$$S = \frac{P^{¥}}{P^{\$}}$$

Purchasing Power Parity and the Law of One Price

If the law of one price were true for all goods and services, the purchasing power parity (PPP) exchange rate could be found from any individual set of prices. By comparing the prices of identical products denominated in different currencies, we could determine the "real" or PPP exchange rate that should exist if markets were efficient. This is the *absolute* version of the theory of purchasing power parity. Absolute PPP states that the spot exchange rate is determined by the relative prices of similar baskets of goods.

The "hamburger standard," as it has been christened by the *Economist* (Exhibit 6.1), is a prime example of this law of one price. Assuming that the Big Mac is indeed identical in all countries listed, the "hamburger standard" serves as one form of comparison of whether currencies are trading at market rates close to the exchange rate implied by Big Macs in local currencies. For example, a Big Mac in Switzerland costs SFr6.30, while the same Big Mac in the United States is \$2.49. This implies a purchasing power parity exchange rate of:

$$\frac{\text{SFr}6.30}{\$2.49} = \text{SFr}2.5301 / \$$$

However, on the date of the survey, the actual exchange rate was SFr1.66/\$. Therefore the Swiss franc is overvalued by:

$$\frac{\text{SFr}2.5301}{\text{SFr}1.66} = 1.5242 \text{ or } \approx \ +52.42\%$$

A less extreme form of this principle would be that with relatively efficient markets, the price of a basket of goods would be the same in each of several markets. Replacing the price of a single product with a price index allows the PPP spot exchange rate (S) between two countries to be stated as follows:

$$S = \frac{PI^{¥}}{PI^{\$}}$$

where $PI^{¥}$ and $PI^{\$}$ are price indices expressed in local currency for Japan and the United States, respectively. For example, if the basket of goods cost ¥1000 in Japan and \$10 in the United States, the PPP exchange rate would be:

$$\frac{¥1000}{\$10} = ¥100 / \$$$

Exhibit 6.1 The Law of One Price: The Big Mac Hamburger Standard

		(1)	(2)	(3)	(4)	(5)
		Big Mac Prices			Actual	Under/over
Country	Currency	In local currency	In dollars	Implied PPP of the dollar	exchange rate 23/4/02	valuation against the dollar, %
United States	Dollar	$ 2.49	2.49	—	—	—
Argentina	Peso	2.50	0.80	1.00	3.13	- 68%
Australia	A$	3.00	1.61	1.20	1.86	–35%
Brazil	Real	3.60	1.54	1.45	2.34	–38%
Britain	£	1.99	2.89	$1.25	$1.45	16%
Canada	C$	3.33	2.12	1.34	1.57	–15%
Chile	Peso	1,400	2.14	562	655	–14%
China	Yuan	10.50	1.27	4.22	8.28	–49%
Czech Republic	Koruna	56.28	1.66	22.60	34.00	–34%
Denmark	DKr	24.75	2.95	9.94	8.38	19%
Euro area	€	2.67	2.38	$0.93	$0.89	-5%
Hong Kong	HK$	11.20	1.44	4.50	7.80	–42%
Hungary	Forint	459	1.69	184	272	–32%
Indonesia	Rupiah	16,000	1.70	6,426	9,430	–32%
Israel	Shekel	12.00	2.51	4.82	4.79	1%
Japan	¥	262	2.02	105	130	–19%
Malaysia	M$	5.04	1.33	2.02	3.80	–47%
Mexico	Peso	21.90	2.36	8.80	9.28	–5%
New Zealand	NZ$	3.95	1.76	1.59	2.24	–29%
Peru	New Sol	8.50	2.48	3.41	3.43	0%
Philippines	Peso	65.00	1.27	26.10	51.00	–49%
Poland	Zloty	5.90	1.46	2.37	4.04	–41%
Russia	Rouble	39.00	1.25	15.66	31.20	–50%
Singapore	S$	3.30	1.81	1.33	1.82	–27%
South Africa	Rand	9.70	0.89	3.90	10.90	–64%
South Korea	Won	3,100	2.38	1,245	1,304	–5%
Sweden	SKr	26.00	2.52	10.44	10.30	1%
Switzerland	SFr	6.30	3.80	2.53	1.66	52%
Taiwan	NT$	70.00	2.01	28.11	34.80	–19%
Thailand	Baht	55.00	1.27	22.09	43.30	–49%
Turkey	Lira	4,000,000	3.02	1,606,426	1,324,500	21%
Venezuela	Bolivar	2,500	2.92	1,004	857.00	17%

(continued)

Exhibit 6.1 The Law of One Price: The Big Mac Hamburger Standard (continued)

		(1)	(2)	(3)	(4)	(5)
		Big Mac Prices				
Country	Currency	In local currency	In dollars	Implied PPP of the dollar	Actual exchange rate 23/4/02	Under/over valuation against the dollar, %
United States	Dollar	$ 2.49	2.49	—	—	—
Aruba	Florin	2.34	1.31	0.94	1.79	–47%
Bahrain	Dinar	0.85	2.24	0.34	0.38	–10%
Belarus	Rouble	2,280	1.31	915.66	1,745	–48%
Colombia	Peso	5,700	2.52	2,289	2,261	1%
Costa Rica	Colon	875	2.49	351.4	351	0%
Croatia	Kuna	14.9	1.80	5.98	8.29	–28%
Dominican Republic	Peso	50.00	2.91	20.08	17.2	17%
Estonia	Kroon	28.5	1.62	11.45	17.6	-35%
Guatemala	Quetzal	16.00	2.03	6.43	7.90	–19%
Iceland	Krona	399	4.14	160.24	96.3	66%
Jamaica	Jamaican	120	2.53	48.19	47.4	2%
Kuwait	Dinar	0.65	2.10	0.26	0.31	–16%
Macau	Pataca	11.2	1.39	4.50	8.03	–44%
Morocco	Dirham	23.00	1.99	9.24	11.53	–20%
Norway	Kroner	35.00	4.09	14	8.56	64%
Oman	Rial	0.90	2.31	0.36	0.39	–7%
Qatar	Riyal	9.00	2.47	3.61	3.64	–1%
Saudi Arabia	Riyal	9.00	2.40	3.61	3.75	–4%
Slovakia	Koruna	63.00	1.35	25.30	46.8	–46%
Slovenia	Tolar	430	1.70	172.69	253	-32%
Suriname	Sur guilder	6,000	2.75	2,410	2,179	11%
Ukraine	Hryvna	8.79	1.65	3.53	5.33	-34%
UAE	Dirham	9.00	2.45	3.61	3.67	–2%
Uruguay	Peso	28.00	1.67	11.24	16.8	-33%
Yugoslavia	Dinar	85.00	1.25	34.14	67.8	–50%

Source: The *Economist*, April 25, 2002 (print edition). Values have been recalculated from published data. Note that the British pound and the Euro Area euro are quoted in U.S. dollars per unit of currency. The U.S. Big Mac price is the average of New York, Chicago, San Francisco and Atlanta.

Column (2) = Column (1) / Column (4)

Column (3) = Column (1) / $2.49

Column (5) = [Column (3) – Column (4)] / Column (4)

Note that as of April 25, 2002 (the date of this Big Mac standard), the majority of exchange rates (40 out of 56) were undervalued compared to the U.S. dollar according to this measure. However, the dollar's strength began to weaken significantly in 2003.

Relative Purchasing Power Parity

If the assumptions of the absolute version of PPP theory are relaxed a bit more, we observe what is termed *relative purchasing power parity.* Relative PPP holds that PPP is not particularly helpful in determining what the spot rate is today, but that the relative change in prices between two countries over a period of time determines the change in the exchange rate over that period. More specifically, if the spot exchange rate between two countries starts in equilibrium, any change in the expected differential rate of inflation between them tends to be offset over the long run by an equal but opposite change in the spot exchange rate.

Exhibit 6.2 shows a general case of relative PPP. The vertical axis shows the percentage appreciation or depreciation of the foreign currency relative to the home currency, and the horizontal axis shows the percentage higher or lower rate of expected inflation in the foreign country relative to the home country. The diagonal parity line shows the equilibrium position between a change in the exchange rate and relative inflation rates. For instance, point P represents an equilibrium point where inflation in the foreign country, Japan, for example, is 4% lower than in the home country, the United States, for example. Therefore, relative PPP would predict that the yen would appreciate by 4% per annum with respect to the U.S. dollar.

The main justification for purchasing power parity is that if a country experiences inflation rates higher than those of its main trading partners, and its exchange rate does not change, its exports of goods and services become less competitive with comparable products produced elsewhere. Imports from abroad become more price competitive with higher-priced domestic

Exhibit 6.2 Purchasing Power Parity (PPP)

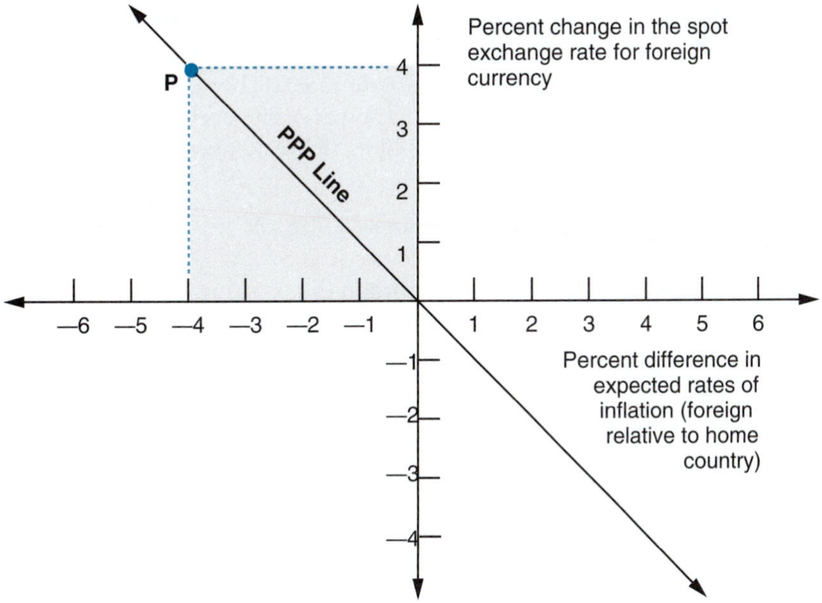

products. These price changes lead to a deficit on current account in the balance of payments unless offset by capital and financial flows.

Empirical Tests of Purchasing Power Parity

Extensive testing of both the absolute and relative versions of purchasing power parity and the law of one price has been done.[1] These tests have, for the most part, not proved PPP to be accurate in predicting future exchange rates. Goods and services do not in reality move at zero cost between countries, and in fact many goods are not "tradeable"—for example, haircuts. Many goods and services are not of the same quality across countries, reflecting differences in the tastes and resources of the countries of their manufacture and consumption.

Two general conclusions can be made from these tests: 1) PPP holds up well over the very long run but poorly for shorter time periods, and 2) the theory holds better for countries with relatively high rates of inflation and underdeveloped capital markets. Global Finance Perspective 6.1 presents one of the most recent and comprehensive studies of purchasing power parity.

Exchange Rate Indices: Real and Nominal

Since any single country trades with numerous partners, we need to track and evaluate its individual currency value against all other currency values in order to determine relative purchasing power. The objective is to discover whether its exchange rate is "overvalued" or "undervalued" in terms of PPP. One of the primary methods of dealing with this problem is the calculation of exchange rate indices. These indices are formed by trade-weighting the bilateral exchange rates between the home country and its trading partners.

The *nominal effective exchange rate index* uses actual exchange rates to create an index, on a weighted average basis, of the value of the subject currency over time. It does not really indicate anything about the "true value" of the currency, or anything related to PPP. The nominal index simply calculates how the currency value relates to some arbitrarily chosen base period, but it is used in the formation of the real effective exchange rate index. The real effective exchange rate index indicates how the weighted average purchasing power of the currency has changed relative to some arbitrarily selected base period. Exhibit 6.3 plots the real effective exchange rate indexes for the United States and Japan over the past 20 years.

The real effective exchange rate index for the U.S. dollar, $E_R^{\$}$, is found by multiplying the nominal effective exchange rate index, $E_N^{\$}$, by the ratio of U.S.
dollar costs, $C^{\$}$, over foreign currency costs, C^{FC}, both in index form:

$$E_R^{\$} = E_N^{\$} \times \frac{C^{\$}}{C^{FC}}$$

1. See for example, Kenneth Rogoff, "The Purchasing Power Parity Puzzle," *Journal of Economic Literature*, June 1996, Volume 34, No. 2, pp. 647–668; and Barry K. Goodwin, Thomas Greenes, and Michael K. Wohlgenant, "Testing the Law of One Price When Trade Takes Time," *Journal of International Money and Finance*, March 1990, pp. 21–40.

Global Finance Perspective **6.1**

Deviations from Purchasing Power Parity in the 20th Century

The recent seminal work by Dimson, Marsh, and Staunton (2002) found that for the 1900–2000 period, relative purchasing power parity generally held. They did, however, note that significant short-run deviations from PPP did occur. "When deviations from PPP appear to be present it is likely that exchange rates are responding not only to relative inflation but also to other economic and political factors. Changes in productivity differentials, such as Japan's post-war productivity growth in the traded-goods sector, can bring similar wealth effects, with domestic inflation that does not endanger the country's exchange rate."

Real Exchange Rate Changes Against the U.S. Dollar, Annually 1900–2000

Country	Geometric mean (%)	Arithmetic mean(%)	Standard deviation (%)	Minimum change (year, %)	Maximum change (year, %)
Australia	–0.6	–0.1	10.7	1931: –39.0	1933: 54.2
Belgium	0.2	1.0	13.3	1919: –32.1	1933: 54.2
Canada	–0.5	–0.4	4.6	1931: –18.1	1933: 12.9
Denmark	0.1	1.0	12.7	1946: –50.3	1933: 37.2
France	–0.4	2.5	24.0	1946: –78.3	1943: 141.5
Germany	–0.1	15.1	134.8	1945: –75.0	1948: 1302.0
Ireland	–0.1	0.5	11.2	1946: –37.0	1933: 56.6
Italy	–0.2	4.0	39.5	1946: –64.9	1944: 335.2
Japan	0.2	3.2	29.5	1945: –78.3	1946: 253.0
The Netherlands	–0.1	0.8	12.6	1946: –61.6	1933: 55.7
South Africa	–1.3	–0.7	10.5	1946: –35.3	1986: 37.3
Spain	–0.4	1.1	18.8	1946: –56.4	1939: 128.7
Sweden	–0.4	0.2	10.7	1919: –38.0	1933: 43.5
Switzerland	0.2	0.8	11.2	1936: –29.0	1933: 53.3
United Kingdom	–0.3	0.3	11.7	1946: –36.7	1933: 55.2

"While real exchange rates do not appear to exhibit a long-term upward or downward trend, they are clearly volatile, and on year-to-year basis, PPP explains little of the fluctuations in foreign exchange rates. Some of the extreme changes [in the table above] reflect exchanges rates or inflation indexes that are not representative, typically (as in Germany) because of wartime controls, and this may amplify the volatility of real exchange rates changes. Given the potential measurement error in inflation indexes, and the fact that real exchange rates involve a ratio of two different price index series, it is all the more striking that, with the exception of South Africa, all real exchange rates appreciate or depreciate annually by no more than a fraction of one percentage point."

Source: Elroy Dimson, Paul Marsh, and Mike Staunton, *Triumph of the Optimists, 101 Years of Global Investment Returns* (Princeton: University Press, 2002) pp. 97–98.

If changes in exchange rates just offset differential inflation rates—if purchasing power parity holds—all the real effective exchange rate indices would stay at 100. If an exchange rate strengthened more than was justified by differential inflation, its index would rise above 100. If the real

Exhibit 6.3 IMF's Real Effective Exchange Rate Indexes for the United States and Japan (1995 = 100)

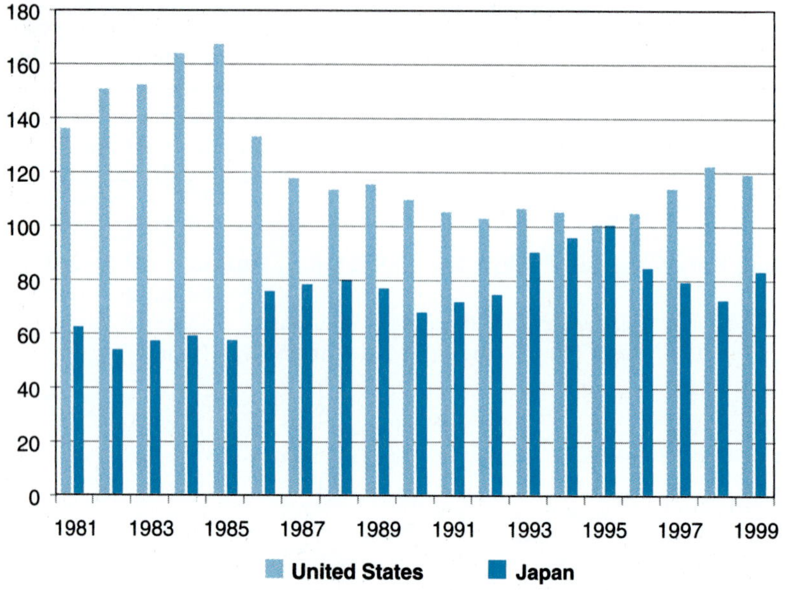

Source: International Financial Statistics, International Monetary Fund, monthly, 1995 = 100.

effective exchange rate index is above 100, the currency would be considered "overvalued" from a competitive perspective. An index value below 100 would suggest an "undervalued" currency.

Exhibit 6.3 shows that the real effective exchange rate has varied considerably from year to year for both the U.S. dollar and the Japanese yen, and the data lends some support to the concept that PPP may hold—even for the long run. For example, the index of the real effective exchange rate for the U.S. dollar rose from a level of 135 in 1981 to a level of 166 in 1985, only to fall to 100 (the index base year) in 1995. The dollar immediately rose again, rising to nearly 122 in 1999 (the last year for which data was available at the time this was written). The Japanese yen has been undervalued every year for which the dollar was overvalued. Beginning with a value of 63 in 1981, the yen rose relatively steadily toward parity in 1995. After 1995, however, the yen returned to its undervalued ways, falling to an index value of 85 in 1999.

Apart from measuring deviations from PPP, a country's real effective exchange rate is an important tool for management when predicting upward or downward pressure on a country's balance of payments and exchange rate, as well as an indicator of the desirability to produce for export from that country.

Exchange Rate Pass-Through

Incomplete exchange rate pass-through is one reason that a country's real effective exchange rate index can deviate for lengthy periods from its PPP-equilibrium level of 100. The degree to which the prices of imported and exported goods change as a result of exchange rate changes is termed *pass-through*. Although PPP implies that all exchange rate changes are passed through by equivalent changes in prices to trading partners, empirical research in the 1980s questioned this long-held assumption. For example, sizeable current account deficits of the United States in the 1980s and 1990s did not respond to changes in the value of the dollar.

To illustrate exchange rate pass-through, assume BMW produces an automobile in Germany and pays all production expense in euros. When the firm exports the auto to the United States, the price of the BMW in the U.S. market should simply be the euro value converted to dollars at the spot exchange rate:

$$P^{\$}_{\text{BMW}} = P^{€}_{\text{BMW}} \times S$$

where $P^{\$}_{\text{BMW}}$ is the BMW price in dollars, $P^{€}_{\text{BMW}}$ is the BMW price in euros, and S is the number of dollars per euro. If the euro appreciated 10% versus the U.S. dollar, the new spot exchange rate should result in the price of the BMW in the United States rising a proportional 10%. If the price in dollars increases by the same percentage change as the exchange rate, the pass-through of exchange rate changes is complete (or 100%).

However, if the price in dollars rises by less than the percentage change in exchange rates (as is often the case in international trade), the pass-through is partial, as illustrated in Exhibit 6.4. The 71% pass-through (U.S. dollar prices rose only 14.29% when the euro appreciated 20%) implies that BMW is absorbing a portion of the adverse exchange rate change. This absorption could result from smaller profit margins, cost reductions, or both. For example, components and raw materials imported to Germany cost less in euros when the euro appreciates. It is also likely that some time may pass before all exchange rate changes are finally reflected in the prices of traded goods, including the period over which previously signed contracts are delivered upon. It is obviously in the interest of BMW to keep the appreciation of the euro from raising the price of its automobiles in major export markets.

The concept of ***price elasticity of demand*** is useful when determining the desired level of pass-through. Recall that the own-price elasticity of demand for any good is the percentage change in quantity of the good demanded as a result of the percentage change in the good's own price:

$$\text{price elasticity of demand} = \varepsilon_p = \frac{\%\Delta Q_d}{\%\Delta P}$$

where Q_d is quantity demanded and P is product price. If the absolute value of ε_p is less than 1.0, the good is relatively "inelastic," while a value greater than 1.0, indicates a relatively "elastic" good.

A German product that is relatively price inelastic, meaning that the quantity demanded is relatively unresponsive to price changes, may often demonstrate a high degree of pass-through. This is so because a higher dollar price in the United States market would have little noticeable effect on the quantity of the product demanded by consumers. Dollar revenue would increase, but euro revenue would remain the same. However, products that are relatively price-elastic would respond

Exhibit 6.4 Exchange Rate Pass-Through

Pass-through is the measure of response of imported and exported product prices to exchange rate changes. Assume the price in dollars and euros of a BMW automobile produced in Germany and sold in the United States at the spot exchange rate is:

$$P^{\$}_{BMW} = P^{€}_{BMW} \times (\$/€) = €35{,}000 \text{ x } \$1.000/€ = €35{,}000$$

If the euro were to appreciate 20% versus the U.S. dollar, from $1.0000/€ to $1.2000/€, the price of the BMW in the U.S. market should theoretically be $42,000. But if the price of the BMW in the U.S. rises by less than 20%—for example, to only $40,000—then the degree of pass-through is only *partial*:

$$\frac{P^{\$}_{BMW,2}}{P^{\$}_{BMW,1}} = \frac{\$40{,}000}{\$35{,}000} = 1.1429, \text{ or a 14.29\% increase}$$

The degree of pass-through is measured by the proportion of the exchange rate change reflected in dollar prices. In this example, the dollar price of the BMW rose only 14.29%, while the euro appreciated 20.0% against the U.S. dollar. The degree of pass-through is partial: 14.29% ÷ 20.00%, or approximately 0.71. Only 71% of the exchange rate change was passed-through to the U.S. dollar price. The remaining 29% of the exchange rate change has been absorbed by BMW.

in the opposite direction. If the 20% euro appreciation resulted in 20% higher dollar prices, U.S. consumers would decrease the number of BMWs purchased. If the price elasticity of demand for BMWs in the United States were greater than one, total dollar sales revenue of BMWs would decline.

Interest Rates and Exchange Rates

We have already seen how prices of goods in different countries should be related through exchange rates. We now consider how interest rates are linked to exchange rates.

The Fisher Effect

The *Fisher effect*, first theorized by economist Irving Fisher, states that nominal interest rates in each country are equal to the required real rate of return plus compensation for expected inflation. More formally, this is derived from $(1+r)(1+\pi)-1$:

$$i = r + \pi + r\pi$$

where i is the nominal rate of interest, r is the real rate of interest, and π is the expected rate of inflation over the period of time for which funds are to be lent. The final compound term, $r\pi$, is frequently dropped from consideration due to its relatively minor value. The Fisher effect then reduces to (approximate form):

$$i = r + \pi$$

The Fisher effect applied to two different countries like the United States and Japan would be:

$$i^{\$} = r^{\$} + \pi^{\$}; \quad i^{¥} = r^{¥} + \pi^{¥}$$

where the superscripts $ and ¥ pertain to the respective nominal (i), real (r), and expected inflation (π) components of financial instruments denominated in dollars and yen, respectively. We need to forecast the future rate of inflation, not what inflation has been. Predicting the future can be difficult.

Empirical tests using ex-post national inflation rates have shown the Fisher effect usually exists for short-maturity government securities such as treasury bills and notes. Comparisons based on longer maturities suffer from the increased financial risk inherent in fluctuations of the market value of the bonds prior to maturity. Comparisons of private sector securities are influenced by unequal creditworthiness of the issuers. All the tests are inconclusive to the extent that recent past rates of inflation are not a correct measure of future expected inflation.

The International Fisher Effect

The relationship between the percentage change in the spot exchange rate over time and the differential between comparable interest rates in different national capital markets is known as the *international Fisher effect*. "Fisher-open," as it is often termed, states that the spot exchange rate should change in an equal amount but in the opposite direction to the difference in interest rates between two countries. More formally:

$$\frac{S_1 - S_2}{S_2} \times 100 = i^{\$} - i^{¥}$$

where $i^{\$}$ and $i^{¥}$ are the respective national interest rates, and S is the spot exchange rate using indirect quotes (an indirect quote on the dollar is, for example, ¥/\$) at the beginning of the period (S_1) and the end of the period (S_2). This is the approximation form commonly used in industry. The precise formulation is:

$$\frac{S_1 - S_2}{S_2} = \frac{i^{\$} - i^{¥}}{1 + i^{¥}}$$

Justification for the international Fisher effect is that investors must be rewarded or penalized to offset the expected change in exchange rates. For example, if a dollar-based investor buys a 10-year yen bond earning 4% interest instead of a 10-year dollar bond earning 6% interest, the investor must be expecting the yen to appreciate vis-à-vis the dollar by at least 2% per year during the 10 years. If not, the dollar-based investor would be better off remaining in dollars. If the yen appreciates 3% during the 10-year period, the dollar-based investor would earn a bonus of 1% higher return. However, the international Fisher effect predicts that with unrestricted capital flows, an investor should be indifferent to whether his bond is in dollars or yen, since investors worldwide would see the same opportunity and remove it via competition.

Empirical tests lend some support to the relationship postulated by the international Fisher effect, although considerable short-run deviations occur. A more serious criticism has been posed, however, by recent studies that suggest the existence of a foreign exchange risk premium for most major currencies. Also, speculation in uncovered interest arbitrage (described later in this chapter) creates distortions in currency markets. Thus the expected change in exchange rates might consistently be more than the difference in interest rates.

The Forward Rate

A *forward rate* is an exchange rate quoted today for settlement at some future date. A forward exchange agreement between currencies states the rate of exchange at which a foreign currency will be *bought forward* or *sold forward* at a specific date in the future (typically 30, 60, 90, 180, 270, or 360 days).

The forward rate is calculated for any specific maturity by adjusting the current spot exchange rate by the ratio of eurocurrency interest rates of the same maturity for the two subject currencies. For example, the 90-day forward rate for the Swiss franc/U.S. dollar exchange rate (F_{90}^{SF}) is found by multiplying the current spot rate ($S^{SF/\$}$) by the ratio of the 90-day euro-Swiss franc deposit rate (i^{SF}) over the 90-day eurodollar deposit rate ($i^{\$}$):

$$F_{90}^{SF/\$} = S^{SF/\$} \times \frac{\left[1 + \left(i^{SF} \times \frac{90}{360}\right)\right]}{\left[1 + \left(i^{\$} \times \frac{90}{360}\right)\right]}$$

Assuming a spot rate of SF1.4800/\$, a 90-day euro Swiss franc deposit rate of 4.00% per annum, and a 90-day eurodollar deposit rate of 8.00% per annum, the 90-day forward rate is SF1.4655/\$:

$$F_{90}^{SF/\$} = \text{SF}1.4800/\$ \times \frac{\left[1 + \left(0.0400 \times \frac{90}{360}\right)\right]}{\left[1 + \left(0.0800 \times \frac{90}{360}\right)\right]} = \text{SF}1.4800/\$ \times \frac{1.01}{1.02} = \text{SF}1.4655/\$$$

The *forward premium* or *discount* is the percentage difference between the spot and forward exchange rate, stated in annual percentage terms. When the foreign currency price of the home currency is used as in this case of SF/\$, the formula for the percent-per-annum premium or discount (denoted *f* here) becomes:

$$f^{SF} = \frac{\text{Spot} - \text{Forward}}{\text{Forward}} \times \frac{360}{\text{days}} \times 100$$

Substituting the SF/\$ spot and forward rates, as well as the number of days forward (90):

$$f^{SF} = \frac{\text{SF}1.4800/\$ - \text{SF}1.4655/\$}{\text{SF}1.4655/\$} \times \frac{360}{90} \times 100 = +3.96\% \text{ per annum}$$

The sign is positive, indicating that the Swiss franc is selling forward at a 3.96% per annum premium over the dollar (it takes 3.96% more dollars to get a franc at the 90-day forward rate).

As illustrated in Exhibit 6.5, the forward premium on the eurodollar forward exchange rate series arises from the differential between eurodollar interest rates and Swiss franc interest rates. Because the forward rate for any particular maturity utilizes the specific interest rates for that term, the forward premium or discount on a currency is visually obvious. The currency with the higher interest rate (in this case, the U.S. dollar) will sell forward at a discount, and the currency with the lower interest rate (in this case, the Swiss franc) will sell forward at a premium.

The forward rate is calculated from three observable data items—the spot rate, the foreign currency deposit rate, and the home currency deposit rate—and is not a forecast of the future spot exchange. It is, however, frequently used by managers within MNEs as a forecast, with mixed results as the following section describes.

Interest Rate Parity (IRP)

The theory of interest rate parity (IRP) provides the linkage between the foreign exchange markets and the international money markets. The theory states: *The difference in the national interest rates for securities of similar risk and maturity should be equal to, but opposite in sign to, the forward rate discount or premium for the foreign currency, except for transaction costs.*

Exhibit 6.6 shows how the theory of interest rate parity works. Assume that an investor has \$1,000,000 and several alternative but comparable Swiss franc (SF) monetary investments. If the investor chooses to invest in a dollar money market instrument, the investor would earn the dollar rate of interest. This results in $(1 + i^{\$})$ at the end of the period, where $i^{\$}$ is the dollar rate of

Exhibit 6.5 Currency Yield Curves and the Forward Premium

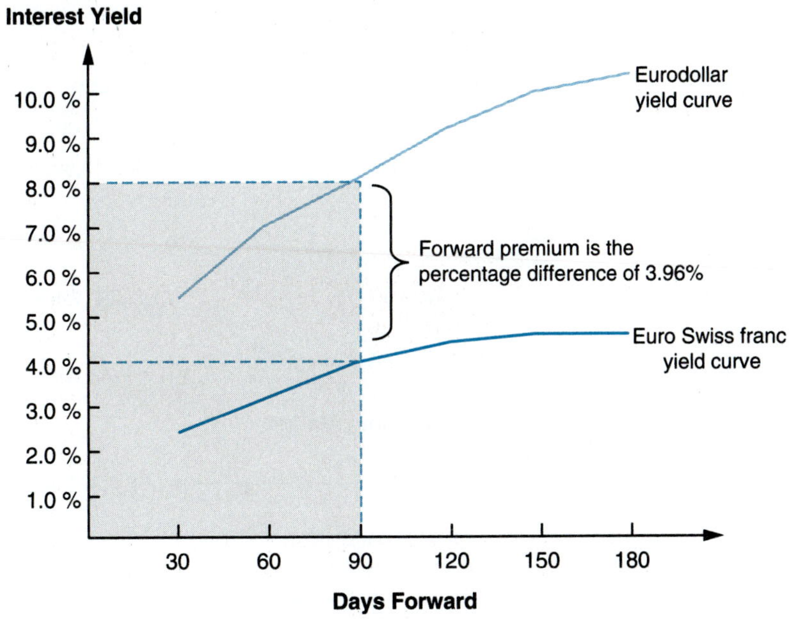

interest in decimal form. The investor may, however, choose to invest in a Swiss franc money market instrument of identical risk and maturity for the same period. This would require that the investor exchange the dollars for francs at the spot rate of exchange, invest the francs in a money market instrument, sell the francs forward (in order to avoid any risk that the exchange rate would change), and at the end of the period convert the resulting proceeds back to dollars.

A dollar-based investor would evaluate the relative returns of starting in the top left corner and investing in the dollar market (straight across the top of the box) compared to investing in the Swiss franc market (going down and then around the box to the top right corner). The comparison of returns would be:

$$(1+i^{\$}) = S^{SF/\$} \times (1+i^{SF}) \times \frac{1}{F^{SF/\$}}$$

where S = the spot rate of exchange and F = the forward rate of exchange. Substituting in the spot rate (SF1.4800/\$) and forward rate (SF1.4655/\$) and respective interest rates ($i^{\$} = 0.02$, $i^{SF} = 0.01$) from Exhibit 6.6, the interest rate parity condition is:

$$(1+0.02) = 1.4800 \times (1+0.01) \times \frac{1}{1.4655}$$

Exhibit 6.6 **Interest Parity Rate (IRP)**

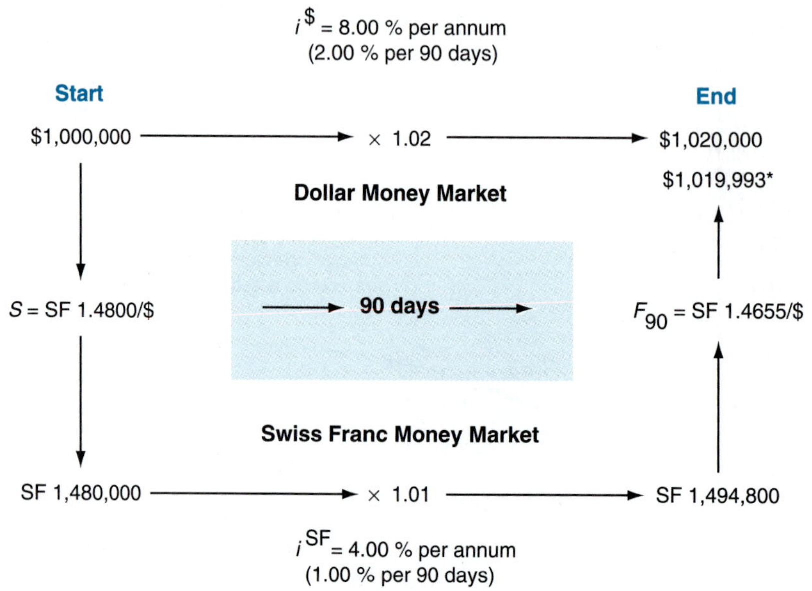

*Note that the Swiss franc investment yields $1,019,993—$7 less on a $1 million investment.

The left-hand side of the equation is the gross return the investor would earn by investing in dollars. The right-hand side is the gross return the investor would earn by exchanging dollars for Swiss francs at the spot rate, investing the franc proceeds in the Swiss franc money market, and simultaneously selling the principal plus interest in Swiss francs forward for dollars at the current 90-day forward rate.

Ignoring transaction costs, if the returns in dollars are equal between the two alternative money market investments, the spot and forward rates are considered to be at *interest rate parity* (IRP). The transaction is "covered" because the exchange rate back to dollars is guaranteed at the end of the 90-day period. Therefore, as in Exhibit 6.6, in order for the two alternatives to be equal, any differences in interest rates must be offset by the difference between the spot and forward exchange rates (in approximate form):

$$\frac{F}{S}=\frac{\left(1+i^{SF}\right)}{\left(1+i^{\$}\right)},\ \text{or}\ \frac{\text{SF}1.4655/\$}{\text{SF}1.4800/\$}=\frac{1.01}{1.02}=0.9902\approx 1\%$$

Covered Interest Arbitrage (CIA)

The spot and forward exchange markets are not, however, constantly in the state of equilibrium described by interest rate parity. When the market is not in equilibrium, the potential for "riskless" or arbitrage profit exists. The arbitrager who recognizes such an imbalance will move to take advantage of the disequilibrium by investing in whichever currency offers the higher return on a covered basis. This is called *covered interest arbitrage* (CIA).

Exhibit 6.7 describes the steps that a currency trader, most likely working in the arbitrage division of a large international bank, would implement to perform a CIA transaction. The currency trader, lets call him Fye Hong, can utilize any of a number of major eurocurrencies that his bank holds to conduct arbitrage investments. The morning conditions indicate to Fye Hong that a CIA transaction that exchanges 1 million U.S. dollars for Japanese yen, invested in a six-month euroyen account and sold forward back to dollars, will yield a profit of $4,638 ($1,044,638 – $1,040,000) over and above that available from a eurodollar investment. Conditions in the exchange markets and euromarkets change rapidly, however, so if Fye Hong waits even a few minutes, the profit opportunity may disappear. Fye Hong executes the following transaction:

Step 1: Convert $1,000,000 at the spot rate of ¥106.00/$ to ¥106,000,000 (see "Start" in Exhibit 6.7).

Step 2: Invest the proceeds, ¥106,000,000, in a euroyen account for six months, earning 4.00% per annum, or 2% for 180 days.

Step 3: Simultaneously sell the future yen proceeds (¥108,120,000) forward for dollars at the 180-day forward rate of ¥103.50/$. This action "locks in" gross dollar revenues of $1,044,638 (see "End" in Exhibit 6.7).

Step 4: Calculate the cost (opportunity cost) of funds used at the eurodollar rate of 8.00% per annum, or 4% for 180 days, with principal and interest then totaling $1,040,000. Profit on CIA ("End") is $4,638 ($1,044,638 – $1,040,000).

Exhibit 6.7 Covered Interest Arbitrage (CIA)

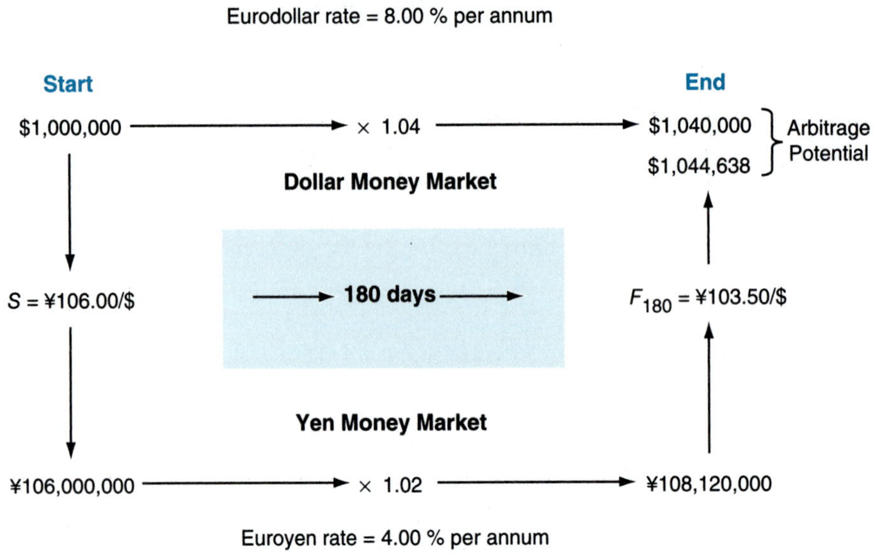

Rule of Thumb: All that is required to make a covered interest arbitrage profit is that interest rate parity is not holding. Depending on the relative interest rates and forward premium, Fye Hong could have started in Japanese yen, invested in U.S. dollars, and sold the dollars forward for yen. The profit would then be denominated in yen. But how should Hong decide which direction to follow around the box in Exhibit 6.7?

The key to determining whether to start in dollars or yen is to compare the differences in interest rates to the forward premium on the yen (the *cost of cover*). For example, in Exhibit 6.7 the difference in 180-day interest rates is 2.00% (dollar interest rates are higher by 2.00%). The premium on the yen for 180 days forward is:

$$f^{¥} = \frac{S-F}{F} \times \frac{360}{180} \times 100 = \frac{¥106.00/\$ - ¥103.50/\$}{¥103.50/\$} \times 200 = 2.42\%$$

In other words, by investing in yen Fye Hong earns 2.42% on the premium when converting yen back to dollars. He earns only 2.00% if he continues to invest in dollars.

Rule of Thumb: When the foreign currency is at a premium:

- If the difference in interest rates is greater than the forward premium on the foreign currency, invest in the higher interest rate currency.
- If the difference in interest rates is less than the forward premium on the foreign currency, invest in the foreign currency.

A similar rule is also valid when the *foreign currency is at a discount.*

- If the difference in interest rates is greater than the forward discount on the foreign currency, invest in the foreign currency (which will be the one with the higher interest rate).
- If the difference in interest rates is less than the forward discount on the foreign currency, invest in the lower interest rate currency.

Using these rules of thumb should enable Fye Hong to choose which direction to follow around the box in Exhibit 6.7. It also guarantees that he will always make a profit if he goes in the right direction. This assumes that the profit is greater than any transaction costs incurred.

This process of covered interest arbitrage drives the international currency and money markets toward the equilibrium described by interest rate parity. Slight deviations from equilibrium provide opportunities for arbitragers to make riskless profits. Such deviations provide the supply and demand forces which will move the market back toward parity (equilibrium).

Covered interest arbitrage opportunities continue until interest rate parity is reestablished, because the arbitragers are able to earn risk-free profits by repeating the cycle as often as possible. Their actions, however, nudge the foreign exchange and money markets back toward equilibrium for the following reasons:

1. Purchase of yen in the spot market and sale of yen in the forward market narrows the premium on the forward yen. This is so because the spot yen strengthens from the extra demand and the forward yen weakens because of the extra sales. A narrower premium on the forward yen reduces the foreign exchange gain previously captured by investing in yen.
2. The demand for yen-denominated securities causes yen interest rates to fall, while the higher level of borrowing in the United States causes dollar interest rates to rise. The net result is a wider interest differential in favor of investing in the dollar.

Uncovered Interest Arbitrage (UIA)

A deviation from covered interest arbitrage is uncovered interest arbitrage (UIA), wherein investors borrow in countries and currencies exhibiting relatively low interest rates and convert the proceeds into currencies that offer much higher interest rates. The transaction is "uncovered" because the investor does not sell the higher yielding currency proceeds forward, choosing to remain uncovered and accept the currency risk of exchanging the higher yield currency into the lower yielding currency at the end of the period. Exhibit 6.8 demonstrates the steps an uncovered interest arbitrager takes when undertaking what is termed the *yen carry trade.*

The "yen carry trade" is an age-old application of UIA. Investors from both inside and outside Japan take advantage of extremely low interest rates in Japanese yen (0.40% per annum) to raise capital. Investors exchange the capital they raise for other currencies like U.S. dollars or euros. They then reinvest these dollar or euro proceeds in dollar or euro money markets, where the funds earn substantially higher rates of return (5.00% per annum in Exhibit 6.8). At the end of the period, a year in this case, they convert the dollar proceeds back into Japanese yen in the spot market. The result is a tidy profit over what it costs to repay the initial loan.

The trick, however, is that the spot exchange rate at the end of the year must not change significantly from what it was at the beginning of the year—at least not move significantly

Exhibit 6.8 Uncovered Interest Arbitrage (UIA): The Yen Carry Trade

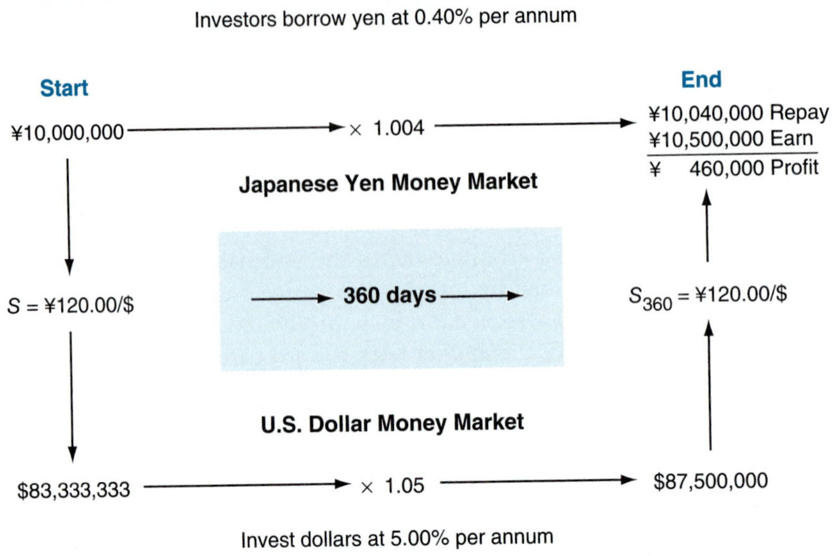

In the yen carry trade, the investor borrows Japanese yen at relatively low interest rates, converts the proceeds to another currency such as the U.S. dollar where the funds are invested at a higher interest rate for a term. At the end of the period, the investor exchanges the dollars back to yen to repay the loan, pocketing the differences as arbitrage profit. If the spot rate at the end of the period is roughly the same as at the start, or the yen has fallen in value against the dollar, the investor profits. If, however, the yen were to appreciate versus the dollar over the period, the investment may result in significant loss.

against the borrower. If the yen were to appreciate significantly against the dollar, as it did throughout 2002, moving from ¥133/$ to ¥118/$, these "uncovered" investors could suffer sizeable losses when they convert their dollars into yen to repay the yen they borrowed; higher return at higher risk.

Equilibrium Between Interest Rates and Exchange Rates

Exhibit 6.9 illustrates the conditions necessary for equilibrium between interest rates and exchange rates. The vertical axis shows the difference in interest rates in favor of the foreign currency, and the horizontal axis shows the forward premium or discount on that currency. The interest rate parity line shows the equilibrium state, but transaction costs cause the line to be a band rather than a thin line. Transaction costs arise from foreign exchange and investment brokerage costs on buying and selling securities. Typical transaction costs in recent years have been in the range of 0.18% to 0.25% on an annual basis. For individual transactions like Fye Hong's arbitrage activity in the previous example, there is no explicit transaction cost per trade; rather, the costs of the bank in supporting Fye Hong's activities are the transaction costs. Point X shows one possible equilibrium position, where a 4% lower rate of interest on yen securities would be offset by a 4% premium on the forward yen.

Exhibit 6.9 Interest Rate Parity (IRP) and Equilibrium

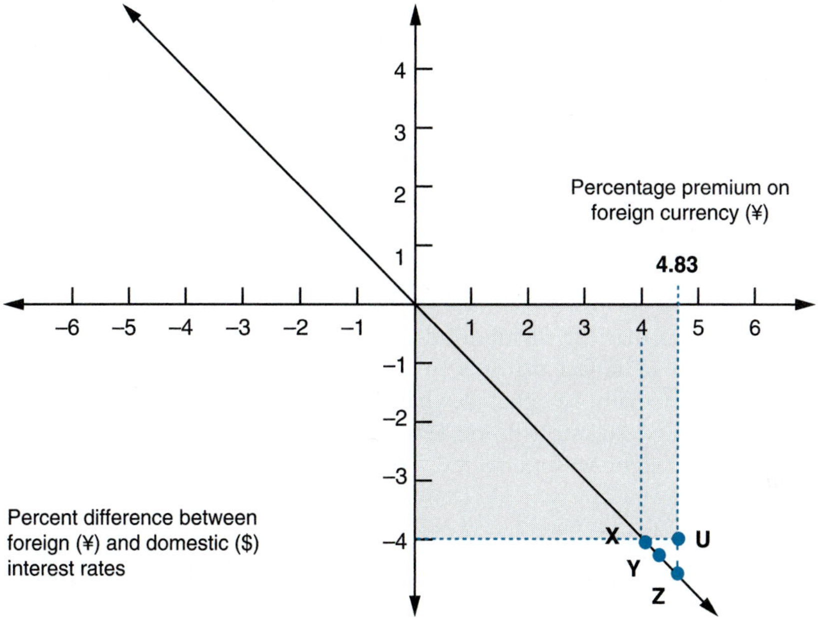

The disequilibrium situation, which encouraged the interest rate arbitrage in the previous CIA example (Exhibit 6.7), is illustrated by point U. It is located off the interest rate parity line, because the lower interest on the yen is –4% (annual basis), whereas the premium on the forward yen is slightly over 4.8% (annual basis). Using the formula for forward premium presented earlier, we find the premium on the yen thus:

$$\frac{¥106.00/\$ - ¥103.50/\$}{¥103.50/\$} \times \frac{360 \text{ days}}{180 \text{ days}} \times 100 = 4.83\%$$

The situation depicted by point U is unstable, because all investors have an incentive to execute the same covered interest arbitrage. Except for a bank failure, the arbitrage gain is virtually risk-free.

Some observers have suggested that political risk does exist, because one of the governments might apply capital controls that would prevent execution of the forward contract. This risk is fairly remote for covered interest arbitrage between major financial centers of the world, especially because a large portion of funds used for covered interest arbitrage is in eurodollars. The concern may be valid for pairings with countries not noted for political and fiscal stability.

The net result of the disequilibrium is that fund flows will narrow the gap in interest rates and/or decrease the premium on the forward yen. In other words, market pressures will cause point U in Exhibit 6.9 to move toward the interest rate parity band. Equilibrium might be reached at point Y, or at any other locus between X and Z, depending on whether forward market premiums are more or less easily shifted than interest rate differentials.

Forward Rate as an Unbiased Predictor of the Future Spot Rate

Some forecasters believe that foreign exchange markets for the major floating currencies are "efficient" and forward exchange rates are unbiased predictors of future spot exchange rates.

Exhibit 6.10 demonstrates the meaning of "unbiased prediction" in terms of how the forward rate performs in estimating future spot exchange rates. If the forward rate is an unbiased predictor of the future spot rate, the expected value of the future spot rate at time 2 equals the present forward rate for time 2 delivery, available now, $E(S_2) = F_1$.

Intuitively this means that the distribution of possible actual spot rates in the future is centered on the forward rate. The fact that it is an unbiased predictor, however, does not mean that the future spot rate will actually be equal to what the forward rate predicts. Unbiased prediction simply means that the forward rate will, on average, overestimate and underestimate the actual future spot rate in equal frequency and degree. The forward rate may, in fact, never actually equal the future spot rate.

The rationale for this relationship is based on the hypothesis that the foreign exchange market is reasonably efficient. Market efficiency assumes that (a) all relevant information is quickly reflected in both the spot and forward exchange markets, (b) transaction costs are low, and (c) instruments denominated in different currencies are perfect substitutes for one another.

Exhibit 6.10 Forward Rate as an Unbiased Predictor for Future Spot Rate

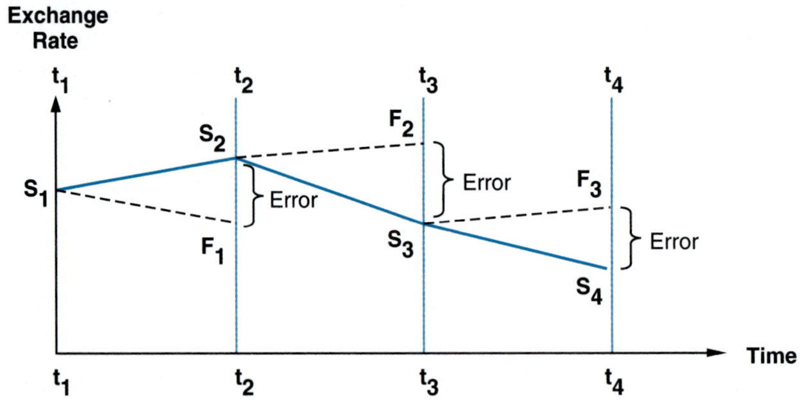

The forward rate available today ($F_{t,t+1}$), time t, for delivery at future time t+1, is used as a "predictor" of the spot rate that will exist at that day in the future. Therefore, the forecast spot rate for time S_{t2} is F_1 ; the actual spot rate turns out to be S_2. The vertical distance between the prediction and the actual spot rate is the forecast error.

When the forward rate is termed an "unbiased predictor of the future spot rate," it means that the forward rate over- or underestimates the future spot rate with relatively equal frequency and amount. It therefore "misses the mark" in a regular and orderly manner. The sum of the errors equals zero.

Empirical studies of the efficient foreign exchange market hypothesis have yielded conflicting results. Nevertheless, a consensus is developing that rejects the efficient market hypothesis. It appears that the forward rate is not an unbiased predictor of the future spot rate and that it does pay to use resources to attempt to forecast exchange rates.

If the efficient market hypothesis is correct, a financial executive cannot expect to profit in any consistent manner from forecasting future exchange rates, because current quotations in the forward market reflect all that is presently known about likely future rates. While future exchange rates may well differ from the expectation implicit in the present forward market quotation, we cannot know today which way actual future quotations will differ from today's forward rate. The expected mean value of deviations is zero. The forward rate is therefore an "unbiased" estimator of the future spot rate.

Tests of foreign exchange market efficiency using longer time periods of analysis conclude that either exchange market efficiency is untestable or, if it is testable, the market is not efficient. Furthermore, the existence and success of foreign exchange forecasting services suggest that managers are willing to pay a price for forecast information, even though they can use the forward rate as a forecast at no cost. The cost of buying this information is, in many circumstances, an "insurance premium" for financial managers who might get fired for using their own forecast, including forward rates, when that forecast proves incorrect. If they bought professional advice that turns out wrong, the fault was not in their forecast!

If the exchange market is not efficient, it would be sensible for a firm to spend resources on forecasting exchange rates. This is the opposite conclusion to the one in which exchange markets are deemed efficient.

Prices, Interest Rates, and Exchange Rates in Equilibrium

Exhibit 6.11 illustrates all of the fundamental parity relations simultaneously, in equilibrium, using the U.S. dollar and the Japanese yen. The forecasted inflation rates for Japan and the United States are 1.0% and 5.0%, respectively—a 4% differential. The nominal interest rate in the U.S. dollar market (one-year government security) is 8%, a differential of 4% over the Japanese nominal interest rate of 4%. The current spot rate, S_1, is ¥104/$, and the one-year forward rate is ¥100/$.

Relation A: Purchasing Power Parity (PPP). According to the relative version of purchasing power parity, the spot exchange rate one year from now, S_2, is expected to be ¥100/$:

$$S_2 = S_1 \times \frac{1+\pi^{¥}}{1+\pi^{\$}} = ¥104 / \$ \times \frac{1.01}{1.05} = ¥100 / \$$$

This is a 4% change and equal, but opposite in sign, to the difference in expected rates of inflation (1% – 5%).

Relation B: The Fisher Effect. The real rate of return is the nominal rate of interest less the expected rate of inflation. Here, the real rate in U.S. dollars is 4% ($r = i - \pi = 8\% - 4\%$) and also 4% in Japanese yen markets (5% – 1%).

Relation C: International Fisher Effect. The forecast change in the spot exchange rate—in this case, 4%—is equal to but opposite in sign to the differential between nominal interest rates:

$$\frac{S_1 - S_2}{S_2} \times 100 = i^{¥} - i^{\$} = -4\%$$

Relation D: Interest Rate Parity (IRP). According to the theory of interest rate parity, the difference in nominal interest rates is equal to, but opposite in sign to, the forward premium. For this numerical example, the nominal yen interest rate is 4% less than the nominal dollar interest rate:

$$i^{¥} - i^{\$} = 1\% - 5\% = -4\%$$

and the forward premium on the yen is a positive 4%:

$$f^{¥} = \frac{S_1 - F}{S_1} \times 100 = \frac{¥104/\$ - ¥100/\$}{¥100/\$} \times 100 = 4\%$$

Relation E: Forward Rate as an Unbiased Predictor. Finally, the one-year forward rate on the Japanese yen, ¥100/$, if assumed to be an unbiased predictor of the future spot rate, also forecasts ¥100/$.

Exhibit 6.11 International Parity Conditions in Equilibrium (Approximate Form)

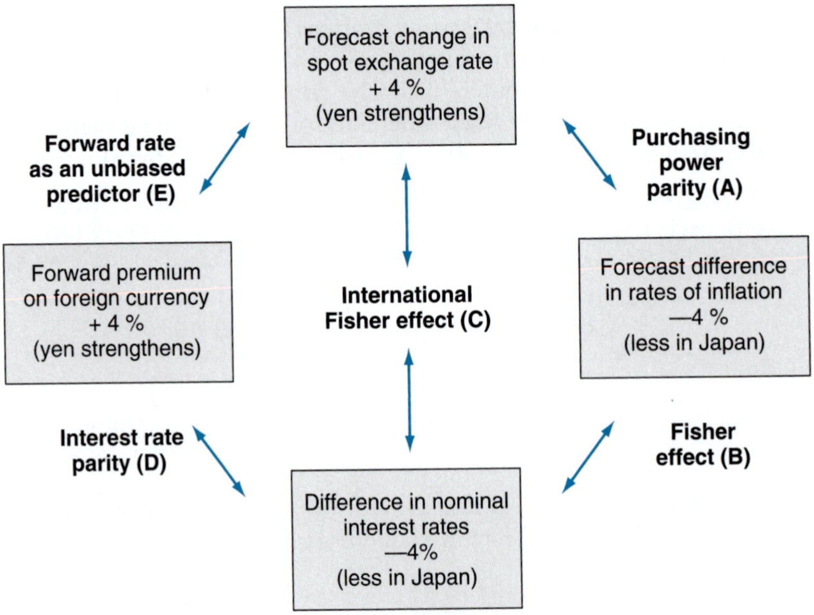

SUMMARY

- Parity conditions have traditionally been used by economists to help explain the long run trend in an exchange rate.
- Under conditions of freely floating rates, the expected rate of change in the spot exchange rate, differential rates of national inflation and interest, and the forward discount or premium are all directly proportional to each other and mutually determined. A change in one of these variables has a tendency to change all of them with feedback to the variable that changes first.
- If the identical product or service can be sold in two different markets and there are no restrictions on its sale or the transportation costs of moving it between markets, its price should be the same in both markets. This is called the *law of one price.*
- The absolute version of the theory of purchasing power parity states that the spot exchange rate is determined by the relative prices of similar baskets of goods.
- The relative version of the theory of purchasing power parity states that if the spot exchange rate between two countries starts in equilibrium, any change in the differential rate of inflation between them tends to be offset over the long run by an equal but opposite change in the spot exchange rate.
- The *Fisher effect*, named after economist Irving Fisher, states that nominal interest rates in each country are equal to the required real rate of return plus compensation for expected inflation.
- The *international Fisher effect*—"Fisher-open," as it is often termed—states that the spot exchange rate should change in an equal amount but in the opposite direction to the difference in interest rates between two countries.
- The theory of interest rate parity (IRP) states that the difference in the national interest rates for securities of similar risk and maturity should be equal to, but opposite in sign to, the forward rate discount or premium for the foreign currency, except for transaction costs.
- When the spot and forward exchange markets are not in equilibrium as described by interest rate parity, the potential for "riskless" or arbitrage profit exists. This is called *covered interest arbitrage* (CIA).
- Some forecasters believe that for the major floating currencies, foreign exchange markets are "efficient" and forward exchange rates are unbiased predictors of future spot exchange rates.

QUESTIONS

1. **Purchasing power parity.** Define the following terms:
   a. The law of one price
   b. Absolute purchasing power parity
   c. Relative purchasing power parity
2. **Nominal effective exchange rate index.** Explain how a nominal effective exchange rate index is constructed.
3. **Real effective exchange rate index.** What formula is used to convert a nominal effective exchange rate index into a real effective exchange rate index?
4. **Real effective exchange rates: Japan and the United States.** Exhibit 6.3 compares the real effective exchange rates for Japan and the United States. If the comparative real effective exchange rate was the main determinant, does Japan or the United States have a competitive advantage in exporting? Which of the two has an advantage in importing? Explain why.

5. **Exchange rate pass-through.** Incomplete exchange rate pass-through is one reason that a country's real effective exchange rate can deviate for lengthy periods from its purchasing power equilibrium level of 100. What is meant by the term *exchange rate pass-through*?

6. **The Fisher effect.** Define the Fisher effect. To what extent do empirical tests confirm that the Fisher effect exists in practice?

7. **The international Fisher effect.** Define the international Fisher effect. To what extent do empirical tests confirm that the international Fisher effect exists in practice?

8. **Interest rate parity.** Define interest rate parity. What is the relationship between interest rate parity and forward rates?

9. **Covered interest arbitrage.** Define the terms *covered interest arbitrage* and *uncovered interest arbitrage*. What is the difference between these two transactions?

10. **Forward rate as an unbiased predictor of the future spot rate.** Some forecasters believe that foreign exchange markets for the major floating currencies are "efficient" and forward exchange rates are unbiased predictors of future spot exchange rates. What is meant by "unbiased predictor" in terms of how the forward rate performs in estimating future spot exchange rates?

PROBLEMS

1. **The Big Mac Hamburger Standard.** With reference to Exhibit 6.1 assume the following changes and calculate the over (+) or under (-) valuation of the local currency:

Country	Big Mac Price	Exchange Rate
United States	$2.80	——
Argentina	Ps7.50	Ps3.60/$
Canada	C$3.50	C$1.63/$
Euro Area	€2.90	$1.02/€
Japan	¥300	¥122/$

2. **Exchange rate pass-through.** Assume that the export price of a Nissan Maxima from Osaka, Japan is ¥3,000,000. The exchange rate is ¥122/$. The forecast rate of inflation in the United States is 2% per year and is 0% per year in Japan.
   a. What is the export price of the Nissan at the beginning of the year expressed in U.S. dollars?
   b. Assuming purchasing power parity holds, what should the exchange rate be at the end of the year?
   c. Assuming 100% pass-through of exchange rate changes, what should be the dollar price of a Nissan at the end of the year?
   d. Assuming 70% pass-through of exchange rate changes, what should be the price of a Nissan at the end of the year?

3. **Argentine pesos.** The Argentine peso was fixed through a currency board at Ps1.00/$. In January, 2002 the Argentine peso was floated. As of January 29, 2003 it had depreciated to Ps3.20/$. During the one year period Argentina's inflation was 20% on an annualized basis. Inflation in the United States was 2.2% annualized.
   a. What should have been the exchange rate in January 2003 if purchasing power parity held?
   b. By what percentage was the Argentine peso undervalued on an annualized basis?
   c. What were the probable causes of undervaluation?

4. **International Fisher effect.** Assume that one-year interest rates are 3% in the United States and 5% in the Euro zone. The spot rate between the euro and the dollar is €1.02/$. Assuming the international Fisher effect holds, what should the €/$ rate be one year hence?

5. **Covered interest arbitrage—Denmark A.** James Chang, a foreign exchange trader at J.P. Morgan Chase, can invest $5 million or the

foreign currency equivalent of the bank's short term funds in a covered interest arbitrage with Denmark. He has the following quotes:

Spot exchange rate:	DKr 7.5000/$
three-month forward rate:	DKr 7.5372/$
three-month dollar interest:	3% per year (0.75% for 90 days)
three-month krone interest:	5% per year (1.25% for 90 days)

Can James Chang make a covered interest arbitrage profit?

6. **Covered interest arbitrage—Denmark B.**
   a. Assume that interest rates in the United States increase to 4% per year (1% for 90 days) but all other rates remain the same. Can James Chang make a 90-day covered interest arbitrage profit?
   b. Assume that interest rates in the Euro zone increase to 6% per year (1.5% for 90 days) but all other rates remain the same, including the original U.S. interest rate of 3% per year. Calculate whether James Chang could make a 90-day covered interest arbitrage profit.

7. **Covered interest arbitrage—Japan I.** Yukiko Miyaki, a foreign exchange trader at Credit Suisse First Boston, wants to invest $800,000, or its yen equivalent, in a covered interest arbitrage between U.S. dollars and Japanese yen. She has the following quotes:

Spot exchange rate:	¥124/$
six-month forward exchange rate:	¥123/$
six-month dollar interest rate:	3.00% per year (1.50% for 180 days)
six-month yen interest rate:	1.00% per year (0.50% for 180 days)

The bank does not calculate transaction costs on any individual transaction because these costs are part of the overall operating budget of the arbitrage department. Explain and diagram the specific steps Yukiko must take to make a covered interest arbitrage profit.

8. **Uncovered interest arbitrage—Japan II.** Yukiko Miyaki observes that the ¥/$ spot rate has been steady and both dollar and yen interest rates have remained relatively fixed over the past week. Therefore, she wonders if she should try an uncovered interest arbitrage and thereby save the cost of forward cover. Many of her research associates—and their computer models—are predicting the spot rate to remain at ¥124/$ at the end of 6 months. Using the same data as in problem 7:
   a. Calculate how much profit she could make if her expectations hold true.
   b. What is the risk she is taking?

9. **International parity conditions in equilibrium.** Assume the following data:

Forecast annual rate of inflation for Canada:	3.62%
Forecast annual rate of inflation for the United States:	3.00%
One-year interest rate for Canada:	5.62%
One-year interest rate for the United States:	5.00%
Spot rate	C$1.60/$
One-year forward rate	C$1.61/$

Diagram and calculate whether international parity conditions hold for Canada and the United States. What is the forecast change in the C$/$ spot exchange rate one year hence?

10. **Mary Smyth—CIA.** Mary Smyth is a foreign exchange dealer for a bank in New York City. She has $1,000,000 (or its Swiss franc equivalent) for a short-term money market investment and wonders if she should invest in U.S. dollars for three months or make a covered interest arbitrage investment in the Swiss franc. She faces the following rates:

Spot exchange rate:	SF1.6000/$
three-month forward rate:	SF1.5800/$
three-month U.S. interest rate:	8.00% p.a. (2.00% per quarter)
three-month Swiss interest rate:	6.00% p.a. (1.50% per quarter)

Where do you recommend Ms Smyth invest? Why?

11. **Mary Smyth—UIA.** Mary Smyth (using the same information in problem 10) decides to seek the full 8.00% return available in U.S. dollars by not covering her forward dollar receipts—an uncovered interest arbitrage (UIA) transaction. Assess this decision.

12. **Mary Smyth—one month later.** One month after the events described in problems 10 and 11, Mary Smyth again has $1,000,000 (or its Swiss franc equivalent) to invest for three months. She now faces the following rates. Should she again enter into a covered interest arbitrage investment?

Spot exchange rate:	SF1.6000/$
three-month forward rate:	SF1.5850/$
three-month U.S. interest rate:	8.00% p.a. (2.00% per quarter)
three-month Swiss rate:	4.80% p.a. (1.20% per quarter)

13. **Langkawi Island Resort.** You are planning a 30-day vacation on Langkawi Island, Malaysia, one year from now. The present charge for a luxury suite plus meals is RM760 per day, and the Malaysian ringgit presently is traded at RM3.8000/$. Hence the dollar cost today for a 30-day stay would be $6,000.

    The hotel has informed you that any increase in its room charges will be limited to any increase in the Malaysian cost of living. Malaysian inflation is expected to be 4% per annum, while U.S. inflation is only 1% per annum.

    a. How many dollars might you expect to need one year hence to pay for your 30-day vacation?

    b. By what percent has the dollar cost gone up? Why?

14. **Covered Interest Arbitrage against the Norwegian Krone.** A foreign exchange trader sees the following prices on his computer screen:

Spot rate, Norwegian krone per dollar:	NKr8.8181/$
3-month forward rate:	NKr8.9169/$
U.S. 3-month treasury bill rate:	2.60% p.a.
Norwegian 3-month treasury bill rate:	4.00% p.a.

    Could the trader profit by placing $500,000 of principal in a covered interest arbitrage operation in Norway?

15. **Frankfurt and New York.** Money and foreign exchange markets in Frankfurt and New York are very efficient. The following information is available:

	Frankfurt	New York
Spot exchange rate	$0.9000/€	$0.9000/€
One-year treasury bill rate	6.50%	3.20%
Expected inflation rate	unknown	2.00%

    a. What do the financial markets suggest for inflation in Europe next year?

    b. Estimate today's one-year forward exchange rate between the dollar and the euro.

16. **Tyrolean rents.** You have just rented a castle in the Tyrolean Alps for a vacation you are planning one year from now. Your landlord wants to preserve his real income in euros, and so the present monthly rent of €24,000/month will be adjusted upward or downward for any change in the Austrian cost of living between now and then. You expect Austrian inflation to be 2% and U.S. inflation to be 4% over the coming year. You believe implicitly in the theory of purchasing power parity, and you note from the *Financial Times* that the current spot exchange rate is $1.08/€. How many U.S. dollars will you need one year from now to pay your first month's rent?

17. **East Asiatic Company—Thailand.** The East Asiatic Company (EAC), a Danish company with subsidiaries all over Asia, has been funding its Bangkok subsidiary primarily with U.S. dollar debt because of the cost and availability of dollar capital as opposed to Thai baht (B) funds. The treasurer of EAC-Thailand is considering a one-year bank loan for $350,000. The current spot exchange rate is B42.84/$, and the dollar-based interest is 8.885% for the one year period.

    a. Assuming expected inflation rates of 4.50% and 2.20% in Thailand and the United States for the coming year respectively. According to purchasing power parity, what would the effective cost of funds be in Thai baht terms?

b. If EAC's foreign exchange advisors believe strongly that the Thai government wishes to push the value of the baht down against the dollar by 5% over the coming year (to promote its export competitiveness in dollar markets), what might the effective cost of funds end up being in baht terms?

c. If EAC could borrow Thai baht at 14% per annum, would this option be more cost-effective than part a or part b above?

18. Maltese Falcon: March 2003–2004. The infamous solid gold falcon, initially intended as a tribute by the Knights of Rhodes to the King of Spain in appreciation for his gift of the island of Malta to the order in 1530, has recently been recovered. The falcon is 14 inches in height and solid gold, weighing approximately 48 pounds. Gold prices in late 2002 and early 2003, primarily as a result of increasing international political tensions, have risen to $440/ounce.

The falcon is currently held by a private investor in Istanbul, who is actively negotiating with the Maltese government for its purchase and prospective return to its island home. The sale and payment are to take place in March of 2004, and the parties are negotiating the price and currency of payment. The investor has decided, in a show of goodwill, to base the sales price only on the falcon's *specie value*—its gold value.

The current spot exchange rate is 0.39 Maltese lira (ML) per U.S. dollar. Maltese inflation is expected to be about 8.5% for the coming year, while U.S. inflation, on the heels of a double-dip recession, is expected to come in at only 1.5%. If the investor bases value in the U.S. dollar, would he be better off receiving Maltese lira in one year—assuming purchasing power parity, or receiving a guaranteed dollar payment assuming a gold price of $420 per ounce?

19. London money fund. Tim Hogan is the manager of an international money market fund managed out of London. Unlike many money funds that guarantee their investors a near-risk-free investment with variable interest earnings, Tim Hogan's fund is a very aggressive fund that searches out relatively high interest earnings around the globe, but at some risk. The fund is pound-denominated.

Tim is currently evaluating a rather interesting opportunity in Malaysia. The Malaysian government has been periodically enforcing substantive currency and capital restrictions since the Asian Crisis of 1997 to protect and preserve the value of the Malaysian ringgit. The current spot exchange rate of M$3.800/$ has been maintained with little deviation since late 1997. Local currency (Malaysian ringgit) time deposits of 180-day maturities are hovering at about 9.600% per annum ($500,000 minimum deposit). The London eurocurrency market, for pounds, is offering only about 4.200% per annum for the same 180-day maturities. The current spot rate on the British pound is $1.6382/£, and the 180-day forward rate is $1.6100/£.

What do you recommend Tim Hogan do about the Malaysian money market opportunity, assuming he is investing £1 million?

20. The Beer Standard. In 1999 the *Economist* magazine reported the creation of an index or standard for the evaluation of currency values in Africa. Beer was chosen as the product for comparison because McDonald's had not penetrated the African continent beyond South Africa, and beer met most of the same product and market characteristics required for the construction of a proper currency index.

Investec, a South African investment banking firm, has replicated the process of creating a measure of purchasing power parity like that of the Big Mac Index of The Economist, for Africa. The index compares the cost of a 375 milliliter bottle of clear lager beer across sub-Sahara Africa. As a measure of purchasing power parity, the beer needs to be relatively homogeneous in qualities across countries, and needs to possess substantial elements of local manufacturing, distribution, and service, in order to actually provide a measure of relative purchasing power.

The beers are first priced in local currency (purchased in the taverns of the local man, and not

The Beer Standard

Country	Beer	Beer Prices: In local currency	In rand	Implied PPP rate	Spot rate 3/15/99	Under or overvalued to rand %
South Africa	Castle	Rand 2.30	2.30	—	—	—
Botswana	Castle	Pula 2.20	2.94	0.96	0.75	______
Ghana	Star	Cedi 1,200	3.17	521.74	379.10	______
Kenya	Tusker	Shilling 41.25	4.02	17.93	10.27	______
Malawi	Carlsberg	Kwacha 18.50	2.66	8.04	6.96	______
Mauritius	Phoenix	Rupee 15.00	3.72	6.52	4.03	______
Namibia	Windhoek	N$ 2.50	2.50	1.09	1.00	______
Zambia	Castle	Kwacha 1,200	3.52	521.74	340.68	______
Zimbabwe	Castle	Z$ 9.00	1.46	3.91	6.15	______

Beer price in rand = price in local currency/spot rate. Implied PPP rate = price in rand/2.30. Under/overvalued to rand = implied PPP rate/spot rate. *The Economist*, May 8, 1999, p. 78.

in the high-priced tourist centers and servers), then converted to South African rand. The prices of the beers in rand are then compared to form one measure of whether the local currencies are undervalued (–%) or overvalued (+%) versus the South African rand.

Use the data in the exhibit and complete the calculation of whether the individual African currencies listed are either overvalued or undervalued.

INTERNET EXERCISES

WWW.

1. **Big Mac Index updated.** Use the *Economist's* web site to find the latest edition of the Big Mac Index of currency over- and undervaluation. (You will need to do a search for "Big Mac Currencies.") Create a worksheet to compare how the British pound, the euro, the Swiss franc, and the Canadian dollar have changed from the version presented in this chapter.

   The Economist http://www.economist.com

2. **Purchasing Power Parity statistics.** The Organization for Economic Cooperation and Development (OECD) publishes detailed measures of prices and purchasing power for its member countries. Go to the OECD's web site and download the spreadsheet file with the historical data for purchasing power for the member countries.

   OECD Purchasing Power http://www.oecd.org/oecd/pages/home/displaygeneral/0,3380,EN-statistics- 513-15-no-no-no-513,00.html

3. **International interest rates.** A number of web sites publish current interest rates by currency and maturity. Use the *Financial Times* web site listed below to isolate the interest rate differentials between the U.S. dollar, the British pound, and the euro for all maturities up to and including one year.

Financial Times Market Data http://www.marketprices.ft.com/markets/currencies/international

Data Listed by the Financial Times:

International money rates (bank call rates for major currency deposits)

Money rates (LIBOR and CD rates, etc.)

10-year spreads (individual country spreads versus the euro and U.S. 10-year treasuries) Note: Which countries actually have lower 10-year government bond rates than the United States and the euro? Probably Switzerland and Japan. Check.

Benchmark government bonds (sampling of representative government issuances by major countries and recent price movements). Note which countries are showing longer maturity benchmark rates.

Emerging market bonds (government issuances, Brady bonds, etc.)

Eurozone rates (miscellaneous bond rates for assorted European-based companies; includes debt ratings by Moodys and S&P)

4. **Emerging market currencies.** Although major currencies like the U.S. dollar and the Japanese yen dominate the headlines, there are nearly as many currencies as countries in the world. Many of these currencies are traded in extremely thin and highly regulated markets, making their convertibility suspect. Finding quotations for these currencies is sometimes very difficult. Using the web page listed below, see how many African currency quotes you can find.

   Emerging Markets http://emgmkts.com

5. **Exchange rate indices.** JP Morgan calculates and maintains indices of many of the world's major currencies' values relative to baskets of other major currencies. Like those published by the IMF, these indices serve as more fundamental and general indicators of relative currency value.

   JP Morgan Currency Indices http://jpmorgan.com/MarketDataInd/Forex/CurrIndex.html

SELECTED READINGS

Cumby, Robert E., and Maurice Obstfeld, "A Note on Exchange Rate Expectations and Nominal Interest Differentials: A Test of the Fisher Hypothesis," *Journal of Finance*, June 1981, pp. 697–703.

Ohno, Kenichi, "Exchange Rate Fluctuations, Pass Through, and Market Share," *IMF Staff Papers*, June 1990, Volume 37, No. 2, pp. 294–310.

Rogoff, Kenneth, "The Purchasing Power Parity Puzzle," *Journal of Economic Literature*, June 1996, Volume 34, No. 2, pp. 647–668.

Chapter 6 APPENDIX

An Algebraic Primer to International Parity Conditions

The following is a purely algebraic presentation of the parity conditions explained in this chapter. It is offered to provide those who wish additional theoretical detail and definition ready access to the step-by-step derivation of the various conditions.

The Law of One Price

The *law of one price* refers to the state in which, in the presence of free trade, perfect substitutability of goods, and costless transactions, the equilibrium exchange rate between two currencies is determined by the ratio of the price of any commodity *i* denominated in two different currencies. For example,

$$S_t = \frac{P_{i,t}^{\$}}{P_{i,t}^{\mathrm{SF}}}$$

where $P_i^{\$}$ and P_i^{SF} refer to the prices of the same commodity i, at time t, denominated in U.S. dollars and Swiss francs, respectively. The spot exchange rate, S_t, is simply the ratio of the two currency prices.

Purchasing Power Parity

The more general form in which the exchange rate is determined by the ratio of two price indexes is termed the absolute version of *purchasing power parity (PPP)*. Each price index reflects the currency cost of the identical "basket" of goods across countries. The exchange rate which equates purchasing power for the identical collection of goods is then stated:

$$S_t = \frac{P_t^{\$}}{P_t^{\mathrm{SF}}}$$

where $P_t^{\$}$ and P_t^{SF} are the price index values in U.S. dollars and Swiss francs at time t, respectively. If the Greek letter π represents the rate of inflation in each country, the spot exchange rate at time $t + 1$ would be:

$$S_{t+1} = \frac{P_t^{\$}\left(1+\pi^{\$}\right)}{P_t^{\mathrm{SF}}\left(1+\pi^{\mathrm{SF}}\right)} = S_t\left[\frac{\left(1+\pi^{\$}\right)}{\left(1+\pi^{\mathrm{SF}}\right)}\right]$$

The change from period t to $t + 1$ is then:

$$\frac{S_{t+1}}{S_t} = \frac{\dfrac{P_t^{\$}\left(1+\pi^{\$}\right)}{P_t^{\mathrm{SF}}\left(1+\pi^{\mathrm{SF}}\right)}}{\dfrac{P_t^{\$}}{P_t^{\mathrm{SF}}}} = \frac{S_t\left[\dfrac{\left(1+\pi^{\$}\right)}{\left(1+\pi^{\mathrm{SF}}\right)}\right]}{S_t} = \frac{\left(1+\pi^{\$}\right)}{\left(1+\pi^{\mathrm{SF}}\right)}$$

Isolating the percentage change in the spot exchange rate between periods t and $t + 1$:

$$\frac{S_{t+1} - S_t}{S_t} = \frac{S_t\left[\frac{(1+\pi^{\$})}{(1+\pi^{SF})}\right] - S_t}{S_t} = \frac{(1+\pi^{\$}) - (1+\pi^{SF})}{(1+\pi^{SF})}$$

This equation is often approximated by dropping the denominator of the right-hand-side if it is considered to be relatively small. It is then stated as:

$$\frac{S_{t+1} - S_t}{S_t} = (1+\pi^{\$}) - (1+\pi^{SF}) = \pi^{\$} - \pi^{SF}$$

Forward Rates

The *forward exchange rate* is that contractual rate which is available to private agents through banking institutions and other financial intermediaries who deal in foreign currencies and debt instruments. The annualized percentage difference between the forward rate and the spot rate is termed the *forward premium*:

$$f^{SF} = \left[\frac{F_{t,t+1} - S_t}{S_t}\right] \times \left[\frac{360}{n_{t,t+1}}\right]$$

where f^{SF} is the forward premium on the Swiss franc, $F_{t,t+1}$ is the forward rate contracted at time t for delivery at time $t + 1$, S_t is the current spot rate, and $n_{t,t+1}$ is the number of days between the contract date (t) and the delivery date ($t + 1$).

Covered Interest Arbitrage (CIA) and Interest Rate Parity (IRP)

The process of *covered interest arbitrage* is when an investor exchanges domestic currency for foreign currency in the spot market, invests that currency in an interest-bearing instrument, and signs a forward contract to "lock-in" a future exchange rate at which to convert the foreign currency proceeds (gross) back to domestic currency. The net return on CIA is:

$$\text{Net Return} = \left[\frac{(1+i^{SF})F_{t,t+1}}{S_t}\right] - (1+i^{\$})$$

where S_t and $F_{t,t+1}$ are the spot and forward rates (\$/SF), i^{SF} is the nominal interest rate (or yield) on a Swiss franc-denominated monetary instrument, and $i^{\$}$ is the nominal return on a similar dollar-denominated instrument.

If they possess exactly equal rates of return, i.e., if CIA results in zero riskless profit, ***interest rate parity*** (IRP) holds, and appears as:

$$\left(1+i^{\$}\right)=\left[\frac{\left(1+i^{\mathrm{SF}}\right)F_{t,t+1}}{S_t}\right]$$

or alternatively:

$$\frac{\left(1+i^{\$}\right)}{\left(1+i^{\mathrm{SF}}\right)}=\frac{F_{t,t+1}}{S_t}$$

If the percent difference of both sides of this equation is found (the percentage difference between the spot and forward rate is the forward premium), then the relationship between the forward premium and relative interest rate differentials is:

$$\frac{F_{t,t+1}-S_t}{S_t}=f^{\mathrm{SF}}=\frac{i^{\$}-i^{\mathrm{SF}}}{i^{\$}+i^{\mathrm{SF}}}$$

If these values are not equal (thus the markets are not in equilibrium), there exists a potential for riskless profit. The market will then be driven back to equilibrium through CIA by agents attempting to exploit such arbitrage potential, until CIA yields no positive return.

Fisher Effect

The *Fisher effect* states that all nominal interest rates can be decomposed into an implied real rate of interest (return) and an expected rate of inflation:

$$i^{\$}=\left[\left(1+r^{\$}\right)\left(1+\pi^{\$}\right)\right]-1$$

where $r^{\$}$ is the real rate of return, and $\pi^{\$}$ is the expected rate of inflation, for dollar-denominated assets. The sub-components are then identifiable:

$$i^{\$}=r^{\$}+\pi^{\$}+r^{\$}\pi^{\$}$$

As with PPP, there is an approximation of this function that has gained wide acceptance. The cross-product term of $r^{\$}\pi^{\$}$ is often very small, and therefore dropped altogether:

$$i^{\$}=r^{\$}+\pi^{\$}$$

International Fisher Effect

The *international Fisher effect* is the extension of this domestic interest rate relationship to the international currency markets. If capital, by way of covered interest arbitrage (CIA), attempts to find higher rates of return internationally resulting from current interest rate differentials, the real rates of return between currencies are equalized (e.g., $r^{\$}=r^{\mathrm{SF}}$):

$$\frac{S_{t+1}-S_t}{S_t}=\frac{\left(1+i^{\$}\right)-\left(1+i^{\mathrm{SF}}\right)}{\left(1+i^{\mathrm{SF}}\right)}=\frac{i^{\$}-i^{\mathrm{SF}}}{\left(1+i^{\mathrm{SF}}\right)}$$

If the nominal interest rates are then decomposed into their respective real and expected inflation components, the percentage change in the spot exchange rate is:

$$\frac{S_{t+1}-S_t}{S_t}=\frac{\left(r^{\$}+\pi^{\$}+r^{\$}\pi^{\$}\right)-\left(r^{\mathrm{SF}}+\pi^{\mathrm{SF}}+r^{\mathrm{SF}}\pi^{\mathrm{SF}}\right)}{1+r^{\mathrm{SF}}+\pi^{\mathrm{SF}}+r^{\mathrm{SF}}\pi^{\mathrm{SF}}}$$

The international Fisher effect has a number of additional implications, if the following requirements are met: 1) capital markets can be freely entered and exited; 2) capital markets possess investment opportunities that are acceptable substitutes; and 3) market agents have complete and equal information regarding these possibilities.

Given these conditions, international arbitragers are capable of exploiting all potential riskless profit opportunities, until real rates of return between markets are equalized ($r^{\$}=r^{\mathrm{SF}}$). Thus the expected rate of change in the spot exchange rate reduces to the differential in the expected rates of inflation:

$$\frac{S_{t+1}-S_t}{S_t}=\frac{\pi^{\$}+r^{\$}\pi^{\$}-\pi^{\mathrm{SF}}-r^{\mathrm{SF}}\pi^{\mathrm{SF}}}{1+r^{\mathrm{SF}}+\pi^{\mathrm{SF}}+r^{\mathrm{SF}}\pi^{\mathrm{SF}}}$$

If the approximation forms are combined (through the elimination of the denominator and the elimination of the interactive terms of r and π), the change in the spot rate is simply:

$$\frac{S_{t+1}-S_t}{S_t}=\pi^{\$}-\pi^{\mathrm{SF}}$$

Note the similarity (identical in equation form) of the approximate form of the international Fisher effect to Purchasing Power Parity discussed previously (the only potential difference is that between *ex post* and *ex ante* (expected) inflation.

Chapter 7

Foreign Exchange Rate Determination

EXCHANGE RATE DETERMINATION IS COMPLEX. CHAPTER 6 DESCRIBED THE INTERNATIONAL PARITY conditions that integrate exchange rates with inflation and interest rates and provided a theoretical framework for both the global financial markets and the management of international financial business. This chapter extends the discussion of exchange rate determination to the other two major schools of thought on the determination of exchange rates: the *balance of payments approach* and the *asset market approach.*

Exhibit 7.1 provides an overview of the many determinants of exchange rates. This "road map" is organized first by the three major schools of thought (parity conditions,

Exhibit 7.1 The Determinants of Foreign Exchange Rates

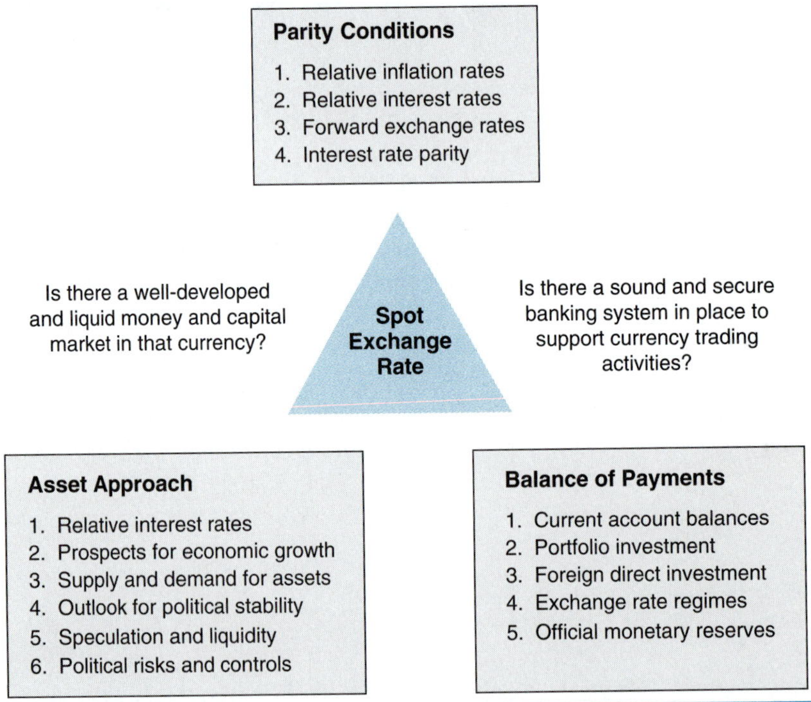

balance of payments approach, asset market approach), and second by the individual drivers within those approaches. At first glance, the idea that there are three sets of theories may appear daunting, but it is important to remember that these are not *competing* theories, but rather *complementary* theories. Without the depth and breadth of the various approaches combined, our ability to capture the complexity of the global market for currencies is lost.

In addition to gaining an understanding of the basic theories, it is equally important to gain a working knowledge of how the complexities of international political economy; societal and economic infrastructures; and random political, economic, or social events affect the exchange rate markets. A few examples:

- *Infrastructure weaknesses* were among the major causes of the exchange rate collapses in emerging markets in the late 1990s. On the other hand, infrastructure strengths help explain why the U.S. dollar continued to be strong, at least until the September 11, 2001, terrorist attack on the United States, despite record balance of payments deficits on current account.
- *Speculation* contributed greatly to the emerging market crises. Some characteristics of speculation are hot money flowing into and out of currencies, securities, real estate, and commodities. Uncovered interest arbitrage caused by exceptionally low borrowing interest rates in Japan coupled with high real interest rates in the United States was a problem in much of the 1990s. Borrowing yen to invest in safe U.S. government securities, hoping that the exchange rate did not change, was popular.
- *Cross-border foreign direct investment* and *international portfolio investment* into the emerging markets dried up during the recent crises.
- *Foreign political risks* have been much reduced in recent years as capital markets became less segmented from each other and more liquid. More countries adopted democratic forms of government. However, recent occurrences of terrorism within the U.S. may be changing perceptions of political risk.

Finally, note that most determinants of the spot exchange rate are also in turn affected by changes in the spot rate. In other words, they are not only linked but mutually determined.

Cash flows, which may be motivated by any and all of these potential exchange rate determinants, eventually show up in the balance of payments (BOP). As described in Chapter 3, the BOP provides a means to account for these cash flows in a standardized and systematic manner. It increases the transparency of the international monetary environment and enables decision-makers to make more rational policy choices, in both the private and public sectors. Therefore, the next section of this chapter describes the basics of the BOP approach to forecasting. An analysis of the asset market approach appears next. Then the chapter details some of the most frequently observed disequilibrium exchange rate situations, as well as discussing the causes of several of the most recent exchange rate crises in emerging markets. The chapter concludes with a description of forecasting exchange rates in practice.

The Balance of Payments (BOP) Approach

A country's BOP can have a significant impact on the level of its exchange rate depending on that country's exchange rate regime. Exhibit 7.2 is a copy of Exhibit 3.1 in Chapter 3; it may serve as a gentle reminder of the fundamental components of the common "balances" tracked by managers and analysts.

Exhibit 7.2 Generic Balance of Payments

A.	***Current Account***	
	1. Net export/imports of goods (*balance of trade*)	
	2. Net exports/imports of services	
	3. Net income (investment income from direct and portfolio investment plus employee compensation)	
	4. Net transfers (sums sent home by migrants and permanent workers abroad, gifts, grants, and pensions)	***A (1–4) = Current Account Balance***
B.	***Capital Account***	
	Capital transfers related to the purchase and sale of fixed assets such as real estate	
C.	***Financial Account***	
	1. Net foreign direct investment	
	2. Net portfolio investment	
	3. Other financial items	***A + B + C = Basic Balance***
D.	***Net Errors and Omissions Account***	
	Missing data such as illegal transfers	***A + B + C + D = Overall Balance***
E.	***Reserves and Related Items***	
	Changes in official monetary reserves including gold, foreign exchange, and IMF position.	

The relationship between the BOP and exchange rates can be illustrated by use of a simplified equation that summarizes BOP data:

Current Account Balance		Capital Account Balance		Financial Account Balance		Reserve Balance		Balance of Payments
$(X - M)$	+	$(CI - CO)$	+	$(FI - FO)$	+	FXB	=	BOP

where:

- X is exports of goods and services,
- M is imports of goods and services,
- CI is capital inflows,
- CO is capital outflows,
- FI is financial inflows,
- FO is financial outflows, and
- FXB is official monetary reserves such as foreign exchange and gold.

The effect of an imbalance in the BOP of a country is somewhat different depending on whether that country has fixed exchange rates, floating exchange rates, or a managed exchange rate system.

Fixed Exchange Rate Countries

Under a fixed exchange rate system, the government bears the responsibility to ensure a BOP near zero. If the sum of the current and capital accounts does not approximate zero, the government is expected to intervene in the foreign exchange market by buying or selling official foreign exchange reserves. If the sum of the first two accounts is greater than zero, a surplus demand for the domestic currency exists in the world. To preserve the fixed exchange rate, the government must then intervene in the foreign exchange market and sell domestic currency for foreign currencies or gold so as to bring the BOP back near zero.

If the sum of the current and capital accounts is negative, an excess supply of the domestic currency exists in world markets. Then the government must intervene by buying the domestic currency with its reserves of foreign currencies and gold. It is obviously important for a government to maintain significant foreign exchange reserve balances to allow it to intervene effectively. If the country runs out of foreign exchange reserves, it will be unable to buy back its domestic currency and will be forced to devalue.

For fixed exchange rate countries, then, business managers use balance of payments statistics to help forecast devaluation or revaluation of the official exchange rate. (Recall from Chapter 2 that a change in fixed exchange rates is technically called "devaluation" or "revaluation," while a change in floating exchange rates is either "depreciation" or "appreciation.")

Thailand serves as a classic example of a country with a fixed exchange rate that experienced an imbalance in its balance of payments. As illustrated in Exhibit 7.3, the Thai current account balance worsened throughout the 1990s. Finally, as a result of a complex mix of both economic, social, and political forces (discussed in further detail later in this chapter), the capital/financial

Exhibit 7.3 Thailand's Deteriorating Balance of Payments, 1991–1998

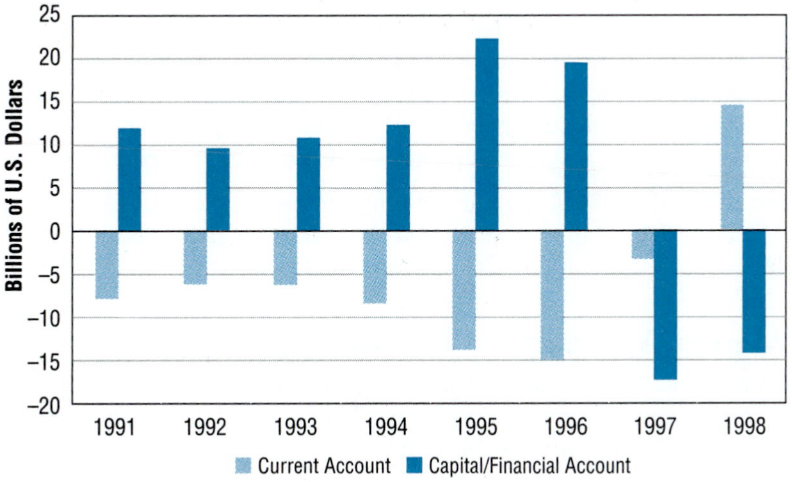

Source: International Monetary Fund, *International Financial Statistics*, Washington D.C., monthly.

account plummeted and the Thai baht was devalued in 1997. The impact of the balance of payments on the currency was significant and sudden.

Floating Exchange Rate Countries

Under a floating exchange rate system, the government of a country has no responsibility to peg its foreign exchange rate. The fact that the current and capital account balances do not sum to zero will automatically (in theory) alter the exchange rate in the direction necessary to obtain a BOP near zero. For example, a country running a sizable current account deficit with a capital and financial accounts balance of zero will have a net BOP deficit. An excess supply of the domestic currency will appear on world markets. As in all cases where goods are in excess supply, the market will rid itself of the imbalance by lowering the price. Thus the domestic currency will fall in value, and the BOP will move back toward zero. Exchange rate markets do not always follow this theory, particularly in the short to intermediate term.

Managed Floats

Although they still rely on market conditions for day-to-day exchange rate determination, countries operating with managed floats often find it necessary to take action to maintain their desired exchange rate values. They therefore seek to alter the market's valuation of a specific exchange rate by influencing the motivators of market activity, rather than through direct intervention in the foreign exchange markets.

The primary action taken by such governments is to change relative interest rates, thus influencing the economic fundamentals of exchange rate determination. In the context of the BOP equation, a change in domestic interest rates is an attempt to alter the term CI–CO, especially the short-term portfolio component of these capital flows, in order to restore an imbalance caused by the deficit in the current account. The power of interest rate changes on international capital and exchange rate movements can be substantial. A country with a managed float that wishes to "defend its currency" may choose to raise domestic interest rates to attract additional capital from abroad. This will alter market forces and create additional market demand for the domestic currency. In this process, the government "signals" exchange market participants that it intends to take measures to preserve the currency's value within certain ranges. The process also raises the cost of local borrowing for businesses, however, so the policy is seldom without domestic critics. For managed float countries, MNE business managers use BOP trends to help forecast changes in government policies on domestic interest rates.

So far we have analyzed the BOP approach to long-term foreign exchange rate determination. As mentioned earlier, there is an alternative approach to exchange rate forecasting called the asset market approach.

The Asset Market Approach to Forecasting

The *asset market approach* assumes that whether foreigners are willing to hold claims in monetary form depends on an extensive set of investment considerations or drivers. These drivers, as previously depicted in Exhibit 7.1, include the following:

1. Relative real interest rates are a major consideration for investors in foreign bonds and short-term money market instruments.

2. Prospects for economic growth and profitability are an important determinant of cross-border equity investment in both securities and foreign direct investment.

3. Capital market liquidity is particularly important to foreign institutional investors. Cross-border investors are interested not only in the ease of buying assets, but also in the ease of selling those assets quickly for fair market value if desired.

4. A country's economic and social infrastructure is an important indicator of that country's ability to survive unexpected external shocks and to prosper in a rapidly changing world economic environment.

5. Political safety is exceptionally important to both foreign portfolio and direct investors. The outlook for political safety is usually reflected in political risk premiums for a country's securities and for purposes of evaluating foreign direct investment in that country.

6. The credibility of corporate governance practices is important to cross-border portfolio investors. A firm's poor corporate governance practices can reduce foreign investors' influence and cause subsequent loss of the firm's focus on shareholder wealth objectives.

7. *Contagion* is defined as the spread of a crisis in one country to its neighboring countries and other countries that have similar characteristics—at least in the eyes of cross-border investors. Contagion can cause an "innocent" country to experience capital flight with a resulting depreciation of its currency.

8. Speculation can both cause a foreign exchange crisis or make an existing crisis worse. We will observe this effect through the three illustrative cases that follow shortly.

Global Finance Perspective 7.1 shows a recent example of how contagion can wreck a seemingly solid economy and currency.

The Asset Market Approach in Highly Developed Countries

Foreign investors are willing to hold securities and undertake foreign direct investment in highly developed countries based primarily on relative real interest rates and the outlook for economic growth and profitability. All the other drivers described in Exhibit 7.1 and detailed previously are assumed to be satisfied.

For example, during the 1981–1985 period, the U.S. dollar strengthened despite growing current account deficits. This strength was due partly to relatively high real interest rates in the United States. Another factor, however, was the heavy inflow of foreign capital into the U.S. stock market and real estate, motivated by good long run prospects for growth and profitability in the United States.

The same cycle was repeated in the United States in the period between 1990 and 2000. Despite continued worsening balances on current account, the U.S. dollar strengthened in both nominal and real terms due to foreign capital inflow motivated by rising stock and real estate prices, a low rate of inflation, high real interest returns, and a seemingly endless "irrational exuberance" about future economic prospects.

This time the "bubble" burst following the September 11, 2001, terrorist attack on the United States. The attack and its aftermath caused a negative reassessment of long-term growth and profitability prospects in the United States (as well as a newly formed level of political risk for

Global Finance Perspective 7.1

Uruguay Infected

Uruguay has been called the Switzerland of Latin America: a stronghold of financial stability in an often chaotic region. Today, however, it is a case study in contagion—the victim of its reckless neighbor across the Rio de la Plata, Argentina.

The warm waters of Uruguay's beaches and its generous tax and banking secrecy laws have long been a magnet for rich Argentines in times of crisis. Foreign investors were attracted to the country's investment-grade status—the only Latin country besides Mexico to enjoy that rank. So Uruguayan assets became an anchor for many Latin American portfolios.

But the impressive track record came to an end in January [2002], when Argentina devalued and defaulted. That country's strict capital controls forced Argentines to dip into their Uruguayan savings, reducing those deposits by 80% since then. In June, Uruguay floated its peso, which promptly fell by 45%. Panicky investors pushed the country's banks to the brink of collapse, and bouts of looting occurred. After the bank run, the central bank on June 29 ordered a four-day bank holiday, its first in 70 years. And the congress swiftly passed legislation to exchange $2.2 billion in fixed-term dollar deposits for government bonds.

Responding to the government's proactive stance, the U.S. made Uruguay a direct loan of $1.5 billion as a bridge until the International Monetary Fund approves its own aid package. Although IMF aid should stem the deposit outflow, nobody can guarantee for how long, and the country's benchmark bonds still trade at default levels.

Although international banks have small exposure in Uruguay—$7.7 billion in March 2002, versus $50 billion in Argentina—the country's rapid demise portends a grim future for the region. The two bright spots left in Latin America, Chile and Mexico, are still little affected by the crisis in the Southern Cone. But the near-collapse of one stalwart economy shows that no nation is safe from the turmoil.

Source: "A Bright Latin Beacon is Snuffed Out," *Business Week*, August 26, 2002, p. 30. Direct quote.

the United States itself). This negative outlook was reinforced by a very sharp drop in the U.S. stock markets based on lower expected earnings. Further damage to the economy was caused by a series of revelations about failures in corporate governance of several large corporations. These failures included accounting overstatement of earnings, insider trading, and self-serving loans by firms to their own executives.

Loss of confidence in the U.S. economy led to a large withdrawal of foreign capital from U.S. security markets. As would be predicted by both the balance of payments and asset market approaches, the U.S. dollar depreciated. Indeed, its nominal rate depreciated by 18% between mid-January and mid-July 2002 relative to the euro alone.

The experience of the United States, as well as other highly developed countries, illustrates why some forecasters believe that exchange rates are more heavily influenced by economic prospects than by the current account. One scholar summarizes this belief using an interesting anecdote:

> *Many economists reject the view that the short-term behavior of exchange rates is determined in flow markets. Exchange rates are asset prices traded in an efficient financial market. Indeed, an exchange rate is the relative price of two currencies and therefore is determined by the willingness to hold each currency. Like other asset prices, the exchange rate is determined by expectations about the future, not current trade flows.*

> *A parallel with other asset prices may illustrate the approach. Let's consider the stock price of a winery traded on the Bordeaux stock exchange. A frost in late spring results in a poor harvest, in terms of both quantity and quality. After the harvest the wine is finally sold, and the income is much less than the previous year. On the day of the final sale there is no reason for the stock price to be influenced by this flow. First, the poor income has already been discounted for several months in the winery stock price. Second, the stock price is affected by future, in addition to current, prospects. The stock price is based on expectations of future earnings, and the major cause for a change in stock price is a revision of these expectations.*
>
> *A similar reasoning applies to exchange rates: Contemporaneous international flows should have little effect on exchange rates to the extent they have already been expected. Only news about future economic prospects will affect exchange rates. Since economic expectations are potentially volatile and influenced by many variables, especially variables of a political nature, the short-run behavior of exchange rates is volatile.*[1]

The asset market approach to forecasting is also applicable to emerging markets. In this case, however, a number of additional variables contribute to exchange rate determination. These variables, as described previously, are illiquid capital markets, weak economic and social infrastructure, political instability, corporate governance, contagion effects, and speculation. These variables will be illustrated in the sections on crises that follow.

Disequilibrium: Exchange Rates in Emerging Markets

Although the three different schools of thought on exchange rate determination (parity conditions, balance of payments approach, asset approach) make understanding exchange rates appear to be straightforward, that is rarely the case. The large and liquid capital and currency markets follow many of the principles outlined so far relatively well in the medium to long term. The smaller and less liquid markets, however, frequently demonstrate behaviors that seemingly contradict theory. The problem lies not in the theory, but in the relevance of the assumptions underlying the theory. An analysis of the emerging market crises illustrates a number of these seeming contradictions.

After a number of years of relative global economic tranquility, the second half of the 1990s was racked by a series of currency crises that shook all emerging markets. The devaluation of the Mexican peso in December 1994 was a harbinger. The Asian crisis of July 1997, the Russian rouble's collapse in August 1998, and the fall of the Argentine peso in 2002 provide a spectrum of emerging market economic failures, each with its own complex causes and unknown outlooks. These crises also illustrated the growing problem of capital flight and short-run international speculation in currency and securities markets. We will use each of the individual crises to focus on a specific dimension of the causes and consequences:

- **The Asian Crisis.** Although this was not the collapse of any one currency, economy, or system, the complex structures combining government, society, and business throughout the Far East provide a backdrop for understanding the tenuous link between business, government, and society.
- **The Russian Crisis.** The loss of the relatively stable rouble, once considered the cornerstone and symbol of success of President Boris Yeltsin's regime, was a death blow to the Yeltsin-led

1. Bruno Solnik, *International Investments* (Addison Wesley, 1996) p. 58. Reprinted with permission.

Russian government and led to the rise of Vladimir Putin. Russian borrowers have found themselves *persona non grata* in the post-1998 period in the global capital markets.

The Argentine Crisis. In 1991, Argentina adopted a currency board structure. The Argentine peso was tied to the U.S. dollar on a one-to-one basis. The resulting austerity program caused by the need to defend its fixed exchange rate caused Argentina to plunge into recession. Starting in 1998 and continuing for the next four years, the austerity program and recession caused increasing political turmoil, capital flight, and eventually the demise of the currency board itself.

Illustrative Case: The Asian Crisis

The roots of the Asian currency crisis extended from a fundamental change in the economics of the region, the transition of many Asian nations from being net exporters to net importers. Starting as early as 1990 in Thailand, the rapidly expanding economies of the Far East began importing more than they exported, requiring major net capital inflows to support their currencies. As long as the capital continued to flow in—capital for manufacturing plants, dam projects, infrastructure development, and even real estate speculation—the pegged exchange rates of the region could be maintained. When the investment capital inflows stopped, however, crisis was inevitable.

The most visible roots of the crisis were in the excesses of capital inflows into Thailand in 1996 and early 1997. With rapid economic growth and rising profits forming the backdrop, Thai firms, banks, and finance companies had ready access to capital on the international markets, finding U.S. dollar debt cheap offshore. Thai banks continued to raise capital internationally, extending credit to a variety of domestic investments and enterprises beyond what the Thai economy could support. As capital flows into the Thai market hit record rates, financial flows poured into investments of all kinds, including manufacturing, real estate, and even equity market margin-lending. As the investment "bubble" expanded, some participants raised questions about the economy's ability to repay the rising debt. The baht came under attack.

Currency Collapse

The Thai government and central bank intervened in the foreign exchange markets directly (using up precious hard currency reserves) and indirectly (by raising interest rates to attempt to stop the continual outflow). The Thai investment markets ground to a halt. This caused massive currency losses and bank failures. On July 2, 1997, the Thai central bank finally allowed the baht to float (or sink in this case). The baht fell 17% against the U.S. dollar and more than 12% against the Japanese yen in a matter of hours. By November, the baht had fallen from Baht25/US$ to Baht40/US$, a fall of about 38%. In the aftermath, the international speculator and philanthropist George Soros was the object of much criticism, primarily by the Prime Minister of Malaysia, Dr. Mahathir Mohamad, for being the cause of the crisis because of massive speculation by his and other hedge funds. Soros, however, was likely only the messenger.

Within days, in Asia's own version of what is called the *tequila effect*, a number of neighboring Asian nations, some with and some without similar characteristics to Thailand, came under speculative attack by currency traders and capital markets. ("Tequila effect" is the term used to describe how the Mexican peso crisis of December 1994 quickly spread to other Latin American currency and equity markets, a form of financial panic termed *contagion*.) The Philippine peso, the Malaysian ringgit, and the Indonesian rupiah all fell in the months following the July baht devaluation (see Exhibits 7.4 and 7.5).

Exhibit 7.4 The Economies and Currencies of Asia, July–November 1997

Weaker Economies	1996 Current Acct (bil U.S.$)	Liabilities to Foreign Banks (bil U.S.$)	Exchange Rate July (per U.S.$)	Exchange Rate November (per U.S.$)	% Change
Indonesia (rupiah)	9.0	29.7	2400	3600	- 33.3 %
Korea (won)	–23.1	36.5	900	1100	- 18.2 %
Malaysia (ringgit)	–8.0	27.0	2.5	3.5	- 28.6 %
Philippines (peso)	–3.0	2.8	27	34	- 20.6 %
Thailand (baht)	–14.7	48.0	25	40	- 37.5 %
Stronger Economies					
China (renminbi)	47.2	56.0	8.4	8.4	+ 0.0 %
Hong Kong (dollar)	0.0	28.8	7.75	7.73	+ 0.0 %
Singapore (dollar)	14.3	55.3	1.43	1.60	- 10.6 %
Taiwan (dollar)	11.0	17.6	27.8	32.7	- 15.0 %

Source: International Monetary Fund, *International Financial Statistics*, Washington D.C., October–November 1997.

Exhibit 7.5 Comparative Daily Exchange Rates Relative to U.S. Dollar

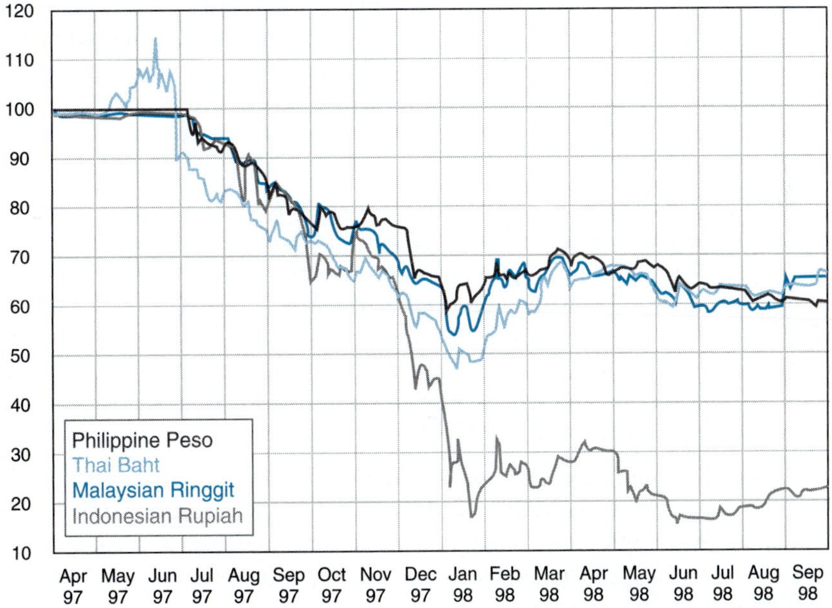

Source: Pacific Currency Exchange, http://pacific.commerce.ubc.ca/xr ©1999 by Prof. Werner Antweiler, University of British Columbia, Vancouver, BC, Canada. Time period shown in diagram: April 1, 1997–September 30, 1998.

In late October 1997, Taiwan caught the markets off-balance with a surprise competitive devaluation of 15%. The Taiwanese devaluation seemed only to renew the momentum of the crisis. Although the Hong Kong dollar survived (at great expense to the central bank's foreign exchange reserves), the Korean won was not so lucky. In November 1997 the historically stable Korean won also fell victim, falling from Won900/US$ to more than Won1100/US$. The only currency that had not fallen besides the Hong Kong dollar was the Chinese renminbi (Rmb), which was not freely convertible. Although the renminbi was not devalued, there was rising speculation that the Chinese government would devalue soon for competitive reasons. It did not devalue, as it turned out.

Causal Complexities

The Asian economic crisis—for it was more than just a currency collapse—had many roots besides traditional balance of payments difficulties. The causes were different in each country; yet there are specific underlying similarities that allow comparison: corporate socialism; corporate governance; and banking stability and management.

Corporate socialism. Although Western markets have long known the volatility of the free market, the countries of the post–World War II Asia have largely known only stability. Because of the influence of government and politics in the business arena, even in the event of failure, it was believed that government would not allow firms to fail, workers to lose their jobs, or banks to close. That was true until the problems reached the size seen in 1997 and business liabilities exceeded the capacities of governments to bail business out. Practices that had persisted for decades without challenge, such as lifetime employment, were now no longer sustainable. The result was a painful lesson in the harshness of the marketplace.

Corporate governance. Little doubt exists that many local firms operating within the Far Eastern business environments were often largely controlled either by families or by groups related to the governing party or body of the country. This tendency has been labeled *cronyism.* Cronyism means that the interests of minority stockholders and creditors are often secondary at best to the primary motivations of corporate management. When management did not focus on "the bottom line," the bottom line deteriorated.

Banking liquidity and management. The banking sector has fallen out of fashion in the past two decades. Bank regulatory structures and markets have been deregulated nearly without exception across the globe. The central role played by banks in the conduct of business, however, has largely been ignored and underestimated. As firms across Asia collapsed, government coffers were emptied and speculative investments made by the banks themselves failed. Without banks, the "plumbing" of business conduct was shut down. Firms could not obtain the necessary working capital financing to manufacture and sell their products or provide their services. This pivotal role of banking liquidity was the focus of the IMF's bail-out efforts.

The Asian economic crisis had global impacts. What started as a currency crisis quickly became a region-wide recession. (The magnitude of economic devastation in Asia is still largely unappreciated by Westerners. At a 1998 conference sponsored by the Milken Institute, a speaker noted that the world's preoccupation with the economic problems of Indonesia was incomprehensible because "the total gross domestic product of Indonesia is roughly the size of North Carolina." The following speaker observed, however, that the last time he had checked, "North Carolina did not have a population of 220 million people.") The slowed economies of the region quickly caused major reductions in world demands for many products, especially commodities. World oil, metal, and agricultural products markets all saw severe price falls as demand fell. These price drops were immediately noticeable in declining earnings and growth prospects for other emerging economies. The problems of Russia in 1998 were reflections of those declines.

Illustrative Case: The Russian Crisis of 1998

The crisis of August 1998 was the culmination of a continuing deterioration in general economic conditions in Russia. During the period from 1995 to 1998, Russian borrowers—both governmental and non-governmental—had gone to the international capital markets for large quantities of capital. Servicing this debt soon became an increasing problem, as dollar debt requires earning dollars to service that debt. The Russian current account—a surprisingly healthy surplus ranging between $15 billion and $20 billion per year—was not, however, finding its way into internal investment and external debt service. Capital flight accelerated, as hard-currency earnings flowed out as fast as they found their way in. Finally, in the spring of 1998, even Russian export earnings began to decline. Russian exports were predominantly commodity-based, and global commodity prices had been on the decline since the onset of the Asian economic crisis in the summer and fall of 1997.

The Russian currency, the rouble, operated under a managed float. This meant that the Central Bank of Russia allowed the rouble to trade within a band. The band, for example, was Rub5.750/$ to Rub6.350/$ in the weeks prior to August 17, 1998. The exchange rate band had been adjusted continually throughout 1996, 1997, and the first half of 1998. Theoretically, the Central Bank allowed the exchange rate and associated band to slide daily at a 1.5% per month rate. Automatically, the Central Bank announced an official exchange rate each day at which it was willing to buy and sell roubles, always within the official band. In the event that the rouble's exchange rate came under pressure at the limits of the band, the Central Bank intervened in the market by buying and selling roubles—usually buying—using the country's foreign exchange and gold reserves. The stability of the rouble in the 1990s was considered the single most observable success of President Boris Yeltsin. But in spite of a $4.3 billion loan from the IMF in July of 1998, the rouble came under intense pressure in August of that year.

The August Collapse

On Friday, August 7, 1998, the Russian Central Bank announced that its hard currency reserves had fallen by $800 million in the last week of July to a level of $18.4 billion on July 31. Prime Minister Sergei Kiriyenko said that Russia would issue an additional $3 billion in foreign bonds to help pay its rising debt, a full $1 billion more than had been previously scheduled. The rouble, however, continued to trade within a very narrow range of Rub6.24/$ to Rub6.26/$.

On Monday, August 10, Russian stocks fell more than 5% as investors feared a Chinese currency (renminbi) devaluation. The Chinese currency was the only Asian currency of size not devalued in 1997 and 1998. Devaluation would aid Chinese exports in cutting into Russian export sales. Analysts worldwide speculated that international markets were waiting to see if the Russian government would increase its tax revenues as it had promised the IMF throughout the year. Russian oil companies were publicly warned by the Russian government to pay past due taxes. (Russian tax revenue collections averaged slightly over $1 billion per month in 1998, less than those of New York City.) By Wednesday of that week, Russian financing choices narrowed further as the government canceled the government debt auction for the third week in a row. On international markets, Russia's outstanding eurobonds due in 2001 sank in price for a sixth straight day, the yield (implicit cost of borrowing) rising 350 basis points to 23.6%. The rouble fell to Rub6.30/$.

Thursday, August 13, saw a series of press releases by senior governmental officials committing the government to stabilizing the markets and assuring the general population that all was in hand:

> *If we thought that devaluation was unavoidable, we would not be taking the measures we are taking now.*
>
> Mikhail Zadornov, Finance Minister

Mr. Zadornov went on to explain that Russia expected an additional $4.3 billion from the IMF in September. Analysts believed that Russia had $23.4 billion due in payments on domestic debt, and $4.5 billion due on foreign debt, throughout the remainder of the year. Despite the statements from Finance Minister Zadornov, the stock and bond markets in Moscow and St. Petersburg plummeted. Rumors regarding the likely collapse of the banking system spread.

On Friday, August 14, the press releases and statements of commitment from senior governmental officials continued. The government stated that the "panic" was psychological, not fiscal, and repeated, as it had in recent days, that it had money to meet its obligations through the fall of the year. "A stable rouble is the anchor of an inflation-free economy," according to Alexander Livshits, deputy head of President Boris Yeltsin's administration. He added that the loss of a stable rouble "will start rocking our ship again. The result is well known—nausea."

The Russian Central Bank continued to trade roubles throughout Friday at Rub6.30/$, but at many unofficial exchanges throughout Moscow the rate was Rub7.00/$ or more. President Yeltsin, in a speech in the ancient city of Novgorode, stated: "There will be no devaluation—that's firm and definite." He went on to add, "That would signify that there was a disaster and that everything was collapsing. On the contrary, everything is going as it should."

"As it should" turned out to mean devaluation. On Monday, August 17, the floodgates were released. Late in the day, the Russian Central Bank announced that the rouble would be allowed to fall by 34% this year, from Rub6.30/$ to about Rub9.50/$. It also postponed the payment of $43 billion in short-term domestic debt to help it through the cash crisis. As a final blow to international markets, the government announced a 90-day moratorium on all repayment of foreign debt, debt owed by Russian banks and all private borrowers, in order to avert a banking collapse.

On Tuesday, August 18, the rouble continued to fall, quickly passing the Rub9.50/$ limit for the rest of the year. Reports from Moscow to Vladivostok quoted trading at between Rub10.00 and Rub12.00 per dollar. International circles debated whether Russia's postponement of debt service was in fact a default.

The currency's fall continued into the following week (see Exhibit 7.6). On Thursday, August 27, Acting Prime Minister Viktor Chernomyrdin traveled to the Ukraine to meet with the visiting head of the IMF, Michael Camdessus. A sense of urgency was felt after the rouble fell from Rub10.0/$ to Rub13.0/$ the previous day alone. In related matters, the Central Bank of Russia, in an attempt to defray criticism of its management of the rouble's devaluation, disclosed that it had expended $8.8 billion in the preceding eight weeks defending the rouble's value. On Friday,

Exhibit 7.6 Daily Exchange Rates: Russian Roubles per U.S. Dollar

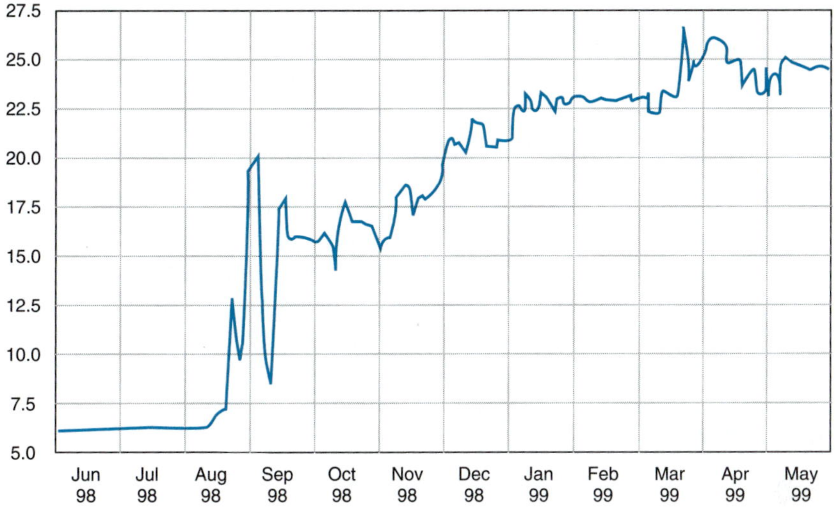

Source: Pacific Currency Exchange, http://pacific.commerce.ubc.ca/xr ©1999 by Prof. Werner Antweiler, University of British Columbia, Vancouver, BC, Canada.

August 28, the Moscow currency exchange closed after 10 minutes of trading as the rouble continued to fall.

The Aftermath

It is hard to say when a crisis begins or ends, but for the Russian people and the Russian economy, the deterioration of the economic conditions continued. As illustrated in Exhibit 7.6, the rouble continued to fall throughout the fall of 1998. In early December, rumors that the Russian state was printing money to make long-overdue payments to state workers and pensioners added insult to injury. The tumbling rouble finally stabilized in January and February of 1999, at a rate of approximately Rub25.0/$.

Spring and early summer of 1999 saw a Russian government battling both within and without to find ways to service its outstanding sovereign and private debts without impoverishing the country further. Domestic bonds issued by the Russian government, rouble bonds, were now in default, with repayment uncertain. The primary task for survival was the servicing of the dollar debt, with Russia's outstanding eurobonds at the top of the list. No sovereign borrower has ever rescheduled or defaulted on outstanding eurobonds.

What is likely of more substantial concern is the toll the crisis has taken on Russian society. For many, the collapse of the rouble and the loss of Russia's access to the international capital markets has brought into question the benefits of a free-market economy, long championed by the advocates of Western-style democracy.

Illustrative Case: The Argentine Crisis of 2002

Now, most Argentines are blaming corrupt politicians and foreign devils for their ills. But few are looking inward, at mainstream societal concepts such as viveza criolla, *an Argentine cultural quirk that applauds anyone sly enough to get away with a fast one. It is one reason behind massive tax evasion here: One of every three Argentines does so—and many like to brag about it.*

"Once-Haughty Nation's Swagger Loses Its Currency," Anthony Faiola, The *Washington Post*, March 13, 2002.

Argentina's economic ups and downs have historically been tied to the health of the Argentine peso. South America's southernmost resident—which oftentimes considered itself more European than Latin American—had been wracked by hyperinflation, international indebtedness, and economic collapse in the 1980s. By early 1991, the people of Argentina had had enough. Economic reform in the early 1990s was a common goal of the Argentine people. They were not interested in quick fixes, but lasting change and a stable future. They nearly got it.

The Currency Board

In 1991 the Argentine peso had been fixed to the U.S. dollar at a one-to-one rate of exchange. The policy was a radical departure from traditional methods of fixing the rate of a currency's value. Argentina adopted a *currency board*, a structure—rather than a mere commitment—to limiting the growth of money in the economy. Under a currency board, the central bank of a country may increase the money supply in the banking system only with increases in its holdings of hard currency reserves. These reserves were in this case U.S. dollars. By removing the ability of government to expand the rate of growth of the money supply, Argentina believed it was eliminating the source of inflation which had devastated its standard of living.

The idea was simple and in many ways elegantly simplistic: limit the rate of growth in the country's money supply to the rate at which the country receives net inflows of U.S. dollars as a result of trade growth and general surplus. It was both a recipe for conservative and prudent financial management, and a decision to eliminate the power of politicians, elected and unelected, to exercise judgement both good and bad. It was an automatic and unbendable rule. And from the beginning, it had shown the costs and benefits of its rigor.

Exhibit 7.7 illustrates the three traditional measures of a country's macroeconomic performance: real growth in Gross Domestic Product (GDP), inflation, and unemployment.

Exhibit 7.7 Argentina's Economic Performance, 1991–2000

	1991	1992	1993	1994	1995	1996	1997	1998	1999	2000
Real GDP growth rate (%)	10.5	9.6	5.8	5.8	–2.8	5.5	8.2	3.9	–3.5	–0.4
Unemployment rate (%)	6.3	7.2	9.1	11.7	15.9	16.3	14.2	14.1	15.5	15.0
Inflation rate (%)	172.0	24.6	10.6	4.3	3.3	0.2	0.5	0.9	–1.2	–0.9

Source: International Monetary Fund, Political Risk Services, Argentina Economic Development Agency.

But Exhibit 7.7 also illustrates the austerity dimension to the currency board structure. Although hyperinflation had indeed been the problem, the "cure" was a restrictive monetary policy that slowed economic growth in the coming years. The first and foremost cost of the slower economic growth had been in unemployment. Beginning with a decade low unemployment rate of 6.3% in 1991, unemployment rose to double-digit levels in 1994 and stayed there. The real GDP growth rate, which opened the decade with booming levels over 10%, settled into recession in late 1998. GDP growth "shrank" in 1999 (–3.5%) and 2000 (–0.4%). Preliminary estimates for 2001 indicated a further deterioration in GDP: –3% for the year.

As part of the continuing governmental commitment to the currency board's fixed exchange rate for the peso, Argentine banks allowed depositors to hold their money in either form—pesos or dollars. This was intended to provide a market-based discipline to the banking and political systems, and to demonstrate the government's unwavering commitment to maintaining the peso's value parity with the dollar. Although considered by many an excellent policy to build confidence, in the end it proved disastrous to the Argentine banking system.

Economic Crisis, 2001

The 1998 recession proved to be unending. Three and a half years later, Argentina was still in recession. By 2001, crisis conditions had revealed three very important underlying problems with Argentina's economy: 1) the Argentine peso was overvalued; 2) the currency board regime had eliminated monetary policy alternatives for macroeconomic policy; and 3) the Argentine government budget deficit—and deficit spending—was out of control.

The Argentine peso. The peso had indeed been stabilized. But inflation had not been eliminated, and the other factors that are important in the global market's evaluation of a currency's value—economic growth, corporate profitability, etc.—had not necessarily always been positive. The inability of the peso's value to change with market forces led many to believe increasingly that it was overvalued, and that the overvaluation gap was rising as time passed.

Argentina's large neighbor to the north, Brazil, had also suffered many of the economic ills of hyperinflation and international indebtedness in the 1980s and early 1990s. Brazil's response, the *real plan*, was introduced in July 1994.[2] The real plan worked, for a while, but eventually collapsed in January 1999 as a result of the rising gap between the real's official value and the market's assessment of its true value.

Brazil was by far Argentina's largest trading partner. With the fall of the Brazilian real, however, Brazilian consumers could no longer afford Argentine exports. It simply took too many real to purchase a peso. In fact, Argentine exports became some of the most expensive in all of South America as other countries saw their currencies slide marginally against the dollar over the decade. But not the Argentine peso.

2. Brazil introduced a new currency at that time, the *real* (*reais*). The real's value was not, however, fixed to the U.S. dollar but pegged to the dollar with a predictable and promised rate of daily devaluation. This allowed the real to weaken commensurate with Brazil's still higher rate of inflation and lower rate of growth, but control its value change over time.

The Currency board and monetary policy. The increasingly sluggish economic growth in Argentina warranted expansionary economic policies, argued many policy-makers in and out of the country. But the currency board's basic premise was that the money supply to the financial system could not be expanded any further or faster than the ability of the economy to capture dollar reserves. This eliminated monetary policy as an avenue for macroeconomic policy formulation, leaving only fiscal policy for economic stimulation.

Government budget deficits. Government spending was not slowing, however. As the unemployment rate grew higher, as poverty and social unrest grew, government—both in the civil center of Argentina, Buenos Aires, and in the outer provinces—was faced with growing expansionary spending needs to close the economic and social gaps. Government spending continued to increase, but tax receipts did not. Lower income led to lower taxes on income.

Argentina then turned to the international markets to aid in the financing of its government's deficit spending. As illustrated in Exhibit 7.8, the total foreign debt of the country began rising dramatically in 1997 and 1998. Only a number of International Monetary Fund capital injections in 2000 and 2001 prevented the total foreign debt of the country from skyrocketing. When the decade was over, however, total foreign debt had effectively doubled, and the economy's earning power had not.

Also seen in Exhibit 7.8 is Argentina's failure to turn the current account toward surplus. Although not surprising given the overvalued currency relative to other major South American neighbors, it was only through running a trade surplus that Argentina could earn additional dollar reserves and allow a loosening of monetary policy constraints.

In the end, the government budget deficit continued to grow. Continuing recession required large fiscal expenditures by federal and local governments. Government spending was increasingly financed by international capital. International investors were beginning to doubt Argentina's ability to repay them.

Social Repercussions

As economic conditions continued to deteriorate, banks suffered increasing runs. Depositors, fearing that the peso would be devalued, lined up to withdraw their money, both Argentine peso cash balances and U.S. dollar cash balances. Pesos were converted to dollars, once again adding fuel to the growing fire of currency collapse. The government, fearing that the increasing financial drain on banks would cause their collapse, closed the banks on December 1, 2001, in an effort to stop the flight of cash and capital out of Argentina. Consumers, unable to withdraw more than $250

Exhibit 7.8 Argentina's Economic Performance, 1991–2000

	1991	1992	1993	1994	1995	1996	1997	1998	1999	2000
Foreign debt (billion $)	65.4	71.9	60.3	69.6	68.2	105.2	123.2	139.0	149.0	123.7
Current account (billion $)	−0.65	−5.49	−8.03	−11.22	−5.30	-6.94	−12.43	−14.55	−11.95	−8.90
Budget balance (billion $)	−1.01	−0.07	−1.58	−1.88	−1.42	−5.24	−4.35	−4.15	−8.13	−6.86

Source: International Monetary Fund, Political Risk Services, Argentina Economic Development Agency.

per week, were instructed to use debit cards and credit cards to make purchases and conduct the everyday transactions required by society.

Riots in the streets of Buenos Aires in December 2001 intensified the need for rapid change. As the new year of 2002 arrived, the second president in two weeks, Fernando de la Rua, was driven from office. He was succeeded by a Peronist, President Adolfo Rodriguez Saa, who lasted all of one week as president before he too was driven from office. President Saa did, however, leave his legacy. In his one week as President of Argentina, President Adolfo Rodriguez Saa declared the largest sovereign debt default in history. Argentina announced it would not be able to make interest payments due on $155 billion in sovereign (government) debt.

Saa was succeeded by Eduardo Duhalde, Argentina's fifth president in a little more than two weeks. A presidential candidate in 1999 and a senator for Buenos Aires province, Duhalde faced a massive task. He was immediately granted emergency powers to try to save what was left to be saved of the Argentine economic system.

Devaluation

On Sunday January 6, 2002, in the first act of his presidency, President Eduardo Duhalde devalued the peso from Ps1.00/$ to Ps1.40/$. It was hoped that once the peso was devalued, the country could calm the nerves of its people.

But the economic pain continued. Two weeks after the devaluation, the banks were still closed. Most of the state governments outside of Buenos Aires, basically broke and without access to financing resources, began printing their own money—*script*—promissary notes of the provincial governments. The provincial governments were left with little choice as the economy of Argentina was nearing complete collapse as people and businesses could not obtain money to conduct the day-to-day commercial transactions of life.

But the notes were only a partial answer. Because the notes were promissary notes of the provincial governments, not the federal government, people and businesses in other provinces would not accept the notes from other provinces. Store shelves stood empty as consumers could buy what was already in the store, but the store in turn could not make acceptable payment to regional, national, or international suppliers. The population itself became somewhat trapped within its own province, as their money was not accepted in the outside world in exchange for goods, services, travel, or anything else.

On February 3, 2002, the Argentine government announced that the peso would be floated. The government would no longer attempt to fix or manage its value to any specific level, allowing the market to find or set the exchange rate. The value of the peso now began a slow but gradual depreciation.[3]

As the year wore on, the country was confronted with issue after issue of social, political, and economic collapse. The banks and bankers were increasingly the target of the ire of the population. As banks collapsed business fell with them. In February and March a growing series of investigations into

3. When a currency that is under a fixed-exchange-rate regime is officially altered downward in value, it is termed a *devaluation*. When a currency that is freely floated on exchange markets moves downward in value, it is termed *depreciation*.

illegal trading and financial fraud covered the Buenos Aires headlines. In February and March 2002 continued negotiations between the IMF and Argentina went through fits and starts as the IMF demanded increasing fiscal reform over the growing government budget deficits and bank mismanagement. The IMF itself became an increasing target of the Argentine population's general discontent.

On March 24 and 25 the peso was once again hit by massive sell-offs. In a country long- considered the wealthiest and most sophisticated in all of South America, the people were increasingly opposed to all politicians, all banks and financial service providers, and in many cases each other. The path of the peso's collapse is illustrated in Exhibit 7.9. In the spring of 2002, Argentina was a country in considerable trouble.

A former Harvard professor and member of the U.S. President's Council of Economic Advisors summed up the hard lessons of the Argentine story:

> *In reality, the Argentines understood the risk that they were taking at least as well as the IMF staff did. Theirs was a calculated risk that might have produced good results. It is true, however, that the IMF staff did encourage Argentina to continue with the fixed exchange rate and currency board. Although the IMF and virtually all outside economists believe that a floating exchange rate is preferable to a "fixed but adjustable" system, in which the government recognizes that it will have to devalue occasionally, the IMF (as well as some outside economists) came to believe that the currency board system of a firmly fixed exchange rate (a "hard peg" in the jargon of international finance) is a viable long-term policy for an economy. Argentina's experience has proved that wrong.*[4]

Exhibit 7.9 The Collapse of the Argentine Peso

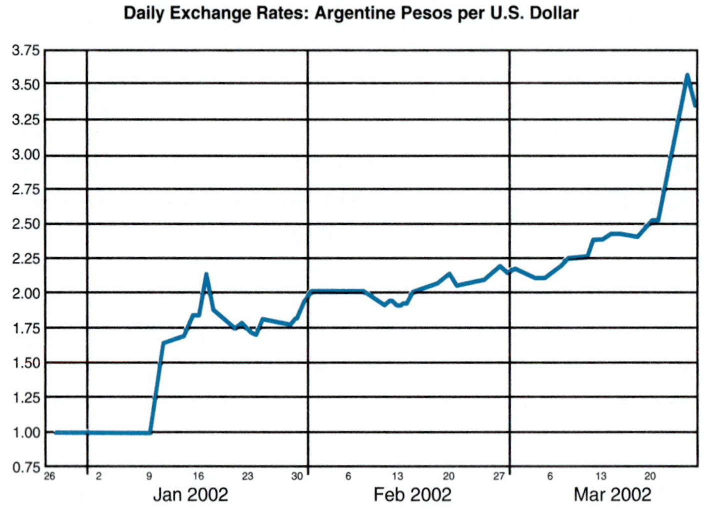

© 2002 by Prof. Werner Antweiler, University of British Columbia, Vancouver BC, Canada. Permission is granted to reproduce the above image provided that the source and copyright are acknowledged. Time period shown in diagram: December 26, 2001–March 26, 2002.

4. Martin Feldstein, "Argentina's Fall," *Foreign Affairs*, March/April 2002.

Exhibit 7.10 summarizes many of the political and economic events surrounding the Argentine collapse.

Exhibit 7.10 A Time Line of Events in the Argentine Crisis

December 10, 1999	Fernando de la Rua is inaugurated as President of Argentina. He inherits a country in the midst of continual recession and increasing financial crisis. The policies of the outgoing president, Carlos Menem, are blamed for the deterioration of the society and the growing culture of corruption.
May 29, 2000	Argentina's government unveils $938 million in government budget cuts in order to meet its fiscal targets of rebalancing the budget.
December 18, 2000	Argentina announces a package of financial borrowing totaling $40 billion, heading off growing concern in the international community that it will default on its international debt.
March 20, 2001	Domingo Cavallo, the architect of the original currency board implemented in 1991, returns to government to take a hand in revitalizing the economy. He later announces a series of deregulations which will save industry some 20% of its costs.
July 18, 2001	Public protests surge as the government of Argentina announces a new series of budget cuts and reductions in public aid programs. The $1.5 billion austerity program is primarily at the request of the International Monetary Fund in order for Argentina to qualify for additional loans.
August 21, 2001	The IMF agrees to $8 billion in financial aid to support Argentina's depleted currency reserves following increasing capital flight.
December 1, 2001	The Argentine government closes the banks.
December 5, 2001	The International Monetary Fund refuses to make a $1.26 billion loan installment to Argentina amid disagreements over the content of the Argentine 2002 government budget.
December 19, 2001	Government declares a state of siege as thousands of unemployed workers riot through the streets of Buenos Aires, demanding food and the resignation of the president.
December 20, 2001	President Fernando de la Rua and his government fall. Rioting in Buenos Aires intensifies.
December 29, 2001	Peronist President Adolfo Rodriguez Saa lasts only one week as president before he too is driven from office. In his one week as President of Argentina, President Adolfo Rodriguez Saa declares the largest sovereign debt default in history: Argentina announces it would not make interest payments on $155 billion in sovereign public debt.
January 1, 2002	Eduardo Duhalde becomes Argentina's fifth president in two weeks. He is immediately granted emergency powers to deal with the growing political and economic crisis.
January 6, 2002	In his first act as president, President Eduardo Duhalde devalues the peso from Ps1.00/$ to Ps1.40/$.
February 1, 2002	The Supreme Court of Argentina, after several weeks of political sparring with the federal government, declares the two-month long bank closure unconstitutional, instructing the government to reopen the banks on Monday February 4.
February 3, 2002	The government, on Sunday, announces a change in the direction of Argentina's economic revisions. The peso is to be floated immediately, ending one month of an official bi-level exchange rate system. The banks are to be closed on Monday and Tuesday. All banking reserves held as U.S. dollars are to be converted to pesos at differing exchange rates. The government pursues the overthrow of the Supreme Court, setting the stage for a constitutional crisis for the country.
March 26, 2002	Peso floated to 3.5/$

Forecasting in Practice

Numerous foreign exchange forecasting services exist, many of which are provided by banks and independent consultants. In addition, some multinational firms have their own in-house forecasting capabilities. Predictions can be based on elaborate econometric models, technical analysis of charts and trends, intuition, and a certain measure of gall.

Whether any of the forecasting services are worth their cost depends partly on our motive for forecasting as well as the required accuracy of the forecast. For example, long-run forecasts of the Japanese yen may be motivated by a multinational firm's desire to initiate a foreign investment in Japan, or perhaps to raise long-term funds denominated in Japanese yen. Or a portfolio manager may be considering diversifying for the long term in Japanese securities. The longer the time horizon of the forecast, the more inaccurate but also the less critical the forecast is likely to be. The forecaster will typically use annual data to display long-run trends in such economic fundamentals as Japanese inflation, growth, and BOP.

Short-term forecasts are typically motivated by a desire to hedge a receivable, payable, or dividend for perhaps a period of three months. In this case, the long-run economic fundamentals may not be as important as technical factors in the marketplace, government intervention, news, and passing whims of traders and investors. Accuracy of the forecast is critical, since most of the exchange rate changes are relatively small even though the day-to-day volatility may be high.

Forecasting services normally undertake fundamental economic analysis for long-term forecasts, and some base their short-term forecasts on the same basic model. Others base their short-term forecasts on technical analysis similar to that conducted in security analysis. They attempt to correlate exchange rate changes with various other variables, regardless of whether there is any economic rationale for the correlation. The chances of these forecasts being consistently useful or profitable depend on whether one believes the foreign exchange market is efficient. The more efficient the market is, the more likely it is that exchange rates are "random walks," with past price behavior providing no clues to the future. The less efficient the foreign exchange market is, the better the chance that forecasters may get lucky and find a key relationship that holds, at least for the short run. If the relationship is really consistent, however, others will soon discover it and the market will become efficient again with respect to that piece of information.

Exhibit 7.11 summarizes the various forecasting periods, regimes, and the authors' suggested methodologies. Opinions, however, are subject to change without notice! (And remember, if the authors could predict the movement of exchange rates with regularity, we surely wouldn't write books.)

Technical Analysis

Technical analysts, traditionally referred to as *chartists*, focus on price and volume data to determine past trends that are expected to continue into the future. The single most important element of technical analysis is that future exchange rates are based on the current exchange rate. Exchange rate movements, similar to equity price movements, can be subdivided into three periods: 1) day-to-day movement, which is seemingly random; 2) short-term movements extending from several days to trends lasting several months; 3) long-term movements, which are characterized by up and down long-term trends. Long-term technical analysis has gained new popularity as a result of

Exhibit 7.11 Exchange Rate Forecasting in Practice

Forecast Period	Regime	Recommended Forecast Methods
SHORT-RUN	Fixed rate	1. Assume the fixed rate is maintained 2. Indications of stress on fixed rate? 3. Capital controls; black market rates 4. Indicators of government's capability to maintain fixed rate? 5. Changes in official foreign currency reserves
	Floating rate	1. Technical methods that capture trend 2. Forward rates as forecasts a. < 30 days, assume a random walk b. 30–90 days, forward rates 3. 90–360 days, combine trend with fundamental analysis 4. Fundamental analysis of inflationary concerns 5. Government declarations and agreements regarding exchange rate goals 6. Cooperative agreements with other countries
LONG-RUN	Fixed rate	1. Fundamental analysis 2. BOP management 3. Ability to control domestic inflation 4. Ability to generate hard currency reserves to use for intervention 5. Ability to run trade surpluses
	Floating rate	1. Focus on inflationary fundamentals and PPP 2. Indicators of general economic health such as economic growth and stability 3. Technical analysis of long-term trends; new research indicates possibility of long-term technical "waves"

recent research into the possibility that long-term "waves" in currency movements exist under floating exchange rates.

The longer the time horizon of the forecast, the more inaccurate the forecast is likely to be. Whereas forecasting for the long run must depend on economic fundamentals of exchange rate determination, many of the forecast needs of the firm are short- to medium-term in their time horizon and can be addressed with less theoretical approaches. Time series techniques infer no theory or causality but simply predict future values from the recent past. Forecasters freely mix fundamental and technical analysis, presumably because forecasting is like horseshoes and hand grenades: Getting close is all that counts!

Cross-Rate Consistency in Forecasting

International financial managers must often forecast their home currency exchange rates for the set of countries in which the firm operates, not only to decide whether to hedge or to make an investment, but also as an integral part of preparing multi-country operating budgets in the home country's currency. These are the operating budgets against which the performance of foreign subsidiary managers will be judged. Checking the reasonableness of the cross rates implicit in individual forecasts acts as a reality check to the original forecasts.

To illustrate, assume the U.S. parent home office forecasts the yen-to-dollar exchange rate a year hence to be ¥120/$ and the U.K. pound sterling rate to be $1.50/£. This creates an implied spot rate one year hence of ¥180/£. However, both the Japanese and the British financial managers, with good reason, have forecast a spot rate one year hence of ¥150/£.

Obviously the two foreign subsidiary managers (forecasting ¥150/£) and the home office (with an implicit forecast of ¥180/£) cannot both be correct. The time to reconcile these conflicting forecasts is the present, not one year hence when managers in Japan or the United Kingdom claim that their performance against budget is better than measured by the U.S. parent. Additionally, checking the reasonableness of implied cross rates is an exercise in improving the accuracy of the forecasting process.

Forecasting: What to Think?

Obviously, with the variety of theories and practices, forecasting exchange rates into the future is a daunting task. Here is a synthesis of our thoughts and experience:

- It appears from decades of theoretical and empirical studies that exchange rates do adhere to the fundamental principles and theories outlined in the previous sections. Fundamentals do apply in the long term. There is, therefore, something of a *fundamental equilibrium path* for a currency's value.
- It also seems that in the short term, a variety of random events, institutional frictions, and technical factors may cause currency values to deviate significantly from their long-term fundamental path. This is sometimes referred to as *noise*. Clearly, therefore, we might expect deviations from the long-term path not only to occur, but to occur with some regularity and relative longevity.

Exhibit 7.12 illustrates this synthesis of forecasting thought. The long-term equilibrium path of the currency—although relatively well defined in retrospect—is not always apparent in the short term. The exchange rate itself may deviate in something of a cycle or wave about the long-term path.

If market participants both agree on the general long-term path and possess *stabilizing expectations*, the currency's value will periodically return to the long-term path. It is critical, however, that when the currency's value rises above the long-term path, most market participants see it as being overvalued and respond by selling the currency—causing its price to fall. Similarly, when the currency's value falls below the long-term path, market participants respond by buying the currency driving its value up. This is what is meant by *stabilizing expectations*: Market participants continually respond to deviations from the long-term path by buying or selling to drive the currency back to the long-term path.

If, however, for some reason the market becomes unstable, as illustrated by the dotted deviation path in Exhibit 7.12, the exchange rate may move significantly away from the long-term path for longer periods of time. Causes of these destabilizing markets, weak infrastructure (such as the banking system), and political or social events that dictate economic behaviors, are often the result of actions by speculators or inefficient or uncompetitive economic outcomes.

Exhibit 7.12 Differentiating Short-Term Noise from Long-Term Trends

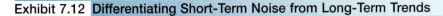

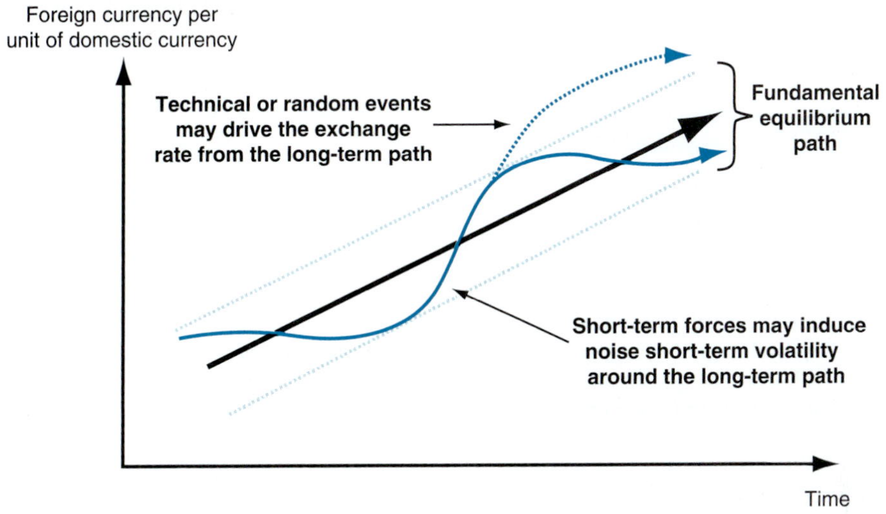

SUMMARY

- The managerial significance of the balance of payments depends upon whether the currency in question is under a floating exchange rate regime or a fixed exchange rate regime.
- Under a fixed exchange rate regime the government bears the responsibility to ensure a BOP near zero. If the BOP deviates significantly from zero, the government is expected to intervene in the foreign exchange market.
- Under a floating-exchange-rate regime, the government bears no responsibility to maintain a BOP near zero. If the BOP deviates significantly from zero, the market will—in theory—automatically alter the exchange rate to attain equilibrium.
- The asset approach to forecasting suggests that whether foreigners are willing to hold claims in monetary form depends partly on relative real interest rates and partly on a country's outlook for economic growth and profitability.
- Longer-term forecasting, longer than one year, requires a return to the basic analysis of exchange rate fundamentals such as BOP, relative inflation rates, relative interest rates, and the long-run properties of purchasing power parity.
- Technical analysts (chartists) focus on price and volume data to determine past trends that are expected to continue into the future.
- Exchange rate forecasting in practice is a mix of both fundamental and technical forms of exchange rate analysis.
- The Asian currency crisis was primarily a balance of payments crisis in its origins and its effects on exchange rate determination. A weak economic and financial infrastructure, corporate governance problems, and speculation were also contributing factors.

- The Russian rouble crisis of 1998 was a complex combination of speculative pressures best explained by the asset approach to exchange rate determination.
- The Brazilian real crisis of 1999 was probably a combination of a disequilibrium in international parity conditions (differential rates of inflation) and balance of payments disequilibrium (current account deficits combined with financial account outflows).

QUESTIONS

1. **Forecasting using the BOP approach.** Explain how a country's BOP can be used to forecast pressure to devalue its exchange rate under a fixed-exchange-rate regime.

2. **BOP approach: forecasting the spot rate under a floating-exchange-rate regime.** Explain how a BOP deficit on current account under a floating-exchange-rate regime creates downward pressure on a country's spot exchange rate. What is the role of a country's government in this case?

3. **BOP approach: forecasting the spot rate under a managed-float-exchange-rate regime.** Explain how a government could seek to influence its spot exchange rate under a managed-float-exchange-rate regime.

4. **Asset market approach to forecasting.** Explain how the asset market approach can be used to forecast future spot exchange rates. How does the asset market approach differ from the BOP approach to forecasting?

5. **Technical analysis.** Explain how technical analysis can be used to forecast future spot exchange rates. How does technical analysis differ from the BOP and asset market approaches to forecasting?

6. **Forecasting services.** Many treasurers subscribe to rather expensive on-line foreign exchange forecasting services even if these services have a dubious record of consistently correct forecasts. What might motivate a treasurer to continue to use a forecasting service?

7. **Cross-rate consistency in forecasting.** Explain the meaning of "cross-rate consistency" as used by MNEs. How do MNEs use a check of cross-rate consistency in practice?

8. **Infrastructure weakness.** Infrastructure weakness was one of the causes of the emerging market crisis in Thailand in 1997. Define infrastructure weakness and explain how it could affect a country's exchange rate.

9. **Infrastructure strength.** Explain why infrastructure strengths have helped to offset the large BOP deficits on current account in the United States.

10. **Speculation.** The emerging market crises of 1997–2002 were worsened because of rampant speculation. Do speculators cause such crises or do they simply respond to market signals of weakness? How can a government manage foreign exchange speculation?

11. **Foreign direct investment.** Swings in foreign direct investment flows into and out of emerging markets contribute to exchange rate volatility. Describe one concrete historical example of this phenomenon during the past 10 years.

12. **Thailand's crisis of 1997.** What were the main causes of Thailand's crisis of 1997? What lessons were learned and what steps were eventually taken to normalize Thailand's economy?

13. **Russia's crisis of 1998.** What were the main causes of Russia's crisis of 1998? What lessons were learned and what steps were taken to normalize Russia's economy?

14. **Argentina's crisis of 2001–2002.** What were the main causes of Argentina's crisis of 2001–2002? What lessons were learned and what steps were taken to normalize Argentina's economy?

PROBLEMS

Use the following economic, financial, and business indicators from the February 3, 2003, issue of the The *Economist* to answer problems 1 through 10.

Forecasting the Pan-Pacific Pyramid: Australia, Japan, and the United States

	Gross Domestic Product				Industrial	Retail	Unem-
		Year		Forecast	Production	Sales	ployment
Country	Rec Qtr	Ago	2002	2003	Rec Qtr	Rec Qtr	Rec Qtr
Australia	3.5%	3.7%	3.7%	3.2%	1.6%	5.4%	6.2%
Japan	3.2%	1.3%	−0.3%	0.2%	6.7%	−1.8%	5.5%
United States	0.7%	2.8%	2.4%	2.5%	2.1%	4.9%	6.0%

	Consumer Prices			Producer Prices		Wages & Earnings	
Country	Year Ago	2002	2003e	Latest	Year Ago	Latest	Year Ago
Australia	3.1%	3.0%	2.7%	1.6%	−0.7%	3.6%	4.0%
Japan	−1.2%	−0.9%	−0.7%	0.3%	−0.8%	−1.9%	−1.9%
United States	1.6%	1.6%	2.1%	1.2%	−1.6%	3.0%	3.7%

	Money	Interest Rates (percent per annum)					
	Supply	3-month money market		2-year	10-year Govt Bonds		Corporate
Country	Growth	Latest	Year Ago	Govt bonds	Latest	Year Ago	Bonds
Australia	10.6%	4.78%	4.28%	4.50%	5.12%	5.86%	5.86%
Japan	2.2%	0.30%	0.30%	0.40%	0.87%	1.53%	0.97%
United States	6.3%	1.25%	1.79%	1.71%	4.00%	4.93%	6.04%

	Trade Balance	Current Account			Trade-Weighted Exchange		Currency
	Last 12 mos	Last 12 mos	2002	2003e	Rate (1990=100)		(per £)
Country	(Billion $)	(Billion $)	(% of GDP)	(% of GDP)	Feb 5th	Year Ago	Feb 5th
Australia	−$5.3	−$14.3	−3.9%	−4.2%	75.8	73.6	2.78
Japan	$92.6	$114.8	2.8%	2.8%	129.7	127.7	197
United States	−$467.0	−$482.2	−4.8%	−5.0%	108.3	124.4	1.65

Source: Data abstracted from The *Economist*, February 3, 2003, pp. Unless otherwise noted, percentages are percentage changes over one year. Rec Qtr = recent quarter. Values for 2003 (2003e) are forecasts.

1. **Current spot rates.** What are the current spot exchange rates for the following cross-rates?
   a. Japanese yen/U.S. dollar
   b. Japanese yen/Australian dollar
   c. Australian dollar/U.S. dollar

2. **Purchasing power parity forecasts.** Using the theory of purchasing power parity, and assuming that forecasted changes in consumer prices are the best measures of expected inflation, forecast the following spot exchanges for one year into the future:
   a. Japanese yen/U.S. dollar
   b. Japanese yen/Australian dollar
   c. Australian dollar/U.S. dollar

3. **International Fisher forecasts.** Using the international Fisher effect, and assuming that the latest 2-year government bond rates are the most appropriate interest rates for applying international Fisher, forecast the following spot exchanges for one year into the future:
   a. Japanese yen/U.S. dollar
   b. Japanese yen/Australian dollar
   c. Australian dollar/U.S. dollar

4. **Implied real interest rates.** Use the latest 2-year government bond rates and the forecast changes in consumer prices to forecast the real interest rates for the following:
   a. Australian dollar
   b. Japanese yen
   c. U.S. dollar

5. **Forecasting with real interest rates.** Using the real interest rates forecast in problem 4 above, forecast the following spot exchange rates one year into the future:
   a. Japanese yen/U.S. dollar
   b. Japanese yen/Australian dollar
   c. Australian dollar/U.S. dollar

6. **Forward rates as forecasts.** Using the 3-month money market interest rates listed, calculate the 3-month forward rates for the following exchange rates:
   a. Japanese yen/U.S. dollar
   b. Japanese yen/Australian dollar
   c. Australian dollar/U.S. dollar

7. **Real economic activity and misery.** One of the common general measures of national economic health is sometimes referred to as the "misery index," the sum of a country's inflation rate and unemployment rate. Using the previously calculated cross-rates (problem 1), calculate each country's misery index and use it as a relative measure for forecasting (in the same way inflation differentials or interest differentials are used to forecast).
   a. Japanese yen/U.S. dollar
   b. Japanese yen/Australian dollar
   c. Australian dollar/U.S. dollar

8. **Balance of payments approach.** Using the trade and current account information provided, forecast the *direction* of spot exchange rate movement one year into the future for the following spot exchange rates:
   a. Japanese yen/U.S. dollar
   b. Japanese yen/Australian dollar
   c. Australian dollar/U.S. dollar

   Now, in addition to the economic and financial data, consider the following graphs of how these three exchange rates have performed in recent years.

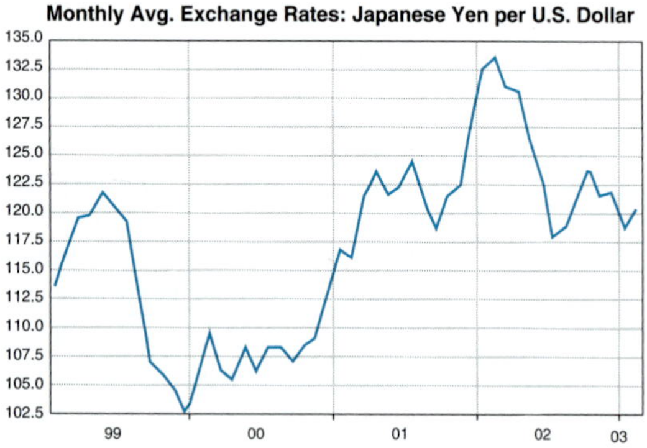

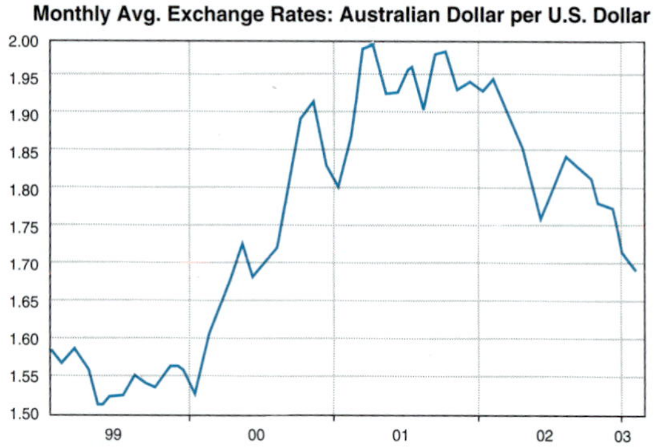

© 2003 by Prof. Werner Antweiler, University of British Columbia, Vancouver BC, Canada. Time period shown in diagram: January 1, 1999–February 12, 2003.

9. **Current accounts and spot rates.** Given what you concluded about the direction of the spot exchange rate in problem 8, does this directional view fit with the recent trend exhibited by the spot exchange rate above for the Japanese yen/U.S. dollar and Australian dollar/U.S. dollar?

10. **Exchange rate trends and bounds.** Using the graphs of the spot exchange rates for the January 1999 through February 2003 period, determine what you believe to be the trend, the mean value, and the upper and lower bounds to their respective rates.

INTERNET EXERCISES

WWW.

1. **Recent economic and financial data.** Use the following web sites to obtain recent economic and financial data used for all approaches to forecasting to presented in this chapter.

   Economist.com http://www.economist.com

   FT.com http://www.ft.com

   EconEdLink http://www.econedlink.org/datalinks/index.cfm

2. **OzForex weekly comment.** The OzForex Foreign Exchange Services web site provides a weekly commentary on major political and economic factors and events that move current markets. Using the web site, see what OzForex expects to happen in the coming week on the three major global currencies—the dollar, yen, and euro.

   OzForex http://www.ozforex.com.au/marketwatch.htm

3. **Exchange rates, interest rates, and global markets.** The magnitude of market data can seem overwhelming on occasion. Use the following Bloomberg markets page to organize your mind and your global data.

   Bloomberg Financial News http://www.bloomberg.com/markets

4. **National Bank of Slovakia and the Slovakia koruna.** The National Bank of Slovakia has been publishing spot and forward rates of selected currencies versus the Slovakia koruna for several years. Using the web site below, compile spot rates, 3-month forward rates, and 6-month forward rates for a recent two-year period. After graphing the data, does it appear that the forward rate has predicted the future direction of the spot rate?

   National Bank of Slovakia http://www.nbs.sk/KL/INDEXA.HTM

5. **Banque Canada and the Canadian dollar forward market.** Use the following web site to find the latest spot and forward quotes of the Canadian dollar against the Bahamian dollar and the Brazilian real.

   Banque Canada http://www.bank-banque-canada.ca/find/exchange.htm

SELECTED READINGS

Levich, Richard, *International Financial Markets: Prices and Policies* (Boston: Irwin McGraw-Hill, 1998).

Krugman, Paul R., and Maurice Obstfeld, *International Economics: Theory and Policy*, Third Edition (New York: Harper Collins, 1994).

PART 3

Foreign Exchange Exposure

PART 3

Part 3 uses the background provided in Part 2 to analyze the task of measuring and managing foreign exchange exposure. Foreign exchange exposure is a measure of the potential that a firm's profitability, cash flow, and market value will change because of a change in exchange rates. A major responsibility of financial managers in multinational enterprises is to manage these currency exposures.

Chapter 8 defines the four different types of foreign exchange exposure; namely, *transaction*, *operating*, *accounting*, and *tax exposure*. It then analyzes why a firm should or should not hedge one or more of these exposures. The rest of this chapter examines *transaction exposure*. This type of exposure measures changes in the value of outstanding financial obligations incurred prior to a change in exchange rates but not due to be settled until a future point in time. Typical exposures are accounts receivable and payable, including their current exposures, as well as backlog and quotation exposures. We use the case of Dayton Manufacturing to illustrate how a firm can hedge transaction exposure. The chapter concludes with an examination of how risk management is conducted in practice and a mini-case illustrating how Lufthansa attempted to hedge the transaction exposure arising from its purchase of Boeing 737s. An appendix to the chapter describes the basics of foreign currency accounting. This is followed by a decision case, Zapa Chemical and BuBa.

Chapter 9 examines how a firm should measure and manage its *operating exposure*. Operating exposure measures the change in the present value of a firm resulting from a change in its future operating cash flows due to an unexpected change in exchange rates. The change in present value depends on the effect of an exchange rate change on the firm's future sales volume, prices, and costs. We use the Carlton case to illustrate the change in its net present value under a variety of scenarios. We then illustrate how a firm can manage operating exposure through such strategic measures as diversifying operations and sources of financing. The chapter concludes with a description of four proactive techniques that are used to manage operating exposure in practice. We also present a mini-case on Toyota's European operating exposure.

Chapter 10 analyzes how a firm should measure and manage its *accounting exposure*. Accounting exposure is the potential for accounting-derived changes in owners' equity and consolidated income that occur because of the need to translate foreign currency–denominated financial statements of foreign subsidiaries into a single currency to prepare worldwide consolidated financial statements. The chapter starts with a description of the current transaction methods used in the United States and worldwide, and then uses Carlton Germany to illustrate the use of each method. We then compare Carlton's transaction exposure with its operating exposure. The chapter continues with an analysis of the use of a balance sheet hedge to offset transaction exposure. It concludes with an analysis of how MNEs can evaluate the performance of foreign subsidiaries whose financial results are affected by exchange rate changes.

apter 8

Transaction Exposure

Foreign exchange exposure is a measure of the potential for a firm's profitability, net cash flow, and market value to change because of a change in exchange rates. An important task of the financial manager is to measure foreign exchange exposure and to manage it so as to maximize the profitability, net cash flow, and market value of the firm.

Types of Foreign Exchange Exposure

What happens to a firm when foreign exchange rates change? The effect can be measured in several ways. Exhibit 8.1 shows schematically the three main types of foreign exchange exposure: transaction, operating, and accounting.

Exhibit 8.1 Conceptual Comparison of Transaction, Operating, and Accounting Foreign Exchange Exposure

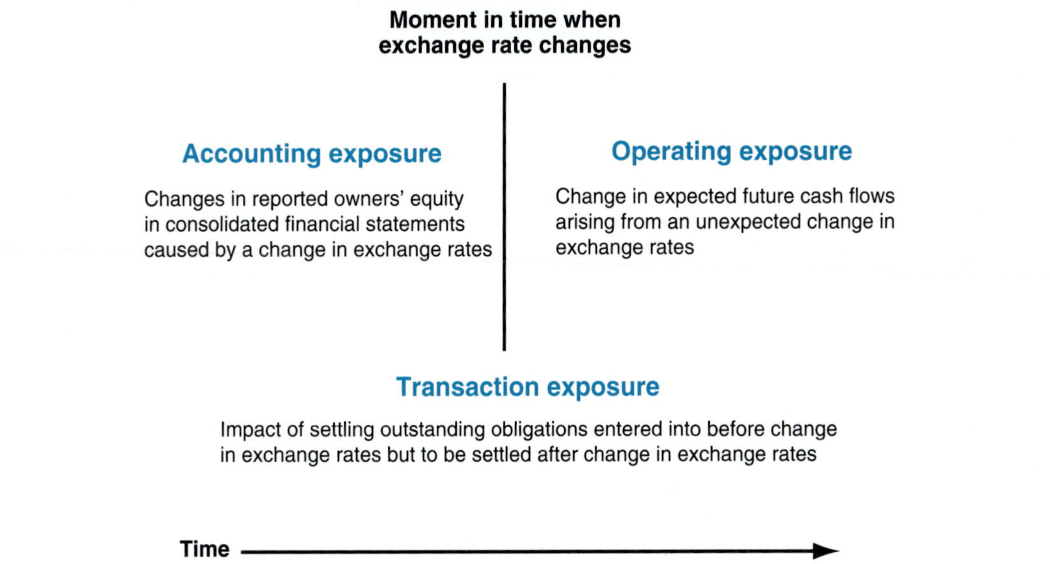
Moment in time when exchange rate changes
Accounting exposure
Changes in reported owners' equity in consolidated financial statements caused by a change in exchange rates
Operating exposure
Change in expected future cash flows arising from an unexpected change in exchange rates
Transaction exposure
Impact of settling outstanding obligations entered into before change in exchange rates but to be settled after change in exchange rates
Time

Transaction Exposure

Transaction exposure measures changes in the value of outstanding financial obligations incurred prior to a change in exchange rates but not due to be settled until after the exchange rates change. Thus it deals with changes in cash flows that result from existing contractual obligations.

Operating Exposure

Operating exposure, also called *economic exposure*, *competitive exposure*, or *strategic exposure*, measures the change in the present value of the firm resulting from any change in future operating cash flows of the firm caused by an *unexpected* change in exchange rates. The change in value depends on the effect of the exchange rate change on future sales volume, prices, and costs.

Transaction exposure and operating exposure exist because of unexpected changes in future cash flows. The difference between the two is that transaction exposure is concerned with future cash flows already contracted for, while operating exposure focuses on expected (not yet contracted for) future cash flows that might change because a change in exchange rates has altered international competitiveness. The purpose of this chapter is to analyze how transaction exposure is measured and managed.

Accounting Exposure

Accounting exposure, also called *translation exposure*, is the potential for accounting-derived changes in owner's equity to occur because of the need to "translate" foreign currency financial statements of foreign subsidiaries into a single reporting currency to prepare worldwide consolidated financial statements.

Tax Exposure

The tax consequence of foreign exchange exposure varies by country. As a general rule, however, only *realized* foreign exchange losses are deductible for purposes of calculating income taxes. Similarly, only *realized* gains create taxable income. "Realized" means that the loss or gain involves cash flows.

Losses from transaction exposure usually reduce taxable income in the year in which they are realized. Losses from operating exposure reduce taxable income over a series of future years. As will be explained in Chapter 10, losses from accounting exposure are not cash losses and so are not deductible. Some steps taken to minimize one or another of the types of exposure—such as entering into a forward exchange contract—create taxable income or loss. Other steps taken to obtain the same protection have no income tax implications. Because tax exposure is determined by the country of domicile of each subsidiary, a MNE needs to plan its foreign exchange management policies to minimize the worldwide after-tax consequences of foreign exchange losses and to maximize after-tax gains. However, since many MNEs manage foreign exchange exposures centrally, gains or losses are often not matched with the country of origin.

As illustrated in Global Finance Perspective 8.1, however, currency exposures do not always result in losses. They may, in fact, occasionally result in gains to the firm—gains that are not the result of the firm's true operations or core competence—from the luck and timing associated with exchange rate changes and currency movements.

Global Finance Perspective 8.1

Amazon.com's Quest for Profits: The Role of Currency Gains/Losses

Jeff Bezos, CEO of Amazon.com, promised that Amazon would turn a profit sometime in 2001. Although most analysts and investors did not believe him, he proved them wrong as Amazon.com reported a positive operating profit of $59 million and a net income of $5 million for the fourth quarter of 2001. He had indeed delivered on his promise.

But one issue primary to all investors is the quality of earnings. Although there are a number of technical components to earnings quality, one of the fundamental questions about reported earnings is whether they are sustainable. Did the earnings arise from operations, or from one-time asset sales, investment gains, or other non-sustainable transactions? In the case of Amazon, there was just one dimension to its quarterly profit return: the $5 million in net income was, at least in part, the result of a one-time foreign currency gain in the quarter of $16 million!

Why Hedge?

MNEs possess a multitude of cash flows that are sensitive to changes in exchange rates, interest rates, and commodity prices. These three financial price risks are the subject of the growing field of *financial risk management*. In this chapter, we will focus on the sensitivity of the individual firm's future cash flows to exchange rates alone.

Definition of Hedging

Many firms attempt to manage their currency exposures through hedging. *Hedging* is the taking of a position, acquiring either a cash flow, an asset, or a contract (including a forward contract) that will rise (fall) in value and offset a fall (rise) in the value of an existing position. Hedging therefore protects the owner of the existing asset from loss. However, it also eliminates any gain from an increase in the value of the asset hedged against. The question remains: What is to be gained by the firm from hedging?

The value of a firm, according to financial theory, is the net present value of all expected future cash flows. The fact that these cash flows are *expected* emphasizes that nothing about the future is certain. If the reporting currency value of many of these cash flows is altered by exchange rates changes, a firm that hedges its currency exposures reduces some of the variance in the value of its future expected cash flows. *Currency risk* can therefore be defined roughly as the variance in expected cash flows arising from unexpected exchange rate changes.

Exhibit 8.2 illustrates the distribution of expected net cash flows of the individual firm. Hedging these cash flows narrows the distribution of the cash flows about the mean of the distribution. Currency hedging reduces risk. Reduction of risk is not, however, the same as adding value or return. The value of the firm depicted in Exhibit 8.2 would be increased only if hedging actually shifted the mean of the distribution to the right. In fact, if hedging is not "free," meaning that the firm must expend resources to undertake hedging activity, then hedging will add value only if the rightward shift is sufficiently large to compensate for the cost of hedging.

Exhibit 8.2 Impact of Hedging on the Expected Cash Flows of the Firm

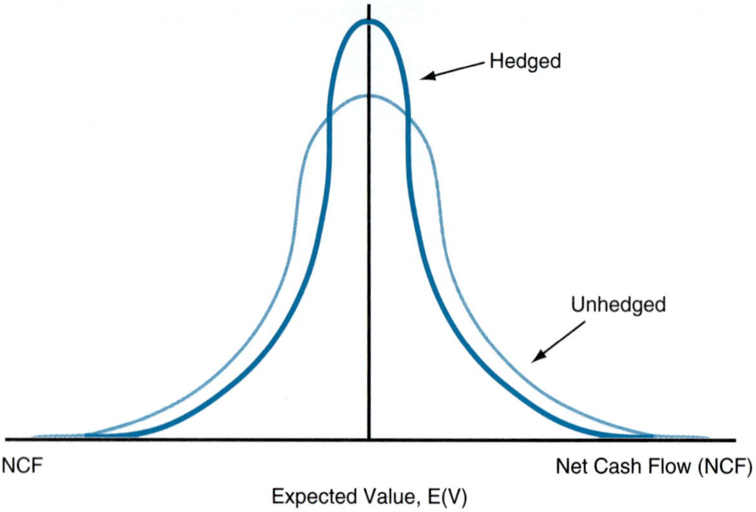

Hedging reduces the variability of expected cash flows about the mean of the distribution. This reduction of distribution variance is a reduction of risk.

Reasons Not to Hedge

Hence the key question: Is a reduction in the variability of cash flows sufficient reason for currency risk management? This question is actually a continuing debate in multinational financial management. Opponents of currency hedging commonly make the following arguments:

- Shareholders are much more capable of diversifying currency risk than the management of the firm. If stockholders do not wish to accept the currency risk of any specific firm, they can diversify their portfolios to manage the currency risk in a way that satisfies their individual preferences and risk tolerance.
- As noted earlier, currency risk management does not increase the expected cash flows of the firm. Currency risk management normally consumes some of a firm's resources and so reduces cash flow. The impact on value is a combination of the reduction of cash flow (which by itself lowers value) and the reduction in variance (which by itself increases value).
- Management often conducts hedging activities that benefit management at the expense of the shareholders. Agency theory frequently argues that management is generally more risk-averse than shareholders. If the firm's goal is to maximize shareholder wealth, then hedging activity is probably not in the best interest of the shareholders.
- Managers cannot outguess the market. If and when markets are in equilibrium with respect to parity conditions, the expected net present value of hedging is zero.

- Management's motivation to reduce variability is sometimes driven by accounting reasons. Management may believe that it will be criticized more severely for incurring foreign exchange losses in its financial statements than for incurring similar or even higher cash costs in avoiding the foreign exchange loss. Foreign exchange losses appear in the income statement as a highly visible separate line item or as a footnote, but the higher costs of protection are buried in operating or interest expenses.
- Efficient market theorists believe that investors can see through the "accounting veil" and therefore have already factored the foreign exchange effect into a firm's market valuation.

Reasons to Hedge

Proponents of hedging cite the following reasons:

- Reduction in risk in future cash flows improves the planning capability of the firm. If the firm can more accurately predict future cash flows, it may be able to undertake specific investments or activities that it might otherwise not consider.
- Reduction of risk in future cash flows reduces the likelihood that the firm's cash flows will fall below a necessary minimum. A firm must generate sufficient cash flows to make debt-service payments in order for it to continue to operate. This minimum cash flow point, often referred to as the point of *financial distress*, lies left of the center of the distribution of expected cash flows. Hedging reduces the likelihood of the firm's cash flows falling to this level.
- Management has a comparative advantage over the individual shareholder in knowing the actual currency risk of the firm. Regardless of the level of disclosure provided by the firm to the public, management always possesses an advantage in the depth and breadth of knowledge concerning the real risks and returns inherent in any firm's business.
- Markets are usually in disequilibrium because of structural and institutional imperfections, as well as unexpected external shocks (such as an oil crisis or war). Management is in a better position than shareholders to recognize disequilibrium conditions and to take advantage of one-time opportunities to enhance firm value through selective hedging. *Selective hedging* refers to the hedging of large, singular, exceptional exposures or the occasional use of hedging when management has a definite expectation of the direction of exchange rates.

Measurement of Transaction Exposure

Transaction exposure measures gains or losses that arise from the settlement of existing financial obligations whose terms are stated in a foreign currency. Transaction exposure arises from:

1. Purchasing or selling on credit goods or services when prices are stated in foreign currencies,
2. Borrowing or lending funds when repayment is to be made in a foreign currency,
3. Being a party to an unperformed foreign exchange forward contract, and
4. Otherwise acquiring assets or incurring liabilities denominated in foreign currencies.

The most common example of transaction exposure arises when a firm has a receivable or payable denominated in a foreign currency. Exhibit 8.3 demonstrates how this exposure is born.

Exhibit 8.3 The Life Span of a Transaction Exposure

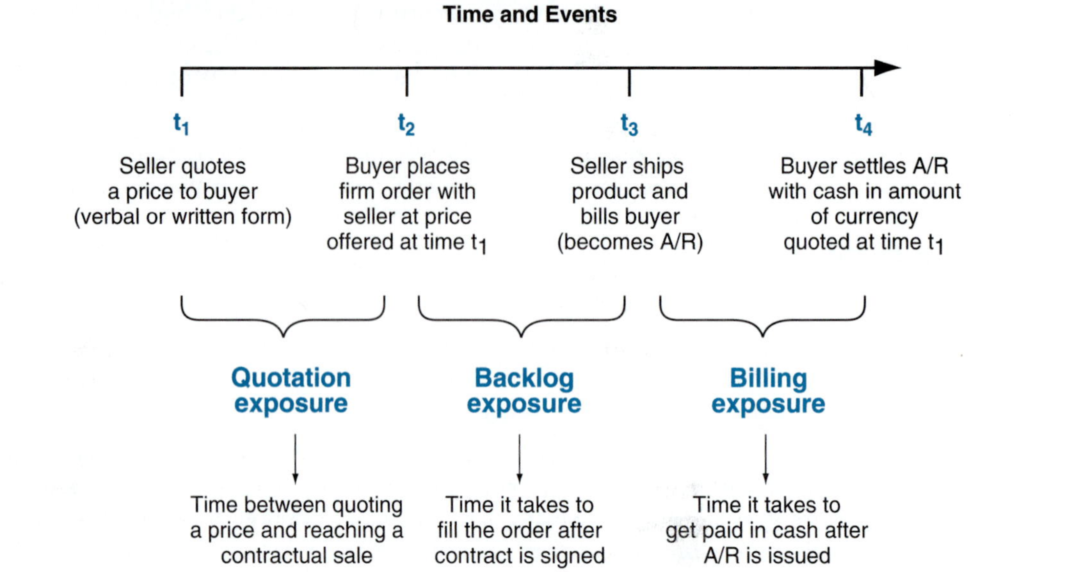
Time and Events
t_1
t_2
t_3
t_4
Seller quotes a price to buyer (verbal or written form)
Buyer places firm order with seller at price offered at time t_1
Seller ships product and bills buyer (becomes A/R)
Buyer settles A/R with cash in amount of currency quoted at time t_1
Quotation exposure
Backlog exposure
Billing exposure
Time between quoting a price and reaching a contractual sale
Time it takes to fill the order after contract is signed
Time it takes to get paid in cash after A/R is issued

The total transaction exposure consists of *quotation*, *backlog*, and *billing exposures.* A transaction exposure is actually created at the first moment the seller quotes a price in foreign currency terms to a potential buyer (t_1). The quote can be either verbal, as in a telephone quote, or in the form of a written bid or even a printed price list. With the placing of an order (t_2), the potential exposure created at the time of the quotation (t_1) is converted into actual exposure, called *backlog exposure* because the product has not yet been shipped or billed. Backlog exposure lasts until the goods are shipped and billed (t_3), at which time it becomes *billing exposure.* Billing exposure remains until actual payment is received by the seller (t_4).

Purchasing or Selling on Open Account

Suppose that a U.S. firm sells merchandise on open account to a Belgian buyer for €1,800,000, payment to be made in 60 days. The current exchange rate is \$1.1200/€, and the U.S. seller expects to exchange the euros received for €1,800,000 × \$1.1200/€ = \$2,016,000 when payment is received.

Transaction exposure arises because of the risk that the U.S. seller will receive something other than the \$2,016,000 expected. For example, if the euro weakens to \$1.0800/€ when payment is received, the U.S. seller will receive only €1,800,000 × \$1.0800/€ = \$1,944,000, or some \$72,000 less than anticipated. If the euro should strengthen to \$1.1500/€, however, the seller receives €1,800,000 × \$1.1500/€ = \$2,070,000, an increase of \$54,000 over the amount expected. Thus exposure is the chance of either a loss or a gain.

The U.S. seller might have avoided transaction exposure by invoicing the Belgian buyer in dollars. Of course, if the U.S. company attempted to sell only in dollars, it might not have obtained the sale in the first place. Avoiding transaction exposure by not having a sale is counterproductive to the well-being of the firm! Even if the Belgian buyer agrees to pay in dollars, transaction exposure is not eliminated. Instead it is transferred to the Belgian buyer, whose dollar account payable has an unknown cost in euros 60 days hence.

Borrowing and Lending

A second example of transaction exposure arises when funds are borrowed or loaned, and the amount involved is denominated in a foreign currency. For example, PepsiCo's largest bottler outside of the United States in 1994 was Grupo Embotellador de Mexico (Gemex). In mid-December, 1994, Gemex had U.S. dollar debt of $264 million. At that time Mexico's new peso ("Ps") was traded at Ps3.45/US$, a pegged rate that had been maintained with minor variations since January 1, 1993, when the new currency unit had been created. On December 22, 1994, the peso was allowed to float because of economic and political events within Mexico, and in one day it sank to Ps4.65/US$. For most of the following January it traded in a range near Ps5.50/US$.

	Debt in U.S.$	*In pesos (at Ps3.45/$)*	*In pesos (at Ps5.50/$)*
Gemex dollar-denominated debt	$264,000,000	Ps910,800,000	Ps1,452,000,000

The pesos needed to repay the dollar debt increased by Ps541,200,000 (Ps1,452,000,000 − Ps910,800,000), or 59%! In U.S. dollar terms, the drop in the value of the pesos caused Gemex to need the peso-equivalent of an additional US$98,400,000 (Ps541,200,000 ÷ Ps5.50/$) to repay. This increase in debt was the result of transaction exposure.

Other Causes of Transaction Exposure

When a firm buys a forward exchange contract, it deliberately creates transaction exposure. This risk is usually incurred to hedge an existing transaction exposure. For example, a U.S. firm might want to offset an existing obligation to purchase ¥100 million to pay for an import from Japan in 90 days. One way to offset this payment is to purchase ¥100 million in the forward market today for delivery in 90 days. In this manner, any change in value of the Japanese yen relative to the dollar is neutralized. If the yen increases in value, an unhedged account payable would cost more dollars, a transaction loss. The forward contract, however, has already fixed the amount of dollars needed to buy the ¥100 million. Thus the potential transaction loss (or gain) on the account payable has been offset by the transaction gain (or loss) on the forward contract.

Note that foreign currency cash balances do not create transaction exposure, even though their home currency value changes immediately with a change in exchange rates. No legal obligation exists to move the cash from one country and currency to another. If such an obligation did exist, it would show on the books as a payable (e.g., dividends declared and payable) or receivable and then be counted as part of transaction exposure. Nevertheless, the foreign exchange value of cash balances does change when exchange rates change. Such a change is reflected in the consolidated statement of cash flows and the consolidated balance sheet, as will be discussed in Chapter 10.

Contractual Hedges

Foreign exchange transaction exposure can be managed by *contractual*, *operating*, and *financial hedges*. The main contractual hedges employ the forward, money, futures, and options markets.

Operating and financial hedges employ the use of risk-sharing agreements, leads and lags in payment terms, swaps, and other strategies to be discussed in later chapters.

The term ***natural hedge*** refers to an off-setting operating cash flow, a payable arising from the conduct of business. A ***financial hedge*** refers to either an off-setting debt obligation (such as a loan) or some type of financial derivative such as an interest rate swap. Care should be taken to distinguish hedges in the same way finance distinguishes cash flows—*operating* from *financing*.

The following case illustrates how contractual hedging techniques may be used to protect against transaction exposure.

Dayton Manufacturing's Transaction Exposure

Scout Finch is the chief financial officer of Dayton Manufacturing, a U.S.-based manufacturer of gas turbine equipment. She has just concluded negotiations for the sale of a turbine generator to Crown, a British firm, for £1,000,000. This single sale is quite large in relation to Dayton's present business. Dayton has no other current foreign customers, so the currency risk of this sale is of particular concern. The sale is made in March with payment due three months later in June. Scout Finch has collected the following financial and market information for the analysis of her currency exposure problem:

- Spot exchange rate: \$1.7640/£
- Three-month forward rate: \$1.7540/£ (a 2.2676% per annum discount on the pound)
- Dayton's cost of capital: 12.0%
- U.K. three-month borrowing interest rate: 10.0% (or 2.5%/quarter)
- U.K. three-month investment interest rate: 8.0% (or 2.0%/quarter)
- U.S. three-month borrowing interest rate: 8.0% (or 2.0%/quarter)
- U.S. three-month investment interest rate: 6.0% (or 1.5%/quarter)
- June put option in the over-the-counter (bank) market for £1,000,000; strike price \$1.75 (nearly at-the-money); 1.5% premium
- June put option in the over-the-counter (bank) market for £1,000,000; strike price \$1.71 (out-of-the-money); 1.0% premium
- Dayton's foreign exchange advisory service forecasts that the spot rate in three months will be \$1.76/£.

Like many manufacturing firms, Dayton operates on relatively narrow margins. Although Ms. Finch and Dayton would be very happy if the pound appreciated versus the dollar, concerns center on the possibility that the pound will fall. When Ms. Finch budgeted this specific contract, she determined that its minimum acceptable margin was at a sales price of \$1,700,000. The *budget rate*, the lowest acceptable dollar per pound exchange rate, was therefore established at \$1.70/£. Any exchange rate below this budget rate would result in Dayton actually losing money on the transaction.

Four alternatives are available to Dayton to manage the exposure:

1. Remain unhedged.
2. Hedge in the forward market.

3. Hedge in the money market.
4. Hedge in the options market.

Unhedged Position

Scout Finch may decide to accept the transaction risk. If she believes the foreign exchange advisor, she expects to receive £1,000,000 × \$1.76 = \$1,760,000 in three months. However, that amount is at risk. If the pound should fall to, say, \$1.65/£, she will receive only \$1,650,000. Exchange risk is not one-sided, however; if the transaction is left uncovered and the pound strengthened even more than forecast by the advisor, Dayton will receive considerably more than \$1,760,000.

The essence of an unhedged approach is as follows:

(Today)	(Three months hence)
Do nothing.	Receive £1,000,000. Sell £1,000,000 spot and receive dollars at that day's spot rate.

Forward Market Hedge

A *forward hedge* involves a forward (or futures) contract and a source of funds to fulfill that contract. The forward contract is entered into at the time the transaction exposure is created. In Dayton's case, that would be in March, when the sale to Crown was booked as an account receivable. Funds to fulfill the contract will be available in June, when Crown pays £1,000,000 to Dayton. If funds to fulfill the forward contract are on hand or are due because of a business operation, the hedge is considered "covered," "perfect," or "square" because no residual foreign exchange risk exists. Funds on hand or to be received are matched by funds to be paid.

In some situations, funds to fulfill the forward exchange contract are not already available or due to be received later, but must be purchased in the spot market at some future date. Such a hedge is "open" or "uncovered." It involves considerable risk because the hedger must take a chance on purchasing foreign exchange at an uncertain future spot rate in order to fulfill the forward contract. Purchase of such funds at a later date is referred to as *covering*. There is an old financial saying that is appropriate for an uncovered forward obligation:

He who sells what isn't his'n
Must buy it back or go to prison![1]

Should Dayton wish to hedge its transaction exposure in the forward market, it will sell £1,000,000 forward today at the three-month forward quotation of \$1.7540 per pound. This is a "covered transaction" in which the firm no longer has any foreign exchange risk. In three

1. This quotation is attributed to Daniel Drew, in Bouck White, *The Book of Daniel Drew* (New York: George H. Doran Company, 1910), p. 180.

months, the firm will receive £1,000,000 from the British buyer, deliver that sum to the bank against its forward sale, and receive \$1,754,000. This certain sum is \$6,000 less than the uncertain \$1,760,000 expected from the unhedged position because the forward market quotation differs from the firm's three-month forecast. However, it would be recorded on Dayton's income statement as a foreign exchange loss of \$10,000 (\$1,764,000 as booked, \$1,754,000 as settled).

The essence of a forward hedge is as follows:

(Today)	(Three months hence)
Sell £1,000,000 forward at \$1.7540/£.	Receive £1,000,000. Deliver £1,000,000 against forward sale. Receive \$1,754,000.

If Scout Finch's forecast of future rates were identical to that implicit in the forward quotation—that is, \$1.7540—expected receipts would be the same whether or not the firm hedges. However, realized receipts under the unhedged alternative could vary considerably from the certain receipts when the transaction is hedged. Belief that the forward rate is an unbiased estimate of the future spot rate does not preclude use of the forward hedge to eliminate the risk of an unexpected change in the future spot rate.

Money Market Hedge

Like a forward market hedge, a *money market hedge* also involves a contract and a source of funds to fulfill that contract. In this instance, the contract is a loan agreement. The firm seeking the money market hedge borrows in one currency and exchanges the proceeds for another currency. Funds to fulfill the contract—that is, to repay the loan—may be generated from business operations, in which case the money market hedge is *covered*. Alternatively, funds to repay the loan may be purchased in the foreign exchange spot market when the loan matures. In this instance, the money market hedge is *uncovered* or *open*.

A money market hedge can cover a single transaction, such as Dayton's £1,000,000 receivable, or repeated transactions. Hedging repeated transactions is called *matching*. It requires the firm to match the expected foreign currency cash inflows and outflows by currency and maturity. For example, if Dayton had numerous sales denominated in pounds to British customers over a long period of time, it would have somewhat predictable U.K. pound cash inflows. The appropriate money market hedge technique would be to borrow U.K. pounds in an amount matching the typical size and maturity of expected pound inflows. Then, if the pound depreciated or appreciated, the foreign exchange effect on cash inflows in pounds would be approximately offset by the effect on cash outflows in pounds from repaying the pound loan plus interest.

The structure of a money market hedge resembles that of a forward hedge. The difference is that the cost of the money market hedge is determined by differential interest rates, while the cost of the forward hedge is a function of the forward rate quotation. In efficient markets, interest rate parity should ensure that these costs are nearly the same, but not all markets are efficient at all times. Furthermore, the difference in interest rates facing a private firm borrowing in two separate national markets may be different than the difference in risk-free government bill rates or Eurocurrency interest rates in these same markets. It is the latter differential that is relevant for interest rate parity.

To hedge in the money market, Ms. Finch will borrow pounds in London at once, immediately convert the borrowed pounds into dollars, and repay the pound loan in three months with the proceeds from the sale of the generator. How much should she borrow? She will need to borrow just enough to repay both the principal and interest with the sale proceeds. The borrowing interest rate will be 10% per annum, or 2.5% for three months. Therefore, the amount to borrow now for repayment in three months is:

$$\frac{£1,000,000}{1+.025} = £975,610$$

Scout Finch should borrow £975,610 now and in three months repay that amount plus £24,390 of interest from the sale proceeds of the account receivable. Dayton would exchange the £975,610 loan proceeds for dollars at the current spot exchange rate of $1.7640/£, receiving $1,720,976 at once.

The money-market hedge, if selected by Dayton, actually creates a pound-denominated liability, the pound loan, to offset the pound-denominated asset, the account receivable. The money market hedge works as a hedge by matching assets and liabilities according to their currency of denomination. Using a simple T-account illustrating Dayton's balance sheet, the loan in British pounds is seen to offset the pound-denominated account receivable:

Assets		*Liabilities and Net Worth*	
Account receivable	£1,000,000	Bank loan (principal)	£975,610
		Interest payable	+ 24,390
	£1,000,000		£1,000,000

The loan acts as a *balance sheet hedge*—a money market hedge in this case—against the pound-denominated account receivable.

To compare the forward hedge with the money market hedge, one must analyze how Dayton's loan proceeds will be utilized for the next three months. Remember that the loan proceeds are received today but the forward contract proceeds are received in three months. For comparison purposes, one must either calculate the future value in three months of the loan proceeds or the present value of the forward contract proceeds. (We will use future value for pedagogical reasons, but correct use of present value would give the same comparative results.)

As both the forward contract proceeds and the loan proceeds are relatively certain, it is possible to make a clear choice between the two alternatives based on the one that yields the higher dollar receipts. This result in turn depends on the assumed rate of investment of the loan proceeds.

At least three logical choices exist for an assumed investment rate for the loan proceeds for the next three months. First, if Dayton is cash-rich, the loan proceeds might be invested in U.S. dollar money market instruments that have been assumed to yield 6% per annum. Second, Scout

Finch might simply use the pound loan proceeds to substitute for an equal dollar loan that Dayton would otherwise have undertaken at an assumed rate of 8% per annum. Third, Scout Finch might invest the loan proceeds in the general operations of the firm, in which case the cost of capital of 12% per annum would be the appropriate rate. The future value of the loan proceeds at the end of three months under each of these three investment assumptions would be as follows:

Received today	*Invested in*	*Rate*	*Full value in three months*
\$1,720,976	Treasury bill	6%/yr or 1.5%/quarter	\$1,746,791
\$1,720,976	Debt cost	8%/yr or 2.0%/quarter	\$1,755,396
\$1,720,976	Cost of capital	12%/yr or 3.0%/quarter	\$1,772,605

Because the proceeds in three months from the forward hedge would be \$1,754,000, the money market hedge is superior to the forward hedge if Scout Finch used the loan proceeds to replace a dollar loan (8%) or to conduct general business operations (12%). The forward hedge would be preferable if Dayton merely invested the pound loan proceeds in dollar-denominated money market instruments at 6% annual interest.

A break-even investment rate can be calculated that would make Dayton indifferent between the forward hedge and the money market hedge. Assume that r is the unknown three-month investment rate, expressed as a decimal, that would equalize the proceeds from the forward and money market hedges. We have:

$$\begin{gathered}(\text{loan proceeds})\ (1 + \text{rate}) = (\text{forward proceeds}),\\ \$1{,}720{,}976\ (1 + r) = \$1{,}754{,}000\\ r = 0.0192\end{gathered}$$

We can convert this three-month (90 days) investment rate to an annual whole percentage equivalent, assuming a 360-day financial year, as follows:

$$0.0192 \times \frac{360}{90} \times 100 = 7.68\%$$

In other words, if Scout Finch can invest the loan proceeds at a rate higher than 7.68% per annum, she would prefer the money market hedge. If she can only invest at a lower rate than 7.68%, she would prefer the forward hedge.

The essence of a money market hedge is as follows:

(Today)	(Three months hence)
Borrow £975,610. Exchange £975,610 for dollars at \$1.7640/£. Receive \$1,720,976 cash.	Receive £1,000,000. Repay £975,610 loan plus £24,390 interest, for a total of £1,000,000.

Options Market Hedge

Scout Finch could also cover her £1,000,000 exposure by purchasing a put option. This technique allows her to speculate on the upside potential for appreciation of the pound while limiting downside risk to a known amount. Given the two quotes shown earlier, Scout Finch could purchase from her bank a three-month put option on £1,000,000 at either 1) an at-the-money (ATM) strike price of \$1.75/£ (and a premium cost of 1.50%), or 2) an out-of-the-money (OTM) strike price of \$1.71/£ (and a premium cost of 1.00%). The cost of the first option with strike price of \$1.75, a strike price that would be considered close to forward-at-the-money, is:[2]

$$(\text{size of option}) \times (\text{premium}) \times (\text{spot rate}) = \text{cost of option},$$
$$£1{,}000{,}000 \times 0.015 \times \$1.7640 = \$26{,}460$$

Because we are using future value to compare the various hedging alternatives, it is necessary to project the premium cost of the option forward three months. Once again one could justify several investment rates. We will use the cost of capital of 12% per annum or 3% per quarter. Therefore the premium cost of the put option as of June would be \$26,460(1.03) = \$27,254. This is equal to \$0.0273 per pound (\$27,254 ÷ £1,000,000).

When the £1,000,000 is received in June, the value in dollars depends on the spot rate at that time. The upside potential is unlimited, the same as in the unhedged alternative. At any exchange rate above \$1.75/£, Dayton would allow its option to expire unexercised and would exchange the pounds for dollars at the spot rate. If the expected rate of \$1.76/£ materializes, for example, Dayton would exchange the £1,000,000 in the spot market for \$1,760,000. Net proceeds would be \$1,760,000 minus the \$27,254 cost of the option, or \$1,732,746.

In contrast to the unhedged alternative, downside risk is limited with an option. If the pound depreciates below \$1.75/£, Scout Finch would exercise her option to sell (put) £1,000,000 at \$1.75/£, receiving \$1,750,000 gross, but \$1,722,746 net of the \$27,254 cost of the option. Although this downside result is worse than the downside of the forward or money market hedges, the upside potential is not limited the way it is with those hedges. Thus, whether the option strategy is superior to a forward or money market hedge depends on the degree to which management is risk-averse.

The essence of the at-the-money (ATM) option market hedge is as follows:

(Today)	(Three months hence)
Buy put option to sell pounds at \$1.75/£. Pay \$26,460 for put option.	Receive £1,000,000. Either deliver £1,000,000 against put, receiving \$1,750,000, or sell £1,000,000 spot if current spot rate is greater than \$1.75/£.

2. Recall from Chapter 5 that currency options are priced on the basis of the forward rate. An option that possesses a strike price that is the same as the forward rate is called forward-at-the-money.

We can calculate a trading range for the pound that defines the break-even points for the option compared with the other strategies. The upper bound of the range is determined by comparison with the forward rate. The pound must appreciate enough above the $1.7540 forward rate to cover the $0.0273/£ cost of the option. Therefore the break-even upside spot price of the pound must be $1.7540 + $0.0273 = $1.7813. If the spot pound appreciates above $1.7813, proceeds under the option strategy will be greater than under the forward hedge. If the spot pound ends up below $1.7813, the forward hedge would be superior in retrospect.

The lower bound of the range is determined by a comparison with the unhedged strategy. If the spot price falls below $1.75/£, Scout Finch will exercise her put option and sell the proceeds at $1.75/£. The net proceeds per pound will be $1.75/£ less the $0.0273 cost of the option, or $1.7221/£. If the spot rate falls below $1.7221/£, the net proceeds from exercising the option will be greater than the net proceeds from selling the unhedged pounds in the spot market. At any spot rate above $1.7221/£, the spot proceeds from the unhedged alternative will be greater.

The same basic calculations, costs, and breakeven points can be determined for the second option, the one with a strike price of $1.71/£. It has a smaller premium cost because it is out-of-the-money (OTM). The cost of the $1.71/£ strike put option = £1,000,000 × 0.010 × $1.7640 = $17,640. In future value terms, $17,640 × 1.03 = $18,169.20 ($0.018169/£). The break-even rate versus the forward rate is $1.7540 + $0.0182 = $1.7722/£. The resulting comparison of the two alternative over-the-counter options appears as follows:

Put option strike price	*ATM option $1.75/£*	*OTM option $1.71/£*
Option cost (future value)	$27,254	$18,169
Proceeds if exercised	$1,750,000	$1,710,000
Minimum net proceeds	$1,722,746	$1,691,831
Maximum net proceeds	Unlimited	Unlimited
Break-even spot rate (upside)	$1.7813/£	$1.7722/£
Break-even spot rate (downside)	$1.7221/£	$1.6918/£

Comparison of Alternatives

The four alternatives available to Scout Finch and Dayton are shown in Exhibit 8.4. The forward hedge yields a certain $1,754,000 in three months. This is equivalent to a money market hedge if the loan proceeds are invested at 7.68% per annum. At any higher rate, such as the 12% cost of capital, the money market hedge is preferable, but at any lower rate, the forward hedge is preferable.

If Scout Finch does not hedge, she can "expect" $1,760,000 in three months. However, this sum is at risk and might be greater or smaller. Under conditions when the forward rate is accepted as the most likely future spot rate, the expected results from an unhedged position are identical to the certain results from the forward hedge. Under such circumstances the advantage of hedging over remaining unhedged is the reduction of uncertainty.

The two put options offer a unique alternative. If the exchange rate moves in Dayton's favor, both options have nearly the same upside potential as the unhedged alternative except for their

Exhibit 8.4 Comparison of Alternative Hedging Strategies for Dayton

Goal: Receive maximum dollars from sale

Unhedged alternative	**Result**
Wait three months then sell £1,000,000 for dollars in the spot market	Receive in three months: 1. An unlimited maximum; 2. An expected $1,760,000; or 3. A zero minimum
Forward market hedge	**Result**
Sell £1,000,000 forward for dollars at once	Certain receipts of $1,754,000 in three months
Money market hedge	**Result**
1. Borrow £975,610 in U.K. at 10% 2. Exchange for $1,720,976 at spot rate 3. Invest in U.S. for three months	Receive $1,720,976 at once. Value in three months depends on U.S. investment assumption: 1. At break-even rate of 7.68%, receive $1,754,000. 2. At cost of capital of 12% receive an expected $1,772,605.
Options market hedge	**Result**
Purchase a three-month put option of £1,000,000 with strike price of $1.75/£ and premium cost of $27,254 (after 3 months)	Receive in three months: 1. An unlimited maximum less $27,254; 2. An expected $1,760,000 less $27,254, or $1,732,746; 3. A minimum of $1,750,000 less $27,254, or $1,722,746.

up-front costs. If, however, the exchange rate moves against Dayton, the put options limit the downside risk to net receipts of either $1,722,746 for the $1.75/£ strike put, or $1,691,831 for the $1.71/£ strike put.

Foreign currency options have a variety of hedging uses beyond the one illustrated here. A put option is useful to construction firms or other exporters when they must submit a fixed price bid in a foreign currency without knowing until some later date whether their bid is successful. A put option can be used to hedge the foreign exchange risk either for the bidding period alone or for the entire period of potential exposure if the bid is won. If the bid is rejected, the loss is limited to the cost of the option. In contrast, if the risk is hedged by a forward contract and the bid is rejected, the forward contract must be reversed or eventually fulfilled at an unknown potential loss or gain. The bidder has been holding what turned out to be an uncovered forward contract.

Strategy Choice and Outcome

The preceding section compared hedging alternatives available to Dayton. Dayton, like all firms attempting to hedge transaction exposure, must decide on a strategy before the exchange rate changes occur. Exhibit 8.5 provides an evaluation of each potential strategy open to Dayton over a range of exchange rates that may occur at the end of the three-month period.

Exhibit 8.5 Valuation of Cash Flows Under Hedging Alternatives for Dayton

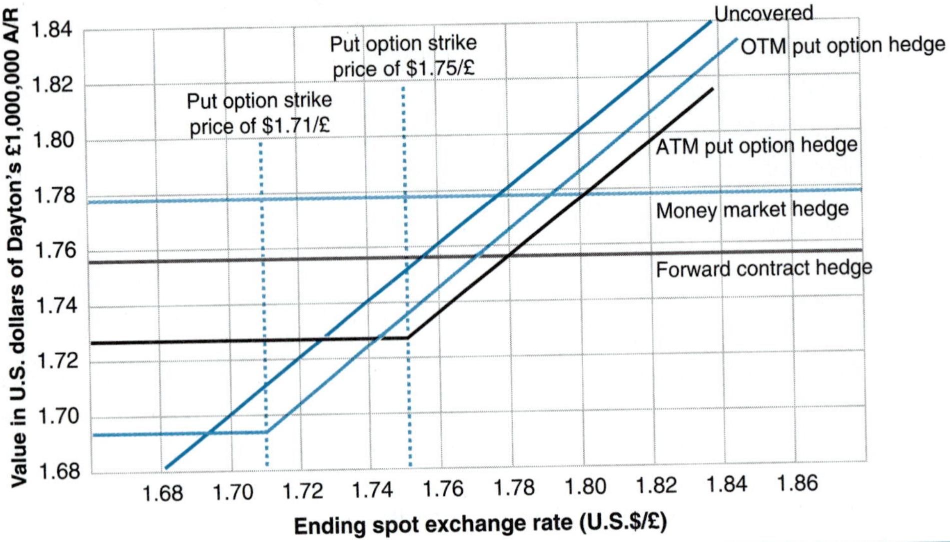

How will Scout Finch of Dayton choose among the alternative hedging strategies? She must select on the basis of two decision criteria: 1) the *risk tolerance* of Dayton, as expressed in its stated policies; and 2) her own *view*, or expectation of the direction (and how far) the exchange rate will move over the coming three-month period.

Dayton's *risk tolerance* is a combination of management's philosophy towards transaction exposure and the specific goals of treasury activities. Many firms believe that currency risk is simply a part of doing business internationally, and therefore start their analysis from an unhedged baseline. Other firms, however, view currency risk as unacceptable, and either start their analysis from a full forward contract cover baseline, or simply mandate that all transaction exposures be fully covered by forward contracts regardless of the value of other hedging alternatives. The treasury in such firms operates as a cost or service center for the firm. On the other hand, if the treasury operates as a profit center, it might tolerate taking more risks.

If management is willing to consider all alternatives, the firm's *view* of likely exchange rate changes aids in the hedging choice. As is evident from Exhibit 8.5, if the exchange rate is expected to move against Dayton, to the left of $1.76/£, the money market hedge is the clearly preferred alternative. At a guaranteed value of $1,772,605, the money market hedge is by far the most profitable choice. If the exchange rate is expected to move in Dayton's favor, to the right of $1.76/£, the choice of the hedge is more complex. Consider the following points:

- If the spot rate is expected to move to the right of $1.77/£, the unhedged alternative always provides the highest U.S. dollar value for the receivable.
- If Scout Finch is worried that her expectations may prove incorrect, the decision to remain unhedged does not assure Dayton of meeting its budgeted exchange rate of $1.70/£. This is

an outcome that the firm cannot afford. The possibility always exists of a major political or economic event disrupting international currency markets unexpectedly.

- If the spot rate is expected to move to the right of \$1.77/£, but not far to the right—for example \$1.78/£—the expected benefits of remaining unhedged versus the risks of remaining unhedged are probably not worth it. The money market hedge is still the preferred choice.
- If the spot rate is expected to move far to the right of \$1.76/£ such as \$1.84/£, the put option potentially would allow Dayton to enjoy the up-side movement and simultaneously provide a safety net of a minimum value if the puts are exercised.
- If the spot rate is expected to move so far to the right that Dayton considers both put options, the choice is one of tradeoffs. The \$1.71/£ strike put option is significantly cheaper, but also provides a lower level of protection (\$1,691,831 minimum net proceeds as opposed to the \$1,722,746 assured by the \$1.75/£ strike put). You get what you pay for. The decision in this case is simplified for Dayton because the OTM put option does not assure Dayton, after premium expenses, of meeting its budgeted exchange rate of \$1.70/£ (or minimum net proceeds of \$1,700,000).

The final choice among hedges (if Scout Finch does expect the pound to appreciate) combines both the firm's risk tolerance, its view, and its confidence in its view. Transaction exposure management with contractual hedges requires managerial judgement.

Management of an Account Payable

The Dayton Manufacturing case as discussed so far assumes a foreign currency denominated receivable. The management of an account payable, where the firm would be required to make a foreign currency payment at a future date, is similar but not identical in form.

If Dayton had a £1,000,000 account payable in 90 days, the hedging choices would appear as follows:

1. *Remain unhedged.* Dayton could wait 90 days, exchange dollars for pounds at that time, and make its payment. If Dayton expects the spot rate in 90 days to be \$1.7600/£, the payment would be expected to cost \$1,760,000. This amount is, however, uncertain; the spot exchange rate in 90 days could be very different from that expected.
2. *Forward market hedge.* Dayton could buy £1,000,000 forward, locking in a rate of \$1.7540/£, and a total dollar cost of \$1,754,000. This is \$6,000 less than the expected cost of remaining unhedged and therefore clearly preferable to the first alternative.
3. *Money market hedge.* The money market hedge is distinctly different for a payable as opposed to a receivable. To implement a money market hedge in this case, Dayton would exchange U.S. dollars spot and invest them for 90 days in a pound-denominated interest-bearing account. The principal and interest in British pounds at the end of the 90-day period would be used to pay the £1,000,000 account payable.

In order to assure that the principal and interest exactly equal the £1,000,000 due in 90 days, Dayton would discount the £1,000,000 by the pound investment interest rate of 8% for 90 days in order to determine the pounds needed today:

$$\frac{£1,000,000}{\left[1+\left(0.08\times\frac{90}{360}\right)\right]}=£980,392.16$$

This £980,392.16 needed today would require \$1,729,411.77 at the current spot rate of \$1.7640/£:

$$£980,392.16\times\$1.7640/£=\$1,729,411.77$$

Finally, in order to compare the money market hedge outcome with the other hedging alternatives, the \$1,729,411.77 cost today must be carried forward 90 days to the same future date as the other hedge choices. If the current dollar cost is carried forward at Dayton's WACC of 12%, the total cost of the money market hedge is \$1,781,294.12:

$$\$1,729,411.77\times\left[1+\left(0.12\times\frac{90}{360}\right)\right]=\$1,781,294.12$$

This is higher than the forward hedge and therefore unattractive.

4. *Option hedge*. Dayton could cover its £1,000,000 account payable by purchasing a call option on £1,000,000. A June call option on British pounds with a near at-the-money strike price of \$1.75/£ would cost 1.5% (premium) or:

$$£1,000,000\times0.015\times\$1.7640/£=\$26,460$$

This premium, regardless of whether the call option is exercised, will be paid up front. Its value carried forward 90 days at the WACC of 12%, as it was in the receivable example, would raise its end of period cost to \$27,254.

If the spot rate in 90 days is less than \$1.75/£, the option would be allowed to expire and the £1,000,000 for the payable purchased on the spot market. The total cost of the call option hedge if the option is not exercised is theoretically smaller than any other alternative (with the exception of remaining unhedged, because the option premium is still paid and lost).

If the spot rate in 90 days exceeds \$1.75/£, the call option would be exercised. The total cost of the call option hedge if exercised is as follows:

Exercise call option (£1,000,000 × \$1.75/£)	\$1,750,000
Call option premium (carried forward 90 days)	+ 27,254
Total maximum expense of call option hedge	\$1,777,254

The four hedging methods of managing a £1,000,000 account payable for Dayton are summarized in Exhibit 8.6. The costs of the forward hedge and money market hedge are certain. The cost of using the call option hedge is calculated as a maximum, and the cost of remaining unhedged is highly uncertain.

As with Dayton's account receivable, the final hedging choice depends on the confidence of Scout Finch's exchange rate expectations, and her willingness to bear risk. The forward hedge provides the lowest cost of making the account payable payment that is certain. If the dollar

Exhibit 8.6 Valuation of Hedging Alternatives for an Account Payable

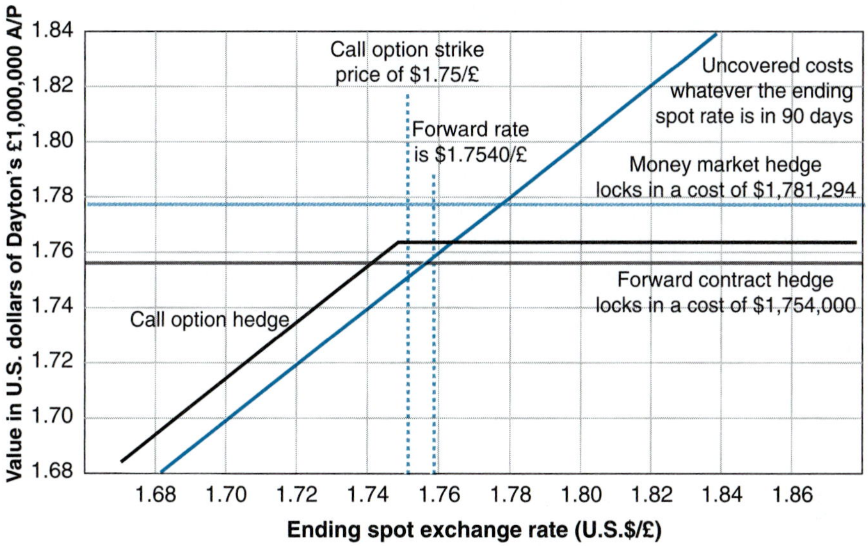

strengthens against the pound, ending up at a spot rate less than $1.75/£, the call option could potentially be the lowest cost hedge. Given an expected spot rate of $1.76/£, however, the forward hedge appears the preferred alternative.

Risk Management in Practice

As many different approaches to exposure management exist as there are firms. A variety of surveys of corporate risk management practices in recent years in the United States, the United Kingdom, Finland, Australia, and Germany indicate no real consensus exists regarding the best approach.[3] The following is our attempt to assimilate the basic results of these surveys and combine them with our own personal experiences in industry.

Which Goals?

The treasury function of most private firms, the group typically responsible for transaction exposure management, is usually considered a cost center. It is not expected to add profit to the firm's bottom line (which is not the same thing as saying it is not expected to add value to the firm). Currency risk managers are expected to err on the conservative side when managing the firm's money. But as illustrated in Global Finance Perspective 8.2, some MNEs have become a bit too aggressive in currency management, according to the IRS.

3. For a recent study of financial risk management by U.S. non-financial firms see: Bodnar, Gordon M., "1998 Wharton Survey of Financial Risk Management by U.S. Non-Financial Firms," *Financial Management*, Volume 24, No. 4, Winter 1998, pp. 70–91.

Global Finance Perspective 8.2

Manipulation of Currency Gains and Losses

The Internal Revenue Service (IRS) of the United States became increasingly concerned in the spring of 2002 about the possible manipulation of corporate earnings—specifically currency-related gains and losses. The government agency detected more and more companies that were creating a "circular flow of funds" in which the parent company and a foreign subsidiary would exchange cash flows for a very short time (in several cases overnight), suffering foreign exchange losses on the transactions. The losses were then used to reduce tax liabilities in the United States. The cash flows exchanged were suspicious because they reflected no underlying business reason. One set of potential solutions under consideration is the elimination of daily calculation of currency gains and losses, as well as requiring all international transactions reported for tax purposes to reflect an underlying business reason.

Which Exposures?

Transaction exposures exist before they are actually booked as foreign currency-denominated receivables and payables. However, many firms do not allow the hedging of quotation exposure or backlog exposure as a matter of policy. The reasoning is straightforward: until the transaction exists on the accounting books of the firm, the probability of the exposure actually occurring is considered to be less than 100%. Conservative hedging policies dictate that contractual hedges be placed only on existing exposures.

An increasing number of firms, however, are actively hedging not only backlog exposures, but also selectively hedging quotation and anticipated exposures. *Anticipated exposures* are transactions for which there are—at present—no contracts or agreements between parties, but which are anticipated on the basis of historical trends and continuing business relationships. Although on the surface this would appear to be overly speculative behavior on the part of these firms, it may be that hedging expected foreign-currency payables and receivables for future periods is the most conservative approach to protect the firm's future operating revenues against unexpected exchange rate changes. Anticipatory hedging programs have been the focus of considerable debate in recent years, particularly the accounting principles that apply to their use. Exhibit 8.7 reports the results of one survey of corporate risk management practices conducted by Bank of America.

Which Contractual Hedges?

As might be expected, transaction exposure management programs are generally divided along an "option-line": those that use options and those that do not. Firms that do not use currency options rely almost exclusively on forward contracts and money market hedges. Many firms with appreciable quantities of transaction exposure actually do no hedging at all.

Proportional hedges. Many MNEs have established rather rigid transaction exposure risk management policies that mandate proportional hedging. These policies generally require the use of forward contract hedges on a percentage (e.g., 50, 60, or 70%) of existing transaction exposures. As the maturity of the exposures lengthens, the percentage forward-cover required decreases. The remaining portion of the exposure is then selectively hedged on the basis of the firm's risk tolerance, view of exchange rate movements, and confidence level.

Exhibit 8.7 Bank of America Corporate FX Risk Management Survey Results

- **Translation Management**
  80% identify this exposure; 15% fully hedge; 15% partially or selectively hedge;
  70% do not hedge; forwards used 73% of the time, options used 27%
- **Transaction Exposure**
  60% identify this exposure; 30% fully hedge; 55% partially or selectively hedge;
  20% do not hedge; forwards used 83% of the time, options used 17%
- **Anticipated Exposure**
  70% identify this exposure; 2% fully hedge; 55% partially or selectively hedge;
  43% do not hedge; forwards used 71% of the time, options used 29%
- **Contingent Exposure**
  52% identify this exposure; 4% fully hedge; 11% partially or selectively hedge;
  85% do not hedge; forwards used 63% of the time, options used 37%
- **Economic Exposure**
  54% identify this exposure; 5% fully hedge;
  95% do not hedge; forwards used 54% of the time, options used 46%
- **Balance Sheet Exposure**
  30% identify this exposure; 6% fully hedge; 15% partially or selectively hedge;
  78% do not hedge; forwards used 74% of the time, options used 26%
- **Income Statement Exposure**
  44% identify this exposure; 6% fully hedge; 33% partially or selectively hedge;
  61% do not hedge; forwards used 66% of the time, options used 34%
- **Firm Hedging Maturities**
  21% of hedges are for maturities of less than six months; 62% are for maturities of six months to one year; 17% are for maturities over one year
- **Functional Currency of Foreign Affiliates**
  33% USD; 66% local currency

Source: "Corporate America: FX Risk Management 1996," Global Capital Markets Group, Bank of America, Monograph 78, Winter 1996/97, pp. 1–3.

Although rarely acknowledged by the firms themselves, the continual use of selective hedging programs is essentially speculation against the currency markets. Significant theoretical questions remain as to whether a firm or a financial manager can consistently predict the future direction of exchange rate movements. One informed observer has noted: "it may occasionally be possible to find money lying in the street, but I would not expect to make a living at it."[4]

Forward points. In addition to having required minimum forward-cover percentages, many firms also require full forward-cover when forward rates "pay them the points." The *points on the forward rate* is the forward rate's premium or discount.

4. Professor Gunter Dufey, University of Michigan, undated.

For example, using the same situation and financial assumptions as in the Dayton case, the forward rate of \$1.7540/£ could be the result of the following 90-day Eurocurrency interest rates on U.S. dollars (6.80% per annum) and British pounds (9.12% per annum):

$$\text{Forward}_{90} = \$1.7640/£ \times \left[\frac{1+\left(0.0680 \times \frac{90}{360}\right)}{1+\left(0.0912 \times \frac{90}{360}\right)}\right] = £1.7540/£$$

Because British pound interest rates are higher than U.S. dollar interest rates, the pound is selling forward at a discount. A firm purchasing a forward contract to sell pounds forward would itself be *paying the points.*

If U.S. dollar interest rates (6.80% per annum) were higher than British pound interest rates (6.00% per annum), the pound would be selling forward at a premium:

$$\text{Forward}_{90} = \$1.7640/£ \times \left[\frac{1+\left(0.0680 \times \frac{90}{360}\right)}{1+\left(0.0600 \times \frac{90}{360}\right)}\right] = £1.7675/£$$

A forward rate of \$1.7675/£ would allow Dayton to lock in an exchange rate for 90 days in the future, which is better than the exchange rate that would be realized even if Dayton received the British pounds today.

Many firms require that when the firm earns the forward points (as shown in this example) that full forward-cover be put in place. Not only is the exchange rate in the firm's favor, it also allows the firm to earn a U.S. dollar effective rate that meets its budget exchange rate, and a hedge choice that is independent of the firm's exchange rate view. Although the favorable forward rate is a result only of interest rate differences, many firms view this as riskless profit.

Bought currency options. A further distinction in practice can be made between those firms that buy currency options (buy a put or buy a call) and those that both buy and write currency options. Those firms that do use currency options are generally more aggressive in their tolerance of currency risk. This is a generalization, however, and in many cases firms that are extremely conservative and risk-intolerant may be hedging all existing exposures with forwards and then additionally hedging a variety of backlog and anticipated exposures with options. The currency options used by MNEs are nearly exclusively over-the-counter in origination and European in pricing style.

Hedgers with some degree of settlement risk may find it in their best interest to purchase protective options with maturities longer than the expected exposure maturity. This allows the hedger to at least recapture some of the option premium investment through resale if the exposure cash flow does indeed not occur as expected. The hedger must then determine if the added benefits of a longer maturity and security in settlement risk coverage are worth the added expense.

Written currency options. Since the writer of an option has a limited profit potential with unlimited loss potential, the risks associated with writing options can be substantial. Firms that write options usually do so to finance the purchase of a second option. For example, a firm such as Dayton, that is long British pounds, may write an out-of-the-money call option on pounds to partially offset the expense of purchasing an at-the-money put option on the same quantity of British pounds. These so-called *complex options* are gaining ever wider use in industry. The most frequently used complex options are *range forwards*, *participating forwards*, *break forwards*, and *average rate options* (see Chapter 24).

If the hedger were actually writing options as part of its exposure management program, it would be beneficial to write relatively short-term options with rapidly deteriorating prices. This technique allows the writer to gain the benefits of the sale, the initial premium, yet in most cases rest assured that time value deterioration will cause the value of the option to drop precipitously soon after sale, making any possible repurchase of the option affordable.

SUMMARY

- MNEs encounter three types of currency exposure: 1) transaction exposure; 2) operating exposure; and 3) accounting (translation) exposure.
- Transaction exposure measures gains or losses that arise from the settlement of financial obligations whose terms are stated in a foreign currency. Transaction exposure arises from 1) purchasing or selling on credit goods or services whose prices are stated in foreign currencies; 2) borrowing or lending funds when repayment is to be made in a foreign currency; 3) being a party to an unperformed forward foreign exchange contract; and 4) otherwise acquiring assets or liabilities denominated in foreign currencies.
- Considerable theoretical debate exists as to whether firms should hedge currency risk. Theoretically, hedging reduces the variability of the cash flows to the firm. It does not increase the cash flows to the firm. In fact, the costs of hedging may potentially lower the firm's cash flows.
- Transaction exposure can be managed by contractual techniques and certain financing strategies. Contractual hedging techniques include forward, futures, money market, and option hedges.
- The choice of which contractual hedge to use depends on the individual firm's currency risk tolerance and its expectation of the probable movement of exchange rates over the transaction exposure period.
- In general, if an exchange rate is expected to move in a firm's favor, the preferred contractual hedges are probably those which allow it to participate in some up-side potential (remaining unhedged or using a currency option), but protect it against significant adverse exchange rate movements.
- In general, if the exchange rate is expected to move against the firm, the preferred contractual hedge is one that locks in an exchange rate, such as the forward contract hedge or money market hedge.
- Risk management in practice requires a firm's Treasury department to identify its goals. Is Treasury a cost center or profit center?
- Treasury must also choose which contractual hedges it wishes to use and what proportion of the currency risk should be hedged. Additionally, Treasury must determine whether the firm should buy and/or sell currency options, a strategy that has historically been risky for some firms and banks.

QUESTIONS

1. **Definitions.**
   a. Define the term *foreign exchange exposure.*
   b. Define the four types of foreign exchange exposure.
2. **Hedging and currency risk.**
   a. Define the term *hedging.*
   b. Define the term *currency risk.*
3. **Arguments against currency risk management.** What are six arguments against a firm pursuing an active currency risk management program?
4. **Arguments for currency risk management.** What are four arguments in favor of a firm pursuing an active currency risk management program?
5. **Transaction exposure.** What are the four main types of transactions from which transaction exposure arises?
6. **Life span of a transaction exposure.** Diagram the life span of an exposure arising from selling a product on open account. On the diagram define and show *quotation, backlog,* and *billing* exposures.
7. **Borrowing exposure.** Give an example of a transaction exposure that arises from borrowing in a foreign currency.
8. **Cash balances.** Explain why foreign currency cash balances do not cause transaction exposure.
9. **Contractual hedges.** What are the four main contractual instruments used to hedge transaction exposure?
10. **Decision criteria.** Ultimately, a treasurer must chose among alternative strategies to manage transaction exposure. Explain the two main decision criteria that must be used.
11. **Proportional hedge.** Many MNEs have established transaction exposure risk management policies that mandate proportional hedging. Explain and give an example of how proportional hedging can be implemented.

PROBLEMS

1. **Lipitor in Indonesia.** Pfizer, the U.S.-based multinational pharmaceutical company, is evaluating an export sale of its extremely effective cholesterol reduction drug, Lipitor, with a prospective Indonesian distributor. The purchase would be for 750 million Indonesian rupiah (Rp), which at the current spot exchange rate of Rp8,800/$ translates into a little more than $85,000. Although not a big sale by Pfizer standards company policy dictates that sales must be settled for at least a minimum gross margin, in this case, a cash settlement of $78,000 on the sale.

   The current 90-day forward rate is Rp9,800/$. Although this rate appeared unattractive, Pfizer had to contact several major banks before even finding a forward quote on the rupiah. The consensus of currency forecasters at the moment, however, is that the rupiah will hold relatively steady, possibly falling to Rp9,400 over the coming 90 to 120 days. Analyze the prospective sale and make a hedging recommendation.
2. **Embraer of Brazil.** Embraer of Brazil is one of the two leading global manufacturers of regional jets (Bombardier of Canada is the other). Regional jets are smaller than the traditional civilian airliners produced by Airbus and Boeing, seating between 50 and 100 people, on average. Embraer has concluded an agreement with a regional U.S. airline to produce and deliver four aircraft one year from now for $80 million. Although Embraer will be paid in U.S. dollars, it also possesses a currency exposure of inputs—it must pay foreign suppliers $20 million for inputs one year from now (but they will be delivering the sub-components throughout the year).

The current spot rate on the Brazilian real (R$) is R$3.40/$, but it has only recently dropped back down to this level after hitting R$3.80/$ only a few months ago. Forward contracts are difficult to acquire and considered expensive. Citibank Brasil has not explicitly provided Embraer a forward rate quote, but has stated that it will probably be pricing a forward off the current 4.00% U.S. dollar eurocurrency rate and the 14.00% Brazilian government deposit note. Advise Embraer on its currency exposure.

3. **Mattel Toys.** Mattel is a U.S.-based company whose sales are roughly two-thirds in dollars (Asia and the Americas) and one-third in euros (Europe). In September Mattel delivers a large shipment of toys (primarily Barbies and Hot Wheels) to a major distributor in Antwerp.

   The receivable, €20 million, is due in 90 days, standard terms for the toy industry in Europe. Mattel's treasury team has collected the following currency and market quotes. The company's foreign exchange advisors believe the euro will be at about $1.0300/€ in 90 days. Mattel's management does not use currency options in currency risk management activities. Advise Mattel on which hedging alternative is probably preferable.

Spot rate	$1.0600/€
Credit Suisse 90-day forward quote	$1.0580/€
Barclays 90-day forward quote	$1.0560/€
Mattel's cost of capital	10.000%
90-day eurodollar interest rate	3.600%
90-day euro euro interest rate	4.600%
90-day dollar borrowing rate	7.600%
90-day euro borrowing rate	8.400%

4. **Hindustan Lever.** Unilever's subsidiary in India, Hindustan Lever, procures much of its toiletries product line from a Japanese company. Because of the shortage of working capital in India, payment terms by Indian importers are typically 180 days or longer. Hindustan Lever wishes to hedge a 8.5 million Japanese yen payable.

   Although options are not available on the Indian rupee (Rs), forward rates are available against the yen. Additionally, a common practice in India is for companies like Hindustan Lever to work with a currency agent who will, in this case, lock in the current spot exchange rate in exchange for a 4.85% fee. Using the following exchange rate and interest rate data, recommend a hedging strategy.

Spot rate, yen/dollar	¥120.60/$
Spot rate, rupees/dollar	Rs47.75/$
180-day forward rate, yen/rupee	¥2.4000/Rs
Expected spot rate in 180 days	¥2.6000/Rs
180-day yen investment rate	1.500%
180-day rupee investment rate	8.000%
Hindustan Lever's cost of capital	12.00%

Tektronix

The following five problems are based on the hypothetical but typical foreign exchange transaction exposures that might be faced by Tektronix, Inc. (Tek), an actual MNE based in Beaverton, Oregon, USA. Tek's sales in the fiscal year ending May 31, 2002, were about $1 billion. Its main products are scientific measuring instruments such as protocol analysers and simulators, network monitoring systems, transmission and cable test products, and a broad range of oscilloscopes. Part of the foreign sales were direct exports from Tek's Beaverton manufacturing and research facility. A second part of sales were passed through Tek's own foreign sales and assembly subsidiaries. A third part of sales were through joint ventures such as in Japan (Sony) and China. Tek also imported components and other materials that were used in the manufacturing operations in Beaverton. Tek's main competitors are Agilent (formerly Hewlett Packard's measuring instruments business), and Siemens (a very large German conglomerate).

5. **Tek—Italian account receivable.** Tek wishes to hedge a €4,000,000 account receivable arising from a sale to Olivetti (Italy). Payment is due in three months. Tek's Italian unit does not have ready access to local currency borrowing, eliminating the money market hedge alternative. Citibank has offered Tek the following quotes:

Spot rate	\$0.9800/€
3-month forward rate	\$0.9850/€
3-month euro interest rate	6.000% per year
3-month put option on euros at strike price of \$0.9800/€	3%
Tek's weighted average cost of capital	12%

a. What are the costs of each alternative?

b. What are the risks of each alternative?

c. Which alternative should Tek choose if it prefers to "play it safe"?

d. Which alternative should Tek choose if it is willing to take a reasonable risk and has a directional view that the euro may be appreciating versus the dollar during the next 3 months?

6. Tek—Japanese account payable. Tek has imported components from its joint venture in Japan, Sony-Tek, with payment of ¥8,000,000 due in 6 months. Citibank has offered Tek the following quotes.

Spot rate	¥125/\$
6-month forward rate	¥122/\$
6-month yen deposit rate	1.5000% per year
6-month dollar interest rate	4.0000% per year
6-month call option on yen at a strike price of ¥125/\$	4%
Tek's weighted average cost of capital	12%

a. What are the costs of each alternative?

b. What are the risks of each alternative?

c. Which alternative should Tek choose if it is willing to take a reasonable risk and has a directional view that the yen may be depreciating versus the dollar during the next 6 months?

7. Tek—British Telecom bidding. Tek has made a £1,000,000 bid to supply and install a network monitoring system for British Telecom in Manchester, U.K. The bid is good for 30 days at which time the winner of the bidding process will be announced. Other bidders are expected to be Agilent, Siemens, and at least two British firms. If Tek wins the bid it will have 60 days to build and install the system. During this 90-day period the £1,000,000 will be accounted for as backlog. Upon delivery and testing of the system British Telecom will make full payment 30 days later. During this month Tek will account for the £1,000,000 as an account receivable. Barclay's Bank (UK) has offered Tek the following quotes:

Spot rate	\$1.5700/£
1-month forward rate	1.5720/£
4-month forward rate	1.5750/£
1-month £ investment rate	4.000% per year
1-month £ borrowing rate	9.000% per year
4-month £ investment rate	4.250% per year
4-month £ borrowing rate	9.200% per year
1-month put option on pound (\$1.58/£ strike)	\$0.006/£ premium
4-month put option on pound (\$1.58/£ strike)	\$0.012/£ premium
Tek's weighted average cost of capital	12%

What should Tek do to hedge this bid?

8. Tek—Swedish price list. Tek offers oscilloscopes and other off-the-shelf products through foreign-currency-denominated price lists. The prices are valid for three months only. One example is a Swedish price list expressed in Swedish kronor. In effect, customers are given a cost-free call option on products with a fixed dollar/krona exchange rate. During a typical three-month period, Tek could expect to sell SKr 5,000,000–SKr 10,000,000 worth of products based on the price list. Since the SKr/\$ exchange rate is likely to change during any three-month period, Tek would like to hedge this transaction exposure (although Tek's Swedish business unit does believe the krona will be weakening versus the dollar in the coming months). Nordea Bank (Sweden) has offered Tek the following quotes:

Spot rate	SKr9.20/\$
3-month forward rate	SKr9.25/\$
3-month krona interest rate	6.15% per year
3-month krona borrowing rate	12.50% per year
3-month dollar interest rate	4.00% per year
3-month put option on krona at strike price of SKr9.20/\$	3.5%
Tek's weighted average cost of capital	12%

a. What are the costs of each alternative for hedging SKr5,000,000?

b. What are the risks of each alternative? How much kronor should Tek hedge if it wants to "play it safe"?

c. Which alternative should Tek choose if it is willing to take a reasonable risk and has a directional view that the Swedish krona will appreciate versus the U.S. dollar during the next 3 months?

9. **Tek—Swiss dividend payable.** Tek's European subsidiaries are formally owned by a holding company, Tek-Switzerland. Thus, the subsidiaries pay dividends to the Swiss holding company, which in turn pays dividends to Tek-Beaverton. Tek has declared a dividend of 5 million Swiss francs payable in three months from Switzerland to Tek-Beaverton. If Tek-Beaverton wishes to hedge this transaction exposure it could utilize the following quotes from Swiss Bank Corporation:

Spot rate	SFr1.50/$
Expected spot rate in 3 months	SFr1.47/$
3-month forward rate	SFr1.52/$
3-month Swiss franc interest rate	5.25% per year
3-month dollar interest rate	4.00% per year
3-month put option on SF at strike price of SFr1.54/$	$0.0150/SFr premium
Tek's weighted average of capital	12%

What are the costs of each alternative for hedging the dividend payable? What are the risks of each alternative? Which alternative should Tek choose? Explain your assumption about Tek's motivation in choosing your suggested alternative.

10. **Northern Rainwear.** Northern Rainwear, Ltd. (Northern), a Canadian manufacturer of raincoats, does not selectively hedge its transaction exposure. Instead, if the date of the transaction is known with certainty, all foreign currency-denominated cash flows must utilize the following mandatory forward contract cover formula:

	Exposure coverage required according to maturity		
If Northern is:	0–90 days	91–180 days	> 180 days
paying the points forward	75%	60%	50%
receiving the points forward	100%	90%	50%

Northern expects to receive multiple payments in Danish kroner over the next year. DKr3,000,000 is due in 90 days; DKr2,000,000 is due in 180 days; and DKr1,000,000 is due in one year. Using the following spot and forward exchange rates, what would be the amount of forward cover required by company policy by period?

Spot rate	DKr4.70/C$
3-month forward rate	DKr4.71/C$
6-month forward rate	DKr4.72/C$
1-year forward rate	DKr4.74/C$

11. **Vamo Road Industries.** Vamo Road Industries of Sarasota, Florida, is completing a new assembly plant near Guatemala City. A final construction payment of Q8,400,000 is due in six months. ("Q" is the symbol for Guatemalan quetzals.) Vamo uses 20% per annum as its weighted average cost of capital. Today's foreign exchange and interest rate quotations are:

Present spot rate	Q7.0000/$
Six-month forward rate	Q7.1000/$
Guatemalan 6-month interest rate	14.00% per annum
U.S. dollar 6-month interest rate	6.00% per annum

Vamo's treasury manager, concerned about the Guatemalan economy, wonders if Vamo should be hedging its foreign exchange risk. The manager's own forecast is as follows:

Highest expected rate	Q8.0000/$, reflecting a significant devaluation
Expected rate	Q7.3000/$
Lowest expected rate	Q6.4000/$, reflecting a strengthening of the quetzal

What realistic alternatives are available to Vamo for making payment? Which method would you select, and why?

12. **Worldwide Travel's Acquisition.** Worldwide Travel, a Honolulu, Hawaii–based 100% privately owned travel company has signed an agreement to acquire a 50% ownership share of Taipei Travel, a Taiwan–based privately owned travel agency specializing in servicing inbound customers from the United States and Canada. The acquisition price is 7 million Taiwan new dollars (NT$7,000,000) payable in cash in 3 months.

    Matt Morita, Worldwide Travel's owner, believes the Taiwan new dollar will either remain stable or decline a little over the next 3 months. At the present spot rate of NT$35/$, the amount of cash required is only $200,000 but even this relatively modest amount will need to be borrowed personally by Matt Morita. Taiwanese interest-bearing deposits by non-residents are regulated by the government, and are currently set at 1.5% per year. He has a credit line with Bank of Hawaii for $200,000 with a current borrowing interest rate of 8% per year. He does not believe that he can calculate a credible weighted average cost of capital since he has no stock outstanding and his competitors are all also privately owned without disclosure of their financial results. Since the acquisition would use up all his available credit, he wonders if he should hedge this transaction exposure. He has the following quotes from Bank of Hawaii:

Spot rate	NT$35.00/$
3-month forward rate	NT$36.00/$
3-month dollar borrowing rate	8.0% per year
3-month NT$ deposit rate	1.5% per year
3-month call options	not available

    Analyze the costs and risks of each alternative, and then make a recommendation as to which alternative Morita should choose.

13. **Seattle Scientific, Inc.** Josh Miller is chief financial officer of a medium-sized Seattle-based medical device manufacturer. The company's annual sales of $40 million have been growing rapidly, and working capital financing is a common source of concern. He has recently been approached by one of his major Japanese customers, Yokasa, with a new payment proposal.

    Yokasa typically orders ¥12,500,000 in product every other month and pays in Japanese yen. The current payment terms extended by Seattle are 30 days, with no discounts given for early or cash payment. Yokasa has suggested that it would be willing to pay in cash—in Japanese yen—if it was given a 4.5% discount on the purchase price. Josh Miller gathered the following quotes from his bank on current spot and forward exchange rates, and estimated Yokasa's cost of capital.

Spot rate	¥120.23/$
30-day forward rate	¥119.73/$
90-day forward rate	¥118.78/$
180-day forward rate	¥117.21/$
Yokasa's WACC	8.850%
Seattle Scientific's WACC	12.500%

    a. What is Seattle Scientific's "cost of hedging" the yen receivable?
    b. How much in U.S. dollars will Seattle Scientific receive 1) with the discount and 2) with no discount but fully covered with a forward contract?
    c. If Josh were to compare the results of part b) in present value terms, which appears to be preferable?

14. **Wilmington Chemical Company.** Wilmington Chemical Company has just purchased a shipment of phosphates from Morocco for 6,000,000 dirhams, payable in six months. Wilmington's cost of capital is 14%. The following quotes are available in the market.

	United States	*Morocco*
6-month interest rate for borrowing	6.00% p.a.	8.00% p.a.
6-month interest rate for investing	5.00% p.a.	7.00% p.a.
Spot exchange rate	$1.00 = 10.00 dirhams	
6-month forward rate	$1.00 = 10.40 dirhams	

Six-month call options on 6,000,000 dirhams at an exercise price of 10.00 dirhams per dollar are available from Bank Al-Maghrub at a premium of 2%. Six-month put options on 6,000,000 dirhams at an exercise price of 10.00 dirhams per dollar are available at a premium of 3%.

Compare and contrast alternative ways that Wilmington Chemical might hedge its foreign exchange transaction exposure. What is your recommendation?

15. **Dawg-Grip, Inc.** Dawg-Grip, Inc., of Georgia just purchased a Korean company that produces plastic nuts and bolts for automobile manufacturers. The purchase price was 7,030 million Won. Won1,000 million has already been paid, and the remaining Won6,030 million is due in six months. The current spot rate is Won1200/$, and the 6-month forward rate is Won1260/$. Additional data:

6-month Korean interest rate	16.00% p.a.
6-month U.S. interest rate	4.00% p.a.
6-month call option on Korean won at W1200/$	3.0% premium
6-month put option on Korean won at W1200/$	2.4% premium

Dawg-Grip can invest at the rates given above, or borrow at 2% per annum above those rates. Dawg-Grip's weighted average cost of capital is 25%. Compare alternate ways that Dawg-Grip might deal with its foreign exchange exposure. What do you recommend and why?

16. **Aqua-Pure.** Aqua-Pure is a U.S.–based company that manufactures, sells, and installs water purification equipment. On April 20 the company sold a system to the city of Nagasaki, Japan, for installation in Nagasaki's famous Glover Gardens (where Puccini's Madame Butterfly waited for the return of Lt. Pinkerton). The sale was priced in yen at ¥20,000,000, with payment due in three months. On the day of the sale the *Financial Times* published the following mid-rates for the yen:

Spot exchange rate	¥118.255/$ (closing mid-rate)
1-month forward rate	¥117.760/$, a 5.04% p.a. premium
3-month forward:	¥116.830/$, a 4.88% p.a. premium
1-year forward	¥112.450/$, a 5.16% p.a. premium

Money rates (% p.a.)	United States	Japan	Differential
1 month	4.8750%	0.09375%	4.78125%
3 months	4.9375 %	0.09375%	4.84375%
12 months	5.1875%	0.31250%	4.87500%

Note: The interest rate differentials vary slightly from the forward discounts on the yen because of time differences for the quotes. The spot ¥118.255/$, for example, is a mid-point range. On April 20 the spot yen traded in London from ¥118.30/$ to ¥117.550/$.

Additional information: Aqua-Pure's Japanese competitors are currently borrowing yen from Japanese banks at a spread of 2 percentage points above the Japanese money rate. Aqua-Pure's weighted average cost of capital is 16%, and the company wishes to protect the dollar value of this receivable.

Three-month options from Kyushu Bank:

Call option on ¥20,000,000 at exercise price of ¥118.00/$: a 1% premium

Put option on ¥20,000,000 at exercise price of ¥118.00/$: a 3% premium

a. What are the costs and benefits of alternative hedges? Which would you recommend. Why?

b. What is the break-even reinvestment rate when comparing forward and money market alternatives?

17. **Botox Watch Company.** Botox Watch Company exports wristwatches to many countries, selling for local currencies to watch stores

and distributors. Botox prides itself on being financially conservative. At least 70% of each individual transaction exposure is hedged, mostly in the forward market but occasionally with options. Botox's foreign exchange policy is such that the 70% hedge may be increased up to a 120% hedge if devaluation or depreciation appears imminent.

Botox has just shipped to its major continental European distributor. It has issued a 90-day invoice to its buyer for €1,560,000. The current spot rate is $0.9650/€; the 90-day forward rate is $0.9460/€. Botox treasurer Harry Weaver has a very good track record in predicting exchange rate movements. He currently believes the euro will weaken against the dollar in the coming 90 to 120 days, possibly to around $0.93/€.

a. Evaluate the hedging alternatives for Botox if Harry is right (Case #1: $0.93/€) and if Harry is wrong (Case #2: $1.00/€). What do you recommend?
b. What does it mean to hedge 120% of a transaction exposure?
c. What would be considered the most conservative transaction exposure management policy by a firm? How does Botox compare?

18. Redwall Pump Company. On March 1, Redwall Pump Company sold a shipment of pumps to Vollendam Dike Company of the Netherlands for €4,000,000, payable €2,000,000 on June 1 and €2,000,000 on September 1. Redwall derived its price quote of €4,000,000 on February 1 by dividing its normal U.S. dollar sales price of $4,320,000 by the then-current spot rate of $1.0800/€.

By the time the order was received and booked on March 1, the euro had strengthened to $1.1000/€, so the sale was in fact worth €4,000,000 × $1.1000/€ = $4,400,000. Redwall had already gained an extra $80,000 from favorable exchange rate movements! Nevertheless Redwall's director of finance wondered if the firm should hedge against a reversal of the recent trend of the euro. Four approaches were possible:

a. Hedge in the forward market. The 3-month forward exchange quote was $1.1060/€ and the 6-month forward quote was $1.1130/€.
b. Hedge in the money market. Redwall could borrow euros from the Frankfurt branch of its U.S. bank at 8.00% per annum.
c. Hedge with foreign currency options. June put options were available at strike price of $1.1000/€ for a premium of 2.0% per contract, and September put options were available at $1.1000/€ for a premium of 1.2%. June call options at $1.1000/€ could be purchased for a premium of 3.0%, and September call options at $1.1000/€ were available at a 2.6% premium.
d. Do nothing. Redwall could wait until the sales proceeds were received in June and September, hope the recent strengthening of the euro would continue, and sell the euros received for dollars in the spot market.

Redwall estimates its cost of equity capital to be 12% per annum. As a small firm, Redwall is unable to raise funds with long-term debt. U.S. T-bills yielded 3.6% per annum. What should Redwall do?

19. Pixel's financial metrics. Leo Srivastava is the Director of Finance for Pixel Manufacturing, a U.S.–based manufacturer of hand-held computer systems for inventory management. Pixel's system combines a low-cost active bar-code used on inventory (the bar-code tags emit an extremely low-grade radio frequency) with custom-designed hardware and software that tracks the low-grade emissions for inventory control.

Pixel has completed the sale of a bar-code system to a British firm, Grand Metropolitan (U.K.), for a total payment of £1,000,000. The following exchange rates were available to Pixel on the following dates corresponding to the events of this specific export sale. Assume each month is 30 days.

Date	Spot Rate ($/£)	Forward Rate ($/£)	Description
Feb 1	1.7850	F_{210} = 1.7771	Price quotation by Pixel (U.S.) to Grand Met (U.K.)
Mar 1	1.7465	F_{180} = 1.7381	Contract signed for the sale totaling £1,000,000
Jun 1	1.7689	F_{90} = 1.7602	Product shipped to Grand Met
Aug 1	1.7840	F_{30} = 1.7811	Product received by Grand Met
Sept 1	1.7290	————	Grand Met makes payment of £1,000,000

a. Pixel's income statement will reflect the sale both as booked sales and as a potential foreign exchange gain (loss). Assume that Leo decides not to hedge this transaction exposure. What is the value of the sale as booked? What is the foreign exchange gain (loss) on the sale?

b. Now assume that Leo decides that he should hedge the exposure with a forward contract. The financial statements will reflect a different set of values when hedged. What is the value of the sale as booked? What is the foreign exchange gain (loss) on the sale if hedged with a forward contract?

20. Scout Finch and Dayton Manufacturing (A). Dayton—the same U.S.-based company as discussed in this chapter, has concluded a second larger sale of three additional gas turbines to Crown (U.K.). Total payment of £3,000,000 is due in 90 days. Scout Finch has also learned that Dayton will be able to borrow in the United Kingdom only at 14% per annum (due to credit concerns of the British banks). Given the following exchange rates and interest rates, what transaction exposure hedge is now in Dayton's best interest?

Spot rate	$1.7620/£
Expected spot rate in 90 days	$1.7850/£
90-day forward rate	$1.7550/£
90-day dollar deposit rate	6.0% per annum
90-day dollar borrowing rate	8.0% per annum
90-day pound deposit rate	8.0% per annum
90-day pound borrowing rate	14.0% per annum
Dayton's WACC	12.0% per annum

Scout has also collected data on two specific options as well:

	Strike rate	*Premium*
90-day put option on £	$1.75/£	1.5%
90-day put option on £	$1.71/£	1.0%

21. Scout Finch and Dayton Manufacturing (B). One year later Scout Finch is still on the job at Dayton. Dayton's business is booming, and sales have now expanded to include exports to Germany and Japan. All export sales are invoiced in the local currency of the buyer. Scout Finch will book the following sales this period:

Domestic sales	$7,300,000 (45-day credit terms)
Export sales	€2,340,000; £1,780,000; ¥125,000,000 (all export terms are 90 days)

Other income statement items are as follows:

Cost of goods sold	65% of sales
G&A expenses	9% of sales
Depreciation	$248,750 per period
U.S. corporate tax	40% of earnings before tax
Shares outstanding	1,000,000

Scout Finch has collected the following spot rates (sales will be booked at these rates), 90-day forward rates, and 90-day forecasts by Dayton's foreign exchange advisor for the three currencies:

Spot	*90-day forward*	*FX advisor forecast*
$1.5900/£	$1.5875/£	$1.5600/£
$1.0560/€	$1.0250/€	$1.0660/€
¥122.43/$	¥120.85/$	¥126.00/$

Using the structure for Dayton's income statement presented in Chapter 8 Appendix Exhibit 8A.1, answer the following questions:

a. If Scout Finch leaves all positions uncovered, and the final spot rates at settlement are exactly what the FX advisor had forecast, what are the foreign exchange gains (losses) for the period, and what are the final net income and earnings per share (EPS) figures?

b. If Scout Finch covers all positions with full forward cover, and the final spot rates at settlement are exactly what the FX advisor forecast, what are the foreign exchange gains (losses) for the period, and the final net income and earnings per share (EPS) figures?

c. If Scout Finch uses a common industry practice of covering all positions 100% with forward cover if the forward rate earns her the points, while covering only half the positions in which she is paying the forward points. What are the foreign exchange gains (losses) for the period and the final net income and earnings per share (EPS) figures, assuming the following final settlement spot rates: \$1.0480/€, \$1.6000/£, ¥122.50/\$?

22. **Siam Cement.** Siam Cement, the Bangkok-based cement manufacturer, suffered enormous losses with the coming of the Asian crisis in 1997. The company had been pursuing a very aggressive growth strategy in the mid-1990s, taking on massive quantities of foreign currency–denominated debt (primarily U.S. dollars). When the Thai baht (B) was devalued from its pegged rate of B25.0/\$ in July 1997, Siam's interest payments alone were over \$900 million on its outstanding dollar debt (with an average interest rate of 8.40% on its U.S. dollar debt at that time).

    Assuming Siam Cement took out \$50 million in debt in June 1997 at 8.40% interest, and had to repay it in one year when the spot exchange rate had stabilized at B42.0/\$, what was the foreign exchange loss incurred on the transaction?

Use the following hypothetical construction project to answer questions 23 through 25.

Aswan Infrastructure Reinvestment. On December 20, 2002, the Egyptian government, backed by new loans from the World Bank, began an infrastructure reinvestment project for the Aswan Dam on the Nile River. First constructed by the British between 1898 and 1902, the Aswan Dam had last been restored in 1960, and was now desperately in need of a significant restoration and overhaul. The total project cost was estimated at 626 million Egyptian pounds (E£), approximately \$135.5 million at the spot exchange rate of E£4.62/\$, and would be completed in a little more than one year.

The project director, Jacques Mayol, had now successfully concluded sub-contract awards to daSilva of Brazil (E£118 million), Fluor Corporation of the United States (E£220 million), and Mitsubishi Industries of Japan (E£288 million). Each company had agreed to accept payment in Egyptian pounds, and given the fixed rate of exchange between the Egyptian pound and the dollar, believed they could manage the currency risk effectively.

		Expected Payments (Egyptian pounds, millions)			
Company	**Spot rate**	**3-months**	**6-months**	**9-months**	**12-months**
daSilva (Brazil)	R\$3.55/\$	28	66	24	—
Fluor Corporation (U.S.)	E£4.62/\$	56	44	120	—
Mitsubishi Industries (Japan)	¥120.64/\$	—	168	38	82

On January 28, 2003, little more than one month later, all involved were shocked when the Egyptian government devalued the Egyptian pound to E£5.35/\$.

23. Aswan project: Mitsubishi's exposure. Mitsubishi Industries of Japan had been willing to agree to receive payments in Egyptian pounds because of the Egyptian government's pegged exchange rate against the dollar and Mitsubishi's ability to access currency derivatives for the yen/dollar exposure.

The contract agreement was passed to Mitsubishi's International Finance Division on January 1, 2003, when the following exchange rate and interest rate quotes were available. [Note that both borrowing rates for this case, when Mitsubishi would be posting the receivable from the Egyptian government as collateral, are relatively high. This is because of the higher associated credit risk assigned by the banks to the Egyptian government, even with the World Bank backing payment.]

Spot rate	¥120.64/$
1-month forward rate	¥120.51/$
3-month forward rate	¥120.24/$
6-month forward rate	¥119.62/$
Expected spot rate, 180 days	¥122.00/$
6-month dollar investing rate	3.40%
6-month dollar borrowing rate	9.60%
6-month yen investing rate	1.25%
6-month yen borrowing rate	6.50%
Mitsubishi's cost of capital	8.00%

6-month call options on the yen:

Strike: ¥119.00/$	Premium: 1.50%
Strike: ¥116.00/$	Premium: 0.80%

6-month put options on the yen:

Strike: ¥122.00/$	Premium: 1.60%
Strike: ¥124.00/$	Premium: 0.90%

Mitsubishi *officially* (meaning all business units use this as their benchmark rate for budgeting purposes) expects the value of the yen to hover around ¥122/$ for most of 2003.

a. Assuming it is the first week of January 2003, advise Mitsubishi on the management of its 6-month exposure.

b. Assuming it is February 2003, and the Egyptian government has now devalued the Egyptian pound, assess the impact on the yen receipts now expected as a result of your analysis in part a.

24. Aswan project: Fluor's exposure. Although the Egyptian pound was set a pegged rate of exchange by the Egyptian government, Fluor was well aware of the currency's recent history (it had actually been devalued in December 2001). As a result, Fluor Corporation had obtained a "forward insurance agreement" from its major bank in New York against all three of its expected future payments. The agreement stated that if the spot exchange rate at settlement differed from E£4.62/$ by more than 8.0% (positive or negative), then the bank would share equally in the gain or loss with Fluor. For this protection, Fluor had paid the bank 0.8% of the current value of all three contracts (paid up-front, at the value of the contracts when written).

a. If Fluor Corporation's weighted average cost of capital is 10.60%, what was the actual amount of the payment for the forward insurance agreement?

b. For the first payment of E£56 million to Fluor, assuming the spot rate at settlement was E£5.58/$ (the Egyptian pound had continued to slide a bit by settlement of the 3-month payment), what was Fluor's total net proceeds from this first payment, including that payment's proportion of the insurance premium paid up-front?

25. Aswan project: daSilva's contingency. daSilva of Brazil had significant experience with currency risk and exchange rates that were theoretically fixed right up until the day they were devalued. The firm had, therefore, built significant "room" into its price quote and resulting contract to try to protect itself against any potential devaluation of the Egyptian pound. (daSilva, like most, were not particularly worried that the Egyptian pound would be re-valued against the dollar.)

Since is frequently difficult—due to intense competition in international markets—to build such a contingency into a competitive price quote. daSilva currently enjoyed a productivity-cost advantage. The combined benefit of recent lean-manufacturing initiatives at daSilva, and the Brazilian recession's impact on labor costs, gave the firm a substantial cost advantage over international competitors. daSilva's financial staff had studied a number of the major currency devaluations experienced globally in the 1990s and had concluded that the average devaluation was roughly 16% to 18%. Although many currencies continued to fall in value over extended periods following the initial devaluation, the staff believed that Egypt, if it did devalue, would follow the stair-step process of periodic devaluation that it had demonstrated in the late 1990s.

Assuming daSilva built a 16% contingency into its Aswan Dam project contract, and assuming the following final effective spot exchange rates over the payment periods, evaluate the effectiveness of daSilva's financial strategy.

Monthly Avg. Exchange Rates: Egyptian Pounds per U.S. Dollar

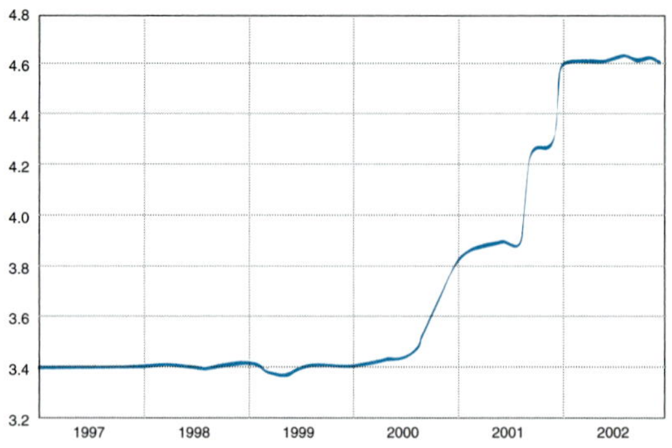

© 2003 by Prof. Werner Antweiler, University of British Columbia, Vancouver BC, Canada. Time period shown in diagram: January 1, 1997–December 31, 2002.

Budget Rates	3 months	6 months	9 months
Brazilian real (R$/$)	3.50	3.50	3.50
Egyptian pound (E£/$)	4.62	4.62	4.62
plus a contingency	+16%	+16%	+16%

Actual Rates	3 months	6 months	9 months
Brazilian real (R$/$)	3.50	3.60	3.70
Egyptian pound (E£/$)	5.58	6.20	6.20
plus a contingency	+16%	+16%	+16%

INTERNET EXERCISES

1. **Dayton: current volatilities.** Scout Finch wishes to price her own options, but needs current volatilities on the euro, British pound, and Japanese yen. Using the following web site, collect spot rates and volatilities in order to price forward-at-the-money put options for Finch's hedging analysis.

   Federal Reserve Bank of New York http://www.ny.frb.org/statistics

2. **Hedging objectives.** Most multinational companies will state the goals and objectives of their currency risk management activities in their annual reports. Beginning with the following firms, collect samples of corporate "why hedge?" discussions for a contrast and comparison discussion.

Nestlé	http://www.nestle.com
Disney	http://www.disney.com
Nokia	http://www.nokia.com
BP	http://www.bp.com

SELECTED READINGS

Bodnar, Gordon M., "1998 Wharton Survey of Financial Risk Management by U.S. Non-Financial Firms," *Financial Management*, Winter 1998, Volume 24, No. 4, pp. 70–91.

Briys, Eric, and Francois de Varenne, "Optimal Hedging and the Partial Loss Offset," *European Financial Management*, November 1998, Volume 4, No. 3, pp. 321–334.

Smith, Clifford W., Jr., Charles W. Smithson, and D. Sykes Wilford, "Financial Engineering: Why Hedge?" in *The Handbook of Financial Engineering*, Clifford W. Smith, Jr., and Charles W. Smithson, eds. (New York: Harper Business, 1990) pp. 126–138.

Stulz, Rene M., "Rethinking Risk Management," *Journal of Applied Corporate Finance*, Fall 1996, Volume 9, No. 3, pp. 8–24.

MINI-CASE

Lufthansa's Purchase of Boeing 737s

In January 1985 Lufthansa, the national airline of Germany, under the chairmanship of Heinz Ruhnau, signed a contract with Boeing (U.S.) for the purchase of 20 Boeing 737 jets. Boeing agreed to deliver the 20 aircraft to Lufthansa's specifications in one year, in January 1986. Lufthansa would have a single payment due on that date of $500 million. Given a spot exchange rate of DM3.2/$ in January 1985, this was an expected purchase of DM1.6 billion.

The Problem

Heinz Ruhnau was quite concerned over the exchange rate exposure that Lufthansa was bearing in this transaction. The U.S. dollar had been steadily appreciating in value against the Deutschemark for several years. Although many currency advisors and analysts had repeatedly stated they believed the dollar to be overvalued, it had continued to climb. Herr Ruhnau agreed with the majority of the currency advisors who believed the dollar would fall soon. Ruhnau also knew, however, that the size of the transaction represented too large a risk to Lufthansa if left unhedged. The current 360-day forward rate was the same as the spot rate, DM3.2/$, as a result of Eurodollar and EuroDeutschemark interest rates being the same.

But Ruhnau was torn between taking the most conservative strategy of locking in a forward contract for the entire amount and following his instincts that the dollar would fall in the coming year. If the dollar did fall, as he expected, he could potentially save Lufthansa millions of Deutschemarks in the completion of the sale. Although Ruhnau did not typically involve himself in currency management issues, the sheer size and significance of this transaction required him to make the final decision.

The Decision

Herr Ruhnau decided to compromise. He would cover one-half of the total exposure, $250 million, with a forward contract at DM3.2/$, and he would leave the other half uncovered. This would allow him to reduce his total exchange rate risk significantly, but still allow him to benefit if the dollar did indeed weaken versus the Deutschemark in the coming year as he expected.

The Outcome

In the end, Ruhnau's expectations proved correct. The dollar did indeed fall in the coming year—to DM2.3/$ by January 1986. (Although most currency analysts had predicted the dollar would fall, most were surprised by the speed and magnitude of this change.) The total cost to Lufthansa for settlement of its payment to Boeing totaled DM 1.375 billion:

Half covered with forward contract:	$250,000,000 × DM3.2/$ = DM800,000,000
Half left uncovered:	$250,000,000 × DM2.3/$ = DM575,000,000
Total:	DM1,375,000,000

The problem with the outcome (Exhibit A) was that the half of the exposure that he had covered with the forward contract had resulted in a cost of DM225,000,000 higher than that left uncovered. As a result, Ruhnau was heavily criticized for his handling of Lufthansa's currency exposure. Ruhnau was accused of recklessly speculating with Lufthansa's money, but the forward contract was seen as speculation, not the amount of the dollar exposure left uncovered. Herr Ruhnau was called before the Minister of Transportation in Germany (the government authority over the national airline) to explain his actions. Discussion of his employment contract, which was due to be renewed, were postponed and eventually he was given only a short renewal. Clearly the concept of speculation takes on a completely different meaning when performance is evaluated with 20/20 hindsight!

Case Questions

1. Do you think Heinz Ruhnau's hedging strategy made sense?
2. To what degree did he limit the upside and downside exposure of the transaction by hedging one-half of it?
3. Do you agree with Ruhnau's critics that he was "speculating"?
4. Is it fair to judge transaction exposure management effectiveness with 20/20 hindsight?

Exhibit A Lufthansa and the DM/$ Exchange Rate, 1982–1986

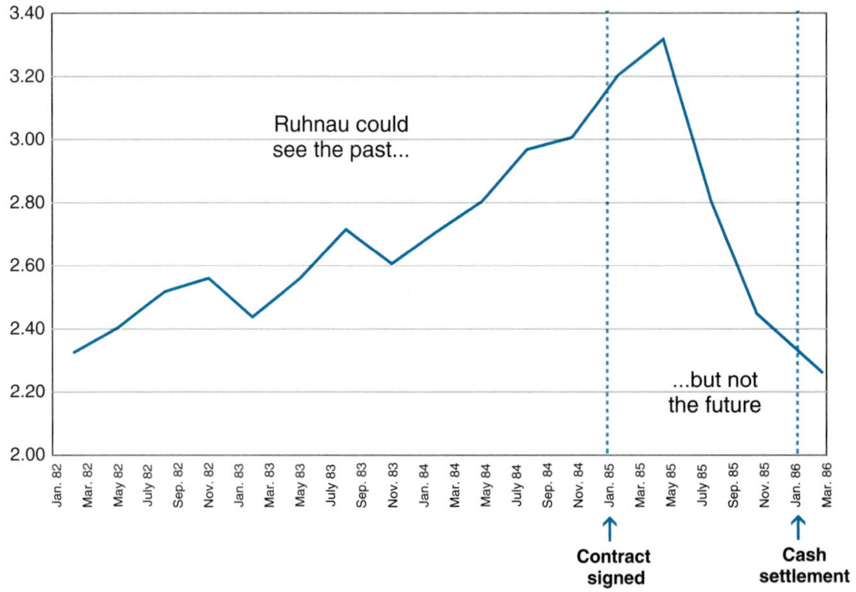

Chapter 8 APPENDIX

Basics of Foreign Currency Accounting

Although we do not claim to provide an accounting text, it is still important to know the basic accounting practices that apply to certain international business practices, including foreign exchange rates. It is also important to know that, in practice, the way in which many foreign-currency denominated transactions are recorded on the firm's books has a significant impact on how the firm views itself as being "exposed" to foreign currency movements.

Accounting for Foreign Currency–Denominated Transactions

In the case of Dayton Manufacturing, on the date that the equipment was shipped to the British buyer, Dayton would record the sale on its books at the spot rate in effect on that date: \$1.7640/£. This would be recorded as an account receivable due Dayton in the amount of:

$$£1,000,000 \times \$1.7640/£ = \$1,764,000$$

This sale is recorded as and expected to yield (according to accounting practices) revenue of \$1,764,000. Exhibit A.1 is an income statement that combines the export sale with sales revenue from domestic sales. If Dayton accepts the transaction risk and remains unhedged, the difference between what was booked and what is finally received would enter Dayton's financial statements (its income statement) as a *foreign exchange gain (loss)*. For example, if Dayton's foreign exchange advisor is correct and the exchange rate at the end of 90 days is \$1.7600/£, the receivable would be settled at that exchange rate, resulting in a foreign exchange loss of:

A/R booked at \$1.7640/£	\$1,764,000
A/R settled at \$1.7600/£	1,760,000
Foreign exchange gain (loss)	(\$ 4,000)

If the foreign exchange advisor is wrong and the spot rate at the end of the 90-day period moves in Dayton's favor to \$1.7800/£, the transaction would be settled for \$1,780,000, and a foreign exchange gain of \$16,000 would be recorded and realized (\$1,780,000 – \$1,764,000 = \$16,000).

Because all foreign currency–denominated transactions must be booked at the spot rate in effect on the date of sale or purchase rather than on the date of settlement, foreign exchange gains and losses are essentially unavoidable for the firm (unless exchange rates were indeed fixed). The only other way to avoid a foreign exchange loss on a foreign currency–denominated sale is to be paid cash at the time of sale. A cash purchase would be converted to domestic currency immediately, and no booking of receivables or foreign exchange gains (losses) required. Under existing U.S. and IASC[5] GAAP (generally accepted accounting principles), these gains and losses are reported in a firm's income statement in the period in which the gain or loss occurs. These amounts are real gains and losses, and represent potential changes to net income and earnings per share (EPS), which the firm may wish to monitor and manage.

5. The International Accounting Standards Committee (IASC) is a body established in 1973 by the leading professional accounting groups of the major industrial countries to formulate and promote the use of a set of global accounting standards, as well as to provide a forum for the harmonization of significant differences in practices across countries.

Exhibit 8A.1 Dayton's Income Statement and Foreign Exchange Gains (Losses)

Spot rate on date of export sale ($/£)	1.7640	1.7640	1.7640
Forward rate, 90 days ($/£)	1.7540	1.7540	1.7540
Ending spot rate, actual ($/£)	1.7600	1.7800	1.7600
Amount of 90-day account receivable (£)	1,000,000	1,000,000	1,000,000

Income Statement (US$)	**Uncovered: FX advisor is correct**	**Uncovered: FX advisor is incorrect**	**Forward cover: Exposure settled at forward rate**
Sales:			
Domestic sales	5,246,000	5,246,000	5,246,000
Export sales (single export)	1,764,000	1,764,000	1,764,000
Less cost of goods sold	(3,340,000)	(3,340,000)	(3,340,000)
Gross profit	3,670,000	3,670,000	3,670,000
Less general & administrative expenses	(565,000)	(565,000)	(565,000)
Less depreciation	(248,750)	(248,750)	(248,750)
Foreign exchange gains (losses)	(4,000)	16,000	(10,000)
Earnings before interest & taxes (EBIT)	2,852,250	2,872,250	2,846,250
Less interest expenses	(646,000)	(646,000)	(646,000)
Earnings before taxes (EBT)	2,206,250	2,226,250	2,200,250
Less U.S. corporate income taxes at 40%	(882,500)	(890,500)	(880,100)
Net income	1,323,750	1,335,750	1,320,150
Shares outstanding	1,000,000	1,000,000	1,000,000
Earnings per share (EPS)	$1.32	$1.34	$1.32

Accounting for Forward Contracts as Hedges

Had Dayton decided not to accept the transaction risk but instead purchased a forward contract (sold pounds forward), the forward contract would lock in a specific exchange rate ($1.7540/£) upon settlement.[6] If the spot exchange rate on the settlement date was that forecast by Dayton's advisor, $1.7600/£, the final settlement details recorded on Dayton's books would be:

Receivable	
A/R booked at $1.7640/£	$1,764,000
A/R settled at spot rate of $1.7600/£	1,760,000
Foreign exchange gain (loss)	($ 4,000)

6. Forward contracts are off-balance sheet liabilities, meaning that they are contractual commitments of the firm that do not result in specific on-balance sheet entries. They are, however, legal liabilities of the firm and are normally discussed in the footnotes to the financial statements in the firm's annual report. Financial Accounting Standard #133 now requires more detailed disclosure of financial contracts such as forward contracts.

Forward Contract	
Forward contract gain (loss)	(\$ 6,000)
(\$1,754,000 – \$1,760,000)	
Total foreign exchange gain (loss)	(\$ 10,000)

The foreign currency–denominated receivable is still settled at a loss of \$4,000; nothing has changed regarding its valuation. The purchase and settlement of the forward contract, however, results in an additional recognition of a \$6,000 currency loss, the difference between the forward rate and the spot rate on the settlement date.

The total receipts resulting from the settlement of the receivable and the forward hedge (often referred to as the *two legs of the hedge position*) are \$1,754,000. The firm receives a net dollar amount equal to that rate dictated by the forward contract. Note that this combined \$10,000 loss is "locked-in," meaning that regardless of the spot rate at the end of the 90-day period, the combined foreign exchange gain (loss) and forward contract gain (loss) will always total a negative \$10,000. If, for example, the spot rate at the end of the 90-day period was \$1.7800/£, the foreign exchange gain on the receivable would be \$16,000, while the loss on the forward contract would total \$26,000 (\$1,754,000 – \$1,780,000), for a net loss of \$10,000 on the hedged exposure. Although the individual gains (losses) change with the ending spot rate, the net position will not (which is why the position was "hedged" to begin with).

Foreign Exchange Gains (Losses) on the Income Statement

As illustrated previously, foreign currency–denominated transactions are booked on the balance sheet of the firm at the spot exchange rate in effect on the date of the entry. If or when the transaction is settled at a later date with a different spot exchange rate, the difference between the settlement rate and the booked exchange rate results in a foreign exchange gain (loss) associated with the transaction. If the total foreign exchange gains (losses) for a firm for the current period are material in the minds of the firm's management and independent auditors, a separate line item identifies the total *currency gains (losses)* for the period on the firm's income statement. If not material, these gains (losses) are customarily included in *other expenses.*

Because the difference between the spot exchange rate and the forward exchange rate results from interest rate differentials between the two country currencies involved, the gains (losses) associated with the use of a forward contract may be categorized as *forward interest expenses.* This expense is ordinarily of significance only when constructing the year-end financial statements for a firm with outstanding foreign currency–denominated transactions.

Hedge Accounting

Hedge accounting has a very specific meaning in corporate financial management. Hedge accounting specifies that gains and losses on hedging instruments be recognized in earnings at the same time as the effects of changes in the value of the items being hedged are recognized, assuming certain criteria are met. If a forward contract was purchased as a hedge of a foreign currency–denominated receivable (as in the case of Dayton), changes in the value of the forward contract would be recognized in Dayton's income only when the changes in the value of the A/R were recognized (typically on settlement).

This approach seems obvious, except for the possibility that the 90-day receivable was created during one year, but would be settled in the following year (after December 31, the firm's end-of-year balance sheet date). Under traditional accounting practices, Dayton would have to value the forward contract and the A/R on December 31 at current market rates (the spot rate of exchange on that date), and recognize those valuation impacts in current income. U.S. accounting practices require the firm to value the forward contract and the receivable independently, and at current market value (marked-to-market).

This procedure is followed for all financial contracts or speculative instruments that any or all firms may enter into. This process alters current income, even though no real cash flow has occurred and neither the receivable nor the forward contract have been closed-out. Separately, the forward premium implied by the forward rate (the difference between the originally booked spot rate and the forward rate) would be allocated as an interest expense (gain) for the current period by a day-count proportion. In this case, 45/90 days of the interest expense on the forward contract would be included in current expenses on the firm's income statement.

Many firms suggest that this practice defeats the purpose of hedging. According to Financial Accounting Standard (FAS) #52, if the transaction and hedge meet certain criteria, recognition of these changes may be deferred until the two legs of the hedge are actually settled.

Meeting the criteria for the application of hedge accounting, however, is difficult for many firms. According to FAS #52, paragraph 21, a foreign currency transaction shall be considered a hedge of an identifiable foreign currency commitment, provided both of the following are met:

1. The foreign currency transaction is designated as, and is effective as, a hedge of a foreign currency commitment.
2. The foreign currency commitment is firm.

The first condition focuses on the ability of the "hedge"—such as a forward contract—to act effectively as a hedge, its value moving in the opposite direction to that of the exposure given a spot exchange rate change. This condition is typically easily met.

The second condition, however, is of a more controversial nature. For a commitment to be considered "firm," the exposure must have some type of financial certainty of occurring. For example, if a firm has sold merchandise to a foreign buyer as in the case of Dayton, a contract exists and the seller can expect to receive the £1,000,000 as agreed. If, however, the receivable resulted from the sale of merchandise to another unit or affiliate of the same firm (for example, to Dayton, U.K.), there must be some basis for expecting the payment to occur in the amount and on the date designated. This requirement is difficult for many firms to meet, since most intra-firm sales and transactions do not have explicit contracts or penalties for non-performance.

In summary, a firm may hedge a currency exposure in any way it deems appropriate. Hedging actions are a managerial decision. However, the way in which the exposure and the hedge are carried on the firm's books and recognized in income is the subject of hedge accounting principles and foreign currency accounting practices in general.

Decision CASE

THUNDERBIRD
THE AMERICAN GRADUATE SCHOOL OF INTERNATIONAL MANAGEMENT

ZAPA Chemical and BuBa

"...there is a tendency in Europe to treat the exchange rate as a type of virility symbol. I, myself, have never felt the need for such a symbol."

British Prime Minister Margaret Thatcher

Stephanie Mayo, currency analyst for ZAPA Chemical of Cleveland, stared at her Reuters screen, her option pricing screen, and then out the window. It was Monday, September 21, 1992, and the markets seemed much calmer this morning. The French had voted *oui* by 50.95% to *non* of 49.05% to approve the Maastricht treaty the previous day. Stephanie was now debating what to do about her put option on Deutschemarks she had been holding for the last month.

The Original Exposure and Rate View

Stephanie had originally been given the exposure for management in mid-August. ZAPA Chemical had sold a specialty chemical distributorship in Stuttgart, Germany. The proceeds of the sale, approximately DM7.6 million, would be brought back to the United States sometime in November. Because of special tax and sales document filings in Germany, it could not yet be determined when exactly the funds would be available for repatriation.

The U.S. dollar had been falling like a rock since late March. The central bank of Germany, the Bundesbank, or as it is affectionately known—"BuBa," had added momentum to the drop when it had increased the German base lending rate by 75 basis points ($^3/_4$ of a percent) to 9.75% on July 16th. By August 17th, when Steph was given the exposure, the DM/$ rate looked as if it had settled down to a historically weak dollar of DM1.4649/$ (see Exhibit 1). At that time Steph had debated whether the dollar was as low as it was going to go, or just hesitating before sliding further. Steph *felt* there were a number of forces which could drive the dollar still lower.

- **The Bundesbank.** The Bundesbank had become very high profile in the last month as German interest rates continued to rise. The Bundesbank was slowing monetary growth to a crawl and driving interest rates up, all in an effort to stop the inflationary forces resulting from reunification. Of the many rumors emanating from the central bank, the ones about further interest rate hikes were the loudest.
- **Dollar-DM Interest Differentials.** The anemic growth of the U.S. economy continued. The U.S. Federal Reserve was attempting to provide needed stimulus through lower interest rates. The United States was now enjoying the lowest interest rates in twenty years. The high interest rates in Germany and the low interest rates in the U.S.,

Exhibit 1 **The Falling Value of the U.S. Dollar versus the Deutschemark (Friday closing, Jan–Aug 1992)**

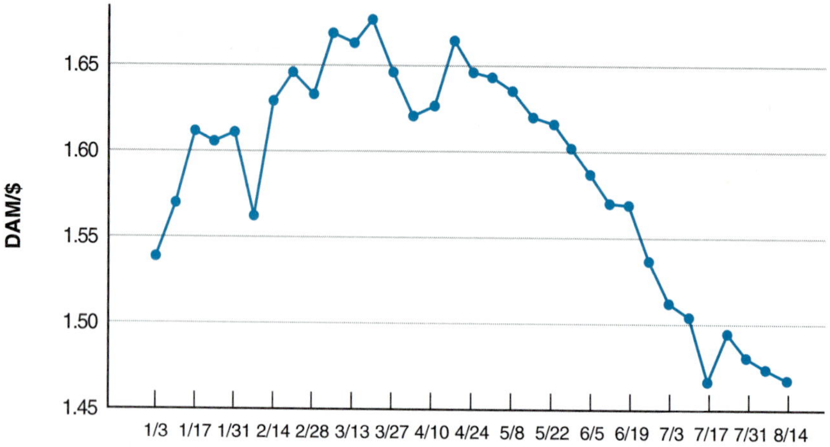

an unusual scenario by any account, was resulting in a massive capital flow from dollar-denominated assets into Deutschemarks.

Three-month Eurodollar deposits were paying 3.3125%, while similar Euro-Deutschemark deposits were paying 9.750%. And there were no signs of either rate moving toward the other.

- **The French Vote on the Maastricht Treaty.** The European Community had now painted itself into a corner with the escalating debate on the willingness of individual countries to actually pursue true European economic integration. The Maastricht Treaty had been signed by the Council of Ministers in December 1991, but had to be ratified by each country. The Treaty had formalized the steps and timetable for the adoption of a single European banking system and currency by the end of the decade. But the Danes had voted no in June 1992, when the French vote was pending. The outcome had been impossible to call. The vote was September 20th.
- **Stress in the European Monetary System (EMS).** Not only were the high German interest rates causing a strengthening of the DM versus the dollar, but for the same reasons, they were putting pressure on all EMS currencies as they tried to maintain their parities with the Deutschemark. The Italian lira and the British pound were both trading at the bottom of their allowable ranges (according to the agreed ranges within the Exchange Rate Mechanism (ERM) of the EMS) versus the Deutschemark.

To top it all off, 1992 was an election year in the United States. In mid-August President George Bush was 18 to 20 percentage points behind Democratic presidential candidate Bill Clinton in the polls. The markets had historically favored and rewarded Republican economic policies as opposed to the policies of the Democrats.

The Risk Tolerance of ZAPA

ZAPA was a rather unusual firm in its approach to currency risk management. Although the parent corporation, ZAPA Oil, did not use foreign currency options for risk management,

ZAPA Chemical used them exclusively. Because of losses caused by forward contracts in the previous year, Zapa's Treasury now used foreign exchange options whenever possible If needed, synthetic forwards were created by simply buying calls and selling puts for the same strike prices and maturities (or vice versa).

ZAPA Chemical considered Treasury a cost-center. Treasury therefore saw its primary responsibility as conservative management of exposures. Profit through currency speculation was not its purpose. In addition to an in-house aversion to forwards, the group could not write uncovered options (with their corresponding unlimited loss potential). The fiasco in 1991 at Allied-Lyons, the British food conglomerate, had sparked an internal review of all activities of international treasury at ZAPA Chemical. Allied-Lyons had suffered losses of $150 million as a result of unwise and uncontrolled currency speculation. Although ZAPA did not in any way mirror Allied-Lyons, the review had resulted in the exclusion of writing uncovered call options, as well as the requirement that the use of new instruments be allowed only after approval of the operating committee. But, all things considered, management was appreciative when the expenses of running the cost-center were lower.

Hedge Decision: August 17th

On August 17th the Deutschemark had traded around the DM1.4649/$ point all day. After discussion with her risk manager, Steph had decided that a safety net was called for. Her logic was relatively simple. First, she believed that the dollar would fall further. Most currency forecasters felt the dollar was already at bottom, but then again, they had said the same thing at the magic DM1.50/$ level. She believed the DM would move in her favor. Secondly, although she held the directional view of dollar-down, she also felt there were too many unknowns to feel secure. Currency volatility would by all guesses increase in the coming 4 to 6 weeks, with uncertainty over Bundesbank policies rising and the French vote on Maastricht forthcoming.

Before making her decision, Steph had reviewed an alternative which was not considered by ZAPA to be a true alternative: the forward. The coming volatility of the markets—and Stephanie felt sure that things would be heating up—posed many uncertainties. Selling the entire DM exposure forward would at least allow her to sleep nights. But there were two distinctly negative characteristics of the forward at this time. First, the huge interest differentials between U.S. dollar and Deutschemark assets resulted in forward rates which were extremely unattractive. The 120-day forward on August 17 was DM1.4957/$. Given the spot rate of DM1.4649/$, this was an annual discount of nearly 6.2%,—expensive protection. By selling the Deutschemarks forward she would be locking in a rate which she sincerely felt was in the wrong direction from that which the spot rate would move. The forward was quite unattractive.

The safety net Steph had chosen was an out-of-the-money (OTM) put option (bank option) on Deutschemarks. Gotham Bank (NY) was willing to sell ZAPA a December put on the DM7.6 million for a premium of 1.40 cents per DM ($0.0140/DM) for a strike of 66 ($0.66/DM or DM1.5152/$). This was a total outlay of $106,400 for the DM December put option. Although seemingly a lot of money, the option price was a paltry 2.1% premium ($0.0140 ÷ $0.6600/DM) for a substantial amount of protection against a dollar rebound.

Steph, as she did with all her major stand-alone exposures, took a look at her option position versus the totally unhedged and total forward cover alternatives. Exhibit 2 reproduces her exposure valuation analysis. The put option's value would parallel the uncovered position, but with the added benefit of a safety net if the spot rate were to actually move in the opposite direction.

Exhibit 2 Hedge Alternatives for ZAPA Chemical's DM Exposure (millions of US$)

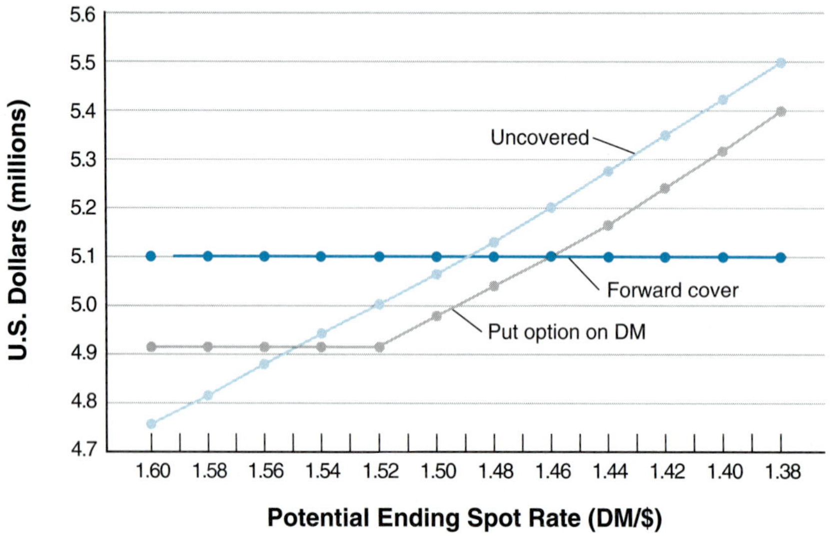

Daily Position Monitoring

Given the size of the position and the tension in the markets, Steph had watched the markets and the DM put option position daily. The next two weeks yielded good news and bad news. The good news was that Steph's intuition had been right on target. The dollar had declined rapidly in the days following her put option purchase, so that the prospective dollar value of the DM7.6 million was rising by the minute. The bad news, however, was that the December 66 put option was also falling in value. As the put option had moved further and further out-of-the-money, the market value of the option (the premium) had fallen.

By September 1st the U.S. dollar was at an all-time low of DM1.39/\$, and the option's premium was approximately 0.50 cents per DM. The potential loss on the option was \$68,400.

$$(\$.0050/\text{DM} - \$.0140/\text{DM}) \times \text{DM}7{,}600{,}000 = (\$68{,}400)$$

Although it was a bit unsettling when expressed in this manner, Steph recognized that this was what the corporate hedger wanted to happen when purchasing an OTM put option for protection. The U.S. dollar declined to approximately DM1.40/\$ and stayed there for the first two workweeks of September. Stephanie watched and waited.

September Turbulence

The week of September 14th had been a literal nightmare. The dollar had fallen, risen, and fallen again. The British pound had been withdrawn from the ERM. The Italian lira had been first devalued by over 7%, then finally withdrawn from the ERM as it came under further pressure. The Spanish peseta had been devalued 5% in the ERM. Other currencies had come under speculative attacks on Friday. The high interest rates in Germany had continued to bleed capital out of the other major European capital markets. Exhibit 3 reviews the roller coaster of events in these turbulent times.

In Great Britain the events of the previous weeks continued to have substantial news value. With the pound still floating freely against the Deutschemark, the long-standing critics of Britain's participation in the EMS were once more making a lot of noise.

The cynics still seemed to have carried the day. Many EC analysts saw the Maastricht Treaty and the idea of economic integration as something of a dead issue. The fundamental economic pressures which had led to the currency events of the first weeks of September were

Exhibit 3 EMS in Crisis: The Events of September 1992

Sept 1	The U.S. dollar falls below DM1.39/$.
Sept 4	The Italian lira trades below the ERM floor. Italian central bank raises discount rate from 13.25% to 15% to protect the lira.
Sept 6	EC finance ministers and central bank governors reaffirm their unwillingness to realign the EMS and promise massive intervention to protect the status quo.
Sept 8	Finland announces that it will no longer fix the markka to the ECU following a week of increasing speculation against the markka. The markka immediately falls against the DM and the dollar. The Swedish krona is hit by speculation as capital flows accelerate out of the Nordic countries into Deutschemark-denominated assets; Swedish monetary authorities begin raising interest rates to protect the krona.
Sept 9	Swedish central bank raises interest rates from 24% to 75% and plans to raise up to ECU 31 billion to protect the krona. Bundesbank is quoted as believing the Italian lira, Spanish peseta, and British pound should be devalued.
Sept 13	The Bundesbank cuts the Lombard borrowing rate, the base bank borrowing rate, by 25 basis points, from 9.75% to 9.50%. It is the first interest rate cut by the Bundesbank in five years. Italy/EMS announce that the Italian lira will be devalued by 7.6%. The Netherlands, Belgium, Austria, and Switzerland announce that their interest rates will be allowed to fall. Sweden announces that it will lower its marginal lending rate, the rate of interest which governs overnight interest rates between banks, to 20%.
Sept 14	The currency markets react favorably, the dollar rising from Friday's close of DM1.44/$ to DM1.49/$, a 2.4% appreciation. The markets wait for more interest rate cuts from the Bundesbank.
Sept 15	Bundesbank president Helmut Schlesinger makes it clear in an interview that the German monetary authority has not changed course towards expansionary policy. The Italian lira finds itself once more under attack as no interest rate cuts follow Sunday's devaluation. Rumors abound that Giuliano Amato, the Italian Prime Minister, is about to resign. The British pound comes under increasing speculative pressure as it falls below the allowed floor value against the Deutschemark.
Sept 16	The Bank of England raises its base lending rate to defend the falling British pound. By afternoon the Bank considers a further rate increase, but instead withdraws from the Exchange Rate Mechanism (ERM) of the EMS. Sweden raises the base lending rate from 75% to 500% to stop speculators from shorting the krona. Currency volatilities and option premiums skyrocket as crisis continues.
Sept 17	The Bundesbank refuses all pressure to cut German interest rates. The Spanish peseta is devalued 5% in the European Monetary System grid. The Italian lira withdraws from the exchange rate mechanism of the EMS. Official trading in the lira is suspended until the following Tuesday. The U.S. dollar falls from the previous day's high against the Deutschemark in response to rumors that the Bundesbank may be waiting to cut interest rates until after Sunday's French vote on Maastricht.
Sept 18	Sweden announces that it will cut the bank borrowing rate from 500% to 50%. The markets remain tense as all is put on hold awaiting the results of the French referendum on Sunday the 20th.
Sept 20	The French vote on the Maastricht Treaty and its proposed monetary unification of the EC.

still present: extremely high interest differentials between Germany and the United States; extreme devaluation pressures on most of the currencies of the EMS versus the Deutschemark.

Steph now wished to reevaluate her put option hedge position on the DM exposure.She knew that the DM7.6 million would be repatriated to the American parent on December 15th. This would match the maturity of the DM put option's expiration. But the massive volatility in the markets in the week before the September 20th vote had sent option values straight up. Steph was wondering whether it would be better to sell her put option and either cover the position with a forward or wait a few days until the markets calmed to replace the put position.

Steph quickly downloaded data on the daily spot rate and the December put option premium value. The graphic results of the comparison are shown in Exhibit 4. The put option premium had closed at 1.95 cents per DM on Friday (September 18th), while the spot and 90-day forward rates were DM1.5015/$ and DM1.5255/$, respectively. 90-day Eurocurrency interest rates had not changed since August. Steph thought she would have to move fast if—and it was a big if—she wished to sell her option while values (and volatilities) were still high.

Exhibit 4 Daily Changes in the DM/$ Spot Rate and the DM Put Option Premium

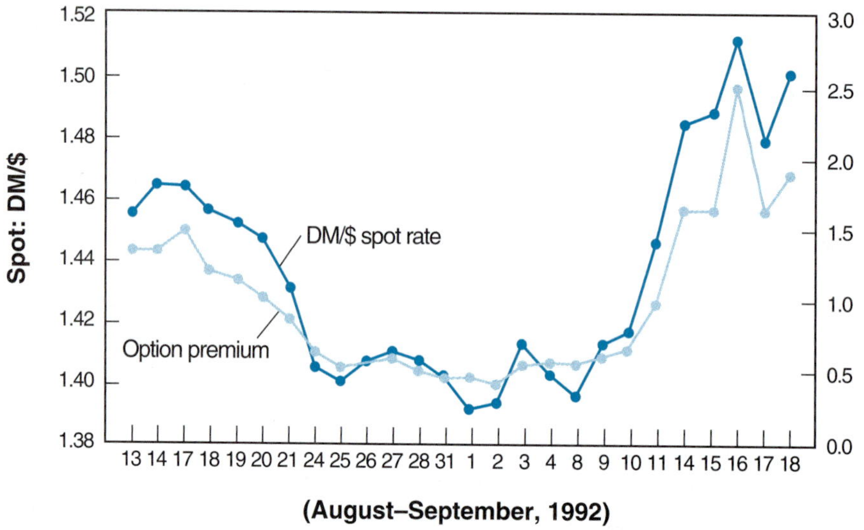

Case Questions

1. Should Stephanie Mayo sell the put option protection already in place? Use the current market rates and prices to defend your logic.
2. How have the events of September altered Stephanie's view of the DM/$ exchange rate?
3. How has the volatility of the put option changed between August and September?
4. If you were the Vice President for Treasury at Zapa, what benchmarks would you use to measure Stephanie's hedging effectiveness? How would this alter Stephanie's hedging?

apter 9

Operating Exposure

THIS CHAPTER EXTENDS THE CONCEPT OF TRANSACTION EXPOSURE, DESCRIBED IN CHAPTER 8, further into time and across the multitudes of future cash flows that create the value of any multinational firm. *Operating exposure*, also called *economic exposure*, *competitive exposure*, and even *strategic exposure* on occasion, measures any change in the present value of a firm resulting from changes in future operating cash flows caused by any unexpected change in exchange rates. Operating exposure analysis assesses the impact of changing exchange rates on a firm's own operations over coming months and years and on its competitive position vis-á-vis other firms. The goal is to identify strategic moves or operating techniques that the firm might wish to adopt to enhance its value in the face of unexpected exchange rate changes.

Operating exposure and transaction exposure are related in that they both deal with future cash flows. They differ in terms of which cash flows management considers and why those cash flows change when exchange rates change.

Attributes of Operating Exposure

Measuring the operating exposure of a firm requires forecasting and analyzing all the firm's future individual transaction exposures together with the future exposures of all the firm's competitors and potential competitors worldwide. A simple example will clarify the point.

A MNE like Eastman Kodak (U.S.) has a number of transaction exposures at any point in time. Kodak has sales in the United States, Japan, and Europe and therefore posts a continuing series of foreign currency receivables (and payables). Sales and expenses that are already contracted for are traditional *transaction exposures*. Sales that are highly probable based on Kodak's historical business line and market share but have no legal basis yet are *anticipated transaction exposures*. (This term is used quite specifically in accounting for foreign exchange rate gains and losses.)

What if the analysis of the firm's exposure to exchange rate changes is extended even further into the future? What are the longer-term exposures of Kodak to exchange rate changes? Future exchange rate changes will not only alter the domestic currency value (U.S. dollars in this case) of the firm's foreign currency cash flows, it will change the quantity of foreign currency cash flows generated as well. Any change in Kodak's cash flows in the future depends on how competitive it is in various markets. Kodak's international competitiveness will in turn be affected by the operating exposures of its major competitors like Fuji (Japan) and Agfa (Germany). The analysis of this longer term—where exchange rate changes are unpredictable and therefore unexpected—is the goal of operating exposure analysis.

From a broader perspective, operating exposure is not just the sensitivity of a firm's future cash flows to unexpected changes in foreign exchange rates, but also its sensitivity to other key macroeconomic variables. This factor has been labeled *macroeconomic uncertainty.* Chapter 6 described the parity relationships among exchange rates, interest rates, and inflation rates. However, these variables are often in disequilibrium with one another. Therefore, unexpected changes in interest rates and inflation rates could also have a simultaneous but differential impact on future cash flows. Global Finance Perspective 9.1 illustrates macroeconomic uncertainty.

Operating and Financing Cash Flows

The cash flows of the MNE can be divided into *operating cash flows* and *financing cash flows.* Operating cash flows arise from intercompany (between unrelated companies) and intracompany (between units of the same company) receivables and payables, rent and lease payments for the use of facilities and equipment, royalty and license fees for the use of technology and intellectual property, and assorted management fees for services provided.

Global Finance Perspective **9.1**

Volvo Car

Volvo Car, a subsidiary of Volvo (Sweden), illustrates a MNE's sensitivity to various macroeconomic variables including exchange rates, interest rates, and prices; i.e., *macroeconomic uncertainty.* Volvo Car produces most of its cars in Sweden but buys most of its inputs from Germany. The company's most important market is the United States. Top management of Volvo Car, as well as most financial analysts, believed that a depreciating Swedish krona versus the U.S. dollar, and an appreciating Swedish krona versus the deutschemark, would be beneficial to Volvo Car. Volvo Car's cash flows were statistically analyzed for their sensitivity to relevant macroeconomic variables. However, three variables explained most of the unanticipated variability of cash flows. The three variables were:

1. The Swedish krona/deutschemark exchange rates. A depreciating krona improved Volvo Car's cash flows.
2. The Swedish krona short-term interest rate. A reduction in this rate improved Volvo Car's cash flow due to increased demand for its cars.
3. German producer prices. An increase in these prices improved Volvo Car's cash flow.

These results reflected the fact that Volvo Car's major competitors were the German prestige car manufacturers BMW, Mercedes, and Audi. Thus measurement of Volvo Car's long-term operating exposure depended on how its competitors were situated with respect to unexpected changes in the same key macroeconomic variables, such as foreign exchange rates, interest rates, and inflation rates. (Since this study, Volvo Car has been acquired by Ford.)

Source: Oxelheim, Lars, and Clas Wihlborg, "Measuring Macroeconomic Exposure: The Case of Volvo Cars," *European Financial Management,* 1995, Volume 1, No. 3, pp. 211–263. This analysis was written before the introduction of the euro.

Financing cash flows are payments for the use of intercompany and intracompany loans (principal and interest) and stockholder equity (new equity investments and dividends). Each of these cash flows can occur at different time intervals, in different amounts, and in different currencies of denomination, and each has a different predictability of occurrence. We summarize intracompany cash flow possibilities in Exhibit 9.1.

Expected Versus Unexpected Changes in Cash Flow

Operating exposure is far more important for the long-run health of a business than changes caused by transaction or accounting exposure. However, operating exposure is inevitably subjective, because it depends on estimates of future cash flow changes over an arbitrary time horizon. Thus it does not spring from the accounting process, but rather from operating analysis. Planning for operating exposure is a total management responsibility because it depends on the interaction of strategies in finance, marketing, purchasing, and production.

An expected change in foreign exchange rates is not included in the definition of operating exposure, because both management and investors should have factored this information into their evaluation of anticipated operating results and market value. From a management perspective, budgeted financial statements already reflect information about the effect of an expected

Exhibit 9.1 Financial and Operating Cash Flows Between Parent and Subsidiary

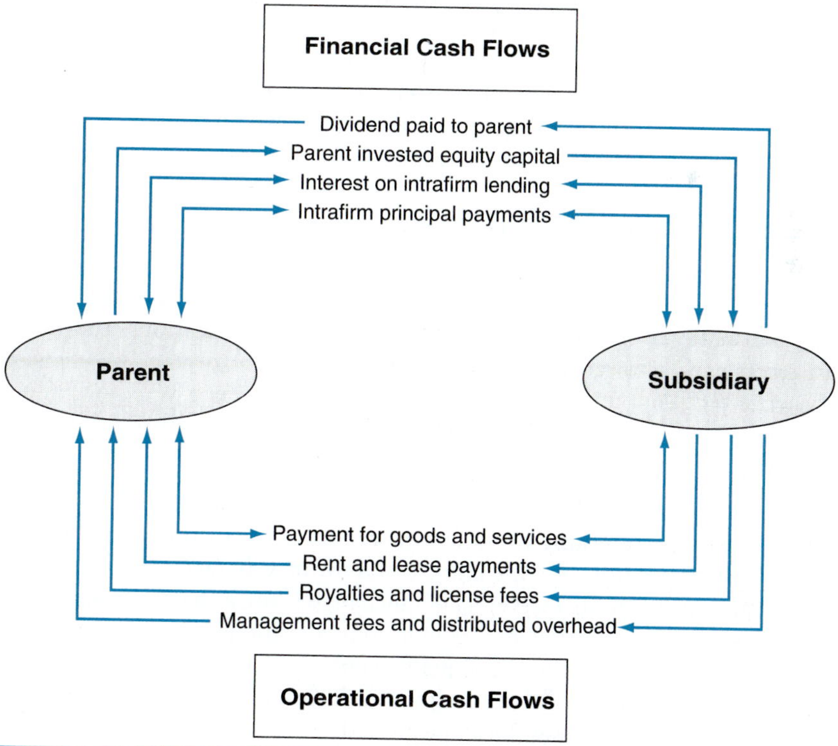

change in exchange rates. For example, under equilibrium conditions the forward rate might be used as an unbiased predictor of the future spot rate. In such a case, management would use the forward rate when preparing the operating budgets, rather than assume the spot rate would remain unchanged.

Another example is that expected cash flow to amortize debt should already reflect the international Fisher effect. The level of expected interest and principal repayment should be a function of expected exchange rates rather than existing spot rates.

From an investor's perspective, if the foreign exchange market is efficient, information about expected changes in exchange rates should be widely known and thus reflected in a firm's market value. Only unexpected changes in exchange rates, or an inefficient foreign exchange market, should cause market value to change.

Measuring the Impact of Operating Exposure

An unexpected change in exchange rates impacts a firm's expected cash flows at four levels, depending on the time horizon used.

Short Run

The first-level impact is on expected cash flows in the one-year operating budget. The gain or loss depends on the currency of denomination of expected cash flows. The currency of denomination cannot be changed for existing obligations, such as those defined by transaction exposure, or even for implied obligations such as purchase or sales commitments. Apart from real or implied obligations, in the short run it is difficult to change sales prices or renegotiate factor costs. Therefore realized cash flows will differ from those expected in the budget. However, as time passes, prices and costs can be changed to reflect the new competitive realities caused by a change in exchange rates.

Medium Run: Equilibrium Case

The second-level impact is on expected medium-run cash flows, such as those expressed in two- to five-year budgets, assuming parity conditions hold among foreign exchange rates, national inflation rates, and national interest rates. Under equilibrium conditions, the firm should be able to adjust prices and factor costs over time to maintain the expected level of cash flows. In this case the currency of denomination of expected cash flows is not as important as the countries in which cash flows originate. National monetary, fiscal, and balance of payments policies determine whether equilibrium conditions will exist and whether firms will be allowed to adjust prices and costs.

If equilibrium exists continuously and a firm is free to adjust its prices and costs to maintain its expected competitive position, its operating exposure may be zero. Its expected cash flows would be realized and therefore its market value unchanged, since the exchange rate change was anticipated. However, it is also possible that equilibrium conditions exist but the firm is unwilling or unable to adjust operations to the new competitive environment. In such a case, the firm would experience operating exposure because its realized cash flows would differ from expected cash flows. As a result, its market value might also be altered.

Medium Run: Disequilibrium Case

The third-level impact is on expected medium-run cash flows assuming disequilibrium conditions. In this case, the firm may not be able to adjust prices and costs to reflect the new competitive realities caused by a change in exchange rates. The firm's realized cash flows will differ from its expected cash flows. The firm's market value may change because of the unanticipated results.

Long Run

The fourth-level impact is on expected long-run cash flows, meaning those beyond five years. At this strategic level, a firm's cash flows will be influenced by the reactions of existing and potential competitors to exchange rate changes under disequilibrium conditions. In fact, all firms that are subject to international competition, whether they are purely domestic or multinational, are exposed to foreign exchange operating exposure in the long run whenever foreign exchange markets are not continuously in equilibrium.

Illustration of Operating Exposure: Carlton, Inc.

To illustrate the consequences of operating exposure we use Carlton, Inc., a hypothetical U.S.-based MNE with headquarters, research, and manufacturing located in Palo Alto, California. Its main products are equipment for the telecommunications industry worldwide. Carlton has 100%-owned manufacturing, sales, and service subsidiaries in Munich, Germany (Carlton Germany), and Sao Paulo, Brazil (Carlton Brazil).

Exhibit 9.2 presents the dilemma facing Carlton as a result of an unexpected change in the value of the euro, the currency of economic consequence for the German subsidiary. Carlton derives much of its reported profits (earnings and earnings per share—EPS—as reported to Wall Street) from its European subsidiary. If the euro unexpectedly falls in value, how will Carlton Germany's revenues change (prices, in euro terms, and volumes). How will its costs change (primarily input costs, in euro terms)? How will competitors respond? We explain the sequence of likely events over the short and medium run in the following section.

Base Case

Carlton Germany manufactures in Germany from European material and labor. Half of production is sold within Europe for euros, and half is exported to non-European countries. All sales are invoiced in euros, and accounts receivable are equal to one-fourth of annual sales. In other words, the average collection period is 90 days. Inventory is equal to 25% of annual direct costs. Carlton Germany can expand or contract production volume without any significant change in per-unit direct costs or in overall general and administrative expenses. Depreciation on plant and equipment is €600,000 per year, and the corporate income tax in Germany is 34%.

The December 31, 2002, balance sheet and alternative scenarios are shown in Exhibit 9.3. We assume that on January 1, 2003, before any commercial activity begins, the euro unexpectedly drops 16.67% in value, from \$1.2000/€ to \$1.0000/€. If no devaluation had occurred, Carlton Germany was expected to perform in 2003 as shown in the base case of Exhibit 9.3, generating a dollar cash flow from operations for Carlton of \$2,074,320.

Exhibit 9.2 Carlton, Inc., and Carlton Germany

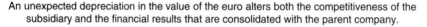

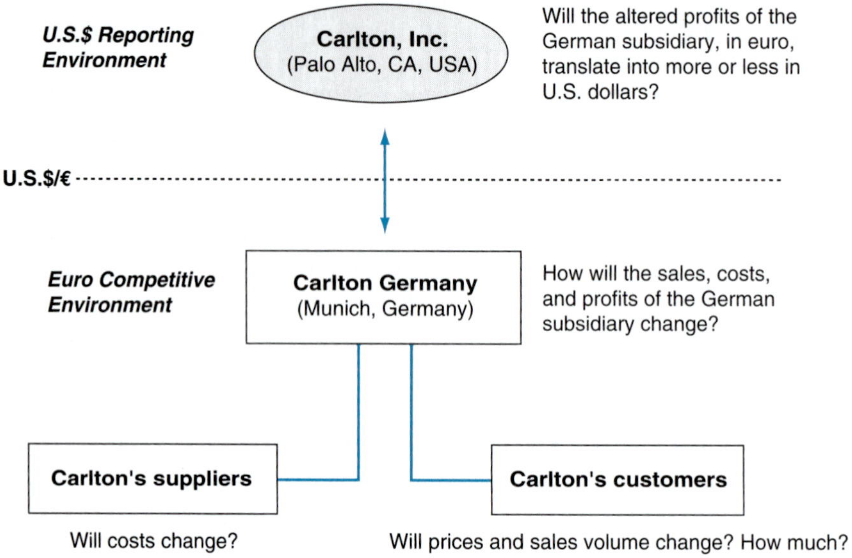
U.S.$ Reporting Environment
Carlton, Inc. (Palo Alto, CA, USA)
Will the altered profits of the German subsidiary, in euro, translate into more or less in U.S. dollars?
U.S.$/€
Euro Competitive Environment
Carlton Germany (Munich, Germany)
How will the sales, costs, and profits of the German subsidiary change?
Carlton's suppliers
Carlton's customers
Will costs change?
Will prices and sales volume change? How much?

An unexpected depreciation in the value of the euro alters both the competitiveness of the subsidiary and the financial results that are consolidated with the parent company.

Operating exposure depends on whether an unexpected change in exchange rates causes unanticipated changes in sales volume, sales prices, or operating costs. Following a euro devaluation, Carlton Germany might choose to maintain its domestic sales prices constant in euro terms, or it might try to raise domestic prices because competing imports are now priced higher in Europe. The firm might choose to keep export prices constant in terms of foreign currencies, in terms of euros, or somewhere in between (partial pass-through). The strategy undertaken depends to a large measure on management's opinion about the price elasticity of demand. On the cost side, Carlton Germany might raise prices because of more expensive imported raw material or components, or perhaps because all domestic prices in Germany have risen and labor is now demanding higher wages to compensate for domestic inflation.

Carlton Germany's domestic sales and costs might also be partly determined by the effect of the euro devaluation on demand. To the extent that the devaluation, by making prices of German goods initially more competitive, stimulates purchases of European goods in import-competing sectors of the economy as well as exports of German goods, German national income should increase. This assumes that the favorable effect of a euro devaluation on comparative prices is not immediately offset by higher domestic inflation. Thus Carlton Germany might be able to sell more goods domestically because of price and income effects and internationally because of price effects.

To illustrate the effect of various post-devaluation scenarios on Carlton Germany's operating exposure, consider three simple cases:

Case 1: Devaluation; no change in any variable.

Case 2: Increase in sales volume; other variables remain constant.

Case 3: Increase in sales price; other variables remain constant.

To calculate the net change in present value under each of the scenarios, we will use a five-year horizon for any change in cash flow induced by the change in the dollar/euro exchange rate.

Case 1: Devaluation; No Change in Any Variable

Assume that in the five years ahead no changes occur in sales volume, sales price, or operating costs. Profits for the coming year in euros will be as expected, and cash flow from operations will be €1,728,600, as shown in Exhibit 9.3. With a new exchange rate of $1.0000/€, this cash flow measured in dollars during 2003 will be €1,728,600 × $1.0000/€ = $1,728,600. Exhibit 9.3 shows that the change in year-end cash flows from the base case is $345,720 for each of the next five years (2003–2007).

Exhibit 9.3 shows that the discounted present value of this series of diminished dollar value cash flows is ($1,033,914).

Case 2: Volume Increases; Other Variables Remain Constant

Assume that sales within Europe double following the devaluation because German-made telecom components are now more competitive with imports. Additionally, export volume doubles because German-made components are now cheaper in countries whose currencies have not weakened. The sales price is kept constant in euro terms because management of Carlton Germany has not observed any change in local German operating costs and because it sees an opportunity to increase market share.

Exhibit 9.3 shows expected cash flow for the first year (2003) would be $3,840,600. This amount, however, is not available, because a doubling of sales volume will require additional investment in accounts receivable and in inventory. Although a portion of this additional investment might be financed by increasing accounts payable, we assume additional working capital is financed by cash flow from operations.

At the end of 2003, accounts receivable will be equal to one- fourth of annual sales, or €6,400,000. This amount is twice receivables of €3,200,000 at the end of 2002, and the incremental increase of €3,200,000 must be financed from available cash. Year-end inventory would be equal to one-fourth of annual direct costs, or €4,800,000, an increase of €2,400,000 over the year-beginning level. Receivables and inventory together increase by €5,600,000. At the end of five years (2007), these incremental cash outflows will be recaptured, because any investment in current assets eventually rolls back into cash.

Assuming no further change in volume, price, or costs, cash inflows for the five years would be as described in Exhibit 9.3. In this instance, the devaluation causes a major drop in first-year cash flow from the $2,074,320 anticipated in 2003 without devaluation to a negative cash flow of $1,759,400. However, the remaining four years' cash flow is substantially enhanced by the operating effects of the devaluation. Over time Carlton Germany generates significantly more cash for its owners. The devaluation produces an operating gain over time, rather than an operating loss.

Exhibit 9.3 Carlton Germany

	A	B	C	D	E	F	G	H
1								
2		Exhibit 9.3 Carlton Germany						
3								
4		Balance Sheet, December 31, 2002						
5		Assets		Liabilities and net worth				
6		Cash	€ 1,600,000	Accounts payable	€ 800,000			
7		Accounts receivable	3,200,000	Short-term bank loan	1,600,000			
8		Inventory	2,400,000	Long-term debt	1,600,000			
9		Net plant and equipment	4,800,000	Common stock	1,800,000			
10				Retained earnings	6,200,000			
11		Total assets	€ 12,000,000	Total liabilities and net worth	€ 12,000,000			
12								
13		**Assumptions**		**Base Case**	**Case 1**	**Case 2**	**Case 3**	
14		Exchange rate, $/€		1.2000	1.0000	1.0000	1.0000	
15		Sales volume (units)		1,000,000	1,000,000	2,000,000	1,000,000	
16		Sales price per unit		€12.80	€12.80	€12.80	€15.36	
17		Direct cost per unit		€9.60	€9.60	€9.60	€9.60	
18		Accounts receivable (% of sales)		25.00%				
19		Inventory (% of direct cost)		25.00%				
20		Cost of capital (annual discount rate)		20.00%				
21		Income tax rate		34.00%				
22								
23		Annual Cash Flows before Adjustments						
24		Sales revenue		€ 12,800,000	€ 12,800,000	€ 25,600,000	€ 15,360,000	
25		Direct cost of goods sold		9,600,000	9,600,000	19,200,000	9,600,000	
26		Cash operating expenses (fixed)		890,000	890,000	890,000	890,000	
27		Depreciation		600,000	600,000	600,000	600,000	
28		Pretax profit		€ 1,710,000	€ 1,710,000	€ 4,910,000	€ 4,270,000	
29		Income tax expense		581,400	581,400	1,669,400	1,451,800	
30		Profit after tax		€ 1,128,600	€ 1,128,600	€ 3,240,600	€ 2,818,200	
31		Add back depreciation		600,000	600,000	600,000	600,000	
32		Cash flow from operations, in euros		€ 1,728,600	€ 1,728,600	€ 3,840,600	€ 3,418,200	
33		Cash flow from operations, in dollars		$ 2,074,320	$ 1,728,600	$ 3,840,600	$ 3,418,200	
34								
35		Adjustments to Working Capital for 2003 and 2007 Caused by Changes in Conditions						
36		Accounts receivable		€ 3,200,000	€ 3,200,000	€ 6,400,000	€ 3,840,000	
37		Inventory		2,400,000	2,400,000	4,800,000	2,400,000	
38		Sum		€ 5,600,000	€ 5,600,000	€ 11,200,000	€ 6,240,000	
39		Change from base conditions in 2003		€ -	€ -	€ 5,600,000	€ 640,000	
40								
41			Year	Year-End Cash Flows				
42			1 (2003)	$ 2,074,320	$ 1,728,600	$ (1,759,400)	$ 2,778,200	
43			2 (2004)	2,074,320	1,728,600	3,840,600	3,418,200	
44			3 (2005)	2,074,320	1,728,600	3,840,600	3,418,200	
45			4 (2006)	2,074,320	1,728,600	3,840,600	3,418,200	
46			5 (2007)	2,074,320	1,728,600	9,440,600	4,058,200	
47								
48				Present Value of Year-End Cash Flows				
49				$ 6,203,487	$ 5,169,572	$ 9,069,593	$ 9,946,379	
50								
51			Year	Change in Year-End Cash Flows from Base Conditions				
52			1 (2003)	na	$ (345,720)	$ (3,833,720)	$ 703,880	
53			2 (2004)	na	(345,720)	1,766,280	1,343,880	
54			3 (2005)	na	(345,720)	1,766,280	1,343,880	
55			4 (2006)	na	(345,720)	1,766,280	1,343,880	
56			5 (2007)	na	(345,720)	7,366,280	1,983,880	
57								
58				Present Value of Incremental Year-End Cash Flows				
59				na	$ (1,033,914)	$ 2,866,106	$ 3,742,892	
60								
61		Key Cell Entries						
62		C11: =SUM(C6:C10), copy to F11		D33: =D32*D14, copy to D33:F33				
63		D18: =C7/D24, copy to D19		D36: =$D18*D24, copy to E36:G37				
64		D24: =D$15*D16, copy to E24:G25		D38: =SUM(D36:D37), copy to E38:G38				
65		D26: Enter as data value, copy to E26:G		D39: =D38 —D38, copy to E39:G39				
66		D27: Enter as data value, copy to E27:G		D42: =D33-D39, copy to E42:G42				
67		D28: =D24-SUM(D25:D27), copy to E28:G28		D43: =D$33, copy to E43:G45				
68		D29: =D21*D28, copy to E29:G29		D46: =D33+D39, copy to E46:G46				
69		D30: =D28—D29, copy to E30:G30		D49: =NPV(D20,D42:D46), copy to E49:G49				
70		D31: =D27, copy to E31:G31		E52: =E42—$D42, copy to F52:G56				
71		D32: =D30+D31, copy to E32:G32		E59: =NPV(D20,E52:E56), copy to F59:G59				
72								
73								
74

The reason that Carlton Corporation is better off in Case 2 following the devaluation is that sales volume doubled, while the per-unit dollar-equivalent sales price fell only 16.67%—the percent amount of the devaluation. In other words, the product faced a price elasticity of demand greater than 1.

Case 3: Sales Price Increases; Other Variables Remain Constant

Assume the euro sales price is raised from €12.80 to €15.36 per unit to maintain the same U.S. dollar-equivalent price (the change offsets the depreciation of the euro). Assume further that volume remains constant in spite of this price increase; that is, customers expect to pay the same dollar-equivalent price and local costs do not change.

Carlton Germany is now better off following the devaluation than it was before because the sales price, which is pegged to the international price level, increased. However, volume did not drop. The new level of accounts receivable would be one-fourth of the new sales level of €15,360,000, or €3,840,000, an increase of €640,000 over the base case. The investment in inventory is $2,400,000, which is the same as the base case because annual direct costs did not change.

Expected dollar cash flow in every year exceeds the cash flow of $2,074,320 that had been anticipated with no devaluation. The increase in working capital causes net cash flow to be only $2,778,200 in 2003, but thereafter the cash flow is $3,418,200 per year, with an additional $640,000 working capital recovered in the fifth year.

The key to this improvement is operating leverage. If costs are incurred in euros and do not increase after a devaluation, an increase in the sales price by the amount of devaluation will lead to sharply higher profits.

Other Possibilities

If any portion of sales revenues were incurred in other currencies, the situation would be different. Carlton Germany might leave the foreign sales price unchanged, in effect raising the euro-equivalent price. Alternatively, it might leave the euro-equivalent price unchanged, thus lowering the foreign sales price in an attempt to gain volume. Of course, it could also position itself between these two extremes. Depending on elasticities and the proportion of foreign to domestic sales, total sales revenue might rise or fall.

If some or all raw material or components were imported and paid for in hard currencies, euro operating costs would increase after the devaluation of the euro. Another possibility is that local (not imported) euro costs would rise after a devaluation.

Measurement of Loss

Exhibit 9.3 summarizes the change in expected year-end cash flows for the three cases and compares them with the cash flow expected should no devaluation occur (Base Case). These changes are then discounted by Carlton's assumed weighted average cost of capital of 20% to obtain the present value of the gain (loss) on operating exposure.

In Case 1, in which nothing changes after the euro is devalued, Carlton incurs an operating loss with a present value of ($1,033,914). In Case 2, in which volume doubled with no price change after devaluation, Carlton experienced an operating gain with a present value of \$2,866,106. In Case 3, in which the euro sales price was increased and volume did not change, the present value of the operating gain from devaluation was \$3,742,892. An almost infinite number of combinations of volume, price, and cost could follow any devaluation, and any or all of them might take effect immediately after a devaluation or only after the passage of some time.

Strategic Management of Operating Exposure

The objective of both operating and transaction exposure management is to anticipate and influence the effect of unexpected changes in exchanges rates on a firm's future cash flows, rather than merely hoping for the best. To meet this objective, management can *diversify* the firm's operating and financing base. Management can also change the firm's operating and financing policies.

The key to managing operating exposure at the strategic level is for management to recognize a disequilibrium in parity conditions when it occurs and to be prepositioned to react in the most appropriate way. This task can best be accomplished if a firm diversifies internationally both its operating and its financing bases. Diversifying operations means diversifying sales, location of production facilities, and raw material sources. Diversifying the financing base means raising funds in more than one capital market and in more than one currency.

A diversification strategy permits the firm to react either actively or passively, depending on management's risk preference, to opportunities presented by disequilibrium conditions in the foreign exchange, capital, and product markets. Such a strategy does not require management to predict disequilibrium, but only to recognize it when it occurs. It does require management to consider how competitors are prepositioned with respect to their own operating exposures. This knowledge should reveal which firms would be helped or hurt competitively by alternative disequilibrium scenarios.

Diversifying Operations

If a firm's operations are diversified internationally, management is prepositioned both to recognize disequilibrium when it occurs and to react competitively. Consider the case where purchasing power parity is temporarily in disequilibrium. Although the disequilibrium may have been unpredictable, management can often recognize its symptoms as soon as they occur. For example, management might notice a change in comparative costs in the firm's own plants located in different countries. It might also observe changed profit margins or sales volume in one area compared to another, depending on price and income elasticities of demand and competitors' reactions.

Recognizing a temporary change in worldwide competitive conditions permits management to make changes in operating strategies. Management might make marginal shifts in sourcing raw materials, components, or finished products. If spare capacity exists, production runs can be lengthened in one country and reduced in another. The marketing effort can be strengthened in export markets where the firm's products have become more price-competitive because of the disequilibrium condition.

Even if management does not actively distort normal operations when exchange rates change, the firm should experience some beneficial portfolio effects. The variability of its cash flows is probably reduced by international diversification of its production, sourcing, and sales because exchange rate changes under disequilibrium conditions are likely to increase the firm's competitiveness in some markets while reducing it in others. In that case operating exposure would be neutralized. Global Finance Perspective 9.2 shows Goodyear's response to the Mexican peso devaluation through a timely shift in operating strategy.

In contrast to the internationally diversified MNE, a purely domestic firm might be subject to the full impact of foreign exchange operating exposure even though it does not have foreign currency cash flows. For example, it could experience intense import competition in its domestic market from competing firms producing in countries with undervalued currencies.

A purely domestic firm does not have the option to react to an international disequilibrium condition in the same manner as a MNE. In fact, a purely domestic firm will not be positioned to recognize that a disequilibrium exists, because it lacks comparative data from its own internal sources. By the time external data are available from published sources, it is often too late to react. Even if a domestic firm recognizes the disequilibrium, it cannot quickly shift production and sales into foreign markets in which it has had no previous presence.

Constraints exist that may limit the feasibility of diversifying production locations. The technology of a particular industry, such as aerospace, may require large economies of scale. High-tech firms, such as Intel, prefer to locate in places where they have easy access to other high-tech suppliers, a highly educated workforce, and one or more leading universities. Their research and development efforts are closely tied to initial production and sales activities.

Diversifying Financing

If a firm diversifies its financing sources, it will be prepositioned to take advantage of temporary deviations from the international Fisher effect. If interest rate differentials do not equal expected changes in exchange rates, opportunities to lower a firm's cost of capital will exist. However, to be able to switch financing sources, a firm must already be well-known in the international investment community, with banking contacts firmly established. Once again, this is not an option for a domestic firm that has limited its financing to one capital market.

Global Finance Perspective 9.2

Goodyear's Response to the Mexican Peso Devaluation

When Goodyear's manager in Mexico heard on his car radio on December 20, 1994, that the peso had crashed, he immediately met with his managers to assess the damage. Within days, he figured that domestic demand for their tires would plunge more than 20 percent, or 3,000 tires a day. His choices: lay off workers or find new export markets—right away, before his warehouse overflowed.

His team members, aided by the Goodyear Tire and Rubber company headquarters in Akron, Ohio, not only found enough export buyers to make up for what turned out to be a 3,500-tire drop in domestic sales. They also found spots to sell 1,600 more, setting an output record at the plant, some 15 miles north of Mexico City. A factory that had imported supplies but exported not a single tire in 1992 now shipped away half its production, mostly to the United States but also to South America and Europe. The company quickly moved from being a net importer to a net exporter.

As we will demonstrate in Chapter 11, diversifying sources of financing, regardless of the currency of denomination, can lower a firm's cost of capital and increase its availability of capital. It could also diversify such risks as restrictive capital market policies, and other constraints if the firm is located in a segmented capital market. This is especially important for firms resident in emerging markets.

Proactive Management of Operating Exposure

Operating and transaction exposures can be partially managed by adopting operating or financing policies that offset anticipated foreign exchange exposures. Four of the most commonly employed proactive policies are:

1. Matching currency cash flows
2. Risk-sharing agreements
3. Back-to-back or parallel loans
4. Currency swaps

Matching Currency Cash Flows

One way to offset an anticipated continuous long exposure to a particular currency is to acquire debt denominated in that currency. Exhibit 9.4 depicts the exposure of a U.S. firm with continu-

Exhibit 9.4 Matching: Debt Financing as a Financial Hedge

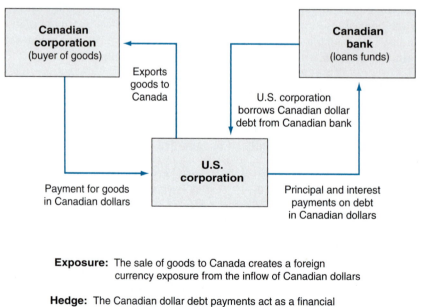

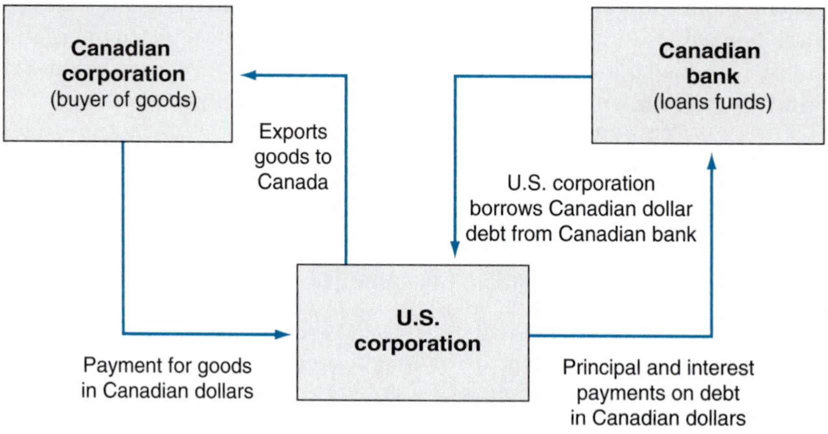

Exposure: The sale of goods to Canada creates a foreign currency exposure from the inflow of Canadian dollars

Hedge: The Canadian dollar debt payments act as a financial hedge by requiring debt service, an outflow of Canadian dollars

ing export sales to Canada. In order to compete effectively in Canadian markets, the firm invoices all export sales in Canadian dollars. This policy results in a continuing receipt of Canadian dollars month after month. If the export sales are part of a continuing supplier relationship, the long Canadian dollar position is relatively predictable and constant. This endless series of transaction exposures could of course be continually hedged with forward contracts or other contractual hedges, as discussed in the previous chapter.

But what if the firm sought out a continual use, an outflow, for its continual inflow of Canadian dollars? If the U.S. firm were to acquire part of its debt-capital in the Canadian dollar markets, it could use the relatively predictable Canadian dollar cash inflows from export sales to service the principal and interest payments on Canadian dollar debt and be cash flow *matched*. The U.S.-based firm has hedged an operational cash inflow by creating a financial cash outflow, and so it does not have to actively manage the exposure with contractual financial instruments such as forward contracts. This form of hedging, sometimes referred to as *matching*, is effective in eliminating currency exposure when the exposure cash flow is relatively constant and predictable over time.

The list of potential matching strategies is nearly endless. A second alternative would be for the U.S. firm to seek out potential suppliers of raw materials or components in Canada as a substitute for U.S. or other foreign firms. The firm would then possess not only an operational Canadian dollar cash inflow, the receivable, but also a Canadian dollar operational cash outflow, a payable. If the cash flows were roughly the same in magnitude and timing, the strategy would be a natural hedge. The term "natural" refers to operating-based activities of the firm.

A third alternative, often referred to as *currency switching*, would be to pay foreign suppliers with Canadian dollars. For example, if the U.S. firm imported components from Mexico, the Mexican firms themselves might welcome payment in Canadian dollars because they are short Canadian dollars in their multinational cash flow network.

Currency Clauses: Risk Sharing

An alternative arrangement for managing a long-term cash flow exposure between firms with a continuing buyer-supplier relationship is risk sharing. *Risk sharing* is a contractual arrangement in which the buyer and seller agree to "share" or split currency movement impacts on payments between them. If the two firms are interested in a long-term relationship based on product quality and supplier reliability and not on the whims of the currency markets, a cooperative agreement to share the burden of currency risk management may be in order.

If Ford's North American operations import automotive parts from Mazda (Japan) every month, year after year, major swings in exchange rates can benefit one party at the expense of the other. (Ford is a major stockholder of Mazda, but it does not exert control over its operations. Therefore, the risk-sharing agreement is particularly appropriate; transactions between the two are both intercompany and intracompany. A risk-sharing agreement solidifies the partnership.) One potential solution would be for Ford and Mazda to agree that all purchases by Ford will be made in Japanese yen at the current exchange rate, as long as the spot rate on the date of invoice is between, say, ¥115/\$ and ¥125/\$. If the exchange rate is between these values on the payment dates, Ford agrees to accept whatever transaction exposure exists (because it is paying in a foreign currency). If, however, the exchange rate falls outside this range on the payment date, Ford and Mazda will share the difference equally.

For example, Ford has an account payable of ¥25,000,000 for the month of March. If the spot rate on the date of invoice is ¥110/$, the Japanese yen would have appreciated versus the dollar, causing Ford's costs of purchasing automotive parts to rise. Since this rate falls outside the contractual range, Mazda would agree to accept a total payment in Japanese yen which would result from a difference of ¥5/$ (i.e., ¥115 – ¥110). Ford's payment would be:

$$\left[\frac{¥25{,}000{,}000}{¥115.00/\$ - \left(\dfrac{¥5.00/\$}{2}\right)}\right] = \frac{¥25{,}000{,}000}{¥112.50/\$} = \$222{,}222.22$$

Ford's total payment in Japanese yen would be calculated using an exchange rate of ¥112.50/$, and saves Ford $5,050.51. At a spot rate of ¥110/$, Ford's costs for March would be $227,272.73. The risk-sharing agreement between Ford and Mazda allows Ford to pay $222,222.22, a savings of $5,050.51 over the cost without risk sharing (this "savings" is a reduction in an increased cost, not a true cost reduction.) Both parties therefore incur costs and benefits from exchange rate movements outside the specified band. Note that the movement could just as easily have been in Mazda's favor if the spot rate had moved to ¥130/$.

The risk-sharing arrangement is intended to smooth the impact on both parties of volatile and unpredictable exchange rate movements. Of course a sustained appreciation of one currency versus the other would require the negotiation of a new sharing agreement, but the ultimate goal of the agreement is to alleviate currency pressures on the continuing business relationship. Risk-sharing agreements like these have been in use for nearly 50 years on world markets. They became something of a rarity during the 1960s when exchange rates were relatively stable under the Bretton Woods Agreement. But with the return to floating exchange rates in the 1970s, firms with long-term customer-supplier relationships across borders have returned to some old ways of maintaining mutually beneficial long-term trade.

Back-to-Back Loans

A *back-to-back loan*, also referred to as a *parallel loan* or *credit swap*, occurs when two business firms in separate countries arrange to borrow each other's currency for a specific period of time. At an agreed terminal date they return the borrowed currencies. The operation is conducted outside the foreign exchange markets, although spot quotations may be used as the reference point for determining the amount of funds to be swapped. Such a swap creates a covered hedge against exchange loss, since each company, on its own books, borrows the same currency it repays. Back-to-back loans are also used at a time of actual or anticipated legal limitations on the transfer of investment funds to or from either country.

The structure of a typical back-to-back loan is illustrated in Exhibit 9.5. A British parent firm wanting to invest funds in its Dutch subsidiary locates a Dutch parent firm that wants to invest funds in the United Kingdom. Avoiding the exchange markets entirely, the British parent lends pounds to the Dutch subsidiary in the United Kingdom, while the Dutch parent lends euros to the British subsidiary in the Netherlands. The two loans would be for equal values at the current spot rate and for a specified maturity. At maturity the two separate loans would each be repaid to

Exhibit 9.5 Using a Back-to-Back Loan for Currency Hedging

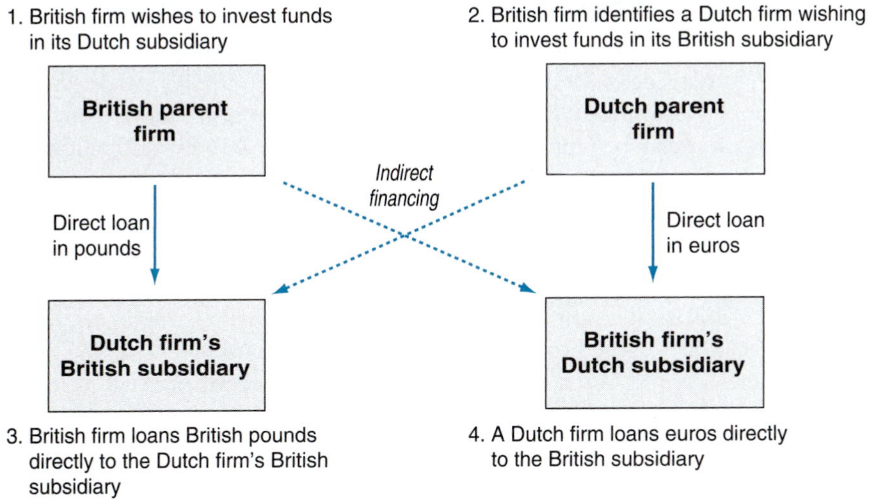
1. British firm wishes to invest funds in its Dutch subsidiary
2. British firm identifies a Dutch firm wishing to invest funds in its British subsidiary
British parent firm
Dutch parent firm
Indirect financing
Direct loan in pounds
Direct loan in euros
Dutch firm's British subsidiary
British firm's Dutch subsidiary
3. British firm loans British pounds directly to the Dutch firm's British subsidiary
4. A Dutch firm loans euros directly to the British subsidiary

The back-to-back loan provides a method for parent-subsidiary cross-border financing without incurring direct currency exposure.

the original lender, again without any need to use the foreign exchange markets. Neither loan carries any foreign exchange risk, and neither loan normally needs the approval of any governmental body regulating the availability of foreign exchange for investment purposes.

Parent company guarantees are not needed on the back-to-back loans because each loan carries the right of offset in the event of default of the other loan. A further agreement can provide for maintenance of principal parity in case of changes in the spot rate between the two countries. For example, if the pound dropped by more than, say, 6% for as long as 30 days, the British parent might have to advance additional pounds to the Dutch subsidiary to bring the principal value of the two loans back to parity. A similar provision would protect the British if the euro should weaken. Although this parity provision might lead to changes in the amount of home currency each party must lend during the period of the agreement, it does not increase foreign exchange risk, because at maturity all loans are repaid in the same currency loaned.

There are two fundamental impediments to widespread use of the back-to-back loan. First, it is difficult for a firm to find a partner, termed a *counterparty*, for the currency, amount, and timing desired. Secondly, a risk exists that one of the parties will fail to return the borrowed funds at the designated maturity—although this risk is minimized because each party to the loan has, in effect, 100% collateral, albeit in a different currency. These disadvantages have led to the rapid development and wide use of the currency swap.

Currency Swaps

A *currency swap* resembles a back-to-back loan except that it does not appear on a firm's balance sheet. As we noted briefly in Chapter 6, the term *swap* is widely used to describe a foreign exchange agreement between two parties to exchange a given amount of one currency for another and, after a period of time, to give back the original amounts swapped. Care should be taken to clarify which of the many different swaps is being referred to in a specific case.

In a currency swap, a firm and a swap dealer or swap bank agree to exchange an equivalent amount of two different currencies for a specified period of time. Currency swaps can be negotiated for a wide range of maturities up to at least ten years. If funds are more expensive in one country than another, a fee may be required to compensate for the interest differential. The swap dealer or swap bank acts as a middleman in setting up the swap agreement.

A typical currency swap first requires two firms to borrow funds in the markets and currencies in which they are best known. For example, a Japanese firm would typically borrow yen on a regular basis in its home market. If, however, the Japanese firm were exporting to the United States and earning U.S. dollars, it might wish to construct a *matching cash flow hedge*, which would allow it to use the U.S. dollars earned to make regular debt-service payments on U.S. dollar debt. If, however, the Japanese firm is not well known in the U.S. financial markets, it may have no ready access to U.S. dollar debt.

One way in which it could, in effect, borrow dollars, is to participate in a *cross-currency swap* (see Exhibit 9.6). The Japanese firm could swap its yen-denominated debt service payments with another firm that has U.S. dollar-debt service payments. This swap would have the Japanese firm "paying dollars" and "receiving yen." The Japanese firm would then have dollar-debt service

Exhibit 9.6 Using a Cross-Currency Swap to Hedge Currency Exposure

Both the Japanese corporation and the U.S. corporation would like to enter into a cross-currency swap that would allow them to use foreign currency cash inflows to service debt.

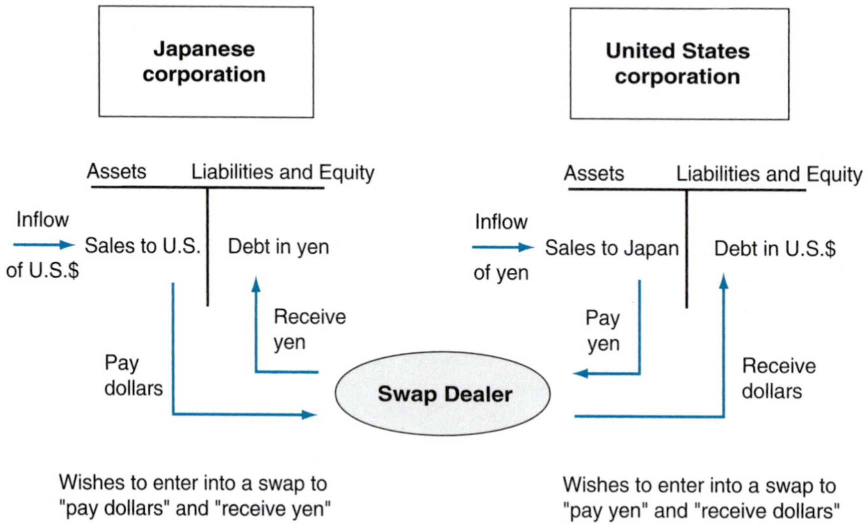

without actually borrowing U.S. dollars. Simultaneously, a U.S. corporation could actually be entering into a cross-currency swap in the opposite direction—"paying yen" and "receiving dollars." The swap dealer is taking the role of a middleman.

Swap dealers arrange most swaps on a *blind basis,* meaning that the initiating firm does not know who is on the other side of the swap arrangement—the *counterparty.* The firm views the dealer or bank as its counterparty. Because the swap markets are dominated by the major money center banks worldwide, the counterparty risk is acceptable. Because the swap dealer's business is arranging swaps, the dealer can generally arrange for the currency, amount, and timing of the desired swap.

Accountants in the United States treat the currency swap as a foreign exchange transaction rather than as debt and treat the obligation to reverse the swap at some later date as a forward exchange contract. Forward exchange contracts can be matched against assets, but they are entered in a firm's footnotes rather than as balance sheet items. The result is that both translation and operating exposures are avoided, and neither a long-term receivable nor a long-term debt is created on the balance sheet. The risk of changes in currency rates to the implied collateral in a long-term currency swap can be treated with a clause similar to the maintenance-of-principal clause in a back-to-back loan. If exchange rates change by more than some specified amount—say, 10%—an additional amount of the weaker currency might have to be advanced.

After being introduced on a global scale in the early 1980s, currency swaps have grown to be one of the largest financial derivative markets in the world. Chapter 14 will provide a detailed explanation of the theory and application of currency swaps in the context of interest rate risk management.

Contractual Approaches: Hedging the Unhedgeable

Some MNEs now attempt to hedge their operating exposure with contractual strategies. Firms like Merck (U.S.) and Eastman Kodak (U.S.) have undertaken long-term currency option positions hedges designed to offset lost earnings from adverse exchange rate changes. This hedging of what many of these firms refer to as *strategic exposure* or *competitive exposure* seems to fly in the face of traditional theory.

The ability of firms to hedge the "unhedgeable" is dependent upon *predictability*: 1) the predictability of the firm's future cash flows and 2) the predictability of the firm's competitor's responses to exchange rate changes. Although the management of many firms may believe they are capable of predicting their own cash flows, few in practice feel capable of accurately predicting competitor response.

Merck is an example of a firm whose management feels capable of both. The company possesses relatively predictable long-run revenue streams due to the product-niche nature of the pharmaceuticals industry. As a U.S.-based exporter to foreign markets, markets in which sales levels by product are relatively predictable and prices are often regulated by government, Merck can accurately predict net long-term cash flows in foreign currencies five and ten years into the future. Merck has a relatively undiversified operating structure. It is highly centralized in terms of where research, development, and production costs are located. Merck's managers feel Merck has no real alternatives but contractual hedging if it is to weather long-term unexpected exchange rate changes. Merck has purchased over-the-counter (OTC) long-term put options on foreign currencies versus the U.S. dollar as insurance against potential lost earnings from exchange rate changes. In Merck's case, the predictability of competitor response to exchange rate changes is less pertinent given the niche-market nature of pharmaceutical products.

Eastman Kodak is another MNE that has in the past undertaken contractual hedging of its operating exposure. Kodak management believes its markets are largely price-driven and is aware that its major competitor, Fuji, has a Japanese cost base. If the U.S. dollar were to strengthen in the medium to long term, Kodak's market share in the United States and in foreign markets would decline. Kodak leadership also believes that whatever sales Kodak loses, its competitors will gain. Kodak has therefore also purchased long-term put options on foreign currencies, which would replace long-term earnings if the value of the U.S. dollar rose unexpectedly.

The magnitude of the option position depends on the nature of desired replacement. For example, if Kodak wished to insure only the lost net earnings from exchange rate–induced losses, the option position would be considerably smaller than a position attempting to replace gross sales revenues. Given the premium expenses associated with long-term put option positions of this type, replacing earnings is preferred to replacing sales.

A significant question remains as to the true effectiveness of hedging operating exposure with contractual hedges. The fact remains that even after feared exchange rate movements and put option position payoffs have occurred, the firm is competitively disadvantaged. The capital outlay required for the purchase of such sizeable put option positions is capital not used for the potential diversification of operations, which in the long run might have more effectively maintained the firm's global market share and international competitiveness.

SUMMARY

- *Foreign exchange* exposure is a measure of the potential for a firm's profitability, net cash flow, and market value to change because of a change in exchange rates. The three main types of foreign exchange risk are operating, transaction, and translation exposures.
- *Operating exposure* measures the change in value of the firm that results from changes in future operating cash flows caused by an unexpected change in exchange rates.
- Strategies for the management of operating exposure emphasize the structuring of firm operations in order to create matching streams of cash flows by currency. This is termed *natural hedging*.
- The objective of operating exposure management is to anticipate and influence the effect of unexpected changes in exchange rates on a firm's future cash flow, rather than being forced into passive reaction to such changes. This task can best be accomplished if a firm diversifies internationally both its operations and its financing base.
- Proactive policies include matching currency of cash flow, currency risk-sharing clauses, back-to-back loan structures, and cross-currency swap agreements.
- Contractual approaches (i.e., options and forwards) have occasionally been used to hedge operating exposure but are costly and possibly ineffective.

QUESTIONS

1. **Definitions.** Define the following terms:
   a. Operating exposure
   b. Economic exposure
   c. Competitive exposure
2. **Operating versus transaction exposure.** Explain the difference between operating exposure and transaction exposure.
3. **Unexpected exchange rate changes.**
   a. Why do unexpected exchange rate changes contribute to operating exposure, but expected exchange rate changes do not?
   b. Explain the time horizons used to analyze unexpected changes in exchange rates.
4. **Macroeconomic uncertainty.** Explain how the concept of macroeconomic uncertainty expands the scope of analyzing operating exposure.
5. **Strategic response.** The objective of both operating and transaction exposure management is to anticipate and influence the effect of unexpected changes in exchange rates on a firm's future cash flows. What strategic alternative policies exist to enable management to manage these exposures?
6. **Managing operating exposure.** The key to managing operating exposure at the strategic level is for management to recognize a disequilibrium in parity conditions when it occurs and to be prepositioned to react in the most appropriate way. How can this task best be accomplished?
7. **Diversifying operations.**
   a. How can a MNE diversify operations?
   b. How can a MNE diversify financing?
8. **Proactive management of operating exposure.** Operating and transaction exposures can be partially managed by adopting operating or financing policies that offset anticipated foreign exchange exposures. What are four of the most commonly employed proactive policies?
9. **Matching currency exposure.**
   a. Explain how matching currency cash flows can offset operating exposure.
   b. Give an example of matching currency cash flows.
10. **Risk sharing.** An alternative arrangement for managing operating exposure between firms with a continuing buyer-supplier relationship is risk sharing. Explain how risk sharing works.
11. **Back-to-back loans.** Explain how back-to-back loans can hedge foreign exchange operating exposure.
12. **Currency swaps.** Explain how currency swaps can hedge foreign exchange operating exposure. What are the accounting advantages of currency swaps?
13. **Contractual hedging.** Eastman Kodak is a MNE that has undertaken contractual hedging of its operating exposure.
    a. How does it accomplish this task?
    b. What assumptions does Kodak make in order to justify contractual hedging of its operating exposure?
    c. How effective is such contractual hedging in your opinion? Explain your reasoning.

PROBLEMS

1. **Carlton Germany—Case 4.** Carlton Germany (Exhibit 9.3) decides not to change its domestic price of €12.80 per unit within Europe, but to raise its export price (in euros) from €12.80 per unit to €15.36 per unit, thus preserving its original dollar equivalent price of $15.36 per unit. Volume in both markets remains the same because no buyer perceives that the price has changed.
   a. What is the impact on cash flow?
   b. What is the impact on working capital needed?
   c. What is the impact on the present value approach to measuring operating exposure?

2. **Carlton Germany—Case 5.** Carlton Germany (Exhibit 9.3) finds that domestic costs increase in proportion to the drop in value of the euro because of local inflation and a rise in the cost of imported raw materials and components. This rise in costs (20%) applies to all cash costs, including direct costs and fixed cash operating costs. However it does not apply to depreciation. Because of the increase in its costs Carlton Germany increases its sales price in euros from €12.80 per unit to €15.36 per unit.
   a. What is the impact on cash flow?
   b. What is the impact on working capital needed?
   c. What is the impact on the present value approach to measuring operating exposure?
3. **Denver Plumbing Company (A).** Denver Plumbing Company exports toilet bowls to China. Sales are currently 1,000,000 units per year at the renminbi equivalent of $24 each. The Chinese renminbi has been trading at Rmb8.2000/$, but a Hong Kong advisory service predicts the renminbi will drop in value next week to Rmb10.0000/$, after which it will remain unchanged for at least a decade.

   Accepting this forecast as given, Denver Plumbing Company faces a pricing decision in the face of the impending devaluation: It may 1) maintain the same renminbi price and in effect sell for fewer dollars, in which case Chinese volume will not change, or 2) maintain the same dollar price, raise the renminbi price in China to offset the devaluation, and experience a 10% drop in unit volume. Direct costs are 75% of the U.S. sales price.
   a. What would be the short-run (one-year) impact of each pricing strategy?
   b. Which do you recommend?
4. **Denver Plumbing Company (B).** Assume the same facts as in Denver Plumbing Company (A). Additionally, financial management believes that if it maintains the same renminbi sales price, volume will increase at 12% per annum for eight years. Dollar costs will not change. At the end of ten years, Denver Plumbing's patent expires and it will no longer export to China. After the renminbi is devalued to Rmb10.00/$, no further devaluations are expected.

   If Denver Plumbing raises the renminbi price so as to maintain its dollar price, volume will increase at only 1% per annum for eight years, starting from the lower initial base of 900,000 units. Again dollar costs will not change and at the end of eight years Denver Plumbing will stop exporting to China. Denver Plumbing's weighted average cost of capital is 10%. Given these considerations, what should be Denver Plumbing's pricing policy? Explain.
5. **Hawaiian Macadamia Nuts.** Hawaiian Macadamia Nuts, based in Hilo, Hawaii, exports Macadamia nuts worldwide. The Japanese market is its biggest export market, with average annual sales invoiced in yen to Japanese customers of ¥1,200,000,000. At the present exchange rate of ¥125/$, this is equivalent to $9,600,000. Sales are relatively equally distributed during the year. They show up as a ¥250,00,000 account receivable on Hawaiian Macadamia Nuts' balance sheet. Credit terms to each customer allow for 60 days before payment is due. Monthly cash collections are typically ¥100,000,000.

   Hawaiian Macadamia Nuts would like to hedge its yen receipts, but it has too many customers and transactions to make it practical to sell each receivable forward. It does not want to use options because they are considered to be too expensive for this particular purpose. Therefore, it has decided to use a "matching" hedge by borrowing yen at 4% per annum.
   a. How much should Hawaiian Macadamia Nuts borrow in yen?
   b. What should be the terms of payment on the yen loan?
6. **Cellini Fashionwear's risk sharing.** Cellini Fashionwear, based in New York City, imports leather coats from Boselli Leather Goods, a reliable and longtime supplier, based in Buenos Aires, Argentina. Payment is in Argentine pesos. When the peso lost its parity with the U.S. dollar in January 2002 it collapsed in value to Ps4.0/$ by October 2002. The outlook was for a further decline in the peso's

value. Since both Cellini Fashionwear and Boselli Leather Goods wanted to continue their longtime relationship they agreed on a risk-sharing arrangement. As long as the spot rate on the date of an invoice is between Ps3.5/$ and Ps4.5/$ Cellini Fashionwear will pay based on the spot rate. If the exchange rate falls outside this range it will share the difference equally with Boselli Leather Goods. The risk-sharing agreement will last for six months, at which time the exchange rate limits will be reevaluated. Cellini Fashionwear contracts to import leather coats from Boselli Leather Goods for Ps8,000,000 or $2,000,000 at the current spot rate of Ps4.0/$ during the next six months.

a. If the exchange rate changes immediately to Ps6.00/$ what will be the dollar cost of six months of imports to Cellini Fashionwear?

b. At Ps6.0/$ what will be the peso export sales of Boselli Leather Goods to Cellini Fashionwear?

7. **Autocars, Ltd.** Autocars, Ltd., of Coventry, England, manufactures British style sports cars, a number of which are exported to New Zealand for payment in pounds sterling. The distributor sells the sports cars in New Zealand for New Zealand dollars. The New Zealand distributor is unable to carry all of the foreign exchange risk, and would not sell Autocar models unless Autocar could share some of the foreign exchange risk. Autocars has agreed that sales for a given model year will initially be priced at a "base" spot rate between the New Zealand dollar and pound sterling set to be the spot mid-rate at the beginning of that model year. As long as the actual exchange rate is within ±5% of that base rate, payment will be made in pounds sterling (that is, the New Zealand distributor assumes all foreign exchange risk). However if the spot rate at time of shipment falls outside of this ±5% range, Autocars will share equally the difference between the actual spot rate and the base rate. For the current model year the base rate is NZ$1.6400/£.

a. What are the outside ranges within which the New Zealand importer must pay at the then-current spot rate?

b. If Autocars ships ten sports cars to the New Zealand distributor at a time when the spot exchange rate is NZ$1.7000/£, and each car has an invoice cost of £12,000, what will be the cost to the distributor in New Zealand dollars? How many pounds will Autocars-receive, and how does this compare with Autocars' expected sales receipts of £12,000 per car?

c. If Autocars ships the same ten sports cars to New Zealand at a time when the spot exchange rate is NZ$1.6500/£, how many New Zealand dollars will the distributor pay? How many pounds will Autocars receive?

d. Does this risk-sharing agreement shift the currency exposure from one party of the transaction to the other?

e. Why is such a risk-sharing agreement of benefit to Autocars? To the New Zealand distributor?

8. **High-Profile Printers, Inc. (A).** High-Profile Printers, Inc. (HPP) of the United States exports computer printers to Brazil, whose currency, the real (symbol R$) has been trading at R$3.40/$. Exports to Brazil are currently 50,000 printers per year at the real equivalent of $200 each. A strong rumor exists that the real will be devalued to R$4.00/$ within two weeks by the Brazilian government. Should the devaluation take place, the real is expected to remain unchanged for six years when its patent expires.

Accepting this forecast as given, HPP faces a pricing decision that must be made before any actual devaluation: HPP may either 1) maintain the same real price and in effect sell for fewer dollars, in which case Brazilian volume will not change, or 2) maintain the same dollar price, raise the real price in Brazil to compensate for the devaluation, and experience a 20% drop in volume. Direct costs in the U.S. are 60% of the U.S. sales price.

What would be the short-run (one-year) implication of each pricing strategy? Which do you recommend?

9. **High-Profile Printers, Inc. (B).** Assume the same facts as in High-Profile Printers (A). HPP

also believes that if it maintains the same price in Brazilian real as a permanent policy, volume will increase at 10% per annum for six years. Dollar costs will not change. At the end of six years HPP's patent expires and it will no longer export to Brazil. After the real is devalued to R$4.00/$ no further devaluation is expected.

If HPP raises the price in real so as to maintain its dollar price, volume will increase at only 4% per annum for six years, starting from the lower initial base of 40,000 units. Again dollar costs will not change, and at the end of six years HPP will stop exporting to Brazil.

HPP's weighted average cost of capital is 12%. Given these considerations, what do you recommend for HPP's pricing policy? Justify your recommendation.

10. **Hedging hogs: Risk-sharing at Harley Davidson.** Harley-Davidson (U.S.) reportedly uses risk-sharing agreements with its own foreign subsidiaries and with independent foreign distributors. Because these foreign units typically sell to their local markets and earn local currency, Harley would like to ease their individual currency exposure problems by allowing them to pay for merchandise from Harley (U.S.) in their local functional currency.

    The spot rate between the U.S. dollar and the Australian dollar on January 1 is A$1.2823/$. Assume that Harley uses this rate as the basis for setting its *central rate* or base exchange rate for the year at A$1.2800/$. Harley agrees to price all contracts to Australian distributors at this exact exchange rate as long as the current spot rate on the order date is within ±2.5% of this rate. If the spot rate falls outside of this range, but is still within ±5% of the central rate, Harley will "share" equally the difference between the new spot rate and the neutral boundary with the distributor.

    a. What are the specific exchange rates at the boundaries of the neutral and risk-sharing zones?
    b. If Harley (U.S.) ships a motorcycle with an invoice of $8500 to Australia, and the exchange rate on the order date is A$1.3442/$, what is the price in Australian dollars?
    c. If Harley (U.S.) ships the same motorcycle to Australia, and the exchange rate on the order date is A$1.2442/$, what is the price in Australian dollars to the foreign distributor?

INTERNET EXERCISES

1. **Operating exposure: Recent examples.** Using the following major periodicals as starting points, find a current example of a firm with a substantial operating exposure problem. To aid in your search, you might focus on businesses having major operations in countries with recent currency crises, either through depreciation or major home currency appreciation.

Financial Times	http://www.ft.com
The Economist	http://www.economist.com
The Wall Street Journal	http://www.wsj.com

2. **SEC Edgar Files.** In order to analyze an individual firm's operating exposure more carefully, it is necessary to have more detailed information available than in the normal annual report. Choose a specific firm with substantial international operations, for example Coca-Cola or PepsiCo, and search the Security and Exchange Commission's Edgar Files for more detailed financial reports of their international operations.

Search SEC EDGAR Archives	http://www.sec.gov/cgi-bin/srch-edgar

Exhibit B Daily Exchange Rates: Japanese Yen per Euro

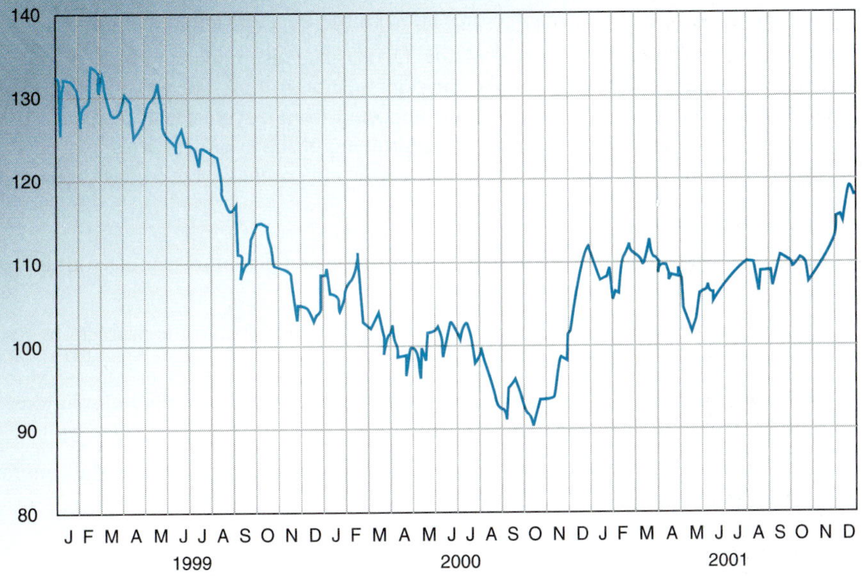

Exhibit B Daily Exchange Rates: British Pounds per Euro

was scheduled to be moved to Valenciennes in 2002. The continuing problem, however, was that it was an assembly facility, meaning that much of the expensive value-added content of the autos being assembled was still based in either Japan or the United Kingdom.

Mr. Shuhei, with the approval of Mr. Okuda, had also initiated a local sourcing and procurement program for the United Kingdom manufacturing operations. TMEM wished to decrease the number of key components imported from Toyota Japan to reduce the currency exposure of the U.K. unit. But again, the continuing problem of the euro's weakness against the British pound, as shown in Exhibit C, reduced the effectiveness of even this solution.

Case Questions

1. Why do you think Toyota waited so long to move much of its manufacturing for European sales to Europe?
2. If Britain were to join the European Monetary Union, would the problem be resolved? How likely do you think it is that Britain will join?
3. If you were Mr. Shuhei, how would you categorize your problems and solutions? What are a short-term and a long-term problem?
4. What measures would you recommend Toyota Europe take to resolve the continuing operating losses?

apter 10

Accounting Exposure

THE PURPOSE OF THIS CHAPTER IS TO ANALYZE THE ACCOUNTING ISSUES THAT ARISE FROM A FIRM operating as a multinational enterprise. The chapter starts with an overview of *translation exposure*, including how foreign subsidiaries are characterized for translation purposes, and the meaning of a *functional currency*. It then continues with a description of the two main translation methods: the *current rate method* and the *temporal method*. This is followed by a specific description of U.S. translation procedures and international translation practices. The next section is a translation example using Carlton Germany and a comparison of its translation exposure with its operating exposure. We then present the techniques used by MNEs today to manage translation exposure, including balance sheet hedges. The chapter ends with an analysis of issues that arise when a MNE evaluates the performance of its foreign subsidiaries. In particular, we analyze how foreign exchange rates impact foreign subsidiary performance, using Carlton Brazil as an example.

Overview of Translation

Accounting exposure, also called *translation exposure*, arises because financial statements of foreign subsidiaries—which are stated in foreign currency—must be restated in the parent's reporting currency for the firm to prepare consolidated financial statements. Foreign subsidiaries of U.S. companies, for example, must restate local euro, pound, yen, etc., statements into U.S. dollars so the foreign values can be added to the parent's U.S. dollar–denominated balance sheet and income statement. This accounting process is called *translation*. *Translation exposure* is the potential for an increase or decrease in the parent's net worth and reported net income caused by a change in exchange rates since the last translation.

Although the main purpose of translation is to prepare consolidated statements, translated statements are also used by management to assess the performance of foreign subsidiaries. Although such assessment might be performed from the local currency statements, restatement of all subsidiary statements into the single "common denominator" of one currency facilitates management comparison.

Translation in principle is quite simple. Foreign currency financial statements must be restated in the parent company's reporting currency for consolidation purposes. If the same exchange rate were used to remeasure each and every line item on the individual statement (income statement and balance sheet), there would be no imbalances resulting from the remeasurement. But if a different exchange rate were used for different line items on an individual statement, an imbalance would result.

Why would we use a different exchange rate in remeasuring different line items? The reason is that translation principles in many countries are often a complex compromise between historical and current market valuation. Historical exchange rates can be used for certain equity accounts, fixed assets, and inventory items, while current exchange rates can be used for current assets, current liabilities, income, and expense items. The question, then, is what—if anything—is to be done with the imbalance? It is taken to either current income or equity reserves.

Translation methods differ by country along two overall dimensions, as well as by individual account. One dimension is a difference in the way a foreign subsidiary is characterized based on its degree of independence of the parent firm. The second dimension is the definition of which currency is most important for the foreign subsidiary's operations.

Subsidiary Characterization

Most countries today specify the translation method used by a foreign subsidiary based on the subsidiary's business operations. For example, a foreign subsidiary's business can be categorized as either an *integrated foreign entity* or a *self-sustaining foreign entity*. An integrated foreign entity is one that operates as an extension of the parent company, with cash flows and general business lines that are highly interrelated with those of the parent. A self-sustaining foreign entity is one that operates in the local economic environment independent of the parent company. The differentiation is important to the logic of translation. A foreign subsidiary should be valued principally in terms of the currency that is the basis of its economic viability.

It is not unusual to find two different foreign subsidiaries of a single company that have different characters. For example, a U.S.-based manufacturer that produces subassemblies in the United States which are then shipped to a Spanish subsidiary for finishing, assembly, and resale in the European Union would likely characterize the Spanish subsidiary as an *integrated* foreign entity. The dominant currency of economic operation is likely the U.S. dollar. That same U.S. parent may, however, also own an agricultural marketing business in Venezuela that has few cash flows or operations related to the U.S. parent company (or U.S. dollar). The Venezuelan subsidiary may purchase almost all materials and expend all costs of operations in Venezuelan bolivar, while selling exclusively in Venezuela. Because the Venezuelan subsidiary's operations are independent of its parent, and its functional currency is the Venezuelan bolivar, it would be classified as a *self-sustaining* foreign entity.

Functional Currency

A foreign subsidiary's *functional currency* is the currency of the primary economic environment in which the subsidiary operates and in which it generates cash flows. In other words, it is the dominant currency used by that foreign subsidiary in its day-to-day operations. It is important to note that the geographic location of a foreign subsidiary and its functional currency may be different. The Singapore subsidiary of a U.S. firm may find that its functional currency is the U.S. dollar (integrated subsidiary), the Singapore dollar (self-sustaining subsidiary), or a third currency such as the British pound (also a self-sustaining subsidiary).

The United States, rather than distinguishing a foreign subsidiary as either integrated or self-sustaining, follows a parallel approach that requires that the functional currency of the subsidiary be determined. Current U.S. translation practices are delineated in *Statement of Financial Accounting Standards Number 52*, usually referred to as FAS #52. It was issued by the Financial Accounting Standards Board (FASB) in December 1981, superseding FAS #8, which had been in effect since 1975. The FASB defines approved accounting practices for U.S. firms.

Management must evaluate the nature and purpose of each of its individual foreign subsidiaries to determine the appropriate functional currency for each. Exhibit 10.1 lists the indicators the FASB uses in determining the functional currency of a foreign subsidiary. If a foreign subsidiary of a U.S.-based company is determined to have the U.S. dollar as its functional currency, it is essentially an extension of the parent company (equivalent to the integrated foreign entity designation used by most countries). If, however, the functional currency of the foreign subsidiary is determined to be different from the U.S. dollar, the subsidiary is considered a separate entity from the parent (equivalent to the self-sustaining entity designation).

Translation Methods

Two basic methods for the translation of foreign subsidiary financial statements are employed worldwide: the *current rate method* and the *temporal method.* Regardless of which method is employed, a translation method must not only designate at what exchange rate individual balance sheet and income statement items are remeasured, but also designate where any imbalance is to be recorded (typically either in current income or in an equity reserve account in the balance sheet). The significance of this decision is that imbalances passed through the income statement affect the firm's current reported income, while imbalances transferred directly to the balance sheet do not.

Current Rate Method

The *current rate method* is the most prevalent in the world today. Under this method, all financial statement line items are translated at the "current" exchange rate, with few exceptions. Line items include:

- *Assets and liabilities.* All assets and liabilities are translated at the current rate of exchange; that is, at the rate of exchange in effect on the balance sheet date.
- *Income statement items.* All items, including depreciation and cost of goods sold, are translated at either the actual exchange rate on the dates the various revenues, expenses, gains, and losses were incurred or at an appropriately weighted average exchange rate for the period.
- *Distributions.* Dividends paid are translated at the exchange rate in effect on the date of payment.
- *Equity items.* Common stock and paid-in capital accounts are translated at historical rates. Year-end retained earnings consist of the original year-beginning retained earnings plus or minus any income or loss for the year.

Gains or losses caused by translation adjustments are not included in the calculation of consolidated net income. Rather, translation gains or losses are reported separately and accumulated in a separate equity reserve account (on the consolidated balance sheet) with a title such as *cumulative*

Exhibit 10.1 Economic Indicators for Determining the Functional Currency

According to the Financial Accounting Standards Board (FASB), the following economic indicators should be used to determine the functional currency of any foreign subsidiary:

a. Cash flow indicators

(1) Foreign currency—Cash flows related to the foreign entity's individual assets and liabilities are primarily in the foreign currency and do not have an impact on the parent company's cash flows.

(2) Parent's currency—Cash flows related to the foreign entity's individual assets and liabilities have a direct impact on the parent's cash flows on a current basis and are readily available for remittance to the parent company.

b. Sales price indicators

(1) Foreign currency—Sales prices for the foreign entity's products are not primarily responsive on a short-term basis to changes in exchange rates but are determined more by local competition or by local government regulation.

(2) Parent's currency—Sales prices for the foreign entity's products are primarily responsive on a short-term basis to changes in exchange rates; for example, sales prices are determined more by worldwide competition or by international prices.

c. Sales market indicators

(1) Foreign currency—There is an active local sales market for the foreign entity's products, although there might also be significant amounts of exports.

(2) Parent's currency—The sales market is mostly in the parent's country or sales contracts are denominated in the parent's currency.

d. Expense indicators

(1) Foreign currency—Labor, materials, and other costs for the foreign entity's products or services are primarily local costs, even though there might also be imports from other countries.

(2) Parent's currency—Labor, materials, and other costs for the foreign entity's products or services, on a continuing basis, are primarily costs for components obtained from the country in which the parent company is located.

e. Financing indicators

(1) Foreign currency—Financing is primarily denominated in foreign currency, and funds generated by the foreign entity's operations are sufficient to service existing and normally expected debt obligations.

(2) Parent's currency—Financing is primarily from the parent or other dollar-denominated obligations, or funds generated by the foreign entity's operations are not sufficient to service existing and normally expected debt obligations without the infusion of additional funds from the parent. Infusion of additional funds from the parent for expansion is not a factor, provided funds generated by the foreign entity's expanded operations are expected to service that additional financing.

f. Intercompany transactions and arrangements indicators

(1) Foreign currency—There is a low volume of intercompany transactions and there is not an extensive interrelationship between the operations of the foreign entity and the parent company. However, the foreign entity's operations may rely on the parent's subsidiaries' competitive advantages, such as patents and trademarks.

(2) Parent's currency—There is a high volume of intercompany transactions and there is an extensive interrelationship between the foreign entity and the parent company. Additionally, the parent's currency generally would be the functional currency if the foreign entity is a device or shell corporation for holding investments, obligations, intangible assets, etc., that could readily be carried on the parent's or an affiliate's books.

translation adjustment (CTA). A multitude of different names are used for this reserve account adjustment. In Spain, for example, the CTA is termed the *diferencias de conversión*. If a foreign subsidiary is later sold or liquidated, translation gains or losses of past years accumulated in the CTA account are reported as one component of the total gain or loss on sale or liquidation. The total gain or loss is reported as part of the net income or loss for the time period in which the sale or liquidation occurs.

The biggest advantage of the current rate method is that the gain or loss on translation does not pass through the income statement but goes directly to a reserve account. This eliminates the variability of reported earnings due to foreign exchange translation gains or losses. A second advantage of the current rate method is that the relative proportions of individual balance sheet accounts remain the same. Hence the process of translation does not distort such balance sheet ratios as the current ratio or the debt-to-equity ratio. The main disadvantage of the current rate method is that it violates the accounting principle of carrying balance sheet accounts at historical cost. For example, foreign assets purchased with dollars and then recorded on a subsidiary's statements at their foreign currency historical cost are translated back into dollars at a different rate. Thus, they are reported in the consolidated statement in dollars at something other than their historical dollar cost.

Temporal Method

Under the temporal method, specific assets and liabilities are translated at exchange rates consistent with the timing of the item's creation. The *temporal method* assumes that a number of individual line item assets such as inventory and net plant and equipment are restated regularly to reflect market value. If these items were not restated but were instead carried at historical cost, the temporal method becomes the *monetary/nonmonetary method* of translation, a form of translation that is still used by a number of countries today. Line items include:

- *Monetary assets* (primarily cash, marketable securities, accounts receivable, and long-term receivables) and *monetary liabilities* (primarily current liabilities and long-term debt) are translated at current exchange rates.
- *Nonmonetary assets* and *liabilities* (primarily inventory and fixed assets) are translated at historical rates.
- *Income statement items* are translated at the average exchange rate for the period, except for items such as depreciation and cost of goods sold that are directly associated with nonmonetary assets or liabilities. These accounts are translated at their historical rate.
- *Distributions.* Dividends paid are translated at the exchange rate in effect on the date of payment.
- *Equity items.* Common stock and paid-in capital accounts are translated at historical rates. Year-end retained earnings consist of the original year-beginning retained earnings plus or minus any income or loss for the year, plus or minus any imbalance from translation, as explained next.

Under the temporal method, gains or losses resulting from remeasurement are carried directly to current consolidated income, and not to equity reserves. Hence foreign exchange gains and losses arising from the translation process do introduce volatility to consolidated earnings.

The basic advantage of the temporal method is that foreign nonmonetary assets are carried at their original cost in the parent's consolidated statement. In most countries, this approach is consistent with the original cost treatment of domestic assets of the parent firm. In practice, however, if some foreign accounts are translated at one exchange rate while others are translated at different rates, the resulting translated balance sheet will not balance. Hence there is a need for a "plug" to remove what has been called the ***dangling debit or credit.*** The true nature of the gain or loss created by use of such a "plug" is open to question. Unrealized foreign exchange gains or losses are included in quarterly primary earnings per share (EPS), thus increasing variability of reported earnings.

U.S. Translation Procedures

As mentioned previously, the United States differentiates foreign subsidiaries on the basis of functional currency, not subsidiary characterization. The result, however, is equivalent. Exhibit 10.2 illustrates the translation procedures used by U.S.-based companies under current U.S. generally accepted accounting practices (GAAP). As shown in Exhibit 10.2:

- If the financial statements of the foreign subsidiary of a U.S. company are maintained in U.S. dollars, translation is not required.
- If the financial statements of the foreign subsidiary are maintained in the local currency and the local currency is the functional currency, they are translated by the current rate method.

Exhibit 10.2 Procedure Flow Chart for United States Translation Practices

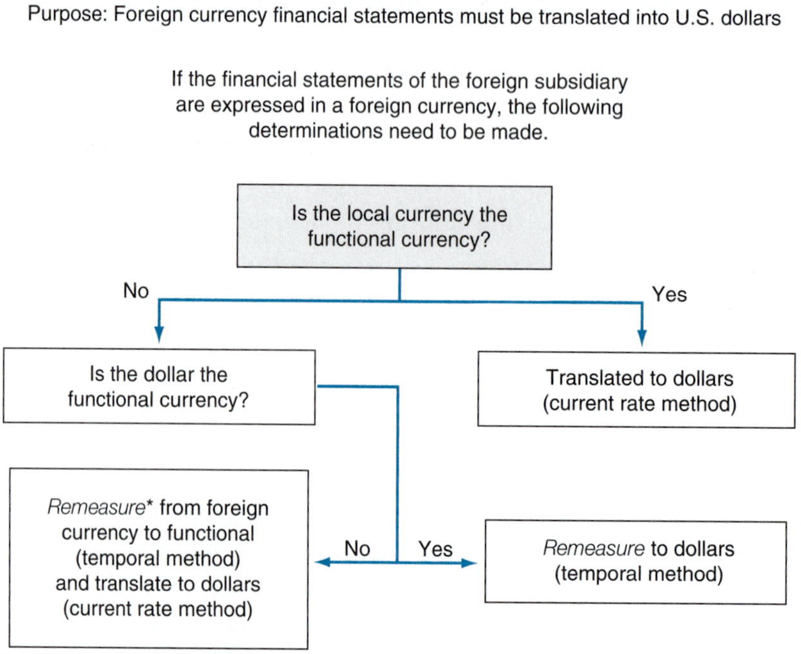
Purpose: Foreign currency financial statements must be translated into U.S. dollars
If the financial statements of the foreign subsidiary are expressed in a foreign currency, the following determinations need to be made.
Is the local currency the functional currency?
No
Yes
Is the dollar the functional currency?
Translated to dollars (current rate method)
*Remeasure** from foreign currency to functional (temporal method) and translate to dollars (current rate method)
No
Yes
Remeasure to dollars (temporal method)

*The term "remeasure" means to translate, as to change the unit of measure, from a foreign currency to the functional currency.

- If the financial statements of the foreign subsidiary are maintained in the local currency and the U.S. dollar is the functional currency, they are remeasured by the temporal method. (Terminology can be tricky; under U.S. accounting and translation practices, use of the current rate method is termed "translation," while use of the temporal method is termed "remeasurement.")
- If the financial statements of foreign subsidiaries of U.S. companies are maintained in the local currency and neither the local currency nor the dollar is the functional currency, then the statements must first be remeasured into the functional currency by the temporal method, and then translated into dollars by the current rate method.

Hyperinflation Countries

FAS #52 has a special provision for translating statements of foreign subsidiaries of U.S. companies operating in countries where cumulative inflation has been approximately 100% or more over a three-year period. Financial statements of these subsidiaries must be translated into the reporting currency using the temporal method.

The rationale is to correct the problem of the "disappearing asset." If the current rate were used, depreciation would be understated relative to replacement costs, profits would be overstated in real terms, and the book value of plant and equipment would eventually nearly disappear from the balance sheet as its value diminished in reporting currency terms. Translating plant, equipment, and depreciation expenses at the historical exchange rate yields a higher asset value in the reporting currency than would use of the current (depreciated) exchange rate. This leads to a less distorted income statement and balance sheet. In effect, FAS #52 declares the functional currency of subsidiaries in hyperinflation countries to be the reporting currency (U.S. dollars for U.S. firms).

The hyperinflation standard has precedence in business practice.

> *When a country is plagued with hyperinflation, it often uses the U.S. dollar or other hard currency as its de facto functional currency for actual transactions regardless of accounting standards. For example, most Israeli retailers in 1982 priced their merchandise in U.S. dollars, not shekels. In the face of triple-digit inflation, they cannot change their prices every other day. The U.S. dollar becomes the unit of account. Also, when an Israeli holds U.S. dollars and the shekel is devalued, his holding in dollars remains the same, whereas if he holds currency in shekels and the shekel is devalued, his holding declines in purchasing power. The U.S. dollar becomes the storehouse of value. Consistent with the mercantile practice of businessmen in highly inflationary economies, the FASB promulgates the accounting standard that the home currency becomes the functional currency when inflation is rampant; otherwise the local currency is the functional currency. Accounting standards-setting simply is patterned after accepted business practice.*[1]

In summary, U.S. translation practices require the parent company to first determine the functional currency of the foreign subsidiary, which then dictates whether the subsidiary's financial statements will be translated by the current rate method or remeasured by the temporal method. A final point of emphasis: The selection of the functional currency is determined by the economic realities of the subsidiary's operations and is not a discretionary management decision on

1. Russell A. Taussig, "Impact of FAS 52 on the Translation of Foreign Financial Statements of Companies in Highly-Inflationary Economies," *Journal of Accounting, Auditing, and Finance*, Winter 1983, pp. 145–146.

preferred procedures or elective outcomes. Since many U.S.-based multinationals have numerous foreign subsidiaries, some U.S. dollar–functional and some foreign currency–functional, foreign currency gains and losses may be both passing through current consolidated income and/or accruing in equity reserves.

International Translation Practices

As illustrated in Exhibit 10.3, many of the world's largest industrial countries—as well as the relatively newly formed International Accounting Standards Committee (IASC)—follow the same basic translation procedure:

- A foreign subsidiary is an *integrated foreign entity* or a *self-sustaining foreign entity.*
- *Integrated foreign entities* are typically remeasured using the *temporal method* (or some slight variation thereof).
- *Self-sustaining foreign entities* are translated at the *current rate method*, also termed the *closing-rate method.*

Translation Example: Carlton Germany

Let us continue the example of Carlton from Chapter 9, focusing here on its European subsidiary. We will also illustrate translation by the temporal method in order to show the very arbitrary nature of a translation gain or loss. Selection of the accounting method is the major factor in determining the magnitude of gain or loss. The example that follows deals with balance sheet translation only. The somewhat more complex procedures for translating income statements are described in international accounting texts.

The functional currency of Carlton Germany is the euro, and the reporting currency of its parent, Carlton Inc., is the U.S. dollar. Assume the following:

1. Plant and equipment and long-term debt were acquired and common stock issued by Carlton Germany some time in the past when the exchange rate was $1.2760/€. Although the euro never traded at this rate against the dollar, the historic deutschemark rate in use at the time the initial investment was made must be converted to a "historic euro rate," which, in effect, backdates euro rates against the deutschemark.
2. Inventory currently on hand was purchased or manufactured during the immediately prior quarter when the average exchange rate was $1.2180/€. At the close of business on Monday, December 31, 2001, the current spot exchange rate was $1.2000/€.
3. When business reopened on January 2, 2002, after the New Year holiday, the euro had dropped 16.67% in value versus the dollar to $1.0000/€.

The example will also look at the consequences had the euro strengthened by 10% overnight to $1.3200/€.

Current Rate Method

The top half of Exhibit 10.4 illustrates translation loss using the current rate method. Assets and liabilities on the pre-depreciation balance sheet are translated at the current exchange rate of

Exhibit 10.3 Comparison of Translation Methods Employed in Selected Countries

Country	Integrated Foreign Entity	Self-Sustaining Foreign Entity
United States	Financial statements are remeasured using the temporal method with adjustments included in current net income.	Current rate method. Translation adjustments are reported as a separate component of shareholders' equity.
International	Temporal method. Translation adjustments are included in net income currently, except that translation adjustments on long-term monetary items may be deferred and amortized over the life of the item.	Current rate method. Translation adjustments are reported as a separate component of shareholders' equity.
Australia	Temporal method. Translation adjustments are included in current net income.	Current rate method. Translation adjustments are reported as a separate component of shareholders' equity.
Canada	Temporal method. Translation adjustments are included in current net income.	Current rate method. Translation adjustments are reported as a separate component of shareholders' equity.
France	Temporal method. Translation adjustments are included in current net income.	Current rate method. Translation adjustments are reported as a separate component of shareholders' equity.
Germany	Temporal method or current rate method is acceptable. Translation adjustments are included in net income currently if the temporal method is used and as a separate component if the current rate method is used.	Same as for Integrated Foreign Entity.
Japan	Temporal method. Adjustments related to foreign subsidiaries are reported separately as an asset or a liability; adjustments related to divisions or branches are included in current net income.	Same as for Integrated Foreign Entity.
Netherlands	Temporal method. Translation adjustments are included in current net income. The current rate method is used if the entity utilizes current value accounting.	Current rate method. Translation adjustments are reported as a separate component of shareholders' equity.
United Kingdom	Temporal method. Translation adjustments are included in current net income.	Current rate method. Translation adjustments are reported as a separate component of shareholders' equity.

Source: Survey of International Accounting Practices, Arthur Andersen & Co., Coopers & Lybrand, Deloitte & Touche, Ernst & Young, KPMG Peat Marwick, and Price Waterhouse, 1991.

\$1.1600/€. Capital stock is translated at the historical rate of \$1.2760/€, and retained earnings are translated at a composite rate that is equivalent to having each past year's addition to retained earnings translated at the exchange rate in effect in that year.

The sum of retained earnings and the cumulative translation adjustment (CTA) account must "balance" the liabilities and net worth section of the balance sheet with the asset side. For this hypothetical text example we have assumed the two amounts used for the December 31, 2001, balance sheet. The assumption does not affect the final measure of the increase in the CTA

Exhibit 10.4 Carlton Germany: Translation Loss Just After Depreciation of the Euro

	A	B	C	D	E	F	G	H	I	J	K	L
1												
2		Exhibit 10.4 Carlton Germany: Translation Loss Just After Depreciation of the euro										
3												
4					December 31, 2001				January 2, 2002			
5			In euros		$/€		Just before depreciation		$/€		Just after depreciation	
6					Current Rate Method							
7		Cash	€ 1,600,000		1.2000		$ 1,920,000		1.0000		$ 1,600,000	
8		Accounts receivable	3,200,000		1.2000		3,840,000		1.0000		$ 3,200,000	
9		Inventory	2,400,000		1.2000		2,880,000		1.0000		$ 2,400,000	
10		Net plant and equipment	4,800,000		1.2000		5,760,000		1.0000		$ 4,800,000	
11			€ 12,000,000				$ 14,400,000				$ 12,000,000	
12												
13		Accounts payable	€ 800,000		1.2000		$ 960,000		1.0000		$ 800,000	
14		Short-term bank loan	1,600,000		1.2000		1,920,000		1.0000		1,600,000	
15		Long-term debt	1,600,000		1.2000		1,920,000		1.0000		1,600,000	
16		Common stock	1,800,000		1.2760		2,296,800		1.2760		2,296,800	
17		Retained earnings	6,200,000		(a)		7,440,000		1.2000	(b)	7,440,000	
18		Translation adjustments (CTA)	---		---		(136,800)		---		(1,736,800)	
19			€ 12,000,000				$ 14,400,000				$ 12,000,000	
20					Temporal Method							
21		Cash	€ 1,600,000		1.2000		$ 1,920,000		1.0000		$ 1,600,000	
22		Accounts receivable	3,200,000		1.2000		3,840,000		1.0000		3,200,000	
23		Inventory	2,400,000		1.2180		2,923,200		1.2180		2,923,200	
24		Net plant and equipment	4,800,000		1.2760		6,124,800		1.2760		6,124,800	
25			€ 12,000,000				$ 14,808,000				$ 13,848,000	
26												
27		Accounts payable	€ 800,000		1.2000		$ 960,000		1.0000		$ 800,000	
28		Short-term bank loan	1,600,000		1.2000		1,920,000		1.0000		1,600,000	
29		Long-term debt	1,600,000		1.2000		1,920,000		1.0000		1,600,000	
30		Common stock	1,800,000		1.2760		2,296,800		1.2760		2,296,800	
31		Retained earnings	6,200,000		(a)		7,711,200		(b)		7,711,200	
32		Translation adjustments (CTA)	---		---		---		(c)		(160,000)	
33			€ 12,000,000				$ 14,808,000				$ 13,848,000	

34
35 **Key Cell Entries for Calculated Values (All other values are entered as data.)**
36 G7: =$C7*E7, copy to G8:G10, K7:K10, G13:G16, K13:K17, G21:G24, K21:K24, G27:G30, and to K27:K30
37 C11: =SUM(C7:C10), copy to G11 and K11 — K31: =G31
38 C19: =SUM(C13:C18), copy to G19 and K19 — C33: =SUM(C27:C32), copy to G33 and K33
39 C25: =SUM(C21:C24), copy to G25 and K25
40 Notes
41 a. Dollar retained earnings before depreciation are the cumulative sum of additions to retained earnings of
42 all prior years, translated at exchange rates in each year. See text for assumptions used in this example.
43 b. Translated into dollars at the same rate as before depreciation of the euro.
44 c. Under the temporal method, the translation loss of $160,000 would be closed into retained earnings via the
45 income statement rather than left as a separate line item shown here. Hence, under the temporal method,
46 ending retained earnings would actually be $7,711,200 — $160,000 = $7,551,200.
47
48

account, because the retained earnings account is carried over at whatever arbitrary amount is assigned for this example.

As shown in the top half of Exhibit 10.4, the "just before depreciation" dollar translation reports an accumulated translation loss from prior periods of $136,800. This balance is the cumulative gain or loss from translating euro statements into dollars in prior years, and it had been carried separately in the CTA account. Statements from 1998 and earlier would have originally been deutschemark statements, translated into euros after January 1, 1999, when the euro was introduced.

After the 16.67% depreciation, Carlton Corp. translates assets and liabilities at the new exchange rate of \$1.0000/€. Equity accounts, including retained earnings, are translated just as they were before depreciation, and as a result the cumulative translation loss increases to \$1,736,800. The increase of \$1,600,000 in this account (from a cumulative loss of \$136,800 to a new cumulative loss of \$1,736,800) is the translation loss measured by the current rate method.

This translation loss is a decrease in equity, measured in the parent's reporting currency, of *net exposed assets*. An *exposed asset* is an asset whose value drops with the depreciation of the functional currency and rises with an appreciation of that currency. "Net" exposed assets in this context means exposed assets minus exposed liabilities. Net exposed assets are positive (that is, "long") if exposed assets exceed exposed liabilities. They are negative ("short") if exposed assets are smaller than exposed liabilities.

Exposure can be measured by creating a "before" and "after" translated balance sheet, as in Exhibit 10.4. A simpler method is to multiply "net exposed assets" by the percentage amount of depreciation. We did this calculation for the current rate method in the left column of Exhibit 10.5, which illustrates that a 16.67% depreciation of the euro means that net exposed assets of \$9,600,000 lose 16.67% of their value, a translation loss of \$1,600,000.

Suppose instead that the euro had appreciated. If, by the end of the year, the euro had appreciated from \$1.2000/€ (to \$1.3200/€), the appreciation would be 10%. The effect of this appears in Panel B of Exhibit 10.5, which starts with the same net exposed assets calculated in Panel A. Under the current rate method, the U.S. parent would have a translation gain of \$960,000.

Temporal Method

Translation of the same accounts under the temporal method shows the arbitrary nature of any gain or loss from translation. This is illustrated in the bottom half of Exhibit 10.4. Monetary assets and monetary liabilities in the pre-depreciation euro balance sheet are translated at the current rate of exchange, but other assets and the equity accounts are translated at their historic rates. For Carlton Germany, the historical rate for inventory differs from that for net plant and equipment because inventory was acquired more recently.

Under the temporal method, translation losses are not accumulated in a separate equity account but passed directly through each quarter's income statement. Thus in the dollar balance sheet translated before depreciation, retained earnings were the cumulative result of earnings from all prior years translated at historical rates in effect each year, plus translation gains or losses from all prior years. In Exhibit 10.4, no translation loss appears in the pre-depreciation dollar balance sheet because any losses would have been closed to retained earnings.

The effect of the 16.67% depreciation is to create an immediate translation loss of \$160,000. This amount is shown as a separate line item in Exhibit 10.4 in order to focus attention on it for this textbook example. Under the temporal method, this translation loss of \$160,000 would pass through the income statement, reducing reported net income and reducing retained earnings. Ending retained earnings would in fact be \$7,711,200 minus \$160,000, or \$7,551,200. Other countries using the temporal method do not necessarily require gains and losses to pass through the income statement.

Put into Excel, 10.5 & 10.7

When translation loss is viewed in terms of changes in the value of exposed accounts, as in the right column of Exhibit 10.5, the loss under the temporal method is 16.67% of net exposed assets of $960,000, or $160,000. If the euro should appreciate 10%, the translation gain to the U.S. parent would be $96,000, as shown at the bottom of the right column in Exhibit 10.5.

Exhibit 10.5 Carlton Germany: Translation Loss Comparison of Euro Depreciation and Appreciation

	A	B	C	D	E
1					
2		Exhibit 10.5 Carlton Germany: Translation Loss Comparison			
3		of euro Depreciation and Appreciation			
4					
5			**Current Rate Method**	**Temporal Method**	
6					
7		**A. Depreciation of the euro from $1.2000/ € to $1.0000/€ (—16.67%)**			
8		**Exposed Assets**			
9		Cash	$ 1,920,000	$ 1,920,000	
10		Accounts receivable	3,840,000	3,840,000	
11		Inventory	2,880,000	not exposed	
12		Net plant and equipment	5,760,000	not exposed	
13		Total exposed assets ("A")	$ 14,400,000	$ 5,760,000	
14		**Exposed Liabilities**			
15		Accounts payable	$ 960,000	$ 960,000	
16		Short-term bank loan	1,920,000	1,920,000	
17		Long-term debt	1,920,000	1,920,000	
18		Total exposed liabilities ("L")	$ 4,800,000	$ 4,800,000	
19		**Gain (loss) if euro depreciates**			
20		Net exposure (A - L)	$ 9,600,000	$ 960,000	
21		Times amount of depreciation	-16.67%	-16.67%	
22		Translation gain (loss)	$ (1,600,000)	$ (160,000)	
23		**B. Appreciation of the euro, from $1.2000/ € to $1.3200/€** (+10%)			
24		**Gain (loss) if euro appreciates**			
25		Net exposure (A - L)	$ 9,600,000	$ 960,000	
26		Times amount of appreciation	10.00%	10.00%	
27		Translation gain (loss)	$ 960,000	$ 96,000	
28					
29		**Key Cell Entries**			
30		C9: ='Exhibit 10.4'!G7, copy to C10:C12			
31		C13: =SUM(C9:C12), copy to D13			
32		D9: ='Exhibit 10.4'!G21, copy to D10			
33		C15: ='Exhibit 10.4'!G13, copy to C16:C17			
34		C18: =SUM(C15:C17), copy to D18			
35		D15: ='Exhibit 10.4'!G27, copy to D16:D17			
36		C20: =C$13-C$18, copy to D20 and to C25:D25			
37		C21: =(1.000-1.2000)/1.2000, copy to D21			
38		C22: =C20*C21, copy to D22 and to C27:D27			
39		C26: =(1.3200-1.2000)/1.2000, copy to D26			
40					
41					

Managerial Implications

In Exhibits 10.4 and 10.5, translation loss or gain is larger under the current rate method because inventory and net plant and equipment, as well as all monetary assets, are deemed exposed. When net exposed assets are larger, gains or losses from translation are also larger.

The managerial implications of this fact are very important. If management expects a foreign currency to depreciate, it could minimize translation exposure by reducing net exposed assets. If management anticipates an appreciation of the foreign currency, it should increase net exposed assets to benefit from a gain.

Depending on the accounting method of the moment, management might select different assets and liabilities for reduction or increase. Thus "real" decisions about investing and financing might be dictated by which accounting technique is required, when in fact the method of reporting should be neutral in its influence on operating and financing decisions.

Comparing Translation Exposure with Operating Exposure

Exhibit 10.6 compares translation gains and losses with operating gains or losses (previously presented in Exhibit 9.3 in Chapter 9) for a currency devaluation. Obviously translation gains or losses can be quite different from operating gains or losses, not only in magnitude but also in sign. A manager focusing only on translation losses, in a situation such as Carlton Germany, might avoid doing business in Germany because of the likelihood of such a loss. The manager might fear losing a bonus tied to reported profits, or possibly losing a job if the investment in Germany were made and the income statement reported severe translation losses back to the home office.

Operating exposure presents an entirely different view of the same situation. As summarized in Exhibit 10.6, Germany and Europe became more (not less) desirable locations for investment because of the *operating* consequences that followed depreciation in two of the three cases shown here. This illustrates the importance of focusing decisions primarily on the operating consequences of changes in exchange rates and only secondarily on the accounting-based measurements of performance.

Exhibit 10.6 Comparison of Translation Exposure with Operating Exposure, Depreciation of Euro from $1.2000/€ to $1.0000/€ for Carlton Germany

Exposure	Amount	Gain or Loss
Translation Exposure (Exhibits 10.4 and 10.5)		
Current rate method	($1,600,000)	**Loss** on translation
Temporal method	($160,000)	**Loss** on translation
Operating Exposure (in present value terms; Exhibit 9.5)		
Case 1: Depreciation of euro	($1,033,914)	**Loss** on operations
Case 2: Volume doubles	$2,866,106	**Gain** on operations
Case 3: Sales price increases	$3,742,892	**Gain** on operations

Global Finance Perspective **10.1**

Subsidiary Valuation

The value contribution of a subsidiary of a multinational to the multinational as a whole is a topic of increasing debate in global financial management. Most multinational companies report the earnings contribution of foreign operations either individually or by region when significant to the total earnings of the consolidated firm.

Changes in the value of a subsidiary as a result of the change in an exchange rate can be decomposed into those specific to the income and the assets of the subsidiary:

$$\Delta \text{ in value of subsidiary} = \Delta \text{ in value of assets} + \Delta \text{ in value of earnings}$$

Subsidiary earnings The earnings of the subsidiary, once remeasured into the home currency of the parent company, contribute directly to the consolidated income of the firm. An exchange rate change results in fluctuations in the value of the subsidiary's income to the global corporation. If the individual subsidiary in question constitutes a relatively significant or material component of consolidated income, the multinational firm's reported income (and earnings per share, EPS) may be seen to change purely as a result of translation.

Subsidiary assets The assets of the subsidiary, remeasured into the reporting currency of the parent company, were the focus of this chapter on Accounting Exposure. Changes in the reporting currency value of the net assets of the subsidiary is passed into consolidated income or equity.

- If the foreign subsidiary was designated as "dollar functional," remeasurement results in a transaction exposure, which is passed through current consolidated income.
- If the foreign subsidiary was designated as "local currency functional," translation results in a translation adjustment and is reported in consolidated equity as a translation adjustment. It does not alter reported consolidated net income in the current period.

One example of how operation, transaction, and translation exposures can become intertwined is in the valuation of a foreign subsidiary, described in detail in Global Finance Perspective 10.1.

Managing Translation Exposure

The main technique to minimize translation exposure is called a *balance sheet hedge*. Some firms have attempted to hedge translation exposure in the forward market. Such action amounts to speculating in the forward market in the hope that a cash profit will be realized to offset the noncash loss from translation. Success depends on a precise prediction of future exchange rates, for such a hedge will not work over a range of possible future spot rates. In addition, such a hedge will increase the tax burden, since the profit from the forward "hedge" (i.e., speculation) is taxable, but the translation loss does not reduce taxable income.

Balance Sheet Hedge Defined

A balance sheet hedge requires an equal amount of exposed foreign currency assets and liabilities on a firm's consolidated balance sheet. If this can be achieved for each foreign currency, net translation exposure will be zero. A change in exchange rates will change the value of exposed liabilities in an equal amount but in a direction opposite to the change in value of exposed assets. If a firm translates by the temporal method, a zero net exposed position is called *monetary balance*.

Complete monetary balance cannot be achieved under the current rate method, because total assets would have to be matched by an equal amount of debt, but the equity section of the balance sheet must still be translated at historic exchange rates.

The cost of a balance sheet hedge depends on relative borrowing costs. If foreign currency borrowing costs, after adjusting for foreign exchange risk, are higher than parent currency borrowing costs, the balance sheet hedge is costly, and vice versa. Normal operations, however, already require decisions about the magnitude and currency denomination of specific balance sheet accounts. Thus balance sheet hedges are a compromise in which the denomination of balance sheet accounts is altered, perhaps at a cost in terms of interest expense or operating efficiency, to achieve some degree of foreign exchange protection.

Balance Sheet Hedge Illustrated

To illustrate a balance sheet hedge, let us return again to the translation exposure previously identified for Carlton Germany and its parent, Carlton Inc. Earlier data from Exhibit 10.4 is restated in a different format in Exhibit 10.7.

Carlton Germany expects the euro to drop 16.67% in value from its year-beginning value to a new exchange rate of $1.0000/€. Under the current rate method, the expected loss is 16.67% of the exposure of $9,600,000, or $1,600,000. Under the temporal method, the expected loss is 16.67% of the exposure of $960,000, or $160,000.

To achieve a balance sheet hedge, Carlton Inc. must either 1) reduce exposed euro assets without simultaneously reducing euro liabilities or 2) increase euro liabilities without simultaneously increasing euro assets. One way to do this is to exchange existing euro cash for dollars. If Carlton Germany does not have large euro cash balances, it can borrow euros and exchange the borrowed euros for dollars. Another subsidiary could borrow euros and exchange them for dollars. That is, the essence of the hedge is for the parent or any of its subsidiaries to create euro debt and exchange the proceeds for dollars.

Current rate method. Under the current rate method, Carlton Germany should borrow as much as €8,000,000. The initial effect of this first step is to increase both an exposed asset (cash) and an exposed liability (notes payable) on the balance sheet of Carlton Germany, with no immediate effect on net exposed assets. The required follow-up step can take two forms: 1) Carlton Germany can exchange the acquired euros for U.S. dollars and hold those dollars itself, or 2) it can transfer the borrowed euros to Carlton Inc., perhaps as a euro dividend or as repayment of intracompany debt. Carlton Inc. could then exchange the euros for dollars. In some countries, of course, local monetary authorities will not allow their currency to be so freely exchanged.

Another possibility would be for Carlton Inc. or a sister subsidiary to borrow the euros, thus keeping the euro debt entirely off Carlton Germany's books. However, the second step is still essential to eliminate euro exposure; the borrowing entity must exchange the euros for dollars or other unexposed assets. Any such borrowing should be coordinated with all other euro borrowings to avoid the possibility that one subsidiary is borrowing euros to reduce translation exposure at the same time as another subsidiary is repaying euro debt. (Note that euros can be "borrowed," by simply delaying repayment of existing euro debt; the goal is to increase euro debt, not borrow in a literal sense.)

Exhibit 10.7 Carlton Germany, Balance Sheet Exposure

Exhibit 10.7 Carlton Germany, Balance Sheet Exposure

	Balance Sheet Account	Current Rate Exposure	Temporal Exposure
Assets			
Cash	€ 1,600,000	€ 1,600,000	€ 1,600,000
Accounts receivable	3,200,000	3,200,000	3,200,000
Inventory	2,400,000	2,400,000	
Net plant and equipment	4,800,000	4,800,000	
Total assets	€ 12,000,000	€ 12,000,000	€ 4,800,000
Exposed assets		€ 12,000,000	€ 4,800,000
Liabilities and Capital			
Accounts payable	€ 800,000	€ 800,000	€ 800,000
Short-term bank loan	1,600,000	1,600,000	1,600,000
Long-term debt	1,600,000	1,600,000	1,600,000
Common stock	1,800,000		
Retained earnings	6,200,000		
Total liabilities and net worth	€ 12,000,000		
Exposed liabilities		€ 4,000,000	€ 4,000,000
Net exposed assets in euros		€ 8,000,000	€ 800,000
Times exchange rate, $/		1.2000	1.2000
Net exposed assets in dollars		$ 9,600,000	$ 960,000.0
Times amount of devaluation		-16.67%	-16.67%
Expected translation gain (loss)		$ (1,600,000)	$ (160,000)

Key Cell Entries

C6: ='Exhibit 10.4'!C7, copy to C7:C9
D6: ='Exhibit 10.4'!K7, copy to D7:D9
E6: ='Exhibit 10.4'!K21, copy to E7
C10: =SUM(C6:C9), copy to D10:E10
D11: =D10
E11: =E10
C13: ='Exhibit 10.4'!C13, copy to C14:C17
D13: ='Exhibit 10.4'!K13, copy to D14:D15
E13: ='Exhibit 10.4'!K27, copy to E14:E15
C18: =SUM(C13:C17)
D19: =SUM(D13:D17), copy to E19
D20: =D10-D19, copy to E20
D22: =D20*D21, copy to E22
D23: =(1.0000-1.2000)/1.2000, copy to E23
D24: =D22*D23, copy to E24

Temporal method. If translation is by the temporal method, only the much smaller amount of €800,000 need be borrowed. As before, Carlton Germany could use the proceeds of the loan to acquire U.S. dollars. However, Carlton Germany could also use the proceeds to acquire inventory or fixed assets in Europe. Under the temporal method, these assets are not regarded as exposed and do not drop in dollar value when the euro depreciates.

When Is a Balance Sheet Hedge Justified?

If a firm's subsidiary is using the local currency as the functional currency, the following circumstances could justify when to use a balance sheet hedge:

- The foreign subsidiary is about to be liquidated, so that the value of its CTA would be realized.
- The firm has debt covenants or bank agreements that state the firm's debt/equity ratios will be maintained within specific limits.
- Management is evaluated on the basis of certain income statement and balance sheet measures that are affected by translation losses or gains.
- The foreign subsidiary is operating in a hyperinflationary environment.

If a firm is using the parent's home currency as the functional currency of the foreign subsidiary, all transaction gains/losses are passed through to the income statement. Hedging this consolidated income to reduce its variability may be important to investors and bond rating agencies.

Choice Between Minimizing Transaction or Translation Exposure

Management will find it almost impossible to offset both translation and transaction exposure at the same time. Reduction of one exposure usually changes the amount of the other exposure. For example, the easiest way to offset translation exposure is to require the parent and all subsidiaries to denominate all exposed assets and liabilities in the parent's reporting currency. For U.S. firms and their subsidiaries, all assets and liabilities would be held in dollars. Such a firm would have no translation exposure, but each subsidiary would have its own transaction exposure.

To illustrate, assume that a U.S. parent instructs its Japanese subsidiary to bill an export to the parent in dollars. The account receivable on the Japanese subsidiary's books is shown as the yen equivalent of the dollar amount, and yen profit is recorded at the time of sale. If, before the parent pays dollars to the Japanese subsidiary, the yen appreciates 5%, the parent still pays only the contracted dollar amount. The Japanese subsidiary receives 5% fewer yen than were expected and booked as profit. Hence the Japanese subsidiary will experience a 5% foreign exchange loss on its dollar-denominated accounts receivable. Lower yen profit will eventually be translated into lower dollar profit when the subsidiary's income statement is consolidated with that of the parent. Eventually the consolidated MNE will show a foreign exchange loss—on dollars!

Similar reasoning will show that if a firm chooses to eliminate transaction exposure, translation exposure might even be increased. The easiest way to be rid of transaction exposure is to require the parent and all subsidiaries to denominate all accounts subject to transaction exposure in its local currency. Thus every subsidiary would avoid transaction gains or losses. However, each subsidiary would be creating net translation exposure by being either long or short in terms of local currency–exposed assets or liabilities. The consolidated financial statement of the parent firm would show translation exposure in each local currency.

As a general matter, firms seeking to reduce both types of exposure usually reduce transaction exposure first. They then recalculate translation exposure (which may have changed), and decide if any residual translation exposure can be reduced without creating more transaction exposure. Taxes complicate the decision to seek protection against transaction or translation exposure. Transaction losses are normally considered "realized" losses and are therefore deductible from pretax income. However, translation losses are only "paper" losses, involving no cash flows, and are not deductible from pretax income. It is highly debatable whether protective techniques that necessitate cash payments, and so reduce net cash flow, should be incurred to avoid noncash losses.

Evaluation of Performance

A MNE must be able to set specific financial goals, monitor progress by all units of the enterprise towards those goals, and evaluate results. It must be able to measure the performance of each of its subsidiaries on a consistent basis, and managers of subsidiaries must be given unambiguous objectives against which they will be judged. The criteria for internal evaluation and control should be designed for the specific purposes of the firm, and not be the byproduct of reports or statements that were initially designed and prepared for financial accounting or for local reporting and tax purposes.

Evaluation is carried out not only by internal management for planning and control purposes, but also by outsiders. Outside evaluation centers around analysis of a firm's official financial statements. Comparing a firm's financial statements with those of its competitors helps managers evaluate their own performance or find how policies of their firms differ from those of other firms. Bankers and rating agencies use financial statements to assess relative strengths and weaknesses of applicants for credit. Security analysts, portfolio managers, and investors use them to help select among competing securities. Government officials use them for a variety of regulatory purposes.

The Financial Goals of the MNE

As introduced in Chapter 1, the MNE must determine for itself the proper balance between three operating financial objectives:

1. Maximization of consolidated after-tax income
2. Minimization of the firm's effective global tax burden
3. Correct positioning of the firm's income, cash flows, and available funds.

These goals—as seen throughout this book—are frequently inconsistent; the pursuit of one goal may result in a less desirable outcome in regard to another goal. Management must continually make decisions about the proper tradeoffs for the MNE. These tradeoffs are not only between the three goals listed earlier, but also frequently about which goals are to be pursued now as opposed to the future.

Consider once again our U.S.-based multinational Carlton Corporation. The explicit goal of management is to maximize shareholder wealth, which within the confines of corporate headquarters is typically interpreted as the maximization of earnings and earnings per share (EPS) growth. In Chapter 21 we will describe the various methods by which management may reposition the profits of a firm to maximize earnings and minimize the global tax liability of the MNE. But repositioning profits by definition means reducing the profits of one individual unit for the benefit of the whole—and logically another unit. How does the MNE design and maintain a performance management system that recognizes the impacts of these "sacrifices" by the individual unit for the benefit of the MNE in total?

Domestic Versus Multinational Control

Managers of foreign subsidiaries must be able to run their own operations efficiently according to achievable objectives. Higher-level management should evaluate their personal success according to criteria that are both clear in a quantitative sense and equitable in considering the nonquantifiable factors of operating in a foreign environment. Furthermore, the criteria by which managers are to be judged must be congruent with the goals of the firm so that managerial action furthers the best long-run interests of the firm. This is much easier said than done, however.

All firms expand and modify their domestic profitability measures when applying them to foreign subsidiaries. In addition, some firms establish foreign subsidiaries for objectives not related to normal corporate profit-oriented goals. Such exceptions include ensuring sources of supply, maintaining a presence in a given market, and conforming with government regulations. Although these goals have some very long-run focus on profits, performance measurement in the short run is not meaningful.

There are four purposes of an internal evaluation system. In order of importance they are:

1. *To ensure adequate profitability.* This is clearly the primary directive of the MNE; profits are the single biggest driver of shareholder wealth creation. All other purposes are secondary to the basic corporate goal of profitability.
2. *To have an early warning system if something is wrong.* Although intuitively appealing, this goal is difficult to implement in practice, because failure to meet targeted results may be due to valid and nonrecurring problems unique to international operations or to the fact that the original target was unrealistic.
3. *To have a basis for allocating resources.* This goal arises primarily in the context of requests from foreign subsidiaries for new funds that total more than the parent has available. Top management needs a fair and equitable means of rationing limited resources while serving overall corporate goals.
3. *To evaluate individual managers.* Managers are often evaluated by criteria in addition to profit contribution, such as their success in developing organizations or in expanding product lines.

Complexities of International Performance Evaluation

Internal financial evaluation of foreign subsidiaries is both unique and difficult. Use of one foreign exchange translation method, in an attempt to measure results in the home currency, will present a different measure of success or of compliance with predetermined goals than use of some other translation method. Even though an internal control system stands independent of such accounting rules as FAS #52, evidence suggests that most firms start with the translation system used for financial reporting. Such a starting point is probably inappropriate when the goal is an effective control system, but it does lessen the cost of an entirely separate reporting procedure.

The results of any control system must be judged against distortions of performance caused by widely differing national business environments. Because many foreign direct investments are made to enhance strategic interaction with the rest of the worldwide system, one cannot evaluate such investments as if they stand alone.

Costs often not attributed to subsidiaries in a formal measurement system include implied costs to the parent of guaranteeing subsidiary loans or holding safety inventory in the home country to serve foreign subsidiaries. Benefits to the worldwide system include profits to the parent or related subsidiaries from additional exports, royalties and management fees, keeping the parent abreast of technological developments in other countries, preempting markets, enlarging economies of scale, and denying such benefits to competing firms.

International measurement systems are distorted by decisions to benefit the world system at the expense of a specific local subsidiary. For example, a subsidiary in a low-interest country may finance another subsidiary in a high-interest country. Although the system benefits, the first subsidiary will have excess interest charges and the second will save on interest. Positioning of funds sometimes requires artificial transfer prices between related subsidiaries for tax, foreign exchange, or liquidity reasons. Management must devise a fair and consistent method of adjusting the basic reports to reflect the "self-sacrifice" of one subsidiary for another.

Additional variables that may invalidate comparisons of reports from subsidiaries in separate countries include nationally imposed barriers on fund remittances, differential rates of inflation, requirements for certain levels of legal reserves financed via earnings retention, customs that call for profit sharing with workers, differing standards between countries over primary corporate goals, and variations in the work ethic and/or labor productivity. By and large, these variables are not significant in differentiating among domestic subsidiaries, but a company that seeks to extend a domestic control system abroad must ponder the significance of the financial data obtained.

Foreign Exchange Rates and Performance Evaluation

The impact of exchange rate movements on the measured performance of foreign subsidiaries is one of the single largest dilemmas facing management of the MNE. This chapter described the process of translating foreign subsidiary foreign currency–denominated financial statements into the home currency of the parent company. As a result of translation, however, it is possible that financial measures of performance may not give true signals as to the profitability—or general success—of the foreign subsidiary.

Consider the two-year income statement summary of Carlton Brazil S.A., described in Exhibit 10.8. By all financial indications on the local level—in Brazilian real—the subsidiary showed good growth in earnings (+14%), earnings before interest, taxes, depreciation, and amortization (EBITDA) (+15%), and income (+38%). The unit's gross margin was maintained at 42%, its return on sales rose from 5% to 6%, all in the face of a tumultuous economic environment.

But from the U.S. parent company's point of view, because of the 34% depreciation of the real, the income generated by the Brazilian subsidiary in U.S. dollar terms fell 9% from the previous year. The evaluation of the performance of a MNE subsidiary like this one involves three different evaluation dimensions:

Exhibit 10.8 Profit and Loss Items, Carlton Brazil S.A. (thousands of Brazilian real)

Income Items	Year 1	Year 2	% Change
Sales	358,640	410,500	14%
Less cost of goods sold	(208,600)	(238,400)	14%
Gross operating profit	150,040	172,100	15%
Gross margin	42%	42%	
Less G&A expenses	(38,600)	(44,380)	
EBITDA	111,440	127,720	15%
Less depreciation and amortization	(58,000)	(58,000)	
EBIT	53,440	69,720	30%
Less interest	(28,000)	(34,500)	
EBT	25,440	35,220	38%
Less Brazilian income tax at 30%	(7,632)	(10,566)	
Net income	17,808	24,654	38%
Return on sales	5%	6%	
Exchange rate (R$/$)	2.17	3.30	–34%
Net income (U.S.$)	$8,206	$7,741	–9%

1. **Management Evaluation.** If the unit is essentially local currency functional, the weight of performance evaluation of local management should be conducted in local currency terms. Growth of sales, control of costs, and maintenance of margins all rely upon the work effort and commitment of local management. If, however, significant operating costs or financing costs are directed from the parent company, either for better or for worse, the performance evaluation system will have to adjust for these corporate-driven decisions which impact financial performance.

2. **Subsidiary Evaluation.** The evaluation of the subsidiary itself as seen through the eyes of the parent company requires a focus on competitiveness in the local market. This is similar to the *project viewpoint* described in the capital budgeting analysis of Chapter 18. Maintenance of gross margin, sales growth, and market share, as compared to similar margins and shares of local competitors, provide a measure of competitiveness on the local level.

3. **Strategic Evaluation.** The role the foreign subsidiary plays within the portfolio of the MNE requires senior management of the parent company level to take the parent viewpoint. This, however, is frequently extremely difficult, requiring management to trade-off short-term profitability (here measured in U.S. dollars) against long-term shareholder wealth creation, as realized in Brazilian real in the business itself. Regardless of local currency performance, the flat earnings in dollar-terms will result in flat consolidated profits as reported to Wall Street. If the MNE's major competitors do not have a similar Brazilian exposure (i.e., they have different operating exposures), Carlton is seen to be underperforming its competitors. Shareholders, and possibly creditors, will require explanations of this underperformance.

Senior strategic and financial management will then have to determine whether the subsidiary is to be liquidated, maintained, or possibly expanded, depending on their perceptions and aspirations for future Brazilian real and U.S. dollar performance.

These three different levels of performance evaluation are inextricably intertwined. By standing in the shoes of local subsidiary management, senior corporate management, and shareholders, it is easy to see how difficult evaluating the performance of foreign subsidiaries is within the MNE. This complexity is compounded by the growth of subsidiaries into more and more emerging markets with their commensurate currency volatility.

Regardless of complexity, however, the ultimate test of a performance measurement system is whether it enables the firm to create shareholder value. If not, the shareholders' expectations will not be met and the share price will underperform the market.

SUMMARY

- Translation exposure results from translating foreign currency–denominated statements of foreign subsidiaries into the parent's reporting currency so the parent can prepare consolidated financial statements. Translation exposure is the potential for loss or gain from this translation process.
- A foreign subsidiary's functional currency is the currency of the primary economic environment in which the subsidiary operates and in which it generates cash flows. In other words, it is the dominant currency used by that foreign subsidiary in its day-to-day operations.
- The two basic procedures for translation used in most countries today are the current rate method and the temporal method.
- Technical aspects of translation include questions about when to recognize gains or losses in the income statement, the distinction between functional and reporting currency, and the treatment of subsidiaries in hyperinflation countries.
- Translation gains and losses can be quite different from operating gains and losses, not only in magnitude but in sign. Management may need to determine which is of greater significance prior to deciding which exposure is to be managed first.
- The main technique for managing translation exposure is a balance sheet hedge. This calls for having an equal amount of exposed foreign currency assets and liabilities.
- Even if management chooses to follow an active policy of hedging translation exposure, it is nearly impossible to offset both transaction and translation exposure simultaneously. If forced to choose, most managers will protect against transaction losses, because these are realized cash losses, rather than protect against translation losses.
- All firms expand and modify their domestic profitability measures when applying them to foreign subsidiaries for purposes of evaluating performance.
- The impact of exchange rate movements on the measured performance of foreign subsidiaries is one of the single largest dilemmas facing management of the MNE.

QUESTIONS

1. **Definitions.** Define the following terms:
   a. Translation exposure
   b. Accounting exposure
   c. Integrated foreign entity
   d. Self-sustaining foreign entity
   e. Functional currency
2. **Functional currency determinants.** Describe the economic indicators that should be used to determine the functional currency of any foreign subsidiary.
3. **Current rate method.** Using the current rate method, define the exchange rate that must be used to translate each of the following line items:
   a. Assets and liabilities
   b. Income statement items
   c. Dividends
   d. Equity items
4. **Temporal method.** Using the temporal method, define the exchange rate that must be used to translate the following line items:
   a. Monetary assets and liabilities
   b. Nonmonetary assets and liabilities
   c. Income statement items
   d. Dividends
   e. Equity items
5. **Gains and losses.**
   a. Explain how gains and losses are accounted for in the calculation of consolidated net income using each translation method.
   b. What are the advantages and disadvantages of accounting for gains and losses in this way?
6. **Hyperinflation.** Under the FAS #52, how do MNEs solve the problem of the "disappearing asset" when translating financial statements of foreign subsidiaries located in countries experiencing hyperinflation? Be sure to define "hyperinflation."
7. **Balance sheet hedge defined.**
   a. Explain what is meant by a "balance sheet hedge."
   b. What is meant by "monetary balance" when translating a foreign subsidiary's balance sheet?
   c. What determines the cost of a balance sheet hedge?
8. **Balance sheet hedge justification.** What are the circumstances that could justify a balance sheet hedge?
9. **Translation versus transaction exposure.** How can a MNE minimize its translation and transaction exposure simultaneously?
10. **Carlton and a strong dollar.** If the U.S. dollar is expected to appreciate relative to the euro, how might this affect the reported consolidated balance sheet and income statement of Carlton Inc.?
11. **Carlton and a weak dollar.** If the U.S. dollar is expected to depreciate relative to the euro, how might this affect the reported consolidated balance sheet and income statement of Carlton Inc.?
12. **Translation versus operating exposure.** How should Carlton react to any differences between gains and losses on operating exposure compared to gains or losses on translation exposure?
13. **Performance evaluation at Carlton Brazil.** Carlton Brazil's financial performance in Year 2 was clearly worse, in U.S. dollar terms, than the previous year. As the managing director of Carlton's Brazilian subsidiary, how would you explain to corporate management the distinction between the translation results and the operating exposure benefits possibly accruing to the business in the future?

PROBLEMS

1. **Translation versus operating exposure: Carlton Germany (A).** Using the facts for Carlton Germany in the chapter, assume the exchange rate on January 2, 2002, in Exhibit 10.4 dropped in value from $1.2000/€ to $0.9000/€ rather than to $1.0000/€. Recalculate Carlton Germany's translated balance sheet for January 2, 2002, with the new exchange rate using the *current rate method.*
   a. What is the amount of translation gain or loss?
   b. Where should it appear in the financial statements?

2. **Carlton Germany (B).** Using the facts for Carlton Germany in the chapter, assume as in problem 1 that the exchange rate on January 2, 2002, in Exhibit 10.4 changed in value from $1.2000/€ to $0.9000/€ rather than to $1.0000/€. Recalculate Carlton Germany's translated balance sheet for January 2, 2002, with the new exchange rate using the *temporal method.*
   a. What is the amount of translation gain or loss?
   b. Where should it appear in the financial statements?
   c. Why does the translation loss or gain under the temporal method differ from the loss or gain under the current rate method?

3. **Carlton Germany (C).** Using the facts for Carlton Germany in the chapter, assume the exchange rate on January 2, 2002, in Exhibit 10.4 changed from $1.2000/€ to $1.500/€. Calculate Carlton Germany's translated balance sheet for January 2, 2002, with the new exchange rate using the *current rate method.*
   a. What is the amount of translation gain or loss?
   b. Where should it appear in the financial statements?

4. **Carlton Germany (D).** Using the facts for Carlton Germany in the chapter, assume as in problem 3 that the exchange rate on January 2, 2002, in Exhibit 10.4 changed from $1.2000/€ to $1.5000/€. Calculate Carlton Germany's translated balance sheet for January 2, 2002, with the new exchange rate using the *temporal method.*
   a. What is the amount of translation gain or loss?
   b. Where should it appear in the financial statements?

Montevideo Products, S.A. *Use the following information to answer questions 5–7.* Montevideo Products, S.A., is the Uruguayan subsidiary of a U.S. manufacturing company. Its balance sheet for January 1 follows. The January 1st exchange rate between the U.S. dollar and the Uruguay peso ($U) is $U20/$.

Montevideo Products, S.A.
Balance Sheet, January 1
(thousands of Uruguay pesos)

Assets	
Cash	$U 60,000
Accounts receivable	120,000
Inventory	120,000
Net plant & equipment	240,000
	$U 540,000
Liabilities and Net Worth	
Current liabilities	$U 30,000
Long-term debt	90,000
Capital stock*	300,000
Retained earnings*	120,000
	$U 540,000

* The capital stock and retained earnings are carried at a historical exchange rate value of $U15.00/$.

5. **Montevideo Products, S.A. (A).** Determine Montevideo's contribution to the translation exposure of its parent on January 1, using the current rate method.

6. **Montevideo Products, S.A. (B).** Calculate Montevideo's contribution to its parent's translation gain or loss using the current rate method if the exchange rate on December 31 is $U22/$. Assume all peso accounts remain as they were at the beginning of the year.

7. **Montevideo Products, S.A. (C).** Calculate Montevideo's contribution to its parent's translation gain or loss using the current rate method if the exchange rate on December 31 is $U12/$. Assume all peso accounts remain as they were at the beginning of the year.

Siam Toys, Ltd. *Use the following information to answer questions 8 and 9.* Siam Toys, Ltd., is the Thai affiliate of a U.S. toy manufacturer. Siam Toys manufactures plastic injection molding equipment for making toy cars. Sales are primarily in the United States and Europe. Siam Toys' balance sheet in thousands of Thai baht (B) as of March 31 is as follows:

Siam Toys, Ltd.

Balance Sheet, March 31 (thousands of Thai baht)

Assets	
Cash	B 24,000
Accounts receivable	36,000
Inventory	48,000
Net plant & equipment	60,000
	B 168,000

Liabilities and Net Worth	
Accounts payable	B 18,000
Bank loans	60,000
Common stock	18,000
Retained earnings	72,000
	B 168,000

Exchange rates for translating Siam Toy's balance sheet into U.S. dollars are:

B30.00/$	March 31 exchange rate, before 25% devaluation. All inventory was acquired at this rate.
B40.00/$	April 1 exchange rate after 25% devaluation.
B20.00/$	Historic exchange rate at which plant and equipment and common stock were acquired.
B34.00/$	Historic exchange rate (weighted average) at which retained earnings were acquired.

8. **Siam Toys, Ltd. (A).** Using the previous data on Siam Toys, assume that the Thai baht dropped in value from B30/$ to B40/$ between March 31 and April 1. Assuming no change in balance sheet accounts between these two days, calculate the gain or loss from translation by both the current rate method and the temporal method. Explain the translation gain or loss in terms of changes in the value of exposed accounts.

9. **Siam Toys, Ltd. (B).** Using the previous data from problem 8, assume that the Thai baht appreciated in value from B30/$ to B25/$ between March 31 and April 1. Assuming no change in balance sheet accounts between these two days, calculate the gain or loss from translation by both the current rate method and the temporal method. Explain the translation gain or loss in terms of changes in the value of exposed accounts.

10. **Egyptian Ingot, Ltd.** Egyptian Ingot, Ltd., is the Egyptian subsidiary of Trans-Mediterranean Aluminium, a British multinational that fashions automobile engine blocks from aluminum. Trans-Mediterranean's home reporting currency is the British pound.

    Egyptian Ingot's December 31 balance sheet follows. At the date of this balance sheet, the exchange rate between Egyptian pounds (£E) and British pounds sterling was £E5.50/UK£.

Egyptian Ingot, Ltd.
Balance Sheet, December 31
(thousands of Egyptian pounds)

Assets	
Cash	£E 16,500,000
Accounts receivable	33,000,000
Inventory	49,500,000
Net plant and equipment	66,000,000
	£E 165,000,000

Liabilities & Net Worth	
Accounts payable	£E 24,750,000
Long-term debt	49,500,000
Invested capital	90,750,000
	£E 165,000,000

a. What is Egyptian Ingot's contribution to the translation exposure of Trans-Mediterranean on December 31, using the current rate method?

b. Calculate the translation exposure loss to Trans-Mediterranean if the exchange rate at the beginning of the following quarter has changed to £E6.00/£.

INTERNET EXERCISES

WWW.

1. **Changing translation practices: FASB.** The Financial Accounting Standards Board promulgates standard practices for the reporting of financial results by companies in the United States. It also, however, often leads the way in the development of new practices and emerging issues around the world. One major issue today is the valuation and reporting of financial derivatives and derivative agreements by firms. Use the FASB's home page and the web pages of several of the major accounting firms and other interest groups around the world to see current proposed accounting standards and the current state of reaction to the proposed standards.

   FASB home page http://raw.rutgers.edu/raw/fasb

   Treasury Management Association http://www.tma.org

2. **Nestlé's financial statements and exchange rates.** Using Nestlé's web page, check current press releases for more recent financial results, including what the company reports as the primary currencies and average exchange rates used for translation of international financial results during the most recent period.

   Nestlé: The World Food Company http://www.nestle.com/press/current

SELECTED READINGS

Ball, Ray, "Making Accounting International: Why, How, and How Far Will It Go?" *Journal of Applied Corporate Finance*, Fall 1995, Volume 8, No. 3, pp. 19–29.

Houston, Carol Olson, "Translation Exposure Hedging Post SFAS No. 52," *Journal of International Financial Management and Accounting*, Summer and Autumn 1990, Volume 2, Nos. 2 and 3, pp. 145–170.

Ruland, Robert G., and Timothy S. Doupnik, "Foreign Currency Translation and the Behavior of Exchange Rates," *Journal of International Business Studies*, Fall 1988, pp. 461–476.

MINI-CASE

Hedging the Euro Away

A specific instance in which management or hedging of translation exposure has become significant is in the protection of consolidated reported earnings. In recent years, a number of major multinational companies have found that they could protect the reported U.S. dollar value of foreign earnings by hedging them.

For example, in 2000 a number of major U.S. multinationals grew increasingly concerned over the sliding value of the euro. Given the significant contribution of European profits earned in euros, the declining value of the euro versus the dollar represented a continuing degradation of potential reported profits. Some, like Coca-Cola Company, hedged the dollar value of their projected euro earnings and suffered no material declines in consolidated earnings as a result. Others, however, like Goodyear and Caterpillar, suffered double-digit percentage reductions in consolidated earnings as a result of the unhedged euro decline (Exhibit A).

Although a number of companies have admittedly been able for a quarter, or a series of quarters, to prevent their consolidated earnings from being hurt by falling foreign currencies, it is still highly controversial for a firm to expend resources and acquire hedging positions with forwards and swaps to hedge accounting results.

Exhibit A **Impact of the Falling Euro on Select U.S.-Based Multinationals**

Company	Operating Income 3rd Qtr 2000 (Millions)	Reduction Because of Euro (Percent)
Goodyear	$ 68	30%
Caterpillar	$294	12%
McDonald's	$910	5%
Kimberly-Clark	$667	2.5%

Source: "Business Won't Hedge the Euro Away," *Business Week*, December 4, 2000.

Case Questions

1. Do you believe multinational firms should hedge their reported earnings? Why or why not?
2. What exactly would a firm have to do in order to hedge the reported earnings of one of its European subsidiaries for the coming quarter?
3. Do you believe an investor should evaluate earnings differently depending on whether the reported earnings were before or after hedging? Why or why not?
4. Does hedging reported earnings reduce their transparency, an increasing concern since the Enron debacle?

PART 4

Financing the Global Firm

PART 4

Part 4 examines how a firm can use the global capital market to minimize its cost of capital and maximize its access to capital. A firm needs to achieve a certain global cost and availability of capital in order to compete successfully in both its domestic and foreign markets.

Chapter 11 starts with a review of how we can compute a firm's *cost of capital*, using Carlton's weighted average cost of capital as an illustration. Next we analyze how a firm can calculate its *equity risk premium*. We then examine the role played by international portfolio investors in determining whether a firm can gain a desired global cost and availability of capital. Next we examine the link between cost and availability of capital; namely, the effect of market liquidity and market segmentation. We continue with a detailed illustrative case showing how Novo Industri, a Danish MNE, was able to gain a global cost and availability of capital despite being located in an illiquid and segmented Danish capital market. We conclude by comparing the cost of capital for MNEs compared to their domestic counterparts. We also present an interesting mini-case on the strategic alliance of Bang & Olufsen and Philips N.V.

Chapter 12 examines how a firm can source its equity in global capital markets. Management must first design a strategy to gain access to the world's most liquid equity markets. Access should improve the liquidity of a firm's equity shares and thereby lower its weighted average cost of capital. An important milestone occurs when a firm cross-lists its shares on one or more foreign stock exchanges. An even more important milestone is for the firm to sell some of its equity to foreign investors. We analyze the barriers a firm must overcome if it is to be successful at cross-listing and selling equity abroad. The chapter concludes with a description of alternative instruments that a firm can use to sell its equity in foreign markets.

Chapter 13 describes how a firm wishing to minimize its cost of capital must maintain a financial structure that balances debt and equity in a manner that is acceptable to its worldwide shareholders and creditors. A MNE, in particular, must consider how to maintain access to global capital markets, reduce risk through international diversification, minimize foreign exchange risk due to raising foreign currency–denominated debt, and meet the expectations of international portfolio investors. A MNE must also consider how to finance its foreign subsidiaries and structure their balance sheets. After a brief description of the Eurocurrency markets, we describe the various debt instruments that a MNE can use to tap global debt markets, including syndicated bank loans, Euronotes, and international bonds. The chapter concludes with an analysis of project financing and a mini-case on project financing in an emerging market—Venezuela.

Chapter 14 explains how financial managers of all firms, whether domestic or multinational, must manage *interest rate risk*. Interest rate risk affects both the liability and asset side of a firm's balance sheet. On the liability side of the balance sheet, a firm's *interest rate risk* is affected by credit risk and repricing risk on floating-rate loans. We describe three important interest rate risk management instruments; namely, *forward rate agreements*, *interest rate futures*, and *interest rate swaps*. We use the Carlton case to illustrate how a firm can swap from a fixed interest rate cash flow obligation to a floating-rate obligation and vice versa. Next we show how Carlton can use a currency swap to switch from floating-rate dollars to fixed rate Swiss francs, and then unwind this swap at a later date. The chapter concludes with an illustrative case of an actual three-way back-to-back cross-currency swap and a mini-case on McDonald's British pound exposure. We also present an appendix covering advanced topics in interest rate management, including forward rate agreements, caps, and floors.

apter 11

Global Cost and Availability of Capital

HOW CAN FIRMS TAP GLOBAL CAPITAL MARKETS FOR THE PURPOSE OF MINIMIZING THEIR COST OF capital and maximizing capital's availability? Why should they do so?

Global integration of capital markets has given many firms access to new and cheaper sources of funds beyond those available in their home markets. These firms can then accept more long-term projects and invest more in capital improvements and expansion. If a firm is located in a country with illiquid and/or segmented capital markets, it can achieve this lower global cost and greater availability of capital by a properly designed and implemented strategy. The dimensions of the cost and availability of capital are illustrated in Exhibit 11.1. The impact of firm-specific characteristics, market

Exhibit 11.1 Dimensions of the Cost and Availability of Capital Strategy

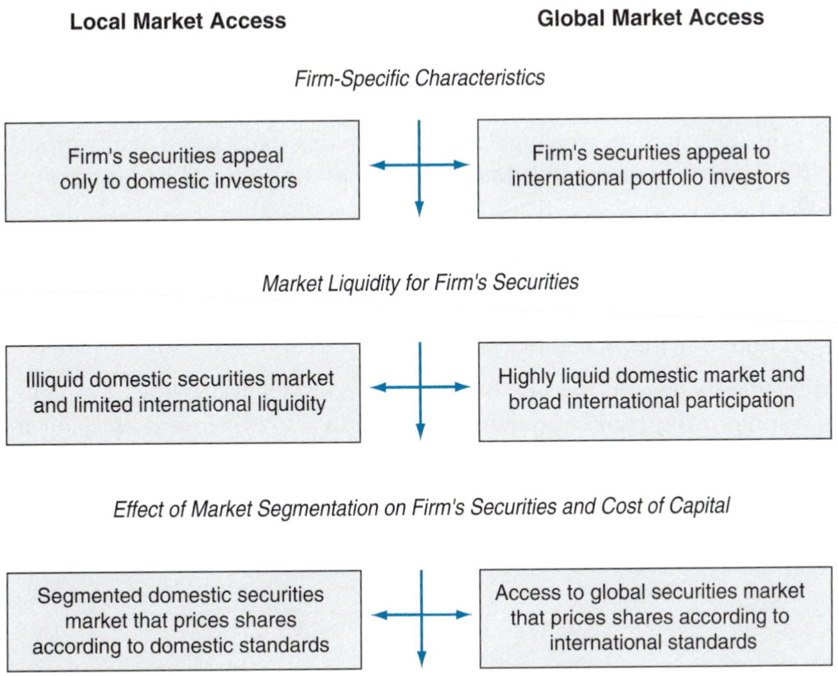

liquidity for the firm's securities, and the definition and effect of market segmentation on the prices of a firm's capital are the subject of most of this chapter.

A firm that must source its long-term debt and equity in a ***highly illiquid domestic securities market*** will probably have a relatively high cost of capital and will face limited availability of such capital, which in turn will lower its competitiveness both internationally and vis-à-vis foreign firms entering its home market. This category of firms includes both firms resident in emerging countries, where the capital market remains undeveloped, and firms too small to gain access to their own national securities markets. Many family-owned firms find themselves in this category because they choose not to utilize securities markets to source their long-term capital needs.

Firms resident in industrial countries with ***small capital markets*** often source their long-term debt and equity at home in these partially liquid domestic securities markets. The firms' cost and availability of capital is better than that of firms in countries with illiquid capital markets. However, if these firms can tap the highly liquid global markets, they can also strengthen their competitive advantage in sourcing capital.

Firms resident in countries with ***segmented capital markets*** must devise a strategy to escape dependence on that market for their long-term debt and equity needs. A national capital market is segmented if the required rate of return on securities in that market differs from the required rate of return on securities of comparable expected return and risk traded on other securities markets. Capital markets become segmented because of such factors as excessive regulatory control, perceived political risk, anticipated foreign exchange risk, lack of transparency, asymmetric availability of information, cronyism, insider trading, and many other market imperfections.

Firms constrained by any of these conditions must develop a strategy to escape their own limited capital markets and source some of their long-term capital abroad. This chapter will first review how a firm calculates its weighted average cost of capital when international portfolio investors are able to invest in its equity and debt securities. Carlton will be our example.

The second section of this chapter analyzes how a firm can attract international portfolio investors to its securities. This ability depends on firm-specific characteristics, a regulatory environment that permits unrestricted cross-border investment flows, and a financial strategy that creates market liquidity and global pricing for the firm's securities, whether or not its domestic market is segmented from other capital markets.

The third section focuses on the link between the cost and availability of capital. Achieving this link requires improving market liquidity for the firm's securities and escaping from a segmented domestic market. If the firm is successful in implementing these strategies, it will reduce its weighted average cost of capital and increase its availability.

The fourth section analyzes whether MNEs have reduced their cost of capital below that of their comparable domestic competitors.

Weighted Average Cost of Capital

A firm normally finds its *weighted average cost of capital* (WACC) by combining the cost of equity with the cost of debt in proportion to the relative weight of each in the firm's optimal long-term financial structure. More specifically:

$$k_{\text{WACC}} = k_e \frac{E}{V} + k_d(1-t)\frac{D}{V}$$

where

k_{WACC}	=	weighted average after-tax cost of capital
k_e	=	risk-adjusted cost of equity
k_d	=	before-tax cost of debt
t	=	marginal tax rate
E	=	market value of the firm's equity
D	=	market value of the firm's debt
V	=	total market value of the firm's securities $(D + E)$

Cost of Equity

The *capital asset pricing model* (CAPM) approach is to define the cost of equity for a firm by the following formula:

$$k_e = k_{rf} + \beta_j(k_m - k_{rf})$$

where

k_e	=	expected (required) rate of return on equity
k_{rf}	=	rate of interest on risk-free bonds (Treasury bonds, for example)
β_j	=	coefficient of *systematic risk* for the firm
k_m	=	expected (required) rate of return on the market portfolio of stocks

Systematic risk is a function of the total variability of expected returns of the firm's stock relative to the market index (k_m) and the degree to which the variability of expected returns of the firm is correlated to the expected returns on the market index. More formally:

$$\beta_j = \frac{\rho_{jm}\sigma_j}{\sigma_m}$$

where β_j (beta) is the measure of systematic risk for security j, ρ (rho) is the correlation between security j and the market; σ_j (sigma) is the standard deviation of the return on firm j; and σ_m (sigma) is the standard deviation of the market return.

Beta will have a value of less than 1.0 if the firm's returns are less volatile than the market, 1.0 if the same as the market, or greater than 1.0 if more volatile—or risky—than the market. CAPM analysis assumes that the required return estimated is an indication of what more is necessary to keep an investor's capital invested in the equity considered. If the equity's return does not reach the expected return, CAPM assumes that individual investors will liquidate their holdings.

Cost of Debt

The normal procedure for measuring the cost of debt requires a forecast of interest rates for the next few years, the proportions of various classes of debt the firm expects to use, and the corporate income tax rate. The interest costs of the different debt components are then averaged according to their proportion in the debt structure. This before-tax average, k_d, is then adjusted for corporate income taxes by multiplying it by the expression (1–tax rate), to obtain $k_d\ (1-t)$, the weighted average after-tax cost of debt.

The weighted average cost of capital is normally used as the risk-adjusted discount rate whenever a firm's new projects are in the same general risk class as its existing projects. On the other hand, a project-specific required rate of return should be used as the discount rate if a new project differs from existing projects in business or financial risk.

Carlton's Weighted Average Cost of Capital

Caitlin Kelly, Carlton's chief financial officer, calculates the weighted average cost of capital to be 12.28%, as shown in Exhibit 11.2.

She believes that Carlton's cost of capital is already at a global level. It is fully competitive with Carlton's main rivals in the telecommunications hardware industry segment worldwide, which are mainly headquartered in the United States, the United Kingdom, Canada, Finland, Sweden, Germany, Japan, and the Netherlands. Their shares are listed on prominent stock exchanges and international portfolio investors can freely trade in their shares. Carlton itself is listed on the very liquid New York Stock Exchange (NYSE). The key to Carlton's favorable global cost and availability of capital is its ability to attract and hold the international portfolio investors that own its stock.

Calculating Equity Risk Premiums in Practice

In practice, calculating a firm's equity risk premium is much more controversial. Although the capital asset pricing model (CAPM) has now become very widely accepted in global business as the preferred method of calculating the cost of equity for a firm, there is rising debate over what numerical values should be used in its application, especially the *equity risk premium*. The equity risk premium is the average annual return of the market expected by investors over and above riskless debt, the term $(k_m - k_{rf})$.

Equity risk premium history. The field of finance does agree that a cost of equity calculation should be *forward-looking*, meaning that the inputs to the equation should represent what is expected to happen over the relevant investment horizon. As is typically the case, however, practitioners use historical evidence as the basis for their forward-looking projections. The current debate begins with a debate over what has actually happened in the past.

Exhibit 11.3 presents the results of a large study completed in 2001 of the equity risk premium in 15 different developed economies for the 1900–2000 period. This century of data is longer

Exhibit 11.2 Calculation of Carlton's Weighted Average Cost of Capital

Cost of Equity (k_e) Inputs:

k_{rf} = 5.000% — k_{rf} is the risk-free rate of interest estimated by using the U.S. government Treasury bond rate.

k_m = 15.000% — k_m is the expected rate of return on the market portfolio held by a well-diversified global investor. Over 40% of Carlton's stock is held by foreign portfolio investors, as part of their globally diversified portfolios. Carlton's U.S. investors also typically hold globally diversified portfolios.

β = 1.2 — β is Carlton's estimate of its own systematic risk using the correlation of Carlton's returns with those of the market (ρ), Carlton's standard deviation (σ_c), and the market's standard deviation (σ_m).

The cost of equity is then:

$$k_e = k_{rf} + \beta\,(k_m - k_{rf}) = 5.000\% + 1.2\,(15.000\% - 5.000\%) = 17.000\%$$

Cost of Debt (k_d) inputs:

k_d = 8.000% — k_d is the before tax cost of debt estimated by observing the current yield on Carlton's outstanding bonds combined with bank debt.

t = 35% — t is the U.S. corporate income tax rate

The after-tax cost of debt is then:

$$k_d\,(1 - t) = 8.000\,(1 - 0.35) = 8.000\,(0.65) = 5.200\%$$

Financial Structure

E/V = 60% — the equity ratio; the percentage of Carlton's securities ($E+D$) that is equity.

D/V = 40% — the debt ratio; the percentage of Carlton's securities ($E+D$) that is debt (bonds and bank loans).

V = 100% — V is the market value of Carlton's securities ($E+D$)

The weighted average cost of capital (k_{WACC}) is then:

$$k_{WACC} = k_e \frac{E}{V} + k_d\left(1 - t\right)\frac{D}{V} = 17.00\%(.60) + 5.20\%(.40) = 12.28\%$$

Exhibit 11.3 Equity Market Risk Premiums in Selected Countries, 1900–2000

Country	Arithmetic Mean Risk Premium	Geometric Mean Risk Premium	Country	Arithmetic Mean Risk Premium	Geometric Mean Risk Premium
Australia	8.0%	6.3%	Netherlands	6.7%	4.7%
Belgium	4.8%	2.9%	South Africa	7.1%	5.4%
Canada	6.0%	4.5%	Spain	4.2%	2.3%
Denmark	3.3%	2.0%	Sweden	7.4%	5.2%
France	7.0%	4.9%	Switzerland	4.2%	2.7%
Germany	9.9%	6.7%	United Kingdom	5.6%	4.4%
Ireland	4.6%	3.2%	United States	7.0%	5.0%
Italy	8.4%	5.0%	World	5.6%	4.9%
Japan	10.3%	6.2%			

Source: Adapted by authors from material presented in *Triumph of the Optimists*, E. Dimson, P. Marsh, and M. Staunton, (Princeton: Princeton University Press, 2002), Chapters 12 and 13. Estimates based on reconstructed data covering the 1900–2000 period of equity market returns over a long-term risk-free bond in the individual market.

by at least 20 years on average by country than what was previously available (the 1900–1920 period was often not covered in previous studies).

There are clearly significant differences in equity returns over time by country. Comparing arithmetic returns, Japan's (10.3%) is clearly the highest, with Germany (9.9%) and Italy (8.4%) following. Denmark, with an average arithmetic return of only 3.3% over risk-free assets for the century is the lowest premium among the listed countries. The United States finished the 20th century with an average arithmetic return of 7.0% per year. The world as defined by the authors of the study had an arithmetic return of 5.6%.

There is less debate regarding the use of arithmetic returns over geometric returns. The mean arithmetic return is simply the average of the annual percentage changes in capital appreciation plus dividend distributions. This is a rate of return calculation with which every business student is familiar. The mean geometric return, however, is a more specialized calculation, which takes into account only the beginning and ending values over an extended period of history. It then calculates the annual average rate of compounded growth to get from the beginning to the end, without paying attention to the specific path taken in between. Exhibit 11.4 provides a simple example of how the two methods would differ for a very short historical series of stock prices.

Arithmetic returns capture the year-to-year volatility in markets, which geometric returns do not. For this reason, most practitioners prefer the arithmetic, as it embodies more of the volatility so often characteristic of equity markets globally. Note that the geometric change will in all but a few extreme circumstances yield a smaller mean return.

The United States looking forward. The debate over which equity risk premium to use in practice was highlighted in this same study by looking at what equity risk premiums are being recommended for the United States by a variety of different sources. As illustrated in Exhibit 11.5, a hypothetical firm with a beta of 1.0 (estimated market risk equal to that of the market) might have a cost of equity as low as 9.000% and as high as 12.800% using this set of alternative values. Note that here the authors used geometric returns, not arithmetic returns.

How important is it for a company to accurately predict its cost of equity? The corporation must annually determine which potential investments it will accept and reject due to its limited capital resources. If the company is not accurately estimating its cost of equity—and therefore its overall cost of capital—it will not be accurately estimating the net present value of potential investments if it uses its own cost of capital as the basis for discounting expected cash flows.

Exhibit 11.4 Arithmetic Versus Geometric Returns: A Sample Calculation

Year	1	2	3	4	5	Mean
Share price	10	12	10	12	14	
Arithmetic change		+20.00%	−16.67%	+20.00%	+16.67%	+ 10.00%
Geometric change		+8.78%	+8.78%	+8.78%	+8.78%	+ 8.78%

Arithmetic change is calculated year by year as $(P_2/P_1 - 1)$. The simple average of the series is the mean. The geometric change is calculated using only the beginning and ending values, 10 and 14, and the geometric root of $[(14/10)^{1/4} - 1]$ is found (the $^{1/4}$ is in reference to four periods of change). The geometric change assumes reinvested compounding, whereas the arithmetic mean only assumes point to point investment.

Exhibit 11.5 Alternative Estimates of Cost of Equity for a Hypothetical U.S. Firm Assuming β=1 and k_{rf} = 4%

Source	Equity Risk Premium ($k_m - k_{rf}$)	Cost of Equity $k_{rf} + \beta\,(k_m - k_{rf})$	Difference From Baseline
Ibbotson	8.800%	12.800%	3.800%
Finance textbooks	8.500%	12.500%	3.500%
Investor surveys	7.100%	11.100%	2.100%
Dimson, et al. (Baseline)	5.000%	9.000%	Baseline

Source: Equity risk premium quotes from "Stockmarket Valuations: Great Expectations," *The Economist*, January 31, 2002.

The Demand for Foreign Securities: The Role of International Portfolio Investors

Gradual deregulation of equity markets during the past three decades not only elicited increased competition from domestic players but also opened up markets to foreign competitors. International portfolio investment and cross-listing of equity shares on foreign markets have become commonplace.

What motivates portfolio investors to purchase and hold foreign securities in their portfolio? The answer lies in an understanding of "domestic" portfolio theory and how it has been extended to handle the possibility of global portfolios. More specifically, it requires an understanding of the principles of portfolio risk reduction, portfolio rate of return, and foreign currency risk. These principles are explained in detail in Chapter 20.

Both domestic and international portfolio managers are asset allocators. Their objective is to maximize a portfolio's rate of return for a given level of risk, or to minimize risk for a given rate of return. International portfolio managers can choose from a larger bundle of assets than portfolio managers limited to domestic-only asset allocations. As a result, internationally diversified portfolios often have a higher expected rate of return, and they nearly always have a lower level of portfolio risk, since national securities markets are imperfectly correlated with one another.

Portfolio asset allocation can be accomplished along many dimensions, depending on the investment objective of the portfolio manager. For example, portfolios can be diversified according to the type of securities. They can be composed of stocks only or bonds only or a combination of both. They also can be diversified by industry or by size of capitalization (small-cap, mid-cap, and large-cap stock portfolios).

For our purposes, the most relevant dimensions are diversification by country, geographic region, stage of development, or a combination of these (global). An example of diversification by country is the Korea Fund. It was at one time the only vehicle for foreign investors to hold South Korean securities, but foreign ownership restrictions have more recently been liberalized. A typical regional diversification would be one of the many Asian funds. These performed exceptionally well until the "bubble" burst in Japan and Southeast Asia during the second half of the 1990s. Portfolios composed of emerging market securities are examples of diversification by stage of development. They are composed of securities from different countries, geographic regions, and stage of development.

The Link Between Cost and Availability of Capital

Carlton's weighted average cost of capital (WACC) was calculated assuming that equity and debt capital would always be available at the same required rate of return even if Carlton's capital budget expands. This is a reasonable assumption, considering Carlton's excellent access through the NYSE to international portfolio investors in global capital markets. It is a bad assumption, however, for firms resident in illiquid or segmented capital markets, small domestic firms, and family-owned firms resident in any capital market. We will now examine how market liquidity and market segmentation can affect a firm's cost of capital. This is followed by an illustrative case showing how NOVO Industri A/S, a Danish firm, was able to overcome the disadvantages of being resident in an illiquid and segmented market.

Improving Market Liquidity

Although no consensus exists about the definition of *market liquidity*, we can observe market liquidity by noting the degree to which a firm can issue a new security without depressing the existing market price, as well as the degree to which a change in price of its securities elicits a substantial order flow.

In the domestic case, an underlying assumption is that total availability of capital to a firm at any time is determined by supply and demand in the domestic capital markets. A firm should always expand its capital budget by raising funds in the same proportion as its optimal financial structure. As its budget expands in absolute terms, however, its marginal cost of capital will eventually increase. In other words, a firm can only tap the capital market for some limited amount in the short run before suppliers of capital balk at providing further funds, even if the same optimal financial structure is preserved. In the long run, this may not be a limitation, depending on market liquidity.

In the multinational case, a firm is able to improve market liquidity by raising funds in the euromarkets (money, bond, and equity), by selling security issues abroad, and by tapping local capital markets through foreign subsidiaries. Such activity should logically expand the capacity of a MNE to raise funds in the short run over what might have been raised if the firm were limited to its home capital market. This situation assumes that the firm preserves its optimal financial structure.

Market Segmentation

If all capital markets are fully integrated, securities of comparable expected return and risk should have the same required rate of return in each national market after adjusting for foreign exchange risk and political risk. This definition applies to both equity and debt, although it often happens that one or the other may be more integrated than its counterpart.

As introduced earlier, capital market segmentation is a financial market imperfection caused mainly by government constraints, institutional practices, and investor perceptions. The most important imperfections are:

- Asymmetric information between domestic and foreign-based investors
- Lack of transparency
- High securities transaction costs

- Foreign exchange risks
- Political risks
- Corporate governance differences
- Regulatory barriers

Market imperfections do not necessarily imply that national securities markets are inefficient. A national securities market can be efficient in a domestic context and yet segmented in an international context. According to finance theory, a market is *efficient* if security prices in that market reflect all available relevant information and adjust quickly to any new relevant information. Therefore the price of an individual security reflects its "intrinsic value" and any price fluctuations will be "random walks" around this value. Market efficiency assumes that transaction costs are low, that many participants are in the market, and that these participants have sufficient financial strength to move security prices. Empirical tests of market efficiency show that most major national markets are reasonably efficient.

An efficient national securities market might very well correctly price all securities traded in that market on the basis of information available to the investors who participate in that market. However, if that market were segmented, foreign investors would not be participants. Thus securities in the segmented market would be priced on the basis of domestic rather than international standards.

In the rest of this chapter and the next chapter we will use the term MNE to describe all firms that have access to a global cost and availability of capital. This includes qualifying MNEs, whether they are located in highly developed or emerging markets. It also includes large firms that are not multinational but have access to global capital markets. They too could be located in highly developed or emerging capital markets. We will use the term *domestic firm* (DF) for all firms that do not have access to a global cost and availability of capital, no matter where they are located.

Availability of capital depends on whether a firm can gain liquidity for its debt and equity securities and a price for those securities based on international rather than national standards. In practice this means that the firm must define a strategy to attract international portfolio investors and thereby escape the constraints of its own illiquid or segmented national market.

The Effect of Market Liquidity and Segmentation

The degree to which capital markets are illiquid or segmented has an important influence on a firm's marginal cost of capital and thus on its weighted average cost of capital. The marginal cost of capital is the weighted average cost of the next currency unit raised. This is illustrated in Exhibit 11.6, which shows the transition from a domestic to a global marginal cost of capital.

Exhibit 11.6 shows that the MNE has a given marginal return on capital at different budget levels, represented in the line MRR. This demand is determined by ranking potential projects according to net present value or internal rate of return. Percentage rate of return to both users and suppliers of capital is shown on the vertical scale. If the firm is limited to raising funds in its domestic market, the line MCC_D shows the marginal domestic cost of capital (vertical axis) at various budget levels (horizontal axis). Remember that the firm continues to maintain the same debt ratio as it expands its budget, so that financial risk does not change. The optimal budget in the

Exhibit 11.6 Market Liquidity, Segmentation, and the Marginal Cost of Capital

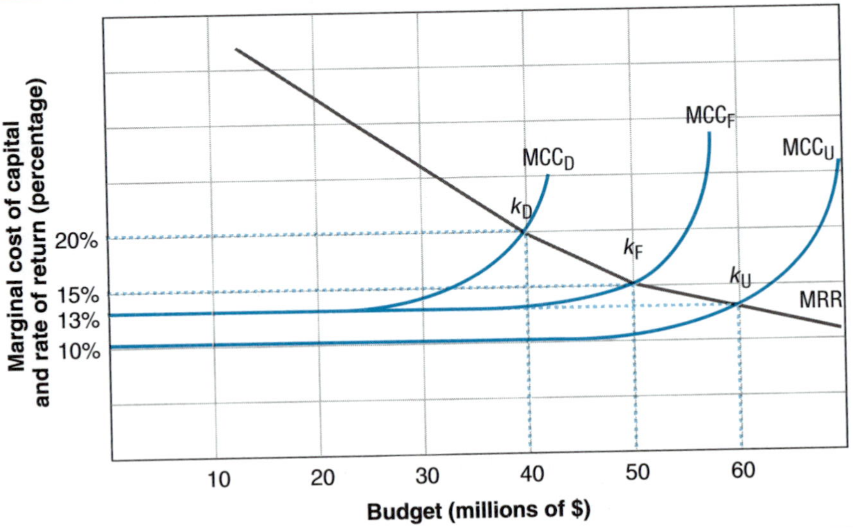

domestic case is \$40 million, where the marginal return on capital (MRR) just equals the marginal cost of capital (MCC_D). At this budget, the marginal domestic cost of capital, k_D, would be equal to 20%.

If the MNE has access to additional sources of capital outside an illiquid domestic capital market, the marginal cost of capital should shift to the right (the line MCC_F). In other words, foreign markets can be tapped for long-term funds at times when the domestic market is saturated because of heavy use by other borrowers or equity issuers, or when it is unable to absorb another issue of the MNE in the short run. Exhibit 11.6 shows that by a tap of foreign capital markets the firm has reduced its marginal international cost of capital, k_F, to 15%, even while it raises an additional \$10 million. This statement assumes that about \$20 million is raised abroad, since only about \$30 million could be raised domestically at a 15% marginal cost of capital.

If the MNE is located in a capital market that is both illiquid and segmented, the line MCC_U represents the decreased marginal cost of capital if it gains access to other equity markets. As a result of the combined effects of greater availability of capital and international pricing of the firm's securities, the marginal cost of capital, k_U, declines to 13% and the optimal capital budget climbs to \$60 million.

Most of the tests of market segmentation suffer from the usual problem for models—namely, the need to abstract from reality in order to have a testable model. In our opinion, a realistic test would be to observe what happens to a single security's price when it has been traded only in a domestic market, is "discovered" by foreign investors, and then is traded in a foreign market. Arbitrage should keep the market price equal in both markets. However, if during the transition we observe a significant change in the security's price uncorrelated with price movements in either of the underlying securities markets, we can infer that the domestic market was segmented.

In academic circles, tests based on case studies are often considered to be "casual empiricism," since no theory or model exists to explain what is being observed. Nevertheless, something may be learned from such cases, just as scientists learn from observing nature in an uncontrolled environment. Furthermore, case studies that preserve real-world complications may illustrate specific kinds of barriers to market integration and ways in which they might be overcome.

Unfortunately, few case studies have been documented in which a firm has "escaped" from a segmented capital market. In practice, escape usually means being listed on a foreign stock market such as New York or London, and/or selling securities in foreign capital markets. We will illustrate something more specific by using the example of Novo Industri A/S, a Danish firm.[1]

Illustrative Case: Novo Industri A/S (Novo)

Novo is a Danish multinational firm that produces industrial enzymes and pharmaceuticals (mostly insulin). In 1977, Novo's management decided to "internationalize" its capital structure and sources of funds. This decision was based on the observation that the Danish securities market was both illiquid and segmented from other capital markets. In particular, the lack of availability and high cost of equity capital in Denmark resulted in Novo having a higher cost of capital than its main multinational competitors, such as Eli Lilly (U.S.), Miles Laboratories (U.S.—a subsidiary of Bayer, Germany), and Gist Brocades (the Netherlands).

Apart from the cost of capital, Novo's projected growth opportunities signaled the eventual need to raise new long-term capital beyond what could be raised in the illiquid Danish market. Since Novo is a technology leader in its specialties, planned capital investments in plant, equipment, and research could not be postponed until internal financing from cash flow became available. Novo's competitors would preempt any markets not served by Novo.

Even if an equity issue of the size required could have been raised in Denmark, the required rate of return would have been unacceptably high. For example, Novo's price/earnings ratio was typically around 5; that of its foreign competitors was well over 10. Yet Novo's business and financial risk appeared to be about equal to that of its competitors. A price/earnings ratio of 5 appeared appropriate for Novo only within a domestic Danish context when Novo was compared with other domestic firms of comparable business and financial risk.

If Denmark's securities markets were integrated with world markets, one would expect foreign investors to rush in and buy "undervalued" Danish securities. In that case, firms like Novo would enjoy an international cost of capital comparable to that of their foreign competitors. Strangely enough, no Danish governmental restrictions existed that would have prevented foreign investors from holding Danish securities. Therefore one must look for investor perception as the main cause of market segmentation in Denmark at that time.

At least six characteristics of the Danish equity market were responsible for market segmentation: 1) asymmetric information base of Danish and foreign investors, 2) taxation, 3) alternative sets of feasible portfolios, 4) financial risk, 5) foreign exchange risk, and 6) political risk.

1. The Novo case material is a condensed version of Arthur Stonehill and Kåre B. Dullum, *Internationalizing the Cost of Capital in Theory and Practice: The Novo Experience and National Policy Implications* (Copenhagen: Nyt Nordisk Forlag Arnold Busck, 1982; and New York: Wiley, 1982). Reprinted with permission.

Asymmetric Information

Certain institutional characteristics of Denmark caused Danish and foreign investors to be uninformed about each other's equity securities. The most important information barrier was a Danish regulation that prohibited Danish investors from holding foreign private sector securities. Therefore Danish investors had no incentive to follow developments in foreign securities markets or to factor such information into their evaluation of Danish securities. As a result, Danish securities might have been priced correctly in the efficient market sense relative to one another, considering the Danish information base, but priced incorrectly considering the combined foreign and Danish information base. Another detrimental effect of this regulation was that foreign securities firms did not locate offices or personnel in Denmark, since they had no product to sell. Lack of a physical presence in Denmark reduced the ability of foreign security analysts to follow Danish securities.

A second information barrier was lack of enough Danish security analysts following Danish securities. Only one professional Danish securities analysis service was published (Børsinformation), and that was in the Danish language. A few Danish institutional investors employed in-house analysts, but their findings were not available to the public. Almost no foreign security analysts followed Danish securities because they had no product to sell and the Danish market was too small (small-country bias).

Other information barriers included language and accounting principles. Naturally, financial information was normally published in Danish, using Danish accounting principles. A few firms, such as Novo, published English versions, but almost none used U.S. or British accounting principles or attempted to show any reconciliation with such principles.

Taxation

Danish taxation policy had all but eliminated investment in common stock by individuals. Until a tax law change in July 1981, capital gains on shares held for over two years were taxed at a 50% rate. Shares held for less than two years, or for "speculative" purposes, were taxed at personal income tax rates, with the top marginal rate being 75%. In contrast, capital gains on bonds were tax-free. This situation resulted in bonds being issued at deep discounts because the redemption at par at maturity was considered a capital gain. Thus most individual investors held bonds rather than stocks. This factor reduced the liquidity of the stock market and increased the required rate of return on stocks if they were to compete with bonds.

Feasible Set of Portfolios

Because of the prohibition on foreign security ownership, Danish investors had a very limited set of securities from which to choose a portfolio. In practice, Danish institutional portfolios were composed of Danish stocks, government bonds, and mortgage bonds. Since Danish stock price movements are closely correlated with each other, Danish portfolios possessed a rather high level of systematic risk. In addition, government policy had been to provide a relatively high real rate of return on government bonds after adjusting for inflation. The net result of taxation policies on individuals, and attractive real yields on government bonds was that required rates of return on stocks were relatively high by international standards.

From a portfolio perspective, Danish stocks provided an opportunity for foreign investors to diversify internationally. If Danish stock price movements were not closely correlated with world stock price movements, inclusion of Danish stocks in foreign portfolios should reduce these portfolio's systematic risk. Furthermore, foreign investors were not subject to the high Danish income tax rates because they are normally protected by tax treaties that typically limit their tax to 15% on dividends and capital gains. As a result of the international diversification potential, foreign investors might have required a lower rate of return on Danish stocks than Danish investors, other things being equal. However, other things were not equal because foreign investors perceived Danish stocks to carry more financial, foreign exchange, and political risk than their own domestic securities.

Financial, Foreign Exchange, and Political Risks

Financial leverage utilized by Danish firms was relatively high by U.S. and U.K. standards but not abnormal for Scandinavia, Germany, Italy, or Japan. In addition, most of the debt was short-term with variable interest rates. Just how foreign investors viewed financial risk in Danish firms depended on what norms they follow in their home countries. We know from Novo's experience in tapping the Eurobond market in 1978 that Morgan Grenfell, its British investment banker, advised Novo to maintain a debt ratio (debt/total capitalization) closer to 50% rather than the traditional Danish 65% to 70%.

Foreign investors in Danish securities are subject to foreign exchange risk. Whether this is a plus or minus factor depends on the investor's home currency, perception about the future strength of the Danish krone, and its impact on a firm's operating exposure. Through personal contacts with foreign investors and bankers, Novo's management did not believe foreign exchange risk was a factor in Novo's stock price because its operations were perceived as being well-diversified internationally. Over 90% of its sales were to customers located outside of Denmark.

With respect to political risk, Denmark was perceived as a stable Western democracy but with the potential to cause periodic problems for foreign investors. In particular, Denmark's national debt was regarded as too high for comfort, although this judgment had not yet shown up in the form of risk premiums on Denmark's Eurocurrency syndicated loans.

The Road to Globalization

Although Novo's management in 1977 wished to escape from the shackles of Denmark's segmented and illiquid capital market, many barriers had to be overcome. It is worthwhile to describe some of these obstacles, because they typify the barriers faced by other firms from segmented markets that wish to internationalize their capital sources.

Closing the information gap. Novo had been a family-owned firm from its founding in the 1920s by the two Pedersen brothers until 1974, when it went public and listed its "B" shares on the Copenhagen Stock Exchange. The "A" shares were held by the Novo Foundation; the "A" shares were sufficient to maintain voting control. However, Novo was essentially unknown in investment circles outside of Denmark. To overcome this disparity in the information base, Novo increased the level of its financial and technical disclosure in both Danish and English versions.

The information gap was further closed when Morgan Grenfell successfully organized a syndicate to underwrite and sell a $20 million convertible Eurobond issue for Novo in 1978. In connection with this offering, Novo listed its shares on the London Stock Exchange to facilitate conversion and to gain visibility. These twin actions were the key to dissolving the information barrier and, of course, they also raised a large amount of long-term capital on favorable terms, which would have been unavailable in Denmark.

Despite the favorable impact of the Eurobond issue on availability of capital, Novo's cost of capital actually increased when Danish investors reacted negatively to the potential dilution effect of the conversion right. During 1979, Novo's share price in Danish kroner (Dkr) declined from around Dkr300 per share to around Dkr220 per share.

The biotechnology boom. During 1979, a fortuitous event occurred. Biotechnology began to attract the interest of the U.S. investment community, with several sensationally oversubscribed stock issues by such start-up firms as Genentech and Cetus. Thanks to the aforementioned domestic information gap, Danish investors were unaware of these events and continued to value Novo at a low price/earnings ratio of 5, compared with over 10 for its established competitors and 30 or more for these new potential competitors.

In order to profile itself as a biotechnology firm with a proven track record, Novo organized a seminar in New York City on April 30, 1980. Soon after the seminar a few sophisticated individual U.S. investors began buying Novo's shares and convertibles through the London Stock Exchange. Danish investors were only too happy to supply this foreign demand. Therefore, despite relatively strong demand from U.S. and British investors, Novo's share price increased only gradually, climbing back to the Dkr300 level by mid-summer. However, during the following months foreign interest began to snowball, and by the end of 1980 Novo's stock price had reached the Dkr600 level. Moreover, foreign investors had increased their proportion of share ownership from virtually nothing to around 30%. Novo's price/earnings ratio had risen to around 16, which was now in line with that of its international competitors but not with the Danish market. At this point, one must conclude that Novo had succeeded in internationalizing its cost of capital. Other Danish securities remained locked in a segmented capital market. Exhibit 11.7 shows that the movement in the Danish stock market in general did not parallel the rise in Novo's share price, nor could it be explained by movement in the U.S. or U.K. stock markets as a whole.

Directed share issue in the United States. During the first half of 1981, under the guidance of Goldman Sachs and with the assistance of Morgan Grenfell and Copenhagen Handelsbank, Novo prepared a prospectus for SEC registration of a U.S. share offering and eventual listing on the New York Stock Exchange. The main barriers encountered in this effort, which would have general applicability, were connected with preparing financial statements that could be reconciled with U.S. accounting principles and the higher level of disclosure required by the SEC. In particular, industry segment reporting was a problem both from a disclosure perspective and an accounting perspective because the accounting data were not available internally in that format. As it turned out, the investment barriers in the U.S. were relatively tractable, although expensive and time consuming to overcome.

The more serious barriers were caused by a variety of institutional and governmental regulations in Denmark. The latter were never designed so that firms could issue shares at market value, since Danish firms typically issued stock at par value with preemptive rights. By this time, however, Novo's share price, driven by continued foreign buying, was so high that virtually nobody in Denmark thought it was worth the price that foreigners were willing to pay. In fact, prior to the time of the

Exhibit 11.7 Novo's B-Share Prices Compared with Stock Market Indices

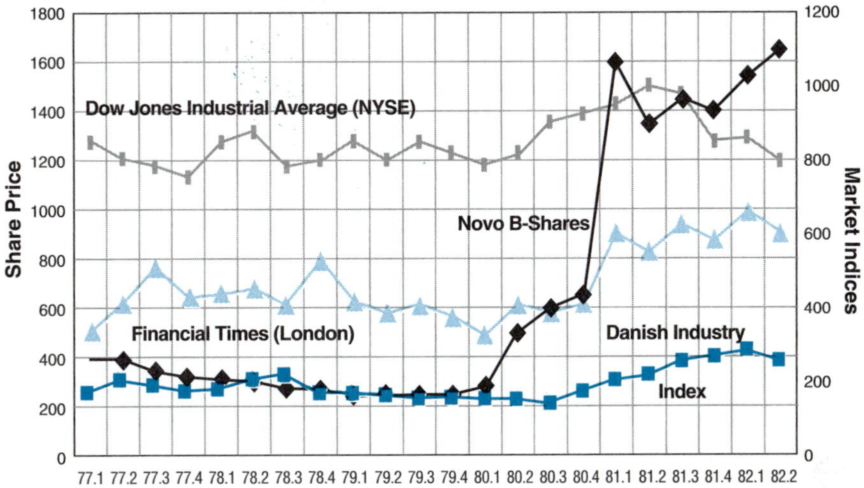

Source: Arthur I. Stonehill and Kåre B. Dullum, *Internationalizing the Cost of Capital: The Novo Experience and National Policy Implications* (London: John Wiley, 1982), p. 73. Reprinted with permission.

share issue in July 1981, Novo's share price had risen to over Dkr1500, before settling down to a level around Dkr1400. Foreign ownership had increased to over 50% of Novo's shares outstanding!

Stock market reactions. One final piece of evidence on market segmentation can be gleaned from the way Danish and foreign investors reacted to the announcement of the proposed $61 million U.S. share issue on May 29, 1981. Novo's share price dropped 156 points the next trading day in Copenhagen, equal to about 10% of its market value. As soon as trading started in New York, the stock price immediately recovered all of its loss. The Copenhagen reaction was typical for an illiquid market. Investors worried about the dilution effect of the new share issue, because it would increase the number of shares outstanding by about 8%. They did not believe that Novo could invest the new funds at a rate of return that would not dilute future earnings per share. They also feared that the U.S. shares would eventually flow back to Copenhagen if biotechnology lost its glitter.

The U.S. reaction to the announcement of the new share issue was consistent with what one would expect in a liquid and integrated market. U.S. investors viewed the new issue as creating additional demand for the shares as Novo became more visible due to the selling efforts of a large aggressive syndicate. Furthermore, the marketing effort was directed at institutional investors who were previously under-represented among Novo's U.S. investors. They had been under-represented because U.S. institutional investors want to be assured of a liquid market in a stock in order to be able to get out, if desired, without depressing the share price. The wide distribution effected by the new issue, plus SEC registration and a New York Stock Exchange listing, all added up to more liquidity and a global cost of capital.

Effect on Novo's weighted average cost of capital. During most of 1981 and the years thereafter, Novo's share price was driven by international portfolio investors transacting on the New York,

London, and Copenhagen stock exchanges. This reduced Novo's weighted average cost of capital and lowered its marginal cost of capital. Novo's systematic risk was reduced from its previous level, which was determined by nondiversified (internationally) Danish institutional investors and the Novo Foundation. However, its appropriate debt ratio level was also reduced to match the standards expected by international portfolio investors trading in the U.S., U.K., and other important markets. In essence, the U.S. dollar became Novo's functional currency when being evaluated by international investors. Theoretically, its revised weighted average cost of capital should have become a new reference hurdle rate when evaluating new capital investments in Denmark or abroad.

Other firms that follow Novo's strategy are also likely to have their weighted average cost of capital become a function of the requirements of international portfolio investors. Firms resident in some of the emerging market countries have already experienced "dollarization" of trade and financing for working capital. This phenomenon might be extended to long-term financing and the weighted average cost of capital.

The Novo experience has been described in hopes that it can be a model for other firms wishing to escape from segmented and illiquid home equity markets. In particular, MNEs based in emerging markets often face barriers and lack of visibility similar to what Novo faced. They could benefit by following Novo's proactive strategy employed to attract international portfolio investors. However, a word of caution is advised. Novo had an excellent operating track record and a very strong worldwide market niche in two important industry sectors, insulin and industrial enzymes. This record continues to attract investors in Denmark and abroad. Other companies would also need to have such a favorable track record to attract foreign investors.

Globalization of Securities Markets

During the 1980s, numerous other Nordic and other European firms followed Novo's example. They cross-listed on major foreign exchanges such as London and New York. They placed equity and debt issues in major securities markets. In most cases, they were successful in lowering their WACC and increasing its availability.

During the 1980s and 1990s national restrictions on cross-border portfolio investment were gradually eased under pressure from the Organization for Economic Cooperation and Development (OECD), a consortium of most of the world's most industrialized countries. Liberalization of European securities markets was accelerated because of the European Union's efforts to develop a single European market without barriers. Emerging nation markets followed suit, as did the former East Bloc countries after the breakup of the Soviet Union. Emerging national markets have often been motivated by the need to source foreign capital to finance large-scale privatization.

At the present time, market segmentation has been significantly reduced, although the liquidity of individual national markets remains limited. Most observers believe that for better or for worse, we have achieved a global market for securities. The good news is that many firms have been assisted to become MNEs because they now have access to a global cost and availability of capital. The bad news is that the correlation among securities markets has increased, thereby reducing, but not eliminating, the benefits of international portfolio diversification. Globalization of securities markets has also led to more volatility and speculative behavior as shown by the emerging market crises of the 1995–2001 period.

In Chapters 12 through 14 we will describe the experiences of firms that have successfully tapped global securities markets and the financial strategies and instruments they have used.

The Cost of Capital for MNEs Compared to Domestic Firms

Is the weighted average cost of capital for MNEs higher or lower than for their domestic counterparts? The answer is a function of the marginal cost of capital, the relative after-tax cost of debt, the optimal debt ratio, and the relative cost of equity.

Availability of Capital

We saw earlier in this chapter that international availability of capital to MNEs, or to other large firms that can attract international portfolio investors, may allow them to lower their cost of equity and debt compared with most domestic firms. In addition, international availability permits a MNE to maintain its desired debt ratio, even when significant amounts of new funds must be raised. In other words, an MNE's marginal cost of capital is constant for considerable ranges of its capital budget. This statement is not true for most domestic firms. They must either rely on internally generated funds or borrow in the short and medium term from commercial banks.

Financial Structure, Systematic Risk, and the Cost of Capital for MNEs

Theoretically MNEs should be in a better position than their domestic counterparts to support higher debt ratios, because their cash flows are diversified internationally. The probability of a firm's covering fixed charges under varying conditions in product, financial, and foreign exchange markets should improve if the variability of its cash flows is minimized.

By diversifying cash flows internationally, the MNE might be able to achieve the same kind of reduction in cash flow variability as portfolio investors receive from diversifying their security holdings internationally. The same argument applies—namely, that returns are not perfectly correlated between countries. For example, in 2000 Japan was in recession but the United States was experiencing rapid growth. Therefore we might have expected returns, on either a cash flow or an earnings basis, to be depressed in Japan and favorable in the United States. A MNE with operations located in both these countries could rely on its strong U.S. cash inflow to cover debt obligations, even if its Japanese subsidiary produced weak net cash inflows.

Despite the theoretical elegance of this hypothesis, empirical studies have come to the opposite conclusion.[2] Despite the favorable effect of international diversification of cash flows, bankruptcy risk was only about the same for MNEs as for domestic firms. However, MNEs faced higher agency costs, political risk, foreign exchange risk, and asymmetric information. These have been identified as the factors leading to lower debt ratios and even a higher cost of long-term debt for MNEs. Domestic firms rely much more heavily on short and intermediate debt, which lie at the low cost end of the yield curve.

2. Lee, Kwang Chul and Chuck C.Y. Kwok, "Multinational Corporations vs. Domestic Corporations: International Environmental Factors and Determinants of Capital Structure," *Journal of International Business Studies*, Summer 1988, pp. 195–217.

Even more surprising, one study found that MNEs have a higher level of systematic risk than their domestic counterparts.[3] The same factors caused this phenomenon as caused the lower debt ratios for MNEs. The study concluded that the increased standard deviation of cash flows from internationalization more than offset the lower correlation from diversification.

As we stated earlier in this chapter, the systematic risk term, β_j, is defined as:

$$\beta_j = \frac{\rho_{jm}\sigma_j}{\sigma_m}$$

where ρ_{jm} is the correlation coefficient between security j and the market; σ_j is the standard deviation of the return on firm j; and σ_m is the standard deviation of the market return. The MNE's systematic risk could increase if the decrease in the correlation coefficient, ρ_{jm}, due to international diversification, is more than offset by an increase in σ_j, the MNE's standard deviation due to the aforementioned risk factors. This conclusion is consistent with the observation that many MNEs use a higher hurdle rate to discount expected foreign project cash flows. In essence, they are accepting projects they consider to be riskier than domestic projects, thus potentially skewing upward their perceived systematic risk. At the least, MNEs need to earn a higher rate of return than their domestic equivalents in order to maintain their market value.

A more recent study found that internationalization actually allowed emerging market MNEs to carry a higher level of debt and lowered their systematic risk.[4] This occurred because the emerging market MNEs are investing in more stable economies abroad, a strategy that lowers their operating, financial, foreign exchange, and political risks. The reduction in risk more than offsets their increased agency costs and allows the emerging market MNEs to enjoy higher leverage and lower systematic risk than their U.S.-based MNE counterparts.

Solving a Riddle: Is the Weighted Average Cost of Capital for MNEs Really Higher than for Their Domestic Counterparts?

The riddle is that the MNE is supposed to have a lower marginal cost of capital (MCC) than a domestic firm because of the MNE's access to a global cost and availability of capital. On the other hand, the empirical studies we mentioned show that the MNE's weighted average cost of capital (WACC) is actually higher than for a comparable domestic firm because of agency costs, foreign exchange risk, political risk, asymmetric information, and other complexities of foreign operations.

The answer to this riddle lies in the link between the cost of capital, its availability, and the opportunity set of projects. As the opportunity set of projects increases, eventually the firm needs to increase its capital budget to the point where its marginal cost of capital is increasing. The optimal capital budget would still be at the point where the rising marginal cost of capital equals the

3. Reeb, David M., Chuck C.Y. Kwok, and H. Young Baek, "Systematic Risk of the Multinational Corporation," *Journal of International Business Studies*, Second Quarter 1998, pp. 263–279.

4. Kwok, Chuck C.Y., and David M. Reeb, "Internationalization and Firm Risk: An Upstream-Downstream Hypothesis," *Journal of International Business Studies*, Volume 31, Issue 4, 2000, pp. 611–630.

declining rate of return on the opportunity set of projects. However, this would be at a higher weighted average cost of capital than would have occurred for a lower level of the optimal capital budget.

To illustrate this linkage, Exhibit 11.8 shows the marginal cost of capital given different optimal capital budgets. Assume that there are two different demand schedules based on the opportunity set of projects for both the multinational enterprise (MNE) and domestic counterpart (DC).

The line MRR_{DC} depicts a modest set of potential projects. It intersects the line MCC_{MNE} at 15% and a \$100 million budget level. It intersects the line MCC_{DC} at 10% and a \$140 million budget level. At these low budget levels the MCC_{MNE} has a higher MCC and probably weighted average cost of capital than its domestic counterpart (MCC_{DC}), as discovered in the recent empirical studies.

The line MRR_{MNE} depicts a more ambitious set of projects for both the MNE and its domestic counterpart. It intersects the line MCC_{MNE} still at 15% and a \$350 million budget. However, it intersects the MCC_{DC} at 20% and a budget level of \$300 million. At these higher budget levels, the MCC_{MNE} has a lower MCC and probably weighted average cost of capital than its domestic counterpart, as predicted earlier in this chapter.

In order to extend this conclusion to the general case, we would need to know under what conditions a domestic firm would be willing to undertake the optimal capital budget despite its increasing the firm's marginal cost of capital. At some point the MNE might also have an optimal capital budget at the point where its MCC is rising.

Empirical studies show that neither mature domestic firms nor MNEs are typically willing to assume the higher agency costs or bankruptcy risk associated with higher MCCs and capital budgets. In fact, most mature firms demonstrate some degree of corporate wealth–maximizing behavior. They are somewhat risk-averse and tend to avoid returning to the market to raise fresh

Exhibit 11.8 The Cost of Capital for MNE and Domestic Counterpart Compared

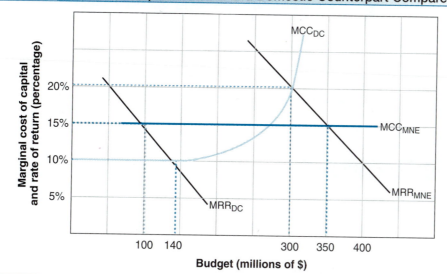

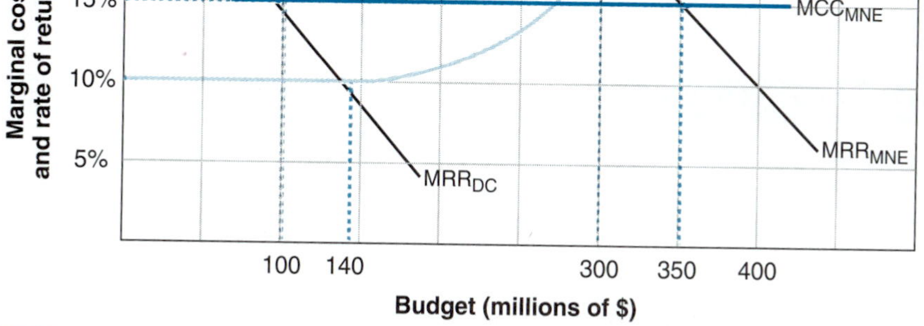

equity. They prefer to limit their capital budgets to what can be financed with free cash flows. Indeed, they have a so-called "pecking order" that determines the priority of which sources of funds they tap and in what order. This behavior motivates shareholders to monitor management more closely. They tie management's compensation to stock performance (options). They may also require other types of contractual arrangements that are collectively part of agency costs.

In conclusion, if both MNEs and domestic firms do actually limit their capital budgets to what can be financed without increasing their MCC, then the empirical findings that MNEs have higher WACC stands. If the domestic firm has such good growth opportunities that it chooses to undertake growth despite an increasing marginal cost of capital, then the MNE would have a lower WACC. Exhibit 11.9 summarizes these conclusions.

Exhibit 11.9 Do MNEs Have a Higher or Lower WACC Than Their Domestic Counterparts?

Is MNE$_{WACC}$ > or < Domestic$_{WACC}$?

$$k_{WACC} = k_e \left[\frac{\text{Equity}}{\text{Value}} \right] + k_d (1\text{-}t) \left[\frac{\text{Debt}}{\text{Value}} \right]$$

Empirical studies indicate that MNEs have a lower debt/capital ratio than domestic counterparts, indicating that MNEs have a higher cost of capital.

And indications are that MNEs have a lower average cost of debt than domestic counterparts, indicating that MNEs have a lower cost of capital.

The cost of equity required by investors is higher for multinational firms than for domestic firms. Possible explanations are higher levels of political risk, foreign exchange risk, and higher agency costs of doing business in a multinational managerial environment. However, at relatively high levels of the optimal capital budget, the MNE would have a lower cost of capital.

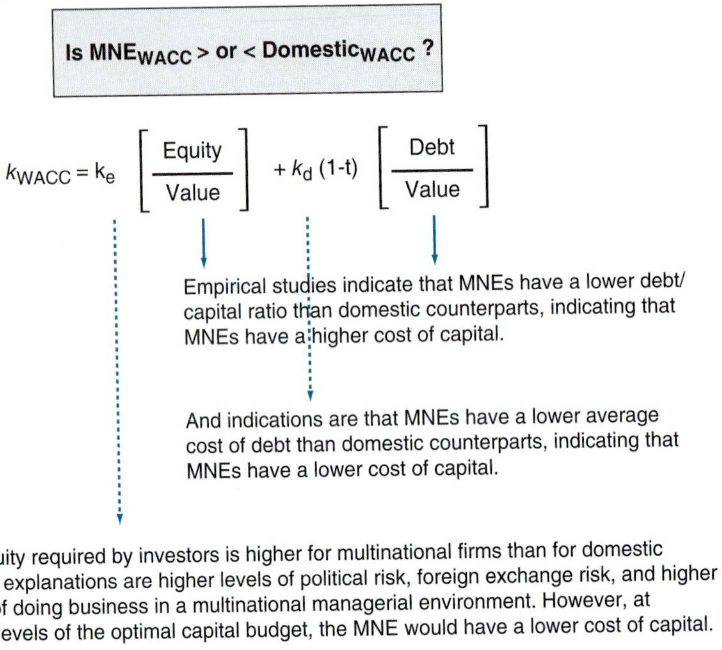

SUMMARY

■ Gaining access to global capital markets should allow a firm to lower its cost of capital. A firm can improve access to global capital markets by increasing the market liquidity of its shares and by escaping from segmentation of its home capital market.

- The cost and availability of capital is directly linked to the degree of market liquidity and segmentation. Firms having access to markets with high liquidity and a low level of segmentation should have a lower cost of capital and greater ability to raise new capital.
- A firm is able to increase its market liquidity by raising debt in the Euromarket, by selling security issues in individual national capital markets and as euroequities, and by tapping local capital markets through foreign subsidiaries. Increased market liquidity causes the marginal cost of capital line to "flatten out to the right." This results in the firm being able to raise more capital at the same low marginal cost of capital, thereby justifying its investing in more capital projects. The key is to attract international portfolio investors.
- A national capital market is segmented if the required rate of return on securities in that market differs from the required rate of return on securities of comparable expected return and risk that are traded on other national securities markets. Capital market segmentation is a financial market imperfection caused by government constraints and investor perceptions. The most important imperfections are: 1) asymmetric information, 2) transaction costs, 3) foreign exchange risk, 4) corporate governance differences, 5) political risk, and 6) regulatory barriers.
- Segmentation results in a higher cost of capital and less availability of capital.
- If a firm is resident in a segmented capital market, it can escape from this market by sourcing its debt and equity abroad. The result should be a lower marginal cost of capital, improved liquidity for its shares, and a larger capital budget. The experience of Novo served as a model for firms resident in small or emerging markets that are partially segmented and illiquid.
- Whether MNEs have a lower cost of capital than their domestic counterparts depends on their optimal financial structures, systematic risk, availability of capital, and the level of the optimal capital budget.

QUESTIONS

1. **Dimensions of the cost and availability of capital.** Global integration has given many firms access to new and cheaper sources of funds beyond those available in their home markets. What are the dimensions of a strategy to capture this lower cost and greater availability of capital?

2. **Benefits.** What are the benefits of achieving a lower cost and greater availability of capital?

3. **Definitions.** Define the following terms:
   a. Systematic risk
   b. Unsystematic risk
   c. Beta (in the Capital Asset Pricing Model)

4. **Equity risk premiums.**
   a. What is an equity risk premium?
   b. What is the difference between calculating an equity risk premium using arithmetic returns and using geometric returns?
   c. In Exhibit 11.3, why are arithmetic mean risk premiums always higher than geometric mean risk premiums?

5. **Portfolio investors.** Both domestic and international portfolio managers are *asset allocators*.
   a. What is their portfolio management objective?
   b. What is the main advantage that international portfolio managers have compared to portfolio managers limited to domestic-only asset allocation?

6. **Dimensions of asset allocation.** Portfolio asset allocation can be accomplished along many dimensions depending on the investment objective of the portfolio manager. Identify the various dimensions.

7. **Market liquidity.**
   a. Define what is meant by the term *market liquidity*.

b. What are the main disadvantages for a firm located in an illiquid market?

c. If a firm is limited to raising funds in its domestic capital market, what happens to its marginal cost of capital as it expands?

d. If a firm can raise funds abroad, what happens to its marginal cost of capital as it expands?

8. **Market segmentation.**

a. Define market segmentation.

b. What are the six main causes of market segmentation?

c. What are the main disadvantages for a firm to be located in a segmented market?

9. **Market liquidity and segmentation effects.** What is the effect of market liquidity and segmentation on a firm's cost of capital?

10. **Novo Industri (A).** Why did Novo believe its cost of capital was too high compared to its competitors? Why did Novo's relatively high cost of capital create a competitive disadvantage?

11. **Novo Industri (B).** Novo believed that the Danish capital market was segmented from world capital markets. Explain the six characteristics of the Danish equity market that were responsible for its segmentation.

12. **Novo Industri (C).**

a. What was Novo's strategy to internationalize its cost of capital?

b. What is the evidence that Novo's strategy succeeded?

13. **Emerging markets.** It has been suggested that firms located in illiquid and segmented emerging markets could follow Novo's proactive strategy to internationalize their own cost of capital. What are the preconditions that would be necessary to succeed in such a proactive strategy?

14. **Cost of capital for MNEs compared to domestic firms.** Theoretically MNEs should be in a better position than their domestic counterparts to support higher debt ratios because their cash flows are diversified internationally. However, recent empirical studies have come to the opposite conclusion. These studies also concluded that MNEs have higher betas than their domestic counterparts.

a. According to these empirical studies, why do MNEs have lower debt ratios than their domestic counterparts?

b. According to these empirical studies, why do MNEs have higher betas than their domestic counterparts?

15. **The "riddle."** The riddle is an attempt to explain under what conditions a MNE would have a higher or lower debt ratio and beta than its domestic counterpart. Explain and diagram these conditions.

16. **Emerging market MNEs.** Apart from improving liquidity and escaping from a segmented home market, why might emerging market MNEs further lower their cost of capital by listing and selling equity abroad?

PROBLEMS

1. **Houston Oil Company.** Houston Oil Company's cost of debt is 7%. The risk-free rate of interest is 3%. The expected return on the market portfolio is 8%. After depletion allowances Houston Oil's effective tax rate is 25%. Its optimal capital structure is 60% debt and 40% equity.

a. If Houston's beta is estimated at 1.1, what is Houston's weighted average cost of capital?

b. If Houston's beta is estimated at 0.8, significantly lower because of the continuing profit prospects in the global energy sector, what is Houston's weighted average cost of capital?

2. **Carlton's cost of capital.** Exhibit 11.2 showed the calculation of Carlton's weighted average cost of capital. Assuming that financial conditions have worsened, and using the following current data, recalculate:

a. Carlton's cost of equity

b. Carlton's cost of debt

c. Carlton's weighted average cost of capital

$k_{rf} = 4.000\%$ $k_m = 9.000\%$ $\beta = 1.3$
$k_d = 7.000\%$ $T = 30\%$ $E/V = 50\%$
$D/V = 50\%$ $V = 100\%$

3. **Sunshine Pipelines, Inc.** Sunshine Pipelines, Inc., a large U.S. natural gas pipeline company, wants to raise $120 million to finance expansion. Sunshine wants a capital structure that is 50% debt and 50% equity. Its corporate combined federal and state income tax rate is 40%.

Sunshine finds that it can finance in the domestic U.S. capital market at the following rates. Both debt and equity would have to be sold in multiples of $20 million, and these cost figures show the component costs, each, of debt and equity if raised half by equity and half by debt.

	Cost of Domestic Equity	Cost of Domestic Debt
Up to $40 million of new capital	12%	8%
$41 million to $80 million of new capital	18%	12%
More than $80 million of new capital	22%	16%

A London bank advises Sunshine that U.S. dollars could be raised in Europe at the following costs, also in multiples of $20 million, while maintaining the 50/50 capital structure:

	Cost of European Equity	Cost of European Debt
Up to $40 million of new capital	14%	6%
$41 million to $80 million of new capital	16%	10%
Above $80 million	24%	18%

Each increment of cost would be influenced by the total amount of capital raised. That is, if Sunshine first borrowed $20 million in the European market at 6% and matched this with an additional $20 million of equity, additional debt beyond this amount would cost 12% in the United States and 10% in Europe. The same relationship holds for equity financing.

a. Calculate the lowest average cost of capital for each increment of $40 million of new capital, where Sunshine raises $20 million in the equity market and an additional $20 million in the debt market at the same time.

b. If Sunshine plans an expansion of only $60 million, how should that expansion be financed? What will be the weighted average cost of capital for the expansion?

4. **Tata's cost of capital.** Tata is a large and successful specialty goods company based in Bangalore, India. It has not yet entered the North American marketplace, but is considering establishing both manufacturing and distribution facilities in the United States through a wholly owned subsidiary. It has approached two different investment banking advisors, Goldman Sachs and Bank of New York, for estimates of what its costs of capital would be several years into the future when it plans to list its American subsidiary on a U.S. stock exchange. Using the following assumptions by the two different advisors, calculate the prospective costs of debt, equity, and the WACC for Tata U.S.

Tata's Cost of Capital

Capital cost component	Symbol	Goldman Sachs	Bank of NY
Risk-free rate of interest	k_{rf}	3.0%	3.0%
Average equity market return	k_m	9.0%	12.0%
Estimated cost of debt, single-A	k_d	7.5%	7.8%
Estimated correlation of Tata with market	ρ_{jm}	0.90	0.85
Estimated standard deviation of Tata's returns	σ_j	24.0%	30.0%
Estimated standard deviation of market's returns	σ_m	18.0%	22.0%
Recommended debt-to-capital structure	D/V	35%	40%
Recommended equity-to-capital structure	E/V	65%	60%
Estimated effective U.S. tax rate	t	35%	35%

5. **Country Equity Risk Premiums.** Using the century of equity market data presented in Exhibit 11.3, answer the following questions:
   a. Which country had the largest differential between the arithmetic mean and geometric mean?
   b. If a Swiss firm were attempting to calculate its cost of equity using this data, assuming a risk-free rate of 2.0% and a security beta of 1.4, what would be its estimated cost of equity using both the arithmetic mean and geometric means for the equity risk premium?
6. **Cargill's cost of capital.** Cargill is generally considered to be the largest privately held company in the world. Headquartered in Minneapolis, Minnesota, the company has been averaging sales of over $50 billion per year over the past five-year period. Although the company does not have publicly traded shares, it is still extremely important for it to calculate its weighted average cost of capital properly in order to make rational decisions on new investment proposals.

	Company A	Company B	Cargill
Company sales	$4.5 billion	$26 billion	$50 billion
Company's beta	0.86	0.78	??
Credit rating	AA	A	AA
Weighted average cost of debt	6.885%	7.125%	6.820%
Debt-to-total capital	34%	41%	28%
Sales	12%	26%	45%

   Assuming a risk-free rate of 2.50%, an effective tax rate of 40%, and a market risk premium of 5.50%, estimate the weighted average cost of capital first for companies A and B, and then estimate what you believe a comparable WACC would be for Cargill.
7. **The Tombs.** You have joined your friends at the local watering hole, The Tombs, for your weekly debate on international finance. The topic this week is whether the cost of equity can ever be cheaper than the cost of debt. One of the group members has torn from Chapter 5 of this book the following table of data about Brazil's economic performance, which then becomes the subject of the analysis.

   Larry argues that "it's all about *expected* versus *delivered*. You can talk about what equity investors expect, but they often find that what is delivered for years at a time is so small—even sometimes negative—that in effect, the cost of equity is cheaper than the cost of debt."

   Mohammed—who goes by Mo—interrupts: "But you're missing the point. The cost of capital is what the investor *requires* in compensation for the risk taken going into the investment. If he doesn't end up getting it, and that was happening here, then he pulls his capital out and walks."

   Curly is the theoretician. "This is not about empirical results; it is about the fundamental concept of risk-adjusted returns. An investor in equities knows he will reap returns only after all compensation has been made to debt-providers. He is therefore always subject to a higher level of risk to his return than debt instruments, and as the *capital asset pricing model* states, equity investors set their expected returns as a risk-adjusted factor over and above the returns to risk-free instruments."

   At this point Larry and Mo simply stare at Curly, pause, and both order another beer. Using the Brazilian data presented, comment on this week's debate at The Tombs.

The Tombs and

Brazilian Economic Performance	1995	1996	1997	1998	1999
Inflation rate (IPC)	23.2%	10.0%	4.8%	−1.0%	10.5%
Bank lending rate (CDI)	53.1%	27.1%	24.7%	29.2%	30.7%
Exchange rate (real/$)	0.972	1.039	1.117	1.207	1.700
Stock market index (Bovespa)	16.0%	28.0%	30.2%	−33.5%	151.9%

	Before Symbol	After Diversification	Diversification
Debt-to-capital ratio	D/V	38%	32%
Equity-to-capital ratio	E/V	62%	68%
Corporate tax rate	t	35%	35%
Correlation of S-C's returns with market	ℓ_{jm}	0.88	0.76
Standard deviation of S-C's returns	σ_j	28.0%	26.0%
Standard deviation of market's returns	σ_m	18.0%	18.0%
Market risk premium	$k_m - k_{rf}$	5.50%	5.50%
Corporate cost of debt	k_d	7.20%	7.00%
Risk-free rate of interest	k_{rf}	3.00%	3.00%

Sushmita-Chen and the Riddle. *Use the information about Sushmita-Chen to respond to problems 8 through 10. Sushmita-Chen is an American conglomerate that is actively debating the impacts of international diversification of its operations on its capital structure and cost of capital. The firm is planning to reduce consolidated debt after diversification.*

8. **Sushmita-Chen's cost of equity.** Senior management at Sushmita-Chen is actively debating the implications of diversification on its cost of equity. Although both parties agree that the company's returns will be less correlated with the reference market return in the future, the financial advisors believe that the market will add an additional 3.0% risk premium for "going international" to the basic CAPM cost of equity. Calculate Sushmita-Chen's cost of equity before and after international diversification of its operations, with and without the hypothetical additional risk premium, and comment on the discussion.

9. **Sushmita-Chen's WACC.** Calculate the weighted average cost of capital for Sushmita-Chen before and after international diversification.
   a. Did the reduction in debt costs reduce the firm's weighted average cost of capital? How would you describe the impact of international diversification on Sushmita-Chen's costs of capital?
   b. Adding the hypothetical risk premium to the cost of equity introduced in problem 8 (an added 3.0% to the cost of equity because of international diversification), what is the firm's WACC?

10. **Sushmita-Chen's WACC and effective tax rate.** Many MNEs have greater ability to control and reduce their effective tax rates when expanding international operations. If Sushmita-Chen was able to reduce its consolidated effective tax rate from 35% to 32%, what would be the impact on its WACC?

INTERNET EXERCISES

1. **International diversification via mutual funds.** All major mutual fund companies now offer a variety of internationally diversified mutual funds. The degree of international composition across funds, however, differs significantly. Use the web sites listed, and any others of interest, to a) Distinguish between international funds, global funds, worldwide funds, and overseas funds; and b) Determine how international funds have been performing, in U.S. dollar terms, relative to mutual funds offering purely domestic portfolios.

Fidelity	http://www.fidelity.com/funds
T. Rowe Price	http://www.troweprice.com

Merrill Lynch	http://www.ml.com
Scudder	http://www.scudder.com
Kemper	http://www.kemper.com

2. **Center for Latin American Capital Markets Research.** Although most of the Latin American markets have suffered significant falls in trading following the Mexican peso crisis of December 1994 and the Brazilian real in January 1999, many of these markets may still be some of the most "undervalued" markets in the world. If you were given the task of investing $1 million in a single equity market in Latin America or South America, which one would you invest in? Use the World Wide Web to find recent market performance statistics to support your choice.

   Center for Latin American Capital Markets Research
   http://www.netrus.net/users/gmorles

3. **Novo Industri.** Novo Industri A/S merged with Nordisk Gentofte in 1989. Nordisk Gentofte was Novo's main European competitor. The combined company, now called Novo Nordisk, has become the leading producer of insulin worldwide. Its main competitor is still Eli Lilly of the United States. Using standard investor information, and the web site for Novo Nordisk and Eli Lilly, determine whether, during the most recent five years, Novo Nordisk has maintained a cost of capital competitive with Eli Lilly. In particular, examine the P/E ratios, share prices, debt ratios, and betas. Try to calculate each firm's actual cost of capital.

Novo Nordisk	http://www.novonordisk.com
Eli Lilly and Company	http://www.lilly.com
BigCharts.com	http://bigcharts.com

4. **Cost of capital calculator.** Ibbotson Associates of Chicago is one of the leading providers of quantitative estimates of the cost of capital across markets. Use the following web site—specifically the Cost of Capital Center—to prepare an overview of the major theoretical approaches and the numerical estimates they yield for cross-border costs of capital.

Ibbotson Associates	http://www.ibbotson.com

SELECTED READINGS

Dimson, Elroy, Paul Marsh, and Mike Staunton, *Triumph of the Optimists: 101 Years of Global Investment Returns* (Princeton N.J., Princeton University Press, 2002), Chapters 12 and 13.

Domowitz, Ian, Jack Glen, and Ananth Madhavan, "Market Segmentation and Stock Prices: Evidence from an Emerging Market," *The Journal of Finance*, June 1997, Volume 52, No. 3, pp. 1059–1085.

Kwok, Chuck C.Y., and David M. Reeb, "Internationalization and Firm Risk: An Upstream-Downstream Hypothesis," *Journal of International Business Studies*, Volume 31, Issue 4, 2000, pp. 611–630.

Reeb, David M., Chuck C. Y. Kwok, and H. Young Baek, "Systematic Risk of the Multinational Corporation," *Journal of International Business Studies*, Second Quarter 1998, pp. 263–279.

Stulz, Rene M., "Does the Cost of Capital Differ Across Countries? An Agency Perspective," *European Financial Management*, 1996, Volume 2, pp. 11–22.

MINI-CASE

Bang & Olufsen and Philips N.V.

One excellent example of financial synergy that lowered a firm's cost of capital was provided by the cross-border strategic alliance of Philips N.V. of the Netherlands and Bang & Olufsen (B & O) of Denmark in 1990. Philips N.V. is one of the largest multinational firms in the world and the leading consumer electronics firm in Europe. B & O is a small European competitor with a nice market niche at the high end of the audiovisual market.

Philips' Motivation

Philips was a major supplier of components to B & O, a situation it wished to continue. It also wished to join forces with B & O in the upscale consumer electronics market where Philips did not have the quality image enjoyed by B & O. Philips was concerned that financial pressure might force B & O to choose a Japanese competitor for a partner. That would be very unfortunate for Philips. B & O had always supported Philips' political efforts to gain EU support to make the few remaining European-owned consumer electronics firms more competitive than their strong Japanese competitors.

B & O's Motivation

B & O was interested in an alliance with Philips to gain more rapid access to its new technology and assistance in converting that technology into B & O product applications. B & O wanted assurance of timely delivery of components at large volume discounts from Philips itself, as well as access to Philip's large network of suppliers under terms enjoyed by Philips. Equally important, B & O wanted to get an equity infusion from Philips to strengthen its own shaky financial position. Despite its commercial artistry, in recent years B & O had been only marginally profitable, and its publicly traded shares were considered too risky to justify a new public equity issue either in Denmark or abroad. It had no excess borrowing capacity.

The Strategic Alliance

A strategic alliance was agreed upon that would give each partner what it desired commercially. Philips agreed to invest Dkr342 million (about $50 million) to increase the equity of B & O's main operating subsidiary. In return, it received a 25% ownership of the expanded company.

When B & O's strategic alliance was announced to the public on May 3, 1990, the share price of Bang & Olufsen Holding, the listed company on the Copenhagen Stock Exchange, jumped by 35% during the next two days. It remained at that level until the Gulf War crisis temporarily depressed B & O's share price. The share price has since recovered and the expected synergies eventually materialized.

In evaluating what happened, we recognize that an industrial purchaser might be willing to pay a higher price for a firm that will provide it some synergies than would a portfolio investor who does not receive these synergies. Portfolio investors are only pricing firm's shares based on the normal risk versus return tradeoff. They cannot normally anticipate the value of synergies that might accrue to the firm from an unexpected strategic alliance partner. The same conclusion should hold for a purely domestic strategic alliance but this example happens to be a cross-border alliance.

Case Questions

1. Why might an industrial purchaser, such as Philips, be willing to pay a higher price for B & O's stock than a typical international portfolio investor?
2. What are the likely synergies that both Philips and B & O expected to achieve through their strategic alliance?
3. What are the advantages and disadvantages to B & O of using a strategic alliance equity infusion from Philips compared to attracting international portfolio investors, assuming that both alternatives would lead to a lower cost and greater availability of capital?

Chapter 12

Sourcing Equity Globally

CHAPTER 11 ANALYZED WHY GAINING ACCESS TO GLOBAL CAPITAL MARKETS SHOULD LOWER A FIRM'S marginal cost of capital and increase its availability by improving the market liquidity of its shares and by overcoming market segmentation. To implement such a lofty goal, it is necessary to start by designing a strategy that will ultimately attract international investors. This means identifying and choosing among alternative paths to access global markets. It also usually requires some restructuring of the firm, improving the quality and level of its disclosure, and making its accounting and reporting standards more transparent to potential foreign investors. The Novo case in Chapter 11 is a good illustration of the steps that need to be taken and barriers that might be faced.

A focus of this chapter is on firms resident in less liquid or segmented markets. These firms need to tap liquid and unsegmented markets in order to attain the global cost and availability of capital. These firms are typically resident in emerging market countries and many of the smaller industrial country markets. Firms in the United States and United Kingdom often have full access to their own domestic liquid and unsegmented markets. Although they too source equity and debt abroad, it is unlikely to have as favorable an impact on their cost and availability of capital. In fact, for them sourcing funds abroad is often motivated mainly by the need to fund large foreign acquisitions rather than existing domestic or foreign operations.

This chapter starts with the design of a strategy to source both equity and debt capital globally. It then describes depositary receipts. These are the most important instruments that facilitate cross-border trading in securities. The chapter then continues with the specifics of cross-listing and selling equity issues abroad. (Selling of debt issues abroad is delayed until the next chapter.) It concludes with an analysis of alternative instruments to source equity abroad.

Designing a Strategy to Source Equity Globally

Designing a capital sourcing strategy requires that management agree upon a long-run financial objective and then choose among the various alternative paths to get there. Exhibit 12.1 is a visual presentation of alternative paths to the ultimate objective of attaining a global cost and availability of capital.

Normally the choice of paths and implementation is aided by an early appointment of an investment bank as official advisor to the firm. Investment bankers are in touch

Exhibit 12.1 Alternative Paths to Globalize the Cost and Availability of Capital

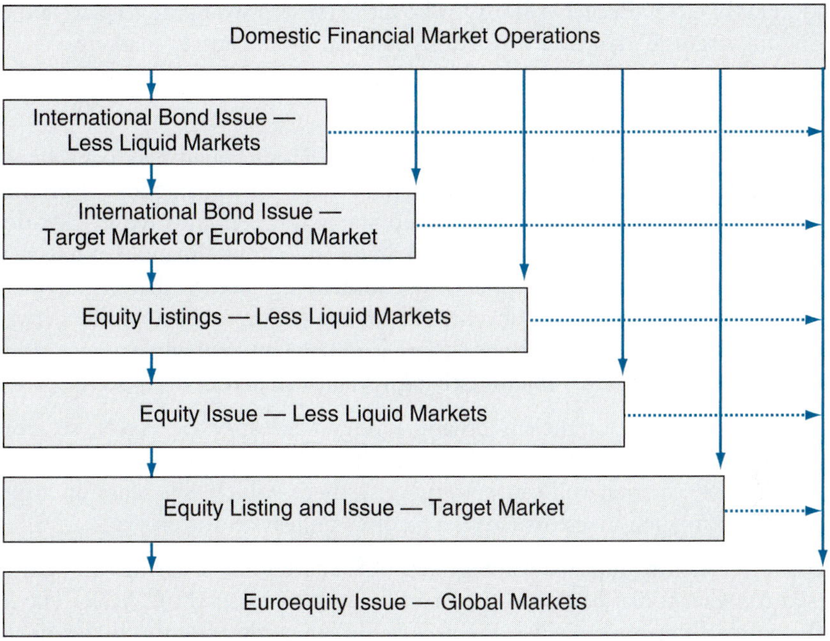

Source: Oxelheim, Stonehill, Randøy, Vikkula, Dullum, and Moden, *Corporate Strategies To Internationalize the Cost of Capital* (Copenhagen: Copenhagen Business School Press, 1998), p. 119.

with potential foreign investors and know what they currently require. They can also help navigate the various institutional requirements and barriers that must be satisfied. Their services include advising whether, if, when, and where a cross-listing should be initiated. They usually prepare the required stock prospectus if an equity issue is desired, help to price the issue, and maintain an aftermarket to prevent the share price from falling below its initial price.

Alternative Paths

Most firms raise their initial capital in their own domestic market (see Exhibit 12.1). Next they are tempted to skip all the intermediate steps and drop to the bottom line, a Euroequity issue in global markets. This is the time when a good investment bank advisor will offer a "reality check." Most firms that have raised capital only in their domestic market are not well known enough to attract foreign investors. Remember from Chapter 11 that Novo was advised by its investment bankers to start with a convertible Eurobond issue and simultaneously cross-list its shares (and the bonds) in London. This was despite Novo's outstanding track record with respect to growth, profitability, and dominance of two worldwide market niches (insulin and industrial enzymes).

Exhibit 12.1 shows that most firms should start sourcing abroad with an international bond issue. This issue could be placed on a less liquid foreign market and be followed by an international bond issue in a target market or in the Eurobond market. The next step might be to cross-list and issue equity in one of the less liquid markets so as to attract international investor attention. The next step could be to cross-list shares on a highly liquid foreign stock exchange such as London (LSE), NYSE, or NASDAQ. The ultimate step would be to place a directed equity issue in a liquid target market or a Euroequity issue in global equity markets.

Depositary Receipts

Depositary receipts (depositary shares) are negotiable certificates issued by a bank to represent the underlying shares of stock, which are held in trust at a foreign custodian bank. *American depositary receipts* (ADRs) are certificates traded in the United States and denominated in U.S. dollars. ADRs are sold, registered, and transferred in the United States in the same manner as any share of stock, with each ADR representing some multiple of the underlying foreign share. This multiple allows the ADRs to possess a price per share conventional for the U.S. market (typically between $20 and $50 per share) even if the price of the foreign share is unconventional when converted to U.S. dollars directly. Exhibit 12.2 illustrates the underlying issuance structure of an ADR.

ADRs can be exchanged for the underlying foreign shares, or vice versa, so arbitrage keeps foreign and U.S. prices of any given share the same after adjusting for transfer costs. For example, investor demand in one market will cause a price rise there, which will cause an arbitrage rise in the other market, even when investors there are not as bullish on the stock.

ADRs convey certain technical advantages to U.S. shareholders. Dividends paid by a foreign firm are passed to its custodial bank and then to the bank that issued the ADR. The issuing bank exchanges the foreign currency dividends for U.S. dollars and sends the dollar dividend to the ADR holders. ADRs are in registered form, rather than in bearer form. Transfer of ownership is

Exhibit 12.2 Mechanics of American Depositary Receipts (ADRs)

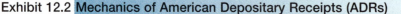

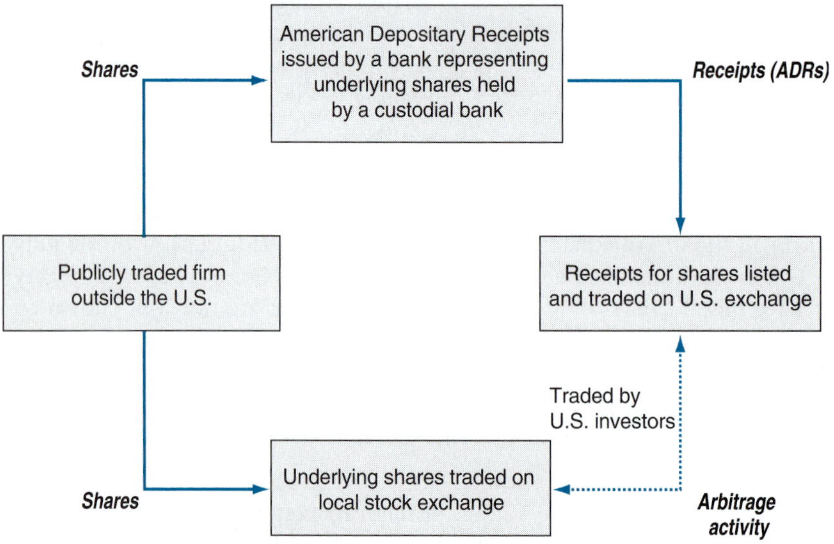

facilitated, because it is done in the United States in accordance with U.S. laws and procedures. In the event of death of a shareholder, the estate need not to go through probate in a foreign court system. Normally, trading costs are lower than when buying or selling the underlying shares in their home market. Settlement is usually faster in the United States. Withholding taxes is simpler, because withholding is handled by the depositary bank.

ADRs are either sponsored or unsponsored. Sponsored ADRs are created at the request of a foreign firm wanting its shares traded in the United States. The firm applies to the Securities and Exchange Commission (SEC) and a U.S. bank for registration and issuance of ADRs. The foreign firm pays all costs of creating such sponsored ADRs. If a foreign firm does not seek to have its shares traded in the United States but U.S. investors are interested, a U.S. securities firm may initiate creation of the ADRs. Such an ADR would be unsponsored, but the SEC still requires that all new ADR programs must have approval of the firm itself.

Exhibit 12.3 summarizes the characteristics of ADRs in the United States. It shows three levels of commitment, distinguished by the necessary accounting standards, SEC registration requirement, time to completion, and costs. Level I ("over the counter" or pink sheets) is the easiest to satisfy. It facilitates trading in foreign securities that have been acquired by U.S. investors but are not registered with the SEC. It is the least costly approach but might have a minimal impact on liquidity.

Level II applies to firms that want to list existing shares on the NYSE, AMEX, or NASDAQ markets. They must meet the full registration requirements of the SEC. This means reconciling their financial accounts with those used under United States GAAP, which raises the cost considerably. Level III applies to the sale of a new equity issued in the United States. It too requires full

Exhibit 12.3 Characteristics of Depositary Receipt Programs Traded in the United States

	Level I	Level II	Level III	144a
Primary exchange	OTC pink sheets	NYSE, AMEX, or NASDAQ	NYSE, AMEX or NASDAQ	PORTAL
Accounting standards	Home country standards	U.S. GAAP	U.S. GAAP	Home country standards
SEC registration	Exempt	Full registration	Full registration	Exempt
Share issuance	Existing shares only (public offering)	Existing shares only (public offering)	New equity capital raised (public offering)	New equity capital raised (private offering)
Time to completion	10 weeks	10 weeks	14 weeks	16 days
Costs	$25,000	$200,000–700,000	$500,000–2,000,000	$250,000–500,000

Foreign securities traded in the U.S. are required to perform periodic reporting under the 1934 Exchange Act, provided that the company's equity securities are held of record by 500 or more persons, of which 300 or more are U.S. residents. This requires quarterly reporting, by filing the form 20-F in U.S. Generally Accepted Accounting Principles. Level I and 144a DRs are eligible for a 12g3-2(b) exemption from this requirement, and only have to supply to the SEC copies of information that the company makes public in its home country. Privately placed Depositary Receipts are also eligible for the 12g3-2(b) exemption. They trade between Qualified Institutional Buyers under SEC Rule 144a, which provides a safe harbor exemption from the registration requirements of the Securities Act of 1933.

Source: Global Offerings of Depositary Receipts, A Transaction Guide (The Bank of New York, 1995), reprinted in Darius P. Miller, "The Market Reaction to International Cross-Listings: Evidence from Depositary Receipts," *Journal of Financial Economics*, 51, 1999, pp. 103–123.

registration with the SEC and an elaborate stock prospectus. This is the most expensive alternative but is the most likely to improve the stock's liquidity and escape from home market segmentation. So-called *144a programs* will be described later in this chapter.

Global Registered Shares (GRSs)

Similar to ordinary shares, Global Registered Shares (GRSs) have the added benefit of being able to be traded on equity exchanges around the globe in a variety of currencies. ADRs, however, are quoted only in U.S. dollars and are traded only in the United States. GRSs can, theoretically, be traded with the sun, following markets as they open and close around the globe around the clock. The shares are traded electronically, therefore eliminating the specialized forms and depositaries required by share forms like ADRs.

Global Registered Shares are not really a recent innovation. They are in fact nearly identical to the structure used for cross-border trading of Canadian company securities in the U.S. for decades. Over 70 Canadian firms are listed on the NYSE, and all of these shares trade as ordinary shares in both their home market in Canada and the U.S. market.

According to the NYSE, dealing fees levied on ADRs cost investors between 3 and 5 cents per share per trade. By comparison, GRSs carry a flat cost of $5 per trade, regardless of the quantity of shares traded. For foreign corporations expecting or hoping to become widely traded securities for large institutional investors, the flat rate per trade for GRSs may increase their cost efficiency. A two-way electronic linkage between the Depositary Trust Company in the United States and the Deutsche Börse Clearing Company in Germany facilitates the efficient quoting, trading, and settlement of shares in the respective currencies as shown in Exhibit 12.4.

Exhibit 12.4 Global Registered Shares (GRS)

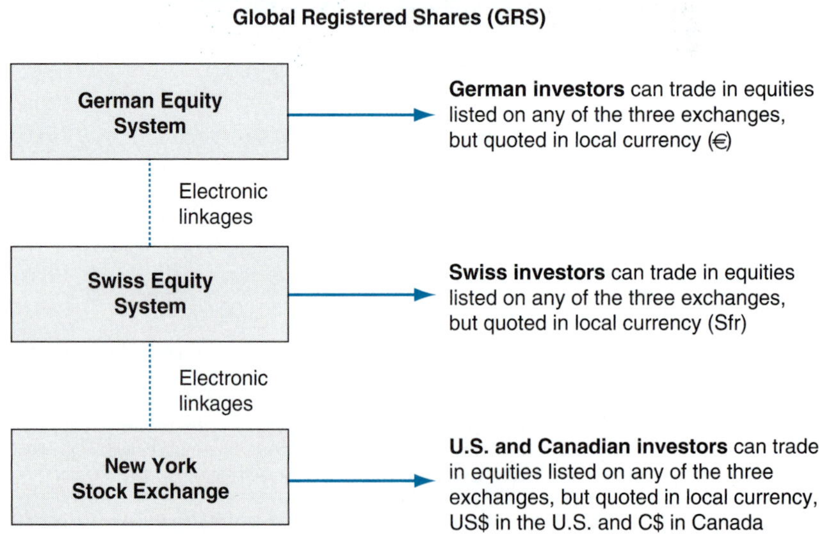
Global Registered Shares (GRS)
German Equity System
German investors can trade in equities listed on any of the three exchanges, but quoted in local currency (€)
Electronic linkages
Swiss Equity System
Swiss investors can trade in equities listed on any of the three exchanges, but quoted in local currency (Sfr)
Electronic linkages
New York Stock Exchange
U.S. and Canadian investors can trade in equities listed on any of the three exchanges, but quoted in local currency, US$ in the U.S. and C$ in Canada

In October 2001, Deutsche Bank (DB) of Germany chose to list on the New York Stock Exchange via Global Registered Shares (GRSs). Many critics argued that by listing through GRSs, Deutsche Bank would experience lower trading in their shares. This lower-trading expectation was based on DaimlerChrysler's GRS experiences in 1998, as described in Global Finance Perspective 12.1.

Foreign Equity Listing and Issuance

According to the alternative paths depicted in Exhibit 12.1, a firm must choose one or more stock markets on which to cross-list its shares and sell new equity. Just where to go depends mainly on the firm's specific motives and the willingness of the host stock market to accept the firm. By

Global Finance Perspective 12.1

The DaimlerChrysler GRS Experience

In November 1998, DaimlerChrysler AG (Germany) surprised the global equity markets by being the first company to list on the NYSE using GRSs rather than ADRS. (Prior to Daimler's merger with Chrysler, it had enjoyed a relatively liquid level of trading on the New York Stock Exchange using ADRs.) The acclaim surrounding the GRS listing was short-lived, however, as evidence grew the following year that trading activity in the combined DaimlerChrysler shares (New York Stock Exchange symbol DCS) was much weaker than hoped. A study conducted by Andrew Karolyi of Ohio State University indicated that only 5% of the transactions in Daimler's shares were traded via the GRS listing on the NYSE.

Average daily trading prior to DaimlerChrysler merger:

Daimler Benz	Frankfurt	$777 million
Chrysler Corporation	New York	$100 million

Average daily trading post-merger for DCX joint listing:

DaimlerChrysler	Frankfurt	$1 billion
DaimlerChrysler GRSs:		
December 1998	New York	$200 million
February 1999	New York	$100 million

Although it is difficult to explain all of the forces at work in DaimlerChrysler's share trading, the factor of listing GRSs rather than ADRs is considered a major one. Another major factor, however, is that the new combined company was actually dropped from the Standard and Poors 500 Index when the index was rebalanced.

Of the ten European companies listing on the NYSE in 2001, only Deutsche Bank chose to use GRSs rather than ADRs. The seven others—including Siemens, BASF, and Novartis—all claim to have seriously considered GRSs, but concluded that the initial costs of ADRs were substantially lower and their liquidity in the U.S. marketplace greater. Although there are few explicit up-front costs associated specifically with GRS listings, traditional German firms have issued much of their equity in bearer form. Before being able to issue GRSs, the firms would need to go through the process of registration of shares for trading via the electronic linkages with New York. Deutsche Bank, as part of its preparations for the 2001 issue, evidently had actually issued registered shares in Frankfurt in 1999.

Source: G. Andrew Karolyi, "DaimlerChrysler AG, the First Truly Global Share," Fisher College of Business, Ohio State University, working paper, May 2002.

cross-listing and selling its shares on a foreign stock exchange, a firm typically tries to accomplish one or more of the following objectives:

1. Improve the liquidity of its existing shares and support a liquid secondary market for new equity issues in foreign markets.
2. Increase its share price by overcoming mis-pricing in a segmented and illiquid home capital market.
3. Increase the firm's visibility and political acceptance to its customers, suppliers, creditors, and host governments.
4. Establish a secondary market for shares used to acquire other firms in the host market.
5. Create a secondary market for shares that can be used to compensate local management and employees in foreign subsidiaries.

Improving Liquidity

Quite often, foreign investors have acquired a firm's shares through normal brokerage channels, even though the shares are not listed in the investor's home market or not traded in the investor's preferred currency. Cross-listing is a way to encourage such investors to continue to hold and trade these shares, thus marginally improving secondary market liquidity. It is usually done through ADRs.

Firms domiciled in countries with small illiquid capital markets often outgrow those markets and are forced to raise new equity abroad. Listing on a stock exchange in the market in which these funds are to be raised is typically required by the underwriters to ensure post-issue liquidity in the shares.

The introductory section of this chapter suggested that firms start by cross-listing in a less liquid market, followed by having an equity issue in that market (see Exhibit 12.1). In order to maximize liquidity, however, the firm ideally should cross-list and issue equity in a more liquid market and eventually offer a global equity issue.

Size of the Market

Exhibit 12.5 describes selected stock exchange size and performance characteristics (2001). The stock exchanges shown are divided into three categories to help identify the illiquid markets and the liquid markets.

In order to maximize liquidity, it is desirable to cross-list and/or sell equity in the "Most Liquid" category. The column entitled "Value of Share Trading" is one indicator of the overall ability of the market to provide liquidity and availability of capital.

- NASDAQ, the NYSE, and the London Stock Exchange (LSE) are clearly the most liquid markets.
- The NYSE, NASDAQ, and the LSE have the largest number of foreign listings—461, 445, and 409, respectively.
- The NYSE has by far the largest market capitalization, $11.0 trillion in 2001.

Exhibit 12.5 Selected Stock Exchange Size Characteristics Categorized by Market Liquidity, End 2001

Exchanges	Type*	Number of Companies Domestic	Foreign	Market Capital of Domestic Companies (millions of U.S.$)	Concentration of 5% Market Value**	Value of Share Trading (millions of U.S.$)
Most Liquid						
NASDAQ	REV	3,618	445	2,739,675	71.9	10,934,569
NYSE	TSV	1,939	461	11,026,587	63.8	10,489,323
London	REV	1,923	409	2,164,716	83.6	4,550,504
Euronext***	REV	1,132	na	1,843,529	76.3	3,179,789
Tokyo	TSV	2,103	38	2,293,842	62.5	1,660,525
Deutsche Börse (Ger)	TSV	748	235	1,071,749	66.1	1,441,633
Spain	TSV	1,458	22	468,203	68.7	842,227
Italy	REV	288	6	527,467	62.8	710,218
Semi-Liquid						
Swiss Exchange	REV	263	149	527,375	82.7	594,936
Taiwan	TSV	584	2	292,621	62.4	544,588
Toronto	TSV	1,261	38	611,493	73.1	459,627
Stockholm	REV	285	20	236,514	67.0	386,730
Korea	TSV	688	0	194,470	76.4	380,586
Australia	TSV	1,334	76	375,131	81.0	244,102
Hong Kong	TSV	857	10	506,073	85.7	241,012
Less Liquid						
Singapore	TSV	424	68	117,338	74.4	71,108
Mexico	REV	167	5	126,258	65.2	69,660
Brazil	TSV	438	3	186,238	67.2	64,606
Thailand	TSV	385	0	35,950	56.9	31,034
Kuala Lumpur	TSV	804	3	118,981	61.4	21,324
Jakarta	TSV	315	0	22,998	64.4	9,529
Buenos Aires	TSV	116	3	33,384	63.2	7,532
Santiago	TSV	248	1	56,310	48.8	4,282
Philippines	TSV	230	2	20,629	64.8	3,148

na = Not available.

Source: World Federation of Exchanges: Statistics, http://www.world-exchanges.org/.

* Type indicates the method by which exchanges define and compile turnover. Trading System View (TSV) counts as turnover only those transactions that pass through their trading systems or take place on the exchange's trading floor. REV exchanges include in their turnover figures all transactions, with no distinction between on- and off-market, or transactions made into foreign markets reported on the national market.

** Market concentration of the 5% of the largest companies by market value compared with the market value of all companies traded on that exchange.

*** In 2001, the three Euronext markets (Amsterdam, Brussels, and Paris) merged into one that is now called just "Euronext."

The number of listed foreign firms on the NYSE is largest among the global exchanges (461), and the individual trading volume of these firms is typically quite large relative to their home markets. For example, Telefonos de Mexico was the most actively traded stock on the NYSE in the mid-1990s. However, the trading volume of the foreign companies listed on the LSE was almost $2.7 trillion compared to $787 million for foreign companies listed on the NYSE (not shown in the exhibit).

Germany and Euronext (merged markets of Amsterdam, Brussels, and Paris) have fairly liquid markets for domestic shares but a much lower level of liquidity for trading foreign shares. On the other hand, Germany (Deutsche Börse) and Euronext are quite appropriate target markets for firms resident in the EU, especially those that have adopted the euro. They are also used as supplementary cross-listing locations for firms that are already cross-listed on LSE, NYSE, or NASDAQ. However, as on NASDAQ, 5% of the listed firms ranked by market value in Germany account for 66.1% of the total market value. Concentration in Euronext is even higher at 76.3% in 2001.

Tokyo has fallen on hard times. It is now only in third place for total market capitalization and in fifth place for trading volume. It is a nearly total flop as a location for foreign firms to gain liquidity and had only 38 foreign firms cross-listed in 2001 compared to 67 in 1996.

The New York Stock Exchange (NYSE) Compared to the London Stock Exchange (LSE)

If we compare the NYSE to the LSE, we note that liquidity in the most actively traded shares is similar, but the NYSE is a more liquid market for the least popular shares. Transaction costs as measured by spreads are lower on the NYSE. The LSE spreads are roughly comparable to the spreads on NASDAQ. On the other hand, the cost of listing and disclosure requirements are less onerous on the LSE than on the NYSE. In terms of fairness, the NYSE is superior, because orders are executed chronologically, whereas on the LSE one has to shop from dealer to dealer. Crisis management by specialists has been more effective in practice on the NYSE than on any other exchange, including LSE. Despite the more favorable liquidity attributes of the NYSE, nearly as many foreign firms list on the LSE as on the NYSE. We must conclude that the ease and cost of listing, lower required disclosure levels, and less frequent reporting requirements have tilted the scale toward the LSE for firms that might have trouble overcoming these barriers. However, for those firms that are willing to pay the price, a listing on the NYSE should improve the liquidity of their shares more than could be achieved with a similar listing elsewhere.

Semi-Liquid and Least Liquid Markets

In the "Semi-Liquid" and "Least Liquid" categories based on trading value, no exchange can provide reasonable liquidity for foreign firms, and local exchanges in this category are not the major source for raising new equity capital even by domestic firms. The "Least Liquid" markets, as expected, offer no value to foreign firms and very little liquidity to their own domestic firms. This is of course why some firms resident in these illiquid markets are dependent on raising equity in more liquid foreign markets. Those that can meet the stringent qualifications of the "Most Liquid" markets would normally opt for that alternative. Others must settle for the "Semi-Liquid" markets.

Although overall market liquidity is shown in Exhibit 12.5, additional characteristics contribute to the liquidity of individual stocks. These include market-making activities, transaction costs, fairness, and crisis management. At one end of the spectrum is the NYSE, where assigned specialists are responsible for ensuring a liquid, low-cost, fair, and orderly market. At the other end of the spectrum is the London Stock Exchange (LSE) where market makers, formerly called jobbers, voluntarily make an active market in some but not all listed shares.

Effect of Cross-Listing and Equity Issuance on Share Price

Cross-Listing

Does merely cross-listing on a foreign stock exchange have a favorable impact on share prices? It depends on the degree to which markets are segmented.

If a firm's home capital market is segmented, the firm could theoretically benefit by cross-listing in a foreign market if that market values the firm or its industry more than does the home market. This was certainly the situation experienced by Novo when it listed on the NYSE in 1981 (see Chapter 11). However, most capital markets are becoming more integrated with global markets. Even emerging markets are less segmented than they were just a few years ago.

Even as early as the period from 1969 to 1982, when markets were more segmented than today, a research study found a positive share price effect for foreign firms that listed on the NYSE, AMEX, or NASDAQ.[1] A more recent study found that share prices increased for foreign firms that cross-listed their shares in ADR form on the NYSE and AMEX during the period from 1982 to 1992.[2] The authors concluded that cross-listing in the United States enhanced share value by reducing the overall effect of segmentation among different national securities markets. A recent and comprehensive study consisted of 181 firms from 35 countries that instituted their first ADR program in the United States over the period from 1985 to 1995.[3] The author measured the stock price impact of the announcement of a cross-listing in the United States and found significant positive abnormal returns around the announcement date. These were retained in the immediate following period. As expected, the study showed that the abnormal returns were greater for firms resident in emerging markets with a low level of legal barriers to capital flows than for firms resident in developed markets. Firms resident in emerging markets with heavy restrictions on capital flows received some abnormal returns, but not as high as those of firms resident in the other markets. This result was due to the perceived limited liquidity of firms resident in markets with too many restrictions on capital flows.

Equity Issuance

It is well known that the combined impact of a new equity issue undertaken simultaneously with a cross-listing has a more favorable impact on stock price than cross-listing alone. This effect occurs because the new issue creates an instantly enlarged shareholder base. Marketing efforts by

1. Alexander, Gordon J., Cheol S. Eun, and S. Janakiramanan, "International Listings and Stock Returns: Some Empirical Evidence," *Journal of Financial and Quantitative Analysis*, June 1988, Volume 23, No. 2, pp. 135–151.
2. Sundaram, Anant K., and Dennis E. Logue, "Valuation Effects of Foreign Company Listings on U.S. Exchanges," *Journal of International Business Studies*, First Quarter 1996, Volume 27, No. 1, pp. 67–88.
3. Miller 1999, op. cit.

the underwriters prior to the issue engender higher levels of visibility. Post-issue efforts by the underwriters to support at least the initial offering price also reduce investor risk.

The study of 181 firms cross-listing in the United States contained 30 firms that initiated new equity issues (Level III ADRs). The author found a statistically significant abnormal return for these firms—even higher than for the firms that just cross-listed (Levels I and II). Furthermore, the highest abnormal return was for Chilean firms (8.23 percent). The Chilean market has one of the highest levels of restrictions affecting foreign investors. Since it is well known that stock prices react negatively to new domestic issues in the United States, something truly significant must be happening when foreign ADRs are sold in the United States.

Even U.S. firms can benefit by issuing equity abroad. A recent study of U.S. firms that issued equity abroad concluded that increased name recognition and accessibility from global equity issues leads to increased investor recognition and participation in both the primary and secondary markets.[4] Moreover, the ability to issue global shares can validate firm quality by reducing the information asymmetry between insiders and investors. Another conclusion was that U.S. firms may seize a window of opportunity to switch to global offerings when domestic demand for their shares is weak. Finally, the study found that U.S. firms announcing global equity offerings have significantly less negative market reactions by about one percentage point than what would have been expected had they limited their issues to the domestic market.

Increasing Visibility and Political Acceptance

MNEs list in markets where they have substantial physical operations. Commercial objectives are to enhance corporate image, advertise trademarks and products, get better local press coverage, and become more familiar with the local financial community in order to raise working capital locally.

Political objectives might include the need to meet local ownership requirements for a multinational firm's foreign joint venture. Local ownership of the parent firm's shares might provide a forum for publicizing the firm's activities and how they support the host country. This objective is the most important one for Japanese firms. The Japanese domestic market has both low-cost capital and high availability. Therefore Japanese firms are not trying to increase the stock price, the liquidity of their shares, or the availability of capital.

Increasing Potential for Share Swaps with Acquisitions

Firms that follow a strategy of growth by acquisition are always looking for creative ways to fund these acquisitions rather than paying cash. Offering their shares as partial payment is considerably more attractive if those shares have a liquid secondary market. In that case, the target's shareholders have an easy way to convert their acquired shares to cash if they do not prefer a share swap. However, a share swap is often attractive as a tax-free exchange.

4. Wu, Congsheng, and Chuck C.Y. Kwok, "Why Do U.S. Firms Choose Global Equity Offerings?", *Financial Management*, Summer 2002, pp. 47–65.

Compensating Management and Employees

If a MNE wishes to use stock options and share purchase compensation plans for local management and employees, local listing would enhance the perceived value of such plans. It should reduce transaction and foreign exchange costs for the local beneficiaries.

Barriers to Cross-Listing and Selling Equity Abroad

Although a firm may decide to cross-list and/or sell equity abroad, certain barriers exist. The most serious barriers are the future commitment to providing full and transparent disclosure of operating results and balance sheets as well as a continuous program of investor relations.

The Commitment to Disclosure and Investor Relations

A decision to cross-list must be balanced against the implied increased commitment to full disclosure and a continuing investor relations program. For firms resident in the Anglo-American markets, listing abroad might not appear to be much of a barrier. For example, the SEC's disclosure rules for listing in the United States are so stringent and costly that any other market's rules are mere child's play. Reversing the logic, however, non-U.S. firms must really think twice before cross-listing in the United States. Not only are the disclosure requirements breathtaking, but a continuous timely quarterly information is required by U.S. regulators and investors. As a result, the foreign firm must provide a costly continuous investor relations program for its U.S. shareholders, including frequent "road shows" and the time-consuming personal involvement of top management.

Disclosure Is a Double-Edged Sword

The U.S. school of thought is that the worldwide trend toward requiring fuller, more transparent, and more standardized financial disclosure of operating results and balance sheet positions may have the desirable effect of lowering the cost of equity capital. As we observed in 2002, lack of full and accurate disclosure and poor transparency worsened the U.S. stock market decline as investors fled to safer securities, such as U.S. government bonds. This action increased the equity cost of capital for all firms.

The other school of thought is that the U.S. level of required disclosure is an onerous, costly burden. It chases away many potential listers, thereby narrowing the choice of securities available to U.S. investors at reasonable transaction costs. 409 as cited earlier, at year-end 2001, 401 foreign firms were listed on the NYSE, whereas 409 foreign firms were listed on the LSE, and 235 foreign firms were listed on the German stock exchange.

A study of 203 internationally traded shares concluded that there is a statistically significant relationship between the level of financial disclosure required and the markets on which the firms chose to list.[5] The higher the level of disclosure required, the less likely that a firm would list in that market. However, for those firms that do list despite the disclosure and cost barriers, the

5. Saudagaran, Shahrokh M., and Gary C. Biddle, "Foreign Listing Location: A Study of MNEs and Stock Exchanges in Eight Countries," *Journal of International Business Studies*, Second Quarter 1995, Volume 26, No. 2, pp. 319–341.

payoff could be needed access to additional equity funding of a large factory or an acquisition in the United States. Daimler Benz took the painful step of cross-listing on the NYSE prior to raising equity in the United States to fund a new auto plant and, as it turned out later, to merge with Chrysler Corporation.

Alternative Instruments to Source Equity in Global Markets

Alternative instruments to source equity in global markets include the following:

- Sale of a directed public share issue to investors in a target market.
- Sale of a Euroequity public issue to investors in more than one market, including both foreign and domestic markets
- Private placements under SEC Rule 144A
- Sale of shares to private equity funds
- Sale of shares to a foreign firm as part of a strategic alliance

Directed Public Share Issues

A *directed public share issue* is defined as one that is targeted at investors in a single country and underwritten in whole or in part by investment institutions from that country. The issue might or might not be denominated in the currency of the target market. The shares might or might not be cross-listed on a stock exchange in the target market.

The $61 million U.S. share issue by Novo in 1981 (Chapter 11) was a good example of a successful directed share issue that both improved the liquidity of Novo's shares and lowered its cost of capital. Novo repeated this success in 1983 with a $100 million share issue at $53 per share (ADR), compared to $36 per share two years earlier.

A directed share issue might be motivated by a need to fund acquisitions or major capital investments in a target foreign market. This is an especially important source of equity for firms that reside in smaller capital markets and that have outgrown that market. A foreign share issue, plus cross-listing, can provide it with improved liquidity for its shares and the means to use those shares to pay for acquisitions.

Nycomed, a small but well-respected Norwegian pharmaceutical firm, was an example of this type of motivation for a directed share issue combined with cross-listing. Its commercial strategy for growth is to leverage its sophisticated knowledge of certain market niches and technologies within the pharmaceutical field by acquiring other promising firms that possess relevant technologies, personnel, or market niches. Europe and the United States have provided fertile hunting grounds. The acquisitions were paid for partly with cash and partly with shares. Norway is too small a home capital market to fund these acquisitions for cash or to provide a liquid enough market to minimize Nycomed's marginal cost of capital.

Nycomed responded to the challenge by selling two successful directed share issues abroad. In June 1989, it cross-listed on the LSE (quoted on SEAQ International) and raised the equivalent of about $100 million in equity from foreign investors there. Then in June 1992, it cross-listed on the NYSE and raised about $75 million with a share issue directed at U.S. investors.

Nycomed eventually merged with Amersham, a British firm, and moved its headquarters to the United Kingdom.

Euroequity Public Issue

The gradual integration of the world's capital markets and increased international portfolio investment has spawned the emergence of a very viable Euroequity market. A firm can now issue equity underwritten and distributed in multiple foreign equity markets, sometimes simultaneously with distribution in the domestic market. The same financial institutions that had previously created an infrastructure for the Euronote and Eurobond markets (to be described in detail in Chapter 13) were responsible for the Euroequity market. The term "Euro" does not imply that the issuers or investors are located in Europe, nor does it mean the shares are sold in the currency "euro." It is a generic term for international securities issues originating and being sold anywhere in the world.

The largest and most spectacular issues have been made in conjunction with a wave of privatizations of government-owned enterprises. The Thatcher government in the United Kingdom created the model when it privatized British Telecom in December 1984. That issue was so large that it was necessary and desirable to sell tranches to foreign investors in addition to the sale to domestic investors. A *tranche* is an allocation of shares, typically to underwriters that are expected to sell to investors in their designated geographic markets. The objective is both to raise the funds and to ensure post-issue worldwide liquidity. Unfortunately, in the case of British Telecom, the issue was, in retrospect, underpriced. Most of the foreign shares, especially those placed in the United States, flowed back to London, leaving a nice profit behind for the U.S. underwriters and investors. Nevertheless, other large British privatization issues followed British Telecom—most notably, British Steel in 1988.

Euroequity privatization issues have been particularly popular with international portfolio investors, because most of the firms are very large, with excellent credit ratings and profitable quasi-government monopolies at the time of privatization. The British privatization model has been so successful that numerous others have followed.

One of the largest Euroequity issues was made by Deutsche Telecom A.G. It was privatized by an initial public offering of $13.3 billion in November 1996.

Even government-owned firms in emerging capital markets have implemented privatization with the help of foreign tranches:

- Telefonos de Mexico, the giant Mexican telephone company, completed a $2 billion Euroequity issue in 1991. U.S.-based Southwestern Bell became a 10% shareholder, as did numerous other foreign institutional and individual investors. Telefonos de Mexico has a very liquid listing on the NYSE.
- One of the largest Euroequity offerings by a firm resident in a "Least Liquid" market was the 1993 sale of shares for $3.04 billion by YPF Sociedad Anónima, Argentina's state-owned oil company. About 75% of its shares were placed in tranches outside of Argentina, with 46% in the United States alone. Its underwriting syndicate represented a virtual who's who of the world's leading investment banks.

It appears that many of the privatized firms have performed well after being privatized. A recent study of privatization concluded that privatized firms showed strong performance improvements without reducing employment security. The firms in the study had been fully or partially privatized via public equity issues during the period from 1961 to 1990. After privatization, the firms increased real sales, raised capital investment levels, improved efficiency, and expanded their employment. With respect to financial performance, their profitability improved, debt levels were lowered, and dividend payments increased.[6]

Private Placement Under SEC Rule 144A

One type of directed issue with a long history as a source of both equity and debt is the private placement market. A *private placement* is the sale of a security to a small set of qualified institutional buyers. The investors are traditionally insurance companies and investment companies. Since the securities are not registered for sale to the public, investors have typically followed a "buy and hold" policy. In the case of debt, terms are often custom designed on a negotiated basis. Private placement markets now exist in most countries.

As noted in Exhibit 12.3, in April 1990 the SEC approved Rule 144A. It permits qualified institutional buyers to trade privately placed securities without the previous holding period restrictions and without requiring SEC registration.

A *qualified institutional buyer* (QIB) is an entity (except a bank or a savings and loan) that owns and invests on a discretionary basis $100 million in securities of non-affiliates. Banks and savings and loans must meet this test but also must have a minimum net worth of $25 million. The SEC has estimated that about 4,000 QIBs exist, mainly investment advisors, investment companies, insurance companies, pension funds, and charitable institutions.

Simultaneously, the SEC modified its Regulation S to permit foreign issuers to tap the U.S. private placement market through an SEC Rule 144A issue, also without SEC registration. A screen-based automated trading system called PORTAL was established by the National Association of Securities Dealers (NASD) to support the distribution of primary issues and to create a liquid secondary market for these unregistered private placements.

Since SEC registration has been identified as the main barrier to foreign firms wishing to raise funds in the United States, SEC Rule 144A placements are proving attractive to foreign issuers of both equity and debt securities. Atlas Copco, the Swedish multinational engineering firm, was the first foreign firm to take advantage of SEC Rule 144A. It raised $49 million in the United States through an ADR equity placement as part of its larger $214 million Euroequity issue in 1990. Since then, several billion dollars a year have been raised by foreign issuers with private equity placements in the United States. However, it does not appear that such placements have a favorable effect on either liquidity or stock price.[7]

6. Megginson, William L., Robert C. Nash, and Mathias Ian Randenborgh, "The Financial and Operating Performance of Newly Privatized Firms: An International Empirical Analysis," *Journal of Finance*, June 1994, pp. 403–452.

7. Boubakri, Narjess, and Jean Claude Cosset, "The Financial and Operating Performance of Newly Privatized Firms: Evidence from Developing Countries," *The Journal of Finance*, June 1998, Volume 53, No. 3, pp. 1081–1110. This same conclusion was reached in the slightly more recent study by Miller 1999, op. cit.

Private Equity Funds

Many mature family-owned firms resident in emerging markets are unlikely to qualify for a global cost and availability of capital even if they follow the strategy suggested in this chapter. Although they might be consistently profitable and growing, they are still too small, too invisible to foreign investors, lacking in managerial depth, and unable to fund the up-front costs of a globalization strategy. For these firms, private equity funds may be a solution.

Private equity funds are usually limited partnerships of institutional and wealthy individual investors that raise their capital in the most liquid capital markets, especially the United States. They then invest the private equity fund in mature, family-owned firms located in emerging markets. The investment objective is to help these firms to restructure and modernize in order to face increasing competition and the growth of new technologies. Sometimes they fund family-owned firms that need to be connected with foreign MNEs, joint venture partners, or strategic alliances. They also can fund privatized government-owned firms.

Private equity funds differ from traditional venture capital funds. The latter usually operate mainly in highly developed countries. They typically invest in high technology start-ups with the goal of exiting the investment with an initial public offering (IPO) placed in those same highly liquid markets. Very little venture capital is available in emerging markets, partly because it would be difficult to exit with an IPO in an illiquid market. The same exiting problem faces the private equity funds, but they appear to have a longer time horizon, they invest in already mature and profitable companies, and they are content with growing companies through better management and mergers with other firms.

The Exxel Group is an example of a successful private equity fund. Its founder and CEO, Juan Navarro, has been called the "buyout king of Argentina." From 1991 to 2002, the firm invested $4.8 billion in 74 companies in Argentina. In line with its mission, the company has continued to pursue full operational control over all acquisitions in order to implement its superior managerial, industrial, and market knowledge to create shareholder value. As illustrated in Global Finance Perspective 12.2, however, even an innovative firm such as the Exxel Group cannot avoid an economic crisis like that suffered by Argentina from 2001 to 2002.

Global Finance Perspective 12.2

Private Equity in Argentina and the Argentine Crisis

It used to be relatively easy for private equity investors to cash out of their Latin American holdings through the public equity markets. But last year [2001], not a single Latin America–based company conducted an initial public offering and only a handful of companies undertook secondary listings. Exxel Group managed to secure a multinational buyer for its stake in the Argentine Supermercados Norte supermarket chain. And in April, when Exxel was struggling to meet interest payments on some $688 million in debt, it executed an impressive exit when it sold its remaining 49% stake in Norte to the French supermarket company Carrefour for $263 million. Selling an Argentine company last year in itself was a notable feat and Exxel's divestment wins *LatinFinance's* private equity deal of the year for its innovative structure.

Source: Adapted from "Cash out to Carrefour," *LatinFinance*, February 2002, anonymous.

Strategic Alliances

Strategic alliances are normally formed by firms that expect to gain synergies from one or more of the following joint efforts. They might share the cost of developing technology or pursue complementary marketing activities. They might gain economies of scale or scope or a variety of other commercial advantages. However, one synergy that may sometimes be overlooked is the possibility for a financially strong firm to help a financially weak firm to lower its cost of capital by providing attractively priced equity or debt financing. This was illustrated in the mini-case on the strategic alliance between Bang & Olufsen and Philips in Chapter 11.

SUMMARY

- Designing a capital sourcing strategy requires management to agree upon a long-run financial objective.
- The firm must then choose among the various alternative paths to get there, including where to cross-list its shares and where and in what form to issue new equity. Elements to consider are:
  - Improve the liquidity of its existing shares by using depositary receipts.
  - Increase its share price by overcoming mis-pricing by a segmented, illiquid home capital market.
  - Support a new equity issue sold in a foreign market.
  - Establish a secondary market for shares used in acquisitions.
  - Increase the firm's visibility and political acceptance to its customers, suppliers, creditors, and host governments.
  - Create a secondary market for shares that will be used to compensate local management and employees in foreign affiliates.
  - If it is to support a new equity issue or to establish a market for share swaps, the target market should also be the listing market.
  - If it is to increase the firm's commercial and political visibility or to compensate local management and employees, it should be the market in which the firm has significant operations.
  - If it is to improve the liquidity of a firm's shares, the major liquid stock markets are New York, London, Tokyo, Frankfurt, and Euronext.
  - Increased commitment to full disclosure.
  - A continuing investor relations program.
  - A firm can lower its cost of capital and increase its liquidity by selling its shares to foreign investors in a variety of forms.
  - Sale of a directed share issue to investors in one particular foreign equity market.
  - Sale of a Euroequity share issue to foreign investors simultaneously in more than one market, including both foreign and domestic markets.
  - Sale of shares to a foreign firm as part of a strategic alliance.

QUESTIONS

1. **Designing a strategy to source equity globally.** Exhibit 12.1 illustrates alternative paths to globalizing the cost and availability of capital. Identify the specific steps in chronological order in Exhibit 12.1 that were taken by Novo Industri (Chapter 11) to gain an international cost and availability of capital.
2. **Depositary receipts—definitions.** Define the following terms:
   a. ADRs
   b. GRSs
   c. Sponsored depositary receipts
   d. Unsponsored depositary receipts
3. **ADRs.** Distinguish between the three levels of commitment for ADRs traded in the United States.
4. **Foreign equity listing and issuance.** Give five reasons why a firm might cross-list and sell its shares on a very liquid stock exchange.
5. **Cross-listing abroad.** What are the main reasons causing U.S. firms to cross-list abroad?
6. **Implementing a strategy to source equity globally.** Using the stock exchange characteristics shown in Exhibit 12.5, design a chronological strategy to source equity globally for a MNE located in the following home markets:
   a. Mexico
   b. Portugal
   c. Hong Kong
   d. Chile
7. **Barriers to cross-listing.** What are the main barriers to cross-listing abroad?
8. **Alternative instruments.** What are five alternative instruments that can be used to source equity in global markets?
9. **Directed public share issue.**
   a. Define "directed public share issue."
   b. Why did Novo choose to make a $61 million directed public share issue in the United States in 1981?
10. **Euroequity public share issue.** Define "euroequity public share issue."
11. **Private placement under SEC Rule 144A.**
    a. What is SEC Rule 144A?
    b. Why might a foreign firm choose to sell its equity in the United States under SEC Rule 144A?
12. **Private equity funds.**
    a. What is a private equity fund?
    b. How do they differ from traditional venture capital firms?
    c. How do private equity funds raise their own capital, and how does this action give them a competitive advantage over local banks and investment funds?
13. **Strategic alliances.**
    a. Why do firms form international strategic alliances?
    b. Why can an international strategic alliance lower a firm's cost of capital?

PROBLEMS

In Chapter 11, we described how Novo Industri A/S (Novo) increased its stock price sevenfold during the April 1980 to July 1981 period. Its strategy was to be discovered by international portfolio investors and sell equity and list in both London and New York. The next six problems ask you to determine just how the dramatic increase in Novo's stock price theoretically should have lowered Novo's cost of capital after the new securities issues in London and New York.

Prior to April 1980, Novo's stock price was determined by the norms of the Danish stock market since nearly all shareholders were Danish, mostly institutional investors. Novo's stock price hovered around Dkr200 with a price-earnings ratio of 5, typical of the Danish stock market. After April 1980 Novo's stock price was increasingly determined by the norms of international portfolio investors, especially from the United States and United Kingdom. By the time that Novo sold its \$61 million equity issue and listed on the New York Stock Exchange, its stock price had increased to Dkr1400 and its P/E ratio to 16, typical of the U.S. and U.K. stock markets.

Problems 1 through 6 relate to Novo. Problems 7 through 10 relate to HangSung, a hypothetical Korean *chaebol* (conglomerate), that also experienced a domestic cost of capital that became an international cost of capital after issuing equity abroad.

1. **Novo's cost of equity prior to April 1980.** Assuming that the following data apply, calculate Novo's cost of equity:

Danish k_{rf} = 10.0%	Denmark purposely maintained high real rates of interest to protect its exchange rate.
Novo's β = 1.0	The Danish market did not distinguish between growth stocks and other industrial stocks; their share prices all moved together.
Danish k_m = 18.0%	The required return on stocks was quite high due to competition with high real interest rates and lack of international diversification by Danish investors caused by Danish legal restrictions.

2. **Novo's WACC prior to April 1980.** Assume that the following data apply:

k_d = 12.0%	Novo's cost of debt
k_e = 18.0%	Novo's cost of equity
E/V = 30%	Novo's equity-to-capital ratio
D/V = 70%	Novo's debt-to-capital ratio
V = 100%	Total market value of Novo's securities, $D + E$
t = 40%	Novo's effective tax rate

   a. What was Novo's weighted average cost of capital?
   b. How did this affect its capital budget?

3. **Novo's cost of equity after April 1981.** Assuming the following data now apply, calculate Novo's cost of equity:

   International k_{rf} = 8.0%

   International β_{Novo} = 0.8

   International k_m = 12.0%

   International portfolio investors dominated the trading activity in Novo's stock. Most of the volume was executed on the New York Stock Exchange. Therefore we use international norms rather than Danish norms.

4. **Novo's WACC after July 1981.** Assume that the following data apply:

k_d = 10.0%	Novo's new cost of debt due to a lower debt ratio
k_e = 11.2%	Novo's cost of equity
E/V = 50%	Novo's equity-to-capital ratio; international investors required a lowered debt ratio than the previous 70%
D/V = 50%	Novo's new lower debt-to-capital ratio
V = 100%	Total market value of Novo's securities, $D + E$
t = 40%	Novo's effective tax rate

   a. What was Novo's weighted average cost of capital?
   b. How did this affect its capital budget?

5. **Novo's cost of equity in 2003.** Answer the following question, assuming the following:

International k_{rf} = 4.0%	Risk-free interest rates had fallen due to the slow economic growth in much of the world.
International β_{Novo} = 0.8	
International k_m = 8.0%	The poor performance of stocks worldwide during the past three years had reduced expected returns.

   What was Novo's cost of equity?

6. **Novo's WACC in early 2003.** Assume that the following data apply:

$k_d = 6.0\%$	Novo's new cost of debt due to overall lower interest rates
$k_e = 7.2\%$	Novo's cost of equity
$E/V = 50\%$	Novo's equity-to-capital ratio
$D/V = 50\%$	Novo's debt-to-capital ratio
$V = 100\%$	Total market value of Novo's securities, $D + E$
$t = 40\%$	Novo's effective tax rate

   a. What was Novo's weighted average cost of capital?
   b. How did this affect its capital budget?

Emerging market conglomerate: HangSung, a Korean *chaebol*. Use the following data to answer problems 7 through 10.

7. **HangSung before equity issue abroad.** Assume the following data applied to HangSung before it raised equity abroad. What was HangSung's cost of equity?

   Korean $k_{rf} = 10.0\%$

   HangSung's $\beta = 1.0$

   Korean $k_m = 14.0\%$

8. **HangSung's WACC before equity issue abroad.** Assume the following data applied to HangSung before it raised equity abroad. What was HangSung's WACC?

$k_d = 12.0\%$	HangSung's cost of debt
$k_e = 14.0\%$	HangSung's cost of equity
$E/V = 20\%$	HangSung's equity-to-capital ratio; Korean *chaebols* have relatively high debt and low equity ratios by international standards
$D/V = 80\%$	HangSung's debt-to-capital ratio
$V = 100\%$	Total market value of HangSung's securities, $D + E$
$t = 30\%$	HangSung's effective tax rate

9. **HangSung after equity issue abroad in 2003.** Assume the following data applied to HangSung after it raised equity abroad. What was HangSung's cost of equity?

   International $k_{rf} = 4.0\%$

   International $\beta_{HangSung} = 0.7$

   International $k_m = 8.0\%$

10. **HangSung after equity issue abroad in 2003.** Assume the following data applied to HangSung after it raised equity abroad.

$k_d = 6.0\%$	HangSung's new cost of debt was lower to due to overall lower interest rates, but also because it had lowered its very high debt ratio
$k_e = 6.8\%$	HangSung's cost of equity
$E/V = 40\%$	HangSung's equity-to-capital ratio
$D/V = 60\%$	HangSung's debt-to-capital ratio
$V = 100\%$	Total market value of HangSung's securities, $D + E$
$t = 30\%$	HangSung's effective tax rate

   a. What was HangSung's WACC in 2003?
   b. How did this affect its capital budget?

INTERNET EXERCISES

1. **American Depositary Receipts.** American Depositary Receipts (ADRs) now make up more than 10% of all equity trading on U.S. stock exchanges. As more companies based outside of the United States list on U.S. markets, the need to understand the principal forces that drive ADR values increases with each trading day. Beginning with Deutsche Morgan Grenfell's detailed description of the ADR process and current ADR trading activity:

   a. Prepare a briefing for senior management in your firm encouraging them to consider internationally diversifying the firm's liquid asset portfolio with ADRs.

b. Identify whether the ADR program level (I, II, III, 144A) has any significance to which securities you believe the firm should consider.

Deutsche Morgan Grenfell	http://www.adr-dmg.com/adr-dmg/welcome.html
Bank of New York	http://www.bankofny.com
JP Morgan's ADR Center	http://adr.com
Stock City	http://www.stockcity.com

2. **Institutional ownership of ADRs.** Use the JP Morgan ADR center web site to find the largest individual owners of major ADRs traded in New York. Include Nokia, Telefonos de Mexico, Toyota, Siemens, and Philips in your search:

JP Morgan's ADR Center	http://adr.com

3. **Cost of capital calculator.** Ibbotson Associates of Chicago is one of the leading providers of quantitative estimates of the cost of capital across markets. Use the following web site—specifically, the *Cost of Capital Center*—to prepare an overview of the major theoretical approaches and the numerical estimates they yield for cross-border costs of capital:

Ibbotson Associates	http://www.ibbotson.com

SELECTED READINGS

Boutchkova, Maria K., and William L. Megginson, "Privatization and the Rise of Global Capital Markets," *Financial Management*, Winter 2000, Volume 29, Issue 4, pp. 31–76.

Foerster, Stephen R., and G. Andrew Karolyi, "The Effects of Market Segmentation and Investor Recognition on Asset Prices: Evidence from Foreign Stock Listing in the United States," *The Journal of Finance*, June 1999, Volume 54, No. 3, pp. 981–1013.

Saudagaran, Shahrokh M., and Gary C. Biddle, "Foreign Listing Location: A Study of MNEs and Stock Exchanges in Eight Countries," *Journal of International Business Studies*, Second Quarter 1995, Volume 26, No. 2, pp. 319–341.

Sundaram, Anant K., and Dennis E. Logue, "Valuation Effects of Foreign Company Listings on U.S. Exchanges," *Journal of International Business Studies*, First Quarter 1996, Volume 27, No. 1, pp. 67–88.

Wu, Congsheng, and Chuck C.Y. Kwok, "Why Do U.S. Firms Choose Global Equity Offerings?", *Financial Management*, Summer 2002, Volume 31, Issue 2, pp. 47-65.

apter 13

Financial Structure and International Debt

WE MUST MODIFY THE DOMESTIC THEORY OF OPTIMAL FINANCIAL STRUCTURE CONSIDERABLY TO encompass the multinational firm. This chapter starts with a brief review of the theory of optimal financial structure. We follow this with an analysis of the complexities involved in finding an optimal financial structure for a MNE. The next section highlights the unique complexities that influence the optimal financial structure for foreign subsidiaries of MNEs. The chapter continues with an analysis of the alternative debt instruments that a MNE can utilize to achieve an optimal financial structure. We follow this with an analysis of how foreign subsidiaries are financed. Then we present a description of the Eurocurrency markets. The chapter concludes with an examination of how MNEs can use a project finance structure to fund large and unique international projects.

Optimal Financial Structure

After many years of debate, most finance theorists are now in agreement about whether an optimal financial structure exists for a firm, and if so, how it can be determined. The great debate between the so-called traditionalists and the Modigliani and Miller school of thought has apparently ended in a compromise. When taxes and bankruptcy costs are considered, a firm has an optimal financial structure determined by that particular mix of debt and equity that minimizes the firm's cost of capital for a given level of business risk. If the business risk of new projects differs from the risk of existing projects, the optimal mix of debt and equity would change to recognize tradeoffs between business and financial risks.

Exhibit 13.1 illustrates how the cost of capital varies with the amount of debt employed. As the debt ratio (defined as total debt divided by total assets at market values) increases, the overall cost of capital (k_{WACC}) decreases because of the heavier weight of low-cost debt $[k_d(1 - t)]$ compared to high-cost equity (k_e). The low cost of debt is, of course, due to the tax deductibility of interest shown by the term $(1 - t)$.

Partly offsetting the favorable effect of more debt is an increase in the cost of equity (k_e), because investors perceive greater financial risk. Nevertheless, the overall weighted average after-tax cost of capital (k_{WACC}) continues to decline as the debt ratio increases, until financial risk becomes so serious that investors and management alike perceive a real danger of insolvency. This result causes a sharp increase in the cost of new debt and equity, thus increasing the weighted average cost of capital. The

Exhibit 13.1 The Cost of Capital and Financial Structure

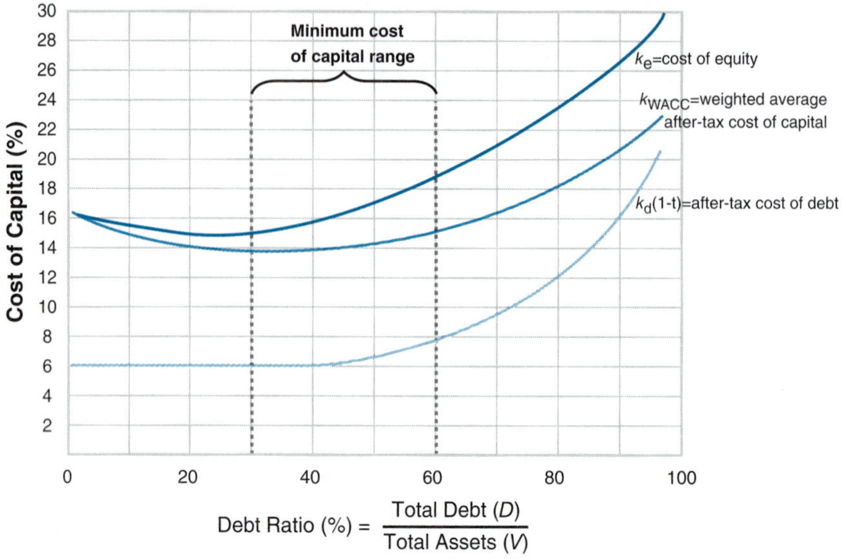

low point on the resulting U-shaped cost of capital curve, which is at 14% in Exhibit 13.1, defines the debt ratio range in which the cost of capital is minimized.

Most theorists believe that the low point is actually a rather broad flat area encompassing a wide range of debt ratios—30% to 60% in Exhibit 13.1—where little difference exists in the cost of capital. They also believe that, at least in the United States, the range of the flat area and the location of a particular firm's debt ratio within that range are determined by such variables as 1) the industry in which it competes, 2) volatility of its sales and operating income, and 3) the collateral value of its assets.

Optimal Financial Structure and the MNE

The domestic theory of optimal financial structures needs to be modified by four more variables in order to accommodate the case of the MNE. These variables, in order of appearance, are 1) availability of capital, 2) diversification of cash flows, 3) foreign exchange risk, and 4) the expectations of international portfolio investors.

Availability of Capital

Chapter 11 demonstrated that access to capital in global markets allows a MNE to lower its cost of equity and debt compared with most domestic firms. It also permits a MNE to maintain its desired debt ratio, even when significant amounts of new funds must be raised. In other words, a multinational firm's marginal cost of capital is constant for considerable ranges of its capital budget. This statement is not true for most small domestic firms, because they do not have access to the national equity or debt markets. They must either rely on internally generated funds or borrow for the short and medium term from commercial banks.

Multinational firms located in countries that have illiquid capital markets are in almost the same situation as small domestic firms, unless they have gained a global cost and availability of capital. They must rely on internally generated funds and bank borrowing. If they need to raise significant amounts of new funds to finance growth opportunities, they may need to borrow more than would be optimal from the viewpoint of minimizing their cost of capital. This is equivalent to saying that their marginal cost of capital is increasing at higher budget levels.

Risk Reduction Through International Diversification of Cash Flows

As explained in Chapter 11, the theoretical possibility exists that multinational firms are in a better position than domestic firms to support higher debt ratios because their cash flows are diversified internationally. The probability of a firm's covering fixed charges under varying conditions in product, financial, and foreign exchange markets should increase if the variability of its cash flows is minimized.

By diversifying cash flows internationally, the MNE might be able to achieve the same kind of reduction in cash flow variability as portfolio investors receive from diversifying their security holdings internationally. Returns are not perfectly correlated between countries.

In contrast, a domestic German firm would not enjoy the benefit of cash flow international diversification but would have to rely entirely on its own net cash inflow from domestic operations. Perceived financial risk for the German firm would be greater than for a multinational firm, because the variability of its German domestic cash flows could not be offset by positive cash flows elsewhere in the world.

As introduced in Chapter 11, the diversification argument has been challenged by empirical research findings that MNEs in the United States actually have lower debt ratios than their domestic counterparts. The agency costs of debt were higher for the MNEs, as were political risks, foreign exchange risks, and asymmetric information.

Foreign Exchange Risk and the Cost of Debt

When a firm issues foreign currency–denominated debt, its effective cost equals the after-tax cost of repaying the principal and interest in terms of the firm's own currency. This amount includes the nominal cost of principal and interest in foreign currency terms, adjusted for any foreign exchange gains or losses.

For example, if a U.S.-based firm borrows Sfr1,500,000 for one year at 5.00% interest, and during the year the Swiss franc appreciates from an initial rate of Sfr1.5000/\$ to Sfr1.4400/\$, what is the dollar cost of this debt ($k_d^{\$}$)? The dollar proceeds of the initial borrowing are calculated at the current spot rate of Sfr1.5000/\$:

$$\frac{\text{Sfr}1{,}500{,}000}{\text{Sfr}1.5000\,/\,\$} = \$1{,}000{,}000$$

At the end of one year, the U.S.-based firm is responsible for repaying the Sfr1,500,000 principal plus 5.00% interest, or a total of Sfr1,575,000. This repayment, however, must be made at an ending spot rate of Sfr1.4400/$:

$$\frac{\text{Sfr}1{,}500{,}000 \times 1.05}{\text{Sfr}1.4400/\$} = \$1{,}093{,}750$$

The actual dollar cost of the loan's repayment is not the nominal 5.00% paid in Swiss franc interest, but 9.375%:

$$\frac{\$1{,}093{,}750}{\$1{,}000{,}000} = 1.09375$$

The dollar cost is higher than expected due to appreciation of the Swiss franc against the U.S. dollar.

This total home-currency cost is actually the result of the combined percentage cost of debt and percentage change in the foreign currency's value. We can find the total cost of borrowing Swiss francs by a U.S. dollar–based firm, $k_d^{\$}$, by multiplying one plus the Swiss franc interest expense, k_d^{Sfr}, by one plus the percentage change in the Sfr/$ exchange rate, s:

$$k_d^{\$} = \left[(1) \times (1 + s)\right] - 1$$

where $k_d^{\text{Sfr}} = 5.00\%$ and $s = 4.1667\%$. The percentage change in the value of the Swiss franc versus the U.S. dollar, when the home currency is the U.S. dollar is:

$$\frac{S_1 - S_2}{S_2} \times 100 = \frac{\text{Sfr}1.5000/\$ - \text{Sfr}1.4400/\$}{\text{Sfr}1.4400/\$} \times 100 = +\ 4.1667\%$$

The total expense, combining the nominal interest rate and the percentage change in the exchange rate, is:

$$k_d^{\$} = \left[(1 + 0.0500) \times (1 + 0.041667)\right] - 1 = 0.09375 \approx 9.375\%$$

The total percentage cost of capital is 9.375%, not simply the foreign currency interest payment of 5%. The after-tax cost of this Swiss franc denominated debt, when the U.S. income tax rate is 34%, is:

$$k_d^{\$}(1 - t) = 9.375\% \times 0.66 = 6.1875\%$$

The firm would report the added 4.1667% cost of this debt in terms of U.S. dollars as a foreign exchange transaction loss, and it would be deductible for tax purposes.

Borrowing with 20/20 hindsight. MNEs have discovered that borrowing foreign currency–denominated bonds on a long-term basis creates considerable exposure to transaction gains or losses. Exhibit 13.2 compares a sample of foreign currency–denominated bonds issued by firms in a wide variety of countries during 1989–1990 as shown in columns (1) and (2). Column (3) shows the firm's expected cost in home currency terms at the time of issuance. Column (4) shows that about 10 years later—June 1, 1999—the realized cost was different from the expected cost (again, in home currency terms). Column (5) shows the difference between expected and realized costs, which were of course due to changes in exchange rates. Note that foreign exchange exposure worked both favorably (negative differences) and unfavorably (positive differences) for the sample firms. And note specifically the disastrous impact of Turkey's currency devaluation on its cost of funds in home currency terms: +73.86%!

Expectations of International Portfolio Investors

The last two chapters highlighted that the key to gaining a global cost and availability of capital is attracting and retaining international portfolio investors. Their expectations for a firm's debt ratio and overall financial structures are based on global norms that have developed over the past 30 years. Because a large proportion of international portfolio investors are based in the most liquid and unsegmented capital markets, such as the United States and the United Kingdom, their expectations tend to predominate and override individual national norms. Therefore, regardless of other factors, if a firm wants to raise capital in global markets, it must adopt global norms that are close

Exhibit 13.2 Costs of Borrowing in Foreign Currency–Denominated Bonds (percentage)

Issuer	(1) Home Country	(2) Date of Issue	(3) Cost of Funds Time of Issue (%)	(4) Cost of Funds as of 6/1/99 (%)	(5) Cost Differences (%)
Deutsche Bank Finance	Germany	5/24/89	9.59	7.24	–2.35
Republic of Austria	Austria	7/10/89	8.46	6.73	–1.73
Den Danske Bank	Denmark	2/16/89	9.93	8.46	–1.47
Electricite de France	France	4/18/89	9.50	8.22	–1.28
Japan Finance Corp.	Japan	4/4/89	9.63	8.70	–0.93
British Telecom Finance	Britain	7/13/89	8.46	8.33	–0.13
Alcan Aluminum Ltd.	Canada	7/20/89	9.89	11.38	+1.49
Finnish Export Credit Ltd.	Finland	2/1/89	9.68	12.16	+2.48
Banca Commerciale Italiana	Italy	3/10/89	9.37	12.07	+2.70
Government of Malaysia	Malaysia	9/19/90	10.29	13.10	+2.81
Kingdom of Thailand	Thailand	8/1/89	8.70	11.87	+3.17
Republic of Turkey	Turkey	8/30/89	10.25	84.11	+73.86

Source: Steven M. Dawson, based on calculation methods in "Eurobond Currency Selection: Hindsight," *Financial Executive*, November 1993, p. 73. "Cost of Funds: Time of Issue" is the expected home currency cost given coupon, new issue price, and maturity. "Cost of Funds as of 6/1/99" is cost in home country currency given the U.S. bank transfer exchange rate at time of each interest or principal payment. Payments after June 1, 1999, are assumed made at the June 1 exchange rate.

to the U.S. and U.K. norms. Debt ratios up to 60% appear to be acceptable. Any higher debt ratio is more difficult to sell to international portfolio investors.

Financial Structure of Foreign Subsidiaries

If we accept the theory that minimizing the cost of capital for a given level of business risk and capital budget is an objective that should be implemented from the perspective of the consolidated MNE, then the financial structure of each subsidiary is relevant only to the extent that it affects this overall goal. In other words, an individual subsidiary does not really have an independent cost of capital. Therefore its financial structure should not be based on an objective of minimizing it.

Financial structure norms for firms vary widely from one country to another but cluster for firms domiciled in the same country. This statement is the conclusion of a long line of empirical studies that have investigated the question from 1969 to the present. Most of these international studies concluded that country-specific environmental variables are key determinants of debt ratios. Among these variables are historical development, taxation, corporate governance, bank influence, existence of a viable corporate bond market, attitude toward risk, government regulation, availability of capital, and agency costs.

Many other institutional differences also influence debt ratios in national capital markets, but firms trying to attract international portfolio investors must pay attention to the debt ratio norms those investors expect. Since many international portfolio investors are influenced by the debt ratios that exist in the Anglo-American markets, there is a trend toward more global conformity. MNEs and other large firms dependent on attracting international portfolio investors are beginning to adopt similar debt ratio standards, even if domestic firms continue to use national standards. Global Finance Perspective 13.1 illustrates one of the recent ways in which equity is injected into subsidiaries, the *equity carve-out*.

Local Norms and the Financial Structure of Local Subsidiaries

Within the constraint of minimizing its consolidated worldwide cost of capital, should a MNE take differing country debt ratio norms into consideration when determining its desired debt ratio for foreign subsidiaries? For definition purposes, the debt considered here should be only that borrowed from sources outside the MNE. This debt would include local and foreign currency loans as well as Eurocurrency loans. The reason for this definition is that parent loans to foreign subsidiaries are often regarded as equivalent to equity investment both by host countries and by investing firms. A parent loan is usually subordinated to other debt and does not create the same threat of insolvency as an external loan. Furthermore, the choice of debt or equity investment is often arbitrary and subject to negotiation between host country and parent firm.

Main advantages of localization. The main advantages of a finance structure for foreign subsidiaries that conforms to local debt norms are as follows:

- A localized financial structure reduces criticism of foreign subsidiaries that have been operating with too high a proportion of debt (judged by local standards), often resulting in the accusation that they are not contributing a fair share of risk capital to the host country. At the other end of the spectrum, a localized financial structure would improve the image of foreign

Global Finance Perspective 13.1

Equity Carve-Outs

The sale of a minority equity interest in a subsidiary, typically 20% or less, is termed an *equity carve-out*. The purpose of equity carve-outs is to raise equity capital for subsidiary operations without risking loss of control. The popular storyline on equity carve-outs has been that firms could increase their share price and their equity capital base without sacrificing control. Evidence from a recent study, however, indicates that this is not the case.

A recent study by McKinsey of 200 major carve-outs in Europe and the United States for the 1990–2001 period found that only 10% of carve-outs raised the parent's share price by more than 12%. And, to make matters worse, in the two years following the initial public offering of subsidiary shares most carve-outs actually destroyed shareholder value. There was, however, one important exception: when the long-term path of the carve-out was to create a fully independent company—a spin-off—the carve-outs significantly outperformed the S&P 500 company returns.

The study found that the long-term ownership of carve-outs demonstrated declining parent control. Five years following the carve-out, only 8% of carve-outs continued to exist as public companies clearly controlled by a parent with 50% or more control (an additional 8% were controlled by parents holding less than 50%). An additional 31% of the carve-outs were held by parents with a stake of less than 25%, and third parties had either acquired or merged with 30% of the carve-outs.

Equity Carve-Outs Five Years Out	
Acquired or merged	39%
Repurchased by parent	11%
De-listed	3%
Independent (>75% public)	31%
Remained parent-controlled	16%
Total	100%

Although there are a variety of reasons for the relative failure of equity carve-outs to build sustainable shareholder value, the primary problem appears to be the basic conflict between giving the subsidiary adequate independence versus the potential competitive conflicts between the subsidiaries and parents (frequently finding themselves bidding against one another in the marketplace).

Source: Abstracted from "When Carve-Outs Make Sense," by André Annema, William C. Fallon, and Marc H. Goedhart, *The McKinsey Quarterly*, 2002, Number 2, and "Doing the Spin-Out," by Patricia Anslinger, Sheila Bonini, and Michael Patsalos-Fox, *The McKinsey Quarterly*, 2000, Number 1, pp. 98–105. Study covered 204 carve-outs with a value exceeding $50 million announced prior to January 1, 1998, for the January 1990 to May 2001 period.

subsidiaries that have been operating with too little debt and thus appear to be insensitive to local monetary policy.

- A localized financial structure helps management evaluate return on equity investment relative to local competitors in the same industry. In economies where interest rates are relatively high as an offset to inflation, the penalty paid reminds management of the need to consider price level changes when evaluating investment performance.
- In economies where interest rates are relatively high because of a scarcity of capital, and real resources are fully utilized (full employment), the penalty paid for borrowing local funds reminds management that unless return on assets is greater than the local price of capital—that is, negative leverage—they are probably misallocating scarce domestic real resources such

as land and labor. This factor may not appear relevant to management decisions, but it will certainly be considered by the host country in making decisions with respect to the firm.

Main disadvantages of localization. The main disadvantages of localized financial structures are as follows:

- A MNE is expected to have a comparative advantage over local firms in overcoming imperfections in national capital markets through better availability of capital and the ability to diversify risk. Why should it throw away these important competitive advantages to conform to local norms established in response to imperfect local capital markets, historical precedent, and institutional constraints that do not apply to the MNE?
- If each foreign subsidiary of a MNE localizes its financial structure, the resulting consolidated balance sheet might show a financial structure that does not conform to any particular country's norm. The debt ratio would be a simple weighted average of the corresponding ratio of each country in which the firm operates. This feature could increase perceived financial risk and thus the cost of capital for the parent, but only if two additional conditions are present:
    1. The consolidated debt ratio is pushed completely out of the discretionary range of acceptable debt ratios in the flat area of the cost of capital curve, shown previously in Exhibit 13.1.
    2. The MNE is unable to offset high debt in one foreign subsidiary with low debt in other foreign or domestic subsidiaries at the same cost. If the international Fisher effect is working, replacement of debt should be possible at an equal after-tax cost after adjusting for foreign exchange risk. On the other hand, if market imperfections preclude this type of replacement, the possibility exists that the overall cost of debt and thus the cost of capital could increase if the MNE attempts to conform to local norms.
- The debt ratio of a foreign subsidiary is only cosmetic, because lenders ultimately look to the parent and its consolidated worldwide cash flow as the source of repayment. In many cases, debt of subsidiaries must be guaranteed by the parent firm. Even if no formal guarantee exists, an implied guarantee usually exists, because almost no parent firm would dare to allow a subsidiary to default on a loan. If it did, repercussions would surely be felt with respect to the parent's own financial standing, with a resulting increase in its cost of capital.

Compromise solution. In our opinion, a compromise position is possible. Both multinational and domestic firms should try to minimize their overall weighted average cost of capital for a given level of business risk and capital budget, as finance theory suggests. However, if debt is available to a foreign subsidiary at equal cost to that which could be raised elsewhere, after adjusting for foreign exchange risk, then localizing the foreign subsidiary's financial structure should incur no cost penalty and yet would also enjoy the advantages listed above.

Financing the Foreign Subsidiary

In addition to choosing an appropriate financial structure for foreign subsidiaries, financial managers of multinational firms need to choose from among alternative sources of funds to finance foreign subsidiaries. Sources of funds available to foreign subsidiaries can be classified as *internal to the MNE* and *external to the MNE.*

Ideally, the choice among the sources of funds should minimize the cost of external funds after adjusting for foreign exchange risk. The firm should choose internal sources in order to minimize worldwide taxes and political risk. Simultaneously, the firm should ensure that managerial motivation in the foreign subsidiaries is geared toward minimizing the firm's consolidated worldwide cost of capital, rather than the foreign subsidiary's cost of capital. Needless to say, this task is difficult if not impossible, and the tendency is to place more emphasis on one variable at the expense of others.

Internal sources of funding. Exhibit 13.3 provides an overview of the internal sources of financing for foreign subsidiaries. In general, although the equity provided by the parent is required, it is frequently kept to legal and operational minimums to reduce risk of invested capital. Equity investment can take the form of either cash or real goods (machinery, equipment, inventory, and the like).

Debt is the preferable form of subsidiary financing, but access to local host country debt is limited in the early stages of a foreign subsidiary's life. Without a history of proven operational

Exhibit 13.3 Internal Financing of the Foreign Subsidiary

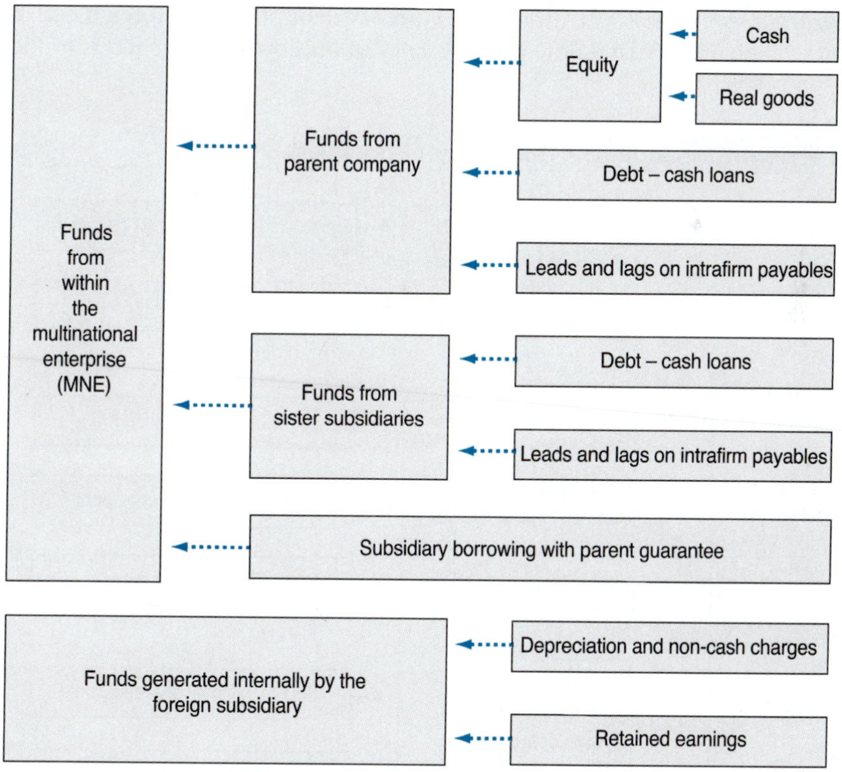

capability and debt service capability, the foreign subsidiary must acquire its debt from the parent company or sister subsidiaries (initially) and from unrelated parties with a parental guarantee (after operations have been initiated).

Once the operational and financial capabilities of the foreign subsidiary have been established, its ability to generate funds internally may become critical for the subsidiary's future growth. In special cases in which the subsidiary may be operating in a highly segmented market, such as an emerging market nation considered to be risky by the international investment and banking communities, the subsidiary's ability to generate its own funds from internal sources is important. These sources combine retained earnings, depreciation, and other noncash expenses. (A *noncash expense* is a deductible item such as depreciation, but the "expense" as a cash flow never leaves the firm.)

External sources of funding. Exhibit 13.4 provides an overview of the sources of foreign subsidiary financing external to the MNE. The sources are first broken down into three categories: debt from the parent's country, debt from countries outside the parent's country, and local equity. Debt acquired from external parties in the parent's country reflects the lenders' familiarity with and confidence in the parent company itself, although the parent is in this case not providing explicit guarantees for the repayment of the debt.

Local currency debt—that is, debt acquired in the host country of the foreign subsidiary's residence—is particularly valuable to the foreign subsidiary that has substantial local currency cash inflows arising from its business activities. Local currency debt provides a foreign exchange financial hedge, matching currency of inflow with currency of outflow. Gaining access to local curren-

Exhibit 13.4 External Financing of the Foreign Subsidiary

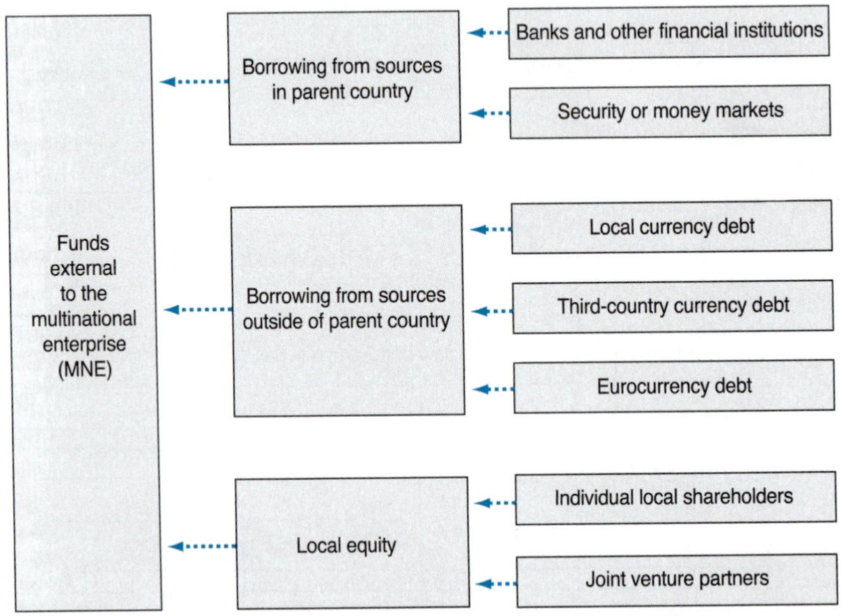

cy debt often takes time and patience by foreign subsidiary management in establishing operations and developing a local market credit profile. And in the case of many emerging markets, local currency debt is in short supply for all borrowers, local or foreign.

The Eurocurrency Markets

The Eurocurrency markets are one of the truly significant innovations in international finance of the past 50 years. These markets have provided a foundation for a series of innovations in both structure and choices in the financing of the MNE.

Eurocurrencies

Eurocurrencies are domestic currencies of one country on deposit in a second country. Eurodollar time deposit maturities range from call money and overnight funds to longer periods. Certificates of deposit are usually for three months or more and in million-dollar increments. A Eurodollar deposit is not a demand deposit; it is not created on the bank's books by writing loans against required fractional reserves, and it cannot be transferred by a check drawn on the bank having the deposit. Eurodollar deposits are transferred by wire or cable transfer of an underlying balance held in a correspondent bank located within the United States. A domestic analogy in most countries would be the transfer of deposits held in nonbank savings associations. These are transferred by having the association write its own check on a commercial bank.

Any convertible currency can exist in "Euro-" form. (Note that this use of the expression "Euro-" should not be confused with the new common European currency called the euro.) The Eurocurrency market includes Eurosterling (British pounds deposited outside the United Kingdom), Euroeuros (euros on deposit outside the euro zone), and Euroyen (Japanese yen deposited outside Japan), as well as Eurodollars. The exact size of the Eurocurrency market is difficult to measure, because it varies with daily decisions by depositors on where to hold readily transferable liquid funds, and particularly on whether to deposit dollars within or outside the United States.

Eurocurrency markets serve two valuable purposes: 1) Eurocurrency deposits are an efficient and convenient money market device for holding excess corporate liquidity and 2) the Eurocurrency market is a major source of short-term bank loans to finance corporate working capital needs, including the financing of imports and exports.

Banks in which Eurocurrencies are deposited are called Eurobanks. A *Eurobank* is a financial intermediary that simultaneously bids for time deposits and makes loans in a currency other than that of the currency of the country in which it is located. Eurobanks are major world banks that conduct a Eurocurrency business in addition to all other banking functions. Thus the Eurocurrency operation that qualifies a bank for the name Eurobank is in fact a department of a large commercial bank, and the name springs from the performance of this function.

History of the Eurodollar Market

The modern Eurodollar market was born shortly after World War II. Eastern European holders of dollars, including the various state trading banks of the Soviet Union, were afraid to deposit their dollar holdings in the United States because these deposits might be attached by U.S. residents with claims against communist governments. Therefore Eastern European holders deposited their dollars in Western Europe, particularly with two Soviet banks: the Moscow Narodny Bank in London and the Banque Commerciale pour l'Europe du Nord in Paris. These banks redeposited the funds in other Western banks, especially in London. Additional dollar deposits were received from various central banks in Western Europe, which elected to hold part of their dollar reserves in this form to obtain a higher yield. Commercial banks also placed their dollar balances in the market for the same reason as well as because specific maturities could be negotiated in the Eurodollar market. Additional dollars came to the market from European insurance companies with a large volume of U.S. business. Such companies found it financially advantageous to keep their dollar reserves in the higher-yielding Eurodollar market.

Although the basic causes of the growth of the Eurodollar market are economic efficiencies, a number of unique institutional events during the 1950s and 1960s helped its growth:

- In 1957, British monetary authorities responded to a weakening of the pound by imposing tight controls on U.K. bank lending in sterling to nonresidents of the United Kingdom. Encouraged by the Bank of England, U.K. banks turned to dollar lending as the only alternative that would allow them to maintain their leading position in world finance. For this they needed dollar deposits.
- Although New York was "home base" for the dollar and had a large domestic money and capital market, international trading in the dollar centered in London, because of that city's expertise in international monetary matters and its proximity in time and distance to major customers.
- Additional support for a European-based dollar market came from the balance of payments difficulties of the United States during the 1960s, which temporarily segmented the U.S. domestic capital market from that of the rest of the world.

Ultimately, however, the Eurocurrency market continues to thrive, because it is a large international money market relatively free of governmental regulation and interference.

International Debt Markets

The international debt markets offer the borrower a variety of different maturities, repayment structures, and currencies of denomination. The markets and their many different instruments vary by source of funding, pricing structure, maturity, and subordination or linkage to other debt and equity instruments. Exhibit 13.5 provides an overview of the three basic categories described in the following sections, along with their primary components as issued or traded in the international debt markets today. The three major sources of debt funding on the international markets are *international bank loans* and *syndicated credits*, the *Euronote market*, and the *international bond market*.

A MNE will normally need debt in a variety of maturities, payment structures, and currencies, therefore often using all three markets in addition to its traditional domestic funding base. The following sections describe the basic attributes of these markets and instruments, as well as their relative advantages and disadvantages for meeting the funding needs of the individual MNE.

Exhibit 13.5 International Debt Markets and Instruments

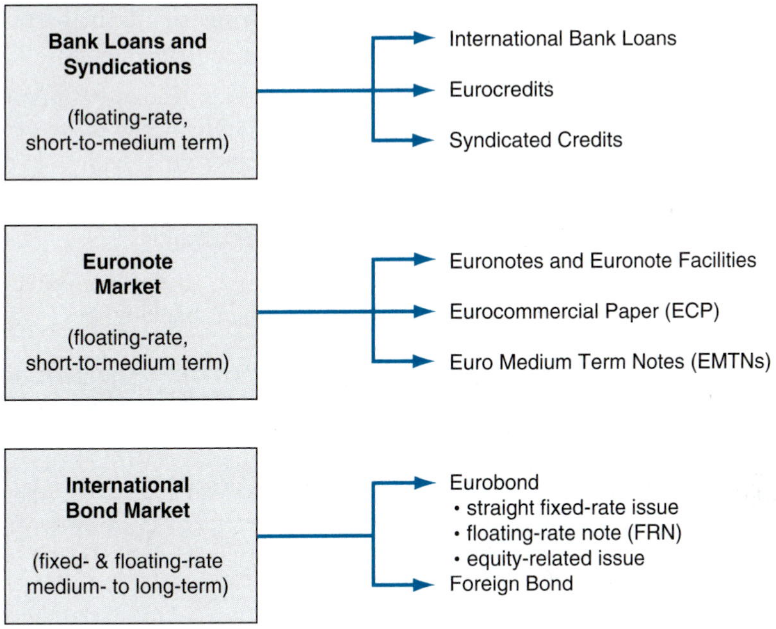

Bank Loans and Syndicated Credits

International bank loans. International bank loans have traditionally been sourced in the Eurocurrency markets. Eurodollar bank loans are also called "Eurodollar credits" or simply "Eurocredits." The latter title is broader, because it encompasses nondollar loans in the Eurocurrency market. The key factor attracting both depositors and borrowers to the Eurocurrency loan market is the narrow interest rate spread within that market. The difference between deposit and loan rates is often less than 1%.

Eurocredits. Eurocredits are bank loans to MNEs, sovereign governments, international institutions, and banks denominated in Eurocurrencies and extended by banks in countries other than the country in whose currency the loan is denominated. The basic borrowing interest rate for Eurodollar loans has long been tied to the *London Interbank Offered Rate* (LIBOR), which is the deposit rate applicable to interbank loans within London. Eurodollars are lent for both short- and medium-term maturities, with transactions for six months or less regarded as routine. Most Eurodollar loans are for a fixed term with no provision for early repayment.

Syndicated credits. The syndication of loans has enabled banks to spread the risk of very large loans among a number of banks. Syndication is particularly important because many large MNEs need credit in excess of a single bank's loan limit. A syndicated bank credit is arranged by a lead bank on behalf of its client. Before finalizing the loan agreement, the lead bank seeks the participation of a group of banks, with each participant providing a portion of the total funds needed. The lead manager bank will work with the borrower to determine the floating-rate base and spread over the base rate, maturity, and fee structure for managing the participating banks. The periodic expenses of the syndicated credit are composed of two elements:

1. The actual interest expense of the loan, normally stated as a spread in basis points over a variable-rate base such as LIBOR. The spread paid over LIBOR by the borrower is considered the risk premium, reflecting the general business and financial risk applicable to the borrower's repayment capability.
2. The commitment fees paid on any unused portions of the credit.

Global Finance Perspective 13.2 illustrates the pricing common to the syndicated loan markets, including interest expenses and the commitment and investment banking fees.

Global Finance Perspective 13.2

Pricing and Structure of a Syndicated Eurocredit

Borrower:	Irish Aerospace, GPA Airbus, GPA Fokker, GPA Jetprop, GPA Rolls
Amount:	US$1.25 billion; Revolving loans/guarantees/letters of credit
Terms:	8 years at 93.75 basis points over LIBOR, with a margin of 7/8% for GPA Airbus drawings
Arranger:	Citicorp Investment Bank
Lead Managers and Underwriters:	Citibank, Chase Investment Bank, Toronto-Dominion Bank, Citibank (Channel Islands) for a syndicate of Japanese leasing companies, Credit Suisse, Societe Generale (London), Amsterdam-Rotterdam Bank, Bank of Nova Scotia, Bank of Tokyo International, Daiwa Bank, IBJ, Irish Intercontinental

A typical syndicated loan of this type would have up-front fees totaling 1.5% of the principal. The fees would be divided between three groups: 1) the lead arranger bank(s), which organizes the loan and participants; 2) the lead managing and underwriting banks, which aid in the syndication of the loan; and 3) the participating banks, which actually provide the capital.

If the 1.5% total fee was subdivided equally among the three groups, the proceeds of the loan after expenses of issuance and arrangement are:

$$\$1,250,000,000 - \left[\left(0.005 + 0.005 + 0.005 \right) \times \$1,250,000,000 \right] = \$1,231,250,000.$$

The debt service payments over the 8-year period prior to principal repayment are LIBOR + 93.75 basis points; assuming an initial LIBOR rate of 9.00% (reset every six months for semi-annual debt service payments):

$$\left[\frac{0.0900 + 0.009375}{2} \right] \times \$1,250,000,000 = \$62,109,375.$$

The effective annual cost is thus:

$$\left[\frac{\$62,109,375}{\$1,231,250,000} \right] \times 2 \times 100 = 10.09\%.$$

The syndicated credit will cost Irish Aerospace 10.09% at the current LIBOR rate of 9.000%.

Euronote Market

The Euronote market is the collective term used to describe short- to medium-term debt instruments sourced in the Eurocurrency markets. Although a multitude of differentiated financial products exists, they can be divided into two major groups—*underwritten facilities* and *non-underwritten facilities.* Underwritten facilities are used for the sale of Euronotes in a number of different forms. Non-underwritten facilities are used for the sale and distribution of *Euro-commercial paper* (ECP) and *Euro medium-term notes* (EMTNs).

Euronote facilities. A major development in international money markets was the establishment of facilities for sales of short-term, negotiable, promissory notes—*euronotes.* Among the facilities for their issuance were revolving underwriting facilities (RUFs), note issuance facilities (NIFs), and standby note issuance facilities (SNIFs). These facilities were provided by international investment and commercial banks. The euronote was a substantially cheaper source of short-term funds than syndicated loans, because the notes were placed directly with the investor public, and the securitized and underwritten form allowed the ready establishment of liquid secondary markets. The banks received substantial fees initially for their underwriting and placement services.

Euro-Commercial paper (ECP). Euro-commercial paper (ECP), like commercial paper issued in domestic markets around the world, is a short-term debt obligation of a corporation or bank. Maturities are typically one, three, and six months. The paper is sold normally at a discount or occasionally with a stated coupon. Although the market is capable of supporting issues in any major currency, over 90% of issues outstanding are denominated in U.S. dollars.

Euro medium-term notes (EMTNs). The Euro medium-term note is the latest major entrant to the world's debt markets. The EMTN effectively bridges the maturity gap between ECP and the longer-term and less flexible international bond. Although many of the notes were initially underwritten, most EMTNs are now non-underwritten.

The rapid initial growth of the EMTN market followed directly on the heels of the same basic instrument that began in the U.S. domestic market when the U.S. Securities and Exchange Commission (SEC) instituted Rule #415, allowing companies to obtain *shelf registrations* for debt issues. What this meant was that once the registration was obtained, the corporation could issue notes on a continuous basis without having to obtain new registrations for each additional issue. This in turn allowed a firm to sell short- and medium-term notes through a much cheaper and more flexible issuance facility than ordinary bonds.

The EMTN's basic characteristics are similar to those of a bond, with principal, maturity, and coupon structures and rates being comparable. The EMTN's typical maturities range from as little as nine months to a maximum of 10 years. Coupons are typically paid semiannually and coupon rates are comparable to similar bond issues. The EMTN does, however, have three unique characteristics. First, the EMTN is a facility, allowing continuous issuance over a period of time, unlike a bond issue, which is essentially sold all at once. Second, because EMTNs are sold continuously, in order to make debt service (coupon redemption) manageable, coupons are paid on set calendar dates regardless of the date of issuance. Finally, EMTNs are issued in relatively small denominations, from $2 million to $5 million, making medium-term debt acquisition much more flexible than the large minimums customarily needed in the international bond markets.

International Bond Market

The international bond market sports a rich array of innovative instruments created by imaginative investment bankers, who are unfettered by the usual controls and regulations governing domestic capital markets. Indeed, the international bond market rivals the international banking market in terms of the quantity and cost of funds provided to international borrowers. All international bonds fall within two generic classifications, *Eurobonds* and *foreign bonds*. The distinction between categories is based on whether the borrower is a domestic or a foreign resident, and whether the issue is denominated in the local currency or a foreign currency.

Eurobonds. A *Eurobond* is underwritten by an international syndicate of banks and other securities firms, and is sold exclusively in countries other than the country in whose currency the issue is denominated. For example, a bond issued by a firm resident in the United States, denominated in U.S. dollars, but sold to investors in Europe and Japan (not to investors in the United States), would be a Eurobond.

Eurobonds are issued by multinational corporations, large domestic corporations, sovereign governments, governmental enterprises, and international institutions. They are offered simultaneously in a number of different national capital markets, but not in the capital market or to residents of the country in whose currency the bond is denominated. Almost all Eurobonds are in bearer form with call provisions and sinking funds.

The syndicate that offers a new issue of Eurobonds might be composed of underwriters from a number of countries, including European banks, foreign branches of U.S. banks, banks from offshore financial centers, investment and merchant banks, and nonbank securities firms.

- **The straight fixed-rate issue.** The straight fixed-rate issue is structured like most domestic bonds, with a fixed coupon, set maturity date, and full principal repayment upon final maturity. Coupons are normally paid annually, rather than semiannually, primarily because the bonds are bearer bonds and annual coupon redemption is more convenient for the holders.
- **The floating-rate note (FRN).** The floating-rate note (FRN) was the new instrument of fashion on the international bond scene in the early 1980s. The FRN normally pays a semiannual coupon which is determined using a variable-rate base. A typical coupon would be set at some fixed spread over LIBOR. This structure, like most variable-rate interest-bearing instruments, was designed to allow investors to shift more of the interest-rate risk of a financial investment to the borrower. It was a popular instrument in the early 1980s when world markets were characterized by relatively high and unpredictable interest rates. Although many FRNs have fixed maturities, a number of major issues since 1985 are perpetuities. The principal will never be repaid. Thus they provide many of the same financial functions as equity.
- **The equity-related issue.** The most recent major addition to the international bond markets is the equity-related issue. The equity-related international bond resembles the straight fixed-rate issue in practically all price and payment characteristics, with the added feature that it is convertible to stock prior to maturity at a specified price per share (or alternatively, number of shares per bond). The borrower is able to issue debt with lower coupon payments due to the added value of the equity conversion feature.

Foreign bonds. A *foreign bond* is underwritten by a syndicate composed of members from a single country, sold principally within that country, and denominated in the currency of that country. The issuer, however, is from another country. A bond issued by a firm resident in Sweden, denominated in dollars, and sold in the United States to U.S. investors by U.S. investment bankers, would be a foreign bond. Foreign bonds have nicknames: foreign bonds sold in the United States are "Yankee bonds," foreign bonds sold in Japan are "Samurai bonds," and foreign bonds sold in the United Kingdom are "Bulldogs."

Unique Characteristics of Eurobond Markets

Although the Eurobond market evolved at about the same time as the Eurodollar market, the two markets exist for different reasons, and each could exist independently of the other. The Eurobond market owes its existence to several unique factors, some of which have changed recently. Three of the original factors still of importance are absence of regulatory interference, less stringent disclosure practices, and favorable tax treatment.

Absence of regulatory interference. National governments often impose tight controls on foreign issuers of securities denominated in the local currency and sold within their national boundaries. However, governments in general have less stringent limitations for securities denominated in foreign currencies and sold within their markets to holders of those foreign currencies. In effect, Eurobond sales fall outside the regulatory domain of any single nation.

Less stringent disclosure. Disclosure requirements in the Eurobond market are much less stringent than those of the Securities and Exchange Commission (SEC) for sales within the United States. U.S. firms often find that the registration costs of a Eurobond offering are less than those of a domestic issue and that less time is needed to bring a new issue to market. Non-U.S. firms often prefer Eurodollar bonds over bonds sold within the United States, because they do not wish to undergo the costs, and disclosure, needed to register with the SEC. However, the SEC has relaxed disclosure requirements for certain private placements (Rule #144A), which has improved the attractiveness of the U.S. domestic bond and equity markets.

Favorable tax status. Eurobonds offer tax anonymity and flexibility. Interest paid on Eurobonds is generally not subject to an income withholding tax. As one might expect, Eurobond interest is not always reported to tax authorities. Eurobonds are usually issued in bearer form, meaning that the name and country of residence of the owner is not on the certificate. To receive interest, the bearer cuts an interest coupon from the bond and turns it in at a banking institution listed on the issue as a paying agent. European investors are accustomed to the privacy provided by bearer bonds and are very reluctant to purchase registered bonds, which require holders to reveal their names before they receive interest. Bearer bond status, of course, is also tied to tax avoidance.

Rating of Eurobonds and Other International Issues

Purchasers of Eurobonds do not rely only on bond-rating services or on detailed analyses of financial statements. The general reputation of the issuing corporation and its underwriters has been a major factor in obtaining favorable terms. For this reason, larger and better-known MNEs, state enterprises, and sovereign governments are able to obtain the lowest interest rates.

Firms whose names are better known to the general public, possibly because they manufacture consumer goods, are often believed to have an advantage over equally qualified firms whose products are less widely known.

Rating agencies, such as Moody's and Standard & Poor's (S&Ps), provide ratings for selected international bonds for a fee. Moody's ratings for international bonds imply the same creditworthiness as for domestic bonds of U.S. issuers. Moody's limits its evaluation to the issuer's ability to obtain the necessary currency to repay the issue according to the original terms of the bond. The agency excludes any assessment of risk to the investor caused by changing exchange rates. Exhibit 13.6 lists Moody's sovereign ceilings for foreign-currency ratings by country in August 1999.

Exhibit 13.6 Moody's Investors Service's Sovereign Ceilings for Foreign-Currency Ratings for Selected Countries (August 1999)

	Bonds and Notes		Bank Deposits			Bonds and Notes		Bank Deposits	
Country	L.T.	S.T.	L.T.	S.T.	Country	L.T.	S.T.	L.T.	S.T.
Argentina	Ba3	P-1	Aaa	P-1	Lithuania	Ba1	NP	Ba2	NP
Australia	Aa2	P-1	Aa2	P-1	Luxembourg	WR	WR	WR	WR
Brazil	B2	NP	Caa1	NP	Malaysia	Baa3	NP	Baa1	NP
Bulgaria	B2	NP	B3	NP	Mexico	Ba2*	NP	B1*	NP
Canada	Aa2	P-1	Aa2	P-1	New Zealand	Aa2	P-1	Aa2	P-1
Cayman Islands	Aa3	P-1	Aa3	P-1	Norway	Aaa	P-1	Aaa	P-1
Chile	Baa1	P-2	Baa1	P-2	Oman	Baa2	P-2	Baa2	P-2
China	A3	P-2	Baa2	P-3	Pakistan	Caa1	NP	Ca	NP
Colombia	Baa3	--	Ba1	NP	Peru	Ba3	NP	B1	NP
Croatia	Baa3	P-3	Ba1	NP	Philippines	Ba1	NP	Ba2	NP
Czech Republic	Baa1	P-2	Baa1	P-2	Poland	Baa3	--	Ba1	NP
Denmark	Aa1	P-1	Aa1	P-1	Romania	B3	NP	Caa1	NP
Euroland	Aaa	P-1	Aaa	P-1	Russia	B3	NP	Ca	NP
Greece	A2	P-2	A2	P-2	Singapore	Aa1	P-1	Aa1	P-1
Hong Kong	A3	P-1	A3	P-1	Slovakia	Ba1	NP	Ba2	NP
Hungary	Baa1	P-2	Baa1	P-2	Slovenia	A3	P-2	A3	P-2
Iceland	Aa3	P-1	Aa3	P-1	South Africa	Baa3	--	Ba1	NP
India	Ba2	NP	Ba3	NP	Sweden	Aa2	P-1	Aa2	P-1
Indonesia	B3	NP	Ca	NP	Switzerland	Aaa	P-1	Aaa	P-1
Israel	A3	P-2	A3	P-2	Taiwan	Aa3	P-1	Aa3	P-1
Japan	Aa1	P-1	Aa1	P-1	Thailand	Ba1	NP	B1	NP

Exhibit 13.6 (continued)

	Bonds and Notes		Bank Deposits			Bonds and Notes		Bank Deposits	
Country	L.T.	S.T.	L.T.	S.T.	Country	L.T.	S.T.	L.T.	S.T.
Kazakhstan	B1	NP	B2	NP	United States	Aaa	P-1	Aaa	P-1
Korea	Baa3	NP	Baa2	NP	Uruguay	Baa3	P-3	Baa3	P-3
Kuwait	Baa1	P-2	Baa1	P-2	United Kingdom	Aaa	P-1	Aaa	P-1
					Venezuela	B2	NP	Caa1	NP

Source: Moody's Investors Services, http://www.moodys.com/repldata/ratings/ratsov.htm.

* Under review for possible up-grading. ** Under review for possible down-grading.

All EU-11 members of the euro (euroland) are rated together. Long-term (L.T.) bond ratings, from highest to lowest: Aaa, Aa, and A are highest grade (investment grade); Baa, Ba, and B are medium-grade (speculative grade); Caa, Ca, and C are poorest grade. Moody's also applies numerical modifiers (1, 2, and 3) within each rating classification, with 1 being in the higher end of the rating grade. Short-term (S.T.) ratings, from highest to lowest: P-1, P-1, P-3, and NP (not prime).

Moody's rates international bonds upon request of the issuer. Based on supporting financial statements and other material obtained from the issuer, it makes a preliminary rating and then informs the issuer who has an opportunity to comment. After Moody's determines its final rating, the issuer may decide not to have the rating published. Consequently a disproportionately large number of published international ratings fall into the highest categories, since issuers about to receive a lower rating do not allow publication.

Moody's review of political risk includes study of the government system, the social environment, and the nation's external relations. Its review of economic risk looks at debt burden, international liquidity, balance of payments flexibility, economic structure, growth performance, economic management, and economic outlook. Moody's also evaluates the bonds of sovereign-supported entities by looking first at their creditworthiness on a standalone basis and then at the extent to which sovereign support either enhances or diminishes the borrower's financial strength. Credit ratings are critical to borrowers and investors alike. A MNE's credit rating determines its cost of funds.

Access to debt capital is, however, in the end, still a function of basic societal norms. Religion itself, may play a part in the use and availability of debt capital. Global Finance Perspective 13.3 illustrates one area rarely seen by Westerners: Islamic finance.

Project Financing

One of the hottest topics in international finance today is project finance. *Project finance* is the arrangement of financing for long-term capital projects, large in scale, long in life, and generally high in risk. This is a very general definition, however, because many different forms and structures fall under this generic heading.

Project finance is not new. Examples go back centuries and include many famous early international businesses such as the Dutch East India Co. and the British East India Company. These entrepreneurial importers financed their trade ventures to Asia on a voyage-by-voyage basis, with

Global Finance Perspective 13.3

Islamic Finance

Muslims, the followers of Islam, now make up roughly one-fourth of the world's population. The countries of the world that are predominantly Muslim create roughly 10% of global GDP, and comprise a large share of the emerging marketplace. Islamic law reaches into many dimensions of the individual and organizational behaviors for its practitioners—including business. Islamic finance, the specific area of our interest, imposes a number of restrictions on Muslims that dramatically alter the funding and structure of Muslim businesses.

Under Islam, the *shari'ah* lays down a series of fundamental beliefs—restrictions in practice—regarding business and finance:

- Making money from money is not permissible
- Earning interest is prohibited
- Profit and loss should be shared
- Speculation (gambling) is prohibited
- Investments should support only *halal* (lawful or legal under Islamic law) activities

For the conduct of business, the key to understanding the prohibition on earning interest is to understand that profitability from investment should arise from the returns associated with carrying risk. For example, a traditional Western bank may extend a loan to a business. The bank is to receive its principal and interest in repayment and return regardless of the ultimate profitability of the business. In fact, the debt is paid off first. Similarly, an individual who deposits his or her money in a Western bank will receive an interest earning on their deposit regardless of the profitability of the bank and the bank's associated investments.

An Islamic bank, however, cannot pay interest to depositors—who are Muslims—under Islamic law. Therefore the depositors in an Islamic bank are actually shareholders (much like credit unions in the West), and the returns they receive are a function of the profitability of the bank's investments. Their returns cannot be fixed or guaranteed, because that would break the principle of profit and loss being shared.

Recently, however, a number of Islamic banking institutions have opened in Europe and North America. A Muslim now can enter into a sequence of purchases that allows them to purchase a home without departing from Islamic principles. The buyer selects the property, which is then purchased by the Islamic bank. The bank in turn resells the house to the prospective buyer at a higher price. The buyer is allowed to pay off the purchase over a series of years. Although the difference in purchase prices is, by Western thinking, implicit interest, this structure does conform to the *shari'ah*. Unfortunately, in both the United States and the United Kingdom, the difference is not a tax deductible expense for the homeowner, as interest would be.

each voyage's financing being like venture capital; investors would be repaid when the shipper returned and the fruits of the Asian marketplace were sold at the docks to Mediterranean and European merchants. If all went well, the individual shareholders of the voyage were paid in full.

Project finance is used widely today by MNEs in the development of large-scale infrastructure projects in China, India, and many other emerging markets. Although each individual project has unique characteristics, most are highly leveraged transactions, with debt making up more than 60% of the total financing. Equity is a small component of project financing for two reasons: first, the simple scale of the investment project often precludes a single investor or even a collection of private investors from being able to fund it; second, many of these projects involve subjects traditionally funded by governments—such as electrical power generation, dam building, highway construction, energy exploration, production, and distribution.

This level of debt, however, places an enormous burden on cash flow for debt service. Therefore, project financing usually requires a number of additional levels of risk reduction. The lenders involved in these investments must feel secure that they will be repaid; bankers are not by nature entrepreneurs and do not enjoy entrepreneurial returns from project finance.

Four basic properties are critical to the success of project financing.

1. **Separability of the project from its investors.** The project is established as an individual legal entity, separate from the legal and financial responsibilities of its individual investors. This not only protects the assets of equity investors; it provides a controlled platform upon which creditors can evaluate the risks associated with the singular project. The ability of the project's cash flows to service all the debt itself assures that the debt service payments will be automatically allocated by and from the project itself (and not from a decision by management within a MNE).

2. **Long-lived and capital-intensive singular projects.** Not only must the individual project be separable and large in proportion to the financial resources of its owners, its business line must be singular in its construction, operation, and size (capacity). The size is set at inception and is seldom, if ever, changed over the project's life.

3. **Cash flow predictability from third-party commitments.** An oil field or electric power plant produces a homogeneous commodity product that can yield predictable cash flows if third-party commitments to take or pay can be established. Nonfinancial costs of production need to be controlled over time, usually through long-term supplier contracts with price adjustment clauses based on inflation. The predictability of net cash inflows to long-term contracts eliminates much of the individual project's business risk, allowing the financial structure to be heavily debt-financed and still safe from financial distress.

   The predictability of the project's revenue stream is essential in securing project financing. Typical contract provisions intended to ensure adequate cash flow normally include the following clauses: quantity and quality of the project's output; a pricing formula that enhances the predictability of adequate margin to cover operating costs and debt service payments; and a clear statement of the circumstances that permit significant changes in the contract, such as force majeure or adverse business conditions.

4. **Finite projects with finite lives.** Even with a longer-term investment, it is critical that the project have a definite ending point at which all debt and equity has been repaid. Because the project is a standalone investment whose cash flows go directly to the servicing of its capital structure, and not to reinvestment for growth or other investment alternatives, investors of all kinds need assurances that the project's returns will be attained in a finite period. There is no capital appreciation, but only cash flow.

Examples of project finance include some of the largest individual investments undertaken in the past three decades, such as British Petroleum's financing of its interest in the North Sea and the Trans-Alaska Pipeline. The Trans-Alaska Pipeline was a joint venture between Standard Oil of Ohio, Atlantic Richfield, Exxon, British Petroleum, Mobil Oil, Philips Petroleum, Union Oil, and Amerada Hess. Each of these projects cost $1 billion or more and represented capital expenditures which no single firm would or could attempt to finance. Yet through a joint venture arrangement, the higher-than-normal risk absorbed by the capital employed could be managed.

SUMMARY

- The domestic theory of optimal financial structures must be modified by four variables in order to accommodate the case of the MNE. These variables are: 1) the availability of capital, 2) diversification of cash flows, 3) foreign exchange risk, and 4) the expectations of international portfolio investors.
- A multinational firm's marginal cost of capital is constant for considerable ranges of its capital budget. This statement is not true for most small domestic firms, because they do not have access to the national equity or debt markets.
- By diversifying cash flows internationally, the MNE may be able to achieve the same kind of reduction in cash flow variability as portfolio investors receive from diversifying their security holdings internationally.
- When a firm issues foreign currency–denominated debt, its effective cost equals the after-tax cost of repaying the principal and interest in terms of the firm's own currency. This amount includes the nominal cost of principal and interest in foreign currency terms, adjusted for any foreign exchange gains or losses.
- Therefore, regardless of other factors, if a firm wants to raise capital in global markets, it must adopt global norms that are close to the U.S. and U.K. norms. Debt ratios up to 60% appear to be acceptable. Any higher debt ratio is more difficult to sell to international portfolio investors.
- A compromise position between minimizing the global cost of capital and conforming to local capital norms (localization) is possible when determining the financial structure of a foreign subsidiary. Both multinational and domestic firms should try to minimize their overall weighted average cost of capital for a given level of business risk and capital budget, as finance theory suggests.
- The debt ratio of a foreign subsidiary is in reality only cosmetic, because lenders ultimately look to the parent and its consolidated worldwide cash flow as the source of repayment. In many cases, debt of subsidiaries must be guaranteed by the parent firm.
- The international debt markets offer the borrower a variety of different maturities, repayment structures, and currencies of denomination. The markets and their many different instruments vary by source of funding, pricing structure, maturity, and subordination or linkage to other debt and equity instruments.
- The three major sources of debt funding on the international markets are international bank loans and syndicated credits, the Euronote market, and the international bond market.
- Eurocurrency markets serve two valuable purposes: 1) Eurocurrency deposits are an efficient and convenient money market device for holding excess corporate liquidity and 2) the Eurocurrency market is a major source of short-term bank loans to finance corporate working capital needs, including the financing of imports and exports.
- Three original factors in the evolution of the Eurobond markets are still of importance: absence of regulatory interference, less stringent disclosure practices, and favorable tax treatment.
- Project finance is used widely today in the development of large-scale infrastructure projects in many emerging markets. Although each individual project has unique characteristics, most are highly leveraged transactions, with debt making up more than 60% of the total financing. Equity is a small component of project financing for two reasons: first, the scale of the

investment project often prevents a single investor or even a collection of private investors from being able to fund it; second, many of these projects are of a kind traditionally funded by governments—such as electrical power generation, dam building, highway construction, and energy exploration, production, and distribution.

QUESTIONS

1. **Objective.** What, in simple wording, is the objective sought by finding an optimal capital structure?
2. **Varying debt proportions.** As debt in a firm's capital structure is increased from no debt to a significant proportion of debt (say, 60%), what tends to happen to the cost of debt, to the cost of equity, and to the overall weighted average cost of capital?
3. **Availability of capital.** How does the availability of capital influence the theory of optimal capital structure for a multinational enterprise?
4. **Diversified cash flows.** If a multinational firm is able to diversify its sources of cash inflow so as to receive those flows from several countries and in several currencies, do you think that tends to increase or decrease its weighted average cost of capital?
5. **Ex-post cost of borrowing.** Exhibit 13.2 in the text shows that Deutsche Bank borrowed funds at a nominal cost of 9.59% per annum, but at a later date that debt was selling to yield 7.24%. Near the other extreme, the Kingdom of Thailand borrowed funds at a nominal cost of 8.70% but after the fact found the debt was sold in the market at a yield of 11.87%. What caused the changes, in this case in opposite directions, and what might management do to benefit (as Deutsche Bank did) rather than suffer (as the Kingdom of Thailand did)?
6. **Local norms.** Should foreign subsidiaries of multinational firms conform to the capital structure norms of the host country or to the norms of their parent's country? Discuss.
7. **Argentina.** In January 2002, the government of Argentina broke away from its currency board system that had tied the peso to the U.S. dollar and devalued the peso from Ps1.0000/$ to Ps1.40000/$. This caused some Argentine firms with dollar-denominated debt to go bankrupt. Should a U.S. or European parent in good financial health "rescue" its Argentine subsidiary that would otherwise go bankrupt because of the nature of Argentine political and economic management in the four or five years prior to January 2002? Assume the parent has not entered into a formal agreement to guarantee the debt of its Argentine subsidiary.
8. **Internal financing.** What is the difference between "internal" financing and "external" financing for a subsidiary? List three types of internal financing and three types of external financing available to a foreign subsidiary.
9. **Eurodollars.** Which of the following are eurodollars and which are not?
   a. A U.S. dollar deposit owned by a German corporation and held in Barclay's Bank in London.
   b. A U.S. dollar deposit owned by a German corporation and held in Chase Manhattan Bank's office in London.
   c. A U.S. dollar deposit owned by a German corporation and held in Sumitomo Bank in Tokyo.
   d. A U.S. dollar deposit owned by a German corporation and held in Citibank in New York.
   e. A U.S. dollar deposit owned by a German corporation and held in the New York branch of Deutsche Bank.
   f. A U.S. dollar deposit owned by a U.S. resident and held in Overseas Banking Corporation in Singapore.
   g. A U.S. dollar deposit owned by a U.S. resident and held in the New York branch of Deutsche Bank.
   h. A deposit of euros in Paribas Bank in Paris.

i. A deposit of euros in Citibank in New York.
j. A deposit of Australian dollars in Paribas Bank in Paris.

10. **Eurodollar deposits.** Why would anyone, individual or corporation, want to deposit U.S. dollars in a bank outside of the United States when the natural location for such deposits would be a bank within the United States?

11. **Define the following terms:**
    a. LIBOR
    b. Euro-LIBOR
    c. Eurocredits
    d. Syndicated bank credits

12. **International debt instruments.** Bank borrowing has been the long-time manner by which corporations and governments borrowed funds for short periods of time. What then, is the advantage over bank borrowing for each of the following:
    a. Syndicated loans
    b. Euronotes
    c. Euro-commercial paper
    d. Euro-medium term notes
    e. International bonds

13. **Euro- versus foreign bonds.** What is the difference between a eurobond and a foreign bond and why do two types of international bonds exist?

14. **Separation.** In project financing, the project is a legal entity separate from the corporations that are the equity owners. Why?

15. **Singular project.** In the context of project financing, what is a "long-lived, capital-intensive, singular project"?

16. **Predictability.** Predictability of future cash flows is essential to induce creditors to participate in project financing. How does financial leverage increase the risk in highly leveraged projects, and how do the creators of investments financed by project financing manage to reduce the volatility of future cash flows?

17. **Infinite lives.** Why do projects with infinite lives and grandiose growth projects not appeal to creditors who would engage in project financing, while those attributes are normally very desirable in a corporate investment?

18. **Maximizing present value.** Do the equity investors in investments based on project financing seek to maximize the present value of their investment, or are they compensated in some other manner?

PROBLEMS

1. **Tuba City Manufacturing, Inc.** Tuba City Manufacturing, Inc, a U.S. multinational company, has the following debt components in its consolidated capital section:

U.S. dollar–denominated 25-year bonds at 6.00%	$10,000,000
U.S. dollar–denominated 5-year euronotes at 4.00%	$4,000,000
Euro–denominated 10-year bonds at 5.00%	€6,000,000
Yen–denominated 20-year bonds at 2%	¥750,000,000
Common stock	$35,000,000
Retained earnings	$15,000,000

Tuba City's finance staff estimates its cost of equity to be 20%. Current exchange rates are:

European euros:	$0.90/€
British pounds sterling:	$1.50/£
Japanese yen:	¥125/$

Income taxes are 30% around the world after allowing for credits. Calculate Tuba City's weighted average cost of capital. Are any assumptions implicit in your calculation?

2. **Pacific Group (USA).** Pacific Group, a private equity firm headquartered out of Houston, Texas, borrows £3,000,000 for one year at 9% interest, and during the year the pound depreciates from $1.6000/£ to $1.5000/£. What is the cost of this debt in dollar-denominated interest?

3. **Hartford Associates (USA).** Hartford Associates, a U.S.-based investment partnership, borrows €80,000,000 at a time when the exchange rate is $0.9000/€. The entire principal is to be repaid in three years, and interest is 6% per annum, paid annually in euros. The euro is expected to depreciate vis-à-vis the dollar at 3% per annum. What is the effective cost of this loan for Hartford?

4. **Quatrefoil Construction Company.** Quatrefoil Construction Company consists of a U.S. parent and wholly owned subsidiaries in Malaysia (Q-Malaysia) and Mexico (Q-Mexico). Selected portions of their non-consolidated balance sheets, translated into U.S. dollars, are shown below.

Q-Malaysia (accounts in ringgits)

Long-term debt	RM 11,400,000
Shareholders' equity	RM 15,200,000

Q-Mexico (accounts in pesos)

Long-term debt	Ps 20,000,000
Shareholders' equity	Ps 60,000,000

Quatrefoil Construction Company (Non-consolidated BalanceSheet— Selected Items Only)

Investment in subsidiaries:	
In Q-Malaysia	$4,000,000
In Q-Mexico	6,000,000
Parent long-term debt	$ 12,000,000
Common stock	5,000,000
Retained earnings	20,000,000

Current exchange rates are:

Malaysia:	RM3.80/$
Mexico:	Ps 10/$

What are the debt and equity proportions in Quatrefoil's consolidated balance sheet?

5. **Grupo Bimbo de Mexico.** Grupo Bimbo, although Mexican by incorporation, evaluates all business results, including financing costs, in U.S. dollars. The company needs to borrow $100,000,000 or the foreign currency equivalent for four years. For all issues, interest is payable once per year, at the end of the year. Available alternatives are:

   a. Sell Japanese yen bonds at par, yielding 3% per annum. The current exchange rate is ¥125/$, and the yen is expected to strengthen against the dollar by 2% per annum.
   b. Sell euro-denominated bonds at par, yielding 7% per annum. The current exchange rate is $0.9200/€, and the euro is expected to weaken against the dollar by 2% per annum.
   c. Sell U.S. dollar bonds at par, yielding 5% per annum.

   Which course of action do you recommend Grupo Bimbo take and why?

6. **Zermatte Air (Switzerland).** Zermatte Air of Switzerland retains $12,000,000 from tickets sold to U.S. dollar holders, after paying fuel and landing costs associated with its frequent flights between Dulles Airport in the United States and Geneva. These funds are currently deposited in Mid-Manhattan Bank in New York City where they are earning 5.00% per annum. Docklands Bank in London pays 5.50% interest on eurodollar deposits, and Zermatte Air decides to move its funds from New York to London.

   a. Show journal entries (debits and credits) on the books of Zermatte Air, Mid-Manhattan Bank, and Docklands Bank to reflect this transfer.
   b. By how much have bank deposits of U.S. banks changed?
   c. What happens if Docklands Bank invests the dollars in long-term U.S. government bonds?

7. **Gas du Ardennes.** Gas du Ardennes, a European natural gas company, is borrowing US$800,000,000 via a Syndicated Eurocredit for six years at 80 basis points over LIBOR. LIBOR for the loan will be reset every six months. The funds will be provided by a syndicate of eight leading investment banks, which will charge up-front fees totaling 1.2% of the principal amount. What is the effective interest cost for the first year if LIBOR is 8.00% for the first six months and 7.00% for the second six months?

8. **River Thames Insurance Company.** River Thames Insurance Company plans to sell $1,000,000 of Euro-Commercial Paper with a 60-day maturity and discounted to yield 6.0%

per annum. What will be the immediate proceeds to River Thames Insurance?

9. **Mediterranean Alliance, S.A.** Mediterranean Alliance, S.A., is raising funds via a euro medium-term note with the following characteristics:
   a. Coupon rate: 8.00% payable semiannually on June 30 and December 31
   b. Date of issuance: February 28, 2003
   c. Maturity: August 31, 2005

   How much in dollars will Mediterranean Alliance, S.A., receive for each $1,000 note sold?

10. **Yunnan Airlines.** Yunnan Airlines, headquartered in Kunming, China, needs US$5,000,000 for one year to finance working capital. The airline has two alternatives for borrowing:
    a. Borrow US$5,000,000 in Eurodollars in London at 9.00% per annum
    b. Borrow HK$39,000,000 in Hong Kong at 7.00% per annum, and exchange these Hong Kong dollars at the present exchange rate of HK$7.8/US$ for U.S. dollars.

    At what ending exchange rate would Yunnan Airlines be indifferent between borrowing U.S. dollars and borrowing Hong Kong dollars?

INTERNET EXERCISES

1. **Sovereign credit ratings criteria.** The evaluation of credit risk and all other relevant risks associated with the multitude of borrowers on world debt markets requires a structured approach to international risk assessment. Check both Standard & Poor's and Moody's criteria described in depth on their web pages to differentiate the various risks (local currency risk, default risk, currency risk, transfer risk, etc.) with major sovereign ratings worldwide:

   Standard & Poor's http://www.ratings.com

   Moody's http://www.moodys.com

2. **Brady bonds and emerging markets.** Emerging markets have repeatedly been beaten down with every major international financial crisis, whether it be the Mexican peso (1994), the Thai baht (1997), the Russian ruble (1998), or the Brazilian real (1999). Use the web sites listed next to prepare an analysis of why these markets come under such severe pressure when a crisis occurs somewhere else around the globe.

   Brady Network http://www.brady.net.com

   Emerging Markets http://www.emdb.com

SELECTED READINGS

Hill, Claire A., "Securitization: A Financing Strategy for Emerging Market Firms," *Journal of Applied Corporate Finance*, Fall 1998, Volume 11, No. 3, pp. 55–65.

Johnson, Greg, and Thomas Funkhouser, "Yankee Bonds and Cross-Border Private Placements," *Journal of Applied Corporate Finance*, Fall 1999, Volume 10, No. 3, pp. 34–45.

Lee, Kwang Chul, and Chuck C.Y. Kwok, "Multinational Corporations vs. Domestic Corporations: International Environmental Factors and Determinants of Capital Structure," *Journal of International Business Studies*, Summer 1988, pp. 195–217.

Rajan, Raghuram, and Luigi Zingales, "Debt, Folklore, and Cross-Country Differences in Financial Structure," *Journal of Applied Corporate Finance*, Winter 1998, Volume 10, No. 4, pp. 102–107.

Wald, John K., "How Firm Characteristics Affect Capital Structure: An International Comparison," *The Journal of Financial Research*, Summer 1999, Volume 12, No. 2, pp. 161–187.

MINI-CASE

The Financing of Petrozuata

In the spring of 1997, a financing team for the Petrolera Zuata (Petrozuata) petroleum project in Venezuela began its tour of financial institutions in New York City. The financing team's goal was very pointed: They must obtain an investment-grade rating (BBB or better) for the proposed Venezuelan project. If they could not, the project would most likely have to be abandoned.

Petrolera Zuata

Petrozuata was a joint venture between Petróleos de Venezuela (PDVSA, Venezuela) and Conoco Incorporated (USA). The project had three distinct components: 1) production of heavy oil from a new oil field in the interior of Venezuela; 2) the transportation of the heavy oil to a coastal export facility via a pipeline to be constructed; and 3) the transportation of the heavy oil to refineries along the U.S. Gulf Coast for refining and processing. The joint venture would hold ownership to the production facilities, pipeline, and export loading facilities. This venture would be both difficult and costly.

In 1997, PDVSA was the second-largest oil company in the world. It was, however, government-owned—and the Venezuelan government was notoriously unstable. PDVSA was composed of the combined elements of Shell, Exxon, Mobil, Gulf, and Conoco, which had been nationalized by the Venezuelan government in 1976. But PDVSA itself, independent of its government ownership, was highly profitable and considered very well managed. It was a solid and capable partner.

Conoco was a subsidiary of Dupont (USA). It was widely recognized as one of the most astute international oil companies. The company had operations in more than 200 countries and possessed particular expertise in the technology and extraction processes necessary for difficult projects like that of Petrozuata. It made a good partner for PDVSA.

Project Financing Concerns

The total cost of the project was estimated at $2.425 billion. The two equity partners, PDVSA (49.9% interest) and Conoco (50.1% interest), would together invest $975 million. This would leave $1.450 billion to be financed through debt.

Petrozuata would use project financing. This meant that in addition to being more highly leveraged than a normal investment or company, it would require that a number of contracts and agreements be put into place prior to the start of project construction in order to reduce or eliminate the various risks the project would face over its economic life. Project financing is typically used when the investment is large, long-term in economic life, and capable of being viewed as economically separable from its owners. This means that the project could provide sufficient cash flow and earnings on its own to repay its own debt, without its owners being held accountable for shortfalls.

The risks associated with a project financing like Petrozuata were typically divided into three categories:

- **Precompletion risks.** Before the project was completed, there would be no operations and therefore no cash flow–generating capability from the investment. During this stage, the two equity partners would be responsible for "covering" cost overruns, unanticipated problems, or any other financial or operational issues that would threaten the timely completion of the project. Types of risk encountered at this stage include technological (the use of a new unproven technology for example) and resource-oriented (the oil field being different or smaller than expected).

- **Postcompletion risks.** Once operating, the project was expected to generate significant volumes of heavy oil that would be more than sufficient to cover its financing and operating costs. The primary postcompletion risks to be considered were those that threatened production, such as pipeline security from terrorist acts, a government coup resulting in a change in direction of PDVSA itself, or events that threatened the value of production—price and quantity of heavy oil sold.
- **Sovereign or political risks.** Petrozuata was resident within the geographic boundaries of Venezuela. The project would then be in varying ways impacted by Venezuelan macroeconomic factors such as inflation, unemployment, currency convertibility, and expropriation by government.

The project financing agreement required many documents. Agreements included long-term labor and supplier contracts to control project operating costs and a long-term sales contract for the oil. Although heavily debated at the time, the idea was to provide a guaranteed sale of the product—the heavy oil—at a long-term assured minimum price. Conoco would guarantee the purchase of the heavy oil, but only at the market price over time, so that if the market price dropped, Petrozuata would be assured of a sale, but not a minimum price on the sale.

The Financing Goal

The Petrozuata financing team wanted to split the debt financing between bank loans, the traditional source of debt for this type of project, and Rule 144A project bonds. Rule 144A bonds were a relatively new security gaining popularity. Their major benefit was that an investor who purchased them had the ability to sell and trade these securities with other qualified investors. Bank loans could not be traded like this. Thus, investors with 144A bonds had more flexibility in managing their portfolio.

A major problem was that the project would have to obtain an investment-grade rating (BBB) in order to issue the 144A bonds. Ordinarily, the ratings agencies would look to the investment rating of the equity partners for this determination. Conoco was single A. PDVSA and Venezuela, however, were rated single B (the credit rating of a country is termed its sovereign rating). As shown in Exhibit A, moving from single B (speculative grade) to triple BBB (investment grade) was a big jump in both quality and cost.

The Deal

The Petrozuata financing team's meetings in New York were highly successful. Potential investors were very impressed by the detail and completeness of the Petrozuata project financing structure. Standard & Poor's awarded the project a BBB rating (investment grade), with Moody's (Baa1) and Duff & Phelps (BBB+) agreeing.

When the financing team asked for preliminary commitments for both bank loans and project bonds, over $5 billion in capital was offered (they needed only $1.5 billion). In the end, the project was financed largely with 144A project bonds at an average interest rate only 1.30% to 1.60% over U.S. Treasury bills. The deal was hailed as the "Deal of the Year for 1997" by *Euromoney* magazine and "Deal of the Decade" by *Project Finance* magazine.

Exhibit A Debt Ratings and Interest Rate Spreads, January 1997

Moody's Rating		Yield	Incremental Spread	Cumulative Spread
AAA		7.13%	—	—
AA	Investment	7.21%	0.08%	0.08%
A	Grade	7.39%	0.18%	0.26%
BBB		7.70%	0.31%	0.57%
BB		8.69%	0.99%	1.56%
B	Speculative Grade	10.17%	1.48%	3.04%

Source: Standard & Poor's, January 17, 1997. *Incremental spread* is the percentage difference from the previous rating level; *cumulative spread* is the cumulative total of incremental spreads.

The Aftermath

Less than one year later, Dupont announced it was selling Conoco. This would reduce Conoco's individual credit rating. The benchmark price of this heavy oil, Mayan crude, fell from $16 per barrel to under $10 per barrel in six months. The Venezuelan economy spiraled out of control, with inflation driving short-term interest rates up from 25% to 70% in six months. The 1998 Venezuelan president election was won by Hugo Chavez, the leader of the largest and most powerful anti-government radical group in the early 1990s. In August 1999, Petrozuata announced a second set of cost overruns on the project of $553 million (the first set in 1998 was approximately $242 million). Total project cost was now $3.22 billion, and the Petrozuata Rule 144A project bonds were trading at a price 3.00% above U.S. Treasuries.

Case Questions

1. Why was getting an investment-grade rating so critical to the financing of the Petrozuata project?
2. Is a project finance venture like Petrozuata of lower or higher risk than if the project had simply been funded by the two joint venture partners as in most investments?
3. Did the Petrozuata finance team oversell the project? Were the economic and political events that followed the financing predictable?
4. Did the investors—the debt providers in particular—not assess the risk of the project appropriately?
5. Given the events of 2002–2003, when widespread strikes crippled the Venezuelan economy—and particularly the oil sector—how should the market view political risk for bonds such as these?

Chapter 14

Interest Rate and Currency Swaps

THIS CHAPTER FINE-TUNES THE ANALYSIS OF THE OPTIMAL FINANCIAL STRUCTURE FOR A MULTINATIONAL enterprise (MNE). In Chapter 13, we analyzed the financial structure of MNEs from the perspective of an optimal capital structure—debt versus equity. In this chapter, we profile the optimal strategies for managing interest rate and currency risks associated with a MNE's capital structure. Our main tools are interest rate and currency swaps. Moreover, many of the same tools we observed earlier in foreign exchange risk management have parallels in interest rate and currency risk management.

The management of financial risks—exchange rates, interest rates, and commodity prices—is a rapidly expanding area of multinational financial management. All three of these financial prices introduce risk into the cash flows of the firm. The identification, measurement, and management of interest rate risk now receive roughly the same level of attention and effort as foreign exchange risk did just a few years ago.

This chapter begins by defining interest rate risk. We then examine its management, including credit risk and repricing risk. Next we illustrate Carlton's floating-rate loan and how it can be managed with forward rate agreements, interest rate futures, and interest rate swaps. The following section illustrates how Carlton can swap to fixed interest rates. After describing currency swaps, we show how Carlton can swap their floating dollar loan into a fixed-rate Swiss franc–denominated loan. Then we examine how Carlton can unwind its swaps. The next section analyses counterparty risk. The chapter concludes with an illustrative case of a three-way, back-to-back cross-currency swap.

Interest Rate Risk

All firms—domestic or multinational, small or large, leveraged or unleveraged—are sensitive to interest rate movements in one way or another. Although a variety of interest rate risks exist in theory and industry, this book focuses on the financial management of the nonfinancial firm. Hence our discussion is limited to the interest rate risks associated with the multinational firm. The interest rate risks of financial firms, such as banks, are not covered here.

The single largest interest rate risk of the nonfinancial firm is debt service. The debt structure of the MNE will possess differing maturities of debt, different interest rate structures (such as fixed versus floating-rate), and different currencies of denomination. Interest rates are currency-specific. Each currency has its own interest rate yield curve and credit spreads for borrowers. Therefore, the multicurrency dimension of interest rate risk for the MNE is a serious concern. As illustrated in Exhibit 14.1, even the interest rate calculations vary on occasion across currencies and countries.

The second most prevalent source of interest rate risk for the MNE lies in its holdings of interest-sensitive securities. Unlike debt, which is recorded on the right-hand side of the firm's balance sheet, the marketable securities portfolio of the firm appears on the left-hand side. Marketable securities represent potential earnings or interest inflows to the firm. Ever-increasing competitive pressures have pushed financial managers to tighten their management of both the left and right sides of the firm's balance sheet.

Whether it is on the left or right side, the reference rate of interest calculation merits special attention. A *reference rate*—for example, U.S. dollar LIBOR—is the rate of interest used in a standardized quotation, loan agreement, or financial derivative valuation. LIBOR, the London Interbank Offered Rate, is by far the most widely used and quoted. It is officially defined by the British Bankers Association (BBA). U.S. dollar LIBOR is the mean of 16 multinational banks' interbank offered rates as sampled by the BBA at approximately 11 a.m. London time in London. Similarly, the BBA calculates the Japanese yen LIBOR, euro LIBOR, and other currency LIBOR rates at the same time in London from samples of banks.

The interbank interest rate market is not, however, confined to London. Most major domestic financial centers construct their own interbank offered rates for local loan agreement purposes. These rates include PIBOR (Paris Interbank Offered Rate), MIBOR (Madrid Interbank Offered Rate), SIBOR (Singapore Interbank Offered Rate), and FIBOR (Frankfurt Interbank Offered Rate), to name but a few.

Management of Interest Rate Risk

The Management Dilemma

Before they can manage interest rate risk, treasurers and financial managers of all types must resolve a basic management dilemma: the balance between risk and return. Treasury has traditionally been considered a service center (cost center) and is therefore not expected to take

Exhibit 14.1 International Interest Rate Calculations

International interest rate calculations differ by the number of days used in the period's calculation and their definition of how many days there are in a year (for financial purposes). The following example highlights how the different methods result in different one-month payments of interest on a $10 million loan, 5.500% per annum interest, for an exact period of 28 days.

			$10 million @ 5.500% per annum	
Practice	**Day Count in Period**	**Days/Year**	**Days Used**	**Interest Payment**
International	Exact number of days	360	28	$42,777.78
British	Exact number of days	365	28	$42,191.78
Swiss (Eurobond)	Assumed 30 days/month	360	30	$45,833.33

From "Hedging Instruments for Foreign Exchange, Money Market, and Precious Metals," Union Bank of Switzerland, 1994, pp. 41–42.

positions that incur risk in the expectation of profit. Treasury activities are rarely managed or evaluated as profit centers. Treasury management practices are therefore predominantly conservative, but opportunities to reduce costs or actually earn profits are not to be ignored. History, however, is littered with examples in which financial managers have strayed from their fiduciary responsibilities in the expectation of profit. Unfortunately, much of the time they have realized only loss. Losses on derivatives by specific companies have already been chronicled in Chapter 7. The many derivative disasters, combined with the wider use of financial derivatives, has helped more and more firms realize the value of well-constructed policy statements such as those in Exhibit 14.2.

Both foreign exchange and interest rate risk management must focus on managing existing or anticipated cash flow exposures of the firm. As in foreign exchange exposure management, the firm cannot undertake informed management or hedging strategies without forming expectations—a directional and/or volatility view—of interest rate movements. Fortunately, interest rate movements have historically shown more stability and less volatility than exchange rates. Financial management has frequently found it valuable to err on the conservative side, adding to the predictability of commitments and cash flows. This conservatism in turn improves the strategic decision-making capability of the firm. Finally, similar to exchange rate risks, the question still exists as to whether stockholders want management to hedge interest rate risk or prefer to diversify the risk away through their ownership of other securities.

Once management has formed expectations about future interest rate levels and movements, it must choose the appropriate implementation, a path that includes the selective use of various techniques and instruments.

Credit Risk and Repricing Risk

Prior to describing the management of the most common interest rate pricing risks, it is important to distinguish between credit risk and repricing risk. *Credit risk*, sometimes termed *roll-over risk*, is the possibility that a borrower's creditworthiness, at the time of renewing a credit, is reclassified by the lender. This can result in changing fees, changing interest rates, altered credit line

Exhibit 14.2 Treasury Policy Statements

The major derivative disasters of the 1990s highlighted the need for the proper construction and implementation of corporate financial management policy statements. Policy statements are, however, frequently misunderstood by those writing and enforcing them. A few helpful fundamentals may be in order.

- *A policy is a rule, not a goal.* A policy is intended to limit or restrict management actions, not set priorities or goals. For example, "thou shalt not write uncovered options" is a policy. "Management will pursue the lowest cost of capital at all times" is a goal.
- *A policy is intended to restrict some subjective decision making.* Although at first glance this aspect seems to indicate that management is not to be trusted, it is actually intended to make management's decision making easier in potentially harmful situations.
- *A policy is intended to establish operating guidelines independently of staff.* Although many policies may appear overly restrictive given the specific talents of financial staff, the fiduciary responsibility of the firm needs to be maintained independently of the specific personnel on board. Changes in personnel frequently place new managers in uncomfortable and unfamiliar surroundings. Errors in judgment may result. Proper policy construction provides a constructive and protective base for management's learning curve.

commitments, or even denial. *Repricing risk* is the risk of changes in interest rates charged (earned) at the time a financial contract's rate is reset.

Consider the following three different debt strategies being considered by a corporate borrower. Each is intended to provide $1 million in financing for a three-year period:

- Strategy 1: Borrow $1 million for three years at a fixed rate of interest.
- Strategy 2: Borrow $1 million for three years at a floating rate, LIBOR + 2%, to be reset annually.
- Strategy 3: Borrow $1 million for one year at a fixed rate, then renew the credit annually.

Although the lowest cost of funds is always a major selection criteria, it is not the only one. If the firm chooses Strategy 1, it assures itself of the funding for the full three years at a known interest rate. It has maximized the predictability of cash flows for the debt obligation. What it has sacrificed, to some degree, is the ability to enjoy a lower interest rate in the event that interest rates fall over the period. Of course, it has also eliminated the risk that interest rates could rise over the period, increasing debt servicing costs.

Strategy 2 offers what Strategy 1 did not: flexibility (repricing risk). It too assures the firm of full funding for the three-year period. This eliminates credit risk. Repricing risk is, however, alive and well in Strategy 2. If LIBOR changes dramatically by the second or third year, the LIBOR rate change is passed through fully to the borrower. The spread, however, remains fixed (reflecting the credit standing that has been locked in for the full three years). Flexibility comes at a cost in this case: the risk that interest rates could go up as well as down.

Strategy 3 offers more flexibility and more risk. First, the firm is borrowing at the shorter end of the yield curve. If the yield curve is positively sloped, as is commonly the case in major industrial markets, the base interest rate should be lower. But the short end of the yield curve is also the more volatile. It responds to short-term events in a much more pronounced fashion than longer-term rates. The strategy also exposes the firm to the possibility that its credit rating may change dramatically by the time for credit renewal, for better or worse. Noting that credit ratings in general are established on the premise that a firm can meet its debt-service obligations under worsening economic conditions, firms that are highly creditworthy (investment-rated grades) may view Strategy 3 as a more relevant alternative than do firms of lower quality (speculative grades). This is not a strategy for firms that are financially weak.

Although the previous example gives only a partial picture of the complexity of funding decisions within the firm, it demonstrates the many ways credit risks and repricing risks are inextricably intertwined. The expression interest rate exposure is a complex concept, and the proper measurement of the exposure prior to its management is critical. We now proceed to describe the interest rate risk of the most common form of corporate debt: floating-rate loans.

Carlton's Floating-Rate Loans

Floating-rate loans are a widely used source of debt for firms worldwide. They are also the source of the single largest and most frequently observed corporate interest rate exposure.

Exhibit 14.3 depicts the costs and cash flows for a three-year floating rate loan taken out by Carlton Corporation. The loan of US$10 million will be serviced with annual interest payments and total principal repayment at the end of the three-year period.

Exhibit 14.3 Carlton Corporation's Costs and Cash Flows in Servicing a Floating-Rate Loan

The expected interest rates and cash flows associated with a three-year $10,000,000 floating-rate loan. Carlton pays an initiation fee of 1.500% of principal up front (which reduces proceeds).

Loan Interest Rates	**Year 0**	**Year 1**	**Year 2**	**Year 3**	
LIBOR (floating)	5.000%	5.000%	5.000%	5.000%	
Spread (fixed)		1.500%	1.500%	1.500%	
Total interest payable		6.500%	6.500%	6.500%	
Interest cash flows on loan					
LIBOR (floating)		($500,000)	($500,000)	($500,000)	
Spread (fixed)		(150,000)	(150,000)	(150,000)	
Total interest		($650,000)	($650,000)	($650,000)	
Loan proceeds (repayment)	$9,850,000			($10,000,000)	
Total loan cash flows	$9,850,000	($650,000)	($650,000)	($10,650,000)	
IRR of total cash flows	7.072%		"all-in-cost" (AIC)		
Sensitivities to LIBOR	**LIBOR (Year 0)**	**LIBOR (Year 1)**	**LIBOR (Year 2)**	**LIBOR (Year 3)**	**AIC***
Baseline case above	5.000%	5.000%	5.000%	5.000%	7.072%
LIBOR rises 25 basis points/yr		5.250%	5.500%	5.750%	7.565%
LIBOR falls 25 basis points/yr		4.750%	4.500%	4.250%	6.578%

* The effective cost of funds (before-tax) for Carlton, the all-in-cost (AIC), is found by determining the internal rate of return (IRR) of the total cash flows associated with the loan. The all-in-cost of the original loan agreement, without fees, is 6.500%.

- The loan is *priced* at U.S. dollar LIBOR + 1.500% (note that the cost of money, interest, is often referred to as *price*). The LIBOR base will be reset each year on an agreed-upon date (say, two days prior to payment). Whereas the LIBOR component is truly floating, the spread of 1.500% is actually a fixed component of the interest payment, which is known with certainty for the life of the loan.

  When the loan is drawn down initially, at time year 0, an up-front fee of 1.500% is charged by the lender. This fee results in a reduction in the net proceeds of the loan by US$150,000. Although the loan agreement states the amount as $10,000,000 and Carlton is required to repay it in full, the actual net proceeds to the firm are only $9,850,000.

- Carlton will not know the actual interest cost of the loan until the loan has been completely repaid. Caitlin Kelly, the CFO of Carlton, may forecast what LIBOR will be for the life of the loan, but she will not know with certainty until all payments have been completed. This uncertainty is not only an interest rate risk, but it is also an actual cash flow risk associated with the interest payment. (A fixed interest rate loan has *interest-rate risk*, in this case opportunity cost, which does not put actual cash flows at risk.)

Exhibit 14.3 illustrates the *all-in-cost* (AIC) of the loan under a number of different sensitivities. The AIC is found by calculating the internal rate of return (IRR) of the total cash flows for repayment. The baseline analysis assumes that LIBOR remains at 5.000% for the life of the loan.

Including the up-front fees, the AIC to Carlton is 7.072% (or 6.500% flat without fees). If, however, LIBOR were to rise steadily over the three-year period by 25 basis points (0.25%) per year, the AIC of the loan would rise to 7.565%. If LIBOR were to fall by the same 25 basis points per year, the AIC would fall to 6.578%. We must remember, however, that only the LIBOR component of the loan price creates cash flow risk.

If Carlton Corporation decided, after it had taken out the loan, that it wished to manage the interest rate risk associated with the loan agreement, it would have a number of management alternatives:

- **Refinancing.** Carlton could go back to its lender and restructure and refinance the entire agreement. This is not always possible and is often expensive.
- **Forward rate agreements (FRAs).** Carlton could lock in the future interest rate payments with FRAs, much the same way that exchange rates are locked in with forward contracts.
- **Interest rate futures.** Although companies rarely use foreign currency futures for foreign exchange risk management, interest rate futures have gained substantially more acceptance. Carlton could lock in the future interest rate payments by taking an interest rate futures position.
- **Interest rate swaps.** Carlton could enter into an additional agreement with a bank or swap dealer in which it exchanged cash flows in such a way that the interest rate payments on the floating-rate loan would become fixed.

Forward Rate Agreements

A *forward rate agreement* (FRA) is an interbank-traded contract to buy or sell interest rate payments on a notional principal. These contracts are settled in cash. The buyer of an FRA obtains the right to lock in an interest rate for a desired term that begins at a future date. The contract specifies that the seller of the FRA will pay the buyer the increased interest expense on a nominal sum (the notional principal) of money if interest rates rise above the agreed rate, but the buyer will pay the seller the differential interest expense if interest rates fall below the agreed rate. Maturities available are typically 1, 3, 6, 9, and 12 months, much like traditional forward contracts for currencies.

For example, Carlton may decide that it wishes to lock in the first interest payment (due at the end of year 1), so it buys an FRA that locks in a total interest payment of 6.500%. If LIBOR rises above 5.000% by the end of year 1, Carlton would receive a cash payment from the FRA seller that would reduce the interest rate to 5.000%. Similarly, if LIBOR were to fall during year 1 to below 5.000% (not what Caitlin Kelly expects to happen), Carlton would make a cash payment to the seller of the FRA, effectively raising its LIBOR payment to 5.000% and the total loan interest to 6.500%.

Like foreign currency forward contracts, FRAs are useful on individual exposures. They are contractual commitments of the firm that allow little flexibility to enjoy favorable movements, such as when LIBOR is falling as described earlier. Firms also use FRAs if they plan to invest in securities at future dates but fear that interest rates might fall prior to the investment date. Because of the limited maturities and currencies available, however, FRAs are not widely used outside the largest industrial economies and currencies.

Interest Rate Futures

Unlike foreign currency futures, *interest rate futures* are relatively widely used by financial managers and treasurers of nonfinancial companies. Their popularity stems from the relatively high liquidity of the interest rate futures markets, their simplicity in use, and the rather standardized interest-rate exposures most firms possess. The two most widely used futures contracts are the Eurodollar futures traded on the Chicago Mercantile Exchange (CME) and the U.S. Treasury Bond Futures of the Chicago Board of Trade (CBOT). Interestingly, the third-largest volume of a traded futures contract in the latter 1990s was the U.S. dollar/Brazilian real currency futures contract traded on the Bolsa de Mercadorias y Futuros in Brazil.

To illustrate the use of futures for managing interest rate risks, we will focus on the three-month Eurodollar futures contracts. Exhibit 14.4 presents Eurodollar futures for two years (they actually trade 10 years into the future).

The yield of a futures contract is calculated from the *settlement price*, which is the closing price for that trading day. For example, a financial manager examining the Eurodollar quotes in Exhibit 14.4 for a March 2003 contract would see that the settlement price on the previous day was 94.76, an annual yield of 5.24%:

$$\text{yield} = (100.00 - 94.76) = 5.24\%$$

Since each contract is for a three-month period (quarter) and a notional principal of $1 million, each basis point is actually worth $2,500 (0.01 × $1,000,000 × 90/360).

If Caitlin Kelly were interested in hedging a floating-rate interest payment due in March 2003, she would need to *sell a future*, or to take a short position. This strategy is referred to as a short position because Caitlin is selling something she does not own (as in shorting common stock). If interest rates rise by March—as Caitlin fears—the futures price will fall and she will be able to close the position at a profit. This profit will roughly offset the losses associated with rising interest payments on her debt. If she is wrong, and interest rates actually fall by the maturity date, causing the futures price to rise, Caitlin will suffer a loss that will wipe out the "savings" derived by making a lower floating-rate interest payment than she expected. So by selling the March 2003 futures contract, she will be locking in an interest rate of 5.24%.

Exhibit 14.4 Eurodollar Futures Prices

Maturity	Open	High	Low	Settle	Yield	Open Interest
June 02	94.99	95.01	94.98	95.01	4.99	455,763
Sept	94.87	94.97	94.87	94.96	5.04	535,932
Dec	94.60	94.70	94.60	94.68	5.32	367,036
Mar 03	94.67	94.77	94.66	94.76	5.24	299,993
June	94.55	94.68	94.54	94.63	5.37	208,949
Sept	94.43	94.54	94.43	94.53	5.47	168,961
Dec	94.27	94.38	94.27	94.36	5.64	130,824

Typical presentation by the *Wall Street Journal*. Only regular quarterly maturities are shown. All contracts are for $1million; points of 100%. Open interest is number of contracts outstanding.

Exhibit 14.5 Interest Rate Futures Strategies for Common Exposures

Exposure or Position	Futures Action	Interest Rates	Position Outcome
Paying interest on future date	Sell a futures (short position)	If rates go up	Futures price falls; short earns a profit
		If rates go down	Futures price rises, short earns a loss
Earning interest on future date	Buy a futures (long position)	If rates go up	Futures price falls; long earns a loss
		If rates go down	Futures price rises, long earns a profit

Obviously interest rate futures positions could be—and are on a regular basis—purchased purely for speculative purposes. Although that is not the focus of the managerial context here, the example shows how any speculator with a directional view on interest rates could take positions in expectations of profit.

As mentioned previously, the most common interest rate exposure of the non-financial firm is interest payable on debt. Such exposure is not, however, the only interest rate risk. As more and more firms aggressively manage their entire balance sheet, the interest earnings from the left-hand side are under increasing scrutiny. If financial managers are expected to earn higher interest on interest-bearing securities, they may well find a second use of the interest rate futures market: to lock in future interest earnings. Exhibit 14.5 provides an overview of these two basic interest rate exposures and the strategies needed to manage interest rate futures.

Interest Rate Swaps

Swaps are contractual agreements to exchange or swap a series of cash flows. These cash flows are most commonly the interest payments associated with debt service, such as the floating-rate loan described earlier.

- If the agreement is for one party to swap its fixed interest rate payment for the floating interest-rate payments of another, it is termed an *interest rate swap*.
- If the agreement is to swap currencies of debt service obligation—for example, Swiss franc interest payments in exchange for U.S. dollar interest payments—it is termed a *currency swap*.
- A single swap may combine elements of both interest rate and currency swaps.

In any case, however, the swap serves to alter the firm's cash flow obligations, as in changing floating-rate payments into fixed-rate payments associated with an existing debt obligation. The swap itself is not a source of capital, but rather an alteration of the cash flows associated with payment. What is often termed the *plain vanilla swap* is an agreement between two parties to exchange fixed-rate for floating-rate financial obligations. This type of swap forms the largest single financial derivative market in the world.

The two parties may have various motivations for entering into the agreement. For example, a very common situation is as follows. A corporate borrower of good credit standing has existing floating-rate debt service payments. The borrower, after reviewing current market conditions and forming expectations about the future, may conclude that interest rates are about to rise. In order to protect the firm against rising debt-service payments, the company's treasury may enter into a swap agreement to *pay fixed/receive floating*. This means the firm will now make fixed interest rate payments and receive from the swap counterparty floating interest rate payments. The floating-rate payments that the firm receives are used to service the debt obligation of the firm, so the firm, on a net basis, is now making fixed interest rate payments. Using derivatives, it has synthetically changed floating-rate debt into fixed-rate debt. It has done so without going through the costs and intricacies of refinancing existing debt obligations.

Similarly, a firm with fixed-rate debt that expects interest rates to fall can change fixed-rate debt to floating-rate debt. In this case, the firm would enter into a *pay floating/receive fixed* interest rate swap. Exhibit 14.6 presents a summary table of the recommended interest rate swap strategies for firms holding either fixed rate debt or floating-rate debt.

The cash flows of an interest rate swap are interest rates applied to a set amount of capital (*notional principal*). For this reason, they are also referred to as *coupon swaps*. Firms entering into interest rate swaps set the notional principal so that the cash flows resulting from the interest rate swap cover their interest rate management needs.

Interest rate swaps are contractual commitments between a firm and a swap dealer and are completely independent of the interest rate exposure of the firm. That is, the firm may enter into a swap for any reason it sees fit and then swap a notional principal that is less than, equal to, or even greater than the total position being managed. For example, a firm with a variety of floating-rate loans on its books may enter into interest rate swaps for only 70% of the existing principal, if it wishes. The reason for entering into a swap, and the swap position the firm enters into, is purely at management's discretion. It should also be noted that the interest rate swap market is filling a gap in market efficiency. If all firms had free and equal access to capital markets, regardless of interest rate structure or currency of denomination, the swap market would most likely not exist. The fact that the swap market not only exists but flourishes and provides benefits to all parties is in some ways the proverbial "free lunch."

Carlton Corporation: Swapping to Fixed Rates

Carlton Corporation's existing floating-rate loan is now the source of some concern to Caitlin Kelly. Recent events have led her to believe that interest rates, specifically LIBOR, may be rising in the three years ahead. Because the loan agreement is relatively new (Carlton is still in the first year of the loan and has yet to make an interest payment), refinancing is considered too expensive

Exhibit 14.6 Interest Rate Swap Strategies

Position	Expectation	Interest Rate Swap Strategy
Fixed rate debt	Rates to go up	Do nothing
	Rates to go down	Pay floating/Receive fixed
Floating-rate debt	Rates to go up	Pay fixed/Receive floating
	Rates to go down	Do nothing

at this point. Caitlin believes that a *pay fixed/receive floating* interest rate swap may be the better alternative for fixing future interest rates now. Upon contacting several of its primary banks, Caitlin is quoted a fixed rate of 5.750% against LIBOR. If Carlton enters into the swap agreement, for the next three years it will receive LIBOR and pay out 5.750% on a notional principal of $10 million. A quick analysis of the combined existing loan and pay fixed/receive floating swap undertaken by Carlton's Treasury group is presented in Exhibit 14.7.

The swap agreement does not replace the existing loan agreement; it supplements it. Carlton is still responsible for making all payments on the floating-rate loan. Note that the swap agreement applies only to the interest payments on the loan and does not include the principal repayment. The portion of the debt service payment that Carlton is concerned about—the LIBOR base rate—would now be offset by the receipt of a cash flow of LIBOR from the swap bank. This arrangement leaves Carlton responsible for payment of the 1.500% fixed spread on the loan plus the fixed payment to the swap bank of 5.750%. These payments combine to create a total fixed interest rate payment of 7.250% on the $10 million debt, as illustrated in Exhibit 14.7.

The question that remains for Caitlin Kelly is whether this is a good deal. Carlton now has a fixed-rate debt of $10 million for three years. If current market rates quoted to Carlton by its lenders are at fixed rates above 7.250%, the answer is yes. Carlton would be well advised to secure the swap agreement now, assuming its goal is to lock in fixed rates of interest for the coming three years.

Currency Swaps

Since all swap rates are derived from the yield curve in each major currency, the fixed- to floating-rate interest rate swap existing in each currency allows firms to swap across currencies. Exhibit 14.8

Exhibit 14.7 Carlton's Interest Rate Swap to Pay Fixed/Receive Floating

Loan Interest Rates	**Variability**	**Year 1**	**Year 2**	**Year 3**
LIBOR (floating)	Could go up or down	–5.000%	–5.000%	–5.000%
Spread (fixed)	Fixed	–1.500%	–1.500%	–1.500%
Total interest payable		–6.500%	–6.500%	–6.500%
Swap Interest Rates				
Pay fixed	Fixed	–5.750%	–5.750%	–5.750%
Receive floating LIBOR	Could go up or down	+5.000%	+5.000%	+5.000%
Combined Loan and Swap Position				
LIBOR on loan	Paying	–5.000%	–5.000%	–5.000%
Spread (fixed)	Paying	–1.500%	–1.500%	–1.500%
Pay fixed on swap	Paying	–5.750%	–5.750%	–5.750%
Receive floating LIBOR on swap	Receiving	+5.000%	+5.000%	+5.000%
Net interest due after swap	Net payment	–7.250%	–7.250%	–7.250%

Note: On the date the interest rate swap agreement is made, the actual LIBOR rates for all years (1, 2, and 3), are unknown. However, on the basis of the expectations of swaps traders, the present value of the floating-rate cash flow streams and fixed-rate cash flow streams are equal on the agreement date.

Exhibit 14.8 Interest Rate and Currency Swap Quotes

	Euro		Swiss franc		U.S. dollar		Japanese yen	
Years	Bid	Ask	Bid	Ask	Bid	Ask	Bid	Ask
1	2.99	3.02	1.43	1.47	5.24	5.26	0.23	0.26
2	3.08	3.12	1.68	1.76	5.43	5.46	0.36	0.39
3	3.24	3.28	1.93	2.01	5.56	5.59	0.56	0.59
4	3.44	3.48	2.15	2.23	5.65	5.68	0.82	0.85
5	3.63	3.67	2.35	2.43	5.73	5.76	1.09	1.12
6	3.83	3.87	2.54	2.62	5.80	5.83	1.33	1.36
7	4.01	4.05	2.73	2.81	5.86	5.89	1.55	1.58
8	4.18	4.22	2.91	2.99	5.92	5.95	1.75	1.78
9	4.32	4.36	3.08	3.16	5.96	5.99	1.90	1.93
10	4.42	4.46	3.22	3.30	6.01	6.04	2.04	2.07
12	4.58	4.62	3.45	3.55	6.10	6.13	2.28	2.32
15	4.78	4.82	3.71	3.81	6.20	6.23	2.51	2.56
20	5.00	5.04	3.96	4.06	6.29	6.32	2.71	2.76
25	5.13	5.17	4.07	4.17	6.29	6.32	2.77	2.82
30	5.19	5.23	4.16	4.26	6.28	6.31	2.82	2.88
LIBOR	3.0313	3.0938	1.3125	1.4375	4.9375	5.0625	0.1250	0.2188

Typical presentation by *The Financial Times*. Bid and ask spreads as of close of London business. US$ is quoted against three-month LIBOR; Japanese yen against six-month LIBOR; Euro and Swiss franc against six-month LIBOR.

lists typical swap rates for the euro, the Swiss franc, the U.S. dollar, and the Japanese yen. These swap rates are based on the government security yields in each of the individual currency markets, plus a credit spread applicable to investment grade borrowers in the respective markets.

Note that the swap rates in Exhibit 14.8 are not rated or categorized by credit ratings. This is so because the swap market itself does not carry the credit risk associated with individual borrowers. We saw that in the previous interest rate swap example when Carlton, which borrowed on its own at LIBOR plus a spread of 1.500% (the spread representing the credit spread specific to the borrower), swapped out of the LIBOR component only. The fixed spread, a credit risk premium, was still borne by the firm itself. For example, lower-rated firms may pay spreads of 3% or 4% over LIBOR, while some of the world's largest and most financially sound MNEs may actually raise capital at rates of LIBOR –0.40%. The swap market does not differentiate the rate by the participant; all swap at fixed rates versus LIBOR in the respective currency.

The usual motivation for a currency swap is to replace cash flows scheduled in an undesired currency with flows in a desired currency. The desired currency is probably the currency in which the firm's future operating revenues (inflows) will be generated. Firms often raise capital in currencies in which they do not possess significant revenues or other natural cash flows. The reason they do so is cost; specific firms may find capital costs in specific currencies attractively priced to them under special conditions. Having raised the capital, however, the firm may wish to swap its repayment into a currency in which it has future operating revenues.

The utility of the currency swap market to a MNE is significant. A MNE wishing to swap a 10-year fixed 6.04% U.S. dollar cash flow stream could swap to 4.46% fixed in euro, 3.30% fixed in Swiss francs, or 2.07% fixed in Japanese yen. It could swap from fixed dollars not only to fixed rates, but also to floating LIBOR rates in the various currencies as well. All are possible at the rates quoted in Exhibit 14.8.

The currency swap market has also been utilized to implement creative financing solutions. Global Finance Perspective 14.1 describes the use of currency swaps to finance student exchanges and economic development in Ecuador. Similar programs have existed in the past to fund and support a variety of environmental preservation programs around the world as well.

Global Finance Perspective **14.1**

Ecuadorian Debt-for-Development

In the early 1990s, several countries introduced unique programs that used some of the basic concepts of cross-currency swaps to both reduce their existing foreign currency debts and promote internal development programs. These countries had borrowed large quantities of U.S. dollar–denominated debt in the prior decade, and were now attempting to find ways in which this debt could be reduced.

Ecuador introduced a debt-for-development program in 1990. This program allowed not-for-profit institutions like universities to exchange their U.S. dollars for local currency–denominated debt—Ecuadorian sucre bonds, in this case. The dollars received from the universities would then be used to pay off the outstanding debt. The universities would then sell the local currency bonds for cash. The cash was then used to run student study programs in Ecuador. The cash could not, however, be exchanged in the currency markets for dollars or any other currency, since this would cause additional downward pressures on the value of the sucre, which Ecuador was trying to avoid.

The mechanics of the swap program were not, however, without risk. For example, Oregon State University would actually purchase the Ecuadorian debt from banks in New York City. They were able to buy these at a discounted rate, say $0.20 per $1.00 of face value debt. (The discount was the result of Ecuador's difficulty in paying off the debt, which was only expected to worsen.) This discounted price then allowed Oregon State to effectively "multiply" its financial resources by a factor of 5 (1/0.2). Oregon State would then present the bonds to the Ecuadorian government in Quito, where the authorities would exchange the dollar-bonds for sucre-bonds. Oregon State would then immediately sell the bonds on the open market for cash. The cash received was substantially larger than what Oregon State could have obtained by simply exchanging U.S. dollars for Ecuadorian sucre in the foreign exchange market.

Other countries introduced similar programs for the same reasons during this time. Costa Rica introduced a debt-for-environment program in which Costa Rican foreign currency debt could be exchanged for local currency resources that could be expended only for environmental projects within Costa Rica. Chile had a number of debt-for-equity swap programs in which debt-holders (e.g., major banks around the world) could exchange their bonds that were now in default for equity shares in Chilean corporations.

Carlton Corporation:
Swapping Floating Dollars into Fixed-Rate Swiss Francs

We return to Carlton Corporation to demonstrate how to use a currency swap. After raising $10 million in floating-rate financing, and subsequently swapping into fixed-rate payments, Carlton decides that it would prefer to make its debt service payments in Swiss francs. Carlton had recently signed a sales contract with a Swiss buyer that will be paying francs to Carlton over the next three-year period. This would be a natural inflow of Swiss francs for the coming three years, and Carlton may decide it wishes to match the currency of denomination of the cash flows through a currency swap.

Carlton Corporation now enters into a three-year *pay Swiss francs and receive U.S. dollars* currency swap. Both interest rates are fixed. Carlton will pay 2.01% (ask rate) fixed Swiss franc interest, and receive 5.56% (bid rate) fixed U.S. dollars.

As illustrated in Exhibit 14.9, the three-year currency swap entered into by Carlton is different from the plain vanilla interest rate swap described above in two important ways:

1. The spot exchange rate in effect on the date of the agreement establishes what the notional principal is in the target currency. The target currency is the currency Carlton is swapping into, in this case the Swiss franc. The $10,000,000 notional principal converts to a Sfr15,000,000 notional principal. This is the principal used to establish the actual cash flows Carlton is committing to making (2.01% × Sfr15,000,000 = Sfr301,500).
2. The notional principal itself is part of the swap agreement. In the interest rate swaps described previously, both interest payment cash flows were based on the same U.S. dollar notional principal. Hence, there was no need to include the principal in the agreement. In a currency swap, however, because the notional principals are denominated in two different currencies, and the exchange rate between those two currencies may change over the life of the swap, the notional principals are actually part of the swap agreement.

At the time of the swap's inception, both positions have the same net present value. Carlton's swap commits it to three future cash payments in Swiss francs. In turn, it will receive three pay-

Exhibit 14.9 Carlton's Currency Swap: Pay Swiss Francs and Receive U.S. Dollars

Swap component	Year 0	Year 1	Year 2	Year 3
Will receive fixed US$ at this rate:		5.56%	5.56%	5.56%
on a notional principal of:	$10,000,000			
Cash flows Carlton will receive:		$556,000	$556,000	$10,556,000
Exchange rate	Sfr.1.5000/$			
Carlton will pay fixed Sfr at rate:		2.01%	2.01%	2.01%
on a notional principal of:	Sfr15,000,000			
Cash flows Carlton will pay:		Sfr301,500	Sfr301,500	Sfr15,301,500

The pay fixed US$ rate of 5.56% is the three-year bid rate in Exhibit 14.8. The receive fixed Swiss franc rate of 2.01% is the three-year ask rate from Exhibit 14.8. Once Carlton determines the notional principal of $10,000,000, the current spot rate is used to determine the notional principal for the Swiss franc side of the swap (or vice versa, depending on Carlton's goals). The present value of each side of the swap at inception is $10,000,000 (Sfr15,000,000).

ments in U.S. dollars. The payments are set. Financial accounting practices will require Carlton to regularly track and value its position, mark-to-market the swap, on the basis of current exchange rates and interest rates. If after the swap is initiated the Swiss franc appreciates versus the dollar, and Carlton is paying francs, Carlton will record a loss on the swap for accounting purposes. (Similarly, the swap dealer's side of the transaction will record a gain.) At the same time, if interest rates in Swiss franc markets rise, and Carlton's swap commits it to a fixed rate of 2.01%, then a gain will result from the interest component of the swap's value. In short, gains and losses on the swap, at least for accounting purposes, will persist throughout the swap's life.

The currency swaps described here are nonamortizing swaps. A nonamortizing swap repays the entire principal at maturity, rather than over the life of the swap agreement. Swap dealers will of course be more than happy to provide the firm with the form of its choice. We use nonamortizing swap examples throughout this chapter for simplicity of presentation.

Carlton Corporation: Unwinding Swaps

As with all original loan agreements, it may happen that at some future date the partners to a swap may wish to terminate the agreement before it matures. If, for example, after one year Carlton Corporation's Swiss sales contract is terminated, Carlton will no longer need the swap as part of its hedging program. Carlton could terminate or *unwind* the swap with the swap dealer.

Unwinding a currency swap requires the discounting of the remaining cash flows under the swap agreement at current interest rates, then converting the target currency (Swiss francs) back to the home currency of the firm (U.S. dollars for Carlton). If Carlton has two payments remaining on the swap agreement of Sfr301,500 and Sfr15,301,500 (an interest-only payment, and a principal and interest payment), and the two-year fixed rate of interest for francs is now 2.000%, the present value of Carlton's commitment in Swiss francs is:

$$PV(Sfr) = \frac{Sfr301,500}{(1.020)^1} + \frac{Sfr15,301,500}{(1.020)^2} = Sfr15,002,912$$

At the same time, the present value of the remaining cash flows on the dollar side of the swap is determined using the current two-year fixed dollar interest rate, which is now 5.500%:

$$PV(\$) = \frac{\$556,000}{(1.055)^1} + \frac{\$10,556,000}{(1.055)^2} = \$10,011,078$$

Carlton's currency swap, if unwound at this time, would yield a present value of net inflows (what it receives under the swap) of $10,011,078 and a present value of outflows (what it pays under the swap) of Sfr15,002,912. If the spot exchange rate is now Sfr1.4650/$, the net settlement of this currency swap will be:

$$Settlement = \$10,011,078 = \frac{Sfr15,002,912}{Sfr1.4650\,/\,\$} = (\$229,818)$$

Carlton makes a cash payment to the swap dealer of $229,818 to terminate the swap. Carlton lost on the swap, largely as a result of the appreciation of the Swiss franc (the interest rates barely changed). Since Carlton had promised to pay in the currency which is now stronger in value—the franc unwinding the swap is costly. The swap, however, was entered into as a hedge rather than as a financial investment.

Counterparty Risk

Counterparty risk is the potential exposure any individual firm bears that the second party to any financial contract will be unable to fulfill its obligations under the contract's specifications. Concern over counterparty risk has risen in the interest rate and currency swap markets as a result of a few large and well-publicized swap defaults. The rapid growth in the currency and interest rate financial derivatives markets has actually been accompanied by a surprisingly low default rate to date, particularly in a global market that is, in principle, unregulated.

Counterparty risk has long been one of the major factors that favor the use of exchange-traded rather than over-the-counter derivatives. Most exchanges, like the Philadelphia Stock Exchange for currency options or the Chicago Mercantile Exchange for Eurodollar futures, are themselves the counterparty to all transactions. This allows all firms a high degree of confidence that they can buy or sell exchange-traded products quickly, and with little concern over the credit quality of the exchange itself. Financial exchanges typically require a small fee of all traders on the exchanges, to fund insurance funds created expressly for the purpose of protecting all parties. Over-the-counter products, however, are direct credit exposures to the firm because the contract is generally between the buying firm and the selling financial institution. Most financial derivatives in today's world financial centers are sold or brokered only by the largest and soundest financial institutions. This structure does not mean, however, that firms can enter continuing agreements with these institutions without some degree of real financial risk and concern.

A firm entering into a currency or interest rate swap agreement retains ultimate responsibility for the timely servicing of its own debt obligations. Although a swap agreement may constitute a contract to exchange U.S. dollar payments for euro payments, the firm that actually holds the dollar debt is still legally responsible for payment. The original debt remains on the borrower's books. In the event that a swap counterparty does not make the payment as agreed, the firm legally holding the debt is still responsible for debt service. In the event of such a failure, the euro payments would be stopped, by the right of *offset* (juxtaposed obligations), and the losses associated with the failed swap would be mitigated.

The real exposure of an interest or currency swap is not the total notional principal, but the mark-to-market values of differentials in interest or currency interest payments (replacement cost) since the inception of the swap agreement. This differential is similar to the change in swap value discovered by unwinding a swap. This amount is typically only 2% to 3% of the notional principal.

Illustrative Case: A Three-Way Back-to-Back Cross-Currency Swap

Individual firms often find special demands for their debt in select markets, allowing them to raise capital at several basis points lower there than in other markets. Thus a growing number of firms are confronted with debt service in currencies that are not normal for their operations. The result has been a use of debt issuances coupled with swap agreements from inception. The three-way borrowing plus swap structure depicted in Exhibit 14.10 between a Canadian province, a Finnish export agency, and a multilateral development bank is a case in point.

The Finnish Export Credit agency (FEC), the Province of Ontario, Canada, and the Inter-American Development Bank all possessed ready access to particular sources of capital but wished debt service in another. The investment banking house of Goldman Sachs as matchmaker brought all parties together and aided in the negotiation of both borrowing rates and swap rates:

- Finnish Export Credit (FEC) had not previously raised capital in the Canadian dollar Euromarkets and would be well received if borrowing there. FEC, however, had a need for increased debt service payments in U.S. dollars at this time, not Canadian dollars.
- Province of Ontario (Canada) needed Canadian dollars but, due to the size of the provincial borrowings in the recent past, it knew that further issues would push up the cost of funds. The province was, however, considered an attractive credit risk by the U.S. dollar market.
- Inter-American Development Bank (IADB), like FEC, had a need for additional U.S. dollar–denominated debt service. It had, however, already raised the majority of its capital in the dollar markets, but it was a welcome newcomer to the Canadian dollar market.

Each borrower determined its initial debt amounts and maturities expressly with the needs of the currency swap in mind. Then, in conjunction with Goldman Sachs, each negotiated the best pricing for its individual debt commitments. Simultaneous with debt issuance and placement, the three parties swapped the proceeds and debt service payment streams for their desired debt profiles. Each party was therefore able to issue debt in the market in which its debt would be well received (thus at lower cost) and then swap into the desired currency. All parties borrowed where they had a comparative advantage and then swapped into their desired currency at a lower all-in-cost than they could have achieved by direct debt issuance in that currency.

Exhibit 14.10 Three-Way Back-to-Back Cross-Currency Swap

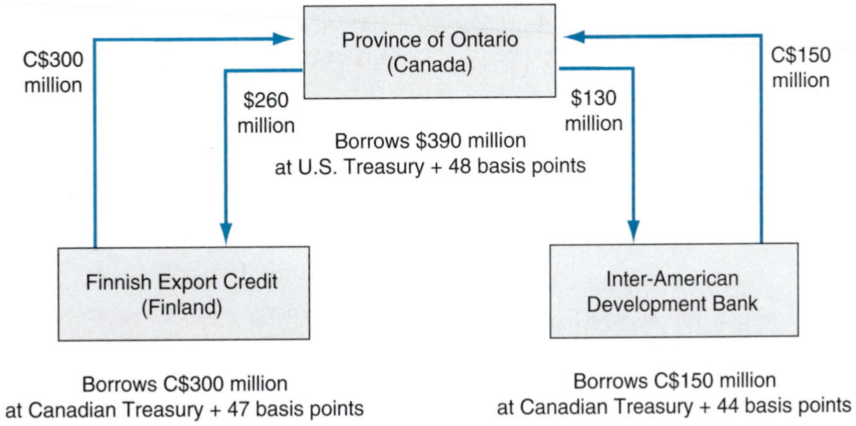

SUMMARY

- The single largest interest rate risk of the non-financial firm is debt service. The debt structure of the MNE will possess differing maturities of debt, different interest rate structures (such as fixed versus floating rate), and different currencies of denomination.
- The increasing volatility of world interest rates, combined with the increasing use of short-term and variable-rate debt by firms worldwide, has led many firms to actively manage their interest rate risks.
- The primary sources of interest rate risk to a multinational nonfinancial firm are short-term borrowing and investing, as well as long-term sources of debt.
- The techniques and instruments used in interest rate risk management in many ways resemble those used in currency risk management: the tried and true methods of lending and borrowing.
- The primary instruments and techniques used for interest rate risk management include forward rate agreements (FRAs), interest rate futures, and interest rate swaps.
- The interest rate and currency swap markets allow firms that have limited access to specific currencies and interest rate structures to gain access at relatively low costs. This in turn allows these firms to manage their currency and interest rate risks more effectively.
- A cross-currency interest rate swap allows a firm to alter both the currency of denomination of cash flows in debt service and the fixed-to-floating or floating-to-fixed interest rate structure.

QUESTIONS

1. **Triumvirate of risks.** Define and explain the three main financial risks facing a multinational enterprise.
2. **Reference rates.** What is an interest "reference rate" and how is it used to set rates for individual borrowers?
3. **Risk and return.** Some corporate treasury departments are organized as service centers (cost centers), while others are set up as profit centers. What is the difference and what are the implications for the firm?
4. **Forecast types.** What is the difference between a specific forecast and a directional forecast?
5. **Policy statements.** Explain the difference between a goal statement and a policy statement.
6. **Credit and repricing risk.** From the point of view of a borrowing corporation, what are credit and repricing risks? Explain steps a company might take to minimize both.
7. **Forward rate agreement.** How can a business firm that has borrowed on a floating-rate basis use a forward rate agreement to reduce interest rate risk?
8. **Eurodollar futures.** The newspaper reports that a given June Eurodollar future settled at 93.55. What was the annual yield?
9. **Defaulting on an interest rate swap.** Smith Company and Jones Company enter into an interest rate swap, with Smith paying fixed interest to Jones, and Jones paying floating interest to Smith. Smith now goes bankrupt and so defaults on its remaining interest payments. What is the financial damage to Jones Company?
10. **Currency swaps.** Why would one company with interest payments due in pounds sterling want to swap those payments for interest payments due in U.S. dollars?
11. **Counterparty risk.** How does organized exchange trading in swaps remove any risk that the counterparty in a swap agreement will not complete the agreement?

PROBLEMS

1. **Andina, S.A.** Andina, S.A., a Chilean company, wishes to borrow $8,000,000 for eight weeks. A rate of 4.00% per annum is quoted by potential lenders in New York, Great Britain, and Switzerland using, respectively, international, British, and the Swiss-Eurobond definitions of interest (day count conventions). From which source should Andina borrow?

2. **Adelaide Corporation.** Adelaide Corporation of Australia seeks to borrow US$30,000,000 in the Eurodollar market. Funding is needed for two years. Investigation leads to three possibilities:

   a. Adelaide Corporation could borrow the US$30,000,000 for two years at a fixed 5% rate of interest.

   b. Adelaide Corporation could borrow the US$30,000,000 at LIBOR + 1.5%. LIBOR is currently 3.5%, and the rate would be reset every six months.

   c. Adelaide Corporation could borrow the US$30,000,000 for one year only at 4.5%. At the end of the first year, Adelaide Corporation would have to negotiate for a new one-year loan.

   Compare the alternatives and make a recommendation.

3. **Raid Gauloises.** Raid Gauloises is a rapidly growing French sporting goods and adventure racing outfitter. The company has decided to borrow €20,000,000 via a euro-euro floating-rate loan for four years. Raid must decide between two competing loan offerings from two of its banks.

   Banque de Paris has offered the four-year debt at euro-LIBOR + 2.00% with an up-front initiation fee of 1.8%. Banque de Sorbonne, however, has offered euro-LIBOR + 2.5%, a higher spread, but with no loan initiation fees up front, for the same term and principal. Both banks reset the interest rate at the end of each year.

   Euro-LIBOR is currently 4.00%. Raid's economist forecasts that LIBOR will rise by 0.5 percentage points each year. Banque de Sorbonne, however, officially forecasts euro-LIBOR to begin trending upward at the rate of 0.25 percentage points per year. Raid Gauloises's cost of capital is 11%. Which loan proposal do you recommend for Raid Gauloises?

4. **Felini Motors.** Felini Motors of Italy recently took out a four-year €5 million loan on a floating-rate basis. It is now worried, however, about rising interest costs. Although it had initially believed interest rates in the Euro-zone would be trending downward when taking out the loan, recent economic indicators show growing inflationary pressures. Analysts are predicting that the European Central Bank will slow monetary growth, driving interest rates up.

   Felini is now considering whether to seek some protection against a rise in euro-LIBOR, and is considering a forward rate agreement (FRA) with an insurance company. According to the agreement Felini would pay to the insurance company at the end of each year the difference between its initial interest cost at LIBOR + 2.50% (6.50%) and any fall in interest cost due to a fall in LIBOR. Conversely, the insurance company would pay to Felini 70% of the difference between Felini's initial interest cost and any increase in interest costs caused by a rise in LIBOR.

   Purchase of the forward rate agreement will cost $100,000, paid at the time of the initial loan. What are Felini's annual financing costs now if LIBOR rises and if LIBOR falls.? Felini uses 12% as its weighted average cost of capital. Do you recommend that Felini purchase the FRA?

5. **John Jones.** John Jones must pay floating-rate interest three months from now. He wants to lock in this interest payment by buying an interest rate futures contract. Interest rate futures for three months from now settled at 93.07, for a yield of 6.93% per annum. If the floating interest rate three months from now is 6.00%, what did John Jones gain or lose? If it is 8.00%, what did John Jones gain or lose?

6. **Cañon Candy Company.** Mary Martin, the treasurer of Cañon Candy Company, believes interest rates are going to rise, so she wants to swap her future floating-rate interest payments for fixed rates. At present, she is paying LIBOR + 2% per annum on $5,000,000 of debt for the next two years, with payments due semiannually. LIBOR is currently 4.00% per annum. Martin has just made an interest payment today, so the next payment is due six months from today.

   Martin finds that she can swap her current floating-rate payments for fixed payments of 7.00% per annum. (Cañon Candy's weighted average cost of capital is 12%, which Martin calculates to be 6% per six-month period, compounded semiannually.)

   a. If LIBOR rises at the rate of 50 basis points per six-month period, starting tomorrow, how much does Martin save or cost her company by making this swap?
   b. If LIBOR falls at the rate of 25 basis points per six-month period, starting tomorrow, how much does Martin save or cost her company by making this swap?

7. **Xavier and Zulu.** Xavier Manufacturing and Zulu Products both seek funding at the lowest possible cost. Xavier would prefer the flexibility of floating-rate borrowing, while Zulu wants the security of fixed-rate borrowing. Xavier is the more creditworthy company. They face the following rate structure. Xavier, with the better credit rating, has lower borrowing costs in both types of borrowing:

	Xavier	Zulu
Credit rating	AAA	BBB
Fixed-rate cost of borrowing	8%	12%
Floating-rate cost of borrowing	LIBOR + 1%	LIBOR + 2%

   Xavier wants floating-rate debt, so it could borrow at LIBOR + 1%. However it could borrow fixed at 8% and swap for floating-rate debt. Zulu wants fixed rate, so it could borrow fixed at 12%. However it could borrow floating at LIBOR + 2% and swap for fixed-rate debt. What should they do?

8. **Carlton's cross-currency swap: Sfr for US$.** Carlton Corporation entered into a three-year cross-currency interest rate swap in the chapter to receive U.S. dollars and pay Swiss francs. Carlton, however, decided to unwind the swap after one year, thereby having two years left on the settlement costs of unwinding the swap after one year. Repeat the calculations for unwinding, but assume that the following rates now apply:

Two-year Swiss franc interest rate	5.20% per annum
Two-year U.S. dollar interest rate	2.20% per annum
Spot exchange rate	SF1.5560/$

9. **Carlton's cross-currency swap: Yen for euros.** Using the same table of swap rates (Exhibit 14.8), assume Carlton enters into a swap agreement to *receive euros and pay Japanese yen*, on a notional principal of €5,000,000. The spot exchange rate at the time of the swap is ¥104/€.

   a. Calculate all principal and interest payments, in both euros and Swiss francs, for the life of the swap agreement. (Use Exhibit 14.9 as a guide.)
   b. Assume that one year into the swap agreement, Carlton decides it wishes to unwind the swap agreement and settle it in euros. Assuming that a two-year fixed rate of interest on the Japanese yen is now 0.80%, a two-year fixed rate of interest on the euro is now 3.60%, and the spot rate of exchange is now ¥114/€: what is the net present value of the swap agreement? Who pays whom what?

10. **Delphi.** Delphi is the U.S.-based automotive parts supplier that was spun off from General Motors in 2000. With annual sales of over $26 billion, the company has expanded its markets far beyond the traditional automobile manufacturers in the pursuit of a more diversified sales base. As part of the general diversification effort, the company wishes to diversify the currency of denomination of its debt portfolio as well. Assume Delphi enters into a $50 million seven-year cross currency interest rate swap to do just that—pay euro and receive dollars. Using the data in Exhibit 14.8 and assuming a spot rate of $1.16/euro:

a. Calculate all principal and interest payments in both currencies for the life of the swap.

b. Assume that three years later, Delphi decides to unwind the swap agreement. If four-year fixed rates of interest in euros have now risen to 5.35%, four-year fixed rate dollars have fallen to 4.40%, and the current spot exchange rate of $1.02/€: what is the net present value of the swap agreement? Who pays what to whom?

INTERNET EXERCISES

WWW.

1. **Current interest rates and yield curves.** Use the New York Federal Reserve Bank's web page for recent interest rates on all maturities of U.S. dollar–denominated debt issues. Historical data is also available, so that it is relatively easy to plot how the Treasury's Constant Maturity yields have changed from week to week and month to month for maturities varying between 3 months and 10 years.

   Federal Reserve Bank of New York http://www.ny.frb.org

   Board of Governors of the Federal Reserve http://www.bog.frb.fed.us/releases/h15/current

2. **The International Swaps & Derivatives Association (ISDA).** The ISDA is the primary global organization attempting to both standardize the use of interest rate and cross-currency swaps and track the market's size. Use ISDA's web site to find out which type of interest rate derivative is growing the fastest.

   International Swaps & Derivatives Association http://www.isda.org

3. **Emerging markets and debt.** The emerging markets of Latin America, Eastern Europe, Africa, and Asia are where many firms are now expanding operations and therefore creating new demands for debt. Use the following web pages to learn more about the instruments and markets of many emerging markets, including the most recent quotes on Brady Bonds, one of the most widely traded emerging market debt instruments in the world.

   Emerging Markets Companion http://www.emgmkts.com

   J.P. Morgan & Company, Inc. http://www.jpmorgan.com

SELECTED READINGS

Brown, Keith C., and Donald J. Smith, "Default Risk and Innovations in the Design of Interest Rate Swaps," *Financial Management*, Summer 1993, Volume 22, No. 2, pp. 94–105.

Ho, T. S., Richard C. Stapleton, and Marti G. Subrahmanyam, "The Risk of a Currency Swap: A Multivariate Binomial Methodology," *European Financial Management*, March 1998, Volume 4, Number 1, pp. 9–28.

Smith, Clifford W., Jr., Charles W. Smithson, and Lee MacDonald Wakeman, "The Market for Interest Rate Swaps," *Financial Management*, Winter 1988, pp. 34–44.

Solnik, Bruno, "Swap Pricing and Default Risk: A Note," *Journal of International Financial Management and Accounting*, Spring 1990, Volume 2, No. 1, pp. 79–91.

MINI-CASE

McDonald's Corporation's British Pound Exposure

McDonald's Corporation has investments in over 100 countries. It considers its equity investment in foreign subsidiaries to be at risk, subject to hedging depending on the individual country, currency, and market.

British Subsidiary as an Exposure

McDonald's parent company has three different pound-denominated exposures arising from ownership and operation of its British subsidiary

- The British subsidiary has equity capital, which is a pound-denominated asset of the parent company.
- In addition to the equity capital invested in the British affiliate, the parent company provides intra-company debt in the form of a four-year £125 million loan. The loan is denominated in British pounds and carries a fixed 5.30% per annum interest payment.
- The British subsidiary pays a fixed percentage of gross sales in royalties to the parent company. This too is pound-denominated. The three different exposures sum to a significant exposure problem for McDonald's.

An additional technical detail further complicates the situation. When the parent company makes an intracompany loan to the British subsidiary, it must designate—according to U.S. accounting and tax law practices—whether the loan is considered to be permanently invested in that country. (Although on the surface it seems illogical to consider four years "permanent," the parent company could continually roll the loan over and never actually repay it.) If it is not considered permanent, the foreign exchange gains and losses related to the loan flow directly to the parent company's profit and loss statement, according to FAS #52. If, however, the loan is designated as permanent, the foreign exchange gains and losses related to the intracompany loan flow only to the CTA (*cumulative translation adjustment*) on the consolidated balance sheet. To date, McDonald's has chosen to designate the loan as permanent. The functional currency of the British affiliate for consolidation purposes is the local currency, the British pound.

Anka Gopi is both the manager for Financial Markets/Treasury at McDonald's and a McDonald's shareholder. She is currently reviewing the existing hedging strategy employed by McDonald's against the pound exposure. The company has been hedging the pound exposure by entering into a cross-currency U.S. dollar/British pound sterling swap. The current swap is a seven-year swap to receive dollars and pay pounds. Like all cross-currency swaps, the agreement requires McDonald's-U.S. to make regular pound-denominated interest payments and a bullet principal repayment (notional principal) at the end of the swap agreement. McDonald's considers the large notional principal payment a hedge against the equity investment in its British subsidiary.

According to FAS #52, a company may elect to take the interest associated with a foreign currency–denominated loan and carry that directly to the parent company's P&L. This has been done in the past, and McDonald's has benefitted from the inclusion of this interest payment.

FAS #133, Accounting for Derivative Instruments and Hedging Activities, issued in June 1998, was originally intended to be effective for all fiscal quarters within fiscal years beginning after June 15, 1999 (for most firms this meant January 1, 2000). The new standard, however, was so complex and potentially of such material influence to U.S.-based MNEs that the Financial Accounting Standards Board has been approached by dozens of major firms and asked to postpone mandatory implementation. The standard's complexity, combined with the workloads associated with Y2K (year 2000) risk controls, persuaded the Financial Accounting Standards Board to delay FAS #133's mandatory implementation date indefinitely.

Anka Gopi wishes to consider the potential impact of FAS #133 on the hedging strategy currently employed. Under FAS #133, the firm will have to mark-to-market the entire cross-currency swap position, including principal, and carry this to *other comprehensive income* (OCI). OCI, however, is actually a form of income required under U.S. GAAP and reported in the footnotes to the financial statements, but not the income measure used in reported earnings per share. Although McDonald's has been carrying the interest payments on the swap to income, it has not previously had to carry the present value of the swap principal to OCI. In Anka's eyes, this poses a substantial material risk to OCI.

Anka Gopi also wishes to reconsider the current strategy. She begins by listing the pros and cons of the current strategy, comparing these to alternative strategies, and then deciding what if anything should be done about it at this time.

Case Questions

1. How does the cross-currency swap effectively hedge the three primary exposures McDonald's has relative to its British subsidiary?
2. How does the cross-currency swap hedge the long-term equity exposure in the foreign subsidiary?
3. Should Anka—and McDonald's—worry about OCI?

Advanced Topics in Interest Rate Risk Management

This appendix extends the analysis of interest rate–risk management foundations presented in Chapter 14 by exploring the potential offered by option-based instruments and techniques. Interest-rate option instruments differ by their market, which may be exchange-traded or interbank (over-the-counter). Interest-rate options that are exchange-traded are actually options on interest rate futures contracts. Interest-rate options that are traded or written over-the-counter are termed *caps*, *floors*, and *collars*.

Interest Rate Caps and Floors

An *interest rate cap* is an option to fix a ceiling or maximum short-term interest-rate payment. The contract is written such that the buyer of the cap will receive a cash payment equal to the difference between the actual market interest rate and the cap strike rate on the notional principal, if the market rate rises above the strike rate. Like any option, the buyer of the cap pays a premium to the seller of the cap up front for this right. The premium is normally stated as an annual percentage consistent with that of the strike rate. An *interest rate floor* gives the buyer the right to receive the compensating payment (cash settlement) when the reference interest rate falls below the strike rate of the floor.

Exhibit 14A.1 lists interest rate cap and floor quotations for the U.S. dollar three-month LIBOR rate and Deutschemark six-month LIBOR. The quotes provide alternative maturities of 2, 3, or 5 years and alternative cap rates for the two shorter maturities, with a single cap and floor rate for the five-year maturity. Each cap and floor has bid and offer quotations so that a buyer could either buy or sell (write) the cap or floor.

Exhibit 14A.1 Interest Rate Cap and Floor Quotations

	U.S. Dollar Caps Versus Three-Month LIBOR		U.S. Dollar Floors Versus Three-Month LIBOR	
Maturity	**Cap Rate**	**Bid-Offer**	**Floor Rate**	**Bid-Offer**
2 years	5.00 %	42–46	4.00 %	42–47
	6.00 %	15–19	5.00 %	149–154
3 years	6.00 %	69–79	4.00 %	54–62
	7.00 %	35–42	5.00 %	190–200
5 years	7.00 %	147–165	5.00 %	245–261

	Deutschemark Caps Versus Six-Month LIBOR		Deutschemark Floors Versus Six-Month LIBOR	
Maturity	**Cap Rate**	**Bid-Offer**	**Floor Rate**	**Bid-Offer**
2 years	6.00 %	35–40	5.50 %	57–63
	6.50 %	19–24	6.00 %	101–107
3 years	6.00 %	93–99	5.50 %	89–96
	6.50 %	60–65	6.00 %	156–161
5 years	6.75 %	172–185	5.50 %	122–145

Source: Adapted from *International Financing Review*, July 31, 1993, Issue 990, p. 83. Bid–offer spreads are stated in basis points. For example, "42–46" is 0.42%–0.46% of the notional principal per annum.

Maturities and Structure

No theoretical limit exists to the specification of caps and floors. Most currency cap markets are liquid for up to ten years in the over-the-counter market, though the majority of trading falls between one and five years. There is an added distinction that is important to understanding cap maturity. It is not the total maturity that is singularly important, but the number of interest rate *resets* involved. For example, a common interest rate cap would be a two-year cap on three-month LIBOR. This means that the total cap agreement will last for two years, in which there will be a total of seven three-month LIBOR interest rate reset dates, or *fixings*. No reset exists for the first three-month period. There are two major types of interest rate caps:

1. *Interest rate guarantee (IRG)*. Provides protection to the buyer for a single period only. Protection is provided to the borrower in the event of a single major variable rate refunding or reinvestment.
2. *Interest rate cap*. Provides protection for an extended period of time—for example, 2 to 5 years—on some interest rate reset. The sub-period reset—for example three-month LIBOR or six-month LIBOR—is called the cap's *tenor*. This protection is discrete, meaning that protection is for the interest rate put into effect on a reset date, and not just any day over the period in which the actual market rate may creep up over the strike rate.

The interest rate cap is the more common of the two and is the subject of the following numerical example.

Cap Valuation

A typical cap written over-the-counter by a bank for a firm would appear as follows:

1. Maturity: 3 years
2. Strike rate: 6.00%
3. Reference rate: three-month U.S. dollar LIBOR
4. Total periods: 12 (4 per year for 3 years)
5. Notional principal: $10,000,000
6. Premium: 79 basis points (0.79%)
7. Fixed borrowing rate: 7.00%

This agreement establishes a cap on all quarterly reset dates for three years. The cap rate is 6.00% per annum. All interest payments made are calculated on the basis of a notional principal of $10,000,000. The up-front cost of the cap, the *premium*, is 79 basis points. If the firm were to borrow at fixed interest, it would pay 7.00%.

The value of a capped interest payment such as this one is actually composed of three different elements: 1) the actual three-month interest payment; 2) the amount of the cap payment to the cap buyer if the reference rate rises above the cap rate; and 3) the annualized cost of the cap. To demonstrate how the cap would work in practice, let us assume that the three-month LIBOR rate on the reset date (the actual reset rate is normally determined two days prior to the next actual payment date) has risen above the strike rate of 6.00% to 6.50%.

1. *Interest rate payment*. Regardless of whether the cap is activated, the buyer of the cap is responsible for making the normal interest payment. The firm owes a payment of three-month U.S. dollar LIBOR of 6.50% on a three-month period of actual 90 days on a notional principal of $10,000,000:

$$\$10,000,000 \times 0.0650 \times \frac{90}{360} = \$162,500$$

2. *Receive cap cash flow.* If the three-month LIBOR rate has risen above the cap rate on the reset date, the cap is activated and the buyer of the cap receives a cash payment from the cap seller equal to the difference between the actual three-month LIBOR rate of 6.50% and the cap rate of 6.00%, a cash payment of the following amount:

$$\$10,000,000 \times \left[(0.0650 - 0.0600) \times \frac{90}{360} \right] = \$12,500$$

3. *Amortized cap premium payment.* But alas, such flexibility and protection comes at a cost: the premium. The cap premium of 0.79% is a single lump-sum payment made at the beginning of the three-year period, and must therefore be annualized in order to calculate the total cost of the capped payment. The fixed rate of interest at which this firm could borrow is 7.00%, and this is therefore the rate of interest used in the amortization of the cap premium over 12 reset periods.

The amortized premium, for 12 periods, discounted at a rate of 7.00% per annum (1.75% per quarter) is found by using the loan amortization formula used in calculating mortgage payments of all kinds:

$$\text{Quarterly premium} = \frac{0.7900\%}{\left[\frac{1}{0.0175} - \frac{1}{0.0175 \times (1.0175)^{12}} \right]} = 0.07356\%$$

This is 0.07356% on a quarterly basis; 0.2942% on an annual basis.[1]

The resulting total or all-in-cost (AIC) of the capped interest payment is 6.2942%, or a maximum of $157,356 every three months:

<u>Cap Component</u>	*Annualized* <u>*Interest Cost*</u>	*Quarterly* <u>*Cash Payments*</u>
#1: Interest payment out-flow	6.5000 %	$ 162,500
#2: Cap cash payment in-flow	6.0000–6.5000 %	–12,500
#3: Cap premium payment out-flow	<u>0.2942 %</u>	<u>+ 7,356</u>
Total Cost or All-in-Cost	6.2942 %	$ 157,356

1. This is the calculation formula for amortized loan payments for a fixed rate of interest. The formula itself is:

$$\text{Period payment} = \frac{\text{present value}}{\left[\frac{1}{r} - \frac{1}{r \times (1+r)^{t}} \right]}$$

where the present value is the current loan amount, t is the number of periods, and r is the rate of interest per period. The resulting amortized mortgage payment services both principal and interest in a single constant cash payment per period.

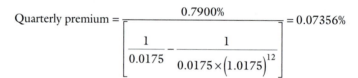

The firm has limited or *capped* its potential interest payments. If three-month LIBOR is below the cap rate of 6.00% on the next reset date, the firm's all-in-cost would be the actual LIBOR payment plus its quarterly premium payment of 0.294%. The premium payment will be made for the life of the cap regardless of whether the cap is exercised.

When the cap is exercised like this, the payment resembles the exchange of a floating for fixed interest payment, a swap. However, unlike a swap, when the reference rate does not rise above the strike rate, the firm continues to make regular interest payments and is not restricted to the swap rate.

In order to understand the motivation of the buyer of the interest rate guarantee or cap, it is useful to see the expected interest payment over a wide range of potential three-month LIBOR rates at the time of the cap agreement initiation. Exhibit 14A.2 compares the unhedged interest payment with the cap-hedged interest payment over a range of potential three-month LIBOR rates. Note that although the effective cap interest payment is slightly higher than 6.00% because of the cap premium that must be paid, it is still significantly cheaper than the unhedged interest payment if three-month LIBOR rates were to rise significantly above the strike rate of 6.00%. If LIBOR does not rise above the cap's strike rate, the presence of the premium of course increases the total cost of debt-service above the totally uncovered position.

If, however, the firm had swapped its three-month LIBOR floating payment for a fixed interest payment of 6.00%, regardless of the actual LIBOR rate on the original reset date, it would be locked in to a 6.00% interest payment. The interest rate cap provides the buyer with insurance against a rise in interest rates, while allowing the firm the opportunity to enjoy lower interest payments if actual market rates do not rise. As was the case with the use of foreign currency options in the management of currency transaction exposures in Chapter 6, a firm would purchase this insurance, this cap, only if it expects not to use it. If the firm held a strong expectation that interest rates would rise above 6.00% by the reset date, it would be better off swapping the floating for a fixed-rate payment.

Interest Rate Floors

Interest rate caps are basically call options on an interest rate, and equivalently, interest rate floors are put options on an interest rate. A *floor* guarantees the buyer of the floor option a minimum interest rate to be received (rate of return on notional principal invested) for a specified reinvestment period or series of periods.

For example, if a firm knows that it will receive a cash inflow in three months, which it must invest, it will want to invest at the highest possible rate. If it fears that interest rates will fall by that time, it may wish to purchase a floor. The floor will guarantee the firm a minimum effective rate of investment. If, when the date of investment arrives, the actual market rate of interest is less than the floor rate, the holder of the floor will receive from the writer of the floor a cash settlement equal to the difference between the actual reference rate and the floor rate.

Floor Valuation

The pricing and valuation of an interest rate floor is the same as that of the interest rate cap. Assume a German firm purchases a two-year interest rate floor of 6.00% as listed in Exhibit 14A.1. The specifications of the firm and its floor would be:

1. Maturity: 2 years
2. Strike rate: 6.00%

Exhibit 14A.2 Profile of an Interest Rate Cap

Exhibit 14A.2 Profile of an Interest Rate Cap

Input data	
Notional principal, $	$10,000,000
Maturity, years	3
Payments per year	4
Fixed borrowing rate, %/yr	7.00%
Cap strike rate, %/yr	6.00%
Premium, basis points	79

Annualized Cost of Cap	
Quarterly premium for cap	0.0736%
Annualized premium rate, %/yr	0.2942%
Cap rate, %/yr	6.0000%
Total cost, %/yr	6.2942%

Profile of an Interest Rate Cap	3-month LIBOR interest rate on reset date, %/year					
	5.00%	5.50%	6.000%	6.294%	7.00%	8.00%
Uncovered interest rate payment, %/year	5.00%	5.50%	**6.00%**	**6.294%**	**7.00%**	**8.00%**
Calculation of capped interest rate payment						
Normal quarterly interest payment	$125,000	$137,500	$150,000	$157,356	$175,000	$200,000
Receive cap cash flow	$0	$0	$0	$7,356	$25,000	$50,000
Cap premium payment outflow, $	$7,356	$7,356	$7,356	$7,356	$7,356	$7,356
Net quarterly cash outflow (All-in-Cost)	$132,356	$144,856	$157,356	$157,356	$157,356	$157,356
Capped interest rate payment, %/year	**5.294%**	**5.794%**	**6.294%**	**6.294%**	**6.294%**	**6.294%**

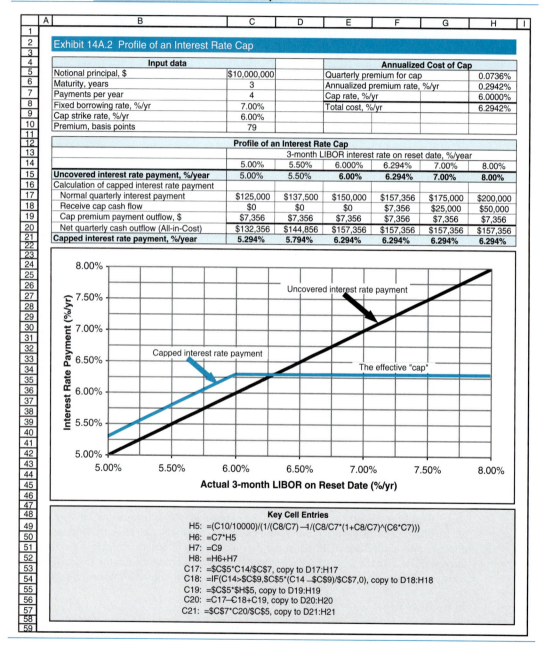

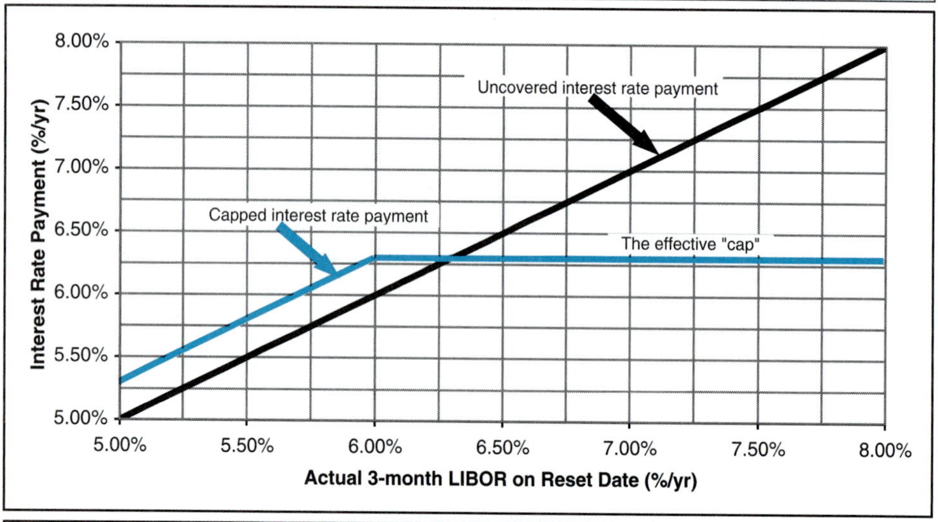

Key Cell Entries

H5: =(C10/10000)/(1/(C8/C7)–1/(C8/C7*(1+C8/C7)^(C6*C7)))
H6: =C7*H5
H7: =C9
H8: =H6+H7
C17: =$C$5*C14/$C$7, copy to D17:H17
C18: =IF(C14>$C$9,$C$5*(C14–$C$9)/$C$7,0), copy to D18:H18
C19: =$C$5*$H$5, copy to D19:H19
C20: =C17–C18+C19, copy to D20:H20
C21: =$C$7*C20/$C$5, copy to D21:H21

3. Reference rate: 6-month DM LIBOR
4. Total periods: 4 (semi-annually for 2 years)
5. Notional principal: DM 5,000,000

6. Floor premium: 107 basis points (1.07%)
7. Fixed investment rate: 6.50%

The firm does not expect interest rates (investment rates available to it) to fall below 6.00%, but wishes some insurance against the possibility. If at the end of a six-month period, however, the six-month DM LIBOR rate has indeed fallen below the floor rate of 6.00% to 5.80%, the interest rate floor is activated (exercised). The valuation of the floor would be decomposed into the same three basic elements as the cap:

1. *Interest rate payment/yield.* Regardless of whether the floor is activated, the firm that bought the floor will invest its funds at the market rate of interest. The firm therefore will earn 5.80%, the six-month DM LIBOR rate, on a notional principal of DM5,000,000:

$$DM5,000,000 \times 0.0580 \times \frac{180}{360} = DM145,000$$

2. *Receive floor cash flow.* Since the reference rate (six-month DM LIBOR) has fallen below the floor strike rate, the floor is activated. The buyer of the floor receives the difference between the floor rate and the reference rate in cash of:

$$DM5,000,000 \times \left[(0.0600 - 0.0580) \times \frac{180}{360} \right] = DM5,000$$

3. *Amortized floor premium payment.* Regardless of whether the floor is activated, the firm must pay for the floor option. The single lump-sum payment of 1.07% made up-front is amortized over the two-year period of six-month reset periods. The rate of interest used for the amortization is the fixed rate of interest available to the firm at the beginning of the period, in this case 6.50%. The premium expense per semi-annual period is:

$$\text{Semi-annual premium} = \frac{1.07\%}{\left[\frac{1}{0.0325} - \frac{1}{0.0325 \times (1.0325)^4} \right]} = 0.2896\%$$

This is 0.2896% on a semi-annual basis, or 0.5792% on an annual basis.

The all-in-yield of the floor-covered interest instrument is then 5.421% per annum, or a minimum return of DM135,520 each six months on a notional principal of DM5,000,000 for the two-year period:

Floor Component	Annualized Interest Yield	Quarterly Cash Flows
#1: Interest payment in-flow	5.800 %	DM 145,000
#2: Floor cash payment in-flow	6.000–5.800 %	5,000
#3: Floor premium payment out-flow	0.579 %	– 14,480
Total Yield or All-in-Yield	5.421 %	$ 135,520

Exhibit 14A.3 illustrates this floor valuation over a range of potential reference rates (six-month DM LIBOR) at the time of the semi-annual reset. Note that although the firm had placed a floor of 6.00% on its reinvestment of DM cash flows, its actual effective yield when the reference rate falls below the floor of 6.00% is 5.421% per annum. This is due to the annu-

Exhibit 14A.3 Profile of an Interest Rate Floor

Exhibit 14A.3 Profile of an Interest Rate Floor

Input data			Annualized Cost of Floor	
Notional principal, DM	5,000,000		Semi-annual premium for floor	0.2896%
Maturity, years	2		Annualized premium rate, %/yr	0.5792%
Payments per year	2		Floor rate, %/yr	6.0000%
Fixed borrowing rate, %/yr	6.50%		Total cost, %/yr	5.4208%
Floor strike rate, %/yr	6.00%			
Floor premium, basis points	107			

Profile of an Interest Rate Floor						
	6-month DM LIBOR interest rate on reset date, %/yr					
	4.00%	5.00%	5.421%	6.00%	7.00%	8.00%
Uncovered interest rate receipt, %/year	**4.00%**	**5.00%**	**5.421%**	**6.00%**	**7.00%**	**8.00%**
Calculation of floor interest rate payment						
Normal semi-annual interest earned, DM	100,000	125,000	135,521	150,000	175,000	200,000
Receive floor cash payment, DM	50,000	25,000	14,479	0	0	0
Floor premium payment outflow, DM	14,479	14,479	14,479	14,479	14,479	14,479
Net quarterly cash outflow (All-in-Cost), DM	135,521	135,521	135,521	135,521	160,521	185,521
Floor interest rate payment, %/year	**5.421%**	**5.421%**	**5.421%**	**5.421%**	**6.421%**	**7.421%**

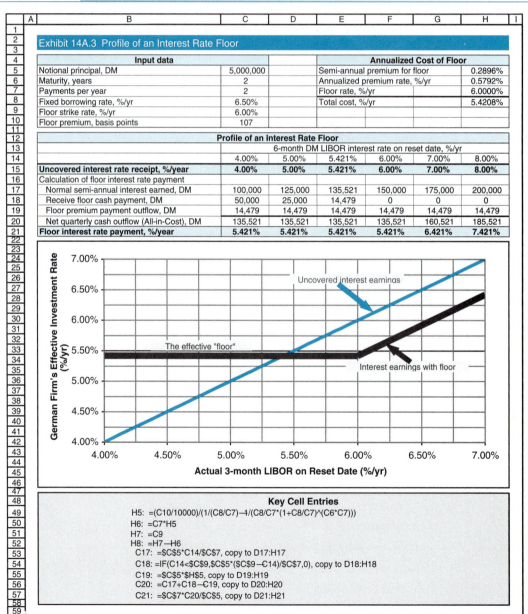

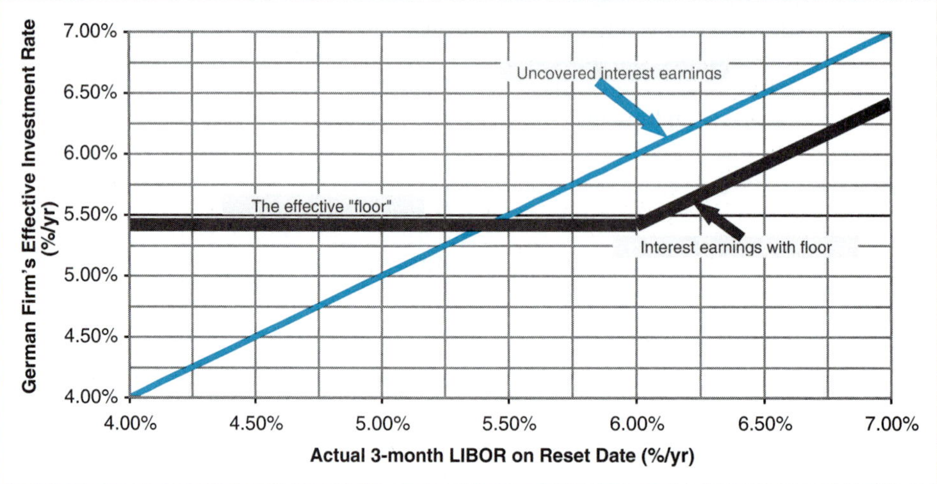

Key Cell Entries

```
H5: =(C10/10000)/(1/(C8/C7)–1/(C8/C7*(1+C8/C7)^(C6*C7)))
H6: =C7*H5
H7: =C9
H8: =H7–H6
C17: =$C$5*C14/$C$7, copy to D17:H17
C18: =IF(C14<$C$9,$C$5*($C$9–C14)/$C$7,0), copy to D18:H18
C19: =$C$5*$H$5, copy to D19:H19
C20: =C17+C18–C19, copy to D20:H20
C21: =$C$7*C20/$C$5, copy to D21:H21
```

alized premium expense. Once again, if the firm truly believed that interest rates would fall far enough to require the use of the floor, they would be better off investing at the fixed rate of 6.50% at the start of the period, rather than purchasing the floor as protection.

Interest Rate Collars

An *interest rate collar* is the simultaneous purchase (sale) of a cap and sale (purchase) of a floor. The firm constructing the collar earns a premium from the sale of one side to cover in part or in full the premium expense of purchasing the other side of the collar. If the two premiums are equal, the position is often referred to as a *zero-premium collar.*

Interest rate collars allow the firm to retain some of the benefit of declining rates while removing the unpleasantness of paying an up-front option premium for the cap. This unpleasantness can be mitigated, or totally eliminated in the case of a zero-cost collar, by the firm simultaneously selling a floor option of a suitable strike rate. For example, using the cap and floor quotations of Exhibit 14A.1, a firm could fund the purchase of a cap against three-month U.S. dollar LIBOR rising above 5.00% in the next two years (paying a premium of 0.46%) by selling a 4.00% floor on three-month U.S. dollar LIBOR for the same two-year maturity (earning a premium of 0.42%). Although not precisely a zero net cost, the up-front net cost of the position is extremely small (0.46%-0.42%=0.04%). This interest rate collar is illustrated in Exhibit 14A.4.

The risk of increased rates has been eliminated by forsaking the advantage of rates declining below the floor, at zero cost. It is important to remember that this means *zero initial cost,* for the firm will still be called on to make payments to the collar seller if rates fall below the floor level. Because the firm may be called on to make payments to the seller, each party to the transaction has credit exposure to the other like a swap. In the extreme case of a zero-cost collar of zero width, the collar becomes a swap. The foreign exchange equivalent of a collar is the simultaneous purchase of a call option and the sale of a put option on the short currency (a synthetic forward for a short foreign currency position).

Swaptions

The purchase of a swap option—a *swaption*—gives the firm the right but not the obligation to enter into a swap on a pre-determined notional principal at some defined future date at a specified strike rate. The firm's treasurer would typically purchase a *payer's swaption,* giving the treasurer the right to enter a swap in which they pay the fixed rate and receive the floating rate. The treasurer would exercise this option if rates had risen above the strike level of the swaption; otherwise, the treasurer would allow the option to expire and take advantage of the lower rate environment.

If exercised, the swaption may be *swap-settled,* settled for cash. In this case, the firm would receive a payment reflecting the intrinsic value of the swap. In the case of cash settlement, this eliminates the ongoing mutual counterparty risk. As with any option, the maximum downside risk for the firm is the initial premium exposure.

Many multinationals increasingly sell swaptions. A U.K.-resident firm would sell a swaption, termed a *receiver's swaption,* struck at an acceptable fixed rate, giving the purchasing bank the right to receive the fixed rate from the firm. The bank would exercise this option if rates had declined below the strike rate.

Exhibit 14A.4 Profile of an Interest Rate Collar

Exhibit 14A.4 Profile of an Interest Rate Collar

Input data	
Notional principal, $	$10,000,000
Maturity, years	2
Payments per year	4
Fixed borrowing rate, %/yr	4.50%
Cap strike rate, %/yr	5.50%
Cap rate, %/yr	5.00%
Premium for cap, basis points	46
Floor strike rate, %/yr	3.50%
Floor rate,, %/yr	4.00%
Premium for floor, basis points	42

Annualized Costs for Cap and Floor	
Quarterly premium for cap	0.0604%
Annualized premium rate, %/yr	0.2418%
Cap strike rate, %/yr	5.5000%
Total cost for cap, %/yr	5.7418%
Semi-annual premium for floor	0.0552%
Annualized premium rate, %/yr	0.2208%
Floor strike rate, %/yr	3.5000%
Total cost for floor, %/yr	3.2792%

Profile of an Interest Rate Collar	Reset interest rate after 3 months, %/yr						
	0.00%	1.00%	3.500%	5.00%	5.50%	6.00%	8.00%
Uncovered interest rate payment	**0.00%**	**1.00%**	**3.50%**	**5.00%**	**5.50%**	**6.00%**	**8.00%**
Calculation of capped interest rate payment							
Normal quarterly interest payment	$0	$25,000	$87,500	$125,000	$137,500	$150,000	$200,000
Receive cap cash payment	$0	$0	$0	$0	$0	$12,500	$62,500
Cap premium payment outflow, $	$6,045	$6,045	$6,045	$6,045	$6,045	$6,045	$6,045
Net quarterly cash outflow (All-in-Cost)	$6,045	$31,045	$93,545	$131,045	$143,545	$143,545	$143,545
Cap interest rate payment	**0.242%**	**1.242%**	**3.742%**	**5.242%**	**5.742%**	**5.742%**	**5.742%**
Calculation of floor interest rate payment							
Normal quarterly interest earned	$0	$25,000	$87,500	$125,000	$137,500	$150,000	$200,000
Receive floor cash payment	$87,500	$62,500	$0	$0	$0	$0	$0
Floor premium payment outflow, $	$5,519	$5,519	$5,519	$5,519	$5,519	$5,519	$5,519
Net quarterly cash outflow (All-in-Cost)	$81,981	$81,981	$81,981	$119,481	$131,981	$144,481	$194,481
Floor interest rate payment	**3.279%**	**3.279%**	**3.279%**	**4.779%**	**5.279%**	**5.779%**	**7.779%**

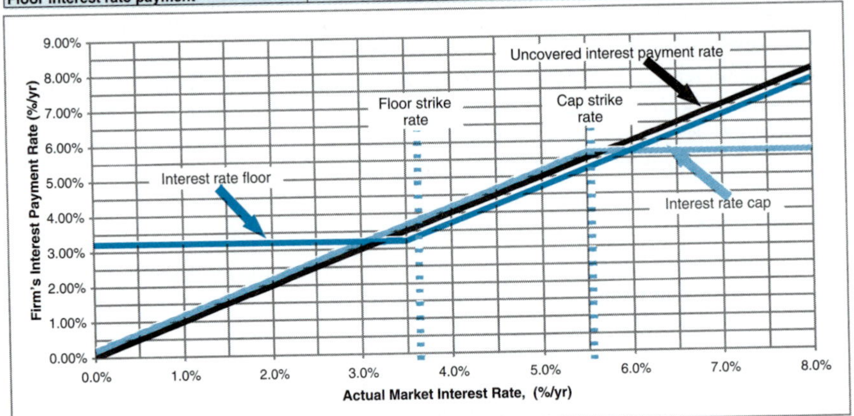

Key Cell Entries

H5: =($C$11/10000)/(1/($C$8/$C$7)-1/($C$8/$C$7*(1+$C$8/$C$7)^($C$6*$C$7)))
H6: =C7:H5
H7: =C9
H8: =H6+H7
H9: =($C$14/10000)/(1/($C$8/$C$7)-1/($C$8/$C$7*(1+$C$8/$C$7)^($C$6*$C$7)))
H10: =C7*H9
H11: =C12
H12: =H11-H10
C21: =$C$5*C$18/$C$7, copy to D21:I21 and C27:I27
C22: =IF(C18>$C$9,$C$5*(C18-$C$9)/$C$7,0), copy to D22:I22
C23: =$C$5*$H$5, copy to D23:I23
C24: =C21-C22+C23, copy to D24:I24
C25: =C24*$C$7/$C$5, copy to D25:I25 and D31:I31
C28: =IF(C18<$C$13,$C$5*($C$12-C18)/$C$7,0), copy to D28:I18
C29: =$C$5*$H$9, copy to D29:I29
C30: =C27+C28—C29, copy to D30:I30

Summary

- Option-based instruments and techniques are commonly employed for interest rate risk management.
- An *interest rate cap* is an option to fix a ceiling or maximum short-term interest rate payment.
- A *interest rate floor* gives the buyer of the floor option a minimum interest rate to be received (rate of return on notional principal invested) for a specified reinvestment period or series of periods.
- An *interest rate collar* is the simultaneous purchase (sale) of a cap and sale (purchase) of a floor.
- The purchase of a swap option—a *swaption*—gives the firm the right but not the obligation to enter into a swap on a pre-determined notional principal at some defined future date at a specified strike rate.

Decision **CASE**

THUNDERBIRD
THE AMERICAN GRADUATE SCHOOL OF INTERNATIONAL MANAGEMENT

British Columbia Hydro

"Treasury cannot be seen as a passive activity," Bell says. "Once we isolated treasury as a separate subset of our business and set some goals for it, it helped our people view problems in a fresh way. If you think of it in terms of opportunities, it may be the biggest profit centre you have got in your company, particularly if you are capital intensive."

Larry Bell, CEO, British Columbia Hydro
Intermarket, September 1989.

British Columbia Hydroelectric and Power Authority (BC Hydro) is a Provincial Crown Corporation, a wholly owned subsidiary of the Province of British Columbia. BC Hydro is the fifth largest Canadian utility, generating, transmitting, and distributing electricity to more than one million customers in British Columbia. The fact that it is a government-owned utility does not change its need to manage treasury operations against financial risks.

BC Hydro has substantial exposure to financial risk. Larry Bell, as Chairman of BC Hydro, was determined to do something about the financial price risks—the movements of exchange rates, interest rates, and commodity prices—facing the firm. It was now March 1988, and the time for discussion had ended and the time for decisions had come.

Financial Exposures

Upon taking over as Chairman of BC Hydro in late 1987, Larry Bell started from the ground up in his analysis of the firm's financial exposures. Bell was formerly British Columbia's Deputy Minister of Finance, and therefore not a newcomer to issues in financial management. His first step was to isolate those major business and financial forces driving net income (revenues and operating costs) and the balance sheet (asset and liability component values).

BC Hydro was—at least by financial standards—relatively simple in financial structure.The firm's revenues came from power sales. Power sales were in turn divisible into residential and small business (60%), and transmission sales (40%). Residential power use was extremely stable, so that 60% of all revenues of BC Hydro were easily predictable. However, the same could not be said of transmission sales. This was power sold to large industrial users, user's who numbered only 80 at that time. The power use of these 80 industrial users was determined by their business needs, and needs were highly cyclical. BC Hydro's sales were predominantly domestic, with only about 5% of all revenues generated from power sales to utilities across the border in the United States.

A06-99-0002

The cost structure of BC Hydro was also relatively simple—debt service. Debt service dominated operating expenses, averaging 55% of operating expenses over the mid-1980s. (Debt service rarely constitutes more than 15% of operating expenses in typical corporate financial structures.) Power generation, however, is extremely capital intensive. The requirements for capital are met primarily by debt.

In 1987 BC Hydro had approximately C$8 billion in debt outstanding. Unfortunately, BC Hydro was a victim of its own attractiveness. It had been a direct beneficiary of the need for U.S.-based investors to diversity their exposures in the late 1970s and early 1980s. It had tapped the U.S. dollar debt markets at extremely attractive rates for the time. But now it was faced with the servicing of this U.S. dollar-denominated debt, a full-half of its total debt portfolio. Much of the U.S. dollar debt had been acquired when the U.S. dollar was weaker (approximately C$1/US$) and both U.S. and Canadian interest rates were higher. As shown in Exhibit 1, the appreciation of the U.S. dollar had resulted in an increase in the Canadian dollar debt equivalent of C$750 million. Equity amounted to approximately C$540 million. BC Hydro was highly leveraged to say the least.

BC Hydro had followed the general principles of conservative capital structure management. It had financed long-term assets with long-term debt. The match of asset and liability maturities was quite good, but the currency of denomination was not. This currency mismatch constituted an enormous potential exposure to the financial viability of the firm.

Isolating the Issues

In early 1988 Chairman Larry Bell called in Bridgewater Associates, a Connecticut financial consulting firm, for help. Bob Prince and Ray Dalio (president) of Bridgewater, along with senior management of BC Hydro and representatives of the BC Ministry of Finance met at Whistler Mountain, British Columbia. The purpose of the retreat was to first identify the primary financial risk issues facing BC Hydro, and secondly purpose preliminary solutions. Chairman Bell encouraged an open exchange of ideas.[1]

Exhibit 1 **Currency Composition and Exchange Rate Impacts on British Columbia Hydro's Liabilities and Net Worth**

Debt and Equity by Currency of Denomination	Initial Values (Canadian Dollars)	March 1988 (Canadian Dollars)
Debt Canadian dollar-denominated	4,000,000,000	4,000,000,000
U.S. dollar-denominated	3,250,000,000	4,000,000,000
Equity	540,000,000	540,000,000
Total liabilities and net worth	7,790,000,000	8,540,000,000
Exchange rate-related gains (losses)		(750,000,000)

Source: BC Hydro and Moodys Canada. Initial values debt are Canadian dollar equivalents, regardless of original currency of denomination, on original date of issuance.

1. *Intermarket*, September 1989, p. 26.

> *We have to do what makes sense economically. We'll deal with the accounting and regulatory hurdles after they've been resolved. If someone w.anted to point out that our legislation wouldn't allow us to trade in futures, that's fine. The legislature sits every year.*

Bell felt that consideration of institutional or legal constraints would prevent the analysis from getting to the core issues. The group proceeded to isolate two basic questions that had to be addressed prior to moving forward:

1. Does BC Hydro want to eliminate all financial risk, or only manage it?
2. BC Hydro is in the business of providing power. Is it also in the business of trading or speculating in the financial markets?

Discussion was heated on these points and ended with no clear agreement initially. Ray Dalio of Bridgewater pushed the discussion by arguing that the interest rate and foreign exchange problems the firm was saddled with were the direct result of a simple basic problem: the lack of a plan.

> *BC Hydro hadn't thought through its financial activities strategically. They were thinking about running their business, not asset-liability management. You can't take that approach in a volatile economic environment.*

The participants agreed to move on to a detailed discussion and analysis of the BC Hydro's financial exposures without resolving these first two issues.

Financial Price Risks

Financial risk management focuses on how the movement of financial prices (interest rates, exchange rates, and commodity prices) affect the value of the firm. Isolating these impacts on any individual firm requires the evaluation of how revenues and costs, both operational and financial, change with movements in these prices. Bridgewater Associates and BC Hydro's staff conducted a number of statistical studies to find what economic forces were at work in the costs and revenues of the firm.

Revenues. The results were quite clear. The 60% of power sales going to the 1.25 million small business and residential consumers was extremely stable, and was therefore insensitive to movements in interest rates, or other business cycle indicators such as unemployment or inflation. In fact residential power use was sensitive primarily to population size. The 40% of power sales to the large industrial users was, however, very cyclical. Closer analysis of the industrial users indicated that these users were sensitive to basic commodity prices (pulp, paper, chemicals mining, etc.). Statistically speaking, transmission sales were found to be heavily dependent on movements in commodity prices (positively related) and industrial production (positively related).

Costs. A closer look at the cost structure of BC Hydro also revealed a number of clear economic forces at work. Operating expenses were dominated by debt service, over 55% of the total. The remaining 45% of operating costs possessed little variable content. Although business conditions for industrial users could decline, the nature of the utility industry still required that operations continue with little change in operating expenses achievable.

Secondly, since 55% of operating expenses were debt service, costs could potentially move directly with interest rates. But BC Hydro's practice over the past decade had been to finance long-term assets with long-term debt, and long-term debt at fixed rates obviously did not move with shorter-cycle interest rate movements. Long-term interest rates were locked in. And interest rates (short-term and long-term rates) had in general been falling in both the United States and Canada since the early 1980s.

Short-term interest rates move with commodity prices. Because increases in commodity prices frequently lead to more inflation, and interest rates and bond yields must in turn move with changes in inflation, significant commodity price increases translated directly into rising interest rates.

It was now clear that if BC Hydro's revenues and cost structures were to be managed against underlying economic or financial forces, protection would be needed against commodity prices. Exhibit 2 illustrates how power sales moved positively with commodity price changes. At the same time, it also shows how short-term interest rates moved with commodity price changes, but long-term interest rates did not. Since BC Hydro was financed nearly exclusively with long-term debt, its present debt structure was not enjoying the fruits of these correlated movements (lower commodity prices and interest rates).

Currency Exposure. BC Hydro was facing an enormous foreign currency exposure. The fact that revenues were 95% Canadian dollar-denominated, while C$4 billion of total longterm debt was a U.S. dollar-denominated, meant that debt-service was completely exposed to currency risk. The firm earned only 5% of its revenues in U.S. dollars, and therefore had no "natural way" of obtaining the foreign currency it needed to service debt. As Exhibit 3 illustrates, although the U.S. dollar had risen versus the Canadian dollar steadily between 1980 and 1986, the Canadian dollar had regained some ground in the past two years.

By 1988 Larry Bell estimated that BC Hydro had realized C$350 million in foreign currency losses on its U.S. dollar debt, all of which passed through current income. The remaining exposure still approached C$400 million depending on the direction of the exchange rate movement. Something had to be done quickly. The urgency of the issue was particularly acute given that the total equity of BC Hydro amounted to only C$540 million! The

Exhibit 2 British Columbia Hydro's Revenue and Cost Sensitivity to Commodity Price Changes

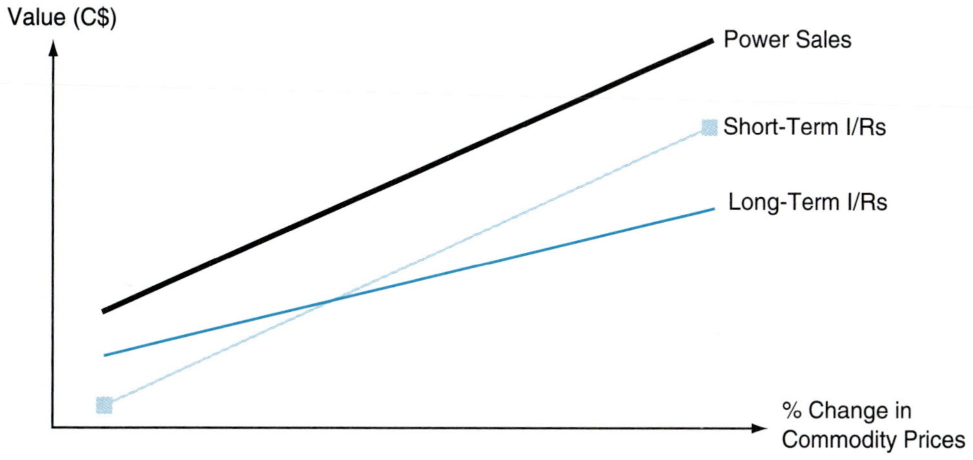

outstanding U.S. dollar debt was to be repaid in single "balloon" payments upon maturity. BC Hydro therefore had an enormous amount of cash flowing into a sinking fund for debt principal repayment. The funds were presently being reinvested in Canadian bonds, yielding short-term current rates on Canadian debt instruments.

Proposed Risk Management Strategies

Several alternative solutions were put forward for both the revenue-cost risks and the foreign currency risks. It seemed the solutions would have to be independently constructed.

The basic revenue-cost mismatch, the fact that BC Hydro held little short-term debt which would parallel the movement of revenues with commodity prices, was attacked first. The obvious solution was to increase the proportion of short-term debt. Although this approach would clearly increase the matching of commodity price cycles, it would do the opposite with regard to asset-liability maturity matching. It was argued that 60% of all power revenues were still very stable, and that the debt structure of the entire utility should not be reworked in order to pursue risk management goals. The critics of the short-term debt approach also emphasized that historical correlations might not hold up in the future. Movements of revenues and short-term interest rates correlated with commodity price movements may not hold true. The debate was heated.

The foreign currency exposure problem was at first glance, simple. The easiest and most risk-averse approach would simply be to buy U.S. dollars forward. There was little risk in that the debt-service schedule was known exactly in terms of amounts and timing, and the resulting forward cover would eliminate the currently risk.

Several senior finance ministry officials suggested a currency-interest rate swap instead. All agreed that both would work equally well. However, they were not certain that as a Crown Corporation they would be allowed to enter into a swap agreement. Late in the afternoon of

Exhibit 3 The Canadian Dollar/U.S. Dollar Exchange Rate, 1980–1987 (C$/US$)

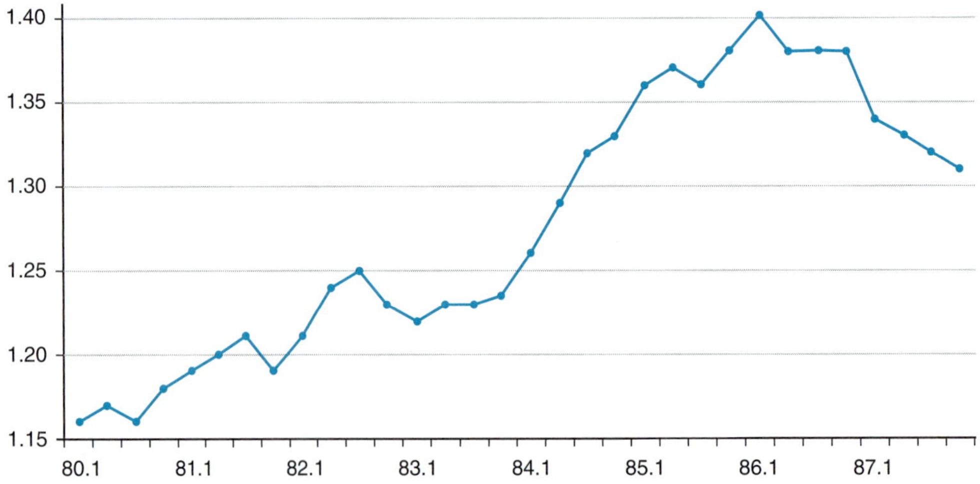

the weekend retreat an additional detail was also recognized, that the signing of a forward contact (or series of forward contracts) to cover the U.S. dollar debt-service would require BC Hydro to recognize and realize (pass through the income statement) the total currency loss remaining, approximately C$500 million. This was obviously unacceptable.

A second alternative put forward by Ray Dalio of Bridgewater Associates was to move all sinking-fund capital out of Canadian dollar bonds into a similar risk category of U.S. dollar-denominated securities. This would result in the security values moving in the opposite direction of the U.S. dollar debt, thus offsetting adverse (or favorable) exchange rate changes; a natural hedge. But, this also meant that BC Hydro, a Crown Corporation, would be intentionally constructing an enormous uncovered foreign currency position. This met with considerable opposition by representatives of the British Columbia Ministry of Finance.

The participants returned from the quiet wilderness setting of Whistler Mountain to the hustle and bustle of Vancouver. It was now March 1988; Larry Bell needed a decision soon.

> *"When I came to BC Hydro, because half our costs are associated with debt servicing, there were significant opportunities that could be shaken loose in a proactive treasury operation," he recalls. "As a manager, I shouldn't run this company unless I exploited all of those opportunities."*

PART 5

Foreign Investment Decisions

PART 5

Part 5 analyzes how a firm transitions from the international trade stage to become a full-blown multinational firm.

Chapter 15 analyzes the theory and strategy that leads a firm to direct foreign investment. The *theory of comparative advantage* is the basis for international trade. However, market imperfections create a rationale for the existence of multinational enterprises. We examine why firms become multinational, where they choose to locate, and how they determine their modes of foreign involvement. An appendix illustrates an example of comparative advantage between Brazil and Thailand.

Chapter 16 shows how to adjust for political risk in foreign investments. It explains how to define, measure, and manage foreign investment risks. We separate risks into three categories: 1) *firm-specific risks*; 2) *country-specific risks*; and 3) *global-specific risks*. Firm-specific risks include the normal business risks that can be revealed through sensitivity analysis, as well as governance risks that stem from goal conflicts with host countries. Country-specific risks stem from host country policies that reduce a firm's ability to transfer freely its funds in and out of the host country. However, country-specific risks also arise from cultural differences and host country protectionism. Global-specific risks arise from terrorism activities, the current anti-globalization movement, environmental concerns, poverty, and cyberattacks. These activities have a negative impact on cross-border supply chain integration and create a need for crisis planning by the MNE. The chapter concludes with an illustrative case of the challenges faced by Starbucks Coffee as a result of the anti-globalization movement. The chapter is followed by a decision case analyzing the potential acquisition of an Indonesian company by Cemex of Mexico.

Chapter 17 describes the global tax environment. It begins with the concepts of tax morality and the importance of tax neutrality to governments as they design how their tax laws could affect a MNE's business decisions. We analyze how tax treaties between countries attempt to provide a level playing field for competing MNEs. Furthermore, different types of taxes, such as the value-added tax, complicate the MNE's goal of minimizing its worldwide tax burden. The chapter continues with a detailed description of how the United States taxes foreign source income of its MNEs. The chapter continues by analyzing how a U.S. MNE should manage its foreign source income in order to minimize its worldwide taxes. The chapter continues with an analysis of tax haven subsidiaries, and concludes with a mini-case on Romanian Telecom's use of a Cyprus subsidiary for profit repositioning and a decision case based on Stanley Works' proposed reincorporation outside of the United States in order to reduce its total tax burden.

Chapter 18 introduces the foreign complexities that you must consider when undertaking a capital budgeting analysis of a foreign project. You learn that a foreign project should be analyzed both from the project's own viewpoint and its parent's viewpoint. An illustrative case, "Cemex Enters Indonesia," illustrates how you should value a foreign project and recognize through sensitivity analysis the various political and foreign exchange risks. The chapter concludes with an introduction to the newly important field of real option analysis, including a mini-case using Carlton's Chinese subsidiary. The chapter includes an appendix devoted to quantitative methods to adjust for risk in foreign investments. The chapter is followed by a decision case on a potential Chinese investment by Sheraton Corporation, the Beijing International Club.

Chapter 19 introduces the increasingly important field of cross-border mergers and acquisitions, which is a viable alternative to a greenfield direct foreign investment. The cross-border acquisition process has three stages. In Stage I you must identify and value a target firm. In Stage II you must negotiate the terms of settlement of the merger or acquisition. In Stage III you must manage the post-settlement in a way that integrates and harmonizes the melding of two different corporate cultures. Corporate governance policies and shareholder rights become important legal and ethical issues that must be recognized during the mergers and acquisitions process. We present a detailed illustrative case, "The Potential Acquisition of Tsingtao Brewery Company, Ltd.," so that you can learn how to evaluate an acquisition as well as make a choice among conflicting valuation results. The chapter is followed by a decision case detailing Gucci's struggle to defend itself against a hostile takeover attempt by LVMH.

Chapter 20 shows how a MNE and an international portfolio investor can reduce their risk through international diversification. Since a MNE needs to attract and retain international portfolio investors in order to gain its global cost and availability of capital, risk reduction through international diversification is important to both parties. Because the theory of international portfolio diversification has a much studied theoretical and empirical base, we use it as the basis for understanding the benefits of diversification, both for MNEs and for investors. Although we build on domestic portfolio theory, we need to add the foreign exchange risk introduced by holding foreign currency–denominated securities in the portfolio. We analyze how to calculate a portfolio's risk and return using the international capital asset pricing model as illustrated by Carlton and Nestlé. We also describe how national markets and assets have performed, as well as the correlation matrix that existed between world equity markets during the twentieth century.

Chapter 15

Foreign Direct Investment Theory and Strategy

THIS CHAPTER ANALYZES THE DECISIONS WHETHER, WHERE, AND HOW TO UNDERTAKE FOREIGN direct investment (FDI). The internationalization process itself begins with international trade. This chapter first reviews the theory of comparative advantage, the theoretical foundation of trade. Only after highlighting the limitations of international trade is it possible to understand why firms move beyond the geographic boundaries of their home country in order to license or manufacture abroad; that is, to engage in *foreign direct investment.*

The second section of the chapter analyzes how market imperfections create a rationale for the existence of multinational enterprises. Here we explain what motivates firms to become multinational. We then demonstrate how key competitive advantages support a firm's strategy to undertake foreign direct investment. We follow this by showing how the OLI Paradigm provides a theoretical foundation for foreign direct investment. Then we analyze how a firm decides where to invest abroad through various types of foreign involvement. At the end of the chapter is a mini-case of how one company pursued the global licensing of its product.

The Theory of Comparative Advantage

The *theory of comparative advantage* provides a basis for explaining and justifying international trade in a model world assumed to enjoy free trade, perfect competition, no uncertainty, costless information, and no government interference. The theory contains the following features:

- Exporters in Country A sell goods or services to unrelated importers in Country B.
- Firms in Country A specialize in making products that can be produced relatively efficiently, given Country A's endowment of factors of production; that is, land, labor, capital, and technology. Firms in Country B do likewise, given the factors of production found in Country B. In this way the total combined output of A and B is maximized.
- Because the factors of production cannot be moved freely from Country A to Country B, the benefits of specialization are realized through international trade.

The way the benefits of the extra production are shared depends on the *terms of trade*, the ratio at which quantities of the physical goods are traded. Each country's share is determined by supply and demand in perfectly competitive markets in the two countries. Neither Country A nor Country B is worse off than before trade, and typically both are better off, albeit perhaps unequally.

An Example of Comparative Advantage

For an example of the benefits of free trade based on comparative advantage, assume that Thailand is more efficient than Brazil at producing both sports shoes and stereo equipment. With one unit of production (a mix of land, labor, capital, and technology), efficient Thailand can produce either 12 shipping containers (ctrs) of shoes or 6 shipping containers of stereo equipment. Brazil, being less efficient in both, can produce only 10 containers of shoes or 2 containers of stereo equipment with one unit of input. These production capabilities are as follows:

	Production Capability	
	Containers of sports shoes	*Containers of stereo equipment*
Thailand has 1,000 production units:	12 containers/unit	6 containers/unit
Brazil has 1,000 production units:	10 containers/unit	2 containers/unit

A production unit in Thailand has an *absolute advantage* over a production unit in Brazil in both shoes and stereo equipment. Nevertheless, Thailand has a larger *relative advantage* over Brazil in producing stereo equipment (6 to 2) than shoes (12 to 10). As long as these ratios are unequal, comparative advantage exists.

Assume that no trade takes place, and each country divides its own production units between shoes and stereo equipment. Each country elects to allocate 300 production units to shoes and 700 production units to stereo equipment, resulting in the production and consumption outcomes in the top half of Exhibit 15.1.

Exhibit 15.1 The Theory of Comparative Advantage: A Numerical Example of Brazil and Thailand

Production if no trade

	Shoe Production	**Stereo Production**
Thailand produces and consumes	300 × 12 = 3,600 ctrs	700 × 6 = 4,200 ctrs
Brazil produces and consumes	300 × 10 = 3,000	700 × 2 = 1,400
Total world production and consumption	6,600 ctrs	5,600 ctrs

Complete specialization

	Shoe Production	**Stereo Production**
Thailand produces only stereo equipment		1,000 × 6 = 6,000 ctrs
Brazil produces only shoes	1,000 × 10 = 10,000 ctrs	
Total world production and consumption	10,000 ctrs	6,000 ctrs

Now assume complete specialization. Thailand produces only stereo equipment and Brazil produces only shoes. World production would be higher for both shoes and stereo equipment, as illustrated by the bottom half of Exhibit 15.1.

Clearly, the world in total is better off, because there are now 10,000 containers of shoes instead of just 6,600. And there are 6,000 containers of stereo equipment instead of just 5,600. But distribution is quite distorted. The Thais now tap only bare feet to their music, and the Brazilians dance through Carnival with good shoes but no recorded music!

Trade can resolve this distribution problem. Assume initially that trade between Thailand and Brazil takes place at the ratio of 2 containers of shoes for 1 container of stereo equipment. This "exchange rate" of 2 containers of shoes for 1 container of stereo equipment is Thailand's "domestic" price; that is, the ratio of trade within Thailand should it produce both items and not engage in international trade. Assume further that Thailand exports 1,800 containers of stereo equipment to Brazil and imports 3,600 containers of shoes from Brazil. The situation would be as depicted in Exhibit 15.2.

At this price, all gains go to Brazil, which consumes 6,400 containers of shoes (instead of 3,000 with no trade) and consumes 1,800 containers of stereo equipment (instead of 1,400 with no trade). Thailand's consumption, 3,600 containers of shoes and 4,200 containers of stereos, is just as it was with no trade. Thailand has gained nothing from trade at this price, although neither has it lost anything!

Assume now that trade takes place at Brazil's "domestic price" of 5 containers of shoes for each container of stereo equipment. This is illustrated in Exhibit 15.3. At Brazil's internal price,

Exhibit 15.2 Trade at Thailand's "Domestic Price"

For each container of stereo equipment exported, Thailand imports 2 containers of shoes from Brazil.

	Shoe Production plus/minus trade	Stereo Production plus/minus trade
Thailand produces 6,000 containers of stereo equipment and exports 1,800 containers	0 + 3,600 = 3,600 ctrs	6,000 – 1,800 = 4,200 ctrs
Brazil produces 10,000 containers of shoes and exports 3,600 containers	10,000 – 3,600 = 6,400	0 + 1,800 = 1,800
World production and consumption	10,000 ctrs	6,000 ctrs

Exhibit 15.3 Trade at Brazil's "Domestic Price"

For each container of stereo equipment exported, Thailand imports 5 containers of shoes from Brazil.

	Shoe Production plus/minus trade	Stereo Production plus/minus trade
Thailand produces 6,000 containers of stereo equipment and exports 1,400 containers	0 + 7,000 = 7,000 ctrs	6,000 – 1,400 = 4,600 ctrs
Brazil produces 10,000 containers of shoes and exports 7,000 containers	10,000 – 7,000 = 3,000	0 + 1,400 = 1,400
World production and consumption	10,000 ctrs	6,000 ctrs

all gains go to Thailand, which now consumes 7,000 containers of shoes (instead of 3,600 with no trade) and 4,600 containers of stereo equipment (instead of 4,200 with no trade). Brazil's consumption, 3,000 containers of shoes and 1,400 containers of stereo, is the same as with no trade. Brazil has gained nothing from trade at this price, although neither has it lost anything.

Now let trade take place at a price in between Thailand's domestic price of 2-to-1 and Brazil's domestic price of 5-to-1. Assume that free bargaining leads to a price of 4-to-1, as seen in Exhibit 15.4.

At any price between the boundaries of 2-to-1 and 5-to-1, both countries benefit from specializing and trading. At a 4-to-1 price, Thailand consumes 2,800 more containers of shoes as well as 200 more containers of stereo equipment than it has consumed with no trade. Brazil consumes 600 more containers of shoes as well as 200 more containers of stereo equipment than it has consumed with no trade. Total combined production of both shoes and stereo equipment has increased through the specialization process, and it only remains for the exchange ratio to determine how this larger output is distributed between the two countries.

Limitations of Comparative Advantage

Although international trade might have approached the comparative advantage model during the nineteenth century, it certainly does not today, for the following reasons:

- Countries do not appear to specialize only in those products that could be most efficiently produced by that country's particular factors of production. Instead, governments interfere with comparative advantage for a variety of economic and political reasons, such as to achieve full employment, economic development, national self-sufficiency in defense-related industries, and protection of an agricultural sector's way of life. Government interference takes the form of tariffs, quotas, and other nontariff restrictions.
- At least two of the factors of production—capital and technology—now flow directly and easily between countries, rather than only indirectly through traded goods and services. This direct flow occurs between related subsidiaries and affiliates of multinational firms, as well as between unrelated firms via loans, and license and management contracts, as we will discuss later in this chapter.
- Modern factors of production are more numerous than in this simple model. Factors considered in the location of production facilities worldwide include local and managerial skills, a

Exhibit 15.4 Trade at a Price Reached by Free Bargaining

For each container of stereo equipment exported, Thailand imports 4 containers of shoes from Brazil.

	Shoe Production plus/minus trade	Stereo Production plus/minus trade
Thailand produces 6,000 containers of stereo equipment and exports 1,600 containers	0 + 6,400 = 6,400 ctrs	6,000 – 1,600 = 4,400 ctrs
Brazil produces 10,000 containers of shoes and exports 6,400 containers	10,000 – 6,400 = 3,600	0 + 1,600 = 1,600
World production and consumption	10,000 ctrs	6,000 ctrs

dependable legal structure for settling contract disputes, research and development competence, educational levels of available workers, energy resources, consumer demand for brand name goods, mineral and raw material availability, access to capital, tax differentials, supporting infrastructure (roads, ports, communication facilities), and possibly others.

- Although the terms of trade are ultimately determined by supply and demand, the process by which the terms are set is different from that visualized in traditional trade theory. They are determined partly by administered pricing in oligopolistic markets.
- Comparative advantage shifts over time, as less developed countries become more developed and realize their latent opportunities. For example, over the past 150 years, comparative advantage in producing cotton textiles has shifted from the United Kingdom to the United States, to Japan, to Hong Kong, to Taiwan, and to China.
- The classical model of comparative advantage did not really address certain other issues, such as the effect of uncertainty and information costs, the role of differentiated products in imperfectly competitive markets, and economies of scale.

Nevertheless, although the world is a long way from the classical trade model, the general principle of comparative advantage is still valid. The closer the world gets to true international specialization, the more world production and consumption can be increased, provided the problem of equitable distribution of the benefits can be solved to the satisfaction of consumers, producers, and political leaders. Complete specialization, however, remains an unrealistic limiting case, just as perfect competition is a limiting case in microeconomic theory.

Supply Chain Outsourcing: Comparative Advantage Today

Comparative advantage is still a relevant theory to explain why particular countries are most suitable for exports of goods and services that support the global supply chain of both MNEs and domestic firms. The comparative advantage of the 21st century, however, is one based more on services, and their cross-border facilitation by telecommunications and the Internet. The source of a nation's comparative advantage is still created from the mixture of its own labor skills, access to capital, and technology.

Many locations for supply chain outsourcing exist today. Exhibit 15.5 presents a geographical overview of this modern reincarnation of trade-based comparative advantage. To prove that these countries should specialize in the activities shown, you would need to know how costly the same activities would be in the countries that are importing these services compared to their own other industries. Remember that it takes a relative advantage in costs, not just an absolute advantage, to create *comparative advantage*. For example, India has developed a highly efficient and low-cost software industry. This industry supplies not only the creation of custom software, but also call centers for customer support and other information technology services. The Indian software industry is composed of both subsidiaries of MNEs and independent companies.

If you own a Compaq computer and call the customer support center number for help, you are highly likely to reach a call center in India. Answering your call will be a knowledgeable Indian software engineer or programmer who will "walk" you through your problem. India has a large number of well-educated, English-speaking, technical experts who are paid only a fraction of the salary and overhead earned by their U.S. counterparts. The overcapacity and low

Exhibit 15.5 Global Outsourcing of Comparative Advantage

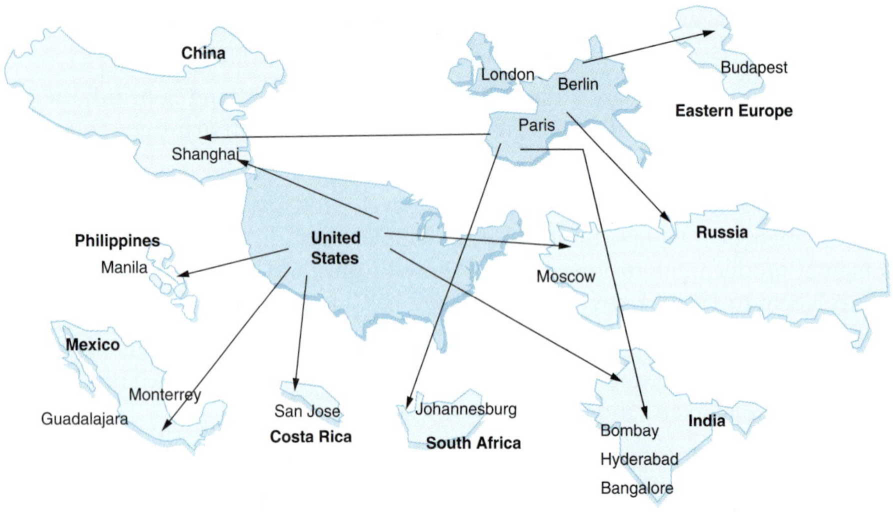

MNEs based in many of th e major industrial countries are outsourcing many of their intellectual functions to providers based in many of the traditional emerging market countries.

cost of international telecommunication networks today further enhances the comparative advantage of an Indian location.

As illustrated by Exhibit 15.6, the extent of global outsourcing is already reaching out to every corner of the globe. From financial back-offices in Manila to information technology engineers in Hungary, modern telecommunications now take business activities to labor, rather than labor migrating to the places of business.

Market Imperfections: A Rationale for the Existence of the Multinational Firm

MNEs strive to take advantage of imperfections in national markets for products, factors of production, and financial assets. Imperfections in the market for products translate into market opportunities for MNEs. Large international firms are better able to exploit such competitive factors as economies of scale, managerial and technological expertise, product differentiation, and financial strength than are their local competitors. In fact, MNEs thrive best in markets characterized by international oligopolistic competition, where these factors are particularly critical. In addition, once MNEs have established a physical presence abroad, they are in a better position than purely domestic firms to identify and implement market opportunities through their own internal information network.

Why Do Firms Become Multinational?

Strategic motives drive the decision to invest abroad and become a MNE. These motives can be summarized under the following five categories:

Exhibit 15.6 Examples of Global Outsourcing of Comparative Advantage in Intellectual Skills

Country	Activity
China	Chemical, mechanical, and petroleum engineering services; business and product development centers for companies like GE
Costa Rica	Call centers for Spanish-speaking consumers in many industrial markets; Accenture has IT support and back-office operations call centers
Eastern Europe	American and IT service providers operate call centers for customer and business support in Hungary, Poland, and the Czech Republic; Romania and Bulgarian centers for German-speaking IT customers in Europe
India	Software engineering and support; call centers for all types of computer and telecom services; medical analysis and consultative services; Indian companies such as Tata, Infosys, and Wipro are already global leaders in IT design, implementation, and support
Mexico	Automotive engineering and electronic sector services
Philippines	Financial and accounting services; architecture services; telemarketing and graphic arts
Russia	Software and engineering services; R&D centers for Boeing, Intel, Motorola, and Nortel
South Africa	Call and user support services for French, English, and German-speaking consumers throughout Europe

Source: Abstracted from "Is Your Job Next," *Business Week*, February 3, 2003.

1. **Market seekers** produce in foreign markets either to satisfy local demand or to export to markets other than their home market. U.S. automobile firms manufacturing in Europe for local consumption are an example of market-seeking motivation.

2. **Raw material seekers** extract raw materials wherever they can be found, either for export or for further processing and sale in the country in which they are found—the host country. Firms in the oil, mining, plantation, and forest industries fall into this category.

3. **Production efficiency seekers** produce in countries where one or more of the factors of production are underpriced relative to their productivity. Labor-intensive production of electronic components in Taiwan, Malaysia, and Mexico is an example of this motivation.

4. **Knowledge seekers** operate in foreign countries to gain access to technology or managerial expertise. For example, German, Dutch, and Japanese firms have purchased U.S.-located electronics firms for their technology.

5. **Political safety seekers** acquire or establish new operations in countries that are considered unlikely to expropriate or interfere with private enterprise. For example, Hong Kong firms invested heavily in the United States, United Kingdom, Canada, and Australia in anticipation of the consequences of China's 1997 takeover of the British colony.

The five types of strategic considerations just described are not mutually exclusive. Forest products firms seeking wood fiber in Brazil, for example, would also find a large Brazilian market for a portion of their output.

In industries characterized by worldwide oligopolistic competition, each of the five strategic motives should be sub-classified into proactive and defensive investments. Proactive investments are designed to enhance the growth and profitability of the firm itself. Defensive investments are designed to deny growth and profitability to the firm's competitors. Examples of the latter are investments that try to preempt a market before competitors can get established there, or attempt to capture raw material sources in order to deny them to competitors.

Sustaining and Transferring Competitive Advantage

In deciding whether to invest abroad, management must first determine whether the firm has a sustainable competitive advantage that enables it to compete effectively in the home market. The competitive advantage must be firm-specific, transferable, and powerful enough to compensate the firm for the potential disadvantages of operating abroad (foreign exchange risks, political risks, and increased agency costs).

Based on observations of firms that have successfully invested abroad, we can conclude that some of the competitive advantages enjoyed by MNEs are: 1) economies of scale and scope arising from their large size; 2) managerial and marketing expertise; 3) superior technology owing to their heavy emphasis on research; 4) financial strength; 5) differentiated products; and sometimes 6) competitiveness of their home markets.

Economies of Scale and Scope

Economies of scale and scope can be developed in production, marketing, finance, research and development, transportation, and purchasing. In each of these areas, there are significant competitive advantages to being large, whether size is due to international or domestic operations. Production economies can come from the use of large-scale automated plant and equipment or from an ability to rationalize production through worldwide specialization. For example, some automobile manufacturers, such as Ford, rationalize manufacturing by producing engines in one country, transmissions in another, and bodies in another and assembling still elsewhere, with the location often being dictated by comparative advantage.

Marketing economies occur when firms are large enough to use the most efficient advertising media to create worldwide brand identification, as well as to establish worldwide distribution, warehousing, and servicing systems. Financial economies derive from access to the full range of financial instruments and sources of funds, such as the Eurocurrency, Euroequity, and Eurobond markets. In-house research and development programs are typically restricted to large firms, because of the minimum-size threshold for establishing a laboratory and scientific staff. Transportation economies accrue to firms that can ship in carload or shipload lots. Purchasing economies come from quantity discounts and market power.

Managerial and Marketing Expertise

Managerial expertise includes skill in managing large industrial organizations from both a human and a technical viewpoint. It also encompasses knowledge of modern analytical techniques and their application in functional areas of business. Managerial expertise can be developed through prior experience in foreign markets. In most empirical studies, multinational firms have been observed to export to a market before establishing a production facility there. Likewise, they have prior experience sourcing raw materials and human capital in other foreign countries either through imports, licensing, or FDI. In this manner, the MNEs can partially overcome the supposed superior local knowledge of host country firms.

Advanced Technology

Advanced technology includes both scientific and engineering skills. It is not limited to MNEs, but firms in the most industrialized countries have had an advantage in terms of access to continuing new technology spin-offs from the military and space programs. Empirical studies have supported the importance of technology as a characteristic of MNEs.

Financial Strength

As discussed in Chapter 11, companies demonstrate financial strength by achieving and maintaining a global cost and availability of capital. This is a critical competitive cost variable that enables them to fund FDI and other foreign activities. MNEs that are resident in liquid and unsegmented capital markets are normally blessed with this attribute. However, MNEs that are resident in small industrial or emerging market countries can still follow a proactive strategy of seeking foreign portfolio and corporate investors.

Small and medium-size firms often lack the characteristics that attract foreign (and maybe domestic) investors. They are too small or unattractive to achieve a global cost of capital. This limits their ability to fund FDI, and their higher marginal cost of capital reduces the number of foreign projects that can generate the higher required rate of return.

Differentiated Products

Firms create their own firm-specific advantages by producing and marketing differentiated products. Such products originate from research-based innovations or heavy marketing expenditures to gain brand identification. Furthermore, the research and marketing process continues to produce a steady stream of new differentiated products. It is difficult and costly for competitors to copy such products, and they always face a time lag if they try. Having developed differentiated products for the domestic home market, the firm may decide to market them worldwide, a decision consistent with the desire to maximize return on heavy research and marketing expenditures.

Competitiveness of the Home Market

A strongly competitive home market can sharpen a firm's competitive advantage relative to firms located in less competitive home markets. This phenomenon is known as the *diamond of national advantage*. The diamond has four components, as illustrated in Exhibit 15.7.[1]

A firm's success in competing in a particular industry depends partly on the availability of factors of production (land, labor, capital, and technology) appropriate for that industry. Countries that are either naturally endowed with the appropriate factors or able to create them will probably spawn firms that are both competitive at home and potentially so abroad. For example, a

1. Porter, Michael, *The Competitive Advantage of Nations* (London: Macmillan Press 1990).

Exhibit 15.7 Determinants of National Competitive Advantage: Porter's Diamond

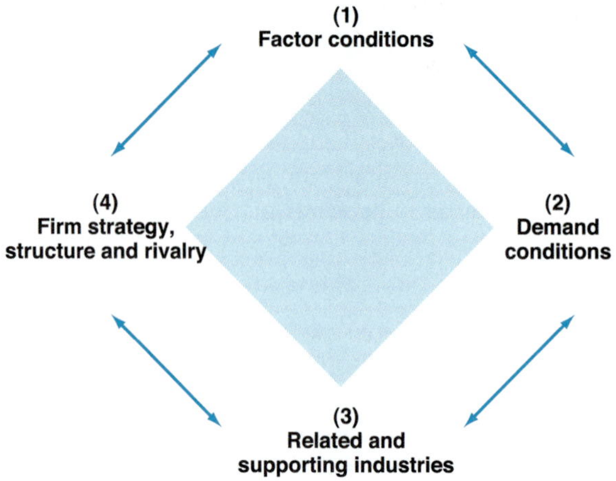

Source: Porter, Michael, "The Competitive Advantage of Nations," *Harvard Business Review*, March–April 1990.

well-educated work force in the home market creates a competitive advantage for firms in certain high-tech industries.

Firms facing sophisticated and demanding customers in the home market are able to hone their marketing, production, and quality control skills. Japan is such a market.

Firms in industries that are surrounded by a critical mass of related industries and suppliers will be more competitive because of this supporting cast. For example, electronic firms located in centers of technical excellence, such as in the San Francisco Bay area, are surrounded by efficient, creative suppliers and enjoy access to educational institutions at the forefront of knowledge.

A competitive home market forces firms to fine-tune their operational and control strategies for their specific industry and country environment. Japanese firms learned how to organize to implement their famous "just-in-time" inventory control system. One key was to use numerous subcontractors and suppliers that were encouraged to locate near the final assembly plants.

In some cases, home country markets have not been large or competitive, but MNEs located there have nevertheless developed global niche markets served by foreign subsidiaries. Global competition in oligopolistic industries substitutes for domestic competition. For example, a number of MNEs resident in Scandinavia, Switzerland, and the Netherlands fall in this category. Some of these are Novo Nordisk (Denmark), Norske Hydro (Norway), Nokia (Finland), L.M. Ericsson (Sweden), Astra (Sweden), ABB (Sweden/Switzerland), Roche Holding (Switzerland), Royal Dutch Shell (the Netherlands), Unilever (the Netherlands), and Philips (the Netherlands).

Emerging market countries have also spawned aspiring global MNEs in niche markets even though they lack competitive home country markets. Some of these are traditional exporters in natural resource fields such as oil, agriculture, and minerals, but they are in transition to becoming MNEs. They typically start with foreign sales subsidiaries, joint ventures, and strategic alliances. Examples are Petrobras (Brazil), YPF (Argentina), and Cemex (Mexico). Another category of firms is those that have been recently privatized in the telecommunications industry. Examples are Telefonos de Mexico and Telebras (Brazil). Still others started as electronic component manufacturers but are making the transition to manufacturing abroad. Examples are Samsung Electronics (Korea) and Acer Computer (Taiwan).

The OLI Paradigm and Internalization

The *OLI Paradigm* (Buckley and Casson, 1976; Dunning, 1977) is an attempt to create an overall framework to explain why MNEs choose FDI rather than serve foreign markets through alternative modes such as licensing, joint ventures, strategic alliances, management contracts, and exporting.[2]

The OLI Paradigm states that a firm must first have some competitive advantage in its home market—"O" or *owner-specific*—that can be transferred abroad if the firm is to be successful in foreign direct investment. Second, the firm must be attracted by specific characteristics of the foreign market—"L" or *location-specific*—that will allow it to exploit its competitive advantages in that market. Third, the firm will maintain its competitive position by attempting to control the entire value chain in its industry—"I" or *internalization*. This leads it to foreign direct investment rather than licensing or outsourcing.

Definitions

The "O" in OLI stands for owner-specific advantages. As described earlier, a firm must have competitive advantages in its home market. These must be firm-specific, not easily copied, and in a form that allows them to be transferred to foreign subsidiaries. For example, economies of scale and financial strength are not necessarily firm-specific, because they can be achieved by many other firms. Certain kinds of technology can be purchased, licensed, or copied. Even differentiated products can lose their advantage to slightly altered versions, given enough marketing effort and the right price.

The "L" in OLI stands for location-specific advantages. These factors are typically market imperfections or genuine comparative advantages that attract FDI to particular locations. These factors might include a low-cost but productive labor force, unique sources of raw materials, a large domestic market, defensive investments to counter other competitors, or centers of technological excellence.

The "I" in OLI stands for internalization. According to the theory, the key ingredient for maintaining a firm-specific competitive advantage is possession of proprietary information and control of the human capital that can generate new information through expertise in research. Needless to say, once again large research-intensive firms are most likely to fit this description.

Why does possession of information lead to FDI? In the words of one of the theory's proponents:[3]

> *Information is an intermediate product par excellence. It is the oil which lubricates the engine of the MNE. There is no proper market for the sale of information created by the MNE and therefore no price*

2. Buckley, Peter J., and Mark Casson, *The Future of the Multinational Enterprise* (London: McMillan, 1976) and John H. Dunning, "Trade Location of Economic Activity and the MNE: A Search for an Eclectic Approach," in *The International Allocation of Economic Activity*, Bertil Ohlin, Per-Ove Hesselborn, and Per Magnus Wijkman, eds. (New York: Holmes and Meier, 1977) pp. 395–418.

3. Rugman, Alan, "Internalization as a General Theory of Foreign Direct Investment: A Reappraisal of the Literature," *Weltwurtschaftliches Archiv*, June 1980, Volume 116, No. 2, pp. 368–369.

for it. There are surrogate prices; for example, those found by evaluating the opportunity cost of factor inputs expended in the production and processing of a new research discovery or by an ex post evaluation of the extra profits generated by that discovery, assuming all other costs to remain the same. Yet there is no simple interaction of supply and demand to set a market price. Instead the MNE is driven to create an internal market of its own in order to overcome the failure of an external market to emerge for the sale of information. This internal market of the MNE is an efficient response to the given exogenous market imperfection in the determination of the price of information. Internalization allows the MNE to solve the appropriability problem by assigning property rights in knowledge to the MNE organization.

The creation of an internal market by the MNE permits it to transform an intangible piece of research into a valuable property specific to the firm. The MNE will exploit its advantage in all available markets and will keep the use of information internal to the firm in order to recoup its initial expenditures on research and knowledge generation. Production by subsidiaries is preferable to licensing or joint ventures since the latter two arrangements cannot benefit from the internal market of an MNE. They would therefore dissipate the information monopoly of the MNE, unless foreign markets were segmented by effective international patent laws or other protective devices.

Minimizing transactions costs is the key factor in determining the success of an internalization strategy. Wholly-owned FDI reduces the agency costs that arise from asymmetric information, lack of trust, and the need to monitor foreign partners, suppliers, and financial institutions. Self-financing eliminates the need to observe specific debt covenants on foreign subsidiaries that are financed locally or by joint venture partners. If a multinational firm has a low global cost and high availability of capital, why share it with joint venture partners, distributors, licensees, and local banks, all of which probably have a higher cost of capital?

The Financial Strategy

Financial strategies are directly related to the OLI Paradigm in explaining FDI, as shown in Exhibit 15.8. Proactive financial strategies can be controlled in advance by the MNE's financial managers. These include strategies necessary to gain an advantage from lower global cost and greater availability of capital and were explained in detail in Part 6. Other proactive financial strategies are negotiating financial subsidies and/or reduced taxation to increase free cash flows, reducing financial agency costs through FDI, and reducing operating and transaction exposure through FDI.

Reactive financial strategies, as illustrated in Exhibit 15.8, depend on discovering market imperfections. For example, the MNE can exploit misaligned exchange rates and stock prices. It also needs to react to capital controls that prevent the free movement of funds and react to opportunities to minimize worldwide taxation.

Where to Invest?

The decision about where to invest abroad is influenced by behavioral factors. The decision about where to invest abroad for the first time is not the same as the decision about where to reinvest abroad. A firm learns from its first few investments abroad and what it learns influences subsequent investments.

Exhibit 15.8 Finance-Specific Factors and the OLI Paradigm

"X" indicates a connection between FDI and finance-specific strategies

	Ownership Advantages	Location Advantages	Internalization Advantages
Proactive Financial Strategies			
1. Gaining and maintaining a global cost and availability of capital			
a. Competitive sourcing of capital globally	X	X	
b. Strategic preparatory cross-listing	X		
c. Providing accounting and disclosure transparency	X		
d. Maintaining competitive commercial and financial banking relationships	X		
e. Maintaining a competitive credit rating	X	X	X
2. Negotiating financial subsidies and/or reduced taxation to increase free cash flow	X	X	
3. Reducing financial agency cost through FDI			X
4. Reducing operating and transaction exposure through FDI	X		
Reactive Financial Strategies			
1. Exploiting undervalued or overvalued exchange rates		X	
2. Exploiting undervalued or overvalued stock prices		X	
3. Reacting to capital control that prevents the free movement of funds		X	
4. Minimizing taxation		X	X

Source: Oxelheim, Lars, Arthur Stonehill, and Trond Randøy, "On the Treatment of Finance Specific Factors Within the OLI Paradigm," *International Business Review 10* (2001), pp. 381–398.

In theory, a firm should identify its competitive advantages. Then it should search worldwide for market imperfections and comparative advantage until it finds a country where it expects to enjoy a competitive advantage large enough to generate a risk-adjusted return above the firm's hurdle rate.

In practice, firms have been observed to follow a sequential search pattern as described in the behavioral theory of the firm. Human rationality is bounded by one's ability to gather and process all the information that would be needed to make a perfectly rational decision based on all the facts. This observation lies behind two behavioral theories of FDI described next: the *behavioral approach* and *international network theory.*

The Internationalization Process

The decision to invest abroad for the first time is often a stage in a firm's development process. The firm first develops a competitive advantage in its home market and eventually finds that it can grow profitably by exporting to foreign markets. Eventually it experiences a stimulus from the external environment, which leads it to consider production abroad.

In a classic study of the foreign investment decision process of 38 market-seeking U.S. firms that had considered investing in Israel, it was observed that the following external stimuli were important:

1. An outside proposal, provided it comes from a source that cannot be easily ignored. The most frequent sources of such proposals are foreign governments, the distributors of the company's products, and its clients, or a powerful member of the firm's board of directors.
2. Fear of losing a market.
3. The "bandwagon" effect: very successful activities abroad of a competing firm in the same line of business, or a general belief that investment in some area is "a must."
4. Strong competition from abroad in the home market.[4]

The sequence and intensity of investigation, including the motivating force, was the major determinant of the FDI decision.

The Behavioral Approach to FDI

The behavioral approach to analyzing the FDI decision is typified by the so-called *Swedish School* of economists.[5] The Swedish School has rather successfully explained not just the initial decision to invest abroad but also later decisions to reinvest elsewhere and to change the structure of a firm's international involvement over time. Based on the internationalization process of a sample of Swedish MNEs, the economists observed that these firms tended to invest first in countries that were not too far distant in psychic terms. *Close psychic distance* defined countries with a cultural, legal, and institutional environment similar to Sweden's, such as Norway, Denmark, Finland, Germany, and the United Kingdom. The initial investments were modest in size to minimize the risk of an uncertain foreign environment. As the Swedish firms learned from their initial investments, they became willing to take greater risks with respect to both the psychic distance of the countries and the size of the investments.

MNEs in a Network Perspective

As the Swedish MNEs grew and matured, so did the nature of their international involvement. Today each MNE is perceived as being a member of an international network, with nodes based in each of the foreign subsidiaries, as well as the parent firm itself. Centralized (hierarchical) control has given way to decentralized (heterarchical) control.[6] Foreign subsidiaries compete with each other and with the parent for expanded resource commitments, thus influencing the strategy and reinvestment decisions. Many of these MNEs have become political coalitions with competing internal and external networks. Each subsidiary (and the parent) is embedded in its host country's network of suppliers and customers. It is also a member of a worldwide network based on its industry. Finally, it is a member of an organizational network under the nominal control of the parent firm.

4. Aharoni, Yair, *The Foreign Investment Decision Process* (Boston: Harvard Graduate School of Business Administration, Division of Research, 1966).
5. Johansen, John, and F. Wiedersheim-Paul, "The Internationalization of the Firm: Four Swedish Case Studies," *Journal of Management Studies*, 1975, Volume 12, No. 3; and Johansen, John, and Jan Erik Vahlne, "The Internationalization of the Firm: A Model of Knowledge Development and Increasing Foreign Market Commitments," *Journal of International Business Studies*, 1977, Volume 8, No. 1.
6. Hedlund, Gunner, "The Hypermodern MNC—A Heterarchy?", *Human Resource Management*, 1994, Volume 25, No. 1, pp. 9–35.

Complicating matters still further is the possibility that the parent itself may have evolved into a transnational firm, one that is owned by a coalition of investors located in different countries.[7]

Asea Brown Boveri (ABB) is an example of a Swedish-Swiss firm that has passed through the international evolutionary process all the way to being a transnational firm. ABB was formed through a merger of Sweden-based ASEA and Switzerland-based Brown Boveri in 1991. Both firms were already dominant players internationally in the electrotechnical and engineering industries. ABB has literally hundreds of foreign subsidiaries, which are managed on a very decentralized basis. ABB's "flat" organization structure and transnational ownership encourage local initiative, quick response, and decentralized FDI decisions. Although overall strategic direction is the legal responsibility of the parent firm, foreign subsidiaries play a major role in all decision making. Their input in turn is strongly influenced by their own membership in their local and worldwide industry networks.

How to Invest Abroad: Modes of Foreign Involvement

The globalization process includes a sequence of decisions regarding where production is to occur, who is to own or control intellectual property, and who is to own the actual production facilities. Exhibit 15.9 provides a roadmap to explain this FDI sequence.

Exhibit 15.9 The FDI Sequence: Foreign Presence and Foreign Investment

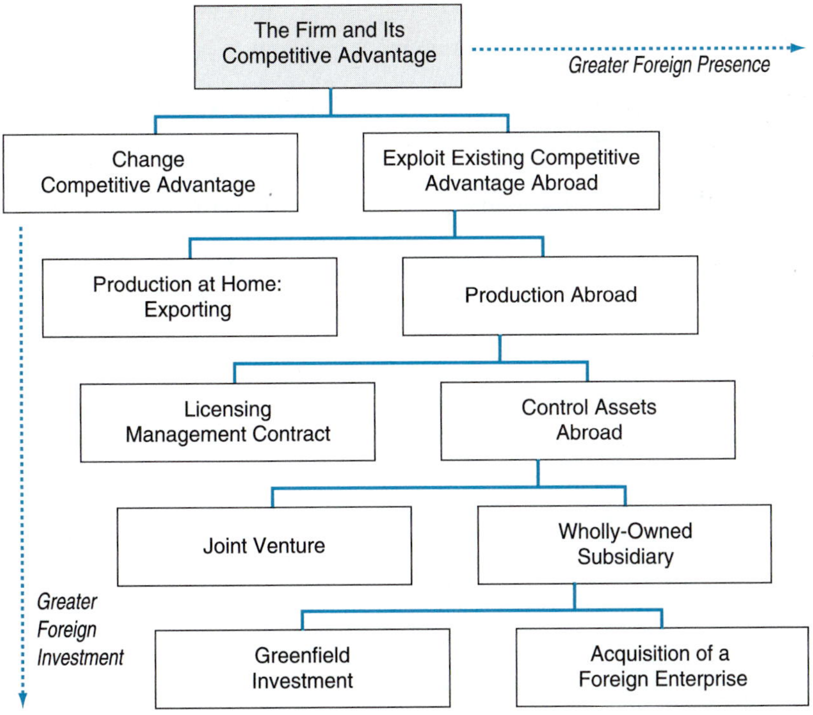

7. Forsgren, Mats, *Managing the Internationalization Process: The Swedish Case* (London: Routledge, 1989).

Exporting Versus Production Abroad

There are several advantages to limiting a firm's activities to exports. Exporting has none of the unique risks facing FDI, joint ventures, strategic alliances, and licensing. Political risks are minimal. Agency costs, such as monitoring and evaluating foreign units, are avoided. The amount of front-end investment is typically lower than in other modes of foreign involvement. Foreign exchange risks remain, however.

The fact that a significant share of exports (and imports) are executed between MNEs and their foreign subsidiaries and affiliates further reduces the risk of exports compared to other modes of involvement. For example, Global Finance Perspective 15.1 shows the extent of exports and imports from U.S.-based MNEs to their foreign subsidiaries and affiliates.

There are also disadvantages. A firm is not able to internalize and exploit the results of its research and development as effectively as if it invested directly. The firm also risks losing markets to imitators and global competitors that might be more cost efficient in production abroad and distribution. As these firms capture foreign markets, they might become so strong that they can export back into the domestic exporter's own market. Remember that defensive FDI is often motivated by the need to prevent this kind of predatory behavior as well as to preempt foreign markets before competitors can get started.

Global Finance Perspective **15.1**

Keeping It in the Family: American Exports to and Imports from American-Owned Affiliates Abroad (billions of US$)

	Intra-company	Inter-company	Total
All countries			
Exports	145.5	24.5	170.0
Imports	123.9	19.4	143.3
Balance	21.6	5.1	26.7
High-income countries			
Exports	129.0	20.8	149.9
Imports	54.0	15.1	129.1
Balance	35.0	5.7	40.7
Middle-income countries			
Exports	28.9	5.4	34.3
Imports	31.5	1.9	33.4
Balance	- 2.6	3.5	0.8
Low-income countries			
Exports	1.6	0.2	1.8
Imports	1.8	0.4	2.2
Balance	- 0.2	- 0.2	- 0.4

Source: Edward M. Graham, Institute for International Economics, as cited in "Globalisation and its critics: A survey of globalisation," *The Economist*, September 29, 2001, p. 9.

Licensing and Management Contracts Versus Control of Assets Abroad

Licensing is a popular method for domestic firms to profit from foreign markets without the need to commit sizable funds. Since the foreign producer is typically wholly owned locally, political risk is minimized. In recent years a number of host countries have demanded that MNEs sell their services in "unbundled form" rather than only through FDI. Such countries would like their local firms to purchase managerial expertise and knowledge of product and factor markets through management contracts, and purchase technology through licensing agreements.

The main disadvantage of licensing is that license fees are likely to be lower than FDI profits, although the return on the marginal investment might be higher. Other disadvantages include:

- Possible loss of quality control
- Establishment of a potential competitor in third-country markets
- Possible improvement of the technology by the local licensee, which then enters the original firm's home market
- Possible loss of opportunity to enter the licensee's market with FDI later
- Risk that technology will be stolen
- High agency costs

MNEs have not typically used licensing of independent firms. On the contrary, most licensing arrangements have been with their own foreign subsidiaries or joint ventures. License fees are a way to spread the corporate research and development cost among all operating units and a means of repatriating profits in a form more acceptable to some host countries than dividends.

Management contracts are similar to licensing, insofar as they provide for some cash flow from a foreign source without significant foreign investment or exposure. Management contracts probably lessen political risk because repatriation of managers is easy. International consulting and engineering firms traditionally conduct their foreign business on the basis of a management contract.

Whether licensing and management contracts are cost-effective compared to FDI depends on the price host countries will pay for the unbundled services. If the price were high enough, many firms would prefer to take advantage of market imperfections in an unbundled way, particularly in view of the lower political, foreign exchange, and business risks. Because we observe MNEs continuing to prefer FDI, we must assume that the price for selling unbundled services is still too low.

Why is the price of unbundled services too low? The answer may lie in the synergy created when services are bundled as FDI in the first place. Managerial expertise is often dependent on a delicate mix of organizational support factors that cannot be transferred abroad efficiently. Technology is a continuous process, but licensing usually captures only the technology at a particular point in time. Most important of all, however, economies of scale cannot be sold or transferred in small bundles. By definition they require large-scale operations. A relatively large operation in a small market can hardly achieve the same economies of scale as a large operation in a large market.

Despite the handicaps, some MNEs have successfully sold unbundled services. An example is sales of managerial expertise and technology to the OPEC countries. In this case, however, the OPEC countries are both willing and able to pay a price high enough to approach the returns on FDI (bundled services) while receiving only the lesser benefits of the unbundled services.

Joint Venture Versus Wholly Owned Subsidiary

A *joint venture* is here defined as shared ownership in a foreign business. A foreign business unit that is partially owned by the parent company is typically termed a *foreign affiliate*. A foreign business unit that is 50% or more owned (and therefore controlled) by the parent company is typically designated a *foreign subsidiary*. A joint venture would therefore typically fall into the categorization of being a foreign affiliate but not a foreign subsidiary.

A joint venture between a MNE and a host country partner is a viable strategy if, and only if, the MNE finds the right local partner. Some of the obvious advantages of having a compatible local partner are as follows:

1. The local partner understands the customs, mores, and institutions of the local environment. A MNE might need years to acquire such knowledge on its own with a 100%-owned greenfield subsidiary (greenfield means from the ground up, as explained in the next section).
2. The local partner can provide competent management, not just at the top but also at the middle levels of management.
3. If the host country requires that foreign firms share ownership with local firms or investors, 100% foreign ownership is not a realistic alternative to a joint venture.
4. The local partner's contacts and reputation enhance access to the host country's capital markets.
5. The local partner may possess technology that is appropriate for the local environment or perhaps can be used worldwide.
6. The public image of a firm that is partially locally owned may improve its sales possibilities if the purpose of the investment is to serve the local market.

Despite this impressive list of advantages, joint ventures are not as common as 100%-owned foreign subsidiaries, because MNEs fear interference by the local partner in certain critical decision areas. Indeed, what is optimal from the viewpoint of the local venture may be sub-optimal for the multinational operation as a whole. The most important potential conflicts or difficulties are these:

1. Political risk is increased rather than reduced if the wrong partner is chosen. Imagine the standing of joint ventures undertaken with the family or associates of Suharto in Indonesia, Hussein in Iraq, or Slobodan Milosevic in Serbia just before their overthrow. The local partner must be credible and ethical or the venture is worse off for being a joint venture.
2. Local and foreign partners may have divergent views about the need for cash dividends, or about the desirability of growth financed from retained earnings versus new financing.
3. Transfer pricing on products or components bought from or sold to related companies creates a potential for conflict of interest.
4. Control of financing is another problem area. A MNE cannot justify its use of cheap or available funds raised in one country to finance joint venture operations in another country.
5. Ability of a firm to rationalize production on a worldwide basis can be jeopardized if such rationalization would act to the disadvantage of local joint venture partners.

6. Financial disclosure of local results might be necessary with locally traded shares, whereas if the firm is wholly owned from abroad, such disclosure is not needed. Disclosure gives nondisclosing competitors an advantage in setting strategy.

Valuation of equity shares is difficult. How much should the local partner pay for its share? What is the value of contributed technology, or of contributed land in a country like China where all land is state-owned? It is highly unlikely that foreign and host country partners have similar opportunity costs of capital, expectations about the required rate of return, or similar perceptions of appropriate premiums for business, foreign exchange, and political risks. Insofar as the venture is a component of the portfolio of each investor, its contribution to portfolio return and variance may be quite different for each.

Greenfield Investment Versus Acquisition

A *greenfield investment* is defined as establishing a production or service facility starting from the ground up, i.e., from a green field. Compared to greenfield investment, a cross-border acquisition has a number of significant advantages. First and foremost, it is quicker. Greenfield investment frequently requires extended periods of physical construction and organizational development. By acquiring an existing firm, the MNE can shorten the time required to gain a presence and facilitate competitive entry into the market. Second, acquisition may be a cost-effective way of gaining competitive advantages such as technology, brand names valued in the target market, and logistical and distribution advantages, while simultaneously eliminating a local competitor. Third, international economic, political, and foreign exchange conditions may result in market imperfections allowing target firms to be undervalued. Many enterprises throughout Asia have been the target of acquisition as a result of the Asian economic crisis's impact on their financial health. Many enterprises were in dire need of capital injections for competitive survival.

Cross-border acquisitions are not, however, without their pitfalls. As with all acquisitions—domestic or international—there are the frequent problems of paying too high a price or suffering a method of financing that is too costly. Meshing different corporate cultures can be traumatic. Managing the post-acquisition process is frequently characterized by downsizing to gain economies of scale and scope in overhead functions. This results in nonproductive impacts on the firm as individuals attempt to save their own jobs. Internationally, additional difficulties arise from host governments intervening in pricing, financing, employment guarantees, market segmentation, and general nationalism and favoritism. In fact, the ability to complete international acquisitions successfully may itself be a test of the MNE's competence in the twenty-first century.

Strategic Alliances

The term *strategic alliance* conveys different meanings to different observers. In one form of cross-border strategic alliance, two firms exchange a share of ownership with one another. A strategic alliance can be a takeover defense if the prime purpose is for a firm to place some of its stock in stable and friendly hands. If that is all that occurs, it is just another form of portfolio investment.

In a more comprehensive strategic alliance, in addition to exchanging stock, the partners establish a separate joint venture to develop and manufacture a product or service. Numerous examples of such strategic alliances can be found in the automotive, electronics, telecommunications, and aircraft industries. Such alliances are particularly suited to high-tech industries, where the cost of research and development is high and timely introduction of improvements is important.

A third level of cooperation might include joint marketing and servicing agreements in which each partner represents the other in certain markets. Some observers believe such arrangements begin to resemble the cartels prevalent in the 1920s and 1930s. Because they reduce competition, cartels have been banned by international agreements and many national laws.

It remains to be seen whether the current wave of strategic alliances with and between firms in the European Union yields partnerships that are stable and durable. It seems as if most firms feel they should be treating the EU internal market as if it were a "United States of Europe." Strategic alliances are a quick way to get EU-wide coverage. This approach is particularly attractive to firms that have historically served the EU markets through exports, licensing, or minor FDI in assembly and service facilities. Specifically, firms located in Norway, Israel, and Switzerland are feeling the pressure to become "insiders." Strategic alliances with EU partners have also been popular with firms from the United States, Japan, Canada, and Australia. It is possible that many of these hurried strategic alliances will be dissolved and be replaced in a more deliberate manner by traditional types of FDI over time.

SUMMARY

- The theory of comparative advantage is based on one country possessing a relative (not absolute) advantage in the production of goods intensive in either land, labor, or capital compared to another country.
- Imperfections in national markets for products, factors of production, and financial assets translate into market opportunities for MNEs.
- Strategic motives drive the decision to invest abroad and become a MNE. Firms could be seeking new markets, raw material sources, production efficiency locations, access to state-of-the-art knowledge, or political safety.
- In order to invest abroad, a firm must have a sustainable competitive advantage in the home market. This must be strong enough and transferable enough to overcome the disadvantages of operating abroad.
- Competitive advantages stem from economies of scale and scope arising from large size, managerial and marketing expertise, superior technology, financial strength, differentiated products, and competitiveness of the home market.
- The OLI Paradigm is an attempt to create an overall framework to explain why MNEs choose FDI rather than serve foreign markets through alternative modes such as licensing, joint ventures, strategic alliances, management contracts, and exporting.
- Finance-specific strategies are directly related to the OLI Paradigm, including both proactive and reactive financial strategies.
- The decision about where to invest is influenced by economic and behavioral factors, as well as the stage of a firm's historical development.
- Psychic distance plays a role in determining the sequence of FDI and later reinvestment. As firms learn from their early investments, they venture further afield and are willing to risk larger commitments.

- The most internationalized firms can be viewed from a network perspective. The parent firm and each of the foreign subsidiaries are members of networks. The networks are composed of relationships within a worldwide industry, within the host countries with suppliers and customers, and within the multinational firm itself.
- Exporting avoids political risk but not foreign exchange risk. It requires the least up-front investment, but it might eventually lose markets to imitators and global competitors that might be more cost-efficient in production abroad and distribution.
- Alternative (to 100%-owned foreign subsidiaries) modes of foreign involvement exist. They include joint venture, strategic alliances, licensing, management contracts, and traditional exporting.
- Licensing enables a firm to profit from foreign markets without a major front-end investment. However, disadvantages include limited returns, possible loss of quality control and potential of establishing a future competitor.
- The success of a joint venture depends primarily on the right choice of a partner. For this reason and a number of issues related to possible conflicts in decision-making between a joint venture and a multinational parent, the 100%-owned foreign subsidiary approach is more common.
- The European Union has recently experienced a surge in cross-border entry through strategic alliances that may not be sustainable. Although some forms of strategic alliances share the same characteristics as joint ventures, they often also include an exchange of stock.

QUESTIONS

1. **Evolving into multinationalism.** As a firm evolves from purely domestic into a true multinational enterprise, it must consider a) its competitive advantages, b) where it wants to locate production, c) the type of control it wants to have over any foreign operations, and d) how much monetary capital to invest abroad. Explain how each of these four considerations is important to the success of foreign operations.

2. **Theory of comparative advantage.** What is the essence of the theory of comparative advantage?

3. **Theory of factor proportions.** What is the essence of the theory of factor proportions?

4. **Market imperfections.** MNEs strive to take advantage of market imperfections in national markets for products, factors of production, and financial assets. Large international firms are better able to exploit such imperfections. What are their main competitive advantages?

5. **Strategic motives for foreign direct investment (FDI).**

   a. Summarize the five main motives that drive the decision to initiate FDI.

   b. Match those motives with the following MNEs:

General Motors (USA)	Royal Dutch Shell (Netherlands/UK)
Kentucky Fried Chicken (USA)	Jardine Matheson (Hong Kong)
Apple Computer (USA)	NEC (Japan)

6. **Competitive advantage.** In deciding whether to invest abroad, management must first determine whether the firm has a sustainable competitive advantage that enables it to compete effectively in the home market. What are the necessary characteristics of this competitive advantage?

7. **Economies of scale and scope.** Explain briefly how economies of scale and scope can be developed in production, marketing, finance, research and development, transportation, and purchasing.

8. **Competitiveness of the home market.** A strongly competitive home market can sharpen a firm's competitive advantage relative to firms

located in less competitive markets. This phenomenon is known as Porter's "diamond of national advantage." Explain what is meant by the "diamond of national advantage."

9. **OLI Paradigm.** The OLI Paradigm is an attempt to create an overall framework to explain why MNEs choose FDI rather than serve foreign markets through alternative modes.
   a. Explain what is meant by the "O" in the OLI Paradigm.
   b. Explain what is meant by the "L" in the OLI Paradigm
   c. Explain what is meant by the "I" in the OLI Paradigm
10. **Financial links to OLI.** Financial strategies are directly related to the OLI Paradigm.
    a. Explain how *proactive* financial strategies are related to OLI.
    b. Explain how *reactive* financial strategies are related to OLI
11. **Where to invest.** The decision about where to invest abroad is influenced by behavioral factors.
    a. Explain the *behavioral approach* to FDI.
    b. Explain the *international network theory* explanation of FDI.
12. **Exporting versus producing abroad.** What are the advantages and disadvantages of limiting a firm's activities to exporting compared to producing abroad?
13. **Licensing and management contracts versus producing abroad.** What are the advantages and disadvantages of licensing and management contracts compared to producing abroad?
14. **Joint venture versus wholly owned production subsidiary.** What are the advantages and disadvantages of forming a joint venture to serve a foreign market compared to serving that market with a wholly owned production subsidiary?
15. **Greenfield investment versus acquisition.** What are the advantages and disadvantages of serving a foreign market through a Greenfield foreign direct investment compared to an acquisition of a local firm in the target market?
16. **Cross-border strategic alliance.** The term "cross-border strategic alliance" conveys different meanings to different observers. What are the different meanings?

PROBLEMS

Comparative Advantage. Problems 1–5 illustrate an example of trade induced by comparative advantage. They assume that China and France each have 1,000 production units. With one unit of production (a mix of land, labor, capital, and technology), China can produce either 10 containers of toys or 7 cases of wine. France can produce either 2 cases of toys or 7 cases of wine. Thus, a production unit in China is five times as efficient compared to France when producing toys, but equally efficient when producing wine. Assume at first that no trade takes place. China allocates 800 production units to building toys and 200 production units to producing wine. France allocates 200 production units to building toys and 800 production units to producing wine.

1. **Production and consumption.** What are the production and consumption of China and France without trade?
2. **Specialization.** Assume complete specialization, where China produces only toys and France produces only wine. What would be the effect on total production?
3. **Trade at China's domestic price.** China's domestic price is 10 containers of toys equals 7 cases of wine. Assume China produces 10,000 containers of toys and exports 2,000 to France. Assume France produces 7,000 cases of wine and exports 1,400 cases to China. What happens to total production and consumption?
4. **Trade at France's domestic price.** France's domestic price is 2 containers of toys equals 7 cases of wine. Assume China produces 10,000 cases of wine. Assume China produces 10,000 containers of toys and exports 400 containers to France. Assume France produces 7,000 cases of wine and exports 1,400 cases to

China. What happens to total production and consumption?

5. **Trade at negotiated mid-price.** The mid-price for exchange between France and China can be calculated as follows:

	Toys		Wine
China's domestic price	10	to	7
France's domestic price	2	to	7
Negotiated mid-price	6	to	7

What happens to total production and consumption?

INTERNET EXERCISES

WWW.

1. **International capital flows: Public and private.** Major multinational organizations (some of which are listed below) attempt to track the relative movements and magnitudes of global capital investment. Using these web pages and others you may find, prepare a two-page executive briefing on the question of whether capital generated in the industrialized countries is finding its way to the less developed and emerging markets. Is there some critical distinction between "less developed" and "emerging?"

The World Bank	http://www.worldbank.org
OECD	http://www.oecd.org
European Bank for Reconstruction	http://www.ebrd.org

2. **Overseas Private Investment Corporation.** The Overseas Private Investment Corporation (OPIC) provides long-term political risk insurance and limited recourse project financing aid to U.S.-based firms investing abroad. Using the organization's web page, answer the following questions:

   a. Exactly what types of risk will OPIC insure against?

   b. What financial limits and restrictions are there on this insurance protection?

   c. How should a project be structured to aid in its approval for OPIC coverage?

   Overseas Private Investment Corp http://www.opic.gov

3. **International management and strategy consultancies.** The management consulting industry has been one of the primary resources utilized by MNEs throughout the world in the 1990s to design and develop their corporate strategies. The following firm web pages provide some insight into the industry, the job opportunities available for professionals in consulting, and some interesting features, such as the Boston Consulting Group's on-line interactive case study.

A.T. Kearney	http://www.atkearney.com
Bain and Company	http://www.rec.bain.com
Booze, Allen & Hamilton	http://www.bah.com
Boston Consulting Group	http://www.bcg.com
McKinsey & Company	http://www.mckinsey.com

SELECTED READINGS

Buckley, Peter J., "The Limits of Explanation: Testing the Internalization Theory of the Multinational Enterprise," *Journal of International Business Studies*, Summer 1988, pp. 181–193.

Buckley, Peter J., and Mark Casson, "An Economic Model of International Joint Venture Strategy," *Journal of International Business Studies*, Special Issue 1996, Volume 27, No. 5, pp. 849–876.

Dunning, John H., "Location and the Multinational Enterprise: A Neglected Factor?," *Journal of International Business Studies*, First Quarter 1998, Volume 29, No. 1, pp. 45–66.

Dunning, John H., "The Eclectic Paradigm of International Production: A Restatement and Some Possible Extensions," *Journal of International Business Studies*, Spring 1988, pp. 1–32.

Wells, Louis T., Jr., "Multinationals and the Developing Countries," *Journal of International Business Studies*, First Quarter 1998, Volume 29, No. 1, pp. 101–114.

MINI-CASE

Benecol's Global Licensing Agreement

In November 1996, a Finnish company by the name of Raisio introduced a revolutionary new product into supermarkets across Finland—a cholesterol-reducing margarine called Benecol. Deriving its name from *bene* from the Latin for "good" and *col* for "cholesterol", the margarine could potentially reduce a regular consumer's blood cholesterol levels by 14–15%. All that was needed was for the consumer to consume a few grams of the margarine roughly three times a day, such as with meals.

Although priced at roughly three times that of most other margarine products, Raisio could not keep store shelves stocked with the level of immediate demand. The global potential for the product was thought to be enormous. Raisio, traditionally a relatively quiet share on the Helsinki Stock Exchange, skyrocketed in the following months.

The problem was that Raisio itself was primarily a regional producer of industrial chemicals and foodstuffs, with margarine being its only retail product. Simultaneously, there were a number of potential competitive products in various stages of pipeline development around the world by large and capable companies like Novartis and Unilever. Raisio quickly came to the conclusion that if it was to reap the benefits of Benecol quickly and effectively in the global marketplace, it would need a global partner.

After continued negotiations, in March of 1997 Raisio signed a global licensing agreement with McNeil Consumer Products, a healthcare products subsidiary of Johnson & Johnson (USA). The global licensing agreement gave exclusive rights to McNeil for the global distribution and sale of all products containing Benecol. The licensing agreement had three key elements, as described in the following exhibit.

Global Licensing: Agreement Between Raisio (Finland) and McNeil Consumer Products (USA)

1. Raisio would provide at an agreed-upon price all stanol ester (the key chemical ingredient of Benecol) that McNeil would use in producing all Benecol-based products.
2. Raisio would receive a royalty calculated as a percentage of the retail sales price of all Benecol products sold in any marketplace outside of Finland (the exact royalty rate was not disclosed, but is thought to be about 5%).
3. Raisio would receive a series of milestone payments from McNeil totaling roughly $60 million over the 1997–1999 period.

The agreement made Raisio responsible for assuring an adequate supply of stanol ester for all McNeil product needs. Raisio would have no other responsibilities under the agreement, other than the usual commitments associated with continued product development, testing, and certification. McNeil would be responsible for product development, manufacturing, regulatory approvals for national and international distribution, and global marketing.

Case Questions

1. How does the global licensing agreement split risk and return, in a financial sense, between Raisio and McNeil?
2. How will the returns to Raisio accrue over the short, medium, and long terms under the agreement, assuming the product is met with relative success?
3. What are some of the possible motivations to Raisio and McNeil behind a *milestone agreement*? Assume the milestone payments are agreed-upon payments from McNeil to Raisio if:
   a. Raisio successfully completes the expansion of its manufacturing capabilities for stanol ester.
   b. McNeil successfully introduces Benecol products in major industrial markets, overcoming regulatory hurdles or reaching specific sales goals.

Chapter 16

Political Risk Assessment and Management

THIS CHAPTER STARTS BY DEFINING POLITICAL RISKS AND CLASSIFYING THEM ON THREE LEVELS, namely *firm-specific*, *country-specific*, or *global-specific*. The next section examines how a MNE can assess political risk by predicting each of these levels of risk. This is followed by a detailed discussion of firm-specific risks related to corporate governance and goal conflict. Then comes an analysis of one of the two main categories of country-specific risk called *transfer risk*. The following section describes the other main category of country-specific risk: culture and institutional risks. This chapter ends with an analysis of global-specific risks, such as terrorism and other actions that are worldwide in origin rather than specific to a particular country.

Defining Political Risk

In order for a MNE to identify, measure, and manage its political risks, it must define and classify these risks. Exhibit 16.1 classifies the political risks facing MNEs as being firm-specific, country-specific, or global-specific:

- *Firm-specific risks*, also known as *micro risks*, are those risks that affect the MNE at the project or corporate level. *Governance risk* due to goal conflict between a MNE and its host government is the main political firm-specific risk. (A MNE also faces business risks and foreign exchange risks, which are covered extensively in other sections of this book).
- *Country-specific-risks*, also known as *macro risks*, are those risks that also affect the MNE at the project or corporate level but originate at the country level. The two main political risk categories at the country level are *transfer risk* and *cultural and institutional risks.* Transfer risk concerns mainly the problem of blocked funds, but also peripherally sovereign credit risk (covered elsewhere in this book). Cultural and institutional risks spring from ownership structure, human resource norms, religious heritage, nepotism and corruption, intellectual property rights, and protectionism.
- *Global-specific risks* are those risks that affect the MNE at the project or corporate level but originate at the global level. Examples are terrorism, the antiglobalization movement, environmental concerns, poverty, and cyberattacks.

Exhibit 16.1 Classification of Political Risks

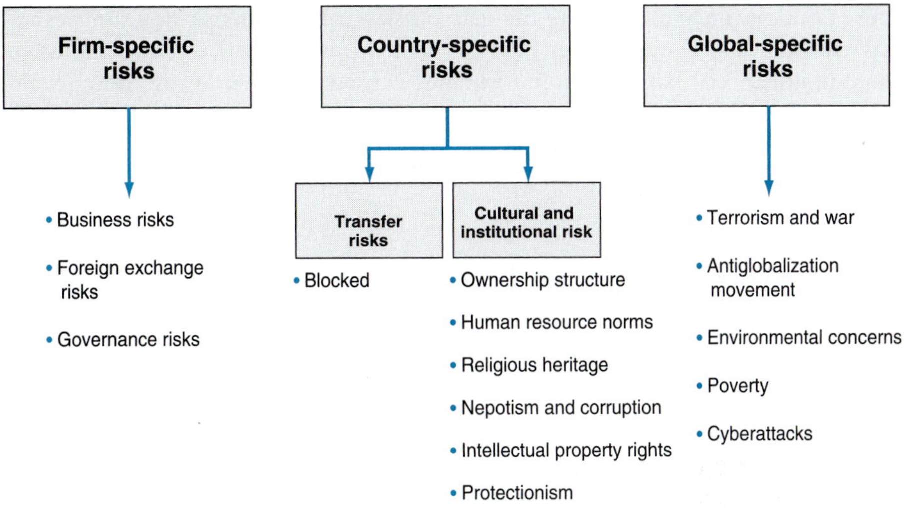

This method of classification differs sharply from the traditional method that classifies risks according to the disciplines of economics, finance, political science, sociology, and law. We prefer our classification system because it is easier to relate the identified political risks to existing and recommended strategies to manage these risks.

Assessing Political Risk

How can multinational firms anticipate government regulations that, from the firm's perspective, are discriminatory or wealth-depriving? Normally a twofold approach is utilized.

At the macro level, firms attempt to assess a host country's political stability and attitude toward foreign investors. At the micro level, firms analyze whether their firm-specific activities are likely to conflict with host-country goals as evidenced by existing regulations. The most difficult task, however, is to anticipate changes in host-country goal priorities, new regulations to implement reordered priorities, and the likely impact of such changes on the firm's operations.

Predicting Firm-Specific Risk (Micro Risk)

From the viewpoint of a multinational firm, assessing the political stability of a host country is only the first step, since the real objective is to anticipate the effect of political changes on activities of a specific firm. Indeed, different foreign firms operating within the same country may have very different degrees of vulnerability to changes in host-country policy or regulations. One does not expect a Kentucky Fried Chicken franchise to experience the same risk as a Ford manufacturing plant.

The need for firm-specific analyses of political risk has led to a demand for tailor-made studies undertaken in-house by professional political risk analysts. This demand is heightened by the observation that outside professional risk analysts rarely even agree on the degree of macro-political risk which exists in any set of countries.

In-house political risk analysts relate the macro risk attributes of specific countries to the particular characteristics and vulnerabilities of their client firms. Mineral extractive firms, manufacturing firms, multinational banks, private insurance carriers, and worldwide hotel chains are all exposed in fundamentally different ways to politically inspired restrictions. Even with the best possible firm-specific analysis, MNEs cannot be sure that the political or economic situation will not change. Thus it is necessary to plan protective steps in advance to minimize the risk of damage from unanticipated changes.

Predicting Country-Specific Risk (Macro Risk)

Macro political risk analysis is still an emerging field of study. Political scientists in academia, industry, and government study country risk for the benefit of multinational firms, government foreign policy decision makers, and defense planners.

Political risk studies usually include an analysis of the historical stability of the country in question, evidence of present turmoil or dissatisfaction, indications of economic stability, and trends in cultural and religious activities. Data are usually assembled by reading local newspapers, monitoring radio and television broadcasts, reading publications from diplomatic sources, tapping the knowledge of outstanding expert consultants, contacting other business persons who have had recent experience in the host country, and finally conducting on-site visits.

Despite this impressive list of activities, the prediction track record of business firms, the diplomatic service, and the military has been spotty at best. When one analyzes trends, whether in politics or economics, the tendency is to predict an extension of the same trends into the future. It is a rare forecaster who is able to predict a cataclysmic change in direction. Who predicted the overthrow of Ferdinand Marcos in the Philippines? Indeed, who predicted the collapse of communism in the Soviet Union and the Eastern European satellites? Who predicted the fall of President Suharto in Indonesia in 1998, or Saddam Hussein in 2003?

Despite the difficulty of predicting country risk, the MNE must still attempt to do so in order to prepare itself for the unknown. A number of institutional services provide updated country risk ratings on a regular basis. A sample of these rating for selected countries is shown in Exhibit 16.2.

Predicting Global-Specific Risk

Predicting global-specific risk is even more difficult than the other two types of political risk. Nobody predicted the surprise attacks on the World Trade Center and the Pentagon in the United States on September 11, 2001. On the other hand, the aftermath of this attack—i.e., the war on global terrorism—increased U.S. homeland security, and the destruction of part of the terrorist network in Afghanistan was predictable. Nevertheless, we have come to expect future surprise terrorist attacks. U.S.-based MNEs are particularly exposed to not only Al Qaeda but also to other unpredictable interest groups willing to use terror or mob action to promote such diverse causes as anti-globalization, environmental protection, and even anarchy.

Since there is a great need to predict terrorism, we can expect to see a number of new indices, similar to country-specific indices, but devoted to ranking different types of terrorist threats, their locations, and potential targets.

Exhibit 16.2 Country Risk Ratings for Selected Countries

Risk ratings	Indonesia	Finland	Brazil	Russia	Mexico
Currency unit	rupiah	euro	real	ruble	peso
Arrangement	floating	EMU	floating	managed float	floating
S&P Rating	CCC+	AA	B+	SD	BB
Moody's Rating	B3	Aaa	B2	B3	B2
Fitch ICA	B–	AAA	B	CCC	BB
Economist Intelligence Unit:					
Rating	D	B	D	D	C
Score	67	35	62	79	53
Euromoney:					
Rank	88	12	76	161	47
Score	36.4	90.9	41.7	20.9	55.2
Institutional Investor:					
Rank	86	14	65	104	49
Score	27.9	82.2	37.4	20.0	46.0
Trend	Negative	Positive	Negative	Negative	Positive
International Country Risk Guide:					
Political	42.0	90.0	66.0	54.0	69.0
Financial	22.0	39.0	31.5	25.5	31.0
Economic	18.0	45.5	33.0	18.5	35.0
Milken Institute Capital Access Index:					
Score	37.8		61.65	57.81	61.65
Quantitative	56.6		52.38	71.15	52.38
Risk measures	26.3		29.41	43.59	31.25
Qualitative	0.0		36.36	31.03	34.76
Overseas Private Invest Corp.	Yes	No	Yes	Yes	No

Adapted by authors from the sources listed above. All values for March 1999. Each of these institutional services has its own regularly updated publications that were used to prepare this table.

Firm-Specific Risks

The firm-specific risks that confront MNEs include business risks, foreign exchange risks, and governance risks. The various business and foreign exchange risks were detailed previously in Chapters 8, 9, and 10. We focus our discussion here on governance risks.

Governance Risks

As introduced in Chapter 1, *governance risk* is the ability to exercise effective control over a MNE's operations within a country's legal and political environment. For a MNE, however, governance is a subject similar in structure to consolidated profitability—it must be addressed for the individual business unit and subsidiary, as well as for the MNE as a whole.

But what is good governance? Like so many other factors which are considered integral to the valuation of companies, corporate governance has been the subject of increasing debate globally. A recent study undertaken by McKinsey found that institutional investors paid on average 28% more for the shares of what the authors of the study classified as well-governed companies in emerging markets.

Many factors contribute to good governance, some (such as the relationship between the CEO and the Chairman) are difficult to quantify. Nevertheless, several useful indicators of a well-governed company are available to shareholders. Ten widely recognized principles are summarized in Exhibit 16.3.

The most important type of governance risk for the MNE on the subsidiary level arises from a goal conflict between bona fide objectives of host governments and the private firms operating within their spheres of influence. Governments are normally responsive to a constituency consisting of their citizens. Firms are responsive to a constituency consisting of their owners and other stakeholders. The valid needs of these two separate sets of constituents need not be the same, but

Exhibit 16.3 The Corporate Governance Top Ten

Accountability

1. **Transparent ownership:** identify major shareholders, director and management shareholders, and cross-holdings.
2. **Board size:** establish an appropriate number of board seats; studies suggest that optimal number is five to nine.
3. **Board accountability:** define board's role and responsibilities in published guidelines, and make them bases for board compensation.
4. **Ownership neutrality:** eschew anti-takeover defenses that shield management from accountability. Notify shareholders at least 28 days before shareholder meetings and allow them to participate on-line.

Disclosure and Transparency

5. **Broad, timely, and accurate disclosure:** fully disclose information on financial and operating performance, competitive position, and relevant details (such as board member backgrounds) in timely manner. Offer multiple channels of access to information and full access to shareholders.
6. **Accounting standards:** use internationally recognized accounting standards for both annual and quarterly reporting.

Independence

7. **Dispersed ownership:** deny any single shareholder or group privileged access to or excessive influence over decision making.
8. **Independent audits and oversight:** perform annual audit using independent and reputable auditor. Insist that independent committees oversee auditing, internal controls, and top management compensation and development.
9. **Independent directors:** allow no more than half of directors to be executives of company; at least half of non-executive directors should have no other ties to company.

Shareholder Equity

10. **One share, one vote:** assign all shares equal voting rights and equal rights to distributed profit.

Source: Paul Coombes and Mark Watson, "Three Surveys on Corporate Governance," *The McKinsey Quarterly*, 2000, Number 4, Special Edition.

governments set the rules. Consequently, governments impose constraints on the activities of private firms as part of their normal administrative and legislative functioning.

Historically, conflicts between objectives of MNEs and host governments have arisen over such issues as the firm's impact on economic development, perceived infringement on national sovereignty, foreign control of key industries, sharing or non-sharing of ownership and control with local interests, impact on a host country's balance of payments, influence on the foreign exchange value of its currency, control over export markets, use of domestic versus foreign executives and workers, and exploitation of national resources. Attitudes about conflicts are often colored by views about free enterprise versus state socialism, the degree of nationalism or internationalism present, or the place of religious views in determining appropriate economic and financial behavior.

The best approach to goal conflict management is to anticipate problems and negotiate understandings ahead of time. Different cultures apply different ethics to the question of honoring prior "contracts," especially when they were negotiated with a previous administration. Nevertheless, pre-negotiation of all conceivable areas of conflict provides a better basis for a successful future for both parties than does overlooking the possibility that divergent objectives will evolve over time. Pre-negotiation often includes negotiating investment agreements, buying investment insurance and guarantees, and designing risk-reducing operating strategies to be used after the foreign investment decision has been made.

Negotiating Investment Agreements

An *investment agreement* spells out specific rights and responsibilities of both the foreign firm and the host government. The presence of MNEs is as often sought by development-seeking host governments as a particular foreign location sought by a MNE. All parties have alternatives and so bargaining is appropriate.

An investment agreement should spell out policies on financial and managerial issues, including the following:

- The basis on which fund flows, such as dividends, management fees, royalties, patent fees, and loan repayments, may be remitted.
- The basis for setting transfer prices.
- The right to export to third-country markets.
- Obligations to build, or fund, social and economic overhead projects, such as schools, hospitals, and retirement systems.
- Methods of taxation, including the rate, the type of taxation, and means by which the rate base is determined.
- Access to host-country capital markets, particularly for long-term borrowing.
- Permission for 100% foreign ownership versus required local ownership (joint venture) participation.
- Price controls, if any, applicable to sales in the host-country markets.
- Requirements for local sourcing versus import of raw materials and components.

- Permission to use expatriate managerial and technical personnel, and to bring them and their personal possessions into the country free of exorbitant charges or import duties.
- Provision for arbitration of disputes.
- Provisions for planned divestment, should such be required, indicating how the going concern will be valued and to whom it will be sold.

Investment Insurance and Guarantees: OPIC

MNEs can sometimes transfer political risk to a home-country public agency through an investment insurance and guarantee program. Many developed countries have such programs to protect investments by their nationals in developing countries.

The U.S. investment insurance and guarantee program is managed by the government-owned Overseas Private Investment Corporation (OPIC). OPIC's stated purpose is to mobilize and facilitate the participation of U.S. private capital and skills in the economic and social progress of less-developed friendly countries and areas, thereby complementing the developmental assistance of the United States. OPIC offers insurance coverage for four separate types of political risk, which have their own specific definitions for insurance purposes:

- *Inconvertibility* is the risk that the investor will not be able to convert profits, royalties, fees, or other income, as well as the original capital invested, into dollars.
- *Expropriation* is the risk that the host government takes a specific step that for one year prevents the investor or the foreign subsidiary from exercising effective control over use of the property.
- *War, revolution, insurrection, and civil strife* coverage applies primarily to the damage of physical property of the insured, although in some cases inability of a foreign subsidiary to repay a loan because of a war may be covered.
- *Business income* coverage provides compensation for loss of business income resulting from events of political violence that directly cause damage to the assets of a foreign enterprise.

Operating Strategies After the FDI Decision

Although an investment agreement creates obligations on the part of both foreign investor and host government, conditions change and agreements are often revised in the light of such changes. The changed conditions may be economic, or they may be the result of political changes within the host government. The firm that sticks rigidly to the legal interpretation of its original agreement may well find that the host government first applies pressure in areas not covered by the agreement and then possibly reinterprets the agreement to conform to the political reality of that country. Most MNEs, in their own self-interest, follow a policy of adapting to changing host-country priorities whenever possible.

The essence of such adaptation is anticipating host-country priorities and making the activities of the firm of continued value to the host country. Such an approach assumes the host government acts rationally in seeking its country's self-interest and is based on the idea that the firm should initiate reductions in goal conflict. Future bargaining position can be enhanced by careful consideration of policies in production, logistics, marketing, finance, organization, and personnel.

Local sourcing. Host governments may require foreign firms to purchase raw material and components locally as a way to maximize value added benefits and to increase local employment. From the viewpoint of the foreign firm trying to adapt to host-country goals, local sourcing reduces political risk, albeit at a tradeoff with other factors. Local strikes or other turmoil may shut down the operation, and such issues as quality control, high local prices (because of lack of economies of scale), and unreliable delivery schedules become important. Often the MNE lowers political risk only by increasing its financial and commercial risk.

Facility location. Production facilities can be located so as to minimize risk. The natural location of different stages of production may be resource-oriented, footloose, or market-oriented. Oil, for instance, is drilled in and around the Persian Gulf, Russia, Venezuela, and Indonesia. No choice exists for where this activity takes place. Refining is *footloose*; a refining facility can be moved easily to another location or country. Whenever possible, oil companies have built refineries in politically safe countries, such as Western Europe, or small islands (such as Singapore or Curaçao), even though costs might be reduced by refining nearer the oil fields. They have traded reduced political risk and financial exposure for possibly higher transportation and refining costs.

Control of transportation. Control of transportation has been an important means to reduce political risk. Oil pipelines that cross national frontiers, oil tankers, ore carriers, refrigerated ships, and railroads have all been controlled at times to influence the bargaining power of both nations and companies.

Control of technology. Control of key patents and processes is a viable way to reduce political risk. If a host country cannot operate a plant because it does not have technicians capable of running the process, or of keeping up with changed technology, abrogation of an investment agreement with a foreign firm is unlikely. Control of technology works best when the foreign firm is steadily improving its technology.

Control of markets. Control of markets is a common strategy to enhance a firm's bargaining position. As effective as the OPEC cartel was in raising the price received for crude oil by its member countries in the 1970s, marketing was still controlled by the international oil companies. OPEC's need for the oil companies limited the degree to which its members could dictate terms. In more recent years, OPEC members have established some marketing outlets of their own, such as Kuwait's extensive chain of Q8 gas stations in Europe.

Control of export markets for manufactured goods is also a source of leverage in dealings between MNEs and host governments. The MNE would prefer to serve world markets from sources of its own choosing, basing the decision on considerations of production cost, transportation, tariff barriers, political risk exposure, and competition. The selling pattern that maximizes long-run profits from the viewpoint of the worldwide firm rarely maximizes exports, or value added, from the perspective of the host countries. Some will argue that if the same plants were owned by local nationals and were not part of a worldwide integrated system, more goods would be exported by the host country. The contrary argument is that self-contained local firms might never obtain foreign market share, because they lack economies of scale on the production side and are unable to market in foreign countries.

Brand name and trademark control. Control of a brand name or trademark can have an effect almost identical to that of controlling technology. It gives the MNE a monopoly on something that may or may not have substantive value but quite likely represents value in the eyes of consumers. Ability to market under a world brand name is valuable for local firms and thus represents an important bargaining attribute for maintaining an investment position.

Thin equity base. Foreign subsidiaries can be financed with a thin equity base and a large proportion of local debt. If the debt is borrowed from locally owned banks, host-government actions that weaken the financial viability of the firm also endanger local creditors.

Multiple-source borrowing. If the firm must finance with foreign source debt, it may borrow from banks in a number of countries rather than just from home country banks. If, for example, debt is owed to banks in Tokyo, Frankfurt, London, and New York, nationals in a number of foreign countries have a vested interest in keeping the borrowing subsidiary financially strong. If the multinational is U.S.-owned, a fallout between the United States and the host government is less likely to cause the local government to move against the firm if it also owes funds to these other countries.

Country-Specific Risks: Transfer Risk

Country-specific risks affect all firms, domestic and foreign, that are resident in a host country. Exhibit 16.4 presents a taxonomy of most of the contemporary political risks that emanate from a specific country location. The main country-specific political risks are *transfer risk* and *cultural and institutional risks.*

Blocked Funds: Transfer Risk

Transfer risk is defined as limitations on the MNE's ability to transfer funds into and out of a host country without restrictions. When a government runs short of foreign exchange and cannot

Exhibit 16.4 Management Strategies for Country-Specific Risks

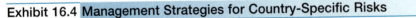

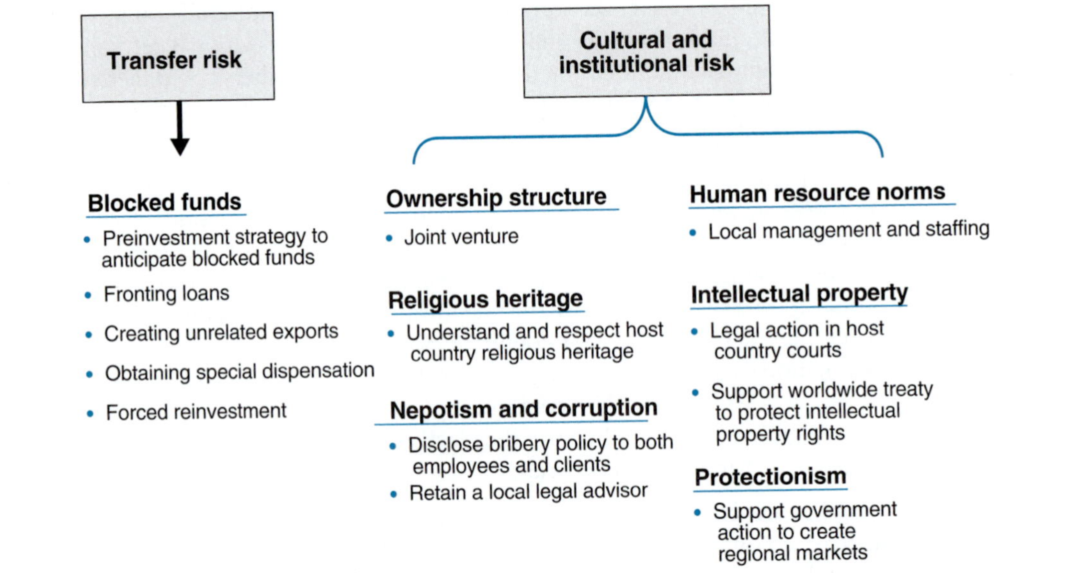

obtain additional funds through borrowing or attracting new foreign investment, it usually limits transfers of foreign exchange out of the country, a restriction known as *blocked funds.* In theory, this does not discriminate against foreign-owned firms, because it applies to everyone; in practice foreign firms have more at stake because of their foreign ownership. Depending on the size of a foreign exchange shortage, the host government might simply require approval of all transfers of funds abroad, thus reserving the right to set a priority on the use of scarce foreign exchange in favor of necessities rather than luxuries. In very severe cases, the government might make its currency nonconvertible into other currencies, thereby fully blocking transfers of funds abroad. In between these positions are policies that restrict the size and timing of dividends, debt amortization, royalties, and service fees.

MNEs can react to the potential for blocked funds at three stages.

1. Prior to making an investment, a firm can analyze the effect of blocked funds on expected return on investment, the desired local financial structure, and optimal links with subsidiaries.
2. During operations a firm can attempt to move funds through a variety of repositioning techniques.
3. Funds that cannot be moved must be reinvested in the local country in a manner that avoids deterioration in their real value because of inflation or exchange depreciation.

Preinvestment Strategy to Anticipate Blocked Funds

Management can consider blocked funds in their capital budgeting analysis. Temporary blockage of funds normally reduces the expected net present value and internal rate of return on a proposed investment. Whether the investment should nevertheless be undertaken depends on whether the expected rate of return, even with blocked funds, exceeds the required rate of return on investments of the same risk class. Pre-investment analysis also includes the potential to minimize the effect of blocked funds by financing with local borrowing instead of parent equity, swap agreements, and other techniques to reduce local currency exposure and thus the need to repatriate funds. Sourcing and sales links with subsidiaries can be predetermined so as to maximize the potential for moving blocked funds.

Moving Blocked Funds

What can a multinational firm do to transfer funds out of countries having exchange or remittance restrictions? At least six popular strategies are used: 1) Providing alternative conduits for repatriating funds (analyzed in Chapter 21); 2) Transfer pricing goods and services between related units of the MNE (also analyzed in Chapter 21); and 3) Leading and lagging payments (described in Chapter 22). Three additional strategies are:

1. Using fronting loans
2. Creating unrelated exports
3. Obtaining special dispensation

Fronting loans. A *fronting loan* is a parent-to-subsidiary loan channeled through a financial intermediary, usually a large international bank. Fronting loans differ from "parallel" or "back-to-back" loans, discussed in Chapter 9. The latter are offsetting loans between commercial businesses arranged outside the banking system. Fronting loans are sometimes referred to as *link financing*.

In a direct intracompany loan, a parent or sister subsidiary loans directly to the borrowing subsidiary, and at a later date the borrowing subsidiary repays the principal and interest. In a fronting loan, by contrast, the "lending" parent or subsidiary deposits funds in, say, a London bank, and that bank loans the same amount to the borrowing subsidiary in the host country. From the London bank's point of view the loan is risk-free, because the bank has 100% collateral in the form of the parent's deposit. In effect the bank "fronts" for the parent—hence the name. Interest paid by the borrowing subsidiary to the bank is usually slightly higher than the rate paid by the bank to the parent, allowing the bank a margin for expenses and profit.

The bank chosen for the fronting loan is usually in a neutral country, away from both the lender's and the borrower's legal jurisdiction. Use of fronting loans increases chances for repayment should political turmoil occur between the home and host countries. Government authorities are more likely to allow a local subsidiary to repay a loan to a large international bank in a neutral country than to allow the same subsidiary to repay a loan directly to its parent. To stop payment to the international bank would hurt the international credit image of the country, whereas to stop payment to the parent corporation would have minimal impact on that image and might even provide some domestic political advantage.

Creating unrelated exports. Another approach to blocked funds that benefits both the subsidiary and host country is the creation of unrelated exports. Because the main reason for stringent exchange controls is usually a host country's persistent inability to earn hard currencies, anything a MNE can do to create new exports from the host country improves the situation and provides a potential means to transfer funds out.

Some new exports can often be created from present productive capacity with little or no additional investment, especially if they are in product lines related to existing operations. Other new exports may require reinvestment or new funds, although if the funds reinvested consist of those already blocked, little is lost in the way of opportunity costs.

Special dispensation. If all else fails and the multinational firm is investing in an industry that is important to the economic development of the host country, the firm may bargain for special dispensation to repatriate some portion of the funds that otherwise would be blocked. Firms in "desirable" industries such as telecommunications, semiconductor manufacturing, instrumentation, pharmaceuticals, or other research and high-technology industries may receive preference over firms in mature industries. The amount of preference received depends on bargaining among the informed parties, the government and the business firm, either of which is free to back away from the proposed investment if unsatisfied with the terms.

Self-fulfilling prophecies. In seeking "escape routes" for blocked funds—or, for that matter, in trying to position funds through any of the techniques discussed in this chapter—the MNE may increase political risk and cause a change from partial blockage to full blockage. The possibility of such a self-fulfilling cycle exists any time a firm takes action that, no matter how legal, thwarts the underlying intent of politically motivated controls. In the statehouses of the world, as in the editorial offices of the local press and TV, MNEs and their subsidiaries are always a potential scapegoat.

Forced reinvestment. If funds are indeed blocked from transfer into foreign exchange, they are by definition "reinvested." In such a situation, the firm must find local opportunities that will maximize rate of return for a given acceptable level of risk.

If blockage is expected to be temporary, the most obvious alternative is to invest in local money market instruments. Unfortunately, in many countries such instruments are not available in sufficient quantity or with adequate liquidity. In some cases, government treasury bills, bank deposits, and other short-term instruments have yields that are kept artificially low relative to local rates of inflation or probable changes in exchange rates. Thus the firm often loses real value during the period of blockage.

If short- or intermediate-term portfolio investments such as bonds, bank time deposits, or direct loans to other companies are not possible, investment in additional production facilities may be the only alternative. Often this investment is what the host country is seeking by its exchange controls, even if the existence of exchange controls is by itself counterproductive to the idea of additional foreign investment. Examples of forced direct reinvestment can be cited from Peru, where an airline invested in hotels and in maintenance facilities for other airlines; from Turkey, where a fish canning company constructed a plant to manufacture cans needed for packing the catch; and from Argentina, where an automobile company integrated vertically by acquiring a transmission manufacturing plant previously owned by a supplier.

If investment opportunities in additional production facilities are not available, funds may simply be used to acquire other assets expected to increase in value with local inflation. Typical purchases might be land, office buildings, or commodities that are exported to global markets. Even inventory stockpiling might be a reasonable investment, given the low opportunity cost of the blocked funds.

Country-Specific Risks: Cultural and Institutional Risks

When investing in some of the emerging markets, MNEs that are resident in the most industrialized countries face serious risks because of cultural and institutional differences. Among many such differences are:

- Differences in allowable ownership structures
- Differences in human resource norms
- Differences in religious heritage
- Nepotism and corruption in the host country
- Protection of intellectual property rights
- Protectionism

Ownership Structure

Historically, many countries have required that MNEs share ownership of their foreign subsidiaries with local firms or citizens. Thus, joint ventures were the only way a MNE could operate in some host countries. Prominent countries that used to require majority local ownership were Japan,

Mexico, China, India, and Korea. This requirement has been eliminated or modified in more recent years by these countries and most others. However, firms in certain industries are still either excluded from ownership completely or must accept being a minority owner. These industries are typically related to national defense, agriculture, banking, or other sectors that are deemed critical for the host nation. Even the United States would not welcome foreign ownership of large key defense-related firms such as Boeing Aircraft.

The risks involved in controlling foreign joint ventures were described in Chapter 15. Potential limitations on a MNE's operating decisions make foreign joint ventures less desirable than 100%-owned foreign subsidiaries, exporting, licensing, contract production, strategic alliances, and other alternative forms of serving foreign markets.

Human Resource Norms

MNEs are often required by host countries to employ a certain proportion of host country citizens rather than staffing mainly with foreign expatriates. It is often very difficult to fire local employees due to host country labor laws and union contracts. This lack of flexibility to downsize in response to business cycles affects both MNEs and their local competitors. It also qualifies as a country-specific risk.

Cultural differences can also inhibit a MNE's staffing policies. For example, it is somewhat difficult for a woman manager to be accepted by local employees and managers in many Middle Eastern countries. The most extreme example of discrimination against women has been highlighted in Afghanistan while the Taliban were in power. Since the Taliban's downfall in late 2001, several women have been suggested for important government roles. It is expected that the private sector in Afghanistan will also reintegrate women into the workforce.

Religious Heritage

The current hostile environment for MNEs in some Middle Eastern countries such as Iran, Iraq, and Syria is being fed by some extremist Muslim clerics who are enraged about the continuing violence in Israel and the occupied Arab territories. However, the root cause of these conflicts is a mixture of religious fervor for some and politics for others. Although it is popular to blame the Muslim religion for its part in fomenting the conflict, a number of Middle Eastern countries, such as Egypt, Saudi Arabia, and Jordan, are relatively passive when it comes to Jihads. Jihads are calls for Muslims to attack the infidels (Jews and Christians). Osama Bin Laden's call for Jihad against the United States has not generated any great interest on the part of moderate Muslims. Indeed one Muslim country, Turkey, has had a secular government for many decades. It strongly supported efforts to rid the world of Bin Laden.

Despite religious differences, MNEs have operated successfully in emerging markets, especially in extractive and natural resource industries, such as oil, natural gas, minerals, and forest products. The main MNE strategy is to understand and respect the host country's religious traditions.

Nepotism and Corruption

MNEs must deal with endemic nepotism and corruption in a number of important foreign investment locations. Indonesia was famous for nepotism and corruption under the now-deposed

Suharto government. Nigeria, Kenya, Uganda, and a number of other African countries have a history of nepotism and corruption since they threw out their colonial governments after World War II. China and Russia have recently launched well-publicized crackdowns on those evils.

Bribery is not limited to emerging markets. It is also a problem in even the most industrialized countries, including the United States and Japan. In fact, the United States has an antibribery law that would imprison any U.S. business executive found guilty of bribing a foreign government official. This law was passed in reaction to an attempt by Lockheed Aircraft to bribe a Japanese Prime Minister.

TI's Corruption Perception Index. Transparency International (TI) publishes a monthly newsletter on corruption in international business. TI's Corruption Perception Index for 2001 is shown in Exhibit 16.5. This index is based on the level of corruption as perceived by persons working for MNEs and financial institutions. Thus it is an index not of actual corruption, but rather of perceptions. The score is based on an integrity ranking, where 10 equals an entirely clean country and zero equals a country in which business transactions are entirely dominated by kick-backs, extortion, bribery, and similar practices. The standard deviation measures the dispersions of opinion.

Managing bribery. MNEs are caught in a dilemma. Should they employ bribery if their local competitors use this strategy? Alternative strategies are:

- Refuse bribery outright, or else demands will quickly multiply.
- Retain a local advisor to diffuse demands by local officials, customs agents, and other business partners.
- Do not count on the justice system in many emerging markets, because Western-oriented contract law may not agree with local norms.
- Educate both management and local employees about whatever bribery policy the firm intends to follow.

Intellectual Property Rights

Rogue businesses in some host countries have historically infringed on the intellectual property rights of both MNEs and individuals. *Intellectual property rights* grant the exclusive use of patented technology and copyrighted creative materials. Examples of patented technology are unique manufactured products, processing techniques, and prescription pharmaceutical drugs. Examples of copyrighted creative materials are software programs, educational materials (textbooks), and entertainment products (music, film, art).

MNEs and individuals need to protect their intellectual property rights through the legal process. However, courts in some countries have historically not done a fair job of protecting intellectual property rights of anyone, much less of foreign MNEs. In those countries, the legal process is costly and subject to bribery.

A worldwide treaty to protect intellectual property rights has recently been ratified by most major countries. China signed the treaty as one of the conditions it needed to meet to join the World Trade Organization (WTO) in 2001. It remains to be seen whether host governments are strong enough to enforce their official efforts to stamp out intellectual piracy. Complicating this

Exhibit 16.5 Transparency International's Corruption Perception Index for 2001

Rank	Country	Score	Std Dev	Rank	Country	Score	Std Dev
1	Finland	9.9	0.6	51	Mexico	3.7	0.6
2	Denmark	9.5	0.7	51	Panama	3.7	0.4
3	New Zealand	9.4	0.6	51	Slovak Republic	3.7	0.9
4	Iceland	9.2	1.1	54	Egypt	3.6	1.5
4	Singapore	9.2	0.5	54	El Salvador	3.6	0.9
6	Sweden	9.0	0.5	54	Turkey	3.6	0.8
7	Canada	8.9	0.5	57	Argentina	3.5	0.6
8	Netherlands	8.8	0.3	57	China	3.5	0.4
9	Luxembourg	8.7	0.5	59	Ghana	3.4	0.5
10	Norway	8.6	0.8	59	Latvia	3.4	1.2
11	Australia	8.5	0.9	61	Malawi	3.2	1.0
12	Switzerland	8.4	0.5	61	Thailand	3.2	0.9
13	United Kingdom	8.3	0.5	63	Dominican Republic	3.1	0.9
14	Hong Kong	7.9	0.5	63	Moldova	3.1	0.9
15	Austria	7.8	0.5	65	Guatemala	2.9	0.9
16	Israel	7.6	0.3	65	Philippines	2.9	0.9
16	United States	7.6	0.7	65	Senegal	2.9	0.8
18	Chile	7.5	0.6	65	Zimbabwe	2.9	1.1
18	Ireland	7.5	0.3	69	Romania	2.8	0.5
20	Germany	7.4	0.8	69	Venezuela	2.8	0.4
21	Japan	7.1	0.9	71	Honduras	2.7	1.1
22	Spain	7.0	0.7	71	India	2.7	0.5
23	France	6.7	0.8	71	Kazakhstan	2.7	1.3
24	Belgium	6.6	0.7	71	Uzbekistan	2.7	1.1
25	Portugal	6.3	0.8	75	Vietnam	2.6	0.7
26	Botswana	6.0	0.5	75	Zambia	2.6	0.5
27	Taiwan	5.9	1.0	77	Cote d'Ivoire	2.4	1.0
28	Estonia	5.6	0.3	77	Nicaragua	2.4	0.8
29	Italy	5.5	1.0	79	Ecuador	2.3	0.3
30	Namibia	5.4	1.4	79	Pakistan	2.3	1.7
31	Hungary	5.3	0.8	82	Tanzania	2.2	0.6
31	Trinidad & Tobago	5.3	1.5	83	Ukraine	2.1	1.1
31	Tunisia	5.3	1.3	84	Azerbaijan	2.0	0.2
34	Slovenia	5.2	1.0	84	Bolivia	2.0	0.6
35	Uruguay	5.1	0.7	84	Cameroon	2.0	0.8
36	Malaysia	5.0	0.7	84	Kenya	2.0	0.7
37	Jordan	4.9	0.8	88	Indonesia	1.9	0.8
40	Costa Rica	4.5	0.7	88	Uganda	1.9	0.6
40	Mauritius	4.5	0.7	90	Nigeria	1.0	0.9
42	Greece	4.2	0.6	91	Bangladesh	0.4	2.9
42	South Korea	4.2	0.7				
44	Peru	4.1	1.1				
45	Poland	4.1	0.9				
46	Brazil	4.0	0.3				
47	Bulgaria	3.9	0.6				
47	Croatia	3.9	0.6				
47	Czech Republic	3.9	0.9				
50	Columbia	3.8	0.9				

Source: Transparency International, http://www.transparency.org/cpi/2001/cp12001.html. Accessed December 2002.

task is the thin line that exists between the real item being protected and look-alikes or generic versions of the same item.

Protectionism

Protectionism is defined as the attempt by a national government to protect certain of its designated industries from foreign competition. Industries that are protected are usually related to defense, agriculture, and "infant" industries.

Defense. Even though the United States is a vocal proponent of open markets, a foreign firm proposing to buy Lockheed Missile Division or other critical defense suppliers would not be welcome. The same attitude exists in many other countries, such as France, which has always wanted to maintain an independent defense capability.

Agriculture. Agriculture is another sensitive industry. No MNE would be foolish enough as to attempt to buy agricultural properties, such as rice operations, in Japan. Japan has desperately tried to maintain an independent ability to feed its own population. Agriculture is the typical "Mother Earth" industry that most countries want to protect for their own citizens.

Infant industries. The traditional protectionist argument is that newly emerging, "infant" industries need protection from foreign competition until they can get firmly established. The infant industry argument is usually directed at limiting imports, but not necessarily MNEs. In fact, most host countries encourage MNEs to establish operations in new industries that do not presently exist in the host country. Sometimes the host country offers foreign MNEs "infant industry" status for a limited number of years. This status could lead to tax subsidies, construction of infrastructure, employee training, and other aids to help the MNE get started. Host countries are especially interested in attracting MNEs that promise to export, either to their own foreign subsidiaries elsewhere or to unrelated parties.

Tariff barriers. The traditional methods for countries to implement protectionist barriers were through tariff and non-tariff regulations. Negotiations under the General Agreements on Tariffs and Trade (GATT) have greatly reduced the general level of tariffs over the past decades. This process continues today under the auspices of the World Trade Organization (WTO). However, many non-tariff barriers remain.

Non-tariff barriers. Non-tariff barriers, which restrict imports by something other than a financial cost, are often difficult to identify because they are promulgated as health, safety, or sanitation requirements. Major types of non-tariff barriers include those shown in Exhibit 16.6.

Strategies to manage protectionism. MNEs have only a very limited ability to overcome host country protectionism. However, MNEs do enthusiastically support efforts to reduce protectionism by joining together in regional markets. The best examples of regional markets are the European Union (EU), the North American Free Trade Association (NAFTA), and the Latin American Free Trade Association (MERCOSUR). Among the objectives of regional markets are elimination of internal trade barriers, such as tariffs and non-tariff barriers, as well as the free movement of citizens for employment purposes. External trade barriers still exist.

The EU is trying to become a "United States of Europe," with a single internal market without barriers. It is not quite there, although the European Monetary Union and the euro have almost eliminated monetary policy differences. The EU still tolerates differences in fiscal policies,

Exhibit 16.6 Types of Non-Tariff Barriers

1. Specific limitations on trade, which either limit the amount of imports directly or establish import procedures that make importing more difficult.
2. Customs and administrative entry procedures, which include inconsistent procedures for valuation, classification of documents, or assessing fees.
3. Unduly stringent or discriminating standards imposed in the name of protecting health, safety, and quality.
4. Governmental participation in trade.
5. Charges on imports.
6. Other nontariff barriers.

Source: Adapted from material in A. D. Cao, "Non-Tariff Barriers to U.S. Manufactured Exports," *Columbia Journal of World Business*, Summer 1980, pp. 93–102.

legal systems, and cultural identities. In any case, the movement toward regional markets is very favorable for MNEs serving those markets with foreign subsidiaries.

Global-Specific Risks

Global-specific risks faced by MNEs have come to the forefront in recent years. Exhibit 16.7 summarizes some of these risks and strategies that can be used to manage them. The most visible recent risk was, of course, the attack by terrorists on the twin towers of the World Trade Center in New York on September 11, 2001. Many MNEs had major operations in the World Trade

Exhibit 16.7 Management Strategies for Global-Specific Risks

Terrorism and War

- Support government efforts to flight terrorism and war
- Crisis planning
- Cross-border supply chain integration

Poverty

- Provide stable, relatively well-paying jobs
- Establish the strictest of occupational safety standards

Anti-Globalization

- Support government efforts to reduce trade barriers
- Recognize that MNEs are the targets

Cyberattacks

- No effective strategy except Internet security efforts
- Support government anti-cyberattack efforts

Environmental Concerns

- Show sensitivity to environmental concerns
- Support government efforts to maintain a level playing field for pollution controls

MNE movement towards multiple primary objectives: profitability, sustainable development, corporate social responsibility

Center and suffered heavy casualties among their employees. In addition to terrorism, other global-specific risks include the antiglobalization movement, environmental concerns, poverty in emerging markets, and cyberattacks on computer information systems.

Terrorism and War

Although the World Trade Center attack and its aftermath, the war in Afghanistan, have affected nearly everyone worldwide, many other acts of terrorism have been committed in recent years. More terrorist acts are expected to occur in the future. Particularly exposed are the foreign subsidiaries of MNEs and their employees. As mentioned earlier, foreign subsidiaries are especially exposed to war, ethnic strife, and terrorism because they are symbols of their respective parent countries.

No MNE has the tools to avert terrorism. Hedging, diversification, insurance, and the likes are not suited to the task. Therefore, MNEs must depend on governments to fight terrorism and protect their foreign subsidiaries (and now even the parent firm). In return, governments expect financial, material, and verbal support from MNEs to support antiterrorist legislation and proactive initiatives to destroy terrorist cells wherever they exist.

Crisis Planning

MNEs can be subject to damage by being in harm's way. Nearly every year one or more host countries experience some form of ethnic strife, outright war with other countries, or terrorism. It seems that foreign MNEs are often singled out as symbols of "oppression," because they represent their parent country, especially if it is the United States.

Cross-Border Supply Chain Integration

The drive to increase efficiency in manufacturing has driven many MNEs to adopt so-called "just-in-time" (JIT) near-zero inventory systems. Focusing on so-called *inventory velocity*, the speed at which inventory moves through a manufacturing process, arriving only as needed and not before, has allowed these MNEs to generate increasing profits and cash flows with less capital being bottled-up in the production cycle itself. This finely tuned supply chain system, however, is subject to significant political risk if the supply chain itself extends across borders.

Supply chain interruptions. Consider the cases of Dell Computer, Ford Motor Company, Dairy Queen, Apple Computer, Herman Miller, and The Limited, in the days following the terrorist attacks of September 11, 2001. An immediate result of the attacks of the morning of September 11 was the grounding of all aircraft into or out of the United States. Similarly, the land (Mexico and Canada) and sea borders of the United States were also shut down and not reopened for several days in some specific sites. Ford Motor Company shut down five of its manufacturing plants in the days following September 11 because of inadequate inventories of critical automotive inputs supplied from Canada. Dairy Queen experienced such significant delays in key confectionary ingredients many of its stores were also temporarily closed.

Dell Computer, with one of the most highly acclaimed and admired virtually integrated supply chains, depends on computer parts and sub-assembly suppliers and manufacturers in both Mexico and Canada to fulfill its everyday assembly and sales needs. In recent years, Dell has carried less than three full days' worth sales of total inventory—by cost of goods value. Suppliers are integrated electronically with Dell's order fulfillment system and deliver required components and subassemblies as sales demands require. But with the closure of borders and grounding of air freight, the company was brought to a near stand-still because of its supply chain's reliance on the ability to treat business units and suppliers in different countries as if they were all part of a single seamless political unit. Unfortunately, that proved not the case with this particular unpredictable catastrophic terrorist event.

As a result of these newly learned lessons, many MNEs are now evaluating the degree of exposure their own supply chains possess in regard to cross-border stoppages or other cross-border political events. These companies are not, however, about to abandon JIT. It is estimated that many U.S. companies alone have saved more than $1 billion a year in inventory carrying costs by using JIT methods over the past decade. This substantial benefit is now being weighed against the costs and risks associated with the post-September 11 supply chain interruptions.

To avoid suffering a similar fate in the future, manufacturers, retailers and suppliers are now employing a range of tactics:

- **Inventory management.** Manufacturers and assemblers are now considering carrying more buffer inventory in order to hedge against supply and production-line disruptions. Retailers, meanwhile, should think about the timing and frequency of their replenishment. Rather than stocking up across the board, companies are focusing on the most critical parts to the product or service, and those components that are uniquely available only from international sources.
- **Sourcing.** Manufacturers are now being more selective about where the critical inputs to their products come from. Although sourcing strategies will have to vary by location, firms are attempting to work more closely with existing suppliers to minimize cross-border exposures and reduce the potential costs with future stoppages.
- **Transportation.** Retailers and manufacturers alike are reassessing their cross-border shipping arrangements. For example, many inputs that currently are carried by passenger flights may be precluded from cohabitation on these flights in the future. Although the mode of transportation employed is a function of value, volume, and weight, many firms are now reassessing whether higher costs for faster shipment balance out the more tenuous their delivery under airline stoppages from labor, terrorist, or even bankruptcy disruptions in the future.

Global Finance Perspective 16.1 illustrates how many of the security policies adopted by the U.S. government also have an impact on the efficiency of supply chain management.

Antiglobalization Movement

During the past decade, there has been a growing negative reaction by some groups to reduced trade barriers and efforts to create regional markets, particularly to NAFTA and the European Union. NAFTA has been vigorously opposed by those sectors of the labor movement that could lose jobs to Mexico. Opposition within the European Union centers on loss of cultural identity, dilution of individual national control as new members are admitted, over-centralization of power in a large bureaucracy in Brussels, and most recently the disappearance of individual national currencies in mid-2002, when the euro became the only currency in 12 of the 15 member nations.

Global Finance Perspective 16.1

International Supply Chain Security: Time Is Money

Many new and evolving border security law and guidelines will have a hand in slowing import processing times at the U.S. border. To protect businesses from these events, U.S. importers must navigate through a variety of new security initiatives, including the following:

- **C-TPAT—The Custom-Trade Partnership Against Terrorism:** A U.S. Customs program designed to encourage companies across the supply chain to voluntarily self-assess and strengthen security practices to protect the U.S. against the risk of terrorist activity via product and conveyance tampering on import shipments.
- **CSI—Container Security Initiative:** A U.S. Customs program focusing on securing ocean-going containers by engaging the authorities of certain foreign ports shipping the highest volumes of container traffic into the U.S. in a way that will facilitate early detection of potential security problems.
- **FAST—Free And Secure Trade:** A joint U.S.-Canada program designed to expedite customs clearance of goods moving across the northern border through specially designated "FAST" lanes for qualified goods by qualified shippers.
- **CIP—Carrier Initiative Program:** A voluntary U.S. Customs and carrier program designed to prevent smuggling of narcotics on air, sea, and land commercial conveyances.
- **BASC—Business Anti-Smuggling Coalition:** A business-led initiative designed to complement the CIP program by combating contraband smuggling via commercial trade and eliminate the contamination of legitimate business shipments by criminal hands.

In addition to these initiatives, a variety of port, maritime, and transportation security legislation has been introduced in the U.S. Congress that could greatly impact the international supply chain of U.S. importers.

Source: Adapted from "The New Era of International Supply Chain Security," *World Trade*, November 2002, pp. 56–57.

The antiglobalization movement has become more visible following riots in Seattle during the 2001 annual meeting of the World Trade Organization. Antiglobalization forces were not solely responsible for these riots, or for subsequent riots in Quebec and Prague in 2001. Other disaffected groups, such as environmentalists and even anarchists, joined in to make their causes more visible.

MNEs do not have the tools to combat antiglobalism. Indeed they are blamed for fostering the problem in the first place. Once again, MNEs must rely on governments and crisis planning to manage these risks.

Environmental Concerns

MNEs have been accused of "exporting" their environmental problems to other countries. The accusation is that MNEs frustrated by pollution controls in their home country have relocated these activities to countries with weaker pollution controls. Another accusation is that MNEs contribute to the problem of global warming. However, that accusation applies to all firms in all countries. It is based on the manufacturing methods employed by specific industries and on consumers' desire for certain products such as large automobiles and sport vehicles that are not fuel-efficient.

Once again, solving environmental problems is dependent on governments passing legislation and implementing pollution control standards. In 2001, a treaty attempting to reduce global warming was ratified by most nations, with the notable exception of the United States. However, the United States has promised to combat global warming using its own strategies. The United States objected to provisions in the worldwide treaty that allowed emerging nations to follow less restrictive standards, while the economic burden would fall on the most industrialized countries, particularly the United States.

Poverty

MNEs have located foreign subsidiaries in countries plagued by extremely uneven income distribution. At one end is an elite class of well-educated, well-connected, and productive persons. At the other end of the spectrum is a very large class of persons living at or below the poverty level. They lack education, social and economic infrastructure, and political power.

MNEs might be contributing to this disparity by employing the elite class to manage their operations. On the other hand, MNEs are creating relatively stable and well-paying jobs for those who were otherwise unemployed and living below the poverty level. Despite being accused of supporting "sweat-shop" conditions, MNEs usually compare favorably to their local competitors. For example, Nike, one of the targeted MNEs, usually pays better, provides more fringe benefits, maintains higher safety standards, and educates their workforce to allow personnel to advance up the career ladder. Of course, Nike cannot manage a country's poverty problems overall, but it can improve conditions for some persons.

Cyberattacks

The rapid growth of the Internet has fostered a whole new generation of scam artists and cranks that disrupt the usefulness of the World Wide Web. This is both a domestic and an international problem. MNEs can face costly cyberattacks by disaffected persons with a grudge because of their visibility and the complexity of their internal information systems.

At this point in time, we know of no uniquely international strategies that MNEs can use to combat cyberattacks. MNEs are using the same strategies to manage foreign cyberattacks as they use for domestic attacks. Once again, they must rely on governments to control cyberattacks.

MNEs have had a difficult time managing these last four global-specific risks. We present an illustrative case featuring the attempts by Starbucks Coffee to manage global-specific risks through heightened corporate social responsibility.

An Illustration of Global-Specific Risks: The Case of Starbucks[1]

Starbucks defines corporate social responsibility as conducting our business in ways that produce social, environmental and economic benefits to the communities in which we operate. In the end, it means being responsible to our stakeholders.

There is growing recognition of the need for corporate accountability. Consumers are demanding more than "product" from their favorite brands. Employees are choosing to work for companies with

1. This illustrative case is adapted from "Planet Starbucks (A)" by Professors Michael H. Moffett and Kannan Ramaswamy, Thunderbird Case Series, A09-03-0007, 2003.

strong values. Shareholders are more inclined to invest in businesses with outstanding corporate reputations. Quite simply, being socially responsible is not only the right thing to do; it can distinguish a company from its industry peers.

Corporate Social Responsibility Annual Report
Starbucks Coffee, Fiscal 2001, p. 3.

Starbucks found itself, somewhat to its surprise, an early target of the anti-globalist movement. Like McDonald's before it, it appeared to be yet another American cultural imperialist, bringing a chain-store sameness to all countries everywhere. Like McDonald's, Starbucks found that its uniquely defined brand and experience did not have to conform to local cultural norms, but could exist alongside traditional practices, creating its own market and successfully altering some consumer behaviors.

Unlike McDonald's, however, Starbucks was the purveyor of a commodity, coffee, which was priced and sold on global markets. Coffee was sourced from hundreds of thousands of small growers in Central and South America, many of which were severely impoverished by all global income and purchasing power standards. As coffee prices plummeted in the late 1990s, companies like Starbucks were criticized both for benefitting from lower cost sourcing and for their unwillingness to help improve the economic conditions of the coffee growers themselves.

Procurement

Coffee was traditionally bought and sold using *market pricing*, buying from wholesalers at a global market price—the so-called New York "C." Since Starbucks purchased only arabica bean premium grade coffee, *green coffee*, it always paid a premium above New York "C." Both New York "C" prices and the premium, however, moved up and down with global market conditions. Traditional robusta bean purchases by mass-market labels were made on the wholesale markets through brokers and buyers.

Starbucks, however, preferred to purchase using *outright pricing*, in which the price was negotiated directly with small and medium-sized farmers, cutting out the segment of the supply chain which the wholesalers (called *coyotes* in Central and South America) usually occupied. In principle, a greater proportion of the price went directly to the producers, assuring a higher return to the small farmer. In addition to the pricing structure, Starbucks was also attempting to break from traditional market practices of always buying in the cash market. The company was moving aggressively to purchase more and more of its coffee under long-term contract guaranteeing prices to growers over multiple crop years.

Coffee Prices

The single biggest problem was the price of coffee itself. As illustrated by Exhibit 16.8, the global price of arabica coffee had been extremely volatile over the previous 20-year period. In fact, arabica beans had been as high as $1.50/lb. (annual average, they had been significantly higher on a daily and weekly basis) as recently as 1994. The price in recent years had plummeted, as more and more coffee production came on to the market creating a substantial excess supply. This was an obvious benefit to coffee consumers, including Starbucks. The growers, however, most of which were small farms of 7 hectares or less, were now receiving prices nearly $0.40/lb., when

Exhibit 16.8 Arabica Bean Coffee Prices, 1981–2001

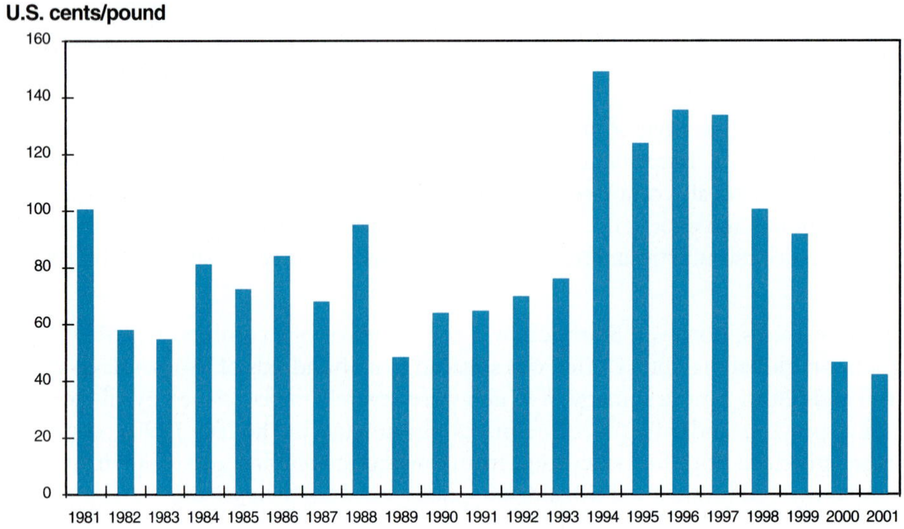

Source: International Coffee Organization (ICO), http://www.ico.org.

average production costs were $0.77/lb. Although this was not any fault or responsibility of Starbucks (it was estimated to use less than 1% of the world's annual coffee crop), the company was criticized as paying less than a living wage to its growers.

By 2001, Starbucks had implemented a multitude of programs to pursue its program for corporate social responsibility (CSR) and pursue sustainable economic development for the people in its supply chain. Although not wishing to own the supply chain, Starbucks strategy was a complex combination of altered business practices in procurement, direct support to the coffee growers, and the formation of brands that would provide conduits for consumers wishing to support CSR initiatives. Exhibit 16.9 provides a brief overview of some of these programs.

Conduit Brand Development

Much of the growing pressure on all multinational companies for sustainable development and social responsibility arose directly from consumer segments. In an effort to provide a direct conduit for these consumer demands, Starbucks initiated a company program called Commitment to Origins "dedicated to creating a sustainable growing environment in coffee originating countries." Under the program, Starbucks had introduced Shade Grown Mexico coffee and Fair Trade Certified coffee.

Shade Grown Mexico coffee was introduced in 1998 in partnership with Conservation International (CI), a non-profit environmental organization. Coffee purchased by Starbucks from CI's Conservation Coffee Program was cultivated under the canopy of shade trees in origin countries. This practice was considered ecologically sound and helped support bio-diversity. Shade Grown Mexico coffee purchases had grown from 304,000 pounds in 2000 to an estimated deliv-

Exhibit 16.9 Starbuck's CSR Programs Focusing on Coffee Growers

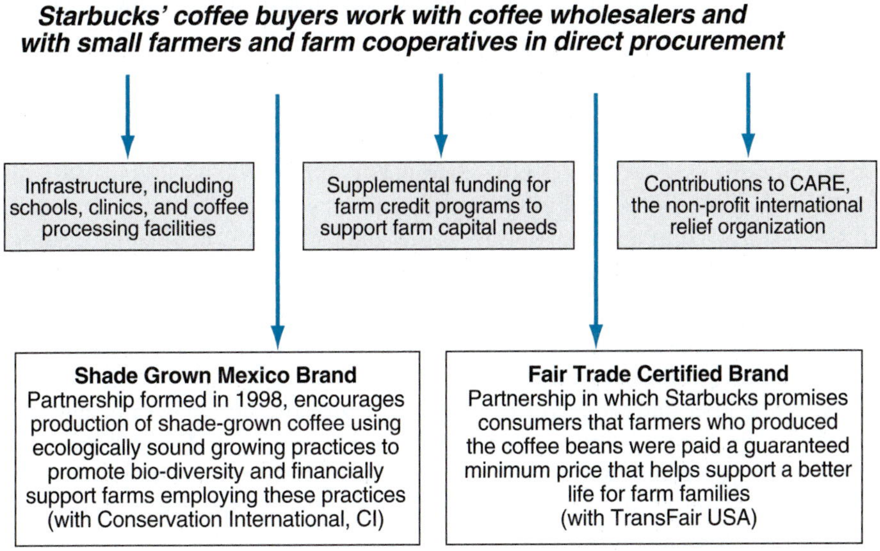
Starbucks' coffee buyers work with coffee wholesalers and with small farmers and farm cooperatives in direct procurement
Infrastructure, including schools, clinics, and coffee processing facilities
Supplemental funding for farm credit programs to support farm capital needs
Contributions to CARE, the non-profit international relief organization
Shade Grown Mexico Brand
Partnership formed in 1998, encourages production of shade-grown coffee using ecologically sound growing practices to promote bio-diversity and financially support farms employing these practices (with Conservation International, CI)
Fair Trade Certified Brand
Partnership in which Starbucks promises consumers that farmers who produced the coffee beans were paid a guaranteed minimum price that helps support a better life for farm families (with TransFair USA)

ery of 1.5 million pounds in 2002.[2] The Shade Grown Mexico coffee had been selectively introduced in Starbucks stores in North America and through online sales at http://starbucks.com.

Beginning in 2000, Starbucks began working with TransFair USA, a non-profit organization that provided independent certification for all Fair Trade coffee in the United States.[3]

> *The concept of Fair Trade addressed the question of the just distribution of the burdens and benefits of trade. The Fair Trade movement argues that when most of the customers' purchasing dollar goes to the retailer, the marketer, the wholesaler, and the speculator and very little goes to the laborer or the farmer, something is wrong with the mutual benefits of the exchanges, particularly when those who provide the product have earnings that do not even cover subsistence costs.*[4]

Although Starbucks introduced Fair Trade coffee in North American stores and promoted it through various brochures and promotions ("Coffee of the Day" monthly), it continued to be heavily criticized for not expanding the program faster. In October 2001, the company expanded its commitments, agreeing to purchase at least one million pounds of Fair Trade–certified coffee meeting its quality requirements in the following 12 to 18 months.

2. Starbucks' commitment to CI was established on an annual basis. Starbucks renewed its partnership in 2000 for a three-year period agreeing to purchase at least $200,000 of shade-grown coffee annually. Starbucks has also noted that growers of Shade Grown Mexico coffee received price premiums of 60% over local coffee prices in fiscal 2001.
3. TransFair USA is associated with Equal Exchange, a Fair Trade organization promoting socially responsible business practices with coffee growers in Central and Latin America.
4. Kohls, John, and Sandra L. Christensen, "The Business Responsibility for Wealth Distribution in a Globalized Political-Economy: Merging Moral Economics and Catholic Social Teaching," *Journal of Business Ethics*, February 2002, p. 12.

Both of these product brand programs allowed consumers wishing to support these sustainable development initiatives to express their interest through purchasing. But Fair Trade–certified coffee was higher cost, by definition, and that cost premium was reflected in the retail price.[5] Both Fair Trade and Shade Grown Mexico coffees were 20% to 25% more expensive compared to Starbucks' traditional blends (whole bean coffee sales).

Starbucks was a regular and growing giver, supporting relief organizations such as CARE, a non-profit international relief organization, as well as providing direct support to farmers and farm communities around the world.[6] For example, Starbucks contributed $43,000 in 2001 to the construction of a health clinic and school in Guatemala and a health clinic in East Timor. The company was also providing aid in a variety of ways to the improvement of coffee-processing facilities in a number of the countries of origin.

Although very aggressive in the eyes of many, the anti-globalization movement continued to focus much of its efforts on Starbucks. Plummeting coffee prices on world markets in 2001 and 2002 had led to more and more pressure on Starbucks to increase the prices it paid to growers. Howard Shultz himself became the increasing target of mail, fax, and email campaigns to pressure Starbucks into more proactive policies for grower income support (see Exhibit 16.10). Although Starbucks had actively pursued a number of corporate social responsibility initiatives, it was accused of polishing its image more than truly working to improve the lives of those its existence depended upon, the coffee growers.

Exhibit 16.10 Cyberattack: The "Starbucks Campaign"

Participate in the Organic Consumers Association
"Global Week of Action Against Starbucks," September 21–28.

In October 2001, Starbucks made a commitment to buy 1 million more pounds of Fair Trade coffee and brew Fair Trade coffee once a month. Don't let Starbucks stop there—Send a Free Fax to demand that Starbucks brew Fair Trade Coffee of the Day EVERY WEEK!

The coffee industry is in crisis. Coffee prices are at an all-time low, remaining below $0.50 since August with no increase in sight. This means that farmers are becoming even more impoverished, going further into debt and losing their land. Meanwhile coffee companies such as Starbucks have not lowered consumer prices but are pocketing the difference, even taking into account the quality premiums in the specialty industry.

The Fair Trade Labeling Organizations International recently released figures that show a total production by groups on the Fair Trade Coffee Register of 165,000,000 pounds in year 2000, whereas total sales were only 30,000,000 pounds. This leaves an additional 135,000,000 pounds of Fair Trade coffee produced by cooperatives that are not receiving a Fair Trade price.

Source: Global Exchange, Global Economy, http://www.globalexchange.org/economy/coffee/starbucks, accessed 10/6/02.

5. Starbucks reported that buyers paid $1.26/lb. for non-organic green and $1.41/lb. for organic green in 2001, when New York "C" prices were hovering at roughly $0.50/pound. Although production costs varied significantly across countries and regions, coffee growers associations estimated average production costs to be $0.80/pound.
6. Starbucks gave $120,000 to CARE in fiscal 2001, bringing its cumulative contributions over time to more than $1.8 million. Starbucks' work with CARE began in 1991.

SUMMARY

- Political risks can be defined by classifying them on three levels; namely, *firm-specific*, *country-specific*, or *global-specific*.
- *Firm-specific risks*, also known as *micro risks*, are those that affect the MNE at the project or corporate level.
- *Country-specific risks*, also known as *macro risks*, are those risks that also affect the MNE at the project or corporate level but originate at the country level.
- *Global-specific risks* are those risks that affect the MNE at the project or corporate level but originate at the global level.
- The main firm-specific risk is *governance risk*, which is the ability to exercise control over the MNE as a whole, globally, and within a specific country's legal and political environment on the individual subsidiary level.
- The most important type of governance risk arises from a goal conflict between bona fide objectives of governments and private firms.
- The main tools used to manage goal conflict are to negotiate an investment agreement; to purchase investment insurance and guarantees; and to modify operating strategies in production, logistics, marketing, finance, organization, and personnel.
- The main *country-specific risks* are *transfer risk*, known as *blocked funds*, and certain cultural and institutional risks.
- Blocked funds can be managed by at least five different strategies. They are: 1) consideration in the original capital budgeting analysis; 2) fronting loans; 3) creating unrelated exports; 4) obtaining special dispensation; and 5) plan on forced reinvestment.
- Cultural and institutional risks emanate from host country policies with respect to ownership structure, human resource norms, religious heritage, nepotism and corruption, intellectual property rights, and protectionism.
- Managing cultural and institutional risks requires the MNE to understand the differences, take legal actions in host country courts, support worldwide treaties to protect intellectual property rights, and support government efforts to create regional markets.
- The main global-specific risks are currently caused by terrorism and war, the anti-globalization movement, environmental concerns, poverty, and cyberattacks.
- In order to manage global-specific risks, MNEs should adopt a crisis plan to protect its employees and property. However, the main reliance remains on governments to protect its citizens and firms from these global-specific threats.

QUESTIONS

1. **Political risk definition.** In order for a MNE to identify, measure, and manage its political risks, it needs to define and classify these risks. Define the following political risks:
   a. Firm-specific risks
   b. Country-specific risks
   c. Transfer risk
   d. Cultural and institutional risk
   e. Global-specific risk
2. **Country risk ratings.** Exhibit 16.2 shows country risk ratings for selected countries. Using Moody's, S&P, and Euromoney rating services, prepare a country risk rating for Argentina.

3. **Governance risk.**
   a. Define "governance risk."
   b. What is the most important type of governance risk?
4. **Investment agreement.** An *investment agreement* spells out specific rights and responsibilities of both the foreign firm and the host government. What are the main financial policies that should be spelled out in an investment agreement?
5. **Investment insurance and guarantees (OPIC)**
   a. What is OPIC?
   b. Against what types of political risks can OPIC insure?
6. **Operating strategies after the FDI decision.** The following operating strategies, among others, are expected to reduce damage from political risk. Explain each one and how it reduces damage.
   a. Local sourcing
   b. Facility location
   c. Control of technology
   d. Thin equity base
   e. Multiple source borrowing
7. **Country-specific risk: definitions. Define the following terms**
   a. Transfer risk
   b. Blocked funds
   c. Sovereign credit risk
8. **Blocked funds.** Explain the strategies that a MNE can use to counter blocked funds.
9. **Cultural and institutional risks.** Identify and explain the main types of cultural and institutional risks, except protectionism.
10. **Strategies to manage cultural and institutional risks.** Explain the strategies that a MNE can use to manage each of the cultural and institutional risks that you identified in Question 9.
11. **Protectionism defined.**
    a. Define protectionism and identify the industries that are typically protected.
    b. Explain the "infant industry" argument for protectionism.
12. **Managing protectionism.**
    a. What are the traditional methods for countries to implement protectionism?
    b. What are some typical non-tariff barriers to trade?
    c. How can MNEs overcome host country protectionism?
13. **Global-specific risks.** What are the main types of political risks that are global in origin?
14. **Managing global-specific risks.** What are the main strategies MNEs can use to manage the global-specific risks you identified in Question 13?
15. **U.S. anti-bribery law.** The United States has a law prohibiting U.S. firms from bribing foreign officials and business persons, even in countries where bribery is a normal practice. Some U.S. firms claim this places the United States at a disadvantage compared to host-country firms and other foreign firms that are not hampered by such a law. Discuss the ethics and practicality of the U.S. anti-bribery law.
16. **FairTrade movement.** How does the FairTrade movement differ from many traditional income redistribution plans used by many countries?
17. **Starbucks' coffee procurement.** Do you think Starbucks should pay a higher price than the market price to its growers, even if there is no significant difference in the quality of the coffee or reliability of production?
18. **Corporate social responsibility.** What is Starbucks' strategy in corporate social responsibility? Is it consistent with shareholder wealth maximization?
19. **Cool Cola Company.** Cool Cola Company, one of the world's major manufacturers of cola soft drinks, is considering the establishment of a very large cola bottling plant in India. Cool Cola expects to sell half its production within India and to export the other half to southeast Asian countries. If the Kashmir conflict could be resolved, Pakistan and even Afghanistan might become important markets.
    a. Prepare an analysis of all the potential areas of goal conflict between Cool Cola and India.

b. Considering your answers to part a, prepare a political risk forecast for Cool Cola's bottling plant in India. Consider the potential for political unrest in India or for war with Pakistan, as well as whether a foreign-owned soft drink plant would be affected by such unrest. Use current periodicals and newspapers to gather your data.

c. Assume Cool Cola Company decides to build a large bottling plant in India. Recommend operating strategies for Cool Cola Company that would reduce its political risk. Include strategies for marketing, production, finance, and organization.

d. Prepare a crisis plan for Cool Cola in India in case political conditions deteriorate.

20. **Divestment—China.** Assume that Cool Cola Company also has a network of soft drink bottling plants throughout China, but political stresses between the United States and China increase to the degree that Cool Cola would like to divest. What should Cool Cola consider in developing a plan that will enable it to divest its investment in bottling plants and distributions systems in China with minimum loss?

INTERNET EXERCISES

WWW.

1. **The World Bank.** The World Bank provides a growing set of informational and analytical resources to aid in the assessment and management of cross-border risk. The Risk Management Support Group has a variety of political risk assessment tools that are under constant development. Visit the following site and compose an executive briefing (one page or less) of what the political risk insurance provided by the World Bank will and will not cover.

   World Bank Risk Management http://www.worldbank.org/business/01risk_manage.html

2. **Global corruption report.** Transparency International (TI) is considered by many to be the leading non-governmental anti-corruption organization in the world today. It has recently introduced its own annual survey analyzing recent developments, identifying ongoing challenges, and offering potential solutions to individuals or organizations. One dimension of this analysis is the Bribe Payers Index. Visit TI's web site to view the latest edition of the Bribe Payers Index.

   Transparency International http://www.globalcorruptionreport.org

3. **Sovereign credit ratings criteria.** The evaluation of credit risk and all other relevant risks associated with the multitude of borrowers on world debt markets requires a structured approach to international risk assessment. Use Standard & Poor's criteria, described in depth on their web page, to differentiate the various risks (local currency risk, default risk, currency risk, transfer risk, etc.) contained in major sovereign ratings worldwide.

   Standard & Poor's http://www.ratings.com/criteria/sovereigns.index

4. **Milken Capital Access Index.** The Milken Institute's Capital Access Index (CAI) is one of the most recent informational indices that helps evaluate how accessible world capital markets are to MNEs and governments of many emerging market countries. According to the CAI, which countries have seen the largest deterioration in their access to capital in the past two years?

   Milken Institute http://www.milken-inst.org

SELECTED READINGS

Godfrey, Stephen, and Ramon Espinosa, "A Practical Approach to Calculating Costs of Equity for Investments in Emerging Markets," *Journal of Applied Corporate Finance*, Fall 1996, Volume 9, No. 3, pp. 80–89.

Hervey, Michael G., "A Survey of Corporate Programs for Managing Terrorist Threats," *Journal of International Business Studies*, Third Quarter 1993, pp. 465–478.

Lee, Suk Hun, "Relative Importance of Political Instability and Economic Variables on Perceived Country Creditworthiness," *Journal of International Business Studies*, Fourth Quarter 1993, pp. 801–812.

Lessard, Donald R., "Incorporating Country Risk in the Valuation of Offshore Projects," *Journal of Applied Corporate Finance*, Fall 1996, Volume 9, No. 3, pp. 52–63.

Decision **CASE**

THUNDERBIRD
THE AMERICAN GRADUATE SCHOOL OF INTERNATIONAL MANAGEMENT

P.T. Semen Gresik

Mismanagement, poor regulation or simple inertia had left more than half of state-owned enterprises "unhealthy." State-appointed managers ran companies like fiefdoms; bloated, failing industries were kept alive more from national pride than economic sense. As 1997 came to a close, 164 state firms were reporting a combined pre-tax profit of just $1.2 billion. Yet state enterprises employed more than 700,000 Indonesians and were worth some $60 billion. They were overseen by touchy ministers and entrenched managers. They were wrapped in a mythology of development. Slimming down or selling off these sacred cows meant playing with fire.

"Anatomy of a Deal," by Jose Manuel Tesoro, *AsiaWeek*, January 22, 1999.

On July 6, 1998, the Indonesian government announced that Cementos Mexicanos (Cemex) was the *preferred bidder* for the largest government-owned cement company—PT Semen Gresik. The first round of bidding had pitted Cemex against Holderbank of Switzerland and Heidelberger of Germany, two of the largest cement manufacturing firms in the world. And a mere seven weeks had passed since the resignation of President Suharto, a turning-point in Indonesia's politics and economics.

In a surprise announcement on August 20, Cemex was informed that its first-round bid would have to be restructured, the primary change being a maximum of 14% of ownership passing from the government to Cemex. Then, as *preferred bidder*, Cemex would wait for the other first-round bidders to submit second bids no later than September 28. If their second bids were superior to that of Cemex's first bid, Cemex would have the right to match theirs if it wished. In the event the second bids did not match that of Cemex, Cemex would automatically be declared the winner. Cemex was also required to bid in the second round. The vice president for finance of Cemex, Hector Medina, and his acquisition staff now had only a few weeks to finalize their position.

Indonesian Privatization

The entire process of selling-off Indonesian state firms was directed by Mr. Tanri Abeng, a former dealmaker in Indonesia's private sector and thought to be well-suited for the position as a result of his lack of ties with politicians. Abeng's background encouraged foreign investors to believe that Indonesia's government was serious about its privatization program. Abeng had

A06-99-0025

previously held positions as the head of Indonesian operations for Union Carbide (United States), Heineken (the Netherlands), and finally the Bakrie Group, a diversified Indonesian conglomerate. After being named State Enterprises Minister in 1997 by then President Suharto, he was given a very ambitious revenue target: raise \$1.5 billion from the sale of stakes in selected Indonesian state-owned enterprises.

Abeng moved quickly, placing 12 government-owned companies up for sale. The 12 included port-operator *Pelindo*, highway and airport operators, mining companies, agricultural plantations, and telecommunications companies—including *Indosat*. These 12 possessed assets of 461 trillion rupiah (Rp), or \$50.6 billion. By early June of 1998 Abeng, had arranged for nine different investment banking firms to act as financial advisors and agents to the 12 companies on the auction block.

Goldman Sachs's Indonesian partner, Bahana, was hired to represent the Indonesian cement producer Semen Gresik. In May, Abeng appointed Goldman Sachs and Lehman Brothers senior advisors to the Indonesian government in its privatization drive. Exhibit 1 summarizes the firms.

The Indonesian privatization drive was the direct result of the economic crisis in which Indonesia was currently mired, and the subsequent promises made by President Suharto to the International Monetary Fund (IMF) in order to obtain economic and financial assistance. The structural reform program agreement signed with the IMF required Indonesia and President Suharto to open the Indonesian economy to outside investors and market forces. Under the terms of the agreement, Indonesia would sell stakes in four firms by the end of 1998, and in all 12 companies by the end of 1999.

The World Bank would supervise the privatization process implemented by the government. In stage one, each bidder—upon the completion of due diligence—would submit a binding offer for shares in the company based on directives given by the government (typically on how much of the government's share was actually up for sale). The winning bid would combine financial, social (employment guarantees), and environmental dimensions. The winning

Exhibit 1 Indonesian Enterprises Slated for Privatization and Their Financial Partners

State-Owned Company	Industry Financial	Adviser
1. Telekomunikasi Indonesia	Telecommunications	Merrill Lynch, Lehman Brothers
2. Indonesia Satellite (Indosat)	Telecommunications	Goldman Sachs
3. Semen Gresik	Cement	Goldman Sachs
4. Tambang Timah	Tin mining	Morgan Stanley, Banque Paribas
5. Aneka Tambang	Gold mining	Morgan Stanley, Banque Paribas
6. Tambang Batubara Bukit Asam	Gold mining	Morgan Stanley, Banque Paribas
7. Jasa Marga	Toll road operator	Lehman Brothers
8. Pelabuhan II (Pelindo II)	Port operator	Goldman Sachs
9. Pelabuhan III (Pelindo III)	Port operator	Credit Suisse First Boston
10. Angkasa Pura II	Airport manager	UBS/SBC Warburg Dillon Read
11. Perkebunan Nusantra IV	Plantation	Jardine Fleming
12. Krakatoa Steel	Steel	Salomon Smith Barney

bidder of stage one would then enter into a provisional sales agreement with the government. Third parties were then allowed to submit bids in a second stage to improve upon the winning bidder's offer. The winning bidder of stage one was then given the right to match the better offer, if it wished, in order to win the bid.

Many of these state-owned enterprises were already publicly traded (minority shares), so that market values did exist for these firms. However, these market capitalizations had been severely degraded following the onslaught of the Asian economic crisis. Markets, in addition to the individual equities traded in these markets, had fallen across Asia. For example, official forecasts for the Indonesian economy expected a 10% fall in total gross domestic product (GDP) for 1998. (The magnitude of this depression and economic collapse is seen when this 10% fall is compared with the deepest recessions in recent U.S. economic history—when GDP fell by a mere 2% during the 1930s.)

Cemex S.A. de C.V.

Founded in 1906, Cementos Mexicanos S.A. (Cemex) is the largest cement manufacturer in the Americas and the third largest cement producer in the world, just behind Holderbank of Switzerland and Lafarge of France. Based in Monterey, Mexico, Cemex has operations in 22 countries and trade relations with over 60 countries worldwide. Cemex is the market leader in Mexico, Spain, Venezuela, Panama, and the Dominican Republic, with a rapidly expanding presence in Colombia, the Caribbean, the southwestern portion of the United States, and most recently the Philippines. Exhibit 2 provides an overview of Cemex's recent financial results. (Appendix 1 provides additional Cemex results.)

Cemex has a corporate strategy which provides much of the impetus for its Asian expansion: 1) to leverage its core cement and ready-mix concrete franchise; 2) to concentrate on developing markets; and 3) to maintain high growth by applying free cash flow toward selective investments that further its geographic diversification. This strategy was focused on repositioning the company from being a dominant regional producer to a true global player in the cement industry.

Most notable regarding Cemex's performance had been its ability to maintain its operating and EBITDA margins over the tumultuous 1990s. Consistently higher than all of its

Exhibit 2 Selected Consolidated Financial Results of Cemex SA (December 31, millions of constant pesos)

	1993	1994	1995	1996	1997
Net sales	25,759	27,687	33,924	35,540	38,464
Operating income	6,269	7,431	8,100	8,482	9,088
Majority net income	4,637	4,951	10,045	10,319	7,725
Earnings per share (EPS)	4.39	4.60	7.81	7.95	6.01
Operating margin (%)	24.4	26.8	23.9	23.8	23.6
EBITDA*	8,120	9,471	10,786	11,483	12,116
EBITDA margin (%)	31.6	34.2	31.8	32.3	31.5

*EBITDA = earnings before interest, taxes, depreciation and amortization.

Source: Cemex, http://www.cemex.com.

European-based global competitors, the source of its efficiencies rested with a capable combination of relatively new vintage capital facilities, pricing-power and market dominance in its primary markets, and a progressive management group and strategy which focused on customer satisfaction and service (a rare concept in cement markets). The bottom line in all commodity-based industries, however, was operating excellence. Cemex consistently attained margins, even in new acquisitions, which competitors could not match. Operating margins expanded by 18% in Spain after Cemex acquired Valenciana and Sanson, and 19% in Venezuela after acquiring Vencemos.

Cemex had little experience in Asia, but it did possess significant experience of its own in surviving an economic crisis. The devaluation of the Mexican peso in December 1994 and the resulting Mexican economic crisis of 1995 had provided Cemex with some in-house insights into enterprise value. Cemex's own price-to-book value had plunged to 1.16 in March 1995 following the fall of the peso, yet Cemex was able to recover remarkably quickly from this discounting by the equity markets. It hoped to use some of these insights into market valuation in expanding its presence in Asia when Asian cement stocks were themselves trading at significant discounts to what their true values likely were.

> *This is most definitely the right time to buy in Asia. The current crisis in Asia has resulted in a fall in value per tonne of capacity for cement companies to US$100 per tonne from US$500 per tonne.*
>
> Lorenzo Zambrano, Chairman, Cemex[1]

Cemex's first direct operating activities in Asia commenced with its acquisition of a 30% stake in Rizal Cement of the Philippines in September 1997 for US$100 million. Although Cemex itself had aspirations of expanding across Asia, and the Asian economic crisis had made many firms throughout the Far East relatively cheap, many analysts had grave concerns over the ability of Cemex to digest more acquisitions in the region rapidly. Nonetheless, Cemex continued to pour over the possibilities in the region, paying significant attention to the movements of its major global competitors.[2] In early 1998 Cemex directed Goldman Sachs to find a company in Indonesia in which the firm might acquire a strategic stake. Exhibit 3 provides an overview of the major cement manufacturing firms across the region, their recent earnings and share price performance, and several measures of cement producer valuation.

Valuation

> *Value, in our opinion, should be the guiding principle in such turbulent times. While stock prices in efficient markets naturally respond to day-to-day changes in life, this should not cloud the fact that the underlying assets possess an intrinsic economic value. When the market price falls below that value, a profit opportunity arises.... Is there value in the Indonesian cement sector and, if there is, when is it going to be realised?*[3]

In addition to most of the traditional valuation techniques (price to earnings, price to free cash flow, earnings per share growth) there are typically additional techniques useful in specific

1. *The Financial Times,* November 7, 1997.
2. Within months of the start of the Asian crisis Holderbank (Switzerland) and Blue Circle (United Kingdom) were both moving on properties in Malaysia and the Philippines, while LaFarge (France) moved to expand into the Philippines and India.
3. "On the Brink of Value Realization," Indosuez W.I. Carr Securities Limited, June 22, 1998, p. 5.

Exhibit 3 Financial Characteristics of Cement Producers in Asia (March 1998)

Firm (Country)	Market Cap (US$ million)	EV/ Capacity	EV/ EBITDA	Price/ FCF	Price/Earnings Per Share (EPS) Earnings	1997	1998E	Share Price Performance Change	12 months	Relative
INDIA										
Associated Cement	460.0	77	12.4	22.1	142.4	56.2	9.2	–84%	3%	6%
Gujarat Ambuja Cement	433.5	128	8.0	11.5	12.4	18.0	18.6	3%	–10%	–8%
India Cement	97.8	64	4.3	4.3	4.9	12.8	12.0	–6%	–8%	–6%
Madras Cement	102.7	73	4.2	3.8	5.8	642.7	572.2	–11%	–59%	–58%
Average		86	7.2	10.4	41.4			–19%	–17%	
INDONESIA										
Indocement	957.9	39	12.6	15.8	(27.9)	(371.1)	(123.8)	improved	38%	82%
Semen Gresik	461.9	53	8.5	11.4	56.0	(90.2)	121.0	improved	–14%	14%
Semen Cibinong	49.5	65	5.5	0.5	(1.1)	2.0	(334.0)	–16800%	–61%	–48%
Average		52	8.9	9.2	9.0			–12%	16%	
THAILAND										
Siam Cement	926.6	190	7.2	4.1	(1.5)	(440.3)	(37.5)	improved	–48%	–23%
Siam City Cement	338.3	97	9.8	10.0	(3.7)	(96.0)	(36.6)	improved	–2%	44%
TPI Polene	71.7	150	15.2	(1.3)	(1.3)	(53.4)	(28.4)	improved	–79%	–68%
Average		146	10.7	4.3	(2.2)			–43%	–16%	
MALAYSIA										
Cement Industries	69.6	26	9.3	11.5	(91.3)	52.7	(2.3)	–104%	–70%	–44%
Kedah Cement	109.4	93	5.1	2.7	4.0	28.3	26.5	–6%	–76%	–55%
Malayan Cement	238.9	45	20.1	11.0	6.7	29.8	10.0	–66%	–56%	–17%
Average		55	11.5	8.4	(26.9)			–67%	–38%	
PHILIPPINES										
Alsons	54.0	40	4.0	4.6	4.4	0.6	0.5	–17%	–74%	–56%
Davao Union Cement	19.3	56	3.0	2.0	1.9	0.4	0.3	–25%	–89%	–81%
Fortune Cement	120.6	96	6.2	7.2	10.0	0.4	0.4	0%	–66%	–44%
Hi Cement	60.3	39	3.1	3.1	5.8	0.7	0.5	–29%	–68%	–47%
Average		58	4.1	4.2	5.5			–74%	–57%	
TAIWAN										
Asia Cement	1,716.2	228	10.1	8.9	13.9	2.3	2.4	4%	–23%	–33%
Taiwan Cement	1,343.7	147	14.1	14.1	25.4	1.2	1.4	17%	–38%	–46%
Average		188	12.1	11.5	19.7			–30%	–40%	
SOUTH KOREA										
Hanil Cement	65.4	25	4.2	3.0	11.5	2,186.5	2,031.0	–7%	–48%	–29%
Ssaangyong Cement	84.8	70	8.0	2.1	11.5	529.2	392.3	–26%	–60%	–45%
Tong Yang Cement	35.5	62	6.0	1.5	6.8	1,151.0	1,061.7	–8%	–59%	–45%
Average		52	6.1	2.2	9.9			–56%	–40%	

All values are estimates for 1998 unless otherwise stated. Market capitalization as of March 2, 1998.
Enterprise Value (EV) calculated as total market capitalization plus net debt.

Source: Constructed by author from Paribas Asia Equity and other sources.

industries. Two such techniques widely used in the cement industry are *enterprise value to capacity* and *enterprise value to EBITDA* (earnings before interest, taxes, depreciation and amortization).

Enterprise value to capacity is a frequently used method of valuation in the cement industry, and is calculated by dividing *enterprise value* (the total of market capitalization and net debt) by the existing installed capacity of the cement producer. Because of standardized technology across countries, EV/ capacity provides a very clear indicator of how different companies may be described as under- or overvalued. Industry experts estimated the *set-up costs* (*replacement cost*) in Asia to be roughly US$160/tonne for a standard 1.5 million metric tons per year (mmt/y) production facility.

Enterprise value to EBITDA is a more common measure of value used across all industries, and focuses on the market's current market capitalization to the current pre-financing and tax based operating earnings of the firm. Similarly, *price to free cash flow* (P/FCF) and *price-to-earnings* (PE) ratios also provide market values to firm cash flows and earnings by more standard methodologies.

As illustrated in Exhibit 3, the lowest EV/capacity in Asia in 1998 were the producers in Indonesia (52), South Korea (52), and Malaysia (55). The lowest EV/EBITDA values were found in a different subset of countries, with the lowest being the Philippines (4.1), South Korea (6.1), and India (7.2). The cement producers of Indonesia and Thailand had suffered negative earnings in 1997 and 1998, although the expectations for 1998 were for significant improvement (but still negative for these two countries). The other manufacturers across the region were still sliding, at least in regard to expected earnings for 1998. Share price performance for cement manufacturers since the inception of the crisis in June 1997 was, however, unambiguously disastrous.

The prospects of the Indonesian cement industry were not clear. In March the Indonesian government announced it would deregulate the local guideline price system (HPS), and the Indonesian Cement Association (ASI) would assume responsibility for supervision of cement distribution and control of cement prices. This was expected to result in price wars as excess supply of cement was expected to continue through the year 2002. Prices could fall by 10% to Rp139,500 per tonne. Because cement is a bulk commodity with high transportation costs, markets are typically geographically defined. Prices therefore vary significantly from one region or country to another.

The Asian currency crisis had led to a significant differentiation—some would say *distortion*—of relative costs and prices across the Asian cement industry. As seen in Exhibit 4, cash

Exhibit 4 Bagged Cement Prices and Cash Costs Across Asia, June 1998

Country	Ex-Factory Price (US$/tonne)	Cash Costs (US$/tonne)	Margin (US$/tonne)	Gross Margin (per tonne)
Pakistan	55	29	26	47%
Malaysia	40	26	14	35%
India	46	27	19	41%
Philippines	39	23	16	41%
Korea	39	28	11	28%
Taiwan	54	30	24	44%
Thailand	38	20	18	47%
Indonesia	16	10	6	38%
Average	41	24	17	40%

Source: Indosuez W.I. Carr Securities, June 12, 1998.

costs ranged from a low of $10/tonne in Indonesia to $30/tonne in Taiwan. At the same time, prices were also the lowest in Indonesia, currently falling to $16/tonne, while Pakistan and Taiwan earned $55 and $54/tonne, respectively. The result was an Indonesian industry which was the lowest cost, but also relatively low in gross margin.

The large discrepancies in costs and prices had led many of the world's largest cement producers to consider something long forgotten, large scale low-cost production and international distribution through exports. For example, the Taiwanese cement market may be quite vulnerable to Indonesian exports. Assuming cash production costs in Indonesia of $10/tonne, loading costs (on both ends) of $2/tonne, and shipping costs to Kaohsiung (Taiwan) from East Java (Indonesia) of $10/tonne, Indonesian exports could severely undercut domestic Taiwanese producers.[4] Several analysts argued that even the United States cement markets may be vulnerable to Indonesian exports if shipping costs between Indonesia and the U.S. could be kept at $35 to $40/tonne. Cement prices in the U.S. hovered just below $75/tonne. Semen Gresik was currently in the process of a significant upgrading of its port facilities to increase its export capabilities. (Appendix 2 provides a discounted cash flow valuation of PT Semen Gresik.)

P.T. Semen Gresik

> *We believe that Gresik would be on the top of the list of acquisition targets for foreign cement players. The partial sell-down of the government's 65% stake will represent a unique opportunity for the foreign players to take a meaningful stake in the Indonesian cement industry (previously closed). However, in our view this foreign interest is dependent on, at a minimum, gaining management control.*[5]

Semen Gresik began producing cement in 1957 by exploiting large and readily accessible limestone deposits in East Java, and was the first government-owned cement producer in Indonesia to go public, issuing 35% of its shares on the Jakarta exchange in July 1991. The ownership structure had not changed since 1991, with 65% of the shares held by the Indonesian government and 35% free float on the Jakarta exchange. The 1998 Indonesian privatization program was focused on maximizing the revenues per share received by the government for some proportion of the 65% held by the government.

Semen Gresik had become the largest Indonesian cement producer in September 1995 when it had purchased Semen Padang (West Sumatra) and Semen Tonasa (South Sulawesi) for a total of $476 million. The three companies still operated separately, maintaining independent administrative structures. Although this added substantial capacity to Semen Gresik's resources, it was also an unpopular government-directed consolidation as fears arose over possibilities of layoffs and reorganizations away from the outer island/provinces.

The Indonesian market, however, like all cements markets around the globe, was regional in nature. The largest markets in Indonesia were Jakarta—dominated by Indocement—and West Java—dominated by Semen Cibinong. Regardless of which region the individual producer dominated, the Asian crisis had hit all the major producers. Indocement and Cibinong were expected to only reach 37% and 27% capacity utilization rates

4. Export cost estimates drawn primarily from Indosuez I.D. Carr Securities, June 12, 1998, p.11.

5. Ibid, p.17.

in 1998, respectively. All producers were expected to see 1998 annual sales volumes fall by roughly 40% from the previous year. Exhibit 5 provides an overview of the major Indonesian cement producers as of July 1998.

Semen Gresik's management of the Asian economic crisis had, however, been relatively successful. As a result of rising input costs (roughly 10% of Gresik's production costs were imported), the firm— all three operational units—had increased its ex-factory prices by over 40% in the spring of 1998, to an average of Rp 229,000 per tonne (US$23/tonne at the then current exchange rate of Rp 10,000/$). Appendices 3 and 4 provide recent and pro forma income statements, cash flows, and balance sheets for Semen Gresik.

Bidding for Semen Gresik

Tari Abeng believed that Semen Gresik was the proper choice to begin the state's privatization program. President Suharto agreed, and allowed Abeng to proceed without interference.[6] The firm was considered one of the best managed government-run enterprises, and had shown

Exhibit 5 Indonesia's Major Cement Manufacturers

	Semen Gresik	Semen Indocement	Semen Cibinong	Andalas
Installed capacity (mmt/y)	17.0	15.5	10.5	1.2
Market share	43%	35%	17%	5%
Dominant market in Indonesia	East Java	Jakarta	West Java	—
1997 sales (mmt)	11.7	9.5	4.6	1.4
1998e sales (mmt)	7.0	5.7	2.8	0.8
Change in sales, 1997 to 1998	–40%	–40%	–39%	–43%
1998e capacity utilization	41%	37%	27%	67%
Costs comparison:				
Production costs (Rp/tonne)	135,478	145,956	155,009	na
Production costs (US$/tonne)	13.6	14.6	15.5	na
Cash costs (Rp/tonne)	115,949	117,844	129,411	na
Cash costs (US$/tonne)	11.6	11.8	12.0	na
Debt in Rupiah (billion)	Rp 1,792	Rp 391	Rp 40	na
Debt in U.S. dollars (million)	$226	$889	$903	na
Primary owner	Government	Private	Private	Government
Minority owner	Market	None	Holderbank	None
Status	Privatizing	Partner?	Stable	Privatizing

na=not available. e= estimated. Costs for Semen Gresik are numerical average of the three primary production facilities.

Source: Deutsche Bank Research, Mexican Special Report, July 6, 1998, p. 5.

6. Krakatoa Steel had actually been the first privatization subject, but had run into a variety of delays resulting in a still-borne privatization program.

some resiliency in the declining business conditions suffered by most in the current crisis. Gresik was not only the largest Indonesian cement producer, it was generally regarded as potentially the most efficient, particularly with so much of its existing capacity using the latest technology, and being of such a recent vintage. Roughly 30% of Semen Gresik's installed capacity had come on-line in 1996 and 1997.

In the midst of rising political tension throughout Indonesia—focused primarily on the push for President Suharto's resignation—Abeng initiated negotiations on May 5 with three of the world's largest cement manufacturers: Holderbank, Heidelberger, and Cemex. Holderbank, fresh off the acquisition of Union Cement (Philippines) and Siam City (Thailand), appeared the most aggressive. Cemex's due diligence team of 30 professionals arrived in Indonesia six days later. On May 17, President Suharto resigned. After a temporary pause in the process, Abeng proceeded with the privatization process. Heidelberg withdrew at this stage, leaving only Cemex and Holderbank to pursue the allotted two-week period of due diligence. On June 19, both companies filed their bids. Holderbank offered $0.96/share, roughly $200 million. The Cemex bid was much higher—$1.38/share—a potential investment of $287 million (both bids were for 207.6 million shares).

At this point Tari Abeng's gamesmanship became apparent. Departing from the original privatization program outlined by the World Bank, Abeng invited both bidders to up their bids at this point without revealing the bids submitted by either party. While Cemex confirmed its existing bid, Holderbank increased its bid to $1.21/share, or $251 million. Cemex was officially declared the winner and the *preferred bidder* for the final stage two.

Cemex's winning stage one bid was actually a complex combination offer:

1. A bid of $1.38/share for 35% of Semen Gresik's shares held by the Indonesian government. Given a current share price of Rp 9,150 (about $0.63/share at the current exchange rate of Rp14,500/$), this represented nearly a 100% premium.
2. An announced intention to purchase an additional 16% of the company's shares on the open market, bringing its total constructed position to 51%.
3. A five-year put option to the Indonesian government to sell its remaining shares to Cemex at a base price of $1.38/share plus an 8.2% annual premium.
4. A one-off payment of $129 million to the Indonesian government in 2006 if Semen Gresik's performance surpassed specific expectations.
5. A contribution of approximately $50 million to the on-going port facilities upgrade and capacity expansion of Semen Gresik (bringing it up to 17.5 mmt/y capacity; see Appendix 5).

This purchase of 207.6 million shares would reap the government approximately $287 million.[7] If the additional 16% were tendered at roughly the same price, the investment for control of Semen Gresik by Cemex would total $417.5 million. This was approximately one-quarter of what Indonesia had promised the IMF to raise through privatization—in just the first of the 12 firm sales.

7. Of P.T. Semen Gresik's total 593,200,000 shares, 35% were publicly traded (207,620,000), and 65% were held by the Indonesian government (385,580,000).

Growing Opposition

Meanwhile, social and political tensions were rising over the falling employment levels of the Indonesian economy. A number of prominent Indonesian government officials raised questions regarding the wisdom of selling valuable Indonesian assets to foreign interests, particularly in light of the control these powers would exert over the companies and their employees. The management of Semen Gresik itself had previously been under pressure to assure employment levels at its Tonasa and Padang subsidiaries (acquired in 1995), and now the prospect of this parent becoming further subordinated itself was not a popular one.

A second area of debate arose over the process itself. A number of prominent bankers in Jakarta were quoted in the press as questioning both the transparency of the process directed by Abeng, and the ethics of the process. At the center of the controversy was whether the investment banking firm— Goldman Sachs—was not actually playing both sides of the street. Goldman Sachs represented both the potential buyer (Cemex) and the seller (the Indonesian government). By mid-July the controversy reached its zenith, the pressure resulting in Goldman Sachs resigning as Cemex's advisor:

> *Goldman Sachs decided to withdraw in the interest of transparency. We didn't think there was anything illegal in what Goldman Sachs was doing. The bank simply wanted to avoid further public debate over its role.*
>
> Sofyan Djalil, Special Assistant to Minister of State Enterprises

Cemex immediately replaced Goldman with Jardine Fleming. Despite the resignation, Goldman Sachs' relationship with Bahana remained controversial. As described by Goldman Sachs, the relationship was "a joint operating agreement with no current cross-ownership." In principle, the problem was one of suspicion in an environment which could not at that time allow suspicion to arise.[8]

A third debate, one which erupted literally days after the culmination of the first stage, was the announcement by the Jakarta Stock Market's watchdog organization—*Bapepam*—of a probe into insider trading in Semen Gresik shares. Evidence put forward to suggest the possibility was that Gresik shares had risen 57% in the month of June while the general market fell. On the day of bid submission (June 19), a record 62 million shares of Gresik were traded, closing above Rp8,700/share for the first time. Bapepam announced that the investigation would focus on the trading activities at Jardine Fleming (now associated with Cemex), Bahana (aligned with Goldman Sachs), and the state-controlled investment bank Danareksa Securities.

Although the bids submitted by the two companies were for shares held by the Indonesian government, and the actual bids submitted secretly, both companies had been quite public in their plans to acquire additional shares sold on the open market in combination with a winning bid. Both firms wished to acquire control of Gresik, and that would have to be done by combining government shares with free-floating shares. The investigation into insider trading continued for months with no violations ever substantiated. The bidding process would continue.

8. The sensitivity of this topic is summarized well by Michael Vatikiotis: "Indonesians cannot be accused of cynicism if they say that these investment banks are guilty of the same kind of collusion and nepotism which brought down the Suharto regime," from "Banking on Big Names," *Far Eastern Economic Review*, 11/19/98.

Indonesia Backs Off

For months rumors had been circulating in West Sumatra that the new owners of Semen Gresik would lay off nearly half the 3,000 employees of Semen Padang's operations. Cemex's acquisition team had, during the due diligence process in which the team had direct contact with present Gresik management and labor, guaranteed that no one would be laid off before the year 2000. Demonstrations intensified in West Sumatra and Jakarta, however, after the first round of bidding. Protests in Jakarta grew in size and fervor, and by late July were occurring nearly daily (eventually resulting in the posting of signs designating a "Demonstration Area"). Rumors that management at Semen Padang paid demonstrators in both West Sumatra and Jakarta were denied by employees.

The governor of West Sumatra then threatened to remove certain land rights and concessions provided to Semen Padang if control of Semen Gresik was allowed to pass to foreign investors. The opposition parties became more and more public with their demands and threats, promising they would occupy the properties of Semen Padang in the event of foreign acquisition. The final tide turned when Azwar Anas, a former army general, former West Sumatra governor, and former CEO of Semen Padang (prior to acquisition in 1995) took the unofficial lead in opposing the privatization. On August 11 Tanri Abeng was called to testify before the Economic Committee of Indonesia's Supreme Advisory Council. Here Abeng finally capitulated to the growing pressure.

> *I was able to grasp that the real reason behind the resistance is purely emotional and cultural. Nothing to do with economics. From there on, I knew, no way. We are fighting a losing battle if we push so hard.*
>
> Tanri Abeng, August 12th

Abeng informed Cemex that the sale of Semen Gresik would have to be restructured and the second round of bidding would be postponed. Speculation on the structure of the new sale intensified, and in a conference call with Morgan Stanley Dean Witter, the Managing Director of Semen Gresik stated that he believed the company would still be sold as one, and not broken up into the individual units (Semen Padang, Semen Tonasa, Semen Gresik). It was also rumored that the winning bidder would be required to make a tender offer to the public minority shareholders at the same price as the bid price, but only if taking more than a 20% position from the government.

Final Bids

On August 20, Tanri Abeng's Office of State Enterprises announced that the government would entertain bids for only 14% of Semen Gresik rather than the original 35% offered, assuring that the government would remain the controlling shareholder after the sale. Tanri Abeng's office informed Cemex that its stage one bid would have to be restructured, keeping its preferred bidder status, and then the second round bids would be accepted. It was now up to Cemex to determine what it wished to do in its restructured stage one bid. Competitor bids were due no later than September 28, a little more than five weeks from now.

Appendix 1

Selected Consolidated Financial Results of Cemex SA (millions of constant pesos)

Income Statement Information	1993	1994	1995	1996	1997	1998
Net Sales	25,729	27,687	33,924	35,540	38,464	42,720
Cost of Sales	15,512	15,968	20,689	21,550	23,571	24,701
Gross Profit	10,217	11,719	13,235	13,990	14,893	18,019
Operating Expenses	3,948	4,288	5,135	5,518	5,805	6,360
Operating Income	6,269	7,431	8,100	8,472	9,088	11,659
Comprehensive Financing Costs	221	(213)	7,498	5,588	1,611	(1,309)
Other Income (Expenses)	(895)	(1,754)	(2,142)	(1,801)	(1,396)	(1,506)
Income Before Taxes & Others	5,595	5,464	13,456	12,259	9,303	8,844
Minority Interest	861	595	1,440	1,256	1,083	391
Majority Net Income	4,637	4,951	10,045	10,319	7,725	7,952
Earnings Per Share (EPS)	4.39	4.60	7.81	7.95	6.01	6.30
Dividends Per Share (DPS)	0.81	0.83	0.87	na	na	1.18
Number of Shares Outstanding	1,056	1,077	1,286	1,303	1,268	1,258
Balance Sheet Information						
Cash and Temporary Investments	2,900	6,385	4,691	4,316	3,862	4,027
Net Working Capital	5,285	6,954	7,498	6,452	5,971	6,320
Property, Plant & Equipment (net)	39,145	53,944	65,337	60,646	60,976	60,805
Total Assets	71,212	104,027	110,738	104,998	103,878	103,551
Short Term Debt	6,073	8,534	11,515	8,609	6,674	10,948
Long-Term Debt	25,455	41,059	40,135	41,757	40,213	31,049
Total Liabilities	35,723	56,546	60,901	59,197	56,198	52,682
Minority Interests	6,845	10,158	11,758	10,562	11,992	12,384
Stockholders Equity, ex Minority	28,644	37,323	38,079	35,239	35,689	38,484
Total Stockholders Equity	35,489	47,481	49,837	45,801	47,681	50,868
Book value per share	27.12	34.65	29.62	27.15	27.80	30.49
Other Financial Data						
Operating Margin	24.4%	26.8%	23.9%	23.8%	23.6%	27.3%
EBITDA Margin	31.6%	34.2%	31.8%	32.3%	31.5%	34.4%
EBITDA	8,120	9,471	10,786	11,483	12,116	14,697
Cash Earnings	4,950	5,873	3,020	4,993	7,316	10,263
Cash Earnings Per Share	4.69	5.45	2.35	3.85	5.70	8.13

Source: Cemex SA , http://www.cemex.com

Appendix 2

Discounted Cash Flow Valuation of the P.T. Semen Gresik Group

Assumptions	Value	Assumptions	Value
Cost of equity calculation:		FX rate (Rp/$)	8,000
Risk-free rate	33.7%	Inflation	29.4%
Equity risk premium	6.0%	Tax rate	30.0%
Beta	1.20	Terminal value growth rate	30.0%
Cost of equity	40.9%	Working capital to sales ratio	14.0%
Cost of debt calculation:		Percentage debt	50%
Cost of local debt	35.0%	Percentage equity	50%
After-tax cost of debt	24.5%	WACC	32.7%

Billions of Rp		**1998**	**1999**	**2000**	**2001**	**2002**
Assumed sales growth rate		*16.0%*	*26.9%*	*20.0%*	*20.0%*	*20.0%*
Net sales		1,842.0	2,337.5	2,805.0	3,366.0	4,039.2
COGS (% of sales)		*46.0%*	*47.0%*	*47.0%*	*47.0%*	*47.0%*
Cost of goods sold		(847.3)	(1,098.6)	(1,318.3)	(1,582.0)	(1,898.4)
Gross profit		994.7	1,238.9	1,486.6	1,784.0	2,140.8
Less selling G & A	15.0%	(276.3)	(350.6)	(420.7)	(504.9)	(605.9)
Operating profit (EBITDA)		718.4	888.2	1,065.9	1,279.1	1,534.9
Less depreciation & amortization		(261.0)	(276.0)	(276.0)	(276.0)	(276.0)
EBIT		457.4	612.2	789.9	1,003.1	1,258.9
Note: Estimated NWC	14.0%	257.9	327.2	392.7	471.2	565.5
For DCF Valuation:						
EBIT		457.4	612.2	789.9	1,003.1	1,258.9
Less taxes	30.0%	(137.2)	(183.7)	(237.0)	(300.9)	(377.7)
Net operating profit after-tax		320.2	428.6	552.9	702.2	881.2
Add depreciation & amortization		261.0	276.0	276.0	276.0	276.0
Less change in NWC		(35.6)	(69.4)	(65.4)	(78.5)	(94.2)
Less capex		(40.0)	(40.0)	-	-	-
Free Cash Flow (FCF)		368.4	411.5	526.5	598.7	685.3
Terminal value						32,996.4
FCF including TV		368.4	411.5	526.5	598.7	33,681.7
Present value factor		0.7536	0.5679	0.4279	0.3225	0.2430
Present value of cash flow		277.6	233.7	225.3	193.1	8,185.4
Cumulative present value		9,115.1				

Enterprise value	9,115.1	Terminal value as % of total EV:	88%
Less net debt	(4,113.5)	Implied Price to EBITDA (1998):	11.7
Less minority interests	(23.1)	Implied Price to FCF (1998):	22.8
Equity value, total	4,978.5		
Shares outstanding (millions)	593.2		
Fair value of equity per share, Rp	8,393	Semen Gresik share price, Rp:	6,500
Exchange rate (Rp/US$)	8,000	Exchange rate (Rp/US$)	8,000
In US dollars	$ 1.05	In US dollars	$ 0.81

The DCF analysis is assumed performed in May of 1998. Cash flows for 1998 are therefore, in reality, not a full year into the future as assumed here.

Appendix 3

P.T. Semen Gresik's Historical and Pro Forma Income and Cash Flows (billion rupiah)

Satement of Income	1996	1997	1998F	1999F
Sales by unit:				
Gresik	625	608	874	1,189
Tonasa	235	465	437	522
Padang	485	495	511	607
Non-cement	17	20	20	20
Total net sales	1,362	1,588	1,842	2,338
Growth in net sales (%)		17%	16%	27%
COGS Gresik	(365)	(377)	(534)	(734)
COGS Tonasa	(144)	(290)	(289)	(345)
COGS Padang	(273)	(286)	(277)	(317)
Total cost of goods sold	(782)	(953)	(1,100)	(1,396)
Gross profit	580	635	742	942
Gross margin (% of net sales)	43%	40%	40%	40%
Less selling, general & admin expenses	(259)	(313)	(284)	(328)
Operating profit	321	322	458	614
Less net interest	(43)	(101)	(279)	(535)
Contributions from subsidiaries	3	4	5	6
Others	5	9	10	10
Non-operating income	(35)	(89)	(264)	(519)
Pretax profit	286	234	194	95
Less Indonesian taxes	(65)	(44)	(29)	(11)
Minorities	(4)	(5)	(6)	(6)
Net profit	217	185	159	78
Return on sales (%)	16%	12%	9%	3%
Effective tax rate (%)	23%	19%	15%	12%

Cash Flow (billion rupiah)	**1996**	**1997**	**1998e**	**1999e**
Profit before interest & taxes	321	322	458	614
Depreciation & amortization	138	180	261	276
Associated adjustments	(3)	(4)	(5)	(6)
Change in net working capital	156	(466)	(96)	(144)
Operating Cash Flow	612	32	618	740
Taxes paid	(65)	(44)	(29)	(11)
Interest paid	(43)	(101)	(279)	(535)
Capitalized interest	(92)	(178)	(187)	(263)
Forex gains (losses)	-	(286)	(674)	-
Cash earnings	412	(577)	(551)	(69)
Dividends paid	(65)	(65)	(74)	-
Net capex (disposal)	(592)	(1,337)	(648)	(60)
Change in share capital	-	-	-	-
Others	(248)	-	-	-
Change in net debt	(493)	(1,979)	(1,273)	(129)
Ending cash (debt)	(1,003)	(2,982)	(4,255)	(4,384)

Source: Barings, March 3, 1998.

Appendix 4

P.T. Semen Gresik's Balance Sheet (billions of rupiah)

Assets	1992	1993	1994	1995	1996	1997
Cash & banks	336	140	52	275	220	461
Accounts receivable	14	5	17	145	179	238
Inventory	30	45	82	175	228	323
Other current	8	19	20	54	81	82
Total current assets	388	209	171	649	708	1,104
Fixed assets	108	109	769	1,471	2,090	2,282
Investments	14	3	6	45	14	14
Other assets	383	649	60	1,186	1,418	2,037
Total assets	893	970	1,006	3,351	4,230	5,437
Liabilities & Net Worth						
Trade payables	-	8	17	41	76	82
Accounts payable	6	21	17	62	309	414
Taxes payable	4	14	4	32	49	51
Other payables	17	4	18	70	47	-
Long-term debt (current)	-	40	79	287	227	93
Notes payable	-	-	-	-	136	-
Current liabilities	27	87	135	492	844	640
Long-term debt	182	181	139	532	900	2,339
Minorities	-	10	11	14	18	20
Share capital	148	148	148	593	593	593
Revaluation surplus	240	240	240	1,252	1,252	1,252
Reserves	293	302	333	468	622	600
Shareholders' funds	681	690	721	2,313	2,467	2,445
Total capital	863	881	871	2,859	3,385	4,804
Net assets (Total assets – current liabilities)	866	883	871	2,859	3,386	4,797

Source: Barings, March 3, 1998.

Appendix 5

Installed Capacity of the P.T. Semen Gresik Group (million metric tons/year)

	1994	1995	1996	1997	1998
Semen Gresik (Java):					
Gresik I	500	500	500	208	208
Gresik II	1,300	1,300	1,300	1,300	1,300
Tuban I	575	2,300	2,300	2,300	2,300
Tuban II	-	-	-	2,300	2,300
Tuban III	-	-	-	-	2,400
Total	2,375	4,100	4,100	6,108	8,508
Semen Padang (Sumatra, acquired 1995):					
Indatung I	254	254	254	254	254
Indatung II	660	660	660	660	660
Indatung III	660	660	660	660	660
Indatung IV	1,620	1,620	1,620	1,620	1,620
Indatung V	-	-	-	-	2,300
Total	3,194	3,194	3,194	3,194	5,494
Semen Tonasa (Sulawesi, acquired 1995):					
Tonasa I	-	-	-	-	-
Tonasa II	590	590	590	590	590
Tonasa III	590	590	590	590	590
Tonasa IV	-	-	2,300	2,300	2,300
Total	1,180	1,180	3,480	3,480	3,480
Total under Gesik Ownership	2,375	8,474	10,774	12,782	17,482
Percent change (%)	32%	257%	27%	19%	37%

Source: Morgan Stanley Dean Witter, June 22, 1998, p. 4, and ING Barings, March 3, 1998, p. 2.

Appendix 6

P.T. Semen Gresik's Share Price and Market Capitalization for Selected Dates (1998)

Date	Share Price (Rp)	Exchange Rate (Rp/$)	Implied Price (US$)	Market Capitalization (Rp)	Market Capitalization (US$)
Feb 3	6775	9,750	$ 0.69	3,997,250	410
March 3	5,600	9,300	$ 0.60	3,304,000	355
June 19	9,150	14,500	$ 0.63	5,398,500	372
July 6	9,150	14,700	$ 0.62	5,398,500	367
July 10	9,150	14,600	$ 0.63	5,398,500	370
Aug 18	10,775	12,000	$ 0.90	6,357,250	530
Aug 21	8,750	12,000	$ 0.73	5,162,500	430
Aug 28	10,500	13,000	$ 0.81	6,195,000	477

Note: Market capitalization on the basis of the following shares outstanding: 593,200,000

Appendix 7

Daily Exchange Rates: Indonesian Rupiah per U.S. Dollar

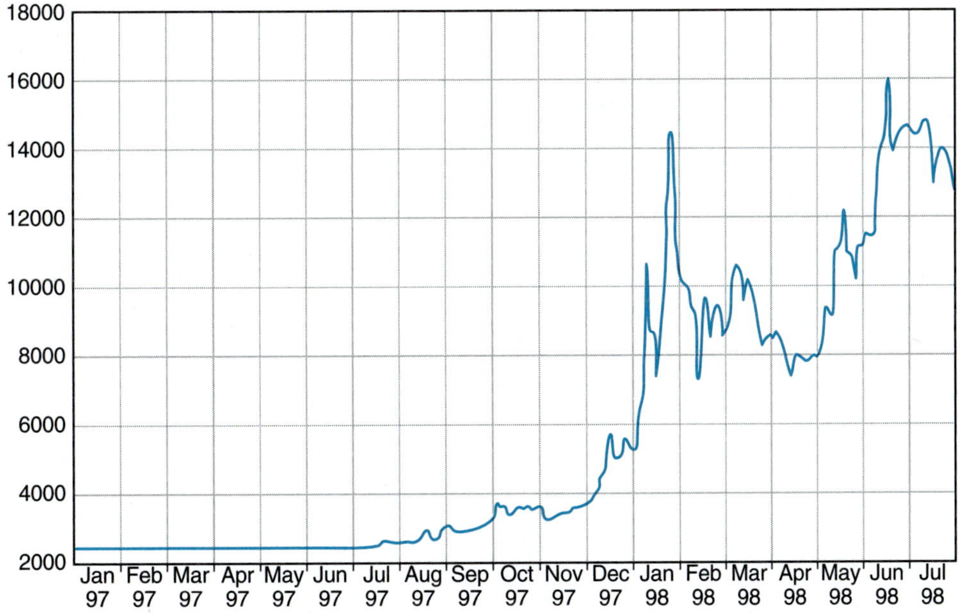

Source: © 1999 by Prof. Werner Antweiler, University of British Columbia, Vancouver, BC, Canada. http://pacific.commerce.ubc.ca. Permission is granted to reproduce the above image provided that the source and copyright are acknowledged.

Appendix 8

P.T. Semen Gresik Share Price, April 1–August 24, 1998

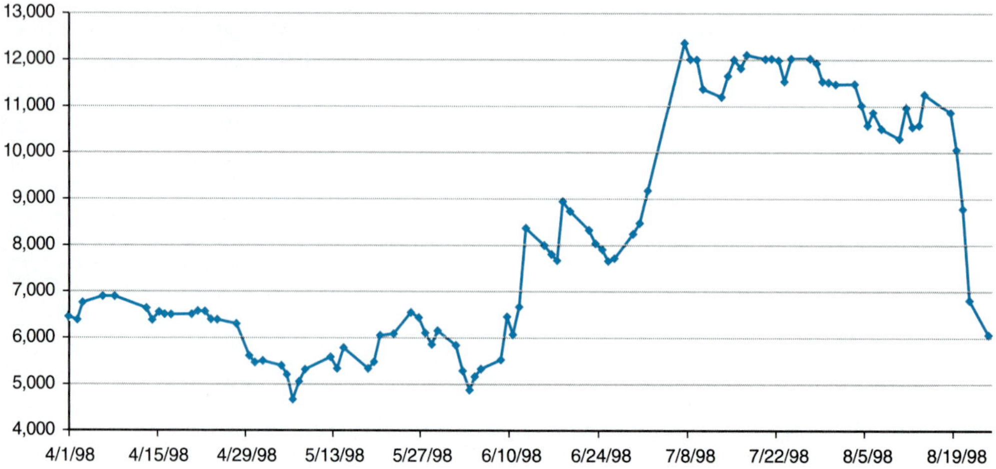

apter 17

Multinational Tax Management

TAX PLANNING FOR MULTINATIONAL OPERATIONS IS AN EXTREMELY COMPLEX BUT VITALLY IMPORTANT aspect of international business. To plan effectively, MNEs must understand not only the intricacies of their own operations worldwide, but also the different structures and interpretations of tax liabilities across countries. The primary objective of multinational tax planning is the minimization of the firm's worldwide tax burden. Managers must not pursue this objective, however, without full recognition that decision making within the firm must always be based on the economic fundamentals of the firm's line of business, and not on convoluted policies undertaken purely for the reduction of tax liability. Taxes have a major impact on corporate net income and cash flow through their influence on foreign investment decisions, financial structure, determination of the cost of capital, foreign exchange management, working capital management, and financial control.

Executives with tax responsibility in a MNE should have a background in public finance so that they can understand the principles of tax neutrality, equity, revenue, and morality. They should have experience in tax law in order to be able to follow the various tax rulings as they apply to international business practice, and they should also be able to read a number of foreign languages to keep abreast of foreign tax rulings. Naturally they should have accounting experience, since a large part of day-to-day tax administration includes decisions about whether specific transactions are tax-deductible or whether a particular transfer price can be defended as an "arm's length" transaction. Needless to say, the ideal international tax executive probably does not exist. Instead, tax planning is effected by group action, with each group member contributing expertise in one or more of the areas just described.

The purpose of this chapter is to provide an overview of the way taxes are applied to MNEs globally, how the United States taxes the global earnings of U.S.-based MNEs, and how U.S.-based multinationals manage their global tax liabilities. Although we use U.S. taxes as illustrations, our intention is not to make this chapter or this book "U.S.-centric." Most of the U.S. practices that we describe have close parallels in other countries, albeit modified to fit their specific national overall tax system.

This chapter begins with a summary of generic tax principles. We explain the dilemma of tax morality and tax neutrality. We then explain how countries adopt either a worldwide or territorial approach to taxation. Next we introduce the existence of a network of bilateral tax treaties. This is followed by a description of the various types of national taxes and how foreign tax credits are granted by most countries to prevent double taxation of their MNEs.

The second third of the chapter focuses on U.S. taxation of foreign source income. This starts by showing how the United States calculates foreign tax credits and what a MNE can do with excess foreign tax credits. This is illustrated by showing how foreign tax credits could be calculated by Carlton, our hypothetical U.S.-based MNE. Next comes a description of four unique U.S. tax features: Subpart F Income, Foreign Branches, Foreign Sales Corporations, and Possessions Corporations.

The final section of the chapter examines tax-haven subsidiaries and international offshore centers. These institutions continue to be highly controversial although they are widely used by MNEs from most countries. However, they are also widely used by "money-launderers," drug dealers, fraudulent scams, and numerous other illegal activities.

Tax Principles

The sections that follow explain the most important aspects of the international tax environments and specific features that affect MNEs. Before we explain the specifics of multinational taxation in practice, it is necessary to introduce two areas of fundamental importance: *tax morality* and *tax neutrality*.

Tax Morality

The MNE faces not only a morass of foreign taxes but also an ethical question. In many countries, taxpayers, corporate or individual, do not voluntarily comply with the tax laws. Smaller domestic firms and individuals are the chief violators. The MNE must decide whether to follow a practice of full disclosure to tax authorities or adopt the philosophy "When in Rome, do as the Romans do." Given the local prominence of most foreign subsidiaries and the political sensitivity of their position, most MNEs follow the full disclosure practice. Some firms, however, believe that their competitive position would be eroded if they did not avoid taxes to the same extent as their domestic competitors. There is obviously no prescriptive answer to the problem, since business ethics are partly a function of cultural heritage and historical development.

Some countries have imposed what seem to be arbitrary punitive tax penalties on MNEs for presumed violations of local tax laws. Property or wealth tax assessments are sometimes perceived by the foreign firm to be excessively large when compared with those levied on locally owned firms. The problem then is how to respond to tax penalties that are punitive or discriminatory.

Tax Neutrality

When a government decides to levy a tax, it must consider not only the potential revenue from the tax, or how efficiently it can be collected, but also the effect the proposed tax can have on private economic behavior. For example, the U.S. government's policy on taxation of foreign-source income does not have as its single objective the raising of revenue. It has multiple objectives that include the following:

- Neutralizing tax incentives that might favor (or disfavor) U.S. private investment in developed countries
- Providing an incentive for U.S. private investment in developing countries
- Improving the U.S. balance of payments by removing the advantages of artificial tax havens and encouraging repatriation of funds
- Raising revenue

The ideal tax should not only raise revenue efficiently but also have as few negative effects on economic behavior as possible. Some theorists argue that the ideal tax should be completely neutral in its effect on private decisions and completely equitable among taxpayers. However, other theorists claim that national policy objectives such as balance of payments or investment in developing countries should be encouraged through an active tax incentive policy. Most tax systems compromise between these two viewpoints.

One way to view neutrality is to require that the burden of taxation on each dollar, euro, pound, or yen of profit earned in home country operations by a MNE be equal to the burden of taxation on each currency equivalent of profit earned by the same firm in its foreign operations. This is called *domestic neutrality*. A second way to view neutrality is to require that the tax burden on each foreign subsidiary of the firm be equal to the tax burden on its competitors in the same country. This is called *foreign neutrality*. The latter policy is often supported by MNEs, because it focuses more on the competitiveness of the individual firm in individual country markets.

The issue of tax equity is also difficult to define and measure. In theory, an *equitable tax* is one that imposes the same total tax burden on all taxpayers who are similarly situated and located in the same tax jurisdiction. In the case of foreign investment income, the U.S. Treasury argues that since the United States uses the nationality principle to claim tax jurisdiction, U.S.-owned foreign subsidiaries are in the same tax jurisdiction as U.S. domestic subsidiaries. Therefore a dollar earned in foreign operations should be taxed at the same rate and the tax paid at the same time as a dollar earned in domestic operations.

National Tax Environments

Despite the fundamental objectives of national tax authorities, it is widely agreed that taxes do affect economic decisions made by MNEs. Tax treaties between nations and differential tax structures, rates, and practices all result in a less than level playing field for the MNEs competing on world markets.

Exhibit 17.1 provides an overview of corporate tax rates as applicable to Japan, Germany, and the United States. The categorizations of income (for example, distributed versus undistributed profits), the differences in tax rates, and the discrimination in tax rates applicable to income earned in specific countries serve to introduce the critical dimensions of tax planning for the MNE.

Nations typically structure their tax systems along one of two basic approaches: the worldwide approach or the territorial approach. Both approaches are attempts to determine which firms, foreign or domestic by incorporation, or which incomes, foreign or domestic in origin, are subject to the taxation of host country tax authorities.

Exhibit 17.1 Comparison of Corporate Tax Rates: Japan, Germany, and the United States

Taxable Income Category	Japan	Germany	United States
Corporate income tax rates:			
Profits distributed to stockholders	37.5%	30.0%	35.0%
Undistributed profits	37.5%	45.0%	35.0%
Branches of foreign corporations	37.5%	42.0%	35.0%
Withholding taxes on dividends (portfolio):			
with Japan	0.0%	15.0%	15.0%
with Germany	15.0%	0.0%	15.0%
with United States	15.0%	5.0%	0.0%
Withholding taxes on dividends (substantial holdings):			
with Japan	0.0%	25.0%	10.0%
with Germany	10.0%	0.0%	5.0%
with United States	10.0%	10.0	0.0%
Withholding taxes on interest:			
with Japan	0.0%	10.0%	10.0%
with Germany	10.0%	0.0%	0.0%
with United States	10.0%	0.0%	0.0%
Withholding taxes on royalties:			
with Japan	0.0%	10.0%	10.0%
with Germany	10.0%	0.0%	0.0%
with United States	10.0%	0.0%	0.0%

* Substantial holdings" for the United States applies only to intercorporate dividend payments. In Germany and Japan, "substantial holdings" applies to corporate shareholders of greater than 25%.

Source: Price Waterhouse Coopers, *Corporate Taxes: A Worldwide Summary,* Information Guide, 1999 edition.

Worldwide approach. The *worldwide approach*, also referred to as the *residential* or *national approach*, levies taxes on the income earned by firms that are incorporated in the host country, regardless of where the income was earned (domestically or abroad). A MNE earning income both at home and abroad would therefore find its worldwide income taxed by its home country tax authorities. For example, a country like the United States taxes the income earned by firms based in the United States regardless of whether the income earned by the firm is domestic or foreign in origin. In the case of the United States, ordinary foreign-sourced income is taxed only as remitted to the parent firm. As with all questions of tax, however, numerous conditions and exceptions exist. The primary problem is that this approach does not address the income earned by foreign firms operating within the United States. Countries like the United States then apply the principle of territorial taxation to foreign firms within their legal jurisdiction, taxing all income earned by foreign firms in their borders as well.

Territorial approach. The *territorial approach*, also termed the *source approach*, focuses on the income earned by firms within the legal jurisdiction of the host country, not on the country of firm incorporation. Countries like Germany that follow the territorial approach apply taxes equally to foreign or domestic firms on income earned within the country, but in principle not on income earned outside the country. The territorial approach, like the worldwide approach, results in a major gap in coverage if resident firms earn income outside the country but are not taxed by the country in which the profits are earned. In this case, tax authorities extend tax coverage to income earned abroad if it is not currently covered by foreign tax jurisdictions. Once again, a mix of the two tax approaches is necessary for full coverage of income.

Tax deferral. If the worldwide approach to international taxation were followed to the letter, it would end the *tax-deferral* privilege for many MNEs. Foreign subsidiaries of MNEs pay host country corporate income taxes, but many parent countries defer claiming additional income taxes on that foreign-source income until it is remitted to the parent firm. For example, U.S. corporate income taxes on some types of foreign-source income of U.S.-owned subsidiaries incorporated abroad are deferred until the earnings are remitted to the U.S. parent. However, the ability to defer corporate income taxes is highly restricted and has been the subject of many tax law changes in the past three decades.

Tax Treaties

A network of bilateral tax treaties, many of which are modeled after one proposed by the Organization for Economic Cooperation and Development (OECD), provides a means of reducing double taxation. Tax treaties normally define whether taxes are to be imposed on income earned in one country by the nationals of another, and if so, how. Tax treaties are bilateral, with the two signatories specifying what rates are applicable to which types of income between themselves alone. Exhibit 17.1's specification of withholding taxes on dividends, interest, and royalty payments between resident corporations of Japan, Germany, and the United States is a classic example of the structure of tax treaties. Note that Germany, for example, imposes a 10% withholding tax on royalty payments to Japanese investors, while royalty payments to U.S. investors are withheld at a 0% rate.

The individual bilateral tax jurisdictions as specified through tax treaties are particularly important for firms that are primarily exporting to another country rather than doing business there through a "permanent establishment." The latter would be the case for manufacturing operations. A firm that only exports would not want any of its other worldwide income taxed by the importing country. Tax treaties define "permanent establishment" and what constitutes a limited presence for tax purposes.

Tax treaties also typically result in reduced withholding tax rates between the two signatory countries, the negotiation of the treaty itself serving as a forum for opening and expanding business relationships between the two countries. This practice is important both to MNEs operating through foreign subsidiaries, earning *active income*, and to individual portfolio investors who are simply receiving *passive income* in the form of dividends, interest, or royalties.

Tax Types

Taxes are classified on the basis of whether they are applied directly to income, called *direct taxes*, or to some other measurable performance characteristic of the firm, called *indirect taxes*. Exhibit 17.2 illustrates the wide range of corporate tax rates in the world today.

Exhibit 17.2 Corporate Tax Rates in Selected Countries (Percentage of Taxable Income)

Country	Tax Rate	Country	Tax Rate	Country	Tax Rate
Antigua and Barbuda	40	Greece	35	Philippines	35
Argentina	30	Guatemala	30	Poland	40
Australia	36	Guyana	45	Portugal	36
Austria	34	Honduras	35	Puerto Rico	20
Azerbaijan	25	Hong Kong	16.5	Qatar	35
Bahamas	0	Hungary	18u/23d	Romania	38
Bahrain	0	India	40	Russian Federation	35?
Barbados	40	Indonesia	30	St. Lucia	33.33
Belgium	39	Ireland	38	Saudi Arabia	45
Belize	35	Isle of Man	20	Singapore	26
Bermuda	0	Italy	37	South Africa	35
Bolivia	25	Ivory Coast	35	Spain	35
Bophutswana	40	Jamaica	33.3	Sri Lanka	35
Botswana	15nm/5m	Japan	37.5	Swaziland	37.5
Brazil	15	Kazakhstan	30	Sweden	28
British Virgin Islands	1/15	Kenya	35	Switzerland	22-46
Brunei Darussalam	30	Korea	28	Taiwan	25
Bulgaria	40	Kuwait	55	Tanzania	35
Cameroon	38.5	Latvia	25	Thailand	30
Canada	38	Liechtenstein	20	Trinidad and Tobago	35
Cayman Islands	0	Lithuania	29	Turkey	25 + 10/20
Channel Islands	20	Luxembourg	33	Uganda	30
Channel Islands, Jersey	20	Malawi	38	United Kingdom	33
Chile	15/35	Malaysia	30	United States	35
China	30	Malta	35	Uruguay	30/30w
Colombia	35	Mauritius	35	Venezuela	34
Congo	49	Mexico	34	Vietnam	25
Costa Rica	30	Morocco	35	Zaire	50
Cote d'Ivoire	35	Namibia	35	Zambia	35
Cyprus	25	Netherlands	35	Zimbabwe	37.5
Czech Republic	39	Netherlands Antilles	39		
Denmark	34	New Caledonia	30		
Dominican Republic	25	New Zealand	33		
Ecuador	25	Nicaragua	30		
Egypt	40	Nigeria	30		
El Salvador	25	Norway	28		
Estonia	26	Oman	50f/7.5r		

Exhibit 17.2 (continued)

Country	Tax Rate	Country	Tax Rate
Fiji	35	Pakistan	35p/30
Finland	28	Panama	34
France	33.33	Papua New Guinea	25r/48nr/50p/35m
Gabon	40	Paraguay	30
Germany	30d/45u	Peru	30
Ghana	35		

Notes: Botswana rates depend on manufacturing (*m*) or non-manufacturing (*nm*). British Virgin Islands assess a 1% tax on foreign-source income of incorporate companies. *d* rate applies to distributed profits, *u* to undistributed profits (e.g., Germany and Hungary). Chile imposes a 35% withholding tax on income remitted to foreign residents from domestic operations. Oman tax rates vary depending on the percentage of capital invested held by foreigners (*f* if over 65%, falling to a minimum tax with 100% Omani ownership). Pakistan charges one rate for publicly traded companies (*p*) and a second rate for all other non-banking companies. Papua New Guinea charges different tax rates depending on residents (*r*), non-residents (*nr*), petroleum companies (*p*), and mining companies (*m*); there is no tax on undistributed profits. Turkey assesses a 25% corporate tax plus an additional withholding tax on distributed profits depending on public or private ownership. Uruguay imposes an additional withholding tax on profits remitted to foreign residents. Representative rates shown only. For actual tax liability calculations, see original source.

Source: PriceWaterhouseCoopers, *Corporate Taxes: A Worldwide Summary*, Information Guide, 1999 edition.

Income tax. Many governments rely on income taxes, both personal and corporate, for their primary revenue source. Corporate income taxes are widely used today. Some countries impose different corporate tax rates on distributed and undistributed income, as in the case of Germany in Exhibit 17.1. Corporate income tax rates vary over a relatively wide range, rising as high as 55% in Kuwait and falling as low as 16.5% in Hong Kong, 15% in the British Virgin Islands, and effectively 0% in a number of offshore tax havens (discussed later in this chapter).

Withholding tax. Passive income (dividends, interest, royalties) earned by a resident of one country within the tax jurisdiction of a second country are normally subject to a withholding tax in the second country. The reason for the institution of withholding taxes is actually quite simple: Governments recognize that most international investors will not file a tax return in each country in which they invest, and the government therefore wishes to ensure that it receives a minimum tax payment. As the term "withholding" implies, the corporation withholds taxes from the payment made to the investor and then turns them over to government authorities. Withholding taxes, a major subject of bilateral tax treaties, generally range between 0% and 25%.

Value-added tax. One type of tax that has achieved great prominence is the *value-added tax*. The value-added tax is a type of national sales tax collected at each stage of production or sale of consumption goods in proportion to the value added during that stage. In general, production goods such as plant and equipment have not been subject to the value-added tax. Certain basic necessities such as medicines and other health-related expenses, education and religious activities, and the postal service are usually exempt or taxed at lower rates. The value-added tax has been adopted as the main source of revenue from indirect taxation by all members of the European Union, most other countries in Western Europe, a number of Latin American countries, Canada, and scattered other countries. A numerical example of value-added tax computation is shown in Exhibit 17.3.

Exhibit 17.3 Value-Added Tax Applied to the Sale of a Wooden Fence Post

This is an example of how a wooden fence post would be assessed for value-added taxes in the course of its production and subsequent sale. A value-added tax of 10% is assumed.

Step 1. The original tree owner sells to the lumber mill, for $0.20, that part of a tree that ultimately becomes the fence post. The grower has added $0.20 in value up to this point by planting and raising the tree. While collecting $0.20 from the lumber mill, the grower must set aside $0.02 to pay the value-added tax to the government.

Step 2. The lumber mill processes the tree into fence posts and sells each post for $0.40 to the lumber wholesaler. The lumber mill has added $0.20 in value ($0.40 less $0.20) through its processing activities. Therefore the lumber mill owner must set aside $0.02 to pay the mill's value-added tax to the government. In practice, the owner would probably calculate the mill's tax liability as 10% of $0.40, or $0.04, with a tax credit of $0.02 for the value-added tax already paid by the tree owner.

Steps 3 and 4. The lumber wholesaler and retailer also add value to the fence post through their selling and distribution activities. They are assessed $0.01 and $0.03 respectively, making the cumulative value-added tax collected by the government $0.08, or 10% of the final sales price.

Stage of production	Sales price	Value added	Value-added tax at 10%	Cumulative value-added tax
Tree owner	$0.20	$0.20	$0.02	$0.02
Lumber mill	$0.40	$0.20	$0.02	$0.04
Lumber wholesaler	$0.50	$0.10	$0.01	$0.05
Lumber retailer	$0.80	$0.30	$0.03	$0.08

Other national taxes. There are a variety of other national taxes, which vary in importance from country to country. The *turnover tax* (tax on the purchase or sale of securities in some country stock markets) and the *tax on undistributed profits* were mentioned before. *Property* and *inheritance taxes*, also termed *transfer taxes*, are imposed in a variety of ways to achieve social redistribution of income and wealth as much as to raise revenue. A number of red-tape charges for public services are in reality user taxes. Sometimes foreign exchange purchases or sales are in effect hidden taxes, inasmuch as the government earns revenue rather than just regulating imports and exports for balance of payments reasons.

Foreign Tax Credits

To prevent double taxation of the same income, most countries grant a *foreign tax credit* for income taxes paid to the host country. Countries differ on how they calculate the foreign tax credit and what kinds of limitations they place on the total amount claimed. Normally foreign tax credits are also available for withholding taxes paid to other countries on dividends, royalties, interest, and other income remitted to the parent. The value-added tax and other sales taxes are not eligible for a foreign tax credit, but are typically deductible from pretax income as an expense.

A *tax credit* is a direct reduction of taxes that would otherwise be due and payable. It differs from a *deductible expense*, which is an expense the taxpayer uses to reduce taxable income before the tax rate is applied. A \$100 tax credit reduces taxes payable by the full \$100, whereas a \$100 deductible expense reduces taxable income by \$100 and taxes payable by $\$100 \times t$, where t is the tax rate. Tax credits are more valuable on a dollar-for-dollar basis than are deductible expenses.

If there were no credits for foreign taxes paid, sequential taxation by the host government and then by the home government would result in a very high cumulative tax rate. To illustrate, assume the wholly owned foreign subsidiary of a MNE earns \$10,000 before local income taxes and pays a dividend equal to all its after-tax income. The host country income tax rate is 30%, and the tax rate of the home country of the parent is 35%. For simplicity, we will assume no withholding taxes. Total taxation with and without allowances for tax credits is shown in Exhibit 17.4.

If tax credits are not allowed, sequential levying of both a 30% host country tax and then a 35% home country tax on the income that remains results in an effective 54.5% tax, a cumulative rate that would render many MNEs uncompetitive with single-country local firms. The effect of allowing tax credits is to limit total taxation on the original before-tax income to no more than the highest single rate among jurisdictions. In the case depicted in Exhibit 17.4, the effective overall tax rate of 35% with foreign tax credits is equivalent to the higher tax rate of the home country (and is the tax rate payable if the income had been earned at home).

The \$500 of additional home country tax under the tax credit system in Exhibit 17.4 is the amount needed to bring total taxation (\$3,000 already paid plus the additional \$500) up to but not beyond 35% of the original \$10,000 of before-tax foreign income.

U.S. Taxation of Foreign Source Income

As we noted previously, the United States applies the *worldwide approach* to international taxation to U.S. multinationals operating globally, but the *territorial approach* to foreign firms operating within its borders. This second part of the chapter focuses on how U.S. tax authorities tax the foreign source income of U.S.-based multinationals.

Exhibit 17.4 Foreign Tax Credits

	Without foreign tax credits	With foreign tax credits
Before-tax foreign income	\$10,000	\$10,000
Less foreign tax at 30%	– 3,000	– 3,000
Available to parent and paid as dividend	\$ 7,000	\$ 7,000
Less additional parent-country tax at 35%	–2,450	
Less incremental tax (after credits)		– 500
Profit after all taxes	\$ 4,550	\$ 6,500
Total taxes, both jurisdictions	\$ 5,450	\$ 3,500
Effective overall tax rate (total taxes paid ÷ foreign income)	54.5%	35.0%

U.S. Calculation of Foreign Tax Credits

Dividends received from U.S. corporate subsidiaries are fully taxable in the United States at U.S. tax rates but with credit allowed for direct taxes paid on income in a foreign country. The amount of foreign tax allowed as a credit depends on five tax parameters:

1. Foreign corporate income tax rate
2. U.S. corporate income tax rate
3. Foreign corporate dividend withholding tax rate for nonresidents (per the applicable bilateral tax treaty between the specific country and the United States)
4. Proportion of ownership held by the U.S. corporation in the foreign firm
5. Proportion of net income distributed; i.e., the dividend payout rate

The five cases depicted in Exhibit 17.5 are based on a foreign subsidiary of a U.S. corporation that earns $10,000 before local taxes. The U.S. corporate income tax rate is 35%. The foreign tax rate is 30% in Cases 1 through 4 and 40% in Case 5.

Case 1: Foreign subsidiary with 100% payout (no withholding tax). Assuming the foreign subsidiary earns $10,000 before local taxes in its overall tax basket, it pays $3,000 in foreign taxes (30% foreign tax rate) and distributes all $7,000 in net income to its U.S. parent (100% payout rate). Because there are no withholding taxes, the U.S. parent receives a net remittance of the full $7,000.

The U.S. parent corporation takes the full before-tax foreign income of the foreign corporation—apportioned by its proportional ownership in the foreign corporation (in this case, 100%)—into its taxable income. This is called *grossing up*.

The U.S. parent then calculates a tentative U.S. tax against the grossed-up foreign income. Assuming a 35% U.S. tax rate, the tentative U.S. tax on a grossed-up income of $10,000 is $3,500. The U.S. parent is then entitled under U.S. tax law to reduce this U.S. tax liability by a *deemed-paid foreign tax credit* for taxes already paid on the same income in the foreign country. The deemed-paid tax credit is calculated as follows:

$$\text{deemed-paid credit} = \frac{\text{dividends received (including withholding tax)} \times \text{creditable foreign taxes}}{\text{after-tax net profits of the foreign corporation}}$$

Creditable taxes are foreign income taxes paid on earnings by a foreign corporation that has paid a dividend to a qualifying U.S. corporation. In order to qualify, a U.S. corporation must own at least 10% of the voting power of the distributing foreign corporation.

The deemed-paid credit in Case 1 is calculated as follows:

$$\text{deemed-paid credit} = \frac{\$7{,}000 \times \$3{,}000}{\$7{,}000} = \$3{,}000$$

The U.S. parent owes an additional $500 in U.S. taxes ($3,500 tentative U.S. tax less the deemed-paid credit of $3,000). The after-tax income earned by the U.S. parent corporation is $6,500, and the overall tax rate on the foreign income is 35% (total taxes of $3,500 on total income of $10,000). Note that although the foreign corporate tax rate was lower (30% to the U.S. 35% rate), the U.S. corporation ends up paying the higher effective rate.

Exhibit 17.5 U.S. Taxation of Foreign Source Income

	A	B	C	D	E	F
1	Exhibit 17.5 U.S. Taxation of Foreign-Source Income					
2	**Baseline Values**	**Case 1**	**Case 2**	**Case 3**	**Case 4**	**Case 5**
3	Foreign corporate income tax rate	30%	30%	30%	30%	40%
4	U.S. corporate income tax rate	35%	35%	35%	35%	35%
5	Foreign dividend witholding tax rate	0%	10%	10%	10%	10%
6	U.S. ownership in foreign firm	100%	100%	100%	40%	40%
7	Dividend payout rate of foreign firm	100%	100%	50%	50%	50%
8	**Foreign Subsidiary Tax Computation**					
9	Taxable income of foreign subsidiary	$ 10,000	$ 10,000	$ 10,000	$ 10,000	$ 10,000
10	Less foreign corporate income tax	$ 3,000	$ 3,000	$ 3,000	$ 3,000	$ 4,000
11	Net income available for distribution	$ 7,000	$ 7,000	$ 7,000	$ 7,000	$ 6,000
12	Retained earnings	$ -	$ -	$ 3,500	$ 3,500	$ 3,000
13	Distributed earnings	$ 7,000	$ 7,000	$ 3,500	$ 3,500	$ 3,000
14	Distribution to U.S. parent company	$ 7,000	$ 7,000	$ 3,500	$ 1,400	$ 1,200
15	Withholding taxes on dividends	$ -	$ 700	$ 350	$ 140	$ 120
16	Net remittance to U.S. parent	$ 7,000	$ 6,300	$ 3,150	$ 1,260	$ 1,080
17	**U.S. Corporate Tax Computation on Foreign-Source Income**					
18	Dividend received (before withholding)	$ 7,000	$ 7,000	$ 3,500	$ 1,400	$ 1,200
19	Add-back foreign deemed-paid tax	$ 3,000	$ 3,000	$ 1,500	$ 600	$ 800
20	Grossed-up foreign dividend	$ 10,000	$ 10,000	$ 5,000	$ 2,000	$ 2,000
21	Tentative U.S. tax liability	$ 3,500	$ 3,500	$ 1,750	$ 700	$ 700
22	Less credit for foreign taxes					
23	Foreign income taxes paid	$ 3,000	$ 3,000	$ 1,500	$ 600	$ 800
24	Foreign withholding taxes paid	$ -	$ 700	$ 350	$ 140	$ 120
25	Total	$ 3,000	$ 3,700	$ 1,850	$ 740	$ 920
26	Additional U.S. taxes due	$ 500	$ -	$ -	$ -	$ -
27	Excess foreign tax credits	$ -	$ 200	$ 100	$ 40	$ 220
28	After-tax income from foreign subsidiary	$ 6,500	$ 6,300	$ 3,150	$ 1,260	$ 1,080
29	**Tax Burden Measurement**					
30	Total taxes paid on remitted income	$ 3,500	$ 3,700	$ 1,850	$ 740	$ 920
31	Effective tax rate on foreign income	35%	37%	37%	37%	46%
32	**Key Cell Entries**					
33	Entries in Column B are to be copied across to Columns C, D, E, and F					
34	B10: =B9*B3	B21: =B20*B4				
35	B11: =B9—B10	B23: =B19				
36	B12: =B11*(1—B7)	B24: =B15				
37	B13: =B11*B7	B25: =SUM(B23:B24)				
38	B14: =B13*B6	B26: =IF(B21>B25,B21—B25,0)				
39	B15: =B14*B5	B27: =IF(B21<B25,B25—B21,0)				
40	B16: =B14—B15	B28: =B20—B25—B26				
41	B18: =B14	B30: =B21+B27				
42	B19: =(B14/B11)*B10	B31: =B30/B20				
43	B20: =SUM(B18:B19)					

Case 2: Foreign subsidiary with 100% payout (10% withholding tax). Assume that the same foreign corporation earns the same income, but now all dividends paid to the U.S. parent corporation are subject to a 10% withholding tax. All other values remain the same as in Case 1.

Although the actual net remittance to the U.S. parent is now lower—\$6,300 instead of \$7,000—the U.S. parent calculates the tentative U.S. tax on a grossed-up dividend of \$7,000.

The tentative U.S. tax liability is again \$3,500. The U.S. corporation can now deduct the amount of the deemed-paid credit (\$3,000) and the full amount of withholding tax (\$700) from its U.S. tax liability. Because the total foreign tax credits of \$3,700 are greater than the tentative U.S. tax of \$3,500, the U.S. parent owes no additional U.S. taxes. The U.S. parent has, in fact, an *excess foreign tax credit* of \$200 (\$3,700 – \$3,500), which it can carry back two years or carry forward five years. The effective foreign tax rate is now 37% as a result of paying higher taxes abroad than would theoretically have been paid at home, including the withholding tax.

Case 3: Foreign subsidiary with 50% payout (10% withholding tax). In this case, we assume that all tax rates remain the same, but the foreign subsidiary chooses to pay out only 50% of net income rather than 100%. As a result, all dividends, withholding taxes, deemed-paid credits, tentative U.S. tax liabilities, foreign tax credits, after-tax income from the foreign subsidiary, and finally total taxes paid are cut in half. The overall effective tax rate is again 37%, higher than what would theoretically have been paid if the income had been earned inside rather than outside the United States.

Case 4: Foreign subsidiary with 50% payout (10% withholding tax). Case 4 illustrates the degree to which these cash flows change when the U.S. parent corporation owns only 40% of the foreign corporation. As illustrated in Exhibit 17.5, the 40% ownership acts only as a "scale factor" in apportioning dividends paid, withholding tax withheld, and tax liabilities and credits resulting. Once again, the U.S. parent corporation has excess foreign tax credits as a result of paying more taxes abroad than it is liable for at home. The overall effective tax rate on the reduced after-tax net income for the foreign subsidiary of \$1,400 is 37%.

Case 5: Foreign subsidiary with 50% payout (40% foreign corporate tax, 10% withholding tax). This fifth and final case illustrates the increasing tax burden on the U.S. parent corporation when the corporate income tax in the foreign country is higher than that in the United States. The combination of a 40% foreign income tax and a 10% withholding tax, even after calculation of deemed-paid foreign tax credits, results in a rising excess foreign tax credit and a substantially higher effective tax rate of 46%. Clearly, when the implications of Case 5 are combined with the number of countries with corporate tax rates higher than that of the United States (see Exhibit 17.1), the tax burden borne by U.S.-based MNEs is a significant competitive concern.

Excess Foreign Tax Credits

If a U.S.-based MNE receives income from a foreign country that imposes higher corporate income taxes than the United States (or combined income and withholding tax), total creditable taxes will exceed U.S. taxes on that foreign income. The result is *excess foreign tax credits.* All firms wish to manage their tax liabilities globally, however, so that they do not end up paying more on foreign-sourced income than they do on domestically sourced income. The proper management of global taxes is not simple, however, and combines three different components: 1) foreign tax credit limitations, 2) tax credit carry-forward/carry-back, and 3) foreign tax averaging.

Foreign tax credit limitation. The amount of credit a taxpayer can use in any year is limited to the U.S. tax on that foreign income. Foreign tax credits cannot be used to reduce taxes levied on domestic income. The total foreign tax creditable in any one year is limited according to the following formula:

$$\text{creditable tax limit} = \frac{\text{total foreign taxable income}}{\text{total taxable income}} \times \text{U.S. tax on total income}$$

This requires the consideration not only of foreign source income, but also of the U.S. tax liabilities associated with the firm's domestic income.

Tax credit carryforward/carryback. Excess foreign tax credits, like domestic tax credits, can be carried forward five years and carried back two years against similar tax liabilities. Unfortunately, since excess foreign tax credits arise from tax differentials, and tax rates typically change slowly, a firm experiencing an excess foreign tax credit one year may experience it year after year.

Tax averaging. The good news is that under U.S. tax law it is possible to offset foreign tax credits derived from one source against foreign tax liabilities from another source, assuming they are derived from the same type of income. This is termed *tax averaging*. In principle, this means that if income is derived from a high-tax country, creating excess foreign tax credits, these credits can in turn be used against a deficit foreign tax credit position formed from repatriating income from a low-tax country.

The primary obstacle to tax averaging is the inability to average across different categories or "baskets" of income. The U.S. tax code specifies a *general limitation income basket*. This is the basket that includes the majority of income derived by U.S. corporations abroad, such as manufacturing, services, and sales income. The U.S. tax code specifies eight other baskets of income into which foreign-source income may fall. For example, a U.S.-based firm cannot average deficit foreign tax credits on active income from a low-tax country against excess foreign tax credits on passive income from a high-tax country. This basket limitation provides fewer incentives for MNEs to position certain types of profits in low-tax countries. Many countries, however, do not restrict the use of foreign tax credits by income category or choose to ignore foreign-source income altogether.

Tax Management at Carlton

Carlton is considering acquiring a profitable telecommunications manufacturing company in Brazil and naming it Carlton Brazil. As part of her due diligence activities, Caitlin Kelly is examining the tax implications of paying dividends to Carlton from its existing subsidiary, Carlton Germany, and simultaneously paying dividends to Carlton from Carlton Brazil.

Exhibit 17.6 summarizes the key tax management issue for Carlton when remitting dividend income back to the United States from Carlton Europe and Carlton Brazil:

- Because corporate income tax rates in Germany (40%) are higher than those in the United States (35%), dividends remitted to the U.S. parent result in excess foreign tax credits. Any applicable withholding taxes on dividends between Germany and the U.S. only increase the amount of the excess foreign tax credit.
- Because corporate income tax rates in Brazil (25%) are lower than those in the United States (35%), dividends remitted to the U.S. parent result in *deficit* foreign tax credits. If there are withholding taxes applied to the dividends by Brazil on remittances to the U.S., this will reduce the size of the deficit but not eliminate it.

Exhibit 17.6 Carlton's Tax Management of Foreign-Source Income

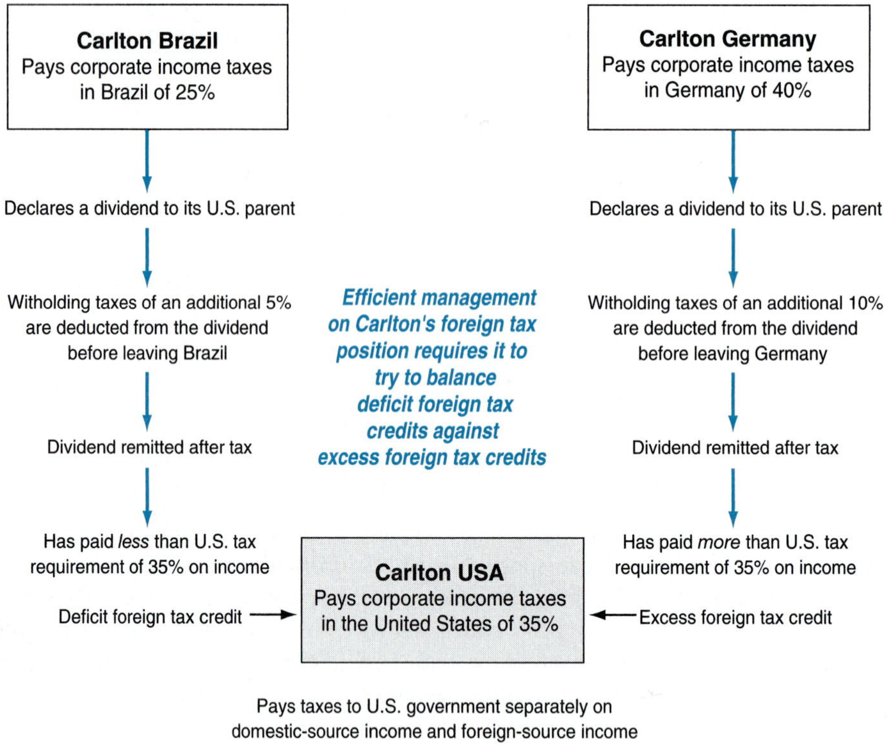

Carlton's management would like to manage the two dividend remittances in order to match the deficits with the credits. The most straightforward method of doing this is to adjust the amount of dividend distributed from each foreign subsidiary so that, after all applicable income and withholding taxes have been applied, Carlton's excess foreign tax credits from Carlton Europe (Germany) exactly match the excess foreign tax deficits from Carlton Brazil. There are a number of other methods of managing the global tax liabilities of Carlton, so-called *repositioning of funds*, which are examined in detail in Chapter 21.

Controlled Foreign Corporations and Subpart F Income

The rule that U.S. shareholders do not pay U.S. taxes on foreign-source income until that income is remitted to the United States was amended in 1962 by the creation of special *Subpart F income.* The revision was designed to prevent the use of arrangements between operating companies and base companies located in tax havens as a means of deferring U.S. taxes and to encourage greater repatriation of foreign incomes.

Subpart F income is subject to immediate U.S. taxation *even when not remitted.* It is income of a type otherwise easily shifted offshore to avoid current taxation. It includes 1) passive income received by the foreign corporation such as dividends, interest, rents, royalties, net foreign currency gains, net commodities gains, and income from the sale of non-income-producing property; 2) income from the insurance of U.S. risks; 3) financial service income; 4) shipping income; 5) oil-related income; and 6) certain related-party sales and service income. Immediate taxation of Subpart F income significantly reduces the potential for U.S. MNEs to abuse the foreign-source income tax deferral privilege.

Branch Versus Locally Incorporated Subsidiary

A MNE normally has a choice whether to organize a foreign subsidiary as a branch of the parent or as a local corporation. Both tax and nontax consequences must be considered. Nontax factors include the locus of legal liability, public image in the host country, managerial incentive considerations, and local legal and political requirements.

One major tax consideration is whether the foreign subsidiary is expected to run at a loss for several years after start-up. If so, it might be preferable to organize originally as a branch operation to permit these anticipated losses to be consolidated in the parent's income statement for tax purposes. For example, tax laws in the United States and many other countries do not permit a foreign corporation to be consolidated for tax purposes, even though it is consolidated for reporting purposes, but do permit consolidation of foreign branches for tax purposes.

A second tax consideration is the net tax burden after paying withholding taxes on dividends. A MNE must weigh the benefit of potential tax deferral of home country taxes on foreign-source income from a fully incorporated foreign subsidiary against the total tax burden of paying foreign corporate income taxes and withholding taxes once the income is distributed to the parent corporation. A foreign branch would pay income taxes to the host country but no withholding taxes when the after-tax income is distributed to its parent.

Foreign Sales Corporations

Over the years, the United States has introduced into U.S. tax laws special incentives dealing with international operations. To benefit from these incentives, a firm may have to form separate corporations for qualifying and nonqualifying activities. The most important U.S. special corporation is a *foreign sales corporation* (*FSC*). FSCs were introduced in the Tax Reform Act of 1984 as a device to provide tax-exempt income for U.S. persons or corporations having export-oriented activities. *Exempt foreign trade income* of an FSC is not subject to U.S. income taxes. Exempt foreign trade income is income from foreign sources that is not effectively connected with the conduct of a trade or business within the United States. Exempt income is limited to 34% of the FSC's total trade income. Exhibit 17.7 illustrates the basic mechanics of how FSCs are used to reduce U.S. tax liabilities on export sales.

A FSC's total foreign trade income is derived from gross receipts from the sale of export property, lease or rental of export property, incidental services provided with the sale or lease of export property, and fees for engineering, architectural, or managerial services. The exempt portion of the FSC's total foreign trade income depends upon the pricing rules used. *Export property* is manufactured, produced, grown, or extracted from the United States by an entity other than the FSC and is sold, leased, or rented outside the United States.

Exhibit 17.7 Foreign Sales Corporations (FSCs)

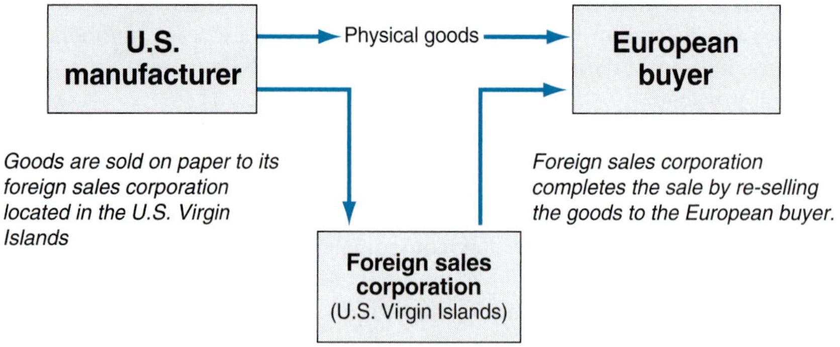

1. The payment by the European buyer is routed through the FSC. The FSC may charge the U.S. parent a commission, or simply pass the full payment on.
2. The tax benefits arise from the fact that up to 34% of the paper profits of the resale are excluded from U.S. taxation.
3. When the FSC pays a dividend to its parent on its profits, the dividend is not taxed by the U.S. tax authorities.

In 1999, the World Trade Organization (WTO) ruled that FSCs were an illegal subsidy worth billions of dollars to thousands of U.S. exporters. Although it is unlikely that FSCs will be discontinued, their role in aiding U.S.-based exporters is increasingly controversial.

Possessions Corporation

A business carried on to a substantial extent in a U.S. possession can be carried on by a separate U.S. corporation, which, if it meets the requirements for a *possessions corporation*, is not subject to U.S. tax on income earned outside the United States unless the income is *received* in the United States. Although technically a U.S. corporation, a possessions corporation is treated like a foreign corporation in nearly every respect. The U.S. pharmaceutical industry, specifically, has made heavy use of Puerto Rican possessions corporations.

Requirements. To qualify as a possessions corporation, a corporation must satisfy the following requirements:

1. It is a domestic U.S. corporation.
2. At least 80% of its gross income is derived from within a U.S. possession.
3. At least 75% of its gross income is derived from the active conduct of a trade or business in a U.S. possession.

Exclusion from gross income. A corporation meeting the previous requirements excludes from U.S. gross income amounts earned outside the United States unless the income is received in the

United States. Thus a possessions corporation should arrange to receive income initially outside the United States, although it may subsequently transfer it from a foreign bank account to a bank account in the United States.

The possessions corporation's income is subject to U.S. tax, but a tax-sparing credit is allowed for U.S. taxes on foreign-source income attributable to the conduct of a trade or business in a U.S. possession and qualified possessions-source investment income. The net result is that nonqualified income is subject to U.S. tax, but possessions income is exempt from tax. The income qualifying for this credit is as follows:

- Income from foreign sources that is attributable to the conduct of a trade or business in a possession.
- Qualified possessions-source investment income that is defined as investment income a) from sources within the possession in which the business is carried on, and b) which the taxpayer establishes is attributable to the funds derived from the business or investment in such possession.

Other investment is taxable in the United States on a current basis. No foreign tax credit is available to possessions corporations except to the extent that a foreign tax is imposed on income subject to U.S. tax but not eligible for the tax-sparing credit. For the U.S. parent company of a possessions corporation, foreign taxes paid with respect to distributions from the possessions subsidiary are neither creditable nor deductible.

Dividends from possessions corporations are eligible for the 100% or 85% dividends-received deduction, regardless of when the income was earned. Thus accumulated earnings from prior years can be repatriated by the possessions corporation to the U.S. parent with little or no U.S. tax.

U.S. Taxation Summary Points

Exhibit 17.8 provides an overview of the primary tax issues facing a U.S.-based MNE:

- *Domestic-source income* and *foreign-source income* are separated. Tax credits or deficits in one category cannot be applied to net positions in the other category.
- Foreign-source income is separated into *active* and *passive* categories. Active income is taxed by U.S. tax authorities only as it is remitted to the U.S. parent. Passive income is taxed as it is earned, regardless of whether it is remitted to the U.S. parent.
- If the remittance of active income from one subsidiary results in an excess foreign tax credit, and the remittance from a second subsidiary results in a foreign tax deficit, the credit may be applied to the deficit if the incomes are of the same "basket" under U.S. tax law.

Although multinational taxation is complex, the global management of tax liabilities is one of the most important financial management tasks facing any MNE. A multinational enterprise that effectively manages its global tax liabilities by reducing its global tax payments creates shareholder value.

Tax-Haven Subsidiaries and International Offshore Financial Centers

Many MNEs have foreign subsidiaries that act as tax havens for corporate funds awaiting reinvestment or repatriation. Tax-haven subsidiaries, categorically referred to as international offshore financial centers, are partially a result of tax-deferral features on earned foreign income allowed by

Exhibit 17.8 U.S. Taxation of a U.S.-Based Multinational Enterprise

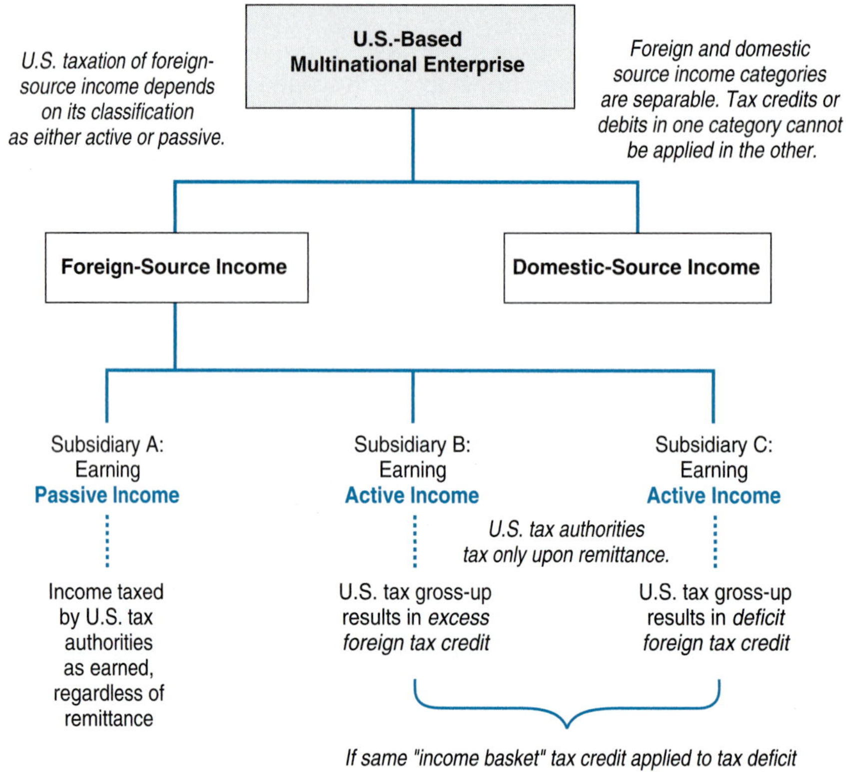

some of the parent countries. Tax-haven subsidiaries are typically established in a country that can meet the following requirements:

- A low tax on foreign investment or sales income earned by resident corporations and a low dividend withholding tax on dividends paid to the parent firm.
- A stable currency to permit easy conversion of funds into and out of the local currency. This requirement can be met by permitting and facilitating the use of Eurocurrencies.
- The facilities to support financial services; for example, good communications, professional qualified office workers, and reputable banking services.
- A stable government that encourages the establishment of foreign-owned financial and service facilities within its borders.

Exhibit 17.9 provides a map of most of the world's major offshore financial centers. The typical tax-haven subsidiary owns the common stock of its related operating foreign subsidiaries, and its equity is typically 100% owned by the parent firm. There might be several tax-haven subsidiaries scat-

Exhibit 17.9 International Offshore Financial Centers

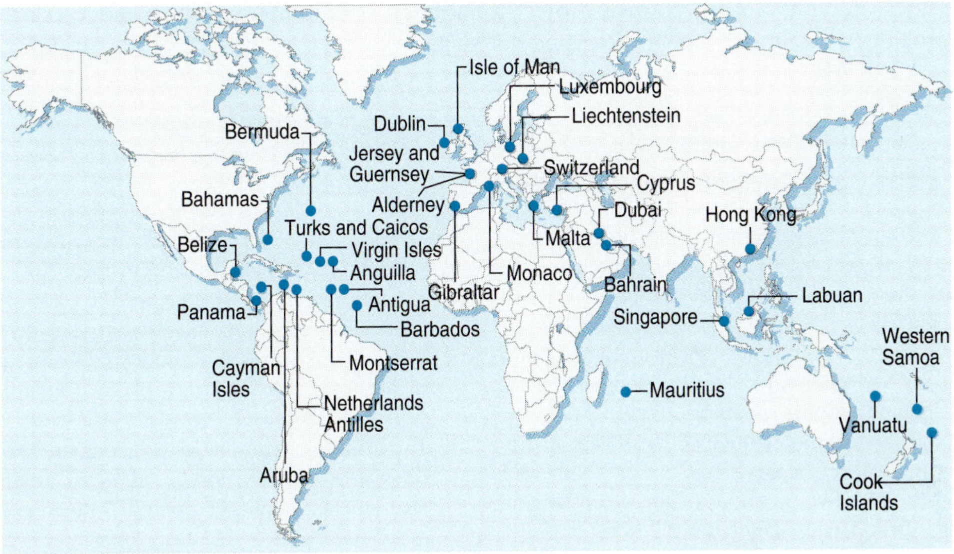

tered around the world. All transfers of funds might go through the tax-haven subsidiaries, including dividends and equity financing. Thus the parent country's tax on foreign-source income, which might normally be paid when a dividend is declared by a foreign subsidiary, could continue to be deferred until the tax-haven subsidiary itself pays a dividend to the parent firm. This event can be postponed indefinitely if foreign operations continue to grow and require new internal financing from the tax-haven subsidiary. Thus MNEs are able to operate a corporate pool of funds for foreign operations without having to repatriate foreign earnings through the parent country's tax machine.

For U.S. MNEs, the tax-deferral privilege of operating through a foreign subsidiary was not originally a tax loophole. On the contrary, it was granted by the U.S. government to allow U.S. firms to expand overseas and place them on a par with foreign competitors that also enjoy similar types of tax deferral and export subsidies of one type or another.

Unfortunately, some U.S. firms distorted the original intent of tax deferral into tax avoidance. Transfer prices on goods and services bought from or sold to related subsidiaries were artificially rigged to leave all the income from the transaction in the tax-haven subsidiary. This manipulation could be done by routing the legal title to the goods or services through the tax-haven subsidiary, even though physically the goods or services never entered the tax-haven country. This maneuver left no residual tax base for either exporting or importing subsidiaries located outside the tax-haven country. Needless to say, tax authorities of both exporting and importing countries were dismayed by the lack of taxable income in such transactions.

One purpose of the U.S. Internal Revenue Act of 1962 was to eliminate the tax advantages of these "paper" foreign corporations without destroying the tax-deferral privilege for those foreign manufacturing and sales subsidiaries that were established for business and economic rather than tax motives. Although the tax motive has been removed, some firms have found these subsidiaries useful as finance control centers for foreign operations. Global Finance Perspective 17.1 provides a categorization of the primary activities of offshore financial centers today.

Global Finance Perspective 17.1

The Activities of Offshore Financial Centers

Offshore financial centers provide financial management services to foreign users in exchange for foreign exchange earnings. The comparative advantage for clients? Several, including very low tax rates, minimal administrative formalities, and confidentiality and discretion. This environment allows wealthy international clients to minimize potential tax liability while protecting income and assets from political, fiscal, and legal risks. There are many vehicles through which offshore financial services can be provided. These include the following:

- Offshore banking, which can handle foreign exchange operations for corporations or banks. These operations are not subject to capital, corporate, capital gains, dividend, or interest taxes or to exchange controls.
- International business corporations, which are often tax-exempt, limited-liability companies used to operate businesses or raise capital through issuing shares, bonds, or other instruments.
- Offshore insurance companies, which are established to minimize taxes and manage risk.
- Asset management and protection allows individuals and corporations in countries with fragile banking systems or unstable political regimes to keep assets offshore to protect against the collapse of domestic currencies and banks.
- Tax planning. Multinationals can route transactions through offshore centers to minimize taxes through transfer pricing. Individuals can make use of favorable tax regimes offered by offshore centers through trust and foundations.

The tax concessions and secrecy offered by offshore financial centers can be used for many legitimate purposes, but they have also been used for illegitimate ends, including money laundering and tax evasion.

Source: "Caribbean Centers: Stricter Rules Change Climate for Offshore Financial Centers," *IMF Survey*, International Monetary Fund, August 5, 2002, p. 252.

SUMMARY

- Nations typically structure their tax systems along one of two basic approaches: the worldwide approach or the territorial approach.
- Both approaches are attempts to determine which firms, foreign or domestic by incorporation, or which incomes, foreign or domestic in origin, are subject to the taxation of host country tax authorities.
- The worldwide approach, also referred to as the residential or national approach, levies taxes on the income earned by firms that are incorporated in the host country, regardless of where the income was earned (domestically or abroad).
- The territorial approach, also termed the source approach, focuses on the income earned by firms within the legal jurisdiction of the host country, not on the country of firm incorporation.

- A network of bilateral tax treaties, many of which are modeled after one proposed by the Organization for Economic Cooperation and Development (OECD), provides a means of reducing double taxation.
- Tax treaties normally define whether taxes are to be imposed on income earned in one country by the nationals of another, and if so, how. Tax treaties are bilateral, with the two signatories specifying what rates are applicable to which types of income between themselves alone.
- The value-added tax is a type of national sales tax collected at each stage of production or sale of consumption goods in proportion to the value added during that stage.
- The United States differentiates foreign source income from domestic source income. Each is taxed separately, and tax deficits or credits in one category may not be used against deficits or credits in the other category.
- If a U.S.-based MNE receives income from a foreign country that imposes higher corporate income taxes than the United States (or combined income and withholding tax), total creditable taxes will exceed U.S. taxes on that foreign income. The result is an excess foreign tax credit.
- All firms wish to manage their tax liabilities globally so that they do not pay more on foreign-source income than they do on domestic-source income.
- Many MNEs have foreign subsidiaries that act as tax havens for corporate funds awaiting reinvestment or repatriation. Because tax havens have the potential to be misused by MNEs and by money launderers, they are carefully watched by all countries' tax authorities.

QUESTIONS

1 **Tax morality.**

a. What is meant by the term "tax morality"?

b. Your company has a subsidiary in Russia, where tax evasion is a fine art. Discuss whether you should comply fully with Russian tax laws or violate the laws as do your local competitors.

2. **Tax neutrality.**

a. Define "tax neutrality."

b. What is the difference between *domestic neutrality* and *foreign neutrality*?

c. What are a country's objectives when determining tax policy on foreign source income?

3. **Worldwide versus territorial approach.** Nations typically structure their tax systems along one of two basic approaches: the *worldwide approach* or the *territorial approach*. Explain these two approaches and how they differ from each other.

4. **Tax deferral.**

a. What is meant by the term "tax deferral"?

b. Why do countries allow tax deferral on foreign source income?

5. **Tax treaties.**

a. What is a bilateral tax treaty?

b. What is the purpose of a bilateral tax treaty?

c. What policies do most tax treaties cover?

6. **Tax types.** Taxes are classified on the basis of whether they are applied directly to income, called *direct* taxes, or to some other measurable performance characteristic of the firm, called *indirect* taxes. Classify each of the following types of taxes as being "direct" or "indirect" or something else.

a. Corporate income tax paid by a Japanese subsidiary on its operating income

b. Royalties paid to Saudi Arabia for oil extracted and shipped to world markets

c. Interest received by a U.S. parent on bank deposits held in London

d. Interest received by a U.S. parent on a loan to a subsidiary in Mexico

e. Principal repayment received by U.S. parent from Belgium on a loan to a wholly owned subsidiary in Belgium

f. Excise tax paid on cigarettes manufactured and sold within the United States

g. Property taxes paid on the corporate headquarters building in Seattle

h. A direct contribution to the International Committee of the Red Cross for refugee relief

i. Deferred income tax, shown as a deduction on the U.S. parent's consolidated income tax

j. Withholding taxes withheld by Germany on dividends paid to a United Kingdom parent corporation

7. **Foreign tax credit.** What is a foreign tax credit? Why do countries give credit for taxes paid on foreign source income?

8. **Tax averaging.** How does tax averaging help or hinder a U.S.-based MNE in managing its global tax liabilities?

9. **Passive versus active income.** What is the difference between passive and active income?

10. **Value-added tax.**
    a. What is a value-added tax?
    b. What are the advantages and disadvantages of a value-added tax?
    c. Although the value-added tax has been proposed numerous times, the United States has never adopted one. Why do you think the United States is so negative on the value-added tax when it is widely used outside the United States?

11. **Subpart F income.** The rule that U.S. shareholders do not pay taxes on foreign source income until that income is remitted to the United States (tax deferral) was amended in 1962 by the creation of special *Subpart F income*.
    a. Why was this revision adopted?
    b. What is Subpart F income?
    c. When is Subpart F income taxed?

12. **Active income.** *Passive* income is included as Subpart F income but *active* income is not. Identify each of the following transactions as either active or passive income when received by a parent MNE.
    a. Royalties received from a wholly owned foreign subsidiary
    b. Royalties received from an unaffiliated foreign company
    c. Royalties received from a foreign branch operation
    d. Profit earned from domestic sales of items manufactured at home
    e. Profit earned from domestic sales of items imported by the parent from a subsidiary
    f. Profit earned from exports of items manufactured at home but sold to a foreign subsidiary
    g. Profit earned by the parent from sale of a building no longer needed
    h. Interest received from domestic treasury bills held by the parent for liquidity purposes
    i. Interest received from a parent loan to a wholly owned subsidiary
    j. Interest received from foreign bank deposits held by the parent as part of its international cash depository system

13. **Branch income.** Branches are often used as the organizational structure for foreign operations that are expected to lose substantial amounts of money in their first years of operation. Why would branches be preferable to wholly owned subsidiaries?

14. **Foreign sales corporation (FSC).** What is a foreign sales corporation? Why are many other countries arguing that U.S. FSCs are illegal under the World Trade Organization's current rules for the conduct of international trade?

15. **Tax haven subsidiary.**
    a. What is meant by the term "tax haven"?
    b. What are the desired characteristics for a country if it expects to be used as a tax haven?
    c. Identify five tax havens.
    d. What are the advantages leading a MNE to use a tax haven subsidiary?
    e. What are the potential distortions of a MNE's taxable income that are opposed by tax authorities in non–tax haven countries?

16. Possessions corporation.

a. Under the U.S. tax code what is a possessions corporation?

b. What are the requirements to qualify as a possessions corporation?

c. What are the advantages to a MNE that operates a possessions corporation?

PROBLEMS

1. U.S. taxation of foreign-source income. Using the structure for calculating U.S. taxes for foreign-source income from Exhibit 17.5, assume a foreign subsidiary has $3,400,000 in gross earnings, U.S. and foreign corporate income taxes are 35% and 28%, respectively, and foreign withholding taxes are 15%.

a. What is the total tax payment, foreign and domestic combined, for this income?

b. What is the effective tax rate paid on this income by the U.S.-based parent company?

c. What would be the total tax payment and effective tax rate if the foreign corporate tax rate was 45% and there were no withholding taxes on dividends?

d. What would be the total tax payment and effective tax rate if the income was earned by a branch of the U.S. corporation?

2. Discovery Bay Airlines (Hong Kong). Discovery Bay Airlines is a U.S.-based air freight firm with a wholly owned subsidiary in Hong Kong. The subsidiary, DBay-Hong Kong, has just completed a long-term planning report for the parent company in San Francisco, in which it has estimated the following expected earnings and payout rates for the years 2002–2005.

The current Hong Kong corporate tax rate on this category of income is 16.5%. Hong Kong imposes no withholding taxes on dividends remitted to U.S. investors (per the Hong Kong-United States bilateral tax treaty). The U.S. corporate income tax rate is 35%. The parent company wants to repatriate 75% of net income as dividends annually.

a. Calculate the net income available for distribution by the Hong Kong subsidiary for the years 2002–2005.

b. What is the amount of the dividend expected to be remitted to the U.S. parent each year?

c. After gross-up for U.S. tax liability purposes, what is the total dividend after tax (all Hong Kong and U.S. taxes) expected each year?

d. What is the effective tax rate on this foreign-sourced income per year?

Discovery Bay–Hong Kong (millions of U.S. dollars)	**2002**	**2003**	**2004**	**2005**
Earnings before interest and taxes (EBIT)	8,000	10,000	12,000	14,000
Less interest expenses	(800)	(1,000)	(1,200)	(1,400)
Earnings before taxes (EBT)	7,200	9,000	10,800	12,600

3. Hintz-Kessels-Kohl (Germany). Hintz-Kessels-Kohl (HKK) is a German-based company that manufactures electronic fuel-injection carburetor assemblies for several large automobile companies in Germany, including Mercedes, BMW, and Opel. The firm, like many firms in Germany today, is revising its financial policies to be in line with the increasing degree of disclosure required by firms if they wish to list their shares publicly in or out of Germany.

HKK's primary problem is that the German corporate income tax code applies a different income tax rate to income depending on whether it is retained (45%) or distributed to stockholders (30%).

Earnings before interest and taxes (EBIT)	€ 580,000,000
Less interest expenses	(96,500,000)
Earnings before taxes (EBT)	€ 483,500,000
Less corporate income taxes	________
Net income	€ ________
Retained earnings	________
Distributed earnings	________

a. If HKK planned to distribute 50% of its net income, what would be its total net income and total corporate tax bills?

b. If HKK were attempting to choose between a 40% and 60% payout rate to stockholders, what arguments and values would management use in order to convince stockholders which of the two payouts is in everyone's best interest?

4. Odessa-Kazakhstan (A). Odessa Petroleum is a U.S.-based multinational petroleum and petrochemical exploration, production, and distribution company. Odessa's subsidiary in Kazakhstan, a new promising area of petroleum exploration that is expecting a major find in the next two-year period. The tax planning staff in the corporate headquarters in the United States wish to estimate tax liabilities and effective tax burdens on this prospective income three years out.

The Kazakhstan currency, the tenge (Tg), is currently trading at Tg155/US$. Although the government claims the tenge is pegged to the dollar, the stability of the currency is highly questionable. Given that inflation in Kazakhstan has been rising (now averaging 20% per year compared to the U.S.'s 3% per year), the tax planning staff would prefer to assume that the currency is likely to weaken over the period.

The government of Kazakhstan requires all petroleum companies operating there to turn over all hard-currency earnings to the government. Since oil is sold on world markets in U.S. dollars, the Kazakhstan subsidiary's income actually begins in U.S. dollars and is then converted to local currency for tax purposes. (When the subsidiary declares a dividend to the parent company, it will have to apply to the government to obtain hard currency, U.S. dollars, for payment to the U.S. parent.)

Odessa has estimated the all-in-cost of production per barrel, as well as the estimated barrels produced, for the years 2003–2005. The forecast oil price (an average for the year), which is a company-wide forecast from the corporate headquarters, is used for projecting revenues.

Odessa-Kazakhstan	**2003**	**2004**	**2005**
Expected price per barrel (US$)	18.50	$19.50	$19.00
Estimated all-in-cost per barrel (US$)	7.50	6.25	4.50
Barrels of oil produced (expected)	1,000,000	10,000,000	15,000,000

The effective Kazakhstan income tax rate is 40% (30% corporate income plus an additional surcharge for the oil industry of 10%); the U.S. corporate tax rate is 35%. In addition, the Kazakhstan tax authorities impose a 20% withholding tax on dividends and interest remitted to foreign resident investors. Kazakhstan has no current set of bilateral tax treaties, applying the same rates to all foreign investors regardless of country of origin. The parent company plans to repatriate 50% of net income as dividends annually. Complete the following basic income statement in order to answer the following questions.

Odessa-Kazakhstan	**2003**	**2004**	**2005**
Expected revenues (US$)			
Expected revenues (Tg)			
Less all-in-production costs (Tg)			
Earnings before tax (EBT)			
Less Kazakhstan corporate income taxes			
Net income of subsidiary			
Retained earnings			
Distributed as dividend to parent			

a. Calculate the expected exchange rate for the 2003–2005 period assuming purchasing power parity.

b. Calculate the net income available for distribution by the Kazakhstan subsidiary for each year in Kazakhstan tenge.

c. What is the amount of the dividend expected to be remitted to the U.S. parent each year, after both income and withholding taxes, in U.S. dollars, assuming the U.S. tax rate is 35%?

d. After gross-up for U.S. tax liability purposes, what is the total dividend after tax (all Kazakhstan and U.S. taxes) expected each year?

e. What is the effective tax rate on this foreign-sourced income per year?

5. **Odessa-Kazakhstan (B).** Odessa Petroleum, the same U.S.-based multinational petroleum and petrochemical company described in Problem #4, has been informed that a major tax bill is about to be passed in Kazakhstan to make it a more attractive country for foreign direct investment. The tax provision will reduce the corporate income tax to 25%, eliminate the 10% petrochemical surcharge, and reduce the withholding tax in dividend payments out of the country to 5%. In addition to the tax changes, Odessa now believes that the exchange rate, regardless of inflation differentials, will remain relatively fixed for the foreseeable future. Assuming all other parameters remain the same, answer the following:

a. Calculate the net income available for distribution by the Kazakhstan subsidiary for each year in Kazakhstan tenge.

b. What is the amount of the dividend expected to be remitted to the U.S. parent each year, after both income and withholding taxes, in U.S. dollars, assuming the US tax rate is 35%?

c. After gross-up for U.S. tax liability purposes, what is the total dividend after tax (all Kazakhstan and U.S. taxes) expected each year?

d. What is the effective tax rate on this foreign-sourced income per year? How has this changed from the previous analysis (Problem 4) before the tax revisions?

6. **Gamboa's tax averaging.** Gamboa Incorporated is a relatively new U.S.-based retailer of specialty fruits and vegetables. The firm is vertically integrated with fruit and vegetable–sourcing subsidiaries in Central America and distribution outlets throughout the southeastern and northeastern regions of the United States. Gamboa's two Central American subsidiaries are in Belize and Costa Rica.

Emilia Gamboa, the daughter of the firm's founder, is being groomed to take over the firm's financial management in the near future. Like many firms of similar size, Gamboa has not possessed a very high degree of sophistication in financial management because of time and cost considerations. Emilia, however, has recently finished her MBA and is now attempting to put some specialized knowledge of U.S. taxation practices to work to save Gamboa money. Her first concern is tax averaging for foreign tax liabilities arising from the two Central American subsidiaries.

Costa Rican operations are slightly more profitable than Belize operations, which is particularly good since Costa Rica is a relatively low-tax country. Costa Rican corporate taxes are a flat 30%, and no withholding taxes are imposed on dividends paid by foreign firms with operations there. Belize has a higher corporate income tax rate, 40%, and imposes a 10% withholding tax on all dividends distributed to foreign investors. The current U.S. corporate income tax rate is 35%.

	Belize	Costa Rica
Earnings before taxes	$1,000,000	$1,500,000
Corporate income tax rate	40%	30%
Dividend withholding tax rate	10%	0%

a. If Emilia Gamboa assumes a 50% payout rate from each subsidiary, what are the additional taxes due on foreign-sourced income from Belize and Costa Rica individually?

How much in additional U.S. taxes would be due if Emilia averaged the tax credits and liabilities of the two units?

b. Keeping the payout rate from the Belize subsidiary at 50%, how should Emilia change the payout rate of the Costa Rican subsidiary in order to most efficiently manage her total foreign tax bill?

c. What is the minimum effective tax rate Emilia can achieve on her foreign-sourced income?

7. **Hazelnut, Incorporated (A).** Jerry Filbert is the vice president of tax planning for the U.S.-based firm, Hazelnut, Inc. Mr. Filbert is attempting to determine what the actual tax liabilities of Hazelnut will be for 2002, given solid forecasts of all expected values (it is now December 15, 2002). Hazelnut (U.S.) has a wholly owned manufacturing subsidiary in Cádiz, Spain.

The Spanish subsidiary, Hazelnut Cádiz, had estimated earnings before tax (EBT) in 2002 of €40 million. The earnings were of two types: manufacturing and sales of chocolate-covered hazelnut candy bars (80% of the total), and dividend income from a wholly-owned subsidiary in Switzerland (20% of the total). The average exchange rate for the year was \$1.06/€. Corporate tax rates in Spain and the United States are both 35%. Dividends distributed from Spain to the United States are subject to a 15% withholding tax. Mr. Filbert was recently told that the Spanish subsidiary will declare an end-of-year dividend of 50% of net income available for distribution.

a. What will be the amount in U.S. dollars of the net dividend remitted?

b. What will be the U.S. tax liability associated with Hazelnut Cádiz' 2002 operations?

8. **Hazelnut, Incorporated (B).** Jerry Filbert now wishes to determine what the actual tax liabilities of Hazelnut are if it creates an offshore holding company in the Cayman Islands, Hazelnut, Ltd (Cayman Islands), for the purpose of owning and operating its manufacturer of chocolate candy and nut bars manufactured in continental Europe, Hazelnut Cádiz (Spain).

The Cayman Island subsidiary would be the sole owner of the Spanish subsidiary. The Spanish subsidiary, whose books are in euros, is expected to close the year out very successfully, with a 32% gross profit margin and a net profit totaling about €1,250,000. The Spanish corporate income tax rate is 35%, with a withholding tax on dividends paid to the Cayman Islands of 25%. (Spain has no bilateral tax treaty with the Caymans resulting in the use of the withholding tax rate from the "non-treaty" category.) Mr. Filbert was a bit surprised to find that the withholding tax rate on dividends paid by Spanish companies to U.S.-based investors was only 10%. He wonders whether the firm made a mistake in restructuring the ownership to be held by the Cayman Island Holding Company.

Hazelnut Cádiz (Spain)	
Gross sales revenue	€ 18,430,000
Less cost of goods sold	(10,500,000)
Gross profit margin	€ ________
Less general and administrative expenses	________
Less depreciation	________
Less interest expense	________
Earnings before tax (EBT)	€ ________
Less corporate income taxes @ 35%	________
Net income	€ ________
Retained earnings	________
Distributed earnings	________

Hazelnut, Ltd., has no other income than the dividends and interest it earns from Hazelnut Cádiz. Its financial statements are recorded in Cayman Island dollars (CI\$). After Hazelnut, Ltd., receives its income from Cádiz, it is expected that approximately 50% of the income will be declared as a dividend back to the U.S. parent company. Current spot exchange rates are \$1.06/€, and CI\$0.83/US\$ (the latter is a fixed rate).

a. Complete the pro forma income statement for Hazelnut Cádiz above. What is the exact amount of dividends, in euros, that will be remitted to the Cayman Islands subsidiary after all taxes, including Spanish withholding taxes?

b. What is the amount of income—in Cayman Island dollars—earned by the Cayman Island subsidiary? What is the amount of income available to be distributed or retained by it?

c. What is the expected tax liability of Hazelnut (U.S.) on the earnings of the Spanish and Cayman Island subsidiaries assuming that 80% of the Spanish subsidiary's income is paid out, and 50% of the Cayman Island subsidiary's income is paid out?

9. **Ballantyne Brand Services (A).** Ballantyne Brand Services is a U.S.-based brand development and management services consultancy. It is privately held, and although now incorporated, was originally a small consulting firm started by Sara Ballantyne. The company signs contracts for services well into the future, and has estimated its income before tax for the 2003–2005 period as follows (note that it has a very large contract already committed for the 2004 year in Australia). All values have been converted to U.S. dollars for tax planning purposes.

Assumptions	2003	2004	2005
US domestic income for tax purposes	$2,500,000	$3,500,000	$2,500,000
Australian earnings before tax	$200,000	$2,000,000	$250,000

The U.S. and Australian corporate income tax rates are 35% and 36%, respectively, in 2003. But the corporate income tax in Australia is scheduled to be reduced to 32% in 2004 and years after that. The reduction in tax rates will also apply to dividend withholding taxes on income remitted outside of Australia, currently 10%, to be reduced to 0% beginning in 2005. Ballantyne intends to remit 75% of all Australian earnings to its parent company each year.

a. What is the net dividend Ballantyne expects to remit to the U.S. parent from its Australian subsidiary in each of the three years?

b. What are the additional U.S. taxes due, or foreign tax credits arising from, the expected dividend remittance to the U.S. parent from Australia?

c. Assuming excess foreign tax credits can be carried forward five years, what is the actual additional tax payment due on the Australian foreign-source income in each year?

d. Assuming carry-forward, what is the cumulative excess foreign tax credits balance at the end of 2005?

e. What is the creditable tax limit on Ballantyne's foreign source income in each year?

10. **Ballantyne Brand Services (B).** Ballantyne Brand Services, the same firm and situation as described in Problem 9, has just been informed by its Australian law firm that the Australian tax revision will not take place as previously expected. The Australian corporate tax rate will stay at 36% for the foreseeable future, and there will be no reduction in the 10% withholding tax on dividend distributions.

a. What is the net dividend that Ballantyne expects to remit to the U.S. parent from its Australian subsidiary in each of the three years?

b. What are the additional U.S. taxes due, or foreign tax credits arising from, the expected dividend remittance to the U.S. parent from Australia?

c. Assuming excess foreign tax credits can be carried forward five years, what is the actual additional tax payment due on the Australian foreign-source income in each year?

d. Assuming carry-forward, what is the cumulative excess foreign tax credits balance at the end of 2005?

INTERNET EXERCISES

1. **Official government tax authorities.** Tax laws are constantly changing, and a MNE's tax planning and management processes must therefore include a continual updating of tax practices by country. Use the following government tax sites to address specific issues related to those countries.

Hong Kong's ownership change to China:	http://www.info.gov.hk/eindex.htm
Ireland's international financial services centre:	http://www.revenue.ie
Czech Republic's tax incentives for investment:	http://www.czech.cz/homepage/busin.htm

2. **Tax practices for international business.** Many of the major accounting firms provide on-line information and advisory services for international business activities as related to tax and accounting practices. Use the following web sites to gain up-to-date information on tax law changes or practices.

Ernst and Young	http://www.ey.com/tax
Deloitte & Touche	http://www.dttus.com
KPMG	http://www.kpmg.com
PriceWaterhouseCoopers	http://www.pwcglobal.com
Ernst & Young	http://www.eyi.com

SELECTED READINGS

Frisch, Daniel J., "Economics of International Tax Policy: Some Old and New Approaches," *Tax Notes*, April 30, 1990, pp. 581–591.

PriceWaterhouseCoopers, *Corporate Taxes: A Worldwide Summary* (New York: PriceWaterhouseCoopers, 2002).

Scholes, Myron S., and Mark A. Wolfson, *Taxes and Business Strategy: A Planning Approach*, (Englewood Cliffs, NJ: Prentice-Hall, 1992), Chapter 14, "Multinational Tax Planning."

Weisfelder, Christine J., "Home Country Taxation and the Theory of International Production," *Journal of International Financial Management and Accounting*, October 1994, Volume 5, No. 3, pp. 193–213.

MINI-CASE

Romanian Communications and Cyprus Offshore

Romanian Communications (RC) was, in early 1998, one of the many telecommunications and network service providers growing rapidly within Eastern Europe. RC was a privately held company, started by two partners who had left the employment of two of the world's largest telecommunications hardware providers to search for more challenging personal growth opportunities in their home country of Romania. Although they possessed the knowledge and capability to provide superior product and services to the Romanian market, they were severely hampered by the lack of established business law in Romania. They had recently created a wholly owned international business subsidiary in Cyprus to try to circumvent this barrier.

Cypriot International Business Companies

The problem confronting RC was very common in the telecom sector. Large levels of investment and network services had to be put into place and operation before revenues of any kind could be generated. This meant that financing the purchase of the equipment was problematic. The vacuum of legal infrastructure in Romania had made it even more difficult, as major lenders were uncomfortable with the level of risk they perceived in the Romanian business and legal climate. The major telecommunication equipment manufacturers would often extend credit of their own to these under-financed firms, vendor financing, but they too found the Romanian system a problem.

But Cyprus was different. Cyprus possessed a well-developed and defined legal environment for Western-style business. Cypriot international business company law allowed the establishment of trading and financing companies that were taxed at only 4.25% of their foreign-source income (all income by international business companies was foreign-source by definition).

Cyprus Offshore

RC Cyprus Offshore was established as the procurement arm of Romanian Communications. It initiated all supplier contacts, negotiated terms including financing for all purchases, and arranged transportation and delivery. As shown in the following exhibit, although the equipment was shipped directly to RC in Romania, the documentation and legal title was passed through Cyprus Offshore.

Cyprus Offshore then re-invoiced RC Romania for the equipment. In addition to the cost of the equipment, the invoice included charges for procurement, negotiations, financing, and import/export services provided by Cyprus Offshore. As a result of these combined charges, the equipment's cost as delivered to RC Romania was significantly higher than what would be termed a normal open-market purchase (often termed an *arm's length price*). Although the owners of RC obviously benefitted from lower combined tax liabilities in Romanian and Cypriot operations combined, the purchases could not have been completed as direct purchases by a Romania-based purchaser.

A second component of the structure was the payment of a technological royalty to RC Cyprus Offshore by RC Romania. The intellectual property and systems designs supplied by RC to Romanian companies was owned by Cyprus Offshore itself. This royalty payment, approximately 5% of the retail sales price on Romanian contracts, served to reduce the tax liabilities of Romanian operations and position it in Cyprus. Once again, the lower Cyprus tax rate of 4.25%, compared to the Romanian rate of 38%, reduced the consolidated tax liabilities of Romanian Communications significantly.

Exhibit A Structure of Romanian Communications' Use of Cypress Offshore

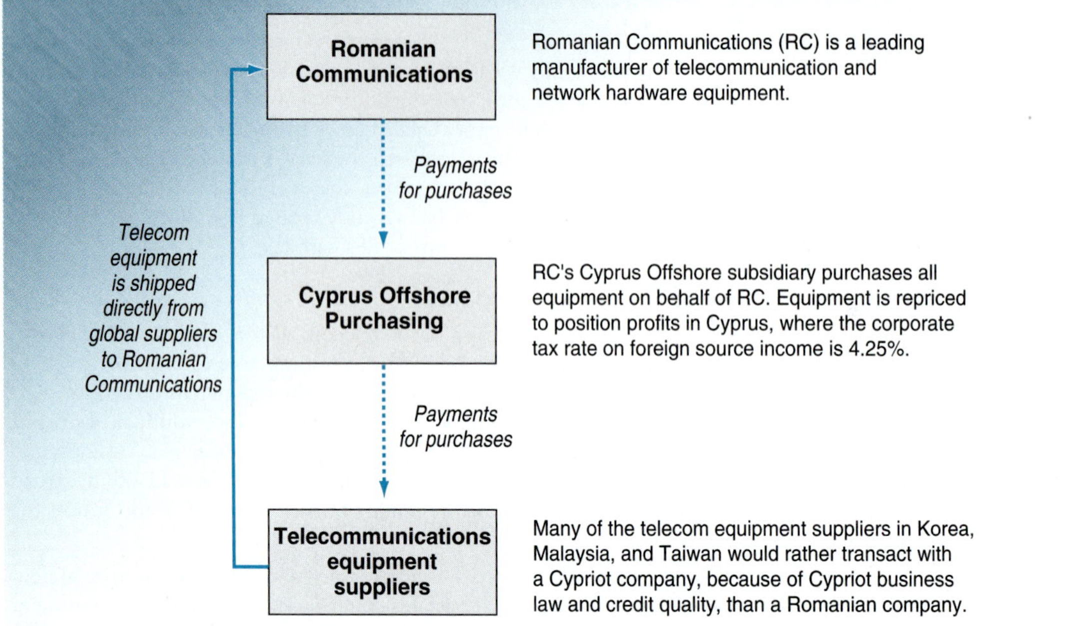
Romanian Communications
Romanian Communications (RC) is a leading manufacturer of telecommunication and network hardware equipment.
Payments for purchases
Telecom equipment is shipped directly from global suppliers to Romanian Communications
Cyprus Offshore Purchasing
RC's Cyprus Offshore subsidiary purchases all equipment on behalf of RC. Equipment is repriced to position profits in Cyprus, where the corporate tax rate on foreign source income is 4.25%.
Payments for purchases
Telecommunications equipment suppliers
Many of the telecom equipment suppliers in Korea, Malaysia, and Taiwan would rather transact with a Cypriot company, because of Cypriot business law and credit quality, than a Romanian company.

Case Questions

1. How does the creation of the Cyprus Offshore business unit, a type of middleman, change the credit quality of the buyer?
2. What benefits and costs accrue to both Romanian and Cypriot government tax authorities as a result of this structure?
3. Although this particular arrangement would be illegal under existing rules and practices among most Western industrial countries, including the United States, do you believe the Cyprus Offshore company as designed serves a useful purpose other than as a method of reducing tax liabilities?

Decision **CASE**

THUNDERBIRD
THE AMERICAN GRADUATE SCHOOL OF INTERNATIONAL MANAGEMENT

Stanley Works and Corporate Inversion

This strategic initiative will strengthen our company over the long term. An important portion of our revenues and earnings are derived from outside the United States, where nearly 50% of our people reside. Moreover, an increasing proportion of our materials are being purchased from global sources. This change will create greater operational flexibility, better position us to manage international cash flows, and help us to deal with our complex international tax structure. As a result, our competitiveness, one of the three legs of our vision to become a Great Brand, will be enhanced. The business, regulatory, and tax environments in Bermuda are expected to create considerable value for share owners. In addition to operational flexibility, improved worldwide cash management, and competitive advantages, the new corporate structure will enhance our ability to access international capital markets, which is favorable for organic growth, future strategic alliances and acquisitions. Finally, enhanced flexibility to manage worldwide tax liabilities should reduce our global effective tax rate from its current 32% to within the range of 23%–25%.

Stanley Works, Form 14A, Securities and Exchange Commission, February 8, 2002

Over and over again courts, have said that there is nothing sinister in so arranging one's affairs as to keep taxes as low as possible. Everybody does so, rich and poor, and all do right, for nobody owes any public duty to pay more than the law demands: taxes are enforced extractions, not voluntary contributions. To demand more in the name of morals is mere cant.

Judge Learned Hand, Commissioner v. Newman, 159 F.2d 848 (CA-2, 1947)

A 37-year employee of Stanley, machinist Stan Piorkowski, said the deal "is going to cost me my retirement." He holds 3,500 shares of Stanley and said taxes on capital gains resulting from the move would cost him between $30,000 and $50,000.

"Stanley Approves Tax Move to Bermuda," *The Washington Post*, May 10, 2002

A06-03-0005

On February 8, 2002, Stanley Works (USA) announced that it would enter into a *corporate inversion*, whereby the company would reincorporate itself as a Bermuda-based corporation. This was termed an *outbound inversion*, as the reincorporation was to move the company's incorporation out of the United States to a foreign country. Currently a U.S.-based corporation with head offices in New Britain, Connecticut, Stanley would make all U.S. operations a wholly owned subsidiary of a new parent company based in Bermuda—Stanley Tools, Ltd. Corporate headquarters—in fact, all company offices and operational centers—would remain in Connecticut. The reasoning was simple: Stanley expected to save close to $30 million annually in corporate income taxes by changing its citizenship. On the date of the announcement, the market value of Stanley increased by $199 million.

But the announcement was met with heated opposition from employees, stockholders, and local, state, and federal authorities. Requiring a 2/3 approval by its stockholders, Stanley suffered through a controversial vote on the move in May 2002 due to confusing corporate communiqués to shareholders, the result of which was the need to schedule a new vote. Stanley now—in August 2002—found itself a lightning rod for public debate on the responsibilities of a corporate citizen and the ethics of tax reduction and patriotism. Many regulators were now accusing the company of treaty shopping. Finally, on August 1 the Majority Whip in the U.S. House of Representatives, Tom Delay (Republican—Texas) had sent a letter to Stanley's CEO and Chairman, John Trani, asking him not to reincorporate in Bermuda. John Trani and his senior management team were now faced with increasing opposition. The senior management wished to reevaluate their previous decision: were the expected tax benefits worth the costs the company was now incurring?

Stanley Works

Stanley Works was founded in New Britain, Connecticut, in 1843 by Frederick Trent Stanley. The company manufactured door bolts and other hardware from wrought iron. Stanley Works is today a Standard & Poor's 500 company, a worldwide leader in the manufacturing and marketing of tools, hardware, and specialty hardware products for home, industrial, and professional use.

Stanley had total revenues of $2.6 billion in 2001 and employed more than 14,000 people worldwide. Stanley's portfolio of businesses included the widely recognized consumer brands of Stanley, Goldblatt, FatMax, Husky, and Mac, in addition to its industrial brands of Stanley, Bostitch, Jensen, Proto, and Vidmar. The company's yellow logo—"Made in the USA"—was instantly recognizable. More than 30% of Stanley's sales were outside of the United States. The company operated distribution and sales operations in more than 30 countries. Stanley Works was traded on the New York Stock Exchange under the symbol SWK.

Corporate Inversion

The purpose of a *corporate inversion* was—for all intents and purposes—to reduce tax liability. The United States taxed U.S.-based multinational companies on their worldwide income. As a U.S.-based company, Stanley paid corporate income taxes on all income generated in the United States (*domestic source income*) and income earned abroad and repatriated or deemed repatriated to the parent company in the United States (*foreign source income*). It was this latter tax on foreign source income which was at the heart of the dilemma for companies like Stanley.

Other countries, for example Germany, taxed only income deemed earned within the country, termed *territorial taxation.* Multinational companies with their parent company located in countries like Germany had lower effective tax burdens imposed by their home country tax structures. Stanley considered this a competitive disadvantage of being U.S.-based.

A third more controversial category was the *offshore tax haven.* Offshore tax havens, countries such as Bermuda, the Cayman Islands, and British Virgin Islands, imposed no taxes on foreign source income and few or negligible taxes on domestic income of multinational companies incorporated there. This provided a literal *tax haven* for a multinational company incorporated in that country, but which had little or no operational or structural presence in that country.

A corporate inversion would result in Stanley's U.S. business being taxed in the United States as before, but since the U.S. business unit would now be a U.S. subsidiary of a foreign corporation—Stanley Tools, Ltd. of Bermuda—Stanley's other income earned around the world would not be taxable by the U.S. government. John Trani and the senior management team at Stanley believed that by reducing their tax payments significantly, they would create greater returns to the shareholders and be able to compete more effectively in the global marketplace in the future.

Inversion Transactions

Corporate inversions were accomplished by three primary transactions: *stock transactions*, *asset transactions* and *drop down transactions.*[1]

- A *stock transaction*, the most common method of inversion, involved the acquisition of the shares of the U.S. parent company by a newly formed foreign parent, e.g., Bermuda-based. The U.S. parent company would survive as a subsidiary of the new foreign parent. The shareholders of the U.S. parent exchanged their shares in U.S. parent stock for stock in the new foreign parent. The U.S.- based corporate group was essentially unchanged as a result of the transaction.
- An *asset transaction*, typically used in smaller company inversions, involved the direct reincorporation of the U.S. parent company in a foreign country. It is typically achieved by merging the U.S. parent company with a foreign-based company. Stockholders then exchange their shares in the U.S. company for shares in the foreign company.
- A *drop down transaction* combines elements of both stock and asset transactions. This is effected by the U.S. parent company transferring its assets to a new foreign corporation. A portion of those assets transferred are then contributed to form the basis of the U.S. subsidiary of the company (the former U.S. parent).

In addition to the specific forms and federal tax implications, any such move would have different state-level tax repercussions depending on the U.S. state of incorporation. All three forms had no real impact on the operations of the company itself. This was the essence of the objection by U.S. tax authorities to outbound inversions—they appeared to be actions taken specifically for tax avoidance purposes only.

1. "Corporate Inversion Transactions: Tax Policy Implications," Office of Tax Policy, Department of the Treasury, United States Government, May 2002, pp. 4–5.

History of Inversions

Corporate inversions were not a new tax strategy. The first outbound inversion of note was that undertaken by the McDermott Company in 1983. McDermott exchanged the shares held by its U.S. stockholders for shares in McDermott International, a Panamanian subsidiary of the company prior to the restructuring. The United States Internal Revenue Service (IRS) had ruled the exchange of shares a taxable event, taxing all of the U.S. shareholders on the sale of their shares as capital gains. This unexpected consequence was thought to be a significant deterrent to future inversions, and the United States Congress soon followed with new tax legislation, Section 1248(i) of the IRS Code, which made it easier for the IRS to construe some inversions as taxable events for U.S. shareholders.

The next major corporate inversion of note was that undertaken by Helen of Troy, a beauty supply company located in Texas, in 1993. This was the first so-called *pure inversion* in that the company set up a completely new company offshore as the corporate headquarters (instead of the sale of the company's shares to an existing company or subsidiary). Management hoped that this strategy would be ruled a reorganization, rather than a taxable sale. The IRS once again, however, ruled the transaction a taxable event: "if US transferors owned, in the aggregate, 50% or more in the vote of value of the transferee foreign corporation immediately after the exchange."

Although the McDermott and Helen of Troy tax rulings were thought to constitute significant deterrents to outbound corporate inversions, more and more companies have considered and, in some cases, completed the reorganization to offshore incorporation. Appendix 1 provides a summary list of U.S.-based companies pursuing expatriation strategies since 1982. As indicated in Appendix 1, the pace quickened in the late 1990s, with companies like Tyco and Ingersoll-Rand moving offshore to reduce tax liabilities.

An additional consideration was the equity market's response to inversions. On average, the market rewarded the announcement of an outbound inversion with a 1.7% appreciation in the company's share price.[2] This share price reaction was thought to represent the present value of cash flow savings resulting from both reduction in taxes due on foreign source income and the reduction of domestic (U.S.) tax savings on domestic income as a result of the restructuring of operations post-inversion. Share price reactions were also larger for firms with steady share price appreciation in the immediate periods prior to inversion announcements—which did not apply to Stanley (see Appendix 4).

Tax Strategy

Stanley, like many other U.S.-based multinational companies, felt increasingly burdened by the U.S. corporate income tax structure. Stanley's U.S. earnings were taxed at the U.S. corporate income tax rate of 35%. This U.S. corporate rate, which had only varied up or down by about 1% over 15 years, had become increasingly high relative to corporate tax rates globally, as many countries reduced corporate tax rates consistently and significantly throughout the 1990s.

But domestic earnings and tax liabilities were only a small part of the story. The problem faced by Stanley and other multinationals was that more and more of their earnings were being generated outside of the United States, and U.S. tax authorities taxed those profits when remitted back to the parent company in the United States. As illustrated in Exhibit 1, if

2. Mihir A. Desai and James R. Hines, Jr., "Expectations and Expatriations: Tracing the Causes and Consequences of Corporate Inversions," *NBER Working Paper 9057*, July 2002, www.nber.org/papers/w9057.

Exhibit 1 Stanley Works U.S. Tax Liabilities Before the Outbound Corporate Inversion

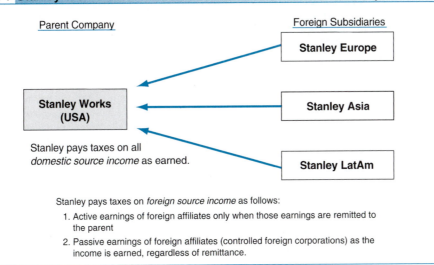

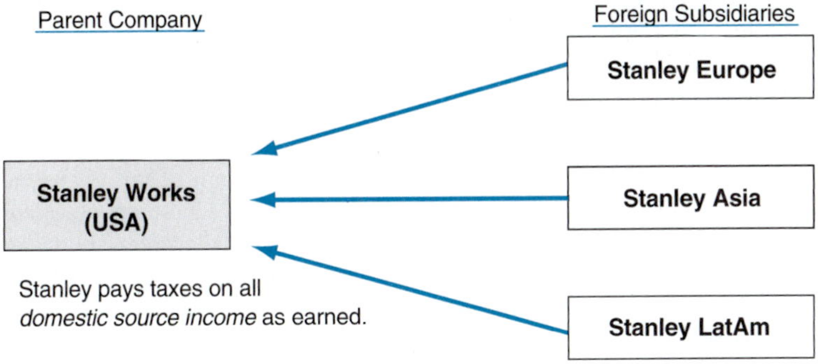

Stanley pays taxes on *foreign source income* as follows:

1. Active earnings of foreign affiliates only when those earnings are remitted to the parent
2. Passive earnings of foreign affiliates (controlled foreign corporations) as the income is earned, regardless of remittance.

Stanley's European operations generated a profit, they would first pay local taxes to the host government in, say, France or Germany, and then additional taxes on those profits when the earnings were remitted back to the U.S. parent.

However, under *Subpart F* of the U.S. Internal Revenue Service Tax Code, Sections 951-964, a U.S. parent company is subject to current U.S. tax on certain income earned by a foreign subsidiary, without regard to whether the income is remitted to the U.S. corporation or not.[3] This income, typically referred to as *Subpart F income*, was income generated by a controlled foreign corporation and earned primarily through ownership of assets, and not through the active production of goods or services. The United States tax authorities taxed this income as earned, rather than waiting to tax it when (or if) it was remitted to the U.S. parent company. This Subpart F provision had been specifically constructed to prevent foreign source income from being permanently parked in offshore tax havens, such as Bermuda, which assessed no corporate income taxes.

The U.S. tax code, however, did have a number of features to either eliminate the potential for double taxation (taxes paid in both Europe and the U.S., for example), or at least lessen the burden. Many of the corporate taxes paid to host governments were credited against potential U.S. tax liabilities. This had proven quite effective when corporate tax rates were 40% and 45% compared to 35% in the United States. But, as many countries lowered their rates to levels of 25% and 28% in the 1990s, the remittance of profits back to the parent in the United States had resulted in additional tax liabilities (bringing a 28% tax rate up to the U.S. rate of 35%).[4]

3. This specifically applied to *controlled foreign corporations* or *CFCs*. A CFC was defined as any foreign corporation with more than 50% of its voting stock owned directly or indirectly by U.S. shareholders. Thus, most foreign subsidiaries of U.S.-based multinationals were classified as CFCs.

4. The problem was frequently much more complex than space here allows. For example, it is quite possible that a host country's tax authorities might recognize a taxable deduction locally which the U.S. tax authorities might not recognize as deductible in the process of recalculating credits and liabilities upon repatriation to the parent. This would once again raise the taxes payable to the U.S. government upon repatriation of foreign source income to the U.S. parent.

Stanley could, of course, keep its profits in the foreign subsidiaries where they were generated and not remit them to the U.S. parent, paying U.S. tax only on the passive earnings on these funds invested offshore. But this too became a problem, as Stanley wished to redistribute the profits generated in one country or region to where it was strategically needed elsewhere in the global business, and not simply reinvest in marginally profitable investments to avoid additional tax obligations.[5]

The specific tax goals of an outbound corporate inversion are: (1) to achieve a more beneficial "territorial" system of taxation for their non-U.S. earnings, and (2) to reduce U.S. tax applicable to earnings generated within the United States.[6] These tax goals are achieved by changing the country of incorporation to an offshore financial center (country) which specifically does not tax foreign source earnings, such as Bermuda, Panama, or the Cayman Islands. As illustrated in Exhibit 2, the reincorporation of Stanley in Bermuda would have a series of significant tax benefits.

- First, Bermuda, as is typical of most offshore financial centers, does not tax foreign source income. (In fact, Bermuda does not have a corporate income tax.) Stanley's profits generated throughout the world could be freely redistributed throughout the global business, including the parent, without creating additional tax liabilities in the country of the parent company (now Bermuda instead of the U.S.).
- Second, the U.S. operations of Stanley would now be conducted as the U.S. subsidiary of a foreign corporation. This would most likely pose restructuring possibilities whereby the U.S. subsidiary would have increasing obligations to the Bermuda parent such as royalties, debt service, licensing fees, etc., which were legitimate deductible expenses in the U.S. but

Exhibit 2 Stanley Works U.S. Tax Liabilities After the Outbound Corporate Inversion

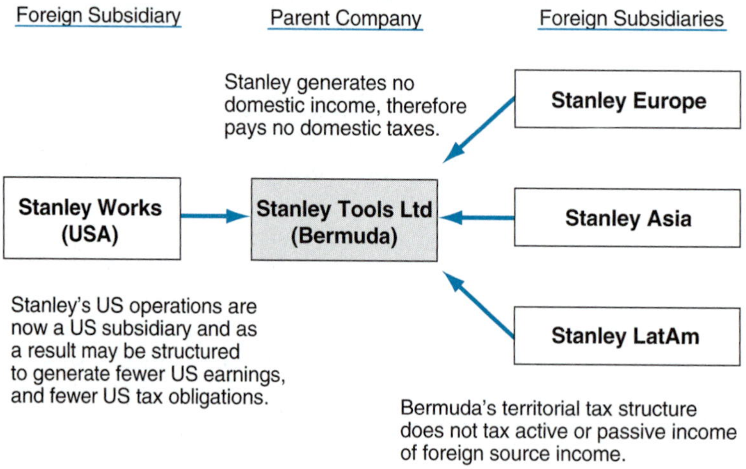

5. If Stanley Europe were to directly distribute profits to Stanley Asia, without going through the U.S. parent, U.S. tax law would treat the distribution as if it had been remitted to the U.S. parent first.
6. "Special Report: Outbound Inversion Transactions," *Tax Notes*, New York State Bar Association Tax Section, July 1, 2002, pp. 127–149.

income to the parent company itself in Bermuda. The result would be a net reduction in U.S. tax liabilities from Stanley's business conducted in the United States.

This second dimension of the tax benefits of corporate inversion is often termed *earnings stripping*. The term refers to the practice of structuring operations within the United States to position as many corporate costs as legally possible to reduce taxable profits within the relatively higher tax environment of the United States.

There was, however, considerable debate as to the actual tax benefits to be gained versus the growing public relations costs of inversion. As illustrated in Exhibit 3, Stanley's effective tax rate (total tax liabilities divided by pre-tax income) had ranged between 35% and 33% in recent years. The inversion was expected to lower the effective tax rate to roughly 24% in the foreseeable future.

Taxable Obligations of Inversion

The outbound inversion would, however, increase the tax obligations of current stockholders. The proposed transaction by Stanley Works was classified as a taxable stock transaction or transfer, in which stockholders exchange their shares in Stanley Works (USA) for Stanley Tools, Ltd. (Bermuda) on a one-to-one basis. The U.S. tax authorities considered the exchange of shares a sale and purchase. The sale would therefore create a taxable capital gain for any stockholder whose cost basis in the stock was below the share price at the time of the exchange.[7] Stanley estimated that the tax impact on stockholders would total roughly $150 million, although accurate information regarding the cost basis of current shareholders was poor.[8]

It was this tax burden imposed on stockholders which had been originally thought to represent an effective deterrent to outbound corporate inversions. Although there was a potential *toll charge*, a tax on the transfer of foreign subsidiaries to the newly formed parent corporation, recent inversions had been able to avoid this tax through specific transaction structures.

Exhibit 3 Stanley Works' Actual and Expected Income Before Inversion (millions)

Income statement item	1999	2000	2001	2002e	2003e
Earnings before tax (EBT)	$231	$294	$302	$363	$420
Taxes	(81)	(99)	(100)	(116)	(134)
Net income	150	194	202	247	286
Effective tax rate	35%	34%	33%	32%	32%
Shares outstanding (millions)	89.9	87.6	87.5	87.6	88.0
Earnings per share (EPS)	$1.67	$2.22	$2.31	$2.82	$3.25

Source: Stanley Works. Values for 2002e and 2003e are consensus estimates before inversion.

7. The depressed share prices in the market as a whole, and in Stanley Works specifically, however, took much of the sting out of this tax bite. In fact, outbound inversions were considered by many experts a strategy to be considered only during times of severe share price falls or depressions.

8. Interestingly Stanley explained this tax liability as "an acceleration of tax that would normally have to be paid by shareholders upon the subsequent disposition of shares at some point in the future." See the frequently asked questions (FAQ) information posted by Stanley in Appendix 3.

But tax liabilities varied across stockholders. Shares held in company 401(k) and other tax-deferred retirement programs were not taxable. Individuals holding shares as investments not in tax-deferred retirement programs, employee or unaffiliated, would suffer significant tax burdens as a result of the inversion (for example, that of Stan Piorkowski quoted on the first page of this case). Shareholder rights groups argued that Stanley was shifting the company's tax liabilities directly onto the backs of its shareholders.

The earnings-per-share (EPS) benefits had been touted by Stanley as a simple reduction in the effective tax rate for the overall organization. For example using the pro form a earnings estimates for 2003 presented in Exhibit 3, Stanley was expected to pay $134 million in taxes in 2003 on $420 million in earnings before tax, as shown in Exhibit 4. This assumed an effective tax rate of 32%. If Stanley were to reincorporate in Bermuda, Stanley estimated the effective tax rate would fall to 24%, yielding a $33 million savings for Stanley and its stockholders.[9]

But in the months following the shareholder vote in May, a number of academics and policy makers raised questions as to the source of the effective tax rate reduction Stanley's management claimed. Many critics of Stanley's inversion proposal noted that Stanley's foreign operations had actually been declining as a proportion of its consolidated business in recent years.

For example, Exhibit 5 presents selected measures of U.S. versus foreign business activities by Stanley for the 1999 to 2001 period. Stanley's foreign net sales had stayed at about 28% of its total net sales in recent years, but actual profitability (earnings before taxes, or EBT) on foreign sales had declined from a high of 13% of total EBT in 1999 to 10% in 2001. Foreign-based earnings were not only a smaller proportion of the total, they were also smaller in absolute earnings in 2001.

This caused substantial debate. If Stanley's foreign sales were not only less profitable before taxes than domestic sales, where were the substantial tax savings to be found which Stanley was claiming as the primary motivation for inversion? Once again, critics argued that Stanley's proposed tax savings would most likely be driven by earnings stripping of U.S. operations post-inversion rather than the tax savings arising from foreign-based earnings.

Exhibit 4 Prospective Changes in Stanley Works' Earnings After Inversion (millions)

	Pro forma 2003 earnings		
	Before	**After**	**Savings**
Earnings before tax	$420	$420	
Tax liability (32%/24%)	(134)	(101)	
Earnings after tax	$286	$319	+ $33
Shares outstanding (millions)	88.0	88.0	
Earnings per share (EPS)	$3.250	$3.625	+ $0.375 or 11.5%

9. Stanley had consistently followed a conservative estimate in its public discussions of a $30 million tax savings, as opposed to the $33 million calculation here.

Exhibit 5 Stanley Works' Foreign and Domestic Sales, Earnings and Assets

Item (millions of US$)	1999	%	2000	%	2001	%
Net Sales						
United States	$1,962.5	71%	$1,984.0	82%	$1,885.2	82%
Foreign	789.3	29%	764.9	28%	739.2	28%
Total	$2,751.8		$2,748.9		$2,624.4	
Earnings Before Taxes						
United States	$201.	0 87%	$267.5	91%	$212.9	90%
Foreign	29.8	13%	26.2	9%	23.8	10%
Total	$230.8		$293.7		$236.7	
Long-Lived Assets						
United States	$442.1	55%	$458.3	58%	$593.5	65%
Foreign	357.5	45%	332.2	42%	320.8	35%
Total	$799.6		$790.5		$914.3	

Source: Stanley Works, Annual Report 2001, p. 57.

Future Acquisitions and Inversion

There were also possible future strategic benefits to Stanley in the field of mergers and acquisitions, especially if the target were a foreign company. One of the most tax-inefficient attributes of a global chain of corporations was the repetitive withholding tax liabilities incurred by multinationals as they moved money across borders in the form of dividends. And these withholding taxes were paid in cash. Withholding tax rates varied from 5% to 30% on the gross amount of the distribution, depending on national tax laws and treaties.

For example, consider the potential situation depicted in Exhibit 6. A Spanish company, Target, is initially a publicly traded company with Spanish stockholders. It pays dividends to its stockholders quarterly. The Spanish tax authorities then tax the stockholders on their dividend earnings.

This situation changes dramatically, however, if Target Company is acquired by Stanley Works (USA). The Spanish stockholders of Target now hold shares in Stanley, a U.S.-based company. Profits generated by Target are now remitted to its US parent, Stanley, but only after the Spanish government has deducted withholding taxes according to the US-Spain tax treaty, e.g., 8%. The dividend distribution from Target to Stanley is foreign source income to Stanley, and fully taxable in the United States. The Spanish stockholder holding Stanley shares now receives his dividend directly from the U.S.-based company, but only after the U.S. tax authorities have applied U.S. corporate income taxes (35%) and withholding taxes (10%) on the dividend distributed in principle from Spain to the U.S. back to Spain. In essence, the profits of the Spanish company, Target, have suffered significant additional tax hits before finding their way back to the Spanish stockholder. And the Spanish stockholder will still be subject to Spanish income taxes on the dividend income.

This potential situation could result in strong Spanish stockholder opposition to potential acquisition by a foreign corporation like Stanley. Stanley is at a competitive disadvantage.

Exhibit 6 Incremental Tax Liabilities of a Spanish Company Being Acquired by Stanley Works

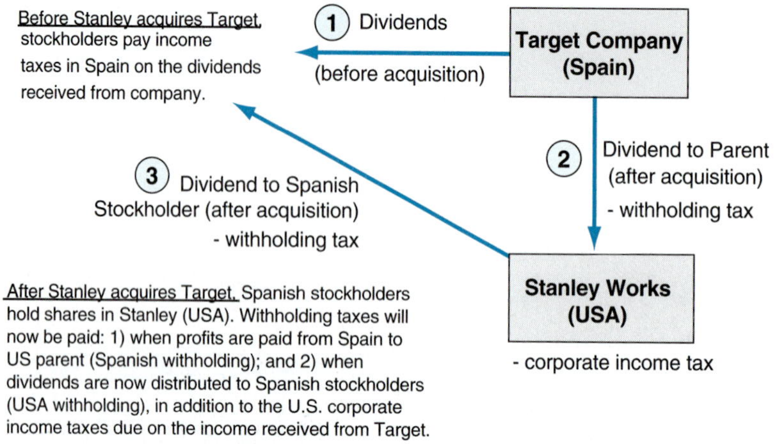
Before Stanley acquires Target, stockholders pay income taxes in Spain on the dividends received from company.
1 Dividends
(before acquisition)
Target Company (Spain)
2 Dividend to Parent (after acquisition) - withholding tax
3 Dividend to Spanish Stockholder (after acquisition) - withholding tax
Stanley Works (USA)
- corporate income tax
After Stanley acquires Target, Spanish stockholders hold shares in Stanley (USA). Withholding taxes will now be paid: 1) when profits are paid from Spain to US parent (Spanish withholding); and 2) when dividends are now distributed to Spanish stockholders (USA withholding), in addition to the U.S. corporate income taxes due on the income received from Target.

However, if Stanley were to undertake an outbound inversion, and now be a resident of a zero or low-tax country such as Bermuda, the tax burdens imposed on the dividend distributions from Target to Stanley to Spanish stockholder are significantly reduced. This is a distinct competitive advantage to Stanley if it intends to undertake a number of future foreign acquisitions.

A final detail regarding Stanley's proposed inversion and the legal construction of its remaining U.S. operations was important. As illustrated in Exhibit 7, the U.S. operations of Stanley would actually be owned by a Barbados wholly owned subsidiary of Stanley-Bermuda.

Exhibit 7 Stanley's Post Inversion Ownership of U.S. Operations

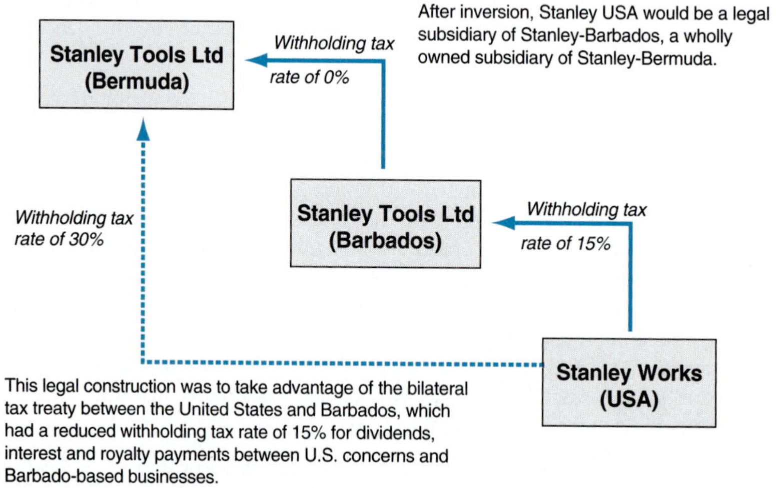
Stanley Tools Ltd (Bermuda)
Withholding tax rate of 0%
After inversion, Stanley USA would be a legal subsidiary of Stanley-Barbados, a wholly owned subsidiary of Stanley-Bermuda.
Withholding tax rate of 30%
Stanley Tools Ltd (Barbados)
Withholding tax rate of 15%
Stanley Works (USA)
This legal construction was to take advantage of the bilateral tax treaty between the United States and Barbados, which had a reduced withholding tax rate of 15% for dividends, interest and royalty payments between U.S. concerns and Barbado-based businesses.

This meant that postinversion, if Stanley USA was required to make dividend, interest, or royalty payments to its parent company, it would be subject to the withholding tax rates as set by the United States–Barbados bilateral tax treaty. These rates, 15% of the amount deemed paid, were half that applicable to a similar transfer of funds between the U.S. unit and the Bermuda parent directly. This feature would also aid in the reduction and simplification of Stanley Tools' global effective tax burden post-inversion.

Potential Law Changes

Stanley also had to consider the possibility that the very tax advantages that it sought to obtain were in danger of being taken away. Congressional tax writers had proposed a number of changes in tax laws to discourage outbound inversions, and had indicated that they were willing to make these new rules retroactive to the dates they were first discussed in Congress—a move to prevent a last-minute wave of inversions. The first of these, on April 11, 2002, caused a drop in Stanley's share price.

Prominent among the tax revision proposals were bills that would deny deductions for the costs of outbound inversions, deny deductions for interest or other charges paid to the newly inverted foreign parent corporation, or bills that would permanently characterize a newly inverted parent as a U.S. corporation, notwithstanding its new country of incorporation, or that would adopt the old British standard that would characterize a corporation's nationality based on the location of its "mind and management," not on its country of incorporation. Based on this latter standard, Stanley would continue to be a U.S. corporation if its corporate headquarters and Board of Directors continued to reside largely in the U.S.

An additional set of proposed tax bills focused on restricting corporate expatriates from receiving federal contracts. According to the Congressional Ways and Means staff, the 10-year cost of revenue losses to corporate expatriates would total more than $4 billion, and include the following specific companies and their prospective tax takes:[10]

- Accenture consulting ($1 billion in federal contracts awarded in fiscal year 2001 alone);
- Foster Wheeler construction (more than $600 million in federal contracts awarded between 1998 and 2002);
- Tyco International, the diversified manufacturer ($400 million per year);
- Ingersoll-Rand, the heavy equipment manufacturer ($40 million per year);
- Cooper Industries, the electrical equipment manufacturer who had just recently completed its corporate inversion ($55 million per year);
- Stanley Works ($30 million per year).

None of these bills had yet advanced far in Congress, and there were outspoken critics of all of them, principally on the basis that the provisions tended to be difficult to limit to inverted companies alone, and the unintended consequences of the bills might do much more damage to US interests abroad than any benefits that might accrue from limiting inversions. Nonetheless, could Stanley risk taking this very unpopular move for benefits that may be more illusory than real?

10. "Corporate Expatriations to Take Center Stage after August Recess," *Tax Notes*, August 5, 2002, 761–763.

Shareholder Approval

The proposed inversion required a two-thirds approval by Stanley's shareholders. In a vote held on May 9, 2002, 57.3 million shares were voted in favor of the proposed reincorporation. This represented 67.2% of outstanding shares, and surpassed (barely) the required 66.6% approval. Within hours, however, the State of Connecticut (itself a shareholder in addition to being the host to corporate headquarters for Stanley) filed a legal challenge to the vote as a result of confusing instructions provided by Stanley to employees holding Stanley shares in their 401k program. Initially, Stanley had sent a letter to employee shareholders explaining that a failure to return the ballot would result in the vote being counted as a "no." This was reversed, however, when in a subsequent letter these same shareholders were told an unreturned ballot would be counted as a "yes."[11]

The Chairman and CEO of Stanley, John Trani, immediately responded to the controversy by announcing that a new vote would be scheduled because "Stanley's integrity is the most important asset of our company. Even the appearance of impropriety is unacceptable." A new vote would be scheduled when possible.[12] Stanley's market value dropped by $252 million.

Patriotism and Inversion

> *How would you like to keep living in your current home, but tell the Internal Revenue Service to go pound sand in Bermuda, because you're a legal resident of that lovely island? You can't, but toolmaker Stanley Works plans to save $30 million a year by moving. So what if our country is at war against terrorism and is spending billions extra for defense and homeland security? That's our problem, not the tax dodgers. Their problem is raising profits to get their stock price higher. What could possibly be more important, since a good stock market is good for America, right?*
>
> Allan Sloan, "The Tax-Free Bermuda Getaway," *Newsweek*, April 15, 2002

John Trani's other worries surrounded the image of Stanley. The move to reincorporate offshore was portrayed by many as unpatriotic—unsupportive of the U.S. government during a time of recession and continuing terrorist threats in the post-September 11th world. In addition to the growing debate in Congress over the increasing use of corporate inversions, there was strong opposition by Stanley workers and their unions to the move. Although Stanley was not doing anything illegal, and was paying its taxes in accordance with current law, the company was portrayed as "working too hard" to avoid future income tax obligations.

> *We will call on Fidelity Investments in Boston, the biggest mutual fund firm in our country, and make it clear that we will not support funds that prop up companies like Stanley Works that want to take from America, but not give back. As investors, we will no longer tolerate the greed of short-term speculators or corrupt insiders, and we will not tolerate companies that overcompensate executives, cheat their employees, lie to their stockholders, or cook their books—no excuses, no exceptions.*
>
> AFL-CIO President John Sweeney
> Speaking to a Wall Street rally, August 1, 2002

11. The latter interpretation was the correct one according to the trustee guidelines established in the Stanley Works 401k program.
12. Ironically, before the new vote could be held, one of Stanley's chief competitors, Cooper Industries Inc., won final approval from its shareholders to move the company's incorporation immediately from the United States to Bermuda. Cooper would officially change its incorporation following close of business on May 21, a matter of days. Ingersoll-Rand, another major competitor, had completed its expatriation transaction in December 2001.

John Trani and his senior management team returned to the conference room. Time was running out. Stanley needed to reschedule the stockholder vote now if it was to continue to pursue corporate inversion. Although everyone agreed there were considerable tax benefits to *being* incorporated outside of the United States, the question remained as to whether the benefits exceeded the costs of *moving* offshore—the outbound inversion itself.

Appendix 1

United States–Based Companies Undertaking Corporate Inversions, 1982–2002

Company	Announcement Date	Corporate Destination	Transaction Detail
McDermott	1983	Panama	Taxable stock transfer
Helen Of Troy	1993	Bermuda	Taxable stock transfer
Triton Energy	1996	Cayman	Taxable stock transfer
Chicago Bridge & Iron	1996	Netherlands	Subsidiary IPO
Tyco	1997	Bermuda	Taxable stock transfer
Santa Fe International	1997	Cayman	
Fruit of the Loom	1998	Cayman	Taxable stock transfer
Playstar	1998	Antigua	F-reorganization
Gold Reserve	1998	Canada	Taxable stock transfer
Xoma	1998	Bermuda	Asset
Transocean	1999	Cayman	Taxable stock transfer
PXRE	1999	Bermuda	Taxable stock transfer
Everest Reinsurance	1999	Bermuda	Taxable stock transfer
White Mountain Insurance	1999	Bermuda	Asset
Trenwick	1999	Bermuda	Asset (M&A related)
Applied Power	2000	Bermuda	Subsidiary spin-off
R&B Falcon	2000	Cayman	Acquired by foreign entity
Foster Wheeler	2000	Bermuda	Taxable stock transfer
Cooper Industries	2001	Bermuda	Taxable stock transfer
Global Marine	2001	Cayman	Taxable stock transfer
Ingersoll Rand	2001	Bermuda	Taxable stock transfer
Nabors Industries	2002	Bermuda	Taxable stock transfer
Noble Drilling	2002	Cayman	Taxable stock transfer
Stanley Tools	2002	Bermuda	Taxable stock transfer
Non-Inversion Transactions			
Seagate Technology	2001	Cayman	*ab initio**
Accenture	2001	Bermuda	*ab initio**

Source: "Expectations and Expatriations: Tracing the Causes and Consequences of Corporate Inversions," Mihir A. Desai and James R. Hines Jr., Working Paper 9057, National Bureau of Economic Research, July 2002.

**ab initio* means "from the beginning."

Appendix 2

Frequently Asked Questions

Question: Will the Stanley Works remain on the New York Stock Exchange?

Answer: Yes, the company will continue to be traded on the New York Stock Exchange using the same symbol (SWK).

Question: Will Stanley World Headquarters relocate?

Answer: No.

Question: How will this affect day-to-day operations?

Answer: There will be essentially no impact on how the company will conduct its daily operations. Corporate offices will remain in the New Britain, Connecticut, location. There will be no change in applicable accounting standards. There are no plants, distribution centers, customer relationships, or vendor relationships that will change because of this transaction.

Question: For shareholders of Stanley common stock, what are the tax implications associated with this transaction?

Answer: For individuals that own stock held in the company 401(k) plan or in a qualified individual retirement account, there will be no tax owed as a result of this transaction.

For shares owned in the Employee Stock Purchase Plan or other shares purchased privately, upon the completion of the Stanley incorporation change, all SWK shares will automatically convert to the right to receive shares in The Stanley Works, Ltd., a Bermuda-based company. Generally, share owners will recognize as gain any appreciation in the market value of SWK shares over their cost basis as a result of such exchange. Assuming continued appreciation in the value of SWK stock, this represents an acceleration of tax that would normally have to be paid by shareholders upon the subsequent disposition of shares at some point in the future.

Additionally, shareholders will not be permitted to recognize any loss realized on SWK shares exchanged where the cost basis of such stock exceeds the fair market value of SWK stock at the time of the exchange. In such a case, the aggregate tax basis in the Bermuda stock received would equal the tax basis of the SWK shares exchanged. Thus, subject to any subsequent changes in the fair market value of the Bermuda based company common shares received, any loss would be preserved.

We urge you to consult your own tax advisors regarding your particular tax consequences of the reorganization.

Question: Are other companies doing this?

Answer: Yes. In fact, Ingersoll-Rand, one of our peer companies, completed their incorporation in December 2001.

Question: What are the benefits of Stanley Works completing the incorporation to Bermuda?

Answer: We believe that reincorporating as a Bermuda company will enable us to realize a variety of potential business, financial and strategic benefits, including, but not limited to, some of the following:

- Enhance our ability to access international capital markets
- Create greater operational flexibility
- Better position the company to manage international cash flows
- Create competitive advantages
- Enhanced flexibility to manage worldwide tax liabilities and reduce global effective tax rate from its current 32% to within the range of 23%–25%.

Question: Will the reincorporation dilute my ownership interest?

Answer: No, the reincorporation will not dilute your ownership interest. Share owners of The Stanley Works will receive the same number of shares of The Stanley Works, Ltd. as they hold in The Stanley Works. These shares will have substantially the same attributes as The Stanley Works common shares.

Question: When do you expect the reincorporation to be completed?

Answer: We expect to complete it by mid-2002.

Question: What will our activities consist of in Bermuda?

Answer: While we will be incorporated in Bermuda, at this point, there are no plans to move any business operations there.

Source: www.stanleyworks.com

Appendix 3

Selected Corporate Income Tax Regimes and Rates, 2002

Country	Tax Regime	Corporate tax rate
Australia	Combination/Exemption	36%
Belgium	Territorial (95% exemption)	40.2% (39%)
Brazil	Worldwide	34%
Canada	Worldwide	26.1% (25%)
Denmark	Worldwide	30%
Finland	Worldwide	29%
France	Worldwide	33.33%
Germany	Territorial	26.375% (25%)
Japan	Worldwide	30%
Mexico	Worldwide	32%
Spain	Worldwide	35%
Sweden	Worldwide	28%
Switzerland	Worldwide	8.5%
United Kingdom	Worldwide	30%
United States	Worldwide	35%

Source: PriceWaterhouseCoopers, *Corporate Taxes, Worldwide Summaries*; Organization for Economic Cooperation and Development (OECD).

Appendix 4

Stanley Works Share Price, January 1, 2002–August 1, 2002

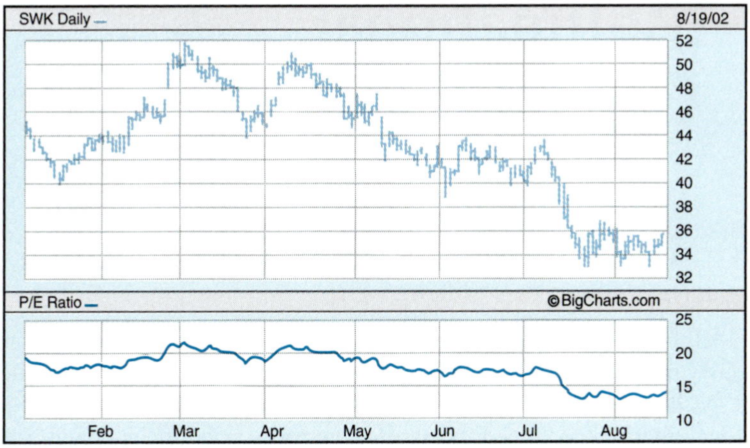

Source: BigCharts.com

Appendix 5

Stanley Works Share Price Relative to the Standard & Poor's 500, January 1, 2002–August 1, 2002

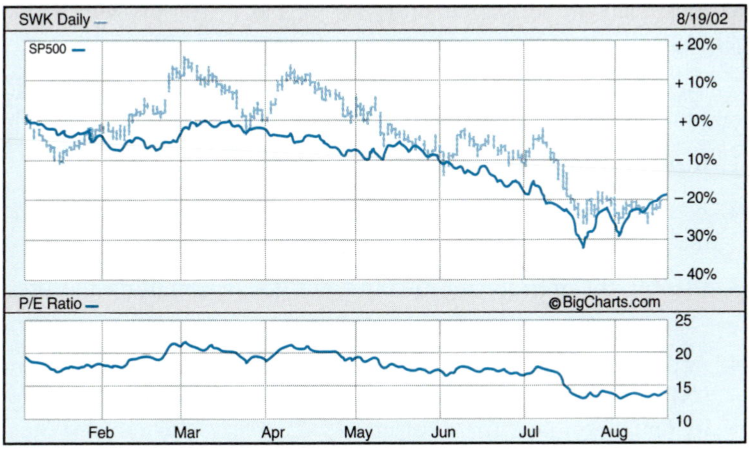

Source: BigCharts.com

Chapter 18

Multinational Capital Budgeting

THIS CHAPTER DESCRIBES IN DETAIL THE ISSUES AND PRINCIPLES RELATED TO THE INVESTMENT IN real productive assets in foreign countries, generally referred to as *multinational capital budgeting*.

Although the original decision to undertake an investment in a particular foreign country may be determined by a mix of strategic, behavioral, and economic decisions, the specific project—as well as all reinvestment decisions—should be justified by traditional financial analysis. For example, a production efficiency opportunity may exist for a U.S. firm to invest abroad, but the type of plant, mix of labor and capital, kinds of equipment, method of financing, and other project variables must be analyzed within the traditional financial framework of discounted cash flows. It must also consider the impact of the proposed foreign project on consolidated net earnings, cash flows from subsidiaries in other countries, and on the market value of the parent firm.

Multinational capital budgeting, like traditional domestic capital budgeting, focuses on the cash inflows and outflows associated with prospective long-term investment projects. Multinational capital budgeting techniques are used in traditional foreign direct investment (FDI) analysis, such as the construction of a manufacturing plant in another country, as well as in the growing field of international mergers and acquisitions.

Capital budgeting for a foreign project uses the same theoretical framework as domestic capital budgeting, with a few very important differences. The basic steps are:

1. Identify the initial capital invested or put at risk.
2. Estimate cash flows to be derived from the project over time, including an estimate of the terminal or salvage value of the investment.
3. Identify the appropriate discount rate for determining the present value of the expected cash flows.
4. Apply traditional capital budgeting decision criteria such as net present value (NPV) and internal rate of return (IRR) to determine the acceptability or priority ranking of potential projects.

This chapter will first describe the complexities of budgeting for a foreign project. Second, we describe the insights gained by valuing a project from both the project's viewpoint and the parent's viewpoint. We then use a hypothetical investment by Cemex of Mexico in Indonesia to describe in detail the process of multinational capital budgeting in practice. We conclude the chapter with an introduction to the concept of real options analysis, an alternative method for evaluating the potential returns to a project or investment.

Complexities of Budgeting for a Foreign Project

Capital budgeting for a foreign project is considerably more complex than the domestic case. Several factors contribute to this greater complexity:

- Parent cash flows must be distinguished from project cash flows. Each of these two types of flows contributes to a different view of value.
- Parent cash flows often depend on the form of financing. Thus we cannot clearly separate cash flows from financing decisions, as we can in domestic capital budgeting.
- Additional cash flows generated by a new investment in one foreign subsidiary may be in part or in whole taken away from another subsidiary, with the net result that the project is favorable from a single subsidiary's point of view but contributes nothing to worldwide cash flows.
- The parent must explicitly recognize remittance of funds because of differing tax systems, legal and political constraints on the movement of funds, local business norms, and differences in the way financial markets and institutions function.
- An array of nonfinancial payments can generate cash flows from subsidiaries to the parent, including payment of license fees and payments for imports from the parent.
- Managers must anticipate differing rates of national inflation because of their potential to cause changes in competitive position, and thus changes in cash flows over a period of time.
- Managers must keep the possibility of unanticipated foreign exchange rate changes in mind because of possible direct effects on the value of local cash flows, as well as indirect effects on the competitive position of the foreign subsidiary.
- Use of segmented national capital markets may create an opportunity for financial gains or may lead to additional financial costs.
- Use of host-government subsidized loans complicates both capital structure and the parent's ability to determine an appropriate weighted average cost of capital for discounting purposes.
- Managers must evaluate political risk because political events can drastically reduce the value or availability of expected cash flows.
- Terminal value is more difficult to estimate because potential purchasers from the host, parent, or third countries, or from the private or public sector, may have widely divergent perspectives on the value to them of acquiring the project.

Since the same theoretical capital budgeting framework is used to choose among competing foreign and domestic projects, it is critical that we have a common standard. Thus all foreign complexities must be quantified as modifications to either expected cash flow or the rate of discount. Although in practice many firms make such modifications arbitrarily, readily available information, theoretical deduction, or just plain common sense can be used to make less arbitrary and more reasonable choices.

Project Versus Parent Valuation

A strong theoretical argument exists in favor of analyzing any foreign project from the viewpoint of the parent. Cash flows to the parent are ultimately the basis for dividends to stockholders, reinvestment elsewhere in the world, repayment of corporate-wide debt, and other purposes that affect the firm's many interest groups. However, since most of a project's cash flows to its parent (or to sister subsidiaries) are financial cash flows rather than operating cash flows, the parent viewpoint usually violates a cardinal concept of capital budgeting—namely, that financial cash flows should not be mixed with operating cash flows. Often the difference is not important because the two are almost identical, but in some instances a sharp divergence in these cash flows will exist. For example, funds that are permanently blocked from repatriation or "forcibly reinvested," are not available for dividends to the stockholders or for repayment of parent corporate debt. Therefore shareholders will not perceive the blocked earnings as contributing to the value of the firm, and creditors will not count on them in calculating interest coverage ratios and other evidence of ability to service debt.

Evaluation of a project from the local viewpoint serves some useful purposes, but it should be subordinated to evaluation from the parent's viewpoint. In evaluating a foreign project's performance relative to the potential of a competing project in the same host country, we must pay attention to the project's local return. Almost any project should at least be able to earn a cash return equal to the yield available on host government bonds with a maturity the same as the project's economic life, if a free market exists for such bonds. Host government bonds ordinarily reflect the local risk-free rate of return, including a premium equal to the expected rate of inflation. If a project cannot earn more than such a bond yield, the parent firm should buy host government bonds rather than invest in a riskier project—or, better yet, invest somewhere else!

Multinational firms should invest only if they can earn a risk-adjusted return greater than locally based competitors can earn on the same project. If they are unable to earn superior returns on foreign projects, their stockholders would be better off buying shares in local firms, where possible, and letting those companies carry out the local projects. Apart from these theoretical arguments, surveys over the past 35 years show that in practice multinational firms continue to evaluate foreign investments from both the parent and project viewpoint.

The attention paid to project returns in various surveys probably reflects emphasis on maximizing reported consolidated net earnings per share as a corporate financial goal. As long as foreign earnings are not blocked, they can be consolidated with the earnings of both the remaining subsidiaries and the parent. As mentioned previously, U.S. firms must consolidate foreign subsidiaries that are over 50% owned. If a firm is owned between 20% and 49% by a parent, it is called an *affiliate*. Affiliates are consolidated with the parent owner on a *pro rata* basis. Subsidiaries less than 20% owned are normally carried as unconsolidated investments. Even in the case of temporarily blocked funds, some of the most mature MNEs do not necessarily eliminate a project from financial consideration. They take a very long-run view of world business opportunities.

If reinvestment opportunities in the country where funds are blocked are at least equal to the parent firm's required rate of return (after adjusting for anticipated exchange rate changes), temporary blockage of transfer may have little practical effect on the capital budgeting outcome, because future project cash flows will be increased by the returns on forced reinvestment. Since large multinationals hold a portfolio of domestic and foreign projects, corporate liquidity is not impaired if a few projects have blocked funds; alternate sources of funds are available to meet all planned uses of funds. Furthermore, a long-run historical perspective on blocked funds does indeed lend support to the belief that funds are almost never permanently blocked. However, waiting for the release of such funds can be frustrating, and sometimes the blocked funds lose value while blocked because of inflation or unexpected exchange rate deterioration, even though they have been reinvested in the host country to protect at least part of their value in real terms.

In conclusion, most firms appear to evaluate foreign projects from both parent and project viewpoints. The parent's viewpoint gives results closer to the traditional meaning of net present value in capital budgeting. Project valuation provides a closer approximation of the effect on consolidated earnings per share, which all surveys indicate is of major concern to practicing managers. To illustrate the foreign complexities of multinational capital budgeting, we analyze a hypothetical market-seeking foreign direct investment by Cemex in Indonesia.

Illustrative Case: Cemex Enters Indonesia[1]

It is early 1998. Cementos Mexicanos, Cemex, is considering the construction of a cement manufacturing facility on the Indonesian island of Sumatra. The project, Semen Indonesia (the Indonesian word for "cement" is *semen*), would be a wholly owned greenfield investment with a total installed capacity of 20 million metric tonnes per year (mmt/y). Although that is large by Asian production standards, Cemex believes that its latest cement manufacturing technology would be most efficiently utilized with a production facility of this scale.

Cemex has three driving reasons for the project: 1) the firm wishes to initiate a productive presence of its own in Southeast Asia, a relatively new market for Cemex; 2) the long-term prospects for Asian infrastructure development and growth appear very good over the longer term; and 3) there are positive prospects for Indonesia to act as a produce-for-export site as a result of the depreciation of the Indonesian rupiah (Rp) in 1997.

Cemex, the world's third-largest cement manufacturer, is a MNE headquartered in an emerging market but competing in a global arena. The firm competes in the global marketplace for both market share and capital. The international cement market, like markets in other commodities such as oil, is a dollar-based market. For this reason, and for comparisons against its major competitors in both Germany and Switzerland, Cemex considers the U.S. dollar its functional currency.

Cemex's shares are listed in both Mexico City and New York (OTC: CMXSY). The firm has successfully raised capital—both debt and equity—outside Mexico in U.S. dollars. Its investor base is increasingly global, with the U.S. share turnover rising rapidly as a percentage of total trading. As a result, its cost and availability of capital are internationalized and dominated by U.S. dollar investors. Ultimately, the Semen Indonesia project will be evaluated—in both cash flows and capital cost—in U.S. dollars.

1. Cemex is a real company. However, the greenfield investment described here is hypothetical.

Overview

A road map of the complete multinational capital budgeting analysis for Cemex in Indonesia is illustrated in Exhibit 18.1. The basic principle is that, starting at the top left, the parent company invests U.S. dollar–denominated capital, which flows clockwise through the creation and operation of an Indonesian subsidiary, which then generates cash flows that are eventually returned in a variety of forms to the parent company—in U.S. dollars. The first step is to construct a set of *pro forma* financial statements for Semen Indonesia, all in Indonesian rupiah (Rp). The next step is to create two capital budgets, the *project viewpoint* and *parent viewpoint.*

Semen Indonesia will take only one year to build the plant, with actual operations commencing in year 1. The Indonesian government has only recently deregulated the heavier industries to allow foreign ownership. The following analysis is conducted assuming that purchasing power parity (PPP) holds for the Rp/US$ exchange rate for the life of the Indonesian project. This is a standard financial assumption made by Cemex for its foreign investments. The projected inflation rates for Indonesia and the United States are 30% per annum and 3% per annum, respectively.

If we assume an initial spot rate of Rp10,000/US$, and Indonesian and U.S. inflation rates of 30% and 3% per annum, respectively, for the life of the project, forecasted spot exchange rates follow the usual PPP calculation. For example, the forecasted exchange rate for year 1 of the project would be:

$$\text{spot rate (year 1)} = \text{Rp}10{,}000/\text{US\$} \times \frac{1+0.30}{1+0.03} = \text{RP}12{,}621/\text{US\$}$$

Exhibit 18.1 A Road Map to the Construction of Semen Indonesia's Capital Budget

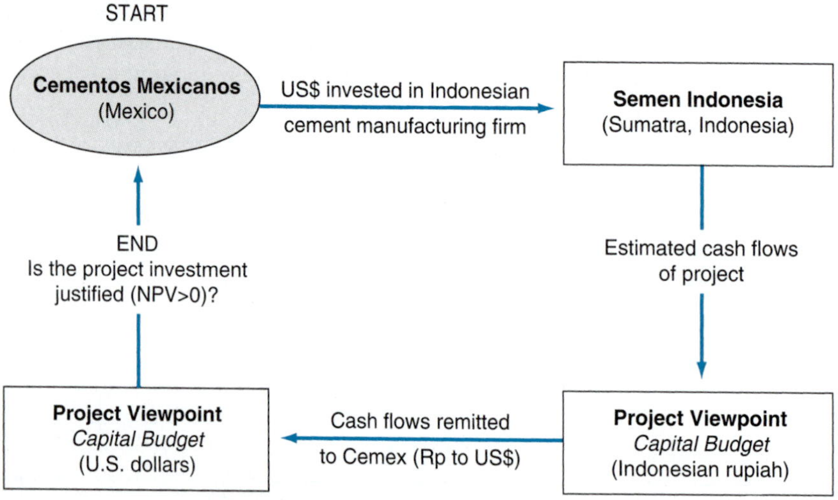

Financial Assumptions

The following series of financial statements are based on these assumptions.

Capital investment. Although the cost of building new cement manufacturing capacity anywhere in the industrial countries is now estimated at roughly \$150/tonne of installed capacity, Cemex believed that it could build a state-of-the-art production and shipment facility in Sumatra at roughly \$110/tonne (see Exhibit 18.2). Assuming a 20 million metric ton per year (mmt/y) capacity, and a year 0 average exchange rate of Rp10,000/\$, this cost will constitute an investment of Rp22 trillion (\$2.2 billion). This figure includes an investment of Rp17.6 trillion in plant and equipment, giving rise to an annual depreciation charge of Rp1.76 trillion if we assume a 10-year straight-line depreciation schedule. The relatively short depreciation schedule is one of the policies of the Indonesian tax authorities meant to attract foreign investment.

Exhibit 18.2 Investment and Financing of the Semen Indonesia Project (all values in thousands unless otherwise noted)

INVESTMENT		FINANCING	
Average exchange rate, Rp/\$	10,000	Equity	Rp 11,000,000,000
Cost of installed capacity, \$/tonne	\$110	Debt	
Installed capacity	20,000	Rupiah debt	2,750,000,000
Investment, US\$	\$2,200,000	US\$ debt, Rp	8,250,000,000
Investment in rupiah	22,000,000,000	Total	Rp 22,000,000,000
Plant and equipment, Rp	17,600,000,000		
Annual depreciation, Rp	1,760,000,000		
COSTS OF CAPITAL: CEMEX			
Risk-free rate	6.000%	Cemex beta	1.500
Credit premium	2.000%	Equity risk premium	7.000%
Cost of debt	8.000%	Cost of equity	16.500%
Cost of debt, after-tax	5.200%	Percent equity	60%
Percent debt	40%	WACC	11.980%
COSTS OF CAPITAL: SEMEN INDONESIA			
Risk-free rate	33.000%	Semen Indonesia beta	1.000
Credit premium	2.000%	Equity risk premium	6.000%
Cost of rupiah debt	35.000%	Cost of equity	40.000%
Cost of debt, after-tax	5.200%	Percent equity	50%
Cost of US\$ debt	38.835%		
Cost of US\$ debt, after-tax	27.184%		
Percent debt	50%	WACC	33.257%

Assumes corporate income tax rates of 35% and 30% in Mexico and Indonesia, respectively. The cost of the US\$ loan is stated in rupiah terms assuming purchasing power parity and U.S. dollar and Indonesian rupiah inflation rates of 3% and 30%, respectively, throughout the subject period.

Financing. This massive investment would be financed with 50% equity, all from Cemex, and 50% debt, 75% from Cemex and 25% from a bank consortium arranged by the Indonesian government. Cemex's own U.S. dollar-based weighted average cost of capital (WACC) was currently estimated at 11.98%. The WACC on a local Indonesian level in rupiah terms for the project itself was estimated at 33.257%. The details of this calculation are discussed later in this chapter.

The explicit debt structures, including repayment schedules, are presented in Exhibit 18.3. The loan arranged by the Indonesian government, part of the government's economic development incentive program, is an eight-year loan, in rupiah, at 35% annual interest, fully amortizing. The interest payments are fully deductible against corporate tax liabilities.

The majority of the debt, however, is being provided by the parent company, Cemex. After raising the capital from its financing subsidiary, Cemex will relend the capital to Semen Indonesia. The loan is denominated in U.S. dollars, 5 years maturity, with an annual interest rate of 10%. Because the debt will have to be repaid from the rupiah earnings of the Indonesian enterprise, the *pro forma* financial statements are constructed so that the expected costs of servicing the dollar debt are included in the firm's *pro forma* income statement. The dollar loan, if the rupiah follows the purchasing power parity forecast, will have an effective interest expense in rupiah terms of 38.835% before taxes. We find this rate by determining the internal rate of return of repaying the dollar loan in full in rupiah (see Exhibit 18.3).

Revenues. Given the current existing cement manufacturing in Indonesia, and its currently depressed state as a result of the Asian crisis, all sales are based on export. The 20 mmt/y facility is expected to operate at only 40% capacity (producing 8 million metric tonnes). Cement produced will be sold in the export market at $58/tonne (delivered). Note also that, at least for the conservative baseline analysis, we assume no increase in the price received over time.

Costs. The cash costs of cement manufacturing (labor, materials, power, etc.) are estimated at Rp115,000 per tonne for 1999, rising at about the rate of inflation, 30% per year. Additional production costs of Rp20,000 per tonne for year 1 are also assumed to rise at the rate of inflation. As a result of all production being exported, loading costs of $2.00/tonne and shipping of $10.00/tonne must also be included. Note that these costs are originally stated in U.S. dollars, and for the purposes of Semen Indonesia's income statement, they must be converted to rupiah terms. This is the case because both ship-loading and shipping costs are international services governed by contracts denominated in dollars. As a result, they are expected to rise over time only at the U.S. dollar rate of inflation (3%).

Semen Indonesia's *pro forma* income statement is illustrated in Exhibit 18.4. This is the typical financial statement measurement of the profitability of any business, whether domestic or international. The baseline analysis assumes a capacity utilization rate of only 40% (year 1), 50% (year 2), and 60% in the following years. Management believes this is necessary since existing in-country cement manufacturers are averaging only 40% of capacity at this time.

Additional expenses in the *pro forma* financial analysis include license fees paid by the subsidiary to the parent company of 2.0% of sales, and general and administrative expenses for Indonesian operations of 8.0% per year (and growing an additional 1% per year). Foreign exchange gains and losses are those related to the servicing of the U.S. dollar–denominated debt provided by the parent and are drawn from the bottom of Exhibit 18.3. In summary, the subsidiary operation is expected to begin turning an accounting profit in its fourth year of operations (2000), with profits rising as capacity utilization increases over time.

Exhibit 18.3 Semen Indonesia's Debt Service Schedules and Foreign Exchange Gains/Losses (millions of Rp and US$)

Spot rate (Rp/$)	10,000	12,621	15,930	20,106	25,376	32,028
Project year	0	1	2	3	4	5
Indonesian loan at 35% for 8 years						
Principal	2,750,000					
Interest payment		(962,500)	(928,921)	(883,590)	(822,393)	(739,777)
Principal payment		(95,939)	(129,518)	(174,849)	(236,046)	(318,662)
Total payment		(1,058,439)	(1,058,439)	(1,058,439)	(1,058,439)	(1,058,439)
Cemex loan at 10% for 5 years						
Principal (US$)	825					
Interest payment (US$)		(82.5)	(69.0)	(54.1)	(37.8)	(19.8)
Principal payment (US$)		(135.1)	(148.6)	(163.5)	(179.9)	(197.8)
Total payment		(217.6)	(217.6)	(217.6)	(217.6)	(217.6)
Scheduled at Rp10,000/$:						
Interest payment		(825,000)	(689,867)	(541,221)	(377,710)	(197,848)
Principal payment		(1,351,329)	(1,486,462)	(1,635,108)	(1,798,619)	(1,978,481)
Total payment		(2,176,329)	(2,176,329)	(2,176,329)	(2,176,329)	(2,176,329)
Actual (at current spot rate):						
Interest payment		(1,041,262)	(1,098,949)	(1,088,160)	(958,480)	(633,669)
Principal payment		(1,705,561)	(2,367,915)	(3,287,494)	(4,564,190)	(6,336,691)
Total payment		(2,746,823)	(3,466,864)	(4,375,654)	(5,522,670)	(6,970,360)
Cfs in Rp on:						
Cemex loan	8,250,000	(2,746,823)	(3,466,864)	(4,375,654)	(5,522,670)	(6,970,360)
IRR of Cfs	38.835%					
Foreign exchange losses on Cemex loan (millions of Rp):						
FX losses on interest		(216,262)	(409,082)	(546,940)	(580,770)	(435,821)
FX losses on principal		(354,232)	(881,453)	(1,652,385)	(2,765,571)	(4,358,210)
Total FX losses on debt		(570,494)	(1,290,535)	(2,1999,325)	(3,346,341)	(4,794,031)

The loan by Cemex to the Indonesian subsidiary is denominated in U.S. dollars. The loan will therefore have to be repaid in U.S. dollars, not rupiah. At the time of the loan agreement, the spot exchange rate is Rp10,000/$. This is the assumption used in calculating the "scheduled" repayments of principal and interest in rupiah. The rupiah, however, is expected to depreciate in line with purchasing power parity. As it is repaid, the "actual" exchange rate will therefore give rise to a foreign exchange loss as it takes more and more rupiah to acquire U.S. dollars for debt service, both principal and interest. The foreign exchange losses on this debt service will be recognized on the Indonesian income statement.

Exhibit 18.4 Semen Indonesia's *Pro Forma* Income Statement (millions of rupiah)

Exchange Rate (Rp/$)	10,000	12,621	15,930	20,106	25,376	32,038
Project year	**0**	**1**	**2**	**3**	**4**	**5**
Sales volume		8,000	10,000	12,000	12,000	12,000
Sales price (US$)		58.00	58.00	58.00	58.00	58.00
Sales price (Rp)		732,039	923,933	1,166,128	1,471,808	1,857,627
Total revenue		5,856,311	9,239,325	13,993,541	17,661,751	22,291,530
Less cash costs		(920,000)	(1,495,000)	(2,332,200)	(3,031,860)	(3,941,418)
Less other production costs		(160,000)	(260,000)	(405,600)	(527,280)	(685,464)
Less loading costs		(201,942)	(328,155)	(511,922)	(665,499)	(865,149)
Less shipping costs		(1,009,709)	(1,640,777)	(2,559,612)	(3,327,495)	(4,325,744)
Total production costs		(2,291,650)	(3,723,932)	(5,809,334)	(7,552,134)	(9,817,774)
Gross profit		3,564,660	5,515,393	8,184,207	10,109,617	12,473,756
Gross margin		61%	60%	58%	57%	56%
Less license fees		(117,126)	(184,787)	(279,871)	(353,235)	(445,831)
Less general and administrative		(468,505)	(831,539)	(1,399,354)	(1,942,792)	(2,674,984)
EBITDA		2,979,029	4,499,067	4,744,982	6,053,589	7,592,941
Less depreciation and amortization		(1,760,000)	(1,760,000)	(1,760,000)	(1,760,000)	(1,760,000)
EBIT		1,219,029	2,739,067	4,744,982	6,053,589	7,592,941
Less interest on Cemex debt		(825,000)	(689,867)	(541,221)	(377,710)	(197,848)
Foreign exchange losses on debt		(570,494)	(1,290,535)	(2,199,325)	(3,346,341)	(4,794,031)
Less interest on local debt		(962,500)	(928,921)	(883,590)	(822,393)	(739,777)
EBT		(1,138,965)	(170,256)	1,120,846	1,507,145	1,861,285
Less income taxes (30%)		------------	------------	------------	(395,631)	(558,386)
Net income		(1,138,965)	(170,256)	1,120,846	1,111,514	1,302,900
Net income (US$)		(90)	(11)	56	44	41
Return on sales		−19%	−2%	8%	6%	6%

EBITDA = earnings before interest, taxes, depreciation, and amortization; EBIT = earnings before interest and taxes; EBT = earnings before taxes. Tax credits resulting from current period losses are carried forward toward next year's tax liabilities. The tax payment for year 3 is zero, and year 4 is less than 30%, as a result of tax loss carry-forwards from previous years. Dividends are not distributed in the first year of operations as a result of losses, and are distributed at a 50% rate in the years 2000–2003. All calculations are exact, but may appear not to add due to reported decimal places and rounding.

Project Viewpoint Capital Budget

The capital budget for the Semen Indonesia project from a project viewpoint is shown in Exhibit 18.5. We find the net cash flow, or *free cash flow,* as it is often called, by summing EBITDA (earnings before interest, taxes, depreciation, and amortization), recalculated taxes, and changes in net

Exhibit 18.5 Semen Indonesia's Capital Budget: Project Viewpoint (millions of rupiah)

Exchange Rate (Rp/$)	10,000	12,621	15,930	20,106	25,376	32,038
Project year	**0**	**1**	**2**	**3**	**4**	**5**
EBITDA		2,979,029	4,499,067	6,504,982	7,813,589	9,352,941
Less recalculated taxes		(893,709)	(1,349,720)	(1,951,495)	(2,344,077)	(2,805,882)
Net operating cash flow		2,085,320	3,149,347	4,553,487	5,469,512	6,547,059
Less additions to NWC		(240,670)	(139,028)	(436,049)	(289,776)	(626,314)
Initial investment	(22,000,000)					
Terminal value						19,686,451
Free cash flow (FCF)	(22,000,000)	1,844,650	3,010,319	4,117,438	5,179,736	25,607,196
NPV	(9,443,538)					
IRR	15.4 %					

NWC = net working capital. NPV = net present value. Discount rate is Semen Indonesia's WACC of 33.257%. IRR = internal rate of return, the rate of discount yielding an NPV of exactly zero. Values in exhibit are exact and are rounded to the nearest million.

working capital (the sum of the net additions to receivables, inventories, and payables necessary to support sales growth).

Note that EBITDA, not EBT, is used in the capital budget, which contains both depreciation and interest expense. Depreciation and amortization are noncash expenses of the firm and therefore contribute positive cash flow. Because the capital budget creates cash flows that will be discounted to present value with a discount rate, and the discount rate includes the cost of debt—interest—we do not wish to subtract interest twice. Therefore, taxes are recalculated on the basis of EBITDA. (This highlights the distinction between an income statement and a capital budget. The project's income statement shows losses the first two years of operations as a result of interest expenses and forecast foreign exchange losses, so it is not expected to pay taxes. But the capital budget, constructed on the basis of EBITDA, before these financing and foreign exchange expenses, calculates a positive tax payment.) The firm's cost of capital used in discounting also includes the deductibility of debt interest in its calculation.

The initial investment of Rp22 trillion is the total capital invested to support these earnings. Although receivables average 50 to 55 days sales outstanding (DSO) and inventories 65 to 70 DSO, payables and trade credit are also relatively long at 114 DSO in the Indonesian cement industry. Semen Indonesia expects to add approximately 15 net DSO to its investment with sales growth. The remaining elements to complete the project viewpoint's capital budget are the terminal value (discussed next) and the discount rate of 33.257% (the firm's weighted average cost of capital).

Terminal value. The terminal value (TV) of the project represents the continuing value of the cement manufacturing facility in the years after year 5, the last year of the detailed *pro forma* financial analysis shown here. This value, like all asset values according to financial theory, is the present value of all future free cash flows that the asset is expected to yield. We calculate the TV as the present value of a perpetual net operating cash flow (NOCF) generated in the fifth year by Semen Indonesia, the growth rate assumed for that net operating cash flow (g), and the firm's weighted average cost of capital (k_{wacc}):

$$\text{terminal value} = \frac{NOCF_5(1+g)}{k_{wacc} - g} = \frac{6,547,059(1+0)}{0.33257 - 0} = \text{Rp}19,686,451$$

or Rp19.686 trillion (Rp 19,686,456,933,000). The assumption that $g = 0$, i.e., that net operating cash flows will not grow past year 5, is probably not true, but it is a prudent assumption for Cemex to make when estimating future cash flows so far into the future.

The results of the capital budget from the project viewpoint indicate a negative net present value (NPV) of Rp9,443,538 million (or about Rp9.4 trillion) and an internal rate of return (IRR) of only 15.4%, compared to the 33.257% cost of capital. These are the returns the project would yield to a local or Indonesian investor in Indonesian rupiah. The project, from this viewpoint, is not acceptable.

Repatriating Cash Flows to Cemex

Exhibit 18.6 now collects all incremental earnings to Cemex from the prospective investment project in Indonesia. As described in the section preceding the case, a foreign investor's assessment of a project's returns depends on the actual cash flows that are returned to it, in its own currency. For Cemex, this means that the investment must be analyzed in terms of U.S. dollar cash inflows and outflows associated with the investment over the life of the project, after-tax, discounted at its appropriate cost of capital.

We build this *parent viewpoint capital budget* in two steps. First, we isolate the individual cash flows, adjusted for any withholding taxes imposed by the Indonesian government and converted to U.S. dollars. (Statutory withholding taxes on international transfers are set by bilateral tax treaties, but individual firms may negotiate lower rates with governmental tax authorities. In the case of Semen Indonesia, dividends will be charged a 15% withholding tax, 10% on interest payments, and 5% license fees.) Mexico does not tax repatriated earnings since they have already been taxed in Indonesia. (The United States does levy a contingent tax on repatriated earnings of foreign source income, as covered in Chapter 17.)

The second step, the actual parent viewpoint capital budget, combines these U.S. dollar after-tax cash flows with the initial investment to determine the net present value of the proposed Semen Indonesia subsidiary in the eyes (and pocketbook) of Cemex. This is illustrated in Exhibit 18.6, which shows all incremental earnings to Cemex from the prospective investment project. A specific peculiarity of this parent viewpoint capital budget is that only the capital invested into the project by Cemex itself, \$1,925 million, is included in the initial investment (the \$1,100 million in equity and the \$825 million loan). The Indonesian debt of Rp 2.75 billion (\$275 million) is not included in the Cemex parent viewpoint capital budget.

Exhibit 18.6 Semen Indonesia's Remittance and Capital Budget: Parent Viewpoint (millions of Rp and US$)

Exchange Rate (Rp/$)	10,000	12,621	15,930	20,106	25,376	32,038
Project year	**0**	**1**	**2**	**3**	**4**	**5**
Dividend Remittance						
Dividends paid (Rp)		—	—	560,423	555,757	651,450
Less withholding tax		—	—	(84,063)	(83,364)	(97,717)
Net dividend remitted (Rp)		—	—	476,360	472,393	553,732
Net dividend remitted (US$)		—	—	23.7	18.6	17.3
License Fees Remittance						
License fees remitted (Rp)		117,126	184,787	279,871	353,235	445,831
Less withholding tax		(5,856)	(9,239)	(13,994)	(17,662)	(22,292)
Net dividend remitted (Rp)		111,270	175,547	265,877	335,573	423,539
Net license fees remitted (US$)		8.8	11.0	13.2	13.2	13.2
Debt Service Remittance						
Promised interest paid (US$)		82.5	69.0	54.1	37.8	19.8
Less withholding tax @ 10%		(8.25)	(6.90)	(5.41)	(3.78)	(1.98)
Net interest remitted (US$)		74.25	62.09	48.71	33.99	17.81
Principal payments remitted (US$)		135.1	148.6	163.5	179.9	197.8

Capital Budget: Parent Viewpoint (millions of US$)

Project year	**0**	**1**	**2**	**3**	**4**	**5**
Dividends		—	—	23.7	18.6	17.3
License fees		8.8	11.0	13.2	13.2	13.2
Debt service		209.4	210.7	212.2	213.9	215.7
Total earnings		218.2	221.8	249.1	245.7	246.2
Initial investment	(1,925.0)					
Terminal value						614.7
Free cash flow (FCF)	(1,925.0)	218.2	221.8	249.1	245.7	860.8
NPV	(925.6)					
IRR	−1.84 %					

NPV calculated using a company determined discount rate of WACC + foreign investment premium of 11.98% + 6.00% = 17.98% (US$ terms).

Parent Viewpoint Capital Budget

Finally, all cash flow estimates are now constructed to form the parent viewpoint's capital budget, detailed in the bottom half of Exhibit 18.6. The cash flows generated by Semen Indonesia from its Indonesian operations, dividends, license fees, debt service, and terminal value are now valued in U.S. dollar terms after-tax.

In order to evaluate the project's cash flows that are returned to the parent company, Cemex must discount these at the corporate cost of capital. Remember that Cemex considers its functional currency to be the U.S. dollar, so it calculates its cost of capital in U.S. dollars. As described in Chapter 11, the customary weighted average cost of capital formula is as follows:

$$k_{\text{WACC}} = k_e \frac{E}{V} + k_d(1-t)\frac{D}{V},$$

k_e = risk-adjusted cost of equity

k_d = before-tax cost of debt

t = marginal tax rate

E = market value of the firm's equity

D = market value of the firm's debt

V = total market value of the firm's securities (E + D)

Cemex's cost of equity is calculated using the capital asset pricing model (CAPM):

$$k_e = k_{rf} + (k_m - k_{rf})\beta_{\text{Cemex}} = 6.00\% + (13.00\% - 6.00\%)1.5 = 16.50\%$$

k_e = risk-adjusted cost of equity

k_{rf} = risk-free rate of interest (U.S. Treasury intermediate bond yield)

k_m = expected rate of return in U.S. equity markets (large stock)

β_{Cemex} = measure of Cemex's individual risk relative to the market

The calculation assumes the current risk-free rate is 6.00%, the expected return on U.S. equities is 13.00%, and Cemex's beta is 1.5. The result is a cost of equity—required rate of return on equity investment in Cemex—of 16.50%.

The investment will be funded internally by the parent company, roughly in the same debt/equity proportions as the consolidated firm, 40% debt (D/V) and 60% equity (E/V). The current cost of debt for Cemex is 8.00%, and the effective tax rate is 35%. The cost of equity, when combined with the other components, results in a weighted average cost of capital for Cemex of:

$$k_{\text{WACC}} = k_e \frac{E}{V} + k_d(1-t)\frac{D}{V} = (16.50\%)(0.60) + (8.00\%)(1-0.35)(0.40) = 11.98\%$$

Cemex customarily uses this weighted average cost of capital of 11.98% to discount prospective investment cash flows for project ranking purposes. The Indonesian investment poses a variety of risks, however, which the typical domestic investment does not.

If Cemex were undertaking an investment of the same relative degree of risk as the firm itself, a simple discount rate of 11.98% might be adequate. Cemex, however, generally requires new investments to yield an additional 3% over the cost of capital for domestic investments, and 6% more for international projects. The discount rate for Semen Indonesia's cash flows repatriated to Cemex will therefore be discounted at 11.98% + 6.00%, or 17.98%. The project's baseline analysis indicates a negative NPV of US$925.6 million (IRR of –1.84%), which means that it is an unacceptable investment from the parent's viewpoint.

Most corporations require that new investments more than cover the cost of the capital employed in their undertaking. It is therefore not unusual for the firm to require a hurdle rate of 3% to 6% above its cost of capital in order to identify potential investments that will literally add value to stockholder wealth. An NPV of zero means the investment is "acceptable," but NPV values that exceed zero are literally the present value of wealth that is expected to be added to that of the firm and its shareholders. For foreign projects, as discussed previously, we must adjust for agency costs and foreign exchange risks and costs.

Sensitivity Analysis: Project Viewpoint

So far, the project investigation team has used a set of "most likely" assumptions to forecast rates of return. It is now time to subject the most likely outcome to sensitivity analyses. The same probabilistic techniques are available to test the sensitivity of results to political and foreign exchange risks as are used to test sensitivity to business and financial risks. Many decision makers feel more uncomfortable about the necessity to guess probabilities for unfamiliar political and foreign exchange events than they do about guessing their own more familiar business or financial risks. Therefore it is more common to test sensitivity to political and foreign exchange risk by simulating what would happen to net present value and earnings under a variety of "what if" scenarios.

Political risk. What if Indonesia should impose controls on the payment of dividends or license fees to Cemex? The impact of blocked funds on the rate of return from Cemex's perspective would depend on when the blockage occurs, what reinvestment opportunities exist for the blocked funds in Indonesia, and when the blocked funds would eventually be released to Cemex. We could simulate various scenarios for blocked funds and rerun the cash flow analysis in Exhibit 18.6 to estimate the effect on Cemex's rate of return.

What if Indonesia should expropriate Semen Indonesia? The effect of expropriation would depend on the following five factors:

1. When the expropriation occurs, in terms of number of years after the business began operation
2. How much compensation the Indonesian government will pay, and how long after expropriation the payment will be made
3. How much debt is still outstanding to Indonesian lenders, and whether the parent, Cemex, will have to pay this debt because of its parental guarantee

4. The tax consequences of the expropriation
5. Whether the future cash flows are forgone

Many expropriations eventually result in some form of compensation to the former owners. This compensation can come from a negotiated settlement with the host government or from payment of political risk insurance by the parent government. Negotiating a settlement takes time, and the eventual compensation is sometimes paid in installments over a further period of time. Thus the present value of the compensation is often much lower than its nominal value. Furthermore, most settlements are based on book value of the firm at the time of expropriation rather than the firm's market value.

Repayment of parent-guaranteed local debt would usually receive first claim on any compensation funds paid. If Cemex had guaranteed Semen Indonesia's debt to Indonesian lenders, they would be paid before Cemex could receive any settlement funds. In fact, the settlement agreement would probably provide for this. Alternatively, Cemex might have refused to guarantee Semen Indonesia's debt, protecting itself in the case of an expropriation, but probably causing Semen Indonesia to pay a higher rate of interest and making the subsidiary less profitable to its parent.

If no compensation agreement is negotiated, Semen Indonesia, as an independently incorporated subsidiary of Cemex, might default on its debt. Cemex would not be obligated for Semen Indonesia's own debt, lacking a parent guarantee. As a practical matter, this is likely to occur only when the subsidiary's debt is borrowed locally, as in the case of Semen Indonesia. If Semen Indonesia had borrowed from, for instance, banks in Singapore, parent Cemex would feel an obligation to repay the debt even if it was not technically obligated.

The tax consequences of expropriation would depend on the timing and amount of capital loss recognized by Mexico. This loss would usually be based on the uncompensated book value of the Indonesian investment. The problem is that there is often some doubt as to when a write-off is appropriate for tax purposes, particularly if negotiations for a settlement drag on. In some ways, a nice clear expropriation without hope of compensation, such as occurred in Cuba in the early 1960s, is preferred to a slow "bleeding death" in protracted negotiations. The former leads to an earlier use of the tax shield and a one-shot write-off against earnings, whereas the latter tends to depress earnings for years, as legal and other costs continue and no tax shelter is achieved.

Foreign exchange risk. The project team assumed that the Indonesian rupiah would depreciate versus the U.S. dollar at the purchasing power parity "rate" (approximately 20.767% per year in the baseline analysis). What if the rate of rupiah depreciation were greater? Although this event would make the assumed cash flows to Cemex worth less in dollars, operating exposure analysis would be necessary to determine whether the cheaper rupiah made Semen Indonesia more competitive. For example, since Semen Indonesia's exports to Taiwan are denominated in U.S. dollars, a weakening of the rupiah versus the dollar could result in greater rupiah earnings from those export sales. This serves to somewhat offset the imported components that Semen Indonesia purchases from the parent company that are also denominated in U.S. dollars. Semen Indonesia is representative of firms today that have both cash inflows and outflows denominated in foreign currencies, providing a partial natural hedge against currency movements.

What if the rupiah should appreciate against the dollar? The same kind of economic exposure analysis is needed. In this particular case, we might guess that the effect would be positive on both local sales in Indonesia and the value in dollars of dividends and license fees paid to Cemex by Semen Indonesia. Note, however that an appreciation of the rupiah might lead to more competition within Indonesia from firms in other countries with now-lower cost structures, lessening Semen Indonesia's sales.

Other sensitivity variables. The project rate of return to Cemex would also be sensitive to a change in the assumed terminal value, the capacity utilization rate, the size of the license fee paid by Semen Indonesia, the size of the initial project cost, the amount of working capital financed locally, and the tax rates in Indonesia and Mexico. Since some of these variables are within control of Cemex, it is still possible that the Semen Indonesia project could be improved in its value to the firm and become acceptable.

Sensitivity Analysis: Parent Viewpoint Measurement

When a foreign project is analyzed from the parent's point of view, the additional risk that stems from its "foreign" location can be measured in at least two ways, *adjusting the discount rates* or *adjusting the cash flows.*

Adjusting discount rates. The first method is to treat all foreign risk as a single problem, by adjusting the discount rate applicable to foreign projects relative to the rate used for domestic projects to reflect the greater foreign exchange risk, political risk, agency costs, asymmetric information, and other uncertainties perceived in foreign operations. However, adjusting the discount rate applied to a foreign project's cash flow to reflect these uncertainties does not penalize net present value in proportion either to the actual amount at risk or to possible variations in the nature of that risk over time. Combining all risks into a single discount rate may thus cause us to discard much information about the uncertainties of the future.

In the case of foreign exchange risk, changes in exchange rates have a potential effect on future cash flows, because of operating exposure. The direction of the effect, however, can either decrease or increase net cash inflows, depending on where the products are sold and where inputs are sourced. To increase the discount rate applicable to a foreign project, on the assumption that the foreign currency might depreciate more than expected, ignores the possible favorable effect of a foreign currency depreciation on the project's competitive position. Increased sales volume might more than offset a lower value of the local currency. Such an increase in the discount rate also ignores the possibility that the foreign currency may appreciate (two-sided risk).

Adjusting cash flows. In the second method, we incorporate foreign risks in adjustments to forecasted cash flows of the project. The discount rate for the foreign project is risk-adjusted only for overall business and financial risk, in the same manner as for domestic projects. Simulation-based assessment utilizes scenario development to estimate cash flows to the parent arising from the project over time under different alternative economic futures.

Certainty regarding the quantity and timing of cash flows in a prospective foreign investment is, to quote Shakespeare, "the stuff that dreams are made of." Due to the complexity of economic forces at work in major investment projects, it is paramount that the analyst realize the subjectivity of the forecast cash flows. Humility in analysis is a valuable trait.

Shortcomings of each. In many cases, neither adjusting the discount rate nor adjusting cash flows is optimal. For example, political uncertainties are a threat to the entire investment, not just the annual cash flows. Potential loss depends partly on the terminal value of the unrecovered parent investment, which will vary depending on how the project was financed, whether political risk insurance was obtained, and what investment horizon is contemplated. Furthermore, if the political climate were expected to be unfavorable in the near future, any investment would probably be unacceptable. Political uncertainty usually relates to possible adverse events that might occur in the more distant future, but that cannot be foreseen at the present. Adjusting the discount rate for political risk thus penalizes early cash flows too heavily while not penalizing distant cash flows enough.

Repercussions to the investor. Apart from anticipated political and foreign exchange risks, MNEs sometimes worry that taking on foreign projects may increase the firm's overall cost of capital because of investors' perceptions of foreign risk. This worry seemed reasonable if a firm had significant investments in Iraq, Iran, Russia, Serbia, or Afghanistan in the 1990s. However, the argument loses persuasiveness when applied to diversified foreign investments with a heavy balance in the industrial countries of Canada, Western Europe, Australia, Latin America, and Asia where, in fact, the bulk of FDI is located. These countries have a reputation for treating foreign investments by consistent standards, and empirical evidence confirms that a foreign presence in these countries may not increase the cost of capital. In fact, some studies indicate that required returns on foreign projects may even be lower than those for domestic projects.

MNE practices. Surveys of MNEs over the past 35 years have shown that about half of them adjust the discount rate and half adjust the cash flows. One recent survey indicated a rising use of adjusting discount rates over adjusting cash flows. However, the survey also indicated an increasing use of multifactor methods—discount rate adjustment, cash flow adjustment, real options analysis, and qualitative criteria—in evaluating foreign investments.[2]

Portfolio Risk Measurement

As we discussed in Chapter 11, the field of finance has distinguished two different definitions of risk: 1) the risk of the individual security (standard deviation of expected return) and 2) the risk of the individual security as a component of a portfolio (*beta*). A foreign investment undertaken in order to enter a local or regional market—market seeking—will have returns that are more or less correlated with those of the local market. A portfolio-based assessment of the investment's prospects would then seem appropriate. A foreign investment undertaken for *resource-seeking* or *production-seeking* purposes may have returns related to those of the parent company or units located somewhere else in the world and have little to do with local markets. Cemex's proposed investment in Semen Indonesia is both *market-seeking* and *production-seeking* (for export). The decision about which approach is to be used by the MNE in evaluating prospective foreign investments may be the single most important analytical decision it makes. An investment's acceptability may change dramatically from one criteria to the other.

For comparisons within the local host country, we should overlook a project's actual financing or parent-influenced debt capacity, since these would probably be different for local investors than they are for a multinational owner. In addition, the risks of the project to local investors

2. Keck, Tom, Eric Levengood, and Al Longield, "Using Discounted Cash Flow Analysis in an International Setting: A Survey of Issues in Modeling the Cost of Capital," *Journal of Applied Corporate Finance*, Fall 1998, Volume 11, No. 3, pp. 82–99.

might differ from those perceived by a foreign multinational owner because of the opportunities a MNE has to take advantage of market imperfections. Moreover, the local project may be only one out of an internationally diversified portfolio of projects for the multinational owner; if undertaken by local investors it might have to stand alone without international diversification. Since diversification reduces risk, the MNE can require a lower rate of return than is required by local investors.

Thus the discount rate used locally must be a hypothetical rate based on a judgment as to what independent local investors would probably demand were they to own the business. Consequently, application of the local discount rate to local cash flows provides only a rough measure of the value of the project as a standalone local venture, rather than an absolute valuation.

Real Option Analysis

The discounted cash flow (DCF) approach used in the valuation of Semen Indonesia, and in capital budgeting and valuation in general, has long had its critics. Investments that have long lives, cash flow returns in later years, or higher levels of risk than those typical of the firm's current business activities are often rejected by traditional DCF financial analysis. More importantly, when MNEs evaluate competitive projects, traditional discounted cash flow analysis is typically unable to capture the strategic options that an individual investment option may offer. This has led to the development of real option analysis. *Real option analysis* is the application of option theory to capital budgeting decisions.

Real options is a different way of thinking about investment values. At its core, it is a cross between decision-tree analysis and pure option-based valuation. It is particularly useful when analyzing investment projects that will follow very different value paths at decision points in time where management decisions are made regarding project pursuit. This wide range of potential outcomes is at the heart of real option theory. These wide ranges of value are volatilities, the basic element of option pricing theory described previously in Chapter 5.

Real option valuation also allows us to analyze a number of managerial decisions that in practice characterize many major capital investment projects:

1. The option to defer
2. The option to abandon
3. The option to alter capacity
4. The option to start up or shut down (switching)

Real option analysis treats cash flows in terms of future value in a positive sense, whereas DCF treats future cash flows negatively (on a discounted basis). Real option analysis is a particularly powerful device when addressing potential investment projects with extremely long life spans, or investments that do not commence until future dates. Real option analysis acknowledges the way information is gathered over time to support decision making. Management learns from both active (searching it out) and passive (observing market conditions) knowledge gathering and then uses this knowledge to make better decisions. The mini-case at the end of this chapter illustrates an application of real option analysis.

SUMMARY

- The proposed greenfield investment in Indonesia by Cemex was analyzed within the traditional capital budgeting framework (base case).
- Foreign complications, including foreign exchange and political risks, were introduced to the analysis.
- Parent cash flows must be distinguished from project cash flows. Each of these two types of flows contributes to a different view of value.
- Parent cash flows often depend on the form of financing. Thus cash flows cannot be clearly separated from financing decisions, as is done in domestic capital budgeting.
- Additional cash flows generated by a new investment in one foreign subsidiary may be in part or wholly taken away from another subsidiary, with the net result that the project is favorable from a single subsidiary point of view but contributes nothing to worldwide cash flows.
- Remittance of funds to the parent must be explicitly recognized because of differing tax systems, legal and political constraints on the movement of funds, local business norms, and differences in how financial markets and institutions function.
- Cash flows from subsidiaries to parent can be generated by an array of nonfinancial payments, including payment of license fees and payments for imports from the parent.
- Differing rates of national inflation must be anticipated because of their importance in causing changes in competitive position and thus cash flows over a period of time.
- A foreign project's capital budgeting analysis should be adjusted for potential foreign exchange and/or political risks associated with the investment.
- A number of alternative methods are used for adjusting for risk, including adding an additional risk premium to the discount factor used, decreasing expected cash flows, and conducting detailed sensitivity and scenario analysis on expected project outcomes.
- Real option analysis is a different way of thinking about investment values. At its core, it is a cross between decision-tree analysis and pure option-based valuation.
- Real option valuation also allows us to evaluate the option to defer, the option to abandon, the option to alter capacity, and the option to start up or shut down a project.

QUESTIONS

1. **Capital budgeting theoretical framework.** Capital budgeting for a foreign project uses the same theoretical framework as domestic capital budgeting. What are the basic steps in domestic capital budgeting?
2. **Foreign complexities.** Capital budgeting for a foreign project is considerably more complex than the domestic case. What are the factors that add complexity?
3. **Project versus parent valuation.**
   a. Why should a foreign project be evaluated both from a project and parent viewpoint?
   b. Which viewpoint, project or parent, gives results closer to the traditional meaning of net present value in capital budgeting?
   c. Which viewpoint gives results closer to the effect on consolidated earnings per share?
4. **Which cash flows?** Capital projects provide both operating cash flows and financial cash flows. Why are operating cash flows preferred for domestic capital budgeting but financial cash flows given major consideration in international projects?

5. **Risk-adjusted return.** Should the anticipated internal rate of return (IRR) for a proposed foreign project be compared to a) alternative home country proposals, b) returns earned by local companies in the same industry and/or risk class, or c) both? Justify your answer.

6. **Blocked cash flows.** In the context of evaluating foreign investment proposals, how should a multinational firm evaluate cash flows in the host foreign country that are blocked from being repatriated to the firm's home country?

7. **Host country inflation.** How should a MNE factor host-country inflation into its evaluation of an investment proposal?

8. **Cost of equity.** A foreign subsidiary does not have an independent cost of capital. However, in order to estimate the discount rate for a comparable host country firm, the analyst should try to calculate a hypothetical cost of capital. As part of this process, the analyst can estimate the subsidiary's proxy cost of equity by using the traditional equation: $k_e = k_{rf} + (k_m - k_{rf})$. Define each variable in this equation and explain how the variable might be different for a proxy host country firm compared to the parent MNE.

9. **Viewpoints.** What are the differences in the cash flows used in a project point-of-view analysis and a parent point-of-view analysis?

10. **Foreign exchange risk.** How is foreign exchange risk sensitivity factored into the capital budgeting analysis of a foreign project?

11. **Expropriation risk.** How is expropriation risk factored into the capital budgeting analysis of a foreign project?

12. **Real option analysis.** What is real option analysis? How is it a better method of making investment decisions than traditional capital budgeting analysis?

PROBLEMS

1. **Sarasota Corporation.** Sarasota Corporation (U.S.) expects to receive cash dividends from a French joint venture over the coming three years. The first dividend, to be paid December 31, 2002, is expected to be €720,000. The dividend is then expected to grow 10.0% per year over the following two years. The current exchange rate (December 30, 2001) is $0.9180/€. Sarasota's weighted average cost of capital is 12%.
   a. What is the present value of the expected euro dividend stream if the euro is expected to appreciate 4.00% per annum against the dollar?
   b. What is the present value of the expected dividend stream if the euro were to depreciate 3.00% per annum against the dollar?

2. **Trefica de Honduras.** Texas Pacific, a U.S.-based private equity firm, is trying to determine what it should pay for a Honduras tool manufacturing firm named Trefica. Texas Pacific estimates that Trefica will generate a free cash flow of 13 million Honduran lempiras (Lp) next year (2003), and that this free cash flow will continue to grow at a constant rate of 8.0% per annum indefinitely.

   A private equity firm like Texas Pacific, however, is not interested in owning a company for long, and plans to sell Trefica at the end of three years for approximately 10 times Trefica's free cash flow in that year. The current spot exchange rate is Lp14.80/$, but the Honduran inflation rate is expected to remain at a relatively high rate of 16.0% per annum compared to the U.S. dollar inflation rate of only 2.0% per annum. Texas Pacific expects to earn at least a 20% annual rate of return on international investments like Trefica.
   a. What is Trefica worth if the Honduran lempira were to remain fixed over the three-year investment period?
   b. What is Trefica worth if the Honduran lempira were to change in value over time according to purchasing power parity?

3. **Baltimore Tile Company.** Baltimore Tile Company (U.S.) is considering investing 50,000,000 rupees (Rs) in India to create a wholly owned tile manufacturing plant to export to the European market. After five years, the subsidiary would be sold to Indian investors for Rs100,000,000. A *pro forma* income statement for the Indian operation predicts the generation of Rs7,000,000 of annual cash flow, as follows:

Annual sales revenue	Rs 30,000,000
Less cash operating expenses	−17,000,000
Less depreciation	−1,000,000
Income before interest and taxes	Rs 12,000,000
Less Indian taxes at 50%	−6,000,000
Net income	Rs 6,000,000
Add back depreciation	+1,000,000
Annual cash flow	Rs 7,000,000

The initial investment will be made on December 31, 2002, and cash flows will occur on December 31 of each succeeding year. Annual cash dividends to Baltimore Tile from India will equal 75% of accounting income.

The U.S. corporate tax rate is 40% and the Indian corporate tax rate is 50%. Because the Indian tax rate is greater than the U.S. tax rate, annual dividends paid to Baltimore Tile will not be subject to additional taxes in the United States. There are no capital gains taxes on the final sale. Baltimore Tile uses a weighted average cost of capital of 14% on domestic investments, but will add 6 percentage points for the Indian investment because of perceived greater risk. Baltimore Tile forecasts the rupee/dollar exchange rate for December 31 on the next six years to be:

Year	Exchange Rate	Year	Exchange Rate
2002	Rs50.00/$	2005	Rs62.00/$
2003	Rs54.00/$	2006	Rs66.00/$
2004	Rs58.00/$	2007	Rs70.00/$

What is the net present value and internal rate of return on this investment?

4. **Berkeley Devices.** Berkeley Devices, Inc., designs components for personal computers. Until the present, manufacturing has been subcontracted to other companies, but for reasons of quality control Berkeley Devices has decided to manufacture itself in Asia. Analysis has narrowed the choice to two possibilities, Penang, Malaysia, and Manila, the Philippines. At the moment only the following summary of expected after-tax cash flows is available. Although most operating outflows would be in Malaysian ringgit or Philippine pesos, some additional U.S. dollar cash outflows would be necessary, as shown.

The Malaysia ringgit currently trades at RM3.80/$ and the Philippine peso trades at Ps50.00/$. Berkeley expects the Malaysian ringgit to appreciate 2.0% per year against the dollar, and the Philippine peso to depreciate 5.0% per year against the dollar. If the weighted average cost of capital for Berkeley Devices is 14.0%, which project looks most promising?

Berkeley in Penang	2002	2003	2004	2005	2006	2007
Net ringgit cash flows	(26,000)	8,000	6,800	7,400	9,200	10,000
Net dollar cash flows	—	(100)	(120)	(150)	(150)	—

Berkeley in Manila	2002	2003	2004	2005	2006	2007
Net peso cash flows	(560,000)	190,000	180,000	200,000	210,000	200,000
Dollar cash outflows	—	(100)	(200)	(300)	(400)	—

End of Year	Unit Demand	Unit Sales Price	Exchange Rate (Korunas/$)	Fixed Cash Operating Expenses	Depreciation
0			32.5		
1	700,000	$ 10.00	30.0	$ 1,000,000	$ 500,000
2	900,000	10.30	27.5	1,030,000	500,000
3	1,000,000	10.60	25.0	1,060,000	500,000

5. **Superior Machine Oil Company.** Privately owned Superior Machine Oil Company is considering investing in the Czech Republic so as to have a refinery source closer to its European customers. The original investment in Czech korunas would amount to K250 million, or $5,000,000 at the current spot rate of K50/$, all in fixed assets, which will be depreciated over ten years by the straight-line method. An additional K100,000,000 ($4,000,000) will be needed for working capital.

   For capital budgeting purposes, Superior assumes sale as a going concern at the end of the third year at a price, after all taxes, equal to the net book value of fixed assets alone (not including working capital). All free cash flow will be repatriated to the United States as soon as possible.

   In evaluating the venture, the table of U.S. dollar forecasts at the top of this page are used.

   Variable manufacturing costs are expected to be 50% of sales. No additional funds need be invested in the U.S. subsidiary during the period under consideration. The Czech Republic imposes no restrictions on repatriation of any funds of any sort. The Czech corporate tax rate is 25% and the United States rate is 40%. Both countries allow a tax credit for taxes paid in other countries. Superior uses 18% as its weighted average cost of capital, and its objective is to maximize present value. Is the investment attractive to Superior?

6. **Tostadas de Baja, S.A.** Tostadas de Baja, S.A., located in the state of Baja California, Mexico, manufactures frozen Mexican food that enjoys a large following in the U.S. states of California and Arizona to the north. In order to be closer to its U.S. market, Tostadas de Baja is considering moving some of its manufacturing operations to southern California. Operations in California would begin in 2003 and have the following attributes:

   a. The 2003 sales price in the United States would average $5 per package, and prices would increase 3% per annum.

   b. 2003 production and sales would be 1 million packets. Unit sales would grow at 10% per annum.

   c. California production costs of an estimated $4 per packet in 2003 would increase by 4% per annum. General and administration expenses would be $100,000 per year. Depreciation expenses would be $80,000 per year.

   d. Tostadas de Baja uses a weighted average cost of capital of 16%.

   e. Tostadas de Baja will assign an after-tax value to its California plant at the end of 2005 equal to an infinite stream of 2005 dividends, discounted at 20% p.a. The higher discount rate is a result of the company's concerns about the political risk of a Mexican firm manufacturing in California.

   f. All production is for sale; hence, production volume equals sales volume. All sales are for cash.

   g. Combined federal and state tax rate is 30% in the United States and 25% in Mexico.

   h. Actual and expected exchange rates, by year, are:

      2002: Ps8.00/$ 2004: Ps10.00/$

      2003: Ps9.00/$ 2005: Ps11.00/$

The California manufacturer will pay 80% of its accounting profit to Tostadas as an annual cash dividend. Mexican taxes are calculated on grossed-up dividends from foreign countries, with a credit for host country taxes already paid. What is the maximum U.S. dollar price Tostadas de Baja should offer in 2003 for the investment?

Santa Clara Electronics. *Use the following problem and assumptions to answer problems 7–10.*

Santa Clara Electronics, Inc., of California exports 24,000 sets of low-density light bulbs per year to Argentina under an import license that expires in five years. In Argentina, the bulbs are sold for the Argentine peso equivalent of \$60 per set. Direct manufacturing costs in the United States and shipping together amount to \$40 per set. The market for this type of bulb in Argentina is stable, neither growing nor shrinking, and Santa Clara holds the major portion of the market.

The Argentine government has invited Santa Clara to open a manufacturing plant so that imported bulbs can be replaced by local production. If Santa Clara makes the investment, it will operate the plant for five years and then sell the building and equipment to Argentine investors at net book value at the time of sale plus the value of any net working capital. (Net working capital is the amount of current assets less any portion financed by local debt.) Santa Clara will be allowed to repatriate all net income and depreciation funds to the United States each year. Santa Clara traditionally evaluates all foreign investments in U.S. dollar terms.

- **Investment.** Santa Clara's anticipated cash outlay in U.S. dollars in 2003 would be:

Building and equipment	\$1,000,000
Net working capital	1,000,000
Total investment	\$2,000,000

  All investment outlays will be made in 2003, and all operating cash flows will occur at the end of years 2004 through 2008.

- **Depreciation and investment recovery.** Building and equipment will be depreciated over five years on a straight-line basis. At the end of the fifth year, the \$1,000,000 of net working capital may also be repatriated to the United States, as may the remaining net book value of the plant.

- **Sales price of bulbs.** Locally manufactured bulbs will be sold for the Argentine peso equivalent of \$60 per set.

- **Operating expenses per set of bulbs.** Material purchases are as follows:

Materials purchased in Argentina (U.S. dollar equivalent)	\$20 per set
Materials imported from Santa Clara—USA	10 per set
Total variable costs	\$30 per set

- **Transfer prices.** The \$10 transfer price per set for raw material sold by the parent consists of \$5 of direct and indirect costs incurred in the United States on their manufacture, creating \$5 of pre-tax profit to Santa Clara.

- **Taxes.** The corporate income tax rate is 40% in both Argentina and the United States (combined federal and state/province).

- **Discount rate.** Santa Clara Electronics uses a 15% discount rate to evaluate all domestic and foreign projects.

7. **Santa Clara Electronics: baseline analysis.** Evaluate the proposed investment in Argentina by Santa Clara Electronics (U.S.). Create a project viewpoint capital budget and a parent viewpoint capital budget. What do you conclude from your analysis?

8. **Santa Clara Electronics: revenue growth scenario.** As a result of the analysis in the previous problem, Santa Clara wishes to explore the implications of being able to grow sales volume by 4% per year. Argentine inflation is expected to average 5% per year, so sales price and material cost increases of 7% and 6% per year, respectively, are thought reasonable. Although material costs in Argentina are expected to rise, U.S.-based costs are not expected to change over the five-year period. Evaluate this scenario for both the project and parent viewpoints. Is the project under this revenue growth scenario acceptable?

9. **Santa Clara Electronics: revenue growth and sales price scenario.** In addition to the assumptions employed in Problem 8, Santa Clara now wishes to evaluate the prospect of being able to sell the Argentine subsidiary at the end of year 5 at a multiple of the business's earnings in that year. Santa Clara believes that a multiple of 6 is a conservative estimate of the market value of the firm at that time. Evaluate the project and parent viewpoint capital budgets.

10. **Santa Clara Electronics: revenue growth, sales price, and currency risk scenario.** One of the new analysts at Santa Clara, a recent MBA graduate, believes that it is a fundamental error to evaluate the Argentine project's prospective earnings and cash flows in dollars, rather than first estimating their Argentine peso (Ps) value and then converting cash flow returns to the U.S. in dollars. She believes the correct method is to use the end-of-year spot rate in 2003 of Ps3.50/$ and assume it will change in relation to purchasing power. (She is assuming U.S. inflation to be 1% per annum, Argentine inflation to be 5% per annum.) She also believes that Santa Clara should use a risk-adjusted discount rate in Argentina that reflects Argentine capital costs (20% is her estimate) and a risk-adjusted discount rate for the parent viewpoint capital budget (18%) on the assumption that international projects in a risky currency environment should require a higher expected return than other lower risk projects. How do these assumptions and changes alter Santa Clara's perspective on the proposed investment?

INTERNET EXERCISES

WWW.

1. **Capital projects and the EBRD.** The European Bank for Reconstruction and Development (EBRD) was established to "foster the transition towards open market-oriented economies and to promote private and entrepreneurial initiative in the countries of central and eastern Europe and the Commonwealth of Independent States (CIS) committed to and applying the principles of multiparty democracy, pluralism and market economics." Use the EBRD web site to determine which projects and companies EBRD is currently undertaking.

   European Bank for Reconstruction and Development — http://www.ebrd.org

2. **Emerging markets: China.** Long-term investment projects such as electrical power generation require a thorough understanding of all attributes of doing business in that country, including import/export restrictions, labor relations, supplier financing, tax rules, depreciation schedules, currency properties and restrictions, and sources of short-term and long-term debt, to name a few. China is currently the focus of investment and market penetration strategies of multinational firms worldwide. Using the web (you might start with the web sites listed here), build a data base on doing business in China, and prepare an update of many of the factors such as average receivables outstanding and currency convertibility discussed in this chapter.

   Ministry of Foreign Trade and Economic Cooperation, PRC — http://www.chinamarket.com.cn

   China Investment Trust & Investment Corporation — http://www.citic.com

   ChinaNet Investment Pages — http://www.business-china.com/invest

SELECTED READINGS

Brealey, Richard A., Ian A. Cooper, and Michael A. Habib, "Using Project Finance to Fund Infrastructure Investments," *Journal of Applied Corporate Finance*, Fall 1996, Volume 9, No. 5, pp. 25–38.

Dixit, Avinash K., and Robert S. Pindyck, "The Options Approach to Capital Investment," *Harvard Business Review*, May/Jun 1995, pp. 105–115.

Godfrey, Stephen, and Ramon Espinosa, "A Practical Approach to Calculating the Cost of Equity for Investments in Emerging Markets," *Journal of Applied Corporate Finance*, Fall 1996, Volume 9, Number 3, pp. 80–89.

Keck, Tom, Eric Levengood, and Al Longfield, "Using Discounted Cash Flow Analysis in an International Setting: A Survey of Issues in Modeling the Cost of Capital," *Journal of Applied Corporate Finance*, Fall 1998, Volume 11, No. 3, pp. 82–99.

MINI-CASE

Carlton's Chinese Market Entry—An Application of Real Option Analysis

Carlton is evaluating the possibility of entering the Chinese market. The senior management team, headed by CEO Charles Darwin, has concluded from a number of preliminary studies (code-named Beagle) performed by a consultant that within three to five years this market could well determine who the major players are to be in Carlton's telecommunications industry. The corporate finance team, headed by the CFO Caitlin Kelly, has concluded a preliminary financial analysis of its own on the basis of the numbers presented by the consultants.

The results of the corporate finance team's expected value analysis were not, however, encouraging. As illustrated in Exhibit A, the expected gross profits of the venture were estimated to be only $10 million.

- Revenues were expected to follow one of two paths—either high (approximately $130 million at a 50% probability) or low ($50 million at a 50% probability). Therefore, using expected value analysis, revenues were estimated at $90 million.
- Costs were expected to be either high ($120 million), medium ($80 million), or low ($40 million), all with an equal 33.3% expected probability of occurrence. The expected value of costs were $80 million.

What made this $10 million gross profit all the more unattractive was that the market development group was requesting an additional $15 million for upfront research and development (R&D). This capital expense could not be justified. The expected total return on the project would then be a negative $5 million: ($15) + $ 10 = ($5). The corporate finance team concluded that the project was not an acceptable investment in its present form.

Darwin was clearly frustrated with the corporate finance team during the presentation of their results. After some heated debate over individual values, Darwin asked what specifically would be learned if the added $15 million in market research and development were actually spent. Would it improve the expected profitability of the project?

After some additional analysis, the corporate finance team concluded that nothing significant would be learned about the market that would change either the probabilities or expected values

Exhibit A Carlton's Analysis of Chinese Market Entry

Revenues	Value in millions	Probability	Expected value in millions
High	$130	0.50	$65.00
Low	50	0.50	25.00
Expected value		1.00	$90.00
Costs			
High	$120	0.33	$40.00
Medium	80	0.33	26.67
Low	40	0.33	13.33
Expected value		1.00	$80.00

Expected value gross profit = revenue – costs = $90 – $80 = $10.

of revenues. However, after the additional R&D expenditure, the team felt certain that the cost of operations would be better known.

Darwin then asked the corporate finance team about an alternative approach to viewing the project:

> *"What if the expenditure of $15 million were looked upon as the purchase of a call option on the project? What I mean is, if we spend the $15 million, we would then have the ability to identify the actual cost associated with undertaking the project. Even though we still would not really know the revenues—we still have business risk—we would be able to decide more intelligently whether to stop or proceed with the project at that point in time."*

As illustrated in Exhibit B, after the investment (or expenditure) of the $15 million in market research and development, the firm would know which of the three cost paths it would be on—high, medium, or low. Regardless of the expected revenue, still assumed to be $90 million, the firm could make an intelligent choice to either stop or proceed at that point. This was, in Darwin's opinion, a much more logical way to pursue the analysis.

Caitlin Kelly and her finance team, however, were still not convinced. Kelly said, "But we would still be spending the $15 million up front and still be looking at the same expected outcomes. I don't see how your approach changes anything."

Darwin continued, "It changes a lot. After spending the $15 million we would know—with added certainty—what the likely outcome would be. If it is either the medium- or low-cost path, we would proceed and end up with a gross operating profit of either $10 or $50 million, depending on revenues. If it is the high-cost path, we would stop all work immediately, before incurring additional operating costs. The expected value, at least according to my calculations, is a positive $20 million."

$$\text{expected value} = (\$15) + [\,(0.333 \times \$0) + (0.333 \times \$10) + (0.333 \times \$50)\,] = \$20$$

It then dawned upon Kelly what Darwin was saying. The purchase of the call option, the expenditure of the $15 million, would allow Carlton to avoid the loss-making option (the

Exhibit B Carlton's Analysis of Chinese Market Entry

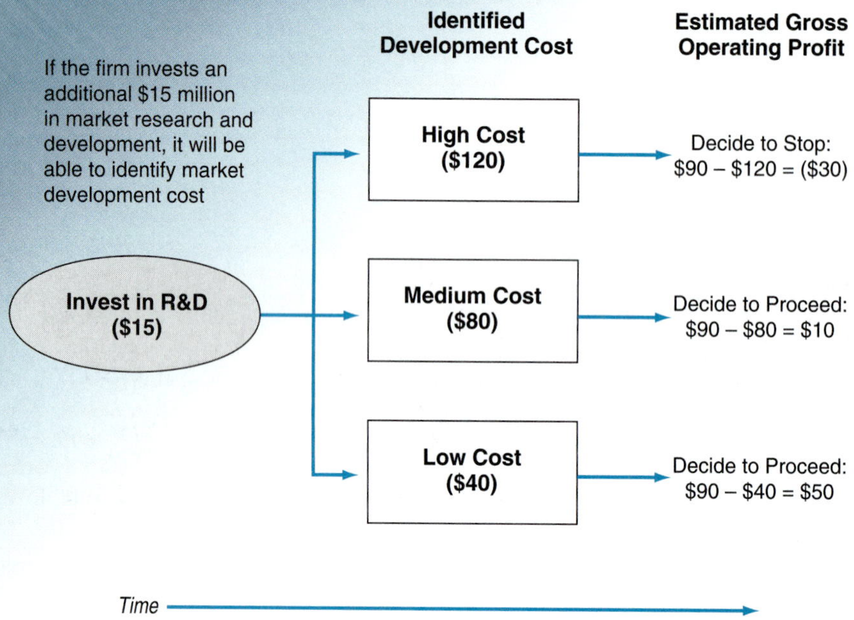

Investing in the market R&D is equivalent to buying a call option. Amounts are in millions.

high-cost path with an expected outcome of negative $30 million), so the high-cost path would enter the calculation of expected value as zero. The purchase of the call option would indeed allow Carlton to undertake the investment, if it wished, only after gaining additional time and knowledge.

Darwin and the senior management team then concluded that they had won the argument (as senior management always does) and approved the project.

The Potential of Real Option Analysis

Real options analysis, like DCF and other investment analysis techniques, is nothing other than a tool. The two techniques are complementary. Management should employ both methods in the analysis of potential investments and gather information from both.

Unlike our example, real option analysis is not ordinarily a simple technique. There is an enormous amount of technical "comfort" required on the part of the analyst in order to implement the technique correctly. Like most techniques derived from financial theory, it is easily abused. Those who will utilize the information provided by real option analysis must be trained in the proper interpretation of its results.

But real option analysis is gaining in use and popularity. Consistent with the example of Carlton, it is often favored first by senior management because it has two characteristics they like.

Its structure acknowledges the time sequence of a project, describing cash inflows and outflows at different points in time. This is more consistent with the way management frequently sees a project unfold. Real option analysis also seems to value "management" by its very nature; it credits the ability of management to gain new information and make good business decisions at the points in time when those decisions must be made.

Case Questions

1. How does real option analysis differ from traditional expected value analysis?
2. How does real option analysis use information gathering differently from discounted cash flow analysis?
3. Recalculate both the expected return analysis and the real option analysis for the Chinese market entry assuming that the revenue probabilities were 25% high and 75% low. Is the project acceptable under either of the decision-making methodologies?

Adjusting for Risk in Foreign Investments

In this chapter, Cemex added a 6% risk premium to its 11.98% domestic cost of capital when evaluating foreign investments. This addition resulted in an arbitrary 17.98% risk-adjusted cost of capital that was then used to calculate the expected rate of return on its proposed Semen Indonesia project from the parent firm's perspective. However, it is possible to design a more sophisticated calculation of the cost of capital that could be selectively risk-adjusted in order to evaluate investments in a variety of international markets, particularly emerging markets like Indonesia.

The risks associated with the prospective Indonesian investment can be subdivided into *two-sided risks* (*symmetric risks*) and *one-sided risks.*[3] Symmetric risks include operating risk, demand markets and pricing risk, and macroeconomic and macro political risks, risk components that can cause the cash flow returns of the investment to be higher or lower than generally expected (most likely). *One-sided risks* (those variables that are likely to result in decreased cash flows only from those expected) include expropriation, cross-border payment restrictions or prohibitions, political chaos, or upheaval. If the prospective Indonesian investment is to be evaluated on a risk-adjusted cost of capital basis, both symmetric and one-sided risks must be incorporated into Cemex's weighted-average cost of capital.

Risk-Adjusting Cemex's Cost of Capital

Cemex needs to adjust both its cost of debt and its cost of equity to reflect the additional risks posed by the Indonesian investment.[4]

Adjusting Debt Costs (Required Returns)

The simplest and most straightforward estimate of the risk premium on risks associated with debt in Indonesia is based on the Indonesian government's cost of borrowing U.S. dollars. The Indonesian government's risk premium would be that additional interest it pays to borrow U.S. dollars in the Eurobond market above that paid by the U.S. Treasury. Since both parties are committing to repayment in the same currency, U.S. dollars, the differential in their debt costs reflects the higher perceived risk associated with repayment of U.S. dollar–denominated debt by the government of Indonesia. These interest rate spreads are termed *sovereign spreads.*[5] Exhibit 18A.1 illustrates sovereign spreads and U.S. dollar borrowing costs by a selected group of emerging market countries, including Indonesia.

The sovereign spread for Indonesia, according to Exhibit 18A.1 is 400 basis points or 4.00%. The risk-free rate of interest applicable to Cemex's prospective Indonesian investment is then:

3. This approach follows that of the following sources: Stephen Godfrey and Ramon Espinosa, "A Practical Approach to Calculating Costs of Equity for Investments in Emerging Markets," *Journal of Applied Corporate Finance*, Fall 1996, Volume 9, No. 3, pp. 80–89; and Donald R. Lessard, "Incorporating Country Risk in the Valuation of Offshore Projects," *Journal of Applied Corporate Finance*, Fall 1996, Volume 9, No. 3, pp. 52–63.

4. There are a number of alternative approaches to cost of capital calculations for international projects and investments. See for example Ibbotson (http://www.ibbotson.com) or Harvey (http://www.duke.edu/_charvey/Country_risk).

5. The sovereign spread used here is from J.P. Morgan for issues outstanding on August 30, 1996. Strangely, sovereign spreads are readily available for emerging market countries, but not for the majority of industrialized nations. Emerging market spreads are found most easily by published spreads on Brady bond issuances (see for example the daily *Financial Times*). Industrialized country governments, however, rarely issue dollar-denominated Eurobonds (and definitely not Brady bonds), making their sovereign spreads much harder to capture empirically.

Exhibit 18A.1 The Cost of Borrowing U.S. Dollars by Selected Emerging Market Countries (1996)

Country	(1) U.S. Treasury Cost of Funds (basis points)	(2) Country's Sovereign Spread (basis points)	(3) Country's U.S. Dollar Total Cost of Funds (basis points)	(percent)
Argentina	600	718	1318	13.18
Brazil	600	610	1210	12.10
Indonesia	600	400	1000	10.00
Mexico	600	597	1197	11.97
Philippines	600	226	826	8.26
Venezuela	600	811	1411	14.11
United States	600	—	600	6.00

Source: Abstracted by authors from Lessard (1996). Original data from J.P. Morgan and the International Finance Corporation's Emerging Stock Markets Factbook, 1996. Column (3) = column (1) + column (2).

$$k_{\mathrm{rf}}^{\mathrm{Indo}} = k_{\mathrm{rf}}^{\mathrm{US}} + \left(\text{Indonesian sovereign spread}\right) = 6.00\% + 4.00\% = 10.00\%$$

If we assume that the project risk of Cemex's prospective Indonesian investment is the same as that of other investments by Cemex, we would add the same credit spread Cemex pays above the risk-free Treasury rate in the United States (200 basis points or 2.00%) to the risk-free rate in Indonesia. This yields a risk-adjusted cost of debt for Cemex's Indonesian investment of:[6]

$$k_{\mathrm{d}}^{\mathrm{Indo}} = k_{\mathrm{rf}}^{\mathrm{Indo}} + \left(\text{credit spread}\right) = 10.00\% + 2.00\% = 12.00\%$$

Although this appears at first glance to be prohibitively high, it does reflect current costs for high-grade Indonesian corporate borrowers in the Eurobond market. And again, this includes the risks associated with borrowing U.S. dollars (the sovereign risk premium) and the risks associated with the project (the credit risk premium).

Adjusting Equity Costs (Required Returns)

Adjusting the required return on equity is not quite as simple as adding a sovereign spread to an existing corporate cost of debt. Again using the capital asset pricing model as the theoretical foundation, we need to find what Lessard calls an *offshore project beta*. In our numerical example here, the *offshore project beta* attempts to measure the risk associated with a U.S.-dollar based company investing in a cement manufacturing facility (the *project* component) in Indonesia (the *offshore* component).

The Offshore project beta. In order to create this new beta (it is too specific to have been previously measured), we utilize one of the basic mathematical characteristics of betas, that

6. This assumption may be a bit heroic. The credit spread of Cemex in the U.S. over U.S. treasuries may not be a good proxy for the credit spread Cemex Indonesia would pay over the dollar risk-free rate in Indonesia.

betas are multiplicative (one beta may be multiplied by a second beta). Assuming that the risk of the project relative to the Indonesian market (a cement plant in Indonesia) is the same *relative risk* as that project would represent in the United States market (a cement plant in the U.S.), we calculate the offshore project beta as the product of Cemex's own beta and the *Indonesia-to-U.S. country beta.*

The *Indonesia-to-U.S. country beta,* β^{Indo}, is rather difficult to empirically estimate because of the limited data on the covariance between U.S. equity markets and Indonesian equity markets. Luckily, an equivalent method of calculating beta is to find the ratio of the standard deviations of each of the individual markets—the United States and Indonesia, in this case—and to then simply multiply this ratio by the correlation coefficient between the two markets. The correlation of the Indonesian equity markets to the U.S. equity markets is here assumed to be 0.26 ($\rho_{\text{Indo, USA}} = 0.26$). This is then multiplied by the ratio of market standard deviations ($\sigma_{\text{Indo}} = 30.55$, $\sigma_{\text{USA}} = 10.08$):[7]

$$\beta^{\text{Indo}} = \frac{\text{Cov}\left(k_{\text{Indo}}, k_{\text{USA}}\right)}{\text{Var}\left(k_{\text{USA}}\right)} = \rho_{\text{Indo, USA}} \frac{\sigma_{\text{Indo}}}{\sigma_{\text{USA}}} = \left[0.26\right]\frac{30.55}{10.08} = 0.7880$$

The country beta for Indonesia is found to be 0.7880. We now multiply this country beta with the beta value for Cemex itself, β_{Cemex}, the same 1.5 value used in the parent company's cost of equity calculation. Cemex's *offshore project beta* for Indonesia is now calculated as 1.182:

$$\beta_{\text{Cemex}}^{\text{Offshore}} = \beta_{\text{Cemex}} \times \beta^{\text{Indo}} = 1.5(0.7880) = 1.182$$

The Equity risk premium. The final input to the CAPM approach is the equity risk premium demanded by a U.S. investor on an Indonesian equity investment, $\text{RPM}_{\text{US}}^{\text{Indo}}$. The offshore project beta calculated in the previous section will now be multiplied by the following risk premium:

$$\text{RPM}_{\text{US}}^{\text{Indo}} = k_{\text{m}} - k_{\text{rf}}^{\text{Indo}}$$

Empirically, we are confronted with making a choice between two approaches. We could infer that the applicable RPM is that found by subtracting the Indonesian risk-free rate of 10.0% (calculated earlier) from the U.S. equity return of 13.0%, a premium of 3.0%. Such a small risk premium for the Indonesian market is, however, troubling. Alternatively, we could use the U.S. market's equity risk premium of 13.0% – 6.0% = 7.0%, and assume this RPM is what would be demanded by a U.S.-based investor when establishing the required return on equity investments in the Indonesian marketplace.[8] We choose the latter.

The Adjusted cost of capital. We now have all of the components for estimating the risk-adjusted cost of equity for Cemex's prospective investment in Indonesia:

7. Godfrey and Espinosa (1996) argue that MNEs are often not interested in their investors' ability to diversify internationally, and therefore the correlation coefficient between country markets should be assumed to be equal to one in this type of analysis. In our opinion, this would tend to rob the approach to international risk measurement of its theoretical foundations, since it would ignore the fact that equity markets in different countries are not perfectly correlated (for example, in this case, the correlation between the United States and Indonesia is 0.26, not 1.00).

8. It should also be noted that the first approach could actually result in a negative premium (for example, Brazil/U.S.), which would be even more troubling.

$$k_{e}^{\text{Indo}} = k_{rf}^{\text{Indo}} + \text{RPM}_{\text{US}}^{\text{Indo}} \beta_{\text{Cemex}}^{\text{Offshore}} = 10.0\% + \left(7.0\%\right)1.182 = 18.274\%$$

With all components in place, the weighted-average cost of capital, adjusted for offshore application to Indonesia, assuming the same 35% effective tax rate as the parent company, is calculated as:

$$k_{\text{WACC}}^{\text{Indo}} = \left(18.274\%\right)\left(0.60\right) + \left(12.000\%\right)\left(1 - 0.35\right)\left(0.40\right) = 14.084\%$$

The relatively surprising result is that the Indonesian risk-adjusted weighted-average cost of capital is only 2.104% higher than the parent company's own cost of capital (14.084% – 11.980%). This is substantially less than if the simple sovereign spread of 4.00% were added to the parent's own cost of capital. This is not to say that this will always be the case. This is not a simple cost of capital plus 3% or 6% premium process. Because the costs of equity are adjusted on the basis of relative volatilities and correlations with the home country capital market, the relative direction and magnitude of the risk-adjusted WACC to that of the parent's is purely an empirical issue on a case-by-case basis.

Adjusting Costs of Capital for Cemex's Portfolio of Potential Projects

But what if Cemex wanted to evaluate projects across a number of emerging markets, and not just Indonesia? It would then need to repeat the capital cost adjustment process just demonstrated for Indonesia across the subject country-set. This calculation, although somewhat cumbersome initially, is quite tractable for Cemex or any other MNE attempting to evaluate a wide spectrum of potential investments globally.

Exhibit 18A.2 presents the needed data for a small set of emerging market countries, including Indonesia, used in the Cemex-Indonesia numerical illustration. The data presented in Exhibit 18A.2 is generally applicable to any U.S.-based or U.S. dollar–based MNE. The

Exhibit 18A.2 Risk-Adjustment Component Inputs for Selected Emerging Countries

Country	(1) Sovereign Spread (basis points)	(2) Market Volatility (%)	(3) Relative to U.S.	(4) Correlation with U.S.	(5) Country Beta to U.S.	(6) Offshore Beta to U.S. Market
Argentina	718	61.63	6.11	0.32	1.9565	2.935
Brazil	610	60.86	6.04	0.40	2.4151	3.623
Indonesia	400	30.55	3.03	0.26	0.7880	1.182
Mexico	597	37.90	3.76	0.22	0.8272	1.241
Philippines	226	34.16	3.39	0.22	0.7456	1.118
Venezuela	811	60.93	6.04	– 0.03	– 0.1813	– 0.272
United States	—	10.08	1.00	1.00	1.0000	1.500

Columns (1), (2), and (4) are from Lessard (1996). Original data from J.P. Morgan and the International Finance Corporation's *Emerging Stock Markets Factbook*, 1996. Correlations are based on 50 months ending December 1995.

Column (3) is the ratio of the individual country's volatility shown in Column (2) divided by U.S. volatility (10.08) shown in column (2). For example, Argentina's relative volatility of 6.11 = 61.63 â 10.08.

Column (5) = Column (3) × Column (4).

Column (6) = Column (5) × U.S. beta of 1.500.

MNE need only contribute its own cost of capital components, plus the appropriate beta value comparable to the industry-specific beta of the prospective investment. (Under most applications, the MNE parent company will simply use its own beta from its home market as a proxy for this relative measure of risk.)

Exhibit 18A.3 summarizes the next step, the calculation of the adjusted cost of equity for Cemex in evaluating prospective investments across the countries listed. As in the previous numerical example, the CAPM approach uses the same basic U.S. Treasury risk-free rate and adds to it the individual country's sovereign risk premium. This country-specific risk-free cost of U.S. dollar debt is then added to the product of the equity market risk premium for the United States (7.000%) and the offshore beta to the U.S. market (Exhibit 18A.2). As Exhibit 18A.3 illustrates, this results in a wide range of adjusted cost of equity estimates across these countries, with the highest in Brazil (37.458%) and the lowest in Venezuela (12.206%). Note that the reason the Venezuelan adjusted cost of equity is so low is a direct result of the negative correlation the Venezuelan equity markets have with U.S. equity markets.

Finally, with the risk-adjusted costs of debt and equity calculated for each country, it is now possible to calculate the weighted-average cost of capital to be applied to each of the individual emerging market countries. Exhibit 18A.4 reports the results of this last step. Clearly this methodology, internally consistent with domestic capital cost estimation, results in substantially different (generally lower) discount rates on foreign projects than the traditional WACC + 3% (or even 6%) rule of thumb utilized by many MNEs in the past.

The adjusted costs of Exhibit 18A.4 do indeed present some surprises. All but one country's cost ends up higher than that of the parent company's 11.98%. The adjusted cost of equity in one country, Venezuela, is actually lower than that in the United States. This is a result of Venezuela's country beta and a negative correlation with U.S. equity market returns. It is critical to remember, however, that the adjusted cost of capital in Venezuela is lower *only*

Exhibit 18A.3 Cemex's Calculated Risk-Adjusted Cost of Equity for Selected Emerging Market Countries

Country	(1) Risk-free US Treasury rate (%)	(2) Sovereign Spread (%)	(3) Adjusted Risk-Free Rate (%)	(4) Equity Risk Premium (%)	(5) Offshore Beta (%)	(6) Adjusted Cost of Equity (%)
Argentina	6.00	7.18	13.18	7.00	2.935	33.723
Brazil	6.00	6.10	12.10	7.00	3.623	37.458
Indonesia	6.00	4.00	10.00	7.00	1.182	18.274
Mexico	6.00	5.97	11.97	7.00	1.241	20.655
Philippines	6.00	2.26	8.26	7.00	1.118	16.088
Venezuela	6.00	8.11	14.11	7.00	–0.272	12.206
United States	6.00	—	6.00	7.00	1.500	16.500

Columns (1) and (2) are drawn from Exhibit 18A.3.
Column (3) = Column (1) + Column (2)
Column (4) is the same U.S. equity market risk premium used in Exhibit 18A.3.
Column (5) is taken from Exhibit 18A.3.
Column (6) = Column 3 + [Column (4) × Column (5)].

Exhibit 18A.4 Cemex's Calculated Risk-Adjusted Cost of Capital for Selected Emerging Market Countries

Country	1) Adjusted Cost of Debt (%)	(2) Adjusted Cost of Equity (%)	(3) Adjusted Cost of Capital (%)	(4) Spread Over U.S. WACC (%)
Argentina	15.180	33.723	24.181	12.201
Brazil	14.100	37.458	26.141	14.161
Indonesia	12.000	18.274	14.084	2.104
Mexico	13.970	20.655	16.025	4.045
Philippines	10.260	16.088	12.321	0.341
Venezuela	16.110	12.206	11.512	–0.468
United States	8.000	16.500	11.980	—

Column (1) and Column (2) from Exhibit 18A.4.
Column (3) = [0.40 × (1 – 0.35) × Column (1)] + [0.60 × Column (2)], where 0.40 and 0.60 are the proportions of debt and equity, respectively, in the weighted-average cost of capital, and the tax rate is assumed to be 35%.
Column (4) = the adjusted cost of capital – United States cost of capital. For example, Argentina's spread over U.S. WACC is 24.181 – 11.980 = 12.201.

when evaluated in the context of Cemex's portfolio of foreign investments and the commensurate correlations with the U.S. dollar markets.

Reservations on the Country-Beta Approach

The *country-beta approach* has a number of implicit assumptions that need to be appreciated by any MNE considering its application. First, as we mentioned previously, if the purpose of the foreign investment is to either source raw material or natural resources, or produce a product for further processing and sale in some other country market, the returns on the specific investment under consideration may have little association with the host-country market and its observable equity returns and correlations. Secondly, beta values are highly sensitive to leverage. If leverage levels and value differ dramatically in the host market from that of the parent company, resulting equity adjustments will be biased. Finally, MNEs operate in specific industry segments, segments that may or may not be typical of the returns and correlations represented by country-level summary statistics.

Decision **CASE**

THUNDERBIRD
THE AMERICAN GRADUATE SCHOOL OF INTERNATIONAL MANAGEMENT

Beijing International Club Corporation (BICC)

"All this helps to make developing Asia the world's most interesting place to do business at present. But it also underlines a crucial point: the region is changing and changing fast. Who would have guessed ten years ago that business people in Beijing would be fighting to join lunch clubs charging a membership fee of $10,000 a year? Both in business and in politics, the only really safe bet is that the future will be different; and that the loser will be those who stand still."

"The Business of Politics," *The Economist*, March 9, 1996

"To succeed in China you have to understand their motives and play their game. As you help them succeed, you have to find ways to achieve your investment objectives."

George Tossan, Assistant Controller Asia Pacific,
Sheraton Asia Pacific Corporation

In April of 1996 George Tossan reviewed the due diligence reports for the Beijing International Club Corporation (BICC) joint venture in Beijing, China. The BICC project was a joint venture (JV) with the Chinese Ministry of Foreign Affairs (MFA) to build a hotel recreation complex in the center of Beijing. George Tossan worked for Sheraton Asia Pacific Corporation (SAPC) which was currently negotiating with Sun Corporation (Hong Kong) to buy out Sun's interest in the JV. George Tossan had just received a telephone call from Hiro Shibano, SAPC's Country Manager for China. Mr. Shibano reported that the Chinese party had expressed their desire to proceed with the JV agreement as soon as possible. In two days George Tossan was due to attend a meeting of SAPC's senior management at which he would present his assessment of Sheraton's investment in BICC.

SAPC's negotiations with Sun Corporation had reached what George Tossan believed to be a reasonable figure for Sun's 31% interest in the venture, $44 million. Additional project funding to complete the remaining construction phases was estimated at $10 million. The key question facing George Tossan was whether the BICC investment represented a sound and prudent entry into actual asset ownership in China. But this question lay in the midst of a host of questions, such as the risks and opportunities of investing in China in principle, whether SAPC's growth strategy would work in China, whether the prospective economics of the JV were truly profitable and whether Sheraton, in the end, would have any exit strategy in the event of impending failure. The JV had already gained a high profile in the head office and George Tossan was worried that the decision would roll forward without careful consideration. George Tossan needed to detail the many issues relevant to a proper assessment of the proposed investment.

Sheraton Asia Pacific Corporation

ITT Sheraton Corporation (Sheraton), a wholly owned subsidiary of ITT Corporation (U.S.), was a worldwide hospitality network focused on quality travel and leisure service. Sheraton owned, leased, managed and franchised nearly 420 luxury, upscale and midscale hotels and resorts in 62 countries. Sheraton's revenues in 1995 were more than US$4 billion, comprised of owned hotel revenue and franchising revenue (initial franchise fees, management fees and continuing fees, advertising, reservation, and frequent traveler programs). The Asia-Pacific Division included 49 properties and more than 16,500 rooms. Separately the Asia region had 35 hotels in 12 countries, while the Pacific region had 14 properties in Australia, New Zealand and the Fiji Islands.

In the 1960s, Sheraton had first expanded into the Asia Pacific region by incorporating SAPC in Hong Kong. SAPC was structured to be the holding and management company in the Asia Pacific region. The first *owned* hotel in the region was the famous Sheraton Hong Kong. By the 1970s SAPC had established strong brand equity in the Sheraton name in the Asia Pacific.

In 1985 SAPC signed the first hotel *management contract* in China for the Great Wall Sheraton (GWS) hotel in Beijing. As the first hotel with foreign management, Great Wall Sheraton was successful soon after it was opened and was recognized as the true five star hotel in the city. To build the brand in China, SAPC had placed their best people in GWS. Several of the GWS expatriates were subsequently promoted to head positions at the SAPC regional level. In 1991 Hiro Shibano, the General Manager of GWS, was named Sheraton's Country Manager for China, with country-wide responsibilities for business development and hotel management issues.

But Sheraton still needed its own ownership entry vehicle. The BICC JV offered such a vehicle, but SAPC had no experience with joint ventures, particularly in China. All hotels signed in China had been on management contracts. When Sun Corporation first approached Hiro Shibano to discuss the 31% sale of ownership in BICC, the superstructure of the hotel had just been completed. The President of SAPC and the Director of Development Asia Pacific were immediately interested as Sheraton had been looking for a flagship hotel to gain entry into the Chinese market. The location of the hotel project was both excellent and attractive. The World Tourism Organization had singled China out to be one of the countries with the fastest growing tourism dollars in the world. Very soon Sheraton's Board had given the approval to pursue the JV in Beijing. The year-long due diligence and negotiations for the memorandum of understanding, management agreement and technical services agreement, began in June 1995.

SAPC Growth Strategy

By 1996, SAPC had five Sheraton-branded managed hotels in some of the major cities of mainland China, namely Beijing, Shanghai, Tianjin, Guilin and Xian. Sheraton announced a 24% increase in gross operating profit in China in 1995, an indication of the market's improving strength.

"We've come a long way since our 1985 contract for the Great Wall Sheraton in Beijing. Great Wall has renewed our contract and Tianjin has extended our contract."

Ed Davie, President of SAPC
Interview with *Times Publishing Limited* on April 22, 1996

In this same interview SAPC made it known that Sheraton was aiming to have 20 hotels in China by the year 2000 and that the group would have an equity investment in at least one property in China by the end of 1996 (a probable reference to BICC). From the report it was interesting to note that between April 1996 and 1999, Sheraton would be opening a total of 15 hotels throughout Asia Pacific, of which four (27% of 15 hotels) would be in China.

Since the opening of its first hotel in Hong Kong in the 1960s, Sheraton had seen the accelerating growth of the travel industry in the Asia Pacific region and enjoyed early entry success as an established and respected brand in the region. SAPC was bullish on the growth potential for business and leisure travel in China. According to the World Tourism Organization China had the highest growth rate of arrivals in the world. To capitalize on a relatively untrodden foreign market, Sheraton saw a lot of intrinsic value in BICC.

Sheraton's senior management believed that the BICC joint venture presented an opportunity to build market power and dominance in China ahead of its competitors. By partnering with the powerful Ministry of Foreign Affairs in a prestigious luxury hotel in Beijing, Sheraton hoped to leverage the relationship to make more deals in other parts of China. The Luxury Collection Hotel in Beijing could be the linchpin for expansion not only in China, but across the Asia Pacific.[1] Thus, the investment in BICC would not be solely evaluated on its stand-alone value, but also on its contribution towards the regional growth strategy of SAPC in total.

Beijing International Club Corporation (BICC)

BICC was incorporated in 1986 between the Ministry of Foreign Affairs (MFA) and Kajira Associates, a Japanese development company, to develop a plot of land owned by MFA in the exclusive embassy district of Beijing. MFA would allow the commercial development of the property in exchange for controlling interest, 51%, of a joint venture. Kajira gained ownership of the remaining 49% for an undisclosed sum paid in U.S. dollars. The JV term was 30 years, subject to extension upon expiration.

The JV land was to be developed in four phases: 1) an office building; 2) luxury hotel; 3) recreation club and apartments; and 4) a shopping mall. The first two phases of development, the mid-sized office building followed by the hotel project, were begun in 1988. In June 1989 the Tiananmen Square demonstrations erupted and all construction projects in Beijing quickly came to a halt. When the political and economic situation in Beijing stabilized in 1991, the office building and hotel construction were resumed. However, Kajira, who had envisioned a mid-priced hotel designed for predominantly Japanese business men and tourists, wished to terminate the JV. Kajira subsequently sold its interest to two Hong Kong development companies—Sun Corporation (40% of the JV) and Chung Corporation (9%).

According to the new JV agreement, Sun Corporation would be the lead project manager (construction phase) as well as provide the management of the hotel and recreation club (oper-

1. Sheraton had three categories of hotels at this time: 1) the *4-Points*, the affordable 4-star chain for business travelers; 2) the *Sheraton*, the 5-star standard; and 3) the *Luxury Collection*, considered to be above 5-star level accommodations.

ational phase). Changes were made to the architectural drawings before construction resumed in 1992 to move from the smaller room Japanese design to the larger room style preferred by most Western business travelers. The luxury hotel was redesigned from 350 rooms to 273. The construction budget was once again revised upwards.

But the troubled relationship between MFA and any partner continued. Sun Corporation had provided an expatriate construction staff of more than 40 on the Beijing site. The MFA employees, numbering more than 200, resented what they considered outside intervention. Continuing conflicts throughout 1994 saw a worsening of the JV relationship. The open hostility worsened to the point that the Sun employees returned to work one morning to find all of their chairs removed, and in a period shortly thereafter, all of the locks had been changed.

Finally in early 1995, due to constant project conflicts and management disagreement with MFA, Sun Corporation decided to sell 31% of its 40% equity position in the JV. Although there were a number of contributing factors to Sun Corporation's decision, the deciding battle had been over the prospective naming of the luxury hotel. The Chinese MFA refused to allow Sun Corporation to use any name—including its own—for the hotel project other than the Beijing International Club Hotel. After nearly a decade of existence, the BICC JV had only completed a 7,000 square meter office building and the superstructure of a hotel.

Sheraton was very interested in purchasing Sun Corporation's stake. Although Sheraton's management would prefer full ownership of the JV, they were only offered a 31% shareholding in the JV by Sun Corporation (Sun would retain a 9% interest). MFA would not give up its 51% majority control. The JV deal was structured to give the second largest shareholder hotel management rights. The proposed final shareholding structure, depicted in Exhibit 1, would be MFA (6 directors), SAPC (3 directors), Sun Corporation (1 director) and Chung Corporation (1 director).

Exhibit 1 Proposed Ownership and Directorship Structure of BICC Joint Venture

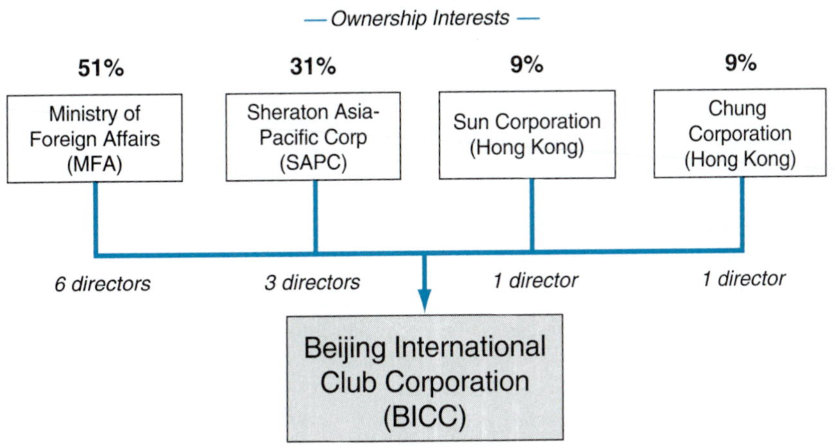

The second largest shareholder—Sheraton Asia-Pacific—would hold management rights to the hotel and recreation club apartments.

Due Diligence

To reduce investment risks, SAPC engaged consultants to perform an extensive due diligence of the following six areas of the proposed JV.[2]

1. **Feasibility.** The feasibility of the investment was examined by Horwath Consulting, an external and independent hospitality consultant. Since there was no precedent investment of similar nature, Horwath applied trajectory demand assumptions, (e.g., based on similar emerging markets, such as Hong Kong's market demands in the 1960s), to forecast occupancy and hotel room rates. From these assumptions the *pro forma* financial analysis was performed (Appendices 1 and 2).
2. **Legal structure.** Legal status of the JV company in terms of its compliance with state regulations, zoning requirements, title clearance and off balance sheet liabilities to the state government. BICC had no outstanding compliance issues.
3. **Investment legacy.** A check on the contractual agreements, past JV agreements, accounting statements, and side payments was made to determine the exact investment made and debt incurred by Sun Corporation to date in the JV. The purpose of this due diligence was to certify the baseline figure before goodwill, which was approximately $33 million proportionately for 31% shareholding.[3]
4. **Audited financial statements.** Audit check on the financial statements and financial health of BICC by Arthur Andersen, LLP. Apart from some missing cars, no significant discrepancies were found.
5. **Estimator's report.** A review of all project expenses incurred to date and estimation of total project costs. BICC's in-house quantity surveyor had estimated the total development cost of the hotel at $72 million. This was certified by the estimator brought in by Sheraton from Hong Kong. MFA agreed to lock in the hotel budget at $72 million, which would be stated in the JV.
6. **Technical specifications.** A technical analysis of all hotel specifications that were not in line with Sheraton's global hotel technical standards. There was a great disparity between Chinese building standards and those of Sheraton. The disparity was particularly acute in the area of fire safety standards. A commitment to upgrade the Chinese standards to meet Sheraton's would be incorporated in the JV agreement.

Investment Risks and Opportunities Considered

As with any company expanding into emerging markets, Sheraton would face an entirely new set of challenges in China. The following issues with possible SAPC responses were identified by George Tossan in the assessment of risks and opportunities of the joint venture:

Issue: Management Control

Although the JV agreement stated that Sheraton would have management rights, it was also clear from many years of troubled JV relationships and Sheraton's year-long negotiations that MFA would retain significant influence. Although there were a number of premier hotels in

2. The due diligence analysis had also been expensive. George Tossan estimated that he had incurred nearly $3 million in consulting fees and expenses related to the BICC due diligence analysis.

3. The proposed $44 million sale price for Sun's 31% interest in the JV was broken down as follows: $33 million for investment made by Sun, Sun's cost of capital for three years, and a negotiated premium—a minimal return.

Beijing, they were owned by private Chinese interests, not MFA. In fact the Chinese MFA did not have any experience in the hospitality industry.

The MFA appointee to BICC was Yang Zhao, an ex-military general, who would be the JV General Manager. A six-member Executive Committee would be formed, on which there would only be two Sheraton appointees (Deputy General Manager and Chief Auditor positions). The number of local employees in BICC would total 220. Clearly, Sheraton input to decision making would be limited and difficult if JV relationships were not handled properly. Exhibit 2 summarizes the proposed management structure.

George Tossan believed the best approach for SAPC would be to first keep the Chinese partner happy and to increasingly influence decisions by emphasizing Sheraton's track record of quality hotels and management. He believed that the way to increase management control was to be selective in the type of conflicts pursued. This would require SAPC to compromise on smaller battles to accommodate their Chinese partner in order to gain ground on other critical issues like management fees, insurance, and hotel service and safety standards. Although there was some concern this might be interpreted as weakness on Sheraton's part, he believed that it was the better path toward achieving SAPC's investment objectives. George Tossan was a bit apprehensive about most of the information flowing from their Chinese partner, since it would be highly filtered. Clearly, the best sources of information would be the Sheraton appointees, the insiders in the JV.

Issue: Different Business Models

> *"While we are corporate citizens, do not forget that we are Party members and that whatever we do, we cannot forsake the principles of the Party."*
>
> Zhao, in an all-staff meeting, 1996

Exhibit 2 Proposed Management Structure of BICC Joint Venture

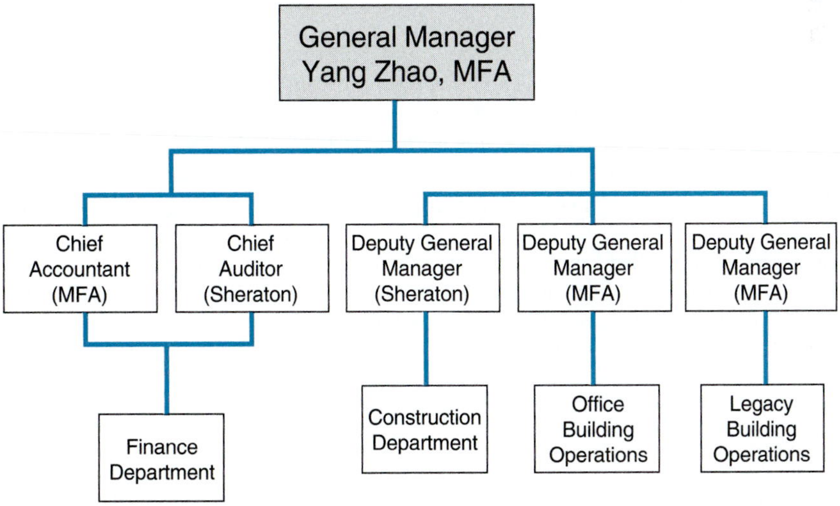

While the Sheraton business model focused on profitability and building *shareholder value*, MFA's business model was closer to that of *corporate wealth* maximization. MFA's stakeholders—labor, government, management, the local community, suppliers and creditors—were treated on par with shareholders. And with MFA being a state entity, governmental and political influence was inevitable. SAPC realized that it was critical to Zhao to keep his staff employed and to secure his own position within the company. Most importantly for MFA, technology transfer and management know-how was the underlying reason to invite foreign equity participation.

SAPC was aware that the two business models would never merge, but that it had to play by the rules of MFA, as the project was on Chinese soil. However as MFA was seeking technology transfer from Sheraton, Tossan believed that SAPC could introduce best practices like cash flow management and project commitment policy to manage the project budget.[4] Also starting early to bring in the hotel expatriate management team to recruit and train new employees would at least ensure that the hotel operations met Sheraton standards.

Issue: Foreign Exchange Risk

As a dollar-based company, Sheraton would be exposed to currency risk in China. The Chinese government set the value of the Chinese currency, the renminbi (Rmb). In addition to stringent currency exchange controls, the local currency, renminbi, was not freely convertible in the foreign exchange markets. In the event of hyperinflation and/or devaluation of the Rmb, Sheraton's investment would be at risk. The last significant change in the Rmb's value had been a devaluation from Rmb7.00/$ to Rmb8.30/$ in 1995, which is where it remained in the spring of 1996.

To eliminate foreign exchange risk, all revenue from operations would be denominated in U.S. dollars. The office building was already leased with rents denominated in dollars, and the JV intended to quote hotel room rates, recreation club and apartment leases, and shopping mall leases all in dollars. It was company practice to maintain all dollar revenues in the bank (Bank of China) until the need arose to exchange dollars for renminbi for payment purposes. Hence George Tossan believed SAPC had minimal foreign exchange risk.

Issue: Political Risk

> *"From technocrats inside the country and joint-venture partners outside, the prophecy is the same, and bleak: Unless China's new hardline leadership can untangle the nation's contradictory economic programs, and revive incentive and productivity, the country's stagnation, inflation and shortages will only worsen. Already, many foreign investors—chilled by the bloody spring revolt—are cutting back operations in China or, worse, simply staying at home."*
>
> Adi Ignatius and Amanda Bennett, *The Wall Street Journal*, 8/3/89, p.1

As a central-controlled country, China would always have high political risk. Especially in Beijing any political change or upheaval would undoubtedly affect the business climate in the city. However it was impossible for foreign companies to predict the risk of another revolt or

4. The BICC project had to date demonstrated a common Chinese business practice of straying from budget. The customary practice was to obtain verbal approval for all expenses, budgeted and non-budgeted. Sheraton had a company-wide program which it termed *project commitment policy*, which emphasized that prior approval was required for all non-budgeted expenditures.

any government policy change. Like most foreign investors Sheraton could only factor a political risk premium in the hurdle rate to evaluate the feasibility of the investment.

Issue: Contract Risk

In China—*guanxi*—or relationships was more critical than having a written contract. The contract laws in the country were unstable and immature compared to those of most Western countries. The basic underpinnings of the *guanxi* system were the twin understandings that one, 'all things are relative,' and two, that 'people are the deciders of all things.' This world view, as opposed to the concept of the rule of law, was a fundamental distinction between how Chinese and Westerners perceive the world. China had never been a nation of laws.

Although Singapore-based arbitration was stated in the JV agreement as a legal device, Sheraton was aware that contracts were not really binding in China. The only way to do business with the Chinese was to have *guanxi*. SAPC was advised that all contracts in China could be terminated after ten years. Hence, even with a JV term of 20 years, there were no real assurances that the partnership would last until the end of the expected term. SAPC's goal was simple; to achieve the strategic mission of the JV before the term expired.

Financial Analysis of BICC

The financial evaluation of BICC posed some specific problems from Sheraton's perspective. Using Horwath Consulting's report on the prospective room and occupancy rates for the increasingly competitive Beijing market, a detailed estimation of the hotel and recreation club and apartments was constructed (Appendix 1). From this a *pro forma* income statement for the JV was generated (Appendix 2). Although some within Sheraton believed the room rates and occupancy estimates a bit aggressive, this would be the premier property in Beijing. According to the *pro forma* financial analysis, the projected profitability of the JV appeared very good.[5]

From the *pro forma* income statement, it was straightforward for Sheraton to project operating cash flows and needed capital expenditures for the JV. The baseline analysis projected cash flows out 10 years to 2006, with additional consideration given the prospective returns generated in a subsequent 10 year period if the JV was renewed. SAPC used a discount rate based on its hurdle rate for the JV of 18%. The rate was the sum of SAPC's weighted average cost of capital (WACC, 10%) and a risk premium for investing in an emerging market such as China (8%). Sheraton's domestic hurdle rate (the required return for any new investment, which was set 2% over the firm's cost of capital) was 12%, and the additional 6% represented a risk premium for strategic investments in emerging markets. The baseline capital budget (Appendix 3) indicated a positive net present value (NPV) and an internal rate of return (IRR) of 26.4%.[6]

But Sheraton's actual capital budgeting process typically focused on the actual cash flows which would be returned to Sheraton or SAPC itself, not on the accounting-based earnings and cash flows shown on the prospective income statement. Sheraton knew that remittance of profits out of China was always a contentious issue with the Chinese, and would most

5. Horwath Consulting assumed that a truly premium-service hotel in Beijing could command approximately $350 per night in 1997, growing at roughly 10% per annum in subsequent years.
6. The BIC valuation presented in Appendix 3 includes Phases I, II, and III, but not Phase IV. Appendix 4, the valuation of the project from the perspective of specific cash flow returns to Sheraton itself, includes Phase IV.

definitely be debated by their JV partner. Sheraton assumed that a large portion of its profits from the JV would most likely be ploughed back into the business to fund the remaining two project phases. Sheraton believed returns would come from the same sources where Sheraton typically earned its living—management fees. Sheraton was typically a manager and operator of hotels, not an owner. It had therefore always reaped the majority of its operational income from management fees. Although an owner in this case, and therefore deserving of dividend distributions, Sheraton was aware of the long-standing difficulties Western investors experienced in actually getting dividend earnings out of China.

The proposed agreement would pay Sheraton a 7% management fee for the luxury hotel operations, and a 5% management fee for the recreation club/apartments management. Both were constructed fees calculated as a percentage of revenues recognized and based on base rates with bonus and escalation clauses for higher occupancy rates. In addition to these management fees, Sheraton would also receive a *technical services fee* totaling roughly $1 million over the first eight full years of operations. Technical services were those safety and quality standards which SAPC's corporate group would continually monitor and maintain to corporate and group standards.

This second form of the multinational capital budgeting process, however, focused just on the cash inflows and cash outflows related to Sheraton itself. From Sheraton's viewpoint, the management fees and dividend distributions were the prospective cash flows returned to SAPC to recover the cash injections into the JV. Although Sheraton would be required to invest $44 million in 1996, Phase III and Phase IV investment outlays would follow in the subsequent years at a steady $2 million per year. The dividend distributions to Sheraton for its 31% were projected to be more than sufficient to cover future capital expenditure commitments required for the completion of Phases III and IV.

Sheraton intended to fund the initial equity of $44 million from its general funds, and the additional investment for Phase III of $10 million (in the form of debt extended from SAPC to the BICC JV) from its earnings from the JV after operations began. Phase IV, of which Sheraton's proportion was an additional $10 million, was also to be funded from operational earnings from the JV itself. With only a 31% share of the JV property, a foreign company would find it impossible to borrow locally in China. In addition, Chinese bank borrowing facilities were not available to Sheraton as it had no current presence except for a representative office in Beijing. The net present value of the baseline analysis indicated a marginally positive project with an internal rate of return of 18.9%. These results are presented in Appendix 4.

Exit Strategy

Since the investment was profitable, Sheraton would want to extend the JV life beyond the remaining 20-year term. SAPC believed that an extension from the regulatory Ministry of Foreign Trade and Economic Cooperation (MOFTEC) would not be difficult if MFA were willing to keep Sheraton as a partner. Although under Chinese contract law practice contracts were potentially not binding beyond 10 years, Sheraton hoped to demonstrate to MFA that it needed Sheraton.

Sheraton had an exit strategy to protect itself against these risks. Although Sheraton brought in technology and management know-how to the JV, the company would be extremely careful not to transfer sufficient technological and managerial skill to the JV that would enable MFA to operate the hotel on its own. In addition to the premise that the Chinese would never catch up with respect to technology and management skills, Sheraton was confident in the value that its global network and reservation system created for the BICC hotel's operation. Even if MFA terminated the JV after 20 years, Sheraton's senior management felt confident that MFA would retain them as operators.

Having given due consideration to the above issues, George Tossan was prepared to present his assessment of the BICC investment.

Appendix 1

Beijing International Club's Projected Earnings

(Thousands of U.S. dollars)	1997	1998	1999	2000	2001	2002	2003	2004	2005	2006
Hotel										
Total number of rooms (year average)	273	273	273	273	273	273	273	273	273	273
Average rate	$300	$306	$312	$318	$325	$331	$338	$345	$351	$359
Percent change		2%	2%	2%	2%	2%	2%	2%	2%	2%
Average occupancy	65%	78%	80%	82%	84%	84%	84%	84%	84%	84%
Room nights sold (in '000s)	16	78	80	82	84	84	84	84	84	84
Total rooms revenue	$4,791	$23,857	$24,881	$26,084	$27,180	$27,724	$28,279	$28,844	$29,421	$30,009
Revenue per available room	$195	$239	$250	$261	$273	$278	$284	$289	$295	$301
Percent change		23%	4%	5%	4%	2%	2%	2%	2%	2%
Room revenue	$4,791	$23,857	$24,881	$26,084	$27,180	$27,724	$28,279	$28,844	$29,421	$30,009
Departmental margin	80%	80%	80%	80%	80%	80%	80%	80%	80%	80%
Room gross profit	$3,833	$19,085	$19,905	$20,867	$21,744	$22,179	$22,623	$23,075	$23,537	$24,008
F&B as % of room revenue	80%	80%	80%	80%	80%	80%	80%	80%	80%	80%
F&B revenue	$3,833	$19,085	$19,905	$20,867	$21,744	$22,179	$22,623	$23,075	$23,537	$24,008
Departmental margin	35%	35%	35%	35%	35%	35%	35%	35%	35%	35%
F&B gross profit	$1,342	$6,680	$6,967	$7,304	$7,611	$7,763	$7,918	$8,076	$8,238	$8,403
Other Hotel ops as % of room sales	15%	15%	15%	15%	15%	15%	15%	15%	15%	15%
Other Hotel operations revenue	$719	$3,579	$3,732	$3,913	$4,077	$4,159	$4,242	$4,327	$4,413	$4,501
Other Hotel operations margin	75%	75%	75%	75%	75%	75%	75%	75%	75%	75%
Other Hotel oper's gross profit	$539	$2,684	$2,799	$2,934	$3,058	$3,119	$3,181	$3,245	$3,310	$3,376
Hotel revenue	$9,343	$46,521	$48,518	$50,864	$53,002	$54,062	$55,143	$56,246	$57,371	$58,518
Total departmental gross profit	5,713	28,449	29,671	31,106	32,413	33,061	33,722	34,397	35,085	35,786
Hotel central costs	(3,000)	(5,000)	(5,150)	(5,305)	(5,464)	(5,628)	(5,796)	(5,970)	(6,149)	(6,334)
Percent change		67%	3%	3%	3%	3%	3%	3%	3%	3%
Hotel EBITDA	$2,713	$23,449	$24,521	$25,801	$26,949	$27,433	$27,926	$28,426	$28,935	$29,452
Days per Year	90	365	365	366	365	365	365	366	365	365

Note: F&B = food and board.

Appendix 1

Beijing International Club's Projected Earnings (continued)

(Thousands of U.S. dollars)	1997	1998	1999	2000	2001	2002	2003	2004	2005	2006
Recreation Club / Apartments										
Number of apartments (year-end)						65	65	65	65	65
Average monthly rate						$12,000	$13,200	$14,520	$15,972	$17,569
Percent growth							10%	10%	10%	10%
Average cccupancy						60%	85%	85%	87%	90%
Room nights sold (in '000s)						4	20	20	21	21
Total rooms revenue						$3,510	$22,183	$24,468	$27,473	$31,262
Departmental margin						90%	90%	90%	90%	90%
Room gross profit						$3,159	$19,965	$22,021	$24,726	$28,136
F&B as % of total rec club revenue						78%	78%	78%	78%	78%
F&B revenue						$94	$1,073	$1,737	$2,317	$2,831
Departmental margin						35%	35%	35%	35%	35%
F&B gross profit						$33	$375	$608	$811	$991
Number of members						200	500	750	900	1,000
Average membership fee						$550	$2,500	$2,700	$3,000	$3,300
Rec club membership fees						$110	$1,250	$2,025	$2,700	$3,300
Other revenues - dues and admission (10% of Rec fees)						$11	$125	$203	$270	$330
Recreation club revenue						$121	$1,375	$2,228	$2,970	$3,630
Recreation club margin						85%	85%	85%	85%	85%
Recreation club gross profit						$94	$1,063	$1,721	$2,295	$2,805
Recreation Club/Apartments Revenue						$3,725	$24,630	$28,433	$32,759	$37,724
Total departmental gross profit						3,286	21,402	24,351	27,831	31,932
Recreation club/apts central costs						(1,000)	(2,000)	(2,060)	(2,122)	(2,185)
Percent change							100%	3%	3%	3%
Recreation club/apts EBITDA						$2,286	$19,402	$22,291	$25,710	$29,747

Appendix 2

Beijing International Club's Pro Forma Income Statement

(Thousands of U.S. dollars)	1997	1998	1999	2000	2001	2002	2003	2004	2005	2006
Hotel revenue	$9,343	$46,521	$48,518	$50,864	$53,002	$54,062	$55,143	$56,246	$57,371	$58,518
Recreation club/apts revenue						3,725	24,630	28,433	32,759	37,724
Office building revenue	720	700	680	670	640	650	640	650	660	660
Other revenue	100	120	110	110	100	90	85	80	75	
Total revenue	$10,163	$47,341	$49,308	$51,644	$53,742	$58,527	$80,499	$85,409	$90,865	$96,902
Hotel EBITDA	2,713	23,449	24,521	25,801	26,949	27,433	27,926	28,426	28,935	29,452
Recreation club/apts EBITDA						2,286	19,402	22,291	25,710	29,747
Office building EBITDA	576	560	544	536	512	520	512	520	528	528
Other EBITDA	70	84	77	77	70	63	60	56	53	—
BICC EBITDA	$3,359	$24,093	$25,142	$26,414	$27,531	$30,302	$47,900	$51,293	$55,225	$59,727
EBITDA	$3,359	$24,093	$25,142	$26,414	$27,531	$30,302	$47,900	$51,293	$55,225	$59,727
Less depreciation	(6,000)	(6,000)	(6,000)	(6,000)	(6,000)	(6,725)	(8,900)	(8,900)	(8,900)	(8,900)
EBIT	$(2,641)	$18,093	$19,142	$20,414	$21,531	$23,577	$39,000	$42,393	$46,325	$50,827
Interest to shareholders' loans	—	(1,470)	(1,890)	(1,890)	(1,890)	(1,890)	(1,890)	(1,890)	(1,890)	(1,890)
EBT	$(2,641)	$16,623	$17,252	$18,524	$19,641	$21,687	$37,110	$40,503	$44,435	$48,937
Less corporate taxes 33%	871	(5,486)	(5,693)	(6,113)	(6,482)	(7,157)	(12,246)	(13,366)	(14,664)	(16,149)
Net profit	$(1,769)	$11,138	$11,559	$12,411	$13,160	$14,530	$24,864	$27,137	$29,772	$32,788
Return on sales (ROS)	-17.4%	23.5%	23.4%	24.0%	24.5%	24.8%	30.9%	31.8%	32.8%	33.8%
Percent change in:										
Revenue		365.8%	4.2%	4.7%	9.0%	13.3%	37.5%	6.1%	6.4%	6.6%
EBITDA		617.2%	4.4%	5.1%	9.5%	14.7%	58.1%	7.1%	7.7%	8.2%
EBIT		–785.2%	5.8%	6.6%	12.5%	15.5%	65.4%	8.7%	9.3%	9.7%
EBT		–729.5%	3.8%	7.4%	13.9%	17.1%	71.1%	9.1%	9.7%	10.1%
Net profit		–729.5%	3.8%	7.4%	13.9%	17.1%	71.1%	9.1%	9.7%	10.1%

Appendix 3

Beijing International Club's Valuation

Project year	**0**	**1**	**2**	**3**	**4**	**5**	**6**	**7**	**8**	**9**	**10**
(Thousands of U.S. dollars)	**1996**	**1997**	**1998**	**1999**	**2000**	**2001**	**2002**	**2003**	**2004**	**2005**	**2006**
EBITDA		$3,359	$24,093	$25,142	$26,414	$27,531	$30,302	$47,900	$51,293	$55,225	$59,727
Less depreciation		(6,000)	(6,000)	(6,000)	(6,000)	(6,000)	(6,725)	(8,900)	(8,900)	(8,900)	(8,900)
EBIT		$(2,641)	$18,093	$19,142	$20,414	$21,531	$23,577	$39,000	$42,393	$46,325	$50,827
Less corporate taxes 33%		871	(5,971)	(6,317)	(6,737)	(7,105)	(7,780)	(12,870)	(13,990)	(15,287)	(16,773)
NOPAT		$(1,769)	$12,122	$12,825	$13,677	$14,426	$15,797	$26,130	$28,403	$31,038	$34,054
Add back depreciation		6,000	6,000	6,000	6,000	6,000	6,725	8,900	8,900	8,900	8,900
Operating Cash Flow		$4,231	$18,122	$18,825	$19,677	$20,426	$22,522	$35,030	$37,303	$39,938	$42,954
Initial investment	$(72,000)										
Changes in NWC 10%		(3,718)	(197)	(234)	(210)	(479)	(2,197)	(491)	(546)	(604)	9,690
Capital expenditure			(22,581)	(6,774)	(2,903)						
Terminal value 10%											297,924
Free Cash Flow	$(72,000)	$513	$(4,655)	$11,817	$16,565	$19,947	$20,324	$34,539	$36,758	$39,334	$350,568
NPV 18%		$53,546									
IRR		26.4%									

Note a: Capex calculation Sheraton		31%	(7,000)	(2,100)	(900)						
BICC		100%	(22,581)	(6,774)	(2,903)						
Note b: TV calculation	2006	2007	2008	2009	2010	2011	2012	2013	2014	2015	2016
Operating CF 10%		47,249	51,974	57,172	62,889	69,178	76,096	83,705	92,076	101,283	111,412
PV factor 18%		0.8475	0.7182	0.6086	0.5158	0.4371	0.3704	0.3139	0.2660	0.2255	0.1911
PV of OCF		40,042	37,327	34,797	32,437	30,238	28,188	26,277	24,496	22,835	21,287
Cumulative PV of OCF $297,924											

Appendix 4

Beijing International Club's Valuation

Project year		0	1	2	3	4	5	6	7	8	9	10
(Thousands of U.S. dollars)		1996	1997	1998	1999	2000	2001	2002	2003	2004	2005	2006
Cash Inflows												
Management fee - hotel ops @7%		$1,000	$654	$3,256	$3,396	$3,561	$3,710	$3,784	$3,860	$3,937	$4,016	$4,096
Management fee - recreation @ 5%								1,186	1,232	1,422	1,638	1,886
Technical services fee			125	125	125	125	125	125	125	125		
Interest income - shareholders' loans				—	—	637	700	700	700	700	700	700
Distributed earnings	31%	(548)	3,453	3,583	3,847	4,079	4,504	7,708	8,412	9,229	10,164	—
Total cash from BIC		$452	$4,232	$6,965	$7,369	$8,402	$9,040	$13,503	$14,329	$15,413	$16,518	$6,682
Cash Outflows												
Initial investment by Sheraton		$(44,000)										
Investment for Phase III			(2,000)	(2,000)	(2,000)	(2,000)	(2,000)					
Investment for Phase IV								(2,000)	(2,000)	(2,000)	(2,000)	(2,000)
Total cash outflow to BIC		$(44,000)	$(2,000)	$(2,000)	$(2,000)	$(2,000)	$(2,000)	$(2,000)	$(2,000)	$(2,000)	$(2,000)	$(2,000)
Net cash flow of BIC		$(43,548)	$2,232	$4,965	$5,369	$6,402	$7,040	$11,503	$12,329	$13,413	$14,518	$4,682
Less withholding tax @ 5%	5%		(212)	(348)	(368)	(420)	(452)	(675)	(716)	(771)	(826)	(334)
Net cash flow after tax		(43,548)	2,020	4,616	5,000	5,982	6,588	10,828	11,613	12,642	13,692	4,348
Terminal value	10%											32,477
PV of Phase IV operations		$10,000										
Net free cash flows after tax (used for discounting)		$(33,548)	$2,020	$4,616	$5,000	$5,982	$6,588	$10,828	$11,613	$12,642	$13,692	$36,825
Present value factor at 18%		1.0000	0.8475	0.7182	0.6086	0.5158	0.4371	0.3704	0.3139	0.2660	0.2255	0.1911
PV of net free cash flow		$(33,548)	$1,712	$3,315	$3,043	$3,085	$2,879	$4,011	$3,645	$3,363	$3,087	$7,036
NPV		$1,630										
IRR		18.91%										

Note a: Terminal value calculation (10 years at a 10% growth rate)		2007	2008	2009	2010	2011	2012	2013	2014	2015	2016
Net cash flow after-tax	10%	5,151	5,666	6,232	6,856	7,541	8,295	9,125	10,037	11,041	12,145
Present value factor at	18%	0.8475	0.7182	0.6086	0.5158	0.4371	0.3704	0.3139	0.2660	0.2255	0.1911
Present value of terminal CFs		4,365	4,069	3,793	3,536	3,296	3,073	2,865	2,670	2,489	2,320
Terminal value (cum PV of CFs)		32,477									

Note b: No corporate tax was payable in Hong Kong as the revenue was offset by losses in other properties.

apter 19

Cross-Border Mergers, Acquisitions, and Valuation

ALTHOUGH THERE ARE MANY PIECES TO THE PUZZLE OF BUILDING SHAREHOLDER VALUE, ultimately it comes down to growth. Chapter 15 described the process of how a MNE will "go global" in search of new markets, resources, productive advantages, and other elements of competition and profit. An increasingly popular route to this global growth and expansion is through *cross-border mergers and acquisitions*. The process of identifying, valuing, and acquiring a foreign firm is the subject of this chapter.

This chapter focuses on identifying and completing a cross-border acquisition transaction. In addition to describing in detail both the valuation techniques employed and the management of the acquisition process, we describe both the theory and the application of calculating discount rates for foreign investments and acquisitions.

Cross-border mergers, acquisitions, and strategic alliances all face similar challenges: *they must value the target enterprise on the basis of its projected performance in its market*. This process of enterprise valuation combines elements of strategy, management, and finance. Strategically, the potential core competencies and competitive advantages of the target firm attract the acquisition. An enterprise's potential value is a combination of the intended strategic plan and the expected operational effectiveness to be implemented post-acquisition.

The first section of this chapter will detail the arguments and identify the trends in cross-border acquisitions. This will focus on the particularly unique factors in the cross-border acquisition environment. Second, we review the acquisition process. The third section explains the corporate governance and shareholder rights issues raised in cross-border acquisitions. In the fourth section, we perform a valuation using an illustrative case, Tsingtao Brewery Company Ltd. of China. We will cover the many different valuation methods employed in industry—and their limitations.

Cross-Border Mergers and Acquisitions

The 1980s and 1990s were characterized by a spate of mergers and acquisitions (M&A) with both domestic and foreign partners. Cross-border mergers have played an important role in this activity. The 1992 completion of the European Union's Internal Market stimulated many of these investments, as European, Japanese, and U.S. firms jockeyed for stronger market positions within the EU. However, the long-run U.S. growth prospects and political safety in the United States motivated more takeovers of U.S. firms by foreign firms, particularly from the United Kingdom and

Japan, than vice versa. This was a reversal of historical trends when U.S. firms were net buyers of foreign firms rather than net sellers to foreign firms.

The latter half of the 1990s saw a number of mega-mergers between multinationals—for example, DaimlerChrysler and Exxon-Mobil—which virtually changed the entire competitive landscapes of their respective global markets. The 1990s also saw the rise of privatization of enterprise in many emerging markets, creating growth opportunities for MNEs to gain access to previously closed markets of enormous potential.

Trends in Cross-Border Mergers and Acquisitions

The number and dollar value of cross-border mergers and acquisitions have grown rapidly in recent years, but the growth and magnitude of activity are taking place in the developed countries, not the developing countries. Exhibits 19.1 and 19.2 show cross-border M&A in the two groups, and the difference is startling.

In Exhibit 19.1, we see that the growth in cross-border mergers and acquisitions within developed countries has been torrid in recent years, particularly within the European Union and the United States. In fact, of the $1,143 billion in activity in 2000, the $586 billion in the EU and the $324 billion in the United States made up 80% of all global cross-border M&A transactions.

Exhibit 19.2 presents evidence of cross-border merger and acquisition activity among the developing countries. At first glance, the growth and magnitudes look impressive. However, on closer examination it is clear that the total of M&A activity in the developing countries in 2000, $86 billion, was only a fraction (8%) of the global total.

Exhibit 19.1 **Cross-Border Mergers and Acquisitions: Developed Countries (billions of U.S. dollars)**

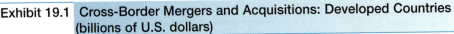

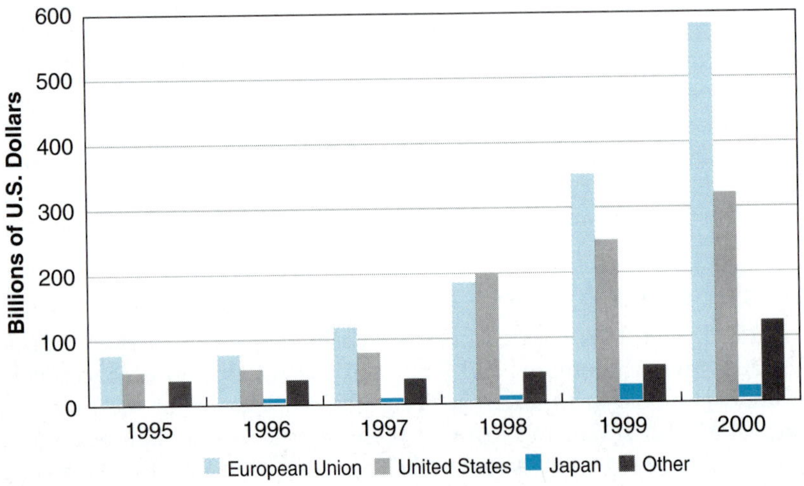

Source: United Nations Center for Trade and Development (UNCTAD).

Exhibit 19.2 Cross-Border Mergers and Acquisitions: Developing Countries (billions of U.S. dollars)

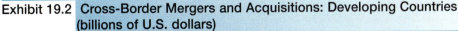

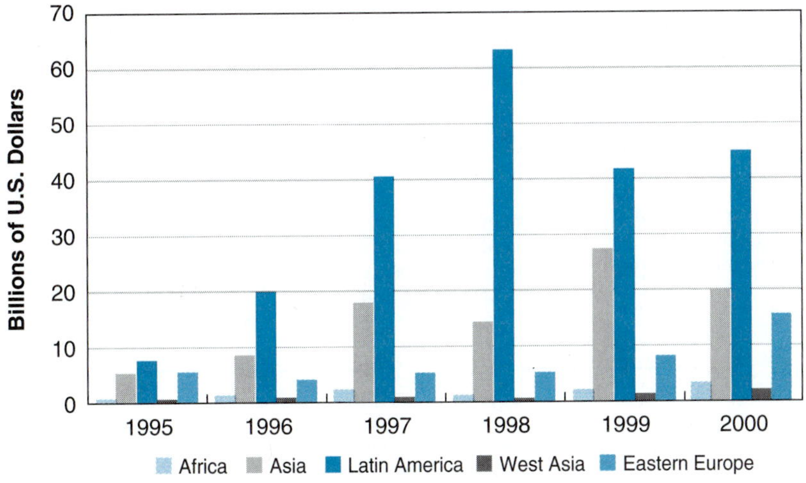

Source: United Nations Center for Trade and Development (UNCTAD).

Among the developing regions of the world, cross-border M&A activity has been focused nearly exclusively on Latin America and Asia. West Asia, Eastern Europe, and particularly Africa—totaling only $20 billion—have largely been bypassed in the international rush to acquire.

There are a variety of reasons for the disparity of occurrence in activity. The most obvious is that measures of activity that are currency-based, like the U.S. dollar valuations in Exhibits 19.1 and 19.2, will arise from acquisitions of MNEs that are traded on exchanges and carry large market capitalizations. Secondly, although the assets owned by MNEs that are operating in much of the developing world may have changed hands, these assets are included in the global holdings of the MNE parent, which is in turn incorporated in its home, a developed country.

The Driving Force: Shareholder Value Creation

What is the true motivation for cross-border mergers and acquisitions? The answer is the traditional one: *to build shareholder value.*

Exhibit 19.3 tries, in a simplistic way, to justify this global expansion. Publicly traded MNEs live and die, in the eyes of their shareholders, by their share price. If the MNE's share price is a combination of the earnings of the firm and the market's opinion of those earnings, the price-to-earnings multiple, then management must strive to grow both.

Management's problem is that it does not directly influence the market's opinion of its earnings. Although management's responsibility is to increase its P/E ratio, this is a difficult, indirect, and long-term process of communication and promise fulfillment. Over the long term, the market—analysts, investors, and institutional stakeholders—will look to the ability of the management

Exhibit 19.3 Building Shareholder Value Means Building Earnings

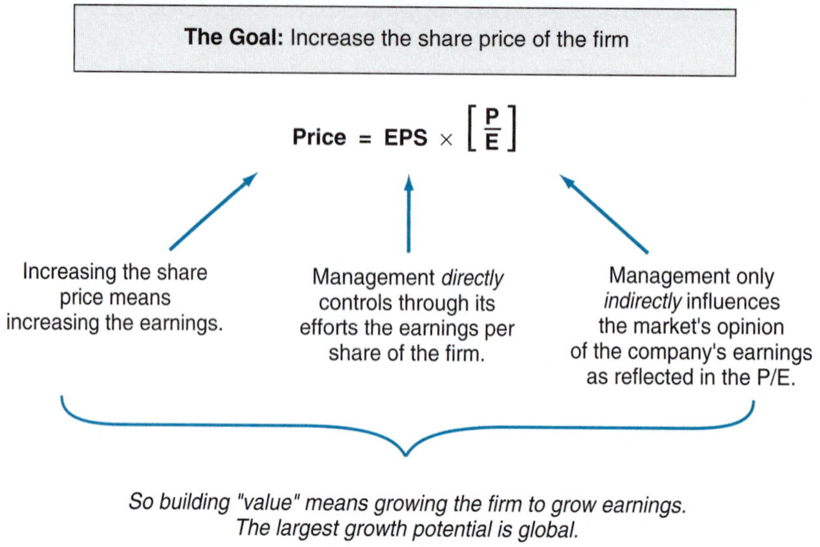

to deliver on the promises made in meetings, advertisements, annual reports, and at the stockholders' meetings. But the opinion of markets as reflected in P/E ratios is infamously fickle. (The astronomic share prices garnered by many dotcom firms in recent years before the bubble burst is the most obvious example.)

The Goal: Increase the share price of the firm
Price = EPS × [P/E]
Increasing the share price means increasing the earnings.
Management *directly* controls through its efforts the earnings per share of the firm.
Management only *indirectly* influences the market's opinion of the company's earnings as reflected in the P/E.
So building "value" means growing the firm to grow earnings.
The largest growth potential is global.

But management does directly affect earnings. Increasing the earnings per share (EPS) is within the direct control of the firm. In many of the developed country markets today, the growth potential for earnings in the traditional business lines of the firm is limited. Competition is fierce; margins are under continual pressure. Senior management of the firm cannot ignore these pressures. Indeed they must continually undertake activities to promote brand, decrease inventory investments, increase customer focus and satisfaction, streamline supply chains, and manage all the other drivers of value in global business. Nevertheless, they must also look outward to build value.

In contrast to the fighting and scraping for market shares and profits in traditional domestic markets, the global marketplace offers greater growth potential—greater "bang for the buck." As Chapter 15 described, there are a variety of paths by which the MNE can enter foreign markets, including greenfield investment and acquisition.

Cross-Border Mergers and Acquisitions Drivers

In addition to the desire to grow, MNEs are motivated to undertake cross-border mergers and acquisitions by a number of other factors. The United Nations Conference on Trade and Development (UNCTAD, formerly the U.N. Centre for Transnational Corporations) has summarized the mergers and acquisitions drivers and forces relatively well in Exhibit 19.4.

Exhibit 19.4 Driving Forces Behind Cross-Border M&A

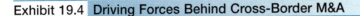

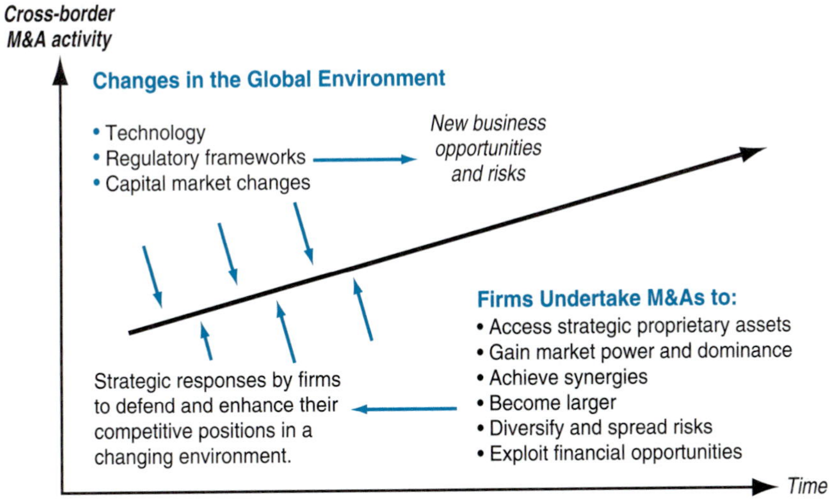

Source: UNCTAD, *World Development Report 2000: Cross-border Mergers and Acquisitions and Development*, figure V.1., p.154.

The drivers of M&A activity are both *macro* in scope (the global competitive environment) and micro in scope (the variety of industry and firm-level forces and actions driving individual firm value). The primary forces of change in the *global competitive environment*—technological change, regulatory change, and capital market change—create new business opportunities for MNEs, which they pursue aggressively.

But the global competitive environment is really just the playing field, the ground upon which the individual players compete. MNEs undertake cross-border mergers and acquisitions for a variety of reasons. As shown in Exhibit 19.4, the drivers are strategic responses by MNEs to defend and enhance their global competitiveness by:

- Gaining access to strategic proprietary assets
- Gaining market power and dominance
- Achieving synergies in local/global operations and across different industries
- Becoming larger, and then reaping the benefits of size in competition and negotiation
- Diversifying and spreading their risks wider
- Exploiting financial opportunities they may possess and others desire

As opposed to greenfield investment, a cross-border acquisition has a number of significant advantages. First and foremost, it is quicker. Greenfield investment frequently requires extended periods of physical construction and organizational development. By acquiring an existing firm, the MNE shortens the time required to gain a presence and facilitate competitive entry into the market. Second, acquisition may be a cost-effective way of gaining competitive advantages such as technology, brand names valued in the target market, and logistical and distribution advantages, while simultaneously eliminating a local competitor. Third, specific to cross-border acquisitions, international economic, political, and foreign exchange conditions may result in market imperfections, allowing target firms to be undervalued. Many enterprises throughout Asia have been the target of acquisition as a result of the Asian economic crisis's impact on their financial health. Many enterprises were in dire need of capital injections from so-called White Knights for competitive survival.

Cross-border acquisitions are not, however, without their pitfalls. As with all acquisitions, domestic or cross-border, there are problems of paying too much or suffering excessive financing costs. Melding corporate cultures can be traumatic. Managing the post-acquisition process is frequently characterized by downsizing to gain economies of scale and scope in overhead functions. This results in nonproductive impacts on the firm as individuals attempt to save their own jobs. Internationally, additional difficulties arise from host governments intervening in pricing, financing, employment guarantees, market segmentation, and general nationalism and favoritism. In fact, the ability to successfully complete cross-border acquisitions may itself be a test of competency of the MNE in the twenty-first century.

The Cross-Border Acquisition Process

Although the field of finance has sometimes viewed acquisition as mainly an issue of valuation, it is a much more complex and rich process than simply determining what price to pay. As depicted in Exhibit 19.5, the process begins with the strategic drivers discussed in the previous section.

The process of acquiring an enterprise anywhere in the world has three common elements: 1) identification and valuation of the target, 2) completion of the ownership change transaction—the *tender*, and 3) management of the post-acquisition transition.

Stage I: Identification and Valuation

Identification of potential acquisition targets requires a well-defined corporate strategy and focus.

Identification. The identification of the target market typically precedes the identification of the target firm. Entering a highly developed market offers the widest choice of publicly traded firms with relatively well-defined markets and publicly disclosed financial and operational data. Emerging markets frequently require the services of acquisition specialists who can aid in the identification of firms—generally privately held or government-owned firms—that not only possess promising market prospects but may be amenable to suitors. Emerging markets pose additional problems, including scant financial data, limited depth of management, government restrictions on foreign purchases, and the fact that few firms are publicly traded. The growth of privatization programs in emerging markets in the latter half of the 1990s did, however, provide a number of new targets for cross-border acquisitions that would have been unavailable in previous times.

Valuation. Once identification has been completed, the process of valuing the target begins. A variety of valuation techniques are widely used in global business today, each with its relative merits. In addition to the fundamental methodologies of discounted cash flow (DCF) and multiples (earnings and cash flows), there are also a variety of industry-specific measures that focus on the

Exhibit 19.5 The Cross-Border Acquisition Process

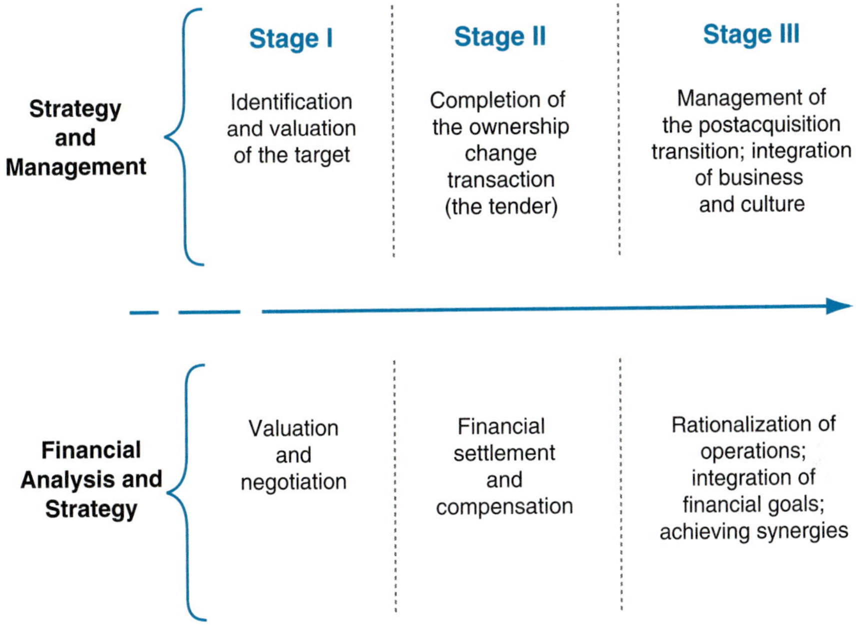

most significant elements of value in business lines. For example, the case of Tsingtao Brewery in China, analyzed later in this chapter, focuses on the valuation of a brewery business. In this industry, the cost per tonne of brewing capacity of the business is an industry-specific valuation method frequently employed. In the field of valuation, "more is better when using valuation methods." The completion of a variety of alternative valuations for the target firm aids not only in gaining a more complete picture of what price must be paid to complete the transaction, but also in determining whether the price is attractive.

Stage II: Settlement of the Transaction

The term *settlement* is actually misleading. Once an acquisition target has been identified and valued, the process of gaining approval from management and ownership of the target, getting approvals from government regulatory bodies, and finally determining method of compensation can be time-consuming and complex.

Tender process. Gaining the approval of the target company has itself been the subject of some of the most storied acquisitions in history. The critical distinction here is whether the acquisition is supported by the target company's management.

Although there is probably no "typical transaction," many acquisitions flow relatively smoothly through a friendly process. The acquiring firm will approach the management of the target company and attempt to convince them of the business logic of the acquisition. (Gaining their support is sometimes difficult, but assuring the target company's management that it will not be replaced is often quite convincing!) If the target's management is supportive they may then recommend to stockholders that they accept the offer of the acquiring company. One problem that does occasionally surface at this stage is that influential shareholders may object to the offer, either in principle or based on price, and therefore feel that management is not taking appropriate steps to protect and build their shareholder value.

The process takes on a very different dynamic when the acquisition is not supported by target company management—the so-called *hostile takeover*. The acquiring company may choose to pursue the acquisition without the target's support and go directly to the target shareholders. In this case, the tender offer is made publicly, although target company management may openly recommend that its shareholders reject the offer. If enough shareholders take the offer, the acquiring company may gain sufficient ownership influence or control to change management. During this rather confrontational process, it is up to the board of the target company to continue to take actions consistent with protecting the rights of shareholders. The board may need to provide rather strong oversight of management during this process, to ensure that management does not take actions consistent with its own perspective but not with protecting and building shareholder value.

Regulatory approval. The proposed acquisition of Honeywell International (a recent merger of Honeywell US and Allied-Signal US) by General Electric (US) in 2001 was something of a watershed event in the field of regulatory approval. General Electric's acquisition of Honeywell had been approved by management, ownership, and U.S. regulatory bodies.

The final stage was the approval of European Union antitrust regulators. Jack Welch, the charismatic chief executive officer and president of General Electric, did not anticipate the degree of opposition that the merger would face from EU authorities. After a continuing series of demands by the EU that specific businesses within the combined companies be sold off to reduce anticompetitive effects, Welch withdrew the request for acquisition approval, arguing that the liquidations would destroy most of the value-enhancing benefits of the acquisition. The acquisition was canceled. This case may have far-reaching affects on cross-border M&A for years to come, as the power of regulatory authorities within strong economic zones like the EU to block the combination of two MNEs—in this case, two U.S.-based MNEs—may foretell a change in regulatory strength and breadth.

Compensation settlement. The last act within this second stage of cross-border acquisition is the payment to shareholders of the target company. Shareholders of the target company are typically paid either in shares of the acquiring company or in cash. If a share exchange occurs, which exchange may be defined by some ratio of acquiring company shares to target company shares (say, 2 shares of acquirer in exchange for 3 shares of target), the stockholder is typically not taxed. The shareholder's shares of ownership have simply been replaced by other shares in a nontaxable transaction.

If cash is paid to the target company shareholder, it is the same as if the shareholder has sold the shares on the open market, resulting in a capital gain or loss (a gain, it is hoped, in the case of an acquisition) with tax liabilities. Because of the tax ramifications, shareholders are typically more receptive to share exchanges so that they may choose whether and when tax liabilities will arise.

A variety of factors go into the determination of type of settlement. The availability of cash, the size of the acquisition, the friendliness of the takeover, and the relative valuations of both acquiring firm and target firm affect the decision. One of the most destructive forces that sometimes arise at this stage is regulatory delay and its impact on the share prices of the two firms. If regulatory body approval drags out over time, the possibility of a drop in share price increases and can change the attractiveness of the share swap. Global Finance Perspective 19.1 illustrates the problems firms confronted recently in settling cross-border acquisition with shares.

Stage III: Post-Acquisition Management

Although the headlines and flash of investment banking activities are typically focused on the valuation and bidding process in an acquisition transaction, post-transaction management is probably the most critical of the three stages in determining an acquisition's success or failure. An acquiring firm can pay too little or too much, but if the post-transaction is not managed effectively, the entire return on the investment is squandered. Post-acquisition management is the stage in which the motivations for the transaction must be realized. Those reasons, such as more effective management, synergies arising from the new combination, or the injection of capital at a cost and availability previously out of the reach of the acquisition target, must be effectively implemented after the transaction. The biggest problem, however, is nearly always melding corporate cultures.

As painfully depicted in the case of British Petroleum (United Kingdom) and Amoco (United States) in Global Finance Perspective 19.2, the clash of corporate cultures and personalities pose both the biggest risk and the biggest potential gain from cross-border mergers and acquisitions. Although not readily measurable like price/earnings ratios or share price premiums, in the end the value is either gained or lost in the hearts and minds of the stakeholders.

Global Finance Perspective **19.1**

Cash or Shares in Payment

One factor influencing not only the number but the method of payment used in cross-border mergers and acquisitions is the equity "altitudes" of many MNEs. One of the major drivers of cross-border M&A growth in 1999 and 2000 was the lofty levels of equity values. Many MNEs found the higher equity prices allowed what the financial press termed "shopping sprees" in which the acquiring firms could afford more M&As as a result of inflated equity prices. This allowed them to bid higher for potential targets and then pay up with their own shares.

But 2001 was different. Falling equity prices in most of the major equity markets of the world made acquisitions much more costly prospects than in the previous years. Shareholders of target firms were no longer interested in being paid in shares, demanding cash payments at significant premiums. (Premiums over the latter half of the 1990s and into 2000 and 2001 averaged between 48% and 55% over existing share values prior to the acquisition offers.)

With slower economies and lower growth prospects, even the banking sectors were increasingly critical of grandiose promises of M&A synergies and benefits in general. As banks and other potential cash providers looked upon potential M&A deals with increasing scrutiny, sources of debt for cash payments also became more scarce. The financing for settlement made cross-border M&A activity much tougher to complete.

Global Finance Perspective 19.2

Clashing Corporate Cultures at British Petroleum and Amoco

A popular joke in Amoco hallways goes: What's the British pronunciation of BP-Amoco? BP—the Amoco is silent.

LONDON—BP and Amoco called it a merger of equals. But over coffee and sandwiches one day in the BP cafeteria here, Amoco Corp. executives discovered that British Petroleum PLC had other plans.

During a conference of 20 top executives from both companies last fall, Rodney Chase, then BP's deputy chief executive, unveiled the blueprint for the merged company. It would be led by BP management, run with BP's structure and infused with BP's do-or-die culture. Anyone who didn't agree was welcome to join the 10,000 other workers who were being fired.

In Chicago during negotiations, Mr. Browne [BP's chief executive] and Amoco Chief Executive Lawrence Fuller wrestled with the question of management control. It was clear that BP would be the acquirer, since it was larger, but Mr. Fuller wondered whether the two companies could combine the "best of both" management worlds. Mr. Browne was unequivocal. "It was not negotiable for us," he said in a recent interview. "We had developed a structure and systems that had worked for us, and we were anxious to apply it to a larger company."

Indeed, at the heart of BP is an unusual management structure and culture that it aims to stamp on other companies. The system grew from the company's near-fatal crisis in 1992, when then-CEO Robert Horton was ousted in a boardroom coup, the company's dividend was cut in half and a single quarter's loss topped $1 billion. The subsequent restructuring essentially turned the company into a giant family of entrepreneurial small businesses.

The system clashed badly with Amoco. More like a classic pyramid, Amoco had strict reporting lines and heavy internal bureaucracy. Managers often spent months negotiating contracts with internal businesses. Amoco's executive suite on the 30th floor in Chicago was a formal corridor of closed doors and strict schedules. BP's fourth-floor suite in London is an open-plan space with glass walls, where top executives breeze in and out of each other's offices.

Company memos began showing up with British spellings, prompting complaints in the BP Amoco newsletter about use of the words "organisation" and "labour." BP jargon was lost on some Amoco executives. In meetings, BP's managers lived on "hard targets" that had to be met, while Amoco talked about "aspirations" that were only occasionally reached. BP raved about "peer groups," while Amoco talked about "strategic-planning councils."

The culture clash came to a head in the cafeteria meeting last fall at BP headquarters. While most managers expected BP would dominate the merged company, few anticipated that its grip would be so strong. During the all-day conference, Amoco managers argued the case for a centralized structure, while their BP counterparts said it wouldn't work. "You're not interested at all in our ideas," said one Amoco executive. Another said: "We weren't prepared for this." Sensing a crisis, Mr. Fuller stood up, a BP executive says, and gave his troops a final order: "We're going to use the BP systems, and that's that."

Abstracted from "Slash and Clash: While BP Prepares New U.S. Acquisition, Amoco Counts Scars," Robert Frank and Steve Liesman, *The Wall Street Journal*, 3/31/99, pp. A1, A8.

Corporate Governance and Shareholder Rights

By takeover bid (tender offer) we mean an unsolicited offer by an unaffiliated third party and/or his group ('Bidder') to acquire enough voting shares of a target company ('Target') in another jurisdiction so that the shares acquired, plus the shares held before the offer was made, give Bidder control in fact or in law of the Target.

"Constraints on Cross Border Takeovers and Mergers,
International Bar Association for International Capital Markets Group,
International Business Lawyer, 1991

One of the most controversial issues in shareholder rights is at what point in the accumulation of shares is the bidder required to make all shareholders a tender offer. For example, a bidder may slowly accumulate shares of a target company by gradually buying shares on the open market over time. Theoretically, this share accumulation could continue until the bidder had 1) the single largest block of shares among all individual shareholders, 2) majority control, or 3) all the shares outright. Every country possesses a different set of rules and regulations for the transfer of control of publicly traded corporations. This market, the *market for corporate control*, has been the subject of enormous debate in recent years.

The regulatory approach taken towards the market for corporate control varies widely across countries. The elements of the regulation of cross-border takeovers typically include the following 10 elements:

1. **Creeping tenders.** Many countries prohibit *creeping tenders*, the secret accumulation of relatively small blocks of stock, privately or in the open market, in a preliminary move towards a public bid. This prohibition is intended to promote public disclosure of bids for takeovers.
2. **Mandatory offers.** Many countries require that the bidder make a full public tender offer to all shareholders when a certain threshold of ownership is reached. This is intended to extend the opportunity to all shareholders to sell their shares at a tender price to a bidder gaining control, rather than have the bidder pay the tender price only to those shareholders it needs to garner control.
3. **Timing of takeovers.** A wide spectrum of different time frames apply to takeover bids. This is typically the time period over which the bid must be left open for each individual tender, withdrawal of tender, or revision of tender. This is to allow bidders and targets alike to consider all potential offers and for information regarding the tender to reach all potential shareholders.
4. **Withdrawal rights.** Most countries allow any security to be withdrawn as long as the bid is open. In some countries a competing bid automatically revokes all acceptances as long as the bid remains open. This is to protect shareholders against tendering their shares early at lower prices than may be garnered by waiting to a later offer by any competing bidder.
5. **Market purchases during bid.** Some countries allow the bidder to purchase shares in the open market during the public tender with public disclosure. Many countries, however, prohibit purchases absolutely during this period. This is done to protect against any potential market manipulation by either bidder or target during the tender period.
6. **Market sales during bid.** Some countries prohibit the sale of the target company's shares by the bidder during the tender offer period. This is to protect against any potential market manipulation by either bidder or target during the tender period.
7. **Limitation of defenses.** Some jurisdictions limit the defensive tactics that a target may take during a public tender offer. In many countries this has not been stated in law, but has been refined through shareholder law suits and other court rulings subsequent to measures taken by target company management to frustrate bidders. This is intended to protect shareholders against management taking defensive measures that are not in the best interests of shareholders.

8. **Price integration.** Most countries require that the highest price paid to any shareholder for their shares be paid to all shareholders tendering their shares during the public tender. Some countries require that this price be also provided to those selling shares to the bidder in the pre-bid purchases as well. Although intended in principle to guarantee equity in price offerings, this is a highly complex provision in many countries that allow two-tier bids and so-called front-end back-end bids.

9. **Proration of acceptances.** Most countries that regulate takeovers require *proration* when a bid is made for less than all the shares and more than that maximum is tendered. Some countries do not allow a bid to be made for less than all the shares once the mandatory offer percentage is reached.

10. **Target responses.** Many countries require that the board of directors of the target company make a public statement regarding their position on a public tender offer within a time frame following the tender. This requirement is intended to disclose the target's opinions and attitudes towards the tender to the existing shareholders. As illustrated in Global Finance Perspective 19.3, the complexity of issues over minority shareholder rights and the constant changes in regulatory policy continue globally.

Cross-Border Valuation

Mergers and acquisitions have long been considered the realm of high-flying investment bankers and deal-making. But this investment banking enterprise requires an enormous work effort of market analysis, competitive evaluation, and financial detail. The due diligence process alone can

Global Finance Perspective 19.3

Vodafone's Hostile Acquisition of Mannesmann

Once a firm has gained majority control of a target, many countries require that the remaining minority shareholders tender their shares. This requirement is to prevent minority shareholders from hindering the decision-making process of the owners, or requiring the owners to continue to take actions or incur expenses to serve a few remaining minority shareholders.

One example of this abuse was the case of Vodafone's acquisition of Mannesmann of Germany in 2000. By August 2001, Vodafone had gained ownership of 99.4% of Mannesmann's outstanding shares. Because minority shareholders holding a total of 7,000 shares refused to sell, and were not required to sell under German law, even though the majority of shareholders had decided to sell the firm, Vodafone was required to continue to hold stockholder's meetings in Germany for their benefit. Under German corporate governance laws, because this was a cross-border acquisition, minority shareholders could not be forced to tender their shares. If, however, the acquisition had been domestic, these same minority shareholders would have been required to sell their shares at the publicly tendered price.

The Vodafone acquisition of Mannesmann is considered by many as a watershed event in continental European mergers and acquisitions history. The acquisition marked the first large-scale cross-border hostile takeover in recent times. After Vodafone's takeover, the German federal government initiated legislation for the governance of acquisitions and a procedure for the future "squeeze-out" of minority shareholders.

be an extremely arduous undertaking. In the end, successful acquisitions require completion of all three stages listed earlier. Relevant strategies are found not in analyzing the financial spreadsheets, but rather in identifying future lines of business and competencies captured and created in the postacquisition enterprise.

Illustrative Case: The Potential Acquisition of Tsingtao Brewery Company Ltd., China

In January 2001, Anheuser Busch (AB) was considering acquiring a larger minority interest in Tsingtao Brewery Company Ltd., China, the largest brewer in China. AB had originally acquired a 5% equity interest (US$16.4 million) in 1993 when Tsingtao had first been partly privatized. Having identified the target (Phase I), AB needed to undertake a valuation of the target's shares (Phase II). Since AB would at best have only an expanded minority interest in Tsingtao, it also needed to assess its prospects for post-acquisition influence on Tsingtao's operations (Phase III).

In 1999, AB had discussed acquiring a larger equity stake in Tsingtao. Negotiations between AB and Tsingtao were unsuccessful because Tsingtao would not offer AB a voice in Tsingtao's operations. However, by the year 2001, Tsingtao needed additional equity capital due to its own success at growing the business. AB considered Tsingtao an even more attractive investment in 2001 than in 1999. The key questions to be answered were:

- The valuation of Tsingtao's share price in an illiquid Chinese equity market (Phase I)
- The percentage of Tsingtao's total equity that could be purchased
- The terms of settling the transaction (Phase II)
- The prospects for AB to contribute its management skills to Tsingtao after the acquisition of a larger equity stake (Phase III)
- The degree of future compatibility between the two corporate cultures
- The potential for future rationalization of operations

AB understood that Tsingtao was also evaluating other alternatives for strengthening its equity position and overall balance sheet. One politically attractive alternative was for Tsingtao to issue additional shares in the Chinese equity markets. Additional support for this alternative came from AB's emergence as a direct competitor in the Chinese brewery market. AB had recently purchased controlling interest (91.8%) in what was now called Budweiser Wuhan International Brewing Company. That company was already expanding AB's operations and market area.

On the other hand, one potentially negative outcome of an equity issue in the illiquid Chinese markets was that it risked diluting share prices. If a new issuance resulted in depressed share prices but did not raise significant amounts of equity, Tsingtao's management and investors would view the initiative as a failure. AB's management believed that despite the potential and competitive barriers, AB could launch a successful acquisition offer for a larger minority stake in Tsingtao, depending on the cash value of its offer and the credibility of its expected post-acquisition contributions to Tsingtao's management, marketing, and operations. It was now time for AB to tender its offer before Tsingtao locked in another alternative to increase its equity.

The Challenge and the Opportunity

Tsingtao Brewery Company Ltd. is the largest brewer in China. The first beer manufacturer in modern times, Tsingtao traced its roots to the Tsingtao Brewery Factory established in 1903 in Qinqdao, China, by German immigrants. But much had changed in a century of Chinese history and development. Tsingtao in January 2001 was a publicly traded company in an increasingly open marketplace. It operated 43 breweries, 2 malt plants, and 49 distribution companies covering 15 provinces in China. It was considered to be the number-one branded consumer product exported from China, selling a variety of brews including Dragon, Phoenix, and Premium. Tsingtao was also China's largest single consumer-product exporter and was continuing to expand, with exports to more than 30 countries. With its two largest rivals, Beijing Yanjing and Guangzhou Zhujiang, Tsingtao was now in a highly competitive market. There were an estimated 800 different breweries in China. Consolidation was the only method of survival.

As illustrated by Exhibit 19.6, Tsingtao was gaining market dominance. The company was gaining the attention of investors inside and outside China. The value proposition for Tsingtao was increasingly clear: It had gained the upper hand in its market through recent acquisitions, acquisitions that would now begin to add earnings with rationalization and modernization through Tsingtao's operational excellence. Tsingtao seemed positioned for strong earnings growth and was increasingly viewed as a potential acquisition target.

Chinese Brewery Consolidation

Chinese per-capita consumption of beer was only 9 liters per person per year, compared to 90 liters in the United States and 154 liters in Germany. But the sheer magnitude of the Chinese market represented an enormous profit potential (or to quote one analyst, "there were simply so many capitas"). China in 2001 was the second-largest beer market in the world after the United States. Tsingtao believed that if it did not move quickly and aggressively, it could lose its opportunity to expand its share of a market poised for growth.

As in most of the maturing beer markets globally, the economies of scale and scope in brewing, distribution, and marketing made it increasingly difficult for small local brewers to survive in China. Survival was not a simple process, however. The Chinese beer market was dominated by the cheapest beer category (85% of beer sales by volume), while the middle market (10%) and premium markets (5%) were somewhat stagnant in sales. Foreign companies like Anheuser Busch

Exhibit 19.6 China's Leading Breweries by Output (thousands of tonnes)

Company	Output	Company	Output
1. Tsingtao Brewery	1,862	6. Sichuan Lanjian Brewery	467
2. Beijing Yanjing Brewery	1,411	7. Shenyang China Resources Brewery	419
3. Zhujiang Brewery	739	8. Chongqing Brewery	406
4. Henan Jin King Brewery	518	9. Hubei Jin Long Quan Brewery	381
5. Harbin Brewery	470	10. Hui Quan Brewery	316

Source: CA$H Securities, http://cash.com.hk.

Exhibit 19.7 Tsingtao's Growth Through Acquisition (millions of Rmb)

Year	Acquisitions	Chinese Brewery Market Share	Capital Expenditures
1996	0	2.1%	30
1997	2	2.1%	245
1998	3	2.5%	384
1999	15	5.1%	1,530
2000	14	8.3%	1,330

(USA) had tried to penetrate the Chinese beer market, but they had gained footholds only in the premium categories with their limited growth potential.

The cheaper beer category was a market niche traditionally filled by small local brewers. The competitive benefits from consolidation for Tsingtao would come from owning and operating these micro-brewers, but not from any significant purchase-and-close strategy. Tsingtao needed to buy them out and make them work. As a result, the firm had undertaken an aggressive acquisition strategy beginning in 1997, resulting in 34 acquisitions in just four years. As illustrated in Exhibit 19.7, however, Tsingtao's growth in market share had come at substantial cost. The capital expenditures on acquisitions alone had totaled more than Rmb3.5 billion. And this did not include the cost of rejuvenating the acquired operations.

By early 2001, Tsingtao was struggling with the post-merger digestion of this acquisition binge, in addition to finding itself under heavy debt-service pressures from the rising debt used to finance the acquisitions. Two other current trends were adding pressure to this debt burden: 1) consolidation had resulted in a series of price wars, putting pressure on operating margins; and 2) the majority of acquired brewers were on the bottom end of the market with high growth potential but low or negative margins when acquired. Management concluded that the company's debt burden—and bright prospects for future earnings and cash flows—made raising additional equity both necessary and feasible.

Tsingtao's Operational Excellence

Tsingtao was known for its operational excellence—it knew brewing and distribution. It had worked constantly throughout the 1990s to increase the efficiency of its operations, specifically in its use of *net working capital.*

Net working capital is the net amount of capital that the firm invests in the actual production and sale of its product. It is calculated as follows:

$$\text{net working capital (NWC)} = (\text{A/R} + \text{inventory}) - (\text{A/P} + \text{OCL})$$

where:

NWC	=	net working capital
A/R	=	accounts receivable
inventory	=	inventories of raw materials, work in process, and finished inventory
A/P	=	accounts payable
OCL	=	other current liabilities, such as accrued taxes and wages

Intuitively, these are the line items of the company's balance sheet that change spontaneously with sales. For example, for Tsingtao to make a sale, it must purchase hops and barley (accounts payable), brew its various beers (inventory), and make sales to distributors (accounts receivable). Net working capital is typically a positive number, because receivables and inventories exceed accounts payable for most firms in most industries (about 99% of the time). (We discuss working capital management in detail in Chapter 22.)

For Tsingtao, the challenge in continuously improving its net working capital structure was complicated by the multitudes of acquisitions of small regional operators. These new acquisitions were often small in scale, low in technology, and frequently relatively inefficient. These new properties represented significant challenges—and opportunities—in improved operations and working capital investments.

Exhibit 19.8 illustrates the enormous progress made by management in improving net working capital in 1999 and 2000. While sales per day had more than doubled from Rmb4.4 million to Rmb9.4 million, total net working capital had actually fallen from a positive Rmb606.2 million

Exhibit 19.8 Tsingtao's Drive to Improve Net Working Capital (NWC)

	A	B	C	D	E	F	G	H	I
1									
2		Exhibit 19.8 Tsingtao's Drive to Improve Net Working Capital (NWC)							
3									
4		**(millions of Rmb)**		1998		1999		2000	
5									
6		Sales		1,597.8		2,253.2		3,448.3	
7		Day's sales (sales/365)		4.38		6.17		9.45	
8									
9		**Components of Net Working Capital**							
10		Accounts receivable		740.9		646.6		681.5	
11		Inventory		359.8		416.8		638.8	
12		Accounts payable		(424.0)		(729.9)		(1,118.8)	
13		Other current liabilities		(70.5)		(203.0)		(205.8)	
14		Net working capital (NWC)		606.2		130.5		(4.3)	
15									
16		NWC/sales		0.38		0.06		(0.001)	
17									
18		**Days Sales of NWC Components**							
19		Accounts receivable		169.3		104.7		72.1	
20		Inventory		82.2		67.5		67.6	
21		Accounts payable		(96.9)		(118.2)		(118.4)	
22		Other current liabilities		(16.1)		(32.9)		(21.8)	
23		Days sales of NWC, total		138.5		21.1		(0.5)	
24									

Row	Cell Entries for Calculated Values
25	**Cell Entries for Calculated Values**
26	D6: ='Exhibit 19.9'!F6, copy to F6 and H6
27	D7: =D6/365, copy to F7 and H7 (i.e., average daily sales = annual sales/365)
28	D14: =SUM(D10:D13), copy to F14 and H14
29	D16: =D14/D6, copy to F16 and H1
30	D19: =D10/D7, copy to D20:D22, F19:F22, and H19:H22
31	D23: =SUM(D19:D22), copy to F23 and H23
32	
33	

* Days sales of NWC components = component

in 1998 to a negative Rmb 4.3 million in 2000. (A negative net working capital level means that the component liability levels exceed the component asset levels. A more intuitive way of understanding negative net working capital is the expression that "the company was receiving money before it was spending money.") The increased efficiency of the business was seen in the net working capital to sales ratio (NWC/sales), which had fallen from 0.38 to near zero (0.001).

Tsingtao's Operating Results

Tsingtao has enjoyed rapid sales growth, both from existing business units and through acquisition. Tsingtao's income statement, shown in Exhibit 19.9, indicates that two measures of gross profitability, gross margin and operating margin, have remained stable over recent years. This is a significant accomplishment, given the many acquisitions made in recent years.

Moving down the income statement, we see the *operating profit margin* slightly declining over time. Beginning at 15.2% in 1998, it dropped to 13.5% in 2000. Although not a large change, this would be noted as a potential problem in the future. Tsingtao is profitable throughout the period shown, but the profit margin is declining. An already low 2.5% in 1998, the *return on sales* (net income/sales) declined to 1.8% in 1999 and 2000.

In general, it appears that Tsingtao has been: 1) growing rapidly; 2) maintaining a gross profit margin that is healthy for its industry—despite taking on 34 acquisitions in the past four years; 3) suffering from higher depreciation and amortization expenses related to modernization and acquisition efforts, respectively; and 4) demonstrating a declining overall profitability as a result.

Measures of Cash Flow

The statement of income for Tsingtao presented in Exhibit 19.9 is based on generally accepted accounting principles. But accounting does not focus on *cash flow*. Financial theory has traditionally defined value as the present value of expected future cash flows. We then need to isolate the *gross* and *free cash flows* of Tsingtao for valuation purposes.

Tsingtao's *statement of cash flows* is a good place to start. The statement of cash flows is constructed in three segments: *operating activities*, *investing activities*, and *financing activities*. Tsingtao's operating activities are illustrated in the top portion of Exhibit 19.10. They begin with earnings before tax, then reduce cash flows by taxes paid (cash taxes), add back depreciation and amortization expenses, and finally add changes in net working capital.

Depreciation and amortization are defined as *non-cash expenses*. *Cash expenses* are for labor or materials purchased by the firm, where cash payments must be paid to the providers of these inputs. Depreciation and amortization are accounting-based expenses (non-cash). *Depreciation* is a charge for investments made in capital equipment. *Amortization* is a charge for investments made in other companies (acquisitions) over and above the value of the assets purchased. Although they are deductible expenses for tax purposes, cash is never paid out by the firm (this is what is meant by the phrase "paid to themselves"). The depreciation and amortization expenses must therefore be added back in for calculation of actual cash flows. As illustrated by Exhibit 19.10, they are significant.

The traditional operating cash flow measure also includes changes in net working capital. An increase in net working capital (positive levels) is an additional investment of capital by the firm. Growth in net working capital therefore reduces the cash flows of the firm. Financial analysts refer

Exhibit 19.9 Tsingtao Brewing Company, Ltd., Statement of Income, 1998–2000 (millions of Rmb)

A	B	C	D	E	F	G	H	I	J	K
1										
2	Exhibit 19.9 Tsingtao Brewing Company Ltd., Statement of Income, 1998 - 2000 (millions of Rmb)									
3										
4	**Income Items**		**Acronym**		**1998**		**1999**		**2000**	
5										
6	Sales				1,597.8		2,253.2		3,448.3	
7	Less cost of goods sold				(1,082.1)		(1,464.9)		(2,245.4)	
8	Gross profit				515.7		788.3		1,202.9	
9	Gross profit margin (%)				32.3%		35.0%		34.9%	
10										
11	Other operating income				8.3		2.9		30.7	
12	Less sales and administration expenses				(280.6)		(482.9)		(768.7)	
13	Operating profit		**EBITDA**		243.4		308.3		464.9	
14	Operating profit margin (%)				15.2%		13.7%		13.5%	
15										
16	Less depreciation and amortization		**D&A**		(132.1)		(180.4)		(257.6)	
17	Earnings before interest and taxes		**EBIT**		111.3		127.9		207.3	
18										
19	Net interest income and expense				(48.1)		(55.0)		(94.0)	
20	Earnings before tax		**EBT**		63.2		72.9		113.3	
21										
22	Less corporate income tax				(21.4)		(29.0)		(34.0)	
23	Profit after tax		**PAT**		41.8		43.9		79.3	
24										
25	Plus net minority interests and other				(2.6)		(3.0)		(18.0)	
26	Net income		**NI**		39.2		40.9		61.3	
27										
28	Return on sales (%)				2.5%		1.8%		1.8%	
29	Revenue growth (%)				10.7%		41.0%		53.0%	
30	Effective tax rate (%)				33.9%		39.8%		30.0%	
31										
32	Shares outstanding, December 31				900.0		900.0		900.0	
33	Earnings per share (Rmb)		**EPS**		0.044		0.045		0.068	
34										
35	*Source:* Tsingtao Brewery Company, Ltd. Operating profit is frequently defined as EBITDA (earnings before interest, taxes, depreciation, and amortization).									
36										
37	**Cell Entries for Calculated Values**									
38	F8: =F6+F7, copy to H8 and J8					F23: =F20+F22, copy to H23 and J23				
39	F9: =F8/F6, copy to H9 and J9					F26: =F23+F25, copy to H26 and J26				
40	F13: =F8+F11+F12, copy to H13 and J13					F28: =F26/F6, copy to H28 and J28				
41	F14: =F13/F6, copy to H14 and J1					H29: =H6/F6-1, copy to J29				
42	F17: =F13+F16, copy to H17 and ·					F30: =–F22/F20, copy to H30 and J30				
43	F20: =F17+F19, copy to H20 and J20					F33: =F26/F32, copy to H33 and J33				
44										
45										
46										

to rising net working capital levels as "capital that is bottled up in the business." In Tsingtao's case, this is literally capital bottled up in its payables, inventories, and receivables for beer sold. As sales grow, net working capital typically rises as well. Tsingtao's sales have been growing very rapidly (primarily through acquisition), but as discussed in the previous section, the firm has also been working aggressively to reduce the net working capital in its many new businesses acquired. The result is an actual reduction in net working capital in 1999 and 2000, adding cash flow back into the business.

Exhibit 19.10 Tsingtao Brewing Company, Ltd., Measures of Cash Flow, 1998–2000 (millions of Rmb)

Exhibit 19.10 Tsingtao Brewing Company Ltd., Measures of Cash Flow, 1998 - 2000 (millions of Rmb)

Row	B	D	F	H	J
4		**Statement of Cash Flows**			
5	Operating Cash Flow Calculation	**Acronym**	**1998**	**1999**	**2000**
6	Earnings before taxes	**EBT**	63.2	72.9	113.3
7	Less corporate income tax		(21.4)	(29.0)	(34.0)
8	Add back depreciation and amortization	**D&A**	132.1	180.4	257.6
9	Less additions to net working capital	**Chg NWC**	(148.3)	475.7	134.8
10	Operating cash flow		25.6	700.0	471.7
12		**Cash Flows for Valuation**			
13	Calculation of NOPAT	**Acronym**	1998	1999	2000
14	Earnings before interest and taxes	**EBIT**	111.3	127.9	207.3
15	Less taxes (recalculated)	**30%**	(33.4)	(38.4)	(62.2)
16	Net operating profit after-tax	**NOPAT**	77.9	89.5	145.1
17	Calculation of Operating Cash Flow				
18	Net operating profit after-tax	**NOPAT**	77.9	89.5	145.1
19	Add back depreciation and amortization	**D&A**	132.1	180.4	257.6
20	Operating cash flow	**OCF**	210.0	269.9	402.7
21	Calculation of Free Cash Flow				
22	Net operating profit after-tax	**NOPAT**	77.9	89.5	145.1
23	Add back depreciation and amortization	**D&A**	132.1	180.4	257.6
24	Less additions to net working capital	**Chg NWC**	(148.3)	475.7	134.8
25	Less capital expenditures	**Capex**	(286.1)	(1,530.0)	(1,330.0)
26	Free cash flow	**FCF**	(224.4)	(784.4)	(792.5)

Cell Entries for Calculated Values

F6: ='Exhibit 19.9'!F20, copy to H6 and J6
F7: ='Exhibit 19.9'!F22, copy to H7 and J7
F8: =-'Exhibit 19.9'!F16, copy to H8 and J8
H9: ='Exhibit 19.8'!D14–'Exhibit 19.8'!F14, copy to J9
F10: =SUM(F6:F9), copy to H10 and J10
F14: ='Exhibit 19.9'!F17, copy to H14 and J
F15: =–$D$15*F14, copy to H15 and J15
F16: =SUM(F14:F15), copy to H16 and J16
F18: =F16, copy to H18 and J18
F19: ='Exhibit 19.9'!F16, copy to H19 and J19
F20: =F18+F19, copy to H20 and J20
F22: =F16, copy to H22 and J22
F23: =F19, copy to H23 and J23
F24: =F9, copy to H24 and J24
F26: =SUM(F22:F25), copy to H26 and J26

Valuation Cash Flows

Financial measures of profit and cash flow used for valuation purposes are significantly different than those measures used for accounting and reporting purposes. For example, the operating cash flow as calculated and recorded on the statement of cash flows is not the measure of cash flow we need for valuation purposes. The lower half of Exhibit 19.10 illustrates the calculation of *net operating profit after-tax (NOPAT)* and *free cash flow (FCF)* for valuation purposes.

- Net operating profit after-tax (NOPAT) is calculated as follows:

  net operating profit after-tax (NOPAT) = EBIT – taxes

  For Tsingtao in 2000, NOPAT was 207.3 – 62.2 = 145.1, or a positive Rmb 145.1 million. This calculation is shown in the lower half of Exhibit 19.10.

- NOPAT is a very powerful financial measure of business performance. It is a cash flow measure of basic business profitability. What it does not contain, however, are the non-cash expenses (depreciation and amortization) and the two areas of investment made by Tsingtao as the company continues to sustain and grow the business (net working capital and capital expenditure).
- Deductions on the income statement for depreciation and amortization must now be added back to NOPAT to calculate the actual cash flows being generated by the firm's operations—*operating cash flow* (OCF). Note that the calculation of operating cash flow for valuation purposes differs from what is termed "operating cash flow" on a statement of cash flows.
- Sustaining the business also alters cash flow. It requires investment in net working capital (NWC) and capital expenditures (capex). Any increase in NWC is a reduction of cash flow; any decrease in NWC is an increase in cash flow. Capital expenditure is any new investment to replace old equipment, to acquire new equipment and technology, or to acquire other businesses, and it reduces available free cash flow.

The addition of these cash flow components to NOPAT creates the desired measure of cash flow for valuation purposes, *free cash flow*:

Free Cash Flow (FCF) = NOPAT + depreciation & amortization – changes in NWC – capex

Tsingtao's free cash flow in 2000 was a negative Rmb792.5 million. The significance of the three adjustments to NOPAT is clear in this case. Although Tsingtao's operations are generating a substantial NOPAT (+145.1), and the addition of depreciation and amortization (+257.6) generates a healthy positive *operating cash flow* (+402.7), and the reduction of net working capital actually adds back a cash flow to the firm (+134.8), Tsingtao's modernization and acquisition strategies as measured by capex have used enormous amounts of cash flow (a negative 1,330.0). The net result is a negative free cash flow for the year 2000 of Rmb792.5 million.

Tsingtao's Discounted Cash Flow Valuation

Now that we have analyzed and decomposed Tsingtao's current financial results, we turn our attention to what its discounted future cash flow will look like. There are three critical components to constructing a discounted cash flow valuation of Tsingtao:

1. Expected future free cash flows
2. Risk-adjusted discount rate
3. Terminal value

Free cash flow forecast. Forecasting Tsingtao's future free cash flows requires forecasting NOPAT, net working capital, and capital expenditures individually.

The source of value of Tsingtao was its operating profits and the recent acquisitions that were expected to grow and improve in both sales and profitability with continued technology and management injections. Sales were expected to grow 25% in 2001, 20% in 2002, 15% in 2003, and 10% in 2004 and 2005. NOPAT is assumed to maintain a level of 4.2% of sales. The entire discounted cash flow valuation is shown in Exhibit 19.11.

Industry experts and analysts had applauded Tsingtao's working capital improvements. The massive improvements and low levels of net working capital achieved by end of year 2000 (essentially

Exhibit 19.11 Discounted Cash Flow Valuation of Tsingtao Brewery Company, Ltd. (millions of Rmb)

Exhibit 19.11 Discounted Cash Flow Valuation of Tsingtao Brewery Company, Ltd. (millions of Rmb)

Row	B	C	E	G	H	I	J	K
4			**Actual**	**1**	**2**	**3**	**4**	**5**
5	**Sales Forecast**	**Assumption**	**2000**	**2001**	**2002**	**2003**	**2004**	**2005**
6	Sales growth rate assumption			25%	20%	15%	10%	10%
7	Sales		3,448.3	4,310.4	5,172.5	5,948.3	6,543.1	7,197.5
8	**Calculation of Discounted Cash Flow Value**							
9	NOPAT	4.2%	145.1	181.0	217.2	249.8	274.8	302.3
10	Depreciation and amortization	7.5%	257.6	276.9	297.7	320.0	344.0	369.8
11	Operating cash flow		402.7	458.0	514.9	569.8	618.8	672.1
12	Less additions to net working capital	1.0%	134.8	(43.1)	(51.7)	(59.5)	(65.4)	(72.0)
13	Less capital expenditures	2.5%	(1,330.0)	(107.8)	(129.3)	(148.7)	(163.6)	(179.9)
14	Free cash flow (FCF)		(792.5)	307.1	333.9	361.7	389.8	420.2
15	Terminal value (and assumed growth rate)	1.0%						4,715.6
16	Expected FCF for discounting			307.1	333.9	361.7	389.8	5,135.8
17	Present value factor (and discount rate)	10.00%		0.9091	0.8264	0.7513	0.6830	0.6209
18	Discounted FCF			279.2	275.9	271.7	266.3	3,188.9
19	Cumulative discounted FCF		4,282.0					
20	Less present value of debt capital		(2,093.0)					
21	Residual equity value		2,189.0					
23	Shares outstanding (millions)		900.0					
24	Equity value (Rmb/share)		2.43					
25	Spot exchange rate (Rmb/HK$)		1.0648					
26	Equity value (HK$/share)		2.28					

Note: The discounted cash flow analysis is based primarily on sales expectations. Sales growth rate assumptions are used to generate sales expectations, which are in turn used for estimates of NOPAT (assumed as 4.2% of sales), depreciation and amortization (assumed as 7.5% of sales), additions to net working capital (assumed 1.0% of sales), and capital expenditures (assumed 2.5% of sales). Free cash flow is discounted at the 10% weighted average cost of capital. The terminal value for this baseline analysis assumes a 1% perpetual growth rate in free cash flow.

Cell Entries for Calculated Values

E7: ='Exhibit 19.9'!J6	G7: =E7*(1+G6)
E9: ='Exhibit 19.10'!J16	H7: =G7*(1+H6), copy to I7:K7
E10: ='Exhibit 19.10'!J19	G9: =$C$9*G7, copy to H9:K9
E11: =E9+E10	G10: =E10*(1+$C$10)
E12: ='Exhibit 19.10'!J24	H10: =G10*(1+$C$10), copy to I10:K10
E13: ='Exhibit 19.10'!J25	G11: =G9:G10, copy to H11:K11
E14: =SUM(E11:E13), copy to G14:K14	G12: =-$C$12*G7, copy to H12:K12
E19: =SUM(G18:K18)	G13: =-$C$13*G7, copy to H13:K13
E21: =E19+E20	G16: =G14, copy to H16:K16
E24: =E21/E23	G17: =1/(1+$C$17)^G4, copy to H17:K1
E26: =E24/E25	G18: =G16*G17, copy to H18:K18

zero net working capital), however, were thought to include most of the improvement possible. With rapid growth forecast, NWC was now expected to be maintained at roughly 1.0% of sales throughout the analysis period.

Capital expenditure forecasts are infamously inaccurate. Most firms, even when not making major acquisitions, have relatively poor capabilities to plan for needed replacement investment or technological upgrades with innovations. Capital expenditures had been enormous in 1999 and 2000 as a result of the 29 acquisitions made in those two years alone. Although few additional acquisitions were planned by Tsingtao beginning in 2001, the capital investment needed to modernize many of the acquired properties would require substantial outlays for years to come. Capital expenditures were therefore estimated to be 2.5% of sales annually through 2005.

Discount rate. The discount rate to be used for Tsingtao's valuation would be the company's weighted average cost of capital. Assuming a 34% corporate tax rate and a pretax cost of debt of 8.00% per year (the cost of Tsingtao's most recent debt), the after-tax cost of debt was estimated at 5.28% per year.

The cost of equity was calculated using the *capital asset pricing model.* With the Hong Kong market as the best indicator of equity valuation, the risk-free rate is 7.000% per year, the equity risk premium is 6.700% per year, and the beta of Tsingtao's H-shares on the Hong Kong stock exchange is 0.80:

$$\text{cost of equity} = k_e^{\text{Tsingtao}} = k_{rf} + \beta\left(k_m - k_{rf}\right) = 7.000 + 0.80\left(13.700 - 7.000\right) = 12.36\%$$

The final component needed for the calculation of Tsingtao's weighted average cost of capital is the weight of debt and equity in its target capital structure. The firm had increased its degree of leverage in recent years, but management and analysts considered a one-third debt and two-thirds equity capital structure appropriate over the long term. Using these weights, Tsingtao's weighted average cost of capital (WACC) was calculated as:

$$\text{WACC} = \left(\frac{\text{Equity}}{\text{Capital}} \times k_e\right) + \left(\frac{\text{Debt}}{\text{Capital}} \times k_d \times \left(1 - \text{tax}\right)\right)$$

Plugging in the 12.36% cost of equity and the 5.28% cost of debt, after tax:

$$\text{WACC} = \left(.667 \times 12.36\%\right) + \left(.333 \times 5.28\%\right) = 10.00\%$$

This weighted average cost of capital is used to discount the future cash flows of Tsingtao for valuation purposes.

Terminal value. The terminal value is always critical in discounted cash flow valuation, because it must capture all free cash flow value flowing indefinitely into the future. Although the cash flows are estimated for the explicit period of 2001 through 2005, Tsingtao's brewery business will most likely continue far into the future (it was already 97 years old). The typical calculation of terminal value uses a constant dividend growth model. Assuming a discount rate of 10.00% (the WACC) and a free cash flow growth rate into the future of 1.0% per year (conservative), we calculate the terminal value in year 5 of the analysis as:

$$\text{terminal value} = \frac{FCF_{2005}(1+g)}{k_{WACC}-g} = \frac{420.2(1+0.0100)}{0.1000-0.0100} = \text{Rmb}4{,}715.6$$

This terminal value, as shown in Exhibit 19.11, enters the discounted cash flow in 2005 and represents all expected free cash flows arising in all years after that.

An alternative method frequently used in valuation analysis is to assume some multiple of net operating cash flow in the final year considered. In this case, assuming a multiple of 10, we might estimate the terminal value for Tsingtao at Rmb4,202 (10 × 420.2). This technique is particularly applicable in leveraged buyouts (LBOs) and private equity ventures where the real value and purpose of the initial purchase is the eventual sale of the enterprise at a future date.

DCF valuation. The present value of all future expected cash flows is the total enterprise value. *Enterprise value* is the sum of the present values of both debt and equity in the enterprise. Tsingtao's equity value is then found by deducting the net debt due creditors and any minority interests. Total equity value divided by total shares outstanding is the fair value of equity per share. The baseline discounted cash flow valuation of Tsingtao is Rmb2.43/share (HK$2.28).

The DCF valuation shown in Exhibit 19.11 is only a starting point. A number of assumptions have been made in order to derive the baseline price of Rmb2.43, and these "value drivers" should be analyzed further using sensitivity analysis. Any such analysis would include the sales growth rate assumptions, all assumed percentage drivers of NOPAT, NWC, capital expenditures, and depreciation and amortization, as well as the discount rate and terminal value growth

Valuation by Multiples of Earnings and Cash Flows

The valuation of businesses of all kinds, small or large, domestic or multinational, goods or services, has long been as much art as science. The use of multiples, in which a ratio for the subject firm is compared to comparable ratios for competitors or recent acquisitions, is one of the more artistic processes. Similar in logic to ratio analysis used in traditional financial analysis, multiples simply present the way the firm stacks up against industry comparables. Some of the most widely used measures include the PE (price/earnings-per-share) ratio, PS (price/sales) ratio, market-to-book (M/B) ratio, and a variety of ratios that compare enterprise value (EV) to either earnings or cash flows. Each of these ratios includes a market-determined value—price—either explicitly in the numerator or in calculating market capitalization. The price is then combined with values taken from the firm's own financials, in the form of either earnings (such as EPS), cash flow (such as FCF), or market capitalization.

PE ratio. The PE ratio is by far the most widely used of the valuation ratios. Simply stated, the PE ratio is an indication of what the market is willing to pay for a currency unit of earnings. But more importantly, it is an indication of how secure the market's perception is about the future earnings of the firm. Coca-Cola has long been a prime example of a MNE whose PE ratio, typically ranging between 35 and 42, is an indicator of how sustainable global earnings and earnings growth are in the eyes of shareholders. Markets do not pay for past or present earnings. An investor purchasing a share today is taking a long position on the basis of what earnings are expected to do in the future—from that moment on.

Because Tsingtao is traded most heavily on the Hong Kong stock exchange, and that exchange is relatively more liquid and open to global investors than the Shanghai stock exchange, we shall focus on the PE ratio calculations and comparisons of the Hong Kong listing for Tsingtao. Tsingtao's earnings per share for 2000 were Rmb61.3 million on 900 million outstanding shares (EPS of Rmb0.068 or HK\$0.0640 assuming an exchange rate of Rmb1.0648/HK\$). The closing share price for 2000 in Hong Kong was HK\$2.20/share. The closing PE ratio for Tsingtao in Hong Kong for 2000 was then:

$$\text{PE ratio}^{\text{Tsingtao}}_{\text{Hong Kong}} = \frac{\text{current share price in HK\$}}{\left[\dfrac{\text{earnings for 2000 in HK\$}}{\text{outstanding shares}}\right]} = \frac{\text{HK\$2.20}}{\left[\dfrac{\text{HK\$57,569,497}}{\text{900,000,000 shares}}\right]} = 34$$

Tsingtao's PE ratio of 34 was quite high compared to the Hong Kong stock exchange's H-share PE average of 12 (a ratio of 2.83:1).

If we recall our earlier statement that "markets do not pay for past or present earnings," then we should also probably calculate Tsingtao's PE ratio not on current earnings but on future earnings. The PE ratio would then be compared to the Hong Kong stock exchange's share prices recalculated on expected earnings. Deutschebank Securities estimated the 2001 forecast PE ratio for Tsingtao as 28.8 compared to its forecast of the Hong Kong H-share market's average of 8.2. This is a ratio of 3.5:1, an even higher relative measure than before. Clearly, regardless of the precise calculation of Tsingtao's PE ratio, the market believes that Tsingtao's earnings would be either relatively riskless compared to the market or significantly higher in the near future.

M/B ratio. The market-to-book (M/B) ratio is nearly as widely used in valuation as the PE ratio. It provides some measure of the market's assessment of the employed capital per share versus what the capital cost. The book value of a firm is the value of common stock as recorded on the firm's balance sheet plus the retained earnings (cumulative capital reinvested from earnings). If the M/B ratio exceeds 1, it implies that the firm's equity is currently valued in excess of what stockholders invested in the firm. Like the PE ratio, the magnitude of the M/B ratio, as compared to its major competitors, reflects the market's perception of the quality of the firm's earnings, management, and general strategic opportunities.

The M/B ratio focuses on equity in both the numerator and denominator and is a mix of market value (numerator) and historical accounting value (denominator). It is calculated as the ratio of share price to book value per share. The M/B ratio for Tsingtao in 2000 is:

$$\text{M / B ratio}^{\text{Tsingtao}} = \frac{\text{current share price}}{\text{book value per share}} = \frac{\text{HK\$2.34 / share}}{\text{HK\$2.35 / share}} = 0.9957 = 1$$

According to this equation, Tsingtao is selling for the historical cost of the capital invested in the business. Under most typical business conditions, a M/B ratio is interpreted as a signal that the company may be "undervalued" and therefore a true investment opportunity.

Other multiples. Two other comparison ratios or multiples may provide additional insights into Tsingtao's value. The 2001 forecast price-to-sales ratio (price per share versus forecast sales per share) for Tsingtao by Deutschebank Securities was 0.56, lower than Hong Kong H-share forecast of 0.85. This ratio would imply an undervaluation of Tsingtao if the other firms in the comparison are truly compatible.

A similar type of ratio, the ratio of 2001 forecast enterprise value (market value of debt and equity, EV) to basic business earnings (EBITDA), for Tsingtao was 7.5 compared to the Hong Kong H-share forecast of 3.7. The higher ratio for Tsingtao implied that its shares were overvalued. Again, the difficulty in interpreting these relative measures of value is in knowing how well Tsingtao compares to the other firms traded as H-shares on the Hong Kong stock exchange.

Summary of Valuation Measures

Exhibit 19.12 summarizes the various measures of Tsingtao's valuation we have discussed. As is often the case in corporate valuations—domestic or cross-border—much of the information is conflicting. What is Tsingtao worth? Value, like beauty, is in the eyes of the beholder.

Exhibit 19.12 Summary of Valuation Measures for Tsingtao Brewing Company, Ltd. (Rmb/share and HK$/share)

Valuation Method	Share Price	Observations
Current market price	Rmb 2.34	Baseline
Discounted cash flow	Rmb 2.43 (wide range)	Implies Tsingtao is undervalued
Price-to-earnings ratio	34 to market's 12	Tsingtao's potential may already be included in the price
Market-to-book ratio	.9957 or 1	Tsingtao is undervalued
Price-to-sales ratio	.56 to market's .85	Tsingtao is undervalued
Enterprise value-to-EBITDA ratio	7.5 to market's 3.7	Tsingtao is overvalued

SUMMARY

- The number and dollar value of cross-border mergers and acquisitions has grown rapidly in recent years, but the growth and magnitude of activity is taking place in the developed countries, not the developing countries.
- As opposed to the fighting and scraping for market share and profits in traditional domestic markets, a MNE can expect greater growth potential in the global marketplace. There are a variety of paths by which the MNE can enter foreign markets, including greenfield investment and acquisition.
- The drivers of M&A activity are both macro (the global competitive environment) and micro in scope (the variety of industry and firm-level forces and actions driving individual firm value).
- The primary forces of change in the global competitive environment—technological change, regulatory change, and capital market change—create new business opportunities for MNEs, which they pursue aggressively.

- The process of acquiring an enterprise anywhere in the world has three common elements: 1) identification and valuation of the target; 2) completion of the ownership change transaction (the tender); and 3) the management of the post-acquisition transition.
- The settlement stage of a cross-border merger or acquisition necessitates gaining the approval and cooperation of management, shareholders, and eventually regulatory authorities.
- Cross-border mergers, acquisitions, and strategic alliances all face similar challenges: They must place a value on the target enterprise on the basis of its projected performance in its market. This process of enterprise valuation combines elements of strategy, management, and finance.
- One of the most controversial issues in shareholder rights is at what point in the accumulation of shares the bidder is required to make all shareholders a tender offer. For example, a bidder might slowly accumulate shares of a target company by gradually buying shares on the open market over time. Theoretically, this share accumulation could continue until the bidder had: 1) the single largest block of shares among all individual shareholders, 2) majority control, or 3) all the shares outright.
- Every country possesses a different set of rules and regulations for the transfer of control of publicly traded corporations. This market, the market for corporate control, has been the subject of enormous debate in recent years.
- A variety of valuation techniques are widely used in global business today, each with its relative merits. In addition to the fundamental methodologies of discounted cash flow (DCF) and multiples (earnings and cash flows), there are also a variety of industry-specific measures that focus on the most significant elements of value in business lines.
- The DCF approach to valuation calculates the value of the enterprise as the present value of all future free cash flows less the cash flows due creditors and minority interest holders.
- The PE ratio is an indication of what the market is willing to pay for a currency unit of earnings. It is also an indication of the market's perception about the future earnings of the firm and its riskiness.
- The market-to-book ratio (M/B) is a method of valuing a firm on the basis of what the market believes the firm is worth, over and above its capital its original capital investment and subsequent retained earnings.
- An illustrative case valuing Tsingtao Brewing Company was analyzed.

QUESTIONS

1. **Cross-border trends.** According to recent trends in cross-border mergers and acquisitions, would you say that many MNEs are moving into emerging markets in a big way?
2. **Shareholder value.** If most bidders pay the owners of the target firm the "true value" of the firm, how does a bidder create value for its own shareholders through the acquisition?
3. **Management and shareholder value.** Why do acquisitions provide management with a greater potential for shareholder value creation than internal growth?
4. **Cross-border drivers.** List and explain at least six drivers of cross-border mergers and acquisitions.
5. **Stages of acquisition.** The three stages of a cross-border acquisition combine all elements of business (finance, strategy, accounting, marketing, management, organizational behavior, etc.), but many people consider finance relevant only in the first stage. List specific arguments why finance is as important as any other business field in stages two and three of a cross-border acquisition.

6. **Shareholder rights.** Why do many national governments create specific laws and processes for one company to acquire the control and ownership of another company? Why not just let the market operate on its own?
7. **Settlement.** What factors are considered when deciding how to settle an acquisition in cash or shares?
8. **Corporate cascades.** Why do some countries object to multiple levels of ownership control? Do minority shareholders get treated any differently in these cascades than without them?
9. **Free cash flow versus profit.** Consider the following statement: Academia always focuses on the present value of free cash flow as the definition of value, yet companies seem to focus on "earnings" or "profits."
   a. Do you think this is true?
   b. What is the basic distinction between cash flow and profit?
   c. How do we convert a measure of profit (say, net income on a profit and loss statement) into a measure of cash flow?
10. **Discounted cash flow valuation.** Discounted cash flow (DCF) valuation requires the analyst to estimate and isolate the expected free cash flows that a specific asset or investment will produce in the future. The analyst then must discount these back to the present.
    a. Are the cash flows and discount rate before or after tax? Do both need to be the same or should one be before tax and the other after tax?
    b. Where does the discount rate for the investment come from? What assumptions should it make about the way the investment will actually be financed?
    c. A very common criticism of DCF is that it punishes future value and therefore is biased against long-term investments. Construct an argument refuting this statement.
11. **Comparables and market multiples.** What valuation information is gained by using market multiples such as PE ratios that is not gained through discounted cash flow analysis?
12. **Market-to-book.** What is the market-to-book ratio, and why is it considered so useful in the valuation of companies?
13. **Tsingtao (A).** Recommend which valuation measure, or combination of valuation methods, Anheuser Busch (AB) should use.
14. **Tsingtao (B).** What share price should AB offer? Is this an opening offer or best offer in negotiations?
15. **Tsingtao (C).** Identify the post-acquisition (Phase III) problems that AB is likely to face if it acquires a larger minority ownership position in Tsingtao.

PROBLEMS

1. **PE valuation of Global.com.** A new worldwide cellular phone company, Global.com (U.S.), is one of the new high-flying telecommunication stocks that are valued largely on the basis of price/earnings multiples. Other firms trading on U.S. exchanges in its similar industry segment are currently valued at PE ratios of 35 to 40. Given the following earnings estimates, what would you estimate the value of Global.com to be?

Last Year EPS	This Year EPS	Next Year EPS
$(1.20)	$0.75	$1.85

2. **Bidding on São Paulo Cellular rights.** A consortium of global telecommunication firms is about to submit a bid to purchase the rights to provide cellular telephone services to central São Paulo. The bid must be submitted and payment made (if awarded the bid) in U.S. dollars, not in Brazilian real (R$). The consortium has finalized the following forecasts of cash flows, exchange rates, and potential discount rates.

São Paulo Cellular Rights

	Year 0	Year 1	Year 2	Year 3
Estimated CF (millions of R$):				
Best case	(1,350)	550	2,000	3,800
Moderate case	(1,350)	550	1,600	3,200
Worst case	(1,350)	550	1,000	1,500
Expected exchange rate (R$/US$):				
Best case	1.70	1.70	1.70	1.70
Moderate case	1.70	1.80	1.90	2.00
Worst case	1.70	2.00	2.20	2.50
Discount rate R$ terms)	32.0%			
Discount rate (US$ terms)	18.0%			

Perform a DCF analysis on the potential investment and propose a final bid for submission.

Private Equity in Latin America—The Soto Group. Use the following information to answer problems 3 through 5. Private equity focuses on purchasing small privately held firms, restructuring them with infusions of capital and professional management, and reselling them several years later (either to another private buyer or through a public offering). This means that the firms' value to the private equity investors is in their terminal value—their value when taken public several years from now.

The Soto Group is a Mexico City–based private equity fund. The Group is evaluating the prospects for purchasing Guga Avionics (Buenos Aires), an aviation operating and management firm with current business operations throughout Argentina and southern Brazil. The Soto Group has, through its due diligence process, acquired the needed financial statements, inventory of assets, and assessment of operations. Soto's valuation staff typically values the potential target on both an *a priori* basis (current structure and management strategy) and an *ex post* basis (expected values after capital and management expertise injections).

***A Priori* Financial Forecast**
Guga Avionics, Buenos Aires, Argentina (millions of Argentine pesos)

	Year 0	Year 1	Year 2	Year 3
Gross revenues	210	235	270	325
Less direct costs	(132)	(144)	(162)	(190)
Gross profit	78	91	108	135
Gross margin	37%	39%	40%	41%
Less G&A	(16)	(17)	(18)	(19)
Less depreciation	(24)	(24)	(24)	(24)
EBIT	38	50	66	92
Less interest	(28)	(30)	(30)	(28)
EBT	10	20	36	64
Less taxes at 30%	(3)	(6)	(11)	(19)
Net profit	7	14	26	45
Return on sales	3%	6%	9%	14%

Soto must also determine what Guga could sell for in three years. Soto has an unbending internal discipline that every firm acquired must be restructured, revitalized, and ready for public sale in three years or less from deal consummation. Given market multiples on the Buenos Aires Bolsa at this time, a value of 18 to 20 times current free cash flow (in year 3) would be considered aggressive. The *a priori* analysis, acquired from Guga Avionics and adjusted by Soto's own valuation and market experts, appears in the preceding exhibit.

The Soto Group believes that it can reduce financing expenses by 25% in years 1 and 2 and by 25% in year 3. It also believes that by using its own operational experience, it can reduce direct costs by 15%, 20%, and 25%, in years 1, 2, and 3, respectively. The big question is revenue enhancement. Guga has done a solid job of promoting and expanding service revenues in the past several years. At most, the Soto Group believes it may be able to expand gross revenues by 5% per annum over current forecasts.

3. **Guga Avionics Valuation (A).** As the lead member of the Soto Group's valuation staff, use this data to find the difference between *a priori* and *ex post* earnings and cash flows?
4. **Guga Avionics Valuation (B).** What is the difference between *a priori* and *ex post* sale value at the end of year 3?
5. **Soto Group and Guga Avionics.** In addition to the current Soto plan, what would you recommend to enhance the profit and cash flow outlook for Guga if acquired?

Tsingtao Brewery Company. Use the spreadsheet analyses of Tsingtao Brewery Company used throughout the chapter to answer Problems 6 through 10.

6. **Tsingtao Brewery Company (A).** As described in the chapter, Anheuser Busch (AB) is interested in further analysis of the potential value represented by the newfound strategic and operational direction of Tsingtao. The baseline analysis assumed some rather aggressive growth rates in sales. AB wishes to find the implications of slower sales growth, say 15% per annum throughout the 2001 to 2005 period, on the discounted cash flow equity value of the company. And, assuming sales growth is indeed slower, AB wishes to determine the compounded impact of a declining NOPAT margin, say 3.6% of sales, rather than the baseline assumption of 4.2% of sales, on equity value. Perform the analysis.
7. **Tsingtao Brewery Company (B).** Returning to the original set of assumptions, AB is now focusing on the capital expenditure and depreciation components of the valuation. Tsingtao has invested heavily in brewery upgrades and distribution equipment in recent years, and hopes that its capital expenditures are largely done. However, AB wants to run a scenario to focus on the possibility that a number of the recent acquisitions may require higher capex levels. What is the impact on Tsingtao's discounted cash flow value if capex expenditures were assumed to be 3.5% of sales rather than the baseline assumption of 2.5%? What is the result of combining that with an assumed depreciation level of 8.5% as opposed to 7.5% (baseline) for the time period of the analysis?
8. **Tsingtao Brewery Company (C).** Return to the original set of assumptions. One of the truly controversial components of all discounted cash flow analyses is the impact terminal value calculations have on equity value. AB wishes to explore the following sensitivities to the DCF valuation:
   a. Assuming no terminal value, what is the DCF equity value per share?
   b. Assuming a terminal value growth rate of 0%, what is the DCF equity value per share? What percentage of the total DCF value is the terminal value?
9. **Tsingtao Brewery Company (D).** One of AB's analysts is quite pessimistic on the outlook for Tsingtao. Although the company did indeed make major strides in reducing net working capital needs in recent years, much of that was accomplished before really tackling the complexity of absorbing many of these new acquisitions. The analyst argues that, at best, sales growth will average 12% for the coming

five-year period and that net working capital will most likely rise to 3% of sales (baseline assumption was 1%). What does this do to the equity valuation of Tsingtao?

10. **Tsingtao Brewery Company (E).** Finally, the valuation staff wants to address a full scenario of what they consider best-case and worst-case analysis, assuming the Baseline analysis is somewhere in between, Moderate.

	Best Case	Baseline	Worst Case
Sales growth	20%	Variable	12%
NOPAT of sales	4.4%	4.2%	3.6%
Depreciation	8.5%	7.5%	6.5%
NWC of sales	0.8%	1.0%	3.0%
Capex of sales	1.5%	2.5%	3.5%
Terminal value growth	2.0%	1.0%	0.0%

Evaluate the best-case and worst-case scenarios for Tsingtao.

INTERNET EXERCISES

WWW.

1. **Intellectual property & valuation.** The late 1990s saw the increase of corporate valuations arising from ownership of various forms of intellectual property, rather than the traditional value arising from goods or services production and sale. Use the following web site to prepare a management brief on the current state of valuing intellectual property.

   Intellectual Property Valuation http://valuationcorp.com

2. **Market Capitalization of Brahma of Brazil.** Brahma is one of the largest publicly traded firms in Brazil. It is listed on both the Bovespa and the New York Stock Exchange (ADRs). Using historical data that can be found on one of these sources, answer the following questions.

   Hoovers http://www.hoovers.com

   Yahoo http://www.yahoo.com

   a. How did Brahma's share price—in both R$ and U.S. dollar terms—react to the January 1999 Brazilian real devaluation?

   b. Would a firm like Brahma be a more or less attractive target of foreign investors after the real's devaluation?

SELECTED READINGS

Bank of America Roundtable on Evaluating and Financing Foreign Direct Investment," *Journal of Applied Corporate Finance*, Fall 1996, Volume 9, No. 3, pp. 64–79.

Lee, Tung-Jean, and Richard E. Caves, "Uncertain Outcomes of Foreign Investment: Determinants of Profits After Large Acquisitions," *Journal of International Business Studies*, Third Quarter 1998, Volume 29, No. 3, pp. 563–582.

Luehrman, Timothy A., "What's It Worth?: A General Manager's Guide to Valuation," *Harvard Business Review*, May 1997.

Luehrman, Timothy A., "Strategy as a Portfolio of Real Options," *Harvard Business Review*, September–October 1998, pp. 89–99.

Decision **CASE**

THUNDERBIRD
THE AMERICAN GRADUATE SCHOOL OF INTERNATIONAL MANAGEMENT

Fashion Faux Pas: Gucci & LVMH

"The brewing battle for Gucci is emblematic of the New Europe that is taking shape with the launch of the common currency and the globalization of industry: two Frenchmen squaring off for control of a Dutch-based Italian company run by a U.S.-educated lawyer and an American designer, and advised by London-based American investment bankers.

"Gucci Watch," *Wall Street Journal*, March 22, 1999.

The Gucci Group N.V. 2000 Annual Report really said it all. Tom Ford, Creative Director, and Domenico De Sole, President and CEO, stood side-by-side facing the camera with eyes of steel. Ford, unshaven and shirt provocatively opened, was the American designer who had single-handedly revitalized the Gucci name. Domenico De Sole, dressed in a dark suit, white shirt, with finely trimmed beard, was the Italian lawyer-turned-businessman who had returned Gucci to profitability and promise. The photograph, of course, by the famous fashion photographer, Annie Leibovitz. These two men represented the defiant spirit of Gucci, a molten mix of high-powered fashion and high-powered finance.

These two men had, in the first six months of 1999, been the centerpiece of one of the most highly contested hostile takeover battles ever seen on the European continent. Under attack by LVMH Möet Hennessey Louis Vuitton, the French luxury goods conglomerate, Gucci had implemented the age-old strategy of "the enemy of an enemy is a friend." Gucci successfully enticed Pinault-Printemps-Redoute of France, a retailer, to act as a white knight, grabbing Gucci from LVMH's clutches. Now, in September of 2001, it appeared this particular chapter of the fashion wars was finally over. But in the end, when all was said and done, had Gucci's shareholders been winners or losers?

Gucci Group N.V.

Guccio Gucci founded Gucci in 1923 after being inspired by extravagant and elegant baggage while working in a London hotel. Gucci's expensive leather goods (shoes, handbags, and ready-to-wear)—and the Gucci red and green logo—became internationally recognized for the next half-century. The Gucci family, however, sold its remaining interest in the company in 1993 after a decade of turmoil and scandal.

Although always considered chic by international standards, the Gucci business lines had grown old in the 1970s and 1980s. Gucci's rebirth in the 1990s was credited, strangely enough, to two Americans, Domenico De Sole and Tom Ford. De Sole was Italian by birth,

A06-02-0007

but had attended Harvard Law School, married an American (gaining U.S. citizenship), and began his climb up the corporate ladder in a Washington D.C. law firm. De Sole first worked for the Gucci family, then eventually headed Gucci America. When control of Gucci passed from Maurizio Gucci and the Gucci family in 1993 to a Bahraini investment bank, Investcorp, De Sole moved to the corporate headquarters in Florence, Italy, to head Gucci International.

Gucci's owner, Investcorp, spun out 49% ownership in October 1995 in an initial public offering in Amsterdam. The original issuance price averaged $22 per share. Investcorp sold its remaining stake six months later for $48 per share. Gucci was now owned by everyone and no one in particular. The company was De Sole's to run.

Upon his arrival in Florence, De Sole found a design team with one real remaining talent, Tom Ford, a transplanted Texan. De Sole allowed Ford a free hand in the revitalization of Gucci's product line and operations, naming him Creative Director in 1994 at the age of 36. In the next five years, Ford successfully transformed what many considered a tired and sad Gucci image into a sexy of-the-moment revolution.

The new Gucci was, by 1999, considered a potential takeover target. Analysts believed the firm was undervalued, well-managed, and possessed significant growth potential. Gucci was also extremely widely held. The Italian fashion house Prada had acquired a 9.5% interest in Gucci in June of 1998, making it the single largest shareholder. Prada's move led to much speculation that it might attempt a takeover. Although silent as to its intentions, Prada's move was later seen as the first move to put Gucci into play.

Creeping Acquisition

On January 6, 1999, LVMH Möet Hennessey Louis Vuitton, the French luxury-goods conglomerate, announced that it had passed the 5% shareholding level in Gucci Group N.V. Because both Gucci and LVMH were traded in the United States in addition to their home markets (Gucci's shares are traded in Amsterdam, LVMH in Paris), US Securities and Exchange Commission regulations applied, requiring public notification of a firm taking a 5% or more stake in another publicly traded company. Gucci's share price in New York moved from $50 to $70 per share (see Appendix 1).

LVMH was inseparable from its President and CEO, Bernard Arnault. Arnault was widely known for his aggressive and persistent drive to continually build the French luxury-goods conglomerate through acquisition. Arnault had pursued a steady strategy of buying up hundreds of small fashion brands and business lines with established brands but lagging results. The acquisitions were then folded into the LVMH conglomerate, building mass and exerting its size in marketing and positioning negotiations globally. Arnault had considered buying Gucci back in 1994, but the asking price, $350 million, had been too much.

LVMH's surprising move on Gucci led quickly to widespread speculation that this was only the first step in a hostile takeover of Gucci. LVMH was ten times the size (by sales) of Gucci. Six days later, LVMH announced that it had acquired an additional 9.5%—the shares previously held by Prada—for $398 million.[1] Two days later, on January 14, LVMH stated, "in the present circumstances it has no intention of making a tender offer" for Gucci.

1. Prada's investment return was impressive. Prada's original investment of $258 million netted a profit of $140 million, a 54% return in approximately six months.

But Bernard Arnault and LVMH were not through yet. On January 26, LVMH confirmed that it had now increased its stake in Gucci to 34.4%. As illustrated in Exhibit 1, Arnault was buying Gucci shares rapidly and globally. Arnault's 34.4% totaled 20.15 million shares and represented an investment estimated at $1.44 billion. This last step was significant, in that under French law, LVMH's home, a company was required to launch a general tender—an offer for all of the shares held publicly—of any company once a 33% share ownership position was attained. US law had no such requirement. Bernard Arnault described his intentions towards Gucci as "not unfriendly."[2]

On Wednesday, February 11, LVMH informed Gucci by letter that it was requesting a shareholder meeting to vote on its proposal to add its own nominee to Gucci's board, expanding it from eight to nine members. Bernard Arnault again assured both Gucci's management and shareholders that his interests were only those of a passive investor—Gucci's largest investor.

> *"I reiterate my complete faith in the creative talent of Tom Ford and in the development strategy implemented by Gucci's management team. Our proposal today is provided for within the statutes of Gucci, allowing LVMH to exercise its rights as a shareholder without altering in any way the independence of the company."*

Gucci's corporate bylaws, as incorporated under Netherlands law, stipulated that a shareholder with a stake of 10% or more was entitled to call a special shareholder meeting to implement board changes. The meeting must then be held within six weeks of the request. Gucci's CEO, Domenico De Sole, publicly admonished Bernard Arnault's moves and characterized the strategy as a "creeping takeover" in which LVMH gradually acquired more and more shares of Gucci until it gained effective control without ever paying existing shareholders any premium for the change in ownership.

The Poison Pill

Gucci reacted quickly and radically. Less than one week later, on February 18, Gucci announced the creation of a new employee stock ownership plan (ESOP) and structure, the

Exhibit 1 LVMH's Creeping Acquisition of Gucci Group

Gucci, total shares outstanding (January 31, 1999)	58,510,700
LVMH's accumulation of shares:	
Purchased on the open market before Jan 19	10,068,185
Purchased from Prada of Italy on Jan 14	5,560,000
Purchased on the NYSE, Jan 19–22	919,800
Purchased on the Amsterdam stock exchange, Jan 19–22	47,000
Purchased from private transactions with Capital Research	3,550,000
Total holdings in Gucci	20,144,985
LVMH's proportional ownership of Gucci	34.4%

2. Details of Tom Ford's contract with Gucci as filed with the US Securities and Exchange Commission included a provision that in the event of any one shareholder gaining a 35% stake in Gucci, Ford could sever his relationship with Gucci and a variety of specified salary, bonus, and stock options could be exercised.

Employee Trust. Gucci granted the Trust the right to purchase up to 37 million newly issued shares. The Trust instantly purchased 20,154,985 shares.

The Trust's ownership in Gucci was now 25.6% (if it exercised its right to purchase all 37 million, its stake in Gucci would rise to 38.7%). This matched LVMH's ownership, and diluted LVMH's position from 34.4% to 26% by the issuance. Gucci had extended an interest-free loan to the Employee Trust to purchase the shares (a Note), with the stipulation that the shares could not be transferred to a third party.[3] Exhibit 2 details the new share structure. A subtle yet significant feature of the ESOP plan was that it did not dilute earnings. Because the ESOP shares were issued to a Trust, the shares carried no dividend rights. The new shares would not be included in Gucci's earnings per share (EPS) calculations.

Gucci CEO De Sole defended the action as necessary. It was not a poison pill in Gucci's opinion. It was instituted in order to prevent a creeping acquisition in which the controlling ownership of Gucci would change hands without all shareholders receiving a payment—a *premium*—for that control. Gucci continued to oppose LVMH's advances on the basis that having a competitor as a part owner and director was not consistent with Gucci's best interests. De Sole went on to invite LVMH to make a public tender:

> *"We are telling them they can make a takeover bid for 100% of the company's shares any time they want.... We've had a lot of contacts with LVMH in the past month. We made it very clear that a minority position held by a major competitor is an impossible situation. It's like Coke having a seat on Pepsi's board."*

LVMH's response was equally as quick and as defiant.

> *"Far from raising new cash, this amounts to creating virtual shares, without putting a cent into the company. They're not issuing shares; they're issuing voting rights to control ... to management."*

One week later, on February 25, LVMH filed suit in the Enterprise Chamber of the Amsterdam Court of Appeals seeking an injunction that would strip the newly issued

Exhibit 2 **Gucci's Share Ownership After the ESOP**

	Prior to ESOP		Post ESOP	
	Shares	Percent	Shares	Percent
LVMH's	20,144,985	34.4%	20,144,985	25.6%
Employee trust*	—	—	20,154,985	25.6%
Free floating shares	38,365,715	65.6%	38,365,715	48.8%
Total shares in Gucci	58,510,700	100.0%	78,665,685	100.0%

* The employee stock ownership plan was authorized to issue up to 37 million shares; 20 million were actually exercised upon initiation of the program.

3. There is some disagreement on the roots of the ESOP plan. The creation of an ESOP was provided for in Gucci's prospectus in its 1995 initial public offering. But Gucci CEO Domenico De Sole reportedly had an American law firm design the specific employee share issuance structure used the previous fall (1998) after Prada of Italy had purchased its 9.5% interest in Gucci. The plan could be triggered on the first sign of a hostile takeover.

Employee Trust share voting rights and bar Gucci's management from issuing new shares. LVMH's argument was that Gucci's management was not acting in the interests of shareholders (of which LVMH was arguably the largest), but rather acting in the best interests of management. LVMH went on to point out that the new share issuance had not raised any capital, and that the shares issues were restricted (could not be sold to a third party, for example, LVMH), preventing employees from redeeming their newly acquired shares for capital.

One week later, the Amsterdam court postponed any decision on the legitimacy of Gucci's defense until May, but did invoke a voting rights injunction on both the newly issued employee shares and LVMH's shares. The court stated that the suspension of LVMH's voting rights was based on the company not acting as a responsible shareholder in that it had failed to fully disclose its intentions. Both sides claimed victory, and the battle moved into a two-week period in which calm was quickly replaced with a new harsher and more personal battle.

The White Knight

Gucci had retained Morgan Stanley Dean Witter's London office in February to aid in its defense strategy. Joseph Perella of Morgan Stanley had immediately contacted Mr. Francois Pinault, the President and CEO of Pinault-Printemps-Redoute (PPR), a French retail conglomerate. Pinault controlled 42.6% of PPR via his personal investment vehicle, Artemis. Pinault had been on an acquisition binge recently, including the famed London auction house Christie's in 1998. Pinault told Morgan Stanley he would think about it.

Pinault flew to New York where he visited Gucci's Fifth Avenue showplace. After returning from New York, he met in London with De Sole of Gucci. In the meeting, De Sole explained Gucci's emerging strategy of becoming a multi-brand luxury-goods company. This goal fit neatly with Pinault's own goal of expanding PPR's business breadth to include luxury goods. Negotiations began immediately, with the two parties discussing the size of PPR's potential investment, managerial implications, and, of course, price.

Francois Pinault, known for his rapid moves, simultaneously undertook the acquisition of Sanofi Beauté, the beauty-products division of the French firm Sanofi. Beauté owned the Yves Saint Laurent brand. Pinault intended to buy the division and resell the business to Gucci.[4]

Exhibit 3 Excerpt from CIBC Oppenheimer's Equity Research on Gucci

Finally, on a fundamental basis, would the acquisition of Gucci by LVMH really make sense anyway? We don't think it would, and here's why. Louis Vuitton (which in imitation of Gucci now has an American designer, Marc Jacobs, and has added a clothing line) really is the jewel in LVMH's crown, and it has seen a renaissance of sorts in the last year or so, but it's still not Gucci in a fashion or design sense. LVMH's other fashion brands, Kenzo, LaCroix, Givenchy (Alexander McQueen), Celine (Narcisco Rodriguez) and Loewe's, are even lesser stars. Gucci and Louis Vuitton would still need to compete against one another—in design, for real estate (whether for owned stores or for space in department stores), and for advertising space (where Gucci excels). So where are the synergies? Frankly, we don't see any.

Source: "Specialty Retailing: Gucci Group NV," CIBC Oppenheimer Equity Research, March 4, 1999, p. 4.

4. Ironically, both Gucci and LVMH had previously considered buying Sanofi's beauty products line. LVMH had come very close, deciding against the purchase only minutes before signing papers making the acquisition. Both Gucci and LVMH had backed away from Sanofi on the basis of price.

Pinault followed the words of his favorite French poet Rene Char, "Think strategically, act primitively."

On March 19, Gucci announced the entry of Francois Pinault's PPR in the role of white knight.[5] Gucci would issue 39 million new shares to PPR for $75 per share ($2.9 billion), giving it a 40% stake in Gucci. PPR would hold four of the nine seats on the Gucci board, and three of the five seats on the newly created strategic and financial committee. LVMH's share in Gucci was once again diluted (as were the shares of all shareholders), falling to 21%, as illustrated in Exhibit 4. Gucci's share price jumped on Friday, March 19, from $70 to $81 per share, a 15.7% increase in one day.[6] See Appendix 2 for share price movements around this date.

Francois Pinault was considered the richest man in France; Bernard Arnault was considered to be the second richest. The entry of Pinault made the issue as much personal as it was business. Pinault made no secret that he saw LVMH as his new competitor:

> *"We want to make Gucci our beachhead for development in the luxury sector and create a rival to LVMH. LVMH was practically a monopoly. There's room for two in this business."*

Arnault and Pinault were very rich, very French, but ultimately very different. The 50-year old Arnault was born into a family real estate business, and a graduate of the elite Ecole Polytechnique. The 62-year old Pinault was a high school dropout, starting from the ground up in a small family partnership running a sawmill. Both had obviously built personal financial empires over many years of hard work. And in a truly French touch, both owned wineries; Pinault owned Chateau Latour and Arnault, in a partnership, Chateau Cheval Blanc.

Morgan Stanley's London offices provided most of the financing behind PPR's entry. Morgan Stanley extended a $3 billion bridge loan to PPR in order for it to purchase the agreed-upon stake in Gucci. $2 billion of the loan was based on a refinancing of existing credit lines held

Exhibit 4 Gucci's Share Ownership After the Strategic Investment of PPR

	Without ESOP Shares		With ESOP Shares	
	Shares	Percent	Shares	Percent
LVMH's	20,144,985	20.7%	20,144,985	17.1%
Employee trust*	——	——	20,154,985	17.1%
PPR's strategic investment	39,007,133	40.0%	39,007,133	33.1%
Free floating shares	38,365,715	39.3%	38,365,715	32.6%
Total shares in Gucci	97,517,833	100.0%	117,672,818	100.0%

* The ESOP shares were typically not included in most discussions of Gucci's new share ownership ("without ESOP shares") structure after the investment by PPR.

5. The move was particularly galling to LVMH as the two parties were scheduled to meet that very day in Amsterdam to search for an amicable solution to LVMH's request for managerial influence at Gucci.
6. The strategic investment agreement contained a five-year *standstill clause* which restricted PPR's holdings to 42% in Gucci. The standstill agreement could only be terminated by either a vote of Gucci's board or by a full public tender offer by a third-party. In the event of a third-party bid, PPR could purchase additional shares only if it were to make a full and open tender offer for all shares outstanding.

by PPR, and the additional $1 billion was funded through the issuance of a convertible bond (issuance led by Morgan Stanley). The bonds were convertible into PPR's ordinary shares.

Within hours, LVMH was once again in the Amsterdam courts asking for injunctions to stop the capital infusion by PPR into Gucci and block Gucci's acquisition of Sanofi's beauty-products division. LVMH now stated that if the PPR transaction was nullified, it could "envision" an offer at $85 per share for those shares needed for control. It did not define *control.* Four days later, the Dutch courts ordered Gucci to consider LVMH's offer(s). Over the following weeks, LVMH sold investments it held in other companies in order to put sufficient funds in place to make additional offers. Over the first two weeks of April 1999, LVMH continued to come forward with alternative offers of a variety of kinds, at one point having four different offers on the table.[7] The fight was increasingly public as both sides continued to make accusations regarding the practices of the other.

On April 20, Gucci's board, hoping to quell the feud, told LVMH that it would be willing to recommend to stockholders an unconditional offer for the company at $88 per share. LVMH responded that the position was untenable because of PPR's continuing stake in the firm.[8]

On April 22, the Amsterdam court heard arguments over the legality of Gucci's defensive maneuvers. The court postponed any ruling until June, putting the debate on ice for a month.[9] During the interim, all parties were busy. LVMH and Gucci continued to wage a public fight in which both urged Gucci shareholders to support their disparate initiatives.

> *More than anyone else, De Sole is looked to as the man who can save the heart of Gucci, keep it from becoming just another profitable listing in a voluminous corporate annual report. He is the man who can salvage the swagger of Gucci as a fashion house founded on Italian craftsmanship and signifying classic Italian chic. And he is the American who can defend Gucci against the French, making sure that the company remains Italian. This is a matter of national pride, supported by folks such as Santo Versace, president of Italy's fashion industry association and the financial brains behind the Versace empire.*
>
> "Gucci's Strong Suit: CEO Domenico Is Defending the Firm Against Takeover Designs," *The Washington Post*, May 6, 1999, by Robin Givhan.

The Amsterdam court released its findings on May 27, upholding PPR's investment in Gucci, but rejecting the poison-pill defense used by Gucci in the issuance of employee shares to the Employee Trust. By most principles, the court's decision signaled a clear defeat for LVMH. Arnault then threatened further legal actions, and also pointed out that LVMH owned 20% of the Gucci Group and expected "to see superior results from Gucci's management."

Gucci and PPR moved quickly. Gucci used the capital injections from PPR to purchase—from Francois Pinault—the Sanofi Beauté division and the Yves Saint Laurent's couture and fragrance business. At PPR's annual shareholder meeting, it was announced that Tom Ford had agreed to

7. Most of the offers had a clause specifically stating that the offers were only applicable if the PPR transaction was nullified and Gucci Creative Director Tom Ford agreed to stay on at Gucci for at least two years following the closure of LVMH's new controlling position.

8. If PPR's investment was canceled, a full bid for Gucci would require LVMH to purchase all shares outstanding which it did not already own, 38,365,715 shares. This assumed the ESOP shares were also canceled. If, however, the PPR investment was not canceled, the share total would rise to 77,372,848 shares, which would double the price.

9. The two principals filled the interval with legal suits and countersuits. Pinault first filed suit in Paris accusing Arnault of libel in a published interview in *Paris Match.* In the interview, Arnault described Pinault's actions as "defrauding minority shareholders." Arnault responded in-kind with a countersuit against Pinault.

stay on at Gucci for at least another four years. The PPR investment was formally approved by 80% of Gucci's shareholders at the regularly scheduled stockholder meeting in July 1999.

The Denouement

The problem Gucci now had was an awkward one. PPR now controlled Gucci in cooperation with Gucci's management. But LVMH still held a 20.7% interest. The question was how to get LVMH out, while simultaneously making good on the long-term promise that stockholders were entitled to a premium when ownership had changed. LVMH, given the intensifying consolidation of luxury goods brands in the European marketplace, wanted to free its $1.4 billion invested in Gucci. Negotiations continued.

- In September 1999, Gucci/PPR and LVMH (with Prada of Italy) once more entered into a bidding war, this time for a third party, the Fendi Italian fashion house. Both parties had offered the same $850 million in the end, but Fendi chose LVMH/Prada over Gucci because Fendi designer Karl Lagerfeld preferred LVMH/Prada's management teams. Prada eventually sold its interest in Fendi to LVMH.
- In May and June 2000, representatives of Francois Pinault and Bernard Arnault tried once again to find a resolution to the ownership impasse. "Impossibility of common ground" was given in late June for breaking off talks.
- All parties were back in court in November 2000 when LVMH charged that Tom Ford and Domenico De Sole were secretly granted Gucci stock options in the spring of 1999 as part of the PPR strategic investment. Gucci denied the charges. The charge was part of a new filing by LVMH in Amsterdam's Enterprise Court claiming that PPR's purchase of the Gucci shares shortchanged minority shareholders and constituted mismanagement. This would be grounds for rescinding the PPR investment. (The Dutch court was rehearing many of the previous arguments as part of a Dutch Supreme Court ruling that the Amsterdam lower court had failed to conduct a thorough investigation of the mismanagement charge prior to its ruling in May of 1999.)
- In March 2001, the Amsterdam Enterprise Court agreed to a new demand for an investigation into Gucci's management practices. The probe was expected to take between three and six months. PPR shares fell 3% on the announcement of the ruling as speculation increased that PPR might eventually have to sell its 40% share in Gucci. The court, however, urged the parties to reach a settlement on their own.

More than two-and-a-half years after it started, it ended. On September 10, 2001, PPR, Gucci, and LVMH reached a termination agreement. LVMH would be able to cash out of Gucci at a profit, and the minority shareholders of Gucci would indeed—finally—reap a premium from the change in ownership.

LVMH's exit. PPR would pay $812 million to raise its stake in Gucci to 53.2% by acquiring 8.6 million Gucci shares from LVMH for $94 per share. This was a $2 premium over the closing price on the Amsterdam close on the previous Friday. This left LVMH with 12% interest in the Gucci Group.

PPR would then offer to buy out all of Gucci's remaining minority shareholders, including LVMH's 12%, in March 2004 at a price set at $101.50 per share.[10] (The assumption was

10. PPR, in order to fund the completion of its takeover of Gucci, announced an additional issuance of 700 million of new shares and 700 million in convertible bonds. Francois Pinault's private investment company Artemis committed to subscribing to both to maintain Pinault's 45% control of PPR.

that LVMH would take PPR up on its offer in March 2004, but many minority shareholders may not.)[11] A member of Gucci's management team termed the exit agreement for LVMH *greenmail*. LVMH in return agreed to forego all legal claims against PPR and Gucci.

Shareholder buyout premium. Gucci agreed to distribute a special dividend of $7 per share to all shareholders except those held by PPR. A number of investment analysts were publicly annoyed, noting that the premium should be at least 15%, or a dividend of about $15 per share, not $7.

Gucci Group continues to refer to LVMH's large investment as an "uninvited acquisition of a 34.4% stock interest in the Company." Gucci consider's PPR's current dominant ownership position as a *strategic investment*.

> *In 2000, our strategy of unparalleled product design and quality, global distribution, and outstanding communication had its natural progression to other brands. For our development in this direction, we are fortunate to have had the partnership of Pinault-Printemps-Redoute (PPR), which in the Spring of 1999, not only brought us the capital to move in this direction, but the cultural breadth to enable us to acquire on proper terms and conditions the pre-eminent French brand, Yves Saint Laurent, and which more recently assisted us in the acquisition of Boucheron.*
>
> President and CEO's Letter to Shareholders,
> Gucci Group N.V. Annual Report 2000, p. 14–15.

11. LVMH arranged a bank securitization of its remaining 12% share holdings against the March 2004 sale, allowing it to receive the money up front and declare a capital gain immediately.

Appendix 1

Gucci Group's Share Price, January–June 1999

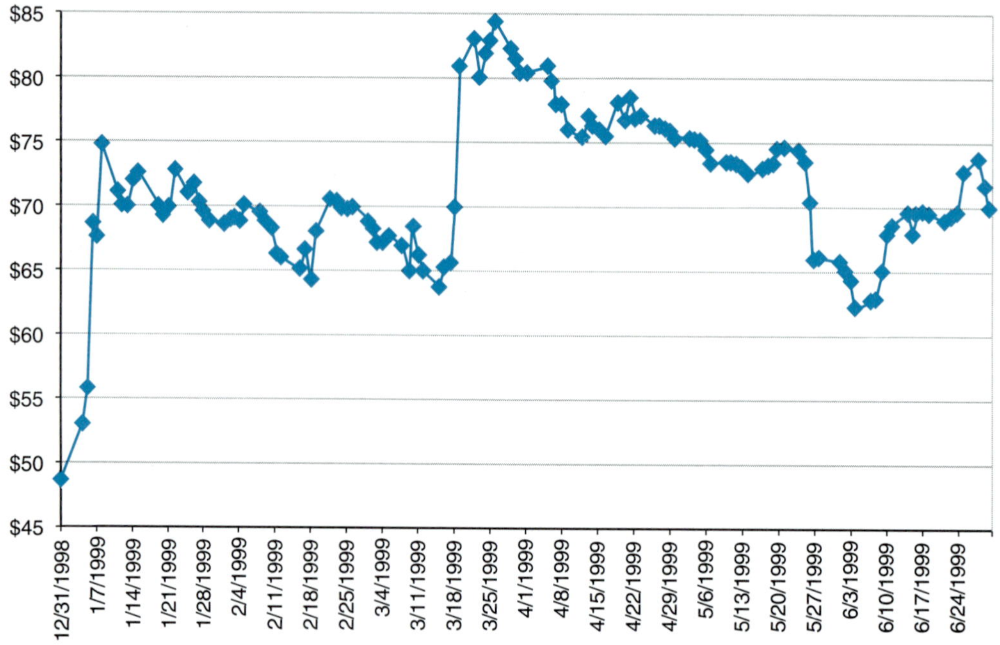

Appendix 2

Gucci Group's Share Price Movements During Key Events of the LVMH Bid

Event	Date (1999)	Closing Day	Share Price	Percent Change in Share Price
LVMH Takes Position in Gucci				
First trading day of year	Jan 4	Mon	$53.00	9.0%
	Jan 5	Tue	55.81	5.3%
	Jan 6	Wed	68.63	23.0%
	Jan 7	Thu	67.44	–1.7%
(Peak price until March)	Jan 8	Fri	74.88	11.0%
	Jan 11	Mon	$71.06	–5.1%
LVMH purchases Prada's 9.5%	Jan 12	Tue	70.06	–1.4%
	Jan 13	Wed	70.00	–0.1%
LVMH: "no intention of tender offer"	Jan 14	Thu	72.00	2.9%
	Jan 15	Fri	72.63	0.9%
PPR Enters as White Knight				
	March 15	Mon	$63.81	–1.8%
	March 16	Tue	65.25	2.3%
	March 17	Wed	65.63	0.6%
	March 18	Thu	70.00	6.7%
Gucci announces PPR investment	March 19	Fri	81.00	15.7%
	March 22	Mon	$83.13	2.6%
	March 23	Tue	80.13	–3.6%
	March 24	Wed	82.00	2.3%
	March 25	Thu	83.00	1.2%
(Peak price until August)	March 26	Fri	84.56	1.9%
Amsterdam Court Makes Final Rulings				
	May 24	Mon	$74.50	–0.3%
	May 25	Tue	73.56	–1.3%
	May 26	Wed	70.50	–4.2%
Court confirms PPR, rejects LVMH	May 27	Thu	65.94	–6.5%
	May 28	Fri	66.13	0.3%

Appendix 3

Time Line of Events in the LVMH-Gucci Controversy

Date	Event
Jan 6, 1999	Gucci is informed that LVMH has increased its holdings in Gucci above 5%.
Jan 12, 1999	Gucci announces that it has not been consulted by LVMH regarding LVMH's stake in Gucci. LVMH increases its stake in Gucci by purchasing Prada's (Italy) 9.5% stake in Gucci.
Jan 13, 1999	Arnault praises Gucci management, CEO De Sole and Creative Director Ford.
Jan 25, 1999	LVMH increases its stake (over previous weeks) to 34.4%. LVMH does not "rule out" additional share purchases.
Feb 10, 1999	Gucci Group receives request from LVMH for special shareholder meeting to approve a request for gaining a seat on Gucci's board.
Feb 18, 1999	Gucci launches a poison pill, an employee stock option plan, which dilutes LVMH's share in Gucci to 26%.
Feb 25, 1999	LVMH files suit in the Enterprise Chamber of the Amsterdam Court of Appeals seeking a stop to the Gucci ESOP defense.
March 1, 1999	Gucci announces a special shareholder meeting, to be held on March 25, in accordance with the Gucci Group's bylaws and a request presented by LVMH for a special shareholder meeting.
March 3, 1999	Amsterdam court postpones any decision on the LVMH suit until a subsequent hearing to be held on April 22, but imposes an injunction on the voting rights held by both the ESOP and LVMH.
March 4, 1999	LVMH withdraws its request for a special shareholder meeting and its nominee to the Supervisory Board of Gucci.
March 19, 1999	Gucci announces that the Pinault-Printemps-Redoute Group has made a strategic investment of $2.9 billion in Gucci. This is to represent 40% of Gucci's capital. PPR signs a 5-year standstill agreement in which PPR agrees not to increase its ownership position in Gucci past 42%. Stock issued to PPR totals 39 million shares at $75 per share, a 13% premium over the average share price of the preceding 10 days. Domenico De Sole and Tom Ford are said to be "fully committed to new alliance."
March 22, 1999	LVMH's request that Gucci's management be removed is denied by the Amsterdam court. Gucci's Supervisory Board is given approval to consider LVMH's proposed $81 per share offered.
April 15, 1999	LVMH publicizes a five-page "Letter to Gucci Shareholders" and other correspondence with Gucci management. LVMH charges Gucci's board with "total lack of good faith and sincerity in negotiations." LVMH again accuses Gucci's management of violating the rights of minority shareholders. LVMH repeats its offer to make a full bid if PPR's investment is canceled.
April 19, 1999	Gucci's board tells LVMH it will recommend to stockholders an unconditional offer for the company at $88 per share. LVMH responds that this position is untenable with PPR's presence.
May 27, 1999	Amsterdam court releases its findings that the PPR investment is legal, but rejects the poisonpill ESOP issuance.
October 1999	Gucci officially acquires Sanofi Beauté from PPR for $1 billion.
Sept 10, 2001	Gucci, LVMH, and PPR reach a termination agreement whereby PPR will buy out LVMH's investment in Gucci and PPR will make a tender offer to all remaining minority shareholders.

Appendix 4

LVMH's Alternative Bids in April 1999

1. If PPR's investment was rescinded, $91/share.
2. $85/share for all outstanding shares, but under which Gucci would help LVMH pass the 50% threshold in share ownership through a reserved capital increase if LVMH obtained a majority of shares held by independent shareholders, but not those of PPR.
3. $85/share under which LVMH would have the same rights and board representation as PPR if it ended up with less than 50%.
4. $85/share including PPR's stake, but only if Gucci helped deliver PPR's stake and guaranteed that most of Gucci's top management stayed on for at least two years.

Source: "Gucci Board Invites Unconditional Bid from LVMH of $88 a Share to End Battle," *Wall Street Journal*, April 20, 1999.

Appendix 5

A Brief Overview of Takeover Laws in Selected European Countries

Great Britain

- Decisions are made by a takeover panel and not appealable to courts
- A final offer is generally final
- Threshold of 30% where an acquirer has to make a full offer

France

- Threshold of 33% beyond which an acquirer has to launch a full offer
- Some defensive measures allowed during a bid
- Regulatory decisions appealable to courts

Germany

- A voluntary takeover code lets companies opt in or out

Netherlands

- Allows companies to adopt a broad array of defenses during a bid
- No rules requiring a company to launch a full offer at a certain threshold

Italy

- Limits the defenses a company can employ during a takeover

Switzerland

- Allows a broad array of defensive steps to a hostile takeover
- An acquirer can force a cash buyout of minority shareholders only after it achieves 98% control

Spain

- Panoply of defenses that can be put in place before a takeover is launched
- Limited defenses after takeover offer is made
- No compulsory buyout of minority shareholders

Source: "Pressure Grows to Unify Europe's Takeover Laws—Mazes of Rules Baffle Investors, Hurt Shareholders," *Wall Street Journal*, December 13, 1999.

Appendix 6

Gucci Group Special Dividend Announcement

GUCCI

GUCCI GROUP

GUCCI Announces Special Dividend of $7 Per Share

Amsterdam, The Netherlands, November 2, 2001: GUCCI Group N.V. (NYSE: GUC; Euronext Amsterdam: GCCI.AS) announces today that the Special Dividend of $7.00 per Common Share to all shareholders, except Pinault-Printemps-Redoute S.A. ("PPR") will be paid on the following schedule:

December 12, 2001	New York registered shares commence trading ex-dividend. Dutch ordinary shares commence trading ex-dividend.
December 14, 2001	Record date for New York registered shares. Gucci Group pays to payment agent (Kas Associatie N.V.) the amount of Distribution due to all shareholders. Kas Associatie and Bank of New York make payments to shareholders as soon as practicable thereafter.

In order to prevent any possibility of arbitrage between the two types of Gucci shares, the Bank of New York will close its books between December 12 and December 14.

The Special Dividend is part of the settlement among Gucci Group, PPR and LVMH Moet Hennessy Louis Vuitton S.A. announced on September 10, 2001, which closed on October 22, 2001.

Gucci Group N.V. is one of the world's leading multi-brand luxury goods companies. Through the Gucci, Yves Saint Laurent, Sergio Rossi, Boucheron, Roger & Gallet, Bottega Veneta, Alexander McQueen, Stella McCartney, Balenciaga and BEDAT & Co brands, the Group designs, produces and distributes high-quality personal luxury goods, including ready-to-wear, handbags, luggage, small leather goods, shoes, timepieces, jewelry, ties and scarves, eyewear, perfume, cosmetics and skin care products. The group directly operates stores in major markets throughout the world and wholesales products through franchise stores, duty free boutiques and leading department stores and specialty stores. The shares of Gucci Group N.V. are listed on the New York Stock Exchange and on the Euronext Amsterdam Stock Exchange,

For media inquiries:
Tomaso Galli
Director of Corporate Communications
Gucci Group N.V.
+39 02 7712 7373
+39 335 737 8435 (mobile)

For investor/analysts inquiries:
Cedric Magnelia/Enza Dominijanni
Gucci Group N.V.
+39 055 759 2456
+44 20 7898 3053

Source: www.guccigroup.com/press.

apter 20

International Portfolio Theory and Diversification

THIS CHAPTER EXPLORES HOW APPLICATION OF PORTFOLIO THEORY CAN REDUCE RISKS OF ASSET portfolios held by MNEs, and risks incurred by MNEs in general from internationally diversified activities. In the first part of the chapter, we extend portfolio theory from the domestic to the international business environment. Then we show how the risk of a portfolio, whether it be a securities portfolio or the general portfolio of activities of the MNE, is reduced through international diversification. The second part of the chapter details the theory and application of international portfolio theory and presents recent empirical results of the risk-return tradeoffs of internationally diversified portfolios. The third and final section explores international diversification's impact on the cost of capital for the MNE.

International Diversification and Risk

The case for international diversification of portfolios can be decomposed into two components: the potential risk reduction benefits of holding international securities, and the potential added foreign exchange risk.

Portfolio Risk Reduction

We first focus only on risk. The *risk* of a portfolio is measured by the ratio of the variance of the portfolio's return relative to the variance of the market return. This is the *beta* of the portfolio. As an investor increases the number of securities in a portfolio, the portfolio's risk declines rapidly at first, then asymptotically approaches the level of *systematic risk* of the market. A domestic portfolio that is fully diversified would have a beta of 1.0. This is illustrated in Exhibit 20.1.

Exhibit 20.1 illustrates portfolio risk reduction for the U.S. economy. It shows that a fully diversified U.S. portfolio is only about 27% as risky as a typical individual stock. This relationship implies that about 73% of the risk associated with investing in a single stock is diversifiable in a fully diversified U.S. portfolio. Although we can reduce risk substantially through portfolio diversification, it is not possible to eliminate it totally, because security returns are affected by a common set of factors—a set we characterize as the market.

The total risk of any portfolio is therefore composed of *systematic risk* (the market) and *unsystematic risk* (the individual securities). Increasing the number of securities in

Exhibit 20.1 Portfolio Risk Reduction Through Diversification

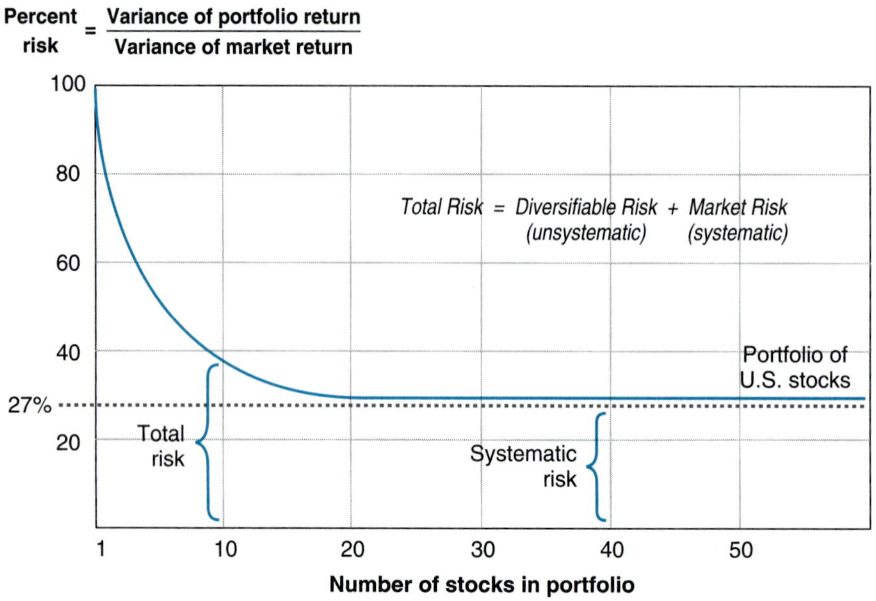

By diversifying the portfolio, the variance of the portfolio's return relative to the variance of the market's return (beta) is reduced to the level of systematic risk—the risk of the market itself.

the portfolio reduces the unsystematic risk component leaving the systematic risk component unchanged.

Exhibit 20.2 illustrates the incremental gains of diversifying both domestically and internationally. The lowest line in Exhibit 20.2 (portfolio of international stocks) represents a portfolio in which foreign securities have been added. It has the same overall risk shape as the U.S. stock portfolio, but it has a lower portfolio beta. This means that the international portfolio's market risk is lower than that of a domestic portfolio. This situation arises because the returns on the foreign stocks are closely correlated not with returns on U.S. stocks, but rather with a global beta. We will return to the concept of a global beta in the third section of this chapter.

Foreign Exchange Risk

The foreign exchange risks of a portfolio, whether it be a securities portfolio or the general portfolio of activities of the MNE, are reduced through international diversification. The construction of internationally diversified portfolios is both the same as and different than creating a traditional domestic portfolio. Internationally diversified portfolios are the same in principle because the investor is attempting to combine assets that are less than perfectly correlated, reducing the total risk of the portfolio. In addition, by adding assets outside the home market, assets that previously

Exhibit 20.2 Portfolio Risk Reduction Through International Diversification

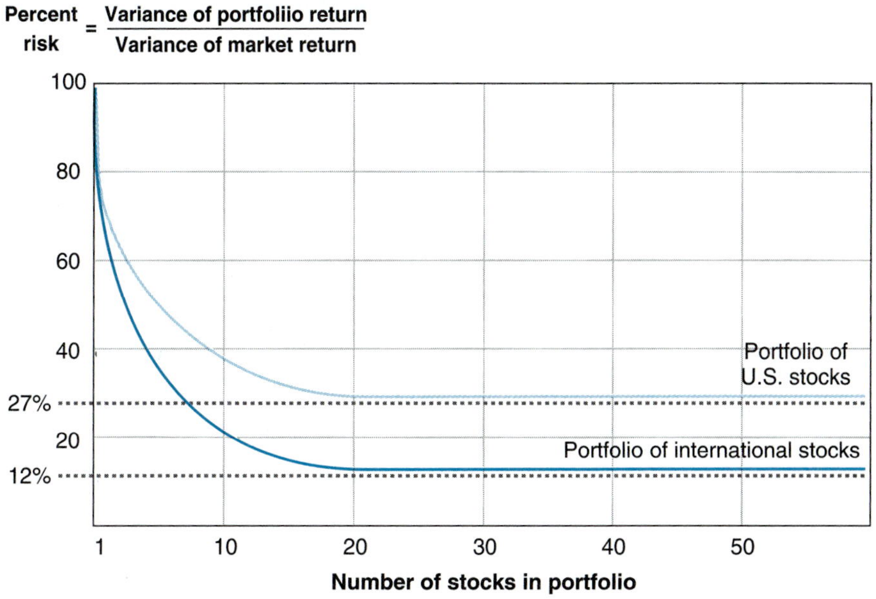

By diversifying the portfolio internationally, the portfolio's beta—the level of systematic risk that cannot be diversified away—is lowered.

were not available to be averaged into the portfolio's expected returns and risks, the investor has now tapped into a larger pool of potential investments.

But international portfolio construction is also different in that when the investor acquires assets or securities outside the investor's home-country market, the investor may also be acquiring a foreign currency–denominated asset. This is not always the case. For example, many U.S.-based investors routinely purchase and hold Eurodollar bonds (on the secondary market only; it is illegal during primary issuance), which would not pose currency risk to the U.S.-based investor, for they are denominated in the investor's home currency. Thus the investor has actually acquired two additional assets—the currency of denomination and the asset subsequently purchased with the currency; one asset in principle, but two in expected returns and risks.

A numerical example can illustrate the difficulties associated with international portfolio diversification and currency risk. A U.S.-based investor takes US$1,000,000 on January 1, 2002, and invests in a share traded on the Tokyo Stock Exchange (TSE). On January 1, 2002, the spot exchange rate is ¥130.00/$. The US$1 million therefore yields ¥130,000,000. The investor uses ¥130,000,000 to acquire shares on the Tokyo Stock Exchange at ¥20,000 per share, acquiring 6,500 shares, and holds the shares for one year.

At the end of one year, the investor sells the 6,500 shares at the market price, which is now ¥25,000 per share; the shares have risen ¥5,000 per share in price. The 6,500 shares at ¥25,000 per share yield proceeds of ¥162,500,000.

The Japanese yen are then changed back into the investor's home currency, the U.S. dollar, at the spot rate of ¥125.00/$ in effect on January 1, 2003. This results in total U.S. dollar proceeds of $1,300,000.00. The total return on the investment is then:

$$\frac{\text{US\$}1{,}300{,}000 - \text{US\$}1{,}000{,}000}{\text{US\$}1{,}000{,}000} = 30.00\%$$

The total U.S. dollar return is actually a combination of the return on the Japanese yen (which in this case was positive) and the return on the shares listed on the Tokyo Stock Exchange (which was also positive). This value is expressed by isolating the percentage change in the share price (r^{shares}) in combination with the percentage change in the currency value ($r^{¥/\$}$):

$$R^{\$} = \left[\left(1 + r^{¥/\$}\right)\left(1 + r^{\text{shares}, ¥}\right)\right] - 1$$

In this case, the value of the Japanese yen, in the eyes of a U.S.-based investor, rose 4.00% (from ¥130/$ to ¥125/$), while the shares traded on the Tokyo Stock Exchange rose 25.00%. The total investment return in U.S. dollars is therefore:

$$R^{\$} = \left[(1 + .0400)(1 + .2500)\right] - 1 = .3000 \text{ or } 30.00\%$$

Obviously the risk associated with international diversification, when it includes currency risk, is inherently more complex than that of domestic investments. You should also see, however, that the presence of currency risk may alter the correlations associated with securities in different countries and currencies, providing portfolio composition and diversification possibilities that domestic investment and portfolio construction may not. Global Finance Perspective 20.1 details the debate among investment funds regarding foreign exchange risk.

In conclusion:

- International diversification benefits induce investors to demand foreign securities (the so-called *buy-side*).
- If the addition of a foreign security to the portfolio of the investor aids in the reduction of risk for a given level of return, or if it increases the expected return for a given level of risk, then the security adds value to the portfolio.
- A security that adds value will be demanded by investors. Given the limits of the potential supply of securities, increased demand will bid up the price of that security, resulting in a lower cost of capital for the issuing firm. The firm issuing the security, the *sell-side*, is therefore able to raise capital at a lower cost.

Internationalizing the Domestic Portfolio

We first review the basic principles of traditional domestic portfolio theory to aid in our identification of the incremental changes introduced through international diversification. We then illus-

Global Finance Perspective 20.1

Should Fund Managers Hedge Currency Risk?

The decline of the euro in 2000, and its impact on globally diversified portfolios, reawakened the debate among portfolio managers as to whether currency components and their risks within the portfolios should be hedged. The decline of the euro over the year 2000, a drop of 19.6%, severely damaged the returns of many international portfolios.

The major international stock index used by most portfolio managers to benchmark performance is the Morgan Stanley Capital International European, Australian, Far Eastern (EAFE) Index. The EAFE index fell 14.17% in 2000. If the currency component of the index was removed (effectively hedged), the index fell only 4.38%.

For example, the Artisan Fund does not practice currency hedging by principle. It believes that the currency risk component of an international portfolio is part and parcel to the principle of international diversification. The problem, however, is that the fund was exposed to the slide of the euro throughout 2000 and its investors suffered. Fund managers who argue against hedging are quick to point out that many of the world's major currencies move in large swings, frequently moving back in the opposite direction, sometimes quickly, in subsequent periods.

Other funds, like Janus Worldwide, used forward contracts and options to completely hedge their portfolios against currency fluctuations. They argue that by removing the currency movements from the portfolio returns, the fund is allowed to focus purely on stock-picking, the traditional competence of the fund manager. For example, Tweedy, Browne Company's Global Fund rose 12.4% in 2000, out-performing 95% of similar international funds sold to U.S.-based investors. According to the fund's manager, currency hedging added approximately 10 percentage points to the performance of the fund.

Still other funds practice selective hedging, removing the risk associated with the currencies which the fund managers and its currency analysts feel are the most at risk in the current period. In the end it is a matter of taste. Similar to the question of whether financial managers should hedge their transaction exposures, the debate over hedging currency components of international portfolios will continue.

trate how diversifying the portfolio internationally alters the potential set of portfolios available to the investor.

The Optimal Domestic Portfolio

Classic portfolio theory assumes a typical investor is risk-averse. This means that an investor is willing to accept some risk but is not willing to bear unnecessary risk. *The typical investor is therefore in search of a portfolio that maximizes expected portfolio return per unit of expected portfolio risk.*

The domestic investor may choose among a set of individual securities in the domestic market. The near-infinite set of portfolio combinations of domestic securities form the *domestic portfolio opportunity set* shown in Exhibit 20.3. The set of portfolios formed along the extreme left edge of the domestic portfolio opportunity set is termed the *efficient frontier*. It represents the optimal portfolios of securities that possess the minimum expected risk for each level of expected portfolio return. The portfolio with the minimum risk among all those possible is the *minimum risk domestic portfolio* (MR_{DP}).

The individual investor will search out the optimal domestic portfolio (DP), which combines the risk-free asset and a portfolio of domestic securities found on the efficient frontier. He or she

Exhibit 20.3 Optimal Domestic Portfolio Construction

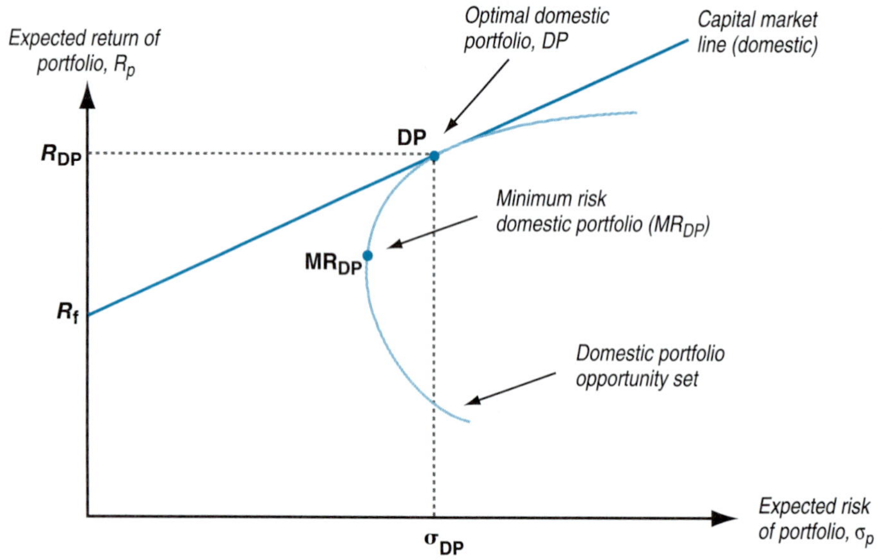

An investor may choose a portfolio of assets enclosed by the *domestic portfolio opportunity set*. The *optimal domestic portfolio* is found at DP, where the capital market line is tangent to the domestic portfolio opportunity set. The domestic portfolio with the minimum risk is designated MR_{DP}.

begins with the risk-free asset with return of R_f (and zero expected risk), and moves out along the security market line until reaching portfolio DP. This portfolio is defined as the optimal domestic portfolio because it moves out into risky space at the steepest slope—maximizing the slope of expected portfolio return over expected risk—while still touching the opportunity set of domestic portfolios. This line is called the *capital market line*, and portfolio theory assumes an investor who can borrow and invest at the risk-free rate can move to any point along this line.

Note that the optimal domestic portfolio is not the portfolio of minimum risk (MR_{DP}). A line stretching from the risk-free asset to the minimum risk domestic portfolio would have a lower slope than the capital market line, and the investor would not be receiving as great an expected return (vertical distance) per unit of expected risk (horizontal distance) as that found at DP.

International Diversification

Exhibit 20.4 illustrates the impact of allowing the investor to choose among an internationally diversified set of potential portfolios. The *internationally diversified portfolio opportunity set* shifts leftward of the purely domestic opportunity set. At any point on the efficient frontier of the internationally diversified portfolio opportunity set, the investor can find a portfolio of lower expected risk for each level of expected return.

It is critical to be clear as to exactly why the internationally diversified portfolio opportunity set is of lower expected risk than comparable domestic portfolios. The gains arise directly from the

Exhibit 20.4 The Internationally Diversified Portfolio Opportunity Set

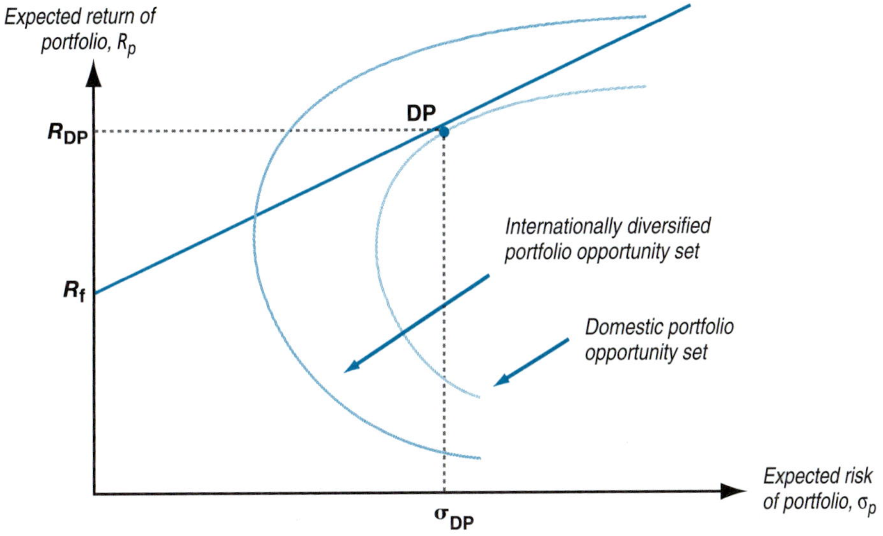

The addition of internationally diversified portfolios to the total opportunity set available to the investor shifts the total portfolio opportunity set left, providing lower expected risk portfolios for each level of expected portfolio return.

introduction of additional securities and/or portfolios that are of less than perfect correlation with the securities and portfolios within the domestic opportunity set.

For example, Sony Corporation is listed on the Tokyo Stock Exchange. Sony's share price derives its value from both the individual business results of the firm and the market in which it trades. If either or both are not perfectly positively correlated to the securities and markets available to a U.S.-based investor, then that investor would observe the opportunity set shift shown in Exhibit 20.4.

The Optimal International Portfolio

The investor can now choose an optimal portfolio that combines the same risk-free asset as before with a portfolio from the efficient frontier of the internationally diversified portfolio opportunity set. The *optimal international portfolio*, IP, is again found by locating that point on the capital market line (internationally diversified) which extends from the risk-free asset return of R_f to a point of tangency along the internationally diversified efficient frontier. We illustrate this in Exhibit 20.5.

The benefits of international diversification are now obvious. The investor's optimal portfolio IP possesses both higher expected portfolio return ($R_{IP} > R_{DP}$) and lower expected portfolio risk ($\sigma_{IP} < \sigma_{DP}$) than the purely domestic optimal portfolio. The optimal international portfolio is superior to the optimal domestic portfolio.

Exhibit 20.5 The Gains from International Portfolio Diversification

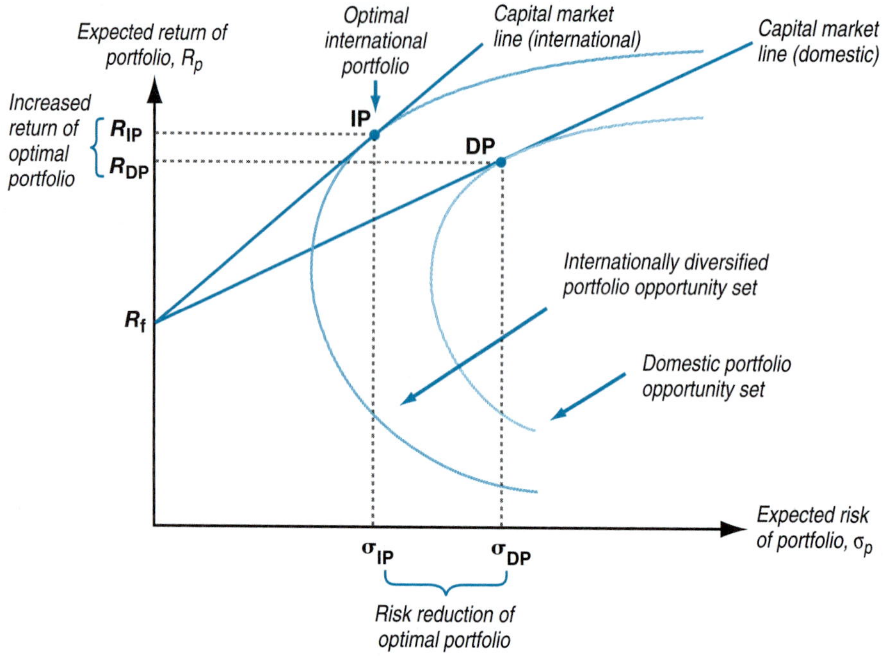

The Calculation of Portfolio Risk and Return

An investor can reduce investment risk by holding risky assets in a portfolio. As long as the asset returns are not perfectly positively correlated, the investor can reduce risk, because some of the fluctuations of the asset returns will offset each other.

Two-asset model. Let us assume Carlton's CFO Caitlin Kelly is considering investing Carlton's marketable securities in two different risky assets, an index of the U.S. equity markets and an index of the German equity markets. The two equities are characterized by the following expected returns (the mean of recent returns) and expected risks (the standard deviation of recent returns):

	Expected return	Expected risk (σ)
United States equity index (US)	14 %	15 %
German equity index (GER)	18 %	20 %
Correlation coefficient ($\rho_{US\text{-}GER}$)	0.34	

If the weights of investment in the two assets are w_{US} and w_{GER} respectively, and $w_{US} + w_{GER} = 1$, the risk of the portfolio (σ_p), usually expressed in terms of the standard deviation of the portfolio's expected return, is given by the following equation:

$$\sigma_p = \sqrt{w_{US}^2\sigma_{US}^2 + w_{GER}^2\sigma_{GER}^2 + 2w_{US}w_{GER}\rho_{US-GER}\sigma_{US}\sigma_{GER}}$$

where $\sigma_{US}{}^2$ and $\sigma_{GER}{}^2$ are the squared standard deviations of the expected returns of risky assets in the United States and Germany (the variances), respectively. The Greek letter *rho*, $\rho_{US\text{-}GER}$, is the correlation coefficient between the two market returns over time.

We now plug in the values for the standard deviations of the U.S. (15%) and Germany (20%) and the correlation coefficient of 0.34. Assuming that Caitlin initially wishes to invest 40% of her funds in the United States (0.40) and 60% of her funds in German equities (0.60), the expected risk of the portfolio will be:

$$\sigma_p = \sqrt{(0.40)^2(0.15)^2 + (0.60)^2(0.20)^2 + 2(0.40)(0.60)(0.34)(0.15)(0.20)}$$

which, when reduced, is:

$$\sqrt{0.0036 + 0.0144 + 0.0049} = 0.151 \approx 15.1\%$$

Note that the portfolio risk is *not* the weighted average of the risks of the individual assets. As long as the correlation coefficient (ρ) is smaller than 1.0, some of the fluctuations of the asset returns will offset each other, resulting in risk reduction. The lower the correlation coefficient, the greater the opportunity for risk diversification.

We obtain the expected return of the portfolio with the following equation:

$$E(R_p) = w_{US}E(R_{US}) + w_{GER}E(R_{GER})$$

where $E(R_p)$, $E(R_{US})$, and $E(R_{GER})$ are the expected returns of the portfolio, the United States equity index, and the German equity index, respectively. Using the expected returns for the United States (14%) and German (18%) equity indexes, we find the expected return of the portfolio to be:

$$E(R_p) = (0.4)(0.14) + (0.6)(0.18) = 0.164 \approx 16.4\%$$

Altering the weights. Before Caitlin finalizes the desired portfolio, she wishes to evaluate the impact of changing the weights between the two equity indexes on the expected risk and expected returns of the portfolio. Using weight increments of 0.5, she graphs the alternative portfolios in the customary portfolio risk-return graphic. Exhibit 20.6 illustrates the result.

The different portfolios possible using different weights with the two equity assets provides Caitlin some interesting choices. The two extremes, the greatest expected return and the minimum expected risks, call for very different weight structures. The greatest expected return is, as we would expect from the original asset expectations, 100% German in composition. The minimum expected risk portfolio, with approximately 15.2% expected risk, is made up of approximately 70% U.S. and 30% German securities.

Exhibit 20.6 Alternative Portfolio Profiles Under Varying Asset Weights

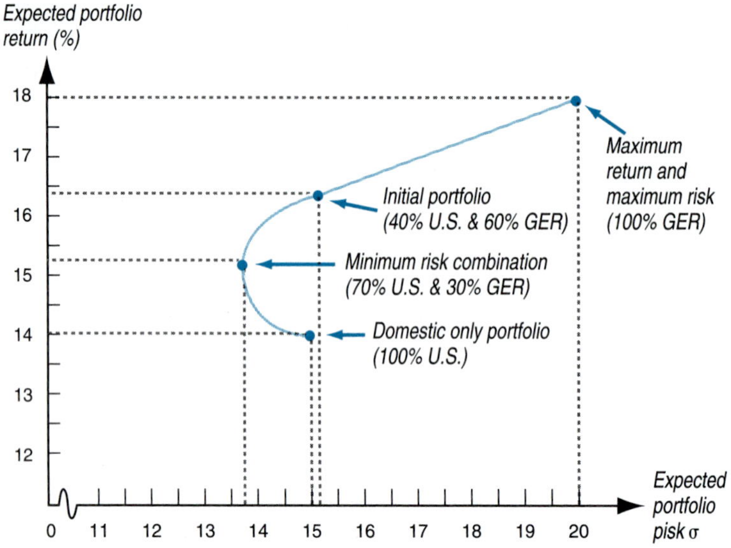

Multiple asset model. We can generalize the previous equations to a portfolio consisting of multiple assets. The portfolio risk is:

$$\sigma_p = \sqrt{\sum_{i=1}^{N} w_i^2 \sigma_j^2 + \sum_{i=1}^{N-1} \sum_{j=i+1}^{N} w_i w_j \rho_{ij} \sigma_i \sigma_j}$$

and the portfolio expected return is:

$$E(R_p) = \sum_{i=1}^{N} w_i E(R_i)$$

where N stands for the total number of assets included in the portfolio.

By allowing investors to hold foreign assets, we substantially enlarge the feasible set of investments; higher return can be obtained at a given level of risk, or lower risk can be attained at the same level of return.

National Markets and Asset Performance

As demonstrated in the previous section, asset portfolios are traditionally constructed using both interest bearing risk-free assets and risky assets. Exhibit 20.7 presents the performance of major individual national markets by asset category—bills, bonds, and equities—for the 21st century (1900–2000). Risks and returns are presented on a real basis.

Exhibit 20.7 Real Returns and Risks on the Three Major Asset Classes, Globally, 1900–2000

Country	Equities (%) Mean	Equities (%) S.D	Bonds (%) Mean	Bonds (%) S.D.	Bills (%) Mean	Bills (%) S.D.
Australia	9.0	17.7	1.9	13.0	0.6	5.6
Belgium	4.8	22.8	0.3	12.1	0.0	8.2
Canada	7.7	16.8	2.4	10.6	1.8	5.1
Denmark	6.2	20.1	3.3	12.5	3.0	6.4
France	6.3	23.1	0.1	14.4	-2.6	11.4
Germany	8.8	32.3	0.3	15.9	0.1	10.6
Ireland	7.0	22.2	2.4	13.3	1.4	6.0
Italy	6.8	29.4	-0.8	14.4	-2.9	12.0
Japan	9.3	30.3	1.3	20.9	-0.3	14.5
The Netherlands	7.7	21.0	1.5	9.4	0.8	5.2
South Africa	9.1	22.8	1.9	10.6	1.0	6.4
Spain	5.8	22.0	1.9	12.0	0.6	6.1
Sweden	9.9	22.8	3.1	12.7	2.2	6.8
Switzerland	6.9	20.4	3.1	8.0	1.2	6.2
United Kingdom	7.6	20.0	2.3	14.5	1.2	6.6
United States	8.7	20.2	2.1	10.0	1.0	4.7

Source: Abstracted from Elroy Dimson, Paul Marsh, and Mike Staunton, *Triumph of the Optimists, 101 Years of Global Investment Returns,* Princeton University Press, 2002, p. 60. "Mean" is arithmetic mean; "S.D." is standard deviation of mean returns. Bond and bill statistics for Germany exclude the years 1922–23; Swiss equities begin 1911.

Exhibit 20.7 demonstrates that, at least for the 100-year period ending in 2000, the risk of investing in equity assets has been rewarded with substantial returns. U.S. equities delivered an inflation-adjusted mean return of 8.7%, versus mean returns of 2.1% on bonds and 1.0% on Treasury bills. But the U.S. market is also not exceptional, and in fact, equity markets in Australia, Germany, Japan, South Africa, and Sweden all exhibited higher mean returns for the century. It is also interesting to note that equity returns for all 16 countries listed demonstrated positive mean returns, the lowest being 4.8% in Belgium, and the highest being 9.9% in Sweden.

As demonstrated by Global Finance Perspective 20.2, however, average performances over extended periods of time can be misleading, as they have a tendency to smooth returns that during the time of the crisis would indeed take an investor's breath away!

The true benefits of global diversification, however, arise from the fact that the returns of different stock markets around the world are not perfectly positively correlated. Because there are different industrial structures in different countries and because different economies do not exactly follow the same business cycle, we expect smaller return correlations between investments in different countries than between investments within a given country.

Exhibit 20.8 reports correlation coefficients between world equity markets for the 1900–2000 period. The correlation coefficients in the lower-left of the exhibit are for the entire period,

Global Finance Perspective 20.2

Equity Market Crises in the Twentieth Century

The largest equity market losses in the past century were primarily related to war and terrorism and their associated economic devastation.

Country	Event	Equity market losses (real returns, %)
U.S.	Terrorist attacks, September 11, 2001	–14%
U.S.	October 1987 stock market crash	–23%
U.S.	Bear market, 2000–2001	–37%
U.S.	Wall Street crash of 1929	–60%
U.K.	Bear market, 1973–1974	–71%
Germany	World War II, 1945–1948	–91%
Japan	World War II, 1944–1947	–97%

Source: Elroy Dimson, Paul Marsh, and Mike Staunton, *Triumph of the Optimists, 101 Years of Global Investment Returns*, Princeton University Press, 2002, p. 58.

Exhibit 20.8 Correlation Coefficients Between World Equity Markets, 1900–2000

Upper-Right: Correlations based on 60 months of real dollar returns, 1996–2000, from FTSE World (Ireland and South Africa) and MSCI (all others).

Lower-Left: Correlations based on 101 years of real dollar returns, 1900–2000.

	Wld	US	UK	Swi	Swe	Spa	Saf	Neth	Jap	Ita	Ire	Ger	Fra	Den	Can	Bel	Aus
Wld		.93	.77	.59	.62	.67	.54	.73	.68	.52	.69	.69	.73	.57	.82	.54	.69
US	.85		.67	.44	.46	.53	.46	.57	.49	.40	.66	.56	.56	.46	.78	.45	.57
UK	.70	.55		.58	.44	.63	.31	.71	.42	.39	.73	.58	.59	.57	.57	.59	.56
Swi	.68	.50	.62		.39	.60	.19	.72	.36	.45	.57	.53	.64	.58	.35	.63	.37
Swe	.62	.44	.42	.54		.63	.38	.63	.34	.49	.27	.76	.76	.44	.61	.29	.44
Spa	.41	.25	.25	.36	.37		.35	.63	.32	.64	.50	.64	.75	.56	.51	.55	.54
Saf	.55	.43	.49	.39	.34	.26		.30	.44	.24	.31	.42	.37	.25	.62	.10	.66
Neth	.57	.39	.42	.51	.43	.28	.29		.39	.59	.63	.74	.77	.64	.55	.70	.46
Jap	.45	.21	.33	.29	.39	.40	.31	.25		.18	.33	.25	.36	.24	.50	.17	.59
Ita	.54	.37	.43	.52	.39	.41	.41	.32	.34		.33	.55	.71	.50	.40	.51	.38
Ire	.58	.38	.73	.70	.42	.35	.42	.46	.29	.43		.42	.45	.49	.54	.57	.50
Ger	.30	.12	–.01	.22	.09	–.03	.05	.27	.06	.016	.03		.83	.61	.57	.59	.46
Fra	.62	.36	.45	.54	.44	.47	.38	.48	.25	.52	.53	.19		.63	.60	.66	.48
Den	.57	.38	.40	.51	.56	.34	.31	.50	.46	.38	.55	.22	.45		.55	.54	.30
Can	.80	.80	.55	.48	.53	.27	.54	.34	.30	.37	.41	.13	.35	.46		.30	.65
Bel	.58	.38	.40	.57	.43	.40	.29	.60	.25	.47	.49	.26	.68	.42	.35		.30
Aus	.66	.47	.66	.51	.50	.28	.56	.41	.28	.43	.62	.04	.47	.42	.62	.35	

Source: Elroy Dimson, Paul Marsh, and Mike Staunton, *Triumph of the Optimists, 101 Years of Global Investment Returns*, Princeton University Press, 2002, p. 115.

1900–2000, while the upper-right of the exhibit are for the 1996–2000 period. The relatively low correlation coefficients among returns for the 16 countries for either period indicates great potential for international diversification. The returns, for the sake of comparison, have all been converted to the same currency basis (in this case, the U.S. dollar) and are corrected for inflation.

As noted by the authors of the study, the correlations seem to be "plausible and linked to geography and distance" as national markets that are contiguous or near-contiguous seemingly demonstrate the higher correlation coefficients for the century. For example, among the lower-left correlation coefficients, the highest correlations are those between the United States and Canada (0.80) and Ireland and the United Kingdom (0.73).

The correlation coefficients among national equity markets in the upper-right of Exhibit 20.8, correlations for the 1996–2000 period, are noticeably higher than those for the entire century. The mean correlation coefficient for the entire century was 0.36, while that of the 1996–2000 period was 0.50. Although only for the most recent time segment, and one in which global equity market performance could have been atypical given the dot-com bubble in select industrial markets, the coefficients do indicate a higher degree of market performance integration.[1]

Additional multiple regression studies undertaken by the authors of the study found that when the 21st century was divided in half "there was no discernible relationship between the two half centuries." They went on to determine that "it would not have been possible to predict correlations for 1950–2000 from those estimated from annual data over the first half-century."[2]

Market Performance Adjusted for Risk: The Sharpe and Treynor Performance Measures

Although the previous two exhibits provided some insights into the long-term historical performance of individual national markets and key assets, they do not provide a complete picture of how returns and risks must be considered in combination. Exhibit 20.9 presents summary statistics for the monthly returns across 18 major equity markets for the 1977–1996 period. In addition to the traditional measures of individual market performance of mean return and standard deviation (for risk), the individual national market's beta to the global portfolio is reported as well as two measures of risk-adjusted returns, the Sharpe and Treynor measures.

Investors should examine returns by the amount of return per unit of risk accepted, rather than in isolation (as in simply mean risks and returns). For example, in Exhibit 20.9, the Hong Kong market had the highest average monthly return at 1.50%, but also the highest risk, a standard deviation of 9.61%. (A major contributing factor to its high volatility was perhaps the political uncertainty about the future of the British colony after 1997.)

To consider both risk and return in evaluating portfolio performance, we introduce two measures in Exhibit 20.9, the *Sharpe measure* (SHP) and the *Treynor measure* (TRN). The Sharpe

1. Elroy Dimson, Paul Marsh, and Mike Staunton, *Triumph of the Optimists, 101 Years of Global Investment Returns* (Princeton University Press, 2002), p. 115–116.
2. Ibid, p. 116.

Exhibit 20.9 Summary Statistics of the Monthly Returns for 18 Major Stock Markets, 1977–1996 (all returns converted into U.S. dollars and include all dividends paid)

	Mean Return (%)	Standard Deviation (%)	Beta (β_i)	Sharpe M. (SHP_i)	Treynor M. (TRN_i)
Australia	1.00	7.44	1.02	0.078	0.0057
Austria	0.77	6.52	0.54	0.055	0.0066
Belgium	1.19	5.53	0.86	0.141	0.0091
Canada	0.82	5.34	0.93	0.076	0.0044
Denmark	0.99	6.25	0.68	0.092	0.0085
France	1.18	6.76	1.08	0.113	0.0071
Germany	0.97	6.17	0.84	0.089	0.0065
Hong Kong	1.50	9.61	1.09	0.113	0.0100
Italy	0.96	7.57	0.89	0.071	0.0061
Japan	1.08	6.66	1.21	0.099	0.0055
Netherlands	1.39	4.93	0.89	0.197	0.0109
Norway	1.00	7.94	1.02	0.073	0.0057
Singapore	1.09	7.50	1.01	0.090	0.0057
Spain	0.83	6.81	0.94	0.060	0.0044
Sweden	1.37	6.67	0.97	0.143	0.0099
Switzerland	1.10	5.39	0.86	0.127	0.0080
United Kingdom	1.35	5.79	1.06	0.162	0.0089
United States	1.01	4.16	0.82	0.143	0.0072
Average	1.09	6.51	0.93	0.107	0.0073

The results are computed with stock market data from Morgan Stanley's *Capital International Perspectives*, monthly.

measure calculates the average return over and above the risk-free rate of return per unit of portfolio risk:

$$\text{Sharpe measure} = SHP_i = \frac{\overline{R}_i - R_f}{\sigma_i}$$

where R_i is the average return for portfolio i during a specified time period, R_f is the average risk-free rate of return, and σ_i is the risk of portfolio i. The Treynor measure is very similar, but instead of using the standard deviation of the portfolio's total return as the measure of risk, it utilizes the portfolio's beta, β_i, the systematic risk of the portfolio, as measured against the world market portfolio:

$$\text{Treynor measure} = TRN_i = \frac{\overline{R}_i - R_f}{\beta_i}$$

The Sharpe measure indicates, on average, how much excess return (above risk-free rate) an investor is rewarded per unit of portfolio risk the investor bears.

Though the equations of the Sharpe and Treynor measures look similar, the difference between them is important. If a portfolio is perfectly diversified (without any unsystematic risk), the two measures give similar rankings because the total portfolio risk is equivalent to the systematic risk. If a portfolio is poorly diversified, it is possible for it to show a high ranking on the basis of the Treynor measure, but a lower ranking on the basis of the Sharpe measure. The difference is attributable to the low level of portfolio diversification. The two measures, therefore, provide complementary but different information.

The mean return for Hong Kong in Exhibit 20.9 was 1.5%. If we assume the average risk-free rate was 5% per year during this period (or 0.42% per month), the Sharpe measure would be calculated as:

$$SHP_{\text{HKG}} = \frac{\overline{R}_i - R_f}{\sigma_i} = \frac{0.015 - 0.0042}{0.0961} = 0.113$$

For each unit (%) of portfolio total risk an investor bore, the Hong Kong market rewarded the investor with a monthly excess return of 0.113% in 1977–1996.

Alternatively, the Treynor measure was:

$$TRN_{\text{HKG}} = \frac{\overline{R}_i - R_f}{\beta_i} = \frac{0.015 - 0.0042}{1.09} = 0.0100$$

Though the Hong Kong market had the second highest Treynor measure, its Sharpe measure was ranked eighth, indicating that the Hong Kong market portfolio was not very well diversified from the world market perspective. Instead, the highest ranking belonged to the Netherlands market, which had the highest Sharpe (0.197) and Treynor (0.0109) measures.

Does this mean that a U.S. investor would have been best rewarded by investing in the Netherlands market over this period? The answer is yes, if the investor were allowed to invest in only one of these markets. It would definitely have been better than staying home in the U.S. market, which had a Sharpe measure of 0.143 for the period. However, if the investor were willing to combine these markets in a portfolio, the performance would have been even better. Since these market returns were not perfectly positively correlated, further risk reduction was possible through diversification across markets.

Are Markets Increasingly Integrated?

It is often said that as capital markets around the world become more and more integrated over time, the benefits of diversification will be reduced. To examine this question, we break the 20-year sample period of 1977–1996 into two halves: 1977–1986 and 1987–1996. Dividing the periods at 1986, the date coincides with the official movement toward a single Europe. At this time, most European Union countries deregulated their securities markets—or at least began the process of removing remaining restrictions on the free flow of capital across the borders.

Exhibit 20.10 Comparison of Selected Correlation Coefficients Between Stock Markets for Two Different Time Periods (dollar returns)

Correlation to United States	1977–86	1987–96	Change
Canada	0.66	0.77	+ 0.11
Denmark	0.26	0.18	– 0.08
France	0.37	0.55	+ 0.18
Germany	0.24	0.42	+ 0.18
Hong Kong	0.13	0.61	+ 0.48
Japan	0.16	0.26	+ 0.10
Singapore	0.31	0.66	+ 0.35
Switzerland	0.38	0.47	+ 0.09
United Kingdom	0.40	0.67	+ 0.27

Correlation coefficients computed from data from Morgan Stanley's *Capital International Perspectives*.

Exhibit 20.10 reports selected stock markets' correlation coefficients with the United States for each subperiod. Only the Danish-U.S. market correlation actually fell from the first to the second period. The Canadian-U.S. correlation rose from an already high 0.66 to 0.77 in the latter period. Similarly, the correlations between the United States and both Singapore and the United Kingdom rose to 0.66 and 0.67, respectively.

The overall picture is that the correlations have increased over time. The answer to the question, "Are markets increasingly integrated?" is most likely "yes." However, although capital market integration has decreased some benefits of international portfolio diversification, the correlation coefficients between markets are still far from 1.0. There are still plenty of risk-reducing opportunities for international portfolio diversification.

The International Capital Asset Pricing Model

We should not leave the subject of international portfolio diversification before turning our discussion to what international portfolio use could mean to a MNE's cost of capital. In Chapter 11, we discussed the common practice of calculating a firm's cost of equity using the capital asset pricing model (CAPM). The question now is how CAPM changes the cost of capital when we introduce an internationally diversified opportunity set of portfolios.

The Capital Asset Pricing Model

As we discussed in Chapter 11, the capital asset pricing model states that the expected return on an equity by an investor is the sum of two components, a risk-free rate of interest and a risk-premium component, which is based on the perceived riskiness of the individual security relative to the market.

$$k_e = k_{rf} + \beta_i \left(k_m - k_{rf}\right)$$

where

k_e = expected (required) rate of return on equity i

k_{rf} = rate of interest on risk-free bonds (Treasury bonds, for example)

β_i = coefficient of systematic risk for the firm

k_m = expected (required) rate of return on the market portfolio of stocks.

This measure of risk, *beta* (β_i), is a measure of how the returns of the individual security, i, are expected to vary and covary with that of the market. Specifically, *beta* is calculated as:

$$\beta_i = \rho_{im}\frac{\sigma_i}{\sigma_m}$$

where *rho* (ρ_{im}), is the correlation coefficient between security i and the market, and σ_i and σ_m are the standard deviations of return of security i and the market, respectively. But what would be the implication for the firm's beta, and therefore its cost of equity, if the investors evaluating its inclusion in their portfolio were using a global portfolio rather than a domestic one?

Nestlé: An Application of the International CAPM

In theory, the primary distinction in the estimation of the cost of equity for an individual firm using an internationalized version of the CAPM is the definition of the "market" and a recalculation of the firm's beta for that market. The case of Nestlé (Switzerland) provides an illustration of the possible impact of this globalization of portfolios.

Nestlé, the Swiss-based multinational firm that produces and distributes a variety of confectionery products, serves as an excellent example of how the international investor may view the global cost of capital differently from a domestic investor.[3]

Estimating the required return on Nestlé, a prospective Swiss investor might assume a risk-free return of 3.3% (index of Swiss government bond issues, in Swiss francs), an average return on a portfolio of Swiss equities of 10.2% (*Financial Times Swiss Index*, in Swiss francs), and a $\beta_{\text{Nestlé}}$ of 0.885. An investor would then expect Nestlé to yield 9.4065% for the coming year.

$$k_e^{\text{Nestlé}} = k_{RF} + \left(k_M - k_{RF}\right)\beta_{\text{Nestlé}} = 3.3 + \left(10.2 - 3.3\right)0.885 = 9.4065\%$$

One problem with this traditional domestic CAPM approach is that it assumes that investors in the Swiss market, and potentially in Nestlé, hold portfolios limited to stocks available in the Swiss market alone—a purely domestic portfolio. If Swiss investors held internationally diversified portfolios instead, both the expected market return k_M, and the beta estimate for Nestlé itself would be defined and determined differently.

3. René Stulz, "The Cost of Capital in Internationally Integrated Markets: The Case of Nestlé," *European Financial Management*, March 1995, Volume 1, No. 1, pp. 11–22.

A Swiss investor can hold a global portfolio, rather than a domestic portfolio. Given the trends toward deregulation and integration of international capital markets, the Swiss investor's portfolio expectations would be more accurately represented by a global portfolio index rather than a purely domestic index.

We follow Stulz's (1995) preference here for describing the internationally diversified portfolio as the global portfolio rather than the world portfolio. The distinction is important. The world portfolio is an index of all securities in the world. However, even with the increasing trend of deregulation and financial integration, a number of securities markets still remain segmented or restricted in their access. Those securities actually available to an investor are the *global portfolio.*

In the case of Nestlé, for the same time period as before, a global portfolio index such as the *Financial Times* index in Swiss francs (FTA-Swiss) would show a market return of 13.7% (as opposed to the domestic Swiss index return of 10.2%). In addition, a beta for Nestlé estimated on Nestlé's returns versus the global portfolio index would be much smaller, 0.585 (as opposed to the 0.885 found previously). An internationally diversified Swiss investor would expect a return on Nestlé of:

$$k_e^{\text{Nestlé}} = k_{RF} + (k_M - k_{RF})\beta_{\text{Nestlé}} = 3.3 + (13.7 - 3.3)0.585 = 9.384\%$$

Admittedly, this is not a lot of difference in the end. Exhibit 20.11 summarizes the values and results of the comparison. However, given the magnitude of change in both the values of the market return average and the beta for the firm, it is obvious that the final result could easily have varied by several hundred basis points. The proper construction of the investor's portfolio and the proper portrayal of the investor's perceptions of risk and opportunity cost are clearly important to identifying the global cost of a company's equity capital.

There are, however, a number of questions regarding the validity of an international or global version of the capital asset pricing model.

Exhibit 20.11 Estimating the Global Cost of Equity for Nestlé (Switzerland)

Domestic Portfolio for Swiss Investor	Global Portfolio for Swiss Investor
k_{RF} = 3.3% (Swiss bond index yield)	k_{RF} = 3.3% (Swiss bond index yield)
k_M = 10.2% (Swiss market portfolio in SF)	k_M = 13.7% (Financial Times global index in SF)
$\beta_{\text{Nestlé}}$ = 0.885 (Nestlé versus Swiss market portfolio)	$\beta_{\text{Nestlé}}$ = 0.585 (Nestlé versus FTA-Swiss index)

$$k_{\text{Nestlé}} = k_{RF} + (k_M - k_{RF})\beta_{\text{Nestlé}}$$

Domestic	Global
Required return on Nestlé:	Required return on Nestlé:
$k_e^{\text{Nestlé}}$ = 9.4065%	$k_e^{\text{Nestlé}}$ = 9.3840%

Source: All values are taken from René Stulz, "The Cost of Capital in Internationally Integrated Markets: The Case of Nestlé," *European Financial Management*, March 1995, Volume 1, No. 1, pp. 11–22.

- There are a multitude of barriers to the free and open movement of capital across boundaries. These barriers prevent professional investors and portfolio managers from responding effectively to new information as it arises regarding the return and risk prospects of individual securities globally.
- As noted previously, there is in reality no way to calculate an international or global portfolio due to the limitations on trading, the illiquidity of many emerging markets, and the incomplete information regarding the equities traded in these markets. (Lack of perfect information is in direct conflict with the underlying assumptions of the CAPM.)
- Unless we believe that purchasing power parity always holds—in both the short term and the long term—there is no single risk-free rate of return globally. The capital asset pricing model uses the risk-free rate as its base, and the international CAPM with its global investor would similarly need a single currency-neutral numeraire to work.

So, at this point in time, the prospect for an operational international or global version of the capital asset pricing model is not good. As markets continue to grow, integrate, and become increasingly transparent, however, its day may come.

SUMMARY

- The total risk of any portfolio is composed of systematic (market) and unsystematic (individual securities) risk. Increasing the number of securities in the portfolio reduces the unsystematic risk component.
- An internationally diversified portfolio has a lower portfolio beta. This means that the portfolio's market risk is lower than that of a domestic portfolio. This situation arises because the returns on the foreign stocks are closely correlated not with returns on U.S. stocks, but rather with a global beta.
- Investors construct internationally diversified portfolios in an attempt to combine assets that are less than perfectly correlated, reducing the total risk of the portfolio. In addition, by adding assets outside the home market, the investor has now tapped into a larger pool of potential investments.
- International portfolio construction is also different, in that when the investor acquires assets or securities outside the investor's home-country market, the investor may also be acquiring a foreign currency–denominated asset.
- The investor has actually acquired two additional assets—the currency of denomination and the asset subsequently purchased with the currency—one asset in principle, but two in expected returns and risks.
- The foreign exchange risks of a portfolio, whether it be a securities portfolio or the general portfolio of activities of the MNE, are reduced through international diversification.
- The individual investor will search out the optimal domestic portfolio (DP), which combines the risk-free asset and a portfolio of domestic securities found on the efficient frontier. The investor begins with the risk-free asset with return of R_f (and zero expected risk) and moves out along the capital market line until reaching portfolio DP.
- This portfolio is called the "optimal domestic portfolio," because it moves out into risky space at the steepest slope—maximizing the slope of expected portfolio return over expected risk—while still touching the opportunity set of domestic portfolios.

- The optimal international portfolio, IP, is found by finding that point on the capital market line (internationally diversified) that extends from the risk-free asset return of R_f to a point of tangency along the internationally diversified efficient frontier.
- The investor's optimal international portfolio IP possesses both higher expected portfolio return ($R_{IP} > R_{DP}$), and lower expected portfolio risk ($s_{IP} < s_{DP}$), than the purely domestic optimal portfolio. The optimal international portfolio is superior to the optimal domestic portfolio.
- Risk reduction is possible through international diversification, because the returns of different stock markets around the world are not perfectly positively correlated.
- A recent study by Dimson et al. found that for the 100-year period ending in 2000, the risk of investing in equity assets had been rewarded with substantial returns. U.S. equities delivered an inflation-adjusted mean return of 8.7%, versus mean returns of 2.1% on bonds and 1.0% on Treasury bills. But the U.S. market is also not exceptional, and in fact, equity markets in Australia, Germany, Japan, South Africa, and Sweden all exhibited higher mean returns for the century.
- Because there are different industrial structures in different countries and because different economies do not exactly follow the same business cycle, we expect smaller return correlations between investments in different countries than between investments within a given country.
- The relatively low correlation coefficients among returns of 18 major stock markets around the world in the 20-year period from 1977 to 1996 indicates great potential for international diversification.
- The overall picture is that the correlations have increased over time.
- Nevertheless, 91 of the 153 correlations (59%) and the overall mean (0.46) were still below 0.5 in 1987–1996. The answer to the question, "Are markets increasingly integrated?" is "yes."
- However, although capital market integration has decreased some benefits of international portfolio diversification, the correlation coefficients between markets are still far from 1.0. There are still plenty of risk-reducing opportunities for international portfolio diversification.
- In theory, the primary distinction in the estimation of the cost of equity for an individual firm using an internationalized version of the CAPM is the definition of the "market" and a recalculation of the firm's beta for that market.

QUESTIONS

1. **Diversification benefits.** How does the diversification of a portfolio change its expected returns and expected risks? Is this in principle any different for internationally diversified portfolios?
2. **Risk reduction.** What types of risk are present in a diversified portfolio? Which type of risk remains after the portfolio has been diversified?
3. **Measurement of risk.** How, according to portfolio theory, is the risk of the portfolio measured precisely?
4. **Market risk.** If all national markets have market risk, is all market risk the same?
5. **Currency risk.** The currency risk associated with international diversification is a serious concern for portfolio managers. Is it ever possible for currency risk to benefit the portfolio's return?
6. **Optimal domestic portfolio.** Define in words (without graphics) how the optimal domestic portfolio is constructed.
7. **Minimum risk portfolios.** If the primary benefit of portfolio diversification is risk reduction,

is the investor always better off choosing the portfolio with the lowest expected risk?

8. **International risk.** Many portfolio managers, when asked why they do not internationally diversify their portfolios, answer that "the risks are not worth the expected returns." Using the theory of international diversification, how would you evaluate this statement?

9. **Correlation coefficients.** The benefits of portfolio construction, domestically or internationally, arise from the lack of correlation among assets and markets. The increasing globalization of business is expected to change these correlations over time. How do you believe they will change and why?

10. **Relative risk and return.** Conceptually, how do the Sharpe and Treynor performance measures define risk differently? Which do you believe is a more useful measure in an internationally diversified portfolio?

11. **International equities and currencies.** As the newest member of the asset allocation team in your firm, you constantly find yourself being quizzed by your fellow group members. The topic this morning is international diversification. One analyst asks you the following question:

    Security prices are driven by a variety of factors, but corporate earnings are clearly one of the primary drivers. And corporate earnings—on average—follow business cycles. Exchange rates, as they taught you back in college, reflect the market's assessment of the growth prospects for the economy behind the currency. So if securities go up with the business cycle, and currencies go up with the business cycle, why do we see currencies and securities prices across the globe not going up and down together?

    Answer her question.

12. **Are MNEs global investments?** Firms with operations and assets across the globe, true MNEs, are in many ways as international in composition as the most internationally diversified portfolio of unrelated securities. Why do investors not simply invest in MNEs traded on their local exchanges and forego the complexity of purchasing securities traded on foreign exchanges?

13. **ADRs versus direct holdings.** When you are constructing your portfolio, you know you want to include Cementos de Mexico (Mexico) in it, but you cannot decide whether you wish to hold it in the form of ADRs traded on the NYSE or directly through purchases on the Mexico City Bolsa.
    a. Does it make any difference in regard to currency risk?
    b. List the pros and cons of ADRs and direct purchases.
    c. What would you recommend if you were an asset investor for a corporation with no international operations or internationally diversified holdings?

PROBLEMS

1. **Investing on the DAX.** Giri Iyer is European analyst and strategist for Tristar Funds, a New York–based mutual fund company. Giri is currently evaluating the recent performance of shares in Pacific Wietz, a publicly traded specialty chemical company in Germany listed on the Frankfurt DAX. The baseline investment amount used by Tristar is $100,000. He gathers the following quotes:

Element	Jan. 1 Purchase	Dec. 31 Sale	Distributions
Share price	€135.00	€157.60	€15.00
Exchange rate	$1.0660/€	$1.1250/€	———

    a. What was the return on the security in local currency terms?
    b. What was the return on the security in U.S. dollar terms?

c. Does this mean it was a good investment for a local investor, a U.S.-based investor, or both?

2. **Portfolio risk and return: Boeing and Unilever.** An investor is evaluating a two-asset portfolio of the following two securities:

Security	Expected Return (percent)	Std. Dev. (percent)
Boeing (U.S.)	18.6	22.8
Unilever (U.K.)	16.0	24.0

a. If the two securities have a correlation of +0.6, what is the expected risk and return for a portfolio that is equally weighted?

b. If the two securities have a correlation of +0.6, what is the expected risk and return for a portfolio that is 70% Boeing and 30% Unilever?

c. If the two securities have a correlation of +0.6, what is the expected risk and return for a portfolio that is optimally weighted? Determine the weights that minimize the combined risk.

3. **Sharpe and Treynor performance measures.** Assume the U.S. dollar returns (monthly averages) shown below for three Baltic republics. Calculate the Sharpe and Treynor measures of market performance.

Country	Mean Return	Standard Deviation	Risk-Free Rate	Beta
Estonia	1.12%	16.00%	0.42%	1.65
Latvia	0.75%	22.80%	0.42%	1.53
Lithuania	1.60%	13.50%	0.42%	1.20

4. **Anglo-American Equity Fund.** An investor is evaluating a two-asset portfolio of the following two securities:

Security	Expected Return (percent)	Std. Dev. (percent)
Anglo Equities	12.5	26.4
American Equities	10.8	22.5

a. If the two equity funds have a correlation of +0.72, what is the expected risk and return for the following three portfolio weightings?

Portfolio A: 75% Anglo, 25% American

Portfolio B: 50% Anglo, 50% American

Portfolio C: 25% Anglo, 75% American

b. Which of the portfolios is preferable? On what basis?

Eastbridge Technology (London Stock Exchange). Eastbridge Technology is an information technology services provider. It currently operates primarily within the European marketplace, and therefore is not active or traded on any North American stock exchange. The company's share price and dividend distributions have been as follows in recent years:

	6/30/00	6/30/01	6/30/02	6/30/03
Share price (£)	37.40	42.88	40.15	44.60
Dividend (£)	1.50	1.60	1.70	1.80
Spot exchange rate ($/£)	1.4650	1.4260	1.4896	1.5546

5. **Eastbridge Technology: British pound-based investors.** Using the previous data, calculate the annual average capital appreciation rate on Eastbridge shares, as well as the average total return (including dividends) to a British pound-based investor holding the shares for the entire period shown.

6. **Eastbridge Technology: U.S. dollar-based investors (A).** Using the previous data, calculate the annual average total return (including dividends) to a U.S. dollar-based investor holding the shares for the entire period shown. Assume an investment of $100,000.

7. **Eastbridge Technology: U.S. dollar–based investors (B).** Using the previous data, but assuming an exchange rate that began at $1.4650/£ in June 2000 and then consistently appreciated versus the U.S. dollar 3.0% per year for the entire period, calculate the annual average total return (including dividends) to a U.S. dollar-based investor holding the shares for the entire period shown.

8. **Nestlé's cost of equity.** This chapter detailed how Nestlé of Switzerland could calculate its cost of equity depending on the nature of the portfolio a potential investor desired to hold. Recalculate Nestlé's cost of equity for a Swiss investor holding a domestic portfolio and a Swiss investor holding a global portfolio with the following updated values:

	Risk-free rate	Market risk premium	Security beta
Swiss investor, domestic portfolio	2.400%	4.880%	0.910
Swiss investor, global portfolio	2.400%	5.600%	0.635

9. **Brazilian investors diversify.** The Brazilian economy in 2001 and 2002 had gone up and down. The Brazilian real (R$) had also been declining since 1999 (when it was floated). Investors wished to diversify internationally—into U.S. dollars, for the most part—to protect themselves against the domestic economy and currency. A large private investor had, in April 2002, invested R$500,000 in Standard & Poor's 500 Indexes, which are traded on the American Stock Exchange (AMSE: SPY). The beginning and ending index prices and exchange rates between the real and the dollar were as follows:

	4/10/02	4/10/03
Share price of SPY (US$)	112.60	87.50
Exchange rate (R$/$)	2.27	3.22

a. What was the return on the index fund for the year to a U.S.-based investor?

b. What was the return to the Brazilian investor for the one-year holding period? If the Brazilian investor could have invested locally in Brazil in an interest-bearing account guaranteeing 12%, would that have been better than the American diversification strategy?

10. **Russian-U.S. equity portfolio.** An investor is evaluating a two-asset portfolio that combines a U.S. equity fund with a Russian equity fund. The expected returns, risks, and correlation coefficients for the coming one-year period are as follows:

Security	Expected Return (percent)	Expected Risk (percent)
U.S. equity fund	10.50	18.60
Russian equity fund	16.80	36.00

Assuming the expected correlation coefficient is 0.52 for the coming year, which weights (use increments of 5% such as 95/5, 90/10) result in the best tradeoff between expected risk and expected return?

INTERNET EXERCISES

WWW.

1. **International diversification via mutual funds.** All major mutual fund companies now offer a variety of internationally diversified mutual funds. The degree of international composition across funds, however, differs significantly. Use the web sites listed here, and any others of interest, to:

   a. Distinguish between international funds, global funds, worldwide funds, and overseas funds

   b. Determine how international funds have been performing, in U.S. dollar terms, relative to mutual funds offering purely domestic portfolios

Fidelity	http://www.fidelity.com/funds
T. Rowe Price	http://www.troweprice.com
Merrill Lynch	http://www.ml.com
Scudder	http://www.scudder.com
Kemper	http://www.kemper.com

2. **Center for Latin American Capital Markets Research.** Because most of the Latin American markets suffered significant declines in market value following the Mexican peso crisis of December 1994, many of these markets may still be some of the most undervalued markets in the world. If you were given the task of investing US$1 million in a single

equity market in Latin America, which one would you choose? Use the Internet to find recent market performance statistics to support your choice.

Center for Latin American Capital http://users.www.netrus.net/gmorles

SELECTED READINGS

Denis, David J., Diane K. Denis, and Keven Yost, "Global Diversification, Industrial Diversification, and Firm Value," *Journal of Finance*, October 2002, Volume 7, No. 5, pp. 1951–1979.

Dimson, Elroy, Paul Marsh, and Mike Staunton, *Triumph of the Optimists: 101 Years of Global Investment Returns* (Princeton N.J., Princeton University Press, 2002), Chapters 8 and 15.

Fama, Eugene, and Kenneth R. French, "Value Versus Growth: The International Evidence," *Journal of Finance*, December 1998, Volume 53, No. 6, pp. 1975–1999.

Guffin, John M., and G. Andrew Karolyi, "Another Look at the Role of the Industrial Structure of Markets for International Diversification Strategies," *Journal of Financial Economics*, December 1998, Volume 50, No. 3, pp. 351–373.

Kim, E. Han, and Vijay Singal, "Are Open Markets Good for Foreign Investors and Emerging Nations?" *Journal of Applied Corporate Finance*, Fall 1997, Volume 10, No. 3, pp. 18–33.

Lins, Karl V., and Henri Serves, "Is Corporate Diversification Beneficial in Emerging Markets?" *Financial Management*, Summer 2002, Volume. 31, Issue 2, pp. 5–31.

Smith, Roy C., and Ingo Walter, "Risks and Rewards in Emerging Market Investments," *Journal of Applied Corporate Finance*, Fall 1997, Volume 10, No. 3, pp. 8–17.

PART 6

Managing Multinational Operations

PART 6

In Part 6, you will learn the intricacies of managing a MNE's ongoing global operations, a task that requires most of a financial manager's attention. Daily attention to the details of everyday operations determines how much value can be added to the shareholders that have approved a MNE's global reach through foreign direct investment as described in Part 5.

Chapter 21 analyzes how a MNE can reposition funds across borders while overcoming political, foreign exchange, tax, and transaction cost constraints. We utilize a hypothetical MNE, Cascade Pharmaceuticals, Inc. (Cascade), to illustrate the importance of unbundling fund transfers. Unbundling means that rather than depending on dividends alone to transfer funds internally, a MNE should utilize other conduits, such as license fees, royalties, and contributions to overhead by foreign subsidiaries. Next we describe the many considerations that financial managers must satisfy in order to set a transfer price on goods and services that are bought and sold between related units of the MNE. The timing of such transfers, called leads and lags, is also analyzed, as well as how Cascade can utilize a re-invoicing center to concentrate foreign exchange transaction risk in one location. The chapter concludes with a mini-case about Ford Ranger in the Asia Pacific.

Chapter 22 analyzes how a MNE can manage its working capital efficiently. We use the case of Cascade to illustrate a MNE's operating cycle. We describe how Cascade can minimize the amount of funds it has tied up in working capital, a goal that is important for maximizing the after-tax return on its invested capital. In addition to managing accounts receivable, MNEs need to manage inventory and cash balances. MNEs manage cash balances through international payments netting systems in order to minimize the funds tied up in cash and the transactions costs incurred every time cash is moved through the banking system. The chapter concludes by showing how Cascade can utilize the banking system to finance its short-term working capital needs. You will learn how a MNE can use its own in-house bank, as well as tapping the commercial banking services offered by both multinational and local host country banks. We then present a mini-case on negotiations between Honeywell and Pakistan International Airways.

Chapter 23 describes all the elements of traditional export and import trade financing. It demonstrates how a MNE or any exporter/importer can reduce the risk of nonpayment on a trade transaction. We describe all the key documents that are needed to accomplish this task. In particular, we present the use and details of letters of credit, drafts, bankers acceptances, and bills of lading. These documents not only reduce the danger of non-payment but also provide a documentary basis for collateralizing short-term trade financing by commercial banks. We document a typical trade transaction showing how the individual documents are linked together. Next we describe the various government programs that are available to help finance exports. The chapter concludes with a description of countertrade. A mini-case is presented detailing the difficulties of importing diapers to Brazil while maintaining price competitiveness.

Chapter 24 presents a series of advanced topics in international financial management. It includes the optimal currency hedging ratio, cross-currency hedging, delta neutral hedging strategies, and second-generation option products. We include an appendix detailing the theory of currency option pricing.

Chapter 21

Repositioning Funds

As originally described in Chapter 1, the MNE is constantly striving to create shareholder value by maximizing the after-tax profitability of the firm. One dimension of this task is to reposition the profits of the firm, as legally and practically as possible, in low-tax environments. Simply put, this repositioning will allow the firm to increase after-tax profits by lowering its tax liabilities with the same amount of sales. Repositioning is also useful when a MNE wishes to redeploy cash flows or funds to more value-creating activities or to minimize exposure to a potential currency collapse or potential political or economic crises. Techniques to reposition funds are particularly important for operations in countries where exchange controls inhibit free foreign exchange transactions.

This chapter examines the various techniques used by MNEs to reposition funds. It starts with a description of a hypothetical U.S.-based MNE, Cascade Pharmaceuticals, Inc. (Cascade), that will be used to illustrate how repositioning funds can create shareholder value. The next section identifies the typical constraints that limit repositioning a MNE's funds internationally. The following section explains how different conduits can be used to "unbundle" the transfer of funds. This is followed by a detailed analysis of transfer pricing as a conduit to reposition funds. This section includes a description of the multiple effects of transfer pricing on a MNE's operating activities, including fund positioning, income taxes, managerial incentives and evaluation, and joint venture partners. The next section identifies additional conduits to reposition funds through license fees, royalties, and shared services. Then we describe international dividend remittances as the traditional "bundled" way of repositioning funds. Next to last we show how a MNE can re-time the transfer of its funds through "leads and lags." The chapter concludes with an analysis of how a re-invoicing center can be used to manage a MNE's accounts receivable and payable in a way that meets the political, foreign exchange, and tax constraints identified at the start of the chapter.

Cascade Pharmaceutical, Inc. (Cascade)

Cascade is a U.S.-based MNE specializing in the manufacture and distribution of generic drugs worldwide. Exhibit 21.1 diagrams Cascade and its three foreign subsidiaries, the currency and tax rates applicable to each entity, and management's conclusions regarding each unit's growth prospects. Cascade's three foreign subsidiaries each present a unique set of concerns for management:

Exhibit 21.1 Cascade Pharmaceutical's Subsidiaries and Their Growth Potentials

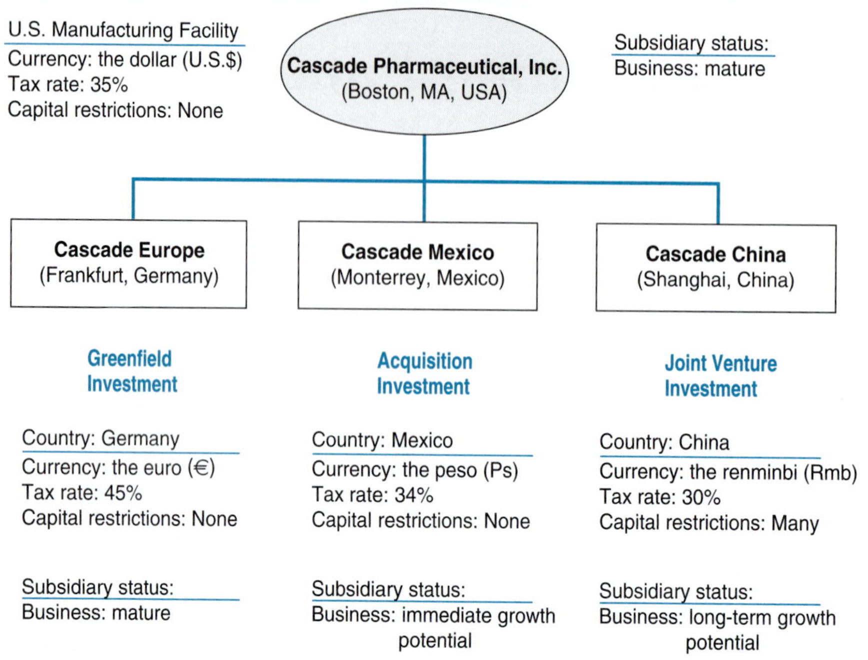

- **Cascade Europe** is operating in a relatively high-tax environment (compared in principle to the tax rate in the parent country, the United States). It conducts transactions in a relatively stable currency—the euro—and is free to move capital into and out of the country (Germany) with few restrictions. The business itself is mature, with few significant growth prospects in the near future.

- **Cascade Mexico** is operating in a medium-tax but historically volatile currency environment. It is subject to no current capital restrictions. Cascade believes the business will have very good growth prospects in the short-to-medium term if it is able to inject additional capital and managerial expertise into the business.

- **Cascade China** a new 50%-owned joint venture with a local partner (a former unit of the Chinese government) is operating in a relatively low-tax environment with a fixed exchange rate (the renminbi is managed within a very narrow band relative to the U.S. dollar). It is subject to a number of restrictions on capital. The business is believed to have the greatest potential of the three subsidiaries—in the long run.

In practice, Cascade's senior management in the parent company (*corporate*) will first determine its strategic objectives for each subsidiary and then design for each a financial management plan for the repositioning of profits, cash flows, and capital. As a result of this process, Cascade will now attempt to pursue the following repositioning objectives by subsidiary:

- **Cascade Europe:** Reposition profits from Germany to the United States, while maintaining the value of the European market's maturity to Cascade
- **Cascade Mexico:** Reposition or in some way manage the capital in Mexico subject to foreign exchange rate risk, while providing adequate capital for immediate growth prospects
- **Cascade China:** Reposition the quantity of funds in and out of China to protect against blocked funds (transfer risk), while balancing the needs of the joint venture partner

Constraints on Positioning Funds

Fund flows between units of a domestic business are generally unimpeded, but that is not the case in a multinational business. A firm operating globally faces a variety of political, tax, foreign exchange, and liquidity considerations that limit its ability to move funds easily and without cost from one country or currency to another. These constraints are the reason multinational financial managers must plan ahead for repositioning funds within the MNE. Advance planning is essential even when constraints do not exist, for at some future date political events may lead to unexpected restrictions.

Political constraints. As described in Chapter 16, political constraints can block the transfer of funds either overtly or covertly. Overt blockage occurs when a currency becomes inconvertible or is subject to government exchange controls that prevent its transfer at reasonable exchange rates. Covert blockage occurs when dividends or other forms of fund remittances are severely limited, heavily taxed, or excessively delayed by the need for bureaucratic approval.

Tax constraints. Tax constraints arise because of the complex and possibly contradictory tax structures of various national governments through whose jurisdictions funds might pass. A firm does not want funds in transit eroded by a sequence of nibbling tax collectors in every jurisdiction through which such funds might flow.

Transaction costs. Foreign exchange transaction costs are incurred when one currency is exchanged for another. These costs, in the form of fees and/or the difference between bid and ask quotations, are revenue for the commercial banks and dealers that operate the foreign exchange market. Although usually a small percentage of the amount of money exchanged, such costs become significant for large or frequent transfers and warrant planning to avoid unnecessary back-and-forth transfers. A subsidiary may remit a cash dividend to its parent at approximately the same time as the parent paid the subsidiary for goods purchased. For example, sending foreign exchange simultaneously in two directions is obviously a sheer waste of corporate resources, but it sometimes occurs when one part of a firm is not coordinated with another.

Liquidity needs. Despite the overall advantage of worldwide cash handling, liquidity needs in each individual location must be satisfied and good local banking relationships maintained. The size of appropriate balances is in part a judgmental decision and one not easily quantified. Nevertheless, such needs constrain a pure optimization approach to worldwide cash positioning.

Conduits for Moving Funds

Multinational firms often *unbundle* their transfer of funds into separate flows for specific purposes. Host countries are then more likely to perceive that a portion of what might otherwise be called *remittance of profits* constitutes an essential purchase of specific benefits that command worldwide values and benefit the host country. Unbundling allows a multinational firm to recover funds from subsidiaries without piquing host country sensitivities over large dividend drains. For example, Cascade might transfer funds from its foreign subsidiaries to the parent by any of the conduits shown in Exhibit 21.2.

The conduits illustrated in Exhibit 21.2 are separable into *before-tax* and *after-tax* groups in the host country. Although not always the focus of intra-unit fund movement, tax goals frequently are a critical determinant for many foreign subsidiary financial structures. An increase in the funds flow (charges) in any of the before-tax categories reduces the taxable profits of the foreign subsidiary if the host country tax authorities acknowledge the charge as a legitimate expense. The before-tax/after-tax distinction is also quite significant to a parent company attempting to repatriate funds in the most tax-efficient method if it is attempting to manage its own foreign tax credit/deficits between foreign units.

An item-by-item matching of remittance to input, such as royalties for intellectual property and fees for patents and advice, is equitable to host country and foreign investor alike, for it allows each party to see the reason for each remittance and to judge its acceptance independently. If all investment inputs are unbundled, part of what might have been classified as residual profits may turn out to be tax-deductible expenses related to a specific purchased benefit. Unbundling also facilitates allocation of overhead from a parent's international division, so-called *shared services*, to each operating subsidiary in accordance with a predetermined formula. Predetermination of the

Exhibit 21.2 Potential Conduits for Moving Funds from Subsidiary to Parent

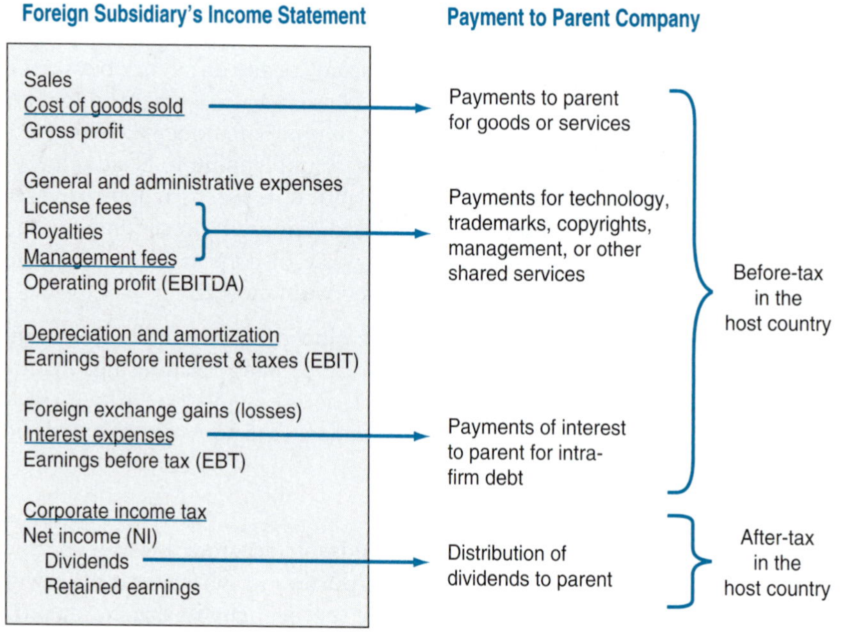

allocation method means a host country is less likely to view a given remittance as capricious and thus inappropriate. Finally, unbundling facilitates the entry of local capital into joint-venture projects, because total remuneration to different owners can be in proportion to the value of the varied contributions of each, rather than only in proportion to the amount of monetary capital they have invested.

Transfer Pricing

The pricing of goods, services, and technology transferred to a foreign subsidiary from a related company, *transfer pricing*, is the first and foremost method of transferring funds out of a foreign subsidiary. These costs enter directly into the cost of goods sold component of the subsidiary's income statement as illustrated in Exhibit 21.2. This is a particularly sensitive problem for MNEs. Even purely domestic firms find it difficult to reach agreement on the best method for setting prices on transactions between related units. In the multinational case, managers must balance conflicting considerations. These include fund positioning and income taxes.

Fund Positioning Effect

A parent wishing to transfer funds out of a particular country can charge higher prices on goods sold to its subsidiary in that country—to the degree that government regulations allow. A foreign subsidiary can be financed by the reverse technique, a lowering of transfer prices. Payment by the subsidiary for imports from its parent or sister subsidiary transfers funds out of the subsidiary. A higher transfer price permits funds to be accumulated in the selling country. Transfer pricing also transfers funds between sister subsidiaries. Multiple sourcing of component parts on a worldwide basis allows switching between suppliers within the corporate family as a device to transfer funds.

Income Tax Effect

A major consideration in setting a transfer price is the income tax effect. MNEs can influence their worldwide corporate profits by setting transfer prices to minimize taxable income in a country with a high income tax rate and maximize income in a country with a low income tax rate. A parent wishing to reduce the taxable profits of a subsidiary in a high-tax environment may set transfer prices at a higher rate to increase the costs of the subsidiary, thereby reducing taxable income. Global Finance Perspective 21.1 illustrates some apparent distortions to transfer prices by U.S. MNEs.

The income tax effect is illustrated in Exhibit 21.3. Cascade Europe is operating in a relatively high-tax environment (German corporate income taxes are 45%). Cascade USA is in a significantly lower tax environment (U.S. corporate income tax rates are 35%), motivating Cascade USA to charge Cascade Europe a higher transfer price on goods produced in the United States and sold to Cascade Europe.

If Cascade USA adopts a high markup policy by "selling" its merchandise at an intracompany sales price of $1,700,000, the same $800,000 of pretax consolidated income is allocated more heavily to low-tax Cascade USA and less heavily to high-tax Cascade Europe. (Note that it is Cascade Pharmaceuticals, Inc., the corporate parent, that must adopt a transfer pricing policy that directly alters the profitability of each of the individual subsidiaries.) As a consequence, total taxes drop by $30,000 and consolidated net income increases by $30,000 to $500,000. Total sales remain constant.

Global Finance Perspective 21.1

Over- and Under-Invoicing

A recent study raises questions over the legitimacy of the invoicing practices of many importers and exporters operating in the United States. The study estimated that MNEs avoided $45 billion in U.S. taxes in the year 2000. Import transactions were examined for over-invoicing, the use of a transfer price to pay more than what is typical for that product or service. Over-invoicing is one method of moving funds out of the United States and into the subject country. Export transactions were examined for under-invoicing, the use of a lower than normal export price to also re-position profits outside the United States.

The study examined approximately 15,000 import commodity code categories and 8,000 export commodity codes to determine the average selling prices—import and export—to determine implied prices. The study first calculated the medium price, lower export quartile price, and upper import quartile price by bilateral transfers (between the United States and nearly 230 individual countries). The following is a sample of some of the more suspicious results.

Over-Priced Imports

Item	From	Unit price
Sunflower seeds	France	$5,519/kg
Toothbrushes	U.K.	$5,655/unit
Hacksaw blades	Germany	$5,485/unit
Razor blades	India	$461/unit
Vinegar	Canada	$5,430/ltr
Flashlights	Japan	$5,000/unit
Sawdust	U.K.	$642/kg
Iron/steel ladders	Slovenia	$15,852/unit
Inkjet printers	Colombia	$179,000/unit
Lard	Canada	$484/kg
Hypodermic syringes	Switzerland	$2,306/unit

Under-Priced Exports

Item	To	Unit price
Truck caps	Mexico	$4.09/unit
Turbojet engines	Romania	$10,000/unit
Cameras (SLRs)	Mexico	$3.30/unit
Soybeans	Netherlands	$1.58/ton
ATM machines	Salvador	$35.93/unit
Bulldozers	Mexico	$527.94/unit
Rocket launchers	Bolivia	$40.00/unit
Toilets, porcelain	Hong Kong	$1.08/unit
Prefabricated buildings	St. Lucia	$0.82/unit
Video projectors	Malta	$28.71/unit
Radial tires—bus	U.K.	$8.46/unit

Source: "U.S. Trade with the World: An Estimate of 2000 Lost U.S. Federal Income Tax Revenues Due to Over-Invoiced Imports and Under-Invoiced Exports," Simon Pak and John Zdanowicz, Florida International University, November 1, 2001, unpublished.

Cascade would naturally prefer the high markup policy for sales from the United States to Europe (Germany, in this case). Needless to say, government tax authorities are aware of the potential income distortion from transfer price manipulation. A variety of regulations and court cases exist on the reasonableness of transfer prices, including fees and royalties, as well as prices set for merchandise. If a government taxing authority does not accept a transfer price, taxable income will be deemed larger than was calculated by the firm, and taxes will be increased.

Section 482 of the U.S. Internal Revenue Code is typical of laws circumscribing freedom to set transfer prices. Under this authority the Internal Revenue Service (IRS) can reallocate gross income, deductions, credits, or allowances between related corporations in order to prevent tax evasion or to reflect more clearly a proper allocation of income. Under the IRS guidelines and subsequent judicial interpretation, the burden of proof is on the taxpaying firm to show that the IRS

Exhibit 21.3 Effect of Low Versus High Transfer Price on Cascade Europe's Net Income (thousands of U.S. dollars)

Low Markup Policy		Cascade USA		Cascade Europe (subsidiary)	Europe and USA combined
Sales		$1,400		$2,000	$2,000
Less cost of goods sold*		(1,000)		(1,400)	(1,000)
Gross profit		$ 400		$ 600	$1,000
Less operating expenses		(100)		(100)	(200)
Taxable income		$ 300		$ 500	$ 800
Less income taxes	35%	(105)	45%	(225)	(330)
Net income		$ 195		$ 275	$ 470
High Markup Policy					
Sales		$1,700		$2,000	$2,000
Less cost of goods sold*		(1,000)		(1,700)	(1,000)
Gross profit		$ 700		$ 300	$1,000
Less operating expenses		(100)		(100)	(200)
Taxable income		$ 600		$ 200	$ 800
Less income taxes	35%	(210)	45%	(90)	(300)
Net income		$ 390		$ 110	$ 500

* Cascade USA's sales price becomes cost of goods sold for Cascade Europe.

has been arbitrary or unreasonable in reallocating income. This "guilty until proved innocent" approach means that MNEs must keep good documentation of the logic and costs behind their transfer prices. The "correct price" according to the guidelines is the one that reflects an *arm's length price*; that is, a price for the sale of the same goods or service to a comparable unrelated customer.

Methods of Determining Transfer Prices

IRS regulations provide three methods to establish arm's length prices: comparable uncontrolled prices, resale prices, and cost-plus calculations. The Organization for Economic Cooperation and Development (OECD) Committee on Fiscal Affairs recommends all three of these methods for use in member countries. In some cases, combinations of these three methods are used.

Comparable uncontrolled price method. A comparable uncontrolled price is regarded as the best evidence of arm's length pricing. Although such a market-determined price is ideal, in practice it is difficult to apply, because of variations in quality, quantity, timing of sale, and proprietary trademarks. Perhaps even more important is the fact that sales between subsidiaries are often of custom-designed items—for instance, a generator sold by Ford U.S. for a European model is unlikely to be sold to, or even usable by General Motors in Europe.

Resale price method. The resale price method, a second-best approach to arm's length pricing, starts with the final selling price to an independent purchaser and subtracts an appropriate markup for the distribution subsidiary. The allowed markup is to cover the distribution subsidiary's costs and profits. This price is then used as the intra-company transfer price for similar but not necessarily identical items. Nevertheless, determination of an appropriate markup is difficult, especially if the distribution subsidiary adds value to the item through subsequent processing or packaging.

Cost-plus method. The cost-plus method sets the allowable transfer price by adding an appropriate profit markup to the seller's full cost, where full cost is the accounting definition of direct costs plus overhead allocation. This method is often used where semifinished products are sold between subsidiaries. Nevertheless, allocation of overhead in determining full cost is always a very subjective matter, especially when joint products are involved, so the method allows room for negotiation.

Other Transfer Pricing Considerations

Many tax authorities allow lower transfer prices when a new market is being established. For example, a manufacturing subsidiary may cut its price to the distribution subsidiary so that the latter can get market penetration. However the price cut must be passed on to the final customer; it cannot be used to accumulate more profits in the distribution subsidiary. Another approach is to negotiate an advance pricing agreement (APA) with both home country and host country tax authorities. APAs take time and expense to negotiate, but they do provide the firm with advance assurance that its transfer pricing policies are acceptable. Without them, a firm may try to follow tax guidelines on transfer prices and still find itself in expensive tax appeals to defend a decision process it thought conformed to the letter of the tax rule.

Managerial Incentives and Evaluation

When a firm is organized with decentralized profit centers, transfer pricing between centers can disrupt evaluation of managerial performance. This problem is not unique to MNEs, but is also a controversial issue in the "centralization versus decentralization" debate in domestic circles. In the domestic case, however, a modicum of coordination at the corporate level can alleviate some of the distortion that occurs when any profit center suboptimizes its profit for the corporate good. Also, in most domestic cases, the company can file a single (for that country) consolidated tax return, so the issue of cost allocation between related companies is not critical from a tax-payment point of view.

In the multinational case, coordination is often hindered by longer and less-efficient channels of communication, the need to consider the unique variables that influence international pricing, and separate taxation. Even with the best of intent, a manager in one country finds it difficult to know what is best for the firm as a whole when buying at a negotiated price from related companies in another county. If corporate headquarters establishes transfer prices and sourcing alternatives, one of the main advantages of a decentralized profit center system disappears: local management loses the incentive to act for its own benefit.

To illustrate, refer to Exhibit 21.3, where an increase in the transfer price led to a worldwide income gain: Cascade's income rose by $195,000 (from $195,000 to $390,000), while Cascade Europe's income fell by only $165,000 (from $275,000 to $110,000), for a net gain of $30,000. Should managers of the European subsidiary lose their bonuses (or even their jobs) because of their "subpar" performance? Bonuses are usually determined by a company-wide formula based in part on the profitability of individual subsidiaries, but in this case Cascade Europe "sacrificed" for the greater good of the whole. Arbitrarily changing transfer prices can create measurement problems.

Specifically, transferring profit from high-tax Cascade Europe to low-tax Cascade USA changes the following for one or both companies:

- Import tariffs paid (importer only) and hence profit levels
- Measurements of foreign exchange exposure, such as the amount of net exposed assets, because of changes in amounts of cash and receivables
- Liquidity tests, such as the current ratio, receivables turnover, and inventory turnover
- Operating efficiency, as measured by the ratio of gross profit to either sales or to total assets
- Income tax payments
- Profitability, as measured by the ratio of net income to either sales or capital invested
- Dividend payout ratio, in that a constant dividend will show as a varied payout ratio as net income changes; alternatively, if the payout ratio is kept constant, the amount of dividend is changed by a change in transfer price
- Internal growth rate, as measured by the ratio of retained earnings to existing ownership equity

Effect on Joint Venture Partners

Joint ventures pose a special problem in transfer pricing, because serving the interest of local stockholders by maximizing local profit may be suboptimal from the overall viewpoint of the MNE. Often the conflicting interests are irreconcilable. Indeed, the local joint venture partner could be viewed as a potential Trojan horse if it complains to local authorities about the MNE's transfer pricing policy.

Flexibility in Transfer Pricing

Although all governments have an interest in monitoring transfer pricing by MNEs, not all governments use these powers to regulate transfer prices to the detriment of MNEs. In particular, transfer pricing has some political advantages over other techniques of transferring funds. Although the recorded transfer price is known to the governments of both the exporting and importing countries, the underlying cost data are not available to the importing country. Thus the importing country finds it difficult to judge the reasonableness of the transfer price, especially for nonstandard items such as specialized components.

Additionally, even if cost data could be obtained, some of the more sophisticated governments might continue to ignore the transfer pricing leak. They recognize that foreign investors must be able to repatriate a reasonable profit by their own standards, even if this profit seems unreasonable locally. An unknown or unproved transfer price leak makes it more difficult for local critics to blame their government for allowing the country to be "exploited" by foreign investors. Thus within the potential and actual constraints established by governments, opportunities may exist for MNEs to alter transfer prices from an arm's length market price. On the other hand, if a host government sours on foreign investment, past transfer price leaks may be exploited to penalize the

Global Finance Perspective 21.2

Transfer Prices and the Japanese Tax Authorities

Foreign companies in Japan became the object of the Tokyo tax man's eyes in the mid-1990s. Tax authorities clamped down on what they claimed were propensities by multinationals to avoid the nation's high corporate taxes by illegally shifting profits of their books in Japan. Japan's National Tax Administration stepped up its hunt for Japanese units of multinational companies that engaged in *transfer-pricing*, a method by which a company artificially depresses the profits it reports in one country by moving those profits onto books in another.

Companies caught engaging in transfer-pricing often face a whopping bill. In 1994, Coca-Cola Co.'s Japan unit announced that it would contest a big claim for back taxes of approximately $140 million. The Japanese unit of Goodyear Tire & Rubber Co. was hit for roughly 600 million yen in 1994. Tax officials purportedly claimed 800 million yen from the Japanese unit of Procter & Gamble Co. in the same year.

Allegations of transfer pricing often arise when tax authorities think the parent company of a foreign company is overcharging its Japanese subsidiary for the use of its products or trademarks. Coca-Cola's case is typical. Coke's Japan unit sells canned drinks developed especially for Japan, such as canned coffees under the name *Georgia*. The only indication that Georgia is a Coke product is the tiny Coca-Cola logo on the side of the can.

Tax authorities said the Japan unit paid too much in royalties—for things like the right to use the logo—to the parent company between 1990 and 1992, effectively shifting profits earned in Japan to the U.S., where taxes were lower. Coca-Cola's Japan unit argued, in a statement released at the time of the claim, that the royalties it paid were "fair and reasonable, given the unmatched value of the Coca-Cola Company's trademarks, manufacturing, marketing and management know-how."

Calculating proper payments for something like a trademark is difficult. Because trademarks aren't traded in the open market, their value is unclear. Japanese tax officials set a figure by examining both the company that's being audited and similar transactions at unrelated companies. This gives auditors a clear idea of what a trademark or an import might be worth in the market and how much a Japanese unit might have overpaid.

foreigners. Global Finance Perspective 21.2 illustrates this transfer pricing problem from a U.S. and Japanese perspective.

License Fees, Royalty Fees, and Shared Services

As illustrated earlier in Exhibit 21.2, unbundled services enter the subsidiary's income statement as expenses, reducing its tax liabilities in-country. They result in an increased taxable income to the parent company.

License and Royalty Fees

License fees are remuneration paid to the owners of technology, patents, trade names, and copyrighted material (including moving pictures, videotapes, compact disks, software, and books). License fees are usually based on a percentage of the value of the product or on the volume of production. As such, they are calculated independently of the amount of sales. *Royalty fees* are similar compensation for the use of intellectual property belonging to some other party. Royalties fees, however, are usually a stated percentage of sales revenue (price times volume), so that the owner is compensated in proportion to the volume of sales.

When license and royalty fees are paid by independent firms they are a straightforward arm's length payment for benefits received. However, license and royalty fees are also paid by subsidiaries to their parents and/or sister subsidiaries. In these instances they also function as a way to reposition funds between subsidiaries and parent. These intracompany licensing and royalty fees can be further differentiated into *management fees* for general expertise and advice, *technical assistance fees* for guidance in technical matters, and *license fees* for use of patented products or processes. Such fees are usually paid for identifiable benefits received by the subsidiaries, in contrast to *shared services*, the distributed overhead charges discussed in the next section, which are for more general benefits. Management and technical assistance fees are usually a fixed charge, either in total for supplying the services for a stated period of time, or on a time-rate basis varying with the number of billable hours devoted to the subsidiary. These fee provisions usually require a subsidiary to pay travel and per diem expenses of the individuals involved.

Shared Services

Shared services charges (often referred to as *distributed charges* or *distributed overhead*) compensate the parent for costs incurred in the general management of international operations and for other corporate services provided to foreign subsidiaries that must be recovered by the parent company. Overhead may be charged for regional cash management, research and development, corporate public relations, legal and accounting costs for the entire enterprise, human resource and organizational development expenditures, or a share of the salaries and other costs of top management. The parent company often levies overhead throughout an entire company as a predetermined percentage of direct labor costs or of sales. The charge may also be based on pro-rata sharing of specific costs that can be matched to the various units.

Licensing Contracts

A MNE must be careful to preserve its rights to receive funds from subsidiaries as royalties, fees, or shared services. The contracts or agreements that establish the terms and amount of payment must be structured carefully and clearly. This is an example of why agency costs are often higher for foreign operations. The following points should be addressed in any licensing contract:

- **Sales price definition.** If payments are calculated as a percentage of the subsidiary's sales price, "net sales price" must be carefully defined. Ideally, net sales price means invoice price net of any trade discounts and excluding packing charges, sales, excise and use taxes, and allowances for freight if that is billed or credited as a separated item to the customer.
- **Coverage.** The royalty or fee should be defined as a given percentage of the net sales price of all licensed products made and used, sold, or otherwise disposed of by the licensee.
- **Time and currency of payment.** A typical arrangement might provide that payments accrue at the time of sale or use, and payment follows on or before the close of the month following the end of the quarter. The currency of payment must be specified so that the location of any foreign exchange risk is clear.
- **Reports.** Each payment should be accompanied by a report describing the number and type of products sold, the customer, and the date of sale. This information is needed to verify accuracy of the amount remitted and to ensure that licensed products are sold only in those geographic or political areas covered by the licensing agreement.

- **Monitoring costs.** During the period of license, licensee personnel will probably visit the licensor's plant or office to acquire expertise, and the licensor will probably visit the licensee to monitor the agreement. The license agreement should specify who will pay for the visits, the amount of payments, and the work pattern (days per week, hours per day, etc.) of such visitors.
- **Nonfinancial issues.** The agreement should specify limitations on the exclusiveness of the license in various geographical areas, sublicensing rights, expiration or termination of the agreement, arbitration or litigation procedures in the case of dispute, disposition of products and/or special tools at the end of the license period, and surrender of trademark rights and blueprints. If the agreement is written in two languages, one of the languages should be established as the controlling text.

Regardless of how well structured and documented intrafirm license and service fees may be, there is no guarantee that local tax authorities will acknowledge their legitimacy. Multinational business is rich with instances in which a host country's tax authorities have denied deductibility of expenses required by the parent company's tax authorities. In this case, the parent company is forced to declare additional taxable profits, increasing its home-country tax liabilities, while being denied tax-deductibility of the expense in the subsidiary. The result is a net increase in the global tax liabilities of the MNE.

International Dividend Remittances

Payment of dividends is the classical method by which firms transfer profit back to owners, be they individual shareholders or parent corporations. Early economists spoke of returns to land, labor, and capital—the latter meaning the cash investment of owners. Implied in this division was the idea that owners contributed only their capital and nothing more—a view perhaps sustained in the early decades of capitalism by the image of owners (all older males) sitting in red leather lounge chairs in a private London club waiting for the ship they financed to return from one of the colonies. In this view, owners had nothing to do with business guidance of their venture. Contemporary views of ownership responsibilities have changed, and international dividend policy now incorporates tax considerations, political risk, and foreign exchange risk, as well as a return for business guidance and technology.

Tax Implications

Host country tax laws influence the dividend decision. Some countries, such as Germany, tax retained earnings at one rate and distributed earnings at a lower rate. Most countries levy withholding taxes on dividends paid to foreign parent firms and investors. Again, most (but not all) parent countries levy a tax on foreign dividends received but allow a tax credit for foreign taxes already paid on that income stream. That said, dividends remain the most tax-inefficient method for repatriating funds, because they are distributed on an after-tax basis. This means that the parent company will frequently be faced with the generation of excess foreign tax credits on a dividend. Remittance of license or royalty fees is on a pretax basis in the foreign subsidiary; the only tax typically applied is that of withholding, at a rate considerably below that of corporate income taxes.

Political Risk

Political risk may motivate parent firms to require foreign subsidiaries to remit all locally generated funds not required to internally finance growth in sales (working capital requirements) and planned capital expansions (*capex* or capital expenditures). Such policies, however, are not universal.

One strategy employed by MNEs in response to potential government restrictions is to maintain a constant dividend payout ratio to demonstrate that an established policy is being carried out consistently. This establishes a precedent for remittance of dividends and removes the perception of some host country governments that dividend distributions are by managerial election. (Even the terminology "declare a dividend" implies managerial discretion.)

Foreign Exchange Risk

If a foreign exchange loss is anticipated, a MNE may speed up the transfer of funds out of the country via dividends. This "lead" is usually part of a larger strategy of moving from weak currencies to strong currencies and can include speeding up intra-firm payments on accounts receivable and payable. However, decisions to accelerate dividend payments ahead of what might be normal must take into account interest rate differences and the negative impact on host country relations. Speeding up or slowing down payments is referred to as *leads and lags* and is addressed in more detail later in this chapter.

Distributions and Cash Flows

Dividends are a cash payment to owners equal to all or a portion of earnings of a prior period. To pay dividends, a subsidiary needs both past earnings and available cash. Subsidiaries sometimes have earnings without cash, because earnings are measured at the time of a sale but cash is received later when the receivable is collected (a typical distinction between accounting profits and cash flow). Profits of rapidly growing subsidiaries are often tied up in ever-increasing receivables and inventory (working capital). Hence rapidly growing foreign subsidiaries may lack the cash to remit a dividend equal to even a portion of earnings.

The reverse may also be true; firms may be receiving cash from the collection of old receivables even when profits are down, because current sales have fallen off or current expenses have risen relative to current sales prices. Such firms might want to declare a dividend in order to remove a bountiful supply of cash from a country, but they lack the earnings against which to charge such payments. For these reasons, a firm must look at both measured earnings and available cash before settling upon a cash dividend policy.

Joint Venture Factors

Existence of joint venture partners or local stockholders also influences dividend policy. The desire to position funds internationally cannot dominate the valid claims of independent partners or local stockholders for dividends. The latter do not benefit from the worldwide success of the MNE parent, but only from the success of the particular joint venture in which they own a share. Firms might hesitate to reduce dividends when earnings falter. They also might hesitate to increase dividends following a spurt in earnings because of possible adverse reaction to reducing dividends later, should earnings decline. Many MNEs insist on 100% ownership of subsidiaries in order to avoid possible conflicts of interest with outside shareholders.

Leads and Lags: Retiming the Transfer of Funds

Firms can reduce both operating and transaction exposure by accelerating or decelerating the timing of payments that must be made or received in foreign currencies. To *lead* is to pay early. A firm holding a "soft" currency or servicing debts denominated in a "hard" currency will lead by using the soft currency to pay the hard currency debts as soon as possible. The object is to pay the currency debts before the soft currency drops in value. To *lag* is to pay late. A firm holding a hard currency and having debts denominated in a soft currency will lag by paying those debts late, hoping that less of the hard currency will be needed. If possible, firms will also lead and lag their collection of receivables, collecting soft foreign currency receivables early and collecting hard foreign currency receivables later.

A firm can lead and lag with related firms (intra-company) or independent firms (inter-company). Assuming that payments will be made eventually, leading or lagging always results in changing the cash and payables position of one firm, with the reverse effect on the other firm.

Intra-Company Leads and Lags

Leading and lagging is more feasible between related firms, because they presumably embrace a common set of goals for the consolidated group. Furthermore, the many periodic payments between units of a MNE provide opportunities for many types of leads or lags. Because opportunities for leading or lagging payments depend on the requirement for payments of this nature, the device is more readily adaptable to a company that operates on an integrated worldwide basis. If each unit functions as a separate and self-sufficient entity, the motivation for leading or lagging diminishes. In the case of financing cash flows with foreign subsidiaries, there is an additional motivation for early or late payments to position funds for liquidity reasons. For example, a subsidiary that is allowed to lag payments to the parent company is in reality "borrowing" from the parent.

Because the use of leads and lags is an obvious technique for minimizing foreign exchange exposure and for shifting the burden of financing, many governments impose limits on the allowed range. Terms allowed by governments are often subject to negotiation when a good argument can be presented. Thus some limits are subject to exceptions. For example, in the past Italy has placed no limit on export and import lags on trade payments with other OECD countries. However, a 180-day limit on export lags and a 5-year limit on import lags was applied to trade with non-OECD countries.

Intercompany Leads and Lags

Leading or lagging between independent firms requires the time preference of one firm to be imposed to the detriment of the other firm. For example, Cascade Europe may wish to lead in collecting its Venezuelan accounts receivable that are denominated in bolivars because it expects the bolivar to drop in value compared with the euro. But why should the Venezuelan customers prepay their accounts payable? Credit in bolivars was part of the inducement for them to purchase from Cascade Europe to begin with. The only way the Venezuelans would be willing to pay their accounts payable early would be for the German creditor to offer a discount about equal to the forward discount on the bolivar or, in equilibrium, the difference between Venezuelan and German interest rates for the period of prepayment. In equilibrium this "discount" would eliminate the benefit to Cascade Europe of collecting the soft currency earlier.

Re-Invoicing Centers

A *re-invoicing center* is a separate corporate subsidiary that serves as a type of middle-man between the parent or related unit in one location and all foreign subsidiaries in a geographic region. Manufacturing subsidiaries sell goods to distribution subsidiaries of the same firm only by selling to a re-invoicing center, which in turn resells to the distribution subsidiary. Title passes to the re-invoicing center, but the physical movement of goods is direct from the manufacturing plant, in this case Cascade USA, to the foreign subsidiary, Cascade Mexico. Thus the re-invoicing center handles paperwork but has no inventory.

As depicted in Exhibit 21.4, the U.S. manufacturing unit of Cascade USA invoices the firm's re-invoicing center—located within the corporate headquarters facilities in Boston—in U.S. dollars. However, the actual goods are shipped directly to Cascade Mexico. The re-invoicing center in turn resells to Cascade Mexico in Mexican pesos. Consequentially, all operating units deal only in their own currency, and all transaction exposure lies with the re-invoicing center.

To avoid accusations of profit-shifting through transfer pricing, most re-invoicing centers resell at cost plus a small commission for their services. The resale price is frequently the manufacturer's price times the forward exchange rate for the date on which payment from the buyer is expected, although other combinations are possible. The commission covers the cost of the re-invoicing center but does not shift profits away from operating subsidiaries.

Exhibit 21.4 Use of a Re-Invoicing Center

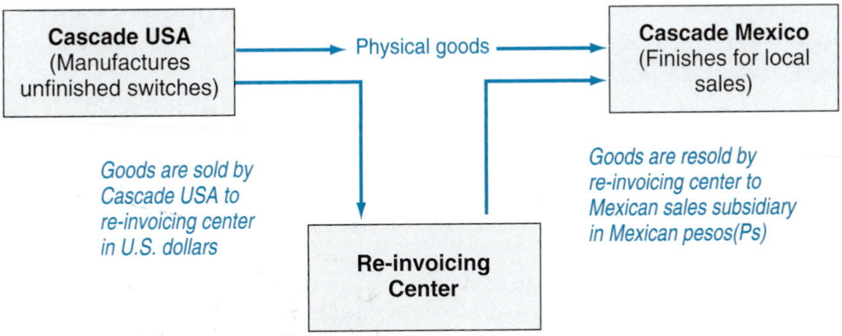

1. Cascade USA ships goods directly to the Mexican subsidiary.
2. The invoice by Cascade USA, which is denominated in U.S. dollars, is passed to the re-invoicing center.
3. The re-invoicing center takes legal title to the goods.
4. The re-invoicing center invoices Cascade Mexico in Mexican pesos, repositioning the currency exposure from both operating units to the re-invoicing center.

Advantages and Disadvantages of Re-Invoicing

There are three basic benefits arising from the creation of a re-invoicing center:

1. **Managing foreign exchange exposure.** The formation of the center allows the management of all foreign exchange transaction exposure for intracompany sales to be located in one place. Re-invoicing center personnel can develop a specialized expertise in choosing which hedging technique is best at any moment, and they are likely to obtain more competitive foreign exchange quotations from banks because they are dealing in larger transactions.
2. **Guaranteeing the exchange rate for future orders.** By guaranteeing the exchange rate for future orders, the re-invoicing center can set firm local currency costs in advance. This enables distribution subsidiaries to make firm bids to unrelated final customers, and to protect against the exposure created by a backlog of unfilled orders. Backlog exposure does not appear on the corporate books because the sales are not yet recorded. Sales subsidiaries can focus on their marketing activities and their performance can be judged without distortion because of exchange rate changes.
3. **Managing intra-subsidiary cash flows.** The center can manage intra-subsidiary cash flows, including leads and lags of payments. With a re-invoicing center, all subsidiaries settle intra-company accounts in their local currencies. The re-invoicing center need only hedge residual foreign exchange exposure.

The main disadvantage is that the benefits may not justify the agency cost. One additional corporate unit must be created, and a separate set of books must be kept. The initial setup cost can be high because existing order-processing procedures must be reprogrammed. The center will have an impact on the tax status and customs duties of all subsidiaries, as well as on the amount of foreign exchange business directed to local banks in each country. Establishment of a re-invoicing center is likely to bring increased scrutiny by tax authorities to be sure that it is not functioning as a tax haven. Consequently a variety of professional costs will be incurred for tax and legal advice, in addition to the costs of personnel operating the center.

SUMMARY

- The MNE is constantly striving to create shareholder value by maximizing the after-tax profitability of the firm. One dimension of this task is to reposition the profits of the firm, as legally and practically possible, in low-tax environments.
- Repositioning profits will allow the firm to increase the after-tax profits of the firm by lowering the tax liabilities of the firm with the same amount of sales.
- In addition to tax management, repositioning is useful when a MNE wishes to move cash flows or funds from where they are not needed to where they may be redeployed in more value-creating activities, or to minimize exposure to a potential currency collapse or potential political or economic crisis.
- IRS regulations provide three methods to establish arm's length prices: comparable uncontrolled prices, resale prices, and cost-plus calculations.
- All three methods are recommended for use in member countries by the Organization for Economic Cooperation and Development (OECD) Committee on Fiscal Affairs. In some cases, combinations of these three methods are used.

- Royalty fees are compensation for the use of intellectual property belonging to some other party. Royalties are usually a stated percentage of sales revenue (price times volume), so that the owner is compensated in proportion to the volume of sales.
- License fees are remuneration paid to the owners of technology, patents, trade names, and copyrighted material (including moving pictures, video tapes, compact disks, software, and books).
- License fees are usually based on a percentage of the value of the product or on the volume of production. As such, they are calculated independently of the amount of sales.
- International dividend policy now incorporates tax considerations, political risk, and foreign exchange risk, as well as a return for business guidance and technology.
- Dividends are the most tax-inefficient method for repatriating funds, because they are distributed on an after-tax basis. This means that the parent company will frequently be faced with the generation of excess foreign tax credits on a dividend.
- Remittance of license or royalty fees is on a pre-tax basis in the foreign subsidiary. The only tax typically applied is that of withholding, at a rate considerably below that of corporate income taxes.
- Firms can reduce both operating and transaction exposure by accelerating or decelerating the timing of payments that must be made or received in foreign currencies.
- To *lead* is to pay early. A firm holding a "soft" currency or that has debts denominated in a "hard" currency will lead by using the soft currency to pay the hard currency debts as soon as possible. The object is to pay the currency debts before the soft currency drops in value.
- To *lag* is to pay late. A firm holding a hard currency and having debts denominated in a soft currency will lag by paying those debts late, hoping that less of the hard currency will be needed. If possible, firms will also lead and lag their collection of receivables, collecting soft foreign currency receivables early and collecting hard foreign currency receivables later.
- A re-invoicing center is a separate corporate subsidiary that serves as a type of middle-man between the parent or related unit in one location and all foreign subsidiaries in a geographic region.

QUESTIONS

1. **Constraints on positioning funds.** Each of the following factors is sometimes a constraint on the free movement of funds internationally. Why would a government impose such a constraint? How might the management of a multinational argue that such a constraint is not in the best interests of the government that has imposed it?
   a. Government-mandated restrictions on moving funds out of the country.
   b. Withholding taxes on dividend distributions to foreign owners.
   c. Dual currency regimes, with one rate for imports and another rate for exports.
   d. Refusal to allow foreign firms in the country to net cash inflows and outflows into a single payment.
2. **Unbundling.** What does this term mean? Why would unbundling be needed for international cash flows from foreign subsidiaries, but not for domestic cash flows between related domestic subsidiaries and their parent?
3. **Conduits.** In the context of unbundling cash flows from subsidiary to parent, explain how each of the following creates a conduit. What are the tax consequences of each?
   a. Imports of components from the parent.

b. Payment to cover overhead expenses of parent managers temporarily assigned to the subsidiary.

c. Payment of royalties for the use of proprietary technology.

d. Subsidiary borrowing of funds on an intermediate or long-term maturity from the parent.

e. Payment of dividends to the parent.

4. **Transfer pricing motivation.** What is a transfer price and can a government regulate it? What difficulties and motives does a parent multinational firm face in setting transfer prices?

5. **Sister subsidiaries.** Subsidiary Alpha in Country Able faces a 40% income tax rate. Subsidiary Beta in Country Baker faces only a 20% income tax rate. At present, each subsidiary imports from the other an amount of goods and services exactly equal in monetary value to what each exports to the other. This method of balancing intra-company trade was imposed by a management keen to reduce all costs, including the costs (spread between bid and ask) of foreign exchange transactions. Both subsidiaries are profitable, and both could purchase all components domestically at approximately the same prices as they are paying to their foreign sister subsidiary. Does this seem like an optimal situation to you?

6. **Correct pricing.** Section 482 of the U.S. Internal Revenue Code specifies use of a "correct" transfer price, and the burden of proof that the transfer price is "correct" lies with the company. What guidelines exist for determining the proper transfer price?

7. **Over- and under-pricing.** Global Finance Perspective 21.1 lists over-priced and under-priced transactions in trade in 22 items with 19 separate countries. In theory, over-pricing would take place in U.S. imports when the country of export had a lower corporate tax rate than the United States, while under-pricing would take place in U.S. exports when the country of import had a higher corporate tax rate than the United States. Using the tax rates in Exhibit 17.2 in Chapter 17, test this hypothesis.

8. **Allocated fees – 1.** What are the differences between a license fee and a royalty fee? Do you think license and royalty fees should be covered by the tax rules that regulate transfer pricing? Why?

9. **Allocated fees – 2.** What is the difference between a "management fee," a "technical assistance fee," and a "license fee?" Should they be treated differently for income tax purposes?

10. **Distributed overhead.** What methods might the U.S. Internal Revenue Service use to determine if allocations of distributed overhead are being fairly allocated to foreign subsidiaries?

11. **Fee treatment.** In the context of unbundling cash flows from subsidiary to parent, why might a host government be more lenient in its treatment of fees than in its treatment of dividends? What difference does it make to the subsidiary and to the parent?

12. **Downstream tax rates.** Exhibit 20.1 in Chapter 20 shows that Argentina, Paraguay, and Uruguay all have a tax rate of 30%, while their neighbor Brazil has a tax rate of only 15%. All four of these River Plate (*Rio de la Plata*) countries trade with each other. What do you imagine happens in terms of the pricing of goods traded between Brazil and its neighbors? Could the tax differential have had anything to do with the roughly 40% drop in the value of the Argentine peso (from Ps1.00/$ to Ps1.70/$ over three days) in January 2002?

13 **Leading foreign payments.** List the motives that might cause a MNE to lead cash payments from one of its foreign subsidiaries to the parent.

14. **Lagging foreign payments.** List the motives that might cause a MNE to lag cash payments to one of its foreign subsidiaries.

15. **Re-invoicing centers.** If Jones Company "sells" its exports to a re-invoicing center in the Netherlands Antilles for dollars, and the Reinvoicing Center resells to a South African buyer for South African rand, what foreign exchange risk is carried by each of the entities? How are the goods shipped? Can Jones Company use the re-invoicing center to avoid income taxes or reposition cash balances?

PROBLEMS

1. **Cascade USA and Cascade Europe (A).** Continuing the analysis presented in Exhibit 21.3 within the chapter, what would be the impact on consolidated net income of Cascade if the European tax authorities implemented a tax reduction to 35%?

2. **Cascade USA and Cascade Europe (B).** Use the same analysis and spreadsheet from question 1 to analyze the impact of a reduction of the German income tax rate to 25%. How should Cascade alter its markup policy to take advantage of the new altered tax environment?

Kowloon Blade Company. Use the following company case to complete problems 3 through 5. Kowloon Blade Company (Hong Kong) exports razor blades to its wholly owned parent company, Cranfield Eversharp (Great Britain). Hong Kong tax rates are 16% and British tax rates are 30%. Kowloon calculates its profit per container as follows (all values in British pounds):

Constructing Price	Kowloon Blade	Cranfield Eversharp
Direct costs	£10,000	£16,100
Overhead	4,000	1,000
Total costs	£14,000	£17,100
Desired markup (15%)	2,100	2,565
Transfer price (sales price)	£16,100	£19,665
Income Statements (assumes a volume of 1,000 units)		
Sales revenue	£16,100,000	£19,665,000
Less total costs	(14,000,000)	(17,100,000)
Taxable income	£2,100,000	£2,565,000
Less taxes (16%)	(336,000)	(30%) (769,500)
Post-tax profit	£1,764,000	£1,795,500
Consolidated profit	£3,559,500	

3. **Kowloon Blade (A).** Corporate management of Cranfield Eversharp is considering repositioning profits within the multinational company. What happens to the profits of Kowloon Blade and Cranfield Eversharp, and the consolidated results of both if the markup at Kowloon was increased to 20% and the markup at Cranfield was reduced to 10%? What is the impact of this repositioning on consolidated tax payments?

4. **Kowloon Blade (B).** Encouraged by the results from the previous problem's analysis, corporate management of Cranfield Eversharp wishes to continue to reposition profit in Hong Kong. It is, however, facing two constraints. First, the final sales price in Great Britain must be £20,000 or less to remain competitive. Secondly, the British tax authorities, in working with Cranfield Eversharp's cost accounting staff, have established a maximum transfer price allowed (from Hong Kong) of £17,800. What combination of markups do you recommend for Cranfield Eversharp to institute? What is the impact of this repositioning on consolidated profits after-tax and total tax payments?

5. **Kowloon Blade (C).** Not to leave any potential tax repositioning opportunities unexplored, Cranfield Eversharp wants to combine the components of Problem 4 with a redistribution of overhead costs. If overhead costs could be reallocated between the two units, but still total £5,000 per unit, and maintain a minimum of £1,750 per unit in Hong Kong, what is the impact of this repositioning on consolidated profits after-tax and total tax payments?

6. **Balanced Tire Company.** Balanced Tire Company manufactures automobile tires for sale to retail outlets in the United States and, through a wholly owned distribution subsidiary, in neighboring Canada. Annual capacity of the U.S. factory is 700,000 tires per year, but present production is only 450,000, of which 300,000 are sold in the United States and 150,000 are exported to Canada. Federal and state income tax rates in both countries add up to 40%.

Within the United States, Balanced Tire sells to retail outlets for the U.S. dollar equivalent of C\$80 per tire. After-tax profit is equivalent to C\$10.80 per tire calculated as follows, with all prices expressed in the Canadian dollar equivalent of U.S. dollars:

Balanced Tire's U.S. profit calculation, expressed in Canadian dollars:

Balanced Tire's U.S. sales price per tire	C$80.00
Less direct labor in U.S.	20.00
Less direct material in U.S.	20.00
Less U.S. manufacturing overhead	12.00
Total manufacturing costs	52.00
U.S. factory margin	28.00
Less selling and administrative costs	10.00
Pre-tax profit per set	18.00
Less 40% U.S. income taxes	7.20
After-tax profit per tire in the U.S.	C$10.80

Direct labor consists of hourly payroll costs for factory workers, and direct material is for raw material purchased in the United States. Manufacturing overhead is a fixed cost that includes supervision and depreciation. Selling and administrative costs are fixed expenses for management salaries, office expenses and rent.

For its exports to Canada, Balanced Tire sells sets to its Canadian subsidiary at a U.S. dollar transfer price equal to C$56 per tire, this being U.S. manufacturing cost of C$52 plus a C$4 profit. Transportation and distribution costs add an additional C$2 per tire, and the tires are resold to Canadian retail outlets for C$80, the same equivalent price as in the United States. This price was arrived at independently, based on the following analysis (table below) of elasticity of demand in Canada:

In making this calculation, Balanced Tire determined that unit demand in Canada was a function only of the sales price. Hence it seemed self-evident to Balanced Tire's management that a transfer price to Canada of C$80 per tire maximized Canada's contribution to profits at a total figure of C$1,980,000.

a. Is Balanced Tire's present pricing strategy for Canada correct?

b. Assume Balanced Tire wants to divide profits on export sales evenly between Canada and the United States so as to avoid difficulties with either tax authority. What final transfer price and unit price in Canada should the firm adopt?

c. If Canada's income tax rate remains 40%, but the United States lowers its tax rate to 25%, should a new transfer price be adopted? What policy issues are involved?

7. **Surgical Tools, Inc.** Surgical Tools, Inc., of Illinois wants to set up a regular procedure for transferring funds from its newly opened manufacturing subsidiary in Korea to the United States. The precedent set by the transfer method or methods is likely to prevail over any government objections that might otherwise arise in future years. The Korean subsidiary manufactures surgical tools for export to all Asian countries. The following *pro forma* financial information portrays the results expected in the first full year of operations.

Balanced Tire

Accounts in Canadian dollars (C$)

Unit sales price in Canada	85.00	80.00	75.00	70.00	65.00
Less import	–56.00	–56.00	–56.00	–56.00	–56.00
Less shipping	–2.00	–2.00	–2.00	–2.00	–2.00
Unit profit before tax	27.00	22.00	17.00	12.00	7.00
Less 40% Canadian tax	–10.80	–8.80	–6.80	–4.80	–5.40
Unit profit after tax	16.20	13.20	10.20	7.20	4.20
Expected unit volume	110,000	150,000	180,000	250,000	400,000
Total profit (000)	1,782	1,980	1,836	1,800	1,680

Maximum profit is at a sales price of C$80.00.

Sales	Won2,684,000,000
Cash manufacturing expenses	1,342,000,000
Depreciation	335,500,000
Pre-tax profit	1,006,500,000
Korean taxes at 28%	281,820,000
Profit after taxes	Won724,680,000
Exchange rate:	Won 1342/$
Korean income tax rate	28%
U.S. income tax rate	34%

Surgical Tool's CFO is pondering the following approaches:

a. Declare a dividend of Won362,340,000, equal to 50% of profit after taxes. The dividend would be taxable in the United States after a gross-up for Korean taxes already paid.

b. Add a license fee of Won362,340,000 to the above expenses, and remit that amount annually. The license fee would be fully taxable in the United States.

8. FinFones, Ltd. FinFones, Ltd., of Helsinki, Finland manufactures automobile and marine telephones, which are sold to wholly owned distribution subsidiaries in many countries of the world. FinFones's CFO has been pondering appropriate transfer prices for sales to subsidiaries in the United States and Japan. Each cellular phone has direct labor costs of €12.50, direct material costs of €6.25, and overhead of €5.00. Phones are sold in Finland for €30.00 each and to FinFones's subsidiaries in the United States and Japan for €30.00 each, and are then resold for the local currency equivalent of €40.00. In the United States an additional US$3 of direct costs per phone are incurred in adjusting the phones for the American network. In Japan, the equivalent expense is ¥250. Current exchange rates and corporate income tax rates are (there are no withholding taxes):

	Exchange rate	Tax rate
Finland	———	30%
United States	$0.90/€	40%
Japan	¥108/€	25%

FinFones's CFO judges that transfer prices to the various subsidiaries could be raised or lowered 20% without causing a tax challenge to FinFones from Finnish, U.S., or Japanese tax authorities. Hence the manager wonders if FinFones should change the transfer price at which it sells to its subsidiaries.

a. What is FinFones's current consolidated after-tax profit per phone sold in the United States? In Japan?

b. For each country, would FinFones gain by raising its transfer price by 20%?

c. For each country, would FinFones gain by lowering its transfer price by 20%?

d. The U.S. dollar might weaken in the aftermath of the extended U.S. recession. How would this expectation influence the recommended transfer price to the United States?

9. Adams Corporation (A). Adams Corporation (U.S.), a recently divested unit of Pfizer and the owner of a series of valuable consumer brands such as Listerine and Halls, owns 100% of Adams Brazil, S.A. This year Adams Brazil, S.A., earned R$52,000,000, equal to $20,000,000 at the current exchange rate of R$2.60/$. The exchange rate is not expected to change.

Adams Corporation wants to transfer half of Brazilian earnings to the United States and wonders if this sum should be remitted 1) by a cash dividend of $10,000,000 or 2) by a cash dividend of $5,000,000 and a royalty of $5,000,000. Brazilian income taxes are 15% and U.S. income taxes are 30%. Which do you recommend and why?

10. Adams Corporation (B). The Brazilian government under President Lula has instituted a new tax policy aimed at encouraging foreign MNEs to come to Brazil but reinvest their profits in the country, rather than pulling them out. Assume that all of the same conditions exist as in the previous problem, but now assume Brazil has instituted the following withholding taxes on dividends, royalties, and licensing fee remittances:

Type of remittance	Withholding tax rate
Dividends	30%
Royalty payments	5%
License fees	5%

Which of the alternatives do you recommend Adams use in remitting the $10 million to Adams (U.S.)?

INTERNET EXERCISES

1. **Transfer pricing.** A number of international banks and consultancies provide ongoing advisory services on transfer pricing. KPMG-United States provides extensive services related to the proper and defensible pricing of products and services both domestically and internationally.

   KPMG-United States http://www.us.kpmg.com/ecs/tp.html

2. **International offshore financial centres (IOFCs).** There are a variety of IOFCs in many parts of the world. Conduct your own survey of their characteristics, qualities, and costs using the following web sites as a beginning.

   British Virgin Islands http://www.elanbvi.com/bviaffil2.html

   Labuan http://www.maybank.com.my/maybank.labuan.htm

   Malta http://www.u-net.com/metcowww

3. **NAFTA and multinational business.** The North American Free Trade Agreement (NAFTA) has enormous impacts on the conduct of business between Canada, the United States, and Mexico. For an update of the variety of regulatory implications and current tariff reduction progress visit the following web site.

   NAFTA Secretariat http://www.nafta-sec-alena.org

SELECTED READINGS

Al-Aaron, Mohammad F., Parvos Adam, and Sed. Akhter, "Transfer Pricing Determinants of U.S. Multinationals," *Journal of International Business Studies*, Third Quarter, 1990, pp. 409–425.

Barrett, M. Edgar, "Case of the Tangled Transfer Price," *Harvard Business Review*, May/June 1977, pp. 20–36, 176–178.

Dewenter, Kathryn L. and Vincent A. Warther, "Dividends, Asymmetric Information, and Agency Conflicts: Evidence from a Comparison of the Dividend Policies of Japanese and U.S. Firms," *Journal of Finance*, June 1998, Volume 53, No. 3, pp. 879–904.

MINI-CASE

Ford Asia-Pacific

Ford Motor Company's Asian Pacific regional headquarters, located in Hiroshima, Japan, had shown only marginal profitability in recent years. The unit's sales within Asia had suffered significantly as a result of the Asian crisis that began in July of 1997, and many of the major Asian retail markets had still not recovered in early 2001. In addition to sales within the region, the business unit also manufactured vehicles for export sales all over the world. One of the most important vehicle lines exported globally was the Ford Ranger pickup truck. The problem was that Ford's current transfer pricing practice made it nearly impossible for Ford Asia Pacific to tell whether the Ford Ranger line was actually making a profit.

The Ranger was manufactured in Thailand by Auto Alliance Thailand (AAT), a joint venture between Ford and Mazda. AAT was responsible for all material procurement, manufacturing, and finished vehicle assembly. AAT then sold the Ranger to Ford Trading Company (FTC), the global sales unit of Ford that served as the link between manufacturing and local distributors. FTC in turn sold the Ranger to the multitudes of distributors in dozens of countries. Ford's problem was how to set prices between the three units.

Ford's transfer pricing, shown in the accompanying exhibit, took the three units in the Ranger supply chain and worked toward the middle. Ford set retail prices for local distributors

Exhibit A The Ford Ranger: Transfer Pricing in Ford, Asia-Pacific

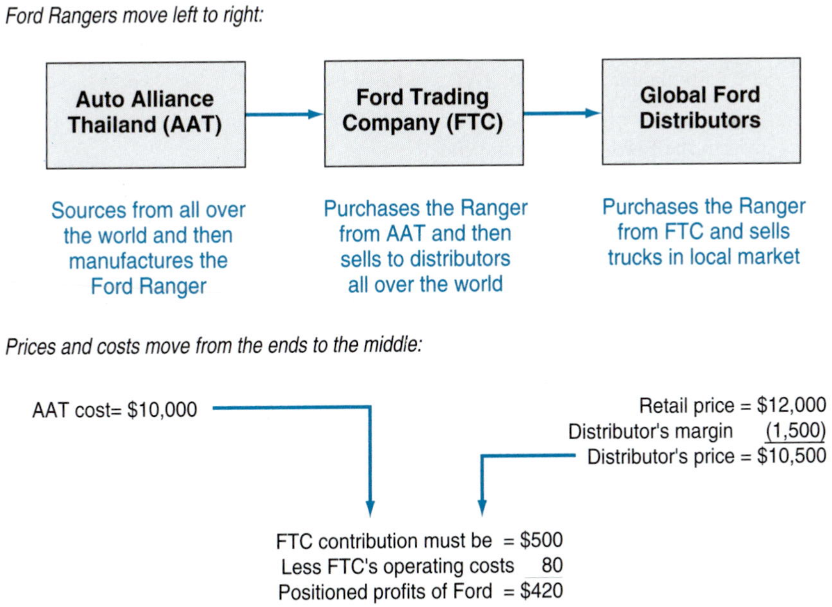
Ford Rangers move left to right:
Auto Alliance Thailand (AAT)
Ford Trading Company (FTC)
Global Ford Distributors
Sources from all over the world and then manufactures the Ford Ranger
Purchases the Ranger from AAT and then sells to distributors all over the world
Purchases the Ranger from FTC and sells trucks in local market
Prices and costs move from the ends to the middle:
AAT cost= $10,000
Retail price = $12,000
Distributor's margin (1,500)
Distributor's price = $10,500
FTC contribution must be = $500
Less FTC's operating costs 80
Positioned profits of Ford = $420

FTC sets the transfer price of the Ford Ranger to its distributors to guarantee them a margin, and simultaneously positions the majority of the value-chain profit in FTC.

twice a year. These prices were to be held. In turn, these prices less a guaranteed margin for local distributors were pushed back down to FTC. On the production end of the supply chain, at AAT, the costs plus margins for Rangers produced in Thailand were set four times a year. The price calculated was then used as the transfer price at which AAT sold the Ranger to FTC. FTC's profits were the residual spread between the price at which it bought from AAT and the price at which it sold to local distributors.

All was well until sales slowed and retailers began discounting prices in an effort to move inventory. These price cuts were then "validated" by Ford, which applied the standard distributor dollar margin to the vehicle even after the price was discounted. The revenue recognized by FTC was then at a lower rate, while the transfer price from the ground up at AAT was the same as before. FTC's profitability was reduced, if not eliminated. Given the role FTC played within the Ford value chain—as a buffer against cost or price pressures—this seemed appropriate.

But it wasn't that simple. FTC in Asia was part of the general business unit of Ford, Asia-Pacific. As Ford, Asia-Pacific came under increasing pressure from Detroit to return to profitability, pressure increased on FTC. Although the structure had been designed to have FTC serve as the locus of profit or loss in the value chain, the "loss" alternative was no longer acceptable. Given the multitude of discounted prices now arising from local distributors all over the world, it was no longer really possible to tell whether the Ford Ranger itself was a profitable vehicle. The question was, "Profitable by whose price?"

Case Questions

1. What possible advantages would Ford gain by positioning all profits and losses within the FTC business unit?
2. What types of incentives or disincentives does the transfer pricing structure described create with manufacturers like AAT and local distributors?
3. What would you suggest Ford do to improve the workings of its transfer pricing structure within the Ford Ranger value chain?

chapter 22

Working Capital Management in the MNE

WORKING CAPITAL MANAGEMENT IN A MULTINATIONAL ENTERPRISE REQUIRES MANAGING *CURRENT assets* (cash balances, accounts receivable, and inventory) and *current liabilities* (accounts payable and short-term debt) when faced with political, foreign exchange, tax, and liquidity constraints. The overall goal is to reduce funds tied up in working capital while simultaneously providing sufficient funding and liquidity for the conduct of global business. Working capital management should enhance return on assets and return on equity. It also should improve efficiency ratios and other performance measures.

This chapter presents working capital management in three segments. The first segment provides a detailed analysis of working capital management. It focuses on how the operating cycle of a business creates working capital needs and explains how this differs from the cash conversion cycle. It also defines the components of working capital and presents management guidelines for the MNE. The second segment of the chapter explores international cash management as practiced by MNEs, include multilateral netting and cash-pooling vehicles. The third and final segment describes how MNEs finance their working capital and cash needs through different forms of banking services offered in the global marketplace, as well as through the MNE's internal banking services.

Working Capital Management

The *operating cycle* of a business generates funding needs, cash inflows and outflows (the *cash conversion cycle*) and foreign exchange rate and credit risks. The funding needs generated by the operating cycle of the firm constitute *working capital*. The operating cycle of a business extends along a time-line from the first point at which a customer requests a price quotation to the final point at which payment is received from the customer for goods delivered. The *cash conversion cycle*, a subcomponent of the operating cycle, is that period of time extending between cash outflow for purchased inputs and materials and cash inflow from cash settlement.

Cascade Mexico's Operating Cycle

The operating and cash conversion cycles for our example, Cascade Mexico, are illustrated in Exhibit 22.1. We can decompose the operating cycle into five different periods, each with business, accounting, and potential cash flow implications.

Exhibit 22.1 Operating and Cash Cycles for Cascade Mexico

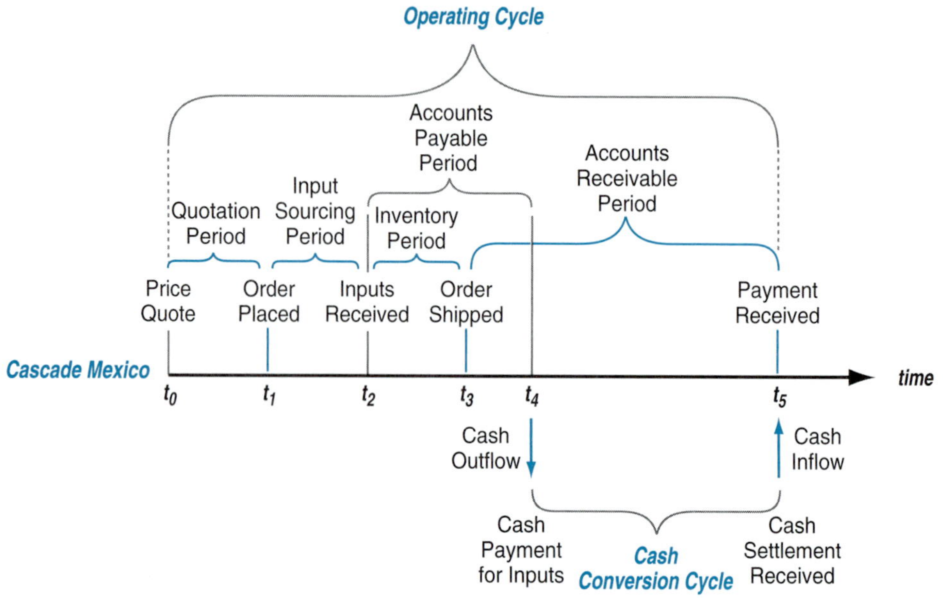

Quotation period. First noted in Chapter 8 when we introduced transaction exposure, the quotation period extends from the time of price quotation, t_0, to the point when the customer places an order, t_1. If the customer is requesting a price quote in foreign currency terms—for instance, in Chilean pesos—Cascade Mexico would now have a potential but uncertain foreign exchange transaction exposure during this period. The quotation itself is not listed on any of the traditional financial statements of the firm, although a firm like Cascade Mexico would keep a worksheet of quotations extended and their time periods.

Input sourcing period. Once the customer has accepted a quotation, the order is placed at time t_1. The buyer and seller sign a contract describing the product to be delivered, likely timing of delivery, conditions of delivery, and price and financing terms. At this time Cascade Mexico would order the material inputs it requires for the manufacture of the product that it does not currently hold in inventory. Depending on the individual sale, the buyer now makes a cash deposit or down payment that constitutes the first actual cash flow associated with the order, a cash inflow to Cascade Mexico. That cash flow initiates the cash conversion cycle for this transaction.

Inventory period. As it receives inputs, Cascade Mexico assembles and manufactures the goods. The length of time during this inventory manufacturing period, from t_1 to t_2, depends on the type of product (off-the-shelf versus custom-built), the supply-chain integration of Cascade Mexico with its various internal and external suppliers, and the technology employed by Cascade itself.

Accounts payable period. As inputs arrive during this period, Cascade lists them as material and component inventories on the left-hand side of its balance sheet, with corresponding accounts payable entries on the right-hand side. If the inputs are invoiced in foreign currencies, from

Cascade, a sister subsidiary, or external suppliers, they constitute foreign currency transaction exposures to Cascade Mexico.

Note that the accounts payable period shown in Exhibit 22.1 begins at the same time as the inventory period t_2, but may extend in time to t_4 after the inventory period ends. If Cascade Mexico's suppliers extend trade credit, Cascade Mexico would have the ability to postpone paying for the inventory for an extended period of time. Of course if Cascade Mexico chooses not to accept trade credit, it can pay for the inputs as delivered or within a few days of delivery. In this case, the accounts payable period would end before the inventory period—the manufacturing period—ends at time t_3. At whatever point in time Cascade Mexico chooses to settle its outstanding accounts payables, it incurs a cash outflow.

Accounts receivable period. When the goods are finished and shipped, Cascade Mexico records the transaction as a sale on its income statement and on its balance sheet as an account receivable. If it is a foreign currency–denominated invoice, the spot exchange rate on that date, t_4, is used to record the sale value in local currency. Cascade would then apply the exchange rate in effect on the date of cash settlement, t_5, in the calculation of any exchange gains and losses associated with the transaction—the transaction exposure.

The length of the accounts receivable period depends on the credit terms Cascade Mexico offers, the buyer's decision to accept trade credit or pay in cash, and country-specific and industry-specific payment practices. At cash settlement, Cascade Mexico receives a cash inflow (finally) in payment for goods delivered. At time t_5 the transaction is concluded and all accounting entries—inventory items, accounts payable, and accounts receivable—are eliminated.

Working Capital Funding

If Cascade Mexico's business continues to expand, it will continually add to inventories and accounts payable (A/P) in order to fill increased sales in the form of accounts receivable (A/R). These three components make up *net working capital* (NWC). The combination is "net" as a result of the spontaneous funding capability of accounts payable; accounts payable provide part of the funding for increased levels of inventory and accounts receivable.

$$\text{net working capital (NWC)} = (\text{A/R} + \text{inventory}) - (\text{A/P})$$

Because both A/R and inventory are components of current assets on the left-hand side of the balance sheet, as they grow they must be financed by additional liabilities of some form on the right-hand side of the balance sheet. A/P may provide a part of the funding. Exhibit 22.2 illustrates Cascade Mexico's net working capital. Note that we do not include cash or short-term debt as part of net working capital, although they are part of *gross working capital.* Cash and short-term debt are not spontaneous. Their determinants are discussed later in this chapter.

In principle, Cascade attempts to minimize its net working capital balance. It reduces A/R if collections are accelerated. It reduces inventories by carrying lower levels of both unfinished and finished goods, and by speeding the rate at which goods are manufactured—reduces so-called *cycle-time.* All of these measures must be balanced with customer costs. Sales could be reduced if inventories were not on hand, or if credit sales were reduced. On the other side of the balance sheet, NWC can be reduced by stretching A/P out. Again, if not done carefully, this could

Exhibit 22.2 Cascade Mexico's Net Working Capital Requirements

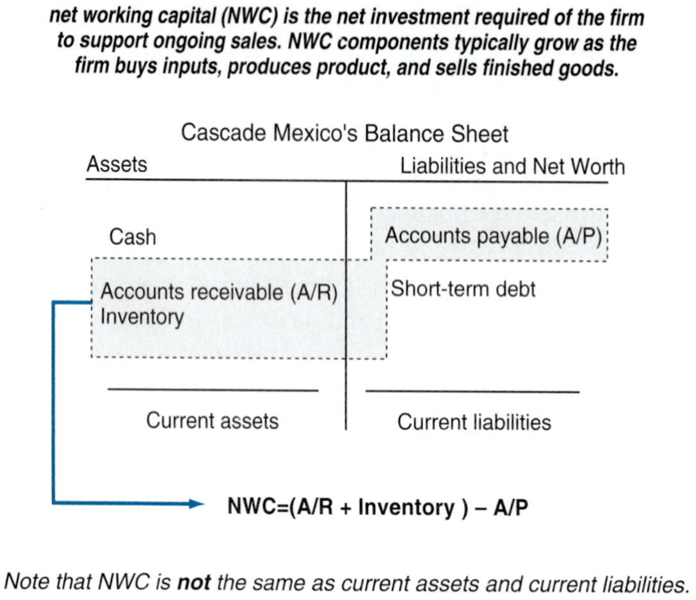
net working capital (NWC) is the net investment required of the firm to support ongoing sales. NWC components typically grow as the firm buys inputs, produces product, and sells finished goods.
Cascade Mexico's Balance Sheet
Assets
Liabilities and Net Worth
Cash
Accounts payable (A/P)
Accounts receivable (A/R)
Inventory
Short-term debt
Current assets
Current liabilities
NWC=(A/R + Inventory) – A/P
Note that NWC is not the same as current assets and current liabilities.

damage the company's relationship with its key suppliers, thereby reducing reliability and supply-chain partnerships.

A/P Versus Short-Term Debt

Exhibit 22.2 also illustrates one of the key managerial decisions for any subsidiary: Should A/P be paid off early, taking discounts if offered by suppliers? The alternative financing for NWC balances is short-term debt.

For example, payment terms in Mexico are quite long by global standards, often extending 60 to 90 days. Monterrey Electronics is one of Cascade Mexico's key suppliers. It delivers a shipment of electronic components and invoices Cascade Mexico Ps180,000. Monterrey Electronics offers credit terms of 5/10 net 60. This means that the entire amount of the A/P, Ps180,000, is due in 60 days. Alternatively, if Cascade Mexico wishes to pay within the first ten days, a 5% discount is given:

$$\text{Ps}180,000 \times (1 - 0.05) = \text{Ps}171,000$$

Cascade Mexico's CFO must decide which is the lower cost method of financing the NWC. Short-term debt in Mexican pesos, because of the relatively higher inflationary conditions common in Mexico, costs 24% per year.

What is the annual cost of the discount offered by Monterrey Electronics? Cascade Mexico is effectively paid 5% for giving up 50 days of financing (60 days less the 10-day period for discounts). Assuming a 365-day count for interest calculation:

$$\frac{365 \text{ days}}{50 \text{ days}} = 7.30$$

To calculate the effective annual interest cost of supplier financing, we must compound the 5% discount for 50 days 7.30 times, yielding a *cost of carry* provided by Monterrey Electronics of:

$$(1 + 0.05)^{7.3} = 1.428, \text{ or } 42.8\% \text{ per annum}$$

Monterrey Electronics is therefore charging Cascade Mexico 42.8% per year for financing. Alternatively, Cascade Mexico could borrow Mexican pesos from local banks in Monterrey for 24% per year, use the funds to pay Monterrey Electronics early, and take the discounts offered. The latter is the obvious choice in this case.

The choice between taking supplier-provided financing and short-term debt is not always purely a matter of comparing interest costs. In many countries, the subsidiaries of foreign MNEs have limited access to local currency debt. In other cases, the subsidiary may be offered funds from the parent company at competitive rates. We will return to this topic, internal banking, in the third section of this chapter.

Days Working Capital

A common method of benchmarking financial management practice is to calculate the NWC of the firm on a "days sales" basis. If the value of A/R, inventories, and A/P on the balance sheet is divided by the annual daily sales (annual sales/365 days), we can summarize the firm's NWC in the number of days of sales NWC constitutes. Exhibit 22.3 provides the results of a survey by *CFO Magazine* in both the United States and Europe in 2001 for the technology hardware and equipment industry segment.

We must use care in viewing the survey results. First, the days sales values are for the consolidated companies, not specific country-level subsidiaries. Therefore the averages could reflect very different working capital structures for individual subsidiaries of the firms listed. Secondly, without knowing the specific business and country areas included, we have difficulty evaluating the short-term financing decisions discussed in the previous section as made by management of the listed firms.

Despite these reservations, there are some clear differences between the U.S. and European averages, as well as between individual firms. The days working capital average for the selected U.S. firms of 29 days is less than half the 75 days for the European sample. A closer look at the subcategories indicates a radically sparse attitude toward inventory among the U.S. firms, averaging 19 days sales. Days sales held in accounts receivable at 53 days on average is nearly 20 days less than the European average of 70. Payables are essentially identical between the two groups. Clearly, European-based technology hardware firms are carrying a significantly higher level of net working capital in their financial structures than comparable U.S.-based firms to support the same level of sales.

Among individual firms, Dell Computer Corporation lives up to its popular billing as one of the most aggressive working capital managers across all industries. Dell's net working capital level

Exhibit 22.3 Days Working Capital for Selected U.S. and European Technology Hardware and Equipment Firms, 2001

Company	Country	Days Working Capital	Days Receivables	Days Inventory	Days Payables
Intel Corporation	U.S.	48	47	21	20
Cisco Systems	U.S.	54	46	20	12
Dell Computer	U.S.	(2)	41	6	49
Texas Instruments	U.S.	34	65	32	63
Applied Materials	U.S.	41	82	52	93
Apple Computer	U.S.	2	48	2	48
Sun MicroSystems	U.S.	58	67	12	21
Gateway	U.S.	0	25	8	33
Average	U.S.	29	53	19	42
ST Microelectronics France- Italy	58	65	52	59	
Nokia	Finland	66	72	31	37
Philips Electronics	Netherlands	71	59	51	39
GN Store Nord	Denmark	100	92	40	32
Spirent	United Kingdom	107	66	63	22
Getronics	Netherlands	51	80	20	49
Infinecon Tech	Germany	75	57	69	51
Average	Europe	75	70	47	41

Source: CFO Magazine, 2001 Working Capital Survey, July 2, 2001, and *CFO Europe Magazine*, 2001 Working Capital Survey, July/August 2001. Days Working Capital = Days Receivables + Days Inventory–Days Payables.

of a negative 2 days indicates exactly what it says—a level of A/P that surpasses the sum of receivables and inventory. Even with that accomplishment, its inventory days of 6 is still three times that of Apple Computer's 2 days in inventory.

Intra-Firm Working Capital

The MNE itself poses some unique challenges in the management of working capital. Many multinationals manufacture goods in a few specific countries and then ship the intermediate products to other facilities globally for completion and distribution. The payables, receivables, and inventory levels of the various units are a combination of intra-firm and inter-firm. The varying business practices observed globally regarding payment terms—both days and discounts—create severe mismatches in some cases.

For example, Exhibit 22.4 illustrates the challenges in working capital management faced by Cascade Mexico. Because Cascade Mexico purchases inputs from Cascade USA, and then uses additional local material input to finish the products for local distribution, it must manage two different sets of payables. Cascade USA sells intra-firm on common U.S. payment terms, net 30 days. Local suppliers in Mexico, however, use payment terms closer to Mexican norms of 60 days net

Exhibit 22.4 Cascade's Multinational Working Capital Sequence

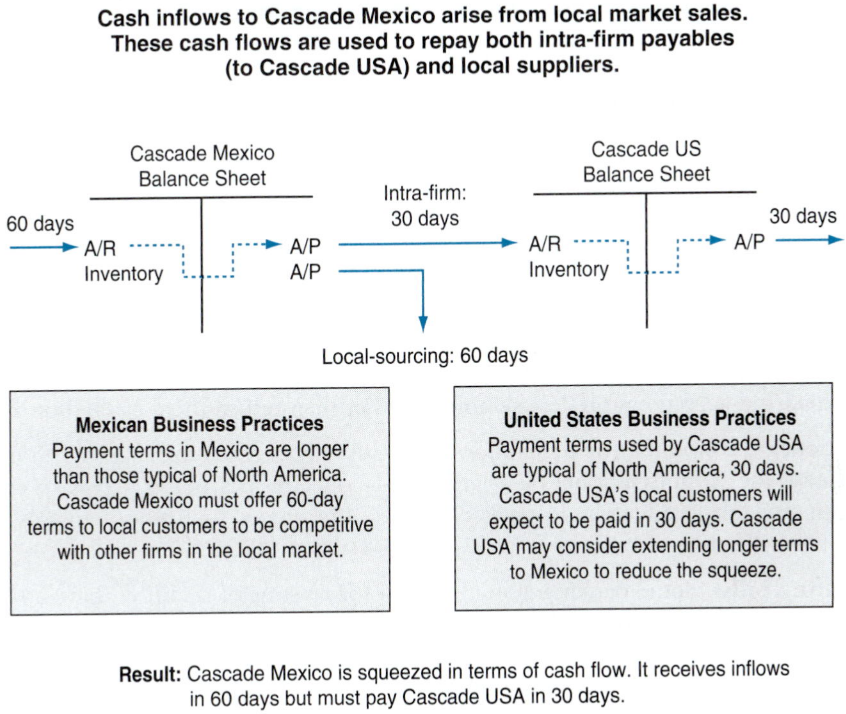
Cash inflows to Cascade Mexico arise from local market sales. These cash flows are used to repay both intra-firm payables (to Cascade USA) and local suppliers.
Cascade Mexico Balance Sheet
60 days
A/R
Inventory
A/P
A/P
Intra-firm: 30 days
Local-sourcing: 60 days
Cascade US Balance Sheet
A/R
Inventory
A/P
30 days
Mexican Business Practices
Payment terms in Mexico are longer than those typical of North America. Cascade Mexico must offer 60-day terms to local customers to be competitive with other firms in the local market.
United States Business Practices
Payment terms used by Cascade USA are typical of North America, 30 days. Cascade USA's local customers will expect to be paid in 30 days. Cascade USA may consider extending longer terms to Mexico to reduce the squeeze.
Result: Cascade Mexico is squeezed in terms of cash flow. It receives inflows in 60 days but must pay Cascade USA in 30 days.

(although this is in many cases still quite short for Mexican practices, which have been known to extend as long as 180 days). Similarly, since the customers of Cascade Mexico are Mexican, they expect the same common payment terms of 60 days. Cascade Mexico is then "squeezed," having to pay Cascade USA much faster than it pays other local suppliers and long before it receives cash settlement from its customers.

In addition to Cascade's need to determine intra-firm payment practices that do not put undue burdens on its foreign subsidiaries, the question of currency of invoice will also be extremely important. If Cascade Mexico sells only domestically, it does not have natural inflows of U.S. dollars or other hard currencies. It earns only Mexican pesos. If Cascade USA then invoices it for inputs in U.S. dollars, Cascade Mexico will be constantly short dollars and will incur continuing currency management costs. Cascade USA should invoice in Mexican pesos and manage the currency exposure centrally (possibly through a re-invoicing center, as discussed in Chapter 21).

Managing Receivables

A firm's operating cash inflow is derived primarily from the collection of accounts receivable. Multinational accounts receivable are created by two separate types of transactions: sales to related subsidiaries and sales to independent or unrelated buyers.

Independent customers. Management of accounts receivable from independent customers requires two types of decisions: In what currency should the transaction be denominated, and what should be the terms of payment? Domestic sales are almost always denominated in the local currency. At issue is whether export sales should be denominated in the currency of the exporter, of the buyer, or of a third country. Competition or custom will often dictate the answer, but if negotiating room exists the seller prefers to price and to invoice in the strongest currency. An informed buyer prefers to pay in the weakest currency.

Payment terms. Terms of payment are another bargaining factor. Considered by themselves, receivables from sales in weak currencies should be collected as soon as possible to minimize loss of exchange value between sales date and collection date. Accounts receivable resulting from sales in hard currencies may be allowed to remain outstanding longer. In fact, if the seller is expecting an imminent devaluation of its home currency, it might want to encourage slow payment of its hard currency receivables, especially if the home government requires immediate exchange of foreign currency receipts into the home currency. An alternative, if legal, would be for the seller to accept the proceeds abroad and keep them on deposit abroad rather than return them to the home country.

In inflationary economies, the demand for credit usually exceeds the supply. Often, however, a large business (be it multinational or a large local concern) has better access to the limited, cheaper credit available locally than do smaller domestic businesses, such as local distributors, retail merchants, or smaller manufacturers.

Self-liquidating bills. Some banking systems, often for reasons of tradition, have a predilection toward self-liquidating, discountable bills. In many European countries, it is easier to borrow from a bank on the security of bills generated from sales (receivables in negotiable form) than on the security of physical inventory. Napoleon is alleged to have had a philosophy that no good French merchant should be required to wait for funds if good merchandise has been sold to good people, provided a document exists showing sales of the items. The document must have the signature of the buyer and the endorsement of the seller and the rediscounting bank. Thus in France it is often possible to reduce net investment in receivables to zero by selling entirely on trade acceptances that can be discounted at the bank.

The European use of discountable bills has a very real rationale behind it. According to European commercial law, based on the "Code Napoleon," the claim certified by the signature of the buyer on the bill is separate from the claim based on the underlying transaction. For example, a bill is easily negotiable, because objections about the quality of the merchandise by the buyer do not affect the claim of the bill holder. In addition, defaulted bills can be collected through a particularly speedy judicial process that is much faster than the collection of normal receivables.

Other terms. In many countries, government bodies facilitate inventory financing in the guise of receivable financing by extending export credit or by guaranteeing export credit from banks at advantageous interest rates. When the term of the special export financing can be extended to match the payment of the foreign purchaser, the foreign purchaser is in effect able to finance its inventory through the courtesy of the exporter's government.

In some environments, credit terms extended by manufacturers to retailers are of such long maturities as to constitute "purchase" of the retailer, such "purchase" being necessary to build an operational distribution system between manufacturer and ultimate customer. In Japan, for example, customer payment terms of 120 days are fairly common, and a manufacturer's sales effort is not competitive unless sufficient financial aid is provided to retailers to make it possible or beneficial for them to buy the manufacturer's product. Financial aid is reported to take the form of outright purchase of the retailer's capital stock, working capital loans, equipment purchase, subsidy or loan, and consideration of payment terms. Such manufacturer-supplied financing is a normal way of doing business in Japan—and contributes to the lack of domestic competition prevalent in that country.

Inventory Management

Operations in inflationary, devaluation-prone economies sometimes force management to modify its normal approach to inventory management. In some cases, management may choose to maintain inventory and reorder levels far in excess of what would be called for in an economic order-quantity model.

Anticipating devaluation. Under conditions in which local currency devaluation is likely, management must decide whether to build up inventory of imported items in anticipation of the expected devaluation. After the devaluation, imported inventory will cost more in local currency terms. One trade-off is a higher holding cost because of the bloated level of inventory and high local interest rates that normally reflect the expected devaluation. A less obvious trade-off is the possibility that local government will enforce a price freeze following devaluation. This freeze would prevent the imported inventory from being sold for an appropriate markup above its now-higher replacement value. Still worse, the devaluation may not occur as anticipated, leaving management holding an excessive level of inventory until it can be worked down. Disposing of excessive inventory will be particularly painful if competitors have followed the same strategy of speculating on imported inventory.

Anticipating price freezes. To circumvent an anticipated price freeze, management can establish the local currency price of an imported item at a high level, with actual sales being made at a discount from this posted price. In the event of a devaluation, sales continue at the posted prices but discounts are withdrawn. This technique circumvents the price freeze only if that freeze is expressed in terms of posted rather than effective price. In any event it provides no protection against competitive price squeezes. An alternative is to sell at the posted price but increase selling, promotion, or other marketing mix activities, which can later be reduced.

If imported inventory is a commodity, another strategy is to purchase it in the forward market. Then if local prices are frozen, the forward contract can be sold abroad for the same currency in which it is denominated. On the other hand, if local price controls are based on a fixed markup over cost, the buyer can exercise the forward contract and import the commodity at the now-higher local currency cost, which becomes the basis for the markup. If options on the commodity are available, the firm can achieve the same benefit. The certain cost of the option should be compared with the uncertain trading gain or loss on the forward contract.

Free-trade zones and free industrial zones. A *free-trade zone* combines the old idea of duty-free ports with legislation that reduces or eliminates customs duties to retailers or manufacturers who structure their operations to benefit from the technique. Income taxes may also be reduced for operations in a free-trade zone. The old duty-free ports were typically in the dock area of major seaports, where goods were held, duty free, until the owner was ready to deliver them within the country. Modern free-trade zones, by comparison, are often located away from a port area. For example, the Italian firm of Olivetti has such a zone in Harrisburg, Pennsylvania.

Free-trade zones function in several ways. As mentioned, they may be a place to offload merchandise for subsequent sale within the country where the zone is located. An example is a storage area for imported Toyota automobiles in the Port of Los Angeles. A large quantity of differentiated models can be held until sold by a dealer, at which time the cars are "imported" into the United States from the free-trade zone. The advantage is that a variety of models can be kept near the point of sale for quick delivery, but import duties need be paid only when the merchandise passes from the zone into California.

In a second type of zone, components are assembled for subsequent sale within the country where the zone is located. An example is the Mercedes assembly line in Alabama. Components are imported into the free-trade zone, where assembly work is finished. The import duty is paid only when the finished car is removed from the zone. Furthermore, the duty is lower than it would be for a finished car, because the charges on components are less than the charge on a finished vehicle.

A third type of zone is a full-fledged manufacturing center with a major portion of its output reexported out of the country. Two examples are Penang, Malaysia, and Madagascar, where such zones are officially designated "Free Industrial Zones." In Penang, companies as diverse as Dell Computers, National Semiconductor, Sony, Bosch, and Trane Air Conditioning manufacture final products. A major portion of production is reexported, avoiding Malaysian customs altogether but providing jobs for Malaysian workers and engineers. The portion of production sold in Malaysia is assessed duties only on the components originally imported. However, the variety of firms permits one to buy from another; Dell buys Pentium chips from Intel and disk drives from Seagate, both of which are located less than a mile from the Dell plant.

International Cash Management

International cash management is the set of activities determining the levels of cash balances held throughout the MNE (cash management) and the facilitation of its movement cross-border (*settlements* and *processing*). These activities are typically handled by the international treasury of the MNE.

Cash Management

The level of cash maintained by an individual subsidiary is determined independent of the working capital management decisions we have discussed. Cash balances, including marketable securities, are held partly to enable normal day-to-day cash disbursements and partly to protect against unanticipated variations from budgeted cash flows. These two motives are called the *transaction motive* and the *precautionary motive.*

Cash disbursed for operations is replenished from two sources: 1) internal working capital turnover and 2) external sourcing, traditionally short-term borrowing. Short-term borrowing can also be "negative," as when the firm uses excess cash to repay outstanding short-term loans. In general, individual subsidiaries of MNEs typically maintain only minimal cash balances necessary to meet the transaction purposes. Efficient cash management aims to reduce cash tied up unnecessarily in the system, without diminishing profit or increasing risk, so as to increase the rate of return on invested assets. All firms, both domestic and multinational, engage in some form of the following fundamental steps:

Planning. A financial manager anticipates cash flows over future days, weeks, or months by preparing a comprehensive cash budget showing expected inflows, outflows, and the net of the two. The net flow increases or decreases expected liquidity. Ideally the cash budget is prepared on a spreadsheet program to allow simulation of alternate liquidity positions should key variables change. The two most common changing variables are sales volume, leading to changes in the amount of inventories and receivables, and changes in average collection period. MNEs have an added variable, changing exchange rates, which cause the quantity of funds paid or received in one currency to change when measured in another. A MNE can prepare three cash budgets: one for each individual national entity, one for each currency used within the system, and one for the worldwide entity as a whole. The latter necessitates agreement on an intra-corporate exchange rate to use for internal budget purposes. This rate is inherently a forecast.

Collection. Cash on its way to the firm should be collected as soon as possible. The normal technique is to shorten the time lag between the date on which a customer remits payment and the date on which the funds clear the banking system and are available for disbursement. Domestic examples include decisions about addresses to which payments are sent and the use of lock boxes, both of which are often determined by the efficiency of the local postal system. Internationally, the country to which payment is directed and the availability of clearing facilities within a multinational banking system are important.

Repositioning. Once cash has been collected, it must be moved within the worldwide organization to the geographic location and specific currency needed. Techniques to reposition cash were the topic of Chapter 21.

Disbursement. A plan must be designed to disburse cash. Steps include avoiding unnecessary early payment (so as to maintain maximum balances with one's own bank), maximizing float (the time it takes for the firm's own checks to clear), and selecting a disbursement bank that will provide a wide range of services and credit. A MNE must decide whether disbursements are to be handled at each local entity or whether they should be managed from a central location and routed through a bank. The currency of disbursement must be determined, although this is normally negotiated beforehand.

Covering cash shortages. Foreign subsidiaries have their own needs, determined by their individual cash budgets. Across the MNE, an anticipated or actual cash shortage in one subsidiary may be covered if that subsidiary borrows locally or if another subsidiary remits funds to the cash-deficit subsidiary. The choice between these two alternatives is often the consequence of the organizational decision to have subsidiaries "stand on their own two feet" or develop an integrated intersubsidiary system of cash management. If the firm chooses short-term borrowing, it must choose the currency to be borrowed; this might be the currency needed or the currency in which future cash flows will be received. The borrowing entity must also be designated, since one subsidiary (presumably in a low real interest rate location) can borrow on behalf of a sister subsidiary (in a higher real interest rate location) and then lend internally to the sister subsidiary.

Investing surplus cash. If a subsidiary generates surplus cash, the MNE must decide whether that subsidiary handles its own short-term liquidity (again, "standing on its own two feet") or whether all surplus funds in the organization should be controlled from a central location.

International Cash Settlements and Processing

Multinational business increases the complexity of making payments and settling cash flows between related and unrelated firms. Over time a number of techniques and services have evolved that simplify and reduce the costs of making these cross-border payments. We focus here on four such techniques: wire transfers, cash pooling, payment netting, and electronic fund transfers.

Wire Transfers

Although there are a variety of computer-based networks for effecting international transactions and settlements, two have come to dominate the international financial sector: CHIPS and SWIFT. The primary distinction among systems is whether they are for secure communications alone or for actual transfer and settlement.

CHIPS. CHIPS, the Clearing House Interbank Payment System, is a computerized network that connects major banks globally. CHIPS is owned and operated by its member banks, making it the single largest privately operated and final payments system in the world. Developed in 1970 when international currency transactions were dominated by the U.S. dollar, CHIPS has continued to dominate the transfer and settlement of U.S. dollar transactions for more than 30 years.

CHIPS is actually a subsidiary of the New York Clearing House, the oldest and largest payments processor of bank transactions. The New York Clearing House was first established in 1853 to provide a central place—a *clearinghouse*—where all banks in New York City could daily settle transactions, such as the many personal checks written by private individuals and corporations, among themselves. CHIPS itself is simply a computer-based evolutionary result of this need. The soundness of the New York Clearing House's activities are obvious considering it managed a large part of the U.S. monetary supply prior to the creation of the Federal Reserve System in 1913. The CHIPS system itself served as the basis for global standards for netting multiple currency payments put into place by the Bank for International Settlements as recently as 1990.

As of November 2001, CHIPS was transferring an average of $1.2 trillion daily. It is estimated that over 95% of interbank transactions in dollars globally occur over CHIPS. Because banks are still the primary financial service provider for MNEs, businesses transferring payments both interfirm and intra-firm globally use banks for effecting the payments, and the banks in turn utilize CHIPS. As illustrated by Exhibit 22.5, the volume of transactions handled by CHIPS grew constantly from 1970 to 1998 without interruption. The post-Asian crisis period of 1998–1999, combined with the introduction of the euro, has reduced the level of these international cash transactions in recent years.

SWIFT. The Society for Worldwide Interbank Financial Telecommunications, SWIFT, also facilitates the wire transfer settlement process globally. Whereas CHIPS actually clears financial transactions, SWIFT is purely a communications system. By providing a secure and standardized transfer process, SWIFT has greatly reduced the errors and associated costs of effecting international cash transfers.

SWIFT currently carries approximately 1.2 billion messages per year, with an average daily transaction value of $6 million. Its financial messaging services are used by over 7,000 financial institutions in 194 countries. In recent years, SWIFT has expanded its messaging services beyond banks to broker-dealers and investment managers. In the mid-1990s, its services gained wider

Exhibit 22.5 Average Daily Dollar Amount Handled by CHIPS (billions of U.S. dollars)

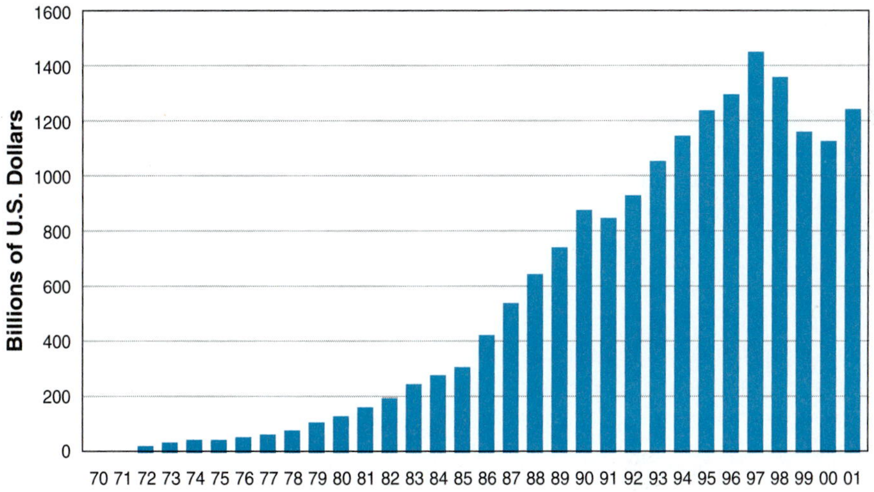

Source: Clearing House Interbank Payment Systems, http://www.chips.org (April 2002).

breadth as SWIFT expanded market infrastructure to payments in treasury, derivatives, and securities and trade services. It is now in the forefront of the evolution of Internet-based products and services for e-payments, expanding beyond banks to non–financial sector customers conducting business-to-business electronic commerce.

Cash Pooling and Centralized Depositories

Any business with widely dispersed operating subsidiaries can gain operational benefits by centralizing cash management. Internationally, the procedure calls for each subsidiary to hold minimum cash for its own transactions and no cash for precautionary purposes. However, the central pool has authority to override this general rule. All excess funds are remitted to a central cash depository, where a single authority invests the funds in such currencies and money market instruments as best serve the worldwide firm.

A central depository provides a MNE with at least four advantages:

1. Obtaining information
2. Holding precautionary cash balances
3. Reducing interest rate costs
4. Locating cost in desirable financial centers

Information advantage. A central depository's size gives it an advantage in obtaining information. The depository should be located in one of the world's major financial centers so information needed for opinions about the relative strengths and weaknesses of various currencies can be obtained easily. Rate of return and risk information on alternative investments in each currency and facilities for executing orders must also be available. The information logic of centralization is that an office that specializes in and operates with larger sums of money can get better information from banks, brokers, and other financial institutions, as well as better service in executing orders.

Funds held in a central pool can be returned quickly to any operating subsidiary needing cash, either by wire transfer or through a worldwide bank credit line. The money center bank wires its branch office in the particular country to advance emergency funds to the local subsidiary. Multinational banks can provide same-day credit for deposits from MNEs or their subsidiaries in the local branches of the banks. Float is reduced and lost payments avoided.

Precautionary balance advantage. A second reason for holding all precautionary balances in a central pool is that the MNE can then reduce the pool in size without any loss in the level of protection. Quad Corporation U.K., for example, has continental subsidiaries in France, Belgium, and Germany. Assume each of these subsidiaries maintains its own precautionary cash balance equal to its expected cash needs, plus a safety margin of three standard deviations of historical variability of actual cash demands. Also assume that cash needs are normally distributed in each country, and the needs are independent from one country to another. Three standard deviations means there exists a 99.87% chance that actual cash needs will be met; that is, only a 0.13% chance that any European subsidiary will run out of cash.

Cash needs of the individual subsidiaries, and the total precautionary cash balances held, are shown in Exhibit 22.6. Total precautionary cash balances held by Quad de France, Quad Belge, and Deutscheland Quad add up to $46,000,000, consisting of $28,000,000 in expected cash needs, and $18,000,000 in idle cash balances (the sum of three standard deviations of individual expected cash balances) held as a safety margin.

What would happen if the three Quad subsidiaries maintained all precautionary balances in a single account with Quad U.K. in London? Because variances are additive when probability distributions are independent (see footnote *b* to Exhibit 22.6), cash needed would drop from $46,000,000 to $39,224,972, calculated as follows:

Centralized cash balance	=	*Sum of expected cash needs*	+	*Three standard deviations of expected sum*
	=	$28,000,000	+	(3 × $3,741,657)
	=	$28,000,000	+	$11,224,972
	=	$39,224,972		

A budgeted cash balance three standard deviations above the aggregate expected cash need requires only $11,224,972 in potentially idle cash, as opposed to the previous cash balance of $18,000,000. Quad saves $6,755,028 in cash balances without reducing its safety.

Interest rate advantage. A third advantage of centralized cash management is that one subsidiary will not borrow at high rates at the same time that another holds surplus funds idle or invests them at low rates. Managers of the central pool can locate the least expensive locations to borrow and the most advantageous returns to be earned on excess funds. When additional cash is

Exhibit 22.6 Decentralized Versus Centralized Cash Depositories

Decentralized cash depositories

Subsidiary	**Expected cash need (A)**	**One standard deviation (B)**	**Cash balance budgeted for adequate protection[a] (A + 3B)**
Quad de France	$10,000,000	$1,000,000	$13,000,000
Quad Belge	6,000,000	2,000,000	12,000,000
Deutscheland Quad	12,000,000	3,000,000	21,000,000
Total	$ 28,000,000	$ 6,000,000	$46,000,000

Centralized cash depository

Subsidiary	**Expected cash need (A)**	**One standard deviation (B)**	**Cash balance budgeted for adequate protection[a] (A + 3B)**
Quad de France	$10,000,000		
Quad Belge	6,000,000		
Deutscheland Quad	12,000,000		
Total	$28,000,000	$ 3,741,657[b]	$39,224,972

[a] Adequate protection is defined as the expected cash balance plus three standard deviations, assuming that the cash flows of all three individual affiliates are normally distributed.

[b] The standard deviation of the expected cash balance of the centralized depository is calculated as follows:

$$\text{Standard deviation} = \sqrt{(1,000,000)^2 + (2,000,000)^2 + (3,000,000)^2} = \$3,741,657$$

needed, the central pool manager determines the location of such borrowing. A local subsidiary manager can avoid borrowing at a rate above the minimum available to the pool manager. If the firm has a worldwide cash surplus, the central pool manager can evaluate comparative rates of return in various markets, transaction costs, exchange risks, and tax effects.

Location. Central money pools are usually maintained in major money centers such as London, New York, Zurich, Singapore, and Tokyo. Additional popular locations for money pools include Liechtenstein, Luxembourg, the Bahamas, and Bermuda. Although these countries do not have strong diversified economies, they offer most of the other prerequisites for a corporate financial center: freely convertible currency, political and economic stability, access to international communications, and clearly defined legal procedures. Their additional advantage as so-called *tax havens* is also desirable.

The need for a centralized depository system means that multinational banks have an advantage over single-country banks in designing and offering competitive services. However, single-country banks can operate in the system if the desired results can still be achieved, for the essence of the operation is centralized information and decisions. MNEs can place actual funds in as many banks as they desire.

Multilateral Netting

Multilateral netting is defined as the process that cancels via offset all or part of the debt owed by one entity to another related entity. Multilateral netting of payments is useful primarily when a large number of separate foreign exchange transactions occur between subsidiaries in the normal course of business. Netting reduces the settlement cost of what would otherwise be a large number of crossing spot transactions.

Multilateral netting is an extension of bilateral netting. Staying with our corporation example, assume Quad Belge owes Deutscheland Quad $5,000,000 and Deutscheland Quad simultaneously owes Quad Belge $3,000,000. A bilateral settlement calls for a single payment of $2,000,000 from Belgium to Germany and the cancellation, via offset, of the remainder of the debt.

A multilateral system is an expanded version of this simple bilateral concept. Assume that payments are due between Quad's European operations at the end of each month. Each obligation reflects the accumulated transactions of the prior month. These obligations for a particular month might be as shown in Exhibit 22.7.

Without netting, Quad Belge, for example, makes three separate payments and receives three separate receipts at the end of the month. If Quad Belge paid its intracompany obligations daily, or even weekly, rather than accumulating a balance to settle at the end of the month, it would gen-

Exhibit 22.7 Multilateral Matrix Before Netting (thousands of U.S. dollars)

The Four European Subsidiaries of Quad Corporation

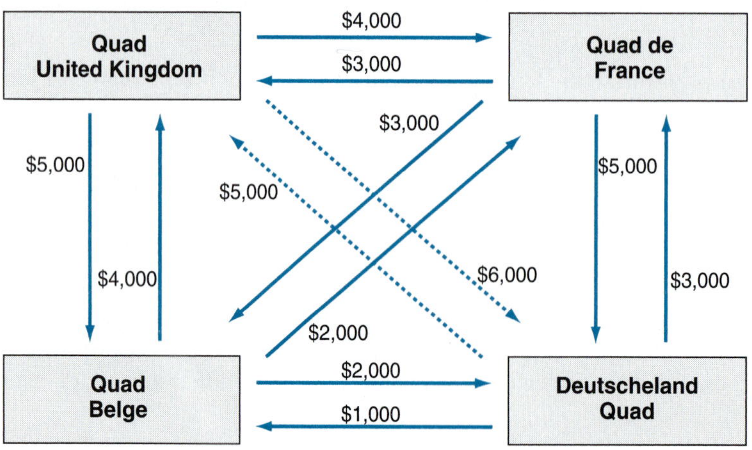

Prior to netting, the four sister subsidiaries of Quad Corporation have numerous intra-firm payments between them. Each payment results in transfer charges.

erate a multitude of costly small bank transactions every day. The daily totals would add up to the monthly accumulated balances shown in the diagram.

In order to reduce bank transaction costs, such as the spread between foreign exchange bid and ask quotations and transfer fees, some MNEs such as Quad establish in-house multilateral netting centers. Other firms contract with banks to manage their netting system. Assume that Quad Europe's net intracompany obligations for a given month can be summarized as in Exhibit 22.8.

Note that payment obligations and expected receipts both add up to $43,000,000, because one subsidiary's debts are another's receivable. If the cost of foreign exchange transactions and transfer fees were 0.5%, the total cost of settlement would be $205,000. Using information from the netting matrix in Exhibit 22.8, the netting center at Quad U.K. can order three payments to settle the entire set of obligations. Quad U.K. will itself remit $3,000,000 to Deutscheland Quad, and Quad de France will be instructed to send $1,000,000 each to Quad Belge and Deutscheland Quad. Total foreign exchange transfers are reduced to $5,000,000, and transaction costs at 0.5% are reduced to $25,000. This is shown in Exhibit 22.9.

Some countries limit or prohibit netting. Others permit netting on a "gross payment" basis only: For a single settlement period, all payments may be combined into a single payment, and all receipts will be received as a single transfer. However, these two payments may not be netted and thus must pass through the local banking system. The reason for such a requirement is usually a desire to subsidize local banks by forcing firms with a significant international business to pay for unnecessary transactions (often these are foreign rather than domestic firms).

Financing Working Capital

All firms need to finance working capital. The normal sources of funds for financing short-term working capital are accounts payable to suppliers and loans against bank credit lines. In some countries, such as the United States, borrowing is done by the firm issuing notes payable to banks and other creditors. In other countries, short-term borrowing is done on an "overdraft" basis. A firm is allowed to overdraw its checking account up to the limit of its credit line. No compensating deposit balances are required, in contrast to the U.S. system, which calls for compensating deposit balances. In all cases, permanent working capital requirements, as opposed to seasonal needs, are at least partially financed with long-term debt and equity.

Exhibit 22.8 Calculation of Quad Europe's Intra-Subsidiary Net Obligations (thousands of U.S. dollars)

	Paying Subsidiary					
Receiving Subsidiary	**U.K.**	**Belgium**	**France**	**Germany**	**Total Receipts**	**Net Receipts (payments)**
Quad U.K.	—	$4,000	$3,000	$5,000	$12,000	($3,000)
Quad Belge	5,000	—	3,000	1,000	9,000	$1,000
Quad de France	4,000	2,000	—	3,000	9,000	($2,000)
Deutscheland Quad	6,000	2,000	5,000	—	13,000	$4,000
Total Payments	$15,000	$8,000	$11,000	$9,000	$43,000	—

Exhibit 22.9 Multilateral Matrix After Netting (thousands of U.S. dollars)

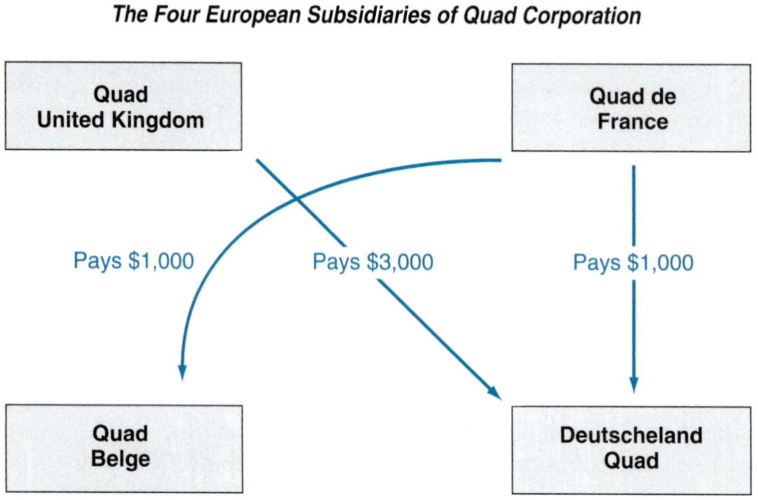

After netting, the four units of Quad Corporation have only three net payments to make among themselves to settle all intra-firm obligations.

The MNE enjoys a much greater choice of banking sources to fund its working capital needs than do domestic firms. Banking sources available to MNEs include in-house banks funded by unrepatriated capital, international banks, and local banks where subsidiaries are located. In-house banks and the various types of external commercial banking offices are described in the remainder of this chapter.

In-House Banks

Some MNEs have found that their financial resources and needs are either too large or too sophisticated for the financial services available in many locations where they operate. One solution to this has been the establishment of an in-house or internal bank within the firm. Such an in-house bank is not a separate corporation; rather, it is a set of functions performed by the existing treasury department. Acting as an independent entity, the central treasury of the firm transacts with the various business units of the firm on an arm's length basis. The purpose of the in-house bank is to provide banking-like services to the various units of the firm. The in-house bank may also be able to offer services to units of the firm that aid in the management of ongoing transaction exposures. Lastly, because it is in-house, credit analysis is not a part of the bank's decision making.

Exhibit 22.10 illustrates how the in-house bank of Cascade Pharmaceuticals, Inc., could work with Cascade Europe and Cascade Mexico. Cascade Mexico sells all its receivables to the in-house bank as they arise, reducing some of its domestic working capital needs. Additional working capital needs are supplied by the in-house bank directly to Cascade Mexico. Because the in-house bank is part of the same company, the interest rates it charges may be significantly lower than what

Exhibit 22.10 Cascade's In-House Bank

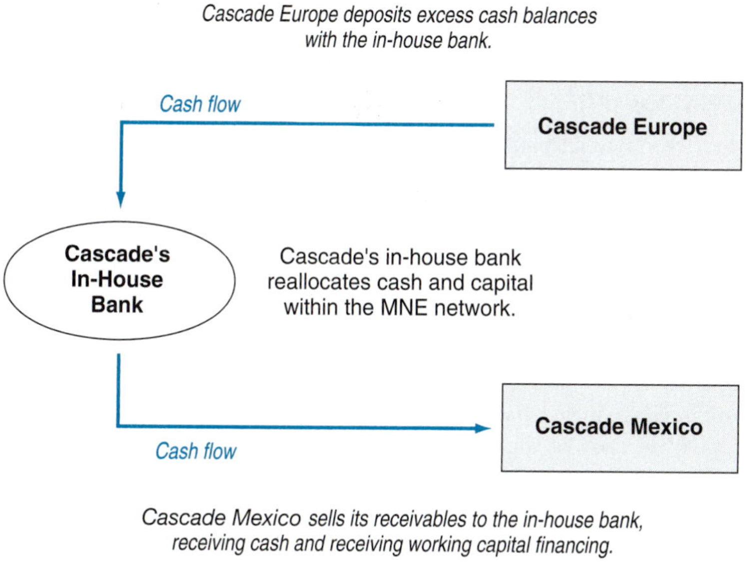
Cascade Europe deposits excess cash balances with the in-house bank.
Cash flow
Cascade Europe
Cascade's In-House Bank
Cascade's in-house bank reallocates cash and capital within the MNE network.
Cascade Mexico
Cash flow
Cascade Mexico sells its receivables to the in-house bank, receiving cash and receiving working capital financing.

Cascade Mexico could obtain on its own. The source of funds for the in-house bank may arise from the deposits of excess cash balances from Cascade Europe. If the in-house bank can pay Cascade Europe a higher deposit rate than it could obtain on its own in Germany, and if the in-house bank can lend these funds to Cascade Mexico at an interest rate lower than it could obtain on its own in Mexico, then both operating units benefit. Assuming the loan rate is greater than the deposit rate, the in-house bank profits by the margin between the two, but this margin or spread must be smaller than would be available from a commercial bank.

How can the in-house bank operate with a smaller spread than a regular commercial bank? First, its costs are lower because it does not have to conform to the stringent capital requirements imposed on commercial banks worldwide. Second, in-house banks do not have the large overhead costs of supporting large dealing rooms, branch networks, retail "storefronts," and other services required for commercial bank competitiveness. Third, they need not assess the creditworthiness of the corporate units with which they deal, since the units are all in the same family. Nor need they provide for credit losses.

In addition to providing financing benefits, in-house banks allow for more effective currency risk management. In the case of Cascade Mexico, the sale of foreign currency receivables to the in-house bank shifts transaction exposure to the bank. The in-house bank is better equipped to deal with currency exposures and has a greater volume of international cash flows, allowing Cascade overall to gain from more effective use of netting and matching. This frees the units of the firm from struggling to manage transaction exposures and allows them to focus on their primary business activities.

There are a variety of different structures for in-house banks. Many firms allow their units to use outside banks if the same services are available at lower cost. This forces the in-house bank to be operationally competitive. Many firms, however, require their units to use the in-house bank in order to ensure the bank an adequate level of activity to take advantage of economies of scale.

Commercial Banking Offices

MNEs depend on their commercial banks to handle most of their trade financing needs, such as letters of credit, and to provide advice on government support, country risk assessment, introductions to foreign firms and banks, and general financing availability. MNEs interact with their banks through a variety of different types of banking offices, many of which perform specialized functions. Therefore it is important for financial managers to understand which bank offices provide which kinds of activities. The main points of bank contact are correspondent banks, representative offices, branch banks, and subsidiaries. In the United States, a more specialized banking facility is available: the Edge Act corporation.

Correspondent banks. Most major banks of the world maintain correspondent banking relationships with local banks in each of the important foreign cities of the world. The two-way link between banks is essentially one of "correspondence," via fax, cable, and mail, and a mutual deposit relationship. For example, a U.S. bank may have a correspondent bank in Kuala Lumpur, Malaysia, and the U.S. bank will in turn be the correspondent bank for the Malaysian bank. Each will maintain a deposit in the other in local currency.

Correspondent services include accepting drafts, honoring letters of credit, and furnishing credit information. Services are centered around collecting or paying foreign funds, often because of import or export transactions. However, a visiting business person can use the home bank's introduction to meet local bankers. Under a correspondent banking relationship, neither of the correspondent banks maintains its own personnel in the other country. Direct contact between the banks is usually limited to periodic visits between members of the banks' management.

For the businessperson, the main advantage of banking at home with a bank having a large number of foreign correspondent relationships is the ability to handle financial matters in many foreign countries through local bankers whose knowledge of local customs should be extensive. The disadvantages are the lack of ability to deposit in, borrow from, or disburse from a branch of one's own home bank, as well as the possibility that correspondents will put a lower priority on serving the foreign banks' customer than on serving their own permanent customers.

Representative offices. A bank establishes a representative office in a foreign country primarily to help bank clients when they are doing business in that country or in neighboring countries. A representative office also functions as a geographically convenient location from which to visit correspondent banks in its region rather than sending bankers from the parent bank at greater financial and physical cost. A representative office is not a "banking office." It cannot accept deposits, make loans, commit the parent bank to a loan, or deal in drafts, letters of credit, or the Eurocurrency market. Indeed, a tourist cannot even cash a travelers check from the parent bank in the representative office.

The basic function of a representative office is to provide information, advice, and local contacts for the parent bank's business clients and to provide a location where businesspersons from either country can initiate inquiries about the parent bank's services. Representative offices introduce visiting executives to local banks and they watch over correspondent banking relationships. They put parent bank customers in contact with local business firms interested in supplying, purchasing, or marketing products or services, and they arrange meetings with government officials if needed to obtain permissions, approvals, or government help. They provide credit analysis of local firms and economic and political intelligence about the country.

A representative office is usually small, often housing one executive, two or three assistants, and clerical help, all of whom work in an office that does not resemble a banking office in the physical sense. The representative and the assistants may have come to the office from the home country, but it is equally likely that they are citizens or permanent residents of the host country. The major advantage of a representative office is that the local representative will have a more precise understanding of the needs of home-country clients than might local correspondents, and they can thus provide data and advice more suitable to their needs. The local representative will be bilingual, if necessary, and can advise visitors about local customs and procedures.

If the parent bank eventually decides to open a local general banking office, the existence of a representative office for some prior period usually provides a valuable base of contacts and expertise to facilitate the change. However, representative offices are not necessarily a prelude to a general banking office, nor need an eventual general banking office be the major reason for opening a representative office. In some countries, such as Mexico, foreign banks are precluded from opening new general banking offices. Thus representative offices are the only possible presence in such countries.

The essential disadvantage of the representative office to the business firm is that it cannot conduct general banking activities. Although it can facilitate such transactions with local correspondents, the process may be slower or more cumbersome than a business firm might wish. Because a representative office is usually small, physical limitations do exist on the services that can be supplied to home office clients.

Branch banks. A foreign branch bank is a legal and operational part of the parent bank, with the full resources of that parent behind it. A branch bank does not have its own corporate charter, its own board of directors, or any shares of stock outstanding. Although for managerial and regulatory purposes it will maintain its own set of books, its assets and liabilities are in fact those of the parent bank. However, branch deposits are not subject to reserve requirements or FDIC insurance (in the case of U.S. banks) unless the deposits are reloaned to the U.S. parent bank.

Branch banks are subject to two sets of banking regulations. As part of the parent, they are subject to home-country regulations. However, they are also subject to regulations of the host country, which may provide any of a variety of restrictions on their operations.

The major advantage to a business of using a branch bank is that the branch will conduct a full range of banking services under the name and legal obligation of the parent. A deposit in a branch is a legal obligation of the parent. Services to customers are based on the worldwide value of the bank/client relationship rather than just on the relationship to the local office. Legal loan limits are a function of the size of the parent, not of the branch.

From the point of view of a banker, the profits of a foreign branch are subject to immediate taxation at home, and losses of a foreign branch are deductible against taxable income at home. A new office expected to have losses in its early years creates a tax advantage if it is initially organized as a branch, even if the intent is to change it eventually to a separately incorporated subsidiary. From an organizational point of view, a foreign branch is usually simpler to create and staff than is a separately incorporated subsidiary.

The major disadvantage of a branch bank is one that accrues to the bank rather than to its customers. The parent bank (not just the branch) may be sued at the local level for debts or other activities of the branch.

Branch banking has been the most important way for U.S. banks to conduct their foreign activities. Foreign branches account for about one-half of all international banking assets held by U.S. banks. Europe is the most important location of U.S. branches with respect to size of assets and historical development. The Caribbean shell branches are also important, but their growth has leveled off in recent years. Asia is growing in importance at the same time as Latin America is declining in terms of assets held.

Banking subsidiaries. A subsidiary bank is a separately incorporated bank, owned entirely or in major part by a foreign parent, that conducts a general banking business. As a separate corporation, the banking subsidiary must comply with all the laws of the host country. Its lending limit is based on its own equity capital rather than that of the parent bank. This limits its ability to service large borrowers; local incorporation also limits the liability of the parent bank to its equity investment in the subsidiary.

A foreign banking subsidiary often appears as a local bank in the eyes of potential customers in host countries and is thus often able to attract additional local deposits. This will especially be true if the bank was independent prior to being purchased by the foreign parent. Management may be local, giving the bank greater access to the local business community. A foreign-owned bank subsidiary is more likely to be involved in both domestic and international business than is a foreign branch, which is more likely to appeal to the foreign business community but may encounter difficulty in attracting banking business from local firms.

Sometimes foreign banks are not allowed to operate a branch in a host country but are allowed to operate a locally incorporated subsidiary. Tax laws may favor subsidiaries over branches, both from the local perspective and from the parent country perspective. Subsidiaries are the second most important organization form for U.S. banks, with about 20% of all international assets held by U.S. banks located in subsidiaries. Over half of the assets of these subsidiaries are located in Europe, particularly in the United Kingdom.

Affiliates. A banking affiliate is a locally incorporated bank owned in part but not necessarily controlled by a foreign parent. The remainder may be owned locally, or by other foreign banks. The affiliated bank itself may be newly formed, or it may be a local bank in which a foreign bank has purchased a part interest.

The major advantage of an affiliated banking relationship springs from any joint venture between parties of different nationalities. The bank acquires the expertise of two or more sets of owners. It maintains its status as a local institution with local ownership and management, but it has continuing and permanent relations with its foreign part owner, including an ability to draw upon the international expertise of that part owner. The major disadvantage is also that common to joint ventures: The several owners may be unable to agree on particular policies important to the viability of the bank.

Edge Act corporations. Edge Act corporations are subsidiaries of U.S. banks, incorporated in the United States under Section 25 of the Federal Reserve Act as amended to engage in international banking and financing operations. Not only may such subsidiaries engage in general international banking, they may also finance commercial, industrial, or financial projects in foreign countries through long-term loans or equity participation. Such participation, however, is subject to the day-to-day practices and policies of the Federal Reserve System.

Edge Act corporations are physically located in the United States. Because U.S. banks used to be prohibited from having branches outside their own state, Edge Act corporations are usually located in states other than the home state in order to conduct international banking activities. Growth in Edge Act banking was greatly facilitated in 1979 when the Federal Reserve Board issued new guidelines that permitted interstate branching by Edge Act corporations. Previously, an Edge Act corporation had to be separately incorporated in each state. By increasing their interstate penetration through Edge Act corporations, the large money center banks are establishing a physical presence in most of the important regional financial centers to prepare for the day when interstate branching without limits will be permitted also for domestic business.

Edge Act corporations generally engage in two types of activities: direct international banking, including acting as a holding company for the stock of one or more foreign banking subsidiaries, and financing development activities not closely related to traditional banking operations.

Edge Act corporations may accept demand and time deposits from outside the United States (as well as from within, if such deposits are incidental to or for the purpose of transactions in foreign countries). Each corporation can also make loans, although commitments to any one borrower cannot exceed 10% of capital and surplus. They can issue or confirm letters of credit; make loans or advances to finance foreign trade, including production loans; create bankers' acceptances; receive items for collection; offer services such as remittance of funds abroad or buying, selling, or holding securities for safekeeping; issue guarantees; act as paying agent for securities issued by foreign governments or foreign corporations; and engage in spot and forward foreign exchange transactions.

Edge Act subsidiaries whose primary activity is international banking can also function as holding companies by owning shares of foreign banking subsidiaries and affiliates. Domestic banks may have branches abroad, but they may not themselves own shares of foreign banking subsidiaries. Thus the Edge Act permits U.S. banks to own foreign banking subsidiaries, either as wholly owned subsidiaries via an intermediary Edge Act corporation or as part of a joint venture with foreign or domestic banks or with other nonbanking institutions.

SUMMARY

- The operating cycle of a business generates funding needs, cash inflows and outflows—the cash conversion cycle—and potentially foreign exchange rate and credit risks.
- The funding needs generated by the operating cycle of the firm constitute working capital. The operating cycle of a business extends along a time-line from the first point at which a customer requests a price quotation to the final point at which payment is received from the customer for goods delivered.

- The cash conversion cycle, a sub-component of the operating cycle, is that period of time extending between cash outflow for purchased inputs and materials and cash inflow from cash settlement.
- The MNE itself poses some unique challenges in the management of working capital. Many multinationals manufacture goods in a few specific countries and then ship the intermediate products to other facilities globally for completion and distribution.
- The payables, receivables, and inventory levels of the various units of a MNE are a combination of intra- and inter-firm. The varying business practices observed globally regarding payment terms—both days and discounts—create severe mismatches, in some cases.
- Financial managers of MNEs must control international liquid assets to maintain adequate liquidity in a variety of currencies while minimizing political and foreign exchange risk.
- In principle, firms attempt to minimize their net working capital balance. A/R is reduced if collections are accelerated. Inventories held by the firm are reduced by carrying lower levels of both unfinished and finished goods and by increasing the rate at which goods are manufactured, reducing so-called cycle-time.
- All firms must determine whether to pay A/P early, taking discounts if offered by suppliers, and finance these payments with short-term debt. Note that cash and short-term debt are not included within net working capital (NWC) itself because they do not spontaneously increase with operations, but must be acquired as part of management's financing choices.
- Multinational business increases the complexity of making payments and settling cash flows between related and unrelated firms.
- Over time, a number of techniques and services have evolved to simplify and reduce the costs of making these cross-border payments. These include wire transfers, cash pooling, payment netting, and electronic fund transfers.
- MNEs can finance working capital needs through in-house banks, international banks, and local banks where subsidiaries are located.
- International banks finance MNEs and service these accounts through representative offices, correspondent banking relationships, branch banks, banking subsidiaries, affiliates, and Edge Act corporations (United States only).

QUESTIONS

1. **The cycle.** The operating cycle of a firm, domestic or multinational, consists of the following four time periods:
   a. Quotation Period
   b. Input Sourcing Period
   c. Inventory Period
   d. Accounts Receivable Period

   For each of these periods, explain whether a cash outflow or a cash inflow is associated with the beginning and the end of the period.
2. **Accounts payable period.** Exhibit 22.1 shows the Accounts Payable Period to be longer than the Inventory Period. Could this be otherwise, and what would be the cash implications?
3. **Payables and receivables.** As a financial manager, would you prefer that the Accounts Payable Period end before, at the same time, or after the beginning of the Accounts Receivable Period? Explain.
4. **Transaction exposure.** Assuming the flow illustrated in Exhibit 22.1, where does transaction exposure begin and end if inputs are purchased with one currency at t_1 and proceeds from the sale are received in another currency at t_5? Is there more than one interval of transaction exposure?
5. **Operating exposure.** Is any operating exposure created during the course of a firm's Operating Cycle?

6. **Accounting exposure.** Is any accounting exposure created during the course of a firm's Operating Cycle?

7. **Reducing NWC.** Assume a firm purchases inventory with one foreign currency and sells it for another foreign currency, neither currency being the home currency of the parent or subsidiary where the manufacturing process takes place. What can the firm do to reduce the amount of net working capital?

8. **Trade terms.** Roberts and Sons, Inc., of Great Britain has just purchased inventory items costing Kronor 1,000,000 from a Swedish supplier. The supplier has quoted terms 3/15, net 45. Under what conditions might Roberts and Sons reasonably take the discount, and when might it be reasonable to wait the full 45 days to pay?

9. **Inventory turnover.** Japanese industry is often praised for its "just-in-time" inventory practice between industrial buyers and industrial sellers. In the context of the "day's receivables" turnover in Exhibit 22.3, what is the comparative impact of the "just-in-time" system in Japan? Are there any risks associated with this system? Do you think this applies equally to Japanese manufacturing firms sourcing raw material and components in Japan and those sourcing similar items from Thailand and Malaysia?

10. **Receivables turnover.** Why might the time lag for intra-multinational firm accounts receivable and payable (i.e., all received or paid to a parent or sister subsidiary) differ substantially from the time lags reported for transactions with non-affiliated companies?

11. **Devaluation risk.** Merlin Corporation of the United States imports raw material from Indonesia on terms of 2/10, net 30. Merlin expects a 36% devaluation of the Indonesian rupiah at any moment. Should Merlin take the discount? Discuss aspects of the problem.

12. **Free trade zones.** What are the advantages of a free trade zone? Are there any disadvantages?

13. **Motives.** Explain the difference between the "transaction motive" and the "precautionary motive" for holding cash.

14. **Cash cycle.** The operating cash cycle of a multinational firm goes from cash collection from customers, cash holding for anticipated transaction needs (the transaction motive for holding cash), possible cash repositioning into another currency, and eventual cash disbursements to pay operating expenses. Assuming the initial cash collection is in one currency and the eventual cash disbursement is in another currency, what can a multinational firm do to shorten its cash cycle and what risks are involved?

15. **Electro-Beam Company.** Electro-Beam Company generates and disburses cash in the currencies of four countries: Singapore, Malaysia, Thailand, and Vietnam. This is different from the single-currency operations for Quad U.K. and its continental subsidiaries described in the chapter. What would be the characteristics you might consider if charged with designing a centralized cash depository system for Electro-Beam Company's southeast Asian subsidiaries?

16. **France.** During the era of the French franc, France imposed a rule on its banks and subsidiaries of international companies operating in France that precluded those subsidiaries from netting cash flow obligations between French and non-French related entities. Why do you suppose the French government imposed such a rule, and what if anything could subsidiaries in France do about it?

17. **Foreign bank office.** What is the difference between a foreign branch and a foreign subsidiary of a home-country bank?

18. **Representative office.** What are the advantages and disadvantages of a bank's foreign representative office and its network of correspondent banks?

PROBLEMS

Hong Kong Tool Company. *Use the following information to complete problems 1 through 4.* Hong Kong Tool Company is a locally owned creator and distributor of master tooling of all kinds. Although the company designs and markets, it does not manufacture itself. Instead, most of the machine tools it sells are manufactured under contract in China (across the border from Hong Kong in Guangdong province), like most other major tool companies in the world. Although privately owned, the company has been trying to clean up its financial performance in the hopes that the family can actually sell the company in the near future. The income statement and balance sheets for Hong Kong Tool Company that follow cover the most recent three-year period.

Income Statements for Hong Kong Tool Company (thousands of HK$)

Income items	Year 1	Year 2	Year 3
Sales revenues (net)	171,275	187,500	244,900
Cost of sales (COS)	(131,295)	(143,810)	(187,225)
Gross profit	39,980	43,690	57,675
Selling and admin. expenses	(27,800)	(29,700)	(36,765)
Operating profit (EBITDA)	12,180	13,990	20,910
Depreciation expenses	(4,650)	(4,800)	(5,700)
Earnings before interest and taxes (EBIT)	7,530	9,190	15,210
Interest expenses	(1,960)	(2,970)	(6,125)
Earnings before taxes (EBT)	5,570	6,220	9,085
Hong Kong corporate tax	(919)	(1,026)	(1,499)
Net income	4,651	5,194	7,586

Balance Sheets for Hong Kong Tool Company (thousands of HK$)

Assets	Year 1	Year 2	Year 3
Cash and marketable securities	6,588	7,750	2,400
Accounts receivable	22,475	24,800	33,325
Inventories	27,125	29,450	42,550
Prepaid expenses	387	925	1,163
Current assets	56,575	62,925	79,438
Net fixed assets	24,025	19,225	18,600
TOTAL ASSETS	80,600	82,150	98,038
Liabilities and Net Worth			
Short-term debt	17,900	18,580	27,774
Accounts payable	14,610	15,500	19,850
Accrued expenses	3,100	3,705	5,108
Current liabilities	35,610	37,785	52,732
Long-term debt	6,240	5,200	3,320
Owners' equity	38,750	39,165	41,986
Total liabilities and net worth	80,600	82,150	98,038

1. **Hong Kong Tool Company: net working capital.** A major initiative pursued by management at Hong Kong Tool in the past three years has been to increase the effectiveness of operations and financing by reducing the total invested capital in the business.
   a. If Hong Kong Tool defines total invested capital as the sum of cash, net working capital (NWC), and net fixed assets, how has total invested capital changed over the past three years?
   b. Net working capital efficiency is also typically measured as the ratio of sales to NWC. Is Hong Kong Tool generating more sales per unit of NWC in year 3 than it did in year 1?
2. **Hong Kong Tool Company: ROIC.** Many firms use different financial performance metrics as indicators of performance and efficiency; Hong Kong Tool prefers return on invested capital (ROIC). If the company defines ROIC as the earnings before interest and taxes (EBIT) divided by total invested capital (cash plus net working capital plus net fixed assets), calculate Hong Kong Tool's ROIC over the past three years.
3. **Hong Kong Tool Company: cash conversion cycle.** Hong Kong Tool is concerned that it may not be actually increasing the efficiency of its cash conversion cycle, the basic components of the total net working capital being utilized by the company. Calculate the number of days of sales represented by each of the components of net working capital for the three-year period. Which components of NWC seem to need additional managerial attention?
4. **Hong Kong Tool Company: DuPont method.** Similar to the evaluation employed in the ROIC analysis in Problem 3, the management of Hong Kong Tool wishes to evaluate the basic income statement and balance sheet components that are driving the company's ROIC. Using the following traditional formulation of the basic DuPont method for financial analysis, decompose the basic elements of Hong Kong Tool's three-year performance.

$$\frac{\text{EBIT}}{\text{Sales}} \times \frac{\text{Sales}}{\text{Invested Capital}} = \begin{array}{c}\text{Return on}\\ \text{invested capital (ROIC)}\end{array}$$

5. **Quinlan Company (France).** The following events take place.

   March 1: Quinlan Company seeks a sale at a price of €10,000,000 for items to be sold to a long-standing client in Poland. To achieve the order Quinlan offered to denominate the order in zlotys (Z), Poland's currency, for Z20,000,000. This price was arrived at by multiplying the euro price by Z2.00/€, the exchange rate on the day of the quote. The zloty is expected to fall in value by 0.5% per month versus the euro.

   April 1: Quinlan receives an order worth Z20,000,000 from that customer. On the same day, Quinlan places orders with its vendors for €4,000,000 of components needed to complete the sale.

   May 1: Quinlan receives the components and is billed €4,000,000 by the vendor on terms of 2/20, net 60. During the next two months Quinlan assigns direct labor to work on the project. The expense of direct labor was €5,000,000.

   July 1: Quinlan ships the order to the customer and bills the customer Z20,000,000. On its corporate books Quinlan debits accounts receivable and credits sales.

   Sept. 1: Quinlan's customer pays Z20,000,000 to Quinlan.

   a. Draw a cash flow diagram for this transaction in the style of Exhibit 22.1 and explain the steps involved.
   b. What working capital management techniques might Quinlan use to better its position vis-à-vis this particular customer?
6. **Shimoda, K.K.** Shimoda, K.K., the Japanese subsidiary of an American company, has

¥100,000,000 in accounts receivable for sales billed to customers on terms of 2/30 n/60. Customers usually pay in 30 days. Shimoda also has ¥60,000,000 of accounts payable billed to it on terms of 3/10 n/60. Shimoda delays payment until the last minute, because it is normally short of cash. Shimoda normally carries an average cash balance for transactions of ¥30,000,000. How much cash could the company save by taking the discount?

7. **Alpine Ski Company.** Alpine Ski Company of Grenoble, France, manufactures and sells in France, Switzerland, and Italy, and also maintains a corporate account in Frankfurt, Germany. Alpine has been setting separate operating cash balances in each country at a level equal to expected cash needs plus two standard deviations above those needs, based on a statistical analysis of cash flow volatility. Expected operating cash needs and one standard deviation of those needs are:

	Expected cash need	One standard deviation
Switzerland	€ 5,000,000	€ 1,000,000
Italy	3,000,000	400,000
France	2,000,000	300,000
Germany	800,000	40,000
	€ 10,800,000	€ 1,740,000

Alpine's Frankfurt bank suggests that the same level of safety could be maintained if all precautionary balances were combined in a central account at the Frankfurt headquarters.

a. How much lower would Alpine Ski Company's total cash balances be if all precautionary balances were combined? Assume cash needs in each country are normally distributed and are independent of each other.

b. What other advantages might accrue to Alpine Ski Company from centralizing its cash holdings? Are these advantages realistic?

8. **Futebal do Brasil, S.A.** Futebal do Brazil, S.A. purchases newly sewn soccer balls from Pakistani manufacturers and distributes them in Argentina, Brazil, and Chile. All operations are through wholly owned subsidiaries. The three subsidiaries have submitted the following daily cash reports, with all amounts in thousands of U.S. dollars, which the Brazilian company uses for cash management purposes. Each of the two foreign subsidiaries is allowed to carry a $1,000,000 cash balance overnight, with the remainder remitted to a U.S. dollar account maintained in São Paulo unless instructed otherwise by the Brazilian financial staff. As a general matter, the cost of moving funds is such that funds should not be moved for one day and then returned the next, but a movement for two days that is then reversed is financially advantageous. The Brazilian headquarters invests surplus cash balances over US$5,000,000 in U.S. money market instruments purchased through the Miami correspondent bank of the firm's Brazilian bank. Anticipated cash flows, in thousands of U.S. dollars, are as below.

Design an advantageous cash movement plan that complies with Futebal do Brazil general policies.

Anticipated Cash Flows (000s)	Companhia Futebal do Brasil	Compañía Fútbal de Argentina	Compañía Fútbal de Chile
Day-end cash balance	$ 6,000	$ 5,000	$ 5,000
Minimum operating balance required:	$5,000	$1,000	$1,000
Expected receipts (+) or disbursements (–):			
+1 day	+3,000	–2,000	+5,000
+2 days	-0-	+1,000	–3,000
+3 days	–5,000	–3,000	+2,000

9. **Earth Technology, Inc.** Earth Technology, Inc. (U.S.), manufactures basic farm equipment in China, Spain, and Iowa. Each subsidiary has monthly unsettled balances due to or from other subsidiaries. At the end of December, unsettled intracompany debts in U.S. dollars were:

Earth Technology —China:	Owes $8 million to Spanish subsidiary
	Owes $9 million to Iowa parent
Earth Technology —Spain:	Owes $5 million to Chinese subsidiary
	Owes $6 million to Iowa parent
Earth Technology —Iowa:	Owes $4 million to Chinese subsidiary
	Owes $10 million to Spanish subsidiary

Foreign exchange transaction spreads average 0.4% of funds transferred.

a. How could Earth Technology net these intracompany debts? How much would be saved in transaction expenses over the no-netting alternative?

b. Before settling the accounts, Earth Technology decides to invest $6,000,000 of parent funds in a new farm equipment manufacturing plant in the new Free Industrial Zone at Subic Bay, the Philippines. How can this decision be incorporated into the settlement process? What would be total bank charges? Explain.

10. **Crystal Publishing Company.** Crystal Publishing Company publishes books in Europe through separate subsidiaries in several countries. On a Europe-wide basis, Crystal Publishing experiences uneven cash flows. Any given book creates a cash outflow during the period of writing and publishing, followed by a cash inflow in subsequent months and years as the book is sold. To handle these imbalances, Crystal decided to create an in-house bank.

At the beginning of April, Crystal's in-house bank held deposits on which it paid 4.8% interest as follows:

From Crystal Germany	€20,000,000
From Crystal Spain	€5,000,000
From Crystal Britain	£12,000,000

At the beginning of April, Crystal's in-house bank advanced funds at an annual rate of 5.4% as follows:

To Crystal France	€12,000,000
To Crystal Italy	€8,000,000
To Crystal Greece	€6,000,000

The exchange rate between pounds sterling and the euro is €1.6000/£.

a. What would be the net interest earnings (i.e., interest earned less interest paid, before administrative expenses), of Crystal's in-house bank for the month of April?

b. If parent Crystal Publishing subsidized the in-house bank for all of its operating expenses, how much more could the in-house bank loan at the beginning of April?

INTERNET EXERCISES

1. **Working capital and export.** There are a variety of governmental and non-governmental organizations which provide working capital funding and management for exporters. Beginning your Internet search with the following sites, determine exactly what funding is available at what cost for exporters?

U.S. Agency for International Development	http://www.usaid.gov/pubs/cbj2003/working_capital.html
U.S. Export-Import Bank	http://www.exim.gov/pubs/pdf/ebd-w-13.pdf

2. **Clearinghouse associations.** The actual process of moving and crediting funds between banks and between firms is often overlooked in academic discussions. Associations like the New York Clearinghouse Association have, however, played major roles in the international financial system for centuries. Use the following web sites to prepare a two-page executive briefing on the role of clearinghouses in history and in contemporary finance. Use the web site for the Clearing House Interbank Payments System (CHIPS) to estimate the volume of international financial transactions.

New York Clearinghouse Association	http://www.theclearinghouse.org
Clearing House Interbank Payments System	http://www.chips.org

SELECTED READINGS

Gentry, James A., Dileep R. Mehta, S. K. Bhattacharya, Robert Cobbaut, and Jean-Louis Scaringella, "An International Study of Management Perceptions of the Working Capital Process," *Journal of International Business Studies*, Spring–Summer 1979, pp. 28–38.

Houpt, James V., "International Trends for U.S. Banks and Banking Markets," Staff Study of the Board of Governors of the Federal Reserve System, No. 156, May 1988.

Srinivasan, VenKat, Susan E. Moeller, and Yong H. Kim, "International Cash Management: State-of-the-Art and Research Directions," *Advances in Financial Planning and Forecasting*, 1990, Volume 4, Part B, pp. 161–194.

"International Working Capital Practices of the Fortune 200," *Financial Practice & Education*, Fall/Winter 1996, Volume 6, Issue 2.

MINI-CASE

Honeywell and Pakistan International Airways

The Space and Avionics Control Group (SAC) of Honeywell Incorporated (US) was quite frustrated in June of 1997. The cockpit retrofit proposal with Pakistan International Airlines had been under negotiation for seven months and over the past weekend a new request had been thrown in—to accept payment in Pakistan rupees, against corporate policy at Honeywell. If an exception was not made, the deal—worth $23.7 million—was most likely dead.

Pakistan International Airlines (PIA)

Pakistan International Airlines Corporation (PIA) was the national flag carrier of the Islamic Republic of Pakistan. Founded in 1954, PIA operated both scheduled passenger and cargo services. The firm was 57% state-owned, with the remaining 43% held by private investors internal to Pakistan.

PIA's fleet was aging. Although the airline had planned a significant modernization program, recent restrictions placed on government spending by the International Monetary Fund (IMF) had killed the program. With the cancellation of the fleet modernization program, PIA now had to move fast to ensure compliance with U.S. Federal Aviation Administration (FAA) safety mandates. If it did not comply with the FAA mandates for quieter engines and upgraded avionics by June 30, 1998, PIA would be locked out of its very profitable U.S. gates. PIA would first retrofit the aircraft utilized on the long-haul flights to the United States, primarily the Boeing 747 classics. Due to SAC's extensive experience with a variety of control systems for Boeing and its recent work on cockpit retrofit for McDonnell Douglas aircraft, SAC felt it was the preferred supplier for PIA. However, SAC had not undertaken Boeing cockpit retrofits to date (no one had), and looked to the PIA deal as an opportunity to build a new competitive base. PIA's insistence on payment in local currency terms was now thought to be a tactic to extract better concessions from SAC and its agent, Makran.

Ibrahim Makran Pvt. LTD

In countries like Pakistan, the use of an agent is often considered a necessary evil. The agent can help to bridge two business cultures and provide invaluable information, but at some cost. Honeywell's agent, Ibrahim Makran Pvt. LTD., based in Hyderabad, was considered one of the most reliable and well-connected in Pakistan. Makran traced its roots back to a long association with the Sperry Aerospace and Marine Group, the precursor to Honeywell's SAC unit (Sperry was acquired in 1986). Makran was also one of the largest import/export trading houses in Pakistan. It was 100% family-owned and managed.

Standard practice in the avionics business was to provide the agent with a 10% commission, although the commission was negotiable. The 10% was based on the final sales and was paid after all payments were received. Typically, it was Makran who spotted the business opportunity and submitted a proposal to SAC Marketing.

After PIA contacted Makran regarding its latest demand, Makran knew that SAC would want to maintain the deal in U.S. dollars. Makran had therefore inquired as to the availability of dollar funds for a deal of this size from Makran's own finance department. The finance department confirmed that it had the necessary U.S. dollar funds to pay SAC but warned that policy was to charge 5% for services rendered and currency risks.

Makran advised SAC that it would be willing to purchase the receivable for an additional 5% (in addition to the 10% commission). Makran's U.S. subsidiary in Los Angeles would credit SAC within 30 days of SAC invoicing Makran. PIA advised Makran that if SAC accepted payment in Pakistan rupees, then local (Pakistan) payment terms would apply. This meant 180 days in principle, but often much longer in practice. The agent also advised SAC that the Pakistan rupee was due for another devaluation. When pressed for more information, Makran simply replied that the company president, the elder Ibrahim Makran, had "good connections."

Pakistan Rupee

A central part of the IMF's austerity program was a devaluation of the Pakistan rupee by 7.86% against the U.S. dollar on October 22, 1996. Now, roughly six months later, there was renewed speculation that another devaluation was imminent in order to limit imports and help the export sector earn badly needed hard currency. Another recent economic setback was that the European Union had ruled Pakistan was guilty of dumping cotton and had imposed antidumping fines on Pakistani cotton. This was a painful blow to the export sector. The current exchange rate of 40.4795 Pakistan rupees (Rp) per dollar was maintained by the Pakistani Central Bank. The parallel market rate—black market rate—was approaching Rp50/US$. At present, there was no forward market for the Pakistan rupee.

Honeywell's Working Capital

Honeywell's finance department was attempting to reduce net working capital and had just concluded a thorough review of existing payment terms and worldwide days sales receivable (DSR) rates. The department's goal was to reduce worldwide DSR rates from 55 to 45 days in the current fiscal year. The Pay for Performance target for the current year (the annual performance bonus system at Honeywell) included net working capital goals. There was concern in the organization that the net working capital goal could prove the obstacle to achieving a bonus despite excellent sales growth. The latest DSR report is shown here.

Exhibit A SAC Control Systems' Average Days Sales Receivables by Region

Region	Actual	Target	Amount
North America	44	40	$31 million
South America	129	70	$2.1 million
Europe	55	45	$5.7 million
Middle East	93	60	$3.2 million
Asia	75	55	$11 million
PIA	264	180	$0.7 million
Boeing	39	30	$41 million
McDonnell Douglas	35	30	$18 million
Airbus Industrie	70	45	$13 million

Notes:

1. U.S.-based airline trading companies distort the actual local payment terms.
2. The spread between individual customers within regions can be extremely large.
3. Some collection activity is assumed. Specific customers are periodically targeted.
4. Disputed invoices are included. Amount is for all products, services, and exchanges.
5. One of the criteria for granting "preferred" pricing is a 30-day DSR. The 10% reduction can be substantial, but typically only motivates the larger customers.

Honeywell payment terms were net 30 from date of invoice. However, payment terms and practices varied dramatically across country and region. Payment terms were generally not published, with the exception of some private reports by credit rating agencies. Honeywell had not in the past enforced stringent credit terms on many customers. For example, neither contracts nor invoices stated any penalties for late payment. Many airlines did pay on time, but others availed themselves of Honeywell's cheap financing.

A review of PIA's account receivable history indicated that they consistently paid their invoices late. The current average DSR was 264 days. PIA had been repeatedly put on hold by the collections department, forcing marketing staff representatives to press the agent who in turn pressed PIA for payment. Honeywell was very concerned about this deal. It had in fact asked for guarantees that PIA would pay promptly. Honeywell's concern was also reflected in the 20% advance payment clause in the contract. Although marketing took the high DSR rate up with PIA and the agent, the current proposed deal was expected to be the same if not worse.

One positive attribute of the proposed contract was that delivery would not occur until one year after the contract was signed. The invoice for the full amount outstanding would be issued at that time. If the expected improvements to the DSR were made in the meantime, maybe the high DSR rate on the PIA deal could be averaged with the rest of Asia. The 20% advance payment would be used to fund the front-end engineering work.

Global treasury at Honeywell was headquartered along with corporate in Minneapolis, Minnesota. Corporate treasury was a profit center and charged 1% commission on all sales. Treasury, however, passed on the currency risk to the business unit. If a local subsidiary required local currency, treasury would try to match those requirements by accepting the A/R in the local currency. They had advised SAC that for many developing countries where Honeywell had little or no activities, such as Pakistan, this was done only on an exception basis. Global treasury also evaluated all deals in present value terms given the extended payment periods, and the corporate cost of capital was set at 12%.

Negotiations

Honeywell now speculated that the local currency request was a result of the 20% advance payment clause. The project was considered one of the riskiest SAC had undertaken, and the 20% advance payment would help reach the group's DSR goals. The DSR was being watched on a daily basis by division management. This project had already been forced to secure group-level approval because it fell below the minimum return on sales target. SAC's management had counted on the deal to make its annual sales targets, and that now seemed in jeopardy. It would need to act soon if it was to reach its targets.

Case Questions

1. Estimate what cash flows in which currencies the proposal would probably yield. What is the expected U.S. dollar value that would, in the end, be received?
2. Do you think the services that Makran is offering are worth the costs?
3. What would you do if you were heading the Honeywell SAC group negotiating the deal?

Chapter 23

International Trade Finance

THE PURPOSE OF THIS CHAPTER IS TO EXPLAIN HOW INTERNATIONAL TRADE (EXPORTS AND IMPORTS) is financed. The contents are of direct practical relevance both to domestic firms that just import or export and to multinational firms that trade with related and unrelated entities.

The chapter begins by explaining the types of trade relationships that exist. Next we explain the trade dilemma: exporters want to be paid before they export and importers do not want to pay until they receive the goods. The next section explains the benefits of the current international trade protocols. This is followed by a section describing the elements of a trade transaction and the various documents that are used to facilitate the trade's completion and financing. The next section identifies international trade risks; namely, currency risk and noncompletion risk. The following sections describe the key trade documents, including letter of credit, draft, and bill of lading. The next section summarizes the documentation of a typical trade transaction. This is followed by a description of government programs to help finance exports, including export credit insurance and specialized banks such as the U.S. Export-Import Bank. Next, we compare the various types of short-term receivables financing and then the use of *forfaiting* for longer-term receivables. The chapter concludes with a detailed analysis of countertrade. Following the chapter is a case study, *Crosswell International's Precious Ultra-Thin Diapers*, that illustrates how an export requires the integration of management, marketing, and finance.

The Trade Relationship

Trade financing shares a number of common characteristics with the traditional value chain activities conducted by all firms. All companies must search out suppliers for the many goods and services required as inputs to their own goods production or service provision processes. Their purchasing and procurement department must determine whether each potential supplier is capable of producing the product to required quality specifications, producing and delivering in a timely and reliable manner, and continuing to work with them in the ongoing process of product and process improvement for continued competitiveness. All must be at an acceptable price and payment terms. This same series of issues applies to potential customers, because their continued business is equally critical to the company's operations and success.

The nature of the relationship between the exporter and the importer is critical to understanding the methods for import-export financing utilized in industry. Exhibit 23.1 provides an overview of the three categories of relationships: unaffiliated unknown, unaffiliated known, and affiliated.

- A foreign importer with which an exporter has not previously conducted business would be considered *unaffiliated unknown*. In this case, the two parties need to enter into a detailed sales contract, outlining the specific responsibilities and expectations of the business agreement. The exporter also needs to seek out protection against the possibility that the importer not make payment in full in a timely fashion.
- A foreign importer with which the exporter has previously conducted business successfully would be considered *unaffiliated known*. In this case, the two parties may still enter into a detailed sales contract, but specific terms and shipments or provisions of services may be significantly looser in definition. Depending on the depth of the relationship, the exporter may seek some third-party protection against noncompletion or conduct the business on an open-account basis.
- A foreign importer that is a subsidiary business unit of the exporter would be an *affiliated* party (sometimes referred to as *intra-firm trade*). Because both businesses are part of the same MNE, the most common practice would be to conduct the trade transaction without a contract or protection against nonpayment. This is not always the case, however. In a variety of international business situations, it may still be in the exporter's best interest to detail the conditions for the business transaction and possibly to protect against any political or country-based interruption to the completion of the trade transaction.

Exhibit 23.1 Alternative International Trade Relationships

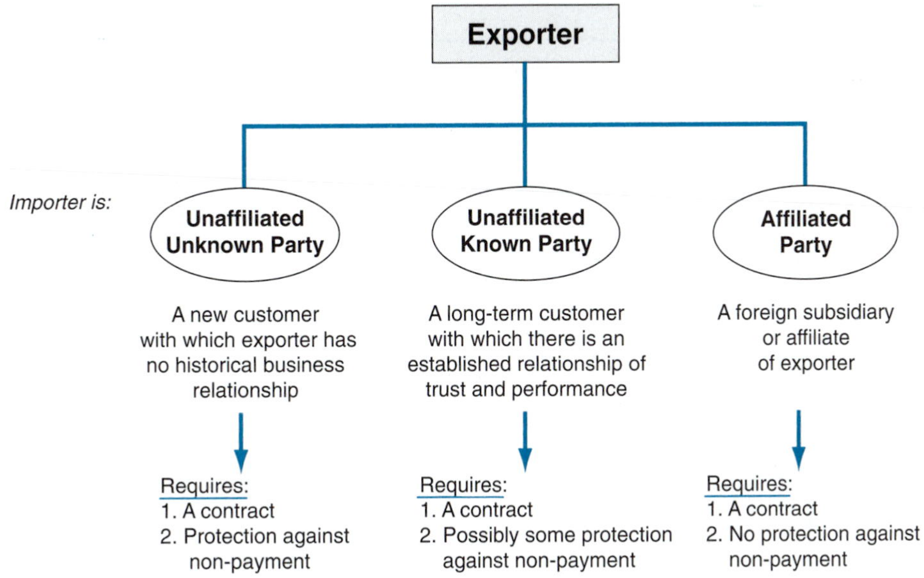

The composition of global trade has changed dramatically over the past few decades. Whereas for centuries international trade was dominated by inter-firm trade (transactions between unaffiliated parties), affiliated party trade has become increasingly dominant during the past 40 years. For example, it is now estimated that over 80% of all international trade as measured by U.S. dollar value conducted off the western coast of the United States is between affiliated parties (such as Honda U.S. and Honda of Japan). Although this practice may make management of these transactions simpler in terms of contracts and trade risks, it increases the complexity of the management of the total value and performance of the MNE.

The Trade Dilemma

International trade must work around a fundamental dilemma. Imagine an importer and an exporter who would like to do business with one another. They live in different countries located far apart. They have never met. They speak different languages. They operate in different political environments. They worship different gods (each capitalizes "God" in the home religion and uses a lowercase "god" for foreign religions!). They come from cultures that have different standards for honoring obligations to other persons and different ways to settle disputes. They both know that if they default on an obligation, the other party will have a hard time catching up to seek redress. Although it might be too harsh to say they don't trust one another, each has perfectly valid reasons for being very cautious in dealing with the other.

Because of the distance between the two, it is not possible to simultaneously hand over goods with one hand and accept payment with the other. The importer would prefer the arrangement at the top of Exhibit 23.2, while the exporter's preference is shown at the bottom.

Exhibit 23.2 The Mechanics of Import and Export

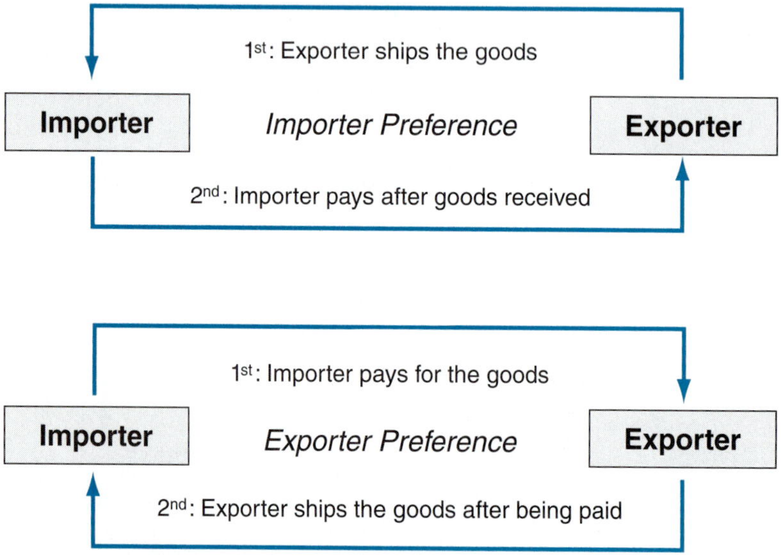

The fundamental dilemma of being unwilling to trust a stranger in a foreign land is solved by using a highly respected bank as intermediary. A greatly simplified view is described in Exhibit 23.3. In this simplified view, the importer obtains the bank's promise to pay on its behalf, knowing that the exporter will trust the bank. The bank's promise to pay is called a *letter of credit.*

The exporter ships the merchandise to the importer's country. Title to the merchandise is given to the bank on a document called an *order bill of lading.* The exporter asks the bank to pay for the goods, and the bank does so. The document to request payment is a *sight draft.* The bank, having paid for the goods, now passes title to the importer, whom the bank trusts. At that time or later, depending on their agreement, the importer reimburses the bank.

Financial managers of MNEs must understand these three basic documents—in part because their firms will often trade with unaffiliated parties, but also because the system of documentation provides a source of short-term capital that can be drawn upon even when shipments are to sister subsidiaries.

Benefits of the System

The three key documents and their interaction will be described later in this chapter. They constitute a system developed and modified over centuries to protect both importer and exporter from the risk of noncompletion and foreign exchange risk, as well as to provide a means of financing.

Exhibit 23.3 The Bank as the Import/Export Intermediary

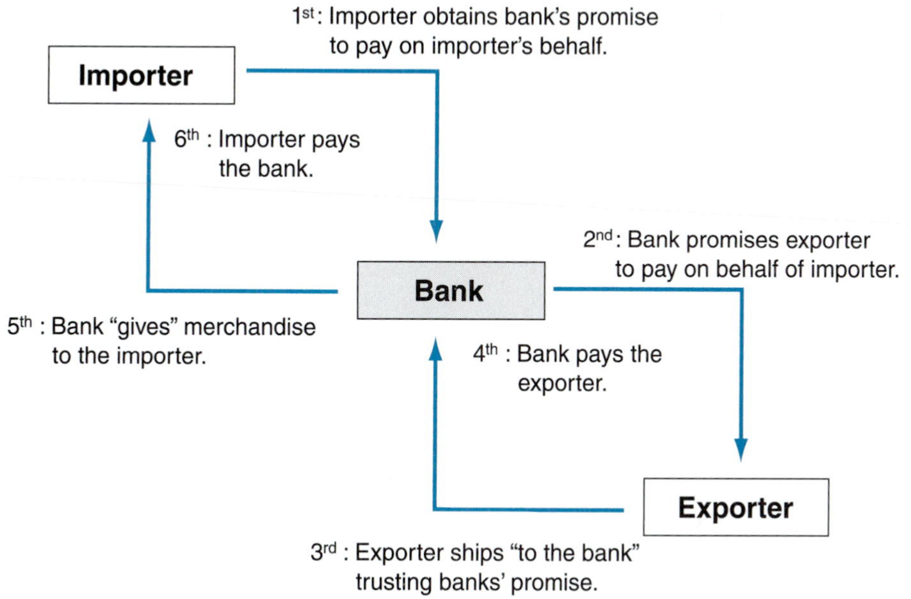

Protection Against Risk of Noncompletion

As stated earlier, once importer and exporter agree on terms, the seller usually prefers to maintain legal title to the goods until paid, or at least until assured of payment. The buyer, however, will be reluctant to pay before receiving the goods, or at least before receiving title to them. Each wants assurance that the other party will complete its portion of the transaction. The letter of credit, sight draft, and bill of lading are part of a system carefully constructed to determine who bears the financial loss if one of the parties defaults at any time.

Protection Against Foreign Exchange Risk

In international trade, foreign exchange risk arises from *transaction exposure.* If the transaction requires payment in the exporter's currency, the importer carries the foreign exchange risk. If the transaction calls for payment in the importer's currency, the exporter has the foreign exchange risk.

Transaction exposure can be hedged by the techniques described in Chapter 8, but in order to hedge, the exposed party must be certain that payment of a specified amount will be made on or near a particular date. The three key documents described in this chapter ensure both amount and time of payment and thus lay the groundwork for effective hedging.

The risk of noncompletion and foreign exchange risk are most important when the international trade is episodic, with no outstanding agreement for recurring shipments and no sustained relationship between buyer and seller. When the import/export relationship is of a recurring nature, as in the case of manufactured goods shipped weekly or monthly to a final assembly or retail outlet in another country, and when it is between countries whose currencies are considered strong, the exporter may bill the importer on open account after a normal credit check. Banks provide credit information and collection services outside of the system of processing drafts drawn against letters of credit.

Financing the Trade

Most international trade involves a time lag during which funds are tied up while the merchandise is in transit. Once the risks of noncompletion and of exchange rate changes are disposed of, banks are willing to finance goods in transit. A bank can finance goods in transit, as well as goods held for sale, based on the key documents, without exposing itself to questions about the quality of the merchandise or other physical aspects of the shipment.

Elements of an Import/Export Transaction

Each individual trade transaction must cover three basic elements: description of goods, prices, and documents regarding shipping and delivery instructions.

Contracts. An import or export transaction is by definition a contractual exchange between parties in two countries that may have different legal systems, monies, languages, religions, or units of measure. Religious practices in countries may have significant impacts on international commercial transactions. In many Islamic countries, for example, interest payments are not allowed and therefore contracts must be constructed carefully to avoid putting parties in conflict with national regulations and religious practices. It is therefore critical to define all terms used in export contracts carefully and fully within the contracts themselves.

All contracts should include definitions and specifications for the quality, grade, quantity, and price of the goods in question. Definitions should be complete and should not use abbreviations. Whenever possible, terms such as "ton" should be defined further to include quantities if possible (2,000 or 2,200 pounds, for example). References in the contract to published prices or catalogs with associated descriptions are often helpful, as are product blueprints or diagrams that include any engineering or other technical details related to expected product qualities and characteristics.

Prices. Price quotations can be a major source of confusion. Price terms in the contract should conform to published catalogs, specify whether quantity discounts or early payment discounts are in effect (and how they are calculated), and state whether finance charges are relevant in the case of deferred payment, transportation charges, insurance fees, or specific surcharges or fees relative to the countries in question.

Documents. Documentation covers a variety of issues of particular importance from a financial management perspective. An importer wishing to take possession of goods at a dock, airport, or any other point of delivery and clear them through customs, must possess certain customs and shipping documents. These typically include bills of lading, commercial invoices, insurance policies, consular invoices, and packing lists.

- A *bill of lading*, or B/L, is issued to the exporter by a common carrier transporting the merchandise. It will be described more fully later in this chapter.
- A signed *commercial invoice* is issued by the exporter and contains a precise description of the merchandise. Unit prices, financial terms of sale, and amount due from the importer are indicated, as are shipping conditions related to charges, such as "FOB" (free on board), "FAS" (free alongside), "CFR" (cost and freight), or "CIF" (cost, insurance, freight).
- *Insurance documents* must be as specified in the contract of sale and must be issued by insurance companies or their agents. The insurance may be issued to the exporter, who must then endorse the policy to the importer, or it may be issued in the name of the importer. Insurance must be of types and for risks specified in the letter of credit.
- *Consular invoices* are issued in the exporting country by the consulate of the importing country to provide customs information and statistics for that country and to help prevent false declarations of value. The consular invoice may be combined with a certificate of origin of the goods.
- *Packing lists* may be required so that the contents of containers can be identified, either for customs purposes or for importer identification of the contents of separate containers. In addition, an *export declaration* prepared by the exporter to assist the government in the preparation of export statistics may be required.

Shipping deadline. Most importers insist on a specified deadline or time interval by which the shipment will be made. If the goods in question are particularly time-sensitive (such as products for seasonal sale), remedies will be included in the sales contract for failure to meet time commitments.

Payment instructions. Which of the parties—the exporter or the importer—is to pay such charges as freight, insurance, import duties, handling fees, taxes, etc., must be specified carefully in the sales contract. The currency in which all payments are to be made between importer and exporter must also be specified clearly. The payment terms state whether cash is to be paid in advance, whether letters of credit are required, and what documents need to be presented against payment, consignments, or payment on open account. These terms must be detailed in the sales contract. The following section on key documents will elaborate on these payment term concepts.

Packaging and marking. Depending on the nature of the goods, proper packaging may be critical to preserving and protecting items being shipped. Proper markings on the inner and outer boxes and containers are needed to conform with customs regulations in countries. These markings typically include clear and conforming invoices of the value of all items for import duty calculation and payment purposes.

Warranties, guarantees, and inspections. Assurances regarding the performance or qualities demonstrated by the goods from the exporter may also be included in the sales contract. This may include not only protection against product defects and proper performance, but protection against any consequential damages from defective parts or performance. In some cases, the importer may wish to have the right to inspect the goods before paying (and even the right to inspect the goods while being manufactured before shipping). These stipulations should of course be delineated in the sales contract.

Included in documents may be *certificates of analysis*, required to ascertain that certain specifications such as weight, purity, or sanitation have been met. These conditions may be required by health or other officials of the importing country—especially in the case of foods and drugs—or they may be insisted on by the importer as assurance that it is receiving what it ordered. The certificates may be issued by government or private organizations, as specified in the letter of credit.

International Trade Risks

In order to understand the risks associated with international trade transactions, it is helpful to understand the sequence of events in any such transaction. Exhibit 23.4 illustrates, in principle, the series of events associated with a single export transaction.

From a financial management perspective, the two primary risks associated with an international trade transaction are *currency risk* (currency of denomination of payment) and *risk of non-completion* (timely and complete payment). Exhibit 23.4 illustrates the traditional business problem of credit management: The exporter quotes a price, finalizes a contract, and ships the goods, losing physical control over the goods based on trust of the buyer or the promise of a bank to pay based on documents presented. The risk of default on the part of the importer is present as soon as the financing period begins, as depicted in Exhibit 23.4.

In many cases, the initial task of analyzing the credit-worthiness of foreign customers is similar to procedures for analyzing domestic customers. If the exporter has had no experience with a foreign customer, but that customer is a large, well-known firm in its home country, the exporter may simply ask for a bank credit report on that firm. The exporter may also talk to other firms that have had dealings with the foreign customer. If these investigations show the foreign customer (and country) to be completely trustworthy, the exporter would likely ship to them on open

Exhibit 23.4 The Trade Transaction Time-Line and Structure

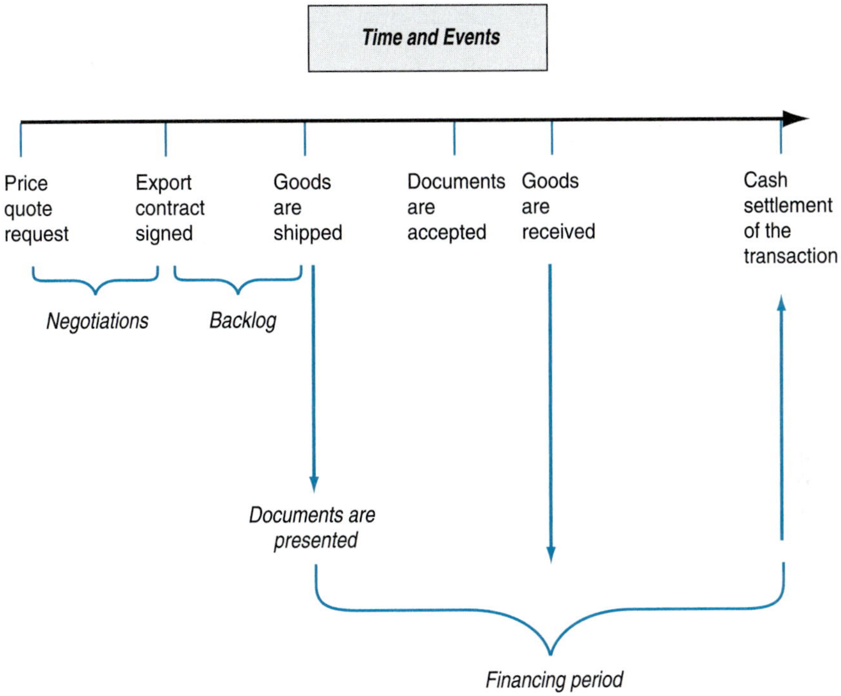

account, with a credit limit, just as they would for a domestic customer. This is the least costly method of handling exports, because there are no heavy documentation or bank charges. However, before a regular trading relationship has been established with a new or unknown firm, the exporter must face the possibility of nonpayment for its exports or noncompletion of its imports. The risk of nonpayment can be eliminated through the use of a letter of credit issued by a creditworthy bank.

The three key documents described in the following pages—the letter of credit, draft, and bill of lading— constitute a system developed and modified over centuries to protect both importer and exporter from the risk of noncompletion of the trade transaction as well as to provide a means of financing. The three key trade documents are part of a carefully constructed system to determine who bears the financial loss if one of the parties defaults at any time.

Letter of Credit (L/C)

A *letter of credit*, abbreviated L/C, is a bank's conditional promise to pay issued by a bank at the request of an importer (the applicant/buyer), in which the bank promises to pay an exporter (the beneficiary of the letter) upon presentation of documents specified in the L/C. An L/C reduces the risk of noncompletion, because the bank agrees to pay against documents rather than actual merchandise. The relationship between the three parties can be seen in Exhibit 23.5.

Exhibit 23.5 Parties to a Letter of Credit (L/C)

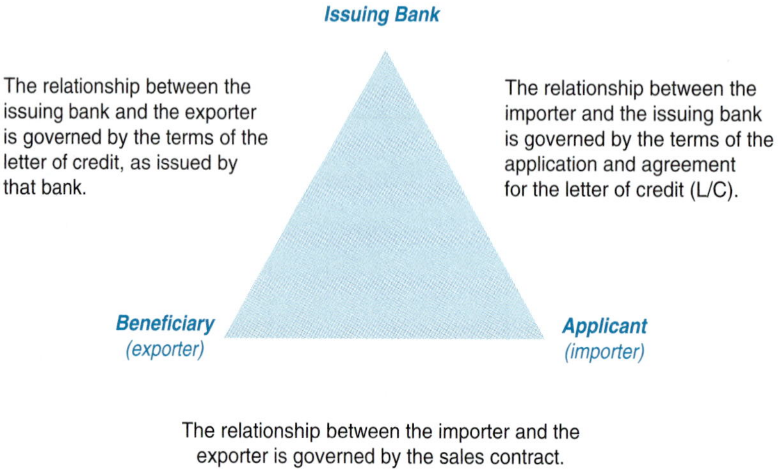

Issuing Bank
The relationship between the issuing bank and the exporter is governed by the terms of the letter of credit, as issued by that bank.
The relationship between the importer and the issuing bank is governed by the terms of the application and agreement for the letter of credit (L/C).
Beneficiary (exporter)
Applicant (importer)
The relationship between the importer and the exporter is governed by the sales contract.

An importer (buyer) and exporter (seller) agree on a transaction and the importer then applies to its local bank for the issuance of an L/C. The importer's bank issues an L/C and cuts a sales contract based on its assessment of the importer's credit-worthiness. The bank might require a cash deposit or other collateral from the importer in advance. The importer's bank will want to know the type of transaction, the amount of money involved, and what documents must accompany the draft that will be drawn against the L/C.

If the importer's bank is satisfied with the credit standing of the applicant, it will issue an L/C guaranteeing to pay for the merchandise if shipped in accordance with the instructions and conditions contained in the L/C.

The essence of an L/C is the promise of the issuing bank to pay against specified documents, which must accompany any draft drawn against the credit. The L/C is not a guarantee of the underlying commercial transaction. Indeed, the L/C is a separate transaction from any sales or other contracts on which it might be based. To constitute a true L/C transaction, all of the following five elements must be present with respect to the issuing bank:

1. The issuing bank must receive a fee or other valid business consideration for issuing the L/C.
2. The bank's L/C must contain a specified expiration date or a definite maturity.
3. The bank's commitment must have a stated maximum amount of money.
4. The bank's obligation to pay must arise only on the presentation of specific documents, and the bank must not be called on to determine disputed questions of fact or law.
5. The bank's customer must have an unqualified obligation to reimburse the bank on the same condition as the bank has paid.

Most commercial letters of credit are *documentary*, meaning that certain documents must be included with any drafts drawn under their terms. Required documents usually include an order bill of lading (discussed in more detail later in the chapter), a commercial invoice, and any of the following: consular invoice, insurance certificate or policy, certificate of origin, weight list, certificate of analysis, and packing list.

Commercial letters of credit are also classified:

- **Irrevocable versus revocable.** An irrevocable L/C obligates the issuing bank to honor drafts drawn in compliance with the credit and can be neither canceled nor modified without the consent of all parties, including in particular the beneficiary (exporter). A revocable L/C can be canceled or amended at any time before payment; it is intended to serve as a means of arranging payment but not as a guarantee of payment.
- **Confirmed versus unconfirmed.** An L/C issued by one bank can be confirmed by another, in which case the confirming bank undertakes to honor drafts drawn in compliance with the credit. An unconfirmed L/C is the obligation only of the issuing bank. An exporter is likely to want a foreign bank's L/C confirmed by a domestic bank when the exporter has doubts about the foreign bank's ability to pay. Such doubts can arise when the exporter is unsure of the financial standing of the foreign bank, or if political or economic conditions in the foreign country are unstable. The essence of an L/C is shown in Exhibit 23.6.

Advantages and Disadvantages of Letters of Credit

The primary advantage of an L/C is that it reduces risk—the exporter can sell against a bank's promise to pay rather than against the promise of a commercial firm. The exporter is also in a more secure position as to the availability of foreign exchange to pay for the sale, since banks are more likely to be aware of foreign exchange conditions and rules than is the importing firm itself. If the importing

Exhibit 23.6 Essence of a Letter of Credit (L/C)

Bank of the East, Ltd.
[*Name of Issuing Bank*]

Date: September 18, 2003
L/C Number 123456

Bank of the East, Ltd. hereby issues this irrevocable documentary Letter of Credit to Jones Company [*name of exporter*] for US $500,000, payable 90 days after sight by a draft drawn against Bank of East, Ltd., in accordance with letter of Credit number 123456.

The draft is to be accompanied by the following documents:

1. Commercial invoice in triplicate
2. Packing list
3. Clean on board order bill of lading
4. Insurance documents, paid for by buyer

At maturity Bank of the East, Ltd. will pay the face amount of the draft to the bearer of that draft.

Authorized Signature

country should change its foreign exchange rules during the course of a transaction, the government is likely to allow already outstanding bank letters of credit to be honored for fear of throwing its own domestic banks into international disrepute. Of course, if the L/C is confirmed by a bank in the exporter's country, the exporter avoids any problem of blocked foreign exchange.

An exporter may find that an order backed by an irrevocable L/C will facilitate obtaining pre-export financing in the home country. If the exporter's reputation for delivery is good, a local bank may lend funds to process and prepare the merchandise for shipment. Once the merchandise is shipped in compliance with the terms and conditions of the credit, payment for the business transaction is made and funds will be generated to repay the preexport loan.

The major advantage of an L/C to the importer is that the importer need not pay out funds until the documents have arrived at the bank that issued the L/C and after all conditions stated in the credit have been fulfilled. The main disadvantages are the fee charged by the importer's bank for issuing its L/C, and the possibility that the L/C reduces the importer's borrowing line of credit with its bank. It may, in fact, be a competitive disadvantage for the exporter to demand automatically an L/C from an importer, especially if the importer has a good credit record and there is no concern regarding the economic or political conditions of the importer's country.

Draft

A *draft*, sometimes called a *bill of exchange* (B/E), is the instrument normally used in international commerce to effect payment. A draft is simply an order written by an exporter (seller) instructing an importer (buyer) or its agent to pay a specified amount of money at a specified time. Thus it is the exporter's formal demand for payment from the importer.

The person or business initiating the draft is known as the *maker*, *drawer*, or *originator*. Normally this is the exporter who sells and ships the merchandise. The party to whom the draft is addressed is the *drawee*. The drawee is asked to *honor* the draft; that is, to pay the amount requested according to the stated terms. In commercial transactions, the drawee is either the buyer, in which case the draft is called a *trade draft*, or the buyer's bank, in which case the draft is called a *bank draft*. Bank drafts are usually drawn according to the terms of an L/C. A draft may be drawn as a bearer instrument, or it may designate a person to whom payment is to be made. This person, known as the *payee*, may be the drawer itself or it may be some other party such as the drawer's bank.

Negotiable Instruments

If properly drawn, drafts can become *negotiable instruments*. As such, they provide a convenient instrument for financing the international movement of the merchandise (freely bought and sold). To become a negotiable instrument, a draft must conform to the following four requirements (Uniform Commercial Code, Section 3104[1]):

1. It must be in writing and signed by the maker or drawer.
2. It must contain an unconditional promise or order to pay a definite sum of money.
3. It must be payable on demand or at a fixed or determinable future date.
4. It must be payable to order or to bearer.

If a draft is drawn in conformity with these requirements, a person receiving it with proper endorsements becomes a *holder in due course.* This is a privileged legal status that enables the holder to receive payment despite any personal disagreements between drawee and maker because of controversy over the underlying transaction. If the drawee dishonors the draft, payment must be made to any holder in due course by any prior endorser or by the maker. This clear definition of the rights of parties who hold a negotiable instrument as a holder in due course has contributed significantly to the widespread acceptance of various forms of drafts, including personal checks.

Types of Drafts

Drafts are of two types: sight drafts and time drafts. A *sight draft* is payable on presentation to the drawee; the drawee must pay at once or dishonor the draft. A *time draft*, also called a *usance draft*, allows a delay in payment. It is presented to the drawee, who accepts it by writing or stamping a notice of acceptance on its face. Once accepted, the time draft becomes a promise to pay by the accepting party (the buyer). When a time draft is drawn on and accepted by a bank, it becomes a *bankers' acceptance*; when drawn on and accepted by a business firm, a *trade acceptance.*

The time period of a draft is referred to as its *tenor.* To qualify as a negotiable instrument, and so be attractive to a holder in due course, a draft must be payable on a fixed or determinable future date. For example, "60 days after sight" is a fixed date, which is established precisely at the time the draft is accepted. However, payment "on arrival of goods" is not determinable, since the date of arrival cannot be known in advance. Indeed, there is no assurance that the goods will arrive at all. The essence of a time draft is illustrated in Exhibit 23.7.

Drafts are also classified as clean or documentary. A *clean draft* is an order to pay unaccompanied by any other documents. When it is used in trade, the seller has usually sent the shipping documents directly to the buyer, who thus obtains possession of the merchandise independent of

Exhibit 23.7 Essence of a Time Draft

Name of Exporter

Date: October 10, 2003
Draft Number 7890

Ninety (90) days after sight of this First of Exchange, pay to the order of Bank of the West [*name of exporter's bank*] the sum of Five-hundred thousand U.S. dollars for value received under Bank of the East, Ltd. letter of credit number 123456.

Signature of Exporter

its payment (on a clean sight draft) or acceptance (on a clean time draft). Clean drafts are often used by multinational firms shipping to their own subsidiaries because matters of trust and credit are not involved. Clean drafts are also used for nontrade remittances; for example, when collection of an outstanding debt is sought. Use of a clean draft puts pressure on a recalcitrant debtor by forcing it to convert an open-account obligation into documentary form. Failure to pay or accept such a draft when presented through a local bank can damage the drawee's reputation.

Most drafts in international trade are *documentary*, which means that various shipping documents are attached to the draft. Payment (for sight drafts) or acceptance (for time drafts) is required to obtain possession of those documents, which are in turn needed to obtain the goods involved in the transaction. If documents are to be delivered to the buyer on payment of the draft, it is known as a *D/P draft*; if the documents are delivered on acceptance, the draft is called a *D/A draft*.

Bankers' Acceptances

When a draft is accepted by a bank, it becomes a bankers' acceptance. As such, it is the unconditional promise of that bank to make payment on the draft when it matures. In terms of quality the bankers' acceptance is practically identical to a marketable bank certificate of deposit (CD). The holder of a bankers' acceptance need not wait until maturity to liquidate the investment, but may sell the acceptance at a discount in the money market, where constant trading in such instruments occurs. The amount of the discount depends entirely on the credit rating of the bank that signs the acceptance or another bank that reconfirms the bankers' acceptance for a fee. The all-in-cost of using a bankers' acceptance compared to other short-term financing instruments is analyzed later in this chapter.

Bill of Lading (B/L)

The third key document for financing international trade is the *bill of lading*, or B/L. The bill of lading is issued to the exporter by a common carrier transporting the merchandise. It serves three purposes: a receipt, a contract, and a document of title.

As a receipt, the bill of lading indicates that the carrier has received the merchandise described on the face of the document. The carrier is not responsible for ascertaining that the containers hold what is alleged to be their contents, so descriptions of merchandise on bills of lading are usually short and simple. If shipping charges are paid in advance, the bill of lading will usually be stamped "freight paid" or "freight prepaid." If merchandise is shipped collect—a less common procedure internationally than domestically—the carrier maintains a lien on the goods until freight is paid.

As a contract, the bill of lading indicates the obligation of the carrier to provide certain transportation in return for certain charges. Common carriers cannot disclaim responsibility for their negligence through inserting special clauses in a bill of lading. The bill of lading may specify alternative ports in the event that delivery cannot be made to the designated port, or it may specify that the goods will be returned to the exporter at the exporter's expense.

As a document of title, the bill of lading is used to obtain payment or a written promise of payment before the merchandise is released to the importer. The bill of lading can also function as collateral against which funds may be advanced to the exporter by its local bank prior to or during shipment and before final payment by the importer.

Characteristics of the Bill of Lading

Bills of lading are either straight or to order. A *straight bill of lading* provides that the carrier deliver the merchandise to the designated consignee only. A straight bill of lading is not title to the goods and is not required for the consignee to obtain possession. Because a straight bill of lading is not title, it is not good collateral for loans. Therefore, a straight bill of lading is used when the merchandise has been paid for in advance, when the transaction is being financed by the exporter, or when the shipment is to a subsidiary.

An *order bill of lading* directs the carrier to deliver the goods to the order of a designated party, usually the shipper. An additional inscription may request the carrier to notify someone else of the arrival. The order bill of lading grants title to the merchandise only to the person to whom the document is addressed, and surrender of the order bill of lading is required to obtain the shipment.

The order bill of lading is typically made payable to the order of the exporter, who thus retains title to the goods after they have been handed to the carrier. Title to the merchandise remains with the exporter until payment is received, at which time the exporter endorses the order bill of lading (which is negotiable) in blank or to the party making the payment, usually a bank. The most common procedure would be for payment to be advanced against a documentary draft accompanied by the endorsed order bill of lading. After paying the draft, the exporter's bank forwards the documents through bank clearing channels to the bank of the importer. The importer's bank in turn releases the documents to the importer after payment (sight drafts), after acceptance (time drafts addressed to the importer and marked D/A), or after payment terms have been agreed upon (drafts drawn on the importer's bank under provisions of an L/C).

Documentation in a Typical Trade Transaction

A trade transaction could conceivably be handled in many ways. The transaction that would best illustrate the interactions of the various documents would be an export financed under a documentary commercial letter of credit, requiring an order bill of lading, with the exporter collecting via a time draft accepted by the importer's bank. Such a transaction is illustrated in Exhibit 23.8.

1. Importer places an order for the goods with exporter, inquiring if exporter would be willing to ship under a letter of credit.
2. Exporter agrees to ship under a letter of credit and specifies relevant information such as prices and terms.
3. Importer applies to its bank, Bank I, for a letter of credit to be issued in favor of exporter for the merchandise importer wishes to buy.
4. Bank I issues the letter of credit in favor of exporter and sends it to Bank X, exporter's bank, or to a correspondent bank in the country of export.
5. Bank X advises exporter of the opening of a letter of credit in the exporter's favor. Bank X may or may not confirm the letter of credit by adding its own guarantee to the document.
6. Exporter ships the goods to the importer.
7. Exporter presents a time draft to Bank X, drawn on Bank I in accordance with Bank I's letter of credit and accompanied by such other documents as required, including the order bill of

Exhibit 23.8 Steps in a Typical Trade Transaction

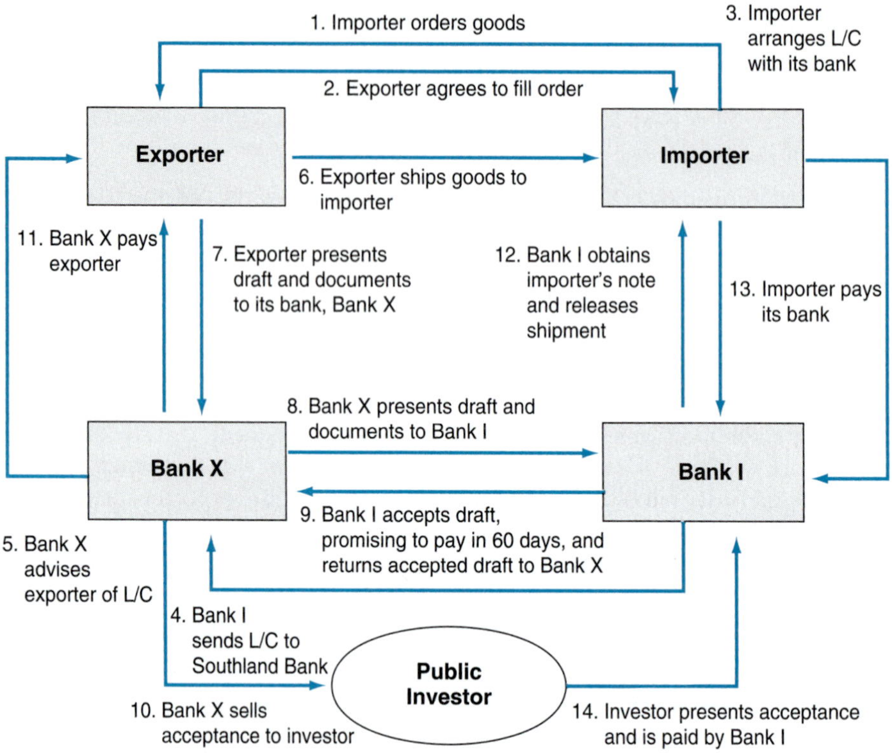

lading. Exporter endorses the order bill of lading in blank (making it a bearer instrument) so that title to the goods goes with the holder of the documents—Bank X at this point in the transaction.

8. Bank X presents the draft and documents to Bank I for acceptance. Bank I accepts the draft by stamping and signing it making it a bankers' acceptance, takes possession of the documents, and promises to pay the now-accepted draft at maturity—for instance, 60 days.

9. Bank I returns the accepted draft to Bank X. Alternatively, Bank X could have asked Bank I to accept and discount the draft; then Bank I would have returned cash less a discount fee rather than the accepted draft to Bank X.

10. Bank X, having received back the accepted draft, now a bankers' acceptance, can choose between several alternatives. Bank X may sell the acceptance in the open market at a discount to a portfolio investor. The investor will typically be a corporation or financial institution with excess cash it wants to invest for a short period of time. Bank X may also hold the acceptance in its own portfolio.

11. If Bank X has discounted the acceptance with Bank I (mentioned in step 9) or has discounted it in the local money market, Bank X will transfer the proceeds less any fees and discount to

exporter. Another possibility would be for the exporter to take possession of the acceptance, hold it for 60 days, and present it for collection. Normally, however, exporters prefer to receive the discounted cash value of the acceptance at once rather than wait for the acceptance to mature and receive a slightly greater amount of cash at a later date.

12. Bank I notifies importer of the arrival of the documents. Importer signs a note or makes some other agreed-upon plan to pay Bank I for the merchandise in 60 days, and Bank I releases the underlying documents so that importer can obtain physical possession of the shipment at once.

13. After 60 days, Bank I receives from importer funds to pay the maturing acceptance.

14. On the same day—the 60th day after acceptance—the holder of the matured acceptance presents it for payment and receives its face value. The holder may present it directly to Bank I, as in the diagram, or return it to Bank X and have Bank X collect it through normal banking channels.

Although this is a typical transaction involving an L/C, few international trade transactions are ever truly typical. Business, and more specifically international business, requires flexibility and creativity by management at all times as illustrated by Global Finance Perspective 23.1. The case study at the end of this chapter presents an application of the mechanics of a real business situation. The result is a classic challenge to management: When and on what basis do you compromise typical procedure in order to accomplish strategic goals?

Global Finance Perspective 23.1

The Letter of Credit Goes On-Line

The landscape of trade finance in Asia is changing, and fast. Given the proliferation of electronic and on-line facilities, traditional trade finance resources such as the letter of credit (LC) stand to be replaced, perhaps totally, in a very short time-frame. More importantly, banks and companies need to change their business mind set in order to accommodate the different type of financing arrangements required by the e-commerce business model. Tai Kah Chye, vice president and Asia head, e-commerce trade and supply chain at JP Morgan, sums up the shift of balance: "The emergence of e-commerce technologies continues to capture the headlines in trade financing. Whilst it is true that e-commerce is not a substitute for financing, it is nonetheless fundamentally changing the way that trade financing has been conducted in the past."

Although the LC is the most conventional trade finance tool, and one that still has a function in the region, its level of usage has declined in some Asian countries. Notes Wenyir Lu, senior vice president and general manager at Bank SinoPac in Taiwan: "In Taiwan, the use of the LC has declined from 50–60% of total trade transactions three years ago to below 30% today." The main reason for the drop in LC usage in countries like Taiwan, Hong Kong, and Singapore is the long processing time: negotiating an LC (from the time of shipment to the time of presentation by the issuing bank) can take over 20 days.

Its easy to pick electronic and on-line application service providers in the market. One is Bolero, a service launched in late 1999 and jointly owned by SWIFT and the Through Transport Club. By standardizing the architecture through which electronic documents are exchanged, Bolero acts as a third-party authenticator of messages, allowing trading parties and banks to exchange documents with confidence. This means that the entire LC cycle can be processed electronically, with greater speed and with less fraud.

Source: Adapted from "The LC Goes On-Line," *Asiamoney*, February 2001, pp. 72–76.

Government Programs to Help Finance Exports

Governments of most export-oriented industrialized countries have special financial institutions that provide some form of subsidized credit to their own national exporters. These export finance institutions offer terms that are better than those generally available from the competitive private sector. Thus domestic taxpayers are subsidizing lower financial costs for foreign buyers in order to create employment and maintain a technological edge. The most important institutions usually offer export credit insurance and a government-supported bank for export financing.

Export Credit Insurance

The exporter who insists on cash or an L/C payment for foreign shipments is likely to lose orders to competitors from other countries that provide more favorable credit terms. Better credit terms are often made possible by means of export credit insurance, which provides assurance to the exporter or the exporter's bank that, should the foreign customer default on payment, the insurance company will pay for a major portion of the loss. Because of the availability of export credit insurance, commercial banks are willing to provide medium- to long-term financing (five to seven years) for exports.

Importers prefer that the exporter purchase export credit insurance to pay for non-performance risk by the importer. In this way, the importer does not need to pay to have an L/C issued and does not reduce its credit line.

Competition between nations to increase exports by lengthening the period for which credit transactions can be insured may lead to a credit war and to unsound credit decisions. To prevent such an unhealthy development, a number of leading trading nations joined together in 1934 to create the Berne Union (officially, the Union d'Assureurs des Credits Internationaux) for the purpose of establishing a voluntary international understanding on export credit terms. The Berne Union recommends maximum credit terms for many items including, for example, heavy capital goods (five years), light capital goods (three years), and consumer durable goods (one year).

Export Credit Insurance in the United States

In the United States, export credit insurance is provided by the Foreign Credit Insurance Association (FCIA). This is an unincorporated association of private commercial insurance companies operating in cooperation with the Export-Import Bank (see later section).

The FCIA provides policies protecting U.S. exporters against the risk of nonpayment by foreign debtors as a result of commercial and political risks. Losses due to commercial risk are those that result from the insolvency or protracted payment default of the buyer. Political losses arise from actions of governments beyond the control of buyer or seller.

Foreign Credit Insurance Association (FCIA) Policies

The FCIA offers short-term policies involving payment terms up to 180 days, and medium-term policies with payment terms from 181 days to 5 years. Coverage up to seven years may be arranged on a case-by-case basis for aircraft, marine, and other sales, if necessary to meet government-supported foreign competition. Coverage is for U.S. goods produced and shipped from the United

States during the policy period and applies to credit sales to a foreign buyer or to export letters of credit opened by a foreign issuing bank.

Generally, commercial coverage ranges from 90% to 95% and political coverage ranges from 95% to 100%, depending on the type of policy and options chosen by the exporter. Premiums depend on a number of variables, including the length of credit terms being offered, the exporter's previous experience with export sales, the risk associated with the countries to which goods are shipped or services are rendered, and the spread of risk covered by the policy.

Export-Import Bank and Export Financing

The Export-Import Bank (also called Eximbank) is another independent agency of the U.S. government, established in 1934 to stimulate and facilitate the foreign trade of the United States. Interestingly, the Eximbank was originally created primarily to facilitate exports to the Soviet Union. In 1945, the Eximbank was re-chartered "to aid in financing and to facilitate exports and imports and the exchange of commodities between the United States and any foreign country or the agencies or nationals thereof."

The Eximbank facilitates the financing of U.S. exports through various loan guarantee and insurance programs. The Eximbank guarantees repayment of medium-term (181 days to 5 years) and long-term (5 years to 10 years) export loans extended by U.S. banks to foreign borrowers. The Eximbank's medium- and long-term, direct-lending operation is based on participation with private sources of funds. Essentially, the Eximbank lends dollars to borrowers outside the United States for the purchase of U.S. goods and services. Proceeds of such loans are paid to U.S. suppliers. The loans themselves are repaid with interest in dollars to the Eximbank. The Eximbank requires private participation in these direct loans in order to: 1) ensure that it complements rather than competes with private sources of export financing; 2) spread its resources more broadly; and 3) ensure that private financial institutions will continue to provide export credit.

The Eximbank also guarantees lease transactions; finances the costs involved in the preparation by U.S. firms of engineering, planning, and feasibility studies for non-U.S. clients on large capital projects; and supplies counseling for exporters, banks, or others needing help in finding financing for U.S. goods.

Trade Financing Alternatives

In order to finance international trade receivables, firms use the same financing instruments as they use for domestic trade receivables, plus a few specialized instruments that are only available for financing international trade. Exhibit 23.9 identifies the main short-term financing instruments and their approximate costs as of March 11, 2003. The next section describes a longer-term instrument called *forfaiting*. The last section illustrates the use of *countertrade*, which is the use of various types of barter to substitute for financial instruments.

Bankers' Acceptances

Bankers' acceptances, described earlier in this chapter, can be used to finance both domestic and international trade receivables. Exhibit 23.9 shows that bankers' acceptances earn a yield comparable to other money market instruments, especially marketable bank certificates of deposit.

Exhibit 23.9 Instruments for Financing Short-Term Domestic and International Trade Receivables

Instrument	Cost or Yield on March 11, 2003 for Three-Month Maturity
Bankers' acceptances*	1.14% yield annualized
Trade acceptances*	1.17% yield annualized
Factoring	Variable rate but much higher cost than bank credit lines
Securitization	Variable rate but competitive with bank credit lines
Bank credit lines (covered by export insurance)	4.25% plus points (fewer points if covered by export credit insurance)
Commercial paper *	1.15% yield annualized

*These instruments compete with three-month marketable bank time certificates of deposit that yielded 1.17% on March 11, 2003.

However, the all-in-cost to a firm of creating and discounting a bankers' acceptance also depends upon the commission charged by the bank that accepts the firm's draft.

The first owner of the bankers' acceptance created from an international trade transaction will be the exporter, who receives the accepted draft after the bank has stamped it "accepted." The exporter may hold the acceptance until maturity and then collect. On an acceptance of, for instance, $100,000 for three months, the exporter would receive the face amount less the bank's acceptance commission of 1.5% per annum:

Face amount of the acceptance	$100,000	
Less 1.5% per annum commission for three months	–375	$(0.015 \times 3/12 \times \$100{,}000)$
Amount received by exporter in three months	$ 99,625	

Alternatively, the exporter may "discount"—that is, sell at a reduced price—the acceptance to its bank in order to receive funds at once. The exporter will then receive the face amount of the acceptance less both the acceptance fee and the going market rate of discount for bankers' acceptances. If the discount rate were 1.14% per annum as shown in Exhibit 23.9, the exporter would receive the following:

Face amount of the acceptance	$100,000	
Less 1.5% per annum commission for three months	–375	$(0.015 \times 3/12 \times \$100{,}000)$
Less 1.14% per annum discount rate for three months	–285	$(0.0114 \times 3/12 \times \$100{,}000)$
Amount received by exporter at once	$ 99,340	

Therefore, the annualized all-in-cost of financing this bankers' acceptance is:

$$\frac{\text{commission} + \text{discount}}{\text{proceeds}} \times \frac{360}{90} = \frac{\$375 + \$285}{\$99{,}340} \times \frac{360}{90} = 0.0266 \text{ or } 2.66\%$$

The discounting bank may hold the acceptance in its own portfolio, earning for itself the 1.14% per annum discount rate, or the acceptance may be resold in the acceptance market to portfolio investors. Investors buying bankers' acceptances provide the funds that finance the transaction.

Trade Acceptances

Trade acceptances are similar to bankers' acceptances, except that the accepting entity is a commercial firm, like General Motors Acceptance Corporation (GMAC), rather than a bank. The cost of a trade acceptance depends on the credit rating of the accepting firm plus the commission it charges. Like bankers' acceptances, trade acceptances are sold at a discount to banks and other investors at a rate that is competitive with other money market instruments (see Exhibit 23.9).

Factoring

Specialized firms, known as *factors,* purchase receivables at a discount on either a non-recourse or recourse basis. *Non-recourse* means that the factor assumes the credit, political, and foreign exchange risk of the receivables it purchases. *Recourse* means that the factor can give back receivables that are not collectable. Since the factor must bear the cost and risk of assessing the credit worth of each receivable, the cost of factoring is usually quite high. It is more than borrowing at the prime rate plus points.

The all-in-cost of factoring non-recourse receivables is similar in structure to acceptances. The factor charges a commission to cover the non-recourse risk—typically 1.5%–2.5%—plus interest deducted as a discount from the initial proceeds.

On the other hand, the firm selling the non-recourse receivables avoids the cost of determining credit worth of its customers. It also does not have to show debt borrowed to finance these receivables on its balance sheet. Furthermore, the firm avoids both foreign exchange and political risk on these non-recourse receivables.

Securitization

The securitization of export receivables for financing trade is an attractive supplement to bankers' acceptance financing and factoring. A firm can *securitize* its export receivables by selling them to a legal entity established to create marketable securities based on a package of individual export receivables. An advantage of this technique is to remove the export receivables from the exporter's balance sheet because they have been sold without recourse.

The receivables are normally sold at a discount. The size of the discount depends on four factors:

1. The historic collection risk of the exporter
2. The cost of credit insurance
3. The cost of securing the desirable cash flow stream to the investors
4. The size of the financing and services fees

Securitization is more cost-effective if there is a large volume of transactions with a known credit history and default profitability. A large exporter could establish its own securitization entity. While the initial setup cost is high, the entity can be used on an ongoing basis. As an alternative, smaller exporters could use a common securitization entity provided by a financial institution, thereby saving the expensive setup costs.

Bank Credit Line Covered by Export Credit Insurance

A firm's bank credit line can typically be used to finance up to a fixed upper limit, such as 80%, of accounts receivable. Export receivables can be eligible for inclusion in bank credit line financing. However, credit information on foreign customers can be more difficult to collect and assess. If a firm covers its export receivables with export credit insurance, it can greatly reduce the credit risk of those receivables. This insurance enables the bank credit line to cover more export receivables and lower the interest rate for that coverage. Of course, any foreign exchange risk must be handled by the transaction exposure techniques described in Chapter 8.

The cost of using a bank credit line is usually the prime rate of interest plus points to reflect a particular firm's credit risk. As usual, 100 *points* equal one percent. In the United States, borrowers are also expected to maintain a compensating deposit balance at the lending institution. In Europe and many other places lending is done on an overdraft basis. An *overdraft* agreement allows a firm to over draw its bank account up to the limit of its credit line. Interest at prime plus points is based only on the amount of overdraft borrowed. In either case, the all-in-cost of bank borrowing using a credit line is higher than acceptance financing, as shown in Exhibit 23.9.

Commercial Paper

A firm can issue *commercial paper*—unsecured promissory notes—to fund its short-term financing needs, including both domestic and export receivables. However, only the large well-known firms with favorable credit ratings have access to either the domestic or euro commercial paper market. As shown in Exhibit 23.9, commercial paper interest rates lie at the low end of the yield curve and compete directly with marketable bank time certificates of deposit.

Forfaiting

Forfaiting is a specialized technique to eliminate the risk of nonpayment by importers in instances where the importing firm and/or its government is perceived by the exporter to be too risky for open account credit. The name of the technique comes from the French *à forfait*, a term that implies "to forfeit or surrender a right."

Role of the Forfaiter

The essence of forfaiting is the non-recourse sale by an exporter of bank-guaranteed promissory notes, bills of exchange, or similar documents received from an importer in another country. The exporter receives cash at the time of the transaction by selling the notes or bills at a discount from their face value to a specialized finance firm called a *forfaiter*. The forfaiter arranges the entire operation prior to the actual transaction taking place. Although the exporting firm is responsible for the quality of delivered goods, it receives a clear and unconditional cash payment at the time of the transaction. All political and commercial risk of nonpayment by the importer is carried by the guaranteeing bank. Small exporters who trust their clients to pay find the forfaiting technique invaluable because it eases cash flow problems.

During the Soviet era, expertise in the technique was centered in German and Austrian banks, which used forfaiting to finance sales of capital equipment to Eastern European "Soviet bloc" countries. British, Scandinavian, Italian, Spanish, and French exporters have now adopted the technique, but U.S. and Canadian exporters are reported to be slow to use forfaiting, possibly because they are suspicious of its simplicity and lack of complex documentation.[1] Nevertheless, some American firms now specialize in the technique, and the Association of Forfaiters in the Americas (AFIA) has more than twenty members. Major export destinations financed via the forfaiting technique are Asia, Eastern Europe, the Middle East, and Latin America.[2]

A Typical Forfaiting Transaction

A typical forfaiting transaction involves five parties, as shown in Exhibit 23.10. The steps in the process are as follows:

Step 1: Agreement. Importer and exporter agree between themselves on a series of imports to be paid for over a period of time, typically three to five years. However, periods up to ten years or as short as 180 days have been financed by the technique. The normal minimum size for a transaction is $100,000. The importer agrees to make periodic payments, often against progress on delivery or completion of a project.

Exhibit 23.10 Typical Forfaiting Transaction

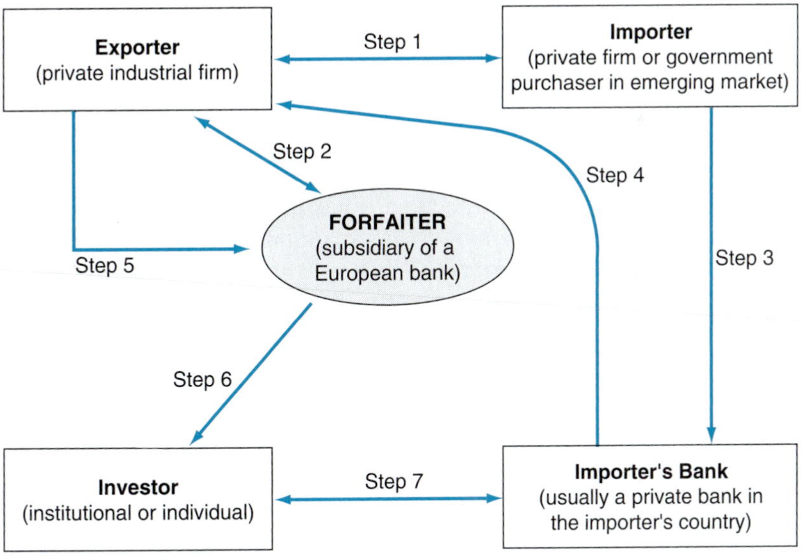

1. *User's Guide—Forfaiting: What is it, who uses it and why?* British-American Forfaiting Company, http://www.tradecompass.com
2. Association of Forfaiters in the Americas (AFIA), 2 Park Avenue, Suite 1522, New York, NY, 10016.

Step 2: Commitment. The forfaiter promises to finance the transaction at a fixed discount rate, with payment to be made when the exporter delivers to the forfaiter the appropriate promissory notes or other specified paper. The agreed-upon discount rate is based on the cost of funds in the Euromarket, usually on LIBOR for the average life of the transaction, plus a margin over LIBOR to reflect the perceived risk in the deal. This risk premium is influenced by the size and tenor of the deal, country risk, and the quality of the guarantor institution. On a five-year deal, for example, with ten semi-annual payments, the rate used would be based on the 2 $^1/_4$ year LIBOR rate. This discount rate is normally added to the invoice value of the transaction so that the cost of financing is ultimately borne by the importer. The forfaiter charges an additional commitment fee ranging from 0.5% per annum to as high as 6.0% per annum from the date of its commitment to finance until receipt of the actual discount paper issued in accordance with the finance contract. This fee is also normally added to the invoice cost and passed on to the importer.

Step 3: *Aval* or Guarantee. The importer obligates itself to pay for its purchases by issuing a series of promissory notes, usually maturing every six or twelve months, against progress on delivery or completion of the project. These promissory notes are first delivered to the importer's bank where they are endorsed (guaranteed) by that bank. In Europe, this unconditional guarantee is referred to as an *aval*, which translates into English as "backing." At this point, the importer's bank becomes the primary obligor in the eyes of all subsequent holders of the notes. The bank's aval or guarantee must be irrevocable, unconditional, divisible, and assignable. Because U.S. banks do not issue avals, U.S. transaction are guaranteed by a standby letter of credit (L/C), which is functionally similar to an aval but more cumbersome. For example, L/Cs can normally be transferred only once.

Step 4: Delivery of notes. The now-endorsed promissory notes are delivered to the exporter.

Step 5: Discounting. The exporter endorses the notes "without recourse" and discounts them with the forfaiter, receiving the agreed-upon proceeds. Proceeds are usually received two days after the documents are presented. By endorsing the notes "without recourse," the exporter frees itself from any liability for future payment on the notes and thus receives the discounted proceeds without having to worry about any further payment difficulties.

Step 6: Investment. The forfaiting bank either holds the notes until full maturity as an investment or endorses and re-discounts them in the international money market. Such subsequent sale by the forfaiter is usually without recourse. The major re-discount markets are in London and Switzerland, plus New York for notes issued in conjunction with Latin American business.

Step 7: Maturity. At maturity, the investor holding the notes presents them for collection to the importer or to the importer's bank. The promise of the importer's bank is what gives the documents their value.

In effect, the forfaiter functions both as a money market firm and as a specialist in packaging financial deals involving country risk. As a money market firm, the forfaiter divides the discounted notes into appropriately sized packages and resells them to various investors having different maturity preferences. As a country risk specialist, the forfaiter assesses the risk that the notes will eventually be paid by the importer or the importer's bank and puts together a deal that satisfies the needs of both exporter and importer.

Success of the forfaiting technique springs from the belief that the aval or guarantee of a commercial bank can be depended on. Although commercial banks are the normal and preferred guarantors, guarantees by government banks or government ministries of finance are accepted in some cases. On occasion, large commercial enterprises have been accepted as debtors without a bank guarantee. An additional aspect of the technique is that the endorsing bank's aval is perceived to be an "off balance sheet" obligation; the debt is presumably not considered by others in assessing the financial structure of the commercial banks.

Countertrade

The word *countertrade* refers to a variety of international trade arrangements in which goods and services are exported by a manufacturer with compensation linked to that manufacturer accepting imports of other goods and services. In other words, an export sale is tied by contract to an import. The countertrade may take place at the same time as the original export, in which case credit is not an issue; or the countertrade may take place later, in which case financing becomes important.

Conventional wisdom is that countertrade takes place with countries having strict foreign exchange controls, countertrade being a way to circumvent those controls; and that countertrade is more likely to take place with countries having low credit-worthiness. One study found to the contrary.[3] The authors found that 1) countries that ban inward foreign direct investment have a significantly higher propensity to engage in countertrade, 2) the higher the level of political risk (i.e., environmental volatility) perceived by foreign investors, the higher the level of countertrade, and 3) the more extensive the degree of state planning, the greater the level of countertrade.

Exhibit 23.11 organizes countertrade into two broad categories—transactions that avoid the use of money, shown along the bottom on the right; and transactions that use money or credit but impose reciprocal commitments, shown along the bottom on the left.

Transactions that avoid the use of money:

- **Simple barter.** *Simple barter* is a direct exchange of physical goods between two parties. It is a one-time transaction carried out under a single contract that specifies both the goods to be delivered and the goods to be received. The two parts of the transaction occur at the same time, and no money is exchanged. Money may, however, be used as the numeraire by which the two values are established and the quantities of each good are determined.
- **Clearing arrangements.** In a *clearing arrangement*, each party agrees to purchase a specific (usually equal) value of goods and services from the other, with the cost of the transactions debited to a special account. At the end of the trading period, any residual imbalances may be cleared by shipping additional goods or by a hard currency payment. In effect, the addition of a clearing agreement to a barter scheme allows for a time lag between barter components. Thus credit facilitates eventual matching of the transactions.
- **Switch trading.** *Switch trading* involves transferring use of bilateral balances from one country to another. For example, an original export from Canada to Romania is paid for with a balance deposited in a clearing account in Romania. Although the clearing account might be

3. Hennart, Jean-Francois, and Erin Anderson, "Countertrade and the Minimization of Transaction Costs: An Empirical Examination," *Journal of Law, Economics, and Organization*, October 1993, pp. 290–313.

Exhibit 23.11 Classification of Forms of Countertrade

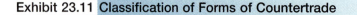

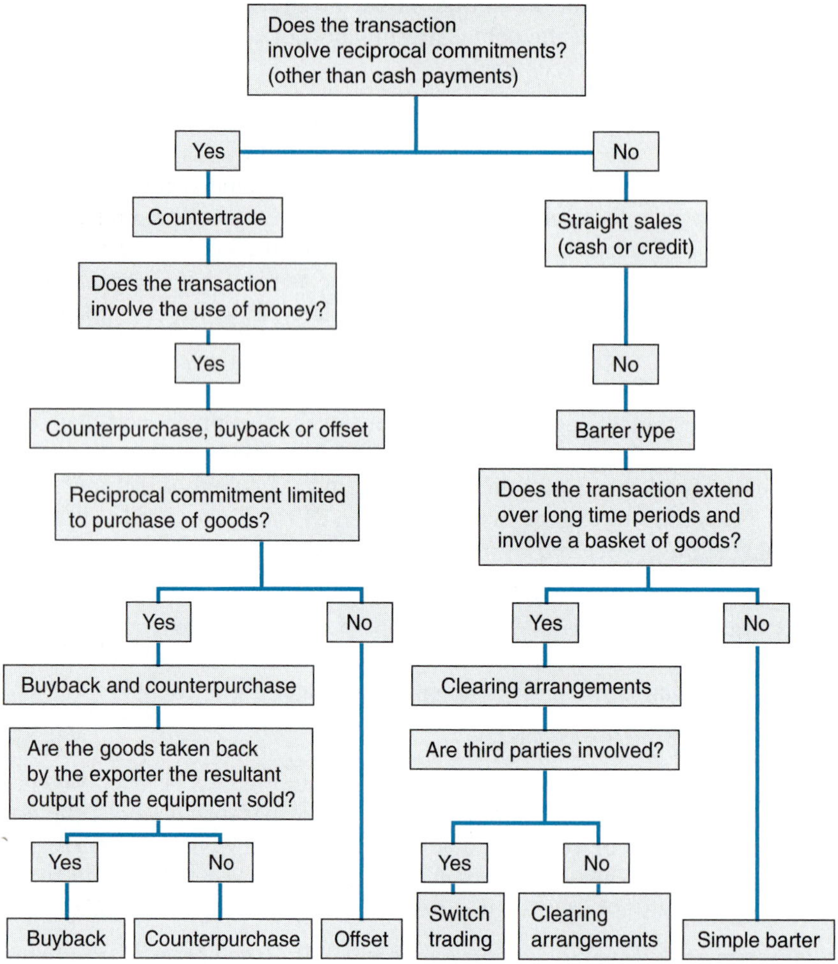

Source: Jean-Francois, Hennart. "Some Empirical Dimensions of Countertrade," *Journal of International Business Studies*, Second Quarter 1990, p. 245. Reprinted with permission.

measured in Canadian dollars or any other currency, the balance can be used only to purchase goods from Romania. The original Canadian exporter might buy unrelated goods from Romania, or it might sell the clearing balance at a discount to a "switch trader," who in turn purchases goods from Romania for sale elsewhere.

Three types of transactions use money or credit but impose reciprocal commitments:

- **Buyback or compensation agreement.** A *compensation agreement*, also called *buyback transaction*, is an agreement by an exporter of plant or equipment to take compensation in the form of future output from that plant. Such an arrangement has attributes that make it, in effect, an alternative form of direct investment. The value of the goods received usually exceeds the value of the original sale, as would be appropriate to reflect the time value of money.

- **Counterpurchase.** A *counterpurchase* involves an initial export, but with the exporter receiving merchandise that is unrelated to items the exporter manufactures. A widely publicized early example was the export of jet aircraft by McDonnell Douglas to Yugoslavia with payment partly in cash and partly in Zagreb hams, wines, dehydrated vegetables, and even some power transmission towers designated eventually for the City of Los Angeles. McDonnell Douglas had the responsibility for reselling the goods received.

- **Offset.** *Offset* refers to the requirement of importing countries that their purchase price be offset in some way by the seller. The exporter may be required to source some of the production locally, to increase imports from the importing country, or to transfer technology.

Reasons for the Growth of Countertrade

In theory, countertrade is a movement away from free multilateral trade. It is a slow, expensive, and convoluted way of conducting trade that often forces firms to set up operations to deal in products very remote from their expertise. The basic problem is that the agreement to take back goods in some form of barter suggests that these goods cannot be sold in the open market for as high a price as is being locked into the countertrade agreement.

Nevertheless, several reasons are advanced in support of countertrade. First, from the perspective of a centrally planned economy, countertrade reduces the risk of fluctuations in export receipts by assuring that future exports will provide foreign exchange roughly equivalent to the cost of the original import.[4] Centrally planned economies have never been competent at marketing their products in foreign countries, perhaps because marketing was not necessary at home. Production plans in these countries are made by a central authority, and the production system does not respond well to sudden changes in export demand. Countertrade provides an assured market for a period of time, and can be negotiated by governmental officials who set economic production quotas, rather than by the managers of individual plants who do not control the availability of resources.

Second, countertrade exports avoid domestic price controls and base prices set by international cartels or commodity agreements. In the case of barter, goods change hands without the explicit use of prices. Consequently any domestic price controls are passed over. Goods can be "sold" abroad at "prices" that are substantially below those charged local customers. Nigeria, Iran, Libya, Indonesia, Iraq, Qatar, and Abu Dhabi are reported to have used barter deals to sell oil below the OPEC cartel agreed-upon price.[5]

Third, because foreign exchange is not created, it need not be turned over to a central bank. Yet the entity that pays for its original imports with mandated countertrade exports in effect earns foreign exchange, which it is able to keep to itself to pay for the import.

4. Hennart, Jean-Francois, "Some Empirical Dimensions of Countertrade," *Journal of International Business Studies*, Second Quarter 1990, p. 247.
5. *Ibid.*, p. 249, quoting *Petroleum Economist*, May 1984.

Fourth, countertrade enables a country to export merchandise of poor design or quality. The merchandise is often sold at a major discount in world markets. Whether this constitutes a discount on the original sale, or even dumping, depends on how that original sale was priced. To the extent that communist and former communist countries have a reputation for poor quality, the marketing of goods in foreign countries by reputable firms gives buyers some assurance of quality and after-sale service.

Survey research indicates that countertrade was most successful for large firms experienced in exporting large, complex products; for firms vertically integrated or that could accommodate countertrade take-backs; and for firms that traded with countries having inappropriate exchange rates, rationed foreign exchange, and import restrictions. Importers who were relatively inexperienced in assessing technology or in export marketing also enjoyed greater success.[6]

SUMMARY

- International trade takes place among three categories of relationships: unaffiliated unknown parties, unaffiliated known parties, and affiliated parties.
- International trade transactions between affiliated parties typically do not require contractual arrangements or external financing. Trade transactions between unaffiliated parties typically require contracts and some type of external financing, such as that available through letters of credit (L/C).
- Over many years, established procedures have arisen to finance international trade. The basic procedure rests on the interrelationship between three key documents: the L/C, the draft, and the bill of lading.
- Variations in each of the three key documents—the L/C, the draft, and the bill of lading—provide a variety of ways to accommodate any type of transaction.
- In the simplest transaction, in which all three documents are used and in which financing is desirable, an importer applies for and receives an L/C from its bank.
- In the L/C, the bank substitutes its credit for that of the importer and promises to pay if certain documents are submitted to the bank. The exporter may now rely on the promise of the bank rather than on the promise of the importer.
- The exporter typically ships on an order bill of lading, attaches the order bill of lading to a draft ordering payment from the importer's bank, and presents these documents, plus any number of additional documents, through its own bank to the importer's bank.
- If the documents are in order, the importer's bank either pays the draft (a sight draft) or accepts the draft (a time draft). In the latter case, the bank promises to pay in the future. At this step, the importer's bank acquires title to the merchandise through the bill of lading, and it then releases the merchandise to the importer against payment or promise of future payment.
- If a sight draft is used, the exporter is paid at once. If a time draft is used, the exporter receives the accepted draft, now a bankers' acceptance, back from the bank. The exporter may hold the bankers' acceptance until maturity or sell it at a discount in the money market.

6. Lecraw, Donald J., "The Management of Countertrade: Factors Influencing Success," *Journal of International Business Studies*, Spring 1989, p. 57.

- The total costs of an exporter entering a foreign market include the transaction costs of the trade financing, the import and export duties and tariffs applied by exporting and importing nations, and the costs of foreign market penetration, which include distribution expenses, inventory costs, and transportation expenses.
- Export credit insurance provides assurance to exporters (or exporters' banks) that should the foreign customer default on payment, the insurance company will pay for a major portion of the loss.
- In the United States, export credit insurance is provided by the Foreign Credit Insurance Association (FCIA), an unincorporated association of private commercial insurance companies operating in cooperation with the Export-Import Bank of the U.S. government.
- The Export-Import Bank of the U.S. government (Eximbank) is an independent agency established to stimulate and facilitate the foreign trade of the United States.
- International trade financing uses the same instruments that are used in domestic trade financing, plus a few instruments that are unique to international trade.
- Countertrade refers to a variety of international trade agreements in which goods and services are exported by a manufacturer with compensation linked to that manufacturer accepting imports of other goods and services.
- Forfaiting is a technique to finance riskier long-term projects that require bank guarantees.

QUESTIONS

1. **Trade dilemma.** What is meant by the term "trade dilemma"?
2. **Basic documents of trade.** What are the three basic documents used in trade with unrelated parties?
3. **Benefits of trade documents.** What are the three main benefits that are derived from using the basic trade documents?
4. **Elements of an import/export transactions.** Each individual trade transaction will need to cover three basic elements (description of goods, prices, and documents regarding shipping and delivery).
   a. What is the role of a "contract"?
   b. What should you be aware of when negotiating price?
   c. What are the typical documents needed for customs and shipping?
5. **Unaffiliated buyers.** Why might different documentation be used for an export to a non-affiliated foreign buyer who is a new customer, as compared to an export to a non-affiliated foreign buyer to whom the exporter has been selling for many years?
6. **Affiliated buyers.** For what reason might an exporter use standard international trade documentation (letter of credit, draft, order bill of lading) on an intra-firm export to its parent or sister subsidiary?
7. **Related party trade.** What reasons can you give for the observation that intra-firm trade is now greater than trade between non-affiliated exporters and importers?
8. **Documents.** Explain the difference between a letter of credit (L/C) and a draft. How are they linked?
9. **Documents.** Explain the difference between a straight bill of lading and an order bill of lading.
10. **Consular invoices and certificates of origin.** Why are consular invoices and certificates of origin often required within the packet of documents prescribed by the letter of credit?
11. **Certificate of analysis.** A shipment of merchandise in international trade often requires a document called a "certificate of analysis." From its name, guess what this document is and why it might be required.

12. **Risks.** What is the major difference between "currency risk" and "risk of non-completion?" How are these risks handled in a typical international trade transaction?

13. **Letter of credit.** Identify each party to a letter of credit (L/C) and indicate its responsibility.

14. **Revocable letter of credit.** Most letters of credit are irrevocable. The bank must honor drafts drawn in accordance with the L/C. However, some letters of credit are revocable. Why would a revocable letter of credit be used?

15. **Confirming a letter of credit.** Why would an exporter insist on a confirmed letter of credit?

16. **Documenting an export of hard drives.** List the steps involved in the export of computer hard disk drives from Penang, Malaysia, to San Jose, California, using an unconfirmed letter of credit authorizing payment on sight.

17. **Documenting an export of lumber from Portland to Yokohama.** List the steps involved in the export of lumber from Portland, Oregon, to Yokohama, Japan, using a confirmed letter of credit, payment to be made in 120 days.

18. **Export credit insurance.**
    a. What is the purpose of export credit insurance?
    b. What is the FCIA?
    c. What types of insurance does FCIA provide?

19. **Export-Import Bank.**
    a. What is the Export-Import Bank in the United States?
    b. What are the functions of the Export-Import Bank?

20. **Countertrade.**
    a. What types of countertrade avoid the use of money?
    b. What types of countertrade use money or credit?
    c. Why is countertrade growing?

PROBLEMS

1. **Bankers' Acceptance: Wisconsin Distillers (A).** Wisconsin Distillers exports beer to Australia and invoices its customers in U.S. dollars. Sydney Wholesale Imports has purchased $1,000,000 of beer from Wisconsin Distillers, with payment due in 6 months. The payment will be made with a bankers' acceptance issued by Charter Bank of Sydney at a fee of 1.75% per annum. Wisconsin Distillers has a weighted average cost of capital of 10%. If Wisconsin Distillers holds this acceptance to maturity. What is its annualized percentage all-in-cost?

2. **Bankers' Acceptance: Wisconsin Distillers (B).** Assuming the facts in problem 1, Bank of America is now willing to buy Wisconsin Distiller's bankers' acceptance for a discount of 6% per annum. What would be Wisconsin Distiller's annualized percentage all-in-cost of financing its $1,000,000 Australian receivable.

3. **Trade Acceptance: Cutler Toyota.** Cutler Toyota buys its cars from Toyota Motors-USA, and sells them to U.S. customers. One of its customers is Green Transport, a car rental firm which buys cars from Cutler Toyota at a wholesale price. Final payment is due to Cutler Toyota in 6 months. Green Transport has bought $200,000 worth of cars from Cutler, with a cash down payment of $40,000 and the balance due in 6 months without any interest charged as a sales incentive. Cutler Toyota will have the Green Transport receivable accepted by Alliance Acceptance for a 2% fee, and then sell it at a 3% per annum discount to Wells Fargo Bank.
    a. What is the annualized percentage all-in-cost to Cutler Toyota?
    b. What are Cutler Transport's net cash proceeds, including the cash down payment?

4. **Trade Acceptance: Sun Microsystems (A).** Assume Sun Microsystems has sold Internet servers to Telecom Italia for €700,000. Payment is due in 3 months and will be made with a trade acceptance from Telecom Italia Acceptance. The acceptance fee is 1.0% per annum of the face amount of the note. This acceptance will be sold at a 4% per annum discount. What is the annualized percentage all-in-cost in euros of this method of trade financing?

5. **Foreign Exchange Acceptance: Sun Microsystems (B).** Assume that Sun Microsystems prefers to receive U.S. dollars rather than euros for the trade transaction described in Problem 4. It is considering two alternatives: 1) It can sell the acceptance for euros at once and convert the euros immediately to U.S. dollars at the spot rate of exchange of $1.00/€; or 2) It can hold the euro acceptance until maturity but sell the expected euro proceeds forward for dollars at the 3-month forward rate of $1.02/€.
   a. What are the U.S. dollar net proceeds received at once from the discounted trade acceptance in alternative 1?
   b. What are the U.S. dollar net proceeds received in three months in alternative 2?
   c. What is the break-even investment rate that would equalize the net U.S. dollar proceeds from both alternatives?
   d. Which alternative should Sun Microsystems choose?

6. **Bank Credit Line With Export Credit Insurance: Hollywood Entertainment (A).** Hollywood Entertainment has sold a combination of films and DVDs to Hong Kong Media Incorporated for US$100,000, with payment due in six months. Hollywood Entertainment has the following alternatives for financing this receivable: 1) Use its bank credit line. Interest would be at the prime rate of 5% plus 150 basis points per annum. Hollywood Enterprises would need to maintain a compensating balance of 20% of the loan's face amount. No interest will be paid on the compensating balance by the bank; 2) Use its bank credit line but purchase export credit insurance for a 1% fee. Because of the reduced risk, the bank interest rate would be reduced to 5% per annum without any points.
   a. What are the annualized percentage all-in-costs of each alternative?
   b. What are the advantages and disadvantages of each alternative?
   c. Which alternative would you recommend?

7. **Hollywood Entertainment (B).** In the situation described above, Hollywood Entertainment has been approached by a factor that offers to purchase the Hong Kong Media Imports receivable at a 16% per annum discount plus a 2% charge for a non-recourse clause.
   a. What is the annualized percentage all-in-cost of this factoring alternative?
   b. What are the advantages and disadvantages of the factoring alternative compared to the alternatives in Hollywood Entertainment (A)?

8. **Forfaiting at Kaduna Oil (Nigeria).** Kaduna Oil of Nigeria has purchased $1,000,000 of oil drilling equipment from Unicorn Drilling of Houston, Texas. Kaduna Oil must pay for this purchase over the next five years at a rate of $200,000 per year due on March 1 of each year.

   Bank of Zurich, a Swiss forfaiter, has agreed to buy the five notes of $200,000 each at a discount. The discount rate would be approximately 8% per annum based on the expected three-year LIBOR rate plus 200 basis points, paid by Kaduna Oil. Bank of Zurich also would charge Kaduna Oil an additional commitment fee of 2% per annum from the date of its commitment to finance until receipt of the actual discounted notes issued in accordance with the financing contract. The first $200,000 promissory note will come due on March 1 in successive years.

   The promissory notes issued by Kaduna Oil will be endorsed by its bank, Lagos City Bank, for a 1% fee and delivered to Unicorn Drilling. At this point Unicorn Drilling will endorse the notes *without recourse* and discount them with the forfaiter, Bank of Zurich, receiving the full $200,000 principal amount.

Bank of Zurich will sell the notes by re-discounting them to investors in the international money market without recourse. At maturity the investor holding the notes will present them for collection at Lagos City Bank. If Lagos City Bank defaults on payment, the investor will collect on the note from Bank of Zurich.

a. What is the annualized percentage all-in-cost to Kaduna Oil of financing the first $200,000 note due March 1, 2004?

b. What might motivate Kaduna Oil to use this relatively expensive alternative for financing?

9. **Andersen Sports (A): Letter of Credit.** Andersen Sports (Andersen) is considering bidding to sell $100,000 of ski equipment to Kim Family Enterprises of Seoul, Korea. Payment would be due in six months. Since Andersen cannot find good credit information on Kim, Andersen wants to protect its credit risk. It is considering the following financing solution.

   Kim's bank issues a letter of credit on behalf of Kim and agrees to accept Andersen's draft for $100,000 due in six months. The acceptance fee would cost Andersen $500, plus reduce Kim's available credit line by $100,000. The bankers' acceptance note of $100,000 would be sold at a 2% per annum discount in the money market. What is the annualized percentage all-in-cost to Andersen of this bankers' acceptance financing?

10. **Andersen Sports (B): Bank Credit Line With Export Credit Insurance.** Andersen could also buy export credit insurance from FCIA for a 1.5% premium. It finances the $100,000 receivable from Kim from its credit line at 6% per annum interest. No compensating bank balance would be required.

    a. What is Andersen's annualized percentage all-in-cost of financing?

    b. What are Kim's costs?

    c. What are the advantages and disadvantages of this alternative compared to the bankers' acceptance financing in Andersen (A)? Which alternative would you recommend?

INTERNET EXERCISES

1. **Letter of credit services.** Commercial banks worldwide provide a variety of services to aid in the financing of foreign trade. Contact any of the many major multinational banks (a few are listed below) and determine what types of letter of credit services and other trade financing services which they are able to provide.

Citibank	http://www.citibank.com
Barclays	http://www.barclays.com
Deutsche Bank	http://www.deutschebank.com
Union Bank of Switzerland	http://www.unionbank.com
Swiss Bank Corporation	http://www.swissbank.com

2. **Export-Import Bank of the United States.** The Eximbank of the United States provides financing for U.S.-based exporters. Like most major industrial country trade-financing organizations, it is intended to aid in the export sale of products in which the buyer needs attractive financing terms. Use the Eximbank's web site to determine the current country limits, fees, and other restrictions which currently apply. (Added note, the Export-Import Bank's web page provides some of the best web site links in international business and statistics.)

Export-Import Bank of the United States	http://www.exim.gov

SELECTED READINGS

Dominguez, Luis V., and Carlos G. Sequeira, "Determinants of LDC Exporters' Performance: A Cross-National Study," *Journal of International Business Studies*, First Quarter 1993, pp. 19–40.

Hennart, Jean-Francois, "Some Empirical Dimensions of Countertrade," *Journal of International Business Studies*, Second Quarter 1990, pp. 243–270.

Lecraw, Donald J., "The Management of Countertrade: Factors Influencing Success," *Journal of International Business Studies*, Spring 1989, pp. 41–59.

MINI-CASE

Crosswell International's Precious Ultra-Thin Diapers

Crosswell International is a U.S.-based manufacturer and distributor of health care products, including children's diapers. Crosswell has been approached by Leonardo Sousa, the president of Material Hospitalar, a distributor of health care products throughout Brazil. Sousa is interested in distributing Crosswell's major diaper product, Precious, but only if an acceptable arrangement regarding pricing and payment terms can be reached. Considerable competition exists in the Brazilian diaper market.

Exporting to Brazil

Crosswell's manager for export operations, Geoff Mathieux, followed up the preliminary discussions by putting together an estimate of export costs and pricing for discussion purposes with Sousa. Crosswell needs to know all of the costs and pricing assumptions for the entire supply and value chain as it reaches the consumer. Mathieux believes it critical that any arrangement that Crosswell enters into results in a price to consumers in the Brazilian marketplace that is both fair to all parties involved and competitive, given the market niche Crosswell hopes to penetrate. This first cut on pricing Precious diapers imported into Brazil is presented in Exhibit A.

Crosswell proposes to sell the basic diaper line to the Brazilian distributor for $34.00 per case, FAS (free alongside ship) Miami docks. This means that the seller, Crosswell, agrees to cover all costs associated with getting the diapers to the Miami docks. The cost of loading the diapers aboard ship, the actual cost of shipping (freight), and the cost of associated documents is $4.32 per case. The running subtotal, $38.32 per case, is termed CFR (cost and freight). Finally, the insurance expenses related to the potential loss of the goods while in transit to final port of destination, export insurance, are $0.86 per case. The total CIF (cost, insurance, and freight) is $39.18 per case, or 97.95 Brazilian real per case, assuming an exchange rate of 2.50 Brazilian real (R$) per U.S. dollar ($). In summary, the CIF cost of R$97.95 is the price charged by the exporter to the importer on arrival in Brazil, and is calculated as follows:

$$\text{CIF} = \text{FAS} + \text{freight} + \text{export insurance} = (\$34.00 + \$4.32 + \$0.86) \times \text{R}\$2.50/\$ = \text{R}\$97.95$$

The actual cost to the distributor in getting the diapers through the port and customs warehouses must also be calculated in terms of what Leonardo Sousa's costs are in reality. The various fees and taxes detailed in Exhibit A raise the fully landed cost of the Precious diapers to R$107.63 per case. The distributor would now bear storage and inventory costs totaling R$8.33 per case, which would bring the costs to R$115.96. The distributor then adds a

Exhibit A Export Pricing for the Precious Diaper Line to Brazil

The Precious Ultra-Thin Diaper will be shipped via container. Each container will hold 968 cases of diapers. The costs and prices below are calculated on a per-case basis, although some costs and fees are assessed by container.

Exports Costs and Pricing to Brazil	**Per Case**	**Rates and Calculation**
FAS price per case, Miami	$34.00	
Freight, loading and documentation	4.32	$4180 per container/968 = $4.32
CFR price per case, Brazilian port (Santos)	$38.32	
Export insurance	0.86	2.25% of CIF
CIF to Brazilian port	$39.18	
CIF to Brazilian port, in Brazilian real	R$97.95	R$2.50/US$ × $39.18
Brazilian Importation Costs		
Import duties	1.96	2.00% of CIF
Merchant marine renovation fee	2.70	25.00% of freight
Port storage fees	1.27	1.30% of CIF
Port handling fees	0.01	R$12 per container
Additional handling fees	0.26	20.00% of storage and handling
Customs brokerage fees	1.96	2.00% of CIF
Import license fee	0.05	R$50 per container
Local transportation charges	1.47	1.50% of CIF
Total cost to distributor in real	R$107.63	
Distributor's Costs and Pricing		
Storage cost	1.47	1.50% of CIF × months
Cost of financing diaper inventory	6.86	7.00% of CIF × months
Distributor's margin	23.19	20.00% of price + storage + financing
Price to retailer in real	R$139.15	
Brazilian Retailer Costs and Pricing		
Industrial product tax (IPT)	20.87	15.00% of price to retailer
Mercantile circulation services tax (MCS)	28.80	18.00% of price + IPT
Retailer costs and markup	56.65	30.00% of price + IPT + MCS
Price to consumer in real	R$245.48	

Diaper Prices to Consumers	**Diapers Per Case**	**Price Per Diaper**
Small size	352	R$ 0.70
Medium size	256	R$ 0.96
Large size	192	R$ 1.28

margin for distribution services of 20% (R$23.19), raising the price as sold to the final retailer to R$139.15 per case.

Finally, the retailer (a supermarket or other retailer of consumer health-care products) would include its expenses, taxes, and markup to reach the final shelf price to the customer of R$245.48 per case. This final retail price estimate now allows both Crosswell and Material Hospitalar to evaluate the price competitiveness of the Precious Ultra-Thin Diaper in the Brazilian marketplace and provides a basis for further negotiations between the two parties.

Mathieux provides the previous export price quotation, an outline of a potential representation agreement (for Sousa to represent Crosswell's product lines in the Brazilian marketplace), and payment and credit terms to Leonardo Sousa. Crosswell's payment and credit terms are that Sousa either pay in full in cash in advance, or with a confirmed irrevocable documentary L/C with a time draft specifying a tenor of 60 days.

Crosswell also requests from Sousa financial statements, banking references, foreign commercial references, descriptions of regional sales forces, and sales forecasts for the Precious diaper line. These last requests by Crosswell are very important for Crosswell to be able to assess Material Hospitalar's ability to be a dependable, creditworthy, and capable long-term partner and representative of the firm in the Brazilian marketplace. The discussions that follow focus on finding acceptable common ground between the two parties and working to increase the competitiveness of the Precious diaper in the Brazilian marketplace.

Crosswell's Proposal

The proposed sale by Crosswell to Material Hospitalar, at least in the initial shipment, is for 10 containers of 968 cases of diapers at $39.18 per case, CIF Brazil, payable in U.S. dollars. This is a total invoice amount of $379,262.40. Payment terms are that a confirmed L/C will be required of Material Hospitalar on a U.S. bank. The payment will be based on a time draft of 60 days, presentation to the bank for acceptance with other documents on the date of shipment. Both the exporter and the exporter's bank will expect payment from the importer or importer's bank 60 days from this date of shipment.

What should Crosswell expect? Assuming Material Hospitalar acquires the L/C and it is confirmed by Crosswell's bank in the United States, Crosswell will ship the goods after the initial agreement—say 15, days—as illustrated in Exhibit B.

Simultaneous with the shipment, in which Crosswell has lost physical control over the goods, Crosswell will present the bill of lading acquired at the time of shipment with the other needed documents to its bank requesting payment. Because the export is under a confirmed L/C, assuming all documents are in order, Crosswell's bank will give Crosswell two choices:

1. Wait the full time period of the time draft of 60 days and receive the entire payment in full ($379,262.40).
2. Receive the discounted value of this amount today. The discounted amount, assuming U.S. dollar interest rate of 6.00% per annum (1.00% per 60 days) is:

$$\frac{\$379{,}262.40}{(1+0.01)} = \frac{\$379{,}262.40}{1.01} = \$375{,}507.33$$

Exhibit B Export Payment Terms on Crosswell's Export to Brazil

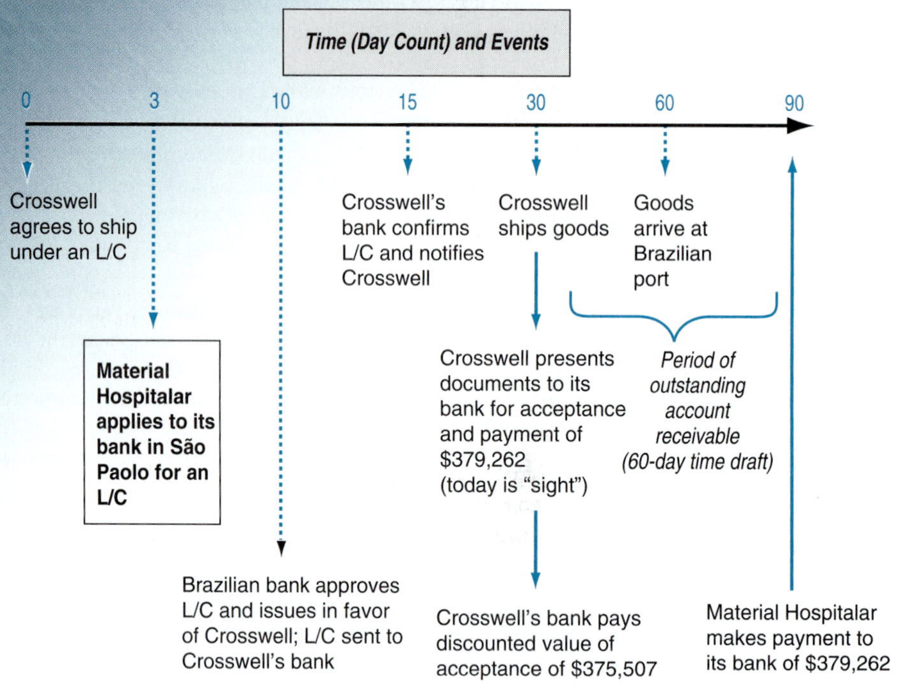

Because the invoice is denominated in U.S. dollars, Crosswell need not worry about currency value changes (currency risk). And because its bank has confirmed the L/C, it is protected against changes or deteriorations in Material Hospitalar's ability to pay on the future date.

What should Material Hospitalar expect? Material Hospitalar will receive the goods on or before day 60. It will then move the goods through its distribution system to retailers. Depending on the payment terms between Material Hospitalar and its buyers (retailers), it could either receive cash or terms for payment for the goods. Because Material Hospitalar purchased the goods via the 60-day time draft and an L/C from its Brazilian bank, total payment of $379,262.40 is due on day 90 (shipment and presentation of documents was on day 30 + 60-day time draft) to the Brazilian bank.

Material Hospitalar, because it is a Brazil-based company and has agreed to make payment in U.S. dollars (foreign currency), carries the currency risk of the transaction.

Crosswell/Material Hospitalar's Concern

The concern the two companies share is that the total price to the consumer in Brazil, R$245.48 per case, or R$0.70/diaper (small size), is too high. The major competitors in the Brazilian market for premium quality diapers, Kenko do Brasil (Japan), Johnson & Johnson (USA), and Procter & Gamble (USA), are cheaper (see Exhibit C). The competitors all manufacture in-country, thus avoiding the series of import duties and tariffs that have added significantly to Crosswell's landed prices in the Brazilian marketplace.

Exhibit C Competitive Diaper Prices in the Brazilian Market (in Brazilian real)

		Price per diaper by size		
Company (Country)	**Brand**	**Small**	**Medium**	**Large**
Kenko (Japan)	Monica Plus	0.68	0.85	1.18
Procter & Gamble (USA)	Pampers Uni	0.65	0.80	1.08
Johnson & Johnson (USA)	Sempre Seca Plus	0.65	0.80	1.08
Crosswell (USA)	Precious	0.70	0.96	1.40

Case Questions

1. How are pricing, currency of denomination, and financing interrelated in the value chain for Crosswell's penetration of the Brazilian market? Can you summarize them using Exhibit B?
2. How important is Sousa to the value chain of Crosswell? What worries might Crosswell have regarding Sousa's ability to fulfill his obligations?
3. If Crosswell is to penetrate the market, some way of reducing its prices will be required. What do you suggest?

Chapter 24

Advanced Topics in International Finance

THIS CHAPTER PROVIDES A MORE RIGOROUS PRESENTATION OF A NUMBER OF TOPICS INTRODUCED in previous chapters, including the determination of the optimal currency hedge ratio, cross-currency "proxy" hedging, delta-neutral hedging strategies, and the construction and use of a number of increasingly accepted second-generation option products such as range forwards and participating forwards.

The Currency Hedge Ratio

The Chapter 8 discussion of transaction exposure management assumed—without discussion—a hedge ratio of 1.0. The *hedge ratio*, frequently termed *beta* (β), is the percentage of an individual exposure's nominal amount covered by a financial instrument such as a forward contract or currency option. Beta is then defined as follows:

$$\beta = \frac{\text{value of currency hedge}}{\text{value of currency exposure}}$$

This section describes the theoretical methodology for the determination of the *optimal hedge ratio*—the *optimal beta.*

The Optimal Hedge

The value of an individual currency position can be expressed as a portfolio of two assets: a spot asset (the exposure) and a hedge asset (a forward, future, or option). The hedge is constructed so that whatever spot value is lost as a result of adverse exchange rate movements (Δ spot) is replaced by an equal but opposite change in the value of the hedge asset, the futures position (Δ futures):

$$\Delta \text{ position value} = \Delta \text{ spot} - \Delta \text{ futures} \approx 0$$

The goal is to formulate the effective hedge which will indeed result in ΔV=0.

The *optimal currency hedge* can be found by minimizing the terminal (end-of-period) variance of the two asset portfolio. The hedge asset amount as a percentage of the exposure is altered to minimize the terminal portfolio variance.

For example, a multinational firm is expecting a foreign currency–denominated payment, an account receivable at a future date, time t_1, which is termed here the spot or *cash position*. The amount of the hedge, however, must be determined now, at time t_0. We can then specify the expected value of this receivable at the future date as:

$$E\left(X_1^{\$}\right) = X_1 \times E\left(S_1\right)$$

where $E(X_1^{\$})$ is the expected value of the foreign currency receivable at time 1;

X_1 is the amount of the foreign currency to be received (in foreign currency)

$E(S_1)$ is the expected spot rate to occur at time 1; it is presently unknown

Note that the present spot rate is not a part of the expected value at the end of the period.

Because it does not know what the exchange rate will actually be on the future date, the firm would like to hedge its foreign currency exposure. It can sign a forward contract that would guarantee it a specific exchange rate for U.S. dollars per unit of foreign currency at time t_1, for whatever amount of foreign currency it wishes. The firm then forms a portfolio of this cash position above and a forward contract as a hedge asset. The expected value of the portfolio, $E(P_1)$, at the end of the period, is:

$$E\left(P_1^{\$}\right) = X_1 E\left(S_1\right) + X_f\left[E\left(F_1\right) - F_0\right]$$

where X_f is the amount of foreign currency sold forward at time 0

F^0 is the current price of the futures contract

$E(F_1)$ is the expected futures price at time 1

This is the expectation now of the portfolio's total value when the receivable is paid in 90 days.

The expected spot rate in 90 days is the only true unknown. The *decision variable* is the amount of the foreign currency that it chooses to sell forward. The question is what is the specific (mathematical) goal that the firm is pursuing when it chooses the amount of the hedge? Answer: to minimize the variance of the expected return. This would translate mathematically into selecting the X_f value that results in the minimum variance of the portfolio's final value.

The variance of the expected portfolio value is:

$$\text{var}\left[E\left(P_1^{\$}\right)\right] = X^2\,\text{var}\left(S_1\right) + X_f^2\,\text{var}\left(F_1\right) + 2XX_f\,\text{cov}\left(S_1, F_1\right)$$

Thus, the quantitative problem at hand is the *minimization* of this variance with respect to the decision variable, X_f:

$$\underset{X_f}{\text{MIN}}\ \text{var}\left[E\left(P_1^{\$}\right)\right] = X^2\,\text{var}\left(S_1\right) + X_f^2\,\text{var}\left(F_1\right) + 2XX_f\,\text{cov}\left(S_1, F_1\right)$$

Differentiating the total variance with respect to X_f, and setting the results equal to zero yields the following:[1]

$$2X_f \operatorname{var}(F_1) = -2X \operatorname{cov}(S_1, F_1)$$

This equation is then solved for the amount of foreign currency to be sold forward (X_f) to minimize the portfolio's terminal variance:

$$X_f = \frac{-2X \operatorname{cov}(S_1, F_1)}{2\operatorname{var}(F_1)} = \frac{-X \operatorname{cov}(S_1, F_1)}{\operatorname{var}(F_1)}$$

Finally, if this equation is rearranged to determine the relative size of the optimal hedge amount to the amount of the original exposure, the *optimal hedge ratio–Beta*, is found:

$$\frac{X_f}{X} = \beta = \frac{-\operatorname{cov}(S_1, F_1)}{\operatorname{var}(F_1)}$$

Optimal Hedge Calculation Example

What are the implications in practice for this theoretical model of the optimal hedge? Assume a U.S.-based firm expects the receipt of DM1,000,000 in 90 days. With this model, the only values necessary for the determination of the optimal hedge percentage, beta, are the variance of the 90-day forward, 0.005573, and the covariance between the spot rate (\$/DM) and the forward rate (\$/DM) of 0.0054998. The optimal hedge ratio is:

$$\beta = \frac{X_f}{X} = \frac{-0.0054998}{0.005573} = -0.986865 \approx 98.69\%$$

This optimal hedge ratio indicates that if the firm wishes to minimize the expected value of the two asset portfolio (spot position and forward position) at the end of the 90 days, it should sell 98.68% of the DM exposure forward, or 0.9868 × DM1,000,000 = DM986,865.

A beta of 1.0 would imply that the entire amount of the exposure (100%) should be sold forward, yet the theoretical model implies a value that is slightly less than 1. Why is that? The reason is that the spot rate and the futures rate are not perfectly correlated. This less than perfect correlation is called *basis risk*. Given that the spot and forward rates for most major currencies typically indicate similar high hedge ratios (0.97 and up), hedgers generally do not bother to evaluate and hedge less than the beta of 1.0 when selling currency forward to eliminate exchange rate risk.

---

1. Differentiation of the entire equation with respect to X_f results in the left-hand side equaling zero, and the first term on the right-hand side also equaling zero. The remaining terms would appear as:

$$0 = 0 + 2X_f \operatorname{var}(F_1) + 2X \operatorname{cov}(S_1, F_1)$$

Cross-Hedging

Sometimes there are no available futures or forward markets for currencies. In these cases, the risk manager might wish to use a substitute or *proxy* for the underlying currency that is available. The methodology used for the determination of the optimal hedge ratio in the previous section is also helpful in the analysis of *proxy-hedging* or *cross-hedging*.

The cross-hedger would likely go through a simple two-step process to determine the optimal cross-hedge: first, find the currency futures most highly correlated with the actual currency of exposure; second, find the optimal hedge ratio using the covariance between the proxy futures and the actual currency as in the previous model. This equation will tell the risk manager the amount of the proxy future that should be purchased to hedge the currency exposure.

Delta Hedging

A slightly more sophisticated currency hedging strategy than the traditional one demonstrated in Chapter 6 is called *delta hedging*. The objective of delta hedging is to construct a position—the combined exposure and hedging instrument—whose market values (not terminal values) will change in opposite directions with changes in the spot exchange rate; it is the value of the position at all times which is being managed, not the value of the position only at termination.

Returning to the basic position valuation principle introduced at the beginning of this chapter: if the hedge is constructed so that the changes in the spot position and hedge position are equal and opposite in currency value at all times in the life-span of the exposure, it is termed *delta-neutral*.

$$\Delta \text{ position value} = \Delta \text{ spot} - \Delta \text{ futures}$$

What is lost (gained) on the spot position as a result of exchange rate changes is exactly offset by the gain (loss) in the market value of the hedge instrument.

A numerical example helps in differentiating this strategy from the generic hedging we have described up to now. Assume a U.S.-based firm has an account payable in 90 days in the amount of £1,000,000. The current exchange rate and interest rate values are the same as those used in Chapter 5 in the explanation of currency option valuation and its corresponding "Greeks."

spot rate	= \$1.7000/£
90-day forward	= \$1.7000/£
strike rate	= \$1.7000/£
U.S. dollar interest rate	= 8.00 % (per annum)
British pound interest rate	= 8.00 % (per annum)
time (days)	= 90
standard deviation (volatility)	= 10.00 %

This call option on British pounds, with strike price of \$1.70/£ (forward at-the-money), has a premium of 3.3 cents/£. The delta of this option is 0.5. This value means that the value of the option, the option premium, will change by (0.5) × (change in spot rate). For example, if the spot rate moves from \$1.70/£ to \$1.71/£, the option premium changes by:

$$\Delta \text{ option premium} = 0.5 \times (\$1.71/£ - \$1.70/£) = \$0.005/£$$

This delta is the focal point of a delta-hedging strategy.

Exhibit 24.1 illustrates how a delta-neutral hedge would be constructed for this exposure. The firm that is short in a foreign currency fears a foreign currency appreciation versus the domestic currency. If the spot rate were to rise to \$1.71/£, while all other values remained the same, the expected cost in U.S. dollars of making the payment would rise from \$1,700,000 to \$1,710,000, an increase of \$10,000.

At the same time, the value of the call option on British pounds—the market price of the option—would rise from 3.3 cents/£ to 3.8 cents/£; or one half-cent per pound purchased. Since the cost of the foreign currency payable has increased one cent per pound and the option's value changes by only one-half cent per pound, if the value of the option position is to offset the change in the exposure, the option contract would need to be for twice the amount of the exposure, or £2,000,000. An option for £2,000,000 would increase in value from the purchase price of \$66,000 to \$76,000 in market value after the spot rate changes. The impact of the exchange rate change has been "neutralized" by the combined position.

Delta-hedging strategies utilize the *total value* of the option (the market value that includes both intrinsic value and time value) as the hedge instrument's value, not simply the *intrinsic value*, which has been utilized throughout previous chapters. Although this is more theoretically correct, delta-hedging has two major drawbacks:

1. Delta-neutral positions such as the example shown here require the purchase of option or other financial derivative contracts, which are often substantially larger in currency amount than the exposure itself. In this case, the option contract is for £2,000,000 in order to hedge an exposure of £1,000,000. Many firms believe this is inherently speculative and overly expensive in capital outlays.
2. Delta-neutral positions must be constantly monitored and frequently rebalanced. For example, after the spot rate in the previous example has moved to \$1.71/£, the delta of the option has now

Exhibit 24.1 Construction and Valuation of a Delta-Neutral Hedging Strategy

(1) Spot Rate	(2) Value of Exposure	(3) US\$ Value of Exposure[a]	(4) Call Option Premium[b]	(5) Option Contract	(6) Market Value[c] of Option[d]
\$1.70/£	£1,000,000	\$1,700,000	\$0.033/£	£2,000,000	\$66,000
\$1.71/£	£1,000,000	\$1,710,000	\$0.038/£	£2,000,000	\$76,000
Change in value:		\$10,000	\$0.005/£		+ \$10,000

a Column (3) = column (1) × column (2).

b Call option strike price of \$1.70/£, 90-day maturity, volatility of 10% per annum, delta = 0.5.

c Option contract size for delta-neutral hedge = exposure/delta = £1,000,000/0.5 = £2,000,000. The delta of the same call option (strike price \$1.70/£) rises to 0.546 after spot rate moves to \$1.71/£.

d Column (6) = column (4) × column (5)

risen to approximately 0.55 from 0.50. In order to maintain a delta-neutral position, the firm needs currency coverage of only £1,818,182 (£1,000,000 ÷ 0.55). It would sell part of the existing option position down to the new delta-neutral position. This procedure requires active management and more frequent transactions, which many firms do not wish to undertake.

Financial Engineering and Risk Management

Financial engineering has come to mean very different things to different people. We use it here to describe the use of the basic financial building blocks (spot positions, forwards, options) to construct positions that provide the user with desired risk and return characteristics. The number of combinations and deviations is indeed infinite.

The following techniques are, however, simply tools. They are a means to an end—foreign currency risk management—and not an end themselves. The purpose of this section is to demonstrate the mechanics of their construction and to highlight for which types of currency exposures they may be appropriate. Many of these products have been developed for a specific risk-management problem, a problem that may or may not be applicable to all firms. With a few notable exceptions, the following products can be acquired either as risk management products from financial institutions or constructed by the firm itself.

Problem: Dayton Manufacturing's 90-Day Account Receivable

Exhibit 24.2 illustrates the problem that is used throughout the remainder of this chapter. A U.S.-based firm possesses a long £1,000,000 exposure—an account receivable—to be settled in 90 days. The firm believes that the exchange rate will move in its favor over the 90-day period (the British pound will appreciate versus the U.S. dollar). Despite having this *directional view* or *currency expectation*, the firm wishes downside protection for the event that the pound were to depreciate instead. Exhibit 24.2 also lists the assumptions and option values used throughout the remainder of this chapter.

The exposure management zones that are of most interest to the firm are the two opposing triangles formed by the uncovered and forward rate profiles. The firm would like to retain all potential area in the upper-right triangle, but minimize its own potential exposure to the bottom-left triangle. The put option's "kinked profile" is consistent with what the firm wishes since it believes the pound will appreciate (dollar will depreciate).

The firm could consider any number of different put option strike prices, depending on what minimum assured value—degree of self-insurance—the firm is willing to accept. Exhibit 24.2 illustrates two different put option alternatives, a forward-ATM put of strike price $1.4700/£, and a forward-OTM put with strike price $1.4400/£. Because foreign currency options are actually priced about the forward rate (see Chapter 5), not the spot rate, the correct specification of whether an option, put or call, is ITM, ATM, or OTM, is in reference to the same maturity forward rate. The forward-OTM put provides protection at lower cost, but also at a lower level of protection.

The Synthetic Forward

At a forward rate of $1.4700/£, the proceeds of the forward contract in 90 days will yield $1,470,000. A second alternative for the firm would be to construct a *synthetic*

Exhibit 24.2 Chapter Problem: Situation, Assumptions, and Option Premiums

		Put Option	Strike Rates	Premium
Spot rate	$1.4790/£			
90-day forward rate	$1.4700/£			
90-day euro-$ interest rate	3.250%	Forward ATM put	$1.4700/£	$0.0318/£
90-day euro-£ interest rate	5.720%	OTM put	$1.4400/£	$0.0188/£
90-day $/£ volatility	11.000%			

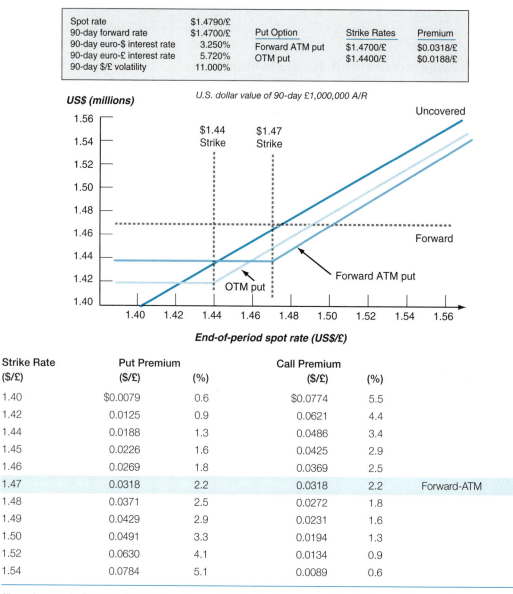

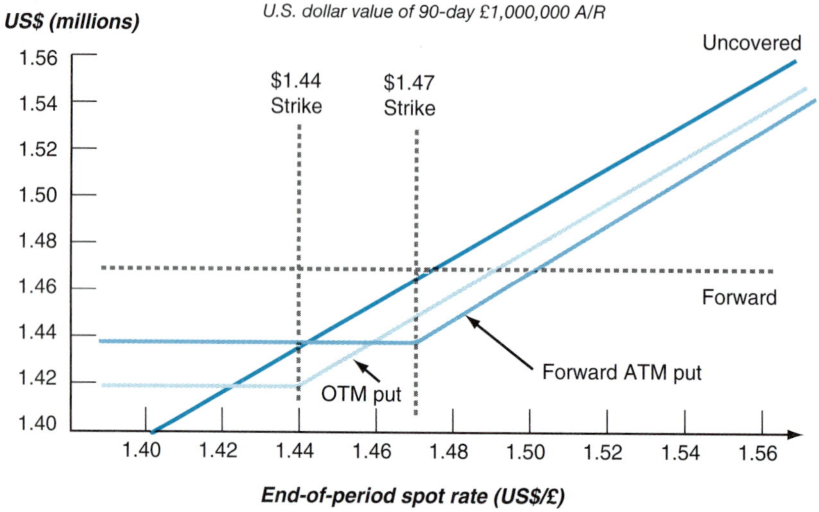

Strike Rate ($/£)	Put Premium ($/£)	(%)	Call Premium ($/£)	(%)	
1.40	$0.0079	0.6	$0.0774	5.5	
1.42	0.0125	0.9	0.0621	4.4	
1.44	0.0188	1.3	0.0486	3.4	
1.45	0.0226	1.6	0.0425	2.9	
1.46	0.0269	1.8	0.0369	2.5	
1.47	0.0318	2.2	0.0318	2.2	Forward-ATM
1.48	0.0371	2.5	0.0272	1.8	
1.49	0.0429	2.9	0.0231	1.6	
1.50	0.0491	3.3	0.0194	1.3	
1.52	0.0630	4.1	0.0134	0.9	
1.54	0.0784	5.1	0.0089	0.6	

All premiums are for European-style options and are calculated using the currency option pricing spreadsheet employed throughout this text. All premiums are rounded to the nearest hundredth of a cent. Premiums are stated in both absolute $/£ terms and as a percentage of the strike price (industry practice).

forward using options. The synthetic forward requires the firm to combine three different elements:

1. Long position in £ (A/R of £1,000,000)
2. Buy a put option on £ bought at a strike price of $1.4700/£, paying a premium of $0.0318/£
3. Sell a call option on £ at a strike price of $1.4700/£, earning a premium of $0.0318/£

The purchase of the put option requires a premium payment, while the sale of the call option earns the firm the premium payment. If both options are struck at the forward rate (forward-ATM), the premiums should be identical and the net premium payment a value of zero.

Exhibit 24.3 illustrates the uncovered position, the basic forward rate hedge, and the individual profiles of the put and call options for the chapter problem. The outcome of the combined position is easily confirmed by simply tracing what would happen at all exchange rates to the left of $1.4700/£, and what would happen to the right of $1.4700/£.

At all exchange rates to the left of $1.4700/£:

1. The firm would receive £1,000,000 in 90 days
2. The call option on pounds sold by the firm would expire out-of-the-money
3. The firm would exercise the put option on pounds to sell the pounds received at $1.4700/£

Exhibit 24.3 Construction of a Synthetic Forward for a Long FX Position

Instruments	Strike Rates	Premium	Notional Principle
Buy a put	$1.4700/£	$0.0318/£	£ 1,000,000
Sell a call	$1.4700/£	$0.0318/£	£ 1,000,000

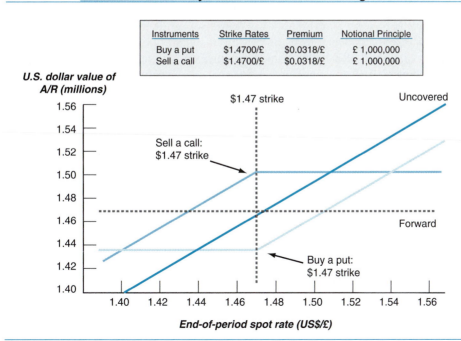

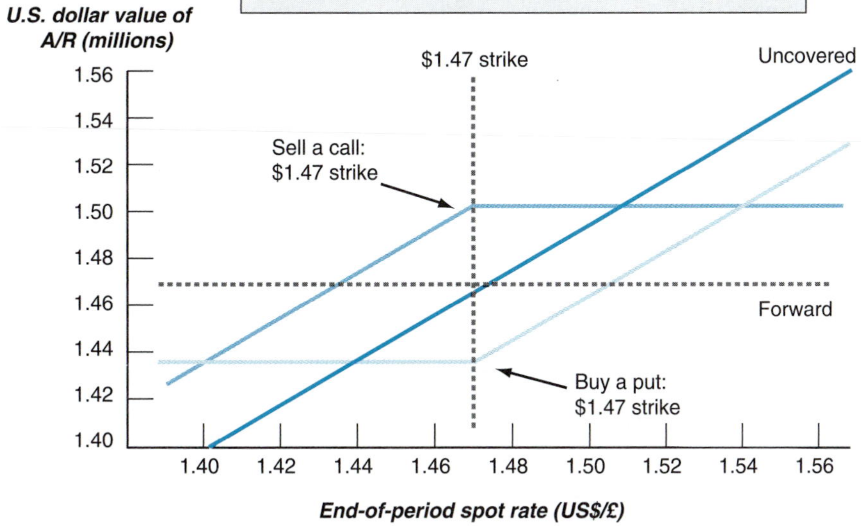

At all exchange rates below \$1.4700/£, the U.S.-based firm would earn \$1,470,000 from the receivable. At all exchange rates to the right of \$1.4700/£:

1. The firm would receive £1,000,000 in 90 days
2. The put option on pounds purchased by the firm would expire out-of-the-money
3. The firm would turn over the £1,000,000 received to the buyer of the call who now exercises the call option against the firm; the firm receives \$1.4700/£ from the call option buyer.

Thus at all exchange rates above or below \$1.4700/£, the U.S.-based firm nets \$1,470,000 in domestic currency. The combined spot-option position has behaved identically to that of a forward contract. A firm with the exact opposite position—a £1,000,00 payable 90 days in the future—could similarly construct a synthetic forward using options.[2]

But why would a firm undertake this relatively complex position in order to simply create a forward contract? The answer is found by looking at the option premiums earned and paid. We have assumed that the option strike prices used were precisely forward-ATM rates, and the resulting option premiums paid and earned were exactly equal. But this need not be the case. If the option strike prices (remember that they must be identical for both options, bought and sold) are not precisely on the forward-ATM, the two premiums may differ by a slight amount. The net premium position may then end up as a net premium earning or a net premium payment. If positive, this amount would be added to the proceeds from the receivable to result in a higher total dollar value received.[3]

Second-Generation Currency Risk Management Products

Second-generation risk-management products are constructed from the two basic derivatives used throughout this book: the forward and the option. We will subdivide them into two groups: 1) the *zero-premium option products*, which focus on pricing in and around the forward rate; 2) the *exotic option products* (for want of a better name), which focus on alternative pricing targets. Although all of the following derivatives are sold as financial products by risk management firms, we will present each as simply the construction of the position from common building blocks, or LEGO®s, as they have been termed, used in traditional currency risk management, forwards and options. As a group, they are collectively referred to as *complex options.*

Zero-Premium Option Products

The primary "problem" with the use of options for risk management in the eyes of the firms is the up-front premium payment. Although the premium payment is only a portion of the total pay-

2. A U.S.-resident firm possessing a future foreign currency–denominated payment of £1,000,000 could construct a synthetic forward in the following way: the firm would 1) pay £1,000,000 in 90 days; 2) buy a call option on pounds at a strike price of \$1.4700/£; and 3) sell a put option on pounds at a strike price of \$1.4700/£.
3. An additional possibility is that the firm finds, for the moment at which the position is taken, that the call option premium earned may actually slightly exceed the put option premium paid. This means that the options market is temporarily out of equilibrium (parity). This is quite possible given the judgement required in the pricing of options (different banks' pricing options do not necessarily use the identical volatilities at all times) and the inherent decentralized structure of the currency and currency option markets.

off profile of the hedge, many firms view the expenditure of substantial funds for the purchase of a financial derivative as prohibitively expensive. In comparison, the forward contract, which eliminates currency risk, requires no out-of-pocket expenditure by the firm (and requires no real specification of expectations regarding exchange rate movements).

Zero-premium option products (or *financially engineered derivative combinations*) are designed to require no out-of-pocket premium payment at the initiation of the hedge. This set of products includes what are most frequently labeled the *range forward* and the *participating forward.* Both of these products: 1) are priced on the basis of the forward rate; 2) are constructed to provide a zero-premium payment up front; 3) allow the hedger to take advantage of expectations of the direction of exchange rate movements.

For the case problem at hand in which the U.S.-resident firm possesses a long position in British pounds, this means that all of the following products are applicable to an expectation that the U.S. dollar will depreciate versus the pound. If the hedger has no such view, they should turn back now (and buy a forward, or nothing at all)!

Ratio Spreads

Before describing the most widely accepted second-generation option products, it is helpful to demonstrate one of the older methods of obtaining a zero-premium option combination: an alternative that leaves the hedger with a large uncovered exposure.

The U.S.-based firm in our chapter problem decides that it wishes to establish a floor level of protection by purchasing a \$1.4700/£ put option (forward-ATM) at a cost of \$0.0318/£ (total cost of \$31,800). This is a substantial outlay of capital up front for the option premium, and the firm's risk management division has no budget funding for this magnitude of expenditures. The firm, feeling strongly that the dollar will depreciate against the pound, decides to "finance" the purchase of the put with the sale of an OTM call option. The firm reviews market conditions and considers a number of call option strike prices that are significantly OTM; strike prices of \$1.5200/£, \$1.5400/£, or further out.

It is decided that the \$1.5400/£ call option, with a premium of \$0.0089/£, is to be written and sold to earn the premium and finance the put purchase. However, because the premium on the OTM call is so much smaller than the forward-ATM put premium, the size of the call option written must be larger. The firm determines the amount of the call by solving the simple problem of premium equivalency:

$$\text{cost of put premium} = \text{earnings call premium}$$

Substituting in the put and call option premiums yields:

$$\$0.0318/£ \times £1{,}000{,}000 = \$0.0089/£ \times £\text{ call}$$

Solving for the size of the call option to be written:

$$\frac{\$31{,}800}{\$0.0089 / £} = £3{,}573{,}034$$

The reason that this strategy is called a *ratio spread* is that the final position, call option size to put option size, is a ratio greater than 1 (£3,573,034 ÷ £1,000,000 or a ratio of about 3.57).

An alternative form of the ratio spread is the *calendar spread*. The calendar spread would combine the 90-day put option with the sale of an OTM call option with a maturity that is longer; for example, 120 or 180 days. The longer maturity of the call option written earns the firm larger premium earnings requiring a smaller "ratio."

As a number of firms using this strategy have learned the hard way, if the expectations of the hedger prove incorrect, and the spot rate moves past the strike price of the call option written, the firm is faced with delivering a foreign currency that it does not have. In this example, if the spot rate moved above $1.5400/£, the firm would have to cover a position of £2,573,034.

The Range Forward

The basic *range forward* has been marketed under a variety of other names, including the *collar*, *flexible forward*, *cylinder option*, *option fence* or simply *fence*, *mini-max*, or *zero-cost tunnel*. The range forward is constructed by:

1. Buying a put option with a strike rate *below* the forward rate, for the full amount of the long currency exposure (100% coverage)
2. Selling a call option with a strike rate *above* the forward rate, for the full amount of the long currency exposure (100% coverage)

The hedger chooses one side of the "range" or spread, normally the downside (put strike rate), which then dictates the strike rate at which the call option will be sold. The call option must be chosen at an equal distance from the forward rate as the put option strike price from the forward rate.

If the hedger believes there is a significant possibility that the currency will move in the firm's favor, and by a sizeable degree, the put-floor rate can be set relatively low in order for the ceiling to be higher or further out from the forward rate and still enjoy a zero net premium. How far down the downside protection is set is a difficult issue for the firm to determine. Often the firm's treasurer will determine at what bottom exchange rate the firm would be able to recover the minimum necessary margin on the business underlying the cash flow exposure, called the *budget rate* (see Chapter 8).

Exhibit 24.4 illustrates the final outcome of a range forward constructed by buying a put with strike price $1.4500/£ paying a premium of $0.0226/£, with selling a call option and strike price $1.4900/£ earning a premium of $0.0231/£. The hedger has bounded the range over which the firm's A/R value moves as an uncovered position, with a put option floor and a sold call option ceiling.

A number of variations on the basic range forward exist. If both strike prices are the same, it is a *synthetic forward* as described in the previous section. If both strike prices chosen are equal to the actual forward rate, the synthetic equals the actual forward contract. This synthetic forward should theoretically have a near zero-net premium. Although the put and call option premiums are in this case not identical, they are close enough to result in a near-zero net premium:

$$\text{net premium} = (\$0.0226/£ - \$0.0231/£) \times £1{,}000{,}000 = -\$500$$

Exhibit 24.4 The Range Forward: Hedging a £1,000,000 Long Position

Instruments	Strike Rates	Premium	Notional Principle
Buy a put	$1.4500/£	$0.0226/£	£1,000,000
Sell a call	$1.4900/£	$0.0231/£	£1,000,000

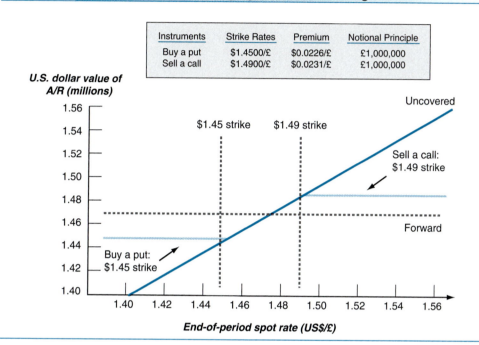

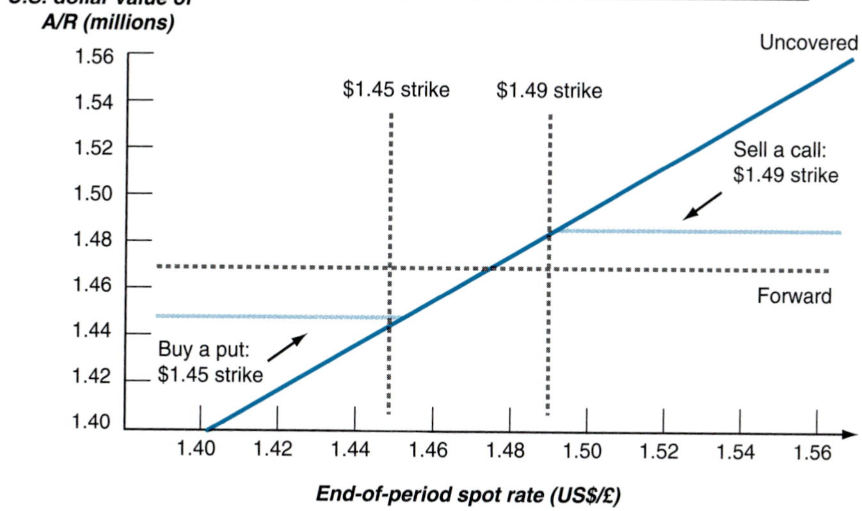

The benefits of the combined position are readily observable, given that the put option premium alone amounts to $22,600. If the strike rates of the options are selected independently of the desire for an exact zero-net premium up front (it must still bracket the forward rate), it is termed an *option collar* or *cylinder option*.

The Participating Forward

The *participating forward*, also called a *zero-cost ratio option* and *forward participation agreement*, is an option combination that allows the hedger to take a position that will share in potential upside movements in the exchange rate, while providing option-based downside protection, all at a zero-net premium. The participating forward is constructed via two steps:

1. Buying a put option with a strike price *below* the forward rate, for the full amount of the long currency exposure (100% coverage)
2. Selling a call option with a strike price that is the same as the put option, for a *portion* of the total currency exposure (less than 100% coverage)

Similar to the range forward, the buyer of a participating forward will normally choose the put option strike rate first. Because the call option strike rate is the same as the put, all that remains is to determine the participation rate, the proportion of the exposure sold as a call option.

Exhibit 24.5 illustrates the construction of a participating forward for the chapter problem. The firm first chooses the put option protection level, in this case \$1.4500/£ with a premium of \$0.0226/£. A call option sold with the same strike rate of \$1.4500/£ would earn the firm \$0.0425/£. The call premium is substantially higher than the put premium because the call option is already in-the-money (ITM). The firm's objective is to sell a call option only on the number of pounds needed to fund the purchase of the put option. The total put option premium is:

$$\text{total put premium} = \$0.0226/£ \times £1{,}000{,}000 = \$22{,}600$$

Which is then used to determine the size of the call option needed to exactly offset the purchase of the put:

$$\$22{,}600 = \$0.0425/£ \times \text{call principal}$$

Solving for the call principal:

$$\text{call principal} = \frac{\$22{,}600}{\$0.0425\ /\ £} = £531{,}765$$

The firm must therefore sell a call option on £531,765 with a strike rate of \$1.4500/£ to cover the purchase of the put option. This mismatch in option principals is what gives the participating

Exhibit 24.5 The Participating Forward: Hedging a £1,000,000 Long Position

Instruments	Strike Rates	Premium	Notional Principle
Buy a put	\$1.4500/£	\$0.0226/£	£1,000,000
Sell a call	\$1.4500/£	\$0.0425/£	£532,000

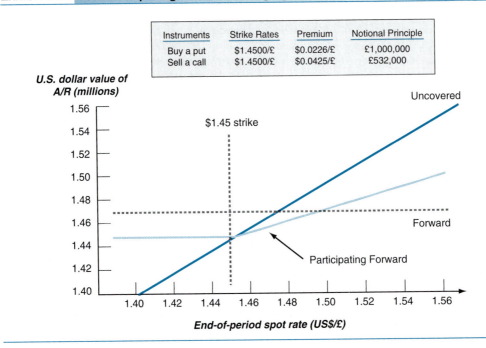

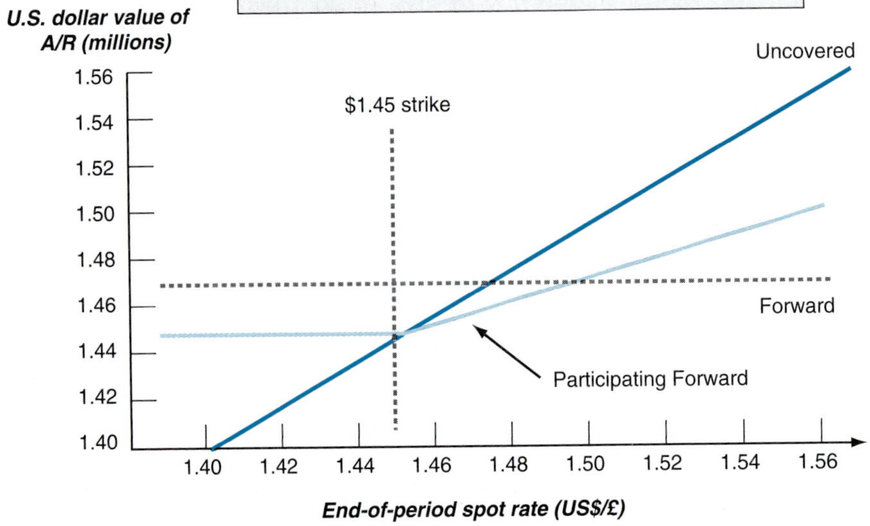

forward its unique shape.[4] The ratio of option premiums, as well as the ratio of option principals, is termed the *percent cover*:

$$\text{percent cover} = \frac{\$0.0226/£}{\$0.0425/£} = \frac{£531{,}765}{£1{,}000{,}000} = 0.5318 \approx 53.18\%$$

The *participation rate* is the residual percentage of the exposure that is not covered by the sale of the call option. For example, if the percent cover is 53.18%, the participation rate would be 1 – the percent cover, or 46.82%. This means that for all favorable exchange rate movements, those above \$1.4500/£, the hedger would "participate" or enjoy 46.8% of the differential. However, like all option-based hedges, downside exposure is bounded by the put option strike rate.

The expectations of the buyer are similar to the range forward, except that the degree of foreign currency bullishness is greater. For the participating forward to be superior in outcome to the range forward, it is necessary for the exchange rate to move further in the favorable direction than for the range forward.

Exotic Options

This second set of instruments offers alternative pricing, timing, or exercise provisions of the product. All of these in some way have altered the valuation principles of the basic option-pricing model; hence the term *exotic*. These products are therefore products only, and not easily reproducible (though generally possible) by the corporate risk manager independently. Their pricing is generally complex and they are generally produced and sold by risk management departments of major multinational banks.

Most exotic options are European-style options whose values change with the direction and the *path* the spot rate follows over their life span (they are in fact often referred to as path-dependent in value). We briefly discuss a few of these exotics: the *knock-out option*, the *average rate option*, *compound option*, and the *chooser option*. This is only a sampling of some of these increasingly complex—even bizarre—option-based instruments. We continue discussing each of these currency derivative products in the context of a U.S.-based firm with a long British pound exposure. But, as they warn spectators during dare-devil exhibitions: don't try this at home.

The Knock-Out Option

The knock-out option, also often referred to as the *down and out option (DAOO)*, *barrier option*, *extinguishable option*, or *activate/deactivate option*, differs markedly from previous products covered. The knock-out option is designed to behave like any option, offering downside protection, but to offer only a limited upside range before crossing a previously specified *barrier* or *knock-out level*, at which it automatically expires. Because the knock-out level is in the upside direction, the

4. Note that if both options had the same strike rate and the same principal, the result would be a positive premium synthetic forward. The positive premium would result from the strike rate which places the call option in-the-money and the put option out-of-the-money. A true net-zero synthetic forward would use a strike rate that was the same as the forward rate.

automatic expiration of the option would occur only after the exchange rate has moved in the expected direction of the hedger (a favorable movement). In return for giving up the full maturity period coverage, the premium of the option—being a shorter-term option—is smaller.

Exhibit 24.6 depicts the knock-out option for the chapter problem, and compares its basic profile with that of the standard put option (strike price \$1.4700/£ at premium \$0.0318/£). The knock-out strike price is also \$1.4700/£ (forward-ATM), with a barrier of \$1.4900/£. The premium of the barrier option is significantly lower, only \$0.0103/£.

The premium of the barrier option is quite sensitive to the specification of the barrier level. The further the barrier is from the forward rate, the less likely the barrier will be crossed and therefore the more likely the option will not automatically expire. In that case, the premium must rise to compensate the writer of the knock-out option for the probability of providing coverage for a longer period of time. As illustrated, the knock-out appears obviously to be the better choice with the same strike price at a lower premium. The problem, however, is that the diagram is not able to illustrate the possibility that the spot rate could rise in the early days of the exposure to \$1.4900/£ or higher, crossing the barrier, and therefore canceling the option protection. The exposure would still have many days left until maturity, during which the spot rate could easily rise or fall in essentially unlimited magnitudes. The standard put option, although higher in premium, will not expire prior to the maturity of the exposure. In the end, the cheaper cost of the knock-out option might prove to be an added cost for a final protection level of zero.

Exhibit 24.6 The Knock-Out Option: Hedging a £1,000,000 Long Position

Instrument	Strike Rates	Premium	Notional Principle
Buy a put	\$1.4700/£ Barrier: \$1.49/£	\$0.0103/£	£1,000,000

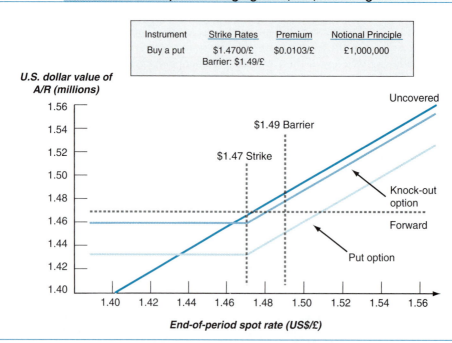

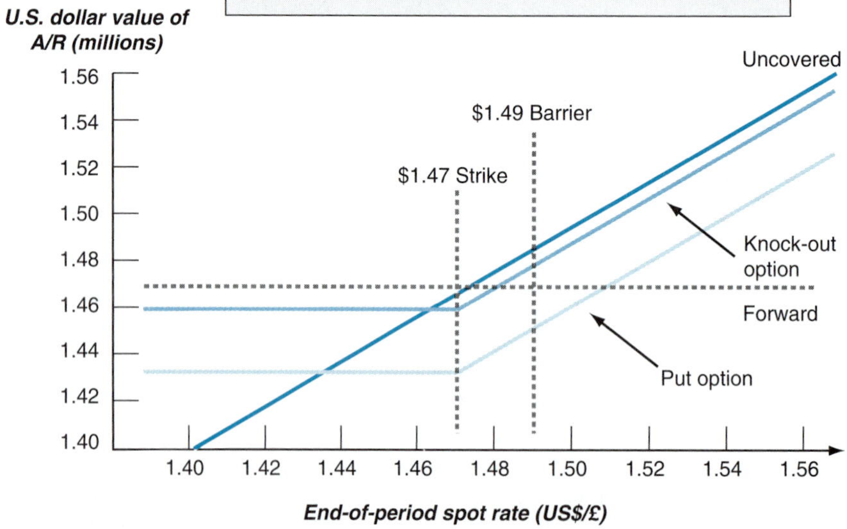

The Average Rate Option

These options are the most recent second-generation (possibly third-generation) currency derivatives. They are normally classified as "path-dependent" currency options because their values depend on averages of spot rates over some prespecified period of time. Here we describe two examples of path-dependent options, the *average rate option* and the *average strike option*:

1. The *average rate option (ARO)*, also known as an *Asian option*, sets the option strike rate up front, and is exercised at maturity if the average spot rate over the period (as observed by scheduled sampling) is less than the preset option strike rate.
2. The *average strike option (ASO)* establishes the option strike rate as the average of the spot rate experienced over the option's life, and is exercised if the strike rate is greater than the end-of-period spot rate.

Like the knock-out option, the average rate option is difficult to depict, because its value depends not on the ending spot rate, but rather the path the spot rate takes over its specified life span. For example, an average rate option with strike price $1.4700/£ would have a premium of only $0.0186/£. The "average rate" would be calculated by weekly observations (12 full weeks, the first observation occurring 13 days from purchase) of the spot rate. Numerous different averages or paths of spot rate movement obviously exist. A few different scenarios aid in understanding how the ARO differs in valuation:

1. The spot rate moves very little over the first 70 to 80 days of the period, with a sudden movement in the spot rate below $1.4700/£ in the days prior to expiration. Although the final spot rate is below $1.4700/£, the average for the period is above $1.4700, so the option cannot be exercised. The receivable is exchanged at the spot rate (below $1.4700/£) and the cost of the option premium is still incurred.
2. The dollar slowly and steadily depreciates versus the pound, the rate rising from $1.4790/£ to $1.48, $1.49, and on up. At the end of the 90-day period, the option expires out of the money, the receivable is exchanged at the favorable spot rate, and the firm has enjoyed average rate option protection at substantially lower premium expense.

A variation on the average rate is the *lookback option*, *with strike* and *without strike*. A *lookback option with strike* is a European-style option with a preset strike rate that on maturity is valued versus the highest or lowest spot rate reached over the option life. A *lookback option without strike* is typically a European-style option that sets the strike rate at maturity as the lowest exchange rate achieved over the period for a call option, or the highest exchange rate experienced over the period for a put option, and is exercised on the basis of this strike rate versus the ending spot rate.

A variety of different types of average rate currency option products are sold by banking institutions, each having a distinct pay-off structure. Because of the intricacy of the path-dependent option's value, care must be taken in the use of these instruments. As in all markets, let the buyer beware.

The Compound Option

The *compound option* is an option to either buy or sell an option on a specific future date. Also referred to as *options on options*, a call compound option gives the buyer the right to buy a specific option on a future date, while a put compound option gives the buyer the right to sell a specific option on a future date. The underlying option—the option the first option is written upon—is fully defined in terms of premium, strike price, amount, and maturity. Because the first option is an option on an option, the up-front premium is substantially smaller.

It is ironic that these "third-generation" currency risk management products are focused on contingent currency exposures, the same exposure for which only a few years ago the simple put and call options were thought appropriate. For example, a firm making a bid on a contract that will result in a substantial exposure in terms of foreign currency cash flows, positive or negative, may be able to cover the bid exposure with a smaller initial premium payment than a standard option would require. It must be remembered, however, that the first premium is to maintain the right to pay (receive) the second premium if the right is exercised. The hedger must be careful and clear as to what cash flows and premiums will be required and at what points in time if the compound option is purchased.

The compound option has two different points in time of maturity. The first, the *near-date* or *first-date*, is the date on which the buyer of the compound option must decide whether the right is to be exercised to buy or sell the underlying option. The second point in time is the *last-date* or *second-date*, on which the actual underlying option expires. Because of this sequencing of time periods, the compound option may in the future be one method firms may use for distant currency exposures that are highly contingent without committing substantial quantities of corporate capital to the payment of option premiums.

The Chooser Option

A final alternative is—at least for the moment—the extreme of option flexibility. The *chooser option* allows the buyer to lock in a specific option strike price, amount, and maturity now, and choose at a later date ("chooser date") whether the option is to be a call option or put option. The primary use of such a hedge instrument is in cases in which the exposure's final net long or net short position is unknown until further into the life of the exposure.

SUMMARY

- The determination of the optimal hedge ratio for an individual exposure can be derived by constructing a two-asset portfolio and minimizing its expected terminal value.
- Alternative hedging methodologies such as delta-hedging and proxy-hedging are often useful and necessary when dealing with exotic currencies or exposures.
- The rapidly developing field of financial engineering allows the corporate treasurer to construct financial positions with financial derivatives that possess desired risk-return profiles to match and manage complex exposures and detailed market expectations.
- Second-generation option products like range forwards and participating forwards allow hedgers to acquire option protection with a zero net up-front premium payment.
- Exotic option products, sometimes called third-generation products, are options that are constructed to provide values and protection that are functions of the path the spot rate takes over the life span of the option, and not simply based on the value at expiration (ending spot rate). The primary benefit is the reduction of the option premium paid by the buyer.

QUESTIONS

1. **The perfect hedge.** A colleague of ours, Gunter Dufey of the University of Michigan, is relatively famous for the following quotation:

   "A perfect hedge is only found in a Japanese garden."

   In light of the discussion of the optimal hedge in this chapter, what do you think this quotation means?

2. **Cross-hedging.** What is the meaning of a cross-hedge or proxy-hedge?

3. **Synthetic forwards (A).** What is the composition of a synthetic forward?

4. **Synthetic forwards (B).** Assume the same values hold as in the chapter problem, with the single exception that the £1,000,000 exposure is a 90-day account payable, not receivable.
   a. Explain precisely how to construct a synthetic forward to cover the exposure.
   b. Explain how you would construct a synthetic forward whose strike prices are set so that the firm would have a positive net premium to pay up front, but would enjoy a slightly better constructed forward rate.

5. **Zero premiums.** Why do you think the net premium payment up front associated with a risk management derivative is so important to many MNEs?

6. **Range forwards.** What is a range forward? What specific expectations would a British MNE need to have if it were constructing a range forward to manage the currency risk associated with a 90-day account payable in U.S. dollars?

7. **Participating forwards.** What is a participating forward? What specific expectations would a British MNE need to have if it were constructing a participating forward to manage the currency risk associated with a 180-day account receivable in euros?

8. **Delta-neutral hedging.** Which is more appropriate for the MNE's accounting purposes, the typical end-of-period currency hedging strategy or the continuing market value hedging strategy used in delta-neutral hedging?

9. **Ratio spreads.** Although the ratio spread can potentially be a very useful risk-management derivative position, it is also considered too risky by many MNEs, to the point that many of their financial policy statements prohibit their treasuries from using them. Why do you think they are sometimes considered too risky?

10. **Financial derivatives: Engineering in emerging markets.** The number of countries allowing domestic banks and other financial service providers to create and sell financial derivatives for risk management is continually growing. Many emerging markets, however, are still confronted with both lack of financial breadth in financial products and regulatory restrictions limiting derivative construction.
    a. What basic financial products and markets are needed to create the currency risk-management derivatives described in this chapter?
    b. Why do you think many emerging markets do not possess these elements?
    c. Why do you think the governments of many emerging markets still prohibit or restrict the growth of either the necessary products and markets or the derivatives themselves?

PROBLEMS

1. **Optimal Hedges.** The optimal hedge ratio (β) was defined and described in the chapter. Calculate the optimal hedge ratio for the following set of assumptions:

U.S.-based MNE exposure, 90-day account receivable	DM1,000,000
Variance of the 90-day forward rate, DM/$	0.0058000
Covariance between the spot and 90-day forward rate, DM/$	-0.0048750

2. **Delta-hedging.** Exhibit 24.2 described a delta-hedging strategy for a U.S.-based MNE with a £1,000,000 90-day account receivable. Assuming the same numerical assumptions as used in Exhibit 24.2, calculate the change in the market value of the put option contract on the following two days assuming the spot rate changes as follows (note that you will also need to use the Option.xls spreadsheet for pricing the currency options):

Spot Rate ($/£)	Days to Maturity	Call Premium ($/£)
1.70	90	0.03302
1.71	89	0.03807
1.73	88	_______
1.69	87	_______

Dayton Manufacturing's pound sterling exposure. *Use the following information to complete problems 3 through 5.* Dayton Manufacturing (US) has a 1 million pound sterling account receivable due in 90 days. Dayton expects the pound to strengthen against the U.S. dollar during that same coming 90-day period, but is unwilling to remain uncovered or to pay a substantial premium for a purchased option up front. It has therefore decided to utilize a participating forward. Current exchange rate and interest rate conditions are as follows:

Spot exchange rate:	$1.4790/£
90-day forward rate:	$1.4000/£
90-day Eurodollar deposit rate:	3.2500%
90-day Euro-sterling deposit rate:	5.7200%
90-day dollar/pound volatility quote:	11.0%

3. **Dayton (A): The range forward.** Construct a range forward that is ±2.5% from the forward rate to manage the currency risk for the £1,000,000 90-day exposure.
   a. What are the two option strikes prices and their respective premiums?
   b. What are the minimum and maximum dollar proceeds Dayton can expect from its range forward hedge?

4. **Dayton (B): The participating forward.** Using the problem's stated assumptions, construct a participating forward with a strike rate of $1.45/£.
   a. What is the participation rate?
   b. What minimum dollar proceeds will the participating forward guarantee Dayton?
   c. What maximum dollar proceeds results from this position for the yen receivable?

5. **Dayton (C): The participating forward.** Using the problem's stated assumptions, construct a participating forward with a strike rate of $1.44/£.
   a. What is the participation rate?
   b. What minimum dollar proceeds will the participating forward guarantee Dayton?
   c. What maximum dollar proceeds results from this position for the yen receivable?

Ikea's yen exposure. *Use the following information about Ikea to answer problems 6 and 7.* Ikea, the Swedish household furnishings firm that has so successfully penetrated the U.S. market, is now betting on a major change in U.S. consumer taste. Ikea believes that many of the simple Japanese furnishing designs will be in demand in the coming year, and is willing to spend nearly $25 million quarterly in new materials and inventory in anticipation of this market trend. It has received its first shipment of merchandise from a Japanese wholesaler, and payment of ¥2.7 billion is due in full in 90 days.

Ikea is considering the use of currency options—specifically net zero premium combinations—to manage the currency risk of the needed payment. Ikea's treasury has a limited budget, so the simultaneous buying and writing of options is the only practical approach for it at this time. Current market conditions are as follows:

Spot exchange rate:	¥108.20/$
90-day forward rate:	¥107.88/$
90-day Eurodollar deposit rate:	3.3750%
90-day Euroyen deposit rate:	2.1875%
90-day yen/dollar volatility quote:	11.8%

6. **Ikea (A): The range forward.** Construct a range forward that is ±2% around the forward rate.
   a. What precisely would Ikea like the spot rate to be at the end of the 90-day period?
   b. If the ending spot exchange rate were $0.0096/¥, what would be the net proceeds to Ikea from the range forward hedge?
   c. What would be the minimum dollar proceeds to Ikea if the spot rate moved against the company?
7. **Ikea (B): The range forward.** Construct and diagram a range forward that is ±3.5% around the forward rate.
   a. What precisely would Ikea like the spot rate to be at the end of the 90-day period?
   b. If the ending spot exchange rate were $0.0096/¥, what would be the net proceeds to Ikea from the range forward hedge?
   c. What would be the minimum dollar proceeds to Ikea if the spot rate moved against the company?

Nokia Oy's acquisition bid. *Use the following information to answer problems 8 through 10.* It was 1997, and Nokia Oy (Finland), the leading manufacturer of cellular telephones and telecommunications equipment in the world, has been increasingly aggressive in its expansion into new markets.

Nokia has decided to make a bid on an assembly and service center in the United States currently owned by Philips (Netherlands) located in Winnetka, Illinois. Although Philips is still operating the facility (albeit at a low capacity rate) the company has decided to withdraw from the U.S. markets due to its continuing financial woes. Nokia wishes to move quickly and take operational control of the facility to avoid the moth-balling costs of shutdown/startup.

The analysts have concluded that the plant, equipment, and facilities, are worth roughly $17 million. Because Philips is planning to get out, the investment bankers think it could be had for less, somewhere between $12 and $14 million. But Nokia's corporate strategy group has argued it is critical that the first bid be acceptable to Philips, otherwise negotiations may drag on; in this case, time was money.

Timo Hakkonen is head of risk management within the treasury group at Nokia's central office in Espoo, Finland. He has been asked in to offer additional advice on the purchase price given the sizeable currency exposure of making a bid in U.S. dollars of $12 to $17 million. Nokia has some U.S. dollar cash flows, but they are not of sufficient magnitude given the timing needs of the potential deal to provide matching protection. The Finnish markka–U.S. dollar exchange rate has been anything but stable over the past few years. Timo's preliminary analysis for the coming 90-day period looked as follows:

Spot exchange rate (today)	FIM 5.6136/$
90-day forward rate	FIM 5.6487/$
90-day Eurodollar deposit rate	3.3750%
90-day Euro-Finmark deposit rate	5.9000%
90-day FIM/$ volatility	14.80%

Most importantly, because of stabilizing economic conditions in Finland (partly because of actions intended to allow its seamless integration in the growing European Union's currency system, the euro, to be introduced in 1999), and the overheating of the U.S. economy with the growing Internet-based dot-com boom, Timo expected the Finnish markka to strengthen in the near term against the dollar.

8. **Nokia (A).** Timo first wishes to price some currency options to provide some protection against a changing FIM/$ exchange rate during the period of the bid.
   a. What would be the premium expense of buying a forward at-the-money option to cover the exposure if Timo assumed a purchase price of $14 million?
   b. What would be the premium expense of that same option if the strike price was set 3% out-of-the-money?
   c. What spot exchange rate at the end of the period would be needed to make the option cover purchases under both part a and part b superior to simply purchasing a forward contract cover for the exposure?
9. **Nokia (B).** Timo has explained to management that the purchase of option cover is beyond the budgetary allotment of Treasury. To finance this cover, he recommends considering a complex option position that would pay for the purchased option with the sale of another option.
   a. Construct a range forward that has strike rates of ±3% around the forward rate, for a $14 million notional principal.
   b. What are the minimum and maximum costs (in Finnish markka) for the dollars if hedged with this range forward?
10. **Nokia (C).** Timo also wishes to explore the possibilities using a participating forward.
    a. Construct a participating forward with a strike rate of FIM5.6/$.
    b. What is the maximum cost (worst case), of acquiring the $14 million needed under the bid?
    c. If the ending spot rate were FIM5.2/$, what would be the cost in Finnish markka under the participating forward?

SUGGESTED READINGS

Kerkvliet, Joe, and Michael H. Moffett, "The Hedging of an Uncertain Future Foreign Currency Payment," *Journal of Financial and Quantitative Analysis*, December 1991, Volume 26, No. 4, pp. 565–578.

Smith, Clifford W., and René M. Stulz, "The Determinants of Firms' Hedging Policies," *Journal of Financial and Quantitative Analysis*, December 1985, Volume 20, No. 4, pp. 390–405.

Stulz, René M., "Optimal Hedging Policies," *Journal of Financial and Quantitative Analysis*, June 1984, Volume 19, No. 2, pp. 127–140.

Currency Option Pricing Theory

The foreign currency option model presented here, the European-style option, is the result of the work of Black and Scholes (1972), Cox and Ross (1976), Cox, Ross, and Rubinstein (1979), Garman and Kohlhagen (1983), and Bodurtha and Courtadon (1987). Although we do not explain the theoretical derivation of the following option-pricing model, the original model derived by Black and Scholes is based on the formation of a riskless hedged portfolio composed of a long position in the security, asset, or currency, and a European call option. The solution to this model's expected return yields the option *premium*.

The basic theoretical model for the pricing of a European call option is:

$$C = e^{-r_f T} SN(d_1) - E_e^{-r_d T} N(d_2)$$

where:

- C premium on a European call
- e continuous time discounting
- S spot exchange rate (\$/foreign currency)
- E exercise or strike rate
- T time to expiration
- N cumulative normal distribution function
- r_f foreign interest rate
- r_d domestic interest rate
- σ standard deviation of asset price (volatility)
- ln natural logarithm

The two density functions, d_1 and d_2, are defined:

$$d_1 = \frac{\ln\left(\frac{S}{E}\right) + \left(r_d - r_f + \frac{\sigma^2}{2}\right)T}{\sigma\sqrt{T}}$$

and:

$$d_2 = d_1 - \sigma\sqrt{T}$$

This expression can be rearranged so the premium on a European call option is written in terms of the forward rate:

$$C = e^{-r_f T} FN(d_1) - e^{-r_d T} EN(d_2)$$

where the spot rate and foreign interest rate have been replaced with the forward rate, *F*, and both the first and second terms are discounted over continuous time, *e*. If we now slightly simplify, we find that the option premium is the present value of the difference between two cumulative normal density functions:

$$C = \left[FN(d_1) - EN(d_2)\right]e^{-r_d T}$$

The two density functions are now defined:

$$d_1 = \frac{\ln\left(\frac{F}{E}\right) + \left(\frac{\sigma^2}{2}\right)T}{\sigma\sqrt{T}}$$

and:

$$d_2 = d_1 - \sigma\sqrt{T}$$

Solving each of these equations for d_1 and d_2 allows the determination of the European call option premium. The premium for a European put option, *P*, is similarly derived:

$$P = \left[F\left(N(d_1) - 1\right) - E\left(N(d_2) - 1\right)\right]e^{-r_d T}$$

The European Call Option: Numerical Example

The actual calculation of the option premium is not as complex as it appears from the preceding set of equations. Assuming the following basic exchange rate and interest rate values, computation of the option premium is relatively straightforward.

spot rate	= \$1.7000/£
90-day forward	= \$1.7000/£
strike rate	= \$1.7000/£
U.S. dollar interest rate	= 8.00 % (per annum)
pound sterling interest rate	= 8.00 % (per annum)
time (days)	= 90
std. dev. (volatility)	= 10.00 %
e (infinite discounting)	= 2.71828

The value of the two density functions are first derived:

$$d_1 = \frac{\ln\left(\frac{F}{E}\right) + \left(\frac{\sigma^2}{2}\right)T}{\sigma\sqrt{T}} = \frac{\ln\left(\frac{1.7000}{1.7000}\right) + \left(\frac{0.1000^2}{2}\right)\frac{90}{365}}{0.1000\sqrt{\frac{90}{365}}} = 0.025$$

and:

$$d_2 = 0.025 - 0.1000\sqrt{\frac{90}{365}} = -0.025$$

The values of d_1 and d_2 are then found in the cumulative normal probability table (see Appendix B to this chapter):

$$N(d_1) = N(0.025) = 0.51; \quad N(d_2) = N(-0.025) = 0.49$$

The premium of the European call with a "forward-at-the-money" strike rate is:

$$C = [(1.7000)(0.51) - (1.7000)(0.49)]2.71828^{-0.08(90/365)} = \$0.033/£$$

This is the call option *premium*, *price*, *value*, or *cost*.

Cumulative Normal Probability Table

The probability that a drawing from a unit normal distribution will produce a value less than the constant d is

$$\text{Prob}(\tilde{z} < d) = \int_{-\infty}^{d} \frac{1}{\sqrt{2\pi}} e^{-z^2/2} dz = N(d)$$

Range of d: $-2.49 \le d \le 0.00$

d	−0.00	−0.01	−0.02	−0.03	−0.04	−0.05	−0.06	−0.07	−0.08	−0.09
−2.40	0.00820	0.00798	0.00776	0.00755	0.00734	0.00714	0.00695	0.00676	0.00657	0.00639
−2.30	0.01072	0.01044	0.01017	0.00990	0.00964	0.00939	0.00914	0.00889	0.00866	0.00842
−2.20	0.01390	0.01355	0.01321	0.01287	0.01255	0.01222	0.01191	0.01160	0.01130	0.01101
−2.10	0.01786	0.01743	0.01700	0.01659	0.01618	0.01578	0.01539	0.01500	0.01463	0.01426
−2.00	0.02275	0.02222	0.02169	0.02118	0.02068	0.02018	0.01970	0.01923	0.01876	0.01831
−1.90	0.02872	0.02807	0.02743	0.02680	0.02619	0.02559	0.02500	0.02442	0.02385	0.02330
−1.80	0.03593	0.03515	0.03438	0.03362	0.03288	0.03216	0.03144	0.03074	0.03005	0.02938
−1.70	0.04457	0.04363	0.04272	0.04182	0.04093	0.04006	0.03920	0.03836	0.03754	0.03673
−1.60	0.05480	0.05370	0.05262	0.05155	0.05050	0.04947	0.04846	0.04746	0.04648	0.04551
−1.50	0.06681	0.06552	0.06426	0.06301	0.06178	0.06057	0.05938	0.05821	0.05705	0.05592
−1.40	0.08076	0.07927	0.07780	0.07636	0.07493	0.07353	0.07215	0.07078	0.06944	0.06811
−1.30	0.09680	0.09510	0.09342	0.09176	0.09012	0.08851	0.08691	0.08534	0.08379	0.08226
−1.20	0.11507	0.11314	0.11123	0.10935	0.10749	0.10565	0.10383	0.10204	0.10027	0.09853
−1.10	0.13567	0.13350	0.13136	0.12924	0.12714	0.12507	0.12302	0.12100	0.11900	0.11702
−1.00	0.15866	0.15625	0.15386	0.15150	0.14917	0.14686	0.14457	0.14231	0.14007	0.13786

(continues)

Range of d: $-2.49 \le d \le 0.00$

d	−0.00	−0.01	−0.02	−0.03	−0.04	−0.05	−0.06	−0.07	−0.08	−0.09
−0.90	0.18406	0.18141	0.17879	0.17619	0.17361	0.17106	0.16853	0.16602	0.16354	0.16109
−0.80	0.21186	0.20897	0.20611	0.20327	0.20045	0.19766	0.19489	0.19215	0.18943	0.18673
−0.70	0.24196	0.23885	0.23576	0.23270	0.22965	0.22663	0.22363	0.22065	0.21770	0.21476
−0.60	0.27425	0.27093	0.26763	0.26435	0.26109	0.25785	0.25463	0.25143	0.24825	0.24510
−0.50	0.30854	0.30503	0.30153	0.29806	0.29460	0.29116	0.28774	0.28434	0.28096	0.27760
−0.40	0.34458	0.34090	0.33724	0.33360	0.32997	0.32636	0.32276	0.31918	0.31561	0.31207
−0.30	0.38209	0.37828	0.37448	0.37070	0.36693	0.36317	0.35942	0.35569	0.35197	0.34827
−0.20	0.42074	0.41683	0.41294	0.40905	0.40517	0.40129	0.39743	0.39358	0.38974	0.38591
−0.10	0.46017	0.45620	0.45224	0.44828	0.44433	0.44038	0.43644	0.43251	0.42858	0.42465
0.00	0.50000	0.49601	0.49202	0.48803	0.48405	0.48006	0.47608	0.47210	0.46812	0.46414
0.00	0.50000	0.50399	0.50798	0.51197	0.51595	0.51994	0.52392	0.52790	0.53188	0.53586
0.01	0.53983	0.54380	0.54776	0.55172	0.55567	0.55962	0.56356	0.56749	0.57142	0.57535
0.20	0.57926	0.58317	0.58706	0.59095	0.59483	0.59871	0.60257	0.60642	0.61026	0.61409
0.30	0.61791	0.62172	0.62552	0.62930	0.63307	0.63683	0.64058	0.64431	0.64803	0.65173
0.40	0.65542	0.65910	0.66276	0.66640	0.67003	0.67364	0.67724	0.68082	0.68439	0.68793
0.50	0.69146	0.69497	0.69847	0.70194	0.70540	0.70884	0.71226	0.71566	0.71904	0.72240
0.60	0.72575	0.72907	0.73237	0.73565	0.73891	0.74215	0.74537	0.74857	0.75175	0.75490
0.70	0.75804	0.76115	0.76424	0.76730	0.77035	0.77337	0.77637	0.77935	0.78230	0.78524
0.80	0.78814	0.79103	0.79389	0.79673	0.79955	0.80234	0.80511	0.80785	0.81057	0.81327
0.90	0.81594	0.81859	0.82121	0.82381	0.82639	0.82894	0.83147	0.83398	0.83646	0.83891
1.00	0.84134	0.84375	0.84614	0.84850	0.85083	0.85314	0.85543	0.85769	0.85993	0.86214
1.10	0.86433	0.86650	0.86864	0.87076	0.87286	0.87493	0.87698	0.87900	0.88100	0.88298
1.20	0.88493	0.88686	0.88877	0.89065	0.89251	0.89435	0.89617	0.89796	0.89973	0.90147
1.30	0.90320	0.90490	0.90658	0.90824	0.90988	0.91149	0.91309	0.91466	0.91621	0.91774
1.40	0.91924	0.92073	0.92220	0.92364	0.92507	0.92647	0.92785	0.92922	0.93056	0.93189
1.50	0.93319	0.93448	0.93574	0.93699	0.93822	0.93943	0.94062	0.94179	0.94295	0.94408
1.60	0.94520	0.94630	0.94738	0.94845	0.94950	0.95053	0.95154	0.95254	0.95352	0.95449
1.70	0.95543	0.95637	0.95728	0.95818	0.95907	0.95994	0.96080	0.96164	0.96246	0.96327
1.80	0.96407	0.96485	0.96562	0.96637	0.96712	0.96784	0.96856	0.96926	0.96995	0.97062
1.90	0.97128	0.97193	0.97257	0.97320	0.97381	0.97441	0.97500	0.97558	0.97615	0.97670
2.00	0.97725	0.97778	0.97831	0.97882	0.97932	0.97982	0.98030	0.98077	0.98124	0.98169
2.10	0.98214	0.98257	0.98300	0.98341	0.98382	0.98422	0.98461	0.98500	0.98537	0.98574
2.20	0.98610	0.98645	0.98679	0.98713	0.98745	0.98778	0.98809	0.98840	0.98870	0.98899
2.30	0.98928	0.98956	0.98983	0.99010	0.99036	0.99061	0.99086	0.99111	0.99134	0.99158
2.40	0.99180	0.99202	0.99224	0.99245	0.99266	0.99286	0.99305	0.99324	0.99343	0.99361

Source: Hans R. Stoll and Robert E. Whaley, *Futures and Options*, Southwestern Publishing, 1993, pp. 242–243. Reprinted with permission.

BIBLIOGRAPHY

Abbott, Ashok B., and K. Victor Chow, "Cointegration Among European Equity Markets," *Journal of Multinational Financial Management*, Vol. 2, No. 3/4, 1993, pp. 167–184.

Abuaf, Niso, "The Nature and Management of Foreign Exchange Risk," *Midland Corporate Finance Journal*, Fall 1986, pp. 30–44.

Abuaf, Niso, and Philippe Jorion, "Purchasing Power Parity in the Long Run," *Journal of Finance*, Mar 1990, pp. 157–174.

Adams, Paul D., and Steve B. Wyatt, "On the Pricing of European and American Foreign Currency Call Options," *Journal of International Money and Finance*, Vol. 6, No. 3, Sep 1987, pp. 315–338,

Adhikari, Ajay, and Rasoul H. Tondkar, "Environmental Factors Influencing Accounting Disclosure Requirements of Global Stock Exchanges," *Journal of International Financial Management and Accounting*, Vol. 4, No. 2, Summer 1992, pp. 75–105.

Adler, Michael, "The Cost of Capital and Valuation of a Two-Country Firm," *Journal of Finance*, Mar 1974, pp. 119–132.

Adler, Michael, and Bernard Dumas, "International Portfolio Choice and Corporation Finance: A Synthesis," *Journal of Finance*, Jun 1983, pp. 925–984.

Adler, Michael, and Bernard Dumas, "Exposure to Currency Risk: Definition and Measurement," *Financial Management*, Spring 1984, pp. 41–50.

Agénor, Pierre-Richard, *Parallel Currency Markets in Developing Countries: Theory, Evidence, and Policy Implications*, Essays in International Finance, No. 188, Princeton: International Financial Section, Department of Economics, 1992.

Aggarwal, Raj, "International Differences in Capital Structure Norms: An Empirical Study of Large European Companies," *Management International Review*, 1981/1, pp. 75–88.

Aggarwal, Raj, "Capital Structure Differences Among Large Asian Companies," *ASEAN Economic Bulletin*, Vol. 7, No. 1, Jul 1990, pp. 39–53.

Aggarwal, Raj, "Distribution of Spot and Forward Exchange Rates: Empirical Evidence and Investor Valuation of Skewness and Kurtosis," *Decision Sciences*, Summer 1990, pp. 588–595.

Aggarwal, Raj, "The Distribution of Exchange Rates and Forward Risk Premia," *Advances in Financial Planning and Forecasting*, Vol. 4, 1990. pp. 43–54.

Aggarwal, Raj, and Luc A. Soenen, "Corporate Use of Options and Futures in Foreign Exchange Management," *Journal of Cash Management*, Nov/Dec 1989, pp. 61–66.

Aggarwal, Reena, Ricardo Leal, and Leonardo Hernandez, "The Aftermarket Performance of Initial Public Offerings in Latin America," *Financial Management*, Spring 1993, pp. 42– 53.

Ahkam, Sharif N., "A Model for the Evaluation of and Response to Economic Exposure Risk by Multinational Companies," *Managerial Finance*, Vol. 21, No. 4, 1995, pp. 7–22.

Ahtiala, Pekka, and Yair E. Orgler, "The Optimal Pricing of Exports Invoiced in Different Currencies," *Journal of Banking and Finance*, Vol. 19, No. 1, Apr 1995, pp. 61–77.

Akhter, Syed H., and Robert F. Lusch, "Environmental Determinants of U.S. Foreign Direct Investment in Developed and Developing Countries: A Structural Analysis," *The International Trade Journal*, Vol. 5, No. 3, Spring 1991, pp. 329–360.

Al-Eryani, Mohammad F., Pervaiz Alam, and Syed Akhter, "Transfer Pricing Determinants of U.S. Multinationals," *Journal of International Business Studies*, 3rd Quarter, 1990, pp. 409–425.

Alexander, Gordon J., Cheol S. Eun, and S. Janakiramanan, "Asset Pricing and Dual Listing on Foreign Capital Markets: A Note," *Journal of Finance*, Mar 1987, pp. 151–158.

Alexander, Gordon J., Cheol S. Eun, and S. Janakiramanan, "International Listings and Stock Returns: Some Empirical Evidence," *Journal of Financial and Quantitative Analysis*, Vol. 23, No. 2, Jun 1988, pp. 135–151.

Aliber, R. Z., and C. P. Stickney, "Accounting Measures of Foreign Exchange Exposure: The Long and Short of It," *Accounting Review*, Jan 1975, pp. 44–57.

Allen, Linda, and Christos Pantzalis, "Valuation of the Operating Flexibility of Multinational Corporation, *Journal of International Business Studies*, Vol. 27, No. 4, Fourth Quarter 1996, pp. 633–653.

Amin, Kaushik, and Robert A. Jarrow, "Pricing Foreign Currency Options Under Stochastic Interest Rates," *Journal of International Money and Finance*, Sep 1991, pp. 310-329.

Anderson, R. W., and J. P. Danthine, "Cross-Hedging," *Journal of Political Economy*, Dec 1981, pp. 1182–1196.

Ang, James S., and Ali M. Fatemi, "A Test of the Rationality of Forward Exchange Rate," *Advances in Financial Planning and Forecasting*, Vol. 4, 1990, pp. 3–22.

Ang, James S., and Tsong-Yue Lai, "A Simple Rule for Multinational Capital Budgeting," *Global Finance Journal*, Fall 1989, pp. 71–75.

Anvari, M., "Efficient Scheduling of Cross-Border Cash Transfers," *Financial Manage-ment*, Summer 1986, pp. 40–49.

Aoi, Joichi, "To Whom Does the Company Belong?: A New Management Mission for the Information Age," *Journal of Applied Corporate Finance*, Winter 1994. pp. 25–31.

Arnold, Jerry L., and William W. Holder, *Impact of Statement 52 on Decisions, Financial Reports, and Attitudes*, Morristown, NJ: Financial Executives Research Foundation, 1986.

Arpan, Jeffrey S., "International Intracorporate Pricing: Non-American Systems and Views," *Journal of International Business Studies*, Spring 1972, pp. 1–18.

Arshanapalli, Bala, and John Doukas, "Integra-tion of Euro-Money Markets," *Journal of Multinational Financial Management*, Vol. 2, No. 3/4, 1993, pp. 107–126.

Arshanapalli, Bala, Jongmo Jay Choi, E. Tyler Clagget, Jr., and John Doukas, "Explaining Premiums and Discounts on Closed-End Equity Country Funds," *Journal of Applied Corporate Finance*, Vol. 9, No. 3, Fall 1996, pp. 109–117.

Babbel, David F., "Determining the Optimum Strategy for Hedging Currency Exposure," *Journal of International Business Studies*, Spring/Summer 1983, pp. 133–139.

Baker, James C., and Laurence J. Beardsley, "Multinational Companies' Use of Risk Evaluation and Profit Measurement for Capital Budgeting Decisions," *Journal of Business Finance*, Spring 1973, pp. 38–43.

Ball, Ray, "Making Accounting International: Why, How, and How Far Will It Go?" *Journal of Applied Corporate Finance*, Vol. 8, No. 3, Fall 1995, pp. 19–29.

Bank for International Settlements, Annual Report, annual issues, Basle.

Bank for International Settlements, "Central Bank Survey of Foreign Exchange and Derivatives Market Activity in April 2004, October 2004.

Bank for International Settlements, Economic Paper No. 41 and *Financial Markets, Institutions and Instruments*, Volume 4, No. 1, 1995.

Bank of America Roundtable on Evaluating and Financing Foreign Direct Investment," *Journal of Applied Corporate Finance*, Fall 1996, Vo. 9, No. 3, pp. 64–79.

Bank of America, "Corporate America: FX Risk Management 1996," Global Capital Markets Group, Monograph 78, Winter 1996–1997.

Barrett, M. Edgar, "Case of the Tangled Transfer Price," *Harvard Business Review*, May/Jun 1977, pp. 20–36, 176–178.

Batten, Jonathan, Robert Mellor, and Victor Wan, "Foreign Exchange Risk Management Practices and Products Used by Australian Firms," *Journal of International Business Studies*, third Quarter 1993, pp. 557–573.

Bauman, Joseph, Steve Saratore, and William Liddle, "A Practical Framework for Corporate

Exposure Management," *Journal of Applied Corporate Finance*, Vol. 7, No. 3, Fall 1994, pp. 66–72.

Baumol, William J., and Burton G. Malkiel, "Redundant Regulation of Foreign Security Trading and U.S. Competitiveness," *Journal of Applied Corporate Finance*, Winter 1993, pp. 19–27.

Bavishi, Vinod B., "Capital Budgeting Practices at Multinationals," *Management Accounting*, Aug. 1981, pp. 32–35.

Bekaert, Gert and Campbell R. Harvey, "Emerging Equity Market Volatility," *Journal of Financial Economics*, Vol. 43, No. 1, Jan. 1997, pp. 29–77.

Belk, P. A., and M. Glaum, "The Management of Foreign Exchange Risk in UK Multinationals: An Empirical Investigation," *Accounting and Business Research*, Vol. 21, No. 81, 1990, pp. 3–13.

Benito, Gabriel R. G., "Ownership Structures of Norwegian Foreign Subsidiaries in Manufacturing," *The International Trade Journal*, Vol. 10, No. 2, Summer 1996, pp. 157–198.

Bergendahl, Göran, "Multi-Currency Netting in a MultiNational Firm," in *International Financial Management*, Göran Bergendahl, ed., Stockholm: Norstedts, 1982, pp. 149–173.

Berkman, Henk, Michael E. Bradley, and Stephen Magan, "An International Comparison of Derivatives Use," *Financial Management*, Vol. 26, No. 4, Winter 1997, pp. 69–73.

Bessembinder, Hendrik, "Forward Contracts and Firm Value: Investment Incentive and Contracting Effects," *Journal of Financial and Quantitative Analysis*, Vol. 26, No. 4, Dec 1991, pp. 519–532.

Biddle, Gary C., and Shahrokh M. Saudagaran, "The Effects of Financial Disclosure Levels on Firms' Choices Among Alternative Foreign Stock Exchange Listings," *Journal of International Financial Management and Accounting*, Vol. 1, No. 1, Spring 1989, pp. 55–87.

Bilson, John F.O., "The Evaluation and Use of Foreign Exchange Rate Forecasting Services," in R.J. Herring, ed., *Management of Foreign Exchange Risk*, Cambridge, U.K.: Cambridge University Press, 1984, pp. 149–179.

Black, Fischer, and Myron Scholes, "The Pricing of Options and Corporate Liabilities," *Journal of Political Economy*, May/Jun 1973, pp. 637–659.

Bodnar, Gordon M., "1998 Wharton Survey of Financial Risk Management by U.S. Non-Financial Firms," *Financial Management*, Volume 24, No. 4, Winter 1998, pp. 70–91.

Bodurtha, James N., D. Chinhyung Cho, and Lemma W. Senbet, "Economic Forces in the Stock Market: An International Perspective," *Global Finance Journal*, Fall 1989, pp. 21–46.

Bodurtha, James N., Jr., and Georges R. Courtadon, "Efficiency Tests of the Foreign Currency Options Market," *Journal of Finance*, Mar 1986, pp. 151–162.

Bodurtha, James N., Jr., and Georges R. Courtadon, "Tests of an American Option Pricing Model on the Foreign Currency Options Market," *Journal of Financial and Quantitative Analysis*, Jun 1987, pp. 153–168.

Bonser-Neal, Catherine, Greggory Brauer, Robert Neal, and Simon Wheatley, "International Investment Restrictions and Closed-End Country Fund Prices," *Journal of Finance*, Jun 1990, pp. 523–548.

Booth, Laurence, and Wendy Rotenberg, "Assessing Foreign Exchange Exposure: Theory and Application using Canadian Firms," *Journal of International Financial Management and Accounting*, Vol. 2, No. 1, Spring 1990, pp. 1–22.

Booth, Laurence David, "Taxes, Funds Positioning, and the Cost of Capital for Multinationals," *Advances in Financial Planning and Forecasting*, Vol. 4, part B, 1990, pp. 245–270.

Boris, C. E. V., "Leverage and Financing of Non-Financial Companies: An International Perspective," *BIS Economic Papers*, No. 27, May 1990.

Boubakri, Narjess and Jean Claude Cosset, "The Financial and Operating Performance of Newly Privatized Firms: Evidence from Developing

Countries," *Journal of Finance*, Vol. 53, No. 3, Jun 1998, pp. 1081–1110.

Boutchkova, Maria K. and William L. Megginson, "Privatization and the Rise of Global Capital Markets," *Financial* , Volume 29, Issue 4, Winter 2000, pp. 31–76.

Braas, Alberic, and Charles N. Bralver, "An Analysis of Trading Profits: How Most Trading Rooms Really Make Money," *Journal of Applied Corporate Finance*, Winter 1990, pp. 85–90.

Bradley, Finbarr, "An Analysis of Call Strategy in the Eurodollar Bond Market," *Journal of International Financial Management and Accounting*, Vol. 2, No. 1, Spring 1990, pp. 23–46.

Brealey, Richard A., Ian A. Cooper, and Michael A. Habib, "Using Project Finance to Fund Infrastructure Investments," *Journal of Applied Corporate Finance*, Fall 1996, Volume 9, No. 5, pp. 25–38.

Brennan, Michael J. and H. Henry Cro, "International Portfolio Investment Flows," *Journal of Finance*, Vol. 52, No. 5, Oct. 1997, pp.. 1851–1880.

Brewer, Thomas L., "Government Policies, Market Imperfections, and Foreign Direct Investment," *Journal of International Business Studies*, 1st Quarter 1993, pp. 101–120.

Briys, Eric, and Francois de Varenne, "Optimal Hedging and the Partial Loss Offset," *European Financial Management*, Vol. 4, No. 3, November 1998, pp. 321–334.

Briys, Eric, and Michel Crouhy, "Creating and Pricing Hybrid Foreign Currency Options," *Financial Management*, Winter 1988, pp. 59–65.

Brown, Keith C., and Donald J. Smith, "Default Risk and Innovations in the Design of Interest Rate Swaps," *Financial Management*, Vol. 22, No. 2, Summer 1993, pp. 94–105.

Buckley, Peter J., "The Limits of Explanation: Testing the Internalization Theory of the Multinational Enterprise," *Journal of International Business Studies*, Summer 1988, pp. 181–193.

Buckley, Peter J., and Mark Casson, "An Economic Model of International Joint Venture Strategy," *Journal of International Business Studies*, Volume 27, Number 5, Special Issue 1996, pp. 849–876.

Burgman, Todd A., "An Empirical Examination of Multinational Corporate Capital Structure," *Journal of International Business Studies,* Third Quarter 1996, pp. 553–570.

Cantor, Richard and Frank Packer, "Sovereign Risk Assessment and Agency Credit Ratings," *European Financial Management*, Vol. 2, 1996.

Capel, Jeanette, "A Real Options Approach to Economic Exposure Management," *Journal of International Financial Management and Accounting*, Vol. 8, No. 2, 1997, pp. 87–113.

Caves, Richard E., "International Corporations: The Industrial Economics of Foreign Investment," *Economica*, February 1971, pp. 1–27.

Carney, William J., "Large Bank Stockholders in Germany: Saviors or Substitutes?," *Journal of Applied Corporate Finance*, Vol. 9, No. 4, Winter 1997, pp. 74–81.

Chan, Su Han, John W. Kensinger, Arthur Keown, and John D. Martin, "When Do Strategic Alliances Create Shareholder Value," *Journal of Financial Economics*, 1997.

Chan, Su Han, John W. Kensinger, Arthur Keown, and John D. Martin, "When Do Strategic Alliances Create Shareholder Value," *Journal of Applied Corporate Finance*, Spring 1999, Vol. 12, No. 1, pp. 82–87.

Chang, Rosita P., Peter E. Koveos, and S. Ghon Rhee, "Financial Planning for International Long-Term Debt Financing," *Advances in Financial Planning and Forecasting*, Vol. 4, part B, 1990, pp. 33–58.

Chase, Carmen D., James L. Kuhle, and Carl H. Walther, "The Relevance of Political Risk in Direct Foreign Investment," *Management International Review*, Vol. 28, No. 3, 1988, pp. 31–38.

Chen, Andrew H., and Sumon C. Mazumdar, "Interest Rate Linkages Within the EMS and

Bank Credit Supply," *European Financial Management*, Vol. 1, No. 1, Mar 1995, pp. 37–48.

Chen, Charles J.P., C. S. Agnes Cheng, Jia He, and Jawon Kim, "An Investigation of the Relationship Between International Activities and Capital Structure," *Journal of International Business Studies*, Third Quarter, 1997, pp. 563–577.

Chen, Howin and Tain-Jy Chen, "Network Linkages and Location Choice in Foreign Direct Investment," *Journal of International Business Studies*, Vol. 29, No. 3, Third Quarter, 1998, pp. 445–468.

Chen, T. J., K. C. John Wei, "Risk Premiums in Foreign Exchange Markets: Theory and Evidence," *Advances in Financial Planning and Forecasting*, Vol. 4, 1990, pp. 23–42.

Chesney, Marc, and Louis Scott, "Pricing European Currency Options: A Comparison of the Modified Black-Scholes Model and a Random Variance Model," *Journal of Financial and Quantitative Analysis*, Sep 1989, pp. 267–284.

Chiang, Thomas C., "Empirical Analysis on the Predictors of Future Spot Rates," *Journal of Financial Research*, Summer 1986, pp. 153–162.

Choi, Frederick D. S., "International Data Sources for Empirical Research in Financial Management," *Financial Management*, Summer 1988, pp. 80–98.

Choi, Frederick D. S., and Arthur Stonehill, "Foreign Access to U.S. Securities Markets: The Theory, Myth and Reality of Regulatory Barriers," *The Investment Analyst*, Jul 1982, pp. 17–26.

Choi, Frederick, Hisaaki Hino, Sang Kee Min, Sang Oh Nam, Junishi Ujiie, and Arthur Stonehill, "Analyzing Foreign Financial Statements: The Use and Misuse of International Ratio Analysis," *Journal of International Business Studies*, Spring/Summer 1983, pp. 113–131.

Choi, Jongmoo Jay, "A Model of Firm Valuation with Exchange Exposure," *Journal of International Business Studies,* Summer 1986, pp. 145–152.

Choi, Jongmoo Jay, "Diversification, Exchange Risk, and Corporate International Investment," *Journal of International Business Studies,* Spring 1989, pp. 145–155.

Choi, Jongmoo Jay, "Accounting Valuation and Economic Hedging of Foreign Inventory Under Exchange and Inflation Risk," in *Advances in Working Capital* , Vol. 2, JAI Press, 1991.

Choi, Jongmoo Jay, and Richard Ajayi, "The Effect of Foreign Debt on Currency Values," *Journal of Economics and Business*, 45, Aug/Oct 1993, pp. 331–340.

Choi, Jongmoo Jay, and Shmuel Hauser, "The Effects of Domestic and Foreign Yield Curves on the Value of American Currency Call Options," *Journal of Banking and Finance*, 14, Mar 1990, pp. 41–53.

Choi, Jongmoo Jay, and Shmuel Hauser, "Forward Foreign Exchange in Continuous-Time Derivative Asset Framework," *Research in Finance*, JAI Press, 1994.

Choi, Jongmoo Jay and Murli Rajan, "A Joint Test of Market Segmentation and Exchange Risk Factor in International Capital Markets," *Journal of International Business Studies*, Volume 28, No. 1, First Quarter 1997, pp. 29–49.

Choi, Jongmoo Jay, and Alan Severn, "On the Effects of International Risk, Segmentation and Diversification on the Cost of Equity Capital: A Critical Review and Synthesis," *Journal of Multinational Financial Management*, Vol. 1, issue 3, 1991, pp. 1–19.

Clark, Terry, Masaaki Kotabe, and Dan Rajaratnam, "Exchange Rate Pass-Through and International Pricing Strategy: A Conceptual Framework and Research Propositions," *Journal of International Business Studies*, Vol. 30, No. 2, Second Quarter 1999, pp. 249–268.

Coase, R. H., "The Nature of the Firm," *Economica*, No. 4, 1937, pp. 386–405.

Cochran, Steven J., and Robert H. Defina, "Can Purchasing Power Parity Help Forecast the Dollar?" *Journal of Forecasting*, Vol. 14, No. 6, Nov 1995, pp. 523–532.

Cochrane, James L., "Helping to Keep U.S. Capital Markets Competitive: Listing World-Class Non-U.S. Firms on U.S. Exchanges," *Journal of International Financial Management and*

Accounting, Vol. 4, No. 2, Summer 1992, pp. 163–170.

Codogne, Lorenzo, "Assessing Bond Market Developments Post-Euro," *Journal of Applied Corporate Finance*, Fall 1998, Vol. 11, No. 3, pp. 66–81.

Cohen, Stephen S., and John Zysman, "Countertrade, Offsets, Barter and Buybacks," *California Management Review*, Winter 1986, pp. 41–56.

Cohn, Richard A., and John J. Pringle, "Imperfections in International Financial Markets: Implications for Risk Premia and the Cost of Capital to Firms," *Journal of Finance*, Mar 1973, pp. 59–66.

Collier, Paul A., E. W. Davis, J. B. Coates, and S. G. Longden, "Policies Employed in the Management of Currency Risk: A Case Study Analysis of US and U.K., *Managerial Finance*, Vol. 18, No. 3, 1992, pp. 41–52.

Collins, J. Markham, "A Market Performance Comparison of U.S. Firms Active in Domestic, Developed and Developing Countries," *Journal of International Business Studies*, Second Quarter 1990, pp. 271–287.

Collins, J. Markham, and William S. Sekely, "The Relationship of Headquarters, Country, and Industry Classification to Financial Structure," *Financial Management*, Autumn 1983, pp. 45–51.

Constand, Richard L., Lewis P. Freitas, and Michael J. Sullivan, "Factors Affecting Price Earnings Ratios and Market Values of Japanese Firms," *Financial Management*, Winter 1991, pp. 68–79.

Contractor, Farok J., "Ownership Patterns of U.S. Joint Ventures Abroad and the Liberalization of Foreign Government Regulations in the 1980s: Evidence from the Benchmark Surveys," *Journal of International Business Studies*, First Quarter 1990, pp. 55–73.

Cooper, Ian, and Evi Kaplanis, "Home Bias and the Cost of Capital for Multinational Firms," *Journal of Applied Corporate Finance*, Vol. 8, No. 3, Fall 1995, pp. 95–104.

Copeland, Thomas, and Yash Joshi, "Why Derivatives Do Not Reduce FX Risk," *Corporate Finance*, May 1996, pp. 35–41.

Cosset, Jean-Claude, and Jean-Marc Suret, "Political Risk and the Benefits of International Portfolio Diversification, *Journal of International Business Studies*, Vol. 26, No. 2, Second Quarter 1995, pp. 301–318.

Cox, J. C., and S. A. Ross, "The Valuation of Options for Alternative Stochastic Processes," *Journal of Financial Economics*, Vol. 3, 1976, pp. 145–166.

Cox, J. C., S. A. Ross, and M. Rubinstein, "Option Pricing: A Simplified Approach," *Journal of Financial Economics*, Vol. 7, 1979, pp. 229–263.

Crum, Roy L., and Lee A. Tavis, "Allocating Multinational Resources When Objectives Conflict: A Problem of Overlapping Systems, *Advances in Financial Planning and Forecasting*, Vol. 4, part B, 1990, pp. 271–294.

Culp, Christopher L., Steve H. Hanke, and Merton H. Miller, "The Case for an Indonesian Currency Board," *Journal of Applied Corporate Finance*, Volume 2, No. 4, Winter 1999, pp. 57–64.

Cumby, Robert E., and Maurice Obstfeld, "A Note on Exchange-Rate Expectations and Nominal Interest Differentials: A Test of the Fisher Hypothesis," *Journal of Finance*, Jun 1981, pp. 697–703.

De Santis, Giorgio and Bruno Gerard, "International Asset Pricing and Portfolio Diversification with Time-Varying Risk," *Journal of Finance*, Volume 52, No. 5, October 1997, pp. 1881–1912.

Denis, David J., Diane K. Denis, and Keven Yost, "Global Diversification, Industrial Diversification, and Firm Value," *The Journal of Finance*, Vol. VII, No. 5, October 2002, pp. 1951–1979.

Dewenter, Kathryn L. and Paul H. Malatesta, "Public Offerings of State-Owned and Privately-Owned Enterprises: An International Comparison," *Journal of Finance*, Vol. 52, No. 4, Aug 1997, pp. 1659–1670.

Dewenter, Kathryn L. and Vincent A. Warther, "Dividends, Asymmetric Information, and Agency Conflicts: Evidence from a Comparison of the Dividend Policies of Japanese and U.S. Firms," *Journal of Finance*, Vol. 53, No. 3, Jun 1998, pp. 879–904.

Dixit, Avinash K., and Robert S. Pindyck, "The Options Approach to Capital Investment," *Harvard Business Review,* May/Jun 1995, pp. 105–115.

Dodd, Mikel T., and James A. Millar, "Financial Structure in Japanese and American Firms: An Indirect Test of Agency Relationships," *Journal of International Financial Management and Accounting,* Vol. 2, nos. 2 and 3, Summer & Autumn 1990, pp. 131–144.

Dominguez, Luis V., and Carlos G. Sequeira, "Determinants of LDC Exporters' Performance: A Cross-National Study," *Journal of International Business Studies*, First Quarter 1993, pp. 19–40.

Domowitz, Ian, Jack Glen, and Ananth Madhavan, "Market Segmentation and Stock Prices: Evidence from an Emerging Market," *Journal of Finance*, Vol. 52, No. 3, June 1997, pp. 1059–1085.

Domowitz, Ian, Jack Glen, and Ananth Madhavan, "International Cross Listing and Order Flow Migration: Evidence from an Emerging Market," *Journal of Finance*, Vol. 53, No. 6, Dec 1998, pp. 2001–2027.

Donaldson, Gordon, "The Corporate Restructuring of the 1980s and its Import for the 1990s," *Journal of Applied Corporate Finance*, Winter 1994, pp. 55–69.

Dotan, Amihud, and Arie Ovadia, "A Capital-Budgeting Decision: The Case of a Multinational Corporation Operating in High-Inflation Countries," *Journal Of Business Research*, Oct 1986, pp. 403–410.

Doukas, John, "Syndicated Euro-Credit Sovereign Risk Assessments, Market Efficiency and Contagion Effects," *Journal of International Business Studies,* Summer 1989, pp. 255–267.

Doukas, John, and Nickolaos G. Travlos, "The Effect of Corporate Multinationalism on Shareholders' Wealth: Evidence from International Acquisitions," *Journal of Finance,* Dec 1988, pp. 1161–1175.

Doukas, John and Christos Pantzalis, "Multinational Firms' Agency Cost of Debt," 1998.

Dufey, Gunter, "Corporate Finance and Exchange, Rate Variations," *Financial Management*, Summer 1972, pp. 51–57.

Dufey, Gunter, and Ian H. Giddy, "International Financial Planning: The Use of Market-Based Forecasts," *California Management Review*, Fall 1978, pp. 69–81; reprinted in Heide V. Wortzel and Lawrence Wortzel, eds., *Strategic Management of Multinational Corporations: The Essentials*, second ed., New York: Wiley, 1991.

Dufey, Gunter, and S. L. Srinivasulu, "The Case for Corporate Management of Foreign Exchange Risk," *Financial Management*, Winter 1983, pp. 54–62.

Dunning, John H., "Trade Location of Economic Activity and the MNE: A Search for an Eclectic Approach," in *The International Allocation of Economic Activity*, Bertil Ohlin, Per-Ove Hesselborn, and Per Magnus Wijkman, eds., New York: Holmes and Meier, 1977, pp. 395–418.

Dunning, John H., "The Eclectic Paradigm of International Production: A Restatement and Some Possible Extensions," *Journal of International Business Studies*, Spring 1988, pp. 1–32.

Dunning, John H., "Location and the Multinational Enterprise: A Neglected Factor?," *Journal of International Business Studies*, Vol. 29, No. 1, First Quarter 1998, pp. 45–66.

Dunning, John H., and Alan M. Rugman, "The Influence of Hymer's Dissertation on the Theory of Foreign Direct Investment," *American Economic Review*, May 1985, pp. 228–232.

Eaker, Mark R., "The Numeraire Problem and Foreign Exchange Risk," *Journal of Finance*, May 1981, pp. 419–427.

Eaker, Mark R., and Dwight Grant, "Optimal Hedging of Uncertain and Long-Term Foreign

Exchange Exposure," *Journal of Banking and Finance*, Jun 1985, pp. 222–231.

Eaker, Mark R., and Dwight M. Grant, "Cross-Hedging Foreign Currency Risk," *Journal of International Money and Finance*, Mar 1987, pp. 85–105.

Economist, "A Survey of Corporate Risk Management," Feb 10, 1996.

Eiteman, David K., "A Model for Expropriation Settlement: The Peruvian-IPC Controversy," *Business Horizons*, Apr 1970, pp. 85–91.

Eiteman, David K., "Multinational Firms and the Development of Penang, Malaysia," *The International Trade Journal*, Vol. XI, No. 2, 1997.

Engel, Charles, and James D. Hamilton, "Long Swings in the Dollar: Are They in the Data and Do Markets Know It?" *American Economic Review*, Sept 1990, pp. 689–713.

Eriksson, Kent, Jan Johanson, Anders Majkgård, and D. Deo Sharma, "Experiential Knowledge and Cost in the Internationalization Process," *Journal of International Business Studies*, Vol. 28, No. 2, Second Quarter 1997, pp. 337–360.

Errunza, Vihang R., "Determinants of Financial Structure in the Central American Common Market," *Financial Management,* Autumn 1979, pp.72–77.

Errunza, Vihang R., "Financing MNC Subsidiaries in Central America," *Journal of International Business Studies,* Fall 1979, pp. 88–93.

Errunza, Vihang, and Ked Hogan, "Macroeconomic Determinants of European Stock Market Volatility," *European Financial Management*, Vol. 4, No. 3, Nov 1998, pp. 361–378.

Errunza, Vihang R., and Lemma W. Senbet, "International Corporate Diversification, Market Valuation, and Size-Adjusted Evidence," *Journal of Finance,* Jul 1984, pp. 727–743.

Errunza, Vihang R., and Lemma W. Senbet, "The Effects of International Operations on the Market Value of the Firm: Theory and Evidence," *Journal of Finance,* May 1981, pp. 401–417.

Eun, Cheol S., and S. Janakiramanan, "Bilateral Cross-Listing and the Equilibrium Security Prices," *Advances in Financial Planning and Forecasting*, Vol. 4, part B, 1990, pp. 59–74.

Fama, Eugene F., "Forward Rates as Predictors of Future Spot Rates," *Journal of Financial Economics*, Oct 1976, pp. 361–377.

Fama, Eugene F., "Forward and Spot Exchange Rates," *Journal of Monetary Economics*, Vol. 14, 1984, pp. 319–338.

Fama, Eugene, and Kenneth R. French, "Value Versus Growth: The International Evidence," *Journal of Finance*, Vol. 53, No. 6, Dec 1998, pp. 1975–1999.

Fatemi, Ali M., "The Effect of International Diversification on Corporate Financing Policy," *Journal of Business Research*, Vol. 16, No. 1, Jan 1988, pp.17–30.

Feiger, George, and Bertrand Jacquillat, "Currency Option Bonds, Puts and Calls on Spot Exchange and the Hedging of Contingent Foreign Earnings," *Journal of Finance*, Dec 1979, pp. 1129–1139.

Finnerty, John D., "Financial Engineering in Corporate Finance: An Overview," *Financial Management*, Winter 1988, pp. 14–32.

Fletcher, Donna J., and Larry W. Taylor, "A Non-Parametric Analysis of Covered Interest Parity in Long-Date Capital Markets," *Journal of International Money and Finance*, Vol. 13, No. 4, Aug 1994, pp. 459–475.

Flood, Eugene, Jr., and Donald R. Lessard, "On the Measurement of Operating Exposure to Exchange Rates: A Conceptual Approach," *Financial Management*, Spring 1986, pp. 25–36.

Foerster, Stephen R. and G. Andrew Karolyi, "The Effects of Market Segmentation and Investor Recognition on Asset Prices: Evidence From Foreign Stock Listing in the United States," *Journal of Finance*, Volume 54, No. 3, June 1999, pp. 981–1013.

Folks, William R., Jr., "Decision Analysis for Exchange Risk Management," *Financial Management*, Winter 1972, pp. 101–112.

Folks, William R., Jr., "Optimal Foreign Borrowing Strategies with Operations in the Forward Exchange Markets," *Journal of Financial and Quantitative Analysis*, Jun 1978, pp. 245–254.

Folks, William R., and Stanley R. Stansell, "The Use of Discriminant Analysis in Forecasting Exchange Risk Movements," *Journal of International Business Studies*, Spring 1975, pp. 33–50.

Fowler, D. J., "Transfer Prices and Profit Maximization in Multinational Enterprise Operations," *Journal of International Business Studies*, Winter 1978, pp. 9–26.

Frankel, J. A., "The Japanese Cost of Finance: A Survey," *Financial Management,* Spring 1991, pp. 95–127.

Frankel, Jeffrey, and Alan MacArthur, "Political vs. Currency Premia in International Real Interest Rate Differentials: A Study of Forward Rates for 24 Countries," *European Economic Review*, Vol. 32, No. 5, Jun 1988, pp. 1083–1114.

Frankel, Allen, and John Montgomery, "Financial Structure: An International Perspective," *Brookings Papers on Economic Activity*, Vol. 1, 1991, pp. 257–297.

Franks, Julian and Colin Mayer, "Corporate Ownership and Control in the U.K., Germany, and France," *Journal of Applied Corporate Finance*, Winter 1997, Vol. 9, No.4, pp. 30–45.

Frenkel, Jacob A., and Richard M. Levich, "Covered Interest Arbitrage: Unexploited Profits?" *Journal of Political Economy*, Apr 1975, pp. 325–338.

Frenkel, Jacob A., and Richard M. Levich, "Transaction Costs and Interest Arbitrage: Tranquil versus Turbulent Periods," *Journal of Political Economy*, Nov/Dec 1977, pp. 1209–1226.

Friend, Irwin, and Ichiro Tokutsu, "The Cost of Capital to Corporations in Japan and the U.S.A.," *Journal of Banking and Finance,* Vol. 11, No. 2, Jun 1987, pp. 313–328.

Frisch, Daniel J., Economics of International Tax Policy: Some Old and New Approaches," *Tax Notes*, Apr 30, 1990, pp. 581–591.

Fry, Clifford, Insup Lee, and Jongmoo Jay Choi, "International Listing and Valuation: The Case of the Tokyo Stock Exchange," *Review of Quantitative Finance and Accounting*, Mar 1994.

Ganitsky, Joseph, and Gerardo Lema, "Foreign Investment Through Debt-Equity Swaps," *Sloan Management Review*, Vol. 29, No. 2, Winter 1988, pp. 21–29.

Garman, Mark B., and Steven W. Kohlhagen, "Foreign Currency Option Values," *Journal of International Money and Finance*, Dec 1983, pp. 231–237.

Géczy, Christopher, Bernadette A. Minton, and Catherine Schrand, "Why Firms Use Currency Derivatives," *Journal of Finance*, Vol. 52, No. 4, Aug 1997, pp. 1323–1354.

Gentry, James A., Dileep R. Mehta, S. K. Bhattacharya, Robert Cobbaut, and Jean-Louis Scaringella, "An International Study of Management Perceptions of the Working Capital Process," *Journal of International Business Studies*, Spring–Summer 1979, pp. 28–38.

Geringer, J, Michael, and Louis Hebert, "Control and Performance of International Joint Ventures," *Journal of International Business Studies,* Summer 1989, pp. 235–254.

Ghertman, Michel, "Foreign Subsidiary and Parents' Roles During Strategic Investment and Divestment Decisions," *Journal of International Business Studies*, Spring 1988, pp. 47–68.

Giddy, Ian H., "An Integrated Theory of Exchange Rate Equilibrium," *Journal of Financial and Quantitative Analysis*, Dec 1976, pp. 863–892,

Giddy, Ian H., "Exchange Risk: Whose View?" *Financial Management*, Summer 1977, pp. 23–33.

Giddy, Ian H., and Gunter Dufey, "The Random Behavior of Flexible Exchange Rates," *Journal of International Business Studies*, Spring 1975, pp. 1–32.

Giddy, Ian H., and Gunter Dufey, "Uses and Abuses of Currency Options," *Journal of Applied Corporate Finance*, Vol. 8, No. 3, Fall 1995, pp. 49–57.

Glassman, Debra, "Exchange Rate Risk and Transactions Costs: Evidence from Bid-Ask Spreads," *Journal of International Money and Finance*, Vol. 6, No. 4, Dec 1987, pp. 479–491.

Glaum, Martin, "Strategic Management of Exchange Rate Risks," *Long Range Planning*, Vol. 23, No. 4, 1990, pp. 65–72.

Gleason, Kimberly C., Ike Mathur, and Lynette Knowles Mathur, "Shareholders' Gains from Corporate Expansion to the Republics of the Former Soviet Union," *Financial Management*, Vol. 28, No. 1, Spring 1999, pp. 61–74.

Godfrey, Stephen, and Ramon Espinosa, "A Practical Approach to Calculating Cost of Equity for Investments in Emerging Markets," *Journal of Applied Corporate Finance,* Vol. 9, No. 3, Fall 1996, pp. 80–89.

Gonzalez, Manolete V., and Edwin Villanueva, "Steering a Subsidiary Through a Political Crisis," *Risk Management*, Oct 1992, pp. 16–27.

Goodman, Stephen, "Foreign Exchange Forecasting Techniques: Implications for Business and Policy," *Journal of Finance*, May 1979, pp. 415–427.

Goodwin, Barry K., Thomas Grennes, and Michael K. Wohlgenant, "Testing the Law of One Price When Trade Takes Time," *Journal of International Money and Finance*, May 1990, pp. 21–40.

Grabbe, J. Orlin, "The Pricing of Call and Put Options on Foreign Exchange," *Journal of International Money and Finance*, Dec 1983, pp. 239–253.

Granick, David, "National Differences in the Use of Internal Transfer Prices," *California Management Review*, Summer 1975, pp. 28–40.

Gruber, W., D. Mehta, and R. Vernon, "The R&D Factor in International Trade and Investment of United States Industries," *Journal of Political Economy*, Feb 1967, pp. 20–37.

Guffin, John M. and G. Andrew Karolyi, "Another Look at the Role of the Industrial Structure of Markets for International Diversification Strategies," *Journal of Financial Economics*, Vol. 50, No. 3, Dec 1998, pp. 351–373.

Gultekin, Mustafa N., N. Bulent Gultekin, and Alessandro Penati, "Capital Controls and International Capital Market Segmentation: The Evidence from the Japanese and American Stock Markets," *Journal of Finance*, Sep 1989, pp. 849–869.

Hamilton, Robert D. and Roger J. Kashlak, "National Influences on Multinational Corporation Control System Selection," *Management International Review*, 2/99, pp. 167–189.

Hanson, Bruce B., "What You Need to Know About Economic Value Added," *Compensation and Benefits Review*, Mar/Apr 1995, pp. 33–36.

Harris, Trevor S., Nahun D. Melumad, and Toshi Shibano, "An Argument Against Hedging by Matching the Currency of Costs and Revenues," *Journal of Applied Corporate Finance*, Fall 1996, Volume 9, No. 3, pp. 90–97.

Harvard Business School, "A Note on Private Equity in Developing Countries," Boston, Ma: Harvard Business School Publishing, Mar 1997.

He, Jia and Lilian Ng, "The Foreign Exchange Exposure of Japanese Multinational Corporations," *Journal of Finance*, Vol. 53, No. 2, April 1998, pp. 733–753.

Hedlund, Gunner, "A Model of Knowledge Management and the N-form Corporation," *Strategic Management Journal*, No. 15, 1994, pp. 73–90.

Hedlund, Gunner, "The Hypermodem MNC-A Heterarchy?" *Human Resource Management*, Vol. 25, No. 1, pp. 9–35.

Hekman, Christine R., "A Financial Model of Foreign Exchange Exposure," *Journal of International Business Studies*, Summer 1985, pp. 83–99.

Hekman, Christine R., "Don't Blame Currency Values for Strategic Errors," *Midland Corporate Finance Journal*, Fall 1986, pp. 45–55.

Hennart, Jean-Francois, "Internalization in Practice: Early Foreign Direct Investment in Malaysian Tin Mining," *Journal of International Business Studies*, Summer 1986. pp. 131–144.

Hennart, Jean-Francois, "Some Empirical Dimensions of Countertrade," *Journal of International Business Studies*, second Quarter 1990, pp. 243–270.

Hennart, Jean-Francois and Erin Anderson, "Countertrade and the Minimization of Transaction Costs: An Empirical Examination," *Journal of Law, Economics, and Organization*, Oct 1993, pp. 290–313.

Hervey, Michael G., "A Survey of Corporate Programs for Managing Terrorist Threats," *Journal of International Business Studies*, Third Quarter, 1993, pp. 465–478.

Hofstede, Geert, Cheryl A. Van Deusen, Carolyn Mueller, Thomas A. Charles and the Business Goals Network, "What Goals Do Business Leaders Pursue? A Study in Fifteen Countries," *Journal of International Business Studies*, Volume 39, Number 4, Fourth Quarter, 2002, pp. 785–803.

Hill, Claire A., "Securitization: A Financing Strategy for Emerging Market Firms," *Journal of Applied Corporate Finance*, Fall 1998, Vol. 11, No. 3, pp. 55–65.

Hirsch, Se'ev, "Multinationals: How Different Are They?" in *The Growth of The Large Multinational Corporation*, G. Y. Bertin, ed., Paris: Centre Nationale de la Recherche Scientifique, 1973.

Ho, T.S., Richard C. Stapleton, and Marti G. Subrahmanyam, "The Risk of a Currency Swap: A Multivariate Binomial Methodology, *European Financial Management*, Vol. 4, No. 1, March 1998, pp. 9–28.

Hodder, James E., "Evaluation of Manufacturing Investments: A Comparison of U.S. and Japanese Practices," *Financial Management*, Spring 1986, pp. 17–24.

Hodder, James E., and Adrian E. Tschoegl, "Some Aspects of Japanese Corporate Finance," *Journal of Financial and Quantitative Analysis*, Jun 1985, pp. 173–191.

Hodder, James E., and Lemma W. Senbet, "International Capital Structure Equilibrium," *Journal of Finance*, Dec 1990, pp. 1495–1516.

Hogue, W. Dickerson, "The Foreign Investment Decision Making Process," *Association for Education in International Business Proceedings*, Dec 29, 1967, pp.1–2.

Holmes, M.C., "Checklist for Foreign Licensing," *Business Lawyer*, Nov 1968, pp. 281–289.

Horaguchi, Haruo, and Brian Toyne, "Setting the Record Straight: Hymer, Internalization Theory and Transaction Cost Economics," *Journal of International Business Studies*, Third Quarter 1990, pp. 487–494.

Houpt, James V., "International Trends for U.S. Banks and Banking Markets," Staff Study of the Board of Governors of the Federal Reserve System, No. 156, May 1988.

Houston, Carol Olson, "Translation Exposure Hedging Post SFAS No. 52," *Journal of International Financial Management and Accounting*, Vol. 2, Nos. 2 and 3, Summer and Autumn 1990, pp. 145–170.

Howton, Shawn D. and Steven B. Perfect, "Currency and Interest Rate Derivatives Use in U.S. Firms," *Financial Management*, Vol. 27, No. 4, Winter 1998, pp. 111–121.

Howe, John S., and Kathryn Kelm, "The Stock Price Impacts of Overseas Listings," *Financial Management*, Autumn 1987, pp. 51–56.

Hu, Henry T.C., "Behind the Corporate Hedge: Information and the Limits of 'Shareholder Wealth Maximization,'" *Journal of Applied Corporate Finance*, Vol. 9, No. 3, Fall 1996, pp. 39–51.

Huang, Roger D., "Expectations of Exchange Rates and Differential Inflation Rates: Further Evidence on Purchasing Power Parity in Efficient Markets," *Journal of Finance*, Mar 1987, pp. 69–79.

Huang, Roger D., and Hans R. Stoll, *Major World Equity Markets: Current Structure and Prospects for Change*, New York: New York University Salomon Center; Monograph Series in Finance and Economics, No. 3, 1991.

Huckins, Nancy White, and Anoop Rai, "Market Risk for Foreign Currency Options: Basle's Simplified Model," *Financial Management*, Vol. 28, No. 1, Spring 1999, pp. 99–109.

Hughes, John S., Dennis E. Logue, and Richard J. Sweeney, "Corporate International Diversification and Market Assigned Measures of Risk and Diversification," *Journal of Financial and Quantitative Analysis*, Nov 1975, pp. 627–637.

Hull, John, and Alan White, "Hedging the Risks from Writing Foreign Currency Options," *Journal of International Money and Finance*, Jun 1987, pp. 131–152.

Hymer, Stephen, and Robert Rowthorn, "Multinational Corporations and International Oligopoly: The Non-American Challenge," in *The International Corporation: A Symposium*, Charles P. Kindleberger, ed., Cambridge, Mass.: MIT Press, 1970, pp. 57–91.

International Monetary Fund, *Balance of Payments Statistics Yearbook*, annual.

"International Working Capital Practices of the Fortune 200," *Financial Practice & Education*, Fall/Winter 1996, Volume 6, Issue 2.

Investing, Licensing and Trading Conditions Abroad, New York: Business International, a reference service that is continually updated.

Jacque, Laurent, and Gabriel Hawawini, "Myths and Realities of the Global Capital Market: Lessons for Financial Managers," *Journal of Applied Corporate Finance*, Fall 1993, pp. 81–90.

Jadlow, Janice Wickstead, "Market Assessment of the Eurodollar Default Risk Premium," *Advances in Financial Planning and Forecasting*, Vol. 4, part A, 1990, pp. 105–122.

Jayaraman, Narayanan, Kuldeep Shastri, and Kishore Tandon, "The Impact of International Cross Listings on Risk and Return: The Evidence from American Depositary Receipts," *Journal of Banking and Finance*, No. 17, pp. 91–103.

Jennergren, L. Peter, and Bertil Nëslund, "Models for the Valuation of International Convertible Bonds," *Journal of International Financial Management and Accounting*, Vol. 2, nos. 2 and 3, Summer and Autumn 1990, pp. 93–110.

Jensen, Michael C., "Agency Cost of Free Cash Flow, Corporate Finance and Takeovers, *American Economic Review*, 76, 1986, pp. 323–329.

Jensen, Michael C., "Value Maximization, Stakeholder Theory, and the Corporate Objective Function," *Journal of Applied Corporate Finance*, Fall 2001, Volume 14, No. 3, pp. 8–21.

Jensen, Michael and W. Meckling, "Theory of the Firm: Managerial Behavior, Agency Costs, and Ownership Structure," *Journal of Financial Economics*, No. 3, 1976, pp. 305–360.

Jesswein, Kurt R., Chuck C. Y. Kwok, and William R. Folks, Jr., "Corporate Use of Innovative Foreign Exchange Risk Management Products," *Columbia Journal of World Business*, Vol. 30, No. 3, Fall 1995, pp. 70–82.

Johansen, John, and F. Weidersheim-Paul, "The Internationalization of the Firm: Four Swedish Case Studies," *Journal of Management Studies*, Vol. 12, No. 3, 1975.

Johnansen, John, and Jan Erik Vahlne, "The Internationalization of the Firm: A Model of Knowledge Development and Increasing Foreign Market Commitments," *Journal of International Business Studies*, Vol. 8, No. 1, 1977.

John, Kose, Lemma Senbet, and Anant Sundaram, "Cross-border Liability of Multinational Enterprises, Border Taxes, and Capital Structure," *Financial Management*, Winter 1991.

Johnson, Greg and Thomas Funkhouser, "Yankee Bonds and Cross-Border Private Placements," *Journal of Applied Corporate Finance*, Fall 1999, Vol. 10, No. 3, pp. 34–45.

Johnson, Robert, and Luc Soenen, "Evaluating the Impact of Investment Projects on the Firm's Currency Exposure," *Managerial Finance*, Vol. 20, No. 7, 1994, pp. 51–58.

Jorion, Philippe and William N. Goetzmann, "Global Stock Markets in the Twentieth Century," *Journal of Finance*, Vol. 54, No. 3, Jun 1999, pp. 953–980.

Jorion, Philippe, "The Exchange-Rate Exposure of U.S. Multinationals," *Journal of Business*, Vol. 63, No. 3, Jul 1990, pp. 331–345.

Jorion, Philippe, and Neal M. Stoughton, "An Empirical Investigation of the Early Exercise Premium of Foreign Currency Options," *Journal of Futures Markets*, Oct 1989, pp. 365–375.

Kaen, Fred R., Evangelos 0. Simos, and George A. Hachey, "The Response of Forward Exchange Rates to Interest Rate Forecasting Errors," *Journal of Financial Research*, Winter 1984, pp. 281–290.

Kanas, Angelos, "Exchange Rate Economic Exposure When Market Share Matters and Hedging Using Currency Options," *Management International Review*, Vol. 36, No. 1, First Quarter 1996, pp. 67–84.

Kaplan, Steven N., "Corporate Governance and Incentives in German Companies: Evidence From Top Executive Turnover and Firm Performance, *European Financial Management*, Vol. 1, No. 1, Mar 1995, pp. 23–36.

Kaplan, Steven, "Corporate Governance and Corporate Performance: A Comparison of Germany, Japan, and the U.S.," *Journal of Applied Corporate Finance*, Winter 1997, Vol. 9, No.4, pp. 86–93.

Karolyi, G. Andrew, "Sourcing Equity Internationally With Depositary Receipt Offerings: Two Exceptions That Prove The Rule," *Journal of Applied Corporate Finance*, Winter 1998, Vol. 10, No. 4, pp. 90–101.

Kaufold, Howard, and Michael Smirlock, "Managing Corporate Exchange and Interest Rate Exposure," *Financial Management*, Autumn 1986, pp. 64–72.

Kawaller, Ira G., "The Imperative of Interest Rate Risk Management," *Treasury Management Association (THA) Journal*, Vol. 15, No. 6, Nov/Dec 1996, pp. 4–7.

Keck, Tom, Eric Levengood, and Al Longfield, "Using Discounted Cash Flow Analysis in an International Setting," *Journal of Applied Corporate Finance*, Fall 1998, Vol. 11, No. 3, pp. 82–99.

Kelly, Marie E. Wicks, and George C. Philippatos, "Comparative Analysis of the Foreign Investment Evaluation Practices by U.S.-Based Manufacturing Multinational Corporations," *Journal of International Business Studies*, Winter 1982, pp. 19–42.

Kemna, Antzellen G. Z., "Case Studies in Real Options," *Financial Management*, Autumn 1993, pp. 259–270.

Kerkvliet, Joe, and Michael H. Moffett, "The Hedging of an Uncertain Future Foreign Currency Cash Flow," *Journal of Financial and Quantitative Analysis*, Vol. 26, No. 4, Dec 1991, pp. 565–578.

Kester, W. Carl, "Capital and Ownership Structure: A Comparison of United States and Japanese Manufacturing Corporations," *Financial Management*, Spring 1986, pp. 5–16.

Khouri, Sarkis J., and K. Hung Chan, "Hedging Foreign Exchange Risk: Selecting the Optimal Tool," *Midland Corporate Finance Journal*, Winter 1988, pp. 40–52.

Kim, E. Han, "Globalization of Capital Markets and the Asian Financial Crisis," *Journal of Applied Corporate Finance*, Fall 1998, Vol. 11, No. 3, pp. 30–39.

Kim, E. Han and Vijay Singal, "Are Open Markets Good for Foreign Investors and Emerging Nations?," *Journal of Applied Corporate Finance*, Fall 1997, Vol. 10, No. 3, pp. 18–33.

Kim, Wi Saeng, and Esmerelda 0. Lyn, "FDI Theories and the Performance of Foreign Multinationals Operating in the U.S.," *Journal of International Business Studies*, First Quarter 1990, pp. 41–54.

Kimura, Yui, "Firm-Specific Strategic Advantages and Foreign Direct Investment Behavior of Firms: The Case of Japanese Semiconductor Firms," *Journal of International Business Studies*, Summer 1989, pp. 296–314.

Kobrin, Stephen J., "The Environmental Determinants of Foreign Direct Manufacturing Investment: An Ex-Post Empirical Analysis," *Journal of International Business Studies*, Fall/Winter 1976, pp. 29–42.

Kobrin, Stephen J., "Political Risk: A Review and Reconsideration," *Journal of International Business Studies*, Spring/Summer 1979, pp. 67–80.

Kogut, Bruce, and Harbir Singh, "The Effect of National Culture on the Choice of Entry Mode," *Journal of International Business Studies,* Fall 1988, pp. 411–432.

Kogut, Bruce, and Udo Zander, "Knowledge of the Firm and the Evolutionary Theory of the Multinational Corporation," *Journal of International Business Studies*, Fourth Quarter, 1993, pp. 625–645.

Kohlhagen, Stephen W., *The Behavior of Foreign Exchange Markets—Critical Survey of the Empirical Literature*, New York: New York University Monograph Series in Finance and Economics, No. 3, 1978.

Kohlhagen, Steven W., "A Model of Optimal Foreign Exchange Hedging Without Exchange Rate Projections," *Journal of International Business Studies*, Fall 1978, pp. 9–19.

Kopits, George F., "Intra-Firm Royalties Crossing Frontier, and Transfer–Pricing Behaviour," *Economic Journal*, Dec 1976, pp. 791–805.

Koveos, Peter, and Bruce Seifert, "Purchasing Power Parity and Black Markets," *Financial Management*, Autumn 1985, pp. 40–46.

Kulatilaka, Nalin, and Alan J. Marcus, "Hedging Foreign Project Risk," *Journal of International Financial Management & Accounting*, Vol. 5, No. 2, Jun 1994, pp. 142–156.

Kunz, Roger M., "Factors Affecting the Value of the Stock Voting Right: Evidence from the Swiss Equity Market," *Financial Management*, Vol. 25, No. 3, Autumn 1996, pp. 7–21.

Kwok, Chuck C. Y., "Hedging Foreign Exchange Exposures: Independent vs. Integrative Approaches," *Journal of International Business Studies*, Summer 1987, pp. 33–52.

Kwok, Chuck C. Y., and LeRoy D. Brooks, "Examining Event Study Methodologies in Foreign Exchange Markets," *Journal of International Business Studies*, Second Quarter 1990, pp. 189–224.

Kwok, Chuck C. Y., and David M. Reeb, "Internationalization, Financial Leverage, and Risks of the Multinational Corporation: An Upstream-Downstream Hypothesis," Paper Presented at the Academy of International Business Annual Conference, Vienna, Austria, 1998.

Kwok, Chuck C.Y., and David M. Reeb, "Internationalization and Firm Risk: An Upstream-Downstream Hypothesis," *Journal of International Business Studies*, Volume 31, Issue 4, 2000, pp. 611–630.

Laurence, Martin, Francis Cai, and Sun Qian, "Weak-Form Efficiency and Causality Tests in Chinese Stock Markets," *Multinational Finance Journal*, Vol. 1, No. 4, Dec 1997, pp. 291–307.

Lecraw, Donald J., "The Management of Countertrade: Factors Influencing Success," *Journal of International Business Studies*, Spring 1989, pp. 41–59.

Lee, Kwang Chul, and Chuck C.Y. Kwok, "Multinational Corporations vs. Domestic Corporations: International Environmental Factors and Determinants of Capital Structure," *Journal of International Business Studies*, Summer 1988, pp. 195–217.

Lee, Suk Hun, "Relative Importance of Political Instability and Economic Variables on Perceived Country Creditworthiness," *Journal of International Business Studies*, Fourth Quarter, 1993, pp. 801–812.

Lee, Tung-Jean, and Richard E. Caves, "Uncertain Outcomes of Foreign Investment: Determinants of Profits After Large Acquisitions," *Journal of International Business Studies*, Vol. 29, No. 3, Third Quarter 1998, pp. 563–582.

Lee, W. Y., and K. S. Sachdeva, "The Role of the Multinational Firm in the Integration of Segmented Capital Markets," *Journal of Finance*, May 1977, pp. 479–492.

Lessard, Donald R., "Incorporating Country Risk in the Valuation of Offshore Projects," *Journal of Applied Corporate Finance*, Vol. 9, No. 3, Fall 1996, pp. 52–63.

Lessard, Donald R., "Evaluating International Projects: An Adjusted Present Value Approach," in *International Financial Management: Theory and Application*, Donald R. Lessard, ed., New York: Wiley, 1985, pp. 570–584.

Lessard, Donald R., "Finance and Global Competition: Exploiting Financial Scope and Coping with Volatile Exchange Rates," *Midland Corporate Finance Journal,* Fall 1986, pp. 6–29.

Lessard, Donald R., "Global Competition and Corporate Finance in the 1990's," *Journal of Applied Corporate Finance*, Winter 1991, pp. 59–72.

Lessard, Donald R., and S. B. Lightstore, "Volatile Exchange Rates Can Put Operations at Risk," *Harvard Business Review*, Jul/Aug 1986, pp.107–114.

Levi, Maurice D., and Piet Sercu, "Erroneous and Valid Reasons for Hedging Foreign Exchange Rate Exposure," *Journal of Multinational Financial Management*, Vol. 1, No. 2, 1991, pp. 19–28.

Levich, Richard M., "Tests of Forecasting Models and Market Efficiency in the International Money Market," in Jacob A. Frenkel and Harry G. Johnson, eds., *The Economics of Exchange Rates*, Reading, MA: Addison-Wesley, 1978, pp.129–158.

Levich, Richard M., "Are Forward Exchange Rates Unbiased Predictors of Future Spot Rates?" *Columbia Journal of World Business*, Winter 1979, pp. 49–61.

Levich, Richard M., "Analyzing the Accuracy of Foreign Exchange Forecasting Services: Theory and Evidence," in Clas Wihlborg and Richard Levich, eds., *Exchange Risk and Exposure: Current Developments in International Financial Development*, Lexington, Mass.: D.C. Heath, 1980.

Lewent, Judy C., and A. John Kearney, "Identifying, Measuring, and Hedging Currency Risk at Merck," *Journal of Applied Corporate Finance*, Winter 1990, pp. 19–28.

Lin, James Wuh, and Jeff Madura, "Optimal Debt Financing for Multinational Projects," *Journal of Multinational Financial Management*, Vol. 3, Nos. 1/2, 1993, pp. 63–73.

Logue, Dennis E., "First We Kill All the Currency Traders," *Journal of Business Strategy*, Vol. 17, No. 2, Mar/Apr 1996, pp. 12–13.

Luehrman, Timothy A., "The Exchange Rate Exposure of a Global Competitor," *Journal of International Business Studies*, Vol. 21. No. 2, 1990, pp. 225–242.

Luehrman, Timothy A., "What's it Worth?: A General Manager's Guide to Valuation," *Harvard Business Review*, May 1997.

Luehrman, Timothy A., "Strategy as a Portfolio of Real Options," *Harvard Business Review*, Sept–Oct 1998, pp. 89–99.

Macey, Jonathan R., and Geoffrey P. Miller, "Universal Banks Are Not the Answer to America's Corporate Governance 'Problem': A Look at Germany, Japan, and the U.S.," *Journal of Applied Corporate Finance*, Vol. 9, Winter 1997, No. 4, pp. 57–73.

Magee, Stephen P., "Currency Contracts, Pass-Through, and Devaluation," *Brookings Papers on Economic Activity*, Vol. 1, 1973, pp. 303–325.

Magee, Stephen P., "U.S. Import Prices in the Currency-Contract Period," *Brookings Papers on Economic Activity*, Vol. 1, 1974, pp. 117–164.

Magee, Stephen P., "Contracting and Spurious Deviations from Purchasing Power Parity," in Jacob A. Frenkel and Harry G. Johnson, eds., *The Economics of Exchange Rates*, Reading, MA: Addison Wesley, 1978, pp. 67–74.

Mahajan, Arvind, and Dileep Mehta, "Swaps, Expectations, and Exchange Rates," *Journal of Banking and Finance*, Mar 1986, pp. 7–20.

Malindretos, John, and Demetri Tsanacas, "Hedging Preferences and Foreign Exchange Exposure Management," *Multinational Business Review*, Vol. 3, No. 2, Fall 1995, pp. 56–66.

Malliaropulos, Dimitrios, "Excess Stock Returns and News: Evidence from European Markets," *European Financial Management*, Vol. 4, No. 1, Mar 1998, pp. 29–46.

Mann, Catherine L., "Prices, Profit Margins, and Exchange Rates," *Federal Reserve Bulletin*, Jun 1986, pp. 366–379.

Manzur, Meher, "An International Comparison of Prices and Exchange Rates: A New Test of

Purchasing Power Parity," *Journal of International Money and Finance*, Mar 1990, pp. 75–91.

Marr, M. Wayne, Robert W. Rogowski, and John L. Trimble, "The Competitive Effects of U.S. and Japanese Commercial Bank Participation in Eurobond Underwriting," *Financial Management*, Winter 1989, pp. 47–54.

Marr, M. Wayne, John L. Trimble, and Raj Varma, "On the Integration of International Capital Markets: Evidence from Euroequity Offerings," *Financial Management*, Winter 1991, pp. 11–21.

Masson, Dubos J., "Planning and Forecasting of Cash Flows for the Multinational Firm: International Cash Management," *Advances in Financial Planning and Forecasting*, Vol. 4, Part B. 1990, pp. 195–228.

McCauley, R. N., and S. A. Zimmer, "Explaining International Differences in the Cost of Capital," *Federal Reserve Bank of New York Quarterly Review*, Summer 1989, pp. 7–28.

Meese, Richard, and Kenneth Rogoff, "Was It Real? The Exchange Rate-Interest Differential Relation over the Modern Floating-Rate Period," *Journal of Finance*, Sep 1988, pp. 933–948.

Megginson, William L., Robert C. Nash, and Matthias Ian Randenbough, "The Financial and Operating Performance of Newly Privatized Firms: An International Empirical Analysis," *Journal of Finance*, Jun 1994, pp. 403–452.

Melino, Angelo, and Stuart M. Turnbull, "Misspecification and the Pricing and Hedging of Long-Term Currency Options," *Journal of International Money and Finance,* Vol. 14, No. 3, Jun 1995, pp. 373–393.

Mian, Shehzad L., "Evidence on Corporate Hedging Policy," *Journal of Financial and Quantitative Analysis*, Vol. 31, No. 3, Sep 1996, pp. 419–439.

Michel, Allen, and Israel Shaked, "Multinational Corporations vs. Domestic Corporations: Financial Performance and Characteristics," *Journal of International Business Studies,* Fall 1986, pp. 89–100.

Miller, Darius P., "The Market Reaction to International Cross-Listings: Evidence from Depositary Receipts," *Journal of Financial Economics*, 51, 1999, pp. 103–123.

Miller, Kent D. and Jeffrey J. Reuer, "Firm Strategy and Economic Exposure to Foreign Exchange Rate Movements," *Journal of International Business Studies*, Vol. 29, No. 3, Third Quarter, 1998, pp. 493–514.

Miller, Merton H., "Some Reflections on Recent Monetary Turmoil in Eastern Europe," *Journal of Applied Corporate Finance*, Vol. 11, No. 3, 1998, pp. 49–54.

Miller, Merton H., "Is American Corporate Governance Fatally Flawed?" *Journal of Applied Corporate Finance*, Winter 1994, pp. 32–39.

Miller, Merton H., "Financial Markets and Economic Growth," *Journal of Applied Corporate Finance*, Fall 1998, Vol. 11, No. 3, pp. 8–15.

Millman, Gregory J., "Financing the Uncreditworthy: New Financial Structures for LDCs," *Journal of Applied Corporate Finance*, Vol. 3, No. 4, Winter 1991, pp. 83–89.

Minor, Michael, "Changes in Developing Country Regimes for Foreign Direct Investment: The Raw Materials Sector, 1968–1985," *Essays in International Business*, No. 8, Columbia: University of South Carolina, Sep 1990.

Mirus, Rolf, and Bemard Yeung, "The Relevance of the Invoicing Currency in Intra-Firm Trade Transactions," *Journal of International Money and Finance*, Vol. 6, No. 4. Dec 1987, pp. 449–464.

Mishra, Chandra S. and David H. Gobeli, "Managerial Incentives, Internalization, and Market Valuation of Multinational Firms, " *Journal of International Business Studies*, Vol. 29, No. 3, Third Quarter 1998, pp. 583–598.

Miyamoto, Arnold, and Stephen Godfrey, "Foreign Exchange Budget Rates: How They Can Affect the Firm," *Journal of Applied Corporate Finance*, Vol. 8, No. 3, Fall 1995, pp. 115–120.

Moffett, Michael H., "The J-Curve Revisited: An Empirical Examination for the United States," *Journal of International Money and Finance*, 1989, pp. 425–444.

Moffett, Michael H., and Jan Karl Karlsen, "Managing Foreign Exchange Rate Economic Exposure," *Journal of International Financial Management and Accounting*, Vol. 5, No. 2, Jun 1994, pp. 157–175.

Moffett, Michael H., and Douglas J. Skinner, "Issues in Foreign Exchange Hedge Accounting," *Journal of Applied Corporate Finance*, Vol. 8, No, 3, Fall 1995, pp. 82–94.

Moxon, Richard W., "The Motivation for Investment in Offshore Plants: The Case of the U.S. Electronics Industry," *Journal of International Business Studies*, Spring 1975, pp. 51–66.

Myers, Randy, "Keeping Score: Where Strategy and Performance Metrics Meet," *CFO*, Oct 1996, pp. 25–50.

Nance, Deana R., Clifford W. Smith, Jr., and Charles W. Smithson, "On the Determinants of Corporate Hedging," *Journal of Finance*, Mar 1993, pp. 267–284.

Nigh, Douglas, "The Effect of Political Events on United States Direct Foreign Investment: A Pooled Time Series Cross-Sectional Analysis," *Journal of International Business Studies*, Spring 1985, pp. 1–17.

Oblak, David J., and Roy J. Helm, Jr., "Survey and Analysis of Capital Budgeting Methods Used by Multinationals," *Financial Management*, Winter 1980, pp. 37–41.

Obstfeld, Maurice, and Alan M. Taylor, "Globalization and Capital Markets," Paper Presented at NBER conference on Globalization in Historical Perspective, Santa Barbara, May 4-5, 2001.

O'Brien, Thomas J., "International Production Location and Pro Forma Financial Hedging of Exchange Rate Risk," *Journal of Applied Corporate Finance*, Fall 1998, Vol. 11, No. 3, pp. 100–108.

O'Donnell, Sharon, "Compensation Design as a Tool for Implementing Foreign Subsidiary Strategy," *Management International Review*, 2/99, pp. 149–166.

Ohmae, Kenichi, "Lies, Damned Lies, and Statistics: Why the Trade Deficit Doesn't Matter in a Borderless World," *Journal of Applied Corporate Finance*, Vol. 3, No. 4, Winter 1991, pp. 98–106.

Ohno, Kenichi, "Exchange Rate Fluctuations, Pass Through, and Market Share," *IMF Staff Papers*, Vol. 37, No. 2, Jun 1990, pp. 294–310.

Olsen, Eric E., and James A. Knight, "Managing for Value," in the *Handbook Of Modern Finance*, Dennis E. Logue, ed., New York: Warren, Gorharn & Lamont, 1996, p. E 10-2.

Oxelheim, Lars, and Clas Wihlborg, "Corporate Strategies in a Turbulent World Economy," *Management International Review*, Vol. 31, No. 4,1991, pp. 293–315.

Oxelheim, Lars, and Clas Wihlborg, "Managing Foreign Exchange Exposure," *Journal of Applied Corporate Finance*, Vol. 3, No. 4, Winter 1991, pp. 73–82.

Oxelheim, Lars, and Clas Wihlborg, "Measuring Macroeconomic-Exposure: The Case of Volvo Cars," *European Financial Management*, Vol. 1, No. 3, 1995, pp. 241–263.

Pan, Ming-Shiun, Angela Y. Liu, and Hamid Bastin, "An Examination of the Short-Term and Long-Term Behavior of Foreign Exchange Rates," *Financial Review*, Vol. 31, No. 3, Aug 1996, pp. 603–622.

Park, Yoon S., "Currency Swaps as a Long-Term International Financing Technique," *Journal of International Business Studies*, Winter 1984, pp. 47–54.

Pedersen, Torben, and Steen Thomsen, "European Patterns of Corporate Ownership," *Journal of International Business Studies*, Vol. 28, No. 4, Fourth Quarter, 1997, pp. 759–778.

Plasschaert, S. R. F., "Transfer Pricing Problems in Developing Countries," in *Multinationals and Transfer Pricing*, A. M. Rugman and L. Eden, eds., New York: St. Martin's Press, 1985, pp. 247–266.

Popper, Helen, "Long-Term Covered Interest Parity: Evidence from Currency Swaps,"

Journal of International Money and Finance, Aug 1993, pp. 439–448.

Prahalad, C.K., "Corporate Governance or Corporate Value Added?: Rethinking the Primacy of Shareholder Value," *Journal of Applied Corporate Finance*, Winter 1994, pp. 40–50.

Pringle, John J., "A Look at Indirect Foreign Exchange Exposure," *Journal of Applied Corporate Finance*, Vol. 8, No. 3, Fall 1995, pp. 75–81.

Prowse, Stephen D., "Institutional Investment Patterns and Corporate Financial Behavior in the U.S. and Japan," *Journal of Financial Economics* Vol. 27, Sept 1990, pp. 43–66.

Prowse, Stephen D., "Corporate Governance in an International Perspective: A Survey of Corporate Control Mechanisms Among Large Firms in the U.S., U.K., Japan, and Germany," Geneva: *Bank for International Settlements Economic Paper No. 41*, and *Financial Markets, Institutions, and Instruments*, Vol. 4, No. 1, 1995.

Rajan, Raghuram, and Luigi Zingales, "Debt, Folklore, and Cross-Country Differences in Financial Structure," *Journal of Applied Corporate Finance*, Winter 1998, Vol. 10, No. 4, pp. 102–107.

Rajan, Raghuram G., and Luigi Zingales, "Which Capitalism? Lessons From the East Asia Crisis," *Journal of Applied Corporate Finance*, Fall 1998, Vol. 11, No. 3, pp. 40–48.

Rajan, Raghuram G., and Luigi Zingales, "What Do We Know About Capital Structure? Some Evidence From International Data," *Journal of Finance*, Vol. 1, No. 1, December 1995, pp. 1421–1460.

Rappaport, Alfred, "Linking Competitive Strategy and Shareholder Value Analysis," *Journal of Business Strategy*, Spring 1987, pp. 58–67.

Ravichandran, R., and J. Michael Pinegar, "Risk Shifting in International Licensing Agreements: A Note," *Journal of International Financial Management and Accounting*, Vol. 2, nos. 2 and 3, Summer and Autumn 1990, pp. 181–195.

Reeb, David M., Chuck C. Y. Kwok, and H. Young Baek, "Systematic Risk of the Multinational Corporation," *Journal of International Business Studies*, Second Quarter 1998, pp. 263–279.

Remmers, Lee, Arthur Stonehill, Richard Wright, and Theo Beekhuisen, "Industry and Size as Debt Ratio Determinants for Manufacturing Internationally," *Financial Management*, Summer 1974, pp. 24–32.

Rezaee, Zabihollah, R. P. Malone, and Russell F. Briner, "Capital Market Response to SFAS Nos. 8 and 52; Professional Adaptation," *Journal of Accounting, Auditing & Finance*, Vol. 8, No. 3, Summer 1993, pp. 313–332.

Rhee, S. Ghon, Rosita P. Chang, and Peter E. Koveos, "The Currency-of-Denomination Decision for Debt Financing," *Journal of International Business Studies*, Fall 1985, pp. 143–150.

Rivoli, Pietra, and Eugene Salorio, "Foreign Direct Investment and Investment Under Uncertainty," *Journal of International Business Studies*, Vol. 27, No. 2, Second Quarter 1996, pp. 335–357.

Rogoff, Kenneth, "The Purchasing Power Parity Puzzle," *Journal of Economic Literature*, Vol. 34, No. 2, Jun 1996, pp. 647–668.

Roll, Richard W., and Bruno H. Solnik, "A Pure Foreign Exchange Asset Pricing Model," *Journal of International Economics*, May 1977, pp. 161–179.

Rugman, Alan, "Internalization Is Still a General Theory of Foreign Direct Investment," *Weltwirtschaftliches Archiv*, Sep 1985.

Rugman, Alan, "Internalization as a General Theory of Foreign Direct Investment: A Reappraisal of the Literature," *Weltwirtschaftliches Archiv*, Vol. 116, No. 2, June 1980, pp. 368–369.

Ruland, Robert G., and Timothy S. Doupnik, "Foreign Currency Translation and the Behavior of Exchange Rates," *Journal of International Business Studies*, Fall 1988, pp. 461–476.

Rummel, R. J., and David A. Heenan, "How Multinationals Analyze Political Risk,"

Harvard Business Review, Jan/Feb 1978, pp. 67–76.

Rutenberg, David P., "Maneuvering Liquid Assets in a Multinational Company: Formulation and Deterministic Solution Proced- ures," *Management Science*, Jun 1970, pp. B-671–684.

Saá-Requejo, Jesus, "Financing Decisions: Lessons from the Spanish Experience," *Financial Management*, Vol. 25, No. 3, Autumn 1996, pp. 44–56.

Sarathy, Ravi, and Sangit Chatterjee, "The Divergence of Japanese and U.S. Corporate Financial Structure," *Journal of International Business Studies*, Winter 1984, pp. 75–89.

Saudagaran, Shahrokh M. and Gary C. Biddle, "Foreign Listing Location: A Study of MNEs and Stock Exchanges in Eight Countries," *Journal of International Business Studies*, Vol. 26, No. 2, Second Quarter 1995, pp. 319–341.

Scott, Robert Haney, "Pegged Exchange Rate System of Macao and Hong Kong," *Multinational Finance Journal*, Vol. 1, No. 2, Jun 1997, pp. 153–168.

Sekely, William S., and J. Markham Collins, "Cultural Influences on International Capital Structure," *Journal of International Business Studies*, Spring 1988, pp. 87–100.

Selling, Thomas I., and George H. Sorter, "FASB Statement No. 52 and its Implications for Financial Statement Analysis," *Financial Analysts Journal*, May/Jun 1983, pp. 3–8.

Shao, Lawrence Peter, and Alan T. Shao, "Capital Budgeting Practices Employed by European Affiliates of U.S. Transnational Companies," *Journal of Multinational Financial Management*, Vol. 3. Nos. 1/2, 1993, pp. 95–109.

Shapiro, Alan C., "Optimal Inventory and Credit Granting Strategies Under Inflation and Devaluation," *Journal of Financial and Quantitative Analysis*, Jan 1973, pp. 37–46.

Shapiro, Alan C., "Evaluating Financing Costs for Multinational Subsidiaries," *Journal of International Business Studies*, Fall 1975, pp. 25–32.

Shapiro, Alan C., "Capital Budgeting for the Multinational Corporation," *Financial Management*, Spring 1978, pp. 7–16.

Shapiro, Alan C., "Financial Structure and Cost of Capital in the Multinational Corporation," *Journal of Financial and Quantitative Analysis*, Jun 1978, pp. 211–226.

Shastri, Kuldeep, and Kishore Tandon, "Valuation of Foreign Currency Options: Some Empirical Tests," *Journal of Financial and Quantitative Analysis*, Jun 1986, pp. 145–160.

Sherman, H. Arnold, "Managing Taxes in the Multinational Corporation," *The Tax Executive*, Winter 1987, pp. 171–181.

Singal, Vijay, "Floating Currencies, Capital Controls, or Currency Boards: What's the Best Remedy for the Currency Crises," *Journal of Applied Corporate Finance*, Vol. 11, Winter 1999, No. 4, pp. 49–56.

Smith, Clifford W., Jr., and Charles W. Smithson, "Financial Engineering: An Overview," in *The Handbook of Financial Engineering*, Clifford W. Smith, Jr., and Charles W. Smithson, eds., New York: Harper & Row, 1990, pp. 3–29.

Smith, Clifford W., Jr., Charles W. Smithson, and Lee MacDonald Wakeman, "The Market for Interest Rate Swaps," *Financial Management*, Winter 1988, pp. 34–44.

Smith, Clifford W., Jr., Charles W. Smithson, and D. Sykes Wilford, "Financial Engineering: Why Hedge?" in *The Handbook of Financial Engineering*, Clifford W. Smith, Jr., and Charles W. Smithson, eds., New York: Harper Business, 1990, pp. 126–138.

Smith, Clifford W., and René M. Stulz, "The Determinants of Firms' Hedging Policies," *Journal of Financial and Quantitative Analysis*, Vol. 20, No. 4, Dec 1985, pp. 390–405.

Smith, Roy C. and Ingo Walter, "Risks and Rewards in Emerging Market Investments," *Journal of Applied Corporate Finance*, Fall 1997, Vol. 10, No. 3, pp. 8–17.

Smithson, Charles W., "A LEGO Approach to Financial Engineering: An Introduction to Forwards, Futures, Swaps, and Options," *Midland Corporate Finance Journal*, Vol. 4, No. 4, 1987, pp. 16–28.

Soenen, L. A., "International Cash Management: A Study of Practices of U.K.-Based Companies," *Journal of Business Research*, Aug 1986, pp. 345–354.

Soenen, L. A., and Raj Aggarwal, "Corporate Foreign Exchange and Cash Management Practices," *Journal of Cash Management*, Mar/Apr 1987, pp. 62–64.

Soenen, Luc A., and Jeff Madura, "Foreign Exchange Management-A Strategic Approach," *Long Range Planning*, Vol. 24, No. 5, Oct 1991, pp. 119–124.

Solnik, Bruno, "Swap Pricing and Default Risk: A Note," *Journal of International Financial Management and Accounting*, Vol. 2, No. 1, Spring 1990, pp. 79–91.

Srinivasan, VenKat, Susan E. Moeller. and Yong H. Kim, "International Cash Management: State-of-the-Art and Research Directions," *Advances in Financial Planning and Forecasting*. Vol. 4. part B, 1990. pp. 161–194.

Stanley, Marjorie T., "Capital Structure and Cost of Capital for the Multinational Firm," *Journal of International Business Studies*, Spring/Summer 1981, pp. 103–120.

Stanley, Marjorie, and Stanley Block, "An Empirical Study of Management and Financial Variables Influencing Capital Budgeting Decisions for Multinational Corporations in the 1980s," *Management International Review*, No. 3, 1983.

Stapleton, Richard C., and Marti Subrahmanyam, "Market Imperfections, Capital Asset Equilibrium, and Corporation Finance," *Journal of Finance*, May 1977, pp. 307–319.

Stonehill, Arthur, and Kåre Dullum, "Corporate Wealth Maximization, Takeovers, and the Market for Corporate Control," *Nationaløkonomisk Tidsskrift* (Denmark), No. 1, 1990, p. 76–96.

Stonehill, Arthur, and Leonard Nathanson, "Capital Budgeting and the Multinational Corporation, *California Management Review*, Summer 1968, pp. 39–54.

Stonehill, Arthur, and Thomas Stitzel, "Financial Structure and Multinational Corporations," *California Management Review*, Fall 1969, pp. 91–96.

Stonehill, Arthur I., Niels Ravn, and Kåre Dullum, "Management of Foreign Exchange Economic Exposure," in *International Financial Management*, Göran Bergendahl, ed., Stockholm: Norstedts. 1982, pp. 128–148.

Stonehill, Arthur, Theo Beekhuisen, Richard Wright, Lee Remmers, Norman Toy, Antonio Parés, Alan Shapiro, Douglas Egan, and Thomas Bates, "Financial Goals and Debt Ratio Determinants: A Survey of Practice in Five Countries," *Financial Management*, Autumn 1975, pp. 27–41.

Stulz, René M, "On the Effects of Barriers to International Investment," *Journal of Finance*, Sep 1981, pp. 923–933.

Stulz, René M., "Optimal Hedging Policies," *Journal of Financial and Quantitative Analysis*, Vol. 19, No. 2, Jun 1984, pp. 127–140.

Stulz, René M, "The Cost of Capital in Internationally Integrated Markets: The Case of Nestlé," *European Financial Management*, Vol. 1, No. 1, Mar 1995, pp. 11–22.

Stulz, René M., "Globalization of Capital Markets and the Cost of Capital: The Case of Nestlé," *Journal of Applied Corporate Finance*, Vol. 8, No. 3, Fall 1995, pp. 30–38.

Stulz, René M., "Does the Cost of Capital Differ Across Countries? An Agency Perspective," *European Financial Management*, Volume 2, 1996.

Stulz, René M., "Rethinking Risk Management," *Journal of Applied Corporate Finance*, Vol. 9, No. 3, Fall 1996, pp. 8–24.

Sundaram, Anant, "International Financial Markets," in the *Handbook of Modern Finance*, Dennis Logue, ed., Warren, Gorham, and Lamont, New York, 1994.

Sundaram, Anant K., and Dennis E. Logue, "Valuation Effects of Foreign Company Listings on U.S. Exchanges," *Journal of International Business Studies*, Vol. 27, No. 1, First Quarter 1996, pp. 67–88.

Swamidass, Paul M., "A Comparison of the Plant Location Strategies of Foreign and Domestic

Manufacturers in the U.S," *Journal of International Business Studies*, Second Quarter 1990, pp. 301–317.

Swanson, Peggy E., and Stephen C. Caples, "Hedging Foreign Exchange Risk Using Forward Foreign Exchange Markets: An Extension," *Journal of International Business Studies*, Spring 1987, pp. 75–82.

Sweeney, Richard J., "Beating the Foreign Exchange Market," *Journal of Finance*, March 1986, pp. 163–182.

Sweeney, Richard J., and Edward J. Q. Lee, "Trading Strategies in Forward Exchange Markets," *Advances in Financial Planning and Forecasting*, Vol. 4, 1990, pp. 55–80.

Tallman, Stephen B., "Home Country Political Risk and Foreign Direct Investment in the United States," *Journal of International Business Studies*, Summer 1988, pp. 219–234.

Taussig, Russell A., "Impact of SFAS No. 52 on the Translation of Foreign Financial Statements of Companies in Highly Inflationary Economies," *Journal of Accounting, Auditing and Finance*, Winter 1983, pp. 142–156.

Terpstra, Vern, and Chwo-Ming Yu, "Determinants of Foreign Investment of U.S. Advertising Agencies," *Journal of International Business Studies*, Spring 1988. pp. 33–46.

Thomadakis, Stavros, and Nilufer Usmen, "Foreign Project Financing in Segmented Capital Markets: Equity Versus Debt," *Financial* , Winter 1991, pp. 42–53.

Tompkins, Robert, "Behind the Mirror," in *From Black-Scholes to Black Holes: New Frontiers in Options*, London: Risk Ltd., 1992, pp. 129–133.

Toy, Norman, Arthur Stonehill, Lee Remmers, Richard Wright, and Theo Beekhuisen, "A Comparative International Study of Growth, Profitability and Risk as Determinants of Corporate Debt Ratios in the Manufacturing Sector," *Journal of Financial and Quantitative Analysis*, Nov 1974, pp. 875–886.

Trevino, Len J., and John D. Daniels, "The Preconditions for Manufacturing Foreign Direct Investment in the United States: An Empirical Assessment," *The International Trade Journal*, Vol. 10, No. 2, Summer 1996, pp. 223–246.

Tucker, Alan, "Foreign Exchange Option Prices as Predictors of Equilibrium Forward Exchange Rates," *Journal of International Money and Finance*, Vol. 6, No. 3, Sep 1987, pp. 283294.

Vernon, Raymond, "International Investment and International Trade in the Product Cycle," *Quarterly Journal of Economics*, May 1966, pp. 190–207.

Vernon, Raymond, "The Product Cycle Hypothesis in a New International Environment," *Oxford Bulletin of Economics and Statistics*, Vol. 41, 1979, pp. 255–267.

Wald, John K., "How Firm Characteristics Affect Capital Structure: An International Comparison," *The Journal of Financial Research*, Vol. *xxii*, No. 2, Summer 1999, pp. 161–187.

Walter, Ingo, "The Mechanisms of Capital Flight," in *Capital Flight and Third World Debt*, edited by Donald R. Lessard and John Williamson, Institute for International Economics,

Washington D.C., 1987, p. 104.

Weinstein, David, E., and Yishay Yafeh, "On the Costs of a Bank-Centered Financial System: Evidence from the Changing Main Bank Relations in Japan," *Journal of Finance*, Vol. 53, No. 2, April 1998, pp. 635–672.

Weisman, Lorenzo, "The Advent of Private Equity in Latin America," *The Columbia Journal of World Business*, Spring 1996, pp. 60–98.

Wells, Louis T., Jr., "Multinationals and the Developing Countries," *Journal of International Business Studies*, Volume 29, No. 1, First Quarter, 1998, pp. 101–114.

Weisfelder, Christine J., "Home Country Taxation and the Theory of International Production," *Journal of International Financial and Accounting*, Vol. 5, No. 3, Oct. 1994, pp. 193–213.

Wheatley, S., "Some Tests of International Equity Integration," *Journal of Financial Economics*, Sep 1989, pp. 177–212.

Wright, Richard, and Sadahiko Suzuki, "Financial Structure and Bankruptcy Risk in Japanese

Companies," *Journal of International Business Studies,* Spring 1985, pp. 97–110.

Wu, Congsheng and Chuck C.Y. Kwok, "Why Do U.S. Firms Choose Global Equity Offerings?," *Financial* , Vol. 31, Issue 2, Summer 2002, pp. 47-65.

Wyatt, Steve B., "On the Valuation of Puts and Calls on Spot, Forward, and Future Foreign Exchange: Theory and Evidence," *Advances in Financial Planning and Forecasting*, Vol. 4, 1990, pp. 81–104.

Yang, Ho C., James W. Wansley, and William R. Lane, "A Direct Test of the Diversification Service Hypothesis of Foreign Direct Investment," *Advances in Financial Planning and Forecasting*, Vol. 4, Part A, 1990, pp. 215–238.

Zaheer, Srilata, "Circadian Rhythms: The Effects of Global Market Integration on the Currency Trading Industry," *Journal of International Business Studies*, Vol. 26, No. 4, Fourth Quarter 1995, pp. 699–728.

Zhang, Peter G., "Professional Forum: An Introduction to Exotic Options," *European Financial* , Vol. 1, No. 1, Mar 1995, pp. 87–95.

Books

Agmon, Tamir, Robert G. Hawkins, and Richard M. Levich, eds., *The Future of the International Monetary System*, Lexington, MA: Lexington Books, 1984.

Aharoni, Yair, *The Foreign Investment Decision Process,* Boston: Harvard Graduate School of Business Administration. Division of Research, 1966.

Ahm, Mark J., and William D. Falloon, *Strategic Risk : How the Global Corporations Manage Financial Risk for Competitive Advantage*, Chicago: Probus, 1991.

Aliber, Robert Z., *The International Money Game*, 5th ed., New York: Basic Books. 1987.

Aliber, Robert Z., *Handbook of International Financial* , Homewood, IL: Dow Jones-Irwin, 1989.

Amihud Y. and R. Levich, eds, *Exchange Rates and Corporate Performance*, Burr Ridge, Ill: Irwin, 1994.

Andersen, Torben Juul, *Currency and Interest Rate Hedging*, 2nd ed., New York: New York Institute of Finance, 1993.

Anderson, Torben Juul, *Euromarket Instruments: A Guide to the World's Large Debt Market*, New York: New York Institute of Finance, 1990.

Balling, Morten, *Financial in the New Europe*, Oxford, UK: Blackwell, 1993.

Beidleman, Carl R., *Financial Swaps*, Homewood, IL: Dow Jones-Irwin, 1985.

BenDaniel, David J., and Arthur H. Rosenbloom, *The Handbook of International Mergers & Acquisitions*, Englewood Cliffs, NJ: Prentice-Hall, 1990.

Bergsten, Fred C., and Shafique Islam, *The United States as a Debtor Country*, Washington, D.C.: Institute of International Economics, 1990.

Bernstein, Peter L., *Against the Gods: The Remarkable Story of Risk*, New York: John Wiley Sons, Inc., 1996.

Bishop, Paul, and Don Dixon, *Foreign Exchange Handbook: Managing Risk and Opportunity in Global Currency Markets*, New York: McGraw-Hill, 1992.

Brewer, Thomas L., *Political Risks in International Business*, New York: Praeger, 1985.

Brown, Brendan, *The Flight of International Capital: A Contemporary History*, New York and London: Croom Helm, 1987.

Buckley, Adrian, *International Investment Value Creation and Appraisal: A Real Options Approach*, Copenhagen: Copenhagen Business School Press, 1998.

Buckley, Adrian, *Multinational Finance*, 2nd edition, Hemel Hempstead, Hertfordshire: UK: Prentice-Hall International (UK), Ltd., 1992.

Buckley, Peter J., and Jeremy Clegg, *Multinational Enterprises in Less Developed Countries*, New York: St. Martin's Press, 1991.

Buckley, Peter J., and Mark Casson, *The Future of the Multinational Enterprise*, London: Macmillan. 1976.

Buckley, Peter J., and Mark Casson, eds., *Multinational Enterprises in the World Economy: Essays in the Honour of John Dunning*, Aldershot, Hants, England: Edward Elgar, 1992.

Business International, *Automating Global Financial* , Morristown, NJ: Financial Executives Research Foundation, 1988.

Butler, Kirt C., *Multinational Finance*, second edition, Cincinnati, OH: Southwestern, 1999.

Carvounis, Chris C., *The United States Trade Deficit of the 1980s*, Westport, CT: Quorum Books, 1987.

Casson, Mark, *The Firm and the Market: Studies on Multinational Enterprises and the Scope of the Firm*, Cambridge, MA: MIT Press, 1987.

Caves, Richard E., *Multinational Enterprises and Economic Analysis*, 2nd ed., Cambridge U.K.: Cambridge University Press, 1996.

Celi, Louis J., and I. James Czechowicz, Export Financing, *A Handbook of Sources and Techniques*, Morristown, NJ: Financial Executives Research Foundation, 1985.

Chance, Don M., *An Introduction to Derivatives*, 3rd ed. Harcourt Brace Publishers, Ft. Worth, 1995.

Chew, Donald H., editor, *Studies in International Corporate Finance and Governance Systems: A Comparison of the U.S., Japan, and Europe*, Oxford, U.K.: Oxford University Press, 1997.

Chorafas, Dimitris N., *Treasury Operations and The Foreign Exchange Challenge*, New York: Wiley, 1992.

Claassen, Emil-Maria, *International and European Monetary Systems*, New York: Praeger, 1990.

Coffey, Peter, *The European Monetary, System Past, Present and Future*, 2nd ed., Dordrecht, Netherlands; Lancaster, U.K.: Kluwer Academic Publishers, 1987.

Coninx, Raymond G. F., *Foreign Exchange Dealer's Handbook*, 2nd ed., Homewood, IL: Dow Jones-Irwin, 1986.

Cooper, Richard N., *The International Monetary System: Essays in World Economics*, Cambridge, MA: MIT Press, 1987.

Copeland, Laurence S., *Exchange Rates and International Finance*, 2nd ed., Workingham, England: Addison-Wesley, 1994.

Copeland, Tom, Tim Koller, and Jack Murrin, *Valuation: Measuring and Managing the Value of Companies*, 2nd ed., New York: Wiley, 1994.

de Vries, Margaret Garritsen, *Balance of Payments Adjustment, 1945-1986: The IMF Experience*, Washington, D.C.: IMF, 1987.

Derivatives Week, *Learning Curves, Volume II: The Guide to Understanding Derivatives, Editors of Derivatives Week*, Institutional Investor, Inc., New York, 1995.

Derivatives Week, *Learning Curves: The Guide to Understanding Derivatives, Editors of Derivatives Week*, Institutional Investor, Inc., New York, 1994.

DeRosa, David F., *Managing Foreign Exchange Risk*, Chicago: Probus, 1991.

Dimson, Elroy, Paul Marsh, and Mike Staunton,*Triumph of the Optimists: 101 Years of GlobalInvestment Returns*, Princeton N.J., Princeton University Press, 2002, Chapters 12 and 13.

Dixit, Avinash K., *Investment Under Uncertainty*, Princeton University Press. Princeton, NJ, 1994.

Donaldson, Gordon, *Strategy for Financial Mobility*, Boston: Graduate School of Business Administration, Harvard University, 1969.

Donaldson, Gordon, and Jay W. Lorsch, *Decision Making At the Top: The Shaping of Strategic Direction*, New York: Basic Books, 1983.

Donaldson, Gordon, *Managing Corporate Wealth: The Operation of a Comprehensive Goals System*, New York: Praeger, 1984.

Dufey, Gunter, and Ian Giddy, *50 Cases in International Finance*, 2nd ed., Reading, MA: Addison-Wesley, 1992.

Dufey, Gunter, and Ian H. Giddy, *The International Money Market*, 2nd ed., Prentice Hall, Englewood Cliffs, NJ, 1994.

Dunning, John H., ed., *Multinational Enterprises, Economic Structure, and International Competitiveness*, New York: Wiley, 1985.

Dunning, John H., *Explaining International Production*, Winchester, MA: Unwin Hyman, 1988.

Eaker, Mark R., Frank J. Fabozzi, and Dwight Grant, *International Corporate Finance*, Ft. Worth: The Dryden Press, 1996.

Eichengreen, Barry, and Peter H. Lindert, *The International Debt Crisis in Historical Perspective*, Cambridge, MA: MIT Press, 1990.

Elfstrom, Gerard, *Moral Issues and Multinational Corporations*, New York: St. Martin's Press, 1991.

Eun, Cheol S. and Bruce G. Resnick, *International Financial* , Boston: Irwin McGraw-Hill, 1998.

Financial Accounting Standards Board, *Foreign Currency Translation, Statement of Financial Accounting Standards No. 52,* Dec 1981, Stamford, CT: Financial Accounting Standards Board, 1981.

Forsgren, Mats, *Managing the Internationalization Process: The Swedish Case*, London: Routledge. 1989.

Forsgren, Mats and Jan Johanson, editors, *Managing Networks in International Business*, Philadelphia: Gordon and Breach, 1992.

Francis, Dick, *The Countertrade Handbook*, Westport, CT: Quorum Books, 1987.

Friedman, Irving, *Reshaping the Global Money System*, Lexington, MA: Lexington Books, 1987.

Ghadar, Fariborz, *New Financial Instruments: Horizons for Risk* , Center for Global Business Studies, Pennsylvania State University, 1996.

Giddy, Ian H., *Global Financial Markets*, Lexington, MA: D.C. Heath, 1994.

Gordon, Sara L., and Francis A. Lees, *Foreign Multinational Investment in the United States: Struggle for Industrial Supremacy,* Westport, CT: Quorum Books, 1986.

Grabbe, J. Orlin, *International Financial Markets,* 2nd ed., New York: Elsevier, 1991.

Graham, Edward, and Paul Krugman, *Foreign Direct Investment in the United States*, Washington, D.C.: Institute for International Economics, 1989.

Haendel, Dan, *Foreign Investment and the of Political Risk*, Boulder, CO: Westview Press, 1979.

Hawawini, Gabriel, and Eric Rajendra, *The Transformation of the European Financial Services Industry: From Fragmentation to Integration*, New York: New York University Salomon Center; Monograph Series in Finance and Economics, No. 4, 1989.

Hirsch, Se'ev, *Location of Industry and International Competitiveness*, Oxford: Oxford University Press, 1967.

Holland, John, *International Financial* , 2nd ed., New York and Oxford, U.K.: Basil Blackwell. 1992.

Howcroft, Barry, and Christopher Storey, *and Control of Currency and Interest Rate Risk*, Chicago: Probus. 1989.

Howe, Donna M., *A Guide to Managing Interest Rate Risk*, New York: New York Institute of Finance, 1991.

Hufbauer, Gary Clyde, Diane T. Berliner, and Kimberly Ann Elliott, *Trade Protection in the United States: 31 Case Studies*, Washington, D.C.: Institute for International Economics, 1986.

Hymer, Stephen H., *The International Operations of National Firms: A Study of Direct Foreign Investment*, Cambridge, MA: MIT Press, 1976.

Ibbotson, Roger G., and Gary P. Brinson, *Global Investing: The Professional Guide to the World's Capital Markets,* McGraw-Hill, Inc., New York, 1993.

Jacque, Laurent, *and Control of Foreign Exchange Risk*, Boston: Kluwer, 1996.

Kester, Carl W., *Japanese Takeovers: The Global Contest for Corporate Control*, Boston: Harvard Business School Press, 1991.

Klein, Robert A. and Jess Lederman, *Derivatives Risk and Responsibility*, Chicago: Irwin Professional Publishing, 1996.

Knickerbocker, Fred T., *Oligopolistic Reaction and the Multinational Enterprise*, Boston: Harvard Graduate School of Business Administration, 1973.

Kobrin, Stephen J., *Managing Political Risk Assessment: Strategic Response to Environmental Change*, Berkeley: University of California Press, 1982.

Korth, Christopher M., ed., *International Countertrade*, Westport. CT: Quorum Books, 1987.

Krugman, Paul R., and Maurice Obstfeld, *International Economics: Theory and Policy*, Third Edition, New York: Harper Collins, 1994.

Lessard, Donald R., *International Financial , Theory, and Application*, 2nd ed., New York: Wiley, 1987.

Levi, Maurice, *International Finance: Financial and the International Economy*, 3rd ed., New York: McGraw-Hill, 1996.

Levich, Richard, *International Financial Markets: Prices and Policies*, Boston: Irwin McGraw-Hill, 1998.

Madura, Jeff, *International Financial* , 5th ed., St. Paul, MN: West, 1998.

Madura, Jeff, *Global Portfolio for Institutional Investors,* Quorum Books, Westbury, CT, 1996.

Marshall, John F., and Vipul K. Bansal, *Financial Engineering: A Complete Guide to Financial Innovation*, New York: New York Institute of Finance, 1992.

Millar, William, and Brad Asher, *Strategic Risk* , New York: Business International, Jan 1990.

Mueller, Gerhard G., Helen Gernon, and Gary Meek, *Accounting: An International Perspective*, Homewood, Ill.: Richard D. Irwin, 1987.

Murphy, John J., *Intermarket Technical Analysis: Trading Strategies for the Global Stock, Bond, Commodity, and Currency Markets*, New York: Wiley, 1991.

Murray, Alan I., and Caren Siehl, *Joint Ventures and Other Alliances: Creating a Successful Cooperative Linkage*, New York: Financial Executive Research Foundation, 1989.

O'Brien, Thomas J., *Global Financial* , John Wiley & Sons, Inc.: New York, 1996.

Oxelheim, Lars, *International Financial Integration*, Berlin: Springer-Verlag, 1990.

Oxelheim, Lars, *The Global Race for Foreign Direct Investment: Prospects for the Future*, Berlin: Springer-Verlag, 1993.

Oxelheim, Lars, *Financial Markets in Transition-Globalization, Investment and Economic Growth,* London and New York: Routledge, 1996.

Oxelheim, Lars, and Clas Wihlborg, *Macroeconomic Uncertainty: International Risks and Opportunities for the Corporation*, Chichester, U.K.: Wiley, 1987.

Oxelheim, Lars, and Clas Wihlborg, *Managing in the Turbulent World Economy-Corporate Performance and Risk Exposure*, Chichester and New York: John Wiley, 1997.

Oxelheim, Lars, Arthur Stonehill, Trond Randøy, Kaisa Vikkula, Kåre Dullum, and Karl-Markus Modén, *Corporate Strategies for Internationalizing the Cost of Capital*, Copenhagen: Copenhagen Business School Press, 1998.

Phylaktis, Kaate, and Mahmeed Pradhan, eds., *International Finance and the Less Developed Countries*, Basingstoke, U.K.: Macmillan, in association with the Department of Banking and Finance, City University Business School, 1990.

Porter, Michael, *The Competitive Advantage of Nations*, London: Macmillan Press, 1990.

PriceWaterhouseCoopers, *Corporate Taxes: A Worldwide Summary*, New York: Price Waterhouse Coopers, 1999.

PriceWaterhouseCoopers, *Corporate Taxes: A Worldwide Summary*, New York: Price Waterhouse Coopers, 2002.

Rappaport, Alfred, *Creating Shareholder Value*, New York: The Free Press: Macmillan, 1986.

Riahi-Belkaoui, Ahmed, *Multinationality and Firm Performance*, London: Quorum Books, 1996.

Rogers, Jerry, ed., *Global Risk Assessments: Issues, Concepts and Applications*, Riverside, CA: Global Risk Assessments, Inc., 1988.

Rugman, A.M. and L. Eden, Editors, *Multinationals and Transfer Pricing*, New York: St. Martins Press, 1985.

Scholes, Myron S. and Mark A. Wolfson, *Taxes and Business Strategy: A Planning Approach*, Englewood Cliffs, N.J.: Prentice-Hall, 1992, Chapters 13 and 14.

Schwartz, Robert J. and Clifford W. Smith, Jr., editors, *Currency and Interest Rate Risk* , New York Institute of Finance, 1990.

Shapiro, Alan C., *Multinational Financial Management*, 6th ed., Boston: Prentice-Hall, 1999.

Simon, Herbert, *Administrative Behavior*, New York: Macmillan, 1947.

Smith, Clifford W., Jr., Charles W. Smithson, and D. Sykes Wilford, *Managing Financial Risk, Institutional Investor Series in Finance*, New York: Harper & Row, 1990.

Smith, Roy C., and Ingo Walter, *Global Financial Services*, New York: Harper-Business, 1990.

Solnik, Bruno, *International Investments*, 4th ed., Reading, MA: Addison-Wesley Longman, 1999.

Stewart, G. Bennet, III, *The Quest of Value*, Harper Business, 1991.

Stoll, Hans R., and Robert E. Whaley, *Futures and Options: Theory and Applications, Current Issues in Finance,* Cincinnati: Southwestern, 1993.

Stonehill, Arthur, and Kåre B. Dullum, *Internationalizing the Cost of Capital in Theory and Practice: The Novo Experience and National Policy Implications,* Copenhagen: Nyt Nordisk Forlag Arnold Busck, 1982; and London: Wiley, 1982.

Sutton, William H., *Trading in Currency Options,* New York Institute of Finance, New York: Simon & Schuster, 1988.

Tavis, Lee A., ed., *Rekindling Development: Multinational Firms and World Debt*, Notre Dame, IN: Notre Dame Press, 1988.

Tucker, Alan L., Jeff Madura, and Thomas C. Chiang, *International Financial Markets*, St. Paul, MN, 1991.

Vanden Bulcke, D., and J. J. Boddewyn, *Investment and Divestment Policies in Multinational Corporations in Europe*, London: Saxon/Teakfield: New York: Praeger, 1979.

Venedikian, Harry M., and Gerald A. Warfield, *Export-Import Financing*, 2nd ed., New York: Wiley, 1986.

Walmsley, Julian, *The Foreign Exchange and Money Markets Guide*, New York: Wiley, 1992.

Williamson, John, *Equilibrium Exchange Rates: An Update*, Washington, D.C.: Institute for International Economics, 1990.

Williamson, John, *Voluntary Approaches to Debt Relief*, Washington, D.C.: Institute for International Economics, 1988.

Williamson, John, and Donald Lessard, eds., *Capital Flight and Third World Debt*, Washington, D.C.: Institute for International Economics, 1987.

Williamson, Oliver, *Markets and Hierarchies*, New York: Free Press, 1975.

Williamson, Oliver, *The Economic Institutions of Capitalism*, New York: Free Press, 1985.

Wunnicke, Diane B., David R. Wilson, and Brooke Wunnicke, *Corporate Financial Risk Management*, New York: Wiley, 1992.

GLOSSARY

A.B. Aktiebolag. Swedish word for incorporated or stock company.

A. G. Aktiengesellschaft. German word for incorporated or stock company.

Accounting exposure. The potential for an accounting-derived change in owners' equity resulting from exchange rate changes and the need to restate financial statements of foreign affiliates in the single currency of the parent corporation so as to create a consolidated financial statement. Also called "translation exposure."

Adjusted present value. A type of present value analysis in capital budgeting in which operating cash flows are discounted separately from (1) the various tax shields provided by the deductibility of interest and other financial charges, and (2) the benefits of project-specific concessional financing. Each component cash flow is discounted at a rate appropriate for the risk involved.

ADR. *See* American Depositary Receipt.

Ad valorem duty. A customs duty levied as a percentage of the assessed value of goods entering a country.

Affiliate. A foreign operation, formed as either a branch or a foreign-incorporated subsidiary. If a firm is owned between 20% and 49% by a parent, it is an affiliate.

Affiliated party. A foreign importer that is a subsidiary business unit of the exporter. Also known as intra-firm trade.

Agency theory. A field of finance arguing that management is generally more risk-averse than shareholders.

All-equity discount rate. A discount rate in capital budgeting that would be appropriate for discounting operating cash flows if the project were financed entirely with owners' equity.

American Depositary Receipt (ADR). A certificate of ownership, issued by a U.S. bank, representing a claim on underlying foreign securities. ADRs may be traded in lieu of trading in the actual underlying shares.

American option. An option that can be exercised at any time up to and including the expiration date.

American selling price (ASP). For customs purposes, the use of the domestic price of competing merchandise in the United States as a tax base for determining import duties. The ASP is generally higher than the actual foreign price, so its use is a protectionist technique.

American terms. Foreign exchange quotations for the U.S. dollar, expressed as the number of U.S. dollars per unit of non-U.S. currency.

Amortization. A charge for investments made in other companies (acquisitions) over and above the value of the assets purchased.

Anticipated exposures. Transactions for which there are—at present—no contracts or agreements between parties, but are anticipated on the basis of historical trends and continuing business relationships.

Antiglobalization movement. A growing negative reaction by some groups to reduced trade barriers and efforts to create regional markets; in particular, to NAFTA and the European Union.

A/P. In international trade documentation, abbreviation for "authority to purchase" or "authority to pay." In accounting, abbreviation for "accounts payable."

Appreciation. In the context of exchange rate changes, a rise in the foreign exchange value of a currency that is pegged to other currencies or to gold. Also called "revaluation."

Arbitrage. A trading strategy based on the purchase of a commodity, including foreign exchange, in one market at one price while simultaneously selling it in another market at a more advantageous price, in order to obtain a risk-free profit on the price differential.

Arbitrageur. An individual or company that practices arbitrage.

Arm's-length price. The price at which a willing buyer and a willing unrelated seller freely agree to carry out a transaction. In effect, a free market price. Applied by tax authorities in judging the appropriateness of transfer prices between related affiliates.

Ask price. The price at which a dealer is willing to sell foreign exchange, securities or commodities. Also called "offer price."

ASP. *See* American selling price.

Asset market approach. A method of long-term foreign exchange rate determination that assumes that whether foreigners are willing to hold claims in monetary form depends on an extensive set of investment considerations of drivers.

At-the-money (ATM). A term that describes an option whose exercise price is the same as the spot price of the underlying currency.

"Aussie." Foreign exchange dealers' nickname for the Australian dollar.

Back-to-back loan. A loan in which two companies in separate countries borrow each other's currency for a specific period of time, and repay the other's currency at an agreed maturity. Sometimes the two loans are channeled through an intermediate bank. Back-to-back financing is also called "link financing," "parallel loan," or "credit swap."

Balance of payments (BOP). A financial statement summarizing the flow of goods, services, and investment funds between residents of a given country and residents of the rest of the world.

Balance of trade. An entry in the balance of payments measuring the difference between the monetary value of merchandise exports and merchandise imports.

Balance on current account. *See* Current account.

Balance sheet hedge. A technique to minimize translation exposure; speculating in the forward market in the hope that a cash profit will be realized to offset the noncash loss from translation.

Bank for International Settlements (BIS). A bank in Basle, Switzerland, that functions as a bank for European central banks.

Bank rate. The interest rate at which central banks for various countries lend to their own monetary institutions.

Bank run. A financial panicking, in which all depositors attempt to withdraw all of their funds simultaneously.

Bankers' acceptance. An unconditional promise of a bank to make payment on a draft when it matures. The acceptance is in the form of the bank's endorsement ("acceptance") of a draft drawn against that bank in accordance with the terms of a letter of credit issued by the bank.

Barter. International trade conducted by the direct exchange of physical goods, rather than by separate purchases and sales at prices and exchange rates set by a free market.

Basic balance. In a country's balance of payments, the net of exports and imports of goods and services, unilateral transfers, and long-term capital flows.

Basis point. One one-hundredth of one percentage point, often used in quotations of spreads between interest rates or to describe changes in yields in securities. 0.01% is one basis point.

Basis risk. That type of interest rate risk in which the interest rate base is mismatched.

B/E. *See* Bill of exchange.

Bearer bond. Corporate or governmental debt in bond form that is not registered to any owner. Possession of the bond implies ownership, and interest is obtained by clipping a coupon attached to the bond. The advantage of the bearer form are its easy transfer at the time of a sale, its easy use as collateral for a debt, and what some cynics call "taxpayer anonymity," meaning that governments find it hard to trace interest payments in order to collect income taxes. Bearer bonds are common in Europe, but are seldom issued any more in the United States. The alternate form to a bearer bond is a registered bond.

Beta. Second letter of Greek alphabet, used as a statistical measure of risk in the Capital Asset Pricing Model. Beta is the covariance between returns on a given asset and returns on the market portfolio, divided by the variance of returns on the market portfolio. *See* Hedge ratio.

BID. Banco Interamericano de Desarrollo. Spanish name for the Inter-American Development Bank.

Bid price. The price that a dealer is willing to pay for (i.e., buy) a foreign exchange or a security.

Bid-ask spread. The difference between a bid (buy) and an ask (offer) quotation.

Big Bang. The October 1986 liberalization of the London capital markets.

Bill of exchange (B/E). A written order requesting one party (such as an importer) to pay a specified amount of money at a specified time to the order of the writer of the bill of exchange. Also called a "draft." *See* Sight draft.

Bill of lading (B/L). A contract between a common carrier and a shipper to transport goods to a named destination. The bill of lading is also a receipt for the goods. Bills of lading are usually negotiable, meaning they are made to the order of a particular party and can be endorsed to transfer title to another party.

BIS. *See* Bank for International Settlements.

B/L. *See* Bill of lading.

Black market. An illegal foreign exchange market.

Blocked funds. Funds in one country's currency that may not be exchanged freely for foreign currencies because of exchange controls.

BOP. *See* Balance of payments.

Border tax adjustments. The fiscal practice, under the General Agreement on Tariffs and Trade, by which imported goods are subject to some or all of the tax charged in the importing country and re-exported goods are exempt from some or all of the tax charged in the exporting country.

Branch. A foreign operation not incorporated in the host country, in contradistinction to a "subsidiary."

Bretton Woods Conference. An international conference in 1944 that established the international monetary system in effect from 1945 to 1971. The conference was held in Bretton Woods, New Hampshire, USA.

Bridge financing. Short-term financing from a bank, used while a borrower obtains medium- or long-term fixed-rate financing from capital markets.

Broker. An individual or firm that buys or sells foreign exchange, or securities, on a commission basis, without itself taking title to what was purchased, on behalf of a customer. A broker is an alternative to a "dealer." *See* Dealer.

Bulldogs. British pound–denominated bonds issued within the United Kingdom by a foreign borrower.

Cable. The U.S. dollar per British pound crossrate.

Call option. The right, but not the obligation, to buy foreign exchange or some other financial contract at a specified price within a specified time. *See* Option.

Capital account. A section of the balance of payments accounts. Under the revised format of the International Monetary Fund, the capital account measures capital transfers and the acquisition and disposal of non-produced non-financial assets. Under traditional definitions, still used by many countries, the capital account measures public and private international lending and investment. Most of the traditional definition of the capital account is now incorporated in IMF statements as the "financial account."

Capital Asset Pricing Model (CAPM). A theoretical model that relates the return on an asset to its risk, where risk is the contribution of the asset to the volatility of a portfolio. Risk and return are presumed determined in competitive and efficient financial markets.

Capital budgeting. The analytical approach used to determine whether investment in long-lived assets or projects is viable.

Capital flight. Movement of funds out of a country because of political risk.

Capital markets. The financial markets in various countries in which various types of long-term debt and/or ownership securities, or claims on those securities, are purchased and sold.

Capital mobility. The degree to which private capital moves freely from country to country seeking the most promising investment opportunities.

Cash budgeting. The planning for future receipts and disbursements of cash.

Cash conversion cycle. The period of time extending between cash outflow for purchased inputs and materials and cash inflow from cash settlement; a subcomponent of the operating cycle. *See* Operating cycle.

Cash flow return on investment (CFROI). A measure of corporate performance in which the numerator is profit from continuing operations less cash taxes and depreciation. This is divided by "cash investment" which is taken to mean the replacement cost of capital employed.

CAPM. *See* Capital Asset Pricing Model.

Certificate of Deposit (CD). A negotiable receipt issued by a bank for funds deposited for a certain period of time. CDs can be purchased or sold prior to their maturity in a secondary market, making them an interest-earning marketable security.

C&F. *See* Cost and freight.

CFC. *See* Controlled foreign corporation.

CFROI. *See* Cash flow return on investment.

Chartists. Financial technical analysts; chartists focus on price and volume data to determine past trends that are expected to continue into the future.

CHIPS. *See* Clearinghouse Interbank Payments System.

Cia. Companía. Spanish word for company.

CIF. *See* Cost, insurance, and freight.

Closing rate method. Another name for the current rate method of creating consolidated financial statements. *See* Current rate method.

CKD. "Completely knocked down." International trade term for components shipped into a country for assembly there. Often used in the automobile industry.

Clearinghouse. An institution through which financial obligations are cleared by the process of netting obligations of various members.

Clearing House Interbank Payments System (CHIPS). A New York-based computerized clearing system used by banks to settle interbank foreign exchange obligations (mostly U.S. dollars) between members.

Collar option. The simultaneous purchase of a put option and sale of a call option, or vice versa. Thus a form of hybrid option.

Commercial risk. In banking, the likelihood that a foreign debtor will be unable to repay its debts because of business (as distinct from political) events.

Common market. An association through treaty of two or more countries that agree to remove all trade barriers between themselves. The best known is the European Common Market, now called the European Union.

Comparative advantage. A theory that everyone gains if each nation specializes in the production of those goods that it produces relatively most efficiently and imports those goods that other countries produce relatively most efficiently. The theory supports free trade arguments.

Compensation agreement. An agreement by an exporter of plant or equipment to take compensation in the form of future output from that plant. Also known as a buyback transaction.

Concession agreement. An understanding or contract between a foreign corporation and a host government defining the rules under which the corporation may operate in that country.

Consolidated financial statement. A corporate financial statement in which accounts of subsidiaries and the parent are added together to produce a statement which reports the status of the worldwide enterprise as if it were a single corporation. Inter-affiliate obligations are eliminated in consolidated statements.

Consolidation. In the context of accounting for multinational corporations, the process of preparing a single "reporting currency" financial statement that combines financial statements of affiliates that are in fact measured in different currencies.

Consortium bank. A banking joint venture, owned by two or more individual banks often of different nationalities. Consortium banks are formed in order to offer loans that are larger than the capacity of any one single bank, as well as to engage in other aspects of international banking.

Contagion. A form of financial panic, in which the devaluation of exchange rates by one country leads to similar devaluations at about the same time by other, often nearby, countries.

Controlled foreign corporation (CFC). A foreign corporation in which U.S. shareholders own more than 50% of the combined voting power or total value. Under U.S. tax law, U.S. shareholders may be liable for taxes on undistributed earnings of the controlled foreign corporation.

Convertible bond. A bond or other fixed-income security which may be exchanged for a number of shares of common stock.

Convertible currency. A currency that can be exchanged freely for any other currency without government restrictions.

Corporate wealth maximization. The corporate goal of maximizing the total wealth of the corporation itself rather than just the shareholders' wealth. Wealth is defined to include not just financial wealth but also the technical, marketing, and human resources of the corporation.

Correspondent bank. A bank that holds deposits for and provides services to another bank, located in another geographic area, on a reciprocal basis.

Cost and freight (C&F). Price, quoted by an exporter, that includes the cost of transportation to the named port of destination.

Cost, insurance, and freight (CIF). Exporter's quoted price including the cost of packaging, freight or carriage, insurance premium, and other charges paid in respect of the goods from the time of loading in the country of export to their arrival at the named port of destination or place of transshipment.

Cost of capital. *See* Weighted average cost of capital.

Counterparty. The opposite party to a double transaction; that is, to a transaction involving an exchange of financial instruments or obligations now and a reversal of that same transaction at some agreed-upon later date. Counterparty risk is the potential exposure any individual firm bears that the second party to any financial contract will be unable to fulfill its obligations under the contract's specifications.

Countertrade. A type of international trade in which parties exchange goods directly rather than for money. Hence a type of barter.

Countervailing duty. An import duty charged to offset an export subsidy by another country.

Country risk. In banking, the likelihood that unexpected events within a host country will influence a client's or a government's ability to repay a loan. Country risk is often divided into sovereign (political, or cultural and institutional) risk and foreign exchange (currency or transfer) risk. Also known as macro risks.

Covered interest arbitrage (CIA). The process whereby an investor earns a risk-free profit by (1) borrowing funds in one currency, (2) exchanging those funds in the spot market for a foreign currency, (3) investing the foreign currency at interest rates in a foreign country, (4) selling forward, at the time of original investment, the investment proceeds to be received at maturity, (5) using the proceeds of the forward sale to repay the original loan, and (6) having a remaining profit balance.

Covering. A transaction in the forward foreign exchange market or money market that protects the value of future cash flows. Covering is another term for hedging. *See* Hedge.

Crawling peg. A foreign exchange rate system in which the exchange rate is adjusted very frequently to reflect prevailing rate of inflation.

Credit risk. Also known as roll-over risk, the possibility that a borrower's credit worth, at the time of renewing a credit, is reclassified by the lender.

Credit swap. *See* Back-to-back loan.

Creditable taxes. Foreign income taxes paid on earnings by a foreign corporation that has paid a dividend to a qualifying U.S. corporation.

Creeping tenders. The secret accumulation of relatively small blocks of stock, privately or in the open market, in a preliminary move towards a public bid; intended to promote public disclosure of bids for takeovers.

Cronyism. The tendency of local firms to be controlled either by families or by groups related to the governing party or body of the country.

Crosslisting. The listing of shares of common stock on two or more stock exchanges.

Cross rate. An exchange rate between two currencies derived by dividing each currency's exchange rate with a third currency. For example, if ¥/$ is 140 and DM/$ is 1.5000, the cross rate between ¥ and DM is ¥140/$ 4 DM1.5000 = ¥93.3333/DM.

CTA account. *See* Cumulative translation adjustment account.

Cumulative translation adjustment (CTA) account. An entry in a translated balance sheet in which gains and/or losses from translation have been accumulated over a period of years.

Currency basket. The value of a portfolio of specific amounts of individual currencies, used as the basis for setting the market value of another currency. Also called currency cocktail.

Currency board. A country's central bank that has committed to backing its monetary base (its money supply) with foreign reserves at all times.

Currency cocktail. *See* Currency basket.

Currency risk. The variance in expected cash flows arising from unexpected exchange rate changes.

Currency swap. A transaction in which two counterparties exchange specific amounts of two different currencies at the outset and then repay over time according to an agreed upon contract that reflects interest payments and possibly amortization of principal. In a currency swap, the cash flows are similar to those in a spot and forward foreign exchange transaction. *See also* Swaps.

Current account. In the balance of payments, the net flow of goods, services, and unilateral transfers (such as gifts) between a country and all foreign countries.

Current rate method. A method of translating the financial statements of foreign affiliates into the parent's reporting currency. All assets and liabilities are translated at the current exchange rate. Also known as the "closing-rate method."

Current/noncurrent method. A method of translating the financial statements of foreign affiliates into the parent's reporting currency. All current assets and current liabilities are translated at the current rate, and all noncurrent accounts at their historical rates.

Dealer. An individual or firm that buys or sells foreign exchange, or securities, for its own account, usually buying at one price and reselling at a higher price to a customer in order to make a profit on the spread between the buying and selling price. A dealer is an alternative to a "broker." *See* Broker. A dealer does not charge a commission for its efforts.

Deductible expense. An expense that the taxpayer uses to reduce taxable income before the tax rate is applied.

Deemed-tax paid. That portion of taxes paid to a foreign government that is allowed as a credit (reduction) in taxes due to a home government.

Delta. The change in an option's price divided by the change in the price of the underlying instrument. Hedging strategies are based on delta ratios.

Demand deposit. A bank deposit that can be withdrawn or transferred at any time without notice, in contradistinction to a time deposit where (theoretically) the bank may require a waiting period before the deposit can be withdrawn. Demand deposits may or may not earn interest. A "time deposit" is the opposite of a demand deposit.

Depository receipts, or depository shares. Negotiable certificates issued by a bank to represent the underlying shares of stock, which are held in trust at a foreign custodian bank.

Depreciation. In the context of foreign exchange rates, a drop in the spot foreign exchange value of a floating currency; i.e., a currency the value of which is determined by open market transactions. *See* Devaluation of currency. In the context of accounting, a periodic charge (expense) that represents the allocation of the cost of a fixed asset to various time periods.

Derivatives. Financial instruments such as stock or currency utilized by a MNE's financial manager in the expectation of profit or speculation, or to reduce corporate cash flow risks.

Deterioration. Same as depreciation.

Devaluation of currency. A drop in the spot foreign exchange value of a currency that is pegged to other currencies or to gold. *See* Depreciation.

Diamond of national advantage. The phenomenon that a strongly competitive home market can sharpen a firm's competitive advantage relative to firms located in less competitive home markets.

Direct quote. The price of a unit of foreign exchange expressed in the home country's currency. The term has meaning only when the "home country" is specified.

Direct taxes. Taxes that are applied directly to income.

Directed public share issue. A share issue that is targeted at investors in a single country and underwritten in whole or in part by investment institutions from that country.

"Dirty" float. A system of floating (i.e., market-determined) exchange rates in which the government intervenes from time to time to influence the foreign exchange value of its currency.

Discount (in foreign exchange market). The amount by which a currency is cheaper for future delivery than for spot (immediate) delivery. The opposite of "discount" is "premium."

DISC. *See* Domestic International Sales Corporation.

Dollarization. The use of the U.S. dollar as the official currency of another country.

Domestic International Sales Corporation (DISC). Under the U.S. tax code, a type of subsidiary formed to export U.S.-produced goods. A portion of the earnings and profits of a DISC is not taxed to the DISC but is instead taxed directly to its shareholders.

D/P. "Documents against payment." International trade term.

Draft. An unconditional written order requesting one party (such as an importer) to pay a specified amount of money at a specified time to the order of the writer of the draft. Also called a "bill of exchange." Personal checks are one type of draft.

Dragon bond. A U.S. dollar denominated bond sold in the so-called "Dragon" economies of Asia, such as Hong Kong, Taiwan, and Singapore.

D/S. "Days after sight." International trade term.

Dumping. The practice of offering goods for sale in a foreign market at a price that is lower than that of the same product in the home market or a third country. As used in GATT, a special case of "differential pricing."

EBITDA. Earnings before interest, taxes, depreciation, and amortization.

Economic exposure. Another name for operating exposure. *See* Operating exposure.

Economic Value Added (EVA). The corporate goal of increasing the value of the capital that investors and shareholders have vested in the operations of the business. "EVA" is a registered trademark of Stern Stewart & Company.

ECU. *See* European Currency Unit.

Edge Act and Agreement Corporation. Subsidiary of a U.S. bank incorporated under federal law to engage in various international banking and financing operations, including equity participations that are not allowed to regular domestic banks. The Edge Act subsidiary may be located in a state other than that of the parent bank.

EEC. *See* European Economic Community.

Effective exchange rate. An index measuring the change in value of a foreign currency determined by calculating a weighted average of bilateral exchange rates. The weighting reflects the importance of each foreign country's trade with the home country.

Efficient frontier. The optimal portfolios of securities that possess the minimum expected risk for each level of expected portfolio return. The portfolio with the minimum risk among all those possible is the minimum risk domestic portfolio.

Efficient market. A market in which all relevant information is already reflected in market prices. The term is most frequently applied to foreign exchange markets and securities markets.

EFTA. See European Free Trade Association.

EMS. See European Monetary System.

Enterprise value. The sum of the present values of both debt and equity in the enterprise.

EOM. "End of month." International trade term.

Equitable tax. A tax that imposes the same total tax burden on all taxpayers who are similarly situated and located in the same tax jurisdiction.

Equity risk premium. The average annual return of the market expected by investors over and above riskless debt.

Euro. The single currency adopted by the 11 members of the European Monetary Union on January 1, 1999, to replace their national currencies. The change over from national currencies to euros took place over three years, so that by January 1, 2002, the individual national currencies were phased out.

Eurobank. A bank, or bank department, which bids for time deposits and makes loans in currencies other than that of the country where the bank is located.

Eurobond. A bond originally offered outside the country in whose currency it is denominated. For example, a dollar-denominated bond originally offered for sale to investors outside of the United States.

Euro-Commercial Paper. Short-term notes (30, 60, 90, 120, 180, 270, and 360 days) sold in international money markets.

Eurocredit. A Eurocurrency-denominated bank loan to a MNE, sovereign government, international institution, or bank.

Eurocurrency. A currency deposited in a bank located in a country other than the country issuing the currency.

Eurodollar. A U.S. dollar deposited in a bank outside the United States. A Eurodollar is one type of Eurocurrency.

Euronote. Short- to medium-term debt instruments sold in the Eurocurrency market.

Euroyen. A yen deposited in a bank outside Japan. A Euroyen is one type of Eurocurrency.

European Currency Unit (ECU). Composite currency created by the European Monetary System to function as a reserve currency numeraire. The ECU is used as the numeraire for denominating a number of financial instruments and obligations.

European Economic Community (EEC). The European common market composed of Belgium, Denmark, France, Germany, Greece, Ireland, Italy, Luxembourg, the Netherlands, Portugal, Spain, and the United Kingdom. Officially renamed the European Union (EU) January 1, 1994.

European Free Trade Association (EFTA). European countries not part of the EEC (EU) but having no internal tariffs. EFTA consists of Austria, Iceland, Finland, Sweden, and Switzerland.

European Monetary System (EMS). A monetary alliance of 15 European countries (same members as the European Union), formed to maintain member exchange rates within specified margins about fixed central rates. As of July 1994, the United Kingdom and Italy are not active members.

European option. An option that can be exercised only on the day on which it expires.

European terms. Foreign exchange quotations for the U.S. dollar, expressed as the number of non-U.S. currency units per U.S. dollar.

European Union (EU). The official name of the former European Economic Community (EEC) as of January 1, 1994.

EVA. See Economic Value Added.

Exchange rate. The price of a unit of one country's currency expressed in terms of the currency of some other country.

Exchange Rate Mechanism (ERM). The means by which members of the EMS maintain their currency exchange rates within an agreed upon range with respect to the other member currencies.

Exchange risk. *See* Foreign exchange risk.

Ex dock. followed by the name of a port of import. International trade term in which seller agrees to pay for the costs (shipping, insurance, customs duties, etc.) of placing the goods on the dock at the named port.

Exercise price. The price paid when an option is exercised. Same as Strike price.

Eximbank. *See* Export-Import Bank.

Exotic options. Products that have altered the valuation principles of the basic option-pricing model.

Export-Import Bank (Eximbank). A U.S. government agency created to finance and otherwise facilitate imports and exports.

Expropriation. Official government seizure of private property, recognized by international law as the right of any sovereign state provided expropriated owners are given prompt compensation and fair market value in convertible currencies.

FAF. "Fly away free." International trade term.

FAQ. "Free at quay." International trade term.

FAS. *See* Free alongside.

FASB #8. A regulation of the Financial Accounting Standards Board requiring U.S. companies to translate foreign affiliate financial statements by the temporal method. FASB #8 was in effect from 1976 to 1981.

FAS #52. A regulation of the Financial Accounting Standards Board requiring U.S. companies to translate foreign affiliate financial statements by the current rate (closing rate) method. FAS #52 became effective in 1981.

FCIA. *See* Foreign Credit Insurance Association.

FDI. *See* Foreign direct investment.

FI. "Free in." International trade term meaning that all expenses for loading into the hold of a vessel are for the account of the consignee.

FIFO. "First in, first out." An inventory valuation approach in which the cost of the earliest inventory purchases is charged against current sales. The opposite is LIFO, or "last in, first out."

Financial account. A section of the balance of payments accounts. Under the revised format of the International Monetary Fund, the financial account measures long-term financial flows including direct foreign investment, portfolio investments, and other long-term movements. Under the traditional definition, still used by many countries, items in the financial account were included in the capital account.

Financial distress point. The point when a firm is at its minimum cash flow, a cash flow sufficient to make debt-service payments in order for it to continue to operate.

Financial engineering. Those basic building blocks, such as spot positions, forwards, and options, used to construct positions that provide the user with desired risk and return characteristics.

Financial hedge. An off-setting debt obligation (such as a loan) or some type of financial derivative such as an interest rate swap.

Firm-specific risk. Risks that affect the MNE at the project or corporate level. Also known as micro risks. The main example is governance risk, due to goal conflict between a MNE and its host government. *See also* Country risks.

Fisher Effect. A theory that nominal interest rates in two or more countries should be equal to the required real rate of return to investors plus compensation for the expected amount of inflation in each country.

Fixed exchange rates. Foreign exchange rates tied to the currency of a major country (such as the United States), to gold, or to a basket of currencies such as Special Drawing Rights.

Flexible exchange rates. The opposite of fixed exchange rates. The foreign exchange rate is adjusted periodically by the country's monetary authorities in accordance with their judgment and/or an external set of economic indicators.

Floating exchange rates, or flexible exchange rates. Foreign exchange rates determined by demand and supply in an open market that is presumably free of government interference.

Floating-rate note (FRN). Medium-term securities with interest rates pegged to LIBOR and adjusted quarterly or semiannually.

FOB. "Free on board." International trade term in which exporter's quoted price includes the cost of loading goods into transport vessels at a named point.

Foreign bond. A bond issued by a foreign corporation or government for sale in the domestic capital market of another country, and denominated in the currency of that country.

Foreign Corrupt Practices Act of 1977. A U.S. law that punishes companies and their executives if they pay bribes or make other improper payments to foreigners.

Foreign Credit Insurance Association (FCIA). Private U.S. insurance association that insures exporters in conjunction with Exim bank.

Foreign currency exchange rate, or exchange rate. The price of one country's currency in units of another currency or commodity (typically gold or silver).

Foreign currency futures contract. Forward contract that calls for future delivery of a standard amount of foreign exchange at a fixed time, place, and price.

Foreign currency translation. The process of restating foreign currency accounts of subsidiaries into the reporting currency of the parent company in order to prepare a consolidated financial statement.

Foreign direct investment (FDI). Purchase of physical assets, such as plant and equipment, in a foreign country, to be managed by the parent corporation. FDI is in contradistinction to foreign portfolio investment.

Foreign exchange market. The physical and institutional structure through which the money of one country is exchanged for that of another country, the rate of exchange between currencies is determined, and foreign exchange transactions are physically completed.

Foreign exchange broker. An individual or firm that arranges foreign exchange transactions between two parties, but is not itself a principal in the trade. Foreign exchange brokers earn a commission for their efforts.

Foreign exchange dealer (or trader). An individual or firm that buys foreign exchange from one party (at a "bid" price), and then sells it (at an "ask" price) to another party. The dealer is a principal in two transactions and makes a profit on the spread between its buying and selling prices.

Foreign exchange option. *See* Option.

Foreign exchange risk or exposure. The likelihood that an unexpected change in exchange rates will alter the home currency value of foreign currency cash payments expected from a foreign source. Also, the likelihood that an unexpected change in exchange rates will alter the amount of home currency needed to repay a debt denominated in a foreign currency.

Foreign exchange rate. The price of one country's currency in terms of another currency, or in terms of a commodity such as gold or silver. *See also* Exchange rates and Foreign exchange.

Foreign sales corporation (FSC). Under U.S. tax code, a type of foreign corporation that provides tax-exempt or tax-deferred income for U.S. persons or corporations having export-oriented activities.

Foreign tax credit. The amount by which a domestic firm may reduce (credit) domestic income taxes for income tax payments to a foreign government.

Forfaiting. A technique for arranging nonrecourse medium-term export financing, used most frequently to finance imports into Eastern Europe. A third party, usually a specialized financial institution, guarantees the financing.

Forward. *See* Outright forward transaction.

Forward exchange contract. An agreement to exchange currencies of different countries at a specified future date and at a specified forward rate.

Forward differential. The difference between spot and forward rates, expressed as an annual percentage.

Forward-forward swap. A swap transaction is which the difference between the buying price and the selling price is equivalent to the interest rate differential—i.e., interest rate parity—between the two currencies.

Forward hedge. A hedge involving a forward (or futures) contract and a source of funds to fulfill that contract. *See* Hedge.

Forward premium or discount. The same as "forward differential."

Forward rate. An exchange rate quoted today for settlement at some future date. The rate used in a forward transaction.

Forward rate agreement (FRA). An interbank-traded contract to buy or sell interest rate payments on a notional principal.

Forward transaction. A foreign exchange transaction agreed upon today but to be settled at some specified future date, often one, two, or three months after the transaction date.

Free alongside (FAS). An international trade term in which the seller's quoted price for goods includes all costs of delivery of the goods alongside a vessel at the port of embarkation.

Freely floating exchange rates. Exchange rates determined in a free market without government interference, in contradistinction to "dirty" float.

Free trade zone. An area within a country into which foreign goods may be brought duty free, often for purposes of additional manufacture, inventory storage, or packaging. Such goods are subject to duty only when they leave the duty-free zone to enter other parts of the country.

Fronting loan. A parent-to-subsidiary loan channeled through a financial intermediary, usually a large international bank. Also known as link financing.

Functional currency. For a foreign subsidiary of a MNE, the currency of the primary economic environment in which the subsidiary operates and in which it generates cash flows.

Global-specific risks. Risks that affect the MNE at the project or corporate level, but that originate at the global level (such as terrorism, environmental concerns, and cyber-attacks).

Governance risk. The ability to exercise effective control over a MNE's operations within a country's legal and political environment.

Greenfield investment. An investment that establishes a production or service facility starting from the ground up.

Grantor. Seller of an option (see writer).

Grossing up. The policy of a parent corporation that takes the full before-tax foreign income of a foreign corporation—apportioned by its proportional ownership in the foreign corporation—into its taxable income.

Hedge. The purchase of a contract (including forward foreign exchange) or tangible good that will rise in value and offset a drop in value of another contract or tangible good. Hedges are undertaken to reduce risk by protecting an owner from loss.

Hedge ratio. The percentage of an individual exposure's nominal amount covered by a financial instrument such as a forward contract or currency option. *See* Beta.

Holder. The buyer of an option. *See* Option.

Hostile takeover. An acquisition not supported by target company management.

Inconvertibility. The risk that the investor will not be able to convert profits, royalties, fees, or other income, as well as the original capital invested, into dollars.

Indication. A bid-offer quote.

Indirect quote. The price of a unit of a home country's currency expressed in terms of a foreign country's currency.

Impossible Trinity. Three attributes of a theoretical ideal currency: exchange rate stability, full financial integration, and monetary independence.

Indirect taxes. Taxes that are applied not directly to income, but instead to some other measurable performance characteristic of the firm.

Intellectual property rights. Rights that grant the exclusive use of patented technology and copyrighted creative materials.

Interest rate parity. A theory that the differences in national interest rates for securities of similar risk and maturity should be equal to but opposite in sign to the forward exchange rate discount or premium for the foreign currency.

Interest rate cap. An option to fix a ceiling or maximum short-term interest-rate payment. There are two major types of interest rate caps: the interest rate guarantee (IRG), which provides protection to the buyer for a single period only, and the interest rate cap, which provides protection for an extended period of time.

Interest rate collar. The simultaneous purchase (sale) of a cap and sale (purchase) of a floor. If the two premiums are equal, the position is often referred to as a zero-premium collar.

Interest rate floor. An option to receive the compensating payment (cash settlement) when the reference interest rate falls below the strike rate of the floor.

Interest rate swap. A transaction in which two counterparties exchange interest payment streams of different character (such as floating vs. fixed), based on an underlying notional principal amount.

Internal rate of return (IRR). A capital budgeting approach in which the discount rate is found that matches the present value of expected future cash inflows with the present value of outflows.

Internalization. A theory that the key ingredient for maintaining a firm-specific competitive advantage in international competition is the possession of proprietary information and control of human capital that can generate new information through expertise in research, management, marketing, or technology.

International Bank for Reconstruction and Development (IBRD, or World Bank). International development bank owned by member nations that makes development loans to member countries.

International Banking Facility (IBF). A department within a U.S. bank that may accept foreign deposits and make loans to foreign borrowers as if it were a foreign subsidiary. IBFs are free of U.S. reserve requirements, deposit insurance, and interest rate regulations.

International Monetary Fund (IMF). An international organization created in 1944 to promote exchange rate stability and provide temporary financing for countries experiencing balance of payments difficulties.

International Monetary Market (IMM). A branch of the Chicago Mercantile Exchange that specializes in trading currency and financial futures contracts.

International monetary system. The structure within which foreign exchange rates are determined, international trade and capital flows are accommodated, and balance of payments adjustments made.

In-the-money (ITM). A term describing an option that would be profitable, excluding the price of the premium, if exercised immediately.

International Fisher Effect. A theory that the spot exchange rate should change by an amount equal to the difference in interest rates between two countries.

International parity conditions. The economic theories that link exchange rates, price levels, and interest rates together.

Intrinsic value. The financial gain obtained if an option is exercised immediately.

Inventory velocity. The speed at which inventory moves through a manufacturing process.

IRR. *See* Internal rate of return.

Joint venture. A business venture that is owned by two or more other business ventures. Often the several business owners are from different countries.

Jumbo loans. Loans of $1 billion or more.

Kangaroo bonds. Australian dollar–denominated bonds issued within Australia by a foreign borrower.

"Kiwi." Foreign exchange dealers' nickname for the New Zealand dollar.

KK. *Kabushiki-Kaishi.* Japanese term for stock company.

Lag. In the context of leads and lags, payment of a financial obligation later than is expected or required.

Lambda. A measure of the sensitivity of an option premium to a unit change in volatility.

Law of one price. States that if the identical product or service can be sold in two different markets, and no restrictions exist on the sale or transportation costs of moving the product between markets, the product's price should be the same in both markets.

L/C. *See* Letter of credit.

Lead. In the context of leads and lags, payment of a financial obligation earlier than is expected or required.

Letter of credit (L/C). An instrument issued by a bank, in which the bank promises to pay a beneficiary upon presentation of documents specified in the letter of credit.

LIBOR. *See* London Interbank Offered Rate (LIBOR).

License fees. Remuneration paid to the owners of technology, patents, trade names, and copyrighted material (including images, videotapes, compact disks, software, and books).

LIFO. "Last in, first out." An inventory valuation approach in which the cost of the latest inventory purchases is charged against current sales. The opposite is FIFO, or "first in, first out."

Limited (Ltd). British English word for a business formed as a corporation.

Link financing. *See* Back-to-back loan.

Lombard rate. The interest rate on a "Lombard loan," which is an advance against the collateral of specified European securities.

London Interbank Offered Rate (LIBOR). The deposit rate applicable to interbank loans in London. LIBOR is used as the reference rate for many international interest rate transactions.

Long position. A position in which foreign currency assets exceed foreign currency liabilities to deliver. The opposite of a long position is a short position.

"Loonie." Foreign exchange dealer's nickname for the Canadian dollar.

Ltd. *See* Limited.

Maastricht Treaty. A treaty among the 12 European Union countries that specified a plan and timetable for the introduction of a single European currency, to be called the "Euro."

Marked to market. A revaluation of contracts using the closing price for the day.

Market pricing. Buying from wholesalers at a global market price.

Managed float. *See* "Dirty" float.

Margin. A deposit made as security for a financial transaction otherwise financed on credit.

Merchant bank. A bank that specializes in helping corporations and governments finance by any of a variety of market and/or traditional techniques. In Europe, merchant banks combine in one institution what in the United States are separated into commercial banks or investment banks. European merchant banks are sometimes differentiated from clearing banks, which tend to focus on bank deposits and clearing balances for the majority of the population.

MFN. *See* Most-favored-nation treatment.

Monetary/nonmonetary method. A method of translating the financial statements of foreign affiliates into the parent's reporting currency. All monetary accounts are translated at the current rate, and all nonmonetary accounts are translated at their historical rates. Sometimes called "temporal method" in the United States.

Money market hedge. Use of foreign currency borrowing to reduce transaction or accounting foreign exchange exposure.

Money markets. The financial markets in various countries in which various types of short-term debt instruments, including bank loans, are purchased and sold.

Monetary assets or liabilities. Assets in the form of cash or claims to cash (such as accounts receivable), or liabilities payable in cash. Monetary assets minus monetary liabilities are called "net monetary assets."

m. n. *Moneda nacional.* Spanish language term for "national money," the local currency.

Most-favored-nation status. A term meaning the same as "normal trade status." *See* Normal trade status.

Multilateral netting. The process that cancels via offset all or part of the debt owed by one entity to another related entity.

Multinational capital budgeting. The investment in real productive assets in foreign countries; focuses on the case inflows and outflows associated with prospective long-term investment projects.

NAFTA. *See* North American Free Trade Agreement.

Natural hedge. An off-setting operating cash flow, a payable arising from the conduct of business. *See* Hedge.

Negotiable instrument. A draft or promissory note that is in writing, signed by the maker or drawer, contains an unconditional promise or order to pay a definite sum of money on demand or at a determinable future date, and is payable to order or to bearer. A "holder in due course" of a negotiable instrument is entitled to payment despite any personal disagreements between drawee and maker.

Nepotism. The practice of showing favor to relatives in preference to other qualified persons in conferring such benefits as the awarding of contracts, granting of special prices, promotions to various ranks, etc.

Net operating profit after tax (NOPAT). Cash flow measure of basic business profitability; EBIT minus taxes.

Net present value. A capital budgeting approach in which the present value of expected future cash inflows is subtracted from the present value of outflows to determine the "net" present value.

Netting. The mutual offsetting of sums due between two business entities. If "A" owes "B" $100, and "B" owes "A" $60, a single payment of $40 from "A" to "B" would eliminate both debts. This would be "netting."

Net working capital (NWC). The net amount of capital that the firm invests in the actual production and sale of its product.

Nominal effective exchange rate index. An index that uses actual exchange rates, on a weighted average basis, of the value of the subject currency over time. Calculates how the currency value relates to some arbitrarily chosen base period; used in the formation of the real effective exchange rate index.

Nominal exchange rate. The actual foreign exchange quotation, in contradistinction to "real exchange rate," which is adjusted for changes in purchasing power.

Nondeliverable forward (NDF). A contract similar to traditional forward contracts, but settled only in U.S. dollars; also, the foreign currency being sold forward or bought forward is not delivered.

Nontariff barrier. Trade-restrictive practices other than custom tariffs. Examples are import quotas, "voluntary" restrictions, variable levies, and special health regulations.

NOPAT. *See* Net operating profit after tax.

Normal trade status. The term currently used to describe what economists used to call "most-favored nation" status. Normal trade status is the application by a country of import duties on the same (i.e., "most favored") basis to all countries accorded such treatment. Any tariff reduction granted in a bilateral negotiation to a specific country will be automatically extended to all other nations that have been granted normal trade status.

North American Free Trade Agreement (NAFTA). A treaty allowing free trade and investment between Canada, the United States, and Mexico.

Note issuance facility (NIF). An agreement by which a syndicate of banks indicates a willingness to accept short-term notes from borrowers and resell those notes in the Eurocurrency markets. The discount rate is often tied to LIBOR.

NPV. *See* Net present value.

N. V. Naamloze vennootschap. Dutch term for stock company or corporation.

O_A. "Open account." Arrangement in which the importer (or other buyer) pays for the goods only after the goods are received and inspected. The importer is billed directly after shipment, and payment is not tied to any promissory notes or similar documents.

Offer. The price at which a trader is willing to sell foreign exchange, securities, or commodities. Also called "ask."

Offshore finance subsidiary. A foreign financial subsidiary owned by a corporation in another country. Offshore finance subsidiaries are usually located in tax-free or low-tax jurisdictions to enable the parent multinational firm to finance international operations without being subject to home country taxes or regulations.

OLI Paradigm. States that a firm must first have some competitive advantage in its home market. "O" for "owner-specific"; "L" for "location-specific"; and "I" for internalization.

One-sided risks. Those variables that are likely to result in decreased cash flows only from those expected (including expropriation, cross-border payment restrictions or prohibitions, political chaos, or upheaval).

OPEC. *See* Organization of Petroleum Exporting Countries.

OPIC. *See* Overseas Private Investment Corporation.

Organization of Petroleum Exporting Countries (OPEC). An alliance of most major crude oil producing countries, formed for the purpose of allocating and controlling production quotas so as to influence the price of crude oil in world markets.

OTC market. *See* Over-the-counter market.

Operating cycle. A cycle from the first point at which a customer requests a price quotation to the final point at which payment is received from the customer for goods delivered. *See also* Cash conversion cycle.

Operating exposure. The potential for a change in expected cash flows, and thus in value, of a foreign affiliate as a result of an unexpected change in exchange rates. Also called "economic exposure," "competitive exposure," or "strategic exposure."

Option. In foreign exchange, a contract giving the purchaser the right, but not the obligation, to buy or sell a given amount of foreign exchange at a fixed price per unit for a specified time period. Options to buy are "calls" and options to sell are "puts."

Order bill of lading. A shipping document through which possession and title to the shipment reside with the owner of the order bill of lading.

Out-of-the-money (OTM). An option that would not be profitable, excluding the cost of the premium, if exercised immediately.

Outright forward transaction (forward). A transaction that requires delivery at a future value date of a specified amount of one currency for a specified amount of another currency.

Outright pricing. Negotiating prices directly with small and medium-sized farmers, eliminating the wholesaler position.

Outright quotation. The full price, in one currency, of a unit of another currency. *See* Points quotation.

Overseas Private Investment Corporation (OPIC). A U.S. government-owned insurance company that insures U.S. corporations against various political risks.

Over-the-counter market. A market for share of stock, options (including foreign currency options), or other financial contracts conducted via electronic connections between dealers. The over-the-counter market has no physical location or address, and is thus differentiated from organized exchanges which have a physical location where trading takes place.

Parallel loan. Another name for a back-to-back loan, in which two companies in separate countries borrow each other's currency for a specific period of time, and repay the other's currency at an agreed maturity.

Parallel market. An unofficial foreign exchange market tolerated by a government but not officially sanctioned. The exact boundary between a parallel market and a black market is not very clear, but official tolerance of what would otherwise be a black market leads to use of the term parallel market.

"Paris. " Foreign exchange dealers' nickname for the French franc.

Parity conditions. In the context of international finance, a set of basic economic relationships which provide for equilibrium between spot and forward foreign exchange rates, interest rates, and inflation rates.

Participation rate. The residual percentage of the exposure that is not covered by the sale of the call option.

Participating forward. A complex option position which combines a bought put and a sold call option at the same strike price to create a net zero position. Also called *zero-cost option* and *forward participation agreement*. ***Pass-through.*** The degree to which the prices of imported and exported goods change as a result of exchange rate changes.

Phi. The expected change in an option premium caused by a small change in the foreign interest rate (interest rate for the foreign currency).

P/N. "Promissory note."

Points. A "point" is the smallest unit of price change quoted, given a conventional number of digits in which a quotation is stated. Deutschemarks per dollar are usually quoted to four decimal points, DM1.5624_$. In this quote, a change from 1.5624 to 1.5625 would be an increase of one point. A 12 point increase would bring the quote to 1.5636.

Points quotation. A forward quotation expressed only as the number of decimal points (usually four decimal points) by which it differs from the spot quotation.

Political risk. The possibility that political events in a particular country will have an influence on the economic well-being of firms in that country. *Also see* Sovereign risk.

Portfolio investment. Purchase of foreign stocks and bonds, in contradistinction to "foreign direct investment."

Possessions corporation. A U.S. corporation, the subsidiary of another U.S. corporation, which for tax purposes is treated as if it were a foreign corporation.

Premium (in foreign exchange market). The amount by which a currency is more expensive for future delivery than for spot (immediate) delivery. The opposite of "premium" is "discount."

Price elasticity of demand. The percentage change in quantity of the good demanded as a result of the percentage change in the good's own price.

Private placementThe sale of a security to a small set of qualified institutional buyers. *See* Qualified institutional buyer.

Project finance. The arrangement of financing for long-term capital projects, large in scale, long in life, and generally high in risk.

Protectionism. A political attitude or policy intended to inhibit or prohibit the import of foreign goods and services. The opposite of "free trade" policies.

Pty. Ltd. "Proprietary Limited." Term used in Australia, Singapore, and other countries for a privately owned corporation.

Purchasing power parity (PPP). A theory that the price of internationally traded commodities should be the same in every country, and hence the exchange rate between the two currencies should be the ratio of prices in the two countries. Relative PPP holds that if the spot exchange rate between two countries starts in equilibrium, any change in the differential rate of inflation between them tends to be offset over the long run by an equal but opposite change in the spot exchange rate.

Put option. An option to sell foreign exchange or financial contracts. *See* Option.

Qualified institutional buyer (QIB). An entity (except a bank or a savings and loan institution) that owns and invests on a discretionary basis at least $100 million in securities of non-affiliates. Banks and savings and loans qualify if they also have a minimum net worth of $25 million.

Quota. A limit, mandatory or "voluntary," set on the import of a product.

Quotation. In foreign exchange trading, the pair of prices (bid and ask) at which a dealer is willing to buy or sell foreign exchange.

Quotation period. The time from a price quotation to the point when a customer places an order.

Range forward. A complex option position which combines the purchase of a put option and the sale of a call option with strike prices equidistant from the forward rate. Also called *flexible forward, cylinder option, option fence, mini-max,* and *zero-cost tunnel.*

Real effective exchange rate index. An index that indicates how the weighted average purchasing power of the currency has changed relative to some arbitrarily selected base period.

Real exchange rate. An index of foreign exchange adjusted for relative price level changes since a base period. Sometimes referred to as "real effective exchange rate," it is used to measure purchasing power–adjusted changes in exchange rates.

Real option analysis. The application of option theory to capital budgeting decisions.

Registered bond. Corporate or governmental debt in a bond form in which the owner's name appears on the bond and in the issuer's records, and interest payments are mailed to the owner. Transfer, as at the time of sale or if the bond is being possessed as collateral for a loan in default, requires power of attorney and the return of the physical bond to a transfer agent. The transfer agent replaces the old bond with a new one registered to the new owner.

Re-invoicing center. A central financial subsidiary used by a multinational firm to reduce transaction exposure by having all home country exports billed in the home currency and then re-invoiced to each operating affiliate in that affiliate's local currency.

Rho. The expected change in an option premium caused by a small change in the domestic interest rate (interest rate for the home currency).

Rembrandt bonds. Dutch guilder-denominated bonds issued within the Netherlands by a foreign borrower.

Reporting currency. In the context of translating financial statements, the currency in which a parent firm prepares its own financial statements. Usually this is the parent's home currency.

Revaluation. A rise in the foreign exchange value of a currency that is pegged to other currencies or to gold. Also called "appreciation."

Risk sharing. A contractual arrangement in which the buyer and seller agree to "share" or split currency movement impacts on payments between them.

Round turn. A complete contract procedure, including buying and selling of the contract.

Royalty fees. Compensation for the use of intellectual property belonging to some other party, usually a stated percentage of sales revenue (price times volume).

"Rules of the Game." The basis of exchange rate determination under the international gold standard during most of the 19th and early 20th centuries. All countries agreed informally to follow the "rule" of buying and selling their currency at a fixed and predetermined price against gold.

SA. *Sociedad Anónima* (Spanish), or *Societe Anonyme* (French). Term meaning corporation.

SACI or SAIC. *Sociedad Anónima de Capital e Industria.* Spanish term for company of capital and industry.

Samurai bonds. Yen-denominated bonds issued within Japan by a foreign borrower.

SARL. Società a Responsabilità Limitada (Italian), or Société a Responsabilité Limitéé (French). Term for company with limited liability.

S/D. "Sight draft." International trade term.

S/D-B/L. "Sight draft and bill of lading attached." International trade term.

SDR. *See* Special drawing right.

S. de R. L. *Sociedad de Responsabilidad Limitada.* Spanish term for limited partnership.

Section 482. The set of U.S. Treasury regulations governing transfer prices.

S. en C. *Sociedad en Comandita.* Spanish term for silent partnership.

Shared services. Charges to compensate the parent for costs incurred in the general management of international operations and for other corporate services provided to foreign subsidiaries that must be recovered by the parent company. Also known as distributed charges or distributed overhead.

Shareholder wealth maximization. The corporate goal of maximizing the total value of the shareholders' investment in the company.

Sharpe measure (SHP). Calculates the average return over and above the risk-free rate of return per unit of portfolio risk.

Shogun bonds. Foreign currency–denominated bonds issued within Japan by Japanese corporations.

Short position. *See* Long position.

Speculation. An attempt to make a profit by trading on expectations about future prices.

Seigniorage. A country's ability to profit from printing its own money.

Selective hedging. The hedging of large, singular, exceptional exposures or the occasional use of hedging when management has a definite expectation of the direction of exchange rates. *See* Hedging.

Selling short. A speculation technique in which an individual speculator sells an asset such as a currency to another party for delivery at a future date.

SIBOR. Singapore interbank offered rate.

Sight draft. A bill of exchange (B/E) that is due on demand; i.e., when presented to the bank. *Also see* Bill of exchange.

SIMEX. Singapore International Monetary Exchange.

"Sing dollar." Foreign exchange dealers' nickname for the Singapore dollar.

Snake. Informal name for European Narrow Margins (or Joint Float) Agreement, in which European governments agreed to keep their currencies within a plus or minus 2.25% trading band around an agreed central value. Superceded by the adoption of the euro and so, is no longer in effect.

Society for Worldwide Interbank Financial Telecommunications (SWIFT). A dedicated computer network providing funds transfer messages between member banks around the world.

Soft currency. A currency expected to drop in value relative to other currencies. Free trading in a currency deemed soft is often restricted by the monetary authorities of the issuing country.

Sovereign risk. The risk that a host government may unilaterally repudiate its foreign obligations or may prevent local firms from honoring their foreign obligations. Sovereign risk is often regarded as a subset of political risk.

SPA. *Societa per Azioni.* Italian term for corporation.

Special Drawing Right (SDR). An international reserve asset, defined by the International Monetary Fund as the value of a weighted basket of five currencies.

Speculation. An attempt to make a profit by trading on expectations about future prices.

Spot rate. The price at which foreign exchange can be purchased (its bid) or sold (its ask) in a spot transaction. *See* Spot transaction.

Spot transaction. A foreign exchange transaction to be settled (paid for) on the second following business day.

Spot transaction (spot). A foreign exchange transaction to be settled (paid for) on the second following business day.

Spread. The difference between the bid (buying) quote and the ask (selling) quote.

Stabilizing expectations. If a currency's value falls below the long-term path, market participants respond by buying the currency and driving its value up.

Strategic alliance. A formal relationship, short of a merger or acquisition, between two companies, formed for the purpose of gaining synergies because in some aspect the two companies complement each other.

Strike price. *See* Exercise price.

Stripped bonds. Bonds issued by investment bankers against coupons or the maturity (corpus) portion of original bearer bonds, where the original bonds are held in trust by the investment banker. Whereas the original bonds will have coupons promising interest at each interest date (say June and December for each of the next 20 years), a given stripped bond will represent a claim against all interest payments from the entire original issue due on a particular interest date. A stripped bond is in effect a zero coupon bond manufactured by the investment banker.

Subpart F. A type of foreign income, as defined in the U.S. tax code, which under certain conditions is taxed in the United States, even though it has not been repatriated to the United States.

Subsidiary. A foreign operation incorporated in the host country and owned 50% or more by a parent corporation. Foreign operations that are not incorporated are called "branches."

Sushi bonds. Eurodollar, or other non-yen denominated, bonds issued by a Japanese corporation for sale to Japanese investors.

Swap. This term is used in many contexts. In general it is the simultaneous purchase and sale of foreign exchange or securities, with the purchase being effected at once and the sale back to the same party to be carried out at a price agreed upon today but to be completed at a specified future date. Swaps include interest rate swaps, currency swaps, and credit swaps. A "swap rate" is a forward foreign exchange quotation expressed in terms of the number of points by which the forward rate differs from the spot rate.

Swaption (swap option). A purchase that gives the firm the right, but not the obligation, to enter into a swap on a predetermined notional principal at some defined future date at a specified strike rate.

Swap transaction (swap). This term is used in many contexts. In general, it is the simultaneous purchase and sale of foreign exchange or securities, with the purchase being effected at once and the sale back to the same party to be carried out at a price agreed upon today but to be completed at a specified future date. Swaps include interest rate swaps, currency swaps, and credit swaps. A "swap rate" is a forward foreign exchange quotation expressed in terms of the number of points by which the forward rate differs from the spot rate.

Swedish School. School of economic thought that applies the behavioral approach to analyzing the FDI decision.

SWIFT. *See* Society for Worldwide Interbank Financial Telecommunications.

"Swissie." Foreign exchange dealers' nickname for the Swiss franc.

Switch trading. Transferring use of bilateral balances from one country to another.

Syndicated loan. A large loan made by a group of banks to a large multinational firm or government. Syndicated loans allow the participating banks to maintain diversification by not lending too much to a single borrower.

Synthetic forward. A complex option position which combines the purchase of a put option and the sale of a call option, or vice versa, both at the forward rate.

Systematic risk. The risk of the market itself; i.e., risk that cannot be diversified away.

T/A. "Trade acceptance." International trade term.

Tariff. A duty or tax on imports that can be levied as a percentage of cost or as a specific amount per unit of import.

Tax averaging. Offsetting foreign tax credits derived from one source against foreign tax liabilities from another source, assuming that they are derived from the same type of income.

Tax credit. A direct reduction of taxes that would otherwise be due and payable. *See also* Deductible expense.

Tax haven. A country with either no or very low tax rates that uses its tax structure to attract foreign investment or international financial dealings.

Tenor. The time period of a draft.

Terms of trade. The weighted average exchange ratio between a nation's export prices and its import prices, used to measure gains from trade. Gains from trade refers to increases in total consumption resulting from production specialization and international trade.

Temporal method. In the United States, term for a codification of a translation method essentially similar to the "monetary/nonmonetary method."

Tequila effect. *See* Contagion. A form of panic whereby the Mexican peso crisis of December 1994 quickly spread to other Latin American currency and equity markets.

Territorial approach to tax structure. This tax structure applies taxes to the income earned by firms within the legal jurisdiction of the host country, not on the country of firm incorporation.

Theory of comparative advantage. *See* Comparative advantage.

Theta. The expected change in an option premium caused by a small change in the time to expiration.

Time draft. *See* Usance draft.

Total Shareholder Return (TSR). A measure of corporate performance based on the sum of share price appreciation and current dividends.

Trade acceptance. A draft accepted by a commercial enterprise, instead of by a bank.

Tranche. An allocation of shares, typically to underwriters that are expected to sell to investors in their designated geographic markets.

Transaction exposure. The potential for a change in the value of outstanding financial obligations entered into prior to a change in exchange rates but not due to be settled until after the exchange rates change.

Transfer pricing. The pricing of goods, services, and technology to a foreign subsidiary from a related company.

Transfer taxes. Property and inheritance taxes, imposed to achieve social redistribution of income and wealth, as well as to raise revenue.

Translation exposure. Another name for accounting exposure. *See* Accounting exposure.

Treynor measure (TRN). Calculates the average return over and above the risk-free rate of return per unit of portfolio risk.

Triangular arbitrage. Arbitrage between three markets.

TSR. *See* Total Shareholder Return.

Two-sided risks. Also known as symmetric risks. Risk components that can cause the cash flow returns of the investment to be higher or lower than generally expected.

Unaffiliated known. A foreign importer with which the exporter has previously conducted business successfully.

Unaffiliated unknownA foreign importer with which an exporter has not previously conducted business.

Unbiased predictor. A theory that spot prices at some future date will be equal to today's forward rates.

Unbundling. Dividing cash flows from an affiliate to a parent into their many separate components, such as royalties, lease payments, dividends, etc., so as to increase the likelihood that some fund flows will be allowed during economically difficult times.

Unsystematic risk. In a portfolio, the amount of risk that can be eliminated by diversification.

Usance draft. A contract that allows a delay in payment. Once accepted, becomes a bankers' acceptance. Once drawn on and accepted by a business firm, becomes a trade acceptance.

Value date. The date when value is given (i.e., funds are deposited) for foreign exchange transactions between banks.

Value-added tax (VAT). A type of national sales tax collected at each stage of production or sale of consumption goods, and levied in proportion to the value added during that stage.

Value today. A spot foreign exchange transaction in which delivery and payment are made on the same day as the contract. Normal delivery is two business days after the contract.

Value tomorrow. A spot foreign exchange transaction in which delivery and payment are made on the next business day after the contract. Normal delivery is two business days after the contract.

VAT. *See* Value-added tax.

Volatility. The standard deviation of daily percentage changes in the underlying exchange rate. Volatility is viewed as historic (drawn from a recent period of time), forward-looking (adjusted upward or downward for expected market swings or events), or implied (calculated by being backed out of the market option premium values traded).

WACC. *See* Weighted average cost of capital.

Weak currency. *Same as* Soft currency.

Weakening. *Same as* depreciation.

Weighted average cost of capital (WACC). The sum of the proportionally weighted costs of different sources of capital, used as the minimum acceptable target return on new investments.

World Bank. *See* International Bank for Reconstruction and Development.

World Trade Organization (WTO). The intragovernmental organization that applies rules to international trade and hears complaints filed by countries that a particular rule has been violated. The World Trade Agreement replaced the General Agreement on Trade and Tariffs (GATT).

Worldwide approach tax structure. This approach to tax structure levies taxes on the income earned by firms that are incorporated in the host country, regardless of where the income was earned (domestically or abroad).

Writer. Seller of an option (same as Grantor).

WTO. *See* World Trade Organization.

Yankee bonds. Dollar-denominated bonds issued within the United States by a foreign borrower.

Yield to maturity. The rate of interest (discount) that equates future cash flows of a bond, both interest and principal, with the present market price. Yield to maturity is thus the time-adjusted rate of return earned by a bond investor.

Y. K. *Yugen-Kaisha*. Japanese term for limited liability company.

Zero coupon bond. A bond that pays no periodic interest, but simply returns a given amount of principal at a stated maturity date. Zero coupon bonds are sold at a discount from the maturity amount to provide the holder a compound rate of return for the holding period.

AUTHOR INDEX

n = footnote to text
r = suggested reading
x = source note to an exhibit

SUBJECT INDEX

Page numbers followed by an n *indicate a footnote.*

Currencies of the World

Country	Currency	Symbol	Subdivision	ISO-4217 Code	Regime
Afghanistan	afghani	Af	100 puls	AFA 004	float
Albania	lek	L	100 qindarka (qintars)	ALL 008	float
Algeria	dinar	DA	100 centimes	DZD 012	composite
American Samoa			*see* United States of America		
Andorra	Andorran Peseta (1/1 to Spanish Peseta) and Andorran Franc (1/1 to French Franc)				
Angola	kwanza	Kz	100 lwei	AOK ---	(replaced)
Angola	kwanza (kwanza reajustado, -2000)	Kz	100 lwei	AON 024	m.float
Angola	kwanza (new kwanza, 2001-)	Kz	100 lwei	AOA 024	m.float
Anguilla	dollar	EC$	100 cents	XCD 951	US-$ (2.7)
Antarctica	each Antarctic base uses the currency of its home country				
Antigua and Barbuda	dollar	EC$	100 cents	XCD 951	US-$ (2.7)
Argentina	austral (-1991)	double dashed A	100 centavos	ARA ---	(replaced)
Argentina	peso (1991-)	$	100 centavos	ARS 032	float
Armenia	dram		100 luma	AMD 051	
Aruba	guilder (a.k.a. florin or gulden)	Af.	100 cents	AWG 533	US-$ (1.79)
Australia	dollar	A$	100 cents	AUD 036	float
Austria (-1998)	schilling	S	100 groschen	ATS 040	euro-13.7603
Austria (1999-)			*see* European Union		
Azerbaijan	manat		100 gopik	AZM 031	
Bahamas	dollar	B$	100 cents	BSD 044	US-$ (1.0)
Bahrain	dinar	BD	1,000 fils	BHD 048	US-$ (lim.flex.)
Bangladesh	taka	Tk	100 paisa (poisha)	BDT 050	composite
Barbados	dollar	Bds$	100 cents	BBD 052	US-$ (2.0)
Belarus (-1999)	ruble	BR		BYB 112	replaced, 1000 BYB = 1 BYR
Belarus (2000-)	ruble	BR		BYR 112	m.float
Belgium (-1998)	franc	BF	100 centimes	BEF 056	euro-40.3399
Belgium (1999-)			*see* European Union		
Belize	dollar	BZ$	100 cents	BZD 084	US-$ (2.0)
Belorussia	old name of Belarus				
Benin	franc	CFAF	100 centimes	XOF 952	French Franc (100.0)
Bermuda	dollar	Bd$	100 cents	BMD 060	US-$ (1.0)
Bhutan	ngultrum	Nu	100 chetrum	BTN 064	Indian Rupee (1.0)
Bolivia	boliviano	Bs	100 centavos	BOB 068	float
Bosnia-Herzegovina	(-1999)	B.H. dinar		100 para	BAD 070
Bosnia-Herzegovina (1999+)	convertible mark	KM	100 fennig	BAM 977	DM (1.0)
Botswana	pula	P	100 thebe	BWP 072	composite
Bouvet Island	*see* Norway				
Brazil	cruzeiro (-1993)		100 centavos	BRE 076	(replaced)
Brazil	cruzeiro (1993-94)		100 centavos	BRR 076	(replaced)
Brazil	real (1994-)	R$	100 centavos	BRL 986	float
British Indian Ocean Territory	legal currency is GBP, but mostly USD is used				
British Virgin Islands			*see* United States		

Country	Currency	Symbol	Subdivision	ISO-4217 Code	Regime
Brunei	ringgit (a.k.a. Bruneian dollar)	B$	100 sen (a.k.a. 100 cents)	BND 096	S$ (1.0)
Bulgaria	leva	Lv	100 stotinki	BGL 100	German Mark (1.0)
Burkina Faso	franc	CFAF	100 centimes	XOF 952	French Franc (100.0)
Burma	now Myanmar.				
Burundi	franc	FBu	100 centimes	BIF 108	composite
Cambodia	new riel	CR	100 sen	KHR 116	m.float
Cameroon (100.0)	franc	CFAF	100 centimes	XAF 950	French Franc
Canada	dollar	Can$	100 cents	CAD 124	float
Canton and Enderbury Islands			*see* Kiribati		
Cape Verde Island	escudo	C.V.Esc.	100 centavos	CVE 132	composite
Cayman Islands	dollar	CI$	100 cents	KYD 136	US-$ (0.85)
Central African Republic (100.0)	franc	CFAF	100 centimes	XAF 950	French Franc
Chad (100.0)	franc	CFAF	100 centimes	XAF 950	French Franc
Chile	peso	Ch$	100 centavos	CLP 152	indicators
China	yuan renminbi	Y	10 jiao = 100 fen	CNY 156	m.float
Christmas Island			*see* Australia		
Cocos (Keeling) Islands			*see* Australia		
Colombia	peso	Col$	100 centavos	COP 170	m.float
Comoros	franc	CF	-	KMF 174	French Franc (75.0)
Congo (100.0)	franc	CFAF	100 centimes	XAF 950	French Franc
Congo, Dem. Rep. (former Zaire)	franc		100 centimes	CDF 180	US-$ (2.50)
Congo, Dem. Rep. (2001-)	franc		100 centimes	CDF 976	float
Cook Islands			*see* New Zealand		
Costa Rica	colon	slashed C	100 centimos	CRC 188	float
Côte d'Ivoire (100.0)	franc	CFAF	100 centimes	XOF 952	French Franc
Croatia	kuna	HRK	100 lipas	HRK 191	float
Cuba	peso	Cu$	100 centavos	CUP 192	US-$ (1.0)
Cyprus +/- 2.25%	pound	£C	100 cents	CYP 196	1.7086 EUR/CYP
Cyprus (Northern)			*see* Turkey		
Czechoslovakia	split into Czech Republic and Slovak Republic on January 1, 1993				
Czech Republic	koruna	Kc (with hacek on c)	100 haleru	CZK 203	float
Denmark	krone (pl. kroner)	Dkr	100 øre	DKK 208	EMS-II
Djibouti	franc	DF	100 centimes	DJF 262	US-$ (177.72)
Dominica	dollar	EC$	100 cents	XCD 951	US-$ (2.7)
Dominican Rep.	peso	RD$	100 centavos	DOP 214	m.float
Dronning Maud Land			*see* Norway		
East Timor			*see* Indonesia		
Ecuador	sucre	S/	100 centavos	ECS 218	m.float
Ecuador			country has adopted the US Dollar		

Currencies of the World (continued)

Country	Currency	Symbol	Subdivision	ISO-4217 Code	Regime
Egypt	pound	£E	100 piasters or 1,000 milliemes	EGP 818	m.float
El Salvador	colon	¢	100 centavos	SVC 222	float
Equatorial Guinea	franc	CFAF	100 centimos	GQE 226	French Franc(100.0)
Eritrea	nakfa	Nfa	100 cents	ERN 232	
Estonia	kroon (pl. krooni)	KR	100 senti	EEK 233	German Mark (8.0)
Ethiopia	birr	Br	100 cents	ETB 230	float
European Union (-1998)	European Currency Unit	ecu		XEU 954	
European Union (1999-)	Euro	€	100 euro-cents	EUR 978	
Faeroe Islands (Føroyar)			*see* Denmark		
Falkland Islands	pound	£F	100 pence	FKP 238	British Pound (1.0)
Fiji	dollar	F$	100 cents	FJD 242	composite
Finland (-1998)	markka (pl. markkaa)	mk	100 penniä (sg. penni)	FIM 246	euro-5.94573
Finland (1999-)			*see* European Union		
France (-1998)	franc	F	100 centimes	FRF 250	euro-6.55957
France (1999-)			*see* European Union		
French Guiana			*see* France		
French Polynesia	franc	CFPF	100 centimes	XPF 953	FFr (18.18)
Gabon (100.0)	franc	CFAF	100 centimes	XAF 950	French Franc
Gambia	dalasi	D	100 butut	GMD 270	float
Gaza			*see* Israel and Jordan		
Georgia	lari		100 tetri	GEL 981	float
Germany (-1998)	deutsche mark	DM	100 pfennig	DEM 276	euro-1.95583
Germany (1999-)			*see* European Union		
Ghana	new cedi	¢	100 psewas	GHC 288	float
Gibraltar	pound	£G	100 pence	GIP 292	British Pound (1.0)
Great Britain			*see* United Kingdom		
Greece (-2000)	drachma	Dr	100 lepta (sg. lepton)	GRD 300	euro-340.750
Greece (2001-)			*see* European Union		
Greenland			*see* Denmark		
Grenada	dollar	EC$	100 cents	XCD 951	US-$ (2.7)
Guadeloupe			*see* France		
Guam			*see* United States		
Guatemala	quetzal	Q	100 centavos	GTQ 320	float
Guernsey			*see* United Kingdom		
Guinea-Bissau (-Apr1997)	peso	PG	100 centavos	GWP 624	m.float
Guinea-Bissau (May1997-) (100.0)	franc	CFAF	100 centimes	XOF 952	French Franc
Guinea	syli	FG	10 francs, 1 franc = 100 centimes	GNS 324	m.float
Guinea	franc			GNF 324	
Guyana	dollar	G$	100 cents	GYD 328	float
Haiti	gourde	G	100 centimes	HTG 332	float
Heard and McDonald Islands			*see* Australia		

Country	Currency	Symbol	Subdivision	ISO-4217 Code	Regime
Honduras	lempira	L	100 centavos	HNL 340	m.float
Hong Kong	dollar	HK$	100 cents	HKD 344	US-$ (7.73 central parity)
Hungary	forint	Ft	-none-	HUF 348	composite
Iceland	króna	IKr	100 aurar (sg. aur)	ISK 352	composite
India	rupee	Rs	100 paise	INR 356	float
Indonesia	rupiah	Rp	100 sen (no longer used)	IDR 360	m.float
International Monetary Fund	Special Drawing Right	SDR		XDR 960	
Iran	rial	Rls	10 rials = 1 toman	IRR 364	US-$ (4750)
Iraq	dinar	ID	1,000 fils	IQD 368	US-$ (0.3109)
Ireland (-1998)	punt or pound	IR£	100 pingin or pence	IEP 372	euro-0.787564
Ireland (1999-)			*see* European Union		
Isle of Man			*see* United Kingdom		
Israel	new shekel	NIS	100 new agorot	ILS 376	m.float
Italy (-1998)	lira (pl. lire)	Lit	no subdivision in use	ITL 380	euro-1936.27
Italy (1999-)			*see* European Union		
Ivory Coast			*see* Côte d'Ivoire		
Jamaica	dollar	J$	100 cents	JMD 388	float
Japan	yen	¥	100 sen (not used)	JPY 392	float
Jersey			*see* United Kingdom		
Johnston Island			*see* United States		
Jordan	dinar	JD	1,000 fils	JOD 400	composite
Kampuchea			*see* Cambodia		
Kazakhstan	tenge		100 tiyn	KZT 398	float
Kenya	shilling	K Sh	100 cents	KES 404	float
Kiribati			*see* Australia.		
Korea, North	won	Wn	100 chon	KPW 408	
Korea, South	won	W	100 chon	KRW 410	float
Kuwait	dinar	KD	1,000 fils	KWD 414	composite
Kyrgyzstan	som		100 tyyn	KGS 417	float
Laos	new kip	KN	100 at	LAK 418	m.float
Latvia	lat	Ls	100 santims	LVL 428	SDR
Lebanon	pound (livre)	L.L.	100 piastres	LBP 422	float
Lesotho	loti, pl., maloti	L, pl., M	100 lisente	LSL 426	South African Rand (1.0)
Liberia	dollar	$	100 cents	LRD 430	US-$ (1.0)
Libya	dinar	LD	1,000 dirhams	LYD 434	SDR (8.5085)
Liechtenstein	*see* Switzerland				
Lithuania	litas, pl., litai		100 centu	LTL 440	Euro (3.4528)
Luxembourg (-1998)	franc	LuxF	100 centimes	LUF 442	euro-40.3399
Luxembourg (1999-)			*see* European Union		
Macao (Macau)	pataca	P	100 avos	MOP 446	HK-$ (1.03)
Macedonia (Former Yug. Rep.)	denar	MKD	100 deni	MKD 807	composite
Madagascar	ariayry = 5 francs	FMG	1 francs = 100 centimes	MGF 450	float
Malawi	kwacha	MK	100 tambala	MWK 454	float
Malaysia	ringgit	RM	100 sen	MYR 458	m.float
Maldives	rufiyaa	Rf	100 lari	MVR 462	m.float

Country	Currency	Symbol	Subdivision	ISO-4217 Code	Regime
Mali	franc	CFAF	100 centimes	XOF 952	French Franc(100.0)
Malta	lira, pl., liri	Lm	100 cents	MTL 470	composite
Martinique			*see* France		
Mauritania	ouguiya	UM	5 khoums	MRO 478	composite
Mauritius	rupee	Mau Rs	100 cents	MUR 480	composite
Micronesia			*see* United States		
Midway Islands			*see* United States		
Mexico	peso	Mex$	100 centavos	MXN 484	float
Moldova	leu, pl., lei			MDL 498	float
Monaco			*see* France		
Mongolia	tugrik (tughrik?)	Tug	100 mongos	MNT 496	float
Montserrat	dollar	EC$	100 cents	XCD 951	US-$ (2.7)
Morocco	dirham	DH	100 centimes	MAD 504	composite
Mozambique	metical	Mt	100 centavos	MZM 508	float
Myanmar	kyat	K	100 pyas	MMK 104	US-$ (5.86of, 200-300bm)
Nauru			*see* Australia		
Namibia	dollar	N$	100 cents	NAD 516	South African Rand (1.0)
Nepal	rupee	NRs	100 paise	NPR 524	composite
Netherlands Antilles	guilder (a.k.a. florin or gulden)		Ant.f. or NAf.	100 cents	ANG 532 US-$ (1.79)
Netherlands (-1998) euro-2.20371	guilder (a.k.a. florin or gulden)		f.	100 cents	NLG 528
Netherlands (1999-)			*see* European Union		
New Caledonia	franc	CFPF	100 centimes	XPF 953	FFr (18.18)
New Zealand	dollar	NZ$	100 cents	NZD 554	float
Nicaragua	gold cordoba	C$	100 centavos	NIO 558	indicators
Niger	franc	CFAF	100 centimes	XOF 952	French Franc(100.0)
Nigeria	naira	double-dashed N	100 kobo	NGN 566	US-$ ((82.0))
Niue			*see* New Zealand		
Norfolk Island			*see* Australia		
Norway	krone (pl. kroner)	NKr	100 øre	NOK 578	float
Oman	rial	RO	1,000 baizas	OMR 512	US-$ (1/2.6)
Pakistan	rupee	Rs	100 paisa	PKR 586	m.float
Palau			*see* United States		
Panama	balboa	B	100 centesimos	PAB 590	US-$ (1.0)
Panama Canal Zone			*see* United States		
Papua New Guinea	kina	K	100 toeas	PGK 598	composite
Paraguay	guarani	slashed G	100 centimos	PYG 600	float
Peru	inti		100 centimos	PEI ---	(replaced)
Peru	new sol	S/.	100 centimos	PEN 604	float
Philippines	peso	dashed P	100 centavos	PHP 608	float
Pitcairn Island			*see* New Zealand		
Poland	zloty	z dashed l	100 groszy	PLN 985	m.float
Portugal (-1998)	escudo	Esc	100 centavos	PTE 620	euro-200.482
Portugal (1999-)			*see* European Union		

Country	Currency	Symbol	Subdivision	ISO-4217 Code	Regime
Puerto Rico			*see* United States		
Qatar	riyal	QR	100 dirhams	QAR 634	US-$ (lim.flex.)
Reunion			*see* France		
Romania	leu (pl. lei)	L	100 bani	ROL 642	float
Russia (-1997)	ruble	R	100 kopecks	RUR 810	(replaced, 1000/1)
Russia (1998-)	ruble	R	100 kopecks	RUB 810	float
Rwanda	franc	RF	100 centimes	RWF 646	SDR (201.8?)
Samoa (Western)			*see* Western Samoa		
Samoa (America)			*see* United States		
San Marino			*see* Italy		
Sao Tome & Principe	dobra	Db	100 centimos	STD 678	m.float
Saudi Arabia	riyal	SRls	100 halalat	SAR 682	US-$ (lim.flex.)
Senegal	franc	CFAF	100 centimes	XOF 952	French Franc(100.0)
Serbia			*see* Yugoslavia		
Seychelles	rupee	SR	100 cents	SCR 690	SDR (7.2345)
Sierra Leone	leone	Le	100 cents	SLL 694	float
Singapore	dollar	S$	100 cents	SGD 702	m.float
Slovakia	koruna	Sk	100 halierov	SKK 703	float
Slovenia	tolar	SIT	100 stotinov (stotins)	SIT 705	m.float
Solomon Island	dollar	SI$	100 cents	SBD 090	composite
Somalia	shilling	So. Sh.	100 centesimi	SOS 706	float
South Africa	rand	R	100 cents	ZAR 710	float
Spain (-1998)	peseta	Ptas	100 centimos	ESP 724	euro-166.386
Spain (1999-)			*see* European Union		
Sri Lanka	rupee	SLRs	100 cents	LKR 144	m.float
St. Helena	pound	£S	100 new pence	SHP 654	GBP (1.0)
St. Kitts and Nevis	dollar	EC$	100 cents	XCD 951	US-$ (2.7)
St. Lucia	dollar	EC$	100 cents	XCD 951	US-$ (2.7)
St. Vincent and the Grenadines	dollar	EC$	100 cents	XCD 951	US-$ (2.7)
Sudan (-1992)	pound		100 piastres	SDP 736	m.float
Sudan (1992-)	dinar		100 piastres	SDP 736	m.float
Suriname	guilder (a.k.a. florin or gulden)	Sur.f. or Sf.	100 cents	SRG 740	m.float
Svalbard and Jan Mayen Islands			*see* Norway		
Swaziland	lilangeni, pl., emalangeni	L, pl., E	100 cents	SZL 748	South African rand (1.0)
Sweden	krona (pl. kronor)	Sk	100 öre	SEK 752	m.float
Switzerland	franc	SwF	100 rappen/centimes	CHF 756	float
Syria	pound	£S	100 piasters	SYP 760	US-$ (11.225)
Tahiti	*see* French Polynesia				
Taiwan	new dollar	NT$	100 cents	TWD 901	
Tajikistan (- 5-Nov-2000)	ruble			TJR 762	replaced, 1000 TJR = 1 TJS
Tajikistan (6-Nov-2000 -)	somoni	100 dirams			TJS 762
Tanzania	shilling	TSh	100 cents	TZS 834	float
Thailand	baht	Bht or Bt	100 stang	THB 764	float
Togo	franc	CFAF	100 centimes	XOF 952	French Franc(100.0)
Tokelau			*see* New Zealand		